THE ROUT'
E[

Epistemology, the philosophy of knowledge, is at the core of many of the central debates and issues in philosophy, interrogating the notions of truth, objectivity, trust, belief, and perception. *The Routledge Companion to Epistemology* provides a comprehensive and up-to-date survey of epistemology, charting its history, providing a thorough account of its key thinkers and movements, and addressing enduring questions and contemporary research in the field. Organized thematically, the *Companion* is divided into ten sections:

- Foundational Concepts
- The Analysis of Knowledge
- The Structure of Knowledge
- Kinds of Knowledge
- Skepticism
- Responses to Skepticism
- Knowledge and Knowledge Attributions
- Formal Epistemology
- The History of Epistemology
- Metaepistemological Issues

Seventy-eight original chapters, each between 5000 and 7000 words and written by a leading epistemologist, provide students with an outstanding and accessible guide to the field. Designed to fit the most comprehensive syllabus in the discipline, this text will be an indispensable resource for anyone interested in this central area of philosophy.

The Routledge Companion to Epistemology is essential reading for students of philosophy.

Sven Bernecker is Professor of Philosophy at the University of California, Irvine. His main areas of research are epistemology, metaphysics, and philosophy of mind. He is the author of *Reading Epistemology* (2006), *The Metaphysics of Memory* (2008), and *Memory: A Philosophical Study* (2010); and editor, with Fred Dretske, of *Knowledge: Readings in Contemporary Epistemology* (2000).

Duncan Pritchard FRSE is Professor of Philosophy at the University of Edinburgh. He works mainly in epistemology and has published widely in this area. His books include *Epistemic Luck* (2005), *The Nature and Value of Knowledge* (with A. Millar & A. Haddock; 2010), *Epistemological Disjunctivism* (2012), and *What is this Thing Called Knowledge?* (Third Edition, 2013).

Routledge Philosophy Companions

Routledge Philosophy Companions offer thorough, high quality surveys and assessments of the major topics and periods in philosophy. Covering key problems, themes and thinkers, all entries are specially commissioned for each volume and written by leading scholars in the field. Clear, accessible and carefully edited and organised, *Routledge Philosophy Companions* are indispensable for anyone coming to a major topic or period in philosophy, as well as for the more advanced reader.

The Routledge Companion to Aesthetics, Third Edition
Edited by Berys Gaut and Dominic Lopes

The Routledge Companion to Philosophy of Religion
Edited by Chad Meister and Paul Copan

The Routledge Companion to the Philosophy of Science
Edited by Stathis Psillos and Martin Curd

The Routledge Companion to Twentieth Century Philosophy
Edited by Dermot Moran

The Routledge Companion to Philosophy and Film
Edited by Paisley Livingston and Carl Plantinga

The Routledge Companion to Philosophy of Psychology
Edited by John Symons and Paco Calvo

The Routledge Companion to Metaphysics
Edited by Robin Le Poidevin, Peter Simons, Andrew McGonigal, and Ross Cameron

The Routledge Companion to Nineteenth Century Philosophy
Edited by Dean Moyar

The Routledge Companion to Ethics
Edited by John Skorupski

The Routledge Companion to Epistemology
Edited by Sven Bernecker and Duncan Pritchard

The Routledge Companion to Philosophy and Music
Edited by Theodore Gracyk and Andrew Kania

The Routledge Companion to Phenomenology
Edited by Søren Overgaard and Sebastian Luft

The Routledge Companion to Philosophy of Language
Edited by Gillian Russell and Delia Graff Fara

The Routledge Companion to Philosophy of Law
Edited by Andrei Marmor

The Routledge Companion to Social and Political Philosophy
Edited by Gerald Gaus and Fred D'Agostino

The Routledge Companion to Ancient Philosophy
Edited by Frisbee Sheffield and James Warren

Forthcoming:

The Routledge Companion to Seventeenth Century Philosophy
Edited by Dan Kaufman

The Routledge Companion to Eighteenth Century Philosophy
Edited by Aaron Garrett

The Routledge Companion to Philosophy of Mental Disorder
Edited by Jakob Hohwy and Philip Gerrans

The Routledge Companion to Islamic Philosophy
Edited by Richard C. Taylor and Luis Xavier López-Farjeat

The Routledge Companion to Philosophy of Literature
Edited by Noël Carroll and John Gibson

The Routledge Companion to Philosophy of Religion, Second Edition
Edited by Chad Meister and Paul Copan

The Routledge Companion to Philosophy of Science, Second Edition
Edited by Stathis Psillos and Martin Curd

The Routledge Companion to Bioethics
Edited by John Arras, Rebecca Kukla, and Elizabeth Fenton

The Routledge Companion to Environmental Ethics
Edited by Benjamin Hale and Andrew Light

PRAISE FOR THE SERIES

The Routledge Companion to Aesthetics

'This is an immensely useful book that belongs in every college library and on the bookshelves of all serious students of aesthetics.'—*Journal of Aesthetics and Art Criticism*

'The succinctness and clarity of the essays will make this a source that individuals not familiar with aesthetics will find extremely helpful.'—*The Philosophical Quarterly*

'An outstanding resource in aesthetics...this text will not only serve as a handy reference source for students and faculty alike, but it could also be used as a text for a course in the philosophy of art.'—*Australasian Journal of Philosophy*

'Attests to the richness of modern aesthetics...the essays in central topics – many of which are written by well-known figures – succeed in being informative, balanced and intelligent without being too difficult.'—*British Journal of Aesthetics*

'This handsome reference volume . . . belongs in every library.'—*Choice*

'The *Routledge Companions to Philosophy* have proved to be a useful series of high quality surveys of major philosophical topics and this volume is worthy enough to sit with the others on a reference library shelf.'—*Philosophy and Religion*

The Routledge Companion to Philosophy of Religion

'. . . a very valuable resource for libraries and serious scholars.'—*Choice*

'The work is sure to be an academic standard for years to come . . . I shall heartily recommend *The Routledge Companion to Philosophy of Religion* to my students and colleagues and hope that libraries around the country add it to their collections.'—*Philosophia Christi*

The Routledge Companion to Philosophy of Science

A *Choice* Outstanding Academic Title 2008

'With a distinguished list of internationally renowned contributors, an excellent choice of topics in the field, and well-written, well-edited essays throughout, this compendium is an excellent resource. Highly recommended.'—*Choice*

'Highly recommended for history of science and philosophy collections.'—*Library Journal*

'This well conceived companion, which brings together an impressive collection of distinguished authors, will be invaluable to novices and experienced readers alike.' —*Metascience*

The Routledge Companion to Twentieth Century Philosophy

'To describe this volume as ambitious would be a serious understatement. . . . full of scholarly rigor, including detailed notes and bibliographies of interest to professional philosophers. . . . Summing Up: Essential.'—**Choice**

The Routledge Companion to Philosophy and Film

'A fascinating, rich volume offering dazzling insights and incisive commentary on every page . . . Every serious student of film will want this book . . . Summing Up: Highly recommended.'—**Choice**

The Routledge Companion to Philosophy of Psychology

'This work should serve as the standard reference for those interested in gaining a reliable overview of the burgeoning field of philosophical psychology. Summing Up: Essential.' —**Choice**

The Routledge Companion to Metaphysics

'The *Routledge Philosophy Companions* series has a deserved reputation for impressive scope and scholarly value. This volume is no exception . . . Summing Up: Highly recommended.'—**Choice**

The Routledge Companion to Nineteenth Century Philosophy

A **Choice** Outstanding Academic Title 2010

'This is a crucial resource for advanced undergraduates and faculty of any discipline who are interested in the 19th-century roots of contemporary philosophical problems. Summing Up: Essential.'—**Choice**

The Routledge Companion to Ethics

'This fine collection merits a place in every university, college, and high school library for its invaluable articles covering a very broad range of topics in ethics[.] . . . With its remarkable clarity of writing and its very highly qualified contributors, this volume is must reading for anyone interested in the latest developments in these important areas of thought and practice. Summing Up: Highly recommended.' —**Choice**

The Routledge Companion to Epistemology

'As a series, the *Routledge Philosophy Companions* has met with near universal acclaim. This expansive volume not only continues the trend but quite possibly sets a new standard. Combining encyclopedic coverage with the scholarly acumen of established leaders in the field, this is an indispensable resource for scholars, students, and libraries. . . . Summing Up: Essential.'—**Choice**

THE ROUTLEDGE COMPANION TO EPISTEMOLOGY

Edited by
Sven Bernecker and Duncan Pritchard

Routledge
Taylor & Francis Group
NEW YORK AND LONDON

First published in paperback 2014

First published 2011
by Routledge
711 Third Avenue, New York, NY 10017

and by Routledge
2 Park Square, Milton Park, Abingdon, Oxon OX14 4RN

Routledge is an imprint of the Taylor & Francis Group, an informa business

© 2011, 2014 Taylor & Francis

The right of the editors to be identified as the authors of the editorial material, and of the authors for their individual chapters, has been asserted in accordance with sections 77 and 78 of the Copyright, Designs and Patents Act 1988.

All rights reserved. No part of this book may be reprinted or reproduced or utilised in any form or by any electronic, mechanical, or other means, now known or hereafter invented, including photocopying and recording, or in any information storage or retrieval system, without permission in writing from the publishers.

Trademark notice: Product or corporate names may be trademarks or registered trademarks, and are used only for identification and explanation without intent to infringe.

Library of Congress Cataloging-in-Publication Data
The Routledge companion to epistemology / edited by Sven Bernecker, Duncan Pritchard.
p. cm. — (Routledge philosophy companions)
Includes bibliographical references.
1. Knowledge, Theory of. I. Bernecker, Sven. II. Pritchard, Duncan.
III. Title: Companion to epistemology.
BD161.R69 2011
121—dc22
2010020537

ISBN: 978-0-415-96219-3 (hbk)
ISBN: 978-0-415-72269-8 (pbk)
ISBN: 978-0-203-83906-5 (ebk)

Typeset in Goudy
by Swales & Willis Ltd, Exeter, Devon

Printed and bound in the United States of America by Publishers Graphics, LLC on sustainably sourced paper.

CONTENTS

Notes on Contributors   xv
Preface   xxv

PART I
Foundational Concepts   1

1. Truth   3
   MICHAEL P. LYNCH

2. Belief   14
   ERIC SCHWITZGEBEL

3. Epistemic Justification   25
   JONATHAN L. KVANVIG

4. Epistemic Rationality   37
   RICHARD FOLEY

5. Epistemic Norms   47
   PASCAL ENGEL

6. Evidence   58
   TIMOTHY MCGREW

7. Disagreement   68
   BRYAN FRANCES

8. Epistemic Relativism   75
   PAUL BOGHOSSIAN

9. Understanding   84
   STEPHEN R. GRIMM

10. Wisdom   95
    DENNIS WHITCOMB

PART II
The Analysis of Knowledge — 107

11 The Basing Relation — 109
RAM NETA

12 The Gettier Problem — 119
STEPHEN HETHERINGTON

13 Fallibilism — 131
TRENT DOUGHERTY

14 Externalism/Internalism — 144
HAMID VAHID

15 Defeasibility Theory — 156
THOMAS GRUNDMANN

16 Evidentialism — 167
DANIEL M. MITTAG

17 Reliabilism — 176
JUAN COMESAÑA

18 Modal and Anti-Luck Epistemology — 187
TIM BLACK

19 Virtue Epistemology — 199
JONATHAN L. KVANVIG

20 Knowledge First Epistemology — 208
TIMOTHY WILLIAMSON

21 The Value Problem — 219
JOHN GRECO

PART III
The Structure of Knowledge — 233

22 Foundationalism — 235
MICHAEL DEPAUL

23 Infinitism — 245
PETER D. KLEIN

24 Coherentism — 257
ERIK J. OLSSON

PART IV
Kinds of Knowledge — 269

25 Inductive Knowledge — 271
    ALEXANDER BIRD

26 A Priori Knowledge — 283
    LAURENCE BONJOUR

27 Perceptual Knowledge — 294
    DAVID SOSA

28 Self-Knowledge — 305
    SANFORD GOLDBERG

29 Testimonial Knowledge — 316
    JENNIFER LACKEY

30 Memory Knowledge — 326
    SVEN BERNECKER

31 Semantic Knowledge — 335
    PETER LUDLOW

32 Scientific Knowledge — 346
    PETER ACHINSTEIN

33 Logical and Mathematical Knowledge — 358
    OTÁVIO BUENO

34 Aesthetic Knowledge — 369
    MATTHEW KIERAN

35 Moral Knowledge — 380
    ROBERT AUDI

36 Religious Knowledge — 393
    LINDA ZAGZEBSKI

PART V
Skepticism — 401

37 Pyrrhonian Skepticism — 403
    RICHARD BETT

38 Cartesian Skepticism — 414
    STEVEN LUPER

39 Skeptical Doubts about Self-Knowledge FRED DRETSKE	425
40 Skepticism about Knowledge of Other Minds ANITA AVRAMIDES	433
41 Skepticism about Inductive Knowledge JOE MORRISON	445
42 Rule-Following Skepticism ALEXANDER MILLER	454
43 Moral Skepticism GEOFFREY SAYRE-MCCORD	464

PART VI
Responses to Skepticism — 475

44 Skepticism and Anti-Realism RICHARD SCHANTZ	477
45 Skepticism and Epistemic Externalism RICHARD FUMERTON	488
46 Skepticism and Semantic Externalism ANTHONY BRUECKNER	500

PART VII
Knowledge and Knowledge Attributions — 511

47 Contrastivism ADAM MORTON	513
48 Contextualism PATRICK RYSIEW	523
49 Relativism and Knowledge Attributions JOHN MACFARLANE	536
50 Epistemic Modals JOSH DEVER	545
51 Pragmatic Encroachment JEREMY FANTL AND MATTHEW MCGRATH	558

CONTENTS

PART VIII
Formal Epistemology — 569

52 Logic and Formal Semantics for Epistemology — 571
JOHN SYMONS

53 Second-Order Knowledge — 586
CHRISTOPH KELP AND NIKOLAJ J.L.L. PEDERSEN

54 Epistemic Closure — 597
PETER BAUMANN

55 Bayesian Epistemology — 609
STEPHAN HARTMANN AND JAN SPRENGER

56 Theories of Belief Change — 621
ANDRÉ FUHRMANN

57 The Knowability Paradox — 639
JOE SALERNO

PART IX
The History of Epistemology — 653

58 Plato — 655
TIMOTHY CHAPPELL

59 Aristotle — 666
RICHARD PATTERSON

60 René Descartes — 678
STEPHEN GAUKROGER

61 John Locke — 687
E. J. LOWE

62 Gottfried Wilhelm Leibniz — 697
NICHOLAS JOLLEY

63 George Berkeley — 707
GEORGE PAPPAS

64 Thomas Reid — 717
RYAN NICHOLS

65 David Hume — 730
HELEN BEEBEE

66 Immanuel Kant ECKART FÖRSTER	741
67 Bertrand Russell WILLIAM DEMOPOULOS	750
68 Ludwig Wittgenstein MARIE MCGINN	763
69 Rudolf Carnap THOMAS UEBEL	774
70 Willard van Orman Quine RICHARD CREATH	786
71 John Langshaw Austin MARK KAPLAN	798

PART X
Metaepistemological Issues — 811

72 Epistemology and the Role of Intuitions WILLIAM G. LYCAN	813
73 Experimental Epistemology JONATHAN M. WEINBERG	823
74 Naturalistic Epistemology KLEMENS KAPPEL	836
75 Evolutionary Epistemology MICHAEL BRADIE	848
76 Pragmatist Epistemology CHERYL MISAK	861
77 Social Epistemology MARTIN KUSCH	873
78 Feminist Epistemology ALESSANDRA TANESINI	885
Index	897

NOTES ON CONTRIBUTORS

Peter Achinstein is the Jay and Jeanie Schottenstein Professor of Philosophy at Yeshiva University, and Professor of Philosophy at Johns Hopkins University. He is the author of numerous articles and books in the philosophy of science, among them *Particles and Waves* (1991), which received a Lakatos Award in 1993, *The Book of Evidence* (2001), and *Evidence, Explanation, and Realism* (2010).

Robert Audi is John A. O'Brien Professor of Philosophy at the University of Notre Dame. He writes in epistemology, philosophy of action, and philosophy of religion as well as in moral and political philosophy. His recent books include *The Architecture of Reason* (2001), *The Good in the Right* (2004), *Practical Reasoning and Ethical Decision* (Routledge, 2006). *Epistemology: A Contemporary Introduction to the Theory of Knowledge* (Routledge, 1998, 2003, 2010), *Moral Perception* (2013), and (as Editor) *The Cambridge Dictionary of Philosophy* (1995, 1999).

Anita Avramides is Reader in the Philosophy of Mind and Southover Manor Trust Fellow in Philosophy at St Hilda's College, Oxford. She is the author of *Meaning and Mind: An Examination of a Gricean Account of Language* and *Other Minds* (Routledge).

Peter Baumann is Professor of Philosophy at Swarthmore College. He received his degrees at the University of Göttingen. Peter also worked at universities in Britain, Germany, and the USA. He is interested in questions concerning knowledge, rationality and related issues. He is the author of *Erkenntnistheorie* (2002, 2006).

Helen Beebee is the Samuel Hall Professor of Philosophy at the University of Manchester, UK. Her publications include "Seeing Causing" (*Proceedings of the Aristotelian Society* 103, 2003), *Hume on Causation* (Routledge, 2006), *The Oxford Handbook of Causation* (co-edited with Christopher Hitchock and Peter Menzies, 2009), and *Metaphysics: The Key Concepts* (co-authored with Nikk Effingham and Philip Goff, 2010).

Sven Bernecker is Professor of Philosophy at the University of California, Irvine. His main areas of research are epistemology, metaphysics and philosophy of mind. He is the author of *Reading Epistemology* (2006), *The Metaphysics of Memory* (2008), and *Memory: A Philosophical Study* (2010); and editor, with Fred Dretske, of *Knowledge: Readings in Contemporary Epistemology* (2000).

NOTES ON CONTRIBUTORS

Richard Bett is Professor of Philosophy and Classics, Johns Hopkins University. He is the author of *Pyrrho, his Antecedents and his Legacy* (2000), and of translations of *Against the Logicians* (2005, with Introduction and Notes). He is also the editor of *The Cambridge Companion to Ancient Scepticism* (2010).

Alexander Bird is Professor of Philosophy at the University of Bristol. He is the author of *Philosophy of Science* (1998), *Thomas Kuhn* (2000), and *Nature's Metaphysics: Laws and Properties* (2007), and numerous articles in the epistemology and metaphysics of science.

Tim Black is Associate Professor of Philosophy at California State University, Northridge. He works mainly in epistemology, history of modern philosophy, and philosophy of mind. He is the editor, with Kelly Becker, of *The Sensitivity Principle in Epistemology* (2012).

Paul Boghossian is Silver Professor of Philosophy at New York University. He works primarily in epistemology and the philosophy of mind, although he has also written about the aesthetics of music and the concept of genocide. He is the author of *Fear of Knowledge: Against Relativism and Constructivism* (2007) and *Content and Justification: Philosophical Papers* (2008); and editor, with Christopher Peacocke, of *New Essays on the A Priori* (2000).

Laurence BonJour is Professor Emeritus of Philosophy at the University of Washington. He is the author of *The Structure of Empirical Knowledge* (1985), *In Defense of Pure Reason* (1998), *Epistemology: Classic Problems and Contemporary Responses* (2002), *Epistemic Justification: Internalism vs. Externalism, Foundations vs. Virtues* (co-authored with Ernest Sosa, 2003), and many papers in epistemology and related areas.

Michael Bradie is Professor of Philosophy at Bowling Green State University. His research interests include the philosophy of biology, the role of metaphors in science, and the role of evolutionary thinking on reshaping our understanding of traditional philosophical problems.

Anthony Brueckner is Professor of Philosophy at the University of California, Santa Barbara. He is the author of *Essays on Skepticism* (2010) and has written papers in epistemology, philosophy of mind, metaphysics, and philosophy of language.

Otávio Bueno is Professor of Philosophy at the University of Miami. His work focuses on the philosophies of mathematics, of logic, and of science. He has published articles, e.g., in *Noûs, Mind, Journal of Philosophical Logic, Synthese, Philosophia Mathematica,* and *Philosophy of Science*. He is the editor, with Øystein Linnebo, of *New Waves in Philosophy of Mathematics* (2009), and, with Susana Nuccetelli and Ofelia Schutte, of *A Companion to Latin American Philosophy* (2010).

Timothy Chappell is Professor of Philosophy at the Open University, Milton Keynes, UK, and author of books including *The Plato Reader* (1996), *Understanding Human Goods* (1998), *Reading Plato's Theaetetus* (2004), and *The Inescapable Self: Western Philosophy since Descartes* (2005), *Ethics and Experience: Life Beyond Moral Theory* (2009), and *The Moral Problem of Demandingness: Collected Essays* (2009).

NOTES ON CONTRIBUTORS

Juan Comesaña is Associate Professor of Philosophy at the University of Arizona. He works mainly in epistemology, and has published widely in this area.

Richard Creath is Professor of Philosophy and of Life Sciences at Arizona State University. He has numerous publications on Carnap and Quine. He is the editor of *Dear Carnap, Dear Van: The Quine-Carnap Correspondence and Related Work* (1990), *The Cambridge Companion to Carnap* (with Michael Friedman, 2008), and is the General Editor of the forthcoming *Collected Works of Rudolf Carnap*.

William Demopoulos is Professor Emeritus of Philosophy at the University of Western Ontario. He works on the philosophy of science, philosophy of mathematics, and the history of analytic philosophy, and he has published widely in these areas. He is the author of *Logicism and its Philosophical Legacy* (2013).

Michael DePaul is Professor of Philosophy at the University of Notre Dame. Formal citations in the article aside, he picked up what he knows about foundationalism from listening to teachers—K. Sayre, G. Pappas, M. Swain, W. Lycan, E. Sosa and most especially R. Chisholm—and talking with colleagues—R. Foley, R. Audi, and A. Plantinga. He is the author of *Balance and Refinement: Beyond Coherentism in Moral Inquiry* (1993).

Josh Dever is Associate Professor of Philosophy at the University of Texas at Austin. He works primarily in philosophy of language and philosophical logic.

Trent Dougherty is Assistant Professor of Philosophy at Baylor University. He is a graduate of the University of Missouri and the University of Rochester. He works in traditional, formal, and virtue epistemology as well as Philosophy of Religion. He is the editor of *Evidentialism and Its Discontents* (2011).

Fred Dretske is Professor Emeritus at both the University of Wisconsin and Stanford University. Presently he is a Senior Research Scholar at Duke University. His books include *Seeing and Knowing* (1969), *Knowledge and the Flow of Information* (1981), *Explaining Behavior* (1988), and *Naturalizing the Mind* (1995). His current interests are consciousness and self-knowledge.

Pascal Engel is Professor of Modern and Contemporary Philosophy at the University of Geneva and Directeur d'Études at L'École des Hautes Études en Sciences Sociales, Paris. Previously, he was Professor of Logic, Language and Knowledge at the University of Paris IV Sorbonne. His books include *The Norm of Truth* (1991), *Truth* (2002), *Ramsey, Truth and Success* (with Jerome Dokic, 2002), and *Philosophy of Psychology* (forthcoming).

Jeremy Fantl is Associate Professor of Philosophy at the University of Calgary. He works mainly on epistemology and metaphysics and is the author, with Matthew McGrath, of *Knowledge in an Uncertain World* (2009). He is the editor, with Ernest Sosa, Jaegwon Kim, and Matthew McGrath, of *Epistemology: An Anthology* (2008).

Richard Foley is Professor of Philosophy and Vice Chancellor of Strategic Planning at New York University. His main research interests focus on epistemology and epistemological issues in related fields. He is the author of *The Theory of Epistemic Rationality*

(1987), *Working Without a Net* (1993), *Intellectual Trust in Ourselves and Others* (2001), and *When Is True Belief Knowledge?* (2012).

Eckart Förster is Professor of Philosophy, German, and the Humanities at the Johns Hopkins University, Baltimore, and Honorary Professor of Philosophy at the Humboldt University Berlin, Germany. He is the author of *Kant's Final Synthesis* (2000) and *The Twenty-Five Years of Philosophy* (2012). He edited and translated (with Michael Rosen) *Kant's Opus postumum* (1993) and is the editor of *The Course of Remembrance and Other Essays on Hölderlin* (by Dieter Henrich, 1997), *Kant's Transcendental Deductions: The Three Critiques and the Opus postumum* (1989), and *Spinoza and German Idealism* (with Yitzhak Y. Melamed, 2012).

Bryan Frances is Associate Professor of Philosophy at Fordham University. He works mainly on epistemology and metaphysics, and is the author of *Scepticism Comes Alive* (2005) and *Philosophical Renegades: The Epistemology of Philosophical Disagreement* (forthcoming).

André Fuhrmann is Professor of Logic and Philosophy of Science in the Department of Philosophy at Goethe University in Frankfurt am Main, Germany. He is the author of *An Essay on Contraction* (1995) and numerous articles in philosophy and logic. He is presently working on a book on the justification of belief changes.

Richard Fumerton is F. Wendell Miller Professor of Philosophy at the University of Iowa. He has wide-ranging research interests, taking in epistemology, history of philosophy, metaphysics, and ethics. He is the author of a number of books, including *Epistemology* (2009), *Realism and the Correspondence Theory of Truth* (2002), *Metaepistemology and Skepticism* (1996), and *Metaphysical and Epistemological Problems of Perception* (1985).

Stephen Gaukroger is Professor of History of Philosophy and History of Science at the University of Sydney, and Chair in Philosophy at the University of Aberdeen. He is the author of several books including *Descartes, An Intellectual Biography* (1995), *Francis Bacon and the Transformation of Early-Modern Philosophy* (2001), *Descartes' System of Natural Philosophy* (2002), *The Emergence of a Scientific Culture: Science and the Shaping of Modernity* (2006), and *Objectivity: A Very Short Introduction* (2012).

Sanford Goldberg is Professor of Philosophy at Northwestern University. He works in the areas of epistemology and the philosophy of mind and language. He is the author of *Anti-Individualism: Mind and Language, Knowledge and Justification* (2007), and *Relying on Others: An Essay in Epistemology* (2010).

John Greco is the Leonard and Elizabeth Eslick Chair in Philosophy at Saint Louis University. He received his Ph.D. from Brown University in 1989. His publications include: *Achieving Knowledge: A Virtue-Theoretic Account of Epistemic Normativity* (2010); *The Oxford Handbook of Skepticism*, ed. (2008); *Sosa and his Critics*, ed. (2004); and *Putting Skeptics in Their Place: The Nature of Skeptical Arguments and Their Role in Philosophical Inquiry* (2000).

NOTES ON CONTRIBUTORS

Stephen R. Grimm is Associate Professor of Philosophy at Fordham University. His main areas of research are epistemology, the philosophy of science, and value theory.

Thomas Grundmann is Professor of Philosophy at Cologne University, Germany. He has published several articles on epistemology and philosophy of mind. Among his books are *Analytische Einführung in die Erkenntnistheorie* (2008), *Der Wahrheit auf der Spur* (2003), and *Analytische Transzendentalphilosophie: Eine Kritik* (1994). In his current research he is working on a priori knowledge, intuitions, thought-experiments and experimental philosophy. He is the editor of *Experimental Philosophy and Its Critics* (with Joachim Horvath, 2012), *Erkenntnistheorie: Positionen zwischen Tradition und Gegenwart* (2003), and *Philosophie der Skepsis* (with Karsten Sthber, 1996).

Stephan Hartmann (Ph.D. (Philosophy) at the University of Giessen, 1995) is Chair of Philosophy of Science in the Faculty of Philosophy, Philosophy of Science and the Study of Religion at the University of Munich, Alexander von Humboldt Professor, and Co-Director of the Munich Center for Mathematical Philosophy (MCMP). He has published extensively on philosophy of science and the use of formal methods in epistemology. His publications include *Bayesian Epistemology* (with Luc Bovens, 2003) and *Bayesian Philosophy of Science* (with Jan Sprenger, forthcoming).

Stephen Hetherington is Professor of Philosophy at the University of New South Wales, in Sydney, Australia. He has written several books, including *Good Knowledge, Bad Knowledge* (2001), *Reality? Knowledge? Philosophy!: An Introduction to Metaphysics and Epistemology* (2003), *Self-Knowledge* (2007), *Yes, But How Do You Know? Introducing Philosophy Through Sceptical Ideas* (2009), and *How to Know: A Practicalist Conception of Knowledge* (2011). He has edited *Epistemology Futures* (2006), *Aspects of Knowing* (2006), and *Epistemology: The Key Thinkers* (2012).

Nicholas Jolley is Professor Emeritus of Philosophy, University of California, Irvine. He is the author of *Leibniz and Locke: A Study of the New Essays on Human Understanding* (1984), *The Light of the Soul: Theories of Ideas in Leibniz, Malebranche, and Descartes* (1990), *Locke: His Philosophical Thought* (1999), and *Leibniz* (2005). He is also the editor of the *Cambridge Companion to Leibniz* (1995) and, with translator David Scott, of *Nicolas Malebranche: Dialogues on Metaphysics* (1997).

Mark Kaplan is Professor of Philosophy at Indiana University. He is the author of *Decision Theory as Philosophy* (1996), as well as articles and book chapters on epistemology, on decision theory, and on the philosophy of J.L. Austin.

Klemens Kappel is Associate Professor of Philosophy at the University of Copenhagen. His research interests are in epistemology, in particular social epistemology, but he has also published in ethics and metaethics.

Christoph Kelp is Junior Research Professor at the Katholieke Universiteit Leuven, Belgium. His research focuses on a variety of issues in epistemology and his publications include papers on virtue epistemology (*Synthese*), contrastivism (*Philosophical Studies*), and the knowability paradox.

NOTES ON CONTRIBUTORS

Matthew Kieran is Professor of Philosophy and the Arts at the University of Leeds. He is the author of *Revealing Art* (2005) and currently researches on issues at the intersection of aesthetics, epistemology and ethics, especially concerning aesthetic virtues and vices.

Peter D. Klein is Professor of Philosophy at Rutgers University. He was one of the developers of the defeasibility theory of knowledge and he argued that it provides an adequate response to some forms of skepticism. Recently, he has defended infinitism as the correct response to the epistemic regress problem.

Martin Kusch is Professor of Philosophy at the University of Vienna. Prior to taking up this appointment he was Professor of Philosophy and Sociology of Science at the Department of History and Philosophy of Science at Cambridge University. He has wide-ranging research interests, including epistemology, philosophy of language and philosophy of the social sciences. His books include *Knowledge by Agreement* (Oxford University Press, 2002) and *A Sceptical Guide to Meaning and Rules* (Acumen, 2006).

Jonathan L. Kvanvig is Distinguished Professor of Philosophy at Baylor University, with prior appointments at the University of Missouri and Texas A&M University. He works on metaphysics, epistemology, philosophy of religion, and philosophy of logic and language. He is the general editor of the *Oxford Studies in Philosophy of Religion* series and his recent books include *The Knowability Paradox* (Oxford University Press, 2006) and *The Value of Knowledge and the Pursuit of Understanding* (Cambridge University Press, 2003).

Jennifer Lackey is Professor of Philosophy at Northwestern University. She is the author of *Learning from Words: Testimony as a Source of Knowledge* (2006, Oxford University Press) and her current research focuses on disagreement, norms of assertion, and the value of knowledge.

E. J. Lowe is Professor of Philosophy at the University of Durham. He works mainly on metaphysics, the philosophy of mind and action, the philosophy of logic, the philosophy of language, and early modern philosophy, and he has published widely in these areas. His recent books include *The Four-Category Ontology* (Oxford University Press, 2006) and *Personal Agency* (Oxford University Press, 2008). He is a General Editor of the *Cambridge Studies in Philosophy* monograph series.

Peter Ludlow is Professor of Philosophy at the Northwestern University. Before moving to Northwestern, Ludlow taught at The University of Toronto, The University of Michigan, The State University of New York at Stony Brook and was Visiting Professor of Philosophy at Syracuse University and Cornell University. He has done interdisciplinary work on the interface of linguistics and philosophy, and has extended that work to topics in metaphysics (e.g. the philosophy of time) and epistemology (e.g. contextualism).

Steven Luper is Professor and Chair of the Department of Philosophy at Trinity University. His main research areas are epistemology and the philosophy of death, and he has published widely in these fields.

NOTES ON CONTRIBUTORS

William G. Lycan is William Rand Kenan, Jr. Professor of Philosophy at the University of North Carolina. He is author of eight books, including *Logical Form in Natural Language* (1984), *Knowing Who* (with Steven Boër, 1986), *Consciousness* (1987), *Judgement and Justification* (1988), and *Real Conditionals* (2001).

Michael P. Lynch is Professor of Philosophy at the University of Connecticut. He is the author of *Truth in Context* (1998), *True to Life* (2004), and *Truth as One and Many* (2009), and *In Praise of Reason* (2012).

John MacFarlane Professor of Philosophy at the University of California, Berkeley. He has written extensively on the philosophy of logic and the philosophy of language, and is currently working on a book on relative truth and its applications.

Marie McGinn is Professor of Philosophy at the University of East Anglia, UK, and Professor Emeritus of Philosophy at the University of York. She works on Wittgenstein, epistemology, philosophy of mind, early analytic philosophy and early modern philosophy. Her books include *Sense and Certainty* (Blackwell, 1989) and *Elucidating the Tractatus* (Oxford University Press, 2006).

Matthew McGrath is Associate Professor of Philosophy at the University of Missouri-Columbia. He works mainly on epistemology and metaphysics and is the author (with Jeremy Fantl) of *Knowledge in an Uncertain World* (Oxford University Press, 2009).

Timothy McGrew is Professor of Philosophy at Western Michigan University. His research interests include the history and philosophy of science, probability, and epistemology. He is the author of *The Foundations of Knowledge* (Littlefield Adams, 1995) and co-author of *Internalism and Epistemology* (Routledge, 2007) and *The Philosophy of Science: An Historical Anthology* (Wiley-Blackwell, 2009) as well as numerous articles in *Mind, The Monist, Analysis, Erkenntnis, British Journal for the Philosophy of Science*, and other journals.

Alexander Miller is Professor of Philosophy at the University of Otago, New Zealand. He works mainly in the areas of philosophy of language and mind, metaethics and metaphysics and has published widely on these topics.

Cheryl Misak is Professor of Philosophy at the University of Toronto, where she also holds the position of Vice-President and Provost. Her primary research interests are in pragmatism, epistemology and moral philosophy. Her books include *Truth, Politics, Morality* (Routledge, 2000) and *Truth and the End of Inquiry* (Oxford University Press, 1990).

Daniel M. Mittag is Assistant Professor of Philosophy at Albion College in Albion, MI. He works in the areas of epistemology and the philosophy of mind.

Joe Morrison works on epistemological issues associated with W.V. Quine, particularly Quine's holism and naturalism. Joe got his PhD in Philosophy from the University of Sheffield in 2008. He is presently a Lecturer in Philosophy at Queen's University, Belfast.

NOTES ON CONTRIBUTORS

Adam Morton is Canada Research Chair in Epistemology and Decision Theory at the University of Alberta. His two most recent books are *The Importance of Being Understood* (Routledge 2002) and *On Evil* (Routledge 2004). He is currently working on a book on the intellectual virtues of limitation-management which has the working title *Of Human Boundedness*.

Ram Neta Professor of Philosophy at the University of North Carolina at Chapel Hill. He specializes in epistemology and is currently at work on a book on the nature of knowledge.

Ryan Nichols is Associate Professor of Philosophy at the California State University, Fullerton. He is a specialist in Early Modern with an emphasis on the Scottish Enlightenment. He recently published two books, *Thomas Reid's Theory of Perception* (OUP, 2007) and *Philosophy Through Science Fiction* (Routledge, 2008).

Erik J. Olsson occupies the Chair in Theoretical Philosophy at Lund University, Sweden. His main published areas of research are epistemology and philosophy of science, but he has also written on metaphilosophy, metaphysics, philosophical logic and the history of logic.

George Pappas is Professor of Philosophy, emeritus, at Ohio State University. He is the author of *Berkeley's Thought* (2000), and of numerous articles on Berkeley, Locke, Hume, and Reid.

Richard Patterson is Professor of Philosophy at Emory University. He is the author of *Image and Reality in Plato's Metaphysics* (Hackett, 1985) and *Aristotle's Modal Logic* (Cambridge, 1995) and a variety of articles in Ancient Philosophy. His commentary on Plato's *Parmenides* is forthcoming as part of the Archelogos Project.

Nikolaj J.L.L. Pedersen is Assistant Professor of Philosophy at Underwood International College, Yonsei University, South Korea. His main research areas are epistemology, metaphysics, truth, and the philosophy of logic and mathematics. He is the editor, with Cory D. Wright, of *Truth and Pluralism: Current Debates* (Oxford University Press, forthcoming) and *New Waves in the Philosophy of Truth* (Palgrave Macmillan, forthcoming).

Patrick Rysiew is Associate Professor of Philosophy at the University of Victoria. His primary research interests are in epistemology, including its points of intersection with certain issues in philosophy of language and psychology.

Joe Salerno is Associate Professor of Philosophy at Saint Louis University. He works on epistemology, metaphysics, and philosophy of language and logic, and has published widely in these areas. He is presently writing a book entitled *Impossible Thoughts* with Berit Brogaard.

Richard Schantz is Professor of Philosophy at the University of Siegen, Germany. He is working in epistemology, in the philosophy of language and mind, and in metaphysics. He is author of *Der sinnliche Gehalt der Wahrnehmung* and of *Wahrheit, Referenz und Realismus*. He is editor of *What is Truth?* and of *The Externalist Challenge*.

NOTES ON CONTRIBUTORS

Eric Schwitzgebel is Professor of Philosophy at University of California, Riverside. His primary current research interests are belief (including "in-between" cases of believing), consciousness (including the inaccuracy of introspective reports), and moral psychology (including the moral behavior of ethics professors).

David Sosa is Professor of Philosophy at the University of Texas at Austin.

Jan Sprenger (Ph.D. (Philosophy) at the University of Bonn, 2008) is Assistant Professor of Philosophy at Tilburg University (since 2008). Jan's work focuses on philosophy of statistics, philosophy of probability, decision theory and formal modeling in social epistemology.

John Symons is Associate Professor of Philosophy at the University of Texas at El Paso. His work spans logic, philosophy of mind, epistemology, and metaphysics but focuses on the problem of emergence. In addition to numerous articles and chapters he is the author or editor of eight books including *On Dennett*, (2002) *The Routledge Companion to Philosophy of Psychology*, (2009) *Logic Epistemology and the Unity of Science* (2004). Since 2002 he has been editor of *Synthese*.

Alessandra Tanesini is Professor of Philosophy at Cardiff University. Her research interests include epistemology, feminism, philosophy of mind and language, and Wittgenstein. She is the author of *An Introduction to Feminist Epistemologies* (Blackwell, 1999) and of *Wittgenstein: A Feminist Introduction* (Polity, 2004).

Thomas Uebel is Professor of Philosophy at the University of Manchester, England. His research concerns the history of analytical philosophy with particular attention to philosophy of science and epistemology and he has published widely on these subjects.

Jonathan M. Weinberg is Associate Professor of Philosophy and a member of the Cognitive Science Program at Indiana University, Bloomington. He received his Ph.D. in Philosophy from Rutgers University in 2002, and has published on epistemology, the philosophy of cognitive science, aesthetics, and experimental philosophy.

Dennis Whitcomb is Associate Professor of Philosophy at Western Washington University. He works primarily on epistemic value and has recently published in *Philosophical Studies*, *Pacific Philosophical Quarterly*, *Philosophy and Phenomenological Research*, and other venues.

Timothy Williamson is Wykeham Professor of Logic at Oxford University, a Fellow of New College, Oxford, a Fellow of the British Academy and Honorary Foreign Member of the American Academy of Arts and Sciences. He has published *Identity and Discrimination* (1990), *Vagueness* (1994), *Knowledge and its Limits* (2000), *The Philosophy of Philosophy* (2007) and over 120 articles.

Hamid Vahid is Professor of Philosophy and the Head of the Analytic Philosophy Faculty at the Institute for Fundamental Sciences in Tehran, Iran.

NOTES ON CONTRIBUTORS

Linda Zagzebski is Kingfisher College Chair of the Philosophy of Religion and Ethics and George Lynn Cross Research Professor at Oklahoma University. She works mainly in the philosophy of religion, epistemology, and virtue ethics, with a particular focus on the intersection of epistemology and ethical theory. She is the author of a number of books, including *Virtues of the Mind* (Cambridge University Press, 1996), and is currently writing a book on epistemic authority.

PREFACE

Epistemology has always been one of the most central and important areas of philosophy, one which overlaps and intersects with all the different regions of our ancient discipline. More recently, however, epistemology has gone from being a solid mainstay of the philosophical landscape to being right at the forefront of contemporary debate. Accordingly, while this volume has been designed to offer the reader a sense of the history of epistemology and of those topics which have always been a constant fixture of epistemological discussion (such as the problem of skepticism), at the same time we have also ensured that it provides an overview of the main cutting-edge issues in the contemporary literature too (such as the problem of disagreement, or experimental epistemology). The result is more than 75 articles, organized within 10 sub-topics and all written by experts in the relevant field, which comprehensively explore both familiar and new topics in epistemology.

Assembling a body of articles of this size is, of course, a substantial undertaking, and we would like to take this opportunity to thank Andrew Beck and Michael Andrews at Routledge, our copy-editor Rachel Hutchings, and Colin Morgan of Swales & Willis who assisted us throughout this process. We are also grateful for the numerous anonymous referees who helped improve the quality of the entries. Last but not least, we would like to thank the contributors to this volume for the care and dedication that they devoted to their entries.

Sven Bernecker & Duncan Pritchard
Irvine, California & Edinburgh, Scotland
May 2010

Part I
FOUNDATIONAL CONCEPTS

1
TRUTH
Michael P. Lynch

Philosophical work on truth tends to cluster around three broad and interrelated questions: Does truth have a nature? What sort of nature does it have? And, how—in the harsh light of the semantic paradoxes—can we formally account for the logical behavior of truth?

This essay will be concerned with the metaphysics of truth—in short, the first two questions. It will survey some traditional theories that think truth is worthy of deep metaphysical investigation, some deflationary accounts that disagree, and some more recent accounts which offer a more pluralist perspective.

Correspondence and Representation

Truth is a famously perplexing idea, but most of us share some common assumptions about it. One such truth about truth is that it is objective. To speak truly is to "say of what is, that it is," as Aristotle put it (1993). Alternatively:

> *Objectivity*: The belief that p is true if, and only if, with respect to the belief that p, things are as they are believed to be.

The most venerable theory of truth, the correspondence theory, uses the Objectivity intuition as a starting point. But like the other traditional theories we'll discuss, it isn't content to end there. It aims to explain the Objectivity truism by giving a general account of the nature of truth. According to that account, beliefs are true just when they correspond to reality. In the early twentieth century, for example, Wittgenstein (1922) and Russell (1966) developed a version of the correspondence theory of truth according to which beliefs (or their propositional contents) were true in virtue of sharing a common structure with the facts. According to this view, beliefs such as the *cat is on the mat* exhibit a certain form; and objects (cats, mats) and relations (*being on*) compose basic facts that also exhibit a logical form or configuration. Thus a belief corresponds as a whole to a fact just when they share the same form or structure.

While this sort of view seems to explain the truth of simple beliefs about cats and mats well enough, it faces problems with other sorts of facts. Consider the truth that there are no unicorns. Is there a negative fact that makes this true? It is unclear whether there are any such facts. Moreover, many philosophers have wondered about the nature of facts themselves. It seems that facts are either constituted by objects and properties (and relations) or they are not. If they are, then for reasons of ontological parsimony, we must be given a serious motivation for taking them to be distinct entities over and above that which composes them. It is difficult to see what really compelling motivation could be supplied. If they are not constituted by objects and their properties, then what is their nature exactly? As Strawson (1950) pointed out, they begin to look suspiciously like the mere shadows of statements.

Partly because of these worries, contemporary theoretical descendents of the traditional correspondence idea express its central truism slightly differently. First, the truth of a belief is defined in terms of the representational features of its component concepts (what I will here call "denotation"). Thus in the case of a belief whose content has the simple predicational structure *a is F*, we get:

> REPRESENT: The belief that a is F is true if and only if the object denoted by <a> has the property denoted by <F>.

The basic thought is that beliefs are true because their components stand in certain representational relations to reality and that reality is a certain way (Devitt, 1997). Adopting machinery made familiar with Tarski (1944; see also Field, 1972) the representationalist then applies this insight to beliefs with more complicated structures. The result is a view according to which the truth of complex beliefs is recursively defined in terms of the truth of simpler beliefs and the rules for logical connectives, while less complex beliefs "correspond to reality" in the sense that their component parts—concepts—themselves represent objects and properties.

The second part of any representational view of truth is a theory of how concepts denote objects and properties. A toy example would be:

> CAUSAL: <cat> denotes cats = cats, cause, under appropriate conditions, mental tokenings of <cat>.

In short, truth is defined in terms of representation, representation is defined in terms of denotation, and denotation is defined as a property that either is, or supervenes on natural relations like those specified in CAUSAL. Thus, if we say that an object or property, which, under appropriate conditions, causes (or its instances cause) mental tokenings of some concept "causally maps" that concept:

> CC (Causal-correspondence): The belief that a is F is true if and only if the object causally mapped by <a> has the property causally mapped by <F>.

There are various objections and challenges one might raise against any particular representational theory of truth. But over and above these theory-specific problems, representational theories all face a problem of scope. This is because such theories have metaphysical implications. Take (CC). It is committed to the idea that the object and properties represented are capable of entering into at least indirect causal interaction with our minds. This sounds reasonable when we concentrate on examples involving ordinary objects like cats and cars. But it is highly implausible as a global principle. Consider propositions such as *two and two are four* or *torture is wrong*. Under the assumption that truth is always and everywhere causal correspondence, it is a vexing question how these true thoughts *can* be true. That two and two are four is unimpeachable, but even granting that numbers are objects, how can any thought of mine be in causal contact with something like a number? Numbers, whatever else they turn out to be, are presumably not objects with which we can causally interact. Moral propositions represent a slightly different puzzle: torture is certainly wrong, but it is difficult to know how wrongness—even if we grant that it is a property—can be a natural property with which we can causally interact.

A representationalist can try to avoid the scope problem by watering down his theory of course: "a belief corresponds to reality just when things are as they are believed to be" would be one example. But that just restates Objectivity, it doesn't explain it. The more substantive the correspondence theory becomes—as when it is seen as part of a larger theory of representation—the more it is vulnerable to the scope problem, and the less plausible it is as a universal theory of the underlying nature of truth.

Pragmatism and Superwarrant

A second familiar truth about truth is that it is the aim, or end, of inquiry. By "inquiry" I mean simply the process of asking and answering questions. Truth—in the sense of true beliefs and judgments—is clearly a goal of this process: unless the situation is highly atypical, when I ask you where my car keys are I want to know where they are—I want the truth. In pursuing inquiry of course, we pursue truth only indirectly by explicitly pursuing reasons and evidence. But we care about giving reasons, supplying justification for our beliefs, because beliefs which are so justified are more likely to be true, even if they aren't guaranteed to be such. And this fact explains why, when we don't know what is true, we steer by the evidence, even if evidence sometimes steers us wrong. That is,

End of Inquiry: Other things being equal, true beliefs are a goal of inquiry.

Where correspondence theories give pride of place to Objectivity, their historical rivals, the coherence and pragmatist accounts of truth, privilege End of Inquiry. Indeed, one of the most well-known versions of the theory, Peirce's pragmatist view of truth, simply identifies truth with that end: "The opinion which is fated to be ultimately agreed to by all who investigate is what we mean by truth" (Peirce, 1878/2001: 206). Rather than saying that we agree on what is true because it is true, Peirce's thought is that what is true is so because we agree on it. No mention is made of our thought's having to represent or correspond to some independent world of objects. There may be such a world, but if so, truth is shorn free of it on this account.

One obvious problem with Peirce's view is that it holds truth hostage to the existence of an actual end of inquiry—a time when all questions are presumably settled. It seems highly unlikely, to put it mildly, that there will be such a time. Hilary Putnam (1981 and 1990) modified the account to avoid this point:

(PT): The proposition that p is true if and only if the proposition that p would be warranted to believe in ideal epistemic circumstances for assessing the proposition that p.

This is a significant improvement over Peirce's view. It isn't committed to the actuality of ideal epistemic circumstances; and it treats such circumstances as tailor-made for each individual belief. But Putnam's view notoriously faces its own problems. One such problem is that the view founders on the so-called conditional fallacy (Plantinga, 1982; Wright, 2001). This is a problem that can plague attempts to define a categorical statement in terms of a subjunctive conditional. How the problem applies here can be brought out if we take the proposition in question in (PT) to be

    (not-I): Ideal epistemic circumstances for assessing this proposition will never obtain.

Substituting (not-I) in for "p" in (PT), we arrive at the conclusion that (not-I) is true if and only if it would be warranted in ideal circumstances for assessing (not-I). But if it were warranted in such circumstances it would be false. So, intuitively, (not-I) can only be true if it is false, if (PT) is our theory of truth.

How might such problems be avoided? One reasonable idea, developed by Crispin Wright (1992) is to define a true proposition not as one that would be warranted to believe in ideal conditions, but as one that is warranted to believe in the ordinary sense and remains warranted no matter how our information is expanded or improved. Call this *superwarrant*. To be superwarranted is to be continually warranted without defeat. Note that the idea of superwarrant does not require an idealized "end of inquiry." A superwarranted belief is one that is warranted by some state of information available to ordinary inquirers, which, in fact, would never be defeated or undermined by subsequent increases of information also available to ordinary inquirers. Moreover, superwarrant is a stable property: if a belief is superwarranted, then it is superwarranted at any stage of inquiry. Thus, a friend of the original pragmatist insight might suggest:

    (SW): A belief is true if and only if it is superwarranted.

Like its rival the correspondence theory, (SW) faces a problem of scope. (SW) implies that it must be feasible to have warrant for any true proposition. If we were to focus on only some kinds of truths, this consequence may not seem too bad. Consider, truths about what is or isn't funny. It is odd to think that a joke is funny even if no one will ever have warrant in believing that it is—in other words, even if nobody ever laughs. Likewise for legal truths. It is difficult to see how a proposition of law might be true even if no evidence is ever available for (or against) it—even in principle. For otherwise, it would be possible for there to be a true proposition of the form "x is illegal" even if no one would ever be warranted in believing that it is, or is not legal. And that in turn means that there could be unknowably illegal actions—actions I might even be doing right now. But that seems absurd.

So an epistemic constraint seems plausible in the case of some normative truths at least. But it seems false when applied across the board. Consider propositions such as *the number of stars in the universe right now is even*; or *it rained 15,000 years ago on this spot*. Surely there could not be evidence for or against such propositions. Yet they might be true. Humility in the face of the size of the universe seems to demand that. And yet (SW) would seem to require us to deny that such propositions can be true.

The basic problem can again be put in terms of a dilemma: Either the pragmatist admits that her theory has an absurd consequence—in this case, the consequence that all truths are at some point warranted—or admits that her view has limited scope.

Deflationary Theories

Traditional accounts such as the correspondence and pragmatist theories take very different truisms about truth as their starting point. But they share a methodology. Both assume that truth's real essence underlies these truisms and explains them. They both try to reduce truth to some other property—such as causal mapping, or superwarrant—thought to constitute truth's real essence.

Many philosophers have come to think that the idea that truth has a real essence is misguided. Deflationary views are so-called because they deflate the pretensions of the more traditional theories. They differ widely in their details, but most share at least two key tenets. First, deflationists hold that the concept of truth is merely a logical device. They generally base this claim on the fact that we are inclined to a priori infer the proposition that snow is white from the proposition that it is true that snow is white and vice versa. As a reflection of this fact, deflationists typically give pride of place in their account of truth to some form of the equivalence or T-schema:

TS: <p> is true if and only if p.

Thus Paul Horwich (1998) for example, holds that our grasp of the concept of truth consists in our inclination to accept the instances of TS. Yet the concept one so grasps, Horwich thinks, is merely a device for generalization; it allows us to generalize over potentially infinite strings of claims. Instead of saying that Tom says that grass is green and grass is green; and Tom says that roses are red and roses are red ... and so on for everything Tom says, I can employ the concept of truth and simply point out that everything Tom says is true. If I had a mind big enough to encompass infinite conjunctions, I wouldn't need the concept of truth. But being human, I do. The truth concept is an instrument that allows us to overcome our natural cognitive shortcomings. And that is all that it is.

So our concept of truth is a logical device; our grasp of that concept is revealed in our grasp of the instances of the T-schema. From this, the deflationist concludes that TS and its instances are the only facts about truth one needs to know in order to understand what truth is. Any other fact about truth can be deduced from them together with relevant non truth-theoretical facts. No further metaphysical investigation is needed to tell us anything about the property.

Deflationists often put this point by saying that the role of the truth concept is expressive not explanatory. Truth does not play a significant explanatory role. By a "significant" explanatory role, I mean that truth doesn't figure in any explanations except in its role as a useful generalization device. This is not to deny that the truth concept can't figure in explanations at all. It can, just so long as the concept in question is the deflationary one—that is, its role is limited to acting as a device for making generalizations over potentially infinite strings of propositions. But for deflationists, the fact that a proposition has the property of truth can't be an essential, primitive part of an explanation for some other phenomena. If it was, we would have reason, pace deflationism, to think that it is worthy of substantive investigation.

These two points—that the concept of truth is a mere logical device and that truth plays no significant explanatory role—jointly constitute the core of the deflationary position. Beyond this point, differences between various deflationary views emerge. Some views, for example, scorn propositions, preferring to talk about sentence truth, while others prefer utterances (Field, 1986; Quine, 1990). Deflationists also differ over how to *justify* our commitment to the instances of TS. Thus some deflationary views take it that TS and its instances are simply the consequence of the fact that the concept of truth is *strongly semantically* transparent: <p> and <<p> is true> are, in non-opaque contexts, synonymous, intersubstitutable or "cognitively equivalent" (Beall, 2005; Field, 1986; Ramsey, 2001). Others deny that the instances of TS need justification (Horwich, 1998). They instead claim that the non-paradoxical instances of TS are themselves epistemically and explanatorily basic, and our grasp of the concept of truth is contained in our implicit acceptance of the non-paradoxical instances.

Whatever its specific form, deflationism is a very attractive view. Its most obvious benefit is its relative ontological simplicity. Since truth is metaphysically transparent, there is one less property we need to have a theory of. It captures the semantic appearances, as it were, without positing any mysterious relation like "correspondence" or "superwarrant." And thus it completely avoids the scope problem. The scope problem only arises for views which specify some property P that all and only true propositions have which makes them true. Deflationists deny there is any such property; or if they do allow there is such a property, it will not be a property that will rule out any particular type of proposition from being true. They allow that any proposition that is fit to figure in an instance of TS can be true.

These are significant benefits. But deflationist theories also have considerable costs. Some of these costs concern problems associated with particular versions of deflationism. Some of these concern how best to state some deflationists' views, or even whether you can coherently state them all (David, 1994); others are about whether some deflationists can account for generalizations about truth and involving truth (Gupta, 1993).

Over and above specific worries about particular deflationary views, however, there are at least two objections to the overall approach worth thinking about. First, there is the question of whether deflationism can account for all the common truths about truth. One such common truism is that truth is normative of belief. That is,

> Norm of belief (NB): It is prima facie correct to believe <p> if and only if <p> is true.

Normative facts are those that are "fraught with ought" in Sellars' phrase. And, arguably, any fact that implies ought-involving facts is a normative fact. It is trivial that, other things being equal, I ought to believe what is correct, and thus by (NB), other things being equal, I ought to believe what is true. Since any claim that implies oughts in this way is presumably normative, (NB) is a normative fact about truth.

Deflationists sometimes respond that Norm of Belief is not really about truth at all (Horwich, 2001). Their argument is that one can derive (NB) from instances of TS together with instances of the premise that

> (B) It is prima facie correct to believe <p> if and only if p.

Thus, it is claimed, (NB) doesn't really display a normative fact about truth. Rather, it simply illustrates how the concept of truth can be used as a logical device—in order to generalize over the instances of schemas like (B) for example.

It should be noted that in order for this point to be persuasive, it must be convincing that instances of (B) are not about truth. But why think they aren't? It isn't sufficient to claim that (B) or its instances do not mention the word "true." Indeed, if (B) were said to be a good paraphrase of (NB), then we would have just as much reason to think (B) was about truth as we do for thinking (NB) is about truth. Good paraphrases carry their ontological commitments with them (otherwise they wouldn't be good paraphrases).

Moreover, it isn't plausible to simply claim that (B) or (NB) is about belief and not about truth. Belief and truth are interrelated concepts—thus it is more plausible to say that (NB) or (B) tell us something about truth *and* belief. They tell us that belief's standard of correctness is truth and that truth is the standard of correctness of belief.

Even putting the above point aside, it is difficult to see why we would accept instances of (B) in the absence of already being committed to (NB). For the list of (B)'s instances is an infinite list of normative prescriptions; a list of little belief norms as it were: it is correct to believe snow is white iff snow is white, correct to believe roses are red iff roses are red and so on. Why should we accept each of these individual norms? Individual normative prescriptions are justified by general normative principles. Consider promising: it is correct to keep your promise to Tom for the same reason that it is correct to keep your promise to Bridget; because it is correct, other things being equal, to keep your promises. So, too, with truth: it is prima facie correct to believe that grass is green for the same reason it is correct to believe that snow is white; because it is prima facie correct to believe what is true. The *general normative principle*—(NB) in this case—is in the epistemic driver's seat. Consequently we are justified in accepting instances of (B) only in virtue of accepting instances of (NB). So even if—as I just argued was implausible—(B) isn't about truth, it can't be used to derive (NB). And, given the close tie previously noted between (NB) and the truism that truth is a worthy goal of inquiry, it seems equally dubious that that normative principle could also be derived from TS alone. And this should hardly be surprising: the normative character of a complex concept like truth is usually thought to be irreducible to its purely descriptive character (see Lynch, 2004).

So one concern we should have about deflationism is whether it can fully account for all our common truths about truth. A less direct but possibly more fundamental worry is this. Deflationists of all varieties must remove truth from the philosopher's toolbox. They must convince us to give up truth as an explanatory notion, by which to explain the *nature* of meaning, or knowledge, or the success of our actions. They must do so because, as noted above, it is sufficient for P to be a real and distinct property if P is part of a significant and informative explanation for some phenomenon Q. When it is, we can say that P is an explanatory property. The thought is a familiar one: something is real if we need to postulate it in order to make sense of something else that is real. Thus, if truth were part of an informative, substantive explanation of some other phenomenon of interest, we'd have good reason to think that there is more to say about it than the deflationist wishes to admit.

This point also bears on one of deflationism's benefits—ontological simplicity. A fact about theory building is that simplifying a theory in one way tends to complicate it in others. That is so here. To mention just one example: while deflationists (may) have a simpler ontology of truth, they do so at the cost of having a more complex theory of the nature of meaning and mental content, or no such theory at all. In particular, as several prominent deflationists have highlighted themselves (Brandom, 2001; Horwich, 1998) they are barred from giving a truth-conditional account of the underlying nature of meaning and content. That is not a problem if a truth-conditional account is mistaken. But it is very much an open issue. And it seems that we should not prejudge a significant issue in linguistics by way of adopting a particular theory of truth.

The fact that deflationists must remove truth from our explanatory toolbox is a significant price to pay for deflationism. Yet the view has significant benefits—chief among them being that it avoids the problems of traditional theories. It would be good, therefore, if we could find a theory that had this benefit but allowed us to retain truth as an explanatory tool.

Functionalism and Pluralism about Truth

Traditional theories get into trouble, recall, because they try to reduce truth to some other property, such as correspondence, which allegedly explains why it is objective, the end of inquiry, and the norm of belief. But such views all end up facing the scope problem. It seems as if, for any given property alleged to be identical with truth, there are propositions we believe are true (or capable of being so) but which lack that property.

In the face of these problems, one thought is to abandon a reductive analysis of truth in favor of a broadly functionalist account, according to which the secret to what truth is lies with what it does. Instead of trying to explain truisms such as Objectivity or End of Inquiry in terms of something more fundamental, the functionalist suggests that we understand them as revealing an aspect of truth's *functional role*. Roughly speaking, "portraying things as they are" and "being the end of inquiry" are part of the truth-role. They are part of what beliefs which have the property of truth do. Likewise with Norm of Belief: making a proposition correct to believe is just part of truth's job. In short, the thought is that the truisms tell us that true propositions are those that have a property that has a certain function in our cognitive economy.

Playing a functional role amounts to satisfying a description, one that picks out certain features possessed by anything that plays the role. Such descriptions are like job descriptions. Writing a job description involves listing the tasks anyone who has that job must do, and specifying how that job relates to others in the immediate economic vicinity. We define the job in terms of its place in a larger network of jobs, all of which are understood in relation to each other, and by weighting some aspects of the job as more important or crucial than others. In the philosophy of mind, where functionalist analyses are commonplace, so-called "analytic" functionalists take job-descriptions for mental properties to be given by our implicit folk beliefs about those properties. In the case of a property like pain, these include truisms like "the threat of pain causes fear" and "if you are in pain, you may say 'ouch'" and "if you are hit in the head, you will probably be in pain" and so on. These platitudes tell us that a property plays the pain-role when it is related to certain other mental, behavioral and experiential properties of an organism.

Likewise, we can take the truth-role to be carved out by our common truths about truth. These truisms form a theoretical structure of sorts—one which illustrates the relationships between true propositions and propositions with various other properties such as warrant, belief, correctness, and so on. These features, as in the parallel case of functional properties in the philosophy of mind, will not be primarily causal in nature, but quasi-logical and explanatory. But the basic suggestion in both cases is the same: the unique relations that truth bears to other properties nonetheless suffice to pin it down by jointly specifying the truth-role.

This allows us to give truth-conditions for the application of the truth concept itself as follows:

(F) For every x, x is true if, and only if, x has a property that plays the truth-role.

Moreover, the functionalist can implicitly define the truth-role itself in terms of those relational features—call them the *truish features*—picked out by our common truths about truth. Thus they can say, for example, that

> T that plays the truth-role if, and only if: P is T if and only if, where P is believed, things are as they are believed to be; other things being equal, it is a worthy goal of inquiry to believe P if P is T; it is correct to believe P if and only if P is T.

One of the chief benefits of a functionalist analysis of the concept of truth is that it opens up a new way of understanding the metaphysics of truth. We saw above that properties like correspondence or superwarrant aren't plausible candidates for the essence of truth. But they may well be excellent candidates to *play the truth-role*. Perhaps something like (CC) plays the truth-role for our beliefs about physical objects and their properties; perhaps something like superwarrant plays it for our normative beliefs. In short, functionalism makes room for a form of *alethic pluralism*, or the idea that different kinds of beliefs might be true—in a certain sense—in different ways.

A pluralist metaphysic of truth has significant implications. One such implication is that it would make room for the anti-deflationary idea that an appeal to truth—and its realizing properties—may be explanatorily useful. One obvious example is the nature of knowledge. If there is more than one property that can play the truth-role, then this fact might help to explain how and why moral knowledge differs in kind from knowledge about the things such as cats and cars.

The functionalist view just described is more a theoretical framework than a full-fledged theory of truth. Individual advocates of the general approach can and do differ over how to fill in the details.

One thing they can differ over is the content of the common truths or platitudes that define the truth-role. Wright, an early advocate of this general approach, for example, has argued that equally or more fundamental than the truisms we've so far canvassed are platitudes linking truth with assertion and negation (Wright, 1992). Others (Cotnoir, 2009) have suggested that the number of platitudes required to demarcate the role is smaller, not larger, suggesting a view closer in spirit to some deflationary accounts.

Another area of significant disagreement concerns what to say about the nature of the truth property itself. Wright's more recent work, for example, can be read as implying that truth is whatever property happens to play the truth-role (Wright, 2001). Thus, if where that role is played by correspondence, truth is correspondence, where it is played by superwarrant, truth is superwarrant. But such a view seems to face significant problems. One such problem concerns its implication for our understanding of validity. According to the standard definition valid inferences preserve a single property—truth. But now consider an inference like:

> Murder is wrong or two and two is five; two and two is not five. Therefore, murder is wrong.

Suppose that (a) "truth" denotes any given property that plays the truth-role and (b) that the truth-role is played by different properties in the moral and mathematical domains. If so, then the above argument does not preserve a single property (Tappolet, 1997), contra our ordinary definition of validity.

So it seems that we should not identify truth with the properties that realize the truth-role. Another suggestion (Lynch, 2001) takes "truth" to denote a higher-order property—the property of having a property that plays the truth-role. This suggestion avoids the problem with mixed inferences—since "truth" would now denote a single property in all domains. But it comes at a price. For the point of the functionalist analysis was to define truth by way of a description of its functional role. That description implies that truth itself is a property that has the features described by our common truths about truth. But the property of having a property that has those features does not itself seem to have those features, contra our original analysis.

One possible way out of this difficulty would be to say that truth just is the property that has the truish features essentially, but to allow that this property is itself *immanent* in its realizing properties (Lynch, 2009). Let us say that where property F is immanent in a property M, it is a priori that F's essential features are a subset of M's features. Since it is a priori that every property's essential features are a subset of its own features, every property is immanent in itself. So immanence, like identity, is reflexive and transitive. But unlike identity, it is non-symmetric. Where M and F are ontologically *distinct* properties—individuated by non-identical sets of essential features and relations—and F is immanent in M, M is not thereby immanent in F.

There is more to say about immanence, but even so briefly described it seems that it might allow the functionalist what she wants. Should a property of a belief such as *corresponding to reality* manifest truth, it will be a priori that the truish features are a subset of that property's features. Roughly put: corresponding to reality is what makes some beliefs true because being true is just part of what it is for some beliefs to correspond to reality.

It remains to be seen whether the functionalist proposal is ultimately successful. But it is promising. By leaving room for pluralism about the properties that play the truth-role, it avoids the scope problem plaguing traditional theories of truth. But by allowing that there is more to say about truth and its realizers than the deflationist allows, it suggests that understanding the metaphysics of truth can shed light on other issues of philosophical interest, such as the nature of knowledge.

References

Aristotle (1993) *Metaphysics*, trans. C. Kirwan, Oxford: Oxford University Press.
Beall, Jc (2005) "Transparent Disquotationalism," in Jc Beall and B. Armour-Garb (eds.) *Deflationism and Paradox*, Oxford: Oxford University Press.
Brandom, Robert (2001) "Explanatory vs. Expressive Deflationism about Truth," in R. Schantz (ed). *What is Truth?*, Berlin: Walter De Gruyter, pp. 103–19.
Cotnoir, A. (2009). "Generic Truth and Mixed Conjunctions: Some Alternatives," *Analysis* 69(2): 473–9.
David, Marian (1994) *Correspondence and Disquotation*, Oxford: Oxford University Press.
Devitt, Michael (1997) *Realism and Truth*, Princeton, NJ: Princeton University.
Field, Hartry (1972) "Tarski's Theory of Truth," *Journal of Philosophy*, 69: 347–75.
—— (1986) "The Deflationary Conception of Truth," in G. MacDonald and C. Wright (eds.) *Fact, Science and Morality*, Oxford: Blackwell, pp. 55–117.
Gupta, Anil (1993) "A Critique of Deflationism," *Philosophical Topics*, 21: 57–81.
Horwich, Paul (2001) "Norms of Truth and Meaning," in Richard Schantz (ed.) *What is Truth?*, Berlin: Walter DeGruyter, pp. 133–45.
—— (1998) *Truth*, 2nd edn, Oxford: Oxford University Press.
Lynch, Michael P. (2001) "A Functionalist Theory of Truth," in M. Lynch (ed.) *The Nature of Truth*, Cambridge, MA: MIT Press.
—— (2004) "Minimalism and the Value of Truth," *Philosophical Quarterly*, 54: 497–517.

—— (2009) *Truth as One and Many*, Oxford: Oxford University Press.
Peirce, Charles (1878) "How to Make our Ideas Clear," *Popular Science Monthly* 12: 286–302; citation here refers to reprint in M. P. Lynch (ed.) *The Nature of Truth*, Cambridge, MA: MIT Press, 2001: 193–210.
Plantinga, Alvin (1982) "How to be an Anti-Realist," *Proceedings and Addresses of the American Philosophical Association*, 56: 37–50.
Putnam, Hilary (1990) *Realism with a Human Face*, Cambridge, MA: Harvard University Press.
—— (1981) *Reason, Truth and History*, Cambridge: Cambridge University Press.
Quine, W. V. O. (1990) *The Pursuit of Truth*, Cambridge, MA: Harvard University Press.
Ramsey, F. P. (2001) "The Nature of Truth," in M. P. Lynch (ed.) *The Nature of Truth*, Cambridge, MA: MIT Press, pp. 433–46.
Russell, Bertrand (1966) "On the Nature of Truth and Falsehood," in his *Philosophical Essays*, London: George Allen & Unwin, pp. 147–59.
Strawson, P. F. (1950) "Truth," *Proceedings of the Aristotelian Society*, supp. vol. 24: 129–56.
Tappolet, Christine (1997) "Mixed Inferences: A Problem for Pluralism about Truth Predicates," *Analysis*, 57: 209–11.
Tarski, Alfred (1944) "The Semantic Conception of Truth and the Foundations of Semantics," *Philosophy and Phenomenological Research*, 4: 343–75.
Wittgenstein, Ludwig (1922) *Tractatus Logico-Philosophicus*, trans. C. K. Ogden, London: Kegan Paul.
Wright, Crispin (1992) *Truth and Objectivity*, Cambridge, MA: Harvard University Press.
—— (2001) "Minimalism, Deflationism, Pragmatism, Pluralism," in M. P. Lynch (ed.) *The Nature of Truth*, Cambridge, MA: MIT Press, pp. 751–88.

Further Reading

Beall, Jc, B. Armour-Garb, and G. Priest (2004) *New Essays on Non-Contradiction*, Oxford: Oxford University Press.
Field, Hartry (2001) *Truth and the Absence of Fact*, Oxford: Oxford University Press.
James, W. (1942) *Pragmatism and the Meaning of Truth*, Cambridge, MA: Harvard University Press.
Künne, W. (2003) *Conceptions of Truth*, Oxford: Oxford University Press. (The best overview of theories of truth available.)
Lynch, Michael P. (1998) *Truth in Context*, Cambridge, MA: MIT Press.

2
BELIEF
Eric Schwitzgebel

To believe something, as contemporary analytic philosophers generally use the term "belief," is to take it to be the case or regard it as true. In this sense, many of our beliefs are quite mundane: I believe that Aristotle is dead, that there's tea in my mug, that I have two arms. To qualify as believing these things, I needn't have given them any extended thought or attention, nor need I be particularly or deeply committed to them, as is sometimes suggested by the ordinary English use of the word belief (as in the phrase "these are my beliefs: . . ."). To be a human thinker or rational agent is, in part, to regard the world and the things in it as having certain features. Believing is just this aspect of being a thinker or agent.

Belief is thus a central concept in epistemology. Standard epistemological accounts of knowledge treat knowledge as a species of belief—justified true beliefs, perhaps, or justified true beliefs that meet some further conditions. Also, epistemic justification, or its absence, is typically regarded as a property, first and foremost, of beliefs. It should be unsurprising if not all accounts of belief advanced by philosophers of mind cohere equally well with the different accounts of knowledge and justification advanced by epistemologists.

Contemporary philosophers generally regard belief as a "propositional attitude," where a "proposition" is just whatever it is that sentences express, such that two sentences that have the same meaning express the same proposition (e.g., "tigers are dangerous" in English and "los tigres son peligrosos" in Spanish) and sentences with different meanings express different propositions (setting aside some complications about indexical terms such as "I" and "today"). Propositional attitudes are just the types of mental states that possess the following canonical formal structure: $S\ A$ that P, where S refers to the subject or individual who has the attitude, A refers to the attitude, and P refers to a proposition canonically expressible as a full sentence (though often in ordinary English abbreviated to a phrase with an implied subject). For example: Davy [the subject] believes [the attitude] that Mars is red [the proposition]; Gerardo [the subject] fears [the attitude] that inflation will spiral out of control [the proposition]; Jieying [the subject] desires [the attitude] that the server brings her piece of pie soon [the proposition]. Of course, what one person believes another may only hope for and a third may intend—different attitudes all toward the same proposition. Discussions of the nature of belief are often embedded in more general discussions of the propositional attitudes, with belief typically serving as the central example.

1. Representational Approaches to Belief

Probably the majority of contemporary philosophers of mind adhere to some form of *representationalism* about belief—they hold that believing P involves having in one's brain or mind a representation with the content P (at least in central, canonical cases of belief; see the discussion of explicit and implicit belief below). This view can be developed in various ways.

1.1. Fodor's Representationalism

Jerry Fodor (1975, 1981, 1987, 1990), for example, regards mental representations as sentences in an internal "language of thought"—an innate language (not learned, like English) in which cognition transpires. Consider "machine language" as an analogy. One (simplified) way of thinking about what a word-processing program does is this: When I open a new document and start typing on my keyboard, it transforms those keyboard inputs into a language-like machine code of sequentially ordered representations or representational tokens. For example, position 1 might contain a machine-language token for "B," position 2 a machine-language token for "e," etc. The computer generates screen displays and printer outputs based on the application of pre-programmed output rules (also in machine language) applied to these stored representations. On some visions of the future of artificial intelligence, we might design intelligent robots that operate in essentially the same way—by the storage of representations in machine language and the manipulation of those representations according to (possibly evolving) machine-language rules.

On Fodor's view, human beings are essentially machines of this sort—with the rules and representations underwriting their behavior not encoded in machine language, of course, but in an innate species-wide language of thought. To represent P is to have present in one's mind a sentence in the language of thought with the content P. To believe that P is to have such a representation in mind in such a way that it is poised to play a "belief-like" role in cognition (as opposed to, say, a desire-like role or an imagination-like role). A representation plays a belief-like role if it is apt to be combined with other belief-like representations in the course of inference (e.g., the representation P might combine with that of "if P then Q" to generate a new representation Q, also held in a belief-like way), in the deliberation over means to obtaining desired ends, etc.

1.2. Dretske's Representationalism

Fred Dretske's representationalism (1988; cf. Millikan 1984, 1993) starts with a consideration of very simple representational systems, such as marine "magnetosome" bacteria. Magnetosome bacteria contain magnets that align with Earth's magnetic field. In the Northern Hemisphere, geomagnetic north is downward and, guided by their magnets, these bacteria propel themselves down into deeper water and sediment and away from the (to them) toxic oxygen near the surface of the ocean. It is easy to imagine how such a system might have evolved. The magnetic system of the magnetosome bacteria, on Dretske's view, *represents* magnetic north, or down, or the direction of oxygen-free environments, because it has the evolved *function of indicating* one or more of those things. (Which *exactly* of these things it represents, Dretske regards as indeterminate due to the simplicity of the organism.) Organisms, especially mobile ones, need to keep track of their environments. Consequently, they evolve systems whose function is to covary with features of their environment—that is, representational systems. On Dretske's view, an organism represents P just in case it contains a system one of whose functions it is to enter state A only if P holds, and that subsystem is in state A. As organisms grow more complex, they develop multiple overlapping and competing representational systems, and they develop the capacity to learn new representational structures. To have beliefs, on Dretske's view, is just to have a sophisticated network of such representational systems, some acquired through associative learning, poised to guide behavior.

1.3. Language-Like vs. Map-Like Representations

Another representational view, developed by David Lewis (1994) and David Braddon-Mitchell and Frank Jackson (1996) characterizes representation as map-like rather than language-like. For epistemologists, there are two key differences between maps and sentences as representational structures.

First, when maps represent something, they generally represent it with a determinate content and in determinate relationships to all the other elements represented. If a to-scale map represents a mountain peak, for instance, it must generally represent it as being in a fairly specific place (to whatever level of precision the mapping system allows) and at various specific distances and directions from all the other map elements. In contrast, linguistic representation much more naturally accommodates high levels of indeterminacy: A language-of-thought sentence might contain the content ("the mountain is north of the river") without specifying in any way how far north or in exactly what direction, even if other related elements of the scene are more precisely known.

Second, language-like representation leaves room at least in principle for inconsistencies or even bald contradictions among representations, while maps cannot (or cannot easily) be self-inconsistent. One might store the sentences "The mountain is 10 km north of the river" and "The river is 15 km south of the mountain," but there is no straightforward way to convey this sort of inconsistency in a map-like structure. Consequently, whenever one changes one aspect of a map, every related aspect changes effortlessly and simultaneously to render the new picture consistent: If one learns that the well is actually 2 km east of the mountain, not 5 km, correcting the position of the well with respect to the mountain in itself constitutes a correction of the position of the well with respect to every other map element also (for example, now the well must be 8 km and not 5 km west of the shore, unless the shoreline is also redrawn). In contrast, changing the sentence "The well is 5 km east of the mountain" to "The well is 2 km east of the mountain" in a language-like system of representation does not automatically change the represented distance between the well and the shore.

1.4. Implicit and Explicit Belief

I believe that the number of planets is less than nine. I also, seemingly, believe that it is less than 10. And less than 11. And less than 137. And less than 2,653,665,401. If I do believe all these things, and if a crude language-like representational view is correct, then I must have a vast, perhaps infinite, number of stored representations concerning the number of planets. And obviously the problem generalizes. Since surely we are not cluttering our minds with so many redundant representations, a crude language-like representational view is unsustainable.

On a map-like view, there is no problem here. A single simple map of the solar system simultaneously specifies, without consuming vast cognitive resources, that the number of planets is less than 9, 10, 11, 137, etc. In contrast, a representationalist with a language-like view may be forced to distinguish between what is sometimes called *explicit* and *implicit* belief (Field 1978; Lycan 1986; Dennett 1987; Fodor 1987). On this view, only explicit beliefs require stored representations. We implicitly believe something (that the number of planets is less than 137, say) when we can swiftly derive it from what we explicitly believe. Or, alternatively, one might say that we simply do *not* believe that the number of planets is less than 137 (explicitly or implicitly), prior to explicitly entertaining that thought, but are merely *disposed* to form that belief (Audi 1994). Such views would seem to predict a sharp and substantial cognitive difference between those beliefs with explicitly coded representations and those without explicitly coded representations, an issue that would appear open to empirical investigation.

2. Dispositional and Interpretational Approaches to Belief

Dispositional and interpretational approaches to belief treat believing not principally as a matter of internal cognitive structure but rather as a matter of an individual's patterns of behavior (or in the case of "liberal dispositionism" something broader than behavior). It may help to gain a sense of the difference between these two classes of views to consider the possibility of a being of unknown origin and structure (Rudolfo, say) who comes to Earth and integrates seamlessly into society, behaving in all respects as an ordinary person does—becoming, say, a lawyer and baseball fan. Is the fact that Rudolfo outwardly behaves just as does an ordinary person by itself sufficient to guarantee that it's accurate to describe him as believing that the Supreme Court has nine members and that the Kansas City Royals may never again make the playoffs? Or do certain facts also have to be true about Rudolfo's internal structure? Is it conceptually possible, even if physically impossible, that Rudolfo be made entirely of undifferentiated balsa wood? Or consider a case like that of Lewis's "mad pain" (1980), but adapted for belief. Consider, that is, a being (Susan) who possesses a representation that, if it were possessed by a normal person, we would describe as having the content "there's a beer in the fridge"; and imagine (if it's possible) that that representation is stored in a belief-like way, but due either to an unusual constitution or damage to other functional systems within Susan, it is never caused by things like seeing beer in the fridge or hearing someone say that there's beer in the fridge and is not at all apt to be deployed in inferences, means-to-end reasoning, etc. In cases like that of Rudolfo and Susan, where patterns of behavior and internal representational structure come apart, advocates of dispositional and interpretational approaches will privilege behavior in the ascription of belief, while advocates of representational approaches will privilege internal structure.

2.1. Dispositional Approaches

Traditional dispositional approaches to belief hold that to believe some particular proposition is to have a certain set of behavioral dispositions. For example, on Ruth Marcus's (1990) view, to believe that P is just to be disposed to act, in appropriate circumstances, as if P were the case. A standard objection to accounts of this sort is that it seems to posit too tight a connection between belief and action—for example, if a person is paralyzed or determined to hide her real opinion. While this objection might be avoided in the case of views like Marcus's by working with the "in appropriate circumstances" condition, most contemporary philosophers attracted to approaches of this general sort address the objection by adopting either *liberal dispositionalism* or *interpretationism*. Liberal dispositionalists about belief (e.g., Price 1969; Schwitzgebel 2002) hold that believing is a matter of having not just outward behavioral dispositions but also some non-behavioral dispositions, such as phenomenal dispositions (dispositions to enter certain conscious or "phenomenal" states such as feeling surprise or entertaining visual or verbal imagery) and/or cognitive dispositions (dispositions to enter other sorts of possibly nonconscious mental states such as making assumptions or drawing implicit conclusions). Although Gilbert Ryle (1949) is widely read as a leading exemplar of traditional behaviorist dispositionalism, on a close reading his view appears to be at least somewhat more liberal than that.

2.2. Interpretational Approaches

Interpretational approaches to belief are similar in spirit to traditional dispositional views, in that what matters in the ascription of belief are patterns of behavior rather than internal structure. On an interpretational view, an individual believes that P just in case the best way to make rational sense of her overall pattern of behavior would involve ascribing to her the belief that P. Daniel Dennett (1978, 1987) and Donald Davidson (1984) are the most prominent advocates of interpretational approaches.

Dennett invites us to imagine the difference between three different ways to predict or explain the behavior of a being. We can take the "physical stance," which involves predicting the being's behavior using the laws of physics—for example, that a diver will trace a roughly parabolic arc to the water. We can take the "design stance," which involves predicting that the being will function as it was designed (possibly by evolution) to function—for example, that a person will begin to sweat as her body temperature rises due to exertion. Or we can take the "intentional stance," which involves predicting that the being will behave rationally given certain beliefs and desires. To be a believer, on Dennett's view, is to be a being for which an interpreter who took merely a physical or design stance to explaining her behavior would be involved either in great complexity or massive error, while taking the intentional stance would yield fairly simple and accurate predictions.

Davidson invites us to imagine encountering a being with a wholly unfamiliar language and then attempting the task of "radical interpretation"—the task of attempting to determine what his words mean. To succeed in such a task would also necessarily, Davidson argues, involve ascribing beliefs and desires in light of which his words make sense. On Davidson's view, to be a believer is to be a being that emits behavior that can be productively interpreted as linguistic, rational, and expressive of beliefs and desires. Both Davidson and Dennett allow that there might be indeterminacy in belief in cases where no single best interpretation is possible: If there are two equally good interpretations, one of which ascribes the belief that P and one of which does not, there is no fact of the matter whether the being believes that P.

Interpretational (and dispositional) approaches need not reject the importance of underlying representations. Dennett (1987), for example, suggests that the reason we may be productively interpretable as having beliefs and desires is precisely because our psychology operates through the manipulation of representations. However, he remains an interpretationist because he treats interpretability, rather than internal structure, as what is most fundamental in ascription of belief. The manipulation of representations is simply the means by which we come to be interpretable.

3. Functionalism

Functionalism has been an influential position in the philosophy of mind since the 1960s, and most of the philosophers described in Sections 1 and 2 are, in a broad sense, functionalists about belief. To be a functionalist about a particular mental state is to hold that possession of that state is possession of a state that plays a particular functional or causal role, where functional or causal role is defined in terms of typical (or normal or actual) causes and effects. So, for example, a simple functional analysis of pain might be as the state, whatever it is, that is apt to be caused by such things as tissue damage and tissue stress and is apt, in turn, to cause such things as avoidance, wincing, and utterance of the phrase "I'm in pain" (in appropriate conditions). A functional analysis of belief that P might be as the state, whatever it is, apt to be produced by such things as perception of P, inference from premises that jointly imply P, and hearing testimony as to the truth of P and that, in turn, is apt to produce such things as inference to Q if P (perhaps together with other believed propositions) straightforwardly implies Q, and performance of action A if P implies that A would achieve a much-desired end and no contrary desires recommend against A. We might distinguish between *token* functionalism (like Putnam's (1975)) from *type* functionalism (like Lewis's (1980)): On token functionalism the relevant state must itself have been caused in the right sort of way and must be apt to produce the right sorts of effects. On type functionalism, the state must be of the type that is apt to be caused in a certain way and to have certain effects, even if that particular instance of the type is not so caused and not prone to have such effects. One might think here of the difference between actual memories and merely apparent memories. To be an actual memory of storming the Bastille, a mental state must have been caused (in part) by one's having stormed the Bastille. To be a merely apparent memory of storming the Bastille, it is sufficient if the mental state is of the same type that is normally caused by storming the Bastille even if it, itself, was not so caused: If functionalism is true of genuine memories, it must be token functionalism (at least on the what-it-was-caused-by side), though perhaps type functionalism will suffice for apparent memories.

Dispositional views are a special case of token functional views, according to which the causes of the mental state in question are not at all constitutive of the state. Davidson's example of "Swampman" (2001)—a being molecule-for-molecule identical to Davidson himself and who arises from a swamp through quantum accident when the swamp is struck by lightning—can help distinguish between token functional views that are also dispositional and those that are more broadly functional. Swampman cannot genuinely remember storming the Bastille. His apparent memory was not caused in the right way. On a dispositionalist view, however, he can have beliefs—at least those beliefs that do not constitutively depend on dispositional manifestations that essentially invoke the past (such as, for example, the disposition to rightly say, "This is the same thing I did two weeks ago"). Interpretational views also fit nicely with token functionalism, though unlike dispositional views they more readily accommodate the constitutive importance of causes.

Representational views tend to be type functional: Representational states are generally viewed as states of the sort typically caused in such-and-such a way and that typically produce such-and-such effects, even if particular tokenings of those states are not caused in the right way and/or are not apt to produce the right effects.

4. Eliminativism

Eliminativism about belief is the view that, literally speaking, people have no beliefs. Just as we now think that the sun does not literally rise up over the horizon (though we still find it convenient to talk that way) and just as we now think that there is no such thing as phlogiston (despite the predictive successes of early chemical theories invoking phlogiston), so also when science is far enough advanced we will come to think of belief as a flawed folk-theoretical term despite the convenience of the term for current practical purposes.

Arguments for eliminativism include Paul and Patricia Churchland's argument that neuroscience has much better long-run promise for predicting and explaining human behavior than does ordinary folk psychology and seems to have no room for concepts like that of belief (P.M. Churchland 1981; P.S. Churchland 1986); Stephen Stich's argument that folk psychology individuates belief states in ways that match poorly with the real causal powers of cognitive states and thus that a mature computational cognitive science will use different mental state individuation principles (Stich 1983; but see Stich 1996 for a partial retraction); and William Ramsey, Stich, and Joseph Garron's (1991) argument that if the mind is built upon a roughly "connectionist" architecture, involving the massive and widely distributed interaction of subsemantic neuron-like nodes, then folk psychological states like belief cannot exist, for they are too discrete in their architecture to play a causal role in such a system.

5. Internalism and Externalism

An *internalist* about a mental state holds that whether a being possesses that mental state constitutively depends entirely on facts internal to that being and not at all on facts about the outside world, such that two beings who are internally identical necessarily do not differ with regard to possession of that state. (Of course, the state may *causally* depend on facts about the outside world.) An externalist about a mental state holds, in contrast, that two internally identical beings could differ with respect to the state in question. A version of the brain-in-a-vat thought experiment can help distinguish internalist from externalist views: Imagine a brain exactly identical to yours, created and sustained in a vat, with its inputs manipulated to exactly mimic the inputs your brain receives—inputs that will of course be conditioned in part on the output signals from the brain, so that over time your and the brain-in-a-vat's internally-defined brain states remain exactly identical. You and the brain in a vat will share all internally defined mental states and differ in most or all externally defined mental states. Question: Does the brain in the vat have beliefs? If it does, does it have exactly the same beliefs you do?

Externalism is often supported by the Twin Earth thought experiment, due to Hilary Putnam (1975; originally intended primarily as a thought experiment about linguistic meaning). Imagine that in another part of the universe there exists a planet molecule-for-molecule identical to Earth, with one exception: Where Earth has water (H_2O), this other planet, Twin Earth, has a chemical (XYZ) that behaves outwardly virtually identically to water. It fills the rivers and oceans, is clear and potable, freezes and boils at the same temperature, etc. In 1750, no chemical test is available that can distinguish these substances. Wayne on Earth believes that there is a glass of water in front of him. Twin Wayne is molecule-for-molecule identical to Wayne (except that he has XYZ rather than water in him, but this point is inessential as can be seen by reflecting on parallel examples involving chemicals not present in the human body). He is also looking at a glass of clear, potable liquid and is disposed to utter a sentence that sounds like "There's a glass of water in front of me." The majority (but not unanimous) view in contemporary philosophy is that Wayne's and Twin Wayne's beliefs differ in their content: One is about water (H_2O), the other about twin water (XYZ). For example, if Wayne were teleported to Twin Earth without his knowledge and uttered the sentence "That's a glass of water" while looking at twin water, his sentence and his corresponding belief would be false, while Twin Wayne's identical sentence and corresponding belief would be true. (For a rather different but equally influential example see Burge 1979.)

6. Atomism vs. Holism

Alan says that redwoods are trees. He also says that saguaro cactuses are trees. Gincy says that redwoods are trees, but would not say that saguaro cactuses are. Although Alan and Gincy both have beliefs about redwoods that they would express with the sentence "Redwoods are trees," do they really believe exactly the same thing about redwoods? Or does the fact that they differ about the status of saguaros imply that they have slightly different concepts of "tree" and so slightly different beliefs about redwoods? *Holists* say that the content of any belief depends on the contents of many nearby beliefs so that people who disagree have for the most part slightly different beliefs even on the topics about which it might seem outwardly that they agree. *Atomists*, in contrast, say that the content of our beliefs is generally not interrelated in that way. For the atomist, the content of a belief may be constitutively related to the content of a few others—for example, the content of the belief expressed by the sentence "Redwoods are trees" may differ between people who would give radically different definitions of "tree"—but generally, normal fluent speakers inclined to endorse the same sentence share exactly the same belief and not slightly different beliefs.

Among the leading atomists are Fodor and Ernest Lepore (1992), who appeal among other things to the intuition that people saying the same sentence are generally expressing the same belief. Atomism also fits nicely with the view (Section 1.1) that belief involves discrete representations in an innate language of thought, where the contents of representational elements are shared between members of the same species. It also fits nicely with "externalist" views according to which belief contents or concepts are largely fixed by physical or social context shared among speakers (see Section 5 above). Among the leading holists are W.V.O. Quine (1951), Davidson (1984), and Dennett (1987). If believing, at root, is a matter of exhibiting complex and intertwining patterns of behavior (as these three hold), subtly different patterns in behavioral dispositions may constitute slightly different belief states even if our belief-ascribing language is too coarse-grained a tool ordinarily to capture those differences in short and convenient sentences.

7. De Re and De Dicto Belief Ascriptions

Kyle sees a shadowy figure walking quickly through the factory late one night and concludes that that person is a thief. Unbeknownst to him, that shadowy figure is the plant manager, a woman of unquestionably upright character, and Kyle would disagree with anyone who asserted that the plant manager is a thief. Does Kyle believe that the plant manager is a thief? It seems that there's a sense in which he does and a sense in which he does not. Philosophers sometimes express this ambiguity by saying that Kyle believes, de re, of the plant manager that she is a thief but does not believe, de dicto, that the plant manager is a thief (Quine 1956).

A usage of a term is *referentially transparent* if coreferential terms can be substituted into the sentence in which it occurs without changing the truth value of the sentence. For example, in the sentence "Cati punched the cashier" the term "cashier" would normally be interpreted as referentially transparent. If it is true that Cati punched the cashier, and if the cashier is also (though Cati doesn't know it) the only guy in town born on July 8, 1962, then it's also true that Cati punched the only guy in town born on July 8, 1962. A usage of a term is *referentially opaque* if the substitution of coreferential terms is not guaranteed to preserve the truth value of the sentence. Belief ascriptions are often interpreted as referentially opaque: We might want to say that Cati believes she punched the cashier but does not believe that she punched the only guy in town born on July 8, 1962—for example, if she's inclined to assert the first and deny the second. De re belief attributions are those with some referentially transparent terms. De dicto belief attributions have no referentially transparent terms.

8. Future Directions

Two emerging issues in the literature on belief which as yet lack a settled canon are the following:

8.1. Self-Knowledge

It seems that we typically know what we believe. How is this possible? One possibility is that we have some sort of self-scanning or self-monitoring device by means of which we detect our beliefs (Armstrong 1968; Nichols and Stich 2003; with qualifications, Goldman 2006). Another possibility is that, on the basis of our knowledge of such things as outward behavior and non-belief-like mental states such as images, we theorize or interpret ourselves as believing (Gopnik 1993; Carruthers 2009). Another possibility is that the self-attribution of beliefs is simply expressive, like the utterance of "ow!" when one feels pain, not requiring introspective or epistemic access to the belief states self-attributed (Bar-On 2004; see Wittgenstein 1953 for the pain example). Or, compatible with the previous view but also separable from it, we might attribute beliefs on the basis of a process that involves considering or detecting facts about the outside world while not considering or detecting facts about our mental states. For example, we might think only about the external matter of whether there will be a third world war in answering the question of whether *we believe* there will be a third world war (Evans 1982; Moran 2001; Byrne 2005; Gordon 2007).

8.2. Dissociations Between Implicit Reactions and Explicit Endorsements

A person might sincerely (or for all she can tell sincerely) affirm the proposition "all the races are intellectually equal" and yet show persistent racist bias in her everyday implicit reactions. Another person might in some sense be well aware that she moved her kitchen trashcan from one location to another and yet still find herself going to the old location to dispose of trash (Zimmerman 2007). Another person might walk out onto a glass skywalk above the Grand Canyon, saying "I know it's perfectly safe" yet trembling with fear (Gendler 2008a). In these sorts of cases, the subject's explicit endorsements conform with one proposition (P, let's call it) and her implicit reactions seem to conform with its negation (not-P). What should we say about the subject's belief?

In recent articles dealing with cases of this sort (though the authors' examples vary in important ways), Zimmerman (2007) and Gendler (2008a, 2008b) have suggested that the subject believes P (that the races are intellectually equal, that the trashcan is in its new location, that the skywalk is safe) and does not believe not-P; Gendler calls the subject's attitude toward not-P "alief." Zimmerman and Gendler stress the extent to which belief is the sort of thing responsive to evidence and open to rational revision. In contrast, Hunter (manuscript), emphasizing everyday patterns of action and reaction, suggests that for at least some such cases the subject believes not-P and does not believe P. Gertler (forthcoming), allowing more than one set of sufficient conditions for believing, suggests that the subject believes P (on one set of sufficient conditions) and also believes not-P (on a different set). Schwitzgebel (2001, manuscript), stressing the mixed overall dispositional patterns in many such cases, suggests that such subjects are generally "in-between" believing P and failing to believe it.

References

Armstrong, D.M. (1968) *A Materialist Theory of the Mind*, New York: Routledge.
Audi, R. (1994) "Dispositional Beliefs and Dispositions to Believe," *Noûs*, 28: 419–34.
Bar-On, D. (2004) *Speaking My Mind*, Oxford: Oxford University Press.
Braddon-Mitchell, D. and Jackson, F. (1996) *The Philosophy of Mind and Cognition*, Oxford: Oxford University Press.
Burge, T. (1979) "Individualism and the Mental," in P.A. French, T.E. Uehling, and H.K. Wettstein (eds.), *Midwest Studies in Philosophy*, 4: 73–121.
Byrne, A. (2005) "Introspection," *Philosophical Topics*, 33 (no. 1): 79–104.
Carruthers, P. (2009) "How We Know Our Own Minds: The Relationship Between Mindreading and Metacognition," *Behavioral and Brain Sciences*, 32: 121–38.
Churchland, P.M. (1981) "Eliminative Materialism and the Propositional Attitudes," *Journal of Philosophy*, 78: 67–90.
Churchland, P.S. (1986) *Neurophilosophy*, Cambridge, MA: MIT Press.
Davidson, D. (1984) *Inquiries into Truth and Interpretation*, Oxford: Clarendon.
—— (2001) *Subjective, Intersubjective, Objective*, Oxford: Clarendon.
Dennett, D.C. (1978) *Brainstorms*, Cambridge, MA: MIT Press.
—— (1987) *The Intentional Stance*, Cambridge, MA: MIT Press.
Dretske, F. (1988) *Explaining Behavior*, Cambridge, MA: MIT Press.
Evans, G. (1982) *Varieties of Reference*, Oxford: Oxford University Press.
Field, H.H. (1978) "Mental Representation," *Erkenntnis*, 13: 9–61.
Fodor, J.A. (1975) *The Language of Thought*, New York: Crowell.
—— (1981) *Representations*, Cambridge, MA: MIT Press.
—— (1987) *Psychosemantics*, Cambridge, MA: MIT Press.
—— (1990) *A Theory of Content*, Cambridge, MA: MIT Press.
—— and Lepore, E. (1992) *Holism*, Cambridge: Blackwell.
Gendler, T.S. (2008a) "Alief and Belief," *Journal of Philosophy*, 105: 634–63.
—— (2008b) "Alief in Action (and Reaction)," *Mind & Language*, 23: 552–85.
Gertler, B. (forthcoming) "Self-Knowledge and the Transparency of Belief," in A. Hatzimoysis (ed.) *Self-Knowledge*, Oxford: Oxford University Press.
Goldman, A.I. (2006) *Simulating Minds*, Oxford: Oxford University Press.

Gopnik, A. (1993) "How We Know Our Own Minds: The Illusion of First-Person Knowledge of Intentionality," *Behavioral and Brain Sciences*, 16: 1–14.
Gordon, R.M. (1995) "Simulation Without Introspection or Inference from Me to You," in M. Davies and T. Stone (eds.) *Mental Simulation*, Oxford: Blackwell.
—— (2007) "Ascent Routines for Propositional Attitudes," *Synthese*, 159: 151–65.
Hunter, D. (manuscript) "Belief, Alienation, and Intention."
Lewis, D. (1980) "Mad Pain and Martian Pain," in N. Block (ed.) *Readings in the Philosophy of Psychology, vol. 1*, Cambridge, MA: Harvard University Press.
—— (1994) "Lewis, David: Reduction of Mind," in S. Guttenplan (ed.) *A Companion to the Philosophy of Mind*, Oxford: Blackwell.
Lycan, W.G. (1986) "Tacit Belief," in R.J. Bogdan (ed.) *Belief: Form, Content, and Function*, Oxford: Clarendon.
Marcus, R.B. (1990) "Some Revisionary Proposals about Belief and Believing," *Philosophy and Phenomenological Research*, 50: 132–53.
Millikan, R.G. (1984) *Language, Thought, and Other Biological Categories*, Cambridge, MA: MIT Press.
—— (1993) *White Queen Psychology and Other Essays for Alice*, Cambridge, MA: MIT Press.
Moran, R. (2001) *Authority and Estrangement*, Princeton, NJ: Princeton University Press.
Nichols, S. and Stich, S.P. (2003) *Mindreading*, Oxford: Oxford University Press.
Price, H.H. (1969) *Belief*, London: Allen & Unwin.
Putnam, H. (1975) *Mind, Language, and Reality*, London: Cambridge.
Quine, W.V.O. (1951) "Two Dogmas of Empiricism," *The Philosophical Review*, 60: 20–43.
—— (1956) "Quantifiers and Propositional Attitudes," *Journal of Philosophy*, 53: 177–86.
Ramsey, W., Stich, S., and Garon, J. (1991) "Connectionism, Eliminativism, and the Future of Folk Psychology," in J.D. Greenwood (ed.) *The Future of Folk Psychology*, Cambridge: Cambridge University Press.
Ryle, G. (1949) *The Concept of Mind*, New York: Barnes & Noble.
Schwitzgebel, E. (2001) "In-Between Believing," *Philosophical Quarterly*, 51: 76–82.
—— (2002) "A Phenomenal, Dispositional Account of Belief," *Nous*, 36: 249–75.
—— (manuscript) "Acting Contrary to Our Professed Beliefs, or the Gulf Between Occurrent Judgment and Dispositional Belief."
Stich, S. (1983) *From Folk Psychology to Cognitive Science*, Cambridge, MA: MIT Press.
—— (1996) *Deconstructing the Mind*, New York: Oxford University Press.
Wittgenstein, L. (1953) *Philosophical Investigations*, trans. G.E.M. Anscombe, New York: Macmillan.
Zimmerman, A. (2007) "The Nature of Belief," *Journal of Consciousness Studies*, 14 (no. 11): 61–82.

3
EPISTEMIC JUSTIFICATION
Jonathan L. Kvanvig

The term 'justification' and its cognates are terms of art in contemporary epistemology, falling on the normative side of the distinction between normative and descriptive aspects of the world. Other terms of this sort within contemporary epistemology are terms such as 'rational,' 'warranted,' 'entitled,' and 'reasonable.' Some theorists treat some of these normative terms as synonymous, while others draw various distinctions among them. All such terms, however, have broader application in ordinary language than just to items of epistemic appraisal, such as beliefs. Affective states, such as hopes and fears, can be rational or irrational; items from the practical sphere, including actions and the intentions that sometimes underlie them, can be warranted or not. Epistemologists typically distinguish the epistemic uses by tying the notions in question to knowledge or in terms of means appropriate to the goal of getting to the truth and avoiding error.

Historically, the most important controversy has been between foundationalist and coherentist responses to the regress argument. The regress argument purports to show that justified beliefs are impossible, and foundationalists block the claim that further reasons must always be available by insisting that justification has a tiered structure, with a foundation of self-justifying beliefs which support the remaining beliefs. Coherentists deny the existence of such self-justifying beliefs, maintaining that justification is a matter of coherence with an appropriate system of information available to the individual in question.

Common to both positions, historically, is an internalist assumption, that justification is a feature of a belief that depends on features internal to the believer and is typically accessible by reflection to the individual holding the belief. In recent times, various versions of externalism have arisen in contrast to such an internalism. The most popular has been reliabilism, which can also be seen as a less radical approach to naturalizing epistemology, an approach recommending less a priori theorizing in epistemology and more concern for scientific inquiry relevant to epistemological questions and issues. The most radical forms of naturalized epistemology recommend replacing traditional epistemological questions with related empirical questions that can be addressed by scientific inquiry alone. Other new approaches to justification also fall under the general externalist umbrella, including forms of modal and virtue epistemology, as well as forms of social epistemology that view internalism as too committed to an individualistic picture of our cognitive lives.

I. The Concept of the Epistemic

The language of justification is widespread in ordinary thought and language, applying to plans, decisions, actions, hopes, wishes, fears, policies, judgments in a court of law, and many other things. The primary epistemological interest in the language of justification is as it applies to beliefs (or degrees of belief), but not just any reason for belief counts toward the epistemic justification of that belief. For example, the offer of money in exchange for belief will give one a reason to hold that belief, but it is not an epistemic reason to hold the belief. The usual approach to explaining why such a reason is not an epistemic reason is to clarify epistemic reasons in terms of means appropriate to the intellectual goal of getting to the truth and avoiding error.

Such reasons are assumed to be doubly defeasible: they can be overridden by nonepistemic concerns and also by acquiring further information. First, a situation might arise in which a catastrophe can only be avoided by holding a belief for which one has no evidence at all. In such a situation, the preponderance of reasons favors holding such a belief, even though such a belief would be epistemically unjustified. Second, one can have epistemic reasons for belief that are undermined by further learning. Statistical reasoning provides examples of such: a given sample, properly obtained, may give one evidence that most people in a given locale will vote for candidate X, and an enlargement of the sample might undermine this conclusion.

II. Skepticism, Foundationalism, and Coherentism

The standard approach to theorizing about justification begins with responses to the regress argument for skepticism. When we are justified in taking some cognitive attitude toward a given claim, we are often so justified by basing that attitude on some other attitude. For example, we might base our belief that Obama won the election in 2008 on our belief that the *New York Times* reported this result and that it is a trustworthy source of information about such matters. In order for this supporting belief to provide an adequate basis for the supported belief, however, it cannot itself be baseless, arbitrary, or unjustified. Once such a requirement is noted, a regress threatens. It appears that an attitude cannot support another attitude in the way required for justification unless the supporting attitude is itself justified. If its justification requires support from some further attitude, regress ensues.

The standard metatheory concerning justification focuses on two primary responses to this regress argument. A foundationalist response attempts to find legitimate stopping points for the regress, and coherentists resist the urge for such legitimate stopping points. Coherentists, however, are not the only theorists who try to resist foundationalist stopping points. Skeptics endorse the conclusion that no attitudes are ever justified, whether by being based on other attitudes or in terms of foundationalist stopping points. Infinitists insist that the regress cannot be stopped, but that the regress isn't vicious and hence doesn't block beliefs from being justified. A further option is that stopping points are needed, but can be arbitrary.

Of these options, the last is the road least traveled. If justification can be stopped at arbitrary points, it is hard to see why we see the need for defenses of any sort regarding the cognitive attitudes that we take (a classic source of such a view is Wittgenstein (1969), where the notion of a "hinge proposition" plays the crucial theoretical role). The infinitist response is usually rejected just as quickly, but it has seen a substantial defense by Peter Klein in recent years (see Klein 1999). From a historical perspective, however, most attempts to evade the skeptical conclusion of the regress argument have been in the form of defending some form of foundationalism. From Aristotle to Descartes and the empiricists, the most common view has been that we can trace the roots of any justified attitude to a legitimate stopping point, either in deliverances of reason or deliverances of the senses.

Foundationalists disagree among themselves, however, about the two crucial aspects of the view. The first is the nature of foundational attitudes themselves. The strongest versions of foundationalism require that the foundations be infallible or metaphysically certain. Weaker versions require something less, perhaps as weak as only having some degree of justification not derived from relationships to other beliefs or cognitive attitudes. Variation occurs as well regarding the connection between the foundations and attitudes supported by the foundations. Strong foundationalists require truth-preserving inferential links between the foundations and what the foundations support, while weaker versions allow weaker connections, such as inductive support or inference to the best explanation or probabilistic support (see Alston 1989). Some versions of foundationalism even embrace coherentist elements, requiring or allowing the support relation to include coherence itself as a justification-enhancing feature (see Chisholm 1966).

From Aristotle to major figures in modern philosophy (Descartes, Locke, Hume, and Berkeley) and the first half of the twentieth century (Russell, Ayers, Carnap), the standard non-skeptical view in epistemology has been foundationalism. At the middle of the twentieth century, however, foundationalism came under severe attack. The criticisms of foundationalism by Wilfrid Sellars are especially important in this regard, who argued against what he called "the myth of the given," insisting that the only thing that can justify a belief is another belief (see Sellars 1963). Over the next 25 years or so, foundationalism had all but disappeared as a theory endorsed by leading epistemologists, with Roderick Chisholm an important and notable exception to this trend (see Chisholm 1966). Instead, the fashionable position was coherentism, the primary alternative to foundationalism.

Coherentism can be understood in terms of a desire to avoid foundationalism. Given the dissatisfaction in the history of epistemology with the arbitrary stopping points and with infinitism, coherentism might appear to require the possibility of justification arising from circular reasoning. Such a view would count as a version of coherentism, but there are no defenders of such a view. Instead, coherentists are better understood as objecting to the regress argument at a different point, the point at which it is assumed that justification involves linear relationships between individual propositional contents. They view justification in a holistic fashion, holding that justification is a matter of fit between an individual belief or attitude and an entire system of beliefs or information. Beliefs are thus not justified by anything comparable to inferential connections that play a central role in the psychology of belief formation, but rather by overall comparative fit with an entire picture of the world. So, whereas foundationalists endorse the assumption of the regress argument that justification requires a chain of reasons of some sort, coherentists resist commitment to any such requirement on justification.

Coherentism incurs two important burdens here. The most obvious is the need to say what the relation of coherence involves, and the second is the need to address the problem of the basing relation. The latter problem arises because of the distinction between holding a belief for which one has good evidence and believing on the basis of, or because of, the evidence for it. For example, one might believe that Bush is a terrible President because of the evidence for it (e.g., facts about the war in Iraq and lack of respect for the Constitution) or because one hates Texans. In the former case, the believing itself is justified, and in the latter case only the content of the belief is justified; in the former case, it is said, doxastic justification is present and in the latter case only propositional justification is present.

By endorsing the idea that justification should be understood in terms of chains of reasons, the foundationalist can understand both propositional justification and doxastic justification in terms of the same chain of reasons. One such account understands propositional justification in terms of existence of an adequate chain of reasons, terminating in foundational stopping points, and doxastic justification in terms of propositional justification plus causation, so that the believing itself is produced or sustained by the very chain of reasons in question.

Holistic coherentists, however, cannot endorse this account of basing, since they refuse to endorse the idea that justification can be defined in terms of chains of reasons. One alternative here is to distinguish between that which justifies the content of the belief (the system in question) and central parts of the system that are not themselves sufficient for the justification of the belief but still play an essential and non-redundant role in the story of why the belief in question is justified by the system in question. If we refer to the first category in terms of *conferrers* of justification and the second in terms of *enablers* of justification, coherentists can understand proper basing in terms of enablers of justification, rather than in terms of conferrers of justification (see Kvanvig 1995).

The other major difficulty facing coherentism is the burden of saying precisely what it is for a belief or attitude to cohere with a system of beliefs or information. A variety of suggestions can be found among coherentists on this point. F.H. Bradley, for example, claimed that a coherent system was one characterized by mutual entailment between all the elements of the system, but recent coherentists such as Laurence BonJour propose less stringent (and much more plausible) requirements, claiming that coherence comes in degrees, where the number of inferential connections within the system enhances degree of coherence and the number and variety of unexplained anomalies diminishes the degree of coherence in the system. BonJour admits, however, that his account of coherence is not fully precise. Others inclined toward coherentism think of its central notion in terms of inference to the best explanation (Harman 1973), but this notion is itself in need of clarification.

One promising approach to this difficulty of explaining the nature of coherence is probabilism. Probabilists take the primary item of epistemic evaluation to be degrees of belief rather than beliefs themselves, and by identifying degrees of belief with subjective probabilities, an elegant account of coherence can be developed in terms of satisfying the axioms of the probability calculus. On this account of coherence, a given degree of belief is justified only if it is part of a system of degrees of belief with which it is probabilistically coherent.

Consider some simple examples. According to the probability calculus, a given claim cannot be more probable than any claim it entails. So, if Joe's subjective probability (degree of belief) in "Billy is a bachelor" is .9, and his subjective probability in "Billy is unmarried" is .95, Joe's degrees of belief are incoherent and thus unjustified. Similarly, if two claims cannot both be true, then the probability calculus tells us that the probability of the disjunction of two such claims is the sum of their individual probabilities. So if Mary's probability for "God exists" is .3, and her probability for "God does not exist" is .7, and yet she is uncertain to some degree about the claim that either God exists or doesn't, Mary's attitudes are probabilistically incoherent and thus unjustified.

One quite popular version of probabilism is a variant of Bayesianism, derived by supplementing this synchronic requirement of probabilistic consistency with a diachronic requirement concerning how one's degrees of belief change over time in order to be justified. This version of Bayesianism requires updating of probabilities in a way tied to Bayes' theorem, using one's prior conditional probabilities to determine one's new unconditional probabilities based on further learning. So, for example, if your new evidence is (only) e, and your conditional probability for p on e was some number n yesterday, then your new probability for p, after learning (just) e, must be n in order to be justified. This updating rule is called "conditionalization."

Besides the attractive formal nature of these probabilistic characterizations of coherence, such views offer some promise of avoiding some epistemic paradoxes. In the lottery paradox, one has sufficient evidence to conclude that one's lottery ticket is a loser, but this same evidence justifies a similar conclusion about each other ticket as well. It thus appears that one is in a position to conclude that no ticket will win, in spite of knowing full well that the lottery is fair and that a winner will soon be announced. The preface paradox begins with a book you've written, one that is long and involved, but where you are justified in believing that each claim made is true. Since the book is complex, however, you are also justified when you caution in the preface that you are confident errors remain in spite of your best efforts. Once again, contradiction looms, since one's information puts one in a position to deduce that the book contains no errors, while being justified in believing the warning of the preface that errors remain.

Probabilist accounts offer some hope here by focusing on degrees of belief and their probabilistic coherence rather than on beliefs themselves. The fundamental reality, according to probabilists, is degree of belief, and if a cognizer in the lottery situation assigns a subjective winning probability of $1/n$ to each ticket in an n-ticket fair lottery, those probabilities are consistent. If we try to use this information to conclude that no ticket will win, we will have to combine these probabilities in some way, perhaps by conjoining each of the claims in question to form the large conjunction *ticket 1 will not win & ticket 2 will not win & . . . . & ticket n will not win*. Such a conjunction, however, will have quite low probability, perhaps blocking the inference to the conclusion that no ticket will win.

The popularity of holistic coherentism played a crucial role in enlarging the space of possibilities explored by epistemologists over the past half century. If a fundamental presupposition of the regress argument can be legitimately questioned, perhaps other presuppositions shared by both coherentists and foundationalists are equally questionable. One source of such questioning was the Gettier problem, which came to be seen by many as a problem in the theory of knowledge calling for more careful scrutiny of assumptions both about the nature of knowledge and about the nature of justification. (The Gettier problem involves counterexamples to the claim that knowledge is justified true belief, and the usual approaches to the problem attempted to find some fourth condition to add to justification, belief, and truth that would fully account for the nature of knowledge.) In particular, a standard assumption shared by both foundationalists and coherentists is that justification should be understood in terms of information that is internal to the cognizer in question.

Recognition of this internalist presupposition involved in the most common responses to the regress argument combined with a growing interest in developing epistemologies that fit well with a naturalistic metaphysics, leading to an interest in naturalized epistemology (see Quine 1969, 1990) and various forms of externalist alternatives to such internalism. Most notable among these externalist alternatives is reliabilism (see Goldman 1986), which has become the most popular theory in recent approaches to the nature of justification and knowledge. The rise of holistic coherentism thus led not only to the waning of foundationalism in epistemology, but also to the rise of an alternative metatheory concerning the nature of justification, a metatheory focusing on the distinction between theories that clarify justification in terms of elements internal to the cognizer in question, and those that clarify justification in terms of elements external to the cognizer in question.

III. Internalism and Externalism

Initial discussion of the distinction between internalist and externalist theories of justification focused on two aspects that continue to have strong influences on current philosophical inquiry. These two aspects are (i) the question of whether internalism requires reflective access to the features that generate justification, and (ii) the question of how the normative aspects of justification ultimately trace to, or supervene on, non-normative dimensions of reality.

As noted already, the idea that things that generate justification are things to which we have access by reflection was presupposed in nearly all the debates over foundationalism and coherentism until the middle part of the twentieth century. A major historical source questioning this presupposition is found in the work of W.V.O. Quine. Quine's attack on standard empiricism involved not only the well-known attack on the analytic/synthetic distinction in the philosophy of language, but also an attack on the idea that the epistemological project could be carried out by rationally reconstructing our conception of the world, without concern for the actual psychological realities involved in generating that picture. In his most trenchant moments, Quine recommended turning epistemology into a subdiscipline of psychology, treating questions about reasons for belief in terms of empirical questions about the causal and explanatory relationship between sensory stimuli and the views that result (Quine 1969).

Such strong proposals threaten to eliminate rather than explain epistemic normativity, but as Goldman (1986) points out, there is a more moderate way to embrace the Quinean concerns about rational reconstruction. Instead of eliminating questions about justification in favor of psychological questions, one may attempt to explain this normative concept in terms of the non-normative features of the world on which the normative supervenes or depends. According to reliabilists such as Goldman, epistemic justification is a matter of holding beliefs produced or sustained by processes or methods that are reliable in terms of getting one to the truth and avoiding error. Such an approach does not substitute some rational reconstruction of our beliefs for an accurate description of how they are produced and sustained, and it does so without eliminating the epistemological project of assessing which ways of forming and holding beliefs are preferable from a purely epistemic point of view.

Such approaches break with the internalist tradition found in the debates between foundationalists and coherentists. In that debate, many theorists (including Descartes, Locke, Chisholm, and BonJour) endorsed the idea that we have a cognitive duty to hold justified beliefs, that we are epistemically blameworthy when we hold beliefs without adequate justification. Such deontology provides a strong motivation for the idea that whether or not a belief is justified must itself be accessible to the person holding the belief, since it is difficult to defend the idea that we can legitimately be blamed for not restricting our beliefs on the basis of an undetectable feature of the belief.

The difficulty for such strong versions of internalism, called "access internalism," is that the theorists who favor such versions typically offer accounts of justification that involve such complicated features that it is implausible to maintain that we can always ascertain by introspection alone whether these features obtain. In the face of such concerns, many adopted a weaker form of internalism, called "mentalism," on which the features on which justification supervenes must themselves be psychological features of the individual in question (Feldman and Conee 2004).

Reliabilists and other externalists disagree with both forms of internalism. Reliabilists, for example, argue that the reliability of a process or method is the central factor in determining epistemic status, and that such reliability is neither introspectively accessible nor a psychological feature of the individual in question. Other recent forms of externalism join reliabilism in objecting to internalism. Virtue epistemologies (Sosa 1991; Zagzebski 1996) argue that the normativity involved in the nature of knowledge involves excellences or virtues of the intellect that are neither psychological states nor introspectively accessible, and modal epistemologies, which appeal to either safety or sensitivity counterfactuals in clarifying the nature of knowledge (where a safety counterfactual is of the form "whenever you would hold the belief, you would not easily be mistaken," and a sensitivity counterfactual is of the form "if the claim in question were false, you wouldn't believe it"). Proper functionalist viewpoints, the most influential proponent of which is Alvin Plantinga (Plantinga 1993), share this rejection of internalism as well.

Here there is a danger of terminological dispute, however. Versions of externalism tend to offer conditions relevant to an account of knowledge, and thus assume that if these conditions can be used to clarify the nature of epistemic justification, that epistemic justification is the kind of thing needed for a belief to be a serious candidate for knowledge. The simplest way to endorse such an idea is to think of epistemic justification as that which turns true belief into knowledge, but ever since Gettier's counterexamples to the claim that knowledge is justified true belief, weaker proposals are the norm. On weaker proposals, epistemic justification is often thought of as one of two conditions which are jointly sufficient to turn true belief into knowledge. Externalists typically offer theories of justification on which justification turns true belief into a serious candidate for knowledge in this way (Zagzebski (1996) is an exception here), but internalists do not always think of justification in such terms. Foley (1993) is explicit in this regard, distancing himself from the idea that justification is needed for knowledge. This difference in assumptions about the target of theorizing may be some evidence that certain disputes between internalists and externalists are merely terminological.

It would be a mistake, however, to try to explain away the entire debate in terms of terminological differences. A more accurate understanding of the dispute can be traced to two different historical traditions underlying current interest in the nature of justification. One source is the ancient tradition tracing to Plato which attempts to understand the difference between knowledge and true belief in terms of some normative notion that can be expressed using the language of justification. The other source is the pragmatist tradition that focuses on a fundamental notion of propriety in belief and action in contrast to the endless disputes over the status of academic skepticism, a notion of propriety that can also be expressed using the language of justification. The differences between the camps are deep and broad, with one camp favoring accounts of justification that center on notions such as responsible and blameless belief, and the other camp favoring accounts that generate objective ties to the way the world is, independently of how we think about it. It is rare, however, to find members of either camp who find no appeal whatsoever in the guiding platitudes and underlying presuppositions of the other camp, and the differences between differing platitudes and presuppositions play out in important ways when considering skeptical scenarios, scenarios in which nearly all of our beliefs are false, as occurs in evil demon worlds, and certain brain-in-the-vat hypotheses. Consideration of such scenarios focuses our attention on the important divide between externalists and internalists on the proper account of the connection between justification and truth. Externalists tend to favor accounts of the interdependence of these notions that yield quite strong claims about the objectivity of any view of the world that is justified, whereas internalists are less sanguine about such claims to objectivity for justification. This problem of the truth connection crystallizes in the form of the new evil demon objection to strongly objective externalist theories. That objection claims that strongly objective externalist theories mistakenly classify most beliefs of denizens of Descartes' evil demon world as unjustified. Such a classification is a mistake according to many internalists since, after all, these denizens could be us, and it is a mistake to think that all or most of our beliefs are unjustified.

IV. Recent Developments

These differences between externalists and internalists on the connection between justification and knowledge and between justification and truth raise anew a central concern found in the pragmatic heritage from which the present interest in justification derives. While academic skepticism dominates much of the history of epistemology, a pragmatic concern about what to do and what to believe leads directly to concern about the nature of justification and to less concern about the intricacies of arguments for and against academic skepticism. The distance between these two approaches is highlighted in the recent developments of "knowledge-first" epistemology, as championed in the enormously influential book by Williamson, *Knowledge and its Limits* (2000), and the value-driven conception of epistemological theorizing. The former approach clarifies the crucial notions of justification and evidence in terms of a prior notion of knowledge, thus illustrating the approach to justification that stresses its connection to knowledge and skepticism. Value-driven approaches have developed in several ways. One way is in terms of a heightened interest in virtue epistemologies (Sosa 1991; Zagzebski 1996; Greco 2000), in part because of the hope that in such epistemologies can be found a good answer to the question first raised by Socrates in the *Meno* as to why knowledge is better than mere true opinion (see Kvanvig 2003). Such a value-driven approach to epistemological theorizing raises difficult questions for many approaches to the nature of justification, especially typical externalist ones. Once we assume that a belief is true, the Socratic concerns from the *Meno* should make us wonder what additional value justification adds, especially for theories that focus on identifying the property of justification with something like objective likelihood of truth. The difficulty here is the swamping problem; that once truth is in the picture, it appears that any value deriving from likelihood of truth is swamped by the value of truth itself. Justification, on such conceptions, thus threatens to add no value to a belief in the presence of truth. Responses to this swamping problem range from denials of the idea that truth is the only intrinsic epistemic value (perhaps justification is itself intrinsically valuable) to attempts to defend a preferred conception of justification in a way that makes its value additive even in the presence of true belief.

The pragmatic source of interest in the theory of justification has led in recent years to a heightened interest in the degree to which justification itself might be affected by practical concerns. This interest comes into the theory of justification through the debate at the intersection of the theory of knowledge and the philosophy of language between contextualists and invariantists regarding the truth conditions for knowledge attributions. Early investigation of such attributions suggested that the word 'knows' functions in English in a contextual way, perhaps in the way deictic items such as 'I,' and 'now' function. In this way, contextualism arose in epistemology, according to which the proposition expressed by an epistemic sentence varies depending on the epistemic standards that are conversationally relevant in the speaker's context. Opposed to contextualism is invariantism, which claims that regardless of conversational context, epistemic vocabulary invariantly yields the same propositional content.

The debate between contextualists and invariantists, itself, may be only indirectly relevant to the theory of justification, but the data involved in the debate impinges directly on the fundamental issue of the connection between justification and truth. Among the mechanisms that affect whether speakers assent to a claim of knowledge seems to be what is at stake if one is wrong. Thus, even when speakers acknowledge that total evidence is unchanged, it is claimed that speakers assent to a knowledge claim when nothing of practical significance is at stake, but resist a knowledge claim when the stakes increase. For example, if getting to the bank to deposit a check doesn't much matter, speakers agree, it is claimed, with a knowledge attribution: "Sue knows that the bank will be open tomorrow." But if the stakes increase—say, a check will bounce if the bank isn't open tomorrow, and that will prompt a foreclosure on one's property—then, it is claimed, people resist. Typical contextualists and invariantists agree that such pragmatic encroachment into matters epistemic is commonplace (see Cohen 1999; DeRose 1992; Hawthorne 2004; Stanley 2005; and Fantl and McGrath 2002). If they are correct, and if there is a connection between such patterns of assent and the nature of knowledge and justification, then the connection between justification and truth is more complicated than any of the approaches common in the literature. A concern to answer the skeptic can lead one to adopt a view on which justification requires truth-guaranteeing evidence. The value-driven, pragmatic source of concern about the nature of justification eschews such a strong connection to truth, but not in favor of the radical break envisaged by those who think justification comes and goes depending on the practical stakes. Externalists typically want an objective likelihood connection between justification and truth, and typical internalists usually endorse the idea that justification is what results from following means appropriate to the goal of getting to the truth and avoiding error. The connection between justified belief and rational action is present for such theorists, to be sure, but in a way akin to the connection in standard decision theory: the practical stakes play a role in the story of rational action since the latter is a function of the former plus the relevant probabilities—the very probabilities that have something to do with epistemic justification. Those defending pragmatic encroachment hold something stronger. Instead of endorsing the traditional idea that the justification of action is directly affected by the practical stakes involved, pragmatic encroachment theorists hold that both the justification of action and the justification of the beliefs relevant to that action are lost when the stakes are raised. One way to express the difference in perspective here on pragmatic encroachment is as follows. Both approaches can grant that rational action is a function of what is at stake and what you know or reasonably believe. Traditional approaches that eschew pragmatic encroachment agree that in cases like the bank case above, the change in practical rationality regarding what is rational to do traces back to a change in the practical stakes involved, and this change is all that needs to be noted to explain the variation in practical rationality. Those arguing for pragmatic encroachment into the epistemic domain of justified belief hold that a change in practical rationality in cases such as the bank case reveals a change both in the practical stakes and in the epistemic condition underlying practical rationality as well.

Such a conclusion in the theory of justification requires significant methodological commitments, however—commitments tying the theory of justification to the concept of justification and thus to the meaning of the term 'justified' (or some related term such as 'rational' or 'reasonable' or 'warranted'), and then tying the meaning in question to what ordinary people would assent to when prompted appropriately. Theorists working under the remaining influence of the traditions of logical positivism and logical empiricism may find these commitments congenial, but more traditional approaches to epistemology will find many opportunities to avoid pragmatic encroachment should they wish to do so. Within the tradition of logical positivism and logical empiricism, appropriate philosophical methodology is tied to concept clarification and meaning explication, and by adopting this perspective on philosophical theorizing, the adequacy of a given epistemology could be tested by eliciting linguistic intuitions about the conditions under which assent or dissent occurs to sentences involving terms involved in that theory. The theory of knowledge could thus be informed by considering whether sentences of the form "S knows that p" would be judged true by ordinary speakers of the language across some range of scenarios, and to the extent that justification is related to knowledge, such results would have implications for the theory of justification as well. The underlying assumptions here have led to two additional recent developments in epistemology and philosophy more generally. First, there is a large and growing interest in experimental philosophy, since, to the degree that a philosophical or epistemological theory depends on linguistic data, one should expect the need for empirical data-gathering as part of the theoretical enterprise. Second, the issue of the role of intuitions and their epistemic standing, whether linguistic intuitions or other kinds of intuitions, has become a focus of continued research over the past couple of decades, whether in support of the conception of philosophy just outlined or in terms of a contrasting account of it (see Williamson 2007).

This issue of the connection between justification and truth, and the degree to which pragmatic factors encroach into this arena, is thus deeply involved in fundamental questions concerning appropriate methods in philosophy. The appeal of pragmatic encroachment theories is much less for those who reject the philosophical methodology described above, but the issues involved hark back to the original source of interest in the theory of justification, since the source of interest in the theory of justification within epistemology traces to a pragmatic concern to address questions of what to do and what to think that go beyond disputes about academic skepticism. Given such a source, some tension should be expected between assumptions about the purely intellectual relationship between truth and key epistemic notions such as knowledge and justification and the pragmatic elements that lead to theorizing about the notion of justification in the first place.

The dispute between internalists and externalists has led to another new direction of theorizing in addition to the value-driven approach. Once internalist assumptions are questioned, it is natural to notice the way in which our understanding of the world is deeply social. Most of what we know is not learned by first-hand experience, but by testimony, and once the questioning of internalist assumptions began, theorists began to wonder whether the social dimension of knowledge and justification, both in terms of the epistemic significance of disagreement between intellectual peers and in terms of whether this dimension is, itself, properly understood on the individualistic assumptions built into internalist conceptions of justification. The historically important conception of testimonial, associated with Hume and on which we learn from testimony on an inductive basis that warrants trusting our sources, is difficult to maintain in the face of the obvious fact that we learn as children from our parents and other teachers long before any such inductive basis is available. In response, one might adopt the view of Thomas Reid that default credulity is warranted in the absence of specific reasons to doubt the word of others. Other theorists, however, view these alternatives as too individualistic and that social conditions enter into the story of justification in a more fundamental way than either of these approaches allows. Wittgenstein and Rorty hold such views, for example, and one type of position along these lines would limit justification to beliefs arrived at in ways found acceptable within one's social community. Even more radical approaches recommend beginning with social knowledge and socially justified attitudes and positions, treating individual justification and knowledge as derivative from, and dependent on, the social realities in question.

References

Alston, W. (1989) *Epistemic Justification*, Ithaca, NY: Cornell University Press.
Chisholm, R. (1966) *The Theory of Knowledge*, Englewood Cliffs, NJ: Prentice-Hall, 3rd edn, 1989.
Cohen, S. (1999) "Contextualism, Skepticism, and the Structure of Reasons," *Philosophical Perspectives 13, Epistemology*, pp. 57–89.
DeRose, K. (1992) "Contextualism and Knowledge Attributions," *Philosophy and Phenomenological Research* 52, pp. 913–29.
Fantl, J. and McGrath, M. (2002) "Evidence, Pragmatics, and Justification," *The Philosophical Review* 111, pp. 67–94.
Feldman, R. and Conee, E. (2004) *Evidentialism*, Oxford: Oxford University Press.
Foley, R. (1993) *Working Without a Net*, New York: Oxford University Press.
Goldman, A. (1986) *Epistemology and Cognition*, Cambridge, MA: Harvard University Press.
Greco, J. (2000) *Putting Skeptics in Their Place*, New York: Cambridge University Press.
Hawthorne, J. (2004) *Knowledge and Lotteries*, Oxford: Oxford University Press.
Klein, P. (1999) "Human Knowledge and the Infinite Regress of Reasons," *Philosophical Perspectives* 13, J. Tomberlin (ed.), pp. 297–325.
Kornblith, H. (ed.) (1994) *Naturalizing Epistemology*, Cambridge, MA: MIT Press.
Kvanvig, J. (1995) "Coherentists' Distractions," *Philosophical Topics* 23, pp. 257–75.
Kvanvig, J. (2003) *The Value of Knowledge and the Pursuit of Understanding*, New York: Cambridge University Press.
Plantinga, A. (1993) *Warrant and Proper Function*, New York: Oxford University Press.
Quine, W.V.O. (1969) "Epistemology Naturalized," in *Ontological Relativity and Other Essays*, New York: Columbia University Press.
Quine, W.V.O. (1990) "Norms and Aims," in *The Pursuit of Truth*, Cambridge: Harvard University Press.
Schmitt, F. (ed.) (1994) *Socializing Epistemology*, London: Rowman & Littlefield.
Sellars, W. (1963) *Science, Perception, and Reality*, London: Routledge & Kegan Paul.
Sosa, E. (1991) *Knowledge in Perspective*, Cambridge: Cambridge University Press.
Stanley, J. (2005) *Knowledge and Practical Interests*, Oxford: Oxford University Press.

Williamson, T. (2000) *Knowledge and Its Limits*, Oxford: Oxford University Press.
Williamson, T. (2007) *The Philosophy of Philosophy*, Oxford: Blackwell.
Wittgenstein, L. (1969) *On Certainty*, Oxford: Oxford University Press.
Zagzebski, L. (1996) *Virtues of the Mind*, Oxford: Oxford University Press.

4
EPISTEMIC RATIONALITY
Richard Foley

One way to delineate the concept of epistemically rational belief is to locate it in relation to other core concepts of epistemology, especially those of knowledge and justified belief. Another is to position the concept within a general theory of rationality, which addresses the rationality of actions, decisions, intentions, plans, and strategies as well as beliefs. The two approaches need not be competitors. They can and should complement one another.

Epistemically Rational Belief, Justified Belief and Knowledge

There is no generally agreed way of understanding the relationships among these three core concepts of epistemology. Some epistemologists use the concepts of justified and epistemically rational belief interchangeably and insist as well that there is a necessary connection between them and the concept of knowledge, whereas others distinguish them and don't insist on a necessary link with knowledge.

The best way to make one's way through these complications is to begin with Edmund Gettier's seminal article, "Is Justified True Belief Knowledge?" (Gettier 1963: 121–3). Gettier assumed that justified belief is one of the necessary conditions of knowledge and then went on to devise a pair of counterexamples to show that knowledge cannot be adequately conceived as justified true belief.

Gettier's article marked the beginning of a search for a fourth condition that could be added to justification, truth, and belief to produce an adequate account of knowledge. Some epistemologists suggested that a special kind of justification is needed. The justification has to be non-defective, in the sense that it does not also justify any falsehood (Chisholm 1977: 102–18; Sosa 1979: 79–92; Sosa 1991: 19–34), or it has to be indefeasible, in the sense it cannot be defeated by the addition of any truth (Audi 1993; Klein 1981; Lehrer 1974; Pollock 1986; Swain 1981).

Others, however, began to wonder whether something less intellectual than justification, traditionally understood, is better suited for understanding knowledge. Justification is traditionally associated with being in a position to generate a defense of one's belief, but in many instances, for example, simple perceptual knowledge, people seem not to be in a position to offer anything resembling a defense of what they know.

An early proposal was that knowledge requires there to be an appropriate causal connection between the fact making a belief true and the person's having that belief (Armstrong 1973; Goldman 1967: 357–72) but this proposal encountered a number of problems, for example, problems accounting for knowledge of mathematics, general facts, and the future.

Nevertheless, in the eyes of many, the causal theory at least had the advantage of shifting the focus away from questions of being able to defend one's beliefs intellectually and towards questions of being in an appropriate relation with one's environment. If a simple causal connection between the fact that makes a belief true and the belief itself wouldn't do, some other relation needed to be found.

One suggestion was that for a true belief to count as knowledge, it must be reliably generated (Goldman 1986). A second idea was that in close counterfactual situations the subject's beliefs about the matter in question must track the truth (Nozick 1981). A third was that the belief must be the product of properly functioning cognitive faculties (Plantinga 1993). There have been important variants of each of these proposals as well (Dretske 1981; Sosa 1991).

These new accounts of knowledge led in turn to new accounts of justification, specifically, externalist ones. For example, Alvin Goldman, who had already argued that knowledge is reliably produced true belief, used the assumption that justification is a necessary condition of knowledge to argue that epistemic justification must also be essentially a matter of one's beliefs having been produced and sustained by reliable cognitive processes (Goldman 1986). Because a cognitive process is reliable only if it is well suited to produce true beliefs in the external environment in which it is operating, this is an externalist account of justification. By contrast, most foundationalists and coherentists are internalists, whose accounts of justification emphasize the ability of individuals to mount defenses of their beliefs.

There is a large literature on the relative advantages and disadvantages of externalism and internalism in epistemology (Alston 1989; Audi 1988: 1–29; Bonjour 1980: 53–71; Fumerton 1988; Goldman 1988; Sosa 1991: 225–44). Much of the literature presupposes that externalists and internalists are defending rival theories, but a more interesting reading of the dispute is that they are not, strictly speaking, competitors at all. They are, rather, principally concerned with different issues.

Externalists are primarily interested in explicating knowledge, but along the way they see themselves as proposing an account of justification, because justification, they stipulate, is that which has to be added to true belief in order to get a serious candidate for knowledge.

Internalists, by contrast, are primarily interested in explicating a sense of justification that captures what is involved in having beliefs that are internally defensible, but along the way they see themselves as also assembling the materials for an adequate account of knowledge, because they too assume that, by definition, justification is one of the necessary conditions of knowledge.

There are, then, these very different ways of thinking about justified belief. Despite their differences, they are easy to conflate, especially since some of the most influential figures in the history of epistemology have thought that internally defensible beliefs guarantee knowledge. Descartes, for example, recommended that one should believe only that which is altogether impossible to doubt, in other words, only that which is internally beyond the possibility of criticism. However, he also thought that by doing so one could be altogether assured of having knowledge.

Descartes' search for an internal procedure that guarantees knowledge proved not to be feasible. The lesson, however, is not that either the internal or external aspect of the Cartesian project has to be abandoned but, rather, that there are different, equally legitimate projects for epistemologists to pursue. One project, expressed figuratively, is that of exploring what is required for one to put one's own intellectual house in proper order, whereas another project is that of exploring what is required for one to stand in a relation of knowledge to one's environment.

It is not unusual for the results of both kinds of projects to be reported using the language of rationality and justification, but the terms have different senses within the contexts of these two projects.

It is thus important for epistemologists to be self-conscious about how they are using the terms *epistemically rational belief* and *justified belief*. It is not realistic to expect universal consistency in usage, but there are constraints. If one insists on stipulating, as some do, that justification is, by definition, a necessary condition of knowledge, it becomes all the more critical to distinguish epistemically rational belief from justified belief, for it should not be assumed that an epistemically rational belief, when true, is necessarily a good candidate for knowledge.

Relaxing the tie between knowledge and epistemic rational belief frees the theory of knowledge from overly intellectual conceptions of knowledge, thus smoothing the way for treatments that acknowledge that most people cannot marshal strong epistemic reasons in defense of some things they know. It likewise frees the theory of epistemic rationality from a preoccupation with the prerequisites of knowledge, which in turn creates a space for questions about the rationality of beliefs to be treated similarly to questions about the rationality of other phenomena. The concept of rational belief ought not to be cordoned off from other notions of rationality as if the conditions that make a belief rational have little to do with the conditions that make a decision, strategy, action, or plan rational.

The General Theory of Rationality

A first step towards locating the concept of epistemically rational belief within a general theory of rationality is to appreciate that rationality is a goal-oriented notion. Whether the question is one of the rationality of beliefs, decisions, intentions, plans, or strategies, what is at issue is the effective pursuit of goals. Questions about the rationality of a decision, for example, are in the first instance questions about how effectively the decision seems to accomplish the decision maker's goals.

The qualifier *seems* is needed, because it is too stringent to insist that a decision is rational only if it actually obtains the goals in question. Rational decisions can turn out badly. Similarly, it is too stringent to insist that a decision is rational only if it is probable that it will achieve the goals in question, since it is sometimes the case that no one could be reasonably expected to see that the decision was likely to have unwelcome consequences. Considerations such as these suggest that a decision (or plan, action, strategy, belief) is rational for an individual if it is rational for the individual to believe that it will satisfy her goals.

An obvious drawback is that this schema makes use of the notion of rational belief, thus leaving one within the circle of notions one wishes to understand. Before addressing this issue, consider a couple of preliminary points.

The first is that reasonability admits of degrees whereas rationality does not. In particular, reasonability varies with the strengths of one's reasons, while the rational is that which is sufficiently reasonable. It is thus possible for more than one of the available options in a situation to be rational for an individual even though there are reasons to prefer some of the options to the others. A decision (plan, strategy, etc.) is rational if it is rational to believe that it will do an acceptably good job of achieving the goals in question. To say that it will do *an acceptably good job* is to say its estimated desirability is sufficiently high, where "estimated desirability" is a matter of what it is rational to believe about its probable effectiveness in promoting the goals and the relative value of these goals (Jeffrey 1983).

A second key point is that when making assessments about the rationality of an individual's decisions (plans, strategies, etc.), the set of goals taken into account can vary. We are sometimes interested in evaluating what it is rational for an individual to do all things considered, and we thus take into consideration all her goals. In other contexts, however, we restrict ourselves to a subset. We might want to evaluate a decision, for example, with respect to only those goals that concern her economic wellbeing. If it is rational for her to believe that A would be an effective means of promoting this subset of goals, we can say that A is rational in an economic sense for her. We can say this even if, with respect to all of her goals, both economic and non-economic, it is not rational to decide in favor of A.

Thus, a more precise way of expressing general schema of rationality is as follows: a decision (plan, strategy, etc.) is rational in sense X for an individual if it is rational for her to believe that the plan will do an acceptably good job of satisfying her goals of type X.

Epistemic vs. Non-epistemic Reasons for Belief

The distinction among different kinds of rationality corresponding to different kinds of goals is especially important in epistemology. In assessing the rationality of beliefs, epistemologists have traditionally been interested in a specific intellectual goal, that of now having true beliefs and not having false beliefs.

This goal has two aspects, either of which could be championed more easily on its own than in tandem with the other. If the goal were only not to have false beliefs, the strategy would be to believe relatively little (so as to avoid acquiring any falsehoods), whereas if the goal were only to have true beliefs, the strategy would be to believe a great deal (so as to avoid missing any truths). The challenge is to balance appropriately the values of accuracy and comprehensiveness.

Note that the goal is not to have accurate and comprehensive beliefs at some future time but, rather, to have them now. To understand the significance of characterizing the goal in this way, imagine that my prospects for having accurate and comprehensive beliefs a year from now would be enhanced by now believing something for which I lack adequate evidence. Suppose, for example, that P involves a more favorable assessment of my intellectual talents than the evidence warrants, but believing P would make me more intellectually confident, which would make me a more dedicated inquirer, which in turn would enhance my long-term prospects of having accurate and comprehensive beliefs. Despite these long-term benefits, there is an important sense of rational belief, indeed the very sense that traditionally has been of interest to epistemologists, in which it is not rational for me to believe P. A way of making this distinction is to say that it is not rational in a purely epistemic sense for me to believe P, where this purely epistemic sense is to be understood in terms of the goal of now having accurate and comprehensive beliefs.

Foundationalists, coherentists, virtue theorists, and others propose accounts of what properties a belief must have in order to be rational in this sense, but despite their differences, they all accept the constraint that their accounts should not make reference to any other notion of rationality. Foundationalists, for example, propose that epistemic rationality is to be understood in terms of basic beliefs and a set of deductive and inductive relations by which other beliefs are supported by the basic ones, and they would view it as a defect if they had to make reference to some other notion of rationality or one of its cognates in characterizing basicality or the support relations. By contrast, coherentists explicate epistemic rationality in terms of a set of deductive and probabilistic relations among beliefs and a set of properties such as conservativeness and explanatory power, but they too would view it a defect if their explication smuggled in any reference to any other notion of rationality. This is similarly the case for other theories of epistemic rational belief.

This characteristic of epistemically rational belief makes it suitable for addressing the principal drawback of the general schema of rationality cited above, namely, that it leaves us within the circle of notions we wish to understand. Because an account of epistemically rational belief does not make use of any other notion of rationality or any of its close cognates, it can provide the schema with an escape route from this circle.

In particular, with an account of epistemically rational belief in hand, the general schema of rationality can be further refined: a decision (plan, action, strategy, etc.) is rational in sense X for an individual just in case it is *epistemically rational* for the individual to believe that the decision (plan, action, strategy, etc.) will do an acceptably good job of satisfying her goals of kind X.

Other kinds of rationality are thus understood in terms of epistemic rationality whereas epistemic rationality does not presuppose any other kind of rationality. Epistemic rationality serves as an anchor for other kinds of rationality.

This schema is perfectly general. It applies to all phenomena (decisions, plans, strategies, etc.) and to all forms of rationality for these phenomena (economic rationality, rationality of all things considered, and so on). Note, however, that the schema implies that beliefs, like decisions, strategies, plans, and intentions, can in principle be assessed in terms of how well they promote other goals. The schema suggests, for example, that if it is epistemically rational for an individual to believe that believing a proposition P would effectively promote her overall constellation of goals, it is rational for her to believe P all things considered.

There is nothing improper about evaluating beliefs in terms of how well they promote the total set of one's goals, and yet we in fact rarely do so. Why is this? Answering this question requires an understanding of the different roles that epistemic and pragmatic reasons for belief play in our intellectual lives.

Discussions and debates about what it is rational to believe often take place in a context of trying to convince someone to believe something. In an effort to persuade, we point out the reasons there are for believing the proposition in question, but insofar as our aim is to get someone to believe something that she does not now believe, the citing of pragmatic reasons is ordinarily ineffective. Even if we convince her that she has good pragmatic reasons to believe a proposition, this is usually not enough to generate belief.

Beliefs are psychological states that purport to represent the world accurately (Searle 1983; Williams 1973). Beliefs that are accurate tend also to be useful, but usefulness is a secondary characteristic. The primary function of beliefs is to represent accurately. Pragmatic reasons for belief reverse this order. They are directed first and foremost at producing a state that is useful, not one that accurately represents. Such reasons, correspondingly, are normally not effective at producing belief. At best they motivate the person to get herself into an evidential situation in which belief eventually will be possible. Think of agnostics who are convinced by Pascal's argument that they have pragmatic reasons to believe in God, since if God does exist, their chances for eternal salvation may be enhanced by such a belief. They thereby resolve to attend church regularly, surround themselves with believers, and read religious tracts in an effort to alter their outlook in such a way that belief in God will become possible for them.

Thus, insofar as our concern is to persuade someone to believe a proposition P, the explanation for why we do not tend to be interested in the pragmatic reasons she has to believe P is straightforward, namely, it is generally pointless to cite such reasons, because they are usually not the kind of reasons that generate belief. Similarly, in our own deliberations about a claim, we ordinarily do not consider what pragmatic reasons we might have for believing it, and the explanation is the same; pragmatic reasons for belief are ordinarily inefficacious, and thus our general practice is to ignore them.

A second reinforcing explanation as to why we ordinarily do not deliberate about pragmatic reasons for belief is that such deliberations are usually redundant. Although in principle there can be pragmatic reasons as well as epistemic reasons for belief, ordinarily our overriding pragmatic reason with respect to beliefs is to have and maintain an accurate and comprehensive stock of beliefs.

We are continually faced with an enormous range of decisions, and because we usually do not know in advance what decisions we will need to make, we usually do not know in advance what information will be required to make them well. This might not be important were it not for the fact that a large number of these decisions need to be made quickly, without the opportunity for deliberation or investigation. In making these decisions, we thus need to draw upon our existing stock of beliefs, and if that stock is either small or inaccurate, we increase the likelihood that our decisions will not be good ones.

So ordinarily, the system of beliefs that is likely to do the best overall job of promoting our total constellation of goals is one that is both comprehensive and accurate. Since epistemically rational beliefs are, by definition, ones that are rational for us insofar as our goal is to have accurate and comprehensive beliefs, it is ordinarily rational, all things considered, that is, when all of our goals are taken into account, to believe those propositions that are epistemically rational for us. Thus, for all practical purposes, taking this phrase literally, we can usually safely ignore pragmatic reasons in our deliberations about what to believe.

To be sure, there are conceivable situations in which our epistemic reasons and our overall reasons for belief are pulled apart. If someone credibly threatens to harm my children unless I come to believe P, then it may be rational for me, all things considered, to find some way of getting myself to believe P whatever my epistemic reasons are. In the vast majority of cases, however, there are pressures that keep what it is rational to believe, all things considered, from being in conflict with what it is epistemically rational to believe.

Beliefs, Degrees of Belief, and the Lottery

Consider two questions. What propositions are epistemically rational to believe? And, with what confidence is it epistemically rational to believe a proposition?

Answering the first of these questions requires an epistemology of belief. Answering the second requires an epistemology of degrees of belief. The two kinds of accounts would seem to be closely related. The first merely classifies belief-like attitudes into a threefold schema (believing, disbelieving, and withholding judgment), whereas the second introduces as many distinctions as are needed to talk about the levels of confidence one has in various propositions, that is, one's degrees of belief in them.

A simple thesis would seem to link the two, namely, it is epistemically rational for S to believe P just in case it is epistemically rational for S to have a degree of confidence in P that is sufficient for belief.

This thesis invites a follow-up question, what degree of confidence is sufficient for belief? The vagueness of belief talk makes it difficult to give a definitive answer to this question, but in other cases we deal with vagueness by stipulation. Indeed, it might not even matter much where we set the threshold as long as we are clear about what we are doing.

On the other hand, some have thought that there are paradoxes lurking here, the most well known of which is the lottery. Two assumptions about epistemically rational belief lead to these worries.

The first is non-contradiction: if it is epistemically rational for S to believe P, it cannot be epistemically rational for S to believe not-P. The second assumption is that epistemically rational belief is governed by a conjunction rule: if it is epistemically rational for S to believe P and epistemically rational for S to believe Q, it is also epistemically rational for S to believe their conjunction (P & Q). If both these assumptions are made, the above linking thesis does lead to paradox.

The argument is relatively simple. Suppose that degrees of belief can be measured on a scale from 0 to 1, with 1 representing subjective certainty. Let the threshold x required for belief be any real number less than 1. For example, let $x = 0.99$. Now imagine a lottery with 100 tickets, and suppose that it is epistemically rational for you to believe that the lottery is fair and that as such there will be only one winning ticket. More exactly, assume that it is epistemically rational for you to believe that (either ticket #1 will win or ticket #2 will win ... or ticket #100 will win). This proposition is logically equivalent to the proposition that it's not the case that (ticket #1 will not win and ticket #2 will not win ... and ticket #100 will not win). Assume you are aware of the equivalence and, as a result, it is also epistemically rational for you to believe this proposition.

Suppose, finally, that you have no reason to distinguish among the tickets concerning their chances of winning. So, it is epistemically rational for you to have 0.99 confidence that ticket #1 will not win, 0.99 confidence that ticket #2 will not win, and so on for each of the other tickets. Then, according to the above linking thesis, it is epistemically rational for you to believe each of these propositions, since it is rational for you to have a degree of confidence in each that is sufficient for belief. But if a conjunction rule governs epistemically rational belief, it is also epistemically rational for you to believe the conjunctive proposition that (ticket #1 will not win and ticket #2 will not win ... and ticket #100 will not win). However, we have already assumed that it is epistemically rational for you to believe the denial of this proposition, since it is rational for you to believe that the lottery is fair. But according to the assumption of non-contradiction, it is impossible for contradictory propositions to be epistemically rational for you. So, contrary to the initial hypothesis, x cannot be 0.99.

A little reflection indicates that x cannot be anything other than 1, since the same problem can arise with respect to a lottery of any size whatsoever. On the other hand, it cannot be a requirement that x be 1, since subjective certainty is not required for belief.

The lottery problem thus seems to show that the problem for the linking thesis has nothing to do with the vagueness of belief. If that were the only problem, it could be dealt with by stipulating some degree of belief as the threshold. The problem, rather, is that there doesn't seem to be any threshold that can be sensibly stipulated.

One's way of dealing with this problem shapes one's epistemology.

One diagnosis is that the problem constitutes a *reductio* against doing epistemology in terms of beliefs *simpliciter* as opposed to degrees of belief. If we were to abandon the epistemology of belief and were content with an epistemology of degrees of belief, the problems of the lottery would be avoided. We simply observe that it is epistemically rational for you to have a high degree of confidence in the relevant individual propositions (the proposition that ticket #1 will lose, that ticket #2 will lose, and so on) but a low degree of confidence in their conjunctions, and leave the matter at that, without trying to decide whether it is epistemically rational to believe *simpliciter* any of these propositions. According to this way of viewing the matter, we shouldn't try to stipulate a threshold of belief. Rather, we should quit talking about what it is rational to believe.

A less desperate approach to the problem, however, is to turn the above argument on its head. Begin with the presumption that the project of formulating an epistemology of belief, at least on the face of it, is a legitimate project. The second premise is the same as above, namely, any theory of epistemically rational belief must either reject the conjunction rule or face absurd consequences. The conclusion, then, is to reject the conjunction rule, which in any event is not very plausible. After all, a conjunction can be no more probable than its individual conjuncts, and often it is considerably less probable.

There are worries associated with denying the conjunction rule, however, the most serious of which is that if we are not required on pains of irrationality to believe the conjunction of propositions that we rationally believe, we might seem to lose some of our most powerful argumentative and deliberative tools. Deductive reasoning in particular might seem to lose much of its force, because without a conjunction rule, one might seem to be at liberty to accept each of the premises of an argument, accept also that the argument is deductively valid, and yet nonetheless deny that one is rationally committed to believing the conclusion.

But this worry is misplaced. Some sort of conjunction rule is indeed essential for deductive argumentation and deliberation, but the relevant rule is one governing such attitudes as presuming, positing, and hypothesizing as opposed to believing. Each of these attitudes is a form of commitment that, unlike belief, is context-relative. One doesn't believe a proposition relative to certain purposes but not believe it relative to others. One either believes it or one doesn't. Presuming, positing, and hypothesizing, by contrast, are not like this. Having such attitudes toward a proposition is a matter of one's being prepared to regard the proposition as true for a certain range of purposes or situations. Moreover, relative to these purposes or situations, the attitudes are conjunctive. If for the purposes of a discussion one assumes (supposes, hypothesizes) P and if for that same discussion one also assumes (supposes, hypothesizes) Q, one is committed within that context to their conjunction, and committed as well to anything their conjunction implies.

Once a conjunction rule for belief is abandoned, the way is open for dealing with the problems of the lottery without paradox and without abandoning the epistemology of belief. In particular, the proper conclusion about the lottery is that it can be rational for one to believe of each ticket that it will lose without thereby being also committed, on pains of irrationality, to believing that no ticket will win.

Still, it might be asked, why have two theories, an epistemology of belief and an epistemology of degrees of belief, when one might do just as well? The quick answer is that one won't do just as well. In a wide range of informative, argumentative, and decision-making activities, we want others to report what they think is true or false about the issues at hand. We don't want them to qualify every assertion, much less indicate their exact degree of confidence in each assertion that they make. We want views to be more economically delivered than this.

In expository books and articles, department reports, financial statements, documentaries, and most other material designed to transfer information, we want and need to be given a black-and-white picture of at least some of the issues. This, of course, is not always feasible. Sometimes the evidence is not sufficiently strong one way or the other to allow the author to take a definite stand, in which case we tolerate a straddling of the fence, that is, a withholding of judgment.

Even so, the overall pattern is clear. If all of the information provided to us by others were finely qualified with respect to the provider's degree of confidence in it, we would soon be overwhelmed. And it is no different with our private deliberations. We don't have finely qualified degrees of confidence for every proposition we consider, but even if we did, we would soon find ourselves overwhelmed if we tried to deliberate about complicated issues on the basis of them (Harman 1988).

Of course, sometimes we want and need probabilities, but even here, we arrive at these probabilities against a backdrop of black-and-white assumptions, that is, against a backdrop of belief. I calculate what to bet before I draw my final card, and I note to myself that the probability of the drawn card's being a heart, given the cards in my hand and the exposed cards of my opponents, is 0.25. Or I note that the probability of the die coming up six is 0.16667, or that the probability of an American male's dying of a heart attack prior to age forty is 0.05. The assignment of each of these probabilities depends on antecedent black-and-white beliefs. I believe that the deck of cards is a standard deck, that the die isn't weighted, and that the statistics on heart attacks were reliably gathered. It might be objected that these background beliefs are so close to certain that we ignore their probabilities, but this is just the point. In most situations, there are so many potentially distorting factors that we ignore most of them. We couldn't possibly keep track of all of them, much less have them explicitly enter into our deliberations.

Taking stands is an inescapable part of our intellectual lives, and the epistemology of belief is the study of such stands. The range of options is restricted to just three: to say yes to a proposition, to say no to it, or to remain neutral on it. The project is then to describe what is a reasonable combination of yes, no, and neutral elements for one to adopt, not for all time but for now.

References

Alston, W. (1989) *Epistemic Justification*, Ithaca, NY: Cornell University Press.
Armstrong, D.M. (1973) *Belief, Truth, and Knowledge*, Cambridge: Cambridge University Press.
Audi, R. (1988) "Justification, Truth and Reliability," *Philosophy and Phenomenological Research* 49.
Audi, R. (1993) *The Structure of Justification*, Cambridge: Cambridge University Press.
Bonjour, L. (1980) "Externalist Theories of Empirical Knowledge," in P. French, T. Uehling, H. Wettstein (eds.), *Midwest Studies in Philosophy*, Vol. V, Minneapolis: University of Minnesota Press.
Chisholm, R. (1977) *Theory of Knowledge*, 2nd edn, Englewood Cliffs, NJ: Prentice-Hall.
Dretske, F. (1981) *Knowledge and the Flow of Information*, Cambridge, MA: MIT Press.
Fumerton, R. (1988) "The Internalism-Externalism Controversy," in J. Tomberlin (ed.) *Philosophical Perspectives*, Vol. 2, Atascadero, CA: Ridgeview.

Gettier, E. (1963) "Is Justified True Belief Knowledge?" *Analysis* XXV, 121–3.
Goldman, A. (1967) "A Causal Theory of Knowing," *The Journal of Philosophy* 64, 335–72.
Goldman, A. (1986) *Epistemology and Cognition*, Cambridge, MA: Harvard University Press.
Goldman, A. (1988) "Strong and Weak Justification," in J. Tomberlin (ed.) *Philosophical Perspectives*, Vol. 2, Atascadero, CA: Ridgeview Publishing Company.
Harman, G. (1988) *Change in View*, Cambridge, MA: MIT Press.
Jeffrey, R. (1983) *The Logic of Decision*, 2nd edn, Chicago, IL: University of Chicago Press.
Klein, P. (1981) *Certainty: A Refutation of Scepticism*, Minneapolis: University of Minnesota Press.
Lehrer, K. (1974) *Knowledge*, Oxford: Oxford University Press.
Nozick, R. (1981) *Philosophical Explanations*, Cambridge, MA: Harvard University Press.
Plantinga, A. (1993) *Warrant: The Current Debate*, Oxford: Oxford University Press.
Pollock, J. (1986) *Contemporary Theories of Knowledge*, Totowa, NJ: Rowman and Littlefield.
Searle, J. (1983) *Intentionality*, New York: Cambridge University Press.
Sosa, E. (1979) "Epistemic Presupposition," in G. Pappas (ed.) *Justification and Knowledge*, Dordrecht: Reidel.
—— (1991) *Knowledge in Perspective*, Cambridge: Cambridge University Press.
Swain, M. (1981) *Reasons and Knowledge*, Ithaca, NY: Cornell University Press.
Williams, B. (1973) "Deciding to Believe," in *Problems of the Self*, New York: Cambridge University Press.

5
EPISTEMIC NORMS
Pascal Engel

1. Epistemic Normativity

When we evaluate our beliefs and our reasonings as justified or unjustified, as good or bad, or as rational or irrational, we make, in a broad sense of the term, normative judgments about them. It is often said that justification itself is a normative notion, and that epistemology is a normative discipline. But the nature of epistemic normativity is elusive, and there are several strands in these debates, many of which are common to the domain of practical or ethical normativity and to the domain of epistemic or cognitive normativity.

(i) *Norms and values.* It is common to distinguish two kinds of normative notions, those which are deontic, formulated in terms of *oughts*, *right* or *wrong*, prescriptions and permissions, and those which are teleological or axiological, formulated in terms of *good*, *bad*, *valuable*, *virtuous* or *defective*. There are important differences between these two kinds of normative properties. The former in general call for actions, can give rise to sanctions, and do not admit degrees, whereas the latter are more a matter of possession by the agent of a certain kind of sensitivity, call for praise or blame, and are comparative. Deontic notions are often associated to "thin" properties, whereas axiological ones are often "thick" properties. One main problem about epistemic normativity is whether it should be formulated in terms of epistemic norms in the deontic sense or in terms of value-based notions and whether one has priority over the other.

(ii) *Norms, rationality, and reasons.* The notion of norm is commonly associated with the notion of rationality, both because norms concern what one ideally ought to do or to think, and because rationality seems to be normative in the sense that it prescribes a certain kind of conduct. But it is not clear in what sense rationality is normative rather than descriptive of agents or believers. There is an important sense in which what rationality requires normatively differs from what one has a *reason* to do or to think. Some think the latter has priority over the former. The "buck passing" account of values in the ethical domain (Scanlon 1998; Skorupski 2010) according to which all normative concepts (including the teleological ones) should be formulated in terms of reasons also concerns epistemic reasons and whether these have priorities over values.

(iii) *Normative regulation.* A normative statement is usually supposed to govern or to guide the actions of those who are subject to it. What kind of guidance or regulation does a norm imply? Mere permissions and recommendations, or strict prescriptions? And to what extent is the agent who obeys a norm supposed to be aware that he is subject to it? To what extent does *ought* imply *can* and, if it does, what is the nature of the normative *can*? This depends in part on whether the normative ought is considered as categorical (prescribing regardless of any goal) or hypothetical (relative to a goal for which a prescription is instrumental).

(iv) *Normative objectivity*. Are norms more like rules or conventions, which depend upon human decisions, or more like universal principles governing the whole domain of thought and action? Are they necessarily plural or can they be unified or ranked along a hierarchy? Are there some basic norms which rule a whole domain? This is closely related to the question of the objectivity of norms and to their ontological status: are there genuine normative facts and properties which make our normative statements true or false or are normative statements mere expressions of our attitudes? Should one be a cognitivist (Wedgwood 2007) or an expressivist (Gibbard 2008) about them? Epistemology itself can be understood as a meta-normative discipline: it not only deals with epistemic norms and values, but it also has, at a meta-level, to evaluate the appropriateness and objectivity of these norms. Are there standards to evaluate our standards, meta-norms about which norms we should adopt? And if there are such meta-norms, how to choose between them? If epistemic norms and values are objective, some must be such that they cannot be evaluated further.

(v) *Naturalization*. Do norms supervene on natural facts? Can they be reduced to these? Unless one adopts a form of non-factualism (Field 2009) or a form of eliminativism (Weinberg et al. 2001), to the effect that the apparent objectivity of normative discourse is illusory and that norms can be reduced to descriptive facts, one has to address the question of the relationship between the normative and the descriptive. The epistemological counterpart of this question concerns how much empirical matters count in epistemology and how much it can depend upon psychology or biology (Kornblith 1982).

Questions (i)–(v) all arise for the practical or ethical domain and one can expect that they can be transposed to the epistemic domain. But there are important asymmetries. In particular there are epistemic norms in the deontic sense, and if they entail specific duties to believe, it is not clear that what we ought to believe or not to believe must issue in actions, for believings are not, in general, things that we do. Moreover, if there are epistemic obligations or duties about beliefs, we must be able to conform to them and to perform certain kinds of actions (*ought* normally implies *can*); but if, as many philosophers think, beliefs are not actions and are not under the control of the will, we cannot conform to such obligations, and their existence is dubious. So it is not clear that responsibility for belief, or the capacity to be subject to praise or blame in the epistemic domain, must rest upon the existence of epistemic duties. These questions lie at the heart of the "ethics of belief" debate (Clifford 1879; James 1905; Feldman 2000). Another reason to deny the parallelism between the practical and the epistemic case is that although the idea of a plurality of ethical values, reasons or norms makes sense in the former, it does not make sense in the latter: there may be many kinds of good reasons for which one does something, but normally a belief is justified only by one kind of reason—its being true or its being supported by evidence. One can believe for practical, rather than for epistemic reasons. But the former are, in comparison to the latter, the wrong kind of reasons. Wishful thinking is a normatively incorrect kind of believing, although it can be correct in the practical domain (if I am indifferent in my choice between A and B, I can choose either, but if I have equal evidence for believing p or q, I must suspend judgment). In spite of important structural analogies between practical and theoretical reasoning (Audi 2000; Kelly 2003), there are important disanalogies. Pragmatism is, in general, the view that practical values and norms can be compared to—and sometimes can override—epistemic norms. But if the normative landscape differs from the practical to the theoretical realm, pragmatism is less plausible.

Because they do not give the same kind of answers to questions (i)–(v), not all epistemologists believe in the existence of epistemic norms. Some think that they reduce to epistemic values and favor a teleological or value-based account of epistemic normativity. Others reduce it to the normativity of rationality or to the normativity of reasons. Yet others reject the very idea of normative authority in the epistemic domain, because they consider that epistemology has to be naturalized, although they do not reject the existence of epistemic values altogether.

2. Norms of Rationality

If there are epistemic norms, what are they? One can understand these, in the first place, as general requirements of rationality flowing from the very nature of belief and of the mental. For instance, two main requirements of rationality are those of coherence and deductive closure:

(a) One ought not to believe p and not p.
(b) One ought to believe that q if one believes that p and that p entails q.

But what is the nature of this *ought*? One can take it as a constraint on rational belief or as a general principle for the interpretation of any believer as a rational being (Davidson 1980; Millar 2006). In this sense the principles of logic, or those of probability theory, are the most general norms for belief, and no subject can be said to have a belief unless these norms can be applied (Davidson 2004). The problem with such very high-profile norms is that they do not seem to be normative at all. For a principle to be genuinely normative, it must have normative force and be able to actually regulate belief. It must also have normative freedom, in the sense that one must have the possibility of violating it. But general or abstract norms of rationality like (a) and (b) have neither of these properties, since they are idealized descriptions of a rational believer: at best they tell us what the constitutive properties of rational belief are, but they offer us no guidance (Railton 2000). Perhaps normative statements like (a) or (b) apply to what it is to have a mind or being interpretable as a thinking being, but they do not prescribe (Schröder 2003; Engel 2008).

Nevertheless ideals of reason or normative requirements like (a) and (b) *can* be violated: one can certainly have contradictory beliefs or fail to draw a conclusion from one's other beliefs. Moreover, one can appreciate the force of the ideal and yet fail to conform to it. If one believes that p, and believes that p entails q, one can fail to infer q, if one has a reason not to believe q. For instance, if you believe that the earth was created in less than a week, and believe that if the earth was created in less than a week, you are rationally required, or committed to believing that the earth was created in less than a week, but certainly you ought not to believe this, since it is false, and you have good reason or justification to believe that it is false. The difference between this latter *ought* and the one which figures in the rational requirement (b) is often expressed in terms of the idea that rational requirements take wide scope:

(a′) You ought (if you believe that p, and that p implies p, believe p).

From (a′) one cannot detach the conclusion 'q', whereas inferences like the above about the origin of the earth take narrow scope:

(a″) If you believe that p, and that if p then q, then you ought to believe that q.

which is invalid. On one conception (Broome 2000) what it takes to be rational always involves wide scope normative requirements, on another (Kolodny 2005) to be rational always implies having a reason and so rationality is only a matter of narrow scope.

Non-detachment is a symptom of the difficulty of applying the ideals of reason to particular cases. We need to know how ideal rational norms like (a) and (b) regulate the epistemic attitudes of agents. Because we are not frictionless beings and can be irrational sometimes, some conclude that rational requirements, in so far as they express the norms of logic, are impotent and that logic has no relevance to actual psychological reasoning (Harman 1986). But still, one can learn logic, and it can improve our reasoning ability, just as one can learn epistemic rules. The problem is how to implement them so that they actually guide our epistemic practices.

3. Epistemic Norms and Epistemic Concepts

Epistemic norms can be formulated as correctness conditions relating a kind of epistemic state with an objective condition (Mulligan 2008), and the relation between these is plausibly understood as a necessary and sufficient condition:

S judges (believes) correctly that p	*iff* the proposition that p is true
S conjectures correctly that p	*iff* it is probable that p
S has a correct interrogative attitude towards p	*iff* it is questionable whether p
S doubts correctly whether p	*iff* it is doubtful whether p
S is correctly certain that p	*iff* if is certain that p

Alternatively we may think of them as "possession conditions" for various kinds of concepts (Peacocke 1992), which are typically associated to the kind of epistemic justification which they provide. Thus perceptual concepts obey different kinds of "normative liaisons" from judgmental concepts or from logical concepts. But such a scheme is bound to be abstract unless one tries to spell out the relation between the correctness condition and the believer (doubter, interrogator). The more plausible proposal is that epistemic norms are conditions of "epistemic permissibility" for beliefs, which issue *mays* rather than *oughts* depending on the kind of epistemic state (Pollock and Cruz 1999):

(c) If it perceptually seems to you that p, then you are *prima facie* rationally permitted to believe that p (*perception*).
(d) If you are permitted to believe that p and that if p then q, then you are *prima facie* rationally permitted to believe q (*deduction*).

(e) If you have observed n As and they have been discovered to be Gs, then you are *prima facie* rationally permitted to believe q (*induction*).
(f) If someone testifies to you that p, then you are *prima facie* rationally permitted to believe p.

Such norms of permission are relative to each kind of epistemic domain (reasoning, perception, testimony, and so forth), they spell out specific epistemic rights or permissions to believe, which are rational and *prima facie*. Let us suppose that they are correctness norms. These raise several kinds of questions.

First, what is the nature of the kind of justification that these norms codify? For (c) at least it is not clear that it is a kind of propositional justification, licensed by a transition from beliefs to belief, since the inputs of perceptual beliefs need not, at least on many views of perception, trade in propositional contents. The relation of *prima facie* rational permission is often called "entitlement" (Burge 1993; Peacocke 2004), and it is meant to capture a kind of default justification. But the exact nature of this entitlement is a matter of controversy.

Second, if we understand (c)–(f) (but (a)–(b) as well) as rules specifying the kinds of circumstances in which an agent is licensed to believe, how do they regulate? If we understand them on the model of rules (such as rules of chess), we can construe these in two ways (Boghossian 2008a): as a conditional proposition specifying a permission (or an obligation) of the form:

If condition C obtains, you may (must) φ.

or (for requirements of the form (a) or (b)) as an imperative of the form

If C, do φ!

The imperative construal does not seem appropriate, since a mere imperative does not wear its normative status on its sleeves: it is only an instruction, and it does not tell us what kind of normative requirement is at issue (permission or obligation? of a practical or of an epistemic kind?). The propositional reading is better in this respect, but it seems overly intellectualistic: in order to obey a norm do we have to believe a proposition which expresses it (one follows, as Wittgenstein says, the rule "blindly")? In addition it faces easily the kind of regress made famous by Lewis Carroll's tortoise (Carroll 1895): for if I need a second propositional norm to obey a norm, I need another to obey the second, etc. Perhaps, as Pollock and Cruz (1999) suggest, the kind of knowledge that we have of epistemic norms is procedural, rather than declarative knowledge of a propositional form.

A further problem which the present proposal faces is that of its common association with the deontological conception of epistemic justification (Chisholm 1977; Alston 1989; Steup 2000). It seems to imply it: a belief is justified if and only if it is held in accordance with correct epistemic norms, and if it respects epistemic obligations. But it is not clear that the existence of epistemic norms entails the deontological conception of justification. The norms could be necessary although insufficient conditions for justification. And in the entitlement sense, they typically do not entail obligations or *oughts*.

For similar reasons, the notion of epistemic norm is often associated to a kind of internalism in epistemology, and to the idea that the subject must have an internal access to his reasons or justifications. But in so far as the norms of kind (a)–(f) are concerned, this need not be the case. Perceptual norms of kind (c) and the entitlement to which they give rise need not, and generally do not, entail the existence of a conscious access of the agent to them. Moreover, the norms can be understood in externalist fashion of the general form:

If p is generated by a reliable cognitive process it is permissible to believe p

(perhaps along the lines of the "J-rules" of justification proposed by Goldman 1986), where the agent need not know about the existence of the reliable process. Nevertheless it becomes hard to say, in this externalist construal of rules and norms, that they can act as *reasons* to believe.

4. The Ur-Norm of Truth

Are epistemic norms diverse, in the way rules, maxims, recipes, or heuristics can be? Even when we conceive them as rules for inquiry, such as Descartes' *rules for the direction of the mind*, they have a certain systematicity (Descartes' rules are guided by a certain conception of intuition as the basic source of knowledge). But can't we say that there is a hierarchy and that some norms enjoy more prominence than others? These, in order to have the proper kind of generality, have to be categorical and expressed in terms of *oughts* rather than in terms of permissions or entitlements, and which we can formulate as above in the manner of correctness conditions. There are three obvious candidates.

The first, along the lines of (a) above is the rationality norm:

(NR) For any p, a belief that p is correct if and only if it is rational

or in categorical terms:

(NR0) One ought to be rational in one's beliefs.

The second one is the norm that evidentialists like Clifford (1879) likes so much, that we ought to believe on the basis of sufficient evidence:

(NE) A belief is correct if and only if it is based on appropriate evidence.

None of these is unproblematic. There are several criteria of rationality. The minimal one is logical coherence or non-contradiction, which can also, if one admits degrees of belief, be expressed through some form of probabilistic coherence. There are also several kinds of concepts of evidence, and the amount of "sufficient" evidence that a subject needs to have is left undetermined by the statement of (NE) (Owens 2000).

A more obvious candidate for the role of general norm for beliefs is the so-called norm of truth for beliefs (Wedgwood 2007; Boghossian 2008b; Shah 2003; Engel 2007) which is usually considered as the best expression of the familiar metaphor that belief has an "aim," which is truth:

(NT) For any p, a belief that p is correct if and only if p is true.

It is natural to interpret this in terms of an *ought* rather than in terms of a *may* statement:

(NTO) For any p, one ought to believe that p if and only if p

which, given that it is a biconditional can be broken into two parts:

(NTOa) For any p, if p one ought to believe that p
(NTOb) For any p, one ought to believe that p only if p

which, respectively, seem to capture what James (1905) calls "the two ways of looking at our duty in matters of opinion: knowing the truth and avoiding error."

(NTB) seems more fundamental than (NR) and (NE). For it seems that when we look for rational beliefs or for belief supported by evidence, it is because these properties enhance their chance of being *true*. A set of beliefs that would be rational but false would be of little help to an inquirer, and evidence is evidence *for* truth. In addition, if belief plausibly is taken, among all propositional attitudes, as the central one (Boghossian 2008a), (NT) seems to enjoy a kind of priority. But even if we grant that (NT) is the Ur-Norm, (NTB) and (NT) in both formulations raise several problems.

In the first place, (NT), like the correctness conditions set up at the beginning of §3 above, seems more or less trivial. Does it say more that to believe that p is to believe that p is true? If so how can it have normative force and a power of prescription? So the objection that a mere analytic principle of rationality cannot create a genuine norm reproduces.

In the second place (NTO) seems clearly wrong. It says that for any proposition which is true, one ought to believe it. But certainly no one is under the obligation, if only under the rational requirement, of believing any true proposition whatsoever. There are too many trivial, uninteresting, or useless propositions which no one cares to believe.

In the third place, even if one takes (NTO) in the second, more plausible, formulation (NTOb), which says that if one ought to believe that p, then p is true, nothing seems to follow, since the first member of the conditional can be either true or false; if it is true, nothing follows about what the subject ought to believe, and if it is false, it just says that the subject lacks an obligation to believing something, which is not the same as a positive obligation to believe (Hattiangadi 2005).

These difficulties illustrate the regulation problem: how can the mere (propositional) statement of a norm wear on its face, as it were, the way in which it should be obeyed? If (NT) is understood in the intellectualist sense as prescribing, on the part of every believer, an intention or goal to accept a belief if and only if it reaches the truth (Velleman 2000), the proposal is too intellectualistic to be convincing: not only does the norm (NT) not need to be explicitly present to the mind of the believer, but it need not be present at all, even tacitly, for there are too many cases where one believes that p without believing it for the sake of truth, but from a desire for it to be true.

A more promising solution to the regulation problem exploits one important feature of ascriptions of belief (Moran 2000; Shah 2003): when one deliberates about whether to believe that p, the best way to do so consists in asking oneself whether p, and a positive answer settles the question. In other words, belief is "transparent" to the truth of the proposition believed. This holds only for conscious, deliberate belief, but it also seems to belong to the very concept of belief. Possessing the concept of belief and understanding what it means to possess it entail obeying what the norm of truth prescribes. This feature may bridge the gap between the abstract statement of the norm (NT) and its realization within a believer's psychology, for a belief may be regulated for truth without being explicitly attended in a deliberation about whether to believe that p (Shah and Velleman 2005; Engel 2007).

5. The Evidential Norm

A more common objection to the truth norm, which is implicit in most attempts to resist the idea that it can have normative force, is based on the suspicion that it presupposes a form of evidentialism, the view according to which one ought to believe that p only for evidential reasons, pertaining to the kind of evidence that one has for p's being true. There are a number of formulations of the evidentialist norm, including (NE) above, Clifford's maxim, and its explicit association with a certain theory of justification according to which a belief that p is epistemically justified if and only if it fits the evidence that one has of p at a given moment (Conee and Feldman 2005).

Whatever its proper formulation can be, evidentialism faces, at least since Pascal's famous wager argument and James' will to believe objection to Clifford, the following challenge: given that our reasons to believe—at least in the sense of our *motivating* reasons—fall short of being our exclusive reasons, it seems perfectly correct to believe that p for (normative) reasons other than truth and evidence, in particular pragmatic or prudential reasons. In this sense, certain kinds of belief behaviors described currently as self-deceptive or irrational can be rational in the practical sense. A wife's observation of lipstick on a husband's collar is an evidential reason for her to believe that the husband is unfaithful but it can coexist with a practical reason to believe that—contrary to evidence—the husband is faithful. More importantly there can be a possibility of weighing epistemic and practical considerations for believing, for instance if the benefit of a not too well evidentially supported belief (say, that one will recover from cancer) outweighs the benefit of believing the contrary (that one's life is threatened). On this view epistemic reasons to believe are only contingently normative, and they can be overridden by reasons to desire to believe; hence the so-called constitutive norms of truth (NT) or of evidence (NE) are not constitutive at all. Where the evidentialist claims that the only permissible attitude towards a proposition p is the attitude that one has towards its truth or its evidence (namely, belief that p), the pragmatist claims that the contrary attitude (belief that not p) or another attitude (say, accepting that not p, or taking a certain prudential stance towards it) is licensed, if a certain goal of the agent favors its being rational (Foley 1993). If so the permissibility norms above become, indeed, very permissive, to the point of being only relative and purely contextual (White 2005).

The trouble with this line of thought, however, is that it is hard to conciliate not only with the existence of asymmetries between epistemic reasons and practical reasons mentioned above (§1), but also that it implies, most implausibly, that many prudential or pragmatic beliefs are under the kind of "manipulative" or "managerial" control which a subject can have when he manages to cause himself or herself to believe something for the sake of a certain practical goal (as, for instance when, knowing that I am prone to be late and forgetful about the time of an important meeting, I set my watch 10 minutes ahead of the actual time, in order to create in myself, when the time arrives and when I look at my watch, the belief that my meeting is forthcoming). But such a kind of managerial control is necessarily indirect, and unable to answer the constitutive reasons for belief by definition. One way or another, pragmatic reasons to believe seem perfectly extrinsic, and the idea that belief has an aim cannot simply be reduced to the idea that it has one purpose or other (Owens 2003; Ryan 2003). The pragmatist, in order to defend the view that there is nothing intrinsic in epistemic norms and reasons for believing, needs to deny the transparency feature of the regulation of belief (Shah 2003; Hieronymi 2005).

6. Epistemic Norms and Epistemic Values

The pragmatist's challenge to the truth and to the evidentialist norms is the strongest form of a worry that epistemic norms might not trade in *oughts*, but in *goals*, or in ends, and that they owe their force not to some categorical imperative or even permission, but to the existence of certain epistemic objectives. The most extreme view of this sort would simply be a kind of relativism, according to which there is nothing more in epistemic norms than certain kinds of *policies*, which one may adopt in one circumstance required by inquiry, but that one may withdraw in another circumstance (Field 2009). A less relativistic view would claim that the *oughts* of thought and reason are not as general and context independent as rationality principles or Ur-epistemic norms, but can be, in some sense, specialized. Some *oughts* might relate to a kind of function that a given role enjoys, such as professional *oughts*: just as the role of a teacher is to teach, or of a lawyer is to defend his clients, the *oughts* of belief might be so specialized (Feldman 2000). And given that there is an obvious connexion between normativity and the performance of a function, which has been exploited by many philosophers who hope to reduce norms to biological functions (Millikan 1996; Papineau 2003) it might promise a short way to naturalistic reduction.

In a different spirit some theorists hold that norms are related to social functions, or to various commitments implicit in human discourse, which are ultimately social (Brandom 1994; Chrisman 2008). But going too much in that direction is unpromising if it is supposed to explain epistemic normativity in expressivist terms. We have a sense, which the cognitivist conception of normativity captures better (Wedgwood 2007; Cuneo 2008), that the *oughts* of belief are more general, and that what thought requires outpasses what the expressivist conception can capture. One way to defend this view consists in reflecting upon the intimate relation that belief has to knowledge. Whether or not one accepts the strong kind of externalism according to which knowledge is a primitive mental state distinct from belief, it makes sense to suggest that the aim of belief is knowledge, and that it is knowledge which gives to epistemic norms their intrinsicness (Williamson 2000). In this sense, it may be that the norm of belief, both in the constitutive sense and in the regulative sense, is a norm for knowledge.

This still does not solve the ontological issue associated to questions (i) and (v) of §1 above. The generality of epistemic norms can be captured through the idea that they are, in some sense, related to values, and one may think that the truth and the evidentialist norm can be translated into the idea that the ultimate aim of belief is truth, because truth is the ultimate cognitive value (Lynch 2005). Although the pragmatist will here agree that the normative concepts are better captured in teleological terms, this need not detract from the irreducibility of the truth goal. Space is then left to understand the normativity of epistemic norms in terms of this goal, and to understand normativity as related to features of our capacities to reach "aptly" the truth goal (Sosa

2007), whatever it is, or to understand it, in a more full-blooded Aristotelian sense, as the achievements of a virtuous agent, in the way a virtue epistemology does (Zagzebski 1996; Hookway 2000). Space is left, too, to the debate between the monist about the cognitive goal, who believes that epistemic achievement is related to only one kind of objective, truth, and the pluralist who allows others goals, like understanding (Kvanvig 2003). There are, indeed, a number of conceptions of epistemic value, which are all candidates at accounting epistemic normativity in teleological terms (Pritchard 2007; Grimm 2009; Haddock et al. 2009, 2010).

But whether or not these teleological accounts are correct, they will have to make sense of two facts: that the evidentialist norms are, in some sense which is yet to be spelled out but which all friends of the idea of an epistemic norm grant, constitutive of the epistemic domain, and that they can guide or regulate inquiry. But it is not clear that the constitutivity claim amounts to the same as the goal claim, and that they can, in either way, be reduced to each other. For it is perfectly possible to accept that the truth and evidentialist norms set general conditions on belief in general, whereas the considerations pertaining to the value of a given belief in various circumstances pertain to inquiry, or the process of formation and acquisition of beliefs. In order to understand the concept of a belief and of an epistemic state in general, one needs to understand the first, but the second, which is relevant to inquiry, need not coincide with the constitutive norms for belief and knowledge. On this view there would be two different kinds of epistemic norms: those which are attached to a believer's understanding of the very concept of belief on the one hand, and those which apply to the exercise of belief in inquiry, on the other hand. The norms for belief apply categorically to any believer, whereas the inquirer attends to a goal and to the complex ways of achieving it. The former may be more normative in the constitutive sense, whereas the latter may be more instrumental and teleological. But it has yet to be spelled out in what sense they are related.

References

Alston, W. P. 1989 *Epistemic Justification*, Ithaca, NY: Cornell University Press.
Audi, R. 2000 *The Architecture of Reason*, Oxford: Oxford University Press.
Boghossian, P. 2008a "Epistemic Rules," *Journal of Philosophy* 105(9): 472–500.
—— 2008b *Content and Justification*, Oxford: Oxford University Press.
Brandom, R. 1994 *Making it Explicit*, Harvard, MA: Harvard University Press.
Broome, J. 2000 "Normative Requirements," in Dancy, J. (ed.) *Normativity*, Oxford: Blackwell, pp. 78–99.
Burge, T. 1993 "Content Preservation," *The Philosophical Review* 102(4): 457–488.
Carroll, L. 1895 "What the Tortoise said to Achilles," *Mind* (new series) 4: 278–80.
Chisholm, R. 1977 *Theory of Knowledge*, 2nd edn, Englewood Cliffs, NJ: Prentice Hall.
Clifford, W. K. 1879 "The Ethics of Belief," in his *Lectures and Essays*, London: Macmillan.
Chrisman, M. 2008 "Ought to Believe," *Journal of Philosophy* 105(7): 346–70.
Conee E. and Feldman, R. 2005 *Evidentialism*, Oxford: Oxford University Press.
Cuneo, T. 2008 *The Normative Web*, Oxford: Oxford University Press.
Davidson, D. 1980 *Essay on Actions and Events*, Oxford: Oxford University Press.
—— 2004 *Problems of Rationality*, Oxford: Oxford University Press.
Engel, P. 2007 "Belief and Normativity," *Disputatio*, II, 23: 179–205.
—— 2008 "Davidson on Epistemic Norms," in C. Amoretti and N. Vassalo (eds.) *Davidson, Truth, Language and Interpretation*, Munich: Ontos Verlag, pp. 123–146.
Feldman, R. 2000 "The Ethics of Belief," Philosophy and Phenomenological Research 60: 667–695. Reprinted in Conee and Feldman 2005.
Field, H. 2009 "Epistemology without Metaphysics," *Philosophical Studies* 143: 249–90.

Foley, R. 1993 *Working Without a Net*, Oxford: Oxford University Press.
Gibbard, A. (2008) "Rational Credence and the Value of Truth," in T. Gendler and J. Hawthorne (eds.) *Oxford Studies in Epistemology* 3, Oxford: Oxford University Press.
Goldman, A. 1986 *Epistemology and Cognition*, Harvard, MA: Harvard University Press.
Grimm, S. 2009 "Epistemic Normativity," in Haddock, A., Millar, A., and Pritchard, D. H. (eds.) *Epistemic Value*, Oxford: Oxford University Press, pp. 243–64.
Haddock, A., Millar, A., and Pritchard, D. H. (eds.) *Epistemic Value*, Oxford: Oxford University Press.
—— 2010 *The Nature and Value of Knowledge: Three Investigations*, Oxford: Oxford University Press.
Harman, G. 1986 *Change in View*, Cambridge, MA: MIT Press.
Hattiangadi, A. 2005 *Oughts and Thoughts*, Oxford: Oxford University Press.
Hieronymi, P. 2005 "The Wrong Kind of Reason," *The Journal of Philosophy* 102(9): 437–57.
Hookway, C. 2000 "Epistemic Norms and Theoretical Deliberation," in Dancy, J. (ed.) *Normativity*, Oxford: Blackwell, pp. 60–77.
James, W. 1905 "The Will to Believe," in *The Will to Believe and Other Essays in Popular Philosophy and Human Immortality*, New York: Dover (1956), pp. 1–31.
Kelly, T. 2003 "Epistemic Rationality and Instrumental Rationality: A Critique," *Philosophy and Phenomenological Research* 66(3), May: 612–40.
Kolodny, N. 2005 "Why be Rational?," *Mind* 114(455): 509–63.
Kornblith, H. 1982 "Epistemic Normativity," *Synthese* 94: 357–76.
Kvanvig, J. 2003 *The Value of Knowledge and the Pursuit of Understanding*, Cambridge: Cambridge University Press.
Lynch, M. 2005 *The Value of Truth*, Cambridge, MA: MIT Press.
Millar, A. 2006 *Understanding People*, Oxford: Oxford University Press.
Millikan, R. G. 1996 *White Queen Psychology*, Cambridge, MA: MIT Press.
Moran, R. 2000 *Authority and Estrangement*, Princeton, NJ: Princeton University Press.
Mulligan, K. 2008 "Intentionality, Knowledge and Formal Objects," *Disputatio* II, 23: 205–28.
Owens, D. 2000 *Reason without Freedom*, London: Routledge.
—— 2003 "Does Belief have an Aim?," *Philosophical Studies* 115(3): 283–305.
Papineau, D. 2003 *The Roots of Normativity*, Oxford: Oxford University Press.
Peacocke, C. 1992 *A Study of Concepts*, Cambridge, MA: MIT Press.
—— 2004 *The Realm of Reason*, Oxford, Oxford University Press.
Pollock, J. and Cruz, J. 1999 *Contemporary Theories of Knowledge*, Tottowa, NJ: Rowman and Littlefield.
Pritchard, D. H. 2007 "Recent Work on Epistemic Value," *American Philosophical Quarterly* 44: 85–110.
Railton, P. 2000 "Normative Force and Normative Freedom," in Dancy, J. (ed.) *Normativity*, Oxford: Blackwell (2000).
—— 2003 *Facts Values and Norms*, Cambridge: Cambridge University Press.
Ryan, S. 2003 "Doxastic Compatibilism and the Ethics of Belief," *Philosophical Studies*, 114: 47–79.
Scanlon, T. 1998 *What We Owe to Each Other*, Harvard: Harvard University Press.
Schröder, T. 2003 "Davidson's Theory of Mind is Non-normative," *Philosopher's Imprint*, 2, 1. http://hdl.handle.net/2027/spo.3521354.0003.001.
Shah, N. 2003 "How Truth Regulates Belief," *The Philosophical Review* 112: 447–82.
—— and Velleman, D. 2005 "Doxastic Deliberation," *The Philosophical Review* 114(4): 497–534.
Skorupski, J. 2010 *The Domain of Reasons*, Oxford: Oxford University Press.
Sosa, E. 2007 *A Virtue Epistemology*, Oxford: Oxford University Press.
Steglich-Petersen, A. 2006 "The Aim of Belief: No Norm Needed," *Philosophical Quarterly* 56(225): 500–16.
Steup, M. 2000 "Doxastic Voluntarism and Epistemic Deontology," *Acta Analytica* 15: 25–56.
Velleman, D. 2000 "The Aim of Belief," in *The Possibility of Practical Reason*, Oxford: Oxford University Press.
Wedgwood, R. 2007 *The Nature of Normativity*, Oxford: Oxford University Press.
Weinberg, J., Nichols, S., and Stich, S. 2001 "Normativity and Epistemic Intuitions," *Philosophical Topics* 29: 429–60.
White, R. 2005 "Epistemic Permissiveness," *Philosophical Perspectives* 19: 445–59.
Williamson, T. 2000 *Knowledge and its Limits*, Oxford: Oxford University Press.
Zagzebski, L. 1996 *Virtues of the Mind*, Cambridge: Cambridge University Press.

6
EVIDENCE
Timothy McGrew

The concept of evidence pervades our lives. In science, history, law, medicine, and innumerable other areas, evidence plays a central, indispensable role. Yet both the analysis of the concept of evidence and the characterization of its role in our cognitive lives are matters of lively philosophical controversy. To understand how these philosophical controversies have arisen, it is helpful to start from non-philosophical concepts and uses of evidence and explore the questions they raise.

Some Characteristics of Evidence

In the common sense of the term, evidence may come in a wide variety of forms. In a case at law, evidence might include a fingerprint, bloodstains, testimony, or a will. In science the paradigm case of evidence is a set of experimental data, but sometimes (as in astronomy or paleontology) the principal data are not directly amenable to experimental manipulation, so observation plays the central role. In history, evidence typically comes in the form of narrative documents, but it might also take the form of a coin, some scraps of papyrus, or a few bits of pottery. In medicine it could consist of anything from an X-ray or a test result to a subjective experience of a certain sort of pain. In a trip to the grocery store it might consist in the redness of a watermelon or the softness and smell of a peach.

Although the examples from these different fields are diverse, they have certain common characteristics. First, evidence is always evidence *for* (or *against*) something: the guilt of the defendant, the truth of a hypothesis, the correctness of a particular historical claim, the presence of a certain disease, or the ripeness and sweetness of a piece of fruit. Second, it comes in a range of strengths. Sometimes we are in a position to compare evidence, to say that some piece of evidence is better evidence for a hypothesis than some other piece is, or that a piece of evidence is better evidence for one hypothesis than it is for some alternative hypothesis. Third, and relatedly, evidence may be more or less direct. Testimony that the defendant expressed dislike of the victim is indirect; eyewitness testimony that the defendant assaulted the victim is more direct, and all else being equal we are inclined to take the latter more seriously. Fourth, small things may give us strong evidence for surprising, antecedently improbable facts. When Robinson Crusoe had spent over twenty years as a castaway without seeing any signs of another human being, he had excellent reason to believe that he was alone on his island; but the sight of a single footprint overturned all of his evidence to the contrary. Fifth, pieces of evidence can typically be combined or opposed. A clinical diagnosis may be confirmed or disconfirmed by a histopathological examination; a will may be called into question by the presentation of written documents apparently revoking it. This is closely related to a sixth point. Pieces of evidence may be weakened in several distinct ways: by being opposed by contrary evidence (a second will), by being undermined (documents revoking the will), or by the introduction of new relevant alternatives. In Charles Dickens's novel *A Tale of Two Cities*, for example, Charles Darnay is falsely accused of treason on the testimony of a witness. The defense attorney's assistant, Sydney Carton, stands up and removes his wig, revealing that he and Darnay are strikingly similar in appearance; the witness's certainty that it was Darnay he saw is shaken by the sudden introduction of the possibility that he actually saw someone else of similar appearance.

Propositional Evidence, Internalism, and Foundationalism

Each of these characteristics gives rise to certain interesting philosophical questions and issues. Take the fact that evidence is always evidence for or against something. How can a fingerprint or a bloodstain be evidence for something? The question is more tricky than it looks. After all, fingerprints by themselves do not say anything, and the sense in which a bloodstain can be said to accuse the defendant is clearly metaphorical. Trying to parse this out, some philosophers have been attracted to the view that, strictly speaking, what counts as evidence is not a set of physical objects or even experiences, but rather a set of believed propositions; the bloodstains, wills, and pains are relevant because somehow they underwrite or legitimate our belief in the relevant propositions *that this smudge is a bloodstain*, or *that the document is the will of the deceased*, or even, in the first person case, *that I am experiencing* **thus**.

The position that evidence is, in the strict sense, always propositional, has many attractions. Propositions can be believed or disbelieved, but fingerprints cannot; to say that one disbelieves a fingerprint seems to be a shorthand for saying that one does not believe that the fact *that this fingerprint is present* (a proposition) indicates *that the defendant is guilty* (another proposition). Propositions can stand in logical relations to one another, can entail each other, can be negated, conjoined, and otherwise logically manipulated. But we can no more create a disjunction between a proposition and a fingerprint than we can divide the number seven by a banana. Treating evidence as propositional provides us with a natural way to discuss the combination of evidence, which we noted above as one of the common features of evidence. And there are tremendous systematic advantages to treating the whole system of our beliefs as a set of propositions, particularly if we want to make use of the machinery of Bayesian probability; for to do this, we must generate a probability distribution across all of the propositions in question. Fingerprints need not apply.

The relationship between evidence and probability is a particularly interesting one. The second feature of evidence we noted at the outset was that it comes in differing strengths. We have various options for representing evidential strength: positive (E is evidence for H), comparative (E_1 is stronger evidence for H than E_2), and numerical (the probability of H, given E, is .95, which would typically be written $P(H|E) = .95$). The numerical representation gives us some simple and intuitive ways of capturing the comparative assessment ($P(H|E_1) > P(H|E_2)$) and the positive assessment ($P(H|E) > P(H)$). These advantages come at a price, since the representation of our beliefs as a massive set of conjunctions, disjunctions, and negations of simple propositions, and of our degrees of rational credibility as a probability distribution of infinitely precise numerical values across that set, cannot be perfectly squared either with introspection or with experimental evidence on human rationality (Kahneman et al. 1982). But there are various devices (e.g. probability intervals) that the devotee of probabilistic accounts of evidence can employ to lessen these difficulties; and just as in logic, some degree of idealization is to be expected in any normative formal reconstruction of our epistemic practices and concepts (see "Bayesian Epistemology," Chapter 55 in this volume).

It might seem that philosophers who take evidence to be propositional have just traded one problem for another. If a bloodstain cannot serve as evidence but the proposition *this is a bloodstain* can, then what serves as evidence for the belief about the bloodstain? If it must always be another proposition, we seem doomed to an infinite regress that never makes contact with experience. But if the bloodstain itself, or even the experience one would describe as one's seeing the bloodstain, can serve to justify the proposition *this is a bloodstain*, then why be squeamish at the outset? Why not admit the stain, or the experience, as evidence in its own right?

One way of addressing this problem is to embrace a form of foundationalism in which certain beliefs, typically beliefs about one's present experiential states, are justified in virtue of the manner in which they are connected with one's experience. The idea of *direct acquaintance* plays a vital role here: on some current conceptions (BonJour 2002; Fumerton 2005; McGrew 1995, 1998), one's foundational beliefs are justified because they express one's acquaintance with aspects of one's experience, and the acquaintance relation brings with it some high epistemic standing. The experience one has on the occasion of seeing the bloodstain provides a significant part of one's justification for the belief that there is a bloodstain. In ordinary language we would go further and say that the experience was evidence. But given the theoretical payoff involved in treating evidence as propositional, it may be worth the small divergence from common usage (see "Foundationalism," Chapter 22 in this volume).

This form of foundationalism is highly controversial, both with respect to the standing of the foundations (do we have such beliefs? do they play the evidential role foundationalists say they do?) and with respect to the support they are supposed to give (can such foundations really give us justification for the wide range of our further beliefs?). It also raises several deep questions about the level of awareness required for something to count as one's evidence, since awareness comes in degrees but the status of a belief as evidence, as opposed to the weight of that evidence, does not appear to be a matter of degree. It resolves the question of whether false propositions, or beliefs in false propositions, can count as evidence (on this conception they cannot); but since this resolution is somewhat controversial, it may be taken either as a merit or as a drawback to acquaintance foundationalism, though it is interesting to note that the requirement that knowledge not be crucially based on a false premise—clearly a related, though not an equivalent, notion—is one of the major ways of addressing the Gettier problem. In any event, these are serious questions that cannot be made to disappear by rejecting foundationalism: the question of the relationship between experience and experiential beliefs remains, for example, regardless of one's stance on the propositional question or one's preferred answer to the epistemic regress problem. And this form of foundationalism has the attraction of isolating and attempting to meet head-on questions about the structure of our knowledge and the justification for our epistemic starting points while preserving a role for experience.

Acquaintance foundationalism is a form of epistemic internalism, and the notion of evidence generally plays a much more significant role in internalist epistemologies than it does in various forms of externalism. It would be overstatement to say that evidence plays no role in externalism, but the role is very different, in part because evidence itself is understood differently by externalists than by internalists. In Timothy Williamson's form of "knowledge first" externalism, for example, one's evidence is simply equated with the set of things one *knows*, where the concept of knowledge is taken to be primitive rather than analyzed into more fundamental concepts (see "Knowledge First Epistemology," Chapter 20 in this volume). In some forms of reliabilism, sensitivity to the evidence (not necessarily propositionally construed) is a means of being justified or warranted. The converse does not generally hold; on some externalist views, one may be justified or warranted without being (in any sense that an internalist would recognize) sensitive to evidence (see "Externalism/Internalism," Chapter 14 in this volume).

Evidentialism and the Objectivity Constraint

A position often espoused by those sympathetic to acquaintance foundationalism, though distinct from it, is known as *evidentialism*: it is the position that the epistemic status of a belief depends wholly on the evidence possessed by the believer. Just what this amounts to depends on the notion of evidence being employed, and accordingly evidentialism comes in both narrow and wide forms depending on whether evidence is taken to consist only of propositions or of a wider range of items. According to a recent version of wide evidentialism, evidence for a belief consists in the internal features of the believer exemplified at the time the belief is held (Conee and Feldman 2004). But the internal features, in this version, are not restricted to beliefs.

One interesting feature of evidentialism, whether wide or narrow, is that it entails a strong objectivity constraint on rational belief, which at a first approximation runs like this:

> Disagreements regarding the epistemic evaluation of any proposition are in principle traceable either to differences in the relevant evidence available to the disagreeing parties or to irrationality on the part of at least one of the disputants.

It might seem at first that this is overly stringent. In everyday life, and even in disciplines such as science and history, reasonable and well-informed people often disagree. Here, however, we have an example of the distance between common and philosophical use of terms like "reasonable" and "well-informed." A defender of the objectivity constraint will reply that someone might be reasonable in an everyday sense but fall far short of the ideal of rationality suggested by the constraint, just as someone can be a fine mathematician without being mathematically omniscient. Similarly, for two people to be "well informed" is not the same thing as for them to possess precisely the same evidence. Yet in some cases of disagreement among experts we at least approximate this situation. It is interesting to note that in those cases, the experts themselves are often more than willing to accuse each other of irrationality, which suggests that they are at least tacitly invoking something like the objectivity constraint (see "Disagreement," Chapter 7 in this volume).

Another objection to the objectivity constraint arises from the suggestion that the facts about what it is rational to believe given one's available evidence might not be perfectly sharp. Here we run into wider issues about the nature of epistemology. On a traditional view, the relationship between one's high-level beliefs and one's evidence is both necessary and a priori in a strong sense: roughly, the evidence logically determines a unique rational response, and that rational response is, in principle, discoverable by reflection alone. There are, of course, cases where the evidence does not specify a numerically precise rational stance. On the basis of the fact (true but somewhat vaguely stated) that more than half of all humans born live are male, and in the absence of any further information bearing on the matter, it would be unreasonable to assign any sharp probability to the gender of some particular child about to be born. But here one may well retain the objectivity constraint and argue that the proper rational response is simply to take a stance that goes no further than the evidence—to expect a male child more strongly than a female, but to remain uncommitted to any more precise position. The vagueness of the evidence will be reflected in the relative lack of detail in the commitment, but it does not follow that there is any vagueness in the *connection* between the evidence and that commitment.

One's position on the objectivity constraint determines a great deal about one's overall epistemology. But there is still room for philosophers who give lip service to the constraint to talk past one another if they are not in agreement regarding the concept of evidence being invoked.

The objectivity constraint leaves open the possibility that two people may possess *nearly* the same evidence, reason unimpeachably from it, and yet arrive at widely differing conclusions. One of the attractions of modeling evidence in probabilistic terms is that we can give models, in probability, of cases where this happens. Since the beliefs we take as unproblematic provide the background in terms of which we make judgments of relevance and independence, it is quite possible for there to be situations where Jack and Jill both learn that E, Jack's probability for H goes up, and Jill's goes down. Even more common is a case where one person does not see any significant relevance of E to H, while another, with a different base of evidence, takes E as highly relevant to H. Looking across the history of science, we see this quite often. The famous Michelson-Morley experiment revealed that, so far as optical experimentation is concerned, the motion of the earth in its revolution around the sun is undetectable. Had the opponents of Galileo been informed of this, they would no doubt have taken it to be highly relevant to the question of the motion of the earth, since the result is exactly what would be predicted if the earth is motionless. By the time the experiment was actually performed in the late nineteenth century, however, a stationary earth was no longer a live option. The immediate impact of the evidence was on the dispute between two types of ether theory, and a few decades later it came to be seen as evidence for Einstein's theory of special relativity. An even more striking case is that of Hanno the Navigator (c. 450 BC), who reported that in his travels to the south he reached a point where the sun seemed to rise and set to the north. Subsequent historians, situated comfortably in the northern hemisphere and generalizing their experience, dismissed his account as impossible. Today that very fact, so implausible that it was unlikely to be invented, is our best piece of evidence that Hanno's report was truthful. But this is because we understand what happens when one crosses the equator.

The example of look-alikes from *A Tale of Two Cities* raises an additional question for the objectivity constraint: does the sudden realization of a heretofore unrecognized possibility count as evidence? No new fact need be introduced for a possibility to be recalled; even Sydney Carton's dramatic gesture merely draws the attention of the court to the fact that sometimes different people resemble each other strikingly, which surely no one would deny. (It is not seriously entertained that the witness might have seen

Carton rather than Darnay, though that suggestion is the means by which the witness's testimony is undermined.) In the history of science it has often happened that the realization of a new possibility radically alters our estimate of the weight of evidence for and against various theories. But the very language we use here—that it alters our estimate *of the weight of evidence*—suggests that we are pre-reflectively inclined to count the realization of a mere possibility not as evidence but, rather, as something that influences our evaluation of the evidence. In that case, however, we might need to interpret the objectivity constraint in such a way that "irrationality" could include the failure to recognize alternative possibilities.

Evidence and Interpretation

The prevalence of disagreement among experts suggests that a great deal depends not simply on one's evidence but on one's interpretation of that evidence. In most circumstances it is fairly clear what counts as evidence and what counts as interpretation, though this distinction, like everything else in philosophy, has been challenged. Questions of interpretation of the evidence are closely linked to questions of inference, and these are among the most difficult and interesting problems in all of philosophy. If one adopts an internalist, foundationalist position, then one is bound to admit that a great deal of interpretation and/or inference goes on below the level of explicit consciousness. This involves some extension of the ordinary meanings of these terms, since interpretation and inference are, in the first instance, self-conscious processes.

In the case of scientific evidence, it is important to remember that inference is almost always accompanied by a certain amount of interpretation. The case of Boyle's Law illustrates this well. By pouring measured amounts of mercury into a J-shaped tube, Boyle was able to obtain data on the compression of the air trapped in the short end. From his data, he concluded that the pressure and the volume vary inversely, that is to say, that P and $1/V$ are in a linear relationship. But Boyle's data points, if plotted with P and $1/V$ for axes, do not fall on this line: a dot-to-dot connection of the points looks a bit like the Mississippi River. Boyle was aware of this and dismissed the variations between his measurements and the theoretical values as the product of error. Today, using regression analysis, we can vindicate his judgment (within bounds—when the pressure is great enough to liquefy the air, the relationship between P and $1/V$ ceases to be even approximately linear); but the fact remains that the data do not quite speak for themselves. This point tells against a naive form of falsificationism according to which even the slightest mismatch between theory and evidence suffices to overturn a theory. But it is a grave exaggeration to claim, as some social constructivists have done, that the existence of an interpretive dimension to scientific inference undermines the objectivity of science (Bloor and Edge 1998).

One popular and plausible way to characterize a wide range of inferential practices is that we are attempting to infer the best explanation of the evidence (Lipton 2004). Some philosophers have gone so far as to suggest that inference to the best explanation is the only primitive rational form of non-deductive inference (Harman 1973; Foster 1985, p. 227). Sir Arthur Conan Doyle's Sherlock Holmes stories are full of ingenious applications of such reasoning, and they are the more interesting since they were explicitly modeled on the real-life abilities of Dr Joseph Bell, an Edinburgh physician who pioneered forensic pathology and played a critical role in the trial and conviction of the notorious wife-murderer Eugene Chantrell in 1878 (Liebow 1982).

Even granting that subconscious interpretation and inference take place, there is a significant problem of characterizing these activities. Philosophers, who cannot agree even on the outlines of a solution to the problem of induction, are nowhere close to a consensus on more complex and less easily codified forms of thought such as explanatory inference and analogical reasoning. Yet these forms of reasoning are pervasive; and it would help a great deal to clarify, and perhaps sometimes to resolve, our disputes if we could at least begin to analyze them in terms of more general forms of non-demonstrative reasoning. Most of the current work in this direction makes use of the probability calculus (Hellman 1997; McGrew 2003, 2005), but the project is relatively new, and there is a great deal more to be done.

It is a curious fact that in other disciplines we manage to get along at least tolerably well without paying terribly close attention to various formulations that the philosophers have proposed. In law, for example, there are established canons of evidence, such as the ancient rule that conviction in a criminal case should be made only on the evidence of at least two independent witnesses; in history, a canon often observed (but perhaps just as often flouted) is that in the absence of direct evidence to the contrary, a historical document deserves the benefit of the doubt with respect to matters of fact it affirms that cannot be independently verified. The two witness rule is sometimes justified by the observation that the testimony of one witness and that of the defendant cancel each other out (Franklin 2001), though by itself this leaves it unclear how many additional witnesses should be required and whether they should all have equal credit. A substantial body of legal theory is devoted to the question of the admissibility and credibility of testimony and documentary evidence. No absolutely rigorous argument is available for such canons, but they are often reasonable rules of thumb, representing a distillation of much experience and providing a hedge against abuses that might otherwise have dire consequences. One need only recall the case of the chemist Antoine Lavoisier, who was executed during the reign of terror upon his denunciation by an academic rival, to realize that there are both prudential and epistemic reasons to require more than the word of one accuser.

Absence of Evidence and Arguments from Silence

Some slogans regarding evidence are not restricted to particular disciplines but crop up in conversation and sometimes in written discussions on a wide variety of issues. One of these comes in two incompatible forms: *Absence of evidence is not evidence of absence* (a statement made popular by Carl Sagan) and *Absence of evidence is evidence of absence*. The first (negative) form is more common, and it is sometimes used in criticism of an argument from ignorance to the effect that one should believe a proposition because its denial has not been proved. It is doubtful whether anyone capable of being swayed by this crude argument could be helped by the slogan. But it is an interesting exercise to determine when the slogan is applicable. The answer appears to be that each version, positive and negative, applies under certain conditions. At a first approximation, we can take the absence of evidence to be evidence of absence—or more broadly and less memorably, we can take the lack of positive evidence for some hypothesis to be evidence against the hypothesis—just in case we have good reason to believe that *if* the hypothesis were true, we *would* have positive evidence. In one of Sir Arthur Conan Doyle's stories, Sherlock Holmes finds the key to a mysterious theft in the fact that a dog did nothing in the night, from which he infers that the thief cannot have been a stranger; for if he had been a stranger, the dog would have been expected to bark during the intrusion. On the other hand, in some cases we would not expect to have positive evidence regardless of whether the hypothesis is true or false. Spontaneous proton decay, if it takes place at all, is an event so rare that our expectation of catching it happening is nearly zero. Consequently, our failure thus far to detect it does not give us much in the way of a reason to reject the theoretical possibility. One advantage of looking at the slogan in probabilistic terms is that the first approximation can be sharpened: ~E is evidence for ~H just in case $P(E|H)/P(E|\sim H) > 1$; and the stronger the inequality, the better the evidence. This formulation has the merit of drawing attention to the fact that E may be strong evidence for H, even when both $P(E|H)$ and $P(E|\sim H)$ are quite small in absolute terms, provided that their ratio is very large.

Related questions about absence of evidence crop up in law and in history. In legal contexts, the question has to do with the weight of negative evidence—testimony from a witness that he did *not* notice something, by contrast with the positive evidence of a witness who testifies to what he *did* see or hear. In history, the question has to do with the weight of the argument from silence, particularly when a writer fails to mention a putative event or fact that should have been known to him. Such arguments from silence are, as a rule, quite weak; there are many examples where reasoning from silence would lead us astray. Marco Polo, who traveled across China and kept an extensive journal of his travels, never mentions the Great Wall of China, or tea, or printed books. Pliny the Younger, who in two of his letters gives a detailed account of the eruption of Vesuvius in AD 79, does not mention that the eruption destroyed the populous towns of Pompeii and Herculaneum. In light of such examples, we should not be too quick to assume that we know what an ancient author would have mentioned had he been aware of it.

Extraordinary Claims and Extraordinary Evidence

Another common slogan, also popularized by Sagan, is that *Extraordinary claims require extraordinary evidence*. Much depends, of course, on what counts as extraordinary, both in a claim and in evidence. It cannot be simply that a claim is unprecedented. At a certain level of detail, almost any claim is unprecedented; but this does not necessarily mean that it requires evidence out of the ordinary to establish it. Consider this claim: "Aunt Matilda won a game of Scrabble Thursday night with a score of 438 while sipping a cup of mint tea." Each successive modifying phrase renders the claim less likely to have occurred before; yet there is nothing particularly unbelievable about the claim, and the evidence of a single credible eyewitness might well persuade us that it is true.

The case is more difficult with respect to types of events that are deemed to be improbable or rare *in principle*, such as miracles. It is generally agreed in such discussions that such events cannot be common and that it requires more evidence to render them credible than is required in ordinary cases (Sherlock 1769). David Hume famously advanced the maxim that *No testimony is sufficient to establish a miracle, unless the testimony be of such a kind, that its falsehood would be more miraculous, than the fact, which it endeavours to establish* (Beauchamp 2000, p. 87), which might have been the original inspiration for the slogan about extraordinary evidence. The proper interpretation of Hume's maxim has been a source of some debate among Hume scholars, but one plausible formulation in probabilistic terms is that

$$P(M|T) > P(\sim M|T) \text{ only if } P(M) > P(T|\sim M),$$

where M is the proposition that a miracle has occurred and T is the proposition describing testimonial evidence that it has occurred. This conditional statement is not a consequence of Bayes's Theorem, but the terms of the latter inequality are good approximations for the terms of the exact inequality

$$P(M) P(T|M) > P(\sim M) P(T|\sim M)$$

when both $P(\sim M)$ and $P(T|M)$ are close to 1. There is, then, a plausible Bayesian rationale for Hume's maxim so long as we understand it to be an approximation.

It does not follow that the maxim will do the work that Hume (arguably) and many of his followers (unquestionably) have hoped it would. Hume appears to have thought that his maxim would place certain antecedently very improbable events beyond the reach of evidence. But as John Earman has argued (Earman 2000), an event that is antecedently extremely improbable, and in this sense extraordinary, may be rendered probable under the right evidential circumstances, since it is possible in principle that

$$P(T|M)/P(T|\sim M) > P(\sim M)/P(M),$$

a condition sufficient to satisfy the rigorous condition underlying Hume's maxim and the slogan about extraordinary events. The maxim is therefore less useful as a dialectical weapon than is often supposed. It may help to focus disagreements over extraordinary events, but it cannot resolve them.

Testimonial Evidence and Independence

Discussions of Hume often segue into discussions of the evidential status of testimony. A repeated theme in the voluminous literature is the value of independent testimony, which is indeed remarkable. The testimony of a number of independent witnesses, none of them particularly reliable, who give substantially the same account of some event, may provide a very strong argument in its favor. Independence is, however, often difficult to establish: it is not sufficient (though it is generally necessary) that the witnesses have not conspired to give the same account. Minor discrepancies of detail are often, and reasonably, taken to establish that witnesses are not simply retailing agreed-upon talking points. Of course, the wider the discrepancies, the less we are able to credit all of the witnesses. But if they agree on the main points, those may be taken to be well established notwithstanding their differences on subsidiary points (Starkie 1876, p. 831).

There is also a substantial philosophical debate on the question of whether testimony provides an independent source of evidence or whether its value should be analyzed in terms of some other form of evidence, such as the perceived correspondence between the testifier's previous statements and the facts. Hume's position is reductive: he insists that the credibility of a testifier is a matter of proportion of truths to total testimonies. It may well be doubted whether this approach could provide a sufficient ground for the reasonable confidence we repose in testimony. The reductive view is more plausible when the set of possible forms of argument to justify reliance on testimony is widened to include explanatory inferences. Whether this move suffices to save the reductive approach to testimonial evidence is still a matter of debate (see "Testimonial Knowledge," Chapter 29 in this volume).

References

Tom Beauchamp, ed. *An Enquiry Concerning Human Understanding: A Critical Edition* (Oxford: Oxford University Press, 2000)

D. Bloor and D. Edge, "Knowing Reality through Knowing Society," *Physics World* 11 (1998): 23

Laurence BonJour, *Epistemology: Classic Problems and Contemporary Responses* (Lanham, MD: Rowman and Littlefield, 2002)

Earl Conee and Richard Feldman, *Evidentialism* (Oxford: Oxford University Press, 2004)

John Earman, *Hume's Abject Failure* (Oxford: Oxford University Press, 2000)

John Foster, *A. J. Ayer* (London: Routledge & Kegan Paul, 1985)

James Franklin, *The Science of Conjecture* (Baltimore, MD: Johns Hopkins University Press, 2001)

Richard Fumerton, *Epistemology* (New York: Blackwell, 2005)

Gilbert Harman, *Thought* (Princeton, NJ: Princeton University Press, 1973)

Geoffrey Hellman, "Bayes and Beyond," *Philosophy of Science* 64 (1997): 191–221

Daniel Kahneman, Amos Tversky, and Slovic, P., *Judgment Under Uncertainty: Heuristics and Biases* (Cambridge: Cambridge University Press, 1982)

Ely Liebow, *Dr. Joe Bell: Model for Sherlock Holmes* (Bowling Green, OH: Bowling Green University Popular Press, 1982)

Peter Lipton, *Inference to the Best Explanation*, 2nd edn (New York: Routledge, 2004)

Tim McGrew, *The Foundations of Knowledge* (Lanham, MD: Littlefield Adams, 1995)

—— "A Defense of Strong Foundationalism," in Pojman (1998)

—— "Confirmation, Heuristics, and Explanatory Reasoning," *British Journal for the Philosophy of Science* 54 (2003): 553–67

—— "Toward a Rational Reconstruction of Design Reasoning," *Philosophia Christi* 7 (2005): 253–98

Louis Pojman, *The Theory of Knowledge: Classical and Contemporary Readings*, 2nd edn (New York: Wadsworth, 1998)

Thomas Sherlock, *The Trial of the Witnesses of the Resurrection of Jesus* (Edinburgh: J. Robertson, 1769)

Thomas Starkie, *A Practical Treatise of the Law of Evidence*, 10th edn (Philadelphia: T. & J. W. Johnson & Co., 1876)

7
DISAGREEMENT
Bryan Frances

What should you do when you discover that someone firmly disagrees with you on some claim P? Suppose you know that someone has seen all your evidence and you have seen all hers. Suppose further that you know that both of you have evaluated that common body of evidence for about the same length of time and with the same care. You also know that she is about as clever, thorough, and open-minded as you are, both generally and with respect to the issues at hand. You know that you have about the same relevant biases. At this point, before you find out her opinion on P, you fully admit that you cannot think of *any* epistemic advantage you have over her when it comes to the topic in question; you admit that she is just as likely to get P's truth-value right as you are. Let us say that under these conditions she is your *recognized epistemic peer* with regard to P (I will relax some of these conditions below). And then after learning all this about her you find out that she thinks P is false, whereas you had already concluded to yourself that P is true.

Two conflicting responses immediately suggest themselves. First, there is the thought that respectful disagreement is common and should be expected among intelligent, reflective people. We all know that everyone makes many mistakes, so there is nothing at all odd in thinking that the one who disagrees with you has just made a mistake this time around. But second, why should you think that your cranium is any more accurate than another's—especially since you just admitted that you have *no* epistemic advantage over her, that she is *just as likely as you* to get P's truth-value right (on trust see Foley 2001)? When you take a "third-person view" of the matter, all you see are two people who are equally placed to determine P's truth-value, and so you should see no reason to think that one of them (viz. you) are the one who got things right this time around.

Here is another interesting case. I initially believe P but then learn about the famous Smith. I fully admit that she is a genius and knows much more than I do about the issues relevant to P. I know that she has all my evidence if not much more. I also know that she is smarter than I am and has thought about and investigated P much more than I have. I know full well that when it comes to the topics germane to P she is not my peer but significantly exceeds me. Prior to finding out her opinion on P, I would have insisted that she is *much more likely* than I am to get P's truth-value right. Let us say that under these conditions she is my *recognized epistemic superior* with regard to P. Then I find out that she firmly believes ~P. In this case, it seems as though you would be pretty foolish to not significantly diminish your confidence in P's truth.

And yet, if this reasoning were right could we have *any* epistemically responsible yet even slightly controversial beliefs? The application to philosophical belief is particularly interesting (see Goldberg 2009; Frances 2010, Forthcoming A; Fumerton 2010;

Kornblith 2010). There are many philosophers who are genuine experts on material composition who flatly deny that baseballs and other ordinary composite things exist. Other philosophers truly believe that there are no beliefs. Some believe that nothing is morally wrong (or right). Many think that fire engines aren't red (or any other color). Some of these philosophers are the best in the world. They look at the evidence as carefully and expertly and competently as anyone, and then with full sobriety contravene common sense. And often enough their claims are based on mostly a posteriori evidence and even have the endorsement of some expert scientists (e.g., error theories about color or character traits). So when faced with their opinion are we supposed to suspend judgment on the claims that fire engines are red—or even that they exist?

I have described just two kinds of disagreement cases: the recognized extreme peer one and the recognized superior genius one. But there is a whole range of philosophically interesting cases of disagreement, which can be introduced in the following illuminating way. I say to myself that P is true, where P might concern any subject matter. In case 1, my five-year-old daughter says ~P. I'm not too worried that I might be mistaken. The fact that she disagrees with me gives me no good reason to doubt my belief. In case 2, a sharp undergraduate who majors in the relevant subject matter says ~P. Provided I know that I know the subject matter significantly better than undergraduates I'm still not too worried that my belief in P is mistaken. In case 3, I discover that one of my colleagues says ~P—but I don't know any details regarding what evidence she has seen or how long she has investigated the matter; all I know is that she is generally about as sharp and careful as I am. This discovery might give me some pause. In case 4, I discover that one of my recognized epistemic peers regarding P and the topics surrounding P says that ~P. Now I'm more worried but not mortified. In case 5, a large group of people I recognize to be genii on the topic all announce that they firmly believe ~P for a variety of reasons and have done so for many years. Now I'm feeling pretty insecure in my belief in P. In case 6, I die, knowingly come face to face with the infallible and truth-telling God, and He says that the truth is definitely ~P. At this point only an idiot would retain his belief in P. Surely at *this* point I have to admit I was wrong—or at least withhold judgment! It seems that there is a scale of degree of blameworthiness. In the situation with the five-year-old, I'm not blameworthy in persisting with my belief (degree zero); in the situation with God I'm an idiot if I retain my belief (just about the highest degree of blameworthiness); these claims are hard to contest. Our issue is whether people in the various "middle" situations, cases 2–5 as well as similar ones, are in a bad *enough* position among this scale to be blameworthy.

Epistemologists have just begun to thoroughly explore these and similar cases, with the main works on the topic published quite recently (on the epistemic peer cases, see Christensen 2007, 2009, Forthcoming; Elga 2007; Feldman 2005, 2006, 2007; Feldman and Warfield 2010; Kelly 2006, 2008; on the epistemic superior cases, see Frances 2010, Forthcoming A, Forthcoming B). Often the best way to introduce a new topic is to articulate what one takes to be some of the central questions concerning that topic. That is the approach I'll take here, focusing primarily on recognized peers and recognized superiors.

1. In what situations, if any, in which I have discovered a disagreement with a recognized epistemic peer or superior (or one of the other "middle" situations) am I epistemically permitted to not at all alter my confidence in my belief in P? Under what conditions can I "stick to my guns"?

2. When I am not epistemically permitted to retain my confidence level in P, how is my confidence level supposed to change in response to the discovery of disagreement? (Note that disagreement isn't always one person believing P while another believes ~P: all we need are different levels of confidence in P's truth.) For instance, do I have to suspend judgment on P entirely or can I merely lower my confidence in P a bit? If the latter, what factors dictate what my new level of confidence in P must be? Moreover, consider two cases. In each I'm fairly confident in P but not certain. In the first case the person who disagrees with me says that she is about as confident in P's falsehood as I am in its truth. In the second case everything is as it was in the first case except she says she is completely certain that P is false. If I am required in the first case to lower my confidence in P, am I required to lower my confidence even more in the second case? And how does the level of expertise of the ~P proponent figure in to what I'm supposed to do (e.g., I know that she's a peer, I know that she's a genius, etc.)? Generally speaking, will there be mathematical epistemic principles governing how my confidence levels should change (see White 2005 for discussion)?
3. When I am epistemically required to alter my confidence in P, what has happened to the epistemic characteristics of my belief that makes this alteration required? For instance, when I learn that the peer or superior disagrees with me, has my level of overall *warrant* decreased enough that I am no longer warranted to have my previous confidence level—where warrant is what needs to be added to true belief in order for it to become knowledge? Or is it that my level of *justification* was lowered enough that my previous confidence level would be unjustified—where justification is the thing that is present in Gettier cases but insufficient for true belief to amount to knowledge? Or do I have to lower my confidence level for some other reason entirely?
4. Does it matter who was on the right track in the first place? For instance, suppose I have made some epistemological blunder in coming to believe P, whereas my opponent has made no blunder in coming to believe ~P (whether or not P happens to be true). Do these facts regarding the epistemic statuses of our *past* matter to what we are supposed to do in reacting to the *present* discovery of the disagreement?
5. When I am epistemically required to alter my confidence in P, am I also required to alter the way I behave regarding whether P is true? For instance, can I still act on the assumption that P is true or must I do something different? And might moral principles come into play here? For instance, if I'm epistemically permitted to not alter my confidence in P, might I nevertheless have a moral obligation to act differently regarding P—perhaps due to a moral obligation to respect others and, if the conditions are right, their opinions? In fact, might I have a moral obligation to not just act differently but alter my confidence in P—so a moral obligation gives birth to an epistemological one?
6. Does it matter what topics the disagreement is about? For instance, are the principles governing how we need to react to disagreements in science different from those regarding morals, religion, philosophy, or art (for the case of religion see van Inwagen 1996, Feldman 2007, and McKim 2001)? Or is it rather that different data gets plugged into the same disagreement principles? Furthermore, will it matter how difficult or simple the question, 'Is P true?' is (e.g., 'Is there dark matter?' vs. 'What is 56×7?')? Finally, what about disagreements concerning how we should respond to disagreement itself? Will plausible principles regarding how we should respond

to disagreement generate paradoxical results when applied to disagreements among epistemologists over those principles themselves (think of the analogous trouble from "revenge sentences" concerning the liar paradox or verificationist principles about meaning applied to themselves)?
7. In the recognized peer case I started out with the view that my peer was just as likely as me to get P's truth-value right. I also began with the idea that we had seen the same evidence, we had gone over it just as carefully as one another, and she was about as intelligent and intellectually careful as me in general. After learning of the disagreement, in what situations am I epistemically permitted to retain *those* beliefs (so set aside what I'm supposed to do with my belief in P)? For instance, if I am epistemically permitted to retain my confidence level in P upon discovering the disagreement with the peer, then am I required to lower my confidence level in my beliefs about my peer's knowledge regarding the topics germane to P's truth—since it looks like I'm now accusing her of definitely making a mistake? And how do we answer these questions in the epistemic superior case?
8. How often do the various cases philosophers consider actually show up in practice? For instance, much of the literature seems to address the case in which we start out believing P but not knowing what others think about P. And then the focus is on what we are supposed to do when we actually encounter someone who believes ~P. But in many real cases we start knowing, at least dispositionally, that there are dozens if not thousands of intelligent people who will believe ~P. In such cases it isn't clear what role the actual encounter with the disagreeing person will play (see discussion below).

Those who have published on the topic of disagreement have spent most of their energies on (1)–(4) and, to a lesser extent, (7). Furthermore, they have focused almost exclusively on the "recognized peer" case described at the beginning of this essay.

If the proponent of ~P is known by you to be the infallible and truth-telling God, then you should not only cease believing P but start to believe ~P—even if you have no hint of why P is false. More realistically, if I start out believing P and not knowing what anyone else thinks about P, I then find out that there are 2,000 experts on the topics relevant to P all of whom I fully admit are my epistemic superiors on P and are much more likely than I am to get P's truth-value right, then I probably should give up my belief in P upon later discovery that 95 percent of them firmly believe ~P in mostly mutual independence from one another. So, in some cases we seem forced to significantly alter our opinions in response to the discovery of disagreement.

However, even in the latter case matters are complicated by the details. For instance, what if P was some bit of fundamental philosophy, such as 'There are non-temporal, non-spatial objects' or 'Moral statements have truth-value'? One might think that even though Fred is aware that expert opinion is firmly against him on P, Fred is epistemically a-okay in sticking with his guns because the epistemic weight attached to relative expertise runs out in some sense when it comes to the truly fundamental claims that are beyond the reach of empirical investigation. Or suppose that P is the claim that $1 + 1 = 2$: in such a case one should perhaps not lower one's opinion that P is true but instead either give up one's belief that the superiors are really superiors or give up the belief that they really believe that $1 + 1 \neq 2$. (However, even this can be challenged: what if the experts who deny that $1 + 1 = 2$ are all the best philosophers of mathematics who have sophisticated error theories that attempt to account for the usefulness of arithmetic while holding that its positive claims are false?) Or suppose that the 5 percent of experts who don't believe ~P all believe P and are generally considered the epistemic superiors of the 95 percent who do believe ~P. In such a case it is hardly obvious that when apprised of all those facts I should give up my belief in P.

It might be wise to separate the question Q1, 'After discovering the disagreement what should his confidence level be?' from the question Q2, 'Given that he has just discovered a recognized epistemic peer/superior who disagrees with him, how should his confidence level change in response to *that* discovery alone?' Here's an argument why. Suppose that before the discovery of the disagreement he has credence in P of 0.85 (roughly, credence $x = 0$ when one is perfectly certain P is false, $x = 1$ when one is perfectly certain P is true, and $x = 0.5$ when one thinks there is a 50/50 chance P is true). Suppose further that the evidence he had at that time, the evidence he based his credence on, was so weak that he should have had a credence of just 0.65. Also suppose that P is fairly theoretical in the sense that his credence is fixed by his evidence alone (and not other epistemic factors). Finally, suppose that principles regarding disagreement discovery dictate that he should lower his credence by 0.20 upon discovery of the disagreement with the recognized peer or superior. The answer to Q1 might be, 'His credence should have been 0.65 to begin with; upon disagreement discovery it should have dropped by 0.20; so he should end up at 0.45.' The answer to Q2 might be, 'He started with credence 0.85 and upon disagreement discovery it should have dropped by 0.20; so he should end up at 0.65.' In any case, one must be careful in formulating the question one is trying to answer.

Three relatively straightforward views address what we are supposed to do upon the discovery of disagreement with a *single* recognized peer (see Christensen 2007, 2009; Elga 2007; Feldman 2005, 2006, 2007; Feldman and Warfield 2010; Frances Forthcoming B; Kelly 2006, 2008; Lackey 2010a, 2010b; White 2005):

(a) Always suspend judgment regarding P's truth-value.
(b) Always stick to your guns, not altering your view one bit.
(c) Always "split the difference" in the sense that if I actually gave P credence x before the discovery of disagreement and I know that my peer gave it y before the discovery, then I should change my credence to the average of x and y.

There is reason to think (b) is incorrect. You start out believing P but not knowing what anyone else thinks about P. If you then encounter 100 recognized peers in succession, each of whom firmly believes that P is false, then if (b) were correct you would be epistemically permitted to stick to your guns even while accumulating the knowledge that 100 out of 100 of your recognized peers think ~P. It would seem that in almost all realistic cases this is the wrong result.

A similar yet weaker argument goes against (a). Suppose I encounter 10 recognized peers in succession each of whom firmly *agrees* with me that P is true. Then the very next recognized peer, the 11th, is discovered to think P is false. If (a) is true then I'm supposed to suspend judgment upon encountering the 11th peer—despite the fact that I've learned that 10 out of 11 of my peers agree with me. Once again, it is hard to imagine a scenario in which this holds.

However, that argument ignores some important wrinkles that are important when working on the topic of disagreement. Consider my position after I have encountered the first 10 recognized peers who agree with me. Next I meet Fred, whom I recognize as the 11th peer regarding P. In order for me to recognize him as what might be called an *extreme* peer, I have to know that we have *all* the same evidence concerning P. But part of my evidence concerning P is that 10 of my recognized peers agree with P. (You might think it isn't strong evidence, but it does appear to be evidence and the person who advocates (a) will think it's evidence.) Thus, Fred has to be aware of *that* fact. That is, he has to know, at that moment just before we tell each other our opinions on P, that 10 out of 10 of his recognized epistemic peers think P is true. Furthermore, he can't have any evidence I lack. So the only thing he knows about peoples' opinions regarding P is what I know: 10 out of 10 of his (and my) peers think P is true. So how on earth can Fred be reasonable in retaining his belief in ~P? Keep in mind that he cannot think, for instance, that he has some stunning new evidence that the 10 others have not seen: since these 10 people who disagree with him are his *recognized peers*, he knows that they have seen *all* his evidence. After I learn of his opinion regarding P I will probably conclude that Fred has not fully appreciated the consequences of the fact that 10 out of 10 of his peers disagree with him. I am free to hold that he is still my peer with respect to the issues surrounding P, but I will conclude that he has made two errors: first, he got P's truth-value wrong; second, he did not adequately follow up on the epistemic consequences of the facts of disagreement. I seem epistemically permitted to retain my belief in P, thereby falsifying (a). And if he isn't my extreme peer but is a moderate peer—so he has all the evidence I have with the exception of the knowledge of the 10 out of 10 peers who believe P—then it still seems clear that I need not suspend judgment.

Option (c), "always split the difference," appears more reasonable than the extreme (a) and (b). Even so, there is an argument against it. As indicated above, in many cases when I come to believe P I am not thinking about what anyone else thinks about P but I am disposed to admit that there are many people who will disagree with me on P—people who are my peers and superiors concerning the relevant topics. I don't have any dispositions regarding any percentages of them who endorse or reject P. If you had asked me, right then while I was coming to accept P, 'Do you think there are other intelligent people who will disagree with you on this issue—people you are happy to admit know about as much or even more than you do on the relevant topics?,' I would have responded affirmatively.

If that's the situation I was in, then when I actually encounter Tom who I judge to be a peer or superior and then discover that he disagrees with me on P, I will probably not feel too much pressure to alter my view. After all, *I already knew* that there were loads of such people. This fact had not explicitly crossed my mind, but I knew it all along in a dispositional way. So, bumping into one of the intelligent disagreeing folks doesn't really change anything for me. Under these conditions, which I suspect are common, there doesn't seem to be much reason for me to change my view when I encounter Tom. If that is right, then (c) is false.

Of course, when I encounter Tom I might become a little reflective. I might think to myself 'Come to think of it, I know perfectly well that there must be *loads* of people smarter than I am who think ~P. Why on earth should I think someone like me has got things right this time around?' If I have become *that* reflective, then suspending judgment looks reasonable if not required. But if this encounter with Tom means that I have to suspend judgment, it won't be because of the fact that *Tom* disagrees with me. Instead, it will be due to the fact that I've reflected on how there must be many people who disagree with me—people I would admit are my approximate peers and even superiors. Tom is fully dispensable: all I really needed in order for the epistemic challenge of recognized disagreement to arise was the reflection Tom happened to cause. In any case, I won't be adjusting my opinion based on the confidence level Tom happens to have; so (c) looks false.

If one has never put a moment's thought into these matters then it is hard to see how one is under any epistemic obligation to go against one's strong natural propensity to follow one's own inclinations. The problem of disagreement doesn't arise unless one is both significantly reflective and respectful of the epistemic abilities and performances of others. But what if you have put some thought into these matters—like you are doing right now? What is stopping you from suspending judgment on P even when practical matters often force you to choose to act on either P or ~P? Are you so weak-willed that you have to put an irrational trust in the inclinations you find in your own head?

References

Christensen, David. Forthcoming. "Disagreement, Question-begging and Epistemic Self-criticism." *Philosopher's Imprint.*
Christensen, David. 2009. "Disagreement as Evidence: The Epistemology of Controversy." *Philosophy Compass* 4: 756–67.
Christensen, David. 2007. "Epistemology of Disagreement: the Good News." *The Philosophical Review* 116: 187–217.
Elga, Adam. 2007. "Reflection and Disagreement." *Noûs* 41: 478–502.
Feldman, Richard. 2007. "Reasonable Religious Disagreements." In Louise Antony (ed.), *Philosophers Without Gods: Meditations on Atheism and the Secular Life*. Oxford: Oxford University Press.
Feldman, Richard. 2006. "Epistemological Puzzles About Disagreement." In Stephen Hetherington (ed.), *Epistemology Futures*. Oxford: Oxford University Press.
Feldman, Richard. 2005. "Respecting the Evidence." *Philosophical Perspectives* 19: 95–119.
Feldman, Richard and Ted Warfield (eds.). 2010. *Disagreement*. Oxford: Oxford University Press.
Foley, Richard. 2001. *Intellectual Trust in Oneself and Others*. Cambridge: Cambridge University Press.
Frances, Bryan. Forthcoming A. "Philosophy Sabotages Knowledge." In an as yet untitled OUP volume on Disagreement edited by Jennifer Lackey and David Christensen.
Frances, Bryan. Forthcoming B. "Discovering Disagreeing Epistemic Peers and Superiors." *International Journal of Philosophical Studies.*
Frances, Bryan. 2010. "The Reflective Epistemic Renegade." *Philosophy and Phenomenological Research.*
Frances, Bryan. 2005. *Scepticism Comes Alive*. Oxford: Oxford University Press.
Fumerton, Richard. 2010. "You Can't Trust a Philosopher." In R. Feldman and T. Warfield (eds.), *Disagreement*. Oxford University Press.
Goldberg, Sandy. 2009. "Reliabilism in Philosophy." *Philosophical Studies* 124: 105–17.
Kelly, Thomas. 2008. "Disagreement, Dogmatism, and Belief Polarization." *Journal of Philosophy* 105: 611–33.
Kelly, Thomas. 2006. "The Epistemic Significance of Disagreement." In John Hawthorne and Tamar Gendler Szabo (eds.), *Oxford Studies in Epistemology*, 1. Oxford: Oxford University Press.
Kornblith, Hilary. 2010. "Belief in the Face of Controversy." In R. Feldman and T. Warfield (eds.), *Disagreement*. Oxford University Press.
Lackey, Jennifer. 2010a. "A Justificationist View of Disagreement's Epistemic Significance." In Adrian Haddock, Alan Millar, and Duncan Pritchard (eds.), *Social Epistemology*. Oxford: Oxford University Press.
Lackey, Jennifer. 2010b. "What Should We Do When We Disagree?" In Tamar Szabó Gendler and John Hawthorne (eds.), *Oxford Studies in Epistemology*, vol. 3. Oxford: Oxford University Press.
McKim, Robert. 2001. *Religious Ambiguity and Religious Diversity*. Oxford: Oxford University Press.
van Inwagen, Peter. 1996. "Is It Wrong, Everywhere, Always, and for Anyone to Believe Anything on Insufficient Evidence?" In Jeff Jordan and Daniel Howard-Snyder (eds.), *Faith, Freedom, and Rationality*. Lanham, MD: Rowman and Littlefield.
White, Roger. 2005. "Epistemic Permissiveness." *Philosophical Perspectives* 19: 445–59.

8
EPISTEMIC RELATIVISM
Paul Boghossian

This essay is about epistemic relativism, relativism about the epistemic domain. Since different views have gone by the name "relativism," epistemic relativism is not a single view, but a family of views. What unites these various views is that, in one way or another, the fact that some item of evidence justifies a given belief is said to be relative to the value of some further parameter. Typically, this further parameter is held to be either the believer's or the assessor's epistemic system or framework. (Compare moral relativism: the fact that some act is wrong is said to be relative to the agent's (or assessor's) moral code or framework.)

In order to focus on the issues that concern us, we will need to make certain assumptions about what epistemic facts are like. Given the state of epistemology these days, most any such assumption is likely to be controversial. However, once we get clear about the relevant issues, it is likely that we will be able to restate our discussion using alternative assumptions.

I will assume that a canonical *epistemic sentence* is a sentence of the form:

(1) S's belief that p is justified iff (a) S bases his belief that p on his (overall) evidence E and (b) E justifies the proposition that p.

I will concentrate on the propositional component:

(2) S's overall evidence E justifies the proposition that p.

I will assume that the notion of justification is a *normative* notion; that when we say that E justifies p we are positively evaluating believing p, given E.

Let us take a particular example. Most of us tend to think of the following epistemic sentence as true:

(3) Its visually seeming to S that there is a cat in front of him, along with S's not possessing any background information that counts against that being the case, justifies the proposition that there is a cat in front of S.

At least on the surface, then, our epistemic discourse suggests that whether a proposition is justified is relative to a thinker's overall evidence and to nothing else.

One type of epistemic relativist thinks that this is wrong, that there is a further parameter involved. He might think that this further dependence is already anticipated by our discourse in a way that might not be apparent on the surface but which would be revealed by a deeper semantical analysis. Or he may think that our discourse is in error on this point and needs to be replaced by a discourse that overtly acknowledges this further dependence. (On the latter view, the epistemic relativist's thought would be akin to Einstein's view that we were wrong to think that two events could simply be simultaneous with one another, independently of a spatio-temporal frame of reference.)

Either way, the epistemic relativist thinks that we should affirm the following two claims (see Boghossian 2007):

(4) There are no facts of the form 'E justifies p,' but only facts of the form 'E justifies p relative to the epistemic system, C, accepted by a given person or community.' (Epistemic Relationism)
(5) There are several mutually incompatible epistemic systems, but no facts by virtue of which one of these is more correct than any of the others. (Epistemic Pluralism)

The Epistemic Pluralism clause is needed because without it Epistemic Relationism could not be guaranteed to have captured a relativistic view (suppose one of these epistemic systems were held to be privileged, the uniquely correct epistemic system relative to which epistemic claims should be assessed). It is possible to see something like this view in the work of Richard Rorty and others (see Rorty 1980; Barnes and Bloor 1982; Lennon 1997).

What motivates this type of relativist? The most important of these motivations can be summarized as follows (for more detailed discussion see Boghossian 2007):

A. How can it just be a fact about the world that such and such information epistemically justifies a given belief? Epistemic facts, if there are any, are normative facts. And there is a general puzzle making sense of absolute normative facts, facts that are binding on anyone whether or not they are aware of them or accept them.

B. If there were absolute normative facts, there would be a big puzzle explaining how we could know about them. Any attempt to know anything relies upon some epistemic system or other—some sort of system of general rules that tells us what justifies what. But it is not possible to justify a view about which epistemic rule is correct by relying on that very rule.

C. History and anthropology teach us that different people have subscribed to different and mutually incompatible epistemic systems. Yet, for the reasons mentioned above under B, it would be impossible to rationally resolve a dispute between these systems.

The proponent of (4) owes us answers to three questions:

(a) What is an epistemic system?
(b) What is it for E's justifying p to obtain relative to such a system?

and

(c) What is it for a person to accept a given epistemic system?

And the most natural package of answers to these questions begins with an answer to (a) that has it that an epistemic system consists of general propositions of the form:

(6) For all e, h: e justifies h iff f(e, h).

The relativist can then say, in answer to (b), that a *particular* statement of the form 'e justifies h' (e.g., S's seeming to see a cat justifies his believing that he sees one) obtains relative to such a system just in case that system, along with the epistemic facts, *entails* 'e justifies h.' And he can also say, in answer to (c), that to *accept* an epistemic system is to believe that its ingredient epistemic principles are true. However, this natural package of answers won't do: it does not lead to a reflectively tenable position.

One problem is that propositions of the form (6) seem to be complete truth-evaluable propositions that state the conditions under which a belief would be absolutely justified. It is, therefore, not open to the relativist to say that he *believes* these propositions to be true, since it is a non-negotiable part of his view that no absolute epistemic principle is ever simply true.

A second problem is that, if the only facts there are are relational facts of the form

E justifies p relative to epistemic system C

then it looks as though the consistent relativist should never assert propositions of the form

(7) *E justifies p*

but only propositions of the form

(8) *E justifies p relative to the system, C, that I accept.*

But the trouble is that while (7) is a properly normative proposition, (8) is just a logical remark about what the epistemic system in question does or does not claim, with no normative force whatsoever. Even someone who wholeheartedly disagreed with system C could agree that, according to C, E justifies p. So, at least on this construal of epistemic relativism, the whole subject of epistemic justification will have been lost, and not just a universalist construal of it. We need to be able to retain genuine normative disagreements in the epistemic domain, if we are not to lose the subject matter. We may call this the Normativity Problem.

Finally, there is a problem making sense of the Pluralist clause. Here, the epistemic relativist's thought is that there are many possible mutually conflicting epistemic systems, but no facts by virtue of which one of them is more correct than any of the others. But there is a serious puzzle seeing how any such claim could be true.

An epistemic system consists of a set of general normative propositions that specify under what conditions beliefs are and are not justified. So, we will have one system, C1, which says that:

If E, then p is justified

and we will have another system, C2, which contradicts it and says:

It is not the case that if E, then p is justified.

In such a circumstance, however, it is very hard to see how the Pluralist clause, which says that all epistemic systems are on a par as far as their correctness is concerned, could be true. For, presumably, either it is the case that E is sufficient for p to be justified, or it is not. If we say, with the relativist, that E is not sufficient for p to be justified, because there are no absolute facts about justification, then C1 makes a false assertion; but C2, which denies that E is sufficient for p's justification, then says something true. How, then, could it possibly be right to say that there can be no fact by virtue of which some of these systems are more correct than any of the others?

Alethic Relativism for Epistemic Sentences

Recent analytic philosophy has seen a great deal of interest in formulations of relativism that emphasize the relativity of the *truth* of propositions of a given domain (Kölbel 2002; MacFarlane 2007; Richard 2008). Applied to our case, the idea would be to accommodate the claim that there are only relational facts about epistemic justification not by saying that we should assert only claims of the form (8), which, when true would be absolutely true, but rather by saying that such non-relativized claims as

(7) *E justifies p*

have only relative truth-values and no absolute ones. In the case of such contents, fixing the facts is not enough to fix a truth-value; in addition, the thinker's or assessor's epistemic system (depending on the details of one's view) must also be specified.

This proposal looks as though it has a shot at solving the Normativity Problem for it allows us to continue judging claims that look normative. But even if it did solve that problem, it would still leave the other two problems untouched. And, it's worth emphasizing, it does not really solve the Normativity Problem either. There are several big problems only two of which can be outlined here (for further discussion see Boghossian forthcoming and Wright 2008).

First, the proposal requires a new notion of propositional content—of a complete judgeable claim—one that, unlike Frege's or Russell's, doesn't have its truth value either essentially or intrinsically. One and the same judgeable content will have different truth-values depending on the context (according to some views, the context of the judgment, and according to others, the context in which the judgment is assessed). But it is unclear that we can make sense of such a notion of a judgeable content.

Suppose I come across a token of "It was hot" written on a blackboard. Should I accept this sentence or reject it? Surely, there is nothing specific enough either to accept or reject. We need to know which place and time were being referred to so that we can attach some determinate truth conditions to the sentence and come up with a view as to whether they were or were not satisfied.

The alethic relativist's proposal is similarly puzzling—perhaps even more so, since as most of its proponents insist, the contents in question are to be assessed relative to the *assessor's* epistemic system rather than the original judger's (see Zimmerman 2007).

Second, if when I judge, "S ought to f" I am judging something that is true relative to my standards and if when you judge "S ought not to f" you are judging something that is true relative to your (different) standards, then we are clearly not disagreeing in any interesting sense.

This should be obvious, but is occasionally denied. Suppose we adopt a relativistic treatment of "It is hot," so that the content I express by "It is not hot" is the *negation* of the content that you express by "It is hot." Still if I uttered my token in NYC referring to the weather in NYC and you uttered yours in Chicago referring to the weather in Chicago, then no matter how much our semantics allows us to say that my content is the negation of yours, we are clearly not disagreeing in any interesting sense.

However, if you and I can't disagree by my saying "S ought to f" and by your saying "S ought not to f," how can we claim to have captured the normative content of normative judgments?

Absolutist Relativism

We have been trying to make sense of the idea that there are no absolute facts about epistemic justification. And we have not succeeded in getting very far.

In examining epistemic relativism, we have been guided by a conception of relativism according to which to be a relativist about a given domain is to hold that there are no absolute facts in that domain. To be a relativist about morality is to hold that there are no absolute facts of the form

> Act A is morally bad

but only such absolute facts as

> Act A is morally bad relative to a particular moral framework.

To be a relativist about epistemic justification is to hold that there are no absolute facts of the form

> e justifies h

but only ones of the form

> e justifies h relative to epistemic system C.

This does seem like a very natural construal of relativism and it conforms extremely well to the only uncontroversial cases of relativism that we know of—namely, the cases of motion, mass, and time order that are familiar from physics (see Boghossian 2007).

Traditionally, however, a rather different idea has also gone under the banner of relativism and we should look at that idea as it might be applied to the domain of epistemology. According to this idea, it's not that there are no absolute facts in a given domain; it's rather that such absolute facts as there are call for different and incompatible actions under different circumstances, where those circumstances are themselves permissible from the standpoint of the domain in question. That's rather abstract, so to illustrate what I have in mind here, let me discuss the case of etiquette.

We are all familiar with the idea that different cultures have different practices when it comes, say, to eating. For example, in the West it is considered impolite to noisily slurp one's noodles, while in Japan it can be considered impolite not to, the noisy slurping being a sign of the eater's satisfaction with the dish before him. How should we understand such a case?

Well, in the first instance the judgments we make are of the form

> (R) It is rude to slurp one's noodles in (our) community C.

The relativization is made explicit.

But how do we now explain how a statement like (R) has normative force? It looks as though it is just a sociological remark about how things are done around here, one with which anyone could agree, even someone who belonged to a culture in which it is not rude to slurp one's noodles. Yet, if I say (R) to someone, a child, for example, I intend my remark to have normative force, to give him or her a reason to stop slurping his or her noodles.

The answer is that we all subscribe to some non-relative, universal moral norm, one that we typically express by saying

> When in Rome do as the Romans do!

or, perhaps more precisely,

> (Etiquette) With respect to certain behaviors, one ought to behave as the members of the community one finds oneself in find it natural to behave.

This normative principle is a non-relative, universally binding principle. Nevertheless, it prescribes acting in different ways depending on one's cultural location. It is our acceptance of this principle that explains how remarks like (R) can have normative force even as it accommodates our tolerance for alternative practices.

We may call this a species of Absolutist relativism, to contrast it with the sort of Thoroughgoing relativism that we have been discussing thus far. And we can imagine generating a version of epistemic relativism that conforms to it. Indeed, one of the most influential versions of epistemic relativism in the contemporary literature is an example of absolutist rather than thoroughgoing relativism.

The case I have in mind is that of Subjective Bayesianism. Bayes' rule (or theorem) prescribes how a thinker ought to update his beliefs in response to incoming evidence. Where $P(A)$ is the prior probability of A and $P(A/B)$ is the conditional probability of A, given B, Bayes' rule states that

$$P(A/B) = \frac{P(B/A) \cdot P(A)}{P(B)}$$

This rule, then, can be used to update one's belief in A given that one has observed B and Bayesianism is the view that doing so is the properly rational way to update one's beliefs.

Any such view has to face the question of how to assign the prior probabilities since Bayes' rule is useless without such an assignment and is itself silent about how that is rationally to be done.

A radical view in this connection has it that you are rationally permitted to assign whatever priors you find it natural to assign.

> (Subjective Priors) For any contingent proposition p and credence value X, there exists a probability function f that assigns X to p, and S is rationally permitted to have that function as his initial credence function.

Subjective Bayesianism is a perfect example of what I have been calling Absolutist relativism. Both Bayes' rule and the doctrine I have labeled Subjective Priors are put forward as absolute non-relative norms that govern rational belief.

But Subjective Bayesianism has what can be thought of as a relativistic upshot. It allows two thinkers to have mutually incompatible views about whether e justifies p, if they have started out with sufficiently different prior assignments to p. And, yet, the view seems untouched by all the arguments that were directed at thoroughgoing versions of relativism (see MacFarlane 2008). So, can't the major controversies about relativism now proceed in this form?

In a sense, this is right. I don't think there is anything straightforwardly incoherent about absolutist versions of relativism per se. But what we should recognize is that the aspiring relativist now has a much harder hand to play.

One of the normative relativist's strongest cards, as noted above, is that it is very hard to see where absolute normative facts could come from. It is very hard to see how such facts could be built into the fabric of the world. His other strong card is that it is also hard to see how one could *know* anything about such facts, even if we could make sense of their existence. These powerful considerations give very strong support for the claim that launches a relativistic outlook, namely, that there are no absolute facts in the relevant normative domain, but only relative ones.

However, on the absolutist way of formulating relativism, where what underlies the relativism is some universally binding non-relative normative principle of some sort, both of these cards are taken away from the relativist. Having committed himself to knowing of the existence of at least one non-relative normative principle, he can no longer avail himself of those powerful considerations.

Instead, he will have to find some way of arguing that, although there are non-relative normative principles and although we are able to know what they are, still there are only the sorts of spare principles that govern etiquette.

This, however, will be a difficult trick to pull off. Once it has been admitted that there are at least some non-relative moral principles in a given domain, it's hard to see how to stop short of the conclusion that there are as many such principles as there intuitively seem to be in that domain. It's morally plausible that you should conform your table manners (and not even all of those) to whatever the local practice is; it's not plausible that you should so conform your views on the treatment of children or the sick.

Once we have admitted that we know of some absolute normative principles, ordinary normative reasoning kicks in to tell us exactly what such principles there are. Viewed in that light, any attempt to assimilate morality to etiquette will seem normatively implausible. What makes the Rome dictum the only dictum you need for etiquette is that it is morally plausible that when it comes to such matters as whether or not to slurp one's noodles, all that really matters is what the local conventions are. But it is not similarly plausible that that is all that matters when it comes to the question whether it is alright to cleanse a region of a particular ethnic minority. Once we allow that there are some absolute moral facts, our usual procedures for determining what such facts there are kick in. And it is very implausible that these procedures will yield the result that what it is morally correct to do in a given situation will depend on which norms are accepted in that situation, or what the agent's inclinations happen to be.

Similar remarks apply to the case of Subjective Bayesianism. The idea that you are rationally permitted to assign whatever priors you please is extremely implausible. It leads to the craziest beliefs counting as justified. It conflicts with whatever hold we have on the intuitive extension of 'justified.'

It's a good question what story the Bayesian could tell about what could rationally constrain the assignment of priors, but that's his problem. Just as it would be implausible to maintain that people are morally permitted to adopt whatever moral rules they find it most natural to adopt, so it is implausible to maintain that they are rationally permitted to adopt whatever initial credence function they find it most natural to adopt.

Epistemic Permissiveness

The tendency of our reflections has been to cast doubt both on thoroughgoing versions of epistemic relativism and on extreme versions of Absolutist relativism. But there is a more subtle position—one we might call, following Roger White, "epistemic permissiveness"—that is not so easily dispatched and that calls for considerably more work (see White 2005).

Even if we agree that there are perfectly absolute, universally binding epistemic norms governing the rationality of our beliefs, we face the question whether those norms imply Uniqueness:

> (Uniqueness) Given one's total evidence, there is a unique rational doxastic attitude that one can take to any proposition.

And here an interesting puzzle arises. On the one hand, Uniqueness seems too strong. Intuitively, as Gideon Rosen has put it (Rosen 2001: 71),

> [i]t should be obvious that reasonable people can disagree, even when confronted with the same body of evidence. When a jury or a court is divided in a difficult case, the mere fact of disagreement does not mean that someone is being unreasonable.

This seems right. To take just a humdrum sort of case: we are familiar with the fact that one person can be more cautious than another in reaching conclusions on the basis of evidence. Of course, extreme caution, as exemplified by the Pyrrhonists, for example, might be thought to be a form of irrationality. But some small variation in caution seems to be permitted by the norms of rationality.

This, however, immediately leads to the conclusion that one person can be rational in concluding p on the basis of evidence e and another rational in suspending judgment on whether p, or perhaps even, under the right circumstances, concluding that not-p. If Marco requires evidence of strength a to believe that p and Paolo requires evidence of strength a´ (a´ > a) to believe that p, and both values of the caution parameter are rationally permissible, and the evidence is of strength a but not a´, then it looks as though Marco is rational in believing that p and Paolo is rational in withholding belief. This is puzzling, however, for it suggests that Marco himself could be rational in withholding belief, even after he has seen the relevant evidence and concluded that p, if he adjusts his caution parameter upwards, so that the belief that p is no longer justified. After all, since by hypothesis both values of the caution parameter are rationally permissible, they are permissible for either thinker.

We will need to think further about this kind of case before it will be clear what we should say about it.

References

Barnes, B. and Bloor, D. (1982) "Relativism, Rationalism and the Sociology of Knowledge," in Hollis, M. and Lukes, S. *Rationality and Relativism*, Cambridge, MA: MIT Press.
Boghossian, P. (forthcoming) "Relativism: New and Old."
Boghossian, P. (2007) *Fear of Knowledge*, Oxford: Oxford University Press.
Kölbel, M. (2002) *Truth Without Objectivity*, London: Routledge.
Lennon, K. (1997) "Feminist Epistemology as Local Epistemology," in *Proceedings of the Aristotelian Society*, 71: 37–54.
MacFarlane, J. (2008) "Boghossian, Bellarmine, and Bayes," *Philosophical Studies*, 141: 391–98.
MacFarlane, J. (2007) "Relativism and Disagreement," *Philosophical Studies*, 132: 17–31.
Richard, M. (2008) *When Truth Gives Out*, Oxford: Oxford University Press.
Rorty, R. (1980) *Philosophy and the Mirror of Nature*, Princeton, NJ: Princeton University Press.
Rosen, G. (2001) "Nominalism, Naturalism, Epistemic Relativism," *Philosophical Perspectives*, 15: 69–91.
White, R. (2005) "Epistemic Permissiveness," *Philosophical Perspectives*, 19(1): 445–59.
Wright, C. (2008) "Fear of Relativism?" *Philosophical Studies*, 141: 5–16.
Zimmerman, A. (2007) "Against Relativism," *Philosophical Studies*, 133: 313–48.

9
UNDERSTANDING
Stephen R. Grimm

Understanding comes in a variety of forms, and many of its forms are highly prized. According to many philosophers of science, for example, understanding is the good at which scientific inquiry aims (e.g., Salmon 1998; Lipton 2004; Strevens 2006). On this way of looking at things, what scientists want, when they begin their inquiries, is not just to acquire a range of true beliefs about the world; rather, their goal is to understand the world (or at least some part of it), where understanding the world involves something more than the acquisition of true beliefs. More generally, understanding is often said to be one of the great goods that makes life worth living. Thus according to value theorists such as James Griffin (1986, ch. 4), understanding stands as one of the few goods that deserves to be thought of as an intrinsic good.

Although questions concerning the value of understanding have recently gained attention (e.g., Elgin 1996; Zagzebski 2001; Kvanvig 2003), in this entry I will mainly focus on the nature of understanding rather than its value. What's more, although the concept of understanding covers a vast amount of ground, in this entry I will focus almost entirely on our understanding of the natural world (broadly understood), and little will be said about how—if at all—the approaches on offer here might relate, for example, to the kind of linguistic understanding we have of concepts or meanings. Likewise, very little will be said about the sort of understanding that we can acquire of human actions—or, more generally, of the products of human actions such as works of art. Although these presumably qualify as part of the natural world in some sense, the way in which we achieve understanding in these areas seems different enough that it deserves to be dealt with separately.

I will approach the nature of understanding in three main steps. First I will ask about the *object* of understanding, second about the *psychology* of understanding, and third about the sort of *normativity* that is constitutive of understanding. Along the way, I will also regularly ask how understanding compares with knowledge in all of these respects. According to some philosophers, for example, understanding differs from knowledge on virtually every point: it has different objects, incorporates a different psychology, and has different normative requirements. Whether these differences are as clear as has been suggested, however, is something I will question as we proceed.

1. Objects of Understanding

As we consider the object of understanding, the first thing to notice is that understanding can apparently take a variety of objects, corresponding to the variety of grammatical complements that are available to the verb "understands." Consider, for example, the following sentences:

(1) Mary understands that her class starts in an hour.
(2) Mary understands the New York City subway system.
(3) Mary understands why the coffee spilled.

With examples along the lines of (1), where "understands" takes a that-clause as its complement, it is commonly thought that the object of understanding is something like a Fregean proposition. As several authors have noted, moreover, ascriptions of understanding along the lines of (1) seem to be more or less synonymous with corresponding ascriptions of knowledge (Brogaard 2008; Kvanvig 2009; Pritchard 2009). Thus on most occasions it seems that we can substitute "S knows that p" for "S understands that p" with little loss of meaning; or, if there is a difference in meaning, it seems to derive from the fact that "understands" has more of a hedging connotation, one that suggests an openness to correction.

As we turn to examples such as (2), however, complications arise, and the comparisons with knowledge become less clear. Consider, for example, what a parallel sentence about knowledge might look like:

(4) Mary knows the New York City subway system.

As Brogaard (2009) and others have pointed out, (4) requires some care because it is ambiguous. Depending on context, at least three different senses of "knows" might be expressed.

First, the claim might be read so that the object of knowledge is the subway system itself, the concrete thing. In this sense, the claim would express some sort of relationship of acquaintance between Mary and the subway system. (Or at least some part of it. This qualification should be understood in what follows. If one wanted to substitute the subway system for an object that is more easily taken in or apprehended, one could substitute a different object, such as (say) one's desktop printer.)

Second, it might be read so that the object of knowledge is a group of propositions. In this sense, (4) would express a relationship of knowledge between Mary and a group of propositions *about* the subway system. Thus someone who has never even laid eyes on the subway system might nonetheless know a great deal about it; its history, its routes, and so on.

For our purposes, however, the most interesting way in which (4) might be read, and the one which helps to shed light on what seems distinctive about the sort of understanding we find in (2), is in yet a third sense. It is this third sense that would be operative, for example, if someone were to say, "Well, Paul (as opposed to Mary) might know a lot *about* the system, but he doesn't really *know* the system." In this sense, when we say that someone knows a lot about X but he doesn't really know X, we are not claiming that the person does not stand in a relationship of acquaintance (or the like) to X. Instead, what we are claiming is that while the person may know a lot about X, nonetheless he doesn't really know how X *works*. That is to say, he doesn't really know how the different parts or elements of X are related to, and depend upon, one another. Thus we might likewise say, for example, "Well, Paul might know a lot about Congress, but he doesn't really *know* Congress." Or: "Paul might know a lot about hydrodynamics, but he doesn't really *know* hydrodynamics."

For the time being, let us think of this sort of knowledge as a kind of *know-how*—that is, knowledge that consists in knowing how a thing works, or how the various parts of a thing relate to and depend upon one another. Now, it might be thought that this sort of knowledge can in fact be reduced to a special kind of propositional knowledge: perhaps, propositions *about* how a thing works. (For proponents of reduction, see Stanley and Williamson 2001; for criticism, see Schaffer 2007). I will have more to say about (and against) this sort of reduction below, but for the moment it will help to explore a different idea, one that draws inspiration from the following sort of question: namely, what is it that might make things as diverse as the New York City subway system, Congress, and hydrodynamics the proper *objects* of know-how? And the key thing to appreciate here, plausibly, is that if know-how implies an apprehension of how a thing works, then it seems to follow that the object of the know-how must be constituted by a structure that can *be* worked—that is, that can be worked to determine how the various elements of the thing relate to, and depend upon, one another. At first blush, then, it seems plausible to think of the object of this third sort of knowledge as a structure or system of some kind; at any rate, the sort of thing with "moving parts"—that is, parts or elements that are open to taking on different values and hence of being worked.

So much for these different ways in which claims along the lines of (4) might be understood. How does this shed light on claims about understanding such as (2)? One promising thought is that the object of understanding in (2) can profitably be viewed along the lines of the object of know-how just described (cf. Zagzebski 2001 and Chang 2009). In other words, the thought is that the object of understanding in (2) can profitably be viewed as a kind of system or structure—something, that is, that has parts or elements that depend upon one another in various ways.

But what sort of structure best fits the bill here? It seems we have at least three possibilities. First, we might say that the object is the actual, concrete structure that makes up something like the subway system: the tracks, cars, switch boxes, and all the rest. Second, we might say that the object here is an abstract representation *of* the system—perhaps in the sense of a model of the system, or perhaps in the sense of structural equations that encode information about how the various aspects (or properties) of the system depend upon one another. Finally, we might say that understanding can take a variety of objects, both concrete and abstract; this would be a pluralist view of the object of understanding.

Although we do not need to try to settle the matter here, it is worth pointing out that the "abstract" view seems to have at least two points in its favor. First, thinking of the object of understanding in cases such as (2) as an abstract representation helps to make sense of the kind of understanding we can enjoy of things that presumably lack a concrete basis. Thus on this way of looking at things we can make ready sense of the claim, for example, that "Bullfinch understands Greek Mythology," or that "Priestly understands phlogiston theory"; on the "concrete" view, it is not at all clear what the object of understanding might be in these cases. Second, the "abstract" view seems to provide us with ready truth-evaluable content, of the sort that our talk about understanding seems to require. Thus we commonly say, for example, that someone's understanding was inaccurate, or flawed, and so on. But it hardly makes sense to speak of something like the subway system itself (the concrete thing) as inaccurate, so this too suggests that the object is not concrete but abstract—a representation of the system, rather than the system itself.

As we turn now to examples such as (3), where someone understands *why* such-and-such occurred, identifying the object of understanding is again not straightforward. It will help to start, at any rate, with a specific example.

Suppose, then, that you are settling into a seat at your local coffee shop. As you turn to look at the table next to you, you notice a woman sitting with a hot cup of coffee. Seconds later, moreover, you see her knee accidentally jostle her table, leading to a messy spill. Without going into the details just yet, suppose for the moment that you now understand why your neighbor's coffee spilled, and that your understanding has something crucially to do with your ability to identify the jostling as the cause of the spill. But what exactly is the object of your understanding here?

The basic problem with trying to answer this question is that while from a grammatical point of view it seems clear that the complement of "understands" is an indirect question, from a metaphysical point of view things get murky. For one thing, it is not clear that questions (indirect or otherwise) even have metaphysical correlates. For another, and even supposing they do, it is not clear what such correlates might be.

Perhaps motivated by concerns along these lines, some philosophers have argued that cases of "understanding why" such as (3) can and should be reduced to cases of "understanding that" (e.g., Kvanvig 2003 and 2009). More exactly, the claim is that ascriptions along the lines of "S understands why such-and-such" in fact express propositions of the form S *understands that p*, where p represents a correct answer to the indirect question embedded in the ascription of understanding. (Alternatively, and perhaps more naturally, one might say not that cases of *understanding why* can be reduced to cases of *understanding that* but rather to cases of *knowledge that*.) On such a reductive analysis, then,

(i) Mary understands why the coffee spilled

just in case

(ii) Mary understands (or knows) that p, where p is a correct answer to the question "Why did the coffee spill?"

One benefit of this proposal is that we now have a natural object for instances of understanding why such as (3): namely, the proposition p, where we can suppose that p is something like *that the coffee spilled because of the jostling*.

But is this really a satisfying reduction? Does (ii) really capture what we find in (i)? To see why these questions should give us pause, note first that it seems we can know a proposition of the sort we find in (ii) in a very ordinary sense of "know" while nonetheless falling short of the sort of accomplishment that we naturally associate with understanding why (cf. Grimm 2009 and de Regt and Dieks 2005). For instance, on the basis of your reliable testimony I might come to believe, and hence know, that the coffee spilled because of the jostling. But possessing this knowledge, it seems, is compatible with a general inability to answer a wide range of questions that intuitively go along with the state of understanding why. Suppose, for example, you ask me whether a more forceful strike by the woman's knee would likewise have led to a spill. Or whether a spill would have occurred had there been no jostle of any kind. Although the achievement we associate with understanding why seems to bring with it the ability to answer questions of this sort, strictly speaking it seems one can have knowledge of the cause—again, based on reliable testimony—without possessing these additional abilities at all.

The "strictly speaking" qualification is important, for the thought here is not that, as a matter of fact, coming to believe a claim along these lines is usually accompanied by an inability to answer questions of this sort. The claim is only that it might be accompanied by such an inability. Moreover, the thought is that when an ability to answer questions of this sort *is* present, this seems to be the result of some sort of additional cognitive work—work that goes above and beyond the sort of work that goes into acquiring knowledge by testimony, for example.

The next section will consider just what sort of additional cognitive work needs to be done here, exactly. In bringing this section to a close, however, we can make one final point: namely, that it is now possible to see ways in which cases of understanding along the lines (2) share certain important, and often ignored, similarities with cases of understanding along the lines of (3). In particular, we can now see that the object of understanding in both cases is more similar than we might have originally supposed.

For notice: if someone understands why the cup spilled rather than remained upright, then presumably she in some way "grasps" or "sees" what it is that makes the difference between these alternatives. In other words, she in some way "grasps" or "sees" what the difference between these alternatives depends on. But if that is the case, then interesting parallels with cases of understanding along the lines of (2) begin to emerge. For just as cases of understanding such as (2) involve "grasping" how the various parts of a system depend upon one another, so too with cases such as (3) we find that understanding arises from "grasping" or "seeing" what the difference between certain alternatives depends upon. Plausibly, then, we might think of the object of understanding in cases such as (3) as a kind of "mini" representational structure, where the structure encodes information *about* how the various elements of the target system depend upon one another. (For highly worked out versions of this general idea, see Pearl 2000, Spirtes et al. 2001, and Woodward 2003).

In both cases such as (2) and cases such as (3), accordingly, the common hallmarks of system or structure seem to be present in the object of understanding, despite the differences in surface grammar. As we turn to the psychological element of understanding, our main concern will be to try to flesh out the notions of "grasping" and "seeing" that have played a recurring role in the discussion so far.

2. Psychology

The psychology of understanding is multi-layered. On the one hand, there is clearly something like an attitude of belief or assent involved. The sort of abstract structures that (at least sometimes) appear to be the object of understanding, after all, presumably represent the world as being a certain way, and if we take the representation to be accurate, we are in some sense assenting to these structures or saying Yes to them—just as when we take a proposition to be true we are in some sense assenting to or saying Yes to it. On the other hand, we have also seen reason to think that an element of belief or assent cannot be all there is to understanding. We can take it to be the case, for example, that a model is accurate—we can assent to it in that sense—and yet we might nonetheless not "grasp" or "see" how the various parts of the model relate to one another, where the element of grasping or seeing seems to involve an additional psychological ability.

Further complications arise, moreover, when we remember that many representations are highly idealized. On the ideal gas model that is typically used to explain Boyle's Law, for example, gas molecules are (inaccurately) represented as point particles, and the long range attractive forces between molecules are ignored. In this case, assenting to the model—in the sense of taking it to be an accurate representation of the world—will often involve subtle qualifications on the part of the assenter.

I will touch on a few of these complications as we proceed, but for the most part in this section I will focus on the element of "grasping" or "seeing" that seems to be so integral to understanding in all its forms. And the main thing I would like to try to do here is to move our understanding of these expressions beyond the level of mere metaphor, in order to try to get a better sense of the sort of psychological ability that lies behind, or perhaps constitutes, the graspings and seeings.

Now, in their primary (non-metaphorical) senses "grasping" is something that hands do, and "seeing" is something for eyes. We speak of manually grasping something, moreover, in at least two different ways: on the one hand to grasp a thing is to seize or take hold of it, as when we grasp (say) a baseball; on the other hand we speak of grasping a thing when we are able to manipulate or tinker with a thing, as when we grasp (say) a simple lever system by manually switching the lever from one position to another. Indeed, in this second, manipulationist sense the notions of (manually) grasping and (visually) seeing go together very naturally: if the system is simple enough, when one grasps or manipulates one part of the system one can then literally "see" the way in which the manipulation influences (or fails to influence) other parts of the system.

Given these two senses in which we might manually grasp a thing, moreover, even though the first sense is perhaps the more common one, it seems that the psychological act of grasping that is of interest to us here can most usefully be thought of along the second, manipulationist lines. In this sense, *mentally* to grasp how the different aspects of a system depend upon one another is to be able to anticipate how changes in one part of the system will lead (or fail to lead) to changes in another part. To "grasp" the way in which something like the spilling of the cup depends on the jostling of the knee in this sense is thus to have an ability to anticipate or "see" what things would have been like, had the knee bump not occurred, or had the bump been less forceful, or had it been a fist bump instead, and so on. (Ceteris paribus, etc. James Woodward's (2003) idea that understanding should be unpacked in terms of having an ability to answer "What if things had been different?" questions is another way to construe this thought.) "Grasping" a structure would therefore seem to bring into play something like a modal sense or ability—that is, an ability not just to register how things are, but also to anticipate how certain elements of the system would behave, were other elements different in one way or another.

We noted at the beginning of this section, however, that the act of grasping or seeing cannot be all there is to understanding. For we might grasp a representation in a straightforwardly assenting way, as when we take the representation to be the sober truth about the system it represents. But we might also grasp the representation in a qualified or non-straightforward way. This sort of qualified assent seems to be at play, for example, when we say things such as "for Priestly, the lighting of the tinder was due to the presence of phlogiston"; or perhaps: "supposing that Priestly was right, the lighting of the tinder was due to the presence of phlogiston"; and so on. Similar qualifications are typically in place when we grasp something like the ideal gas model, or when we learn to apply this model to Boyle's Law. Thus we learn to say: supposing that the gases were point particles, or supposing that no intermolecular forces were present, then *this* is how the system would behave. In these cases, we seem to assent to a representation only with certain qualifications in place, or with certain presuppositions in mind.

Of course, this leaves us with a variety of interesting questions (for example, how does our grasp of how the target system *would* behave, if certain properties were otherwise, help us to understand the system as it actually is?), but these will have to be set aside here as we turn instead to ask about the last element of understanding identified at the outset: namely, the sort of normativity that is constitutive of understanding. (For more on the notion of "grasping" see Grimm 2009.)

3. Normativity

As we consider the sort of normativity that is constitutive of understanding, it will help to look again to accounts of knowledge as a kind of template.

When we are evaluating whether a belief amounts to knowledge, we can ask two different sorts of normative questions. On the one hand, we can ask whether the belief is *subjectively appropriate*, where subjective appropriateness has to do, roughly, with whether the belief "fits" with the rest of the person's evidence (where "evidence" can be construed broadly to include the person's experiences as well as his or her beliefs). On the other hand, we can ask whether someone's belief is *objectively appropriate*, where objective appropriateness has to do, roughly, with whether the belief is, as a matter of fact, reliably oriented to the truth. (Fogelin 1994 and Greco 2000 helpfully emphasize these two different types of evaluations.)

On the standard way of looking at things, moreover, both sorts of appropriateness are required for a belief to amount to knowledge. When it comes to understanding, however, opinions differ. According to some theorists, for example, while there are objective appropriateness conditions on understanding, they are noticeably different—and apparently less strict—than the conditions on knowledge (e.g., Elgin 2004 and 2009). According to others, only subjective appropriateness really matters to understanding—a view which makes the achievement of understanding almost entirely an "internal affair."

To see why one might think that only subjective appropriateness really matters to understanding, consider the following variation on our earlier coffee shop case. Suppose that while you are watching your neighbor spill her coffee, a visiting shaman is sitting in another corner of the shop, taking the whole scene in. He notices the jostling, sees the cup spill, and all the rest. From his point of view, however, it was not the jostling that caused the spill but, rather, the fact that he willed the cup to spill seconds before (perhaps he thinks he has powers of telekinesis or something comparable).

Suppose moreover that the shaman has good, albeit misleading, reasons to believe he has such powers (perhaps people have always humored him in the past). In that case, it seems that it will be subjectively appropriate for him to believe that it was his powers that made the difference to the spill. We can also imagine that he not only assents to this claim but that he "grasps" how the spill depended on his powers in the way sketched above. For example, he will "grasp" or "see" that, in the absence of his willing the spill would not have occurred (ceteris paribus). But now: what should we say about the shaman? Does he understand or fail to understand why the cup spilled?

Although I take it that in one sense it seems obvious he does not understand why the cup spilled, it is worth noting that there is at least some conceptual pressure to think otherwise. Consider, for example, Lynne Rudder Baker's suggestion that: "Understanding is more comprehensive than knowledge. To understand something is to know what it is and to make reasonable sense of it" (Baker 2003, p. 186). If Baker is right, and understanding something amounts to knowing what is the case (this way of putting things changes Baker's "knowing what a thing is" formula slightly, but seems to be the same idea) and to making reasonable sense of what is the case, then it would seem to follow that the shaman *does* understand. Again, we can suppose that the shaman's story about the spill makes excellent sense to him, in light of the rest of what he believes; alternatively, it "fits" with the rest of what he believes, and so on. Looked at charitably, we can even recognize the shaman's achievement as a genuine cognitive accomplishment. The various kinds of "seeing" or "grasping" we have just described do not come for free, after all, and someone who has made reasonable sense of a thing, given the rest of what he believes, has indeed accomplished something. And what kind of name do we have for this sort of "seeing" or "grasping"-based accomplishment if not understanding?

Rather than try to downplay or ignore this sort of accomplishment, however, following Wesley Salmon we might instead try to introduce a distinction. (Here, I am indebted in particular to Salmon's 1998 distinction between "cosmological" and "mechanical" understanding.) Let us think of *subjective understanding* as the kind of understanding one achieves by grasping a representation of the world (a model, perhaps, or an explanatory story of some kind) that fits or coheres with one's "world picture." On the other hand, let us think of *objective understanding* as the kind of understanding that comes not just from grasping a representation of the world that fits with one's world picture, but also from grasping a (more or less) *correct* representation of the world. Objective understanding therefore entails subjective understanding but goes beyond it, requiring that the grasped representation in fact obtains.

This therefore suggests that there are at least two normative conditions on objective understanding. First, that the representation of the world that is grasped be correct (more or less). And second, that the attitude of assent or grasping be subjectively appropriate, given the rest of the person's evidence.

But are there other normative conditions on objective understanding? As noted earlier, when we look at knowledge we find that believing the truth with subjective appropriateness is not enough; in addition, the belief must be securely connected to the truth in some way. We might think of this as the "anti-luck" condition on knowledge. According to Jonathan Kvanvig (2003, 2009) and Duncan Pritchard (2009), however, understanding is compatible with luck in a way that knowledge is not. For both, then, the objective appropriateness conditions on understanding are different than the objective appropriateness conditions on knowledge.

Kvanvig first argued for this claim by means of the following example. (See Kvanvig 2003, pp. 197–98; for another example along these lines, where we have a case of fortunate dyslexia, see Kvanvig 2009, p. 8, typescript.) Suppose you come across a book detailing the Comanche dominance of the southern plains of North America from the seventeenth to the nineteenth centuries (Kvanvig 2003, p. 197). But suppose as well that while all of the contents of the book are true they are only "accidentally" so. Perhaps, for example, the book was put together as a joke by someone who did no research at all, but just happened to get everything right.

Now suppose you read the book carefully and come to grasp (in an assenting way) the central explanations offered by the book: for example, suppose you come to grasp that the Comanches dominated in part because of their superior horsemanship. According to Kvanvig, what we have here is a "grasp" that genuinely amounts to a case of understanding, even though one would fail to know the corresponding propositions. (Where the corresponding propositions would apparently include things like: *that the Comanches dominated because of their superior horsemanship.*) One would not know these propositions, according to Kvanvig, because it would be a mere matter of luck that an accurate book landed in your hands, and luck rules out knowledge.

According to Pritchard, however, while Kvanvig is right to claim that there can be lucky understanding, Kvanvig overstates the case because he fails to distinguish between two different types of epistemic luck: on the one hand, what Pritchard calls "Gettier-style" epistemic luck, and on the other hand what he calls "environmental luck." On Pritchard's view, Gettier-style epistemic luck occurs when something intervenes "betwixt belief and fact," as when your belief that there is a sheep in the field turns out to be right, but only because you happened to be looking at a sheep-like dog, rather than the (hidden-from-view) sheep itself. With environmental luck, by contrast, although nothing comes between belief and fact, the environment itself conspires to take away knowledge. The barn façade case is the classic example of this sort of luck—one in which there is a direct causal path between one's belief that there is a barn nearby and the corresponding fact, but where the presence of nearby fake barns makes the fact that one believed the truth seem like a matter of luck.

On Pritchard's view, moreover, while it is right to say that understanding is compatible with environmental epistemic luck, it is wrong to say that understanding is compatible with Gettier-style epistemic luck. Unlike Kvanvig, Pritchard takes it to be obvious that a bunch of made-up facts, even if they turn out to be accurate, cannot grant one a genuine understanding of how the world works. Nevertheless, Pritchard claims that objective understanding can survive *environmental* luck. Suppose, for example, that the history book you happen to consult is the product of rigorous scholarship, but that the majority of the books that you might easily have consulted are full of lies (perhaps you live in an Orwellian regime of some kind). In this case, Pritchard suggests, one can acquire genuine understanding from the book even while genuine knowledge is ruled out.

Despite their differences, one point on which Kvanvig and Pritchard therefore agree is that understanding is not a species of knowledge, because while luck is not compatible with knowledge, it *is* compatible with understanding—either because, as Kvanvig has it, understanding is compatible with both Gettier-style and environmental luck, or because, as Pritchard claims, understanding is at least compatible with environmental luck. Put in terms of an objective normative condition: if Pritchard is right, then there needs to be at least a non-deviant connection between the grasping and the thing grasped; if Kvanvig is right, the connection can be as deviant as one might like.

It is not entirely clear, however, that the cases proposed by Kvanvig and Pritchard really establish that understanding is not a species of knowledge. (See Grimm 2006 and Brogaard 2008 for extended criticism.) For one thing, the claim that luck is not compatible with knowledge can be overstated. As Alvin Goldman (1999) and John Hawthorne (2004) have emphasized, in a "weak" sense of knowledge, all it takes to qualify as a knower with respect to some question is to believe the correct answer to the question; how the correct answer was arrived at seems irrelevant. Perhaps similarly, then, to qualify for a "weak" sense of understanding, all one needs to do is to be able to answer "why questions" successfully, where one might have come by this ability in a lucky way. In any case, it is unclear why, as Kvanvig seems to think, someone who can answer a broad range of "why questions" about a subject would count as understanding that subject while someone who is able to answer a similar range of questions would not qualify as a knower.

For another thing, the sort of *know-how* that we emphasized in Section 2—wherein someone "grasps" or "sees" how the various parts of a system depend upon one another—might also be thought to be compatible with luck, a point which would further undercut the assumption that knowledge as a genus is inimical to luck. After all, and to adopt one of Kvanvig's points, what we seem to "focus on," when we evaluate whether someone has know-how, is whether the person in fact has the ability in question, not how he or she came by the ability. Thus I might be happy to grant, for example, that Paul knows how to fix my computer, even if I later come to learn that he came by this knowledge in a lucky way. But then if, when we think about understanding, we similarly focus not on the etiology of the ability but rather on the ability itself (the "grasping" or "seeing"), then this would not show that understanding is not a species of knowledge. Instead, it would only show that understanding is like know-how: that is, that it is a kind (or species) of knowledge where the focus is on the ability at issue rather than on the circumstances that gave rise to that ability.

Acknowledgments

Thanks to Daniel Breyer, Adam Carter, Catherine Elgin, Daniel Fogal, Bryan Frances, Georgi Gardner, Emma Gordon, Allan Hazlett, Guy Longworth, Daniel McKaughn, Mark Newman, Duncan Pritchard, Todd Stewart, and Linda Zagzebski.

References

Baker, Lynne Rudder. 2003. "Third Person Understanding." In *The Nature and Limits of Human Understanding*. Ed. A. Sanford. London: Continuum.
Brogaard, Berit. 2008. "I Know. Therefore, I Understand." Manuscript.
——. 2009. "What Mary Did Yesterday: Reflections on Knowledge-Wh." *Philosophy and Phenomenological Research* 78: 439–67.
Chang, Hasok. 2009. "Ontological Principles and the Intelligibility of Epistemic Activities." In *Scientific Understanding: Philosophical Perspectives*. Eds. H. deRegt, S. Leonelli, and K. Eigner. Pittsburgh: Pittsburgh University Press.
De Regt, Henk, and Dennis Dieks. 2005. "A Contextual Approach to Scientific Understanding." *Synthese* 144: 137–70.
Elgin, Catherine. 1996. *Considered Judgment*. Princeton, NJ: Princeton University Press.
——. 2004. "True Enough." *Philosophical Issues* 14: 113–31.
——. 2009. "Is Understanding Factive?" In *Epistemic Value*. Eds. A. Haddock, A. Millar, and D. Pritchard. New York: Oxford University Press.
Fogelin, Robert. 1994. *Pyrrhonian Reflections on Knowledge and Justification*. New York: Oxford University Press.
Goldman, Alvin. 1999. *Knowledge in a Social World*. New York: Oxford University Press.
Greco, John. 2000. *Putting Skeptics in Their Place*. New York: Cambridge University Press.
Griffin, James. 1986. *Well-Being*. Oxford: Clarendon Press.
Grimm, Stephen. 2006. "Is Understanding a Species of Knowledge?" *British Journal for the Philosophy of Science* 57: 515–35.
——. 2009. "Reliability and the Sense of Understanding." In *Scientific Understanding: Philosophical Perspectives*. Eds. H. de Regt, S. Leonelli, and K. Eigner. Pittsburgh: Pittsburgh University Press.
——. Forthcoming. "Understanding and the Goal of Explanation." *Studies in the History and Philosophy of Science*.
Hawthorne, John. 2004. *Knowledge and Lotteries*. New York: Oxford University Press.
Kvanvig, Jonathan. 2003. *The Value of Knowledge and the Pursuit of Understanding*. New York: Cambridge University Press.
——. 2009. "The Value of Understanding." In *Epistemic Value*. Eds. A. Haddock, A. Millar, and D. Pritchard. New York: Oxford University Press.
Lipton, Peter. 2004. *Inference to the Best Explanation*. 2nd edn. New York: Routledge.
Pearl, Judea. 2000. *Causality: Models, Reasoning, and Inference*. New York: Cambridge University Press.
Pritchard, Duncan. 2009. "Knowledge, Understanding and Epistemic Value." In *Epistemology*. Ed. A. O'Hear. Royal Institute of Philosophy supp. 64. New York: Cambridge University Press.

Salmon, Wesley. 1998. "The Importance of Scientific Understanding." In his *Causality and Explanation*. New York: Oxford University Press.

Schaffer, Jonathan. 2007. "Knowing the Answer." *Philosophy and Phenomenological Research* 75: 383–403.

Spirtes, Peter, Clark Glymour, and Richard Scheines. 2001. *Causation, Prediction, and Search*. 2nd edn. Cambridge: MIT Press.

Stanley, Jason and Timothy Williamson. 2001. "Knowing How." *Journal of Philosophy* 98: 411–44.

Strevens, Michael. 2006. "Scientific Explanation." In *The Encyclopedia of Philosophy*. 2nd edn. Ed. D. Borchert. New York: Macmillan.

Woodward, James. 2003. *Making Things Happen*. New York: Oxford University Press.

Zagzebski, Linda. 2001. "Recovering Understanding." In *Knowledge, Truth, and Duty*. Ed. M. Steup. New York: Oxford University Press.

10
WISDOM

Dennis Whitcomb

> Men, in whom the principal part is the mind, ought to make their principle care
> the search after wisdom, which is its true source of nourishment.
> Descartes (in Haldane and Ross 1931: 205)

First of all: why wisdom? Why should epistemologists theorize about *that*? Well, there are several reasons. For one, people sometimes write about wisdom as if it were an epistemic good, and these people do not seem to be misguided. For instance, Wayne Riggs uses "wisdom" as a term of art for the highest epistemic good, whatever that good is (Riggs 2003: 215). This use of "wisdom" is telling, because it is no random selection. It is not strange to use "wisdom" as a term of art for the highest epistemic good, whereas it would be strange to use e.g., "toothpaste" as a term of art for the highest epistemic good.

The second reason for epistemologists to theorize about wisdom derives from connections between epistemology and psychology. As several theorists have pointed out, some parts of psychology study epistemically valuable phenomena such as intelligence, creativity, and rationality (Goldman 1986; Bishop and Trout 2004). It would behoove us epistemologists to pay attention to this work, since it addresses some of the very same issues as our own work. And as it turns out, there is a body of psychological work on wisdom, and that work widely recognizes the standing of wisdom as a particularly high-grade intellectual state (Sternberg and Jordan 2005). This body of work may well be on to something. That is the second reason why we epistemologists should theorize about wisdom.

The third reason is that the history of philosophy features rich veins of material that take wisdom to be a central epistemic achievement. This material includes work by Plato and Aristotle, their medieval followers, and the moderns who followed them in turn. Strangely, though, it seems to have petered out by the twentieth century. It is as if twentieth-century epistemologists inherited a big set of interconnected issues from the ancients and their followers, and arbitrarily chose to theorize about some of those issues much more than others. Wisdom falls into the neglected category, so our theorizing about it has some catching up to do.

The fourth reason for epistemologists to theorize about wisdom is that wisdom is connected to several issues in applied epistemology. For instance, it is connected to the design of educational curricula. In pursuing this connection, Goldman (1999) argues that educational curricula should be centered on the cultivation of true belief. But perhaps they should be centered on different epistemic aims instead, such as knowledge or understanding or *wisdom* (Norman 1996; Sternberg 2001). In trying to resolve this issue, it would be helpful to have at hand a theory of the nature of wisdom.

The fifth reason for epistemologists to theorize about wisdom has to do with certain large-scale debates about the structure of epistemic value. In *Virtues of the Mind*, Zagzebski claims that consequentialist accounts of epistemic value have difficulty making sense of the epistemic value of wisdom, and that her own virtue-theoretic theory does better at the task (Zagzebski 1996: 28–29, 50). It is worth getting straight on the merits of this claim, and theorizing about wisdom can help us do that.

For all of these reasons, epistemologists should theorize about wisdom. In this chapter I will do as much, first by critically surveying the extant work on the nature of wisdom, and then by arguing for a particular view on the matter.

The philosophical literature features three main sorts of views about the nature of wisdom. In the *Apology* Socrates seems to view wisdom as some sort of epistemic humility or accuracy. Aristotle (and many of his followers) take wisdom to come in two forms, the practical and the theoretical, the former of which is a capacity for good judgment about how to act and the latter of which is deep knowledge or understanding. Others still follow Aristotle only part way, taking wisdom as a practical matter only. Let us call these three sorts of views *Apologetic*, *Twofold*, and *Practical* views. I'll survey the central views of these three sorts; then I'll argue for a particular version of the twofold view.

Apologetic Views

In Plato's *Apology* the oracle says that Socrates is the wisest of all men; Socrates tests the prophecy; he finds his interlocutors deeply ignorant and unaware of that fact. Socrates alone *knows* he is ignorant—which shows, perhaps, that the oracle was right.

This story suggests that wisdom is some sort of epistemic humility or accuracy (Ryan 2007). Pursuing the humility theme, perhaps one is wise to the extent that one knows the facts about what one fails to know. Pursuing the accuracy theme, perhaps one is wise to the extent that one knows both the facts about what one knows, and the facts about what one fails to know. (These themes aren't restricted to ancient philosophy; variations on them sometimes arise in contemporary psychology. See Kitchener and Brenner 1990 and Kunzmann and Baltes 2005.)

How plausible are these themes? Not very. Suppose that a being has vast amounts of knowledge, indeed God-like knowledge. Such a being would not be epistemically humble (at least not in the sense we've just identified), but might be wise nonetheless. Now suppose that a person knows very little—just enough to barely scrape by in life—plus many or all the facts about what she does and does not know. Despite being epistemically accurate, such a being needn't be wise. Nor could we guarantee that she is wise by simply replacing her ignorance with knowledge. Suppose she knew a vast array of trivial facts, for instance the facts about the precise distances between each two grains of sand on the earth. She might know these trivial facts and additionally know the facts about what she does and does not know; but for all that, she might still be unwise. Wisdom is therefore neither epistemic humility, nor epistemic accuracy, nor even epistemic accuracy combined with large amounts of knowledge.

Practical Views

Lots of people have practical views about wisdom (Nozick 1989; Ryan 1996, 1999; Sternberg 1998). What makes these views *practical* views of wisdom is that they all take wisdom to be some sort of practical knowledge or ability. Let me clarify this by discussing some of the particular views.

Let's start with Sharon Ryan's views. In two illuminating papers she advocates one, and then later another, theory according to which wisdom is a compound state the most central aspect of which is knowing how to live well. In the first of these papers, she argues that to be wise is to (i) be a free agent who (ii) knows how to live well and (iii) does live well, whose (iv) living well is caused by her knowledge of how to live well.

In the second paper, she drops the first, third, and fourth of these conditions. There are good reasons for doing so. A wise and free agent who is suddenly metaphysically enslaved does not thereby cease to be wise; therefore, wise agents need not be free. Wise agents need not live well either: it may turn out that, through ceaseless bad luck, their wise choices always bring about tragedies. Alternatively, wise people may be akratic or evil, and on those grounds fail to live well despite their wisdom (I'll say more about these possibilities momentarily).

So there are several ways in which wise people can fail to live well. And if wise people need not live well, then *ipso facto* they need not live well *via* their knowledge of how to live well. All that remains of Ryan's original account, then, is the epistemic condition—the condition according to which wise people know how to live well.

Her second paper combines this condition with another, and argues for the view that to be wise is to (i) know how to live well, while also (ii) having an appreciation of the true value of living well. The latter condition—the "appreciation condition," we'll call it—seems to have it that being wise requires valuing or desiring the good life.

But why should we think this appreciation condition holds, i.e. that wisdom requires valuing or desiring the good life? Deeply depressed people may desire and value nothing other than sitting in dark rooms alone. But can't they nonetheless be wise?

Consider a wise person who knows how to live well and values and desires the good life. Suppose that at some point in this person's life, he is beset by a fit of deep depression due to a medication he had to take to cure an otherwise terminal illness. It seems unfair to this person to say that his medication destroys his wisdom. Isn't his depression bad enough on its own? Can't his doctor rightly avoid mentioning wisdom loss when discussing the medicine's risks?

Our unfortunate medicine-taker could still retain all of his knowledge, including all of his knowledge of how to live well. People might still go to him for good advice; and with poking and prodding, they might even get it. He might even be a stereotypical wise sage, sitting on a mountain and extolling deep aphorisms. Should his visitors feel slighted because he is deeply depressed? Should they think that they have not found a wise man after all, despite the man's knowledge and good advice?

I certainly wouldn't think that. If I ran across such a person, I'd take his advice to heart, wish him a return to health, and leave the continuing search for sages to his less grateful advisees. And I would think he was wise despite his depression-induced failure to value or desire the good life. So I think that wisdom does not require valuing or desiring the good life.

And just as this argument from depression sheds doubt on the appreciation condition, so too does a similar argument from evil. Consider Mephistopheles, that devil to whom Faust foolishly sells his soul. Mephistopheles knows what advice will bring Faust to lead a bad life, and that is precisely the advice that he gives him. But then, it stands to reason that Mephistopheles also knows what advice will bring Faust to lead a *good* life. So, it stands to reason that Mephistopheles knows how to live well. Despite this knowledge, the life Mephistopheles lives is bad, and so is the life he brings Faust to live. Mephistopheles is sinister, fiendish, and wicked. But whatever he is, he is not a fool. He is, it seems, wise but evil.

If it helps, we can recall that the devil was once an angel (or so the legend goes, of course). Should we say that the devil was wise as an angel but, through no loss of knowledge, became unwise in his attempt to take over the throne and his subsequent fall? That seems no more plausible than the view that the depression-inducing medication destroys the sage's wisdom, despite not destroying any of the sage's knowledge. It seems, then, that wisdom can coexist both with depression and with evil, but that wise people who are depressed or evil do not meet Ryan's appreciation condition. The compatibility of wisdom and depression, and of wisdom and evil, shows that the appreciation condition does not hold.

Yet surely there is something right in the idea that wisdom requires some kind of practical knowledge, such as knowledge of how to live well. Thus we should consider views on which wisdom just amounts to as much, that is, on which wisdom is a kind of practical knowledge. One such view simply says that being wise is identical to knowing how to live well. Other such views theorize in terms of knowledge-that as opposed to knowledge-how. For example, some views might claim that to be wise is to know all the elements in some appropriate set of central moral and prudential truths. Other views still might claim that to be wise is to *believe*, or perhaps *justifiedly believe*, all of those same moral and prudential truths. And of course, some of these various views may be reducible to others, for instance if know-how is a species of knowledge-that (Stanley and Williamson 2001). But regardless of whether any of these views reduce to any of the others, it is worth inquiring into whether any of them are true.

Views in this neighborhood have been advocated by Robert Nozick and Richard Garrett. According to Nozick, wisdom is that "knowledge or understanding" which "you need . . . in order to live well and cope with the central problems and avoid the dangers in the predicament(s) human beings find themselves in" (Nozick 1989: 267–268). Similarly, Garrett claims that "wisdom is that understanding and those justified beliefs which are essential to living the best life" (Garrett 1996: 230).

So Nozick and Garrett both take practical views of wisdom: they both take wisdom to consist in knowledge or justified belief, or understanding of one variety or another, or some combination of these things, where these things concern living well. But they both add an important twist: they take the relevant beliefs and understandings to be those beliefs and understandings that are *essential to* living well.

But plausibly, there are multiple sets of beliefs (or understandings etc.) such that possessing any one of those sets of beliefs (or understandings etc.) is sufficient for living well, given that all of the extra-doxastic conditions for living well are also met. And this entails that there *is no* set of beliefs (or understandings etc.) that is essential to living the best life. Nozick and Garrett's views therefore render it impossible to be wise. The upshot is that the practical views we have considered thus far—Nozick's, Garrett's, and Ryan's—are implausible.

Do any other practical views do better? Perhaps. If we drop the condition about essential-ness that plagues Nozick's and Garrett's views, and we also drop the appreciation condition that plagues Ryan's view, then we are left with the view that wisdom is a kind of practical knowledge or belief: knowledge of how to live well, or perhaps some sort of moral or prudential propositional knowledge or belief. Such a view captures much of the spirit of the other practical views we have considered so far, and it does not have their problems. We can thus reasonably take it to be the best practical view of wisdom.

But despite being the best practical view, it is problematic. To see why, pick what you think is the best sort of knowledge to have, except the know-how or knowledge-that featured in the best practical theory. This sort of knowledge may be fundamental metaphysical or epistemological knowledge; or it may be some more scientific sort of knowledge; or it may be any other sort of knowledge. Whatever it is, call it "the best non-practical knowledge."

Now, consider two people, A and B, with equal amounts of the knowledge featured in the best practical view. Suppose that A has much more of the best non-practical knowledge than does B. Suppose, even, that A has all of the best non-practical knowledge, and that B has very little or none of it. Is A wiser than B?

I would certainly say so. But if in this case A is wiser than B, then wisdom cannot just be practical knowledge. Hence the best practical view of wisdom is implausible; it runs aground on the fact that we can gain wisdom without gaining practical knowledge.

But now let us ask another question: is B more foolish than A? B does, after all, have just as much practical knowledge as A. Why should lacking the best *non*-practical knowledge, be it deep scientific or philosophical knowledge or anything else, render him *foolish*? Doesn't everyone, or at least almost everyone, lack deep philosophical and scientific knowledge? And aren't most people nonetheless not particularly foolish?

It does not seem right to call B more foolish than A. But this leaves us in a bind. For foolishness is in some sense the absence of wisdom. And if foolishness is the absence of wisdom, and foolishness is no more present in B than in A, then A is not wiser than B. Thus in taking B to be no more foolish than A, we ought to also take A to be no wiser than B.

But earlier, when we asked not about foolishness but about wisdom, we wanted to say that A *is* wiser than B. So it has turned out that different things happen when we ask different questions about the case of A and B. When we ask about "wisdom" we think that A is wiser than B, but when we ask about "foolishness" we think that A is not wiser than B. What is going on here? Is it that we tacitly hold contradictory beliefs about wisdom, or what?

The answer, I think, is that there are two kinds of wisdom, the practical and the theoretical. Theoretical wisdom is something like deep knowledge or understanding, and practical wisdom is something like knowledge of how to live well. Somehow, foolishness-talk in our case leads us to interpret "wisdom" as "practical wisdom," whereas wisdom-talk in our case leads us to interpret "wisdom" as "theoretical wisdom." Our responses to the case, then, are not so much contradictory as they are concerned with two different varieties of wisdom.

I'll say more about these two varieties of wisdom later. But first I should point out that Aristotle took wisdom to come in both practical and theoretical varieties, and that many of his followers have done so as well. Maybe these theorists are on to something; let us examine their views.

Twofold Virtue Theories

Aristotle operated with at least two distinct concepts that are not unreasonable to express with the word "wisdom." In several places (especially Book 6 of the *Nicomachean Ethics*), he discusses the intellectual virtues, two of which are "sophia" and "phronesis."

These terms are typically translated as "theoretical wisdom" and "practical wisdom," respectively.

Aristotle views theoretical wisdom as the highest cognitive state or the best position one can be in epistemically. It consists in "episteme," or what most translators call "scientific knowledge," that is properly grounded in "nous," which is something like immediate comprehension of the most fundamental principles in virtue of which all other principles hold. It seems reasonable, then, to call sophia "theoretical wisdom."

Phronesis is a faculty for good practical reasoning. The person with phronesis—that is practical wisdom—has the ability to make good judgments. He, therefore, has a general knowledge not only of what ends are good for him, but also of what means are good for producing those ends. Phronesis is somewhat similar to knowledge of how to live well; and it seems to be quite reasonably translated as "practical wisdom."

Zagzebski, following Aristotle, countenances something like phronesis as a faculty of good judgment and calls it "practical wisdom"; she also recognizes a more intellectualized form of wisdom, which she calls "theoretical wisdom." She takes practical wisdom to be a virtue consisting in good judgment about what to do and what to believe. She takes theoretical wisdom to be a particularly high intellectual good, and to be quite distinct from practical wisdom. It is, she thinks, a species of the sort of understanding that has to do with unificatory insight. On her view, this sort of understanding is not propositional, i.e. it is not any sort of attitude directed at any sort of proposition or propositions. It is instead directed at non-propositional structures in reality such as paintings or domains of inquiry. She does not take theoretical wisdom to be *identical* to this sort of understanding. Rather, she takes it to be the species of this sort of understanding that "is a matter of grasping the whole structure of reality" (Zagzebski 1996: 49–50). Finally, she claims that virtue epistemologies are particularly well-positioned to make sense of the epistemic value of understanding and wisdom. Her basic reason for thinking as much seems to be that understanding and wisdom are literally properties of *persons*, not persons' cognitive states, and that virtue theories take properties of persons as the primary objects of evaluation. Zagzebski thus uses her theory of wisdom, and theory of understanding in which it is embedded, to support a virtue theoretic approach to the whole domain of epistemic value.

But I don't think it is true that virtue epistemologies are particularly well-positioned to theorize about wisdom. For, as we will see below, some theories of wisdom that are *not* virtue theoretic are superior to Aristotle's and Zagzebski's own theories. But before getting into that, it is worth exploring some of the details of Aristotle and Zagzebski's own theories.

First, some remarks on Aristotle on theoretical wisdom. His *sophia* is a form of knowledge through deduction from first principles that one grasps via *nous*. This "grasping" amounts to something like rational intuition. So for Aristotle, every theoretically wise person rationally intuits first principles. But that seems wrong. A person can be theoretically wise through deep empirical knowledge of physics. Such knowledge does not require rational intuition; hence we should reject Aristotle's account of theoretical wisdom.

His account of practical wisdom does not fare any better. He takes it that people have practical wisdom if and only if those people are virtuous. And he takes it that akratic people are not virtuous. But consider the wise sage who is forced into heroin addiction. This sage's practical wisdom is not destroyed by this addiction. But since addiction is a form of akrasia, Aristotle is committed to the view that this sage's addiction *does* destroy his virtue, and therefore his practical wisdom as well. Thus we should reject Aristotle's account of practical wisdom. (Of course, we could re-translate Aristotle's terms "sophia" and "phronesis" instead of rejecting his theory. But I'll leave that aside.)

In addition to rejecting Aristotle's accounts of theoretical and practical wisdom, we should also reject Zagzebski's account of practical wisdom. She thinks that all practically wise people make good choices most of the time. But the cases we discussed above concerning depression, evil, and addiction show that the choices of practically wise people needn't be mostly good ones.

What about Zagzebski's account of theoretical wisdom? About this account I have just two things to say. First, it would be nice to further develop her remarks about grasping the structure of reality—those remarks seem to be on to something. Second and more critically, it is wrong to think that this account of theoretical wisdom is of particular help to virtue-theoretic approaches to epistemology. For, when we try to further develop Zagzebski's account of theoretical wisdom, we end up with a theory that does just as well at serving the purposes of those of us who take epistemic value to have a consequentialist structure. Or so I'll now argue.

Twofold Consequentialism

Virtue-theoretic accounts of wisdom entail that all practically wise people reliably act wisely. For if wisdom is a virtue, then no more could a wise person not reliably act wisely, than could a courageous person not reliably act courageously. In both instances, and with virtues generally, possessing the virtue guarantees reliably acting from it.

But, as I've argued, practically wise people need not reliably act wisely. Therefore, virtue-theoretic accounts of wisdom are mistaken. I'm going to try to replace them with a consequentialist twofold view. This view is consequentialist not in attempting to locate the epistemic value of wisdom in its consequences but, rather, in taking wisdom to be partly *constitutive* of the epistemically good consequences. Various phenomena such as evidence gathering, research program design, library book acquisition policy, and educational curricula can be epistemically evaluated according to the extent to which they produce the epistemically good ends, one of which is wisdom. Wisdom is an epistemic end. Now to the nature of this epistemic end.

Statement of the Theory

There are two kinds of wisdom: practical and theoretical. To be practically wise is to know how to live well. To be theoretically wise is to have deep understanding.

Knowing how to obtain one's ends is not alone sufficient for practical wisdom, because if one can get whatever one wants but does not have any idea what to get in order to live well, then one does not know how to live well. Knowing what ends to obtain in order to live well is not sufficient for practical wisdom either. For even if one knows, of every set of ends the fulfilling of which is sufficient for living well, *that* its fulfilling is sufficient for living well, one may nonetheless not know how to fulfill any of those sets of ends. And, if one does not know how to fulfill any of those sets of ends, then one does not know how to live well. If one knows how to live well, then, one thereby knows both (a) of at least some of the sets of ends the fulfilling of which is sufficient for living well, that the fulfilling of those sets of ends is sufficient for living well, and (b) of at least some of the means sufficient for bringing about those sets of ends, that those means are sufficient for bringing about those sets of ends.

Theoretical wisdom is a form of understanding, and a particular form of it, namely deep understanding. Thus it is to be contrasted with understanding-that and also with unificatory-insight understanding of a shallow variety. It is a kind of explanatory knowledge, because it consists in knowledge of the principles that explain things in a relevant domain.

For instance, to have theoretical wisdom in chemistry is to have a systematic knowledge of the fundamental chemical structures, and of the laws governing their interaction. In virtue of having such knowledge, one is able to explain a wide variety of particular, token chemical phenomena that occur in labs and in the real world. One knows the fundamental chemical principles in virtue of which these token chemical phenomena obtain, and one cognitively subsumes these token phenomena, or at any rate *can* cognitively subsume these phenomena, under the fundamental principles that explain them. It is this fundamental knowledge and ability to subsume particular facts under it that constitutes unificatory insight. The more fundamental one's explanatory knowledge in a domain is, then, the more theoretically wise one is with respect to that domain. (Here, I gloss over complicated literatures on explanation and understanding; see Pitt 1988, Strevens 2008, and Grimm forthcoming.)

That, at first pass at least, is what wisdom is. It is a twofold phenomenon concerning, on the one hand, knowledge of how to live well and, on the other hand, explanatory knowledge of the fundamental truths in a domain. Let us call this theory "twofold consequentialism."

Argument for the Theory

In arguing for twofold consequentialism I'll lay out some adequacy conditions on theories of wisdom, and I'll make a case that twofold consequentialism does the best job of meeting those conditions, among the extant theories. The conditions are as follows:

1. *Advice*: Theories of wisdom should explain why wise people tend to be able to give good advice.

There is within popular culture an image of the wise man as the sage to whom we can go for deep insight about what we should do. The existence of this image suggests that wisdom and the ability to give good advice are importantly related. Furthermore, we generally think of wise people as good people to go to when we are in need of advice. So, the advice condition is a reasonable one.

And it is a condition that twofold consequentialism meets. If wisdom entails or is in some other significant way related to knowing how to live well, then it stands to reason that wise people are able to give good advice. For their knowledge of how to live well can, if combined with the right background information, bring them to know what their advisees should do.

Thus the view that wisdom features knowledge of how to live well explains why wise people are able to give good advice. And twofold consequentialism takes one kind of wisdom, practical wisdom, as identical to knowing how to live well. Therefore, twofold consequentialism explains why wise people—or better, *practically* wise people—can give good advice.

2. *Anti-Wickedness*. Theories of wisdom should explain why wise people tend to not be wicked.

Many theorists suggest that it is impossible for wise people to be wicked (Aristotle, Zagzebski 1996; Ryan 1996; Sternberg 2003: 88). The only argument for this view that I know of is the argument from the claim that wisdom is a virtue. According to that argument, virtues are reliably acted on by whomever possesses them, wisdom is a virtue by which one knows how to live well, and reliably acting so as to live well is incompatible with being wicked; put together, these claims entail that wise people cannot be wicked.

As I argued above, this virtue-theoretic line of thought is not persuasive. The devil is evil but nonetheless wise. He was wise as an angel, and through no loss of knowledge but, rather, through some sort of affective restructuring tried and failed to take over the throne. And mere affective changes accompanied by no loss of knowledge should not remove one's wisdom. So, wisdom and evil are compatible.

Nonetheless, every writer about wisdom that I know of subscribes to some sort of anti-wickedness condition, at least tacitly. Furthermore, it is hard to think of actual characters in the history of literature and film, or even in our own personal lives, who are both wise and wicked. Save sinister characters like Goethe's Mephistopheles and perhaps Machiavelli, I can't think of any such characters. I conclude from these observations that if one is wise, it is unlikely that one is also evil. Theories of wisdom should explain or at least be consistent with the fact that this relationship between wisdom and evil holds.

And twofold consequentialism does as much. For if one knows how to live well, then it stands to reason that one *will* live well, to the extent that one can. Of course, one may be so devilishly evil that one knows how to live well and quite purposely does not do it. But this case seems unlikely, in the same way that it seems unlikely that a person who knows how to walk well would, through strange desires, nonetheless walk badly. Given the view that wisdom somehow features knowledge of how to live well, then, it seems unlikely that a wise person—or better—a *practically* wise person—would be evil.

3. *Anti-Foolishness*. Theories of wisdom should explain why foolishness is in some sense the absence of wisdom.

Theorists talk all the time as if it were true that foolishness is the absence of wisdom (Ryan 1999; Sternberg 2003). Furthermore, foolish action can be characterized as action that is not informed by wisdom. The view that foolishness is the absence of wisdom goes some way towards explaining why this is so. The anti-foolishness condition is, therefore, a reasonable one.

And, twofold consequentialism meets it. This is because knowing how to live well makes it likely that one, in fact, does live well, at least to the extent that one can, given one's circumstances. The view that wisdom, or practical wisdom, is knowledge of how to live well, therefore, explains why it is likely that wise people, in fact, live well. But the fool's life is not a good life. Thus the view that wisdom, or practical wisdom, amounts to knowledge of how to live well would lead us to predict that practically wise people do not live foolishly. And that, in turn, would lead us to predict that practically wise people are not fools; which, itself, helps explain why foolishness is the absence of wisdom.

4. *Difficulty*. Theories of wisdom should explain why wisdom is hard to get.

We don't think of ordinary people as particularly wise. Furthermore, there is empirical evidence suggesting that high degrees of wisdom are, in fact, a rare phenomenon (Kunzmann and Baltes 2005). So the difficulty condition is a reasonable one.

And twofold consequentialism meets it. Deep knowledge is hard to get. Therefore, theoretical wisdom is hard to get. Furthermore, it is hard to know how to live well, or at least, hard to have high levels of knowledge of how to live well. So practical wisdom, at least in high levels, is also hard to get.

5. *Explanation of other theories.* Theories of wisdom should identify what is plausible about the theories with which they disagree.

The folks who have theorized about wisdom are all quite smart and well-informed. It would be strange for such people to be totally off the mark. They ought to get at least *some* things right. A proper theory of wisdom should identify these things.

Twofold consequentialism does as much: it can locate something right within apologetic views, practical views, and twofold views of the virtue-theoretic variety. First of all, it is difficult for one to live well if one is bad at recognizing what one knows and what one does not know. People who are bad at recognizing these things are bad at decision making, which is itself an important aspect of living well. Twofold consequentialism, therefore, predicts that practically wise people should tend to be epistemically humble and accurate in the senses suggested in the *Apology*. Furthermore, twofold consequentialism recognizes a certain kind of wisdom, practical wisdom, that is identical to the thing that according to practical theorists constitutes wisdom *simpliciter*. Practical theories are right in recognizing practical wisdom as a part of wisdom; where they go wrong is in thinking that it is *all* there is to wisdom. So twofold consequentialism identifies something right within practical views as well. Finally, twofold consequentialism explains what is right in virtue-theoretic twofold views. It does so by sharing their recognition of two sorts of wisdom, and by countenancing similar views about both of those sorts of wisdom.

6. *Explanation of particular cases.* Theories of wisdom should explain, for each case in which one is wise or not wise, *why* one is in that case wise or not wise.

It is, at least in part, through explaining the facts about particular cases that theories give us insight and understanding. And giving us insight and understanding are what theories are supposed to do; it is what they are *for*. Thus, in order to do what they are supposed to do, theories should explain particular cases. Theories of wisdom are no exception; they should explain why one is wise, when one is wise, and why one is not wise, when one is not wise.

Now, a theory can explain only what it is consistent with. And every theory other than twofold consequentialism is inconsistent with the facts about wisdom in at least some case or other. As a result, every theory other than twofold consequentialism fails to meet the *explanation of particular cases* condition.

Twofold consequentialism, however, is consistent with the facts about wisdom in particular cases, as far as I can tell. Moreover, twofold consequentialism *explains* the facts about particular cases, as far as I can tell. For instance, it explains the facts about the cases of A and B we discussed above. And it explains why the epistemically accurate person who knows trivialities need not be wise—for this person need not have deep understanding, and need not know how to live well. With these cases and the others we discussed throughout the chapter, twofold consequentialism explains why people are wise when they are wise, and why they are unwise when they are unwise. None of the other theories do as much. As a result of all this, twofold consequentialism meets the *explanation of particular cases* condition, and it is unique in doing as much.

What is more, twofold consequentialism does not do *worse* than any of the other extant theories on any of the *other* conditions I have outlined. Indeed, on some of those other conditions, including the anti-wickedness condition, it does even better than some of those other theories. On balance then, twofold consequentialism seems to be the best theory of wisdom we've got.

Acknowledgments

Thanks to Allan Hazlett, Dan Howard-Snyder, Peter Kivy, Ned Markosian, and Duncan Pritchard for helpful comments on drafts of this paper.

References

Bishop, Michael and J.D. Trout. 2004. *Epistemology and the Psychology of Human Judgment*. Oxford University Press.
DePaul, Michael and Linda Zagzebski (eds). 2003. *Intellectual Virtue*. Oxford University Press.
Garrett, Richard. 1996. "Three Definitions of Wisdom." In Lehrer et al. 1996.
Goldman, Alvin I. 1986. *Epistemology and Cognition*. Harvard University Press.
——. *Knowledge in a Social World*. Oxford University Press.
Grimm, Stephen. Forthcoming. "Understanding." In *The Routledge Companion to Epistemology*, ed. Bernecker and Pritchard.
Haldane, Elizabeth and G.R.T. Ross (eds.). 1931. *The Philosophical Works of Descartes*. Cambridge University Press.
Kitchener, Karen and Helene Brenner. 1990. "Wisdom and Reflective Judgment: Knowing in the Face of Uncertainty." In Sternberg 1990.
Kunzmann, Ute and Paul Baltes. 2005. "The Psychology of Wisdom." In Sternberg and Jordan 2005.
Lehrer, Keith, B. Lum, B.A. Slichta, and N.D. Smith (eds.). 1996. *Knowledge, Teaching, and Wisdom*. Kluwer.
Norman, Andrew. 1996. "Teaching Wisdom." In Lehrer et al. 1996, pp. 253–265.
Nozick, Robert. 1989. *The Examined Life*. Touchstone Press.
Pitt, Joseph (ed.). 1988. *Theories of Explanation*. Oxford University Press.
Riggs, Wayne. 2003. "Understanding 'Virtue' and the Virtue of Understanding." In Depaul and Zagzebski 2003.
Ryan, Sharon. 1996. "Wisdom." In Lehrer et al. 1996.
——. 1999. "What is Wisdom?" *Philosophical Studies* (93): 119–139.
——. 2007. "Wisdom." *Stanford Encyclopedia of Philosophy*.
Stanley, Jason and Timothy Williamson. 2001. "Knowing How." *Journal of Philosophy* 98 (8): 411–444.
Sternberg, Robert (ed.). 1990. *Wisdom: Its Nature, Origins, and Development*. Cambridge University Press.
——. 1998. "A Balance Theory of Wisdom." *Review of General Psychology* 2: 347–365.
——. 2001. "Why Schools Should Teach for Wisdom: The Balance Theory of Wisdom in Educational Settings." *Educational Psychologist* (36/4): 227–245.
——. 2003. *Wisdom, Intelligence, and Creativity Synthesized*. Cambridge University Press.
Sternberg, Robert and Jennifer Jordan (eds.). 2005. *A Handbook of Wisdom: Psychological Perspectives*. Cambridge University Press.
Strevens, Michael. 2008. *Depth*. Harvard University Press.
Zagzebski, Linda. 1996. *Virtues of the Mind*. Cambridge University Press.

Part II
THE ANALYSIS OF KNOWLEDGE

11
THE BASING RELATION
Ram Neta

Sometimes, when you believe something, there are *reasons for which* you believe it, or equivalently, *reasons on the basis of which* you believe it. For instance, I believe that I should not buy oil futures, and the reason for which I believe it is that the recessionary downward pressures on global demand for oil are not going to be mitigated any time soon. I believe that Pluto is not a planet, and the reason for which I believe it is that I was so informed by widely respected science journalists (I can't recall whether in print or on radio, or both). I believe that Tom Stoppard is still alive, and the reason for which I believe it is that I have heard nothing of his death, which I surely would have had he died.

When epistemologists today use the phrase "the basing relation," they mean to denote a relation that obtains between a creature's *belief*, on the one hand, and the *reasons for which* she holds that belief, on the other hand. Now, what I have just offered might fail to be a unique designation of the basing relation, since there might be lots of relations that obtain between a creature's belief and the reasons for which she holds that belief. Which of these relations is the particular relation denoted by the phrase "the basing relation"? It is that relation *the obtaining of which* makes it the case that the reasons that stand on one side of the relation are *the reasons for which* the creature holds the belief that stands on the other side of the relation. In other words, the basing relation is that relation which is such that, when it obtains between a belief B and a reason R for which the belief is held, its obtaining is what makes it the case that R is the reason (or at least *a* reason) for which B is held. Epistemological theorizing about the basing relation is supposed to explain precisely what that particular relation *is*.

In theorizing about the basing relation, it is important to distinguish between something's being a *reason for which* a creature believes something, and its being a *reason why* a creature believes something. It is plausible that every instance of the former is an instance of the latter, but *not* vice-versa. The reason why I believe the suspect to be guilty is that he reminds me of someone I intensely dislike. But this is not, we may suppose, a reason for which I believe the suspect to be guilty (unless, of course, I happen to have reason to think that people who remind me of people that I intensely dislike are especially likely to be guilty of this particular crime).

Again, in theorizing about the basing relation, it is important to distinguish between something's being a reason for which a creature believes something, and its being a reason for the creature to believe something. It is plausible that there are instances of the former that are instances of the latter, and also vice-versa: sometimes, the reasons for which you believe something are also reasons for you to believe it, and sometimes, the reasons for you to believe something are also reasons for which you believe it. But it is equally plausible that there are instances of the former that are *not* instances of the latter, and also vice-versa. The reason for which I believe the suspect to be guilty is that his fingerprints were all over the murder weapon. But this is not a reason for me to believe that the suspect is guilty, because the murder weapon was a metal doorknob that had just been removed from the front door of the suspect's residence—a doorknob that the suspect would certainly have touched on many occasions whether or not he committed the crime. A reason for me to believe that the suspect is guilty is that his DNA was all over the victim. But this is not a reason for which I believe the suspect to be guilty, since (let us suppose) I have an irrational disregard for DNA evidence.

To sum up the points just made: a reason for which someone believes something is always a reason why she believes it, but not all reasons why someone believes something are reasons for which she believes it. A reason for which someone believes something is sometimes, but not always, a reason for her to believe it. And a reason for someone to believe something is sometimes, but not always, a reason for which she believes it. Together, these points place substantial constraints on any adequate theory of the basing relation: a creature's belief B can stand in the basing relation to a reason R *only if* R is the reason why the creature holds B, and *only if* R is the right sort of thing to be a reason for a creature to hold B. We might put this same point by saying that B is based on R only if R does both of the following two things: (i) R rationally supports holding B and, (ii) R explains why B is held.

In theorizing about the basing relation, we want to get clear on what sorts of things can stand in that relation to each other. The basing relation is, we have said, a relation between a creature's belief, on the one hand, and the reasons for which the creature holds the belief, on the other. To understand the basing relation fully, we must understand each of these relata. What are beliefs? And what are reasons for which beliefs are held? While each of these two questions has generated many different responses, the controversy surrounding the second question has been particularly active in recent years. In particular, epistemologists have recently been concerned to say whether the reasons for which creatures hold beliefs are mental events or states (see Swain 1979; Pappas 1979; Davidson 1983; Pollock 1986; Bergmann 2007; Pryor 2007; Turri 2009), or whether they are instead (typically extra-mental) facts (see Unger 1975; McDowell 1994; Collins 1997; Hyman 1999; and Dancy 2000). Ordinary language might seem to suggest the latter answer: I specify the reason for which I believe that I should not buy oil futures by specifying an extra-mental fact, namely, that the recessionary downward pressures on global demand for oil are not going to be mitigated any time soon. But, by itself, this ordinary language argument for the view that reasons are facts carries little weight. From the fact that I specify an extra-mental fact in stating the reason for which I believe that I should not buy oil futures, it doesn't follow that I mean to offer that fact itself as identical to the reason for which I hold this belief. And second, even if I do mean to offer the fact itself as the reason for which I hold my belief, it doesn't follow that I would be correct in so doing.

A full account of the basing relation would have to say something about the nature of its relata. But in what follows, I will avoid this topic to the extent that I can; I will discuss the theoretical options concerning the nature of the basing relation itself, pausing only briefly to consider the interaction between our account of the basing relation, and our account of its relata.

I will organize the discussion that follows around four questions that are central to contemporary theorizing about the basing relation. Answering any one of these questions in the affirmative does not, by itself, commit one to answering any other in the affirmative (or the negative), nor does answering any one of them in the negative commit one to answering any other in the negative (or the affirmative).

I. Is the Basing Relation an Inferential Relation?

If you infer a conclusion q from a premise set P, then the basing relation obtains between your belief that q, and a reason for which you hold that belief. If someone were to ask you for what reason do you believe that q, you could truthfully reply by mentioning P. (Of course, from the fact that you could truthfully answer this question by mentioning P, it doesn't follow that the premise set P is *itself* the reason, or even a reason, on which your belief that q is based. For all I've said, the reason on which your belief that q is based is *your belief* that all the elements of P are true. And for all I've said, the reason on which your belief that q is based is *the fact* described by the premise set P. As I said, I intend to avoid here the issue of the ontology of the reasons that stand on one side of the basing relation.) So inferring q from P is sufficient for there to be a basing relation between your belief that q, on the one hand, and your reason for holding that belief (a reason that you can specify by appeal to P), on the other hand.

But is inferring q from P a *necessary* condition for there to be such a basing relation? Most theorists of the basing relation would answer this question in the negative. But there are important exceptions. For instance, in discussing the epistemology of perceptual belief, Burge writes: "The normative transition from perception to belief is not a piece of reasoning. If perceptual representations were reasons for perceptual belief, such transitions should count as reasoning. But they do not" (Burge 2003: 528). Now, why does Burge think that "if perceptual representations were reasons for perceptual belief, such transitions [from perception to belief] should count as reasoning"? He does not say why he thinks this, but the only reason I can think of is that Burge is supposing that, for a belief to be based on a reason *just is* for the belief to be formed by inference from the reason. If that is indeed Burge's view (and it is hard for me to see what else could account for his reasoning in the passage I've quoted above), then Burge, unlike most philosophers, thinks that inference is not merely sufficient for basing, but it is necessary as well.

II. Is the Basing Relation a Causal Relation?

If R is a *reason for which* you hold belief B, then it follows that R is a *reason why* you hold belief B. But must R also be a *cause* of your holding belief B? In other words, if the basing relation holds between R and B, must there also be a causal relation between R and B? Is the basing relation itself a causal relation?

Most contemporary theorists of the basing relation would answer both of the last two questions in the affirmative (see, e.g., Harman 1970; Goldman 1979; Swain 1979; Alston 1988; Moser 1989; Huemer 2001). They think that the basing relation is itself a causal relation; a fortiori, if the basing relation holds between R and B, then a causal relation holds between R and B.

Although this "causal view" (as I shall henceforth call it) of the basing relation is widely accepted today, it is seldom argued for. Perhaps this is because of the enormous influence exercised by the argument given in Davidson (1963). In that article, Davidson argues as follows. It is possible for someone to have a reason R for performing action A, and to perform A for the reason R. But it is also possible for someone to have reason R for performing A, and to perform A *without* doing so for the reason that R. In both cases, the agent has R, and the agent performs A. The difference between the two cases is that, in one, the agent A's for the reason R, and in the other, she doesn't. But what could this distinction amount to? Davidson finds no answer to this question other than to say that, in the first case, R *causes* the agent to perform A. Thus, Davidson concludes, the reason for which someone acted is a cause of her action. Just as many contemporary philosophers accept Davidson's argument for this causal view about the relation between an action and the reason for which it is performed, it seems likely that many contemporary philosophers are inclined to accept an analogous argument in favor of a causal view of the epistemic basing relation. And perhaps it is the widespread contemporary appeal of this Davidsonian argument that accounts for the currently widespread popularity of a causal view of the basing relation.

But we should note that Davidson's argument founders on the problem of the so-called "deviant causal chain," a problem that Davidson himself noted. The problem, so far as it concerns reasons for action, is this: it is possible for an agent to have a reason R for performing action A, and to perform A, and for R to cause their performance of A, without R being a reason for which the agent performed A. For example:

> A climber might want to rid himself of the weight and danger of holding another man on a rope, and he might know that by loosening his hold on the rope he could rid himself of the weight and danger. The belief and want might so unnerve him as to cause him to loosen his hold, and yet it might be the case that he never chose to loosen his hold, nor did he do it intentionally.
>
> (Davidson 1973)

According to Davidson's discussion of the case, the climber has a reason to loosen his hold on the rope, and the reason causes him to loosen his hold on the rope, but it is nonetheless not the reason for which the climber loosens his hold on the rope. So it follows that, even when an agent has a reason R for performing action A, and R causes the agent to perform A, this is not sufficient for R to be a reason for which the agent performed A. But now notice that if this is true, then causation does not, after all, fully account for the difference between the two sorts of cases described above (one in which the agent performs A for the reason R, and the other in which the agent performs A, and has R, but does not perform A for the reason R). And if causation does not fully account for the difference between the two sorts of cases, then why should we believe that whatever it is that does fully account for the difference between the two sorts of cases will so much as involve causation? Just as this worry—popularly known as the problem of ruling out the "deviant causal chain"—confronts Davidson's argument for a causal view of reasons for action, so too an analogous worry confronts the analogous argument for a causal view of the basing relation.

Now, none of this suggests that the causal view of the basing relation is *false*. As Huemer (2001) points out, most ordinary causal relations (e.g., breaking) are such that we do not know how to provide non-circular necessary and sufficient conditions for the obtaining of these relations, but of course it does not follow that these ordinary relations are not causal. So the considerations offered above do not show that the causal view of the basing relation is false. All that they show is that, unless it is supplemented with a solution to the problem of the deviant causal chain, the Davidson-style argument for the causal view of the basing relation is not a compelling argument. So the causal view of the basing relation may, for all we've said, be true, even if the Davidson-style argument for it mooted above does not show as much.

Some philosophers have attempted to supplement the Davidson-style argument for the causal view with a solution to the problem of the deviant causal chain. For instance, Schlosser (2007), in defending a causal view of reasons for action, attempts to solve the problem of the deviant causal chain by claiming that, when an agent performs A for the reason that R, the causal chain from R to A holds *in virtue of* R's content. But it is not obvious just how this solves the problem: do not the climber's beliefs and desires cause his nervousness, and hence his loosening of the rope, in virtue of their content? Wedgwood (2007), in defending a causal view of the basing relation that obtains in inference, attempts to solve the problem of the deviant causal chain by claiming that, when an agent infers a conclusion from a premise, the agent's belief in the premise causes the agent to believe the conclusion by virtue of the *epistemic support* that the premise gives the conclusion. But this cannot explain what sort of causal connection obtains between an agent's belief in the premise and in the conclusion of a *bad* inference (namely, one in which the premise does not actually lend support to the conclusion, but the agent infers the conclusion from the premise nonetheless). It is not yet clear, therefore, whether any solution to the problem of the deviant causal chain can be found. But, as mentioned above, this does not refute the causal view of the basing relation; it merely undermines one argument for that view.

Some philosophers (e.g., Jacobsen 1993; Korcz 2000; Lehrer 1971 and 2000; Kvanvig 2003) have argued that the causal view of the basing relation is false. For instance, Kvanvig (2003) argues against a causal view of reasons for action, and then claims that we should expect a causal view of the basing relation to be false as well, on the grounds that we should expect there to be a unified theory of the relation that obtains between an action and the reasons for which it is done, and of the relation that obtains between a belief and the reasons for which it is held. And Lehrer (1971) argues against the causal view of the basing relation (specifically, as developed by Harman (1970), who takes basing to involve a causal-explanatory relation between one's belief and the reasons for which it is held) by means of a now famous putative counterexample to that view, a counterexample generally known as the "Gypsy Lawyer" case, which goes as follows:

> The example involves a lawyer who is defending a man accused of committing eight hideous murders. The murders are similar in character, in each case the victim is an Oxford philosophy student who has been choked to death with a copy of *Philosophical Investigations*. There is conclusive evidence that the lawyer's client is guilty of the first seven murders. Everyone, including the lawyer, is convinced that the man in question has committed all eight crimes, though the man himself says he is innocent of all.
>
> However, the lawyer is a gypsy with absolute faith in the cards. One evening he consults the cards about his case, and the cards tell him that his client is innocent of the eighth murder. He checks again, and the cards give the same answer. He becomes convinced that his client is innocent of one of the eight murders. As a result he studies the evidence with a different perspective as well as greater care, and he finds a very complicated though completely valid line of reasoning from the evidence to the conclusion that his client did not commit

the eighth murder. (He could not have obtained an eighth copy of *Philosophical Investigations*.) This reasoning gives the lawyer knowledge....

However, the emotional factors are so powerful and the reasoning so complicated that no one else is convinced. They all have an overwhelming desire to believe that the murderer of all eight victims has been found. Indeed, and this is the crucial point, if it were not for his unshakable faith in the cards, the lawyer himself would be swayed by those emotional factors and would doubt that his client was innocent of the eighth murder. It is only because of his faith in the cards that the reasoning gives him knowledge.

(Lehrer 1971: 311–12)

What causes the lawyer to believe in his client's innocence, according to Lehrer, is his faith in the cards, and not the complicated line of reasoning that the lawyer discovers upon reviewing the evidence. But the lawyer's belief in his client's innocence is based on the complicated line of reasoning, since it is that reasoning that gives the lawyer knowledge of his client's innocence. Thus, Lehrer concludes, basing need not involve causation.

Lehrer's example of the Gypsy Lawyer is intended to serve as a counterexample to the causal view of the basing relation. But it is controversial whether it is in fact a counterexample. Many philosophers (e.g., Goldman 1979; Audi 1983; Pollock 1986) do not share Lehrer's intuitive judgment that the Gypsy Lawyer's belief in his client's innocence is based on the complicated line of reasoning that the lawyer discovers upon examining the evidence, and so do not regard the case of the Gypsy Lawyer as a case of basing without causation.

III. Is the Basing Relation a Relation of Counterfactual Dependence?

Though many philosophers have denied Lehrer's claim that the Gypsy Lawyer case is a case of basing without causation, Marshall Swain has accepted Lehrer's judgment that the Gypsy Lawyer case involves basing without causation. Consequently, Swain attempts to rescue what he takes to be the good idea lurking in the causal view of the basing relation by developing a theory of the basing relation according to which it is a kind of counterfactual dependence (where the counterfactual dependence in question can be, and typically is, realized by causation, but it can also be realized in some noncausal way). According to Swain (1979), S's belief that h is based upon the set of causal reasons R at a time $t =_{df}$

1. S believes that h at t; and
2. for every member r_j of R, there is some time t_n (which may be identical with or earlier than t) such that

    S has (or had) r_j at t_n; and either
    - (b, i) there is a causal chain from S's being in reason state r_j at t_n to S's believing that h at t, or
    - (b, ii) S's being in reason state r_j at t_n is a genuine overdeterminant of S's believing that h at t, or
    - (b, iii) S's being in reason state r_j at t_n is a pseudo-overdeterminant of S's believing that h at t.

Each of clauses (b, i), (b, ii), and (b, iii) requires clarification. What is it for there to be a "causal chain" from one thing to another thing, or for one thing to be a "genuine overdeterminant" of another thing, or for one thing to be "a pseudo-overdeterminant" of another thing? Here's what Swain tells us:

(Causal chain) Where $c, d_1, d_2, \ldots, d_n, e$ is a sequence of distinct occurrent events (but not necessarily a temporal sequence, and where c and e may be the only members), this sequence is a causal chain if and only if:

(a) if c had not occurred, d_1 would not have occurred
(b) for each n, if d_{n-1} had not occurred, then d_n would not have occurred, and
(c) if d_n had not occurred, then e would not have occurred.

(Genuine overdeterminant) Where c and e are occurrent events, c is a genuine overdeterminant of e if and only if: There is some set of occurrent events $D = [d_1, d_2, \ldots, d_n]$ (possibly having only one member) such that:

(a') if c had not occurred and if any member d_i of D had occurred, but no other members of D had occurred, and if e had occurred anyway, then there would have been a causal chain of distinct actually occurrent events from d_i to e; and
(b') if no member of D had occurred, and if c and e had occurred anyway, then there would have been a causal chain of distinct actually occurrent events from c to e.

(Pseudo-overdeterminant) Where c and e are occurrent events, c is a pseudo-overdeterminant of e if and only if:

(a") there is no causal chain from c to e; and
(b") there is some set of occurrent events $D = [d_1, d_2, \ldots, d_n]$ (possibly having only one member) such that there is a causal chain from each d_i in D to e, and if no member of D had occurred, but c and e had occurred anyway, then there would have been a causal chain from c to e.

To summarize Swain's view: for S's belief that h is based upon the set of causal reasons R at a time t is for S's belief to be counterfactually dependent upon R in any of the three ways detailed above: very roughly, for the belief to be caused by R, or for R to be one of its causal overdeterminants, or for it to be such that it would have been caused by R had the actual causal chain not obtained. Notice how this account of basing addresses Lehrer's example of the Gypsy Lawyer. Although the Gypsy Lawyer's belief in his client's innocence is not caused by his discovery of the complicated line of reasoning made available by the evidence, his discovery of that line of reasoning nonetheless pseudo-overdetermines his belief: if the lawyer had not read the cards, but had nonetheless discovered the complicated line of reasoning and had also believed in his client's innocence, then there would have been a causal chain from the lawyer's discovery of the complicated line of reasoning to the lawyer's belief in his client's innocence. So, on Swain's view, the Gypsy Lawyer case is one in which the lawyer's belief in his client's innocence is based on the complicated line of reasoning that the lawyer discovers, even if it is not caused by the lawyer's discovery of that line of reasoning.

Swain's theory of the basing relation has excited considerable controversy (see, e.g., Kvanvig 1985, 1987; Lemke 1986; Korcz 1997; and Lehrer 2000: 196–7). One worry about Swain's theory of the basing relation should already be familiar from our discussion of the causal view of basing: the existence of a causal chain from reason to belief does not suffice for the belief to be based on the reason, and that is because the causal chain may be deviant. But Tolliver (1982) raises a different sort of worry about Swain's theory—a worry about whether satisfying the pseudo-overdetermination condition suffices for basing. I will quote the clear summary description of the case in Korcz (2006):

> Suppose a physics student has learned that from the period of a pendulum . . . one can calculate its length and vice versa. The student measures a particular pendulum and discovers that it has length L, and calculates that it must have period P. The student also has two general beliefs about pendulums, namely (1) that if x is a pendulum of period P, then x is a pendulum of length L, and (2) that if x is a pendulum of length L, then x is a pendulum of period P. We may suppose that it is clear in this case that the student's belief about the period is based (at least in part) on her belief about its length, but her belief about its length is not based on her belief about the period. But . . . the student's belief about the period pseudo-overdetermines her belief about the length of the pendulum, and hence gets counted, on Swain's theory, as the basis of her belief about the length of the pendulum. This is so because . . . if the actual cause of the student's belief about the length had not occurred, and if the student still had both her belief about the period and her belief about the length, then her belief about the period would have caused her belief about the length.
>
> (Korcz 2006: section 2)

Tolliver's example shows that pseudo-overdetermination, as defined by Swain, does not suffice for basing. It is an open question whether Swain could refine his definition of pseudo-overdetermination to accommodate examples of this kind.

IV. Is the Basing Relation a Relation That Obtains Only if the Agent Has Appropriate Beliefs About the Relation Between the Relata?

Tolliver is one of several philosophers (also see Longino 1978; Tolliver 1982; Audi 1986) who take the basing relation to require the believer to have certain sorts of beliefs about the epistemic relations between her belief and the reasons upon which it is based. I will say that these philosophers hold a "doxastic view" of the basing relation. For instance, on Tolliver's account,

> S bases her belief that b on reason r at time t if and only if:
>
> (i) S believes that b at t and S believes that r at t,
> (ii) S believes that the truth of r is evidence for the truth of b, and
> (iii) where S's estimate of the likelihood of b equals h (0 < h < 1) at t, if S were to come to believe that r for the first time at t, then S's estimate of the likelihood of the proposition "the likelihood of b is greater than or equal to h" would be greater at t then it was prior to t.

This particular account of basing is subject to a number of objections. For example, suppose that Jones has always believed that a particular analgesic is effective because it has always seemed to him to work whenever he took it. One day, he reads a scientific study that has shown both that this analgesic is effective, and that consumers of analgesics are typically terrible judges of the effectiveness of the analgesics that they have taken. Jones continues to believe that the analgesic is effective, but now his belief is based not on its always having seemed to him to work whenever he took it (having read the scientific study, he now discounts his own introspective evidence concerning the effectiveness of the analgesic). Rather, his belief is based on the scientific study that purports to show that the analgesic is effective. But suppose that, before reading the scientific study, his estimate of the likelihood of the analgesic's effectiveness was .95, whereas now, after reading the scientific study, his estimate of its likelihood is .85, and so naturally his estimate of the likelihood of the proposition "the likelihood of the analgesic's being effective is greater than or equal to .85" is now lower than it was prior to his reading the scientific study. Thus, after he reads the scientific study, Jones's belief that the analgesic is effective does not satisfy clause (iii) of Tolliver's account of basing. Nonetheless, his belief in the analgesic's effectiveness is based on the scientific study. This suffices to show that clause (iii) is too strong a requirement on basing.

We might think that a proponent of the doxastic view of basing might avoid these problems confronting Tolliver's account by simply weakening, or perhaps simply dropping, clause (iii) of the account. Unfortunately, clause (ii) itself has been subject to some prominent objections. Consider, for instance, the following objections that Alston (1988) poses to the doxastic view of basing defended in Audi (1986):

> My belief that you are upset may be based on various aspects of the way you look and act without my consciously believing that these features provide adequate support for that belief; in a typical case of this sort I have no such belief simply because I am not consciously aware of which features these are; I do not consciously discriminate them. And even where I am more explicitly aware of the ground, I may not consciously believe anything at all about support relations. It is very dubious that very small children, for example, ever have such support beliefs; and yet surely a small child's belief that the kitten is sick can be based on her belief that the kitten is not running around as usual.
>
> (Alston 1988)

Proponents of the doxastic view of basing might reply to these objections by claiming that the relevant meta-belief might somehow refer (de re) to an epistemic support relation without itself employing any epistemic concepts. Alternatively, they might say that the relevant meta-belief is one that the subject *would* hold under appropriate conditions, whether or not she actually does hold it. (Lehrer (1965) develops a version of this latter view, according to which the reason for which one believes that p is the reason that one would give if asked to justify one's belief that p.) But it remains to be seen whether such a proposal can be fleshed out.

Worries about the doxastic view of basing, and worries about the causal view, inspired Korcz (2000) to develop a view that effectively disjoins the two views: on Korcz's theory, a creature's belief can be based on a reason r *either* by being appropriately caused by r, *or* by virtue of the creature's having the appropriate sorts of meta-beliefs. (Much of the detail in Korcz's account goes into specifying what counts as an appropriate cause, or an appropriate sort of meta-belief.) We cannot do justice to Korcz's theory in the small space of this survey, but the theory itself is the most fully developed account of the basing relation published in the decade preceding this survey. Contemporary work on the basing relation must therefore grapple with it.

References

Alston, William. 1988. "An Internalist Externalism." *Synthese* 74: 265–83.
Audi, Robert. 1983. "The Causal Structure of Indirect Justification." *Journal of Philosophy* 80(7): 398–415.
——. 1986. "Belief, Reason and Inference." *Philosophical Topics* 14: 27–65.
Bergmann, Michael. 2007. "Is Klein an Infinitist about Doxastic Justification?" *Philosophical Studies* 134: 19–24.
Burge, Tyler. 2003. "Perceptual Entitlement." *Philosophy and Phenomenological Research* 67: 503–48.
Collins, Arthur. 1997. "The Psychological Reality of Reasons." *Ratio* 10: 108–23.
Dancy, Jonathan. 2000. *Practical Reality*. Oxford University Press: Oxford.
Davidson, Donald. 1963. "Actions, Reasons, and Causes." *Journal of Philosophy* 60: 685–700.
——. 1973. "Freedom to Act" in Honderich 1973.
——. 1983. "A Coherence Theory of Truth and Knowledge" in LePore 1983.
Goldman, Alvin. 1979. "What is Justified Belief?" in Pappas 1979b.
Harman, Gilbert. 1970. "Knowledge, Reasons, and Causes." *Journal of Philosophy* 67: 841–55.
Honderich, Ted, ed. 1973. *Essays on Freedom of Action*. Routledge and Kegan Paul: London.
Huemer, Michael. 2001. *Skepticism and the Veil of Perception*. Rowman and Littlefield: Lanham, MD.
Hyman, John. 1999. "How Knowledge Works." *Philosophical Quarterly* 49: 433–51.
Jacobson, Anne. 1993. "A Problem for Causal Theories of Reasons and Rationalizations." *Southern Journal of Philosophy* 31: 307–21.
Korcz, Keith. 1997. "Recent Work on the Basing Relation." *American Philosophical Quarterly* 34: 171–91.
——. 2000. "The Causal-Doxastic Theory of the Basing Relation." *Canadian Journal of Philosophy* 30: 525–50.
——. 2006. "The Epistemic Basing Relation" in the *Stanford Encyclopedia of Philosophy*, http://www.science.uva.nl/~seop/entries/basing-epistemic/
Kvanvig, Jonathan. 1985. "Swain on the Basing Relation." *Analysis* 45: 153–8.
——. 1987. "On Lemke's Defence of a Causal Basing Requirement." *Analysis* 47: 162–7.
——. 2003. "Justification and Proper Basing" in Olsson 2003.
Lehrer, Keith. 1965. "Knowledge, Truth and Evidence." *Analysis* 107: 168–75.
——. 1971. "How Reasons Give us Knowledge, or the Case of the Gypsy Lawyer." *Journal of Philosophy* 68: 311–13.
——. 2000. *Theory of Knowledge*. Westview Press: Boulder, CO.
Lemke, Lory. 1986. "Kvanvig and Swain on the Basing Relation." *Analysis* 46: 138–44.
LePore, Ernest, ed. 1983. *Truth and Interpretation: Perspectives on the Philosophy of Donald Davidson*. Basil Blackwell: Oxford.
Longino, Helen. 1978. "Inferring." *Philosophy Research Archives* 4: 19–26.
McDowell, John. 1994. *Mind and World*. Harvard University Press: Cambridge, MA.
Moser, Paul. 1989. *Knowledge and Evidence*. Cambridge University Press: Cambridge.
Olsson, Erik. 2003. *The Epistemology of Keith Lehrer*. Kluwer Publishing Company: Dordrecht.
Pappas, George. 1979a. "Basing Relations" in Pappas 1979b.
——. 1979b. *Justification and Knowledge*. D. Reidel: Dordrecht.
Pollock, John. 1986. *Contemporary Theories of Knowledge*. Rowman and Littlefield: Savage, MD.
Pryor, James. 2007. "Reasons and That-Clauses." *Proceedings of the Aristotelian Society* 106(3): 327–44.
Schlosser, Markus. 2007. "Basic Deviance Reconsidered." *Analysis* 67: 186–94.
Swain, Marshall. 1979. "Justification and the Basis of Belief" in Pappas 1979b.
Tolliver, Joseph. 1982. "Basing Beliefs on Reasons." *Grazer Philosophische Studien* 15: 149–61.
Turri, John. 2009. "The Ontology of Epistemic Reasons." *Noûs* 43(3): 490–512.
Unger, Peter. 1975. *Ignorance*. Oxford University Press: Oxford.
Wedgwood, Ralph. 2007. "The Normative Force of Reasoning." *Noûs* 40: 660–86.

12
THE GETTIER PROBLEM
Stephen Hetherington

1. Introduction

In 1963, Edmund Gettier published an article containing two brief fictional stories, each intended to disprove a well-entrenched philosophical definition of knowledge. His article had a striking impact among epistemologists: a subsequent plethora of articles and sections of books gave us the broader concept of *a Gettier case*. Philosophers became adept at describing such cases, deepening Gettier's challenge. As there has been no general agreement on how to solve that challenge, epistemologists talk of *the Gettier problem*. Can we understand knowledge's nature rigorously, in a "Gettier-proof" way?

2. The Justified-True-Belief Analysis of Knowledge

At stake is our understanding of *propositional* knowledge. This is knowledge of truths or facts—described by phrases of the form "knowledge that *p*," with "*p*" replaced by an indicative sentence (such as "Kangaroos have no wings"). Usually, when epistemologists talk of knowledge they refer to propositional knowledge. And, prior to Gettier's challenge, philosophers accepted or presumed some version of this three-part analysis of such knowledge:

> The person has a more or less confident *belief*. The belief is *true*. It is well *justified* (for example, by being based upon good evidence, such as from observation, testimony, or reasoning).

This is generally called the *justified-true-belief* analysis of knowledge (for short: JTB). It requires each of those three conditions to be satisfied; and once all of them *are* satisfied together, the result is knowledge.

JTB aims to delineate a *form* of theory able to absorb comparatively specific analyses, either of all knowledge or of particular kinds of knowledge. Even analyses seemingly different to JTB could be instances of it. Most commonly, these incorporate further analyses, of some or all of belief, truth, and justification. (Thus, some sections below discuss justification.) The goal is to understand every possible instance of knowledge. Gettier's challenge spurred epistemologists to seek increasingly detailed accounts of knowledge. Chisholm (1966/1977/1989) was an influential exemplar of the post-1963 tendency; Ayer (1956: ch. 1) exemplified the pre-1963 approach.

3. Three Gettier Cases

This section presents three representative Gettier cases, including Gettier's own two.

(i) *The job/coins* (Gettier 1963). Smith and Jones have applied for a particular job. But Smith has been told by the company president that Jones will be hired. Smith combines that testimony with his observational evidence of there being ten coins in Jones's pocket. (He had counted them—an odd but imaginable circumstance.) He infers the belief that whoever will get the job has ten coins in their pocket. For convenience, call that belief *b*. It enjoys a reasonable amount of evidential support—from some testimony, observation, and reasoning. Belief *b* is also true—yet not in the way Smith was expecting it to be true. For *he* will get the job, and *he* has ten coins in his pocket. (Neither of those circumstances was known by Smith.) Does he thereby *fail* to know that the person who will get the job has ten coins in his pocket? Surely so (thought Gettier): belief *b* is true and justified—but not knowledge. Hence, JTB is false: this case establishes that being true and justified is not *sufficient* for being knowledge.

But if JTB is false, with what should it be replaced? (Gettier himself made no suggestions.) Epistemologists generally accept JTB's three conditions as being individually *necessary* to knowing, even if not jointly sufficient. What is overlooked by JTB? Which feature of the job/coins case prevents belief *b* from being knowledge? What smallest imaginable alteration to the case would allow belief *b* to become knowledge?

Those questions also arise for other Gettier cases, such as the following two. Epistemologists try to understand the lack of knowledge common to *all* possible such cases. (Sections 7 through 11 will present some attempts at this understanding.)

(ii) *The lucky disjunction* (Gettier 1963). Smith possesses good evidence that Jones owns a Ford. Smith also has a friend, Brown. Where *is* Brown? Smith does not know. Still, on the basis of accepting that Jones owns a Ford, Smith infers—and accepts—these three propositions:

> Either Jones owns a Ford, or Brown is in Boston.
> Either Jones owns a Ford, or Brown is in Barcelona.
> Either Jones owns a Ford, or Brown is in Brest-Litovsk.

No insight into Jones's location guides Smith's reasoning. Realizing that he has good evidence for the first disjunct (regarding Jones) in each of those three disjunctions, he treats this evidence as supporting each disjunction as a whole. Seemingly, he is right about that. (These are inclusive disjunctions, not exclusive: each can accommodate the truth of *both* its disjuncts.) Moreover, one of these disjunctions is true. The second is true because, as good luck would have it, Brown *is* in Barcelona—even though, as bad luck would have it, Jones does not own a Ford. (The evidence for his doing so, although good, was misleading.) Accordingly, Smith's belief that either Jones owns a Ford or Brown is in Barcelona is true. And good evidence supports it. But is it knowledge?

(iii) *The fake barns* (Goldman 1976). Henry is driving in the countryside, looking at objects in fields. He sees what looks like a barn. So, he believes—correctly—that he is seeing a barn. Yet he does not realize that the neighborhood contains many fake barns—mere barn façades, looking like real barns when viewed from the road. If Henry had been looking at one of these, he would have been deceived into believing that he was seeing a barn. He was not doing this. Consequently, his belief is justified and true. But is it knowledge?

In none of those cases (or in any relevantly similar ones), say almost all epistemologists, is the belief knowledge. (Note that some epistemologists do not regard the fake-barns case as a genuine Gettier case. There is some vagueness in the concept of a Gettier case. Section 13 will clarify this case.)

4. Two Categories of Gettier Case

Each Gettier case is either *helpful* or *dangerous* (Hetherington 1999; 2001: ch. 3). Helpful cases include Gettier's own two. The fake-barns case is a dangerous one.

In any helpful Gettier case, the justified true belief is attained partly *because* of the case's odd circumstance. The oddity helps to bring about the pleasing combination of truth, belief, and justification. Without quite that oddness, maybe that justified true belief would not have emerged. The person would not be even *that* close (however close it is) to having knowledge by having this combination.

Each dangerous Gettier case likewise includes an odd circumstance. This one, however, remains only a *threat* to the existence of the justified true belief (which combination comes about without the odd circumstance's help). If that circumstance was not present, the belief would be justified and true in the way it is—but with all else being normal. As it is, the belief is only *close* to not being both true and justified in the way it is.

5. Two Basic Features of Gettier Cases

Some characteristics unite Gettier cases. Each contains a belief that is true and well justified without (according to most epistemologists) being knowledge. The following two features also help to constitute Gettier cases:

(1) *Fallibility*. The justificatory support is *fallible*. It indicates strongly—without proving conclusively—that the belief is true.
(2) *Luck*. Within each case, the well-but-fallibly justified belief is true.

Nevertheless, there is significant *luck* in how the belief combines being true with being justified.

In Gettier's job/coins case, Smith's evidence supports belief *b* well but fallibly. It cannot entirely eliminate the possibility of *b*'s being mistaken. Actually, *b* is true—but due to good luck, not in a normal way. It is made true by circumstances—*Smith* getting the job; there being ten coins in *his* pocket—overlooked by his evidence.

6. The Generality of Gettier Cases

Because JTB aims to be true of *any* possible case of knowledge, it is false if there is even one possible Gettier situation empty of knowledge. Yet Gettier situations are rare: few actual beliefs are "Gettiered." Did Gettier therefore show only that *not all* justified true beliefs are knowledge? Might JTB be *almost* correct—accurate about almost all possible instances of knowledge? But epistemologists generally regard Gettier cases as showing that being justified and true is *never* enough to make a belief knowledge. Why?

It is because epistemologists wish to understand knowledge in *all* its possible manifestations. JTB can be regarded as attempting to know knowledge's inviolable *essence*—so that if JTB misdescribes even one instance's inner nature it misdescribes every instance's inner nature. What, exactly and deeply, distinguishes knowing from not knowing?

And so (we wonder) where, precisely and fundamentally, is the boundary between Gettier cases and other situations? We call various belief-forming situations "everyday" or "ordinary." Accordingly, we might suggest that all "normally" justified true beliefs (unlike "Gettiered" ones) are instances of knowledge. Yet do we know what makes a situation ordinary? To the extent that we do not understand what makes something a Gettier situation, we do not understand what it takes for a situation to be normal—and thereby able to contain knowledge.

7. Attempted Solutions: Infallibility

Section 5 mentioned two key aspects—fallibility and luck—of Gettier situations. In this section and the next, we consider those aspects. Is knowing incompatible with fallibility (this section) or luck (section 8)?

There have long been philosophers who doubt that fallible justificatory support is enough to convert a true belief into knowledge. ("If you know it, there must have been *no* possibility of your being mistaken about it.") Descartes (1641[1911]) most famously expressed that sort of doubt. Contemporary advocates have included Lehrer (1971), Unger (1971), and possibly Dretske (1971). The *Infallibility Proposal* would strengthen JTB by requiring *infallibly* strong justification within knowledge.

For instance, because (in the job/coins case) Smith's justification supported belief *b* only fallibly, the possibility remained open of that belief's being mistaken. Due to this possibility, the belief is not knowledge. As to the fake-barns case, an infallibilist will claim that the potential for mistake is particularly real, given the actual fake barns. Again there is a lack of knowledge, because fallible justification is being used.

That is the Infallibility Proposal. Yet throughout our lives we probably never possess infallible justificatory support. If so, the Infallibility Proposal implies us never being knowers. This is a *skepticism* about our ever having knowledge. But most epistemologists favor a non-skeptical conception of knowledge. Can they solve Gettier's challenge *without* adopting the Infallibility Proposal?

8. Attempted Solutions: Eliminating Luck

Section 5 also highlighted the *lucky* way in which each Gettier case's belief is both justified and true. Need this luck be eliminated if the belief is to be knowledge? The *Eliminate Luck Proposal* claims so.

It is common to call upon this idea when reacting initially to Gettier cases. Unger (1968) developed the idea somewhat: A belief is not knowledge if it is true courtesy of a relevant *accident*. Pritchard (2005: ch. 6) expands upon that idea: In too many similar possible situations with a particular Gettier case's same belief, formed in the same way, that belief is false. Thus, the belief is true only luckily—and therefore not knowledge.

Care is needed here. If we seek to eliminate *all* luck from the production of a justified true belief, again we endorse infallibilism. If no luck remains open, the justification renders the belief's truth inescapable; which makes the belief infallibly justified. And (as section 7 explained) few epistemologists will find this an illuminating response to Gettier cases.

Alternatively, we might say that such cases contain too *much* luck. (Pritchard would claim that there are too *many* similar possible situations where the actual belief is false in spite of resting upon the same evidence.) But how much luck *is* too much? There is scant epistemological commentary about what degree of luck precludes knowledge. A specter of irremediable vagueness haunts the Eliminate Luck Proposal.

Understandably, therefore, detailed analyses of knowledge focus less on delineating dangerous *degrees* of luck than on characterizing substantive *kinds* of luck that are claimed to drive away knowledge. Are Gettier situations *structured* in ways that amount to a kind of luck precluding knowledge's presence? Most attempts to solve Gettier's challenge pursue that idea indirectly. Sections 9 through 11 will discuss a few suggestions. (Section 13 will return directly to the theme of luck. See also Tim Black's "Modal and Anti-Luck Epistemology," Chapter 18 in this volume.)

9. Attempted Solutions: Eliminating False Evidence

On the *No False Evidence Proposal*, the failing within Gettier cases is the evidence's being partly mistaken. To the extent that falsity guides the person's forming her belief, she will be lucky to derive one which is true. And (as section 8 indicated) some epistemologists regard a lucky derivation of a true belief as no way of knowing that truth.

In the job/coins case, Smith's evidence includes the false belief that Jones will get the job. Without that evidence (and with nothing else changing within the case), presumably Smith would not have inferred belief *b*. He should have *no* belief about who would get the job (because he would have lacked all evidence on the matter). He would thereby have lacked the justified and true belief *b* which fails to be knowledge. Should JTB be modified, to say that knowledge is a justified true belief well supported by evidence, *none* of which is false?

Epistemologists have noticed problems with that No False Evidence Proposal.

First, as Feldman (1974) explained, there seem to be Gettier cases where no false evidence is used. Imagine Smith's not believing, falsely, "Jones will get the job." Imagine, instead, his believing, "The company president *told me* that Jones will get the job." (He could have formed the first belief. He just happens not to do so.) This alternative belief is true. It also provides belief *b* with as much justification as the false belief provided. So (if all else remains constant within the case), again Smith has a true belief *b* which is well-although-fallibly justified, yet which might well not be knowledge.

Second, the No False Evidence Proposal could imply an unwelcome skepticism. Quite possibly, there is always *some* false evidence being relied upon, at least implicitly, as we form beliefs. If you do not wholly remove falsity (such as by isolating it from the evidence you are using), then—on the No False Evidence Proposal—there is a danger of that falsity preventing those other beliefs from being knowledge.

Unsurprisingly, therefore, some epistemologists, such as Lehrer (1965), offer a less demanding modification of JTB. Perhaps what is needed for knowing is an absence only of *significant and ineliminable* falsehoods from one's evidence. (Here is what that means. False beliefs which you are—but need not have been—using as evidence are *eliminable* from your evidence. False beliefs whose absence would seriously weaken your evidence are *significant* within that evidence.) That turns the No False Evidence Proposal into the

No False Core Evidence Proposal. This says that if the only falsehoods in your evidence are ones you could discard without seriously weakening it, then (all else being equal) your justification is adequate for giving you knowledge. We might use the proposal to infer that the failing within each Gettier case is that some significant falsehood *is* essential to the case's evidence.

In the same spirit, we might regard the failing as the falsehood's functioning as an unstated lemma or assumption (rather than an explicit belief), underwriting or supplementing the overtly used evidence. This would give us a *No False Core Assumption Proposal* (Lycan 2006).

One problem for those proposals is their potential vagueness. How easy, precisely, must it be to eliminate the false evidence or assumption if knowledge is to be present? Just how weakened, exactly, can evidence or underlying assumptions become—through elimination of false elements—before the support being provided is too weak to be making a true belief knowledge? No answer to these questions is manifest.

10. Attempted Solutions: Eliminating Defeat

Section 9 wondered whether the failing within Gettier cases is a matter of the evidence's *including* or relying upon some core *falsehood*. Epistemologists also ask whether the failing is a matter of some pertinent *truth* being *overlooked* by the "Gettiered" evidence.

That idea is often called a *defeasibility* analysis of knowledge. It can also be termed the *No Defeat Proposal*. (For more on that, see "Defeasibility Theory," by Thomas Grundmann, Chapter 15 in this volume.) The basic thought is that JTB should be modified thus: What is needed in knowing that p is an absence from the inquirer's context of *defeaters* of her evidence for p. What is a defeater? A truth t defeats evidence e, as support for a belief, if adding t to e would produce new evidence $e+$ which definitely does *not* justify that belief well enough to satisfy JTB's justification condition.

But that proposal (like section 9's No False Core Evidence—or Assumption—Proposal) faces a fundamental problem of vagueness. Defeaters defeat by weakening evidence's justificatory force: as more and stronger defeaters are overlooked by a body of evidence, that evidence is correlatively weakened. How weak, exactly, can justification for a belief become before it is too weak to sustain the belief's being knowledge? This question (which, in some form, arises for all proposals allowing knowledge's justificatory component to be satisfied by fallible support) is yet to be answered by epistemologists as a group. Applied to the No Defeat Proposal, it is the question, raised by Lehrer and Paxson (1969) and Lycan (1977), of how much of one's environment needs to be noticed by one's evidence if knowledge is to be present. How strict should we be about this?

11. Attempted Solutions: Eliminating Inappropriate Causality

Within Gettier situations, is the justified true belief *caused*—generated, brought about—too oddly or abnormally to be knowledge? The *Appropriate Causality Proposal* claims so (Goldman 1967).

Consider simple "everyday" perceptual knowledge. Part of its being produced is a normal causal pattern's generating a belief. If you use your eyes in a standard way, a belief might form in a standard way, reporting what you observed. That belief will thereby be justified standardly. And it will be true in a standard way—made *true* by the same aspect of the world causing it to *exist*.

Within the job/coins case, however, such normality is absent. Smith's belief *b* is made true by the facts of his getting the job and of there being ten coins in his own pocket. But these do not help to cause *b*'s *existence*. (That belief is caused by Smith's conversation with the mistaken company president and his observation of Jones's coins.) Should JTB be modified, to say that a justified true belief is knowledge only if those aspects of the world making it true are appropriately involved in creating it?

Here are two worries about that Appropriate Causality Proposal.

First, some objects of knowledge might lack causal influence. Perhaps a truth about numbers, such as that $2 + 2 = 4$, exerts no causal effect upon your believing that $2 + 2 = 4$—because numbers do not act causally. (Numerals, such as specific marks on paper being interpreted in actual minds, might do so. Yet these could merely be *representations* of numbers.) Consequently, the Appropriate Causality Proposal would explain, at most, empirical or observational knowledge.

Second, does the Appropriate Causality Proposal explain even empirical knowledge? Especially when reasoning is involved, indirectness is part of any causal process resulting in a belief. How much indirectness is too much, if the belief is to be knowledge?

Imagine that Smith's being about to be offered the job *is* part of the causal explanation of the company president's telling him that Jones would get the job. The president, with his mischievous sense of humor, wished to mislead Smith. Suppose also that Smith's having ten coins in his own pocket made a jingling noise, subtly making him think of coins in pockets, leading him to investigate Jones's pocket. Given all this, the facts (concerning Smith) which make belief *b* true *are* involved causally in creating *b*. Is the Appropriate Causality Proposal thereby satisfied—so that (in this altered job/coins case) belief *b* is now knowledge? Or is this *still* a Gettier case where *b* fails to be knowledge? If so, *why* is this new causal ancestry too inappropriate to allow *b* to be knowledge?

Often, philosophers talk of *deviant* causal chains. But how clear is that phrase? How deviant can a causal chain (resulting in belief-formation) become before it is too deviant to be bringing knowledge into existence? As in sections 9 and 10, we encounter a conceptual problem of vagueness.

12. Attempted Dissolutions: Questioning Intuitions

Sections 9 through 11 described proposals for solving Gettier's challenge directly. Each proposal modifies JTB, to explain knowledge's not being present within Gettier cases. Why is it important to explain that? The standard epistemological answer is that everyone has a strong *intuition* that knowledge is absent from each Gettier case. That intuition reflects our shared concept of knowledge, accurately indicating pertinent details of that concept.

Yet some epistemologists prefer to *dissolve* the Gettier challenge. One such dissolution questions whether those intuitions about Gettier cases are so widespread. If they are not, reliance upon them might be more a choice than an obligation for epistemologists.

That possibility was made pressing by Weinberg et al. (2001). Their empirical research included asking a wider range of people—not only fellow philosophers and students—about Gettier cases. The ideas behind that research are discussed elsewhere in this volume. (See Jonathan Weinberg's "Experimental Epistemology" (Chapter 73) and William Lycan's "Epistemology and the Role of Intuitions" (Chapter 72).) The resulting suggestion is that the usual epistemological reaction to Gettier situations ("Clearly, knowledge is absent!") is not as widespread as epistemologists assume it is.

They might reply that those who do not regard knowledge as absent from Gettier cases are not evaluating the cases *properly*. But why would intuitions of epistemologists and their students be especially accurate? If it is because these people reflect more than others upon knowledge, their reactions might not, after all, be *intuitions* about Gettier cases. Comparatively reflective *theories* of knowledge could be guiding these reactions.

For example, maybe the usual epistemological interpretation manifests a commitment to a technically demanding concept of knowledge (Kirkham 1984), one used especially by critically reflective philosophers. If that concept feels intuitive to them, this could reflect their professional training. If epistemologists continue insisting that knowledge must be "Gettier-proof," possibly they are talking about something—knowledge—which is unattainable for most inquirers. Kaplan (1985) argues that if knowledge must conform to the usual epistemological interpretation of Gettier cases, knowledge is also not something about which inquirers should care. He advocates seeking something less demanding than knowledge.

13. Attempted Dissolutions: Knowing Luckily

Here is an alternative possible reaction: Maybe knowledge itself could be less demanding, even while remaining a worthy object of inquiry. Towards that end, we may conceive of knowledge by reinterpreting the *luck* within Gettier cases (Hetherington 1998). This *Knowing Luckily Proposal* would reinstate JTB's sufficiency, dissolving Gettier's challenge by regarding any "Gettiered" belief as an especially fallible—because interestingly lucky—instance of knowledge. The proposal analyzes Gettier's job/coins case, for instance, along the following lines.

In forming belief b, Smith is lucky to be gaining a belief which is true in the way it is (via features of Smith)—*given* how his evidence (entirely about Jones) indicates the belief's being true. Because the evidence is misleading about the *specific* way b is true, there is luck ("Gettier-luck") in that evidence's leading Smith to form a belief b which is true *at all*, in *some* way. That luck is combinatorial—reflecting how the situation combines (i) the belief b's existing, with both (ii) b's being true in the particular way it is (via Smith), and (iii) what the evidence (about Jones) implies about what is making b true. Nonetheless, even given what the evidence says about Jones, it is not misleading about the fact of b's *being* true. Hence, the luck is not, as it happens, in the fact *that* b is true. The evidence misleads only about substantive details of *how* b is true. Could belief b be knowledge, albeit luckily so? Could Smith have knowledge luckily, by having a justified true belief luckily?

Here is how. We might allow a Gettiered belief to be knowledge *that* p without being knowledge of substantive details of *how*, in particular, it is that p. Philosophers will be loath to admit that knowledge can be like this, given their own quests always to know-that-it-is *by* knowing-how-it-is. Yet much knowledge can arise in that "trusting" way, such as when learning that p from an expert without gleaning many, even any, details of how it is that p. Gettier cases slightly complicate that picture: "Gettier-luck" is (1) knowing that p without knowing substantive details of how it is that p, because (2) one is *misled* by one's evidence as to substantive details of how it is that p. Because of (2), in Gettier cases at best one would know more "shallowly," less understandingly, than if only (1) was satisfied. Still, although experts typically and helpfully give us (1) without

(2), they *could* sometimes give us both—knowledge-that-*p*-is, while misleading us as to how-it-is-that-*p*-is. Imagine hearing a mathematician speaking on the radio, reporting a mathematical truth *m*; one that is new to you. She explains *m* via a simplified "proof" which is needed if a non-specialist (such as you) is even to understand *m*'s content—but which a specialist would find misleading in its analysis of the constitutive details of how it is that *m*. Accordingly, you remain somewhat mistaken as to precisely *how* it is that *m* obtains. We might regard this as your not *understanding* how *m* obtains: perhaps you could not construct or even comprehend a proof unveiling how *m* obtains (Welbourne 2001: 20–1). Possibly, nevertheless, you would now know simply *that m* obtains.

How does that suggestion apply to the fake-barns case? With an apt indeterminacy: As section 3 noted, this might not *be* a Gettier case. (a) It is not, *if* Henry's evidence, being normal, does not mislead as to how it is true that he is seeing a barn. In that event, although he is lucky to *have* the knowledge (because he is lucky to have the evidence), the knowledge is normal *in itself*, once its constituents (such as the evidence) are present. (b) If this *is* a Gettier case, that is because Henry's evidence misleads by indicating implicitly that the neighborhood is normal and that his belief is true because, in part, of that normality. Even then, Henry's belief could be knowledge—albeit luckily so, being made true by the smaller *part* of the neighborhood (the barn itself) explicitly noticed in his evidence.

In either (a) or (b), then, knowledge is possible—either normally or luckily. Naturally, many epistemologists find it puzzling to talk of knowing luckily. Presumably, little (if any) knowledge would be accepted as being lucky in that way—a belief's being justified and true in a "Gettiered" way. And because we encounter little (if any) such knowledge, our lives leave us unused to thinking of knowledge as able to be constituted so luckily. Consequently, to the extent that the luck involved in such cases reflects the statistical unlikelihood of their occurring, we should *expect* little (if any) knowledge to be present in that lucky way. (Otherwise, this would be a *normal* way for knowledge to be present; the knowledge would not be present *luckily*.)

Nonetheless, *some* knowledge might be present luckily. Ordinarily, it seems, when good evidence for a belief accompanies its being true, this combination of good evidence and true belief occurs (unlike in the job/coins case) without notable luck being needed for its occurring. Ordinary knowledge is thereby constituted, with that absence of notable luck being part of what supposedly *makes* ordinary knowledge ordinary. Again, though, is it impossible for knowledge *ever* to be constituted luckily? The Knowing Luckily Proposal claims that such knowledge is possible even if, at most, uncommon. The proposal distinguishes between knowing that *p* in a comparatively ordinary way and knowing that *p* in a comparatively lucky way. (And the proposal refines a conception of knowledge as able to be present fallibly-because-failably within Gettier cases: Hetherington 1999, 2001: ch. 3.)

We might also wonder whether knowledge that *p* which is only luckily present in that way has a comparatively poor *quality* or *grade* as knowledge that *p*. *Normally*, knowledge is of a higher quality or grade—being less flawed, by being less luckily present. But must all knowledge be of a normal quality as knowledge that *p*? Could we sometimes, even if rarely, know less well that *p*? The Knowing Luckily Proposal permits this interpretive possibility. Accordingly, we could embed that Proposal within a *Gradualism Proposal*, allowing that any particular *p* could be known more *or* less well (Hetherington 2001, 2005, 2006a). Shades of luck might be one such dimension of epistemic gradability:

With all else being equal, an instance of knowledge that p would be better purely as knowledge that p when constituted less luckily.

Is that too odd a way to talk of knowledge? How are we to answer this question? With intuitions? Whose? Perhaps we should look beyond intuitions anyway, when seeking what could well be a deeply *theoretical* understanding (Weatherson 2003). Thus, we meet anew section 12's questions about methodologies for making epistemological progress.

For example, even in talking about luck in an epistemologically usual way, could we be applying a mistaken theory? Lackey (2008) questions existing analyses of the constitutive nature of luck. Perhaps epistemologists should wonder whether they are reflecting a real understanding of luck when claiming that knowledge is never constituted luckily. This section has gestured at how to begin conceiving of knowledge as able, at least occasionally, to be constituted luckily.

14. Gettier Cases and Analytic Epistemology

Since 1963, responding to Gettier cases has often been central within analytic epistemology. Partly, this reflects many epistemologists' assumptions that the Gettier problem provides a paradigmatic test case of a *method* which has long been central to analytic philosophy. That method involves the considered manipulation and modification of definitional models or theories, reacting to clear counterexamples to those models or theories.

JTB purported to provide a definitional analysis of what it is to know. Then Gettier cases emerged, apparently as successful counterexamples to the sufficiency of JTB's analysis. That interpretation of the cases rested upon epistemologists' claims to have reflective-yet-intuitive insight into the absence of knowledge from Gettier situations. These claims of intuitive insight were treated as decisive data, akin to favored observations. The claims were respected accordingly. It was assumed that any modification of JTB needs to accommodate them. So, the entrenchment of Gettier's challenge at the core of analytic epistemology hinged upon the following two assumptions: (1) JTB fails to accommodate the data of those intuitions; and (2) any analytical modification of JTB needs to rectify that failing. Epistemologists proceeded to apply that analytical method, vigorously and repeatedly.

Nevertheless, post-1963 analytic epistemology has contained expressions of frustration at seemingly insoluble difficulties accompanying the many responses to Gettier's disarmingly simple paper. Precisely how should the theory JTB be revised, in accord with the relevant data? Exactly which data are relevant anyway? We have found room for dispute and uncertainty here. For example, we noticed a persistent problem of *vagueness* confronting attempts to revise JTB. We might therefore wonder whether a complete analytical definition of knowledge is possible (Hetherington 2006b: sections 1–6).

That possibility is especially pressing, given that philosophers are yet to agree on how to understand vagueness. On one approach, it is a matter of being unable to *know* where to draw a clearly accurate line between instances of X and instances of non-X (for a vague X, such as being bald or being tall). On that interpretation, a dividing line exists—but we remain ignorant of its location. To many philosophers, that idea sounds regrettably odd when the vague phenomenon is baldness, say. ("Really? You claim that there is an exact—yet unknowable—dividing line, in terms of the number of hairs on a person's head, between being bald and not being bald?")

However, should philosophers react with such incredulity when the phenomenon is that of knowing, and when the possibility of its vagueness is prompted by discussions of Gettier's challenge? Most epistemologists remain convinced that their standard reaction to Gettier cases reflects a definite difference between knowing and not knowing. Yet where exactly is that dividing line? As we have observed, epistemological answers to this question generally characterize that boundary in terms of degrees and kinds of justification. Accordingly, the threats of vagueness we noticed in some earlier sections might be a problem for many. In particular, those forms of vagueness could afflict our *knowing* that Gettier cases reveal a difference between knowledge and non-knowledge. Epistemologists continue regarding the cases in that way. But *do* they know what it is that Gettier cases show about knowledge?

The Gettier challenge has therefore become a test case for analytically inclined philosophers. The following questions have become progressively more pressing with each failed attempt to convince epistemologists that (in a given article, talk, or book) the correct analysis of knowledge has been reached. Will an adequate understanding of knowledge ever emerge from an analytical balancing of theories of knowledge against relevant data such as intuitions? Must any theory of the nature of knowledge answer to intuitions prompted by Gettier cases? What conception of knowledge is at stake? What form should a theory of knowledge take? How precise should it be? Need an understanding of knowledge be logically or conceptually exhaustive? (The methodological model of theory-being-tested-against-data suggests a scientific parallel. Yet need scientific understanding always be logically or conceptually exhaustive?) So, uncertainty continues as to whether Gettier's challenge has been fully understood, let alone solved. Conceptual possibilities still abound—even the possibility that, really, there is *no* Gettier problem.

References

Ayer, A. J. (1956) *The Problem of Knowledge*, London: Macmillan.
Chisholm, R. M. (1966/1977/1989) *Theory of Knowledge*, Englewood Cliffs, NJ: Prentice Hall.
Descartes, R. (1641 [1911]) "Meditations on First Philosophy," in E. S. Haldane and G. R. T. Ross (eds. and trans.), *The Philosophical Works of Descartes*, Vol. I, Cambridge: Cambridge University Press.
Dretske, F. (1971) "Conclusive Reasons," *Australasian Journal of Philosophy* 49: 1–22.
Feldman, R. (1974) "An Alleged Defect in Gettier Counterexamples," *Australasian Journal of Philosophy* 52: 68–9. Reprinted in Moser (1986).
Gettier, E. L. (1963) "Is Justified True Belief Knowledge?" *Analysis* 23: 121–3. Reprinted in Roth and Galis (1970) and Moser (1986).
Goldman, A. I. (1967) "A Causal Theory of Knowing," *The Journal of Philosophy* 64: 357–72. Reprinted, with revisions, in Roth and Galis (1970).
—— (1976) "Discrimination and Perceptual Knowledge," *The Journal of Philosophy* 73: 771–91. Reprinted in Pappas and Swain (1978).
Hetherington, S. (1998) "Actually Knowing," *The Philosophical Quarterly* 48: 453–69.
—— (1999) "Knowing Failably," *The Journal of Philosophy* 96: 565–87.
—— (2001) *Good Knowledge, Bad Knowledge: On Two Dogmas of Epistemology*, Oxford: Clarendon Press.
—— (2005) "Knowing (How It Is) That P: Degrees and Qualities of Knowledge," in C. de Almeida (ed.), *Perspectives in Contemporary Epistemology*, Veritas, 50: 129–52.
—— (2006a) "How To Know (That Knowledge-That Is Knowledge-How)," in S. Hetherington (ed.), *Epistemology Futures*, Oxford: Clarendon Press.
—— (2006b) "Introduction: The Art of Precise Epistemology," in S. Hetherington (ed.), *Aspects of Knowing: Epistemological Essays*, Oxford: Elsevier.
Kaplan, M. (1985) "It's Not What You Know That Counts," *The Journal of Philosophy* 82: 350–63.
Kirkham, R. L. (1984) "Does the Gettier Problem Rest on a Mistake?" *Mind* 93: 501–13.
Lackey, J. (2008) "What Luck Is Not," *Australasian Journal of Philosophy* 86: 255–67.

Lehrer, K. (1965) "Knowledge, Truth and Evidence," *Analysis* 25: 168–75. Reprinted in Roth and Galis (1970).
—— (1971) "Why Not Scepticism?" *The Philosophical Forum* 2: 283–98. Reprinted in Pappas and Swain (1978).
—— and Paxson, T. D. (1969) "Knowledge: Undefeated Justified True Belief," *The Journal of Philosophy* 66: 225–37. Reprinted in Pappas and Swain (1978).
Lycan, W. G. (1977) "Evidence One Does not Possess," *Australasian Journal of Philosophy* 55: 114–26.
—— (2006) "On the Gettier Problem problem," in S. Hetherington (ed.), *Epistemology Futures*, Oxford: Clarendon Press.
Pritchard, D. (2005) *Epistemic Luck*, Oxford: Clarendon Press.
Unger, P. (1968) "An Analysis of Factual Knowledge," *The Journal of Philosophy* 65: 157–70. Reprinted in Roth and Galis (1970).
—— (1971) "A Defense of Skepticism," *The Philosophical Review* 30: 198–218. Reprinted in Pappas and Swain (1978).
Weatherson, B. (2003) "What Good are Counterexamples?" *Philosophical Studies* 115: 1–31.
Weinberg, J., Nichols, S., and Stich, S. (2001) "Normativity and Epistemic Intuitions," *Philosophical Topics* 29: 429–60.
Welbourne, M. (2001) *Knowledge*, Montreal and Kingston: McGill-Queen's University Press.

Further Reading

Hetherington, S. (1996a) *Knowledge Puzzles: An Introduction to Epistemology*, Boulder, CO: Westview Press. (Includes an introduction to JTB, plus several responses to Gettier's challenge.)
—— (1996b) "Gettieristic Scepticism," *Australasian Journal of Philosophy* 74: 83–97. (How, as standardly interpreted, Gettier cases may be used skeptically.)
—— (forthcoming) *How to Know: A Practicalist Conception of Knowledge*, Wiley-Blackwell. (Chapter 3 includes an expanded dissolution of the Gettier problem.)
Keefe, R. and Smith, P. (eds.) (1996) *Vagueness: A Reader*, Cambridge, MA: MIT Press. (Historical and contemporary analyses of the nature and significance of vagueness.)
Moser, P. K. (ed.) (1986) *Empirical Knowledge: Readings in Contemporary Epistemology*, Totowa, NJ: Rowman & Littlefield. (Includes some influential papers on Gettier cases.)
Pappas, G. S. and Swain, M. (eds.) (1978) *Essays on Knowledge and Justification*, Ithaca, NY: Cornell University Press. (Mainly on the Gettier Problem.)
Roth, M. D. and Galis, L. (eds.) (1970) *Knowing: Essays in the Analysis of Knowledge*, New York: Random House. (Includes some noteworthy papers on Gettier's challenge.)
Shope, R. K. (1983) *The Analysis of Knowing: A Decade of Research*, Princeton, NJ: Princeton University Press. (Presents many Gettier cases; discusses several proposed analyses.)
Williamson, T. (2000) *Knowledge and Its Limits*, Oxford: Clarendon Press. (Includes arguments against responding to Gettier cases by analyzing knowledge: Introduction, ch. 1.)

13
FALLIBILISM
Trent Dougherty

> There is a world of difference between fallible knowledge and no knowledge.
> C.S. Peirce

Introduction

Fallibilism in epistemology is neither identical to nor unrelated to the ordinary notion of fallibility. In ordinary life we are forced to the conclusion that human beings are prone to error. The epistemological doctrine of fallibilism, though, is about the consistency of holding that humans have knowledge while admitting certain limitations in human ways of knowing. As will be seen, making the content of the basic intuition more precise is both somewhat contentious and the key to an adequate definition of fallibilism. Before moving on to this project I will address a few preliminary issues. Then, after canvassing some prevailing views I will address two concerns. First, I will address the concern that prevailing views do not adequately take into account fallible knowledge of necessary truths and are thus not fully general accounts of fallible knowledge. Second, I will address probabilistic accounts of fallibilism. I will suggest that a simple, adequate account of fallibilism is possible.

The Root Intuition

One might well wonder what the root cause of the need for a fallibilist doctrine is. It is we knowing agents which are *fallible knowers*. So the root need for fallibilism might seem to be some shortcoming in us mere mortals. But it's not clear that this is the case. For it seems that *any* being which comes to know things the way we do—through experience, broadly construed to include what it's like to have a rational insight—will be fallible knowers. So remove from a typical human what Russell called "medical limitations." That is, idealize away the need for food, rest, (and any other such limitations) and grant logical omniscience. If they are perfectly rational agents—and they ought to be, we've idealized them in all respects relevant to rationality then doxastic voluntarism—the thesis that an agent can choose their beliefs—will be false for them. That is, they will always be compelled by their evidence. There is no reason to think that these beings are any less subject to Cartesian demon worries. They are no more capable of stepping outside their heads and examining the thought-to-world fit of their beliefs than we are. They will be fully aware that it is a genuine broadly logical possibility that they could have all the same experiences and yet be mistaken in this belief (we will discuss necessary truths later). More generally, *they are fully captive to the convincing power of their experiences* (what Plantinga (1993: 193) calls "impulsional evidence"). We can express this by saying that they have *fallible reasons*. As we will see shortly, this seems to be the core notion that theorists have been trying to explicate.

Cognates

Above, I used the terms "fallible knowledge," "fallible knowers," and "fallible reasons." In light of the discussion just above, it seems best to take fallible *reasons* as the basic notion and define the others in terms of it. So *fallible knowers* are agents who know what they know on the basis of fallible reasons. *Fallible knowledge* will be knowledge on the basis of fallible reasons. Thinking of it this way will allow us to have maximum flexibility of expression with minimum confusion. The most general schemas to be filled in below, then, will be as follows.

> Fallibilism = df The thesis that all human knowledge is on the basis of fallible reasons.
> S fallibly knows that p = df S knows that p on the basis of fallible reasons.

Knowledge and Justification

Above, I have spoken exclusively of knowledge. But of course there is a natural usage of "fallible justification" which mimics our use of "fallible knowledge." In fact, as justification is the more basic notion, it might seem better to treat fallibilism as a doctrine about justification rather than knowledge. In principle I'd prefer it this way myself, but (i) it has historically been discussed in terms of knowledge, and (ii) the application to justification is straightforward.

> JF Fallibilism about Justification = df The thesis that all human justification is on the basis of fallible reasons.
> FJ S is fallibly justified in believing that p = df S is justified in believing that p on the basis of fallible reasons.

Thus, in characterizing fallibilism, I will speak of it in terms of knowledge and canvass the more concentrated reflections of the latter half of the twentieth century.

Characterizing Fallibilism

Traditional Accounts

Plausibly, fallibilism is as old as the Stoics. Sextus Empiricus records that Carneades held a kind of fallibilism (*Outlines of Pyrrhonism* and *Against the Logicians*). However, modern reflection began with Peirce. Peirce was concerned in the first instance with scientific knowledge but, clearly, was concerned with knowledge in general as well. Haack describes the lie of the land well:

> It is clear from Peirce's critique of Descartes' epistemology, where fallibilism is introduced as the way to avoid both of the supposedly exhaustive

alternatives of Cartesian dogmatism, on the one hand, and outright skepticism, on the other, that he takes fallibilism to be an epistemological position intermediate between dogmatism and skepticism.

(1979: 47)

Fallibilism is conceived here as a golden mean between two extremes. The skeptical extreme is not hard to characterize: knowledge is impossible for human beings. We might intuitively think of this as an extreme of "under-affirming" propositions. But there are also various ways of, as it were, "over-affirming." This represents a family of "dogmatic" extremes. Dogmatism is variously conceived as insistence on certainty, indubitability, infallibility, incorrigibility, or ignoring skeptical arguments.

What I will do for now is display the definitions from the leading theorists of the latter half of the twentieth century (starting off thematically with Peirce) offering a few brief observations along the way. Later, I will defend a view that does justice to the best of them.

> Peirce (c.1897): "We can never be absolutely sure of anything" (quoted in Haack 1979: 44).

Comments The OED credits Peirce with introducing the term, including a rather poetic statement. Here is the whole of the entry.

> The principle that propositions concerning empirical knowledge cannot be proved c1897 C. S. PEIRCE *Coll. Papers* (1931) I. I. iii. 61 Fallibilism . . . only says that people cannot attain absolute certainty concerning questions of fact. *Ibid.* 70 Fallibilism is the doctrine that our knowledge is never absolute but always swims, as it were, in a continuum of uncertainty and of indeterminacy. 1941 *Mind* L. 81 Fallibilism which denies intuitive or certain knowledge even of common-sense propositions.

Unlike most recent fallibilists, Peirce couched his view in terms of certainty. I will argue in the end that Peirce's is the best characterization, and capable of explaining what is appealing about other plausible accounts.

> Haack (1979: 52): "Every proposition is either such that believing it does not necessarily entail that it is true, or one might have believed otherwise."

Comments She gives a formal account: (F*) $\forall p(\sim\Box(Bp \supset p) \vee \Diamond B\sim p)$. The definition needs to be somewhat complicated, because there are some odd propositions such as *Someone believes something* which are such that they could not be false if someone believed them. She takes dogmatism to be the view that there are some propositions which are both *self-guaranteeing* $\Box(Bp \supset p)$ as well was *indubitable* $\sim\Diamond B\sim p$. Thus (F*) is equivalent to the negation of the conjunction of those properties in an existential claim which she takes to be the core Cartesian content.

Mott (1980: 177ff.) points out that (F*) is logically equivalent to $\forall p\Diamond Bp$, and objects that "we must surely grant that fallibilism has more to say than that we are capable of believing anything" (179). But, as I will argue, this is remarkably close to the core notion of fallibilism, for Haack comments: "His [the fallibilist's] point is, rather, that our liability to believe a proposition doesn't depend [logically] in any direct way on its truth-value" (1979: 50).

> Feldman (1981): "(F) S can know that p even if it is possible that S is mistaken in believing that p" (266). "(F1) It is possible for S to know that p even if S does not have logically conclusive evidence to justify believing that p" (266). "What it amounts to is the claim that people can know things on the basis of nondeductive arguments. That is, they can know things on the basis of inductive, perceptual, or testimonial evidence that does not entail what it is evidence for" (267).

Comments Feldman sets aside his first definition as potentially misleading. The problem, he says, is that it is consistent with the interpretation that entails a denial of the factiveness (truth-entailingness) of knowledge or with the mere assertion that contingent truths can be known. If we give at least a competent reading where both operators are alethic, then it merely says that it is possible to know a contingent proposition. However, if we take the modal as epistemic, then it might have a very plausible interpretation. The epistemic modal couldn't, of course, be given the standard interpretation—that p is epistemically possible iff its negation is not entailed by something in our corpus of knowledge. For consider the definition of epistemic possibility: e-$\Diamond$p = df ~$\exists$q(Kq $\wedge$ q $\to$ ~p). Now Feldman's proposal on an epistemic reading is that fallibilism is the thesis that $\Diamond$(Kp $\wedge$ e-$\Diamond$~p). So to get the full reading of it we need to substitute ~p for p in the def of e-$\Diamond$ above. Doing so, we get e-$\Diamond$~p iff ~$\exists$q(Kq and q $\to$ ~~p). Then Feldman's definition would look like this. $\Diamond$(Kp $\wedge$ ~$\exists$q(Kq and q $\to$ ~~p). But clearly there *is* some q such that S knows it and it entails ~~p, namely p! Thus neither the reading of (F) with both modals as alethic, nor the reading with the latter with the standard interpretation of the epistemic modal gives an adequate account of fallibilism. In the final section on probability, we will consider another way of reading the epistemic modal which will make sense of (F) in a way that actually makes it superior to (F1).

> Jeffrey (1985 (1992)): In "Probability and the Art of Judgment" (originally 1985, reprinted in the 1992 book of the same name) Jeffrey describes a view called "radical probabilism" which asserts that knowledge is consistent with probability. He describes the view in the introduction to the book as follows: "it doesn't insist that probabilities be based on certainties: it can be probabilities all the way down, to the roots" (1992: 11).

Comments Jeffrey laid the foundations for radical probabilism in his 1968 essay "Probable Knowledge" (also reprinted in his 1992) and Chapter 11 of his *The Logic of Decision*, originally published in 1965, second edn 1983, but the material derives from his 1957 PhD dissertation at Princeton under Hempel. That it is a form of fallibilism in our sense is shown by the way he positions it between dogmatism and skepticism (1992: 44–48). I shall have more to say below about how Jeffery's insights are key to the best unified account of fallibilism.

> Cohen (1988): "A fallibilist theory allows that S can know q on the basis of r where r only makes q probable" (91). "Any theory of knowledge that endorses the principle that S knows q on the basis of reason r only if r entails q, is

doomed to a skeptical conclusion. Fallibilist theories reject this entailment principle thereby avoiding this immediate skeptical result" (91).

Comments Here we see the coming together of fallibilism as antiskeptical as in Peirce, and as having as its main content the possibility of knowledge with non-entailing or merely probabilifying support as in Feldman. Cohen points out that the fallibilist move to avoid a skepticism grounded in requiring entailing evidence for knowledge leads naturally to a new skeptical problem from closure. We'll look at this more below in the section on closure.

> Carrier (1993: 367, 370): There is no proposition such that S knows that they are not mistaken regarding p.

Comments Many of Carrier's ideas are refuted in advance by Feldman. In the article, Carrier is defending his view from a threat posed by a closure principle on knowledge. He rejects closure (a) for reasons that confuse epistemic justification with practical rationality and (b) *simply* because to accept the closure principle, he thinks, would force a choice between skepticism and dogmatism. Cohen (1988) discusses the possibility of the fallibilist preserving closure by accepting a kind of contextualism about knowledge.

> David Lewis (1996) writes, concerning fallibilism: "If you claim that S knows that P, and yet you grant that S cannot eliminate a certain possibility in which not-P, it certainly seems as if you have granted that S does not after all know that P. To speak of fallible knowledge, of knowledge despite uneliminated possibility of error, just sounds contradictory" (549).

Comments With typical gusto, Lewis attempts to create in the reader a sense of desperation for a solution he is prepared to offer and which might seem radical if times did not call for such desperate measures. Lewis's solution is to "go contextual" and take knowledge to rule out all "relevant" possibilities. Lewis thinks that it is obvious that knowledge requires infallibility and that fallibilism is "mad" (550) but not quite as mad as skepticism. Lewis's comments here have sparked much discussion. Rysiew (2001) argues that the problem is resolved through consideration of the pragmatics of language. Stanley (2005) seeks to save fallibilism by urging that it is not committed to the rectitude of such utterances in the first place, criticizing Rysiew (2001). Dougherty and Rysiew (2009) defend fallible knowledge claims. Dodd (2009) favors Dougherty and Rysiew (2009) over Stanley (2005), but offers some challenges. Dougherty and Rysiew (2010) seek to meet these challenges.

> Hetherington (1999: 566): *General*: "FailK1: one's knowledge that p is failable, if and only if (1) one knows that p but (2) one might have failed to do so."
> Hetherington (1999: 567): *Particular*: "FailK2: a person x knows failably that p, if and only if (1) x knows that p, and (2) there is an accessible possible world where (i) p is false (but x believes that p, with the same good evidence for p he has here), or (ii) x fails to believe that p (even though p is true and he has the same good evidence for p as he has here), or (iii) x fails to have the same good evidence for p as he has here (but he still believes that p, and p is true)."

THE ANALYSIS OF KNOWLEDGE

Comments Notice that as stated this is an account of "failable" knowledge, not "fallible" knowledge. The reason he introduces this terminology is that he thinks that philosophers are too tied to using "fallibilism" for empirical propositions only, but the standard accounts don't extend to necessary truths (since they are entailed by anything (even nothing)). However, I don't think it wise to capitulate on this, so I include his failabilist theory here as a fallibilist one.

Reed (2002) thinks the cases where S doesn't believe p are irrelevant (Reed 2002: 147–148) because there is a class of cases where the *reason* I don't believe has an intuitive connection not to fallibility, but rather, say, to stubbornness. It's not clear that this isn't intuitively connected to fallibilism since stubbornness is one of the ways we go wrong, but further discussion of the point would be laborious. He says essentially the same about clause (iii) of FailK2. He says "It simply is a different cognitive situation when S's belief that *p* is not based on justification *j* and thus does not affect S's knowledge that *p* when the belief is in fact based on *j*" (Reed 2002: 155, n21). It's not clear (a) what Reed means by "cognitive situation" or (b) why being in a different one makes the fact irrelevant. As will be seen shortly, Reed's initial particular view is almost identical with Hetherington's. Both Hetherington and Reed do a lot of work in their clarification and commentary on their principles.

> Pryor (2000: 518): "A fallibilist is someone who believes that we can have knowledge on the basis of defeasible justification, justification that does not guarantee that our beliefs are correct."
> Pryor (2000: 520): The "fallibilist is only acknowledging that the considerations which support our perceptual beliefs are defeasible and ampliative . . . they don't *entail* that [say] there's a hand . . ."

Comments I only want to note here that it's clear that Pryor is squarely in the Feldman-Cohen camp on the definition of fallibilism.

> Reed (2002): *General*: "Fallibilism is the philosophical view that conjoins two apparently obvious claims. On one hand, we are *fallible*. We make mistakes—sometimes even about the most evident things. But, on the other hand, we also have quite a bit of *knowledge*. Despite our tendency to get things wrong occasionally, we get it right much more of the time" (143).
> Reed (2002): *Particular A*: (FK5) S fallibly knows that *p* = df (1) S knows that *p* on the basis of justification *j* and yet (2) S's belief that *p* on the basis of *j* could have failed to be knowledge (149).
> Reed (2002): *Particular B*: (FK6) S fallibly knows that *p* = df (1) S knows that *p* on the basis of justification *j* and yet (2) S's belief that *p* on the basis of *j* could have been either (i) false or (ii) accidentally true.

Comments First, fallibilism should be, and clearly has historically been, a thesis about the *compatibility* of knowledge with some kind of fallibility thesis. That we have a lot of knowledge might be some kind of datum or constraint on philosophical theorizing, but it is no part of philosophy to assert such generalizations. Similar remarks apply to the statement that we do in fact make mistakes. All that's needed to get skeptical worries going is that we *could* make mistakes, even under the best sorts of circumstances. This is why I preferred to take the root fallibilist notion as *fallible reasons* rather than *fallible people*. People who managed to make no factual errors would still have fallible knowledge if their reasons were fallible reasons.

As mentioned above, Reed's first precisification—Particular A—is essentially the same as that of Hetherington (1999). The main difference with Particular B is that Reed focuses on possible Gettierization (broadly construed). Reed's main purpose in revising the standard definition was that it apparently doesn't capture the sense in which even correct beliefs regarding necessary truths might be fallible. His "or it could have been lucky" modification to Hetherington (1999) does capture a certain class of these cases, for we might make certain pairs of mistakes that "cancel out" to arrive at a true belief that some theorem is true (see Reed 2002: 149). This belief is a fallible one, though it couldn't have been mistaken. How is it fallible? It was based on mistakes. (Note that this doesn't require a luck-based account of Gettierization. It would work just as well on a no-essential-dependence on a falsehood account (see Feldman 2003: chapter 3).

Reed's account just doesn't smack of the kinds of worries that are at the root of the fallibilist's concern. As I've stated above and will consider in greater detail below, the sorts of concerns fallibilists seem to be worried about are more standard threats to knowledge from evil demon type scenarios. Reed's example is one in which our reasoning is flawed. Fallibilism has developed historically in concern over cases where our reasons are as good as they could be, the sorts of cases involved in Cartesian demon scenarios, not Gettier cases. In evil demon scenarios, the problem is with the *way* we know—being convinced by some kind of experience (and recall that each deductive proof consists of basic, intuitive steps). As a result, we could be convinced of anything under the right circumstances, including necessary falsehoods.

> Stanley (2005): "Fallibilism is the doctrine that someone can know that p, even though their evidence for p is logically consistent with the truth of not-p" (127).

Comment Stanley is right in line with the Feldman-Cohen model of fallibility of reasons in terms of non-entailment. This leads back nicely to a consideration of some of the problems that arise for such fallibilists.

Closure, Skepticism, and Dogmatism(s)

From the beginning, there has been a tendency to treat fallibilism as an alternative to either dogmatism or skepticism. Recall Haack's point earlier about Peirce seeing fallibilism as a mean between the extremes of skepticism and dogmatism. Carrier (1993: 363) also thinks along these lines. But it is much better to think of fallibilism as consistent with either dogmatism or skepticism. The relationship between these views comes out best when considering the issue of closure.

I'll consider the problem of necessary truths below, but there's a clear consensus view that fallible knowledge is knowledge based on non-entailing reasons. To say that φ entails ψ is to say that it is not metaphysically possible for φ to be true and yet ψ not be true. The denial of entailment is to say that it *is* possible for φ to be true and yet ψ not be true, $\Diamond(\varphi \wedge \sim\psi)$. So as soon as we allow that one might know p on the basis of evidence E even when it's not the case that E entails p we are faced with the class of propositions which are consistent with the evidence but inconsistent with what we take the evidence to support. This class includes all sorts of skeptical hypotheses. If our evidence E entailed p, then anything incompatible with p would be incompatible with E (via Modus Tollens). But once we become fallibilists we countenance non-entailing evidence. Some fallibilists will allow that I can know that I see a zebra on the basis of perceptual evidence alone. And yet the skeptical hypothesis that it's really just a cleverly painted mule is consistent with my evidence and inconsistent with my commonsense belief. In this way, fallibilists face a closure-generated skeptical threat. It will be easy to show why this is the case by briefly considering the relationship between the three positions in a closure-based skeptical argument. It will be easiest to grasp the dialectic by taking a particularized form of the closure argument rather than attempting a fully general statement. It's not hard to see how the argument generalizes.

Closure-based Skeptical Argument

1. I know that's a zebra.
2. I know that if that's a zebra, it's not a cleverly painted mule.
3. If 1 & 2, then I can know that's not a cleverly painted mule.
4. But I can't know it's not a cleverly painted mule (how on Earth could I know that?!)
5. So I don't know it's a zebra after all (since the entailment is obvious to me).

In this way, it can be easy to talk oneself into a skeptical position. Premise 3 is stated in such a way to avoid detailed consideration of what a final closure principle would look like (but see David and Warfield 2008). The skeptic accepts this dialectic, the dogmatist insists that she *does* in fact know it's not a cleverly disguised mule (without offering other considerations). This seems to leave the non-skeptical, non-dogmatic fallibilist in the position of choosing between contextualism and a denial of closure, neither of which are very attractive. Cohen (1988) argues, persuasively, that though fallibilism avoids certain kinds of skeptical arguments, it doesn't by itself avoid the closure argument, and so he takes the contextualist route. Carrier (1993) takes the closure-denying route. Feldman (1981) seems to be a fallibilist dogmatist, and Pryor (2000) clearly is (Pryor attributes the position to Moore and the dishonorific term "dogmatism" seems to be warranted by the refusal to offer non-question-begging reasons against the skeptic, see also Carrier (1993: 367) and Haack (1979: 47).) Jeffrey (1992: 45) seems to see Descartes' insistence on certainty as central to dogmatism. But one could be a fallibilist skeptic by arguing that closure holds, contextualism is false, and rejecting dogmatism.

A Fully General Fallibilism: The Ever-Present Possibility of Misleading, Compelling Experience

Sometimes, etymology is utterly misleading. In the present case, however, I think it is illuminating. The root for "fallible" doesn't have as its immediate connotation "error" but, rather, "deceit" (that deceit entails error is not an objection). A common phrase used to illustrate it is "Nisi fallit me animus," which means "Unless my mind deceives me." Variations on the phrase in Latin have one's senses deceiving one. But this leads to a fruitful play on words, for "animus" can also mean "spirit" as in "evil spirit" as in Cartesian demon! I mentioned in several places above the role Cartesian skeptical worries played in the formation of fallibilism. I now bring those considerations together into the following insight.

> *Cartesian Insight* Fallibilism arises out of three facts: (i) All our knowledge is ultimately grounded in our *experiences*, broadly construed to include what it's like to have rational insights, (ii) our experiences generally *compel* belief, (iii) for *any* p, it is metaphysically possible that our experiences lead us to believe that p (a Cartesian demon could cause us to have experiences which would compel our assent to anything she chose), without regard for the truth of p or our ability to discriminate whether the experiences are veridical or not.

Hetherington comes very close to this when he says "That skeptical reasoning [the uneliminated possibility of deception by an evil demon] is meant to reveal a problem with the *kind*, not simply the amount, of fallibilist evidence that Descartes is purportedly using" (2002: 91). And remember that Hetherington and Reed are both animated by the desire to give an account of fallibilism that covers necessary truths, which it seems the traditional Feldman-Cohen account does not. Peirce also sees the possibility of deception as the root of fallibilism about necessary truths: "How does any individual here know but that I am a hypnotist, and that when he comes out of my influence he may see that twice two is four is merely his distorted idea?" (quoted in Haack 1979: 44). So it's plausible that even the fallibility of belief in necessary truths is captured by deception worries. It may not *in fact* be possible that I am mistaken, yet I still cannot be *certain* that any belief is true because I cannot discriminate between episodes of veridical experience and deceptive experience.

This shows what is right after all in Haack's most general treatment of fallibilism when she says that the fallibilist's point is "that our liability to believe a proposition doesn't depend [logically] in any direct way upon its truth value" (1979: 50). Indeed, her penultimate candidate for a definition of fallibilism is (F4) $\forall p \Diamond Bp$, we might believe *anything*!

So I think there is considerable merit to the Cartesian insight concerning fallibilism. It remains, however, to distill the Cartesian insight into a particular account of fallible knowledge. I will now put forward the following suggestions for how to do that.

> DFD S fallibly knows that p = df (i) S knows that p, but (ii) S cannot discriminate between (1) a veridical experience caused in the right way by (or otherwise appropriately related to) the fact that p, (2) an altogether misleading experience, and (3) an experience deviantly caused by (or otherwise inappropriately related to) the fact that p (like a benevolent spirit causing in you the impression of a truth of a theorem for which you have no proof).

Or perhaps more simply:

> DFC S fallibly knows that p = df (i) S knows that p, but (ii) S cannot be certain that p (if for no other reason than that S can't tell for sure that she's not being deceived).

My suggestions are not specifically intended to be original or distinct. My hope is just to take the family of ideas surrounding the Cartesian Insight and distill them into the simplest and most illuminating form. I said above that intuitive fallibilism was the thesis that all human knowledge is on the basis of fallible reasons. Then I offered the following definition.

S fallibly knows that p = df S knows that p on the basis of fallible reasons.

With the following connector,

S's belief B that p is fallible knowledge iff S fallibly knows p.

fallibilism can be defined as follows:

Fallibilism = df The thesis that all human knowledge is fallible knowledge (knowledge based on fallible reasons).

Fallibilism could also be relativized to domains if one thought that some human knowledge was possibly infallible. This definition could lead to skepticism, if knowledge entailed the ability to discriminate between veridical and deceptive experiences (the conditional implicit in the definition would then be trivially true), but non-skeptical fallibilism would be defined thus.

Non-skeptical Fallibilism = df The thesis that, possibly, there is some fallible knowledge.

A very sympathetic reading of Hetherington's or Reed's position can bring their accounts in line with the Cartesian Insight. Reed's own example relies on an error that could easily have been avoided, whereas the Cartesian worry is about knowledge in cases where our reasons are as good as they could (humanly) possibly be. But if the lack of a proper connection between justification and truth is glossed in such a way as to focus on basic sources of belief, then there is something to the "it could have failed to be knowledge" account pioneered by Hetherington and pruned by Reed.

Probability

I think there is something to the Cartesian Insight concerning fallibilism and so I think there's something to DFD and DFC. However, it would be nice to salvage the core of the Feldman-Cohen account adopted also by Pryor and Stanley and many others and even to wed it to the earliest accounts in Peirce—"We can never be absolutely sure of anything"—and that of Jeffrey's probable knowledge. I think this can be done by appeal to the notion of epistemic probability.

As noted above, Cohen takes the non-entailing evidence account to be equivalent to some probability account. Here's one reason to think the probabilistic account is more basic. Suppose you have E as evidence for p. Suppose further that E entails p. Still, your grip on E might be less than maximal, so the total probability of p might still be less than one, even though your evidence entails your conclusion. This point was driven home by Jeffrey (in all the works cited thus far). For example, suppose you see a man in a yellow hat down by the dock in the fog and thus acquire *There was a man with a yellow hat on the dock* as basic evidence. This entails that there was a man down by the dock and that there was a yellow-hatted person down by the dock. Yet because of the fog, you're not certain it wasn't a green hat, or a woman dressed as a man. Thus even though your evidence entails the latter propositions, they are not certain for you because they are not grounded in a simple, vivid sense impression. Eventually, justification bottoms out

FALLIBILISM

in experiential grounds often unmediated by beliefs about the nature of your experience (and thus it would be wrong to say that my evidence consists in such propositions as *I am appeared to yellow-hatted-manly* or *I'm having a foggy experience as of a man in a yellow hat*. This is just the kind of mythical given Jeffrey opposed). In keeping with these themes I'll shortly propose a very simple probabilistic account of fallibilism. First, though, I need to treat Reed's attempt at a probabilistic account.

> (FK7) S fallibly knows that p = df (1) S knows that p on the basis of justification j where (2) j makes probable the belief that p in the sense that S's belief belongs to the class of beliefs which have the same (type) j and most, but not all, of which are true.

There are too many questions about Reed's proposal to consider in detail here, but here are some starters. 1. How does it not grossly succumb to the generality problem regarding types of justification (he mentions bases as varied as "reason" and *modus ponens*)? 2. What does it mean to have *modus ponens* as a justification? 3. How can this possibly work on a relative frequency model of probability which Reed endorses (think recently disenvatted brain)? Also, it wouldn't capture the fact that we're still fallible in those laudable worlds where we contingently get everything right, since all the frequencies of all the classes would be 1. Fortunately, there is a better way to give a probabilistic account of fallible knowledge.

Epistemic Probability and Necessary Truths

Help is to be found in turning to an intuitive notion of evidential probability. Plantinga (1993) contains many convincing arguments that epistemic probability comes apart from logical probability. That no exception has ever been found to Goldbach's conjecture clearly counts in favor of its being true. The fact that many great mathematicians think it must be true also counts in its favor. So in a very sensible sense, we have some limited but clearly inconclusive evidence for Goldbach's conjecture. That its logical probability is 1 or 0 needn't bother us, since in epistemic matters, the logical probability is not relevant unless it is known, just as that the physical probability of some empirical proposition is 1 is not relevant to epistemic probability unless that fact is known. Thus, we can sensibly say that the epistemic probability of Goldbach's conjecture is greater than 0 but less than 1. Applying that notion, we have the following.

> FP Fallibilism is the thesis that, necessarily, any belief we might have has an epistemic probability less than one.

Or alternatively,

> FC Fallibilism is the thesis that we cannot be certain of anything.

Fallible knowledge would then be defined thus.

> FKP S fallibly knows that p = df (i) S knows that p, but (ii) the evidential probability of p for S is less than 1.
> FKC S fallibly knows that p = df (i) S knows that p, but (ii) S cannot be certain that p.

Finally, Dougherty and Rysiew (2009, 2010) give an alternative to the standard epistemic reading of "might." They state that the right way to think of epistemic possibility is non-zero evidential probability. This makes FP equivalent to

FP* Fallibilism is the thesis that any of our beliefs might (epistemically) be false.

This would give, then, this final definition of fallible knowledge.

FK* S fallibly knows that p = df (i) S knows that p, but (ii) p might (epistemically) be false.

Ironically, this is Feldman's (1981) original proposal (p. 266). I mentioned in my comments on it that on an alternative epistemic reading of the modal it might prove satisfactory after all. I think I've shown there's a plausible case for that now. Note that it will *ordinarily* be conversationally inappropriate to *say* "I know that p, but p might be false" even if it's true, since this would ordinarily mislead an interlocutor to infer that the possibility was an epistemically significant one; one that might constitute a knowledge defeater. This is also discussed in Dougherty and Rysiew (2009, 2010).

References

Carrier, L.S. (1993) "How to Define Nonskeptical Fallibilism," *Philosophia* 22(3–4): 361–372.
Cohen, S. (1988) "How to Be a Fallibilist," in J. Tomberlin (ed.), *Philosophical Perspectives 2: Epistemology*, Atascadero, CA: Ridgeview Publishing Co.
David, M. and T. Warfield. (2008) "Knowledge-Closure and Skepticism," in Q. Smith (ed.), *Epistemology: New Essays*, Oxford: Oxford University Press.
Dodd, D. (2010) "Confusion about Concessive Knowledge Attributions," *Synthese* 172(3): 381–396.
Dougherty, T. and P. Rysiew. (2009) "Fallibilism, Epistemic Possibility, and Concessive Knowledge Attributions," *Philosophy and Phenomenological Research* Vol. LXXVIII No. 1, January 2009.
——. (2010) "Clarity about Concessive Knowledge Attributions," *Synthese*. Forthcoming.
Feldman, R. (1981) "Fallibilism and Knowing that One Knows," *The Philosophical Review*, 90(2): 266–282.
——. (2003) *Epistemology*, Upper Saddle River, NJ: Prentice Hall.
Jeffrey, R. (1992) *Probability and the Art of Judgment*, Cambridge: Cambridge University Press.
——. (1985) "Probability and the Art of Judgment," in P. Achinstein and O. Hannaway (eds), *Observation, Experimentation, and Hypothesis in Modern Physical Science*, Cambridge, MA: MIT Press.
——. (1983 (orig. 1965)) *The Logic of Decision*, 2nd Edn, Chicago, IL: University of Chicago Press.
Haack, S. (1979) "Fallibilism and Necessity," *Synthese*, 41(1): 37–63.
Hetherington, S. (1999) "Knowing Failably," *Journal of Philosophy*, 96: 565–587.
——. (2002) "Fallibilism and Knowing That One Is Not Dreaming." *Canadian Journal of Philosophy*, 32: 83–102.
Lewis, D. (1996) "Elusive Knowledge," *Australasian Journal of Philosophy*, 74: 649–667.
Mott, P. (1980) "Haack on Fallibilism." *Analysis*, 40(4) (Oct.): 177–183.
Plantinga, A. (1993) *Warrant and Proper Function*, Oxford: Oxford University Press.
Pryor, J. (2000) "The Skeptic and the Dogmatist," *Noûs* (34)4: 517–549.
Reed, B. (2002) "How to Think About Fallibilism," *Philosophical Studies*, 107: 143–157.
Rysiew, P. (2001) "The Context-Sensitivity of Knowledge Attributions," *Noûs* 35(4): 477–514.
Sextus Empiricus. See Loeb Classical Library, Series No. 291, *Against the Logicians*, and Series no. 273, *Outlines of Pyrrhonism*.
Stanley, J. (2005) "Fallibilism and Concessive Knowledge Attributions," *Analysis* 65(2): 126–131.

Further Reading

Howard-Snyder, D., Howard-Snyder, F., and Feit, N. (2003) "Infallibilism and Gettier's Legacy," *Philosophy and Phenomenological Research*, 66(2): 304–327. (Connects the concept of fallibilism with a historically important aspect of epistemology.)

Kaplan, M. (2006) "If you know, you can't be wrong," in S. Hetherington (ed.), *Epistemology Futures*, Oxford University Press, 180–198. (Shows how disjunctivist theories are irrelevant to the issue and how an historically important kind of thought stemming from Austin might impact reflection on fallibilism.)

Levi, I. (1980) *The Enterprise of Knowledge: An Essay on Knowledge, Creedal Probability and Chance*, Cambridge, MA: MIT Press. (Gives a critique of Peirce and Jeffrey that distinguishes between different types of fallibilism with a focus on the distinction between belief measures and belief dynamics.)

14
EXTERNALISM/ INTERNALISM
Hamid Vahid

The externalism/internalism debate in contemporary epistemology arises out of concerns for a proper explication of the concept of epistemic justification. Internalists maintain that something can confer justification on an agent's belief only if it falls within his or her perspective on the world. Different versions of internalism result from how the notion of perspective is to be understood. Externalism, by contrast, allows, at least, some justifying factors of a belief to be external to the agent's cognitive perspective. The internalism/externalism question in epistemology should not be confused with an identically named dispute in the philosophy of mind where externalist theories of mental content, according to which the contents of an individual's thoughts do not supervene on her intrinsic properties, currently enjoy something like the status of orthodoxy. This has led to an interesting question (which we shall not address here) as to whether content externalism favors any side of the internalism/externalism divide (Goldberg 2007).

The internalism/externalism controversy reflects fundamental intuitions at the heart of our pre-theoretic concept of justification. After identifying the two basic elements in an agent's epistemic situation, the agent's perspective and the objective circumstances, on which the questions of justification turn, I shall try to delineate the contours of internalism, examine its different varieties and review the main objections that have been leveled against it. Following this, a number of putative problems with externalism will be investigated. The distinction between internalism and externalism will then be glossed in the light of responses to the problem of skepticism. I will conclude by examining the possibility of hybrid positions within the debate.

1. Elements of a Theory of Justification and the Internalism/Externalism Divide

Although internalist and externalist accounts of both knowledge and justification have been proposed, it is the concept of justification that has been the main focus of the debate. Epistemic justification is usually thought of as that species of justification that (in conjunction with certain requirements to handle Gettier-type cases) turns a true belief into knowledge. It differs, however, from truth in being defeasible and a matter of degree, and in being a function of an agent's perspective. Accordingly, at an intuitive level, every epistemic situation involving a cognizer forming a belief can be diagnosed with regard to its perspectival and objective dimensions. The perspectival dimension is characterized in terms of the phenomenology of the cognizer's epistemic situation, how things appear from his or her perspective and the epistemically relevant factors available to the agent. "Availability" is an epistemic notion suggesting cognitive accessibility. Equally relevant to the perspectival dimension of justification is how responsibly an agent behaves vis-à-vis the evidence available to her when forming a belief, that is, whether her beliefs are based on the total evidence she possesses.

The objective dimension, on other hand, is construed in terms of how things actually are independently of the cognizer. In evaluating an agent's belief, we want to know if there is, so to speak, a "good fit" between her cognitive powers and the world so that her representations reliably match what they represent. This concern is what underlies our intuition that there is an intimate link between truth and justification (but see Ginet 1975; Pollock 1974). Indeed, it is widely believed that epistemic justification is distinct from other species of justification such as moral or pragmatic justification in that it is intended to serve the so-called "truth goal," that is, the goal of believing truth and avoiding falsity. Commensurate with the two dimensions, justification will be both a function of how things appear from the cognizer's perspective as well as how things in actual fact are. While the internalist view is naturally geared towards the perspectival character of epistemic justification, externalism seeks to highlight its objective dimension. On most internalist views, how things are need not play any role in the justification of one's beliefs.

2. Internalism: Prospects and Problems

Given the preceding remarks, one can characterize internalism in general as claiming that only what is within an agent's perspective can determine the justification of her beliefs. Depending on how the notion of "being within an agent's perspective" is to be understood, the following versions of internalism can be identified.

A) *Mentalism*

The most natural interpretation of the general internalist thesis is, perhaps, one according to which only the *internal* states of an agent at a given time determine whether her beliefs are justified. These internal states are usually identified with the relevant mental states of the agent. Thus, the mentalist claims that one's justification in holding a belief supervenes on one's mental states so that no two people can be in identical mental states while one is, but the other is not, justified in holding a particular belief (Conee and Feldman 2001). An externalist, on this account, is someone who maintains that two people can be in the same present mental states while one has a justified belief and the other does not. Since mentalism remains neutral on the question whether these mental states need be accessible to an agent if they are to confer justification on her beliefs it does not seem to do justice to the intuitions that drive paradigm internalist positions. Consequently, many epistemologists are disinclined to view it as a genuine form of internalism (for another, non-standard, version of internalism see McDowell 1995).

B) Access Internalism

While mentalism puts a metaphysical gloss on the notion of "being within an agent's perspective," it is possible to construe it epistemically and take the general internalist thesis as saying that only those factors to which an agent has some sort of unproblematic access, in the sense of falling within his sphere of awareness, can play the role of justifiers for his beliefs. Thus understood, internalism accords no special status to mental states as such. It so happens that many such states are those to which we have unproblematic access. It is important to note that the "access" of "access internalism" is not just any knowledge or justified belief but should, rather, be analyzed as involving direct or introspective knowledge (or justified belief).

Access internalism comes in different varieties or strengths depending on how one construes the type of access as well its objects. Starting with the former, a strong form of internalism emerges if an agent is required to be actually aware of the conditions that constitute justification. Weaker versions would result from loosening the accessibility condition requiring the cognizer only to be able to access the justifiers of his belief. So, while a strong version of internalism restricts the justifying factors to what an agent already knows or justifiably believes, weaker versions enlarge that to include what the cognizer can come to know on reflection. Different strengths of internalism also emerge if one focuses, not on the kind of access, but on the type of its objects, that is, the accessible items. These objects of awareness can be usefully divided into two distinct groups: (i) the justifying factors, and (ii) their epistemizing features, that is, the features in virtue of which they justify the beliefs in question.

A particularly strong form of access internalism (SAI) results if one requires that, for our beliefs to be justified, we should not only be aware of their justifying factors or grounds but also of their adequacy, that is, of how those factors support the justification of the beliefs in question. This is the version of internalism that most internalists have in mind when they insist that the cognitive accessibility requirement should enable an agent to find out, with regard to any possible belief he holds, whether the belief is justified (e.g., BonJour 1985: 55). Some of these internalists uphold a truth-conducive conception of justification, and, thus, require that one should not only know (justifiably believe) what one's reasons are but also why one's beliefs are probable on one's reasons (Bonjour 1985). Others, however, deny that epistemic justification is truth-conducive (Chisholm 1989: 76; Foley 1987).

Defenders of SAI take their analysis of justification to be in accord with the traditional epistemological quest for good (adequate) reasons for one's beliefs. For what motivated the traditional concern to regard knowledge, as opposed to, say, lucky guessing, as epistemically valuable, was that, in addition to true belief, knowledge requires good reasons or evidence. The issue becomes particularly salient if one takes a first-person point of view and asks oneself whether one's beliefs are justified. Insofar as one's concern is to know whether one's beliefs are more likely to be true, rather than being merely hunches, there does not seem to be any adequate way of figuring this out other than by asking oneself what reasons one has for the beliefs in question and how good they are.

To defend this claim, internalists often appeal to the following sort of scenarios (BonJour 1985). Consider an agent, Norman, who is a reliable clairvoyant and spontaneously and forcefully finds himself with beliefs emanating from this source. He accepts these beliefs without bothering to find out if they are true and possesses no available evidence for or against the reliability of such power or for his possessing it. Now, from an objective point of view, Norman is a reliable register of information about his environment in just the same way that a thermometer reliably registers information about its environmental climate. However, from Norman's perspective his beliefs are no different from mere hunches or arbitrary convictions. They obtain purely as a result of some nomological relation between him and his environment. But why, says the internalist, should the holding of such a relation, entirely outside Norman's ken, render his beliefs epistemically justified? Even though such beliefs are invariably true, from Norman's subjective perspective, it is an accident that they are, which is why it would be irrational and irresponsible for Norman to decide to act on his clairvoyant beliefs. The moral of the story, which is what motivates SAI, is that it would be implausible to expect of reasons that fall outside the cognitive grasp of an agent to confer justification on his pertinent beliefs.

Before proceeding to examine SAI, it is worth considering a once popular argument according to which SAI follows directly from the requirements of a deontological conception of justification (e.g., BonJour 1985). On such an account of justification, to say that a belief is deontologically justified is to say that in holding that belief, the agent has flouted no (subjective) epistemic obligations, and is, thus, subject to no blame or disapproval. But, goes the argument, if it is freedom from blameworthiness that is supposed to constitute the justification of a belief, then this can only be the case if the agent knows or is aware of what his epistemic obligations are. One cannot be rightfully blamed for failing to take into account obligations that fall entirely outside one's ken. This implies that the factors that form the bases of justified beliefs (justifiers) must be internal to the agent in the sense of being reflectively accessible to (knowable by) him.

This line of reasoning is, however, no longer popular. Laurence BonJour himself is now inclined to reject it on the ground that epistemic blameworthiness is neither necessary nor sufficient for epistemic justification. Following William Alston (1988a) he invokes, what he calls, epistemic poverty cases where, despite doing all that can be reasonably expected of agents, they form their beliefs on less than adequate evidence (BonJour and Sosa 2003). However, even setting aside this problem, it is far from clear that the above argument supports the internalist thesis. For all that it entails is that an agent must have *some* way of coming to know what the justifiers of his beliefs are (without specifying any particular mode of knowledge or access). Without further assumptions, it does not follow from this fact that the pertinent evidence for a belief should be reflectively accessible to a cognizer (Goldman 1999).

2.1. *Access Internalism: Problems with Intension*

Thus far, we have been trying to draw the contours of internalism and examine its motivations and rationales. But coming up with a definition is not the same thing as claiming that internalism is a defensible position. Indeed, reasons have been advanced to show that internalism is an untenable position.

A) *A Sellarsian Dilemma*

Let us recall that according to SAI an agent's belief p is justified only if he justifiably believes that (i) the ground (e) of his belief obtains, and that (ii) e adequately supports p. However, as Alston (1986) and others have noted, the second requirement of SAI engenders an infinite regress. For if in order to be justified in believing that p, I must be justified in believing that my evidence e adequately supports p, the justification of this latter (higher-order) belief would, in turn, require that it is based on further evidence e_1 and that I justifiably believe that that e_1 adequately supports my belief that e adequately supports p and so on ad infinitum. The ensuing regress not only involves an infinite number of beliefs, but an infinite number of beliefs of ever-increasing complexity (Fumerton 1995: 89).

In the face of this problem, the only way out, it seems, is to follow Alston (1988b), drop the higher-order requirement and be content with a weak version of internalism that only requires an agent to be aware of the grounds of his beliefs and recognize them as such. But the resulting position is too weak to be regarded as a species of internalism. To avoid both the regress problem for internalism and its collapse into externalism, an internalist should find a different mode of access to the adequacy of his reasons that would allow him to avoid these pitfalls. Consider, as an example, the so-called relation of acquaintance that some internalists have claimed to be distinct from any intentional propositional attitude (Fumerton 1995). The idea is that an agent's belief that p is justified if he is directly acquainted with his belief p, with the fact that p and with the correspondence holding between that belief and that fact. What is claimed to be distinctive about the relation of acquaintance is that one can be acquainted with a fact while lacking the conceptual resources to represent that fact in thought. Accordingly, being non-intentional and non-propositional, this mental act requires no further justification, thus, giving rise to no regress while satisfying the basic internalist requirement by allowing the character of an agent's evidence, in virtue of which his belief is justified, to be cognitively given to him.

Setting aside worries about the viability of the idea of acquaintance itself, the latter part of this claim is questionable. For, as BonJour observes, if we are to think of the direct apprehension of evidence as being non-propositional and non-judgmental, then it would involve "no claim or assertion regarding [the] character [of the cognizer's evidence], so that who thus has such an apprehension is apparently not thereby aware *that* it has such-and-such features, then in what way is his belief *that* he has [evidence] with those features justified by that apprehension?" (BonJour and Sosa 2003: 19). The thought is that this particular relation of direct acquaintance, thus understood, between an agent and the justification-conferring grounds of his beliefs provides no guarantee that the agent conceives of those grounds as being relevant to the justification of the beliefs in question.

The preceding remarks provide a dilemma for an internalist: Either the internalist requirement of access involves conceiving of the justifier of a belief as being relevant to its justification, in which case a vicious regress ensues, or it does not, in which case internalism would lose its motivation for imposing such a constraint as the agent's epistemic situation would be no different from his position on an externalist view. BonJour (BonJour and Sosa 2003) traces the original source of this dilemma to Wilfred Sellars (1963) (cf. Bergmann 2006). Although BonJour himself defends SAI, he does not think that this makes him vulnerable to the regress charge (BonJour 2006). He claims that although in addition to grasping one's belief and its ground, one should also recognize the fit between the two, this recognition is not itself an independent judgment requiring further independent justification. As Bergmann (2006: 35–8) has argued, however, it is unclear whether BonJour succeeds in escaping the regress.

B) Internalist Good Reasons

SAI theorists, as we saw, take the central rationale of their position to involve the idea of an agent having good reasons for thinking that his beliefs are true. For those internalists, such as BonJour, who advocate a truth-conducive conception of epistemic justification, these reasons must be both internal to the individual's first-person perspective as well being objectively truth-conducive. The question is whether internalist reasons can combine these two features. For, recalling BonJour's epistemic poverty cases, it seems that internalists want a sort of epistemic justification that is more objective than deontological justification and epistemic blamelessness. This means that the objective goodness of internalist reasons cannot be analyzed in terms of an agent blamelessly *taking* them to be good or adequate from his own perspective. After all, the agent might be in an epistemic poverty situation and could even be blamelessly unaware of his predicament. It follows from this that what determines the adequacy of an agent's reasons might include factors that fall outside his reflective purview and might, thus, be external to him (BonJour and Sosa 2003: 164). Of course, as pointed out earlier, not all internalists commit themselves to the truth conducivity of epistemic justification. Richard Foley (1987), for example, has propounded an internalist and radically subjective account of justification (rationality) according to which it is egocentrically rational for an agent to believe a proposition only if he would think on deep reflection that believing it is conducive to having an accurate and comprehensive belief system.

2.2. Access Internalism: Problems with Extension

Thus far we have been concerned with the question whether a coherent and internally stable account of the intension of "internalism" can be provided. We shall now focus on the extension of this concept and investigate the scope of internalist knowledge and justified belief.

A) Unsophisticated Epistemic Agents

It is rather uncontroversial that young children and individuals with limited cognitive abilities do have knowledge and justified beliefs about the world and their environments. But, by hypothesis, they lack the resources (and might even lack the necessary concepts) to follow the type of arguments and complicated reasoning that the internalists take to constitute good reasons for the obtaining of such knowledge and beliefs. Internalists often concede that they are unable to account for this fact though they also deny that these individuals have knowledge and justified beliefs in an externalist sense (BonJour and Sosa 2003: 34).

B) Non-reflective Justification and Over-intellectualization

Where the previous objection is concerned with cognitively unsophisticated individuals, it is far from obvious that even ordinary cognizers are in possession of any acceptable internalist justification. Consider, for example, the case of our most basic beliefs about our environment. If any of our perceptual beliefs are to be justified, this will presumably be because they are grounded in our justified beliefs about how things appear to us in perception (and, on some views, grounded in our sensory experiences). On an internalist account of justification, knowing how one is justified in holding such beliefs is tantamount to knowing the mechanism through which facts about the world can be derived from facts about perceptual appearances. This is a deep philosophical problem and there is hardly any consensus among epistemologists regarding its resolution. To expect ordinary cognizers to be in possession of such explanations seems gratuitous (BonJour and Sosa 2003: 34).

The root cause of the problem, I believe, is that the internalist approach in epistemology seems to suggest an over-intellectualized and deliberative picture of our belief-forming activities. We are led to think that, when forming a belief, we are in full control of the choices that we make vis-à-vis our epistemic resources; that, for example, we are free to decide which body of evidence to ignore and what grounds to take as justification-conferring. But many of our beliefs are not formed in such a deliberative manner. Often we find ourselves holding beliefs that are involuntary and unreflective with some of them being justified.

3. Externalism: Some Varieties

Of the two dimensions of epistemic justification mentioned earlier, it is the objective dimension that externalism seeks to highlight. Thus, although externalist views have appeared in many forms, what they all have in common is the denial of the central thesis of internalism, namely, the view that we must be able to reflect on the justification-conferring grounds of our beliefs and their adequacy if they are to be justified. On an externalist account, some (or perhaps all) of the factors contributing to the justification of an agent's beliefs can fall outside his perspective and, thus, be unavailable to him on reflection.

The best way to get a feel for the externalist thesis is to review some of the earlier and later versions of externalist theories. Some of these theories are concerned with the explication of knowledge rather than justification like the causal theory of knowledge. In an early response to the Gettier problem, Alvin Goldman (1967) proposed a causal account of knowledge that did not involve a justification clause, but required rather that there be an appropriate causal relation between an agent's belief and its truth maker. As long as the relation in question in fact obtains, the agent can be said to have knowledge, regardless of whether it is accessible to him on reflection. The causal theory soon fell out of favor, setting the stage for the introduction of a more interesting account of knowledge due to Robert Nozick (1981), which construed knowledge as belief that is counterfactually sensitive to its truth value, that is, tracks its truth. It is quite plausible to see the tracking theory as a direct descendent of the causal theory of knowledge, especially if one adopts a counterfactual analysis of causation.

The paradigm example of an externalist theory, however, is Goldman's (1986) process reliabilism which seeks to provide an externalist account of both knowledge and justification. In its simplest form, process reliabilism is basically the view that justification (knowledge) arises from reliable cognitive processes. Another variant of reliabilism is the so-called reliable indicator theory according to which a belief is justified in case it is based on reasons that are reliable indicators of truth (Alston 1985). Dubbed by Goldman as a "historical" theory, process reliabilism makes the positive epistemic status of a belief a function of its history and of how it has been formed. It is, thus, an externalist theory par excellence as it does not require of a cognizer to know or be aware that his belief-forming processes are reliable. As long as a belief is formed by a reliable process it is justified. A more recent version of externalism (which is actually a variation on the reliability theme) is Alvin Plantinga's proper function theory (1993).

3.1. Problems with Externalism

Each of the preceding theories has been criticized on the basis of its particular features, but I shall concentrate on their externalist character, and, for the sake of concreteness, pick out the simple version of Goldman's reliability theory as a paradigm externalist theory of epistemic justification.

A) Changing the Subject

Externalist theories of justification accommodate our intuitions regarding the objective character of epistemic justification, as justification, on such accounts, is clearly truth-conducive. Goldman (1986), for example, presents his reliability theory in a framework of rules and says that a belief is justified if it is permitted by a right system of justification-rules (J-rules). A system R of J-rules is said to be right if and only if R permits certain (basic) psychological processes whose instantiation would result in a truth-ratio of beliefs that meets some specified high threshold. The internalists, however, are unimpressed, for they think that this leaves out what is philosophically interesting about the concept of justification (as it is traditionally understood). For from a first-person perspective the justification of our beliefs is supposed to provide us with assurance for truth, whereas on an externalist account, all that matters for justification is the satisfaction of certain conditions that might not be accessible to us on reflection. Thus, possessing externalist knowledge (justification) does not seem to be relevant to our understanding of how we know the things we know and providing assurance for our beliefs (Fumerton 1995; Stroud 1989). By denying the accessibility requirement, the externalists have, in effect, changed the subject matter of epistemology.

B) The Internalist Character of "No-Defeater" Requirement

Consider the following version of BonJour's clairvoyant example. Again, Norman is a reliable clairvoyant who has no reason available to him that his clairvoyant beliefs are reliably produced. But suppose he has strong reasons (say, scientific evidence) that such beliefs cannot be reliably produced under the circumstances in question. Norman's beliefs, it seems, are intuitively unjustified despite being reliably produced. To accommodate such cases, reliabilists supplement the reliability requirement by a "no-defeater" condition so that a belief is said to be justified if (i) it is reliably produced, and (ii) the agent is not in possession of any negative reason against the reliability of the relevant cognitive process (Goldman 1986). Externalists are inclined to regard the added qualification as an intuitively obvious and natural reaction to cases typified by the Norman example (Bergmann 2006). Internalists, however, have been quick to highlight the internalist character of such negative no-defeater requirements, thereby denying that the qualified version of reliabilism is purely externalist. They claim that what lies behind the intuitive obviousness of the added clause is actually the internalist intuition that it is epistemically irrational and irresponsible to hold beliefs that are, from an agent's perspective, unlikely to be true. So if the externalists are willing to incorporate a negative internalist requirement into their account of epistemic justification, there is no reason why they should not let the same intuitions motivate positive internalist requirements (BonJour 2006).

C) Demon World Scenarios

A particularly acute problem for externalism concerns the epistemic status of beliefs in the so-called demon scenarios that are primarily intended to highlight the perspectival character of epistemic justification. Consider a possible world that is indistinguishable from the actual world as far as our experiences are concerned, but in which a demon has seen to it that our perceptual beliefs are invariably false. Since the demon world is indistinguishable from the actual world, perceptual beliefs in that world should enjoy as much justification as they do in the actual world. But these beliefs are, by hypothesis, not reliably formed, and are thus, according to the reliability theory, unjustified.

In an early response, referring to his notion of right J-rules, Goldman (1986) suggests that "rightness" is a rigid designator, but it is rigidified as a function of reliability in normal worlds, not reliability in the actual world. Normal worlds are those consistent with our general beliefs about the actual world. So, what matters about belief-producing processes in the demon world is whether they are reliable in normal worlds, which seems to be the case. However, Goldman (1988) goes on to abandon the normal worlds theory because of the problems that came to be associated with the very notion of "normal worlds." Instead, he suggests a modified version of reliabilism by effectively bifurcating the sense of "justification" and recognizing two legitimate conceptions of justification, namely, "weak" and "strong" justification. On the strong conception, a justified belief is a well-formed belief, while, on the weak conception, a justified belief is a blameless, non-culpable though ill-formed belief. Given the above apparatus, one can say that since the beliefs in the demon world are unreliably produced, they are not strongly justified, but, being blameless and non-culpable, they are weakly justified.

Although Goldman rightly seeks to present a theory of justification that incorporates both the elements of truth conducivity as well as the subject's perspective, there are internal problems with his account stemming mostly, I believe, from the fact that he also wants the emerging notions of justification to be opposing ones (Vahid 2005). Setting these problems aside, however, Goldman's attempt to bifurcate justification into strong and weak senses, if not simply an ad-hoc maneuver, is at least a significant retreat from his pure externalist approach to justification. In fact Goldman's wavering attitude in handling the internalist intuitions highlighted by the demon scenarios can only be matched by his volatile attitude towards the deontological theory. In his official statement of the pure reliability theory of justification, he presents it within a deontological framework characterizing "justifiedness . . . as a deontic notion" (Goldman 1986: 25). But in his subsequent attempt to handle the problem of demon scenarios, when distinguishing between weak and strong senses of justification, he regards his weak, rather than strong, justification as a species of deontological justification (Goldman 1988: fn. 3). More recently, he has rejected the deontological conception of justification and described his strategy as simply exploring what an acceptance of this thesis entails (Goldman 1999: 211).

The problems become, if anything, more compounded when, in a more recent analysis of the demon scenarios, he seemingly abandons the strong/weak framework in favor of objective/subjective conceptions of justification (Goldman 2001). A belief, he says, is objectively justified if it results from appropriate processes (e.g., reliable processes).

This seems to correspond with his earlier strong justification. A belief is, on the other hand, subjectively justified if it is produced by, what the agent regards as, appropriate processes. This does not, however, seem to be equivalent to his weak notion of justification. And, indeed, he approvingly refers to Foley's egocentric rationality as "[t]he most systematic development of a subjectivist account of justification" (Goldman 2001: fn. 8). This all looks rather puzzling but, most of all, it highlights the unfeasibility of upholding a purely externalist account of epistemic justification (cf. BonJour and Sosa 2006: 156–70).

4. Internalism, Externalism and the Problem of Skepticism

Both the internalist and externalist responses to skepticism have been taken by their opponents as *reductio ad absurdum* of these positions. The internalist approach is claimed to be implausible because it sets itself such high standards for the possibility of knowledge that they can hardly be satisfied, thus, significantly narrowing the scope of knowledge and justified belief. The externalist response, on the other hand, is regarded as inadequate because, the internalists say, it makes the obtaining of knowledge and justified beliefs too easy (cf. Cohen 2002). A reliabilist, for example, would say that if my beliefs are in fact reliably produced, then I can have knowledge and justified beliefs regardless of whether I know that the pertinent cognitive processes are reliable. To internalists, this attitude looks more like a refusal to meet the skeptical challenge than an adequate response to it. For, if, as in an externalist account, the agent has no reason to think that his beliefs are true or reliable, how could he claim that these beliefs amount to knowledge? He cannot even explain how he knows that he is not in a skeptical situation. Rather, the internalists claim, to possess anti-skeptical potentials, an agent's reasons must be such that he can always tell whether his beliefs are justified or not.

I think the attitudes of both the internalists and the externalists towards skepticism would be best understood against the backdrop of the much older debate between realists and idealists. Our commonsense conception of reality construes it as being wholly independent of our beliefs and thoughts, and thus as leaving a gap between those beliefs and the world. As these beliefs seem to transcend what is given to us in experience, however firmly we hold them and however coherently they stick to one another, there always remains the possibility of a mismatch between them and what they are supposed to represent. This makes it impossible to tell for sure whether our beliefs are true or false, or so the skeptic claims. It is precisely at this juncture that an idealist (phenomenalist) response presents itself as a viable alternative. If what lies at the root of our predicament is the gap between what appears to us in experience and a reality to which we have no independent access, then the easiest way to close the gap is to identify physical objects with the contents of our experiences, or, equivalently, reduce object statements to those about our experiences. Why bother about a reality that is forever beyond our reach? All that can be of (epistemic) significance is that to which we would have immediate cognitive access.

The gap between the contents of our beliefs and the world can be equally construed in terms of justification rather than truth. The idea being that however carefully we may have gone about forming our beliefs in the light of available experience or evidence, our impression of the epistemic status of those beliefs might be totally unlike what they in fact are. For example, despite all the evidence to the contrary, our beliefs might have been formed or grounded in an entirely unreliable way due to the influence of a demon or super-scientist intent on deceiving us. This would deprive us of the ability to determine or to tell, at any time, whether our beliefs are justified or unjustified. One way (perhaps the only way) to block this possibility, and, thus, be able to tell, at any time, whether our beliefs are justified, would be to confine their grounds to those whose presence is detectable by the subject on reflection.

One can thus view the internalism/externalism controversy as resulting from the projection of the motivations behind the realism/idealism debate onto an epistemic plane, where it is now evidence and justifying grounds, rather than physical objects and facts, that become the appropriate objects of cognition and awareness. Just as the phenomenalists were willing to confer the status of an object on something only insofar as it was perceivable, the internalists are led to admit something as a justifying ground insofar as it is reflectively accessible to the cognizer. Just as, on the idealist picture, the inaccessible, external reality drops out as irrelevant, on the internalist account of justification the external and inaccessible grounds become epistemically obsolete.

5. Epistemic Pluralism: Resolving the Controversy?

In order to accommodate counterexamples to their theses, epistemologists of both the internalist and externalist stripes have been forced to propound mixed theories of epistemic justification. This was evident in Goldman's attempt to bifurcate justification and the same holds in the case of Sosa's (1991) theory of virtue perspectivism that is intended to improve on simple or pure reliabilism.

Sosa introduces a number of important distinctions to deal with various problems that his theory is designed to solve. One such distinction is that between "aptness" and "justification." An apt belief is one that is produced by a reliable or virtuous faculty in the environment in which it is operating. A justified belief, on the other hand, is construed in terms of the notion of an "epistemic perspective" which is, in turn, cashed out as consisting of meta-beliefs concerning the faculty (responsible for producing the target belief) and its reliability. According to Sosa, it is in virtue of this epistemic perspective that a body of beliefs is rendered justified (rather than merely apt). This seems to suggest that justification is a matter of having reasons for one's beliefs and an internal concept, and it can plausibly be seen as a way of accommodating internalist concerns. Commensurate with this distinction, Sosa makes another distinction between animal knowledge (which requires only apt belief) and reflective knowledge (requiring both apt and justified belief).

Given pluralistic frameworks like Goldman's and Sosa's, an internalist may have no qualms in regarding, say, unsophisticated epistemic agents as having either knowledge or justified belief or both in, say, an externalist "apt" sense while attributing the internalist reflective knowledge or justification to other agents with more sophisticated cognitive abilities. This is, in fact, the line that BonJour (BonJour and Sosa 2003: 35–41) has been advocating in his recent writings. Whether this pluralistic approach is a genuine way of resolving the internalism/externalism dispute is moot. Nonetheless, the fact that the possibility of epistemic pluralism has been taken seriously speaks to our powerful intuitions regarding the perspectival and objective dimensions of epistemic justification.

References

Alston, W. (1985) "Concepts of Epistemic Justification," repr. in Alston (1989), pp. 81–115.
—— (1986) "Internalism and Externalism in Epistemology," repr. in Alston (1989), pp. 185–226.
—— (1988a) "The Deontological Conception of Epistemic Justification," repr. in Alston (1989), pp. 115–53.
—— (1988b) "An Internalist Externalism," repr. in Alston (1989), pp. 227–45.
—— (1989) *Epistemic Justification*, Ithaca, NY: Cornell University Press.
Bergmann, M. (2006) *Justification without Awareness*, Oxford: Oxford University Press.
BonJour, L. (1985) *The Structure of Empirical Knowledge*, Cambridge, MA: Harvard University Press.
—— (2006) "Replies," *Philosophical Studies* 131: 743–59.
—— and Sosa, E. (2003) *Epistemic Justification*, Malden, MA: Blackwell.
Chisholm, R. (1989) *Theory of Knowledge*, 3rd edition, Englewood Cliffs, NJ: Prentice Hall.
Cohen, S. (2002) "Basic Knowledge and the Problem of Easy Knowledge," *Philosophy and Phenomenological Research* 65: 309–29.
Conee, E. and Feldman, R. (2001) "Internalism Defended," repr. in Kornblith (2001).
Foley, R. (1987) *The Theory of Epistemic Rationality*, Cambridge, MA: Harvard University Press.
Fumerton, R. (1995) *Metaepistemology and Skepticism*, Lanham, MD: Rowman and Littlefield.
Ginet, C. (1975) *Knowledge, Perception, and Memory*, Dordrecht, Holland: D. Reidel.
Goldberg, S. (2007) *Internalism and Externalism in Semantics and Epistemology*, Oxford: Oxford University Press.
Goldman, A. (1967) "A Causal Theory of Knowing," *Journal of Philosophy* 64: 355–72.
—— (1986) *Epistemology and Cognition*, Cambridge, MA: Harvard University Press.
—— (1988) "Strong and Weak Justification," repr. in (1992) *Liaisons*, Cambridge, MA: MIT Press.
—— (1999) "Internalism Exposed," *Journal of Philosophy* 96: 271–93.
—— (2001) "The Unity of Epistemic Virtues," repr. in (2002) *Pathways to Knowledge*, Oxford: Oxford University Press.
Kornblith, H. (ed.) (2001) *Epistemology: Internalism and Externalism*, Oxford: Blackwell.
McDowell, J. (1995) "Knowledge and the Internal," *Philosophy and Phenomenological Research* 55: 877–93.
Nozick, R. (1981) *Philosophical Explanations*, Cambridge, MA: Harvard University Press.
Plantinga, A. (1993) *Warrant and Proper Function*, New York: Oxford University Press.
Pollock, J. (1974) *Knowledge and Justification*, Princeton, NJ: Princeton University Press.
Sellars, W. (1963) "Empiricism and the Philosophy of Mind," in *Science, Perception and Reality*, London: Routledge and Kegan Paul.
Sosa, E. (1991) *Knowledge in Perspective*, Cambridge: Cambridge University Press.
Stroud, B. (1989) "Understanding Human Knowledge in General," in Clay and Lehrer (eds.) *Knowledge and Skepticism*, Boulder, CO: Westview Press.
Vahid, H. (2005) *Epistemic Justification and the Skeptical Challenge*, London: Palgrave Macmillan.

15
DEFEASIBILITY THEORY
Thomas Grundmann

Human reasons, methods and sources of belief-production are fallible. In many cases that is obviously true. Sense experience can be deceptive under adverse circumstances. Inductively supported predictions can fail. But Quine (1953) was the first to argue that this fallibility is a ubiquitous phenomenon. New information about the respective subject matter or about the relevant sources of beliefs facilitates an ongoing error correction. For this reason, the human cognitive system is open for such defeating information and usually adapts to it by revising its beliefs. This can happen by simply withholding a belief or by replacing it with a new belief that is incompatible with the former belief. Defeating information is itself fallible. Hence, there can be misleading defeaters, which might be revised in the light of further information. So, defeaters are themselves, in principle, defeasible. Defeaters have an effect on the epistemic status of a belief. They wholly or partly remove the rationality (i.e. the justification or warrant) that individual beliefs formerly did possess. Defeaters are thus local "removers of rationality." It is neither sufficient nor necessary for defeaters to be psychologically effective (i.e. to bring about a belief revision). A belief can, on the one hand, be given up due to irrational factors (prejudice, affect), without its epistemic status having changed. On the other hand, a belief can lose its epistemic status due to counterevidence even if a subject dogmatically continues to hold on to it. Defeaters determine how beliefs would change if their possessor were fully rational. Thus, they determine how the relevant beliefs *should* change.

What Is the Target of Defeaters?

When the epistemic status of some beliefs is challenged, the target is not the relevant beliefs simpliciter, but either their justification, or what turns a true belief into knowledge (i.e. its warrant). Gettier (1963) made it evident that justification and warrant are not the same. There can be justified true beliefs that are not cases of knowledge because the connection between their justification and their truth is merely accidental. However, many epistemologists assume that warrant contains justification as a component (but see Dretske 1991). If that is correct, it would follow from the defeasibility of justification that warrant is also defeasible.

However, there is also the view that warrant is defeasible in a completely different way (independently of the justification condition), namely by means of factive (also: external, propositional) defeaters (Plantinga 2000; Lackey 2008). This view is motivated by the *defeasibility theory* of knowledge that was designed to solve the Gettier problem (Lehrer and Paxson 1969). Here is a typical Gettier case: Yesterday I saw someone steal a book in the library who looked like Tom Grabit. Now, it really was Tom Grabit. So my respective belief is true and justified by perception. Let us further assume that Tom Grabit has an identical twin who is indistinguishable for me and who was in the library at the same time. In this case, it is very plausible to say that I do not know that Tom Grabit stole the book. The simple defeasibility theory now claims that I would only have knowledge if my justification were not defeated by any additional true pieces of information. This theory can easily explain why I have no knowledge in the Grabit case. If I were to find out that Tom Grabit has an indistinguishable twin brother who was in the library at the same time, I would no longer be justified in believing that Tom Grabit stole the book. From my perspective, my perception would simply leave it open whether it was Tom or his twin brother. But the simple defeasibility theory has a decisive flaw. A variant of the Grabit case can demonstrate this. Assume that everything is as described in the above case, except that Tom Grabit's identical twin does not exist. Moreover Tom Grabit's mother comes up with the tall tale that Tom Grabit has a kleptomaniac twin brother and Tom, himself, was not even in town yesterday. If I were to get the true information that Tom's mother testified this, the justification of my belief that Tom Grabit stole the book would then be defeated. But this potential defeater is misleading and cannot therefore override my actual knowledge. For this reason, advocates of the defeasibility theory have tried to exclude true pieces of information that are misleading defeaters. Only if true pieces of information are available which would be genuine defeaters, knowledge is prevented. Klein (1996) explains the difference as follows: Misleading defeaters are such that they only attain their power to defeat by motivating an inference to a false proposition, for example that Tom Grabit really does have a kleptomaniac twin brother. And it is this false proposition that actually brings about the effective defeat. According to the defeasibility theory, defeasibility by means of false additional information is, however, irrelevant to the presence of knowledge.

Even refined versions of the defeasibility theory pose various problems. To name just one: The conditions they specify are not always sufficient for knowledge. Let us consider a typical lottery case. I believe I have drawn a blank. Suppose that this is true and I am also justified in believing it since the probability of drawing a blank is very high in regular lotteries. Knowing the exact probability, say 0.9999, is not a defeater for my justification, since this probability has a very high value of close to 1. And neither is there another fact on the horizon that—if I knew it—would challenge the justification of my belief. Nevertheless, we would not say that I know I have drawn a blank. A probability of less than 1 simply seems to be insufficient for knowledge.

At the end of the day, the defeasibility theory claims that knowledge is only present if there are no facts that—if they were known—would be genuine defeaters of the relevant justification. Some epistemologists (Plantinga 2000: 359; Lackey 2008) now go one step further and claim that these facts, even when they are unknown, constitute factive, warrant defeaters. They prevent (like the existence of Tom Grabit's twin brother) the occurrence of knowledge that otherwise (without these facts) would have been present. However, it isn't unproblematic to speak of defeaters in such cases. Defeaters are facts that remove or neutralize an epistemic status which actually existed before. This diachronic condition is, however, not satisfied in the case of factive defeaters. They prevent the occurrence of knowledge without removing a previously existing epistemic status. So, there are no factive defeaters. Defeaters directly defeat justification and only indirectly defeat warrant (insofar as warrant includes justification).

How Do Defeaters Work?

The defeat of justification can come about in three different ways (Pollock 1986: 38f.; Bergman 2006: 159, fn. 12): 1. The justification of a belief can be neutralized when there is a *rebutting* defeater against the truth of the previously justified belief. 2. The justification of a belief can also be removed when there is an *undercutting* defeater against the justifying power of the evidence for the belief in question. 3. Finally, the justification of a belief can be overridden when there is a *reason-defeating* defeater against the truth of the reason for the belief. The following example illustrates the difference: You travel through a particular country district and up to now you have only seen animals that you believe to be brown cows. That inductively justifies your belief that the cows belonging to your friend Jim, who lives in this district, are also brown. The justification of your belief can now be defeated in the following three different ways: 1. While you visit Jim at his farm it turns out that he does not possess brown cows, but only black and white ones (rebutting defeater). 2. On your further trips through this district you realize that your observations so far have not been representative. Many farmers in the district also possess black and white cows. For this reason, your observations no longer inductively justify the belief that Jim possesses brown cows (undercutting defeater). 3. You find out that your original perceptual beliefs were false. You haven't seen any brown cows, only cleverly disguised black and white ones. Someone has played a joke on you. What you took for a reason turned out to be false (reason-defeating defeater).

What Is the Nature of Defeaters?

Apart from factive defeaters, which were rejected above as defeaters in the strict sense, it seems plausible that defeaters are mental states (experiences, beliefs), which are themselves justified or entitled and thus have a positive epistemic status, that is, count as *evidence* (Alston 2002). The epistemic status of pieces of evidence and defeaters (understood as counterevidence) should thus be symmetrical. If unjustified beliefs cannot confer justification, then unjustified beliefs cannot remove or override any justification either (this argument is critically discussed by Bergmann 2006: 166). But that seems to be intuitively inadequate. Defeaters do not need to possess any positive epistemic status. There are, to wit, also purely *doxastic defeaters* (Plantinga 2000: Ch. 11; Bergmann 2006: Ch. 6; Lackey 2008: 44f.). On the other hand, there are also successful defeaters that do not even have to be believed, i.e. *normative defeaters* (Goldman 1979; Lackey 2008).

What is a *doxastic defeater*? If S has a belief that q that speaks for his belief that p being false or being based on an unreliable source, then the justification of S's belief p is overridden even if q is in fact false or does not itself have a positive epistemic status (Lackey 2008: 44). Here is an example: John remembers reliably that he was the victim of a violent crime as a small boy. But to calm him down, his parents tell him the false story that he had a very vivid imagination as a child and so just imagined such things. If John believes what his parents tell him, then his belief that he was the victim of a violent crime is thereby automatically defeated and thus no longer justified. This seems to be a fairly intuitive claim.

Normative defeaters must be distinguished from doxastic defeaters. The former can be characterized as follows: If S—in the light of the available evidence—*ought* to acquire a belief that q that suggests that his belief that p is false or is based on an unreliable source, then the justification of his belief that p is overridden (Lackey 2008: 45). A normative defeater is a reason that S has for adopting a belief that speaks against his belief that p. It might involve a psychological reason, but it need not. S's reason might just as well be a fact. Here is an example of the former case: A detective believes that a female suspect whom he likes very much is innocent. Later, he acquires evidence that speaks for her guilt. But the detective ignores this evidence and continues to believe in the suspect's innocence even without having arguments or further evidence to invalidate the incriminating evidence. In this case, the justification of the detective's belief in the innocence of the suspect is defeated by the evidence which he possesses. However, to be available in the relevant sense, it need not necessarily be evidence that is really contained in the cognitive perspective of the epistemic subject. It is presumably sufficient (although the intuitions are not indisputable here) that the subject would have noticed this evidence if his cognitive capacities had been functioning properly (i.e. as they should function rationally). A further example can clarify this issue: Imagine that a head of government is assassinated. His ministers decide to pretend that the bullet killed someone else, in order to avoid a looming revolution. They have the news spread on TV that the attempt failed and that a secret agent was killed by mistake. However, a journalist manages to report accurately to his newspaper the actual events that he has witnessed, and his true story is then published in the newspaper. Jill reads this story in the newspaper and arrives at the true and justified belief that the head of government has been assassinated. However, Jill should have also paid attention to the news on TV. By not taking note of such easily available information, she is ignoring relevant, although in fact misleading, defeaters for her belief. For this reason, she is no longer justified in believing that the head of government has been assassinated (cf. Harman 1973: 143f. who, however, cites the case as an example against knowledge and not against justification). The preceding examples suggest that both unjustified beliefs (as doxastic defeaters) and easily available evidence (normative defeaters) are sufficient, but in each case not necessary, for defeating justification.

No-Defeater Conditions

Conditions for justification are frequently given for prima facie justification only. Hence defeaters are thereby completely disregarded. However, if one has the intention to give necessary conditions that jointly suffice for justification, one must positively exclude defeaters. A belief is epistemically justified if and only if (i) it is adequately produced from an epistemic point of view (here the conditions can vary depending on the respective account of prima facie justification) and (ii) no (undefeated) defeaters are present. If one takes into account that there can be doxastic as well as normative defeaters, the fully explicit definition of justification reads as follows:

> (J) A belief is epistemically justified if and only if (i) it is adequately produced from an epistemic point of view and (ii) neither (undefeated) doxastic nor (undefeated) normative defeaters are present.

However, this definition poses a problem. While doxastic defeaters can be explained simply in terms of the actual beliefs of the epistemic subject, and hence the concept of justification need not occur within the definiens, normative defeaters have to be understood as proper defeaters. At any rate, it is not enough to say that normative defeaters are epistemically adequate mental states, for they could also be external facts. In addition, in all cases the condition must be added that there are no further defeater-defeaters. If, however, justification were to be defined in terms of justified defeaters, then definition (J) would become *circular*. The justification of a belief would then be defined in terms of the concept of justification. This problem can only be avoided, it seems, if the presence of normative defeaters is understood as a malfunctioning of our cognitive capacities. In such cases, our cognitive capacities just did not function as they should. An example: Let us assume that I believe, on the basis of memory, that a certain book has a green cover. However, when I look at the book, it looks blue to me. If, in the face of perceptual evidence to the contrary, I stick to my belief, then its justification is defeated by a normative defeater. Now, this must not be understood to mean that the relevant perceptions have a special epistemic status that applies negatively to my belief. One might rather say that my belief-producing cognitive capacity should adjust my belief to the relevant perceptions. If it does not do that, it is malfunctioning. Plantinga (1993, 2000) was the first to claim that the proper functioning of cognitive capacities is a necessary condition for a positive epistemic status. He believes that normative functions can in general only be explained by a divine design plan. However, there are also naturalistic accounts that explain normative functions reductively in terms of their evolutionary or learning history (Millikan 1993; Grundmann 2009). This teleological approach can now be used to solve the above mentioned problem of the definition circle (cf. in this sense Bergman 2006: Ch. 6). The clause on normative defeaters in (J) can now be replaced by a clause on the proper functioning of our cognitive capacities. We then obtain:

(J*) A belief is epistemically justified if and only if (i) it is adequately produced from an epistemic point of view and (ii) no (undefeated) doxastic defeaters are present and (iii) no malfunctions have occurred in the belief-producing cognitive capacities.

Defeaters and the Controversy between Internalists and Externalists

In epistemology, internalists roughly take the view that truths about justification depend solely on the (introspectively accessible) psychological perspective of the respective epistemic subject. In contrast, externalists take the view that justification also depends on facts outside of the subject's perspective, i.e. on facts in the external world. The most common externalist position is reliabilism. According to this view, a belief is epistemically justified if and only if it has been produced by a reliable process that tends to produce more true than false beliefs. BonJour (1980) has pointed out very early on that an unmodified reliabilism does not accommodate defeaters, and surely there can be defeaters against reliably produced beliefs. For this reason, reliability of belief-production is not sufficient for justification. According to BonJour, every modification of reliabilism that accommodates defeaters by adding further no-defeater conditions is purely ad hoc. It does not, from an externalist point of view, give a systematic explanation of why these conditions should be added. In his view, the existence of defeaters therefore decides the controversy in favor of internalism.

Why are internalism and defeaters such a good match? The examples discussed above clearly indicate that defeaters do not have to be reliably produced, but can depend on nothing more than the subjective perspective. It will suffice for the justification of my belief *m* being defeated if I have other beliefs or experiences that speak against the truth or against the reliable production of my belief *m*. The internalist can easily explain why that is so. In her view, the justification of a belief solely depends on the fact that her subjective perspective speaks in favor of the truth of the belief and, respectively, that her belief is internally rational. If her perspective is changed by the occurrence of defeaters in such a way that this perspective no longer speaks for the truth of the belief, then the belief is no longer justified from the internalist point of view.

However, the externalist can also explain the role of defeaters, for example when she advocates what is known as *evidential reliabilism* (Bergman 2006: 165; Hofmann 2009). According to this view, a belief is justified if and only if (i) it is generated by a reliable belief-producing mechanism and (ii) the perspective of the epistemic subject (her total evidence) speaks for the truth of this belief. Evidential reliabilism thus combines externalist and internalist aspects. As soon as the epistemic subject acquires defeaters, condition (ii) is violated and the belief thereby loses its justification. However, evidential reliabilism raises a problem that similarly applies to the internalist approach. If there are external facts that have the status of normative defeaters (as the existence of TV reports in Harman's example), then such external defeaters simply cannot be explained on this account. According to evidential reliabilism there is only one source of defeaters, namely an internal lack of rationality.

However, externalist proper-function theories can solve even this problem. According to such theories (Plantinga 2000; Bergman 2006), a belief *m* is justified if and only if it is produced by cognitive capacities which (i) function properly, (ii) aim at truth and (iii) are reliable in the environment for which they are either designed or selected. On these accounts, the belief *should* be sensitive to internal defeaters (if there are beliefs or experiences that speak against the truth or reliability of the belief in question) as well as external defeaters (if facts are available that speak against the truth or the reliability of the belief in question). If the cognitive system does not satisfy this condition, then it is no longer functioning properly and thus the relevant belief loses its justification.

Defeater-Defeaters

Defeaters are themselves never ultima facie justified, but always defeasible by further defeaters (defeater-defeaters). Therefore, misleading defeaters can at best be neutralized, but at worst it is also possible that genuine error corrections in turn will be revised. The former case can be illustrated by a further development of the example of Tom Grabit and his mother. My true and justified belief that Tom Grabit stole a book from the library is defeated by his mother's false testimony. However, this misleading defeater could in turn be neutralized by the additional information that Tom Grabit's mother is a notorious liar. I would then have an undercutting defeater for my first-order defeater. Here is an example for the latter possibility: Harry took part in the Allied invasion of Normandy and remembers that he was there in October 1944 when a certain village on the western front was captured by the Allies. For this reason he justifiably believes that he captured this village in October 1944. In fact, Harry is wrong. The village was not captured until November. When Harry learns from a military book that the village was not captured until November, his false belief is corrected by means of a rebutting defeater. Later on, Harry reads in a journal that the author of the book is incompetent and notorious for faking historical facts. Thus, his first-order defeater is neutralized by a second-order undercutting defeater, although the truth about the seizure of the village is actually in the book.

It is an interesting question with respect to defeater-defeaters whether the original justification of a belief can be regained through a successful defeat of a defeater (see Jäger 2005). In order to discuss this question, let us focus on an example from religious epistemology. Philosophers such as Alston and Plantinga assume that religious experience can provide us with basic justification (i.e. a justification that does not depend on other beliefs) of theistic beliefs about God's existence. In an enlightened society such as ours this justification is challenged by a variety of defeaters, e.g. by arguments from natural evil which is supposed to be incompatible with the existence of an omniscient, omnipotent and benevolent God (rebutting defeater), or by projection theories that explain religious beliefs as products of unreliable psychological projections (undercutting defeater). Now, if these defeaters against the justification of theistic beliefs were themselves successfully defeated, then the theistic beliefs would become once again justified. But would their regained justification depend on the epistemic status of the relevant defeater-defeaters? Or could the theistic beliefs once again count as basically justified after going through a process of criticism and criticism of that criticism? The correct answer seems to be the following: It depends on which kinds of defeaters and defeater-defeaters do the relevant epistemic work. More specifically, one must distinguish between two types of cases:

First case: If the basic justification of theistic beliefs is defeated by an argument from the natural evil, and if this challenge against the assumption of God's existence is in turn defeated by a positive proof of God's existence, then the theistic belief is, in the end, no longer basic, but justified by this very proof. More generally: If a rebutting defeater is neutralized by another rebutting defeater, the justification of the original belief now positively depends on the rebutting defeater-defeater.

Second case: As in the first case, the justification of the theistic belief is defeated by a rebutting defeater (an argument from the natural evil). But this time it is shown that the existence of natural evil is not sufficient evidence against the existence of God after all (undercutting defeater). In this case the defeater-defeater neutralizes the defeater of the theistic belief without speaking positively for the truth of this belief. Here, although the defeater-defeater facilitates the restoration of the theistic belief and is thereby causally enabling, the positive justification solely relies on the supposed original religious experience. It is only this religious experience that would speak for the truth of the theistic belief. So, it is perfectly possible that the source of the original basic justification becomes effective again after the relevant defeater-defeaters have done their work (pace Jäger 2005).

The Significance of Indefeasible Justification

In the philosophical tradition (especially before Quine 1953), it was a widely held view that certain types of beliefs are absolutely indefeasibly justified. Above all, beliefs about one's own current feelings ("Right now I have a feeling of type φ"), beliefs about simple mathematical facts ("3 + 2 = 5"), and beliefs about logical facts ("All Fs are F") were taken to have this privileged epistemic status. But on closer scrutiny this view turns out to be an untenable dogma. To begin with, indefeasibility and infallibility are not the same thing. Infallible reasons are such that beliefs on which they are based cannot be false. Now, even if there were infallible reasons, they would in principle still be defeasible by misleading defeaters. Conversely, infallibility does not follow from indefeasibility. For example, if we were permanently deceived by an evil demon or a mad neuroscientist then our beliefs would all be radically flawed and fallible. But the situation of deception would be so ingeniously constructed that we would never acquire defeaters to correct our false beliefs. Examples such as the following show that even beliefs about one's own current feelings might be revised in the light of further information: In some American student fraternities there are isolated cases of rather martial practices. They include, for example, the custom of branding the Greek initials of the fraternity on newcomers' backsides with a branding iron. Such a newcomer expects this kind of procedure, pulls his trousers down and sees the glowing iron. But in fact, without him being able to see what is going on, the student is only patted with an ice-cold metal rod. Afterwards, he reports that he felt a terrible heat for a few seconds. In this case, his expectation has changed his belief about his own feeling. Such an error can easily be corrected in the light of further introspective and testimonial information. In the case of mathematical judgments, calculation errors can never be ruled out despite the utmost care. As soon as we notice them, we tend to correct our previous mathematical beliefs. Even in the case of logical facts our judgment is defeasible, as the following example shows (cf. Williamson 2007: 85–7): The statement "All bachelors are bachelors" has the logical form of "All Fs are F" and thus counts as logically true. But this judgment is defeasible by considerations of the following kind: Somebody could (mistakenly) believe that sentences of the type "All Fs are F" imply the existence claim "There is at least one F." If, at the same time, she (mistakenly) believes that there are no bachelors, then she would have a doxastic defeater for her belief that "All bachelors are bachelors."

Even if the absolute indefeasibility of beliefs cannot be sustained on any account, one could still plead for a somewhat weaker indefeasibility claim, namely that beliefs resting on certain sources cannot be defeated by information resting on a different source. In this case, these sources of justification would be *negatively autonomous* (Audi 2002). So one could hold the view that, for instance, introspective beliefs are only defeasible by further introspective beliefs or testimonial reports of introspective beliefs, but not by empirical information from a purely third-person perspective. Or one could hold the view that a priori beliefs are only defeasible by other a priori beliefs, but not by empirical information (Kitcher 2000). But even these weaker indefeasibility claims seem to be false. James believes that he has a slight headache. However, he has hypochondriac tendencies and often falsely believes that he has minor ailments when he actually has none. Let us further assume that a computer tomography of James' relevant brain areas does not show the brain activity that is typical for pain. In this case, the doctor has a defeater from the third-person perspective for Jim's introspective belief that he has a slight headache. Empirical defeaters are also conceivable in the case of a priori calculations. Let us assume that you have calculated that $3 + 2 = 5$. Just for the fun of it, you want to check the result empirically, so you put two things and then three things together and then count them. Let us assume that the result is always "six," no matter how often you repeat the counting. Let us also assume that no one else arrives at a different result and that there are no discernible sources of error in play. Then, at the latest, the justification of your mathematical calculation would have been empirically defeated (Casullo 2003: 94f.).

Do any serious philosophical consequences arise out of the unlimited defeasibility of all beliefs? On the one hand, it has been claimed over and over again by certain philosophers that indefeasibility is constitutive of some sources of justification as, e.g. introspection or a priori justification. On the other hand, classic foundationalists typically assumed that basic beliefs are characterized by their indefeasibility. Yet both claims seem to be false. Introspective and a priori justification are not distinguished by their strength, but only by the peculiarity of their source (Casullo 2003). Moreover, foundationalist theories of justification are entirely compatible with the defeasibility of all beliefs since foundationalism only claims that there are positively justified beliefs that do not depend for their justification on any other beliefs. But this does not imply that the independent justification must be indefeasible in the light of further information. Theories that combine basic justification with the defeasibility of this justification are thus referred to as *moderate foundationalism*.

Dialectical Defeaters

An isolated thinker acquires defeaters for the justification of her belief if this belief no longer rationally fits into her cognitive perspective, or if she does not sufficiently take into account available external evidence and in this respect does not behave cognitively as she should. However, defeaters also play a central role in the debates about controversial claims between different thinkers. In this case, dialectic defeaters constitute objections and counterobjections that one antagonist presents to the other. How does this dialectic role of defeaters fit in with what has been said so far? When the opponent in such a debate presents an objection to the proponent's claim, this objection can affect the epistemic status of the proponent's claim in three different ways. Either the proponent accepts the objection by believing it. Then the dialectic objection is transformed into a doxastic defeater. Or the proponent simply ignores the objection. Then the proponent is behaving like a dogmatist who blinds himself to objections, and the objection becomes a normative defeater. Or the proponent rejects the objection on the basis of further considerations. In this case she is trying to neutralize the defeater with a defeater-defeater.

The Default and Challenge Model of Justification

Certain epistemic contextualists (Sellars 1956; Brandom 1995; Williams 2001: 36, 150f.) emphasize the epistemic primacy of social and dialectic responsibilities. For them, a belief is epistemically justified *by default* as long as there are no undefeated normative dialectic defeaters (constituted by motivated challenges). The absence of certain dialectic defeaters would then already be sufficient for the justification. Thus, the epistemic subject must only adduce positive reasons for his belief when substantiated defeaters have been introduced into the debate. According to this view, positive reasons would then only be needed as defeater-defeaters. The Default and Challenge model of justification has the indubitable advantage of avoiding unrealistic constraints on justification. So, every claim does not first have to be defended by further reasons (which can quickly lead to a regress), and nor does the mere consideration of error possibilities (naked challenge) suffice to generate a genuine defeater. Therefore, real defeaters are only present when something makes the objections likely to be true. In other words, normative defeaters are required for the relevant dialectic challenges.

But the Default and Challenge model operates with conditions that are obviously too weak for the status of positive justification. It does not follow from the fact that a belief is incontestable in certain social contexts (i.e. not challenged by anyone for good reasons) that these beliefs are actually justified. Otherwise, an unlimited form of relativism would threaten. For example, racist beliefs would then be justified in the context of the race biology of Nazi Germany. And in the context of astrology, the belief that the constellation of the stars influences our lives would also be justified. However, in other contexts these same beliefs would clearly not be justified. Williams circumvents this objection by adding a further (externalist) condition on the justification of a belief: it must also be based on an objectively reliable source. But even this quite substantial modification of the model does not yet suffice to establish adequate conditions for justified belief. That is to say, even when all normative defeaters are rejected for good reasons, a belief can still lose its justification when the subject has other (unjustified) beliefs that are incompatible with the truth or the reliability of the belief in question. In other words, there can still be doxastic defeaters. For this reason, a theory of justification that crucially focuses on the social practice of asking for and giving of reasons is not fully adequate.

References

Alston, W. 2002: Plantinga, Naturalism, and Defeat, J. Beilby (ed.), *Naturalism Defeated?*, Ithaca/London, pp. 176–203.
Audi, R. 2002: The Sources of Knowledge, P. Moser (ed.), *The Oxford Handbook of Epistemology*, Oxford, pp. 71–94.
Bergman, M. 2006: *Justification without Awareness*, Oxford.
BonJour, L. 1980: Externalist Theories of Empirical Knowledge, *Midwest Studies in Philosophy* 5, pp. 53–73.
Brandom, R. 1995: Knowledge and the Social Articulation of the Space of Reasons, *Philosophy and Phenomenological Research* 55, pp. 895–908.
Casullo, A. 2003: *A Priori Justification*, Oxford.
Dretske, F. 1991: Two Conceptions of Knowledge, *Grazer Philosophische Studien* 40, pp. 15–30.
Gettier, E. 1963: Is Justified True Belief Knowledge?, *Analysis* 26, pp. 144–6.
Goldman, A. 1979: What is Justified Belief?, G. Pappas (ed.), *Justification and Knowledge*, Dordrecht, pp. 1–23.
Grundmann, T. 2009: Reliabilism and the Problem of Defeaters, *Grazer Philosophische Studien* 79, pp. 65–76.
Harman, G. 1973: *Thought*, Princeton.
Hofmann, F. 2009: Introspective Self-Knowledge of Experience and Evidence, *Erkenntnis* 71, pp. 19–34.
Jäger, C. 2005: Warrant, Defeaters, and the Epistemic Basis of Religious Belief, M. Parker and T. Schmidt (eds.), *Science and Religion*, Tübingen.
Kitcher, P. 2000: A Priori Knowledge Revisited, P. Boghossian and C. Peacocke (eds.), *New Essays on the A Priori*, Oxford, pp. 65–92.
Klein, P. 1996: Warrant, Proper Function, Reliabilism, and Defeasibility, Jonathan Kvanvig (ed.), *Warrant in Contemporary Epistemology*, Lanham, pp. 97–130.
Lackey, J. 2008: *Learning from Words. Testimony as a Source of Knowledge*, Oxford.
Lehrer, K. & Paxson, T. 1969: Knowledge: Undefeated Justified True Belief, *Journal of Philosophy* 66, pp. 225–37.
Millikan, R.G. 1993: In Defense of Proper Functions, Millikan: *White Queen Psychology and Other Essays for Alice*, Cambridge, Mass., pp. 13–29.
Plantinga, A. 1993: *Warrant and Proper Function*, Oxford.
Plantinga, A. 2000: *Warranted Christian Belief*, Oxford.
Pollock, J.L. 1986: *Contemporary Theories of Knowledge*, London.
Quine, W.V. 1953: Two Dogmas of Empiricism, Quine, *From a Logical Point of View*, Cambridge, Mass., pp. 20–46.

Sellars, W. 1956: Empiricism and the Philosophy of Mind, H. Feigl and M. Scriven (eds.), *Minnesota Studies in the Philosophy of Science* 1, Minneapolis.
Williams, M. 2001: *Problems of Knowledge*, Oxford.
Williamson, T. 2007: *The Philosophy of Philosophy*, Oxford.

Further Reading

Bergman, M. 2006: *Justification without Awareness*, Oxford, Ch. 6, pp. 153–77 (Very comprehensive presentation and defense of doxastic defeaters.)

Lackey, J. 2008: *Learning from Words. Testimony as a Source of Knowledge*, Oxford, pp. 44–7, 251–77 (Very good on the demarcation of factive, doxastic and normative defeaters as well as on the role of defeaters in the generation of knowledge.)

Plantinga, A. 2000: *Warranted Christian Belief*, Oxford, ch. 11, pp. 357–73 (Defeaters from the viewpoint of proper function epistemology.)

16
EVIDENTIALISM
Daniel M. Mittag

Evidentialism holds that one's evidence entirely determines what one is epistemically justified in believing. Advocates include John Locke, David Hume, W. K. Clifford, and Bertrand Russell, among others. Though evidentialism has therefore been historically prominent, much of the recent interest in evidentialism stems from the challenges posed to it by newer, competing theories of epistemic justification, such as reliabilism. Roughly, reliabilism understands epistemic justification to be determined not by one's evidence but, rather, by the reliability of the cognitive process used to generate the belief. (See *Reliabilism*, Chapter 17 of this volume.) Given both its bearing on such competing theories and its initial pretheoretical plausibility, evidentialism deserves close consideration.

Two leading contemporary advocates of evidentialism are Richard Feldman and Earl Conee. In their classic article "Evidentialism" they formulate evidentialism as a thesis concerning the justification of all of the doxastic attitudes. One is justified in taking a doxastic attitude towards some proposition at time t just in case it "fits" the total evidence one has at t (Feldman and Conee 1985: 15). Whether one is epistemically justified in believing p, epistemically justified in disbelieving p, or epistemically justified in suspending judgment with respect to p is entirely a matter of the evidence one has at the time of evaluation.

It will help to simplify the discussion if we restrict Feldman and Conee's explicit thesis to the justification of belief. Doing so gives us the following central evidentialist thesis.

> A person S is epistemically justified in believing proposition p at time t if and only if believing p fits the total evidence S has at t.

Most treatments of evidentialism have focused on this narrower evidentialist commitment. Since what we say concerning it can be extended naturally to all of the doxastic attitudes, nothing will be lost by taking it as our focus here.

Evidentialism invokes three key notions: what *evidence* is, what it is for one to *have* something as evidence, and what it is for believing a proposition to *fit* the evidence one has. A complete evidentialist theory will provide philosophically satisfactory accounts of each. By attending to them, one can formulate various, widely divergent versions of evidentialism. Moreover, in the absence of an account, it is unclear what implications evidentialism has concerning cases. It is therefore crucial for the evidentialist to provide at least partial analyses of its constituent notions.

Motivating Evidentialism

When we think about what it takes for one to believe reasonably or justifiably, we think that one has to have good reasons (or, more accurately, adequate reason for thinking the proposition in question is true). In addition, when one does have excellent reason to think p is true, we think that one is in a position to believe p justifiably. In short, reasons seem to be absolutely central to epistemic justification. This provides some initial, pretheoretical support for evidentialism since having evidence for p just is having reason to think p is true.

Of course this initial support can only take a theory so far. Ultimately, the theory needs to correctly explain individual cases and to withstand criticism. Conee and Feldman argue that evidentialism succeeds on both counts, citing the extent to which it succeeds as one of the main strengths of evidentialism (2004: 64).

Jonathan Adler (2002) presents a more ambitious argument for a version of evidentialism. He argues that the requirement to believe only what one's evidence supports is derived from the very concept of belief. Roughly, Adler argues that one cannot "in full awareness" believe *p and I do not have adequate evidence for p* (pp. 31–32). One must at least take oneself to have adequate evidence for believing p if one is "fully aware" of one's belief that p. Furthermore, one must believe p if, "in full awareness," one takes oneself to have adequate evidence for p. Adler argues that these restrictions are not due to mere psychological limitations. The necessity here is conceptual. According to him, this shows "that in first-person awareness we recognize the demands of belief" (p. 52). So, the very concept of belief demands that one ought to believe p only if one has adequate evidence for p. (See Conee (2002) for critical discussion of this argument.)

Developing Evidentialism

A Preliminary Distinction

Note that believing p can fit your evidence even if you have never considered p and thus do not believe it. Evidentialism implies that you would be justified in believing p. As this makes clear, evidentialism is not a theory about when *one's believing* is justified; it is a theory about what makes one *justified in believing* a proposition. As it is sometimes put, evidentialism is a thesis regarding *propositional justification*, not a thesis regarding *doxastic justification*. In order to be doxastically justified in believing p, believing p needs to fit one's evidence, and one needs to believe p on the basis of that justifying evidence.

The following consideration illustrates that we need this distinction. Just as believing p might fit your evidence even though you do not believe p, you might believe the proposition your evidence supports, but you might believe it for bad reasons. You might believe it as a result of wishful thinking, for example. Here something is going wrong, and something is going right. You are believing in accordance with your evidence (p is propositionally justified for you), but you are believing for the wrong reasons (your belief that p is not doxastically justified).

Evidence

Ordinarily, we would take DNA left at the scene of a crime or fingerprints on a murder weapon to be evidence. We count these things as evidence because we take them to be relevant to the question of who committed the crime. However, the evidentialist thesis does not pertain to these sorts of external states of affairs. The relevant sort of evidence the thesis invokes is restricted to mental states or to propositions. (See *Evidence*, Chapter 6 of this volume, and Kelly 2006.) What sorts of mental states qualify as evidential states capable of conferring justification (or which propositions count as evidence one has) varies from account to account.

On the traditional coherentist view, only beliefs can justify. Accordingly, one possible view restricts evidence to beliefs (or the propositional contents of beliefs). Traditional coherence theories, however, seem unable to account for the role experience plays in justification (BonJour 1999: 124–130; Plantinga 1993: 82; Sosa 1991: 184–186). We take one's experiences to provide one with reason to believe certain propositions. It is reasonable, after all, to think my present experience that is just like the experience of seeing a cat provides evidence for the current presence of a cat (perhaps only when combined with certain background information). Similarly, one might think an apparent memory derives some degree of justification from its accompanying phenomenology—i.e., its "seeming to be true." If so, the accompanying phenomenology is evidence for the truth of that apparent memory. Similar reasoning can lead one to classify other mental states as evidence.

Timothy Williamson (2000) rejects the foregoing conceptions of evidence. He argues instead for the radical thesis that one's evidence consists of all and only the propositions one knows. (See *Knowledge First Epistemology*, Chapter 20 of this volume.) Since considering the details of his careful arguments here would take us too far astray, see Brueckner (2005) and Hawthorne (2005) for discussion.

Having Evidence

Recall that the basic evidentialist thesis states that one is epistemically justified in believing p at t if and only if believing p fits the total evidence one has at t. This obviously entails that only *one's own* evidence is relevant to determining what one is justified in believing. And we have seen from the previous section that only mental states or propositions count as evidence. Setting aside for ease of exposition in this section the view that evidence consists of propositions (e.g., the propositional contents of mental states rather than the mental states themselves), these two restrictions suggest one available interpretation of having evidence. On this option the evidence one has at t includes all and only one's (evidential) mental states at t. Both one's occurrent (evidential) mental states and one's nonoccurrent (evidential) mental states will count as evidence one has on this account.

This understanding of having evidence is clearly inadequate, however. To see this, consider the following example. Joe loves diners and visits them frequently. He prefers to eat nowhere else. Over the years he has come to have overwhelming evidence that most diners serve eggs. It seems his belief is well justified. Yet when Joe was a child he visited a diner named Tillman's Diner that did not serve eggs. (The chef and owner was vehemently against them.) He had tried to order eggs, only to be rudely directed to the sign on the wall stating 'NO EGGS.' This upset Joe, and the incident now lies deeply buried in his long-term memory. Though it is retrievable, it would take a prolonged, directed process (e.g., psychotherapy) for him to recall it. If a fellow diner fanatic were now casually to mention Tillman's Diner to Joe and ask him whether it serves eggs, Joe might form the belief that Tillman's Diner *does* serve eggs on the basis of his well-justified belief that most diners serve eggs.

It seems Joe's occurrent belief that Tillman's Diner serves eggs would be eminently reasonable. Yet the present account cannot deliver the result that his belief is justified. This is because his stored memory of the incident defeats his evidence for the belief, and the proposal counts that stored memory belief as evidence he has.

An alternative account holds that only one's *occurrent* mental states count as evidence one has. This nicely entails that Joe's deeply hidden memory is irrelevant to the justification of his belief that Tillman's Diner serves eggs. Yet the restriction to occurrent mental states seems to be too restrictive. After all, it entails that when Joe is not in a diner or entertaining any occurrent beliefs about diners, his (nonoccurrent) belief that most diners serve eggs is not justified. He would have no occurrent mental states that bear on the issue. If it is right that many nonoccurrent beliefs are well justified, then it seems any plausible account of having evidence must include some nonoccurrent mental states. Further, it seems that when I consciously entertain the belief that George Washington was the first President of the United States, that (occurrent) belief is justified, and its justification does not depend on my consciously recalling any supporting evidence at all. If this is right, the present account of having evidence must be rejected. (See Feldman (1988), however, for a defense of the restriction to occurrent mental states.)

It is clear that the correct account of having evidence must lie somewhere between these two extremes. We want to count some, but not all, nonoccurrent mental states as evidence one has. For example, one might propose that the evidence one has includes just one's occurrent mental states and those nonoccurrent mental states that are easily available to one upon reflection. It is unclear whether one can specify what is "easily" available in a plausible and principled way, and other proposals along these lines likely face similar difficulties. However, since 'easily available' is vague, it is worth emphasizing that mere vagueness in the account is not reason to reject it. 'Justification' itself is vague; so we should expect vagueness in its analysis.

Feldman (1988) argues the serious difficulty facing this conception of having evidence is that the way in which one is prompted to recall an event affects how easily it is able to be recalled. He is careful to distinguish this objection from objections concerning vagueness, and he provides the following example to illustrate the difficulty.

> If I ask my childhood friend if he remembers the time we spray-painted my neighbor's dog, I may get an embarrassed 'Yes.' If I ask him if he remembers any of our childhood pranks, this one may fail to come to mind. Is the fact that we spray-painted the dog easily accessible? There seems to be no clear answer.
>
> (Feldman 1988: 94)

At the time Feldman took this to be sufficient reason to look elsewhere for an account of having evidence. But, again, it looks like the options at either extreme are unsatisfactory; so it looks like the evidentialist somehow has to address the kinds of difficulties more moderate conceptions of having evidence face.

More recently, Conee and Feldman (2008: 88–89) have argued in favor of some moderate view that includes certain nonoccurrent mental states as evidence one has. They acknowledge the difficulty involved in providing a detailed account of having evidence along these lines but argue that it does not provide reason to reject evidentialism. They state that it only "makes clear a way in which some familiar terms of epistemic evaluation are vague or obscure" (89). As alluded to above, this is a promising position to take. Nevertheless, a more complete analysis of having evidence is desirable.

Evidential Support

Evidentialism is consistent with any theory of the structure of justification. So, for example, it is amenable to foundationalist, coherentist, and infinitist treatments. Here I set the disputes between these theories concerning the structure of justification aside in order to focus on a related issue concerning evidential support which all evidentialist theories face. This is the issue of what relation a proposition must bear to one's evidence in order for that proposition to be justified by that evidence.

An evidentialist has available a variety of options for understanding this relation of evidential support. One available view holds that believing a proposition fits one's evidence just in case that proposition is made objectively likely by that evidence. On this view, if one's evidence entails (or makes highly probable) that some proposition is true, then one is justified in believing that proposition. However, this implies that one is justified in believing all of the logical consequences of one's justified beliefs, even extremely complex propositions one cannot understand. This seems wrong. Moreover, some logical connections between propositions are too complex for one to grasp—those requiring a complex mathematical proof, for example. So while one might understand the proposition entailed by one's evidence, one might have no idea how or why one's evidence entails it. Again, this seems to imply one is not justified in believing the proposition in question on the basis of one's evidence. (Goldman (1986: 89–93) and Boghossian (2003: 226–227) develop objections of this latter sort.)

These problems with a purely logical conception of evidential support motivate the inclusion of some subjective requirement. It is instructive to consider one flawed account that includes such a requirement. One might propose that believing p fits one's evidence, e, just in case p is made objectively likely by e and one believes this is so. The problem concerns the requirement that one believe e makes probable p. The condition is at once both too weak and too strong. The condition is too weak because one may believe (truly) that e makes probable p for bad reasons. This shows that in order to confer justification the belief about one's evidence would at least need to be justified, but this threatens a regress. Furthermore, if one believes for bad reasons that e makes probable p, one might not be appreciating the fact that e makes probable p, and this is the sort of thing the doxastic condition was supposed to capture.

The condition that one believes e makes probable p is too strong because it seems to over-intellectualize justification. Small children lack the concept of probability and thus are unable to form the belief. Yet it seems reasonable to think they do have many justified beliefs. More generally, nonreflective individuals can have many justified perceptual beliefs even though they do not form beliefs about their experiences making probable those beliefs about the world. Some may not have any beliefs even approximating this content. For these reasons, one need not believe e makes probable p in order for believing p to fit e.

These difficulties with the above account of evidential support illustrate the challenges facing an account that retains the objective probabilistic requirement while imposing some additional subjective condition. If this kind of account is to succeed, it needs to relativize to the individual which propositions made probable by a body of evidence one is justified in believing, and it needs to do so without over-intellectualizing justification or requiring some additional mental state itself in need of justification. One might, then, require that one be *reflectively able* to grasp or appreciate the fact that one's evidence makes probable the proposition. However, even if we understand this making probable relation broadly so as not to require one to possess the concept of probability, it is unclear whether this alternative will avoid all of the problems developed for the earlier account. In particular, it is unclear whether it will deliver the result that small children have many justified beliefs. Suffice it to say, developing a precise account of support that blends objective and subjective considerations is difficult.

Conee and Feldman (2008: 94–98) argue for a different, but related approach. They affirm the view that a proposition is supported by one's evidence when it is part of the "best available explanation" of that evidence (98). Thus, for them evidential support is fundamentally a relation of best explanation, and the qualification that the explanation be available to one might help to relativize to the individual which propositions are part of the best explanation of a body of evidence. We have seen that this is desirable. An analysis of the relevant sense of availability has yet to be provided.

Objections

One Ought Not to Follow One's Evidence

Sometimes we ought not to believe what our evidence supports. For example, a mentally fragile individual might have overwhelming evidence for the proposition that his lover has been cheating on him. But if he were to follow his evidence and believe this, he would murder his lover before killing himself. Clearly, he ought not to believe his spouse is cheating on him. He has overriding practical and moral considerations not to follow his evidence.

These sorts of cases do not conflict with evidentialism, as defined above. Evidentialism is not a thesis about what is in one's interest to believe or what one has a moral duty to believe, even though W. K. Clifford's evidentialism does have this moral dimension (Clifford 1879). Neither is evidentialism a thesis about what one ought to believe, all things considered. Evidentialism is merely a thesis about what one *epistemically* ought to believe. This example only illustrates how sometimes epistemic, practical, and moral considerations conflict (Feldman and Conee 1985: 22–23). The evidentialist appraisal of the case holds that he *epistemically* ought to believe his lover is cheating on him, not that he ought to believe this, all things considered.

Nishi Shah (2006) provides independent support for the view that the evidentialist has the correct position on this case. He argues on the basis of the transparency of belief that only evidence for the truth of p can be a reason for believing p. If this is right, then the practical and moral considerations, even if known, cannot be reasons for the subject not to believe his lover is cheating on him. Non-evidential considerations cannot be reasons for belief. (For a reply, see Steglich-Petersen (2008).)

An Evidence-Gathering Requirement

Evidentialism is a synchronic theory of epistemic justification. It claims epistemic justification concerns what one should *now* believe, given one's *present* evidence. However, some argue that the justification of a belief depends, at least in part, on the inquiry that led to the belief. Even if one now has justifying evidence for p, if one should have discovered (and could have very easily discovered) evidence that defeats one's present justification for p, one ought not to believe p.

Evidentialists can allow that there is a sense in which this is true, but they have to deny that this 'ought' is an epistemic ought (or, perhaps, is the central epistemic ought to which epistemic justification is attuned). Feldman, for example, understands the "central" epistemological question to concern what one should believe in the interim, until one inquires further (2004: 188). He allows that there are other questions about when one ought to gather more evidence and, more generally, how one ought to go about evidence-gathering, but these further questions are decided by prudential or moral considerations rather than by epistemic considerations (2004: 189). They should be carefully distinguished from questions regarding epistemic justification (Feldman 2003: 48). (However, see DeRose (2000) for critical discussion.)

Forgotten Evidence

A further objection stems from the widespread occurrence of one's forgetting the evidence that one once had for some proposition. The objection is best appreciated by considering two sorts of cases. According to the first, when one originally came to believe p one had good evidence for it, but one has since forgotten that supporting evidence. One might think one can nevertheless continue to believe justifiably, even without coming to possess any additional evidence. Evidentialism appears unable to account for this.

According to the second sort of case, when one originally came to believe p one did not have supporting evidence for p. One came to believe p for very bad reasons. At the time one formed the belief, therefore, it was neither propositionally nor doxastically justified. Yet suppose that one has since forgotten all of the evidence against p and also why one originally formed the belief. Since it doesn't seem as though in the interim one *has* to have gained some additional evidence *for* p, one might think that the subject of the second case remains unjustified in believing p. The evidentialist might agree. But notice that the relevant beliefs in both cases appear to be on an evidential par; neither belief seems to be supported by adequate evidence. The objection is that a justificatory difference between the two cases nevertheless exists, and evidentialism is unable to account for this difference.

The details of the cases proposed along these lines are crucial. For example, we tend to have beliefs about the reliability of our memory beliefs, and, we think, reasonably so. If the subject has good reason to think her memory beliefs (of the relevant kind) are generally reliable, then she is justified in so believing. And if she believes that her memory beliefs (of the relevant kind) are generally reliable, she has evidence for p after all. In the absence of special reason to think the memory belief is mistaken, the memory belief will be justified. If, on the other hand, the subject lacks any beliefs about the reliability of her memory beliefs (or does not have supporting evidence to believe that they are reliable), the stored memory belief could well be unjustified. If one genuinely has no evidence for p, it is hard to see why one *would* be justified in believing p, contrary to the objector's claim regarding the first case.

If we restrict the discussion to retrieved memory beliefs that one comes to occurrently believe, evidentialists can handle the cases in a different way. One might think the phenomenology that often accompanies the retrieval of a memory belief is itself some evidence for its truth. In short, they *seem* to one to be true, and this can provide some degree of justification. If the phenomenology is present in both cases above (while the subject does not have outweighing evidence against p), she is justified in believing p, after all. Importantly, however, she is only justified in believing p to the degree provided by that accompanying phenomenology. Whether this is enough to provide a complete explanation of particular cases will, again, depend on the details of those cases. Evidentialism at least has the resources to provide reasonable appraisals.

Conclusion

The fundamental idea that justification depends in some way on evidence or reasons is intuitively plausible and withstands objections. The hybrid theories recently proposed by Juan Comesaña (forthcoming) and Alvin Goldman (forthcoming) reflect this. Both theories blend elements of reliabilism and evidentialism, theories usually thought to be in conflict. What is important to emphasize about these theories here is that they both require that a belief fit one's evidence in order to be justified, even if they depart from the strict evidentialist thesis that has been the subject of this chapter.

Of course, hybrids are motivated by claiming faults with pure versions of a view. This highlights the project facing evidentialists. Given that evidentialism is a broad thesis that can be developed in many ways, the task is to develop a specific, detailed interpretation of the central evidentialist thesis that retains its initial plausibility and withstands objections.

References

Adler, J. (2002) *Belief's Own Ethics*, Cambridge, MA: MIT Press.
Boghossian, P. (2003) "Blind reasoning," *Proceedings of the Aristotelian Society, Supplementary Volume*, 77: 225–248.
BonJour, L. (1999) "The dialectic of foundationalism and coherentism," in J. Greco and E. Sosa (eds.) *The Blackwell Guide to Epistemology*, Malden, MA: Blackwell.
Brueckner, A. (2005) "Knowledge, evidence, and skepticism according to Williamson," *Philosophy and Phenomenological Research*, 70: 436–442.
Clifford, W. K. (1879) "The ethics of belief," in L. Stephen and F. Pollack (eds.) *Lectures and Essays*, Vol. II, London: Macmillan and Co.
Comesaña, J. (forthcoming) "Evidentialist reliabilism," *Noûs*.
Conee, E. (2002) "Review of Jonathan Adler, *Belief's Own Ethics*," *Notre Dame Philosophical Reviews*. Online. Available HTTP: <http://ndpr.nd.edu/review.cfm?id=1083> (accessed September 30, 2009).
—— and Feldman, R. (2004) *Evidentialism: Essays in Epistemology*, Oxford: Oxford University Press.
—— and —— (2008) "Evidence," in Q. Smith (ed.) *Epistemology: New Essays*, Oxford: Oxford University Press.
DeRose, K. (2000) "Ought we to follow our evidence?," *Philosophy and Phenomenological Research*, 60: 697–706.
Feldman, R. (1988) "Having evidence," in D. Austin (ed.) *Philosophical Analysis*, Dordrecht: Kluwer Academic Publishers.
—— (2003) *Epistemology*, Upper Saddle River, NJ: Prentice Hall.
—— (2004) "The ethics of belief," in E. Conee and R. Feldman *Evidentialism: Essays in Epistemology*, Oxford: Oxford University Press.
—— and Conee, E. (1985) "Evidentialism," *Philosophical Studies*, 48: 15–34.
Goldman, A. (1986) *Epistemology and Cognition*, Cambridge, MA: Harvard University Press.
—— (forthcoming) "Toward a synthesis of reliabilism and evidentialism? Or: evidentialism's troubles, reliabilism's rescue package," in T. Dougherty (ed.) *Evidentialism and Its Discontents*, Oxford: Oxford University Press.
Hawthorne, J. (2005) "Knowledge and evidence," *Philosophy and Phenomenological Research*, 70: 452–457.
Kelly, T. (2006) "Evidence," in E. Zalta (ed.) *The Stanford Encyclopedia of Philosophy*. Online. Available HTTP: <http://plato.stanford.edu/entries/evidence/> (accessed September 30, 2009).

Plantinga, A. (1993) *Warrant: The Current Debate*, New York: Oxford University Press.
Shah, N. (2006) "A new argument for evidentialism," *The Philosophical Quarterly*, 56: 481–498.
Sosa, E. (1991) *Knowledge in Perspective*, New York: Cambridge University Press.
Steglich-Petersen, A. (2008) "Does doxastic transparency support evidentialism?," *Dialectica*, 62: 541–547.
Williamson, T. (2000) *Knowledge and Its Limits*, Oxford: Oxford University Press.

17
RELIABILISM
Juan Comesaña

1. Introduction

The reliabilist theory of epistemic justification is one of the most influential theories in recent epistemology. In this chapter I present reliabilism, starting with its origins as a theory of knowledge and considering the main problems that it faces, together with some of the main solutions to those problems that have been proposed in the literature.

2. A Brief History of Reliabilism

In a short note that didn't attract much attention until *after* reliabilist theories were explicitly defended in the 1970s, Ramsey (1931) wrote:

> I have always said that a belief was knowledge if it was (i) true, (ii) certain, (iii) obtained by a reliable process.

We can recognize here perhaps a version of the justified true belief account of knowledge, except that Ramsey talks about the reliability of the process that produced the belief rather than about justification (although it may be that Ramsey is combining the belief and justification conditions in his (ii), and thus appealing to reliability *in addition* to appealing to justification). The next big moment in our brief history involves Edmund Gettier. After Gettier published his counterexamples to the justified true belief account of knowledge (Gettier 1963) many philosophers embarked in a search for a fourth condition which, added to the traditional three, was to be sufficient for knowledge. The history of that search is well-known (see Shope 1983). But other philosophers took a different tack: instead of looking for a fourth condition to *add* to the justification condition, they examined the possibility of *replacing* the justification condition. What is missing in subjects in Gettier-style situations, these philosophers thought, is some connection between the belief and the facts that make the belief true. If that connection is present, moreover, then the subject has knowledge, regardless of whether or not his belief is "justified" as that notion is traditionally understood. Thus, Armstrong (1973) proposed a theory according to which a non-inferential belief amounts to knowledge just in case it has some properties that are nomically connected to its truth. In a similar vein, Goldman (1967) proposed a causal theory of knowledge, according to which (very roughly) a belief constitutes knowledge just in case the fact that p is causally connected (in the right way) with the belief that p. An interesting variant of these theories construes the relation in question not directly as a physical relation, but rather as a certain kind of modal correlation between the belief and the facts. For instance, Dretske (1971) anticipated Nozick (1981) in proposing that a crucial condition for a subject S to know that p is that, if p were true, S wouldn't believe that p. Other proposals along these lines include Sosa (1999) and Williamson (2000) (for critical examination of these proposals, see Comesaña 2007).

As said above, what all these proposals have in common is that they jettison the justification condition in favor of a condition that requires that there be some kind of relation between belief and reality. Reliabilism as a theory of epistemic justification is born when that *replacement* thesis is abandoned in favor of an *explanation* thesis—when reliability is seen as what justification *consists in*, as opposed to a condition that is independent of justification.

3. An Initial Formulation of Reliabilism About Justification

That change takes place in the seminal work on reliabilism as a theory of justification: Goldman (1979). In that work, Goldman proposes a recursive definition of justification along the following lines:

S is justified in believing that p at t if and only if:

(i) S's belief that p at t results from a belief-independent cognitive belief-forming process that is unconditionally reliable; or
(ii) S's belief that p at t results from a belief-dependent cognitive belief-forming process that is conditionally reliable and all the input-beliefs are justified.

To understand the definition we need to explain what Goldman means by a cognitive belief-forming process (simply "process" in what follows), what the distinction between belief-dependent and belief-independent processes amounts to, and what it is for a process to be conditionally and unconditionally reliable.

A process is a psychological mechanism that produces beliefs under certain conditions. A process can be represented by a *function* whose outputs are the propositions produced by the mechanism and whose inputs are the conditions under which the mechanism operates (we can, without fear of generating confusion, talk about the inputs and outputs of the processes themselves). Belief-dependent processes will include among its inputs other beliefs of the agent, whereas belief-independent processes will not. A process is unconditionally reliable if and only if it issues in mostly true beliefs, whereas a belief-dependent process is conditionally reliable if and only if it issues in mostly true beliefs if the input beliefs are true.

4. Problems and Refinements

4.1. Justification Without Reliability? The New Evil Demon Problem

Consider the Cartesian skeptical scenario according to which there is a powerful evil demon who is deceiving me with respect to most of the propositions that I believe. According to the traditional description of this skeptical scenario, what the demon does is to arrange things so that the world appears to me to be exactly the same way that it would appear to me if all of my beliefs about the world were true, when they are in fact false. Thus, in the skeptical scenario I am not typing on a computer, but my total experience is still the same as it is right now, and so on and so forth for most of my other beliefs.

Philosophers disagree regarding whether the possibility of skeptical scenarios like these can form the basis for any powerful skeptical argument. But skepticism is not our concern right now. Consider not *our* epistemic predicament, but that of a victim of a skeptical scenario. Regardless of what we think about ourselves, such a victim of course lacks knowledge (if only because most of his beliefs are false, but not only because of that). But ask yourself not whether the victim has knowledge, but whether he has *justified beliefs*. The answer will depend, of course, on the particular epistemic nature of the victim in question. But if the victim is undergoing an experience just like mine right now and, on the basis of that experience, believes that he is typing on a computer, then surely at least that belief of him will be justified. In general, if the victim is a responsible epistemic agent (that is, if he doesn't commit fallacies, takes experience at face value, etc.), then his beliefs will be just as justified as those of his non-victimized counterpart. This is not to say, of course, that there cannot be victims that are unjustified, but it is to say that the mere fact that they are the victims of a skeptical scenario doesn't guarantee that they are unjustified.

So victims of a skeptical scenario may very well have justified beliefs. But those beliefs are, for the most part, false. It seems to follow that the processes that formed those beliefs were not reliable—they certainly didn't tend to produce mostly true beliefs. If those processes are unreliable, then reliabilism has the consequence that those victims can never have justified beliefs, irrespective of the details of how they came to form those beliefs. This is what Sosa called the "new evil demon" problem. It's *new* because the problem is not Descartes' skeptical argument, but rather the apparent consequence of reliabilism that no victim of skeptical scenarios can ever be justified.

The new evil demon problem has been associated with Cohen (1984), and it has been repeatedly wielded as perhaps the main symptom of everything that's wrong with reliabilism—see, for instance, Pollock (1984), Feldman (1995), and Foley (1985). For friends of reliabilism, the new evil demon problem has proven to be an important reason to modify their theory. Goldman himself, for instance, has reacted to the problem in no less than three different ways (to be considered below).

Sosa (1991) makes an important point in discussing the new evil demon problem. Victims of an evil demon live in worlds where the processes that we use to form our beliefs seem to be unreliable, and they have justified beliefs despite using *those very same processes*. But there might well be creatures who inhabit worlds where the only way to acquire information about the environment is to use processes that would be unreliable if used here (one could argue that the evil demon world is precisely one of those worlds). For instance, there are worlds where when things look round they are square. In those worlds, believing that there is a round thing in front of you whenever something appears round tends to produce false beliefs, while believing that there is a square thing in front of you when it appears round tends to produce true beliefs. Some philosophers (including Sosa (1991) and Bergmann (2006)) think that subjects in those worlds whose beliefs are produced by processes like the latter do have justified beliefs. Some solutions to the new evil demon problem do not have this consequence. Let us now review some of those solutions.

Goldman (1979) actually considered a benevolent-demon world example which is similar in some respects to the kind of cases that Sosa urged us to consider alongside the new evil demon problem. The benevolent demon arranges things so that wishful thinking is reliable. What are we to say, then, of a subject who engages in wishful thinking in the benevolent demon world? Goldman was ambivalent. One possibility that he considered was that the wishful thinker was not justified, because the reliability of the process in question should be evaluated, not with respect to the world of the wishful thinker but, rather, with respect to the actual world. Given that wishful thinking is not actually reliable, the beliefs of the wishful thinker are not justified even if they are produced by processes that are reliable in his world. (Goldman considered that idea not as a theory of justification, but as a theory of justification-attributions. I ignore the complications that this difference raises.) Now, bracketing for the moment any concerns about the consequences that this theory has for the wishful thinker and similar cases, notice that it has the right consequence for the new evil demon problem. For the processes used by those victims of the evil demon that have justified beliefs are actually reliable (or, at least, the objection does not rely on their not being so), and so a theory according to which a belief is justified provided that it was produced by processes that are actually reliable will not succumb to the new evil demon problem.

But let us now go back to the wishful thinker and cases similar to his. Because of obfuscating connotations of wishful thinking, let us concentrate instead on the case of inhabitants of a world where, due to fundamental physical and physiological differences, things that appear round are square (and, maybe, vice-versa). Inhabitants of this world are wired-up so that they believe that there is a square whenever something appears round to them. This appearance–belief transition is, for them, as basic as the usual transition is for us, and nothing in their other experiences or collective inquiries ever gives them (what would of course be misleading) reasons to think that there is anything wrong with proceeding in this way. Let us also suppose that proceeding like this is the only way for them to know about real squares—if they instantiated instead our usual appearance to belief transitions, then nothing in their other experiences or collective inquiries will ever give them a clue that they are making a fundamental mistake. What are we to say about such creatures? If we insist that justification is proportional to the reliability of the process that produces the belief in the actual world, then we are bound to say that their beliefs are unjustified—but, as mentioned before, many epistemologists believe that there is at least some sense in which they are justified. Call this the "alien cognizers" problem for reliabilism (the name comes from Bergmann (2006)). If, on the other hand, we say that justification is proportional to the reliability of the process that produces the belief in whichever world that belief is held, then we are bound to say that the beliefs of any victim of an evil demon are unjustified. The new evil demon problem and the alien cognizers problem pull reliabilism in opposite directions. We'll come back to this issue.

Goldman (1986) proposes a different solution to the new evil demon problem: the "normal worlds" approach (in that book Goldman also reconsiders and rejects the actual world proposal). According to this proposal, the reliability of a process should be evaluated with respect to *neither* the actual world *nor* the world where the belief is held but, rather, with respect to *normal worlds*, which are worlds that are, in their general features, the way we take the actual world to be. This proposal solves the new evil demon problem insofar as we take the actual world to be one where the processes used by justified victims are reliable. But it does nothing to alleviate the doubts of friends of the alien cognizers problem. And it also has more serious problems. It seems to offer a radically subjectivist account of justification, for the justificatory status of beliefs is, in effect, determined by our general beliefs about the world.

Goldman (1988) proposed to solve the new evil demon problem by positing an ambiguity in "justified." In one sense of the word (the "strong" sense), justification answers to the original reliabilist definition in Goldman (1979), but in another, weak sense, a belief is justified just in case it is non-culpably held. The beliefs of victims of an evil demon can never be strongly justified, but they might well be weakly justified. As Sosa (1991) points out, however, this solution doesn't distinguish between justified victims of an evil demon and those who have been brainwashed into holding preposterous beliefs. None of them are culpable in holding their beliefs, but justified victims of an evil demon are more than non-culpable: there is something epistemically positive about how they formed their beliefs, not merely the lack of something epistemically negative.

Elsewhere (Comesaña (2002), building on work by Sosa—Sosa (1993) and Sosa (2001)), I advanced a proposal that aims at taking care of both the new evil demon problem and the alien cognizers problem. Let us first note that, according to many, "actual" is a term whose proper semantics is two-dimensional—thus, to put it in terminology that comes from Chalmers (1996), associated with the term "actual" there is a two-dimensional intension which can be thought of as a function from possible worlds to functions from possible worlds to truth-values. Associated with any utterance of "It is actually true that p" there is a primary intension, which determines a proposition that is true at a world w just in case p obtains in w, and a secondary intension, which determines a proposition which is true in a world w just in case p obtains in the world of utterance. So, for instance, the primary intension of "It is actually the case that Mount Everest is the mountain with the highest altitude in the world" determines a necessarily true proposition, but its secondary intension determines a contingently true proposition. According to my proposal, the reliability of a process should indeed be evaluated in the actual world, as the position that Goldman (1979) considered suggests, but bearing in mind that "actual" must be given a two-dimensional semantics. Thus, there is a sense in which victims of an evil demon can be justified, although it is also true that, on this view, there is a sense in which they can never be (this captures the sense in which victims of an evil demon cannot have knowledge even if their justified beliefs are true). This view also takes care of the alien cognizers problem, insofar as it has the consequence that there is a sense in which they can be justified (their beliefs may be arrived at by processes which are reliable in their world, and, thus, they can have knowledge), even though it is also true that there is a sense in which they are not justified (the sense in which victims of an evil demon and ourselves are). These two senses associated with "justification," however, are not independent of each other (like Goldman's weak and strong notions of justification), but, rather, are related to each other in the same way in which, following Kaplan (1989), we can say that the character of an indexical is related to its content.

4.2. Reliability Without Justification?

The new evil demon problem challenges the necessity of reliability for justification. An equally influential problem challenges the sufficiency of reliability for justification. The *locus classicus* for that challenge is BonJour (1980). In that paper, BonJour presents a number of cases involving subjects whose beliefs are formed by processes which, although actually unreliable, are stipulated to be reliable in the subject's world (so far, this is just like the case of the alien cognizers, but we'll see that there is a crucial difference). In some cases, the subjects in question have reason to believe that the processes that produce their beliefs are unreliable. BonJour's most famous case, however, concerns a subject that is not like that. Here is BonJour's description of the case:

> Norman, under certain conditions that usually obtain, is a completely reliable clairvoyant with respect to certain kinds of subject matter. He possesses no evidence or reasons of any kind for or against the general possibility of such a cognitive power, or for or against the thesis that he possess it. One day Norman comes to believe that the President is in New York City, though he has no evidence either for or against this belief. In fact, the belief is true and results from clairvoyant power, under circumstances in which it is completely reliable.

Goldman (1979) had already considered the problems raised by subjects who have reasons to believe that the processes that produced their beliefs are unjustified, and proposed to add a clause to the reliabilist definition of justification to take care of those problems. The proposed clause adds as a necessary condition for a subject being justified in believing that p that there be no reliable process available to the subject such that, if the subject were to use that process (in addition to the ones actually used), then he would no longer believe that p. In Goldman (1986) the analogous condition is added that the subject should not have a reason to think that his belief is unreliably caused.

The addition of a negative clause might help with the cases where the subjects have reasons to believe that the target belief was unreliably caused. But BonJour's idea is that the case of Norman is not like this, for Norman does not have any reason to believe that his belief was unreliably caused. Indeed, BonJour explicitly says that Norman has no evidence one way or the other regarding the reliability of clairvoyance, or even whether he is clairvoyant. Now, this claim by BonJour could well be challenged: after all, Norman suddenly finds himself believing that the President is in New York City, with no clue as to where the belief came from. Presumably, there are reasons to doubt that beliefs whose provenance is completely obscure to us were caused by reliable processes.

So it's not entirely clear that Goldman's original negative clause cannot take care of Norman's case as well. But there is still reason to think that some other modification to reliabilism is needed. For, even if the fact (if it is indeed a fact) that Norman has reasons to believe that his belief about the President was not produced by a reliable process is *one* of the things that is epistemically wrong with Norman, it could well be that there is more than one thing that is epistemically wrong with Norman. Indeed, it is arguably the fact that the clairvoyantly produced beliefs *just pop into Norman's head* that makes them unjustified (this is the crucial difference with the case of the alien cognizers). Elsewhere (Comesaña forthcoming) I have argued that the way to take care of BonJour's objection to reliabilism (and to externalist theories more generally) is to combine reliabilism with evidentialism. Evidentialism, as defended by Earl Conee and Richard Feldman (see, for instance, Conee and Feldman 2004), is the thesis that adopting a doxastic attitude (for instance, belief) with respect to a proposition is justified for a subject at a time if and only if adopting that attitude fits the evidence that that subject has at that time. If evidentialism is left at that, however, it is a radically incomplete theory, for we would naturally want to know what makes it the case that adopting a certain attitude towards a proposition *fits* a certain body of evidence. I suggest that we should adopt a reliabilist understanding of this notion of fit. The resulting theory looks like this:

S is justified in believing that p at t if and only if p was produced by a process R which includes some evidence e and:

(i) e doesn't include any beliefs of S and R is unconditionally reliable; or
(ii) e includes beliefs of S, all of these beliefs are justified, and R is conditionally reliable.

This version of reliabilism has the consequence that Norman's beliefs are not justified, because they are produced by processes that don't include any evidence. If what is motivating the idea that Norman is not justified is the fact that the clairvoyant beliefs *just pop into his head* (and not just that Norman has reasons to believe that his clairvoyantly acquired beliefs are not justified), then this version of reliabilism takes care of that problem.

4.3. What is Reliability? The Generality Problem

Only *types* of processes can straightforwardly be said to have a meaningful reliability ratio associated with them. *Token* processes issue in only one belief. If the belief is true, then that token process is perfectly reliable, whereas if it is false, the token process is perfectly *un*reliable. A process-type, by contrast, can be more or less reliable depending on the ratio of true to false beliefs that all the tokens of that type produce (this assumes that we are taking a truth-ratio approach to reliability, as is standardly done in the literature, but see section 4.4 for a problem for this approach, as well as for a suggested solution). When reliabilists say that the justificatory status of a belief depends, ultimately, on the reliability of the processes that led to that belief, therefore, they must mean to refer to process-types. But *any token-process belongs to indefinitely many types of processes, each one of which may have a different reliability ratio*. For instance, the process that created my belief that I am facing a computer screen belongs to all of these types: visual process, visual process while I am not using glasses, visual process while I am not using or needing glasses, perceptual process, process that issues in a true belief, process that occurs in Wisconsin, etc. The reliability problem for the reliabilist is best understood as a challenge: the challenge of finding a principled way of selecting, for each token-process of belief formation, the type whose reliability ratio must be high enough in order for the belief to be justified. Goldman (1979) was aware of the problem, and it has been forcefully pushed by Conee and Feldman (1998).

Many different solutions have been proposed for the generality problem, which has proven to be resilient. Heller (1995) proposed a contextualist "dissolution" of the problem according to which reliabilists should resist trying to come up with a principled way of singling out one of the indefinitely many types as the one that has to be evaluated for reliability, for the context of attribution of justification takes care of that. Among the proposals that tackle the problem head on (as opposed to denying that there is one), one of the most influential ones has been that of Alston (1995). According to Alston, the type of process whose reliability determines whether the target belief is justified or not is the type describing the function that is actually operative in the formation of the belief. Thus, if the psychological process that created the belief is insensitive to the exact geographical location where the process takes place, then the reliability of the type that mentions that kind of information is irrelevant to the justificatory status of the belief. The main question that this proposal raises is whether it singles out a unique process-type or whether, as Conee and Feldman (1998) argue, it still leaves us with a multitude of types of differing reliability.

As I said, many other solutions have been proposed, but most of them share with Alston's the characteristic of leaving it open that the strictures that they put in place fail to single out a unique process-type. I have argued (see Comesaña 2006) that *any* plausible epistemological theory will face an analog of the generality problem. Therefore, either the problem is worse than we thought (because it shows not only that reliabilism is an inappropriate epistemological theory but, more generally, that there are no appropriate epistemological theories) or there is a solution to the generality problem. In either case, there is no *special* problem for reliabilism.

Consider a theory that is usually presented as an internalist alternative to reliabilism: evidentialism. As Conee and Feldman (1985) present this theory, a subject S is justified in adopting doxastic attitude D towards proposition p at time t if and only if adopting D towards p fits the evidence that S has at t. Now, given this definition of justification, it could well happen that a subject has a justified true belief, is not in a Gettier-type situation and yet still fails to have knowledge—because, despite the fact that the evidence that he has justifies believing the proposition in question, he doesn't believe it on the basis of that evidence but rather, say, out of wishful thinking. Conee and Feldman recognize this, and add a definition of well-foundedness to their definition of justification:

S's doxastic attitude D towards p at t is well-founded if and only if:

1. having D toward p is justified for S at t; and
2. S has D toward p *on the basis of* some body of evidence e, such that
    (a) S has evidence e at t; and
    (b) having D towards p fits e; and
    (c) there is no more inclusive body of evidence e' had by S at t such that having D toward p does not fit e'.

Now, once we recognize the necessity of relying on something like the notion of basing one's belief on some evidence (as is done in the evidentialist definition of well-foundedness) we can appeal to that very notion in solving the generality problem for reliabilism. Thus, incorporating the modifications made in sections 4.1 and 4.3, I propose the following as a reliabilist definition of justification that is able to deal with the generality problem (I called the resulting position "Evidentialist reliabilism"):

Evidentialist reliabilism: A belief that p by S is justified if and only if:

1. S has evidence e;
2. the belief that p by S is based on e; and either
    (a) e doesn't include any beliefs of the subject and the type *producing a belief that p based on evidence e is actually reliable*; or
    (b) e includes other beliefs of S, all of those beliefs are justified and the type *producing a belief that p based on evidence e is actually conditionally reliable*.

Evidentialist reliabilism solves the generality problem insofar as it provides a process-type whose reliability determines the justification of the belief produced by the token of that type that produced the belief in question. It remains to be seen, of course, whether the resulting theory is adequate in other respects, but objectors cannot now complain that no single type has been selected in a non-principled way.

4.4. What is Reliability? The Lottery Problem

Somewhat surprisingly, an issue that has not received much attention in the literature on reliabilism is the question of what it means, exactly, for a process to be reliable. Insofar as this question is taken up, a truth-ratio answer is generally given. More precisely, the following seems to be the characterization of reliability that most reliabilists take for granted:

> A type T is reliable if and only if most of the actual and close counterfactual tokens of T produce true beliefs.

However, if that is what it takes for a type to be reliable, then there is a range of cases that would constitute counterexamples to reliabilism (Adler (2005) is dedicated to this problem, and it was raised also in Cohen (1988)). Suppose that both Smith and Jones have bought one ticket each in a large fair lottery. The day the result is announced, Smith believes that his ticket lost based solely on the basis that it is one ticket in, say, a million. Jones, on the other hand, believes that his ticket lost based on reading about the result in the newspaper. If we are going by the above definition of reliability, then the relevant type associated with Smith's belief is more reliable than the relevant type associated with Jones' belief (newspapers print typos more often than once in a million cases). It is not part of the official characterizations of reliabilism that we have offered so far that the higher the reliability of the relevant type the higher the justification of the belief, but this is a natural way for a reliabilist to deal with the fact that justification comes in degrees. But the problem is that we judge Jones to be the one that is better justified than Smith, not the other way around (indeed, some philosophers go as far as believing that Smith cannot know that his ticket lost based on the evidence on which he believes it).

If we adopt the modifications to reliabilism offered in the previous section, there is a different but natural way of explaining what it means for a type to be reliable, in terms of conditional probability (Alston (1998) proposed to understand reliability in terms of conditional probability, and Comesaña (2009) develops this idea):

> A type of the form *believing that p based on e* is reliable if and only if the conditional probability of p given e is sufficiently high.

Let s be the proposition that Smith's ticket is a loser, j the proposition that Jones' ticket is a loser, m the proposition that Smith's ticket is one in a million in a fair lottery, and n the proposition that the newspaper announced that a ticket other than Jones' won the lottery. It is easy to verify that (given plausible assumptions about the newspaper's error rate) the conditional probability of j given n is *higher* than the conditional probability of s given m, which gives us the comparative result that we were looking for.

Conceiving of the relevant type as always including some evidence and of reliability as defined in terms of conditional probability also allows us to bypass the distinction between unconditional and conditional reliability that Goldman relied on in order to capture the difference between derived and basic beliefs. The reliabilist definition of justification that we arrive at is therefore the following:

S is justified in believing that *p* if and only if:

1. S has evidence *e*;
2. S bases his belief that *p* on *e*; and
3. the actual conditional reliability of *p* given *e* is high enough.

5. Conclusion

In this chapter we have presented a reliabilist theory of epistemic justification. We have also seen that such a theory is subject to some serious problems. But reliabilism is a resourceful theory, and plausible answers can be given to the most pressing problems.

References

Adler, J. (2005), "Reliabilist Justification (or Knowledge) as a Good Truth-Ratio," *Pacific Philosophical Quarterly* 86(4), pp. 445–458.
Alston, W. (1988), "An Internalist Externalism," *Synthese* 74, pp. 265–283.
Alston, W. (1995), "How to Think about Reliability," *Philosophical Topics* 23, pp. 1–29.
Armstrong, D. (1973), *Belief, Truth and Knowledge*, Cambridge University Press.
Bergmann, M. (2006), *Justification without Awareness*, Oxford University Press.
BonJour, L. (1980), "Externalist Theories of Empirical Knowledge," *Midwest Studies in Philosophy* V, pp. 53–73.
Chalmers, D. (1996), *The Conscious Mind*, Oxford University Press.
Cohen, S. (1984), "Justification and Truth," *Philosophical Studies* 46, pp. 279–295.
Cohen, S. (1988), "How to Be a Fallibilist," *Philosophical Perspectives* (2), pp. 91–123.
Comesaña, J. (2002), "The Diagonal and the Demon," *Philosophical Studies* 110, pp. 249–266.
Comesaña, J. (2006), "A Well-Founded Solution to the Generality Problem," *Philosophical Studies* 129, pp. 127–147.
Comesaña, J. (2007), "Knowledge and Subjunctive Conditionals," *Philosophy Compass* 2(6), pp. 781–791.
Comesaña, J. (2009), "What Lottery Problem for Reliabilism?" *Pacific Philosophical Quarterly* 90(1), pp. 1–20.
Comesaña, J. (forthcoming), "Evidentialist Reliabilism," *Noûs*.
Conee, E. and Feldman, R. (1985), "Evidentialism," *Philosophical Studies* 48, reprinted with an "Afterword" in Conee and Feldman (2004), pp. 83–107.
Conee, E. and Feldman, R. (1998), "The Generality Problem for Reliabilism," *Philosophical Studies* (89), pp. 1–29.
Conee, E. and Feldman, R. (2004), *Evidentialism*, Oxford University Press, New York.
Dretske, F. (1971), "Conclusive Reasons," *Australasian Journal of Philosophy* 49, pp. 1–22.
Feldman, R. (1995), "Reliability and Justification," *The Monist* 68, pp. 159–174.
Foley, R. (1985), "What's Wrong With Reliabilism?" *The Monist* 68, pp. 188–202.
Gettier, E. (1963), "Is Justified True Belief Knowledge?" *Analysis* 23, pp. 121–123.
Goldman, A. (1967), "A Causal Theory of Knowing," *Journal of Philosophy* 64(12), pp. 357–372.
Goldman, A. (1979), "What is Justified Belief?" in G. Pappas (ed.), *Justification and Knowledge*, Reidel, Dordrecht, pp. 1–23.
Goldman, A. (1986), *Epistemology and Cognition*, Harvard University Press.
Goldman, A. (1988), "Strong and Weak Justification," *Philosophical Perspectives* 2, pp. 51–69.
Heller, M. (1995), "The Simple Solution to the Generality Problem," *Noûs* 29(4), pp. 501–515.
Kaplan, D. (1989), "Demonstratives," in H. W. J. Almog and J. Perry (eds.), *Themes from Kaplan*, Oxford University Press.
Nozick, R. (1981), *Philosophical Explanations*, Harvard University Press.

Pollock, J. (1984), "Reliability and Justified Belief," *Canadian Journal of Philosophy* 14, pp. 103–114.
Ramsey, F. (1931), "Knowledge," in *The Foundations of Mathematics and Other Logical Essays*, Routledge & Kegan Paul.
Shope, R. (1983), *The Analysis of Knowing*, Princeton University Press.
Sosa, E. (1991), *Knowledge in Perspective*, Cambridge University Press.
Sosa, E. (1993), "Proper Functionalism and Virtue Epistemology," *Noûs* 27(1), pp. 51–65.
Sosa, E. (1999), "How Must Knowledge Be Modally Related to What Is Known?" *Philosophical Topics* 26(1/2), pp. 373–384.
Sosa, E. (2001), "Goldman's Reliabilism and Virtue Epistemology," *Philosophical Topics* 29(1/2), pp. 383–400.
Williamson, T. (2000), *Knowledge and its Limits*, Oxford University Press.

18
MODAL AND ANTI-LUCK EPISTEMOLOGY
Tim Black

1. Gettier Cases and Anti-Luck Epistemology

The influence of Edmund Gettier's "Is Justified True Belief Knowledge?" (1963) seems to extend to every corner of epistemology. Gettier's counterexamples to the tripartite account of knowledge, according to which to know is to have a justified true belief, involve epistemic agents whose beliefs are true simply as a matter of luck. These counterexamples are widely, perhaps universally, taken to show that an epistemic agent can be justified in holding the true belief that p but nonetheless fail to know that p. It has thus become a tenet of orthodox epistemology that no belief, not even if it is true and we are justified in holding it, can amount to knowledge if it is true simply as a matter of luck.

In one of Gettier's counterexamples, Smith is justified in believing both that Jones will get the job that both he and Smith have applied for and that Jones has ten coins in his pocket. From these two beliefs, Smith justifiedly infers that

(C) the man who will get the job has ten coins in his pocket.

Smith's inferential belief, let us suppose, is true. Still, Smith's belief does not count as knowledge: although Jones will *not* get the job, "by the sheerest coincidence, and entirely unknown to Smith," *he* (Smith) will get the job, and *he* has ten coins in his pocket (Gettier 1963: 123). Although Smith comes to hold his belief that C in a way that is very reliable and which provides him with reasons that would in normal circumstances be identical to the reasons why his belief is true, his belief is based in this instance on reasons that are *different* from those that make it true. Smith's inferential belief that C, then, is true simply as a matter of luck, and hence fails to count as knowledge.

Now, while it is helpful to think about Gettier cases in terms of luck, in that it helps us to understand what keeps their protagonists from knowing, it is less helpful than it might be. What exactly does it mean to say that Smith's belief is true simply as a matter of luck? It seems that there are two ways in which one might respond to this question.

First, there is the thought that justification—that is, the kind of justification that Smith has for believing that C—matters epistemically. The thought, in other words, is that if S is to know that p, then her believing that p must represent an appropriate response to the evidence. To respond appropriately, S must first avail herself of a sufficient amount of the relevant evidence, which will somehow indicate which belief, if any, it supports. S must then respond doxastically in the way her evidence directs her to respond, and she must respond in this way *because* her evidence directs her to do so. Given that her evidence indicates that it supports the truth of p, and given that S believes that p because her evidence supports the truth of p, she is justified in believing that p. We can spell out this notion of justification as follows (cf. Kornblith 1983; BonJour 1985; Greco 1990; and Riggs 1998):

> S is justified in believing that p if and only if (a) she avails herself of a sufficient amount of the relevant evidence, where the relevant evidence is any that bears on the truth or falsity of p, (b) she conducts a reasonably thorough reflective examination of her evidence, (c) her evidence, so far as she can tell on the basis of her reflective examination, is appropriately connected to the fact that p, and (d) S forms a belief that p on the basis of her evidence for p.

Corresponding to this conception of justification is a conception of luck:

> S's belief that p is true simply as a matter of luck if and only if (a) S is justified in believing that p, (b) her justification for p—that is, the evidence that figures into her being justified in believing that p—is *not* appropriately connected to the fact that p; but (c) p is nevertheless true.

One might hope to eliminate this sort of luck by making sure that one's justification for p is appropriately connected to the fact that p. Yet it has proven notoriously difficult to do this. Indeed, some have been led to conclude that it cannot be done. Such a conclusion appears attractive not only in the light of Gettier cases, where S's belief is true for reasons that are different from those on which her belief is based, but also in the light of cases in which S's belief is true for reasons that are quite closely related indeed to those on which her belief is based.

Suppose, then, that S holds a ticket in a fair lottery with a large number of participants and long odds. S forms the belief, on the basis of considerations involving the extremely low probability that her ticket is a winner, that her ticket is a loser. Suppose further that a winner has been selected and that S has not won; her ticket is in fact a loser. Here again, as in the Gettier case discussed above, S comes to believe that her ticket is a loser in a very reliable way. Yet, while Smith's reasons in the Gettier case are different from those that make his belief true, S's belief in the lottery case is based on reasons that are closely related to those that make it true: The fact that there's an extremely low probability that S's ticket is a winner not only serves as the basis of her belief, but it also has much to do with her belief being true. Even in this case, however, we are reluctant to say of S that she knows that her ticket is a loser. Her belief seems true simply as a matter of luck. It does seem difficult, then, to ensure that our justification is appropriately connected to the facts.

Some feel, however, that the sort of luck highlighted by Gettier cases and by lottery cases does not concern the connection between the facts and our beliefs' justification. Rather, they concern the connection between the facts and our beliefs *themselves*. Thus, the protagonists in Gettier cases and in lottery cases fail to have knowledge because their beliefs are true simply as a matter of luck, where this means that their beliefs themselves are not appropriately connected to the facts.

But how should we characterize this new conception of luck? Duncan Pritchard helpfully suggests that our protagonists' beliefs are true as a matter of *veritic epistemic luck*, which he characterizes in the following way: "It is a matter of luck that the agent's belief is true," where

> this demands that the agent's belief is true in the actual world, but that in a wide class of nearby possible worlds in which the relevant initial conditions are the same as in the actual world—and this will mean, in the basic case, that the agent at the very least forms the same belief in the same way as in the actual world [...]—the belief is false.
>
> (Pritchard 2005: 146)

So, for example, Smith's belief is veritically epistemically lucky because while it is true in the actual world, it is false in too many of the nearby possible worlds in which Smith forms the belief that C in the same way as in the actual world. To avoid being veritically epistemically lucky, Smith's belief must be true not only in the actual world, but also in a sufficient proportion of the nearby possible worlds in which he forms the belief that C in the same way as in the actual world. Theories that address the issue of veritic epistemic luck are *modal epistemologies*, according to which a belief counts as knowledge only if there is a modal connection—that is to say, a connection not only in the actual world, but also in other non-actual possible worlds—between the belief and the facts of the matter. A bit more concretely, a modal epistemology might say that a belief counts as knowledge only if it is true not only in the actual world, but also in a certain proportion of worlds within a specified set or range of non-actual possible worlds.

The difficulty here, of course, is with "a sufficient proportion": in order to eliminate veritic epistemic luck, in *what* proportion of the relevant nearby possible worlds must Smith's belief that C be true? In trying to answer this question, epistemologists start from at least two places. Each of these two places corresponds to a distinct way of giving expression to the anti-luck intuition involved in this understanding of the problematic cases. First, to say that Smith's belief is true simply as a matter of luck might be to say that there is nothing about Smith's circumstances, in which his belief happens to be true, that ensures that he will believe that C—even if C had been false, Smith might nonetheless have believed that C. This way of giving expression to our anti-luck intuition corresponds to epistemologies known as *sensitivity* theories, which we will consider in Section 2.

Next, to say that Smith's belief is true simply as a matter of luck might be to say that there is nothing about that which led Smith to believe that C that ensures that C will be true—it might have been that Smith's circumstances are just as they actually are, but that his belief that C is *false*. This way of giving expression to our anti-luck intuition corresponds to modal epistemologies known as *safety* theories, which we consider in Section 3.

2. Sensitivity Theories

Robert Nozick (1981) famously suggests that S knows that p only if S's belief that p is sensitive to the truth, that is, only if S would not believe that p if p were false (cf. Dretske 1971). In evaluating sensitivity's counterfactual condition, we consider the nearest possible world in which p is false—that is, the state of affairs, or the world, in which p is false, but that is otherwise as similar to the actual state of affairs as it can be—and then to determine whether, in that world, S believes that p. If S does believe that p in that world, then her belief that p is insensitive, and she does not know that p. If S does not believe that p in that world, her belief is sensitive, and she can therefore know that p.

As Nozick points out, sensitivity theories, unlike the tripartite account, allow us to get the right result in Gettier cases. According to sensitivity theories, Smith doesn't know that C because his belief that C is true simply as a matter of luck: In the nearest possible world in which the man who'll get the job does *not* have ten coins in his pocket—which, let's suppose, is a world in which Jones has ten coins in his pocket but Smith, who'll get the job, has only nine coins in his pocket—Smith nonetheless believes that the man who'll get the job *does* have ten coins in his pocket (see Nozick 1981: 173).

Sensitivity theories also help with the lottery case, where the difficulty is to explain why we consider S's belief to be true simply as a matter of luck even when it's true for reasons that are closely related to those on which it is based. According to sensitivity accounts, we consider S's belief to be true simply as a matter of luck, and thus as failing to count as knowledge, because in the nearest possible world in which S's ticket is *not* a loser, she still believes that her ticket *is* a loser. Thus, in spite of the fact that S's belief is based on strong probabilistic reasons, and in spite of the fact that her belief is true for reasons that are closely related to those on which it is based, her belief is nevertheless insensitive.

Sensitivity theories almost immediately face a problem, however, which arises from their treatment of a certain anti-skeptical argument:

1. I know that I have hands.
2. I know that my having hands entails that I'm not a handless brain-in-a-vat (that is, a handless brain floating in a vat of nutrients and electrochemically stimulated so as to generate perceptual experiences that are exactly similar to those that I am now having in what I take to be normal circumstances).
3. If I know *both* that I have hands *and* that my having hands entails that I'm not a handless brain-in-a-vat, then I know that I'm not a handless brain-in-a-vat.
4. Therefore, I know that I'm not a handless brain-in-a-vat.

Sensitivity theories have trouble with this argument in two ways. First, there is the complaint that while sensitivity theories allow us to say that (1) is true, they force us to deny (4). (1) is true because my belief that I have hands is both true and sensitive—the nearest possible world in which I have no hands is a world in which, let's say, I lost my hands in some unfortunate accident; but I do not believe in that world that I have hands, for I clearly see that I have no hands. (4) is false, however, because even if my belief that I'm not a handless brain-in-a-vat is true, it is *insensitive*—in the nearest possible world in which I *am* a handless brain-in-a-vat, I still believe that I'm *not* a handless brain-in-a-vat, since in that world everything appears to me just as it does in this world.

Moreover, this sort of result suggests that sensitivity theorists will reject (3), which is an instance of a very plausible epistemic closure principle:

If S knows that p and that p entails q, then S knows that q.

MODAL AND ANTI-LUCK EPISTEMOLOGY

We feel the intuitive pull of this principle in cases like the present one. Surely, it seems, if I know that I have hands, I also know that certain incompatible skeptical hypotheses are false, hypotheses like the one according to which I am a handless brain-in-a-vat. So, since sensitivity theories seem both to lead to the rejection of a very plausible closure principle and to offer no direct response to the skeptic—that is, no response according to which we know that certain skeptical hypotheses are false—many epistemologists are reluctant to adopt them.

Yet this is not the end of the story, for Nozick revises his theory in order "to take explicit account of the ways and methods of arriving at belief" (1981: 179), where we can rely on a standard taxonomy of methods which includes perception, memory, testimony, and intuition:

S knows that p if and only if

a. p is true;
b. S believes, via method or way of coming to believe M, that p;
c. if p weren't true and S were to use M to arrive at a belief whether (or not) p, then S wouldn't believe, via M, that p; and
d. if p were true and S were to use M to arrive at a belief whether (or not) p, then S would believe, via M, that p.

Nozick provides the following example in support of this revision: "A grandmother sees her grandson is well when he comes to visit; but if he were sick or dead, others would tell her he was well to spare her upset" (Nozick 1981: 179). When her grandson is well, the grandmother believes on the basis of seeing him that he is well. But if he were not well, she would use another method—Nozick stipulates that she would use testimony—in forming a belief as to whether her grandson was well. In that case, however, her belief would be *false*. Yet, as Nozick says, the fact that she *would* use another method "does not mean that she doesn't know he is well (or at least ambulatory) when she sees him" (Nozick 1981: 179). This suggests that the only worlds that are relevant to S knowing that p are worlds in which, in arriving at the belief that p, she forms her belief in the same way as in the actual world.

Moreover, given Nozick's revised sensitivity condition, although Nozick himself failed to notice this, worlds in which I am a handless brain-in-a-vat need not be relevant to whether I know that I'm not a handless brain-in-a-vat. In those worlds, one might argue, my belief is produced by a method that is different from the one that produces my belief in the actual world (see Black 2002). Thus, Nozick's revised sensitivity condition gives us room to say that I know both that I have hands and that I'm not a handless brain-in-a-vat. Sensitivity theories, at least those willing to make the sort of revision recommended by Nozick, need neither embrace skepticism nor deny the epistemic closure principle. (Roush's (2006) sensitivity-based theory, which utilizes a probabilistic interpretation of the counterfactuals in Nozick's account, is also meant to allow for knowledge to be closed under known entailment.)

Yet there are cases that cause trouble even for Nozick's revised theory. Keith DeRose provides two such cases. First, take my belief that

(F) I don't falsely believe that I have hands.

It certainly seems that I know that F, yet my belief that F is insensitive, for I would hold that belief even if F were false (see DeRose 1999: 196–197). In DeRose's second case, I believe that

(D) I'm not an intelligent dog who's always incorrectly thinking that I have hands.

Here too, it seems that I know that D in spite of the fact that my belief that D is insensitive (see DeRose 1999: 196–197).

In responding to these cases, DeRose says,

> We *don't* . . . judge ourselves ignorant of P where not-P implies something we take ourselves to know to be false, without providing an explanation of how we came to falsely believe this thing we think we know. Thus, *I falsely believe that I have hands* implies that I don't have hands. Since I do take myself to know that I have hands (*this* belief isn't insensitive), and since the above italicized proposition doesn't explain how I went wrong with respect to my having hands, I'll judge that I do know that proposition to be false.
>
> (DeRose 1999: 197)

DeRose here suggests the following weakened sensitivity condition:

(WES) S knows that p only if *either* S sensitively believes that p *or*, where $\sim p$ implies some q and S knows that $\sim q$, $\sim p$ fails to explain how S might come to hold the false belief that $\sim q$.

Note that the second disjunct of (WES)'s consequent—call it (EXP)—has three components:

(EXP)(i) $\sim p$ implies some q,
     (ii) S knows (in the actual world) that $\sim q$, and
     (iii) $\sim p$ fails to explain how S might come to hold the false belief that $\sim q$.

The introduction of (EXP) allows us to hand down the proper verdict in each of the two problematic cases. In the quoted passage, DeRose explains how (EXP) helps us to get the right result in the first case. (EXP) helps in the second case as well, for (i) *I'm an intelligent dog who's always incorrectly thinking that I have hands* implies *I don't have hands*, (ii) I know that I have hands, and (iii) my being such a dog fails to explain how I might come to hold the false belief that I have hands. (For an extended discussion of this sort of proposal, see Black and Murphy 2007.)

Still, there are objections. Juan Comesaña suggests that (WES) has trouble dealing with Ernest Sosa's Garbage Chute Case:

> I throw a trash bag down the garbage chute of my condo. Some moments later I believe, and know, that the trash bag is in the basement. If the trash bag were not in the basement, however, that would be because it is stuck somewhere in the chute, and I would still believe that it is in the basement.
>
> (Comesaña 2007: 783, adapted from Sosa 2000)

MODAL AND ANTI-LUCK EPISTEMOLOGY

Comesaña maintains that (WES) has trouble dealing with this case when *q* is *The trash bag is in the basement*. The relevant instance of (EXP) is this:

(i) *The trash bag is not in the basement* entails *the trash bag is not in the basement*,
(ii) I know that the trash bag is in the basement, and
(iii) *The trash bag is not in the basement* fails to explain how I might come to hold the false belief that *the trash bag is in the basement*.

Comesaña maintains that (iii) is false. He says that "the closest situation w[h]ere the trash bag is not in the basement is one that *does* explain why I would still falsely believe that it is in the basement (because it is a situation where the trash bag *misleadingly* appears to be in the basement)" (Comesaña 2007: 786). Given this, and given that I insensitively believe that the trash bag is in the basement, (WES) says that I fail to know that the trash bag is in the basement.

Yet (iii) is *true* in Comesaña's case. Moreover, when (iii) *is* false, we do *not* know that the trash bag is in the basement. Either way, (WES) is in the clear. First, in Comesaña's Garbage Chute Case, (iii) is true; that is, ~T, *the trash bag is not in the basement*, *does* fail to explain how I might come to hold the false belief that T, *the trash bag is in the basement*. Note that in the closest situations in which ~T, the fact that ~T occupies no position in the causal history of my belief that T, for I am in no way acquainted with the fact that ~T. I neither see nor hear that the trash bag isn't in the basement, and no one tells me (anything which would suggest) that it isn't in the basement. In the closest situations in which ~T, I come to believe that T *in spite of* the fact that ~T, and so we shouldn't say that ~T explains how I might come to hold the false belief that T. In this instance, then, (iii) is in fact true, which means that the Garbage Chute Case, at least when we configure that case as one in which *q* is *The trash bag is in the basement*, doesn't count against (WES).

Next, consider a case in which (iii) is *not* true, that is, a case in which ~T *does* explain how I might come to hold the false belief that T. Suppose that the condo's janitor likes to trick its tenants. When there's a problem with the garbage chute, he says there isn't a problem. When my trash bag fails to make it to the basement, he tells me that the garbage chute is unobstructed and working fine. The fact that my trash bag didn't make it to the basement helps to explain how I come to hold the false belief that it *did* make it to the basement. In this case, though, (WES) renders the correct verdict: It says that I don't know that the trash bag is in the basement. After all, if it weren't in the basement, the janitor would tell me that it was. (WES) is therefore in the clear both in the case Comesaña presents—since (iii) is true in that case—and in a case in which (iii) is false—since I fail in that case to know that T. (For an extended discussion of this sort of reply to Comesaña's objection, see Murphy and Black 2007.)

3. Safety Theories

The anti-luck intuition that we have in response to Gettier cases and lottery cases might also take the following form: to say that S's belief that *p* is true simply as a matter of luck is to say that there is nothing about that which led S to believe that *p* that ensures that *p* will be true—it might have been that S's circumstances are just as they actually are, but that her belief that *p* is *false*. This way of giving expression to our anti-luck intuition corresponds to modal epistemologies known as *safety* theories. Ernest Sosa, who introduced a safety condition on knowledge, gives expression to such a condition as follows:

> Call a belief by S that p "safe" iff: S would believe that p only if it were so that p. (Alternatively, a belief by S that p is "safe" iff: S would not believe that p without it being the case that p; or, better, iff: as a matter of fact, though perhaps not as a matter of strict necessity, not easily would S believe that p without it being the case that p.)
>
> (Sosa 1999: 142)

Pritchard, whose anti-luck epistemology revolves around a safety condition, provides some of the details that are left implicit in Sosa's formulation: If S knows a contingent proposition, *p*, then in most nearby possible worlds, S believes that *p* only when *p* is true (see, for example, Pritchard 2005: 71). In evaluating S's belief in accordance with a safety principle, we consider all of the nearby possible worlds in which S believes that *p*. If in most of those worlds *p* is true, then S's belief that *p* is safe. If, on the other hand, S's belief that *p* is false in too many of those worlds, S's belief is not safe.

Like sensitivity accounts, safety accounts yield the right result in Gettier cases. Suppose once again that although Smith is justified in holding the true belief that C, he does not *know* that C. Smith's belief is true simply as a matter of luck since "by the sheerest coincidence, and entirely unknown to Smith," *he* (Smith) will get the job, and *he* has ten coins in his pocket (Gettier 1963: 123). The safety condition yields the right result here: Smith doesn't know that C because C is false in too many nearby possible worlds in which he believes that C.

But there are cases which suggest that the safety condition, as it is formulated above, is inadequate.

FELON: A man has been accused of murder. The man's mother holds the true belief that her son is innocent, and she holds this belief on the basis of excellent evidence in its favor, including reliable forensic evidence about the cause of the victim's death. It seems, then, that the mother knows that her son is not the murderer.
Yet while her son is not in fact the murderer, he very nearly was—he intended to murder the victim but before he could act on his intention, the victim, let's say, died of a heart attack. Moreover, in too many of the nearby worlds in which the man's mother believes that he is not the murderer, he *is* the murderer and her belief that her son is innocent is generated simply by her intense love for her son.
(Pritchard 2005: 153; Armstrong (1973: 208–209) discusses a similar case, attributing it to Gregory O'Hair)

Again, our intuition here is that the mother knows that her son is innocent. After all, she is well aware of excellent forensic evidence in favor of the claim that he's innocent. According to safety, however, at least as it's formulated above, the mother does *not* know that her son is innocent, for in too many of the nearby possible worlds in which she believes that her son is innocent, her son did in fact murder the victim.

This sort of case highlights the need to make it more difficult for a world to count as one of the relevant nearby possible worlds. It suggests in particular that the safety condition ought to make additional demands which concern the methods that epistemic agents use in forming their beliefs:

(SAFETY II) If S knows a contingent proposition, *p*, then in most nearby possible worlds *in which S forms her belief about p in the same way as she forms her belief in the actual world*, S believes that *p* only when *p* is true.

Safety II handles FELON, for in most of the nearby possible worlds in which the mother forms her belief about her son's innocence *on the basis of excellent evidence in favor of that belief*, her son did not murder the victim.

Yet Safety II faces difficulties of its own. Suppose once again that S holds a ticket in a fair lottery with a large number of participants. Of course, we are reluctant to say of S that she knows that her ticket is a loser. Nonetheless, S's belief satisfies the conditions set out in Safety II—in *most* nearby possible worlds in which she believes that her ticket is a loser, and in which she forms her belief as she does in the actual world, namely, on the basis of her belief that it is highly likely that her ticket is a loser, her ticket is in fact a loser. "The problem," Pritchard (2005: 163) says, "seems to be that the agent's belief, whilst meeting [Safety II], is still veritically lucky since, given the nearness of the possible worlds in which the agent wins the lottery (and thus where forming her belief on the basis of the odds leads her astray), it is still a matter of luck that her belief happens to be true."

What is required at this point, according to Pritchard, is a third, stronger version of the safety principle, one that increases the proportion of the relevant nearby possible worlds in which S's belief must be true:

(SAFETY III) If S knows a contingent proposition, *p*, then in *nearly all (if not all)* nearby possible worlds in which S forms her belief about *p* in the same way as she forms her belief in the actual world, S believes that *p* only when *p* is true.

Safety III handles the lottery case. S fails to know that her ticket is a loser, according to Safety III, because in too many of the nearby possible worlds in which she believes that her ticket is a loser, and in which she forms her belief in the same way she does in the actual world, her ticket is *not* a loser.

Indeed, Pritchard's main argument for Safety III—and for its "nearly all (if not all)" qualification—comes in terms of the lottery puzzle:

> The agent who forms her belief that she has lost the lottery purely on the basis of the odds involved lacks knowledge because her belief, whilst true and matching the truth in most nearby possible worlds in which she forms her belief in the same way as in the actual world, does not match the truth in a *small cluster* of nearby possible worlds in which what she believes is false (i.e. where she wins the lottery).
>
> (Pritchard 2005: 163, my emphasis)

But what if her belief fails to match the truth in an *even smaller cluster* of nearby possible worlds? In such a case, Safety III might count her as knowing that she has lost the lottery. But this is counterintuitive, perhaps because we are reluctant to count the agent as knowing if there is *even one* nearby possible world in which her belief fails to match the truth.

Moreover, John Greco (2007: 301) maintains that Pritchard's Safety III is ambiguous between *strong safety*—"In close worlds, always if S believes *p* then *p* is true. Alternatively, in close worlds never does S believe p and p is false"—and *weak safety*—"In close worlds, usually if S believes p then p is true. Alternatively, in close worlds, almost never does S believe p and p is false." Safety III says that S *knows* that she has lost the lottery when it is read as *weak* safety, but that S does *not* know that she's lost the lottery when it's read as *strong* safety.

All of this leads us away from Safety III, and to the final version of the safety principle that we will see in this entry, a revision which Pritchard calls SP**:

(SP**) S's belief is safe if and only if in most nearby possible worlds in which S continues to form her belief about the target proposition in the same way as in the actual world, and in all very close nearby possible worlds in which S continues to form her belief about the target proposition in the same way as in the actual world, the belief continues to be true (see Pritchard 2007: 290–292).

SP** handles the lottery case in what seems to be a fairly unobjectionable way.

Still, some cases might weigh against SP**. Consider the following case:

EXPERIMENT: I am participating in a psychological experiment, in which I am to report the number of flashes I recall being shown. Before being shown the stimuli, I consume a glass of liquid at the request of the experimenter. Unbeknownst to either of us, I have been randomly assigned to the control group, and the glass contains ordinary orange juice. Other experimental groups receive juice mixed with one of a variety of chemicals which hinder the functioning of memory without a detectable phenomenological difference. I am shown seven flashes and judge, truly and knowingly, that I have been shown seven flashes. Had I been a member of one of the experimental groups to which I was almost assigned, I would have been shown only six flashes but still believed that I had been shown seven flashes due to the effects of the drug. It seems that in the actual case I know that the number of flashes is seven despite the envisaged possibility of my being wrong. And yet these possibilities are as similar in other respects as they would have to be for the experiment to be well designed and properly executed.

(Neta and Rohrbaugh 2004: 400)

SP** seems to count my belief in EXPERIMENT as unsafe and thus as something other than knowledge.

Yet for this unacceptable result to hold up, the worlds in which I am assigned to a non-control group and in which I am impaired must be very close to the actual world. Safety theorists might be able convincingly to argue, however, that such worlds are not *very* close to the actual world. For one thing, the very fact that I am impaired in these worlds might make it the case that they are too far away from the actual world to count as being very close to it; safety theorists might argue that the only *very* close worlds in this case are worlds in which I am assigned to the control group and in which I drink ordinary orange juice. In worlds like that, though, it seems that my belief that I have been shown seven flashes continues to be true. If this sort of response to EXPERIMENT is effective, then my belief that I have been shown seven flashes can still count both as safe and as an instance of knowledge.

Incidentally, EXPERIMENT seems also to count against sensitivity theories—if I had not been shown seven flashes, if I had been shown only six flashes, I nevertheless would have believed that I had been shown seven flashes. Yet sensitivity theorists, at least those who subscribe to a condition like (WES), can provide a response to EXPERIMENT that is similar to the one provided by safety theorists. Sensitivity theorists, like safety theorists, might argue that a world cannot count as being very close to the actual world unless it is a world in which I am assigned to the control group and drink ordinary orange juice. In this case, however, the hypothesis that I have been shown only six flashes fails to explain how in very close possible worlds, I might come to hold the false belief that I have been shown seven flashes. If this sort of response to EXPERIMENT is effective, my belief that I have been shown seven flashes can both satisfy the conditions set out in (WES) and count as an instance of knowledge.

4. Concluding Remarks

Modal epistemologies—sensitivity theories and safety theories—do much to let us know what it is for a belief to be true simply as a matter of luck, and thus what is required in order to eliminate this sort of luck. We have seen this demonstrated in the way that modal epistemologies handle Gettier cases, lottery cases, and cases of several other sorts. Perhaps, though, there are still other cases in which it seems that we hold beliefs that are true simply as a matter of luck. Yet rather than showing that modal epistemologies are on the wrong track, those cases might simply be suggesting ways in which such epistemologies might be improved or "highlight[ing] the vagueness inherent in the extension of philosophically interesting terms" (Pritchard 2007: 290). Modal epistemologies therefore seem quite promising—indeed, given that such epistemologies do an excellent job of characterizing epistemic luck and of setting forth the conditions that must be met if such luck is to be eliminated, it rather seems that modal epistemologies represent the right approach to some central issues in the theory of knowledge.

References

Armstrong, D. M. (1973). *Belief, Truth and Knowledge* (Cambridge: Cambridge University Press).
Black, Tim. (2002). "A Moorean Response to Brain-in-a-Vat Scepticism," *Australasian Journal of Philosophy* 80: 148–163.
—— and Peter Murphy. (2007). "In Defense of Sensitivity," *Synthese* 154: 53–71.
BonJour, Laurence. (1985). *The Structure of Empirical Knowledge* (Cambridge, MA: Harvard University Press).
Comesaña, Juan. (2007). "Knowledge and Subjunctive Conditionals," *Philosophy Compass* 2: 781–791.
DeRose, Keith. (1999). "Solving the Skeptical Problem," *Skepticism: A Contemporary Reader*, Keith DeRose & Ted A. Warfield, eds. (New York: Oxford University Press): 183–219.
Dretske, Fred (1971). "Conclusive Reasons," *Australasian Journal of Philosophy* 49: 1–22.
Gettier, Edmund. (1963). "Is Justified True Belief Knowledge?" *Analysis* 23: 121–123.
Greco, John. (1990). "Internalism and Epistemically Responsible Belief," *Synthese* 85: 245–277.
——. (2007). "Worries about Pritchard's safety," *Synthese* 158: 299–302.
Kornblith, Hilary. (1983). "Justified Belief and Epistemically Responsible Action," *The Philosophical Review* 92: 33–48.
Murphy, Peter and Tim Black. (2007). "Comments on Juan Comesaña's 'Knowledge and Subjunctive Conditionals'," On-Line Philosophy Conference 2, http://experimentalphilosophy.typepad.com/2nd_annual_online_philoso/files/murphy_and_black_on_comesana.doc.
Neta, Ram and Guy Rohrbaugh. (2004). "Luminosity and the Safety of Knowledge," *Pacific Philosophical Quarterly* 85: 396–406.
Nozick, Robert. (1981). *Philosophical Explanations* (Cambridge, MA: Harvard University Press).
Pritchard, Duncan. (2005). *Epistemic Luck* (Oxford: Clarendon).
——. (2007). "Anti-Luck Epistemology," *Synthese* 158: 277–297.

Riggs, Wayne D. (1998). "What are the 'Chances' of Being Justified?" *The Monist* 81: 452–472.
Roush, Sherrilyn. (2006). *Tracking Truth: Knowledge, Evidence, and Science* (New York: Oxford).
Sosa, Ernest. (1999). "How to Defeat Opposition to Moore," in James E. Tomberlin, ed., *Philosophical Perspectives 13, Epistemology*: 141–153.
——. (2000). "Skepticism and Contextualism," *Philosophical Issues* 10: 1–18.

19
VIRTUE EPISTEMOLOGY
Jonathan L. Kvanvig

I. History

Virtue epistemology constitutes an approach to epistemological issues and problems that can be traced to Ernest Sosa's seminal paper, "The Raft and the Pyramid" (Sosa 1980). Sosa in turn credits the idea for a virtue epistemology to the rise of interest since the 1950s in virtue approaches to ethics, which have an Aristotelian source. Sosa's initial idea was to use virtue notions to provide a unified account of knowledge, and this goal constrains what Sosa counts as an intellectual virtue. The central component in such approaches to virtue epistemology is that of a reliable cognitive faculty, and epistemologists who have followed Sosa's lead here focus on faculties such as vision, reasoning powers, introspection, and memory as primary examples of intellectual virtues.

This approach contrasts with the approach taken by Linda Zagzebski (1996). The publication of her book is another major event in the history of virtue epistemology, and it favors a somewhat different conception of an intellectual virtue. Zagzebski argued that a truly Aristotelian understanding of the intellectual virtues focuses more on character traits such as openmindedness and intellectual courage. Such a conception of the intellectual virtues leads one away from the reliabilist notion adopted by Sosa, and makes it more difficult to use such a notion of an intellectual virtue in service of the standard epistemological project of clarifying the natures of knowledge and justification (even though Zagzebski herself offers such a theory). (Note that while Zagzebski uses the language of reliability, it is not the truth-conducive notion central to reliabilist approaches to epistemological issues. It remains true, however, that character traits of interest in epistemology have something to do with the epistemic goal of getting to the truth and avoiding error, even if not truth-conducive in the sense required by Sosa and his followers.)

Thinking of the intellectual virtues in terms of character traits might lead one in different directions than those of traditional epistemology, and one of the results of thinking about the role of the virtues in intellectual life has been such a broadening of projects that are nonetheless within the scope of epistemological concern, echoing a criticism by Jonathan Kvanvig (1992) that prospects for virtue epistemology look much better outside the domain of traditional epistemological concerns than within it. Lorraine Code, for example, argues for orienting epistemology in terms of the concept of epistemic responsibility, and thus focuses more on the role of agency in inquiry and on the moral and social dimensions of intellectual life (Code 1987). James Montmarquet agrees that the distinctive notion in epistemology to which an understanding of the intellectual virtues is central is the notion of responsibility, and he models the notion of doxastic responsibility on the notion of moral responsibility, conceiving the former as a particular kind of the latter (Montmarquet 1993). His primary interest is thus not with traditional epistemological positions and puzzles but, rather, with the project of attempting to ascertain the cognitive conditions that underlie morally responsible action itself. Roberts and Wood, for a third example, pursue the issue of the role of the virtues in the intellectual life as such, independently of any question concerning the nature of knowledge or justification or an attempt to solve the skeptical challenge (Roberts and Wood 2007). Thus, even though it is possible for the character trait conception of an intellectual virtue to be put in service of traditional epistemology, a primary effect of this conception of a virtue is an expansion of the issues and problems that become the targets of philosophical reflection of a particularly epistemological sort.

II. Traditional Epistemology and the Virtues

The leading figures in the attempt to employ virtue notions in service of traditional epistemology are Sosa, John Greco, and Zagzebski. Sosa views the value of appeals to virtue as a way of solving certain problems with traditional foundationalist and coherentist approaches to the nature of knowledge and justification. The central problem for such approaches is the Scatter Problem, the need for an ever-increasing body of epistemic principles to account for the justification of beliefs by subjects much different in kind from us. Aliens, for example, might have cognitive powers and abilities wholly different from our own, and yet use such capacities to acquire knowledge. A satisfying theory will need to explain the underlying unity here rather than rest content with mere proliferation of additional principles every time a new kind of being is considered, and Sosa maintains that the ability to provide such a unified explanation is a primary motive for virtue epistemology.

Sosa defines a virtue this way: "One has an intellectual virtue or faculty relative to an environment E if and only if one has an inner nature I in virtue of which one would mostly attain the truth and avoid error in a certain field of propositions F, when in certain conditions C" (1991: 284). In light of this conception of a virtue, Sosa holds that primary epistemic evaluation applies to aspects of inner natures as such, and secondary evaluation to the products of such virtues, thus identifying knowledge and justification with the products of such virtues.

Early criticism of Sosa's proposal focused in the way in which it ignores the central notion of epistemic responsibility (Code 1987; Montmarquet 1993). Greco's virtue theory aims at remedying this difficulty without abandoning the general conception Sosa outlines. Greco identifies epistemically responsible belief with subjective justification, and argues that one and the same account of the virtues is capable of giving an account of both subjective justification and knowledge. Greco's account of a virtue is quite similar to Sosa's, holding that intellectual virtues are "innate faculties or acquired habits that enable a person to arrive at truth and avoid error in some relevant field" (2002: 287). He maintains that knowledge requires subjective justification that gives rise to objectively reliable belief, and that such justification is present when the underlying character involves the virtues as understood above. Thus, knowledge is identified in terms of beliefs grounded in the intellectual virtues, and the result is a combination of reliable belief and epistemically responsible belief.

Zagzebski, however, rejects the account of the intellectual virtues employed by Sosa and Greco. She defines a virtue as "a deep and enduring acquired excellence of a person, involving a characteristic motivation to produce a certain desired end and reliable success in bringing about that end" (1996: 137). Though she uses the language of reliability in this definition—a reliability that attaches to the motivation in question—careful reading of her claims about reliability require a weaker interpretation in terms of a role such character traits play in getting to the truth and avoiding error. She agrees with Montmarquet's criticism, for example, that openmindedness is not truth-conducive, and hence not a character trait the underlying motivation of which guarantees any reliability for resulting beliefs. Nonetheless, she maintains that the concept of a virtue so defined can be used to clarify the nature of knowledge as well as that of justification. Knowledge, according to Zagzebski, is a belief arising out of an act of intellectual virtue, and justification is a matter of avoiding in belief what a virtuous person wouldn't believe in like circumstances (so that a justified belief is one that a virtuous person might believe in like circumstances).

III. Expanding Epistemology through the Virtues

The leading figures in the attempt to use virtue notions in addressing epistemological issues but without any explicit attempt to characterize their efforts in terms of the primary topics and issues of traditional epistemology are Code, Montmarquet, Kvanvig, and Roberts and Wood.

Kvanvig argues that traditional epistemological discussion is in the grips of a Cartesian perspective which focuses on synchronic and individualistic issues. He argues that given such a perspective, no interesting role will be found for the virtues in attempting to resolve traditional epistemological matters concerning the nature of knowledge and justification. He suggests, however, that the problem could be with the perspective itself rather than with the virtues, and that if a more social and diachronic perspective were taken, the virtues would become much more important to epistemological inquiry. The expanded perspective would involve the variety of factors that play a role in progress toward cognitive ideality, both for individuals and groups. An investigation of the path toward cognitive ideality would involve the role of cognitive exemplars in the ubiquitous process of mimicry and imitation that plays as significant a role in cognitive life as it does in other aspects of life. In addition, a social perspective on cognitive matters will need to address questions concerning the epistemic superiority of certain corporate attempts to find the truth and avoid error over other such attempts, and there is no doubt that corporate attempts that attend to intellectual virtues in determining the various roles that individuals will play in the corporate scheme will be better epistemically than those that do not.

Code and Montmarquet focus more explicitly on the relationship between the virtues and the concept of responsibility. Code identifies the virtue of being epistemically responsible as the chief cognitive virtue, and claims that the methods and approaches of traditional epistemology are unlikely to provide an adequate conception of the intellectual life and the role of the virtues in it. She thus views traditional epistemology as too concerned with analyzing the concepts of justification and knowledge, and argues instead for an approach that focuses on cognitive character itself, the relationship between the normative dimensions in both ethics and epistemology, and the social and communal aspects of the intellectual life.

Montmarquet similarly focuses on the concept of responsibility and argues that an appeal to the virtues is necessary for a proper understanding of the way in which epistemic matters affect morally responsible action. He thus generates an account of subjective justification that plays two roles. First, it is defined in terms of the intellectual virtues, especially the virtues of epistemic conscientiousness, impartiality, sobriety, and courage, and second, it yields a notion that is the distinctive epistemic component in an account of morally responsible action. Should it turn out that this notion of justification is not the sort that traditional epistemologists are concerned with, this fact by itself need not be of special concern to Montmarquet, since the project isn't oriented toward these traditional epistemological concerns. What is needed, rather, is an account of doxastic responsibility that plays the role an epistemic condition needs to play in an explanation of moral responsibility.

Roberts and Wood eschew traditional epistemological concerns as well. They view the concerns of traditional epistemology as unnecessarily abstract and argue instead for an approach to epistemology that is "regulative," one that attempts to generate guidance for epistemic practice and thus to "change the world." The strategy for achieving such a goal is to characterize the habits of mind relevant to successful epistemic practice, and thus the central focus of their work is on characterizing the particular habits or virtues of successful cognizers, habits such as love of knowledge, firmness, courage and caution, humility, autonomy, generosity, and practical wisdom. Throughout these discussions, the goal aimed at is that of edifying the reader by instilling an interest in and admiration of the virtues in question.

Finally, a significant theme has emerged in the discussion of virtue epistemology questioning the focus of epistemology on the concept of knowledge and related concepts. Though these concepts are still important, several have argued for a more central place for other cognitive achievements such as wisdom and understanding (Kvanvig 1992, 2003b; Zagzebski 1996; Roberts and Wood 2007), with the idea that changing or expanding the focus of epistemology in this way will present a deeper appreciation of the theoretical significance of the intellectual virtues in our theories of cognitive achievements.

IV. Difficulties for Virtue Epistemology

The critical literature on virtue epistemology has focused primarily on those approaches that have attempted to address the issues of traditional epistemology rather than on the attempts to expand epistemological inquiry in a way that finds a central place for the virtues. This fact is not surprising, given the longer history of traditional approaches to the discipline and the way in which success at such projects is easier to assess. The difficulties for virtue approaches to traditional epistemological concerns depend on whether the virtues are conceived as acquired character traits or as faculties or powers useful in the search for truth.

A. *Knowledge, Justification and Acquired Character Traits*

In the theory of justification, challenges to the necessity of virtues conceived in terms of acquired character traits arise first by noticing that individuals themselves can have justified beliefs even if they have acquired few to no virtues. Small children, for example, are justified in believing that Mommy is present on the basis of perceptual abilities alone, regardless of whether the child has had enough time and experience to develop character traits of the virtuous sort. In order to accommodate this point, virtue theories of the sort in question must resort to counterfactuals. In Zagzebski's case, as noted already, the counterfactual concerns what a virtuous person might believe in like circumstances.

Counterfactual theories are pervasive in philosophy, but have an extensive track record of susceptibility to counterexamples. Shope (1978) names the mistake responsible for such susceptibility "the conditional fallacy," and though his characterization of the fallacy is very complex, the usual characterization of the fallacy is that one shouldn't try to analyze anything in terms of counterfactuals. This lesson plays out in the literature on Zagzebski's theory, since it is easy to imagine beliefs that a virtuous person simply wouldn't have, but which less virtuous people can have adequate evidence to believe. For example, consider the claim that a novice in terms of virtue might reasonably believe: "I am a novice with no acquired character traits at this point that would count as virtues." It is hard to see how an intellectually virtuous person could hold such a belief, given the complete lack of self-understanding that would be required for a virtuous person to believe it (see Johnson 2003).

This counterexample is part and parcel of a more general problem for virtue theories, whether in epistemology or ethics. There are things appropriate to believe or do where the appropriateness in question must be explained in terms of defects of the person in question. Such difficulties lead in ethics to views that emphasize, not what a virtuous person would do in my circumstances, but what my better self would hold about the action performed or the belief held (see Smith 2004). But there is a version of this difficulty rooted in the conditional fallacy that even better-self theories cannot accommodate (see Kvanvig 1992, 2003a; Kvanvig and Menzel 1990). For justification attaches both to beliefs as well as to propositions that one does not believe. For example, one can have adequate evidence for thinking that Bush is one of the worst Presidents in history, but be unable to form that opinion out of fear or desire to please one's parents. Moreover, in the usual case of an irrational belief, the explanation for the irrationality in question adverts to the justification the person in question has for the denial of the claim that is believed. In some cases of having propositional justification for something not believed, the justification in question would be destroyed by coming to believe the claim in question. For example, one might know that one has only squared single-digit numbers, and thus have adequate evidence for the claim that one has never considered the claim that twelve squared is one hundred forty-four. No one can believe such a claim, however, without destroying the evidence for the claim. The fact that justification attaches both to beliefs and to propositions thus threatens any virtue theory that attempts to characterize justification in terms of what a virtuous person would or might believe and even what one's better self holds about what one should believe, since any such believing would destroy any evidence in its favor. One's better self can't approve of believing the claim, since that would be to approve of adopting an attitude that would be unjustified. But if one's better self doesn't approve of holding the belief, we have no way to explain, on such a theory, how the claim in question is justified. One could revise the better-self theory so that it determines justificatory status in terms of an approving attitude toward one's present lack of attitude, but that won't distinguish between cases where the proposition is justified and cases in which the evidence is counterbalanced and no attitude toward the proposition is needed or important. That is, the improved better-self theory still won't be able to distinguish between propositional justification and propositional neutrality in some cases, and so fails for that reason.

It is this problem of propositional justification that leads Zagzebski away from the traditional epistemological concern with the nature of justification toward a more expanded epistemological approach, one in which she claims that it is time to abandon the traditional project and to take a different approach (see Zagzebski 2000), one that will make room for a virtue theory of justification of the sort she proposes, even if it isn't a theory of the sort of justification that has been the target of traditional epistemological concern.

Difficulties have been noted as well for the attempt to characterize the nature of knowledge in terms of acquired virtues. The principal challenge is the same here as one already seen concerning justification. Small children and animals have knowledge, but it is difficult to account for this knowledge on the basis of acquired character traits (see Greco 2000). Moreover, ordinary perceptual beliefs, even in those epistemic sophisticates with a full panoply of acquired character traits that count as virtues, do not appear to require or involve these acquired virtues. Such difficulties, just as those encountered in the theory of justification, create strong pressure for those who think of the virtues in terms of acquired character traits to focus on expanding the kinds of inquiry and projects beyond those of traditional epistemology.

B. *Knowledge, Justification, and Faculties or Powers*

Viewing the virtues in terms of faculties or powers successfully aimed at truth can help with some of these problems, but not with all of them. For example, this alternative view of the virtues certainly helps with the problem arising from the existence of individuals who have not yet acquired any useful character traits, and it also helps avoid the problem that arises from simple perceptual knowledge. In these cases, justification and knowledge are present, but without any need for acquired virtues. It is less problematic, however, to claim that such justification and knowledge depend on the presence of faculties or powers typically successful in getting one to the truth.

Even so, problems remain. Such virtue theories are versions of reliabilism, and all such theories are plagued by what Sosa calls the New Evil Demon Problem (Sosa 1980). Inhabitants of evil demon worlds have no faculties or powers that are typically successful in getting them to the truth, but it is less plausible to hold that they have no justified beliefs. They don't have knowledge, since that requires the truth of what they believe, but the fallibilist position that justified false beliefs are possible is just the sort of theoretical underpinning needed to insist that their beliefs are justified even though nearly always mistaken.

Moreover, conceiving of the virtues in terms of faculties or powers doesn't help at all with the problem of accounting for propositional justification. Such positions begin by explaining the nature of a property that attaches to beliefs (one produced by virtuous faculties or powers), but something different must be said in order to account for that property that attaches to propositions that are not believed. One natural idea here is to turn to counterfactuals, claims concerning what beliefs would be justified if they were held. But this natural suggestion raises precisely the same problems we noted earlier concerning the attempt of those appealing to acquired character traits to explain propositional justification.

These difficulties in the theory of justification do not arise, however, when appealing to faculties or powers to explain the nature of knowledge. Hence, the most promising avenue for such a virtue theory is in the domain of knowledge. The challenges that arise here focus more on perceived inadequacies of any reliabilist account of knowledge, including problems of clairvoyance and other purported powers that one has good reason to think do not exist. Such cases show that merely having a belief that results from a power or faculty that typically gets one to the truth is not sufficient for knowledge (when the belief in question is true) and thus threaten certain versions of virtue epistemology (e.g., Sosa 1991). But such problems do not threaten the view that the activity of the virtues is necessary for knowledge.

There is some pressure, however, to try to specify a role for the virtues that is both necessary and sufficient for knowledge. Noted as early as Plato's *Meno* is the point that the value of knowledge exceeds that of true belief. Socrates and Meno discuss the value of a guide who knows the way when one's goal is to get to Larissa, and Socrates points out that a guide with true opinion will do just as well. In response, Meno wonders why we prize knowledge over true opinion and, indeed, what the difference is (*Meno*, 97c-d). This conversation is instructive, for Meno is exactly right that we do prize knowledge over true opinion, and one of the virtues of virtue epistemology is found in the hope that such an approach can explain this value. To the extent, however, that the role the virtues play here is not sufficient to close the gap between true belief and knowledge, to that extent virtue epistemology fails to account for the difference in value. Hence, in recent literature, virtue theories have attempted to state a condition involving the virtues that is both necessary for knowledge and sufficient for it in the presence of true belief. Greco, for example, insists that the belief is true *because* it arises from the virtues, that the virtues not only produce the belief in question but are part of the explanation of why the belief is true (see Greco 2000); and Sosa's more recent (2007) requires that a belief be true *because* competent (Sosa 2007: 23).

Such a view has a difficult time dealing with the variety of Gettier examples in the literature. Greco devotes considerable effort to attempting to show that it can account for the fake barn case (the case in which one doesn't know that what one is looking at is a barn because it is the only real barn in an area littered with fake barns that one can't discriminate from real barns). In such a case, one's perceptual powers operate as they normally do, but do not generate knowledge. Greco's explanation is that the belief in question isn't true because of the faculty in question, but because of other factors (perhaps because one happened not to select a fake barn for perceptual attention). While it is true that the complete explanation of why the belief is true can't be given without reference to other factors, that is true as well in any case of ordinary perceptual knowledge. So it isn't clear that ordinary judgments about causation and explanation are sufficient to underwrite the claim that the barn belief isn't true because of the powers or abilities in question and yet that an ordinary belief that, for example, there is a car parked in my driveway, is true because of my perceptual abilities.

Moreover, there are other Gettier cases that are much more difficult for virtue theorists of this sort to handle. In the Tom Grabit case, you see Tom steal a book from the library. But you don't know that Tom stole the book, because Tom's mother tells the police investigating the crime that Tom was in Hawaii and it must have been his twin brother Buck who stole the book. You don't know because of this defeating information (of which you are unaware). There are variations on this opening theme, variations that differ concerning this lack-of-knowledge verdict. In one version, the police don't need to take the mother's testimony seriously even for a moment. They've had long experience with her lying to protect Tom, and know that there is no twin. In such a case, the defeating information is misleading information, and doesn't undermine your knowledge (see Lehrer and Paxson 1969). In other cases, however, the police have to treat her remarks seriously, and might take months of investigation to determine whether the alibi stands, and in such cases, your knowledge is undermined by the testimony of the mother. In all cases, however, you have a true belief, and the "because" relation between your perceptual powers and the truth of your belief is precisely the same in all these variants of the Tom/Buck case. And yet, in some cases you know and in some you don't.

Besides having difficulty accounting for the nature of knowledge, faculty-based virtue approaches face problems accounting for the value of knowledge as well. A primary concern here is the Swamping Problem (Zagzebski 1996; Kvanvig 1998, 2003a), according to which the value of truth swamps the value of additional features added to true belief which have no value except value instrumentally related to truth. Just as a superb espresso is no better as an espresso because produced by a machine that usually produces superb espressos, so a true belief becomes no more valuable from a purely intellectual point of view by adding some feature that is merely instrumentally valuable in getting one to the truth. Zagzebski argues, for example, that virtues *qua* faculties are only extrinsically valuable, by tending to generate true beliefs, whereas a more agent-based, motivational view of the virtues makes the value of the virtues intrinsic and fundamental, enhancing the value of the states that result from such motives.

The prospects, then, for a virtue explanation of the nature of knowledge that also completely explains the value of knowledge over that of true belief are not promising. Virtue accounts of knowledge might go some distance to explaining this distinctive value of knowledge, but not the entire way (see Kvanvig 2003b). Even so, if the virtues are necessary for knowledge (in spite of being insufficient even in the presence of true belief), that result would be a major accomplishment on the part of virtue epistemology.

V. Future Prospects

Even if some contribution by virtue epistemology to traditional epistemological concerns can be sustained through defenses of the necessity of the virtues for knowledge, this contribution does not exhaust the prospects for further contributions. The expansion of legitimate epistemological inquiry beyond the topics prompted by the concerns of the skeptic—namely, those of knowledge and justification—brings with it the possibility and perhaps even plausibility of further contributions by virtue theorists to our understanding of the intellectual life. It is, of course, not possible to evaluate in some generic way the prospects of such, for any evaluation will need to be project-specific. It is fair to conclude, however, that we have not yet seen the full extent of the contributions to such understanding that appeals to the intellectual virtues can provide.

References

Code, Lorraine. 1987. *Epistemic Responsibility*. Hanover, NH: University Press of New England.
Greco, John. 2000. "Two Kinds of Intellectual Virtue," *Philosophy and Phenomenological Research* 60: 179–184.
———. 2002. "Virtues in Epistemology," *Oxford Handbook of Epistemology*, ed. Paul Moser. New York: Oxford University Press.
Johnson, Robert. 2003. "Virtue and Right," *Ethics* 113.4: 810–834.

Kvanvig, Jonathan. 1992. *The Intellectual Virtues and the Life of the Mind*. Savage, MD: Rowman & Littlefield.
——. 1998. "Why Should Inquiring Minds Want to Know?" *The Monist* 81.3: 426–451.
——. 2003a. "Propositionalism and the Perspectival Character of Justification," *American Philosophical Quarterly* 40.1: 3–18.
——. 2003b. *The Value of Knowledge and the Pursuit of Understanding*. Cambridge: Cambridge University Press.
—— and Christopher Menzel. 1990. "The Basic Notion of Justification," *Philosophical Studies* 59: 235–261.
Lehrer, Keith and Thomas D. Paxson, Jr. 1969. "Knowledge: Undefeated Justified True Belief," *The Journal of Philosophy* 66.8: 225–237.
Montmarquet, James. 1993. *Epistemic Virtue and Doxastic Responsibility*. Lanham, MD: Rowman & Littlefield.
Roberts, Robert C. and W. Jay Wood. 2007. *Intellectual Virtues: An Essay in Regulative Epistemology*. Oxford: Oxford University Press.
Shope, Robert. 1978. "The Conditional Fallacy in Contemporary Philosophy." *Journal of Philosophy* 75: 397–413.
Smith, Michael. 2004. *Ethics and the A Priori: Selected Essays on Moral Psychology and Meta-Ethics*. Cambridge: Cambridge University Press.
Sosa, Ernest. 1980. "The Raft and the Pyramid: Coherence versus Foundations in the Theory of Knowledge," *Midwest Studies in Philosophy* V: 3–25.
——. 1991. *Knowledge in Perspective*. Cambridge: Cambridge University Press.
——. 2007. *A Virtue Epistemology*. Oxford: Oxford University Press.
Steup, Matthias, ed. 2001. *Knowledge, Truth, and Duty*. Oxford: Oxford University Press.
Zagzebski, Linda. 1996. *Virtues of the Mind*. Cambridge: Cambridge University Press.
——. 2000. "Responses," *Philosophy and Phenomenological Research* 60.1: 207–219.

20
KNOWLEDGE FIRST EPISTEMOLOGY
Timothy Williamson

Introduction

"Knowledge first" is a slogan for epistemology that takes the distinction between knowledge and ignorance as the starting point from which to explain other cognitive matters. It reverses the direction dominant in much twentieth-century epistemology, which treated belief as explanatorily prior to knowledge, attempting to analyze knowledge as belief that meets further conditions, such as truth and justification. By contrast, a knowledge first epistemologist might treat believing something as treating it as if one knew it.

The most striking difference between knowledge and belief is that knowledge entails truth while belief does not. There is false belief but no false knowledge. Some people *believe* that Africa is a single country, but since it is false that it is a single country, they do not *know* that it is a single country. They just believe falsely that they know that Africa is a single country. In this sense, all knowledge but not all belief is successful. Thus knowledge first epistemology gives explanatory priority to success. This does not mean that belief first epistemology gives priority to failure. Rather, it gives explanatory priority to conditions that are neutral between success and failure: some beliefs constitute knowledge, others are false.

Most epistemologists agree that while knowing entails believing truly, believing truly does not entail knowing. Someone does not know something he believes truly on the say-so of his guru, who invents things to tell him at random without regard to their truth or falsity. Although merely believing truly involves a sort of success—getting the answer right—it also involves, unlike knowing, a sort of cognitive malfunction. Thus knowledge is a more full-blooded success condition than true belief. Knowledge first epistemology understands cases of cognitive malfunctioning in terms of their deviation from cases of cognitive functioning, as opposed to treating the two kinds of case more symmetrically.

Similar contrasts arise in the philosophy of action, where intentionally doing something is the full-blooded success condition. It stands to the world-to-mind direction of fit as knowing stands to the mind-to-world direction of fit. Believing corresponds to trying, the neutral condition that obtains in both cases of success and cases of failure. Falsely believing corresponds to trying and failing. Merely believing truly without knowing corresponds to trying and doing the intended thing but not as intended: for instance, you hit the intended target because your intention so agitated you that your trigger finger slipped. Knowledge first epistemology corresponds to a philosophy of action that understands cases of trying to do something without intentionally doing it in terms of their deviation from cases of intentionally doing it, again as opposed to treating the two kinds of case more symmetrically.

We cannot reasonably expect to decide between the two directions of explanation on the basis just of such abstract characterizations of the difference. Rather, we must explore the strengths and weaknesses of each approach in application to more specific problems.

The Analysis of Knowledge

One traditional aim of epistemology was to provide an "analysis of knowledge." Sometimes this meant analyzing the *concept* of knowledge, perhaps by providing a more complex sentence synonymous with "S knows that P" and thereby breaking the concept down into its constituent concepts, expressed by the constituent phrases of the complex sentence. At other times what it meant was analyzing the underlying *nature* of knowledge, which might be done without providing such a synonym, since that nature might have to be discovered through arduous investigation, without having already been written into the structure of our concepts or the meanings of our words. Either way, an analysis of knowledge was supposed to provide a non-circular statement of necessary and sufficient conditions for S to know that P. A paradigm candidate for such an analysis of knowledge is the once-popular "JTB" account, on which S knows that P if and only if S has a justified true belief that P.

Notoriously, the JTB analysis was refuted by Edmund Gettier, who gave examples to show that having a justified true belief is not sufficient for knowing. In the following decades, many attempts were made to repair the JTB analysis, by adding further conditions or modifying the justification condition. In each case, most epistemologists regard the attempted repair as unsuccessful, because it falls to other counter-examples, although some proposed analyses still have supporters. One reaction to this depressing track record is that it only shows that we must go on looking; analyzing knowledge was never going to be an easy task. Another reaction is that the track record constitutes good inductive evidence that there is no such analysis to be found: knowledge is not a combination of belief and other conditions more basic than knowledge itself; belief is not prior to knowledge. To decide between these contrasting reactions, we must widen the terms of the debate.

Was there ever good reason to *expect* non-circular necessary and sufficient conditions for knowledge? On some theories of concepts, all concepts are built up out of a small basic stock of simple concepts. A typical motivation for such a theory is empiricist; the simple concepts are supposed to have a peculiarly direct relation to experience. The concept of knowledge is not a promising candidate to be one of those few simple building-blocks. However, such theories of concepts are very hard to sustain on current evidence; very few words in natural languages seem to have that sort of semantic complexity. Nor do epistemologists usually make explicit appeal to theories of concepts in defending the program of seeking analyses of the concept of knowledge. Although very general presuppositions about the nature of concepts may have helped to motivate the idea that conceptual analysis is the goal of philosophy, they do not now provide good reason to expect a non-circular analysis of the concept of knowledge.

Another suggested reason is this. We already have some non-trivial *necessary* conditions for knowledge, such as truth and belief. Why then can't knowledge be analyzed as true belief plus whatever must be added to true belief to get knowledge? As it stands, "whatever must be added to true belief to get knowledge" is a circular specification, since it explicitly mentions knowledge; the problem is that we have been given no reason to expect that the circularity can be eliminated. The usual analogy here is with color concepts. Although being colored is a non-trivial necessary condition for being red, that gives us no reason to expect being red to have an analysis as being colored plus whatever must be added to being colored to get being red, under a different specification of the latter that does not mention red.

A third suggested reason is this. According to *internalist* theories of mind, a purely mental state has no necessary consequences for the world outside the mind: a brain in a vat can be in the same purely mental states as someone who is perceiving and acting on the environment in the normal way. On this view, knowing that it is snowing is not a purely mental state, because it has the non-mental necessary consequence that it *is* snowing. By contrast, believing that it is snowing has no obvious non-mental necessary consequences, and so might yet count as a purely mental state. One might therefore expect the hybrid, impurely mental state of knowing that it is snowing to be analyzable into purely mental components (such as believing that it is snowing) and purely non-mental components (such as it being true that it is snowing). However, such internalism about the mind is ill-supported. Many states that would ordinarily be regarded as mental have necessary consequences for the external world. For instance, loving Mary and hating Mary seem to be mental states, but being in those states has the necessary consequence that your apparently normal causal connections to Mary are not totally illusory. There are strong arguments for *semantic externalism*, on which the content of intentional states such as belief typically depends on causal connections between the thinker and the environment, so that those states have necessary consequences for the external world. For instance, if all the causal connections (direct and indirect) of one's "snow" beliefs had been with masses of tiny flying moths that just look like snow, they would not really have been beliefs that it was snowing; they would have been beliefs in a different proposition about that other phenomenon instead.

Faced with such examples, internalists might retort that such states are not *purely* mental. Indeed, they might be forced to concede that hardly any of the mental states we explicitly attribute in natural language are purely mental. The purely mental states become hypothetical constructs. Even granted that someone who believes that it is snowing is also in various internal states without necessary consequences for the external world, it is unclear why any of those internal states should count as mental. In saying what is peculiarly mental in the states of loving or hating Mary and of believing that it is snowing, it is natural to focus on their *aboutness*: loving or hating Mary is about Mary (she is the one on whom the requitedness or unrequitedness of the emotion depends); believing that it is snowing is about snow (it is the stuff on which the truth or falsity of the belief depends). That is the *point* of such states. Take away their aboutness and you take away what is most mental in them. Yet their necessary aboutness was what made them non-internal. Thus the internalist strategy of postulating internal states to be the underlying purely mental states treats as inessential exactly those features that seem central to the mentality of ordinary "impure" mental states.

Far from compromising "pure" mentality, semantic externalism arguably articulates a deep insight into the nature of mentality. But if mental states are typically ways of relating to one's environment, the truth-entailing nature of knowledge is no obstacle to its being a mental state in a quite unstretched sense. Knowing that it is snowing essentially involves awareness of one's environment in a way that mere believing that it is snowing does not: but that enhanced awareness hardly makes knowing *less* mental than believing. On this view, knowing is just as mental a state as believing. Its mental consequences are not exhausted by believing, or even by justified believing. Such externalism about mental attitudes themselves, not just their contents, is a natural development of knowledge first epistemology. If knowing is not an impure mental state, the argument lapses for expecting it to be analyzable into purely mental and purely non-mental components. Further challenges to the conception of knowing as a mental state will be discussed in later sections.

The arguments that knowledge must be analyzable all rest on highly contentious assumptions. Further inductive evidence for its unanalyzability comes from the track record of failure in programs for analyzing other philosophically central properties and relations, such as meaning and causation. Although such programs often give interesting partial results, attempts to state strictly necessary and sufficient conditions in non-circular terms typically lead to a regress of ever more complex analyses and ever more complex counter-examples. This further reduces the probability that knowledge has such an analysis in terms of belief. Of course, it also reduces the probability that belief has such an analysis in terms of knowledge.

Knowledge first epistemology challenges the project of analyzing knowledge in another way too. Analyses are supposed to be non-circular. In particular, the inclusion of the justification condition in analyses such as JTB presupposes that it is suitably independent of knowledge itself. As will appear later, knowledge first epistemology questions that independence.

Problems of Access

A salient feature of the state of knowing is that one is not always in a position to know whether one is in it. For example, if you are a victim of a clever hoaxer who makes it appear to you to be raining when it isn't, then, for all you are in a position to know, you know that it's raining. Really, you don't know that it's raining, but you are not in a position to know that you don't know that it's raining. Arguably, one can also know without being in a position to know that one knows (see below). Whether one knows is not fully open to introspection. If core mental states such as believing, desiring and feeling sensations *are* fully open to introspection, that would be a new reason to deny that knowing is a "pure" mental state.

Our limited access to whether we know might be used as an objection to knowledge first epistemology in other ways too. Some want epistemology to be *operational*, in the sense of providing rules for rational inquiry such that one is always in a position to know whether one is complying with them. A classic example of a non-operational rule is the useless advice "Believe what is true!"; if you knew what was true, you wouldn't need the advice. By contrast, the rule "Proportion your belief to the evidence!" sounds more useful; it seems to have a better chance of being operational. Non-operational epistemology has a third-personal aspect; it evaluates the agent's epistemic status as it were from the standpoint of an external observer, with access to information unavailable to the agent. Operational epistemology is first-personal in a corresponding sense. Whether one knows is a question for non-operational epistemology, whereas questions of rationality, justification and evidence seem to belong to operational epistemology. This suggests an objection to knowledge first epistemology: the inapplicable should not have priority over the applicable.

The reply on behalf of knowledge first epistemology is that states fully open to introspection and fully operational rules are an illusion. Any non-trivial state is such that one can be in it without being in a position to know that one is in it. An argument for that conclusion goes like this. Call a state *luminous* if whenever one is in it one is in a position to know that one is in it. For any non-trivial state, one can change from being in it to not being in it through a very gradual process. Since our powers of discrimination are limited, in the last moments of the process at which one is still in the state, one cannot discriminate how one is (in the relevant respects) from how one is in the first moments at which one is no longer in the state. In the former moments, one is in the state without being in a position to know that one is in it. Consequently, the state is not luminous (this can all be made more precise). Thus any luminous state is trivial. In particular, states of believing, desiring, and feeling sensations are non-luminous because non-trivial. One can feel pain without being in a position to know that one feels pain. One can believe something without being in a position to know that one believes it. Equally, since knowing is a non-trivial state, one can know something without being in a position to know that one knows it.

In many cases, there are other independent arguments for the non-luminosity of those states. For instance, postulating unconscious beliefs and desires might help to explain someone's actions. It is not even clear that one is always in at least as good a position to determine whether one believes something as to determine whether one knows it. For instance, someone who has just slowly and painfully lost her religious faith might be in a better position to know that she does not know that there is a god than she is to know that she does not believe that there is a god. Although one is *often* in a position to know without observing oneself "from the outside" whether one believes, desires or feels something, one is also often in a position to know without such further observation whether one knows something.

If no non-trivial mental states are fully open to introspection, then the fact that knowing is not fully open to introspection does not make it less mental than believing, desiring, and feeling sensations. Similarly, if one is always in a position to know whether one is complying with an operational rule, then the state of complying with that rule is luminous, and therefore trivial, in which case the rule itself must be trivial. Thus a fully operational epistemology is an impossible ideal. Even matters of rationality, justification and evidence are non-luminous.

The widespread temptation to conceive an agent's evidence as consisting of their present subjective states might, itself, result from the assumption that agents must always be in a position to know what evidence they have. If one rejects that assumption, one can take seriously a straightforward conception of agents' total evidence as comprising the total content of their knowledge (E = K), a view much closer to the way scientists treat evidence—and a characteristic thesis of knowledge first epistemology.

The equation E = K has controversial implications for skepticism. Skeptics often argue that we cannot know whether we are in an everyday scenario or a corresponding skeptical scenario, because we have the same evidence in each. Even some anti-skeptics concede such sameness of evidence. But a defender of common sense can contest that assumption. In the everyday scenario, I know that I have hands. In the skeptical scenario, I lack hands and therefore do not know that I have them. Thus my knowledge differs between the two scenarios. Given E = K, that difference in my knowledge constitutes a difference in my evidence: the skeptical argument rests on a false premise. Part of my cognitive deprivation in the skeptical scenario is that I am not aware that I have less evidence than in the everyday scenario. Of course, that does not exhaust the skeptic's resources. The skeptical argument can be reworked in various ways. Nevertheless, once one is alert to the way in which skeptical reasoning can conceal such unargued epistemological assumptions, one is better placed to dispute the reasoning.

Questions of justification and rationality concern doing the best one can on one's limited evidence; given E = K, that means doing the best one can on one's limited knowledge. If so, they are not prior to questions of knowledge. What you are justified or rational in believing depends on what you know. Thus the occurrence of a justification or rationality condition in an analysis of knowledge risks circularity.

Such externalism about evidence also has implications for the epistemology of philosophy itself. Philosophers have implicitly tended to conduct their reasoning as though their evidence were restricted to data on which all the rival theories can agree. For example, if B denies that there are macroscopic physical objects, then A might cite as evidence not the "question-begging" non-psychological fact that there are rocks but only the psychological fact that we have an "intuition" that there are rocks. Of course, if A is trying to change B's mind, it is normally pointless for A to cite as evidence facts that B denies. However, if A's goal is to find the truth on some matter for herself, not to persuade B of it, why shouldn't she use her knowledge that there are rocks, rather than just her knowledge that she has an intuition that there are rocks. The non-psychological fact might be far more relevant than the psychological one to her question. That might sound like dogmatically rejecting B's point of view. However, the alternative strategy of using only universally accepted evidence is hopeless, since there is virtually no such evidence. Some philosophers will deny that anyone has an intuition that there are rocks, perhaps because they are eliminativists about such mental states, while accepting that there are rocks. To engage in philosophy is to engage in controversy. Of course, that does not mean that there are no constraints. E=K says that your evidence comprises what you do know, not what you believe you know. That it is often hard to recognize the difference in practice might be an inescapable aspect of our cognitive predicament: even the epistemology of philosophy must be non-operational.

Reasons for Action

Here is yet another objection to knowledge's being a mental state. Genuine mental states play a role in causal explanations of rational action. Such explanations cite the agent's beliefs and desires. They do not cite the agent's knowledge as such, for even if some of those beliefs do in fact constitute knowledge, that is irrelevant to their role in causing the action. If you want a drink of water and believe that your glass contains water, then other things being equal you will drink from your glass, whether or not you really know that it contains water. But if believing screens out knowing in the causal explanation of action, then knowing has no serious claim to be a mental state over and above believing.

One problem with that argument is its assumption that causal explanations of action are always of action "at the next instant." If any time elapses from when the agent is in the original mental states of interest to when the action is completed, the difference between knowing and believing might matter causally. In the example above, if a teetotaler falsely believes a glass of gin to contain water, he might spit the gin out as soon as he tastes it without drinking any; that is far less likely to happen if he knows the glass to contain water. Even true belief tends to be less persistent than knowledge, since true beliefs can depend on false ones in ways that knowledge cannot; the former are therefore more vulnerable than the latter to abandonment through discovery of such false assumptions before the action has been completed. Thus believing does not always screen out knowing in the causal explanation of action.

From a normative perspective, knowing is arguably *more* relevant to rational action than believing is. Suppose that, in deciding whether to take certain pills, I treat as a reason for taking them that they will alleviate my hay fever symptoms. If you point out that I don't know whether they will alleviate my symptoms, you reveal a defect in my decision-making with respect to that premise. By contrast, if I do know that the pills will alleviate my symptoms, my decision-making is not defective with respect to that premise. Mere belief in the premise is not what matters, since that is consistent with the belief's being both false and irrational. If I don't know the premise but have strong evidence that I do know it, that may be a good excuse for having treated it as a reason, but that does not make the decision-making non-defective, otherwise no excuse would be needed. In some cases of extreme urgency, I may rely on premises that I know myself not to know even though they are highly probable on my evidence. The urgency is another excuse for defective reasoning; it does not remove the defect. To do that, I might have to replace the premise that the medicine will alleviate my symptoms by the premise, which I might know, that it is highly probable on my evidence that the medicine will alleviate my symptoms. Such a view of reasons for action is another natural development of knowledge first epistemology.

Belief and Assertion

If one was never willing to treat "P" as a reason for doing anything, even when one believed "If P, the house is on fire," then one's commitment to "P" would be too weak to count as belief. Given the connection between knowledge and reasons for action, it follows that if one believes that P, one is willing to make decisions in a way that is non-defective only if one knows that P. This suggests a simpler cognitive norm: believe that P only if you know that P. Call that *the knowledge rule for belief* (KRB).

Versions of Moore's paradox confirm KRB. Something is wrong with believing "It's raining and I don't know that it's raining," even though the belief could very easily be true. Although the two conjuncts are logically consistent with each other, the second undermines the first. KRB explains how. It tells me to believe the conjunction only if I know the conjunction. But I cannot know the conjunction, for to know it I must know the first conjunct ("It's raining"), in which case the second conjunct is false, making the whole conjunction false and therefore unknown. Thus in believing "It's raining and I don't know that it's raining," one automatically violates KRB. If KRB is not in force, it is quite unclear what is wrong with believing such conjunctions.

If a justified belief is one that satisfies the norms for belief, then by KRB only knowledge constitutes justified belief. In particular, there are no justified false beliefs. This might rescue the letter of the JTB account of knowledge from Gettier, since his counterexamples rely on the assumption that there are justified false beliefs, which generate justified true beliefs because the deceived subject can competently deduce true conclusions from false premises and thereby extend his justification from the latter to the former.

However, KRB certainly does not rescue the spirit of JTB. Gettier treated the notion of justification as proponents of JTB had intended; they made truth an independent condition precisely because they did not think that it followed from the other two. KRB makes JTB effectively circular as an analysis of knowledge, since the relevant norm invokes knowledge. Given KRB, the sense of "justification" that Gettier shared with proponents of JTB seems to involve excuse as much as justification: a "justified" false belief is a belief for which the agent has a good excuse, which may consist in strong but misleading evidence that the belief constitutes knowledge.

In the sense in which only knowledge constitutes full justification, one can also define a graded sense of justification, using the equation $E = K$. For the probability of a proposition on one's evidence becomes its probability conditional on the total content of one's knowledge. That probability can be interpreted as one's degree of justification to believe the proposition. The structure of such evidential probabilities can be explored through mathematical models of epistemic logic, sometimes with unexpected results. For example, one can know something even if the probability on one's own evidence that one knows it is close to zero.

Assertion is an analog for speech of belief. It has an analog of KRB, the knowledge rule for assertion (KRA): assert that P only if you know that P. Just as Moore-paradoxical beliefs provide evidence for KRB, so Moore-paradoxical assertions provide evidence for KRA. Moreover, KRA can be supported by a wide range of linguistic data. As with KRB, opponents of KRA tend to object that it sets an unrealistically high standard. For proponents of KRA, such objections, too, mistake excuses for justifications. If the anti-luminosity argument is correct, one can violate *any* non-trivial norm for assertion or belief without being in a position to know that one is violating it.

Both KRA and KRB are natural developments of knowledge first epistemology, for they imply that even central non-truth-entailing cognitive attitudes such as asserting and believing depend normatively on knowing.

Perception and Memory

Knowing is not the only truth-entailing attitude. If one perceives that it is raining, it is raining. If it is not raining, one at most seems to oneself to perceive that it is raining. Similarly, if one remembers that it was raining, it was raining. If it was not raining, one at most seems to oneself to remember that it was raining. Perceiving and remembering are further instances of truth-entailing mental attitudes, if knowing is already one.

Arguably, perceiving and remembering entail not just truth but knowledge: if one perceives that it is raining, one knows that it is raining; if one remembers that it was raining, one knows that it was raining. Objections to these claims focus on cases in which one's perceptual or memory apparatus is in fact functioning properly, but misleading evidence casts doubt on whether it is functioning properly. However, it is not clear in such cases that one perceives or remembers that P without knowing that P. One may perceive the rain without perceiving *that* it is raining, or remember the rain without remembering *that* it was raining, if one fails to recognize the rain as rain. Alternatively, if one does recognize the rain as rain, presumably one does know that it is or was raining. That the misleading evidence casts doubt on whether one knows does not mean that one does not know.

If perceiving and remembering are knowledge-entailing mental attitudes, a wider conjecture suggests itself: that knowing is the most general truth-entailing mental attitude, the one you have to a proposition if and only if you have any truth-entailing mental attitude to it at all. The defense of such a conjecture requires interpreting "mental attitude" appropriately: for example, having forgotten that P had better not count as a mental attitude towards the proposition that P. At least, very many truth-entailing attitudes are closely related to knowing. If you are conscious or aware that P, you know that P; if you learn, discover, or recognize that P, you come to know that P. These examples illustrate how hard it is to imagine a cognitive life in which knowing plays no part. It would be a life in which one was never conscious or aware that something was the case, and never perceived, remembered, learned, discovered, or recognized that something was the case.

Knowledge first epistemology has important similarities to *disjunctivist* accounts of perception, which are sophisticated modern versions of "naive realism." Disjunctivists often explain failure (illusion, hallucination) in terms of its relation to success (genuine perception), rather than treating the two cases on a par. Typically, they also hold that there is a mental state (in an unstretched sense) that one is in when and only when one is genuinely perceiving: one *takes in* the world. Consequently, they deny that one's mental state can be exactly the same in cases of failure as in cases of success, with the only difference consisting in external causal relations inessential to that state. They might well agree that one has more perceptual evidence in the good case than in the bad case: it is just that sometimes, when one is in the bad case, for all one knows one is in the good case. Furthermore, disjunctivists are often sympathetic to the claim that perceiving that P entails knowing that P. To a first approximation, therefore, disjunctivism about perception is simply knowledge first epistemology as applied to perception. However, some qualifications are needed.

First, disjunctivism is usually advanced as a theory about perception in its own right, without appeal to wider claims of knowledge first epistemology.

Second, disjunctivism takes its name from ideas like this: a state of having things perceptually appear to one a certain way is a disjunction of two radically different disjuncts; *either* one is in the successful state *or* one is in the unsuccessful state. The impression is sometimes given that the two disjuncts are being characterized independently of each other, which would undermine the explanatory priority of the first disjunct over the second. However, there is little prospect of grouping together all instances of having it perceptually appear to one that P without perceiving that P except under such a negative characterization; the second disjunct is not really being characterized independently of the first and the supposedly disjunctive state. The strictly *disjunctive* aspect of disjunctivism might be its least defensible feature. But even if the letter of disjunctivism is rejected, its spirit is retained in the idea that success in perception cannot be analyzed as a combination of success-neutral perceptual appearances with external causal perceptions inessential to the subject's mental state.

Third, some disjunctivist accounts focus on object perception (seeing a tree) rather than fact perception (seeing that it is a tree). Object perception is less "epistemic" than fact perception. A cat can look at a king without knowing that he is a king. Here the relation to knowledge first epistemology is less direct. Nevertheless, the emphasis on the explanatory priority of successful cognitive engagement with the external world remains similar.

The extensive analogies between perception and memory raise the question of disjunctivism about memory. So far, such a view has been less fully explored.

Further Themes

Knowledge first epistemology has many more applications. One issue is the nature of consciousness. While opponents often regard knowledge first epistemology as false to what conscious experience is like, as shown by arguments from illusion, proponents reply that many states of consciousness do *seem* essentially to involve external objects and facts; thus when those states are as they seem, they *do* essentially involve external objects and facts, just as states of conscious knowledge and perception do. In cases of illusion, even our states of consciousness are not always as they seem. That is just what the anti-luminosity argument predicts: conscious subjects are sometimes not in a position to know what states of consciousness they are in.

Another application of knowledge first epistemology is to questions about what determines the content of mental attitudes: for instance, what constitutes mental reference to one object rather than another? A central role is often assigned to a principle of charity that prefers assignments of content that maximize the subject's true beliefs. However, assigning true beliefs to a subject might not be an interpretive virtue when those beliefs do not constitute knowledge. This suggests using instead a principle of charity that maximizes the subject's knowledge rather than true belief.

Knowledge first epistemology is still an alien way of thinking to many philosophers, despite its roots in naive realism and common sense. Much of its detailed working out has been very recent, and all the issues raised in this chapter require extensive further investigation. Knowledge first epistemology is contributing a further stage to the development of externalist ideas over past decades. The process is likely to continue.

Further Reading

Austin, J.L. (1964) *Sense and Sensibilia*, Oxford: Oxford University Press. (Classic defense of common sense about perception and bridge between earlier and later versions of knowledge first epistemology.)

Gettier, E. (1963) "Is Justified True Belief Knowledge?" *Analysis* 23: 121–3. (The classic article.)

Gibbons, J. (2001) "Knowledge in Action," *Philosophy and Phenomenological Research* 62: 579–600. (Defense of knowledge constraint on reasons for action.)

Greenough, P. and Pritchard, D. (eds) (2009) *Williamson on Knowledge*, Oxford: Oxford University Press. (Extensive collection of critical essays on *Knowledge and its Limits*, with replies.)

Haddock, A. and Macpherson, F. (eds) (2008) *Disjunctivism: Perception, Action, Knowledge*, Oxford: Oxford University Press. (Large collection of papers for and against.)

Hawthorne, J. (2004) *Knowledge and Lotteries*, Oxford: Clarendon Press. (Examination of puzzles about chance and shifting standards, using knowledge first ideas.)

—— and Stanley, J. (2008) "Knowledge and Action," *Journal of Philosophy* 105: 571–90. (Defense of knowledge norm.)

Hinton, J.M. (1973) *Experiences*, Oxford: Clarendon Press. (Early version of disjunctivism about perception.)

Martin, M.G.F. (2002) "The Transparency of Experience," *Mind and Language* 17: 376–425. (Disjunctivism about experience.)

—— (2004) "The Limits of Self-Awareness," *Philosophical Studies* 120: 37–89. (Disjunctivism about perception.)

McDowell, J. (1998). *Meaning, Knowledge and Reality*, Cambridge, Mass.: Harvard University Press. (Collection of his papers, with many themes related to knowledge first epistemology, including disjunctivism.)

Phillips Griffiths, A. (ed.) (1967) *Knowledge and Belief*, Oxford: Oxford University Press. (Anthology with pieces by John Cook Wilson and H.A. Prichard advocating an earlier form of knowledge first epistemology.)

Snowdon, P. (1980–1) "Perception, Vision, and Causation," *Proceedings of the Aristotelian Society* sup. vol. 81: 175–92. (Disjunctivism about perception.)

Unger, P. (1975) *Ignorance: A Case for Scepticism*, Oxford: Oxford University Press. (Early source of linguistic evidence for knowledge first ideas.)
Williamson, T. (2000) *Knowledge and its Limits*, Oxford: Oxford University Press. (Development of a knowledge first epistemology along the lines presented here.)
—— (2007) *The Philosophy of Philosophy*, Oxford: Blackwell. (A knowledge first epistemology of philosophy, with discussion of knowledge maximization.)

21
THE VALUE PROBLEM
John Greco

The problem of explaining epistemic value (or explaining the value of knowledge) has been with us for a long time. It is one of the perennial problems of philosophy, going back at least as far as Plato's *Meno*. Besides being important in its own right, the problem is related to other issues in epistemology (or the theory of knowledge).

For example, Jonathan Kvanvig has argued that the value problem is closely tied to another perennial problem in the theory of knowledge: that of explaining what knowledge is. Specifically, if an answer to the question "What is knowledge?" makes it difficult to see why knowledge is valuable, then that very fact counts against that answer. On the other hand, if an answer to the "What is knowledge?" question makes it easy to see why we value knowledge, then that counts in favor of that answer. Ideally, an adequate account of knowledge will explain both *what knowledge is* and *why knowledge is valuable* (Kvanvig 2003). (Linda Zagzebski (1996) makes the point in even stronger terms, arguing that any adequate theory *must* explain the value of knowledge. In contrast, Duncan Pritchard (2007, 2008b) makes the point in weaker terms, arguing that an adequate theory must explain only *the intuition* that knowledge is valuable. Accordingly, Pritchard allows for "revisionary" answers to the value problem; i.e. answers that explain why we think knowledge is valuable, even if that thought ultimately harbors an illusion.)

Relatedly, Linda Zagzebski has argued that the value problem makes trouble for many contemporary theories of knowledge. She argues that, in principle, a popular version of externalism in epistemology cannot account for the value of knowledge. This is the so-called "Swamping Problem" for reliabilism (Kvanvig 2003; Zagzebski 1996). Duncan Pritchard has also argued that thinking about the value problem throws light on the internalism/externalism debate in epistemology, but in a different way. Specifically, Pritchard argues that externalist theories do not give knowledge the sort of value that internalists want knowledge to have. This explains internalist dissatisfaction with externalist theories, Pritchard argues, as well as the skeptical inclination of many internalist philosophers (Pritchard 2008a).

Some philosophers have argued that reflection on the value problem motivates a radical shift in the focus of epistemological theorizing. The thought here is that, properly understood, knowledge does not in fact have the special value that epistemologists presuppose. Thus Mark Kaplan argues that distinctive epistemic value resides in justification rather than knowledge, and so epistemology ought to focus on the former rather than the latter (Kaplan 1985). In a similar vein, Kvanvig and Pritchard argue that understanding rather than knowledge has a distinctive epistemic value, and so the focus of epistemology ought to be understanding (Kvanvig 2003; Pritchard 2009).

Finally, Timothy Williamson suggests that reflection on epistemic value motivates a different sort of shift in epistemological theorizing. Since the advent of "Gettier problems," which show that traditional accounts of knowledge are inadequate, epistemologists have offered more and more complicated analyses of what knowledge is. Williamson's thought is that these complicated analyses can all be rejected, and precisely because they make it hard to see why knowledge should be valuable. The moral of post-Gettier epistemology, Williamson argues, is that we should give up trying to analyze knowledge at all. Better to take knowledge as a primitive of epistemological theorizing, and to explain other epistemic concepts, and presumably epistemic value, in terms of knowledge (Williamson 2000).

A Problem from Plato's Meno

Recent controversies notwithstanding, there is a strong presumption among philosophers and non-philosophers alike that knowledge is especially valuable. But why should that be? Why is knowledge valuable? According to a popular slogan, "Knowledge is power." This slogan suggests that knowledge is valuable because it allows us to *do* things. For example, knowing "how the world works" allows us to manipulate things, or perhaps even to manipulate people. More generally, knowledge helps us to achieve our goals. The suggestion in the popular slogan, then, is that knowledge has *practical* value.

That much seems perfectly right, but it does not fully explain the value that we think knowledge has. One reason is that the slogan remains vague. Even if knowledge does have practical value, we want to know why and in what sense. We want to know the details. But a second reason the slogan falls short is that we think knowledge has value *over and above* the value of mere opinion, and even mere true opinion, which also have practical value. Plato makes this point in the *Meno*. The man who wants to go to Larissa, Plato tells us, gets there just as well by having a true opinion about which road to take as by having knowledge about which road to take. But we think that, even so, knowledge is more valuable than true opinion. But then why should that be so? Why should knowledge be more valuable than true opinion, if their practical value is the same? Again, we do not yet have a complete answer to our question about the value of knowledge. Put somewhat differently, we do not yet fully understand why we value knowledge in the way that we do.

This is "the *Meno* problem," or the problem of explaining why knowledge is more valuable than mere true belief. We may also think of the problem as a kind of puzzle. The puzzle begins by noting three plausible thoughts (employed already above) that we have about knowledge:

1. The value of knowledge resides in its practical value: we value knowledge because it gives us power to do things.
2. But true opinion has all the practical value that knowledge has: believing the truth is just as good as knowing the truth, as far as getting things done is concerned.
3. And yet knowledge seems to be *more* valuable than true belief—we think that knowledge has value *over and above* the value of true opinion.

The puzzle is that not all three of these thoughts can be true: at least one thought needs to be revised, but it is not obvious which we should choose.

Philosophers have endorsed each of the options available here. Denying (1), some philosophers have argued that knowledge has a non-practical value that mere true belief and other close relatives of knowledge lack (for example, Greco 2003, 2008, 2009; Riggs 2002; Sosa 1991, 2007). We will look more closely at a version of this approach below, when we consider the position that knowledge is a kind of achievement, and that, as such, knowledge is "valuable for its own sake."

Denying (2), some philosophers have argued that knowledge does, after all, have greater practical value than mere true opinion. This seems to be Socrates' answer in the *Meno*, when he suggests that knowledge is "tethered" or "tied down" in a way that mere true opinion is not. A more recent defense of this position is found in Williamson, when he argues that knowledge is more stable than mere true belief. Consider again the man who wants to get to Larissa. If the man merely believes that a particular road will get him there, he might give up and turn around if things start to look otherwise. That is, even if his belief is *true*, he might give up on it if he gets misleading evidence that the road does not go to Larissa, for example if the road takes an unexpected turn. The man who knows, however, is less likely to be fooled by such misleading evidence (Williamson 2000).

Finally, other philosophers have denied that knowledge really is more valuable than mere true opinion (hence they deny (3)). Some who have taken this third option have argued that true opinion has all the value we want (Sartwell 1992). Others who have taken this third option have argued that something else, rather than knowledge, really does have special and greater value over both knowledge and true opinion. As we have already seen, Kvanvig and Pritchard take this option (e.g. Kvanvig 2003; Pritchard 2009).

Refining the Meno Problem

Problems about epistemic value tend to multiply. In fact, we have already seen various versions of the problem and hinted at some others. Thus we may ask:

> The General Value Problem: Why (how, in what way) is knowledge valuable?
> The *Meno* Problem: Why is knowledge more valuable than true opinion?
> The Secondary Value Problem: Why is knowledge more valuable than *any* of its proper parts? Why is knowledge more valuable than that which falls short of knowledge?
> The Tertiary Value Problem: Why is knowledge *distinctively* valuable? That is, why does knowledge have a special value, over and above its practical value?

In addition to these, one might think that there is a fourth problem:

> The Quaternary Value Problem: Why is knowledge more valuable than anything in the neighborhood?

Notice that the different value problems above share a common structure. Each of them asks a question of the form:

> Why is *knowledge* of greater value than *non-knowledge of some sort*?

Different versions of the value problem can be generated, then, by substituting different *contrast classes* into the above structure. Thus we have:

> The General Value Problem: Why is knowledge more valuable *than non-knowledge in general*?
> The *Meno* Problem: Why is knowledge more valuable *than true opinion*?
> The Secondary Value Problem: Why is knowledge more valuable than *any of its proper parts*?
> The Quaternary Value Problem: Why is knowledge more valuable than *anything in the neighborhood*?

Further disambiguations of our questions are possible as well. Thus we can disambiguate along all of the following dimensions:

a. by contrast class (as above)
b. by quantity or quality:

> Why is knowledge more valuable *by degree* than . . .?
> Why is knowledge more valuable *in kind* than . . .? (this is the Tertiary Value Problem)
> Why is knowledge of more "*over-all*" value than . . .?

c. by quantifier:

> Why is *all* knowledge more valuable than . . .?
> Why is knowledge *typically* more valuable than . . .?
> Why is *some* knowledge more valuable than . . .?

d. by distribution:

> Why is knowledge *as a class* more valuable than non-knowledge of some sort *as a class*?
> Why is knowledge *that p* more valuable than non-knowledge of some sort *that p*?

Finally, we might disambiguate our questions in yet another way: by interpreting the sort of "why question" that they are asking. Thus one kind of why question asks for what Aristotle called a "formal" cause. This sort of question asks about a thing's nature or essence. A different sort of why question asks for what Aristotle called an "efficient" cause—it asks for how a thing is related to other things. Notice that the two kinds of "why question" ask for different kinds of explanation. Thus we have the following disambiguation:

e. by "why question":

> *What sort of thing is knowledge*, such that knowledge is of greater value than non-knowledge of some sort?
> *How is knowledge effectively related to other things*, such that knowledge is of greater value than non-knowledge of some sort?

THE VALUE PROBLEM

Looking at these various ways in which we can disambiguate the value problem, we might note that there is both bad news and good news. The bad news is that our various distinctions cut across each other, and so the value problem quickly multiplies into a fairly large number of distinct questions. But there is good news as well. First, the answers to some of our questions quite clearly depend on the answers to others. Perhaps most obviously, any answer that explains why *all* knowledge has value of a sort, will also explain why *some* knowledge has value of that sort. So not all of our distinctions generate distinct value problems in the sense that each requires a distinct solution.

Second, not all of the value problems that we have identified are equally compelling or pressing. For example, consider the question: Why does knowledge typically have a special value over and above that which falls short of knowledge? It seems that this question deserves an answer—that it is a compelling question in that sense. But this is not clearly the case for all of our questions. For example: Why are all cases of knowledge that p more practically valuable than all cases of non-knowledge that p? We might think that this question is not compelling at all, for we might think that it is not *true* that all cases of knowledge that p are more practically valuable than all cases of non-knowledge that p. For example, consider my recently acquired knowledge that the phrase "coffee shop" has ten letters. This knowledge is of little if any practical value, and so is plausibly not *more* practically valuable than a mere true belief that "coffee shop" has ten letters.

What makes a version of the value problem more or less compelling? Notice that each problem takes the form of a question, and that each question has a presupposition. For example, the question "Why is knowledge valuable?" carries the presupposition that knowledge *is* valuable. The question "Why is knowledge more valuable than any of its proper parts?" carries the presupposition that knowledge *is* more valuable than any of its proper parts. A version of the value problem will be more or less compelling, I want to suggest, depending on whether its presupposition is more or less plausible.

Consider now an interesting and potentially disturbing phenomenon: A person's intuitions about how to answer the value problem might affect how he or she goes on to disambiguate the problem on further analysis. For example, suppose you think, pre-theoretically, that knowledge is more valuable than non-knowledge because it is of more *practical value*. In that case, you are likely to interpret relevant quantifiers as being about typical cases. Why so? Because it is implausible that *every* case of knowledge has more practical value than every case of non-knowledge, or that *every* case of knowledge that p has more practical value than every case of non-knowledge that p.

But suppose you think, pre-theoretically, that knowledge has some *distinctive* value that non-knowledge lacks. In that case, you are more likely to interpret the relevant quantifiers as universal. For it will be natural to think that distinctive value goes with knowledge *as a kind*. And if knowledge does have distinctive value as a kind, then it is at least plausible that every instance of its kind will have that value.

Here is another example of how initial judgments can affect subsequent theorizing. Suppose again that you think (pre-theoretically) that knowledge is more valuable than non-knowledge because it is of more *practical value*. In that case you are likely to interpret the "why question" as asking for an efficient cause: *How is knowledge effectively related to other things*, such that knowledge is typically of greater practical value than non-knowledge? On the other hand, suppose you think (pre-theoretically) that knowledge is more valuable *in kind* than non-knowledge? In that case you are likely to take the "why question" as asking for a formal cause: *What sort of thing is knowledge*, such that knowledge is more valuable in kind than non-knowledge?

Is this disturbing, implying that philosophers must inevitably talk past each other, depending on their original pre-theoretical intuitions about how to solve an ambiguous problem? Or is this just one more instance (no more disturbing than any other) of a more general hermeneutic circle? In either case, it is mistaken to think that we are moving from less refined to more refined versions of the same question as we move, for example, from the General Value Problem to the *Meno* Problem, or from the Secondary Value Problem to the Tertiary Value Problem. Rather, we are at least sometimes shifting questions, or asking different questions altogether. Perhaps a better understanding is this: There are many versions of the value problem, many of which are compelling enough to deserve an answer. A fully adequate answer to "the value problem" will have to say something about all of these.

A Virtue-Theoretic Solution to the Value Problems

We turn now to a recently popular solution to the value problem, or the problem of explaining the value of knowledge (e.g. Greco 2003, 2009; Riggs 2002; Sosa 1991, 2007). The proposed solution employs two important ideas. The first is that knowledge is a kind of success from ability. Put differently, knowledge is a kind of achievement. Hence:

> In cases of knowledge, S has a true belief *because* S's belief is produced by ability.

Alternatively:

> When S knows that p, S's having a true belief that p (rather than a false belief or no belief at all) is to be explained by S's cognitive abilities. More exactly, it is to be explained by the fact that S has exercised some cognitive ability, such as reliable perception, or reliable memory, or sound reasoning.

The second important idea is that, in general, success from ability is more valuable than lucky success. Put differently, we value achievements over lucky successes. What is more, we think that achievements have a distinctive value that mere lucky successes lack. Achievements have "final value," meaning that they are *valuable for their own sake*.

Putting these two ideas together, we get elegant solutions to both the *Meno* Problem and the Tertiary Value Problem: Knowledge is more valuable than mere true belief, in that knowledge has a final value that mere true belief does not. Additionally, we get a solution to the Secondary Value Problem: Knowledge is more valuable than *any* of its proper parts, and even more value than *the sum* of its parts. This is because belief that is true and produced by ability is not as valuable as belief that is true *because* produced by ability. Only achievements (knowledge included) have this latter structure.

The proposed account has at least two major advantages. First, it is extremely elegant, both in the way that it explains the value of knowledge, and in the way that it explains the relationship between the value of knowledge and the nature of knowledge. In effect, the explanation is simply this:

1. Achievements are finally valuable.
2. Knowledge is a kind of achievement.

Therefore,

3. Knowledge is finally valuable.

The second advantage of the account is that it places knowledge in a broader, familiar normative domain. In any arena in which human beings are capable of success from ability, we will find similar practices of crediting, criticizing, evaluating for success, etc. To the extent that we understand these broader practices, our account of knowledge and its value is thereby informed by that understanding.

Knowledge, Understanding and Wisdom

Is every case of knowledge more valuable than anything in the neighborhood? Intuitively, the answer is "No," because understanding that p is more valuable than merely knowing that p. More generally, understanding is more valuable than knowledge and wisdom is more valuable than understanding.

We can accommodate these intuitions on the "Knowledge as Achievement" account by wedding it to a traditional (Aristotelian) account of understanding and wisdom. Specifically, understanding has been traditionally understood as knowledge of causes, or knowing the answer to "Why" and "How" questions. In this same tradition, wisdom is understood as understanding of the highest (or most important) things.

Wedding this tradition to the present account of the value of knowledge, we can say the following: Understanding and wisdom are also achievements, and therefore have final value. But wisdom has more final value than mere understanding and understanding has more final value than mere knowledge. That is, in each case the former is more valuable *for its own sake* than the latter. Understanding and wisdom are *greater* achievements. We might still say, however, that *some* knowledge is more valuable than anything in the neighborhood. That is, understanding and wisdom are.

Some Objections to the Knowledge as Achievement Account

Duncan Pritchard has raised the following objection to the proposed account of the value of knowledge.

> [T]he real weak point for this proposal lies with the achievement thesis. In particular, on closer analysis it turns out that knowledge is not a cognitive achievement at all. This is because one can possess knowledge without exhibiting a cognitive achievement, and exhibit a cognitive achievement while lacking knowledge.
> (Pritchard 2008a; see also Pritchard 2008b and 2009)

Some Cognitive Achievements Are Not Knowledge

The argument that some cognitive achievements are not knowledge comes in two steps. First, Pritchard asks us to consider the following case of Archie, who seems to exhibits a genuine achievement.

> Archie . . . selects a target at random, skilfully fires at this target and successfully hits it because of his skill . . . Suppose, however, that unbeknownst to Archie

> there is a forcefield around each of the other targets such that, had he aimed at one of these targets, he would have missed. It is thus a matter of luck that he is successful, in the sense that he could very easily have not been successful.
>
> (Pritchard 2009)

According to Pritchard, Archie's success in hitting the target is from ability, even if (unknown to him) he hits the one genuine target in the area.

The second step in Pritchard's argument is to draw an analogy to standard Barn Façade cases. In those cases, epistemologists tend to agree, the person in question does not know that he sees a real barn. Thus consider the following Barn Façade case from Pritchard.

> Barney forms a true belief that there is a barn in front of him by using his cognitive abilities ... The twist in the tale, however, is that, unbeknownst to Barney, he is in fact in "barn façade county" where all the other apparent barns are fakes. Intuitively, he does not have knowledge in this case because it is simply a matter of luck that his belief is true.
>
> (Pritchard 2009)

Since the archery and barn façade cases are in all relevant respects analogous, Pritchard argues, we must allow that Barney's success is from ability and that he exhibits a genuine achievement. But then, of course, Pritchard's first conclusion follows: there are cases of cognitive achievement that are not cases of knowledge.

Some Cases of Knowledge Are Not Cases of Achievement

A number of philosophers have argued that some cases of knowledge are not cases of achievement. Here we may consider a case of testimonial knowledge from Jennifer Lackey.

> Having just arrived at the train station in Chicago, Morris wishes to obtain directions to the Sears Tower. He looks around, randomly approaches the first passerby that he sees, and asks how to get to his desired destination. The passerby, who happens to be a Chicago resident who knows the city extraordinarily well, provides Morris with impeccable directions to the Sears Tower.
>
> (Lackey 2007)

The argument is straightforward: Morris's true belief in the Sears Tower case is best explained by the cognitive abilities of the testifier, and to that extent the achievement is his rather than Morris's. Testimonial knowledge, then, gives us knowledge without achievement in the relevant sense.

Pritchard's Anti-luck Virtue Epistemology

In the face of objections to the Knowledge as Achievement account, Pritchard offers an alternative explanation of the value of knowledge. On Pritchard's account, knowledge remains a kind of success from ability, but this does not have the result that knowledge is always an achievement or that knowledge is always valuable (see Pritchard 2008a and 2009).

There are two elements to Pritchard's account of knowledge: an anti-luck condition and an ability condition. We need the anti-luck component, Pritchard argues, in order to rule out the sort of luck that is present in standard Gettier cases and in Barn Façade cases. Once we have incorporated an appropriate anti-luck condition, however, we only need a modest ability condition. According to Pritchard, knowledge requires that true belief is "in substantial part due to ability" but not necessarily "because of ability." The idea here is that ability must be involved in the production of true belief, but need not play the central role in explanation that the Knowledge as Achievement view requires. According to Pritchard, then, knowledge is non-lucky cognitive success that is in substantial part due to ability.

It should now be clear how Pritchard's account handles the cases we saw in the previous section. Since the present account weakens the ability condition, it can allow that there is knowledge in the Sears Tower case and in many other cases of belief from testimony. Since the account includes a separate anti-luck condition, it continues to handle standard Gettier cases and Barn Façade cases. Therefore, Pritchard argues, his account of knowledge solves both of the problems raised for the Knowledge as Achievement account. Moreover, Pritchard argues, this new account of knowledge yields a compelling explanation of the value of knowledge. In short, we may reject the presupposition that *all* knowledge is valuable, and replace it with the idea that all cognitive achievement is valuable. Our pre-theoretical intuitions about the value of knowledge are thus explained but not preserved. That is, we have an explanation of why we might *think* all knowledge is valuable—we are apt to confuse knowledge with cognitive achievement. Closer consideration convinces us that not all knowledge is cognitive achievement and not all cognitive achievement is knowledge, although knowledge is typically a cognitive achievement, and therefore typically has the associated distinctive value. Moreover, Pritchard argues, there is something in the neighborhood—a species of understanding—that *is* a kind of cognitive achievement and therefore always has a distinctive value (Pritchard 2009).

Pritchard's alternative account of knowledge and its value has much to recommend it. However, it does have a significant disadvantage when compared to the Knowledge as Achievement account. Namely, the account is less elegant in two ways. First, Anti-luck Virtue Epistemology invokes independent ability and anti-luck conditions. Moreover, within that account the two conditions lack any unifying theoretical motivation. Rather, they are proposed because they are needed to handle different kinds of cases. In that respect, the account is *ad hoc*. Second, Anti-luck Virtue Epistemology must adopt a revisionary solution to the value problem. That is, it requires that we *explain away* various pre-theoretically plausible intuitions about the value of knowledge, including the intuition that all knowledge is distinctively valuable.

Neither of these liabilities constitutes an objection to Anti-luck Virtue Epistemology. Rather, they are theoretical costs that might or might not be offset by advantages elsewhere.

In light of these costs, however, we should see what can be said for the Knowledge as Achievement account in response to the objections that were raised against it earlier.

Knowledge as Achievement Revisited

First, what can be said in face of the objection that some cases of knowledge are not cases of achievement? More specifically, what should we say about the Sears Tower case? Some philosophers have not found the case convincing, and in particular they have suggested that the case is under-described (for example, Greco 2009; Riggs 2009). Most significantly, are we to understand the case so that Morris is exercising his cognitive abilities in evaluating the testimony he receives? Or does Morris simply accept "willy-nilly" whatever the testifier says? In either case, we seem not to have a counter-example to the Knowledge as Achievement thesis. More specifically, either Morris's abilities regarding the evaluation of testimony are involved or they are not. If they are, then Morris's true belief is from ability and constitutes an achievement on his part. If they are not, then we should reject the claim that Morris has knowledge in the case.

The preceding diagnosis of the Sears Tower case seems available but not demanded. But considering other cases of achievement supports the diagnosis made here. Thus consider the following case from soccer.

> Ted receives a brilliant, almost impossible pass, and then scores an easy goal as a result. In the case we are imagining, it is the athletic abilities of the passer that stand out. The pass was brilliant, its reception easy.

Now compare this case with another:

> Ted is playing in a soccer game, but not paying attention. Never seeing the ball, a brilliant pass bounces off his head and into the goal.

In the first case, we are happy to say that the goal constitutes an achievement on Ted's part. Not so in the second case. Here Ted was involved in the goal in a way, but not in the right sort of way. The principled explanation is this: Credit for an achievement, gained in cooperation with others, is not swamped by the able performance of others. It is not even swamped by the outstanding performance of others. So long as one's own efforts and abilities are appropriately involved, one gets credit for the achievement in question. And now the application to the testimony case is obvious: The fact that Morris's true belief is produced in cooperation with the testifier should not undermine our judgment that Morris's true belief is an achievement on his part. So long as Morris's cognitive abilities are involved in the right sort of way, he gets credit for the achievement in question (Greco 2009).

In response to this sort of consideration, Pritchard offers a different analogy that he thinks is more apt: An expert archer puts his arms around the novice to help aim and shoot the arrow. In this sort of case, Pritchard argues, it is wrong to say that the novice gets credit for an achievement (Pritchard 2009). In response, I do not see how this analogy is more apt than the soccer analogy. But in any case, it is not obviously more apt. At the very least, a diagnosis of the various cases that preserves the Knowledge as Achievement account is available.

What about the claim that not all cognitive achievement amounts to knowledge? Strictly speaking, this claim is irrelevant, since the view only requires that knowledge is *a kind* of cognitive achievement. It would not matter that there are other cognitive achievements as well. Thus, consider again our explanation that all knowledge has final value:

1. Achievements are finally valuable.
2. Knowledge is a kind of achievement.

Therefore,

3. Knowledge is finally valuable.

Premise 2 does not identify knowledge with cognitive achievement, but rather makes it an instance of that kind. Nevertheless, Pritchard claims that Barn Façade cases present examples where S exhibits a cognitive achievement that *falls short of* knowledge. If he is right, then the present account does not answer a version of the Tertiary Problem—it won't be the case that knowledge has a distinctive value over anything that falls short of knowledge.

Several strategies for preserving the Knowledge as Achievement account remain available, however. First, one might adopt a revisionary strategy similar to Pritchard's: Deny the presupposition that knowledge is always more valuable than that which falls short of knowledge, in favor of the presupposition that knowledge is typically more valuable than that which falls short of knowledge. Barn Façade cases could then be plausibly considered as atypical. Alternatively, one might admit that there is achievement and final value in the Barn Façade case, but insist that we value knowledge *more* for its own sake than we value cognitive achievement that falls short of knowledge for its own sake. Knowledge would then stand to true belief from ability as (a) understanding stands to knowledge and (b) wisdom stands to understanding.

The strategy I prefer, however, is to insist on a disanalogy between the Archery case and the Barn Façade case. On this alternative, we deny that Barney's success is from ability and that it thereby constitutes a genuine achievement.

But how can we plausibly deny the analogy between the two cases? The first step is to note that abilities are always understood as being relative to an environment. When we say that Jeter has the ability to hit baseballs, for example, we mean that he has this ability relative to environments typical for playing baseball. Presumably, Jeter *lacks* the ability to hit baseballs relative to some environments, such as in war zones where he would be too distracted. Once we are clear about this point, however, we might insist that, relative to Barn Façade County, Barney does not have the ability to perceptually discriminate barns from non-barns. And if he does not *have* the ability relative to that environment, then his success in that environment is not *from* ability.

The second step is to note that abilities are always understood in terms of the interests and purposes associated with the ability in question. For example, the ability to hit baseballs is understood in terms of the interests and purposes involved in playing baseball—the sorts of manifestation conditions that are relevant, and the sorts of results that are relevant, must be understood in those terms. But then there is a relevant difference between the Archie case and the Barney case: The interests and purposes at play in archery do not require the ability to discriminate between targets with forcefields and "genuine" targets. So long as you have the ability to hit the target you are aiming at, you have the relevant ability. But then Archie *does* have the relevant archery abilities, even relative to his odd environment. And so Archie's success in hitting his target *is* success from ability.

By contrast, the interests and purposes associated with knowledge attribution do require that one be able to discriminate between cases that p and cases that not-p. But then Barney does *not* have the relevant cognitive ability, relative to his odd environment. And so Barney's success in believing the truth is not success from ability.

Finally, consider a different sport, Archery*. In Archery* the goal of the contest is to first identify a good target and then shoot it. Suppose Archie lacks the first ability but picks out a good target by luck and shoots it with skill. In this case we would *not* credit him with an Archery* achievement, and precisely because he lacks the sort of ability we are interested in when evaluating for Archery* success. Or suppose he is properly skilled but running out of time. He randomly picks out a target, which lucky for him is a good one, and shoots it. Again, in this case we might properly withhold credit for an achievement, and precisely because he has not manifested the right sort of ability (Greco 2009).

Pritchard responds to this sort of consideration by, in effect, insisting that there will be cases of "lucky" achievement, and therefore cases of cognitive achievements that fall short of knowledge.

> [W]hile it is undoubtedly true that abilities should be understood relative to suitable environments, however that point is to be understood it must be compatible with the fact that it can be a matter of luck *that one is in a suitable environment to exercise one's ability in the first place* [my emphasis]. Critically, however, that is just to allow that the presence of environmental luck is compatible with one exercising one's normal abilities . . . hence however one relativizes abilities to suitable conditions one must allow that environmental luck —and thus environmental *epistemic* luck—is compatible with the exercise of the target ability.
>
> (Pritchard 2009)

But this last does not follow. From the premise that *environmental* luck is compatible with the exercise of cognitive ability, it does not follow that environmental *epistemic* luck is so compatible. That is, it does not follow that the sort of environmental luck that is compatible with the exercise of ability (i.e. luck that one is in a suitable environment to exercise one's ability in the first place) will also be the sort of luck that excludes knowledge. In effect, this is just what the Knowledge as Achievement account denies, when it claims that the sense in which luck is incompatible with knowledge *just is* the sense in which, more generally, luck is incompatible with success from ability. More specifically, luck regarding what environment one is in, and whether that environment is suitable to the exercise of one's ability, does not exclude achievement once in a suitable environment.

Do the replies to objections in this section make the Knowledge as Achievement account less elegant? No, because they do not *add* conditions to the previous, beautifully elegant account. Rather, they merely *explicate* those conditions in independently motivated ways—ways that we would have to anyway to understand what it is to have an ability, and what it is for success to be from ability, more generally.

Accordingly, we may conclude that the Knowledge as Achievement account of the nature and value of knowledge remains viable. It has resources to plausibly address various kinds of counter-example regarding the nature of knowledge, and can at the same time explain the value of knowledge in a non-revisionary way. It also remains the most *elegant* explanation of both the nature and value of knowledge, and of understanding and wisdom as well.

Acknowledgments

I would like to thank Duncan Pritchard and John Turri for their comments on earlier versions of the paper. Thanks also to Irem Kurtsal Steen, and to participants at the "Epistemic Goodness" conference, held at the University of Oklahoma in the spring of 2009.

References

Greco, J. (2003) "Knowledge as Credit for True Belief" in M. DePaul and L. Zagzebski (eds.) *Intellectual Virtue: Perspectives from Ethics and Epistemology*, Oxford: Oxford University Press.

Greco, J. (2008) "The Value Problem" in A. Haddock, A. Millar, & D. H. Pritchard (eds.) *The Value of Knowledge*, Oxford: Oxford University Press.

Greco, J. (2009) *Achieving Knowledge*, Cambridge: Cambridge University Press.

Kaplan, M. (1985) "It's Not What You Know That Counts", *Journal of Philosophy* 82: 350–63.

Kvanvig, J. (2003) *The Value of Knowledge and the Pursuit of Understanding*, Cambridge: Cambridge University Press.

Lackey, J. (2007) "Why We Don't Deserve Credit for Everything We Know", *Synthese* 158: 345–61.

Pritchard, D. H. (2007) "Recent Work on Epistemic Value", *American Philosophical Quarterly* 44: 85–110.

Pritchard, D. H. (2008a) "Radical Scepticism, Epistemic Luck and Epistemic Value", *Proceedings of the Aristotelian Society* (Supplementary Volume) 82: 19–41.

Pritchard, D. H. (2008b) "The Value of Knowledge" in E. Zalta (ed.) *The Stanford Encyclopedia of Philosophy*. URL = http://plato.stanford.edu/archives/fall2008/entries/knowledge-value/

Pritchard, D. H. (2009) *The Value of Knowledge*, manuscript.

Riggs, W. (2002) "Reliability and the Value of Knowledge", *Philosophy and Phenomenological Research* 64: 79–96.

Riggs, W. (2009) "Two Problems of Easy Credit", *Synthese* 169: 201–16.

Sartwell, C. (1992) "Why Knowledge is Merely True Belief", *The Journal of Philosophy* 89, 4: 167–80.

Sosa, E. (1991) *Knowledge in Perspective: Selected Essays in Epistemology*, Cambridge: Cambridge University Press.

Sosa, E. (2007) *A Virtue Epistemology: Apt Belief and Reflective Knowledge*, vol. 1, Oxford: Oxford University Press.

Williamson, T. (2000) *Knowledge and Its Limits*, Oxford: Oxford University Press.

Zagzebski, L. (1996) *Virtues of the Mind: An Inquiry into the Nature of Virtue and the Ethical Foundations of Knowledge*, Cambridge: Cambridge University Press.

Part III
THE STRUCTURE OF KNOWLEDGE

22
FOUNDATIONALISM
Michael DePaul

Epistemic foundationalism is a thesis about the structure of the beliefs having an epistemic property, such as being known, rational, or justified. The structure is indicated by the foundation metaphor. In a building constructed of blocks, many blocks are supported by other blocks, but some blocks are not supported by any other blocks. Blocks that are not supported by other blocks form the foundation, supporting the rest of the structure, i.e., all the superstructure blocks. Every block in the structure is either part of the foundation or part of the superstructure. Hence, the weight of every superstructure block is eventually carried by one or more foundation blocks.

Foundationalists about an epistemic property hold that the beliefs having that property are structured like the blocks in a building. Thus, e.g., foundationalists regarding justification recognize that many of our justified beliefs depend for their justification on other justified beliefs we hold. But they also insist that some of our justified beliefs do not depend for their justification on any other justified beliefs. These beliefs are *basic* or *foundational*. Finally, such foundationalists hold that every one of our justified beliefs is either basic or part of the superstructure, with all superstructure beliefs eventually justified by one or more basic beliefs.

Epistemic properties are evaluative, involving assessment of beliefs from a distinctive epistemic perspective marked by a concern for such epistemic goods as believing what is true and not believing what is false. Accordingly, we might roughly characterize knowledge as true belief that is not true by accident and rational belief as belief that seems—from the believer's perspective—to have been formed in a way that is likely to yield true beliefs and not false beliefs. There is less agreement about the property of epistemic justification, but one major alternative conceives of it as fulfilling an intellectual obligation to try to believe truths while avoiding falsehoods; according to another conception, justification is an historical property that beliefs have if they were produced by a cognitive process that reliably yields true beliefs.

Let's now state more formally the three elements of epistemic foundationalism. First some handy abbreviations:

> Let S be a person; B and $B_1, B_2, B_3, \ldots$ be beliefs; P and $P_1, P_2, P_3, \ldots$ be propositions, and BP be the belief that P, BP_1 the belief that P_1, etc. E stands for an epistemic property and *SE* shall be the set of all S's beliefs that have E.

Here's a definition of a concept that's useful for defining foundationalism:

Let T be the relation, or disjunction of relations, between beliefs that transmits E from one belief to another. (For example, T, or one disjunct of T, might be the relation of being-formed-as-a-result-of-being-deduced-from. Hence, according to the cogito, Descartes' belief "I exist" stands in T to his belief "I think.")

T is transitive: if B_1 stands in T to B_2, and B_2 stands in T to B_3, then B_1 stands in T to B_3.

We can now formulate three theses that together constitute foundationalism regarding an epistemic property.

Foundations Thesis: Some of the beliefs in SE do not have E in virtue of standing in T to any other beliefs in SE. Such beliefs are *basic* (or *foundational*).

Dependence Thesis: Some of the beliefs in SE have E in virtue of standing in T to other beliefs in SE. Such beliefs are *superstructure beliefs* (or *non-basic*).

Closure Thesis: All of the superstructure beliefs in SE have E in virtue of standing in T to one or more basic beliefs in SE. (Compare Sosa 1980.)

Foundationalism regarding a specific epistemic property, E, can be fleshed out in various ways. Foundationalists must explain which beliefs are basic and how these beliefs come to have E and also specify T and explain how it transmits E; different views about these matters are possible. We shouldn't expect all versions of foundationalism regarding E to be equally plausible. Moreover, as we've noted, there are a number of epistemic properties. We shouldn't expect the most plausible version of foundationalism concerning E to be analogous to the most plausible version for a different epistemic property. Maybe no version of foundationalism is plausible for some epistemic properties.

It's important, therefore, to realize that foundationalism is not the name of one single epistemological theory. There are many distinct foundationalist views. One should be suspicious, then, of anyone who writes or speaks of foundationalism writ large, without specifying exactly the version of foundationalism at issue. I obviously cannot address all the possible versions of foundationalism regarding all the different epistemic properties. I'll limit myself to some versions of foundationalism regarding epistemic justification. Henceforth, unless I indicate otherwise, by "foundationalism" I mean foundationalism regarding justification.

Before proceeding, let's note one important non-epistemic form of foundationalism. Most of us have many beliefs we hold on the basis of other beliefs because we have inferred them from these other beliefs. But we also have beliefs not held on the basis of other beliefs. If you ask me my phone number, for example, I just form a belief that such and such is my phone number. No other belief serves as a reason, good or bad, for my belief about my phone number—the belief just pops into my head. One might conjecture, then, that our beliefs have a foundational structure, with some being basic because they are not, as a matter of psychological fact, based upon other beliefs, while all other beliefs are eventually based on such psychologically basic beliefs. This view isn't an epistemic foundationalism: no evaluative, epistemic properties are involved. The beliefs that are psychologically basic for a person might be utterly unjustified; indeed, they can be downright mad. The same holds for the "inferences" some benighted people make from their psychologically basic beliefs. It does not matter for the kind of foundationalism we have just identified, since it only concerns the psychological relations structuring a person's beliefs. I'll follow philosophers who mark the distinction between psychological foundationalism and epistemic foundationalism by using the terms 'basic' and 'properly basic': the former indicates merely that a belief is basic within a person's system of beliefs while the latter indicates the belief is justified but does not depend for its justification on any other belief.

Returning to epistemic foundationalism, the foundations and closure theses are clearly the most controversial parts. Why think some beliefs are justified on their own, independently of their relations to other justified beliefs? And why think that all justified beliefs must eventually derive their justification from properly basic beliefs? One historically significant answer is provided by the epistemic regress argument, which runs as follows. Begin with some belief, B_1, that S is justified in holding. What justifies B_1? In many cases there will be another belief or beliefs that justify B_1, perhaps because S deduced B_1 from them. Let's assume the simple case, where B_1 is justified by one other belief, B_2. If B_2 is not justified, it could hardly justify B_1. So what justifies B_2? Presumably S can provide some reason for B_2 as well, some other belief or beliefs that justify it. Assume the simple case again: B_2 is justified by B_3. By now you can probably see where this is going. There are only three possible ways for the chain of justifying beliefs (or reasons) to continue. First, it might go on forever. Second, it might loop back on itself, that is, S might use beliefs that have already appeared in the chain again. And finally, the chain might simply end. Those who accept that the series of justifying beliefs goes on forever are known as *infinitists*. (For a defense of infinitism see Klein 1999.) *Coherentists* hold that the chain loops back on itself. Foundationalists hold that the chain ends at some point, arguing that this is the only viable possibility for such a justificatory chain.

Why don't foundationalists think the chain can go on forever? We are finite beings, so we clearly do not have infinitely many beliefs. Hence, we simply could not go on indefinitely justifying beliefs with different beliefs we already hold. Therefore the chain of reasons cannot be infinitely long.

Why don't foundationalists think the chain can loop back on itself? S obviously cannot justify B by citing that very same belief. The problem might not leap out as clearly in a case where S has cited some other beliefs in between, but the problem must remain. If S is justified in believing B_1 by B_2, and justified in believing B_2 by B_3, and justified in believing B_3 by B_4, but the justification S has for B_4 is nothing but B_1, then S doesn't really have an adequate justification for B_1. If B_1 needs to be justified to begin with, then B_1 can hardly supply that justification either at the first step or further down the line for the simple reason that it stands in need of justification itself! Or so the argument goes. Real coherentists complain that this misrepresents their view, arguing that they reject the "linear" conception of justification, which sees justification as transmitted from belief to belief via evidential relations. They instead conceive of justification as a property a whole system of beliefs has in virtue of the relations of mutual support interconnecting the beliefs that comprise the system (see Bonjour 1976: 285–86). But notice that, on this view, coherentism looks like a non standard version of foundationalism with no superstructure beliefs; all justified beliefs are properly basic since justification is not transferred to them from other justified beliefs. They are justified in virtue of their membership in a coherent system of beliefs (see Sosa 1980). Unfortunately I do not have space to say more about this issue.

Only foundationalism remains; the regress of justification must stop someplace. The beliefs that end the regress would, of course, have to be justified. If they were not, how could they possibly justify other beliefs? But these special beliefs must not derive their justification from any other justified beliefs; otherwise we would be off again on the regress. So there must be some foundational beliefs and the chain of justification for any belief must eventually terminate in one or more of these special beliefs. This is the only viable possibility.

But you might already be having doubts about foundationalism. If B cannot be justified by B itself, how could B be justified on its own? Indeed, is there any substantial difference between claiming that B is justified by B and claiming that B is justified on its own? Such questions are encouraged by the characterization of properly basic beliefs as "self-justifying," which one sometimes sees. The building metaphor suggests how foundationalists should respond. Foundation blocks in a building are not supported by any other blocks, but they are neither un-supported nor self-supporting. They obviously are supported in virtue of something. Similarly, foundationalists who have their wits about them will claim that although properly basic beliefs are not justified by other beliefs, they are justified *in virtue of something*. Foundationalists don't think that just any belief could be properly basic. These will be special beliefs. Consider the belief that everything is identical to itself, which is a likely candidate for being properly basic. It seems "self-evident"; a person who understands it can see that it is true. Foundationalists could explain that it is justified in virtue of this special feature. As we will see, there are a number of other special features beliefs might have that foundationalists could cite to explain the justification of properly basic beliefs. They only deny that properly basic beliefs are justified by other justified beliefs.

Let's now examine a specific example that illustrates how foundationalists think the regress plays out. I'll take a very simple example and first describe a fairly traditional foundationalist account. I'll then describe a couple of more contemporary, and I think more plausible, foundationalist accounts.

I look into my bedroom on a sunny afternoon. There is no philosopher's funny business going on. I clearly see Pingus, my cat, sitting on the windowsill, and form the belief that Pingus is on the windowsill. What justifies my belief? Here's one traditional answer: My belief that Pingus is on the windowsill is justified by my belief that I see Pingus on the windowsill. Sounds promising. This much is certainly true: if I do *see* Pingus on the windowsill, then Pingus *is* on the windowsill. Seeing, like perceiving in general, is factive: One cannot see, or perceive, that P unless P is true. So my belief that I see Pingus on the windowsill could serve to justify my belief that Pingus is on the windowsill.

But what justifies my belief that I see Pingus on the windowsill? It's natural to cite my sensory experience here. Visual sensation has its own peculiar character distinct from other kinds of conscious experience. We typically believe we are *seeing* something because of our *visual* sensations. We can distinguish among our visual sensations, and what we believe we see is determined by the specific character of our visual experience. Thus, I might say, what justifies my belief that I see Pingus on the windowsill is my belief that I have a visual sensation as of seeing Pingus on the windowsill. My belief that I have a "Pingus seeing" kind of experience may not guarantee that I see Pingus—I could be dreaming after all—but my belief about my visual sensation certainly seems relevant to the truth of my belief that I see Pingus. So, for now, let's allow that my belief that I am having a Pingus seeing sort of visual sensation justifies my belief that I see Pingus.

What justifies my belief that I am having that particular kind of visual sensation? A typical foundationalist answer is that beliefs about our own current conscious experiences, such as sensations, are properly basic. This answer immediately raises a question: in virtue of what are beliefs about our own current experiences justified if not their relations with other beliefs? One traditional response is that beliefs about our current experiences are justified because they are infallible, i.e., they cannot be mistaken. I might be mistaken that Pingus is on the windowsill—it might be my other tiger cat, Luigi, who looks much like Pingus. I might be mistaken that I am seeing anything at all because I am dreaming of Pingus or hallucinating. But many traditional foundationalists hold my belief that I have a visual experience of the type I then actually have, specifically, the Pingus seeing type, simply can't be mistaken. Other traditional foundationalists claim beliefs about our current conscious states are properly basic because they are indubitable (cannot be doubted), incorrigible (cannot be overturned by further information), or certain (no other belief is more reasonable). There are likely other possibilities. The basic idea shared by these traditional views is that we have some kind of privileged access to our own conscious experiences, and hence our beliefs about these experiences need no support from any other beliefs to be justified. Traditional foundationalists were likely mistaken in thinking our beliefs about our current conscious experiences are infallible or incorrigible or absolutely certain. It's possible to imagine cases where we make mistakes about our own experiences (see Pollock 1986). Nevertheless, it still seems we have some sort of special access to our own conscious experiences. There is, so to speak, nothing between us and the experience, so we're in an ideal position to form beliefs. Hence, the claim that such beliefs are properly basic retains considerable plausibility. So it's plausible that my belief that I am having a Pingus seeing kind of experience is properly basic.

This traditional foundationalist account of how the regress ends is not beyond question. But clearly it isn't guilty of holding properly basic beliefs justify themselves or that they are justified, but not in virtue of anything at all. The account claims properly basic beliefs are justified because they have a very special, and very strong, justificatory status: they concern something to which we have a kind of special, privileged access.

Let's now consider an objection to this foundationalist account. If foundational beliefs need to have such a strong positive epistemic status, aren't equally strong connections between beliefs required for justification to be transmitted? If BP must be infallible, or nearly so, to be properly basic, must not the truth of P_1 guarantee the truth of P_2, or nearly guarantee it, for BP_1 to justify BP_2? Alternatively, if we need privileged access to P for BP to be properly basic, shouldn't we have to "see" that P_1 guarantees the truth of P_2 for BP_2 to be justified by BP_1? The problem is, if we set the requirements for justification and justification transmission this high, we might be able to identify some few properly basic beliefs and explain how they are justified independently of any other beliefs, but we will not be able to use those beliefs to justify many other beliefs. In fact, the account I sketched of the justification of my belief that Pingus is on the windowsill won't even work: that I have an experience as of seeing Pingus obviously doesn't *guarantee* that I'm in fact seeing Pingus.

This criticism doesn't faze some foundationalists. They continue to hold the requirements for properly basic beliefs and justification transmission to be extremely high, and either accept the skeptical consequence that very few of our ordinary beliefs are justified or soldier on, attempting to find an argument that will forge a strong enough link between properly basic beliefs and our ordinary beliefs for the former to justify the latter (see, e.g., Fumerton 2000 and BonJour 2000). But few contemporary foundationalists accept such extremely demanding versions of foundationalism. We'll next examine some less demanding foundationalist positions. But I should first note that many critics seem to identify foundationalism with very demanding versions of foundationalism (Rorty 1979 provides an influential example). Perhaps this identification is understandable given the historical prominence of the demanding forms, beginning at least with Descartes. These critics reject foundationalism on such grounds as that virtually no beliefs are infallible or that no beliefs are unrevisable in the light of further information or that foundationalism is ultimately a skeptical position because too few beliefs are properly basic to allow us to justify the things we ordinarily believe about the world. Such criticisms don't impact most contemporary foundationalists, since they have modest views about what's required for a belief to be properly basic and for the transmission of justification.

So how might a modest foundationalist account for the justification of my belief that Pingus is on the windowsill? Compared to the novella provided by more traditional foundationalists, this will be a short story. If we reflect on cases like the one where I look into the sunny bedroom and believe that Pingus is on the windowsill, it becomes apparent that the traditional foundationalist's account is overly complicated. It does not correspond with the way we actually form such beliefs. When we look at an object in normal conditions, and form a belief about the thing or some perceptible quality it has, for example, a belief that there's Pingus or that Pingus is a tabby, we typically don't start with a belief about the nature of our visual experience, infer a belief that we are seeing something, and then infer the relevant belief about the thing we see. We just have a certain visual experience and form a belief. In fact, in the usual case, where we are not being extraordinarily reflective or introspective, we will not have any beliefs at all about the nature of our visual experience or that we are seeing this or that. Indeed, we all go for days at a time without forming any beliefs about the nature of our visual experiences or that we are seeing this or that—we are much too busy forming beliefs about the ordinary objects around us.

How are these observations relevant to the justification of my belief that Pingus is on the windowsill? Let's begin by distinguishing between two ways in which we can think of a belief being justified. Suppose that I have impeccable evidence for P, and that this evidence is constituted by my belief B_1. Suppose further that I do believe that P, but that as a matter of empirical fact, my belief that P in no way depends upon B_1. I've never even considered how P relates to B_1. Instead, I believe P because I had a drug induced hallucination in which an angel descended from the clouds and solemnly swore to me that P. In this case, there is one clear sense in which BP is not justified—it's silly of me to believe something in the way I believe P. But there is another sense in which BP is justified—I do, after all, have good evidence for BP. The first sense of justification evaluates my holding some particular belief in the way I actually hold it. The second sense instead focuses on the proposition I believe and evaluates whether the evidence I have at my disposal supports that proposition. To avoid confusion, I will use 'justified belief' for the first type of justification and 'justifiable belief' for the second.

If we are concerned with justification rather than justifiability, the traditional foundationalist account immediately appears problematic. How could my believing that Pingus is on the windowsill be justified in virtue of my belief that I have a Pingus seeing type of experience when I don't actually believe I'm having such an experience? The belief that I have such an experience might be relevant to the *justifiability* of my belief that Pingus is on the windowsill, since, if challenged to justify the latter belief, I might eventually come to form the former belief and use it to answer the challenge in the traditional foundationalist way. But when it comes to *justification* it seems clear that the only things that could be relevant to the belief's status as justified or unjustified are things that actually played an epistemically significant role in the formation or maintenance of the belief. (I include maintenance because a belief might now be justified in virtue of now being based on reasons acquired *after* it was initially formed.)

If I believe that P_1, infer P_2 from P_1, and come to believe P_2 as a result, then BP_2 will depend for its justification on BP_1. But if I have some belief that was neither formed nor is sustained by any inference, then that belief cannot depend for its justification on any other belief, that is, it will have to be properly basic to be justified. In the example we've been considering I immediately formed the belief that Pingus is on the windowsill in response to my visual experience. I certainly did not infer it from any other beliefs I had, in particular, beliefs about what I was seeing or what sorts of visual experiences I was having. So according to the contemporary foundationalist account, my belief that Pingus is on the windowsill is properly basic. It is justified, but does not depend for its justification on any other belief that I hold. But what explains the justification of my basic belief that Pingus is on the windowsill? We might not form beliefs about our current experiences very often, but when we do traditional foundationalists have a good story to tell about their justification. The beliefs about ordinary things that we form on the basis of perceptual experiences, which contemporary foundationalists regard as properly basic, lack the awe inspiring epistemic credentials traditional foundationalists claim for their foundations. We have no sort of privileged access to the ordinary things we perceive. In virtue of what, then, are our basic perceptual beliefs about these things justified?

Recall that a beliefs' status as justified, as opposed to justifiable, depends upon the things that play an epistemically significant role in the formation or maintenance of that belief. For my belief that Pingus is on the windowsill, my visual experience is the most salient thing. I formed the belief because I was having a particular type of visual experience, a visual experience as of seeing Pingus on the windowsill. If I had been having a different type of visual experience, say an experience as of seeing an empty windowsill, I wouldn't have been justified in believing Pingus is on the windowsill. This suggests one possible explanation contemporary foundationalists might give of why my belief is justified: it was formed in response to the appropriate sort of visual experience for that belief. The idea is not that the belief is justified by a *belief* about the nature of my experience. Rather, the belief is justified in virtue of its being formed in response to an experience of that nature. This account preserves the foundational status of the belief—it does not derive its justification from some other justified belief—, makes it clear that the belief is justified in virtue of something—so its epistemic status is not left mysterious—, and finally, explains the justification of the belief in terms of the way in which it was actually formed. We'll call this view *experiential foundationalism*.

It would be irresponsible to go farther without at least mentioning an important objection to both experiential foundationalism and traditional versions of foundationalism. All these versions of foundationalism hold that some significant foundational beliefs are justified in virtue of the conscious experiences that lead the person to form the belief. Traditional foundationalists hold that our beliefs about our current sensory experiences are justified in virtue of our current sensory experiences. Experiential foundationalists hold that our ordinary perceptual beliefs about ordinary things are justified in virtue of our current sensory experiences. These versions of foundationalism hold that beliefs about different things—experiences in the one case and ordinary objects in the other—are justified by these experiences, but they agree that the beliefs are justified in virtue of the experiences. They are able to maintain that these beliefs are, nevertheless, properly basic because the beliefs are justified in virtue of their relations to *experiences*, not their relations to other justified *beliefs*. The objection comes in the form of a dilemma: If sensory experiences have content that is proposition like, then it is possible to see how they might stand in the sort of logical or evidential relation that is necessary to justify a belief. But if these experiences are proposition like, they represent the world as being one way rather than another. They might be mistaken. Hence, it would seem that these experiences themselves need to be justified, or something like it, before they could justify beliefs. But if the experiences need to be justified, we have not really reached the foundations. So suppose the content of sensory experience is not proposition like. Then these experiences are off the hook as far as needing justification is concerned. They are just brute states of awareness that it makes no sense to think of as justified or unjustified. Now the problem shifts to their relation to beliefs. They cannot stand in anything like a logical or evidential relation to a belief. Experiences could, of course, stand in temporal or causal relations to beliefs, but it is difficult to see why a belief would be *justified* by a certain experience just because it followed or was caused by that experience. This is obviously a formidable objection to the versions of foundationalism I've described so far. That does not mean it is decisive, but I do not have the space to consider possible foundationalist responses. I will, instead, move on to describe a different type of contemporary foundationalism. (The objection is found in Sellars 1963. For a response see BonJour 2000.)

Here is a familiar story about the justification of my belief that Pingus is on the windowsill, which is a version of foundationalism although it usually is not presented as such. Rather than looking at the specific character of the sensory experience that led me to form the belief that Pingus is on the windowsill this account focuses on the reliability of the psychological process that was responsible for me having the sensory experience I had and then forming the belief I formed. In circumstances of the kind in which I actually formed my belief, this process would produce a very large proportion of true beliefs. The belief is justified because it was produced by a *reliable* belief-forming process. It is important that this account does not hold my belief to be justified by a *belief* that it was formed in a reliable way. If it held that, my belief that Pingus is on the windowsill would not be properly basic—its justification would depend upon another belief. Reliabilism entails that my belief about Pingus is foundational because this belief does not depend for its justification on any other belief; it is justified in virtue of being produced by a reliable belief-forming process. We'll call this view *reliabilist foundationalism* (see Goldman 1979).

One advantage claimed for reliabilist foundationalism is that it would not hold our perceptual beliefs to be justified if the experiences that ground them did not reliably match reality. So suppose we have fallen into the clutches of a Cartesian demon or are brains in a vat. Experiential foundationalism entails that our perceptual beliefs are, nonetheless, justified since we would be forming beliefs about the world around us on the basis of the right kinds of sensory experiences—even though nearly all the beliefs so formed would be false! Reliabilist foundationalism can deny that these beliefs are justified because they are unreliable. Many see this as an advantage for reliabilism. Experiential foundationalists won't agree. They think their account gives the intuitively correct answer about demon worlds and brain in vat scenarios, that is, that those living in such extraordinary circumstances are justified in believing the world is as it seems to them. Why think these beliefs are justified when they're so massively mistaken? One answer is that our similar beliefs formed in the actual world are quite obviously justified, and the denizens of demon worlds and brain nourishing vats would be forming their beliefs on the basis of conscious experiences that are exactly the same as ours. This answer clearly proceeds from the experiential foundationalist's basic presupposition that beliefs are justified or not in virtue of the conscious experiences of the believer. And this is not a presupposition shared by the reliabilist foundationalist. But that doesn't show the presupposition is false, any more than the experiential foundationalist's failure to share the reliabilist's presuppositions shows that they are false. We've here reached a deep disagreement that may be irresolvable.

Let's take stock. First, since I have been working with a perceptual belief as an example for some time, it is important to recall that it is just an example. The three versions of foundationalism we've examined would want to say similar things about other kinds of beliefs. Thus, if we were talking about a memory belief I formed, for example, that I cleaned Pingus' litter box this morning—yuck!—the traditional foundationalist would want to trace its justification back to a belief about the nature of the memory experience I was having, the experiential foundationalist would take my belief that I cleaned the litter box to be basic and justified directly in virtue of my having the particular kind of memory experience I was having, and the reliabilist foundationalist would cite the reliability of the psychological process that produces my memory beliefs.

Second, our discussion of these three forms of foundationalism implicitly recognized that they (like other forms of foundationalism) range along two dimensions. The first has to do with how demanding the form of foundationalism is about the epistemic status of properly basic beliefs and what's required for the transmission of justification. Some traditional forms of foundationalism are extremely demanding, requiring infallibility for foundations and a guarantee of truth for the transmission of justification. More contemporary versions of foundationalism tend to be less demanding. Reliabilist foundationalism can theoretically be demanding or lax depending upon how reliable the process that formed a belief must be for the belief to be justified. The second dimension along which the theories range is the degree of justification at issue. Strong versions of foundationalism are obviously concerned with a very high degree of justification, typically at least justification that is sufficient for knowledge. Given how demanding they are about the foundations and the transmission of justification, it is easy to see why traditional foundationalists think they have shown our beliefs are so highly justified. Other forms of foundationalism tend to be more moderate or modest. Experiential foundationalists in particular are likely to claim properly basic beliefs have only some low level of justification and then try to explain how these beliefs can acquire a higher level of justification if further conditions are met. Interestingly, some foundationalists hold that coherence can increase the level of justification had by basic beliefs that have a low level of justification on their own.

Third, many versions of traditional foundationalism tend to see the justificatory status of our beliefs as being determined strictly by our beliefs, while other versions of foundationalism appeal to other things in their accounts. All versions of foundationalism obviously see the regress of justification tracing along beliefs and ending with foundational beliefs. The contrast emerges when you ask what justifies these beliefs. Many traditional foundationalists seek to explain why these beliefs are justified by citing some characteristic of the beliefs themselves: a paradigm of this approach is provided by accounts that claim properly basic beliefs must be infallible, where what makes a belief infallible is the nature of the proposition believed. Belief about our own conscious experiences cannot be mistaken simply because they are beliefs about our conscious experiences—there is no need to compare the belief with the experience. Contemporary versions of foundationalism see things other than beliefs as being relevant. Experiential foundationalism holds foundational beliefs to be justified in virtue of their relation to the experiences in response to which they were formed. Reliabilist foundationalism holds them to be justified in virtue of the reliability of the psychological process that produced them. So while many traditional foundationalists think that if you had a complete list of all the propositions a person believes you could determine which of the person's beliefs were justified (or perhaps justifiable), contemporary foundationalists hold that you need to know more—you need to know about the person's experience or psychology—to determine which of the person's beliefs are justified.

References

BonJour, L. (1976) "The Coherence Theory of Empirical Knowledge," *Philosophical Studies* 30 281–312.
—— (2000) "Toward a Defense of Empirical Foundationalism," in DePaul 2000.
DePaul, M. (ed.) (2000) *Resurrecting Old-Fashioned Foundationalism*, Lanham, MD: Rowman and Littlefield.
Fumerton, R. (2000) "Classical Foundationalism," in DePaul 2000.
Goldman, A. (1979) "What is Justified Belief?" in G. Pappas (ed.) *Justification and Knowledge*, Dordrecht: Reidel.
Klein, P. (1999) "Human Knowledge and the Infinite Regress of Reasons," *Philosophical Perspectives* 13: 297–332.
Pollock, J. (1986) *Contemporary Theories of Knowledge*, Totowa, NJ: Rowman and Littlefield.
Rorty, R. (1979) *Philosophy and the Mirror of Nature*, Princeton, NJ: Princeton University Press.
Sellars, W. (1963) "Empiricisim and the Philosophy of Mind," in *Science, Perception, and Reality*, London: Routledge and Kegan Paul.
Sosa, E. (1980) "The Foundations of Foundationalism," *Noûs* 14: 547–64.

Further Reading

Audi, R. (1993) *The Structure of Justification*, Cambridge: Cambridge University Press. (An extended defense of a moderate version of foundationalism regarding justification.)
Chisholm, R. (1977) *Theory of Knowledge*, 2nd. edn., Englewood Cliffs, NJ: Prentice Hall. (A classic statement of a sophisticated version of foundationalism that includes coherentist elements and a number of different epistemic properties.)
Foley, R. (1987) *The Theory of Epistemic Rationality*, Cambridge, MA: Harvard University Press. (An extended development of a subjective foundationalist theory of rationality conceived as distinct from justification.)
Sosa, E. "The Raft and the Pyramid: Coherence Versus Foundations in the Theory of Knowledge," *Midwest Studies in Philosophy* 5: 3–25. (Compares and contrasts foundationalism and coherentism.)

23
INFINITISM
Peter D. Klein

Introduction

Infinitism, along with coherentism and foundationalism, is a view about the structure of reasons and reasoning that is designed to provide a solution to the epistemic regress problem. The regress problem can be put this way: Suppose we give a reason, r_1, for holding one of our beliefs, b. Then, we are asked for our reason for holding r_1, and we provide the reason, r_2. Then, we are asked for our reason for r_2, and we give r_3. Now, either this process could go on indefinitely, which seems to suggest that nothing has been gained by providing a reason because there is always another one needed; or, if some reason repeats, it seems that we have argued in a circle and that no such argument could provide a good basis for accepting b; or, if at some point there is no further reason, it seems that the stopping point is arbitrarily held because there is no reasonable basis for holding it. The problem is that, contrary to strong pre-theoretical intuitions, there seems to be no point in giving reasons for our beliefs.

Infinitism holds that there is no reason that can be given for any belief which is so privileged that it is immune to further interrogation. There are circumstances in which even the most commonplace reasons require further reasons. Even so, knowledge based upon such reasoning is possible, and giving reasons does increase the warrant for our beliefs.

The primary purpose of this chapter is to sketch the case for infinitism. It has three main steps.

First, I will discuss the way in which the regress problem was originally conceived by the Pyrrhonians and Aristotelians. The upshot will be that given two presuppositions that underlie the regress problem as originally conceived, the Pyrrhonian response, namely that reasoning is unable to resolve disputes, is highly plausible.

Second, I will discuss three challenges to the Pyrrhonian response. The first challenge arises from various forms of foundationalism including what I call 'austere reliabilism' and 'embellished reliabilism.' I will argue that these forms of foundationalism fail to adequately address the normative basis motivating the regress argument. The second challenge originates with contemporary coherentism. I will argue that contemporary coherentism is not a viable response because it is subject to the same objections that apply to foundationalism. That leaves infinitism, the third challenge, as the only viable, non-skeptical response.

Third, I will sketch infinitism, point to some of its advantages, and try to show that the primary objections to it miss the mark.

THE STRUCTURE OF KNOWLEDGE

1. The Traditional Problem

The traditional regress problem was known to Aristotle, who wrote this in the *Metaphysics*:

> There are ... some who raise a difficulty by asking, who is to be the judge of the healthy man, and in general who is likely to judge rightly on each class of questions. But such inquiries are like puzzling over the question whether we are now asleep or awake. And all such questions have the same meaning. These people demand that a reason shall be given for everything; for they seek a starting point, and they seek to get this by demonstration, while it is obvious from their actions that they have no such conviction. But their mistake is what we have stated it to be; they seek a reason for things for which no reason can be given; for the starting point of demonstration is not demonstration.
>
> (Aristotle 1941b: 1011a2–14)

Even though Aristotle is speaking about "demonstration," and there is a special meaning that he would sometimes attach to that concept involving syllogistic reasoning from intuited first principles, his point here is that reasoning, in general, reaches an end because there are some privileged starting points "for which no reason can be given" because "the starting point of demonstration is not demonstration." No reason *can* be given because reasoning presupposes something not inferred—namely the premises that provide the basis for the reasoning.

This argument still motivates foundationalism. Here is a redacted paragraph from William Alston's *Epistemic Justification* that faithfully renders his general point:

> The argument [for foundationalism] is that the original belief [the one that requires justification] will be mediately justified only if every branch [of the justificatory tree] ... terminates in an immediately justified belief. Positively, it is argued that on this condition the necessary conditions for the original belief's being mediately justified are satisfied, and negatively it is argued that if any branch assumes any other form, they are not.
>
> (Alston 1989: 54)

Alston goes on to say that this argument "gives stronger support to foundationalism than any other regress argument" (Alston 1989: 55).

The foundationalists' response is an answer to the skeptics' use of the regress argument whose classical formulation is due to Sextus Empiricus:

> The later Skeptics hand down Five Modes leading to suspension, namely these: the first based on discrepancy, the second on the regress *ad infinitum*, the third on relativity, the fourth on hypothesis, the fifth on circular reasoning. That based on discrepancy leads us to find that with regard to the object presented there has arisen both amongst ordinary people and amongst the philosophers an interminable conflict because of which we are unable either to choose a thing or reject it, and so fall back on suspension. The Mode based upon regress *ad infinitum* is that whereby we assert that the thing adduced as a proof of the matter proposed needs a further proof, and this again another,

and so on *ad infinitum*, so that the consequence is suspension [of assent], as we possess no starting-point for our argument. The Mode based upon relativity ... is that whereby the object has such or such an appearance in relation to the subject judging and to the concomitant percepts, but as to its real nature we suspend judgment. We have the Mode based upon hypothesis when the Dogmatists, being forced to recede *ad infinitum*, take as their starting-point something which they do not establish but claim to assume as granted simply and without demonstration. The Mode of circular reasoning is the form used when the proof itself which ought to establish the matter of inquiry requires confirmation derived from the matter; in this case, being unable to assume either in order to establish the other, we suspend judgement about both.
(Empiricus 1976: I: 166–69)

There are five modes mentioned in the passage from Sextus Empiricus. The modes of relativity and discrepancy are crucial to understanding the *reductio* put forth by Sextus because those modes are designed to show that neither a judgment based on how things appear nor a judgment based upon what we collectively believe (either qua "philosophers" or qua "ordinary" persons) is so privileged that it does not need to be supported by further reasoning. As we will see, considerations similar to those motivating the modes of relativity and discrepancy form part of the motivation for infinitism.

The foundationalists' answer to the skeptical conclusion is that there must be some beliefs that cannot be justified by further reasoning because, as they see it, reasoning cannot create epistemic warrant, so warrant *must* be present in some basic beliefs. From the foundationalists' perspective, the problem is typically not *whether* there is sufficient warrant for knowledge, it is, rather, *how* sufficient warrant arises and is transferred.

This is clear, for example, from Aristotle's rather dismissive attitude towards skepticism manifested in the citation above, and even in the carefully constructed answer in the *Posterior Analytics* designed to show that *if* some knowledge is the result of demonstration, then some knowledge must not be the result of demonstration. There he argues that either the series of demonstrations is finite or infinite. It must be finite because "one cannot traverse an infinite series" (Aristotle 1941a: 72b10). But if it terminates, it cannot terminate in another belief that requires a demonstration because the conclusion would not be "properly" known and "rests on the mere supposition that the premises are true" (Aristotle 1941a: 72b14). It cannot be finite and circular because the premises in a demonstration must be "prior to and better known than the conclusion" and "the same things cannot be simultaneously both prior and posterior to one another" (Aristotle 1941a: 72b25–28). Thus, *if* there is demonstrative knowledge, then there must be non-demonstrative knowledge.

Near the end of the *Posterior Analytics* Aristotle does provide a sketch of how such non-demonstrative knowledge reliably originates with sensation and ends with rational insight. The details of Aristotle's proto-reliabilist sketch are not important at this point, although I will return to it and a general discussion of reliabilism in section 2. What is important here is to understand how the foundationalists use the regress argument.

The Regress Argument as Used by Foundationalism

1. Reasoning has only three possible structures: it is finite and has a beginning point, it is circular, or it is infinite.

2. Circular reasoning is not acceptable because a belief would have to be epistemically prior to itself.
3. Reasoning infinite in length could not be carried out by humans.
4. Thus, if there is knowledge that results from reasoning, the reasoning must be finite in length.
5. The beginning points of the reasoning must be known (otherwise it would be mere supposition).
6. Thus, if there is reasoning that results in knowledge, there must be some beliefs (the beginning points) that are known by some process other than reasoning.

The conclusion is the basic claim made by the foundationalist, namely, if there is some knowledge that is the result of reasoning, some knowledge is not the result of reasoning. Note the hypothetical nature of the conclusion. As mentioned above, although almost all foundationalists eschew skepticism, a foundationalist need not hold that there is knowledge in any specific area, or even in general. There can be and have been skeptical foundationalists: Hume, for example. There can be non-skeptical foundationalists: Locke, and of course Aristotle, for example.

I think it is fair to say that there are two core presuppositions underlying the regress argument as put forth by foundationalists without which the argument could not succeed:

Non-Originating Principle: Reasoning, alone, cannot produce epistemic warrant.

Inheritance Principle: Reasoning can transmit the requisite epistemic warrant for knowledge from other beliefs.

For the sake of the discussion, the Pyrrhonians can accept the hypothetical in step 6 (above) as well as the two principles, but they would invoke the modes of relativity and discrepancy in order to show that there are no legitimate firm beginning points. Aristotle might be right that in practice we do not push for reasons beyond those that are taken for granted by all of the participants in a discussion, but skeptics would argue that such contextually based agreements do not indicate the presence of a belief that has the requisite epistemic warrant because at other times and in other circumstances, different agreements are, or can be, made. In addition, skeptics would point out that beliefs based upon perception are person and circumstance relative. That's not to say that reasons for holding such beliefs can't be located; rather, it is to say that they are not privileged in the way required by foundationalism.

The skeptics would point out that the inheritance and non-originating principles are telling against infinitism and coherentism because if reasoning cannot originate epistemic warrant, then neither view can explain how warrant arises in the first place. Each belief in the potentially infinite reasoning process is warranted on the condition that the previous belief is warranted, but that previous belief is warranted only if the previous one is, etc. So, how does warrant originate? (see Dancy 1985: 55). Similarly, even if the beliefs in a set of coherent beliefs are mutually warranting—each increasing the warrant of the other—the question of how the beliefs obtain warrant to begin with still remains.

The upshot, from the Pyrrhonian point of view, is withholding beliefs. To them, what initially looked like a good argument for foundationalism, when examined more carefully, actually provides a basis for a skeptical attitude towards beliefs because the origin of warrant remains mysterious.

2. Responses to the Skeptics' Use of the Regress Argument

Aristotle was not content with his response to skepticism quoted in the previous section (Aristotle 1941b: 1011a2–14). As mentioned earlier, in the *Posterior Analytics* he provides the sketch of another type of response, namely, one designed to provide a basis for explaining the origin of warrant. Here is a somewhat redacted and interpolated quotation that remains true to the basic Aristotelian view. (I have indicated exact quotes with double quotation marks):

> In order for us to acquire the basic beliefs "we must possess a capacity of some sort" which is "a characteristic of all animals, for they all possess a congenital discriminative capacity which is called sense perception. But though sense perception is innate in all animals, in some the sense-impression comes to persist, in others, it does not." In those animals in which sense perception persists, there "comes to be what we call memory, and out of frequently repeated memories of the same thing develop experience . . . [and] from experience . . . originate the skill of the craftsman and the knowledge of the man of science".
>
> (Aristotle 1941a: 99b33–100a8)

The essence of this form of foundationalism is what I call 'austere reliabilism' with regard to basic beliefs that acquire their warrant simply in virtue of having the right kind of causal history. What makes this form of reliabilism "austere" is that although reasoning can produce new knowledge, reasoning neither creates new types of epistemic warrant nor augments the amount of warrant, it merely transmits the warrant inherent in basic beliefs. (See Goldman 1979 for a contemporary form of austere reliabilism.)

'Embellished reliabilism' does not adhere strictly to the two principles mentioned in the previous section because it allows that reasoning can produce either a new type of epistemic warrant or augment the amount of epistemic warrant inherent in basic beliefs. Nevertheless, embellished reliabilism, like austere reliabilism, holds that some beliefs have a type of epistemic warrant that obtains because of the way in which such "basic" beliefs arise. But once the basic beliefs, or those inferred from them, become members of a set of beliefs that have been subjected to careful self-reflection—including reflection about the reliability of our (or, in a Cartesian mode, my) epistemic capacities—a different type of (or at least more) warrant can arise. Here is a passage from Ernest Sosa that makes that very point:

> Admittedly, there is a sense in which even a supermarket door "knows" when someone approaches, and in which a heating system "knows" when the temperature in a room rises above a certain setting. Such is "servo-mechanic" knowledge. And there is an immense variety of animal knowledge, instinctive or learned, which facilitates survival and flourishing in an astonishingly rich diversity of modes and environments. Human knowledge is on a higher plane of sophistication, however, precisely because of its enhanced coherence and comprehensiveness and its capacity to satisfy self-reflective curiosity. Pure reliabilism is questionable as an adequate epistemology for such knowledge.
>
> (Sosa 1991: 95)

It is not my purpose here to examine either austere ("pure") or embellished reliabilism in detail and I grant that this taxonomy might be difficult to apply in some cases. Nevertheless, it should be clear that although the embellished form of reliabilism does recognize the normative imperative to provide reasons for some of our beliefs, both forms fail to *fully* recognize the fundamental intuition informing the regress—namely, that any belief for which one can produce reasons is better or differently warranted than a belief for which one cannot produce reasons.

If good reasoning cannot be circular, and if being able to provide reasons for our beliefs is importantly epistemically better than not being able to do so, then infinitism is the only solution to the regress argument—other than skepticism. To see that, take any proposed "basic" belief in the regress. Call it "E." One can ask the following question: In virtue of what is E a proper ending point? If no answer is forthcoming, then it clearly appears arbitrary to believe E without a reason because up to that point reasons were needed. Why should the regress end at E rather than at some earlier step or at some possible later step?

Suppose that the answer is that E is the appropriate ending belief in virtue of E's having some foundational property, F. Then, the next question becomes obvious: Does E's possessing F make it more likely that E is true than it would be if E did not possess F?

The imperative to produce an answer strikes me as obvious. Consider what I have called elsewhere a "Wednesday Foundationalist" who holds that a belief formed by any person on Wednesday has the austere form of warrant (Klein 2007a: 15). No one is such a foundationalist because there is absolutely no reason to believe that Wednesday-beliefs are any better than, say, Friday- or Sunday-beliefs. What foundationalists typically put forth as the F-property in virtue of which E beliefs are foundational is such that E's possessing F readily provides a basis for believing that E is likely to be true.

Once the question is asked about whether E's possessing F is truth conducive, there are four possible responses: It can be ignored, or "yes," "no," or "I don't know." I take it that ignoring the question is to fail to grasp the normative imperative underlying the regress argument, and the "no" and the "I don't know" answers place S's acceptance of E in jeopardy. Once the question is asked and understood, the only answer that at least preserves all of E's warrant is "yes." But, then, a reason for believing E has been given and the regress has continued.

Let me note in passing that this argument against foundationalism, if sound, works against the current forms of emergent coherentism as well—and emergent coherentism strikes me as the only plausible form. The other form—what I call transference coherentism—was probably never held since it takes individual beliefs to be the primary bearers of warrant and leads to circular reasoning. That logically possible but completely unsatisfying view was well disposed of by Aristotle and the Pyrrhonians.

Emergent coherentism is best exemplified by BonJour (BonJour 1985: 87–110). In this view, it is *sets* of beliefs that are the primary bearers of warrant. All beliefs in the appropriate type of coherent set are warranted simply in virtue of being members of that set. Thus, warrant is not transferred from one belief to another—rather, warrant emerges as a result of the mutual support provided by the beliefs in the set.

As Ernest Sosa has pointed out, this form of coherentism shares a formal structure with foundationalism (Sosa 1980). Using the terminology I am employing, the emergent coherentist takes the foundational property F to be E's being a member of a set of beliefs that is coherent (and perhaps has other features as well). In other words, emergent coherentism can be seen as one-step foundationalism because all beliefs are foundational. (Perhaps some are relatively "more foundational" than others because they are more important to the coherence of the set. But they all gain their initial warrant because they are members of the appropriate type of set.) But once the foundational property, F, is identified as "being a member of a set of coherent beliefs," the question arises about whether E's being a member of such a set is truth-conducive. Without a positive answer to that question, acceptance of the coherent set seems arbitrary. The regress has continued.

Now, it could be objected (1) that this very general argument against foundationalism (and emergent coherentism) conflates an important distinction between a belief itself *being* justified with the meta-belief that the belief is justified and (2) that knowledge only requires that the belief be justified (see Alston 1976).

To assess the force of the objection, it is important to distinguish two senses of belief and the concomitant two senses in which a belief is justified. In one sense, "belief" refers to the propositional content of a belief as in "that belief is true" or "her belief was implied by what she said earlier." In the other sense, "belief" can refer to the belief-state as in "she had that belief for many years" or "her belief was caused by a reliable process." The concomitant distinction regarding "justified belief" is between the proposition being justified for someone, that is, propositional justification, and the believing (i.e., the state of believing) being justified, that is, doxastic justification (see Firth 1978).

The objection mentioned above would be valid only with regard to propositional justification. There is a clear distinction between a proposition, say p, being justified and the meta-proposition 'p is justified' being justified. Any argument that conflated the distinction is built upon a pun. I grant that in order for p to be justified for a person, it is not required that 'p is justified' is justified for that person.

Nevertheless, it is crucial to note that what is required for knowledge is that S's believing that p be justified (even if the believing is only a dispositional state). For even if p is true, believed, and propositionally justified for S, S could fail to know that p because either S believed p for the wrong reasons or no reasons whatsoever (as in a guess). The regress argument and any possible responses are concerned with whether the belief that p is doxastically justified sufficiently for the belief to rise to the level of knowledge.

Once the question is raised concerning whether E's possessing F makes it more likely that E is true than it would be if E did not possess F, it is S's entitlement to continue to believe that p that is being questioned. If S is not able to defend the "yes" answer to the question, some adjustment of S's entitlement to believe E and every belief that depends upon E is called for. It might not be required that S give up E because E (as opposed to any of the contraries of E) might possess the kind or amount of epistemic warrant that austere reliabilism would attribute to it, but those views that recognize the importance of having reasons for our beliefs when their epistemic credentials are challenged (i.e., embellished reliabilism, coherentism, and infinitism) would require some recalibration of S's entitlement to believe that p.

In other words, the "meta-question" concerning whether E's possessing F makes it more likely that E is true is directly relevant to determining whether S's believing that E is warranted. It is only austere reliabilists who will not grant this point. For them, the belief that E is fully epistemically warranted just in case it is produced by an appropriate process. As mentioned above, the normative force behind the regress argument is simply that having reasons for believing a proposition adds a type of epistemic warrant. Lacking a reason is problematic only when seen from the standpoint of normative epistemology in which knowledge is taken to be the most highly prized form of true belief—where, of course, it is the believing that is prized, not the propositional content (see Plato 1980: 97a–98b).

3. Infinitism

Brief sketch

The upshot of the argument up to this point is that either we have to reduce what it takes to be the most highly prized form of true belief to something akin to austere reliabilism or it appears that there is no privileged belief which is immune to interrogation. The first alternative simply ignores the normative intuition underlying the regress. But a major obstacle to accepting infinitism remains. Recall the two principles that motivated foundationalism: the Inheritance Principle and the Non-Originating Principle.

Together they rule out infinitism. For even if we had infinite time to produce reasons, it still seems mysterious, if not downright impossible, that some belief could ever be warranted because reasoning alone cannot warrant a belief. Coupled with the fact that compared to an infinitely enduring being, we live but a nanosecond, the upshot seems to be that the Pyrrhonians were right after all. Suspension of belief is the only apt attitude.

The answer to these worries and the key to understanding infinitism is that neither of the principles, though they motivate and imply foundationalism, is required by all accounts of epistemic warrant. Having reasons for a belief does add a type of warrant for holding it. Indeed, having reasons for a belief is required for it to be the most highly prized form of true belief. In other words, although there is some type of epistemic warrant that a belief acquires in virtue of its etiology, having a reason for the belief provides a different type of warrant for believing it. I say "different type" of warrant rather than just "more warrant" because no matter how reliable the process is that produced the belief, the belief does not rise to the status of the most highly prized form of true belief unless there are good reasons for holding it. So, although there is one form of warrant that does not originate with reasoning, another form of warrant does. Thus, the Non-Originating Principle is false. Having reasons for a belief provides it with a new type of warrant. In addition, the inheritance principle is, at best, misleading since it seems to imply that the warrant required for knowledge is transmitted by reasoning. But the reason, r, for a belief, b, can provide b with a type of warrant that r, as yet, does not possess because no reason for r has yet been given or located. So b could be known without r being known.

The infinitist will take the belief that p to be doxastically justified for S only if S has engaged in providing "enough" reasons along the path of reasons. S would be completely doxastically justified if every reason in the path were provided. But since it takes some time to discover and offer reasons, even though a *proposition* might be completely justified (if there is a suitable endless path of reasons), no *belief* could ever be completely doxastically justified. Nothing is ever completely settled in the sense that it is beyond interrogation, but as S engages in the process of providing more reasons for her beliefs they become better justified—not because S is getting closer to completing the task but, rather, because S has added some warrant for her belief. How far forward in providing reasons S needs to go in order to acquire knowledge seems to me to be a matter of the pragmatic features of the epistemic context—just as which beliefs are being questioned and which can be taken as reasons is at least partially contextually determined (see Fantl 2003; Klein 2005a, 2005b, 2007a, 2007b).

Responses to Some Objections to Infinitism

Infinitism has not been taken as a serious contender among the answers to the regress problem because there seem to be obvious, clear objections. But I think these objections to infinitism miss the mark. Let us consider five of them:

1. The Finite Mind Objection

Aristotle correctly observed that beings with a finite mind cannot traverse an infinitely long inference path because each inference takes some time. But infinitism—or at least the kind that makes proper use of the distinction between propositional and doxastic justification—does not require that an infinite set of reasons be produced or located in order for a belief to rise to the level of the most highly prized form of true belief. Knowledge requires being able to provide enough reasons for our believing. It does not require completing a task with an infinite number of steps.

What constitutes "enough" reasons requires careful elaboration and I have not done that here. Such an elaboration would include a discussion of the role of the contextual considerations that make further questioning either necessary because a legitimate question has been raised and understood or frivolous because the amount of added warrant that further investigation would produce is minuscule. Those issues are beyond the scope of this essay.

2. The No-Starting Point Objection

The Pyrrhonians said that the process of reasoning endorsed by infinitism could not succeed in justifying a belief sufficiently for us to adopt it because "we possess no starting-point for our argument." That objection has an intuitive tug only if we thought that knowledge could be produced by reasoning only if all of the positive epistemic properties required for belief rising to the level of knowledge had to be present in the reasons for the belief. But I hope I have dispelled their intuitive appeal by showing how reasoning can produce a new type of warrant that is not inherited from the offered reason.

3. Skepticism

Some philosophers have argued that knowledge entails certainty, where certainty includes at least having finally settled the matter. And they would point out that infinitism makes that kind of certainty impossible and, thus, infinitism leads to skepticism. There are two replies to this objection.

First, as I mentioned earlier, there are both skeptical and non-skeptical forms of foundationalism. There would be skeptical forms of coherentism if no belief set held by creatures like us could be sufficiently coherent to satisfy the requirements of knowledge. In a similar vein, there certainly could be skeptical forms of infinitism that held that the normative requirements of justification simply cannot be fulfilled. The fact that a theory of justification leads to skepticism might provide a basis for looking more carefully at whether the theory is correct, but that, alone, does not strike me as a sufficient reason for rejecting the theory.

Second, the form of infinitism that I am defending does not lead to skepticism. It is a form of fallibilism that eschews certainty as a requirement for knowledge, where certainty is construed as requiring that the degree of epistemic warrant necessary for knowledge makes the belief immune to further interrogation. Indeed, I think this form of infinitism can explain why certainty is taken to be both a relative notion as when we say that one belief is more certain than another, and an absolute notion as when we say that a belief is certain only if there is no belief that is more certain. It can also explain why absolute certainty cannot be obtained because any belief can always be made a little more certain by producing more reasons along the path of reasons while at the same time it can explain how a belief can be certain enough to rise to the level required by knowledge (see Klein 2005c).

4. Infinitism Really Endorses a Form of Arbitrary Foundationalism

It has been claimed that (1) infinitism is really a form of an unjustified (arbitrary) foundationalist view, and (2) that a "bad" reason, r, could justify a belief, b. (See Bergmann 2007 for the objection and Klein 2007b for a full response.) That infinitism is not a form of foundationalism should be clear because it eschews the fundamental claim endorsed by foundationalists, namely, that there are some beliefs immune to further interrogation.

The answer to (2) is more complex. There are several distinct factors that could make a reason, r, "bad" for believing b:

(i) A reason, r, could be "bad" because it was not formed in a reliable manner. Such a bad reason could not transfer the kind of warrant required by the austere reliabilist to b by reasoning, and consequently, neither b nor r would be knowledge—even according to the infinitist. In other words, the infinitist can embrace the reliabilists' basic insight that a belief must be properly caused in order to be knowledge. So, in this sense r could not be "bad" and lead to knowledge.

(ii) A reason, r, could be "bad" because there is *no* further reason for it. But note that in such a case, r couldn't have been formed reliably because the belief that b was reliably formed is a good reason for thinking b is true. Hence, what was said with regard to (i) applies here as well.

(iii) A reason, r, could be "bad" because S does not have available an answer to the question as to why she believes that r is likely to be true. In such a case, although b has gained some warrant because r was produced as a reason for believing b, b's degree of warrant would diminish. That strikes me as just what a theory of justification should dictate. We are a bit better off by possessing r as a reason for b than we would be if we had no reason for believing b, but we are not completely in the epistemic clear.

(iv) A reason, r, could be "bad" because it is false or there is a defeater of the reason for r. If it is false, there is a defeater of the inference from the "bad" reason (namely, ~r). Infinitism, per se, is an account of only the justification condition in knowledge; an infinitist can include a no-defeater condition in the necessary conditions for knowledge. So, such a "bad" reason could not lead to knowledge.

(I should add parenthetically that I think on some occasions a false belief can lead to knowledge and, hence, such useful falsehoods are not "bad" reasons, but those considerations are irrelevant here because those false beliefs could appear in chains of reasons endorsed by foundationalists (see Klein 2008).)

5. The Something from Nothing Objection

An anonymous reviewer of this chapter poses this question:

> **Q**: Can a belief B be warranted (to at least some degree) by being based on a belief in reason R1 if both of the following are true: (i) the belief in reason R1 is not reliably formed and (ii) the believer has no reason for thinking the belief in reason R1 is likely to be true?

The reviewer writes that a 'yes' answer "seems completely implausible" and that I seem committed to a "no" answer. I suppose that a 'yes' answer seems so implausible because if B can be warranted (at least partially) on the basis of R1, when R1 isn't warranted at all, it seems that some warrant is originating from nothing. The reviewer's point is that if the correct answer to Q is 'no,' then the Non-Originating Principle is true.

He/she writes:

> Klein doesn't directly answer Q in the paper, though he says that under these circumstances, a belief in R1 couldn't transfer the kind of warrant required by the austere reliabilist and so B couldn't amount to knowledge. So I think we should assume that Klein thinks that B couldn't be warranted to any degree at all by being so based and that R1 couldn't transfer any degree of warrant at all under conditions (i) and (ii).

I agree that R1 couldn't *transfer* any degree of warrant under conditions (i) and (ii) because R1 has no warrant to transfer. But the reviewer is wrong in thinking that "B isn't warranted at all by being so based." To repeat, a basic claim of infinitism is that reasoning can originate warrant. When we locate a reason for a belief, we have provided that belief with some warrant which the reason might not (yet) possess. Warrant hasn't originated from nothing. It has originated through the process of locating and citing the reason. Of course, B falls short of being knowledge because "R1 was not reliably formed" is a defeater of R1's justification for B, and, as mentioned above, B lacks the kind of warrant that the reliabilists require of a belief.

Conclusion

I conclude that neither foundationalism nor coherentism provides an adequate non-skeptical response to the epistemic regress problem. Only infinitism does.

References

Alston, W. (1976) "Two Types of Foundationalism," *Journal of Philosophy*, 73: 165–85.
—— (1989) *Epistemic Justification*, Ithaca, NY: Cornell University Press.
Aristotle (1941a) *Posterior Analytics* in McKeon, R. (ed.), *The Basic Works of Aristotle*, New York: Random House.
Aristotle (1941b) *Metaphysics* in McKeon, R. (ed.), *The Basic Works of Aristotle*, New York: Random House.

Bergmann, M. (2007) "Is Klein an Infinitist About Doxastic Justification?" *Philosophical Studies*, 134(1): 19–24.
BonJour, L. (1985) *The Structure of Empirical Knowledge*, Cambridge, MA: Harvard University Press.
Dancy, J. (1985) *Introduction to Contemporary Epistemology*, Oxford: Basil Blackwell.
Empiricus, S. (1976) all citations are to Bury, R.G., *Outlines of Pyrrhonism*, Cambridge, MA: Harvard University Press.
Fantl, J. (2003) "Modest Infinitism," *Canadian Journal of Philosophy*, 33(4): 537–62.
Firth, R. (1978) "Are Epistemic Concepts Reducible to Ethical Concepts?" in A. Goldman and J. Kim (eds) *Values and Morals*, Dordrecht: D. Reidel Publishing Co.
Goldman, A. (1979) "What is Justified Belief?" in G.S. Pappas (ed.) *Justification and Knowledge*, Dordrecht: D. Reidel Publishing Company, 1–23.
Klein, P.D. (2005a) "Infinitism Is the Solution to the Epistemic Regress Problem," in M. Steup and E. Sosa (eds) *Contemporary Debates in Philosophy*, Malden, MA: Blackwell Publishers, 131–40.
—— (2005b) "Reply to Ginet," in M. Steup and E. Sosa (eds) *Contemporary Debates in Philosophy*, Malden, MA: Blackwell Publishers, 149–52.
—— (2005c) "Infinitism's Take on Justification, Knowledge, Certainty and Skepticism," *Perspectives in Contemporary Epistemology*, (a special edition of *Veritas*), 50(4): 153–172.
—— (2007a) "Human Knowledge and the Infinite Progress of Reasoning," *Philosophical Studies*, 134(1): 1–17.
—— (2007b) "How to Be an Infinitist about Doxastic Justification," *Philosophical Studies*, 134(1): 25–29.
—— (2008) "Useful False Beliefs," in Quentin Smith (ed.) *Epistemology: New Essays*, Oxford University Press, 25–61.
Plato (1980) *Meno*, translated by G. M. A. Grubbe, Indianapolis, IN: Hacket.
Sosa, E. (1980) "The Raft and the Pyramid: Coherence Versus Foundations in the Theory of Knowledge," *Midwest Studies in Philosophy*, 5(1): 3–26.
—— (1991) *Knowledge in Perspective*, Cambridge: Cambridge University Press.

Further Reading

Fumerton, R. (1995) *Metaepistemology and Skepticism*, Lanham, MD: Rowman & Littlefield.
Ginet, C. (2005a) "Infinitism is not the Solution to the Regress Problem," in M. Steup and E. Sosa (eds) *Contemporary Debates in Philosophy*, Malden, MA: Blackwell Publishers, 140–49.
—— (2005b) "Reply to Klein," in M. Steup and E. Sosa (eds) *Contemporary Debates in Philosophy*, Malden, MA: Blackwell Publishers, 153–55.
Klein, P.D. (1998) "Foundationalism and the Infinite Regress of Reasons," *Philosophy and Phenomenological Research*, 58(4): 919–25.
—— (1999) "Human Knowledge and the Infinite Regress of Reasons," *Philosophical Perspectives*, ed. J. Tomberlin, 13, 297–325.
—— (2000) "Why Not Infinitism?" in R. Cobb-Stevens (ed.) *Epistemology: Proceedings of the Twentieth World Congress in Philosophy*, Bowling Green: Philosophy Documentation Center, 5: 199–208.

24
COHERENTISM
Erik J. Olsson

1. The Regress Problem

Traditionally, a person cannot know something to be true without having good reasons for believing that thing to be true. If Karen knows that she will pass tomorrow's exam, she must have good reasons for thinking that she will pass. But consider Karen's reasons for thinking she will pass. They will presumably consist of other beliefs Karen has, for example, beliefs about her previous track-record, how well she has prepared herself this time, and so on. Surely, these other beliefs will also have to be items of knowledge in order for her belief that she will pass the exam to be such an item.

Why is that? Well, otherwise her knowledge that she will pass the exam will be based on something that falls short of being known. But things that fall short of being known are things of which we are ignorant, and knowledge, as Nicholas Rescher (1979: 76) has pointed out, cannot be based on ignorance. So, the reasons upon which Karen's knowledge that she will pass the exam is based must themselves be cases of knowledge. So, Karen must have good reasons for thinking those reasons true as well. Moreover, those reasons for her reasons must, by the same token, be items of knowledge, or they would be things of which Karen is ignorant, and so on.

The conclusion is that any knowledge claim requires a never-ending chain of reasons and reasons for reasons. This seems very strange indeed. One is inclined to think that such a chain of propositions that provide reasons for other propositions is somehow impossible. If so, knowledge is also impossible. But knowledge is possible, or so we think. So we have a contradiction. This is the infamous regress problem.

There are various ways to respond to the regress, the traditionally most popular one being some form of foundationalism. According to this proposal, the regress ends once we reach a privileged set of basic beliefs. Infinitism represents another approach to the regress. The infinitist strategy is to question the premise that an infinite chain of reasons need to be epistemically defective. Our concern however will be with coherentist responses to the regress.

On one interpretation, the coherentist response to the regress involves licensing circular chains of reasons. On this picture, A can be a reason for B which is a reason for C which is a reason for A. If this is acceptable, what we have is a chain of reasons that is never-ending in the sense that for each belief in the chain there is a reason for that belief also in the chain. And yet there is obviously no problem of infinity, potential or actual. On one understanding of coherentism, this is the proper response to the regress problem.

Yet this response invites an immediate objection. While there are indeed kinds of circularity that are non-vicious—recursive definitions in mathematics come to mind—justificatory circles do not belong to those kinds. If someone claims C and is asked why she believes it, she might utter B as her reason. If asked why she believes B, she might assert A. But given a request to justify her belief in A, she might, at this point, not refer back to C which is still in doubt. If she did so nonetheless, her move would have no justificatory force whatsoever. Hence, the coherentist solution to the regress problem, thus construed, fails miserably.

Is this the end of coherentism as a solution to the regress problem? Not really. The coherentist might deny that she has ever intended to suggest that circular reasoning is legitimate. Her take on the regress is, rather, to question the premise that justification should proceed in a linear fashion where reasons are given for reasons, and so on. This assumption presupposes that what is, in a primary sense, justified are individual beliefs. This, says the coherentist, is simply wrong: what is primarily justified are not individual beliefs but total belief systems. Particular beliefs are justified in a secondary or derived sense, if they form part of a justified belief system. This is a coherence approach because what makes a belief system justified, on this view, is its coherence, i.e. the extent to which the member beliefs mutually support or agree with each other etc. A belief system is justified if it is coherent to a sufficiently high degree. This, in essence, is Laurence BonJour's (1985) solution to the regress problem. In later works BonJour has distanced himself from the coherence theory altogether (see, for example, BonJour 1999).

This looks much more promising than the circularity theory. If epistemic justification is holistic in this sense, then a central assumption behind the regress is indeed false, and so the regress never gets started. The approach is interestingly related to Quine's influential holism and web of belief metaphor (Quine and Ullian 1970). Even so, this holistic approach raises many new questions that the coherentist will need to respond to.

First of all, the proposal that a singular belief is justified merely in virtue of being a member of a justified totality does not seem very plausible. Conceivably, a belief can be member of a sufficiently coherent system without itself adding to the coherence of that system. Surely, a belief will have to *contribute* to the coherence of the system in order to become justified by that system. A particular belief needs, in other words, to *cohere with* the system of which it is a member if that belief is to be considered justified. A detailed theory of coherence as a relation, i.e. of what it means for a given belief to cohere with a system of beliefs, can be found in Keith Lehrer's epistemological work. (See, for instance, Lehrer 1990, 1997 and 2000, and Olsson 2003 for a discussion. For an alternative theory of relational coherence, see Olsson 1999.) Bender (1989) is a particularly useful critical review of BonJour's and Lehrer's coherence theories. Another obvious issue raised by this holistic response to the regress concerns the concept of coherence itself and what it involves. To this subject matter we now turn.

2. Defining Coherence

The purpose of this section is mainly to survey some of the classical definitions of coherence and, in doing so, raise some general questions which any reasonably precise theory of coherence will need to answer in one way or the other. Finally, we will also look at some more recent attempts to explicate that elusive concept.

In his 1934 book on idealism, Cambridge philosopher A. C. Ewing put forward a much-cited definition of coherence. In his view, a coherent set is characterized partly by consistency and partly by the property that every belief in the set follows logically from the others taken together. On this picture, a set such as {p, q, p&q} would, if consistent, be highly coherent, as each element follows by logical deduction from the rest in concert.

While Ewing should be credited for having provided a precise definition of an intangible idea, his proposal must be rejected on the grounds that it defines coherence too narrowly. Few sets that occur naturally in everyday life satisfy the second part of his definition, that is, the requirement that each element follow logically from the rest when combined. Consider, for instance, the set consisting of proposition A, B and C, where:

A = "John was at the crime scene at the time of the robbery."
B = "John owns a gun of the type used by the robber."
C = "John deposited a large sum of money in his bank account the next day."

Many of us would consider this set to be coherent, and yet it does not satisfy Ewing's definition. A, for instance, does not follow logically from B and C taken together: that John owns a gun of the relevant type and deposited money in his bank the day after does not logically imply him being at the crime scene at the time of the crime.

From that perspective, C. I. Lewis's definition of coherence is more promising. According to Lewis, whose proposal can be seen as a refinement of Ewing's basic idea, a set is coherent just in case every element in the set is supported by all the other elements taken together, where "support" is understood in a weak probabilistic sense: A supports B if and only if the probability of B is raised on the assumption that A is true. It is easy to see that Lewis's definition is wider than Ewing's, so that more sets will turn out to be coherent on the former than on the latter. (There are some uninteresting limiting cases for which this is not true. For instance, a set of tautologies will be coherent in Ewing's but not in Lewis's sense.)

To illustrate, let us go back to the example with John. Here one could argue that A, while not being logically entailed by B and C, is nevertheless supported by those sentences taken together. Assuming that John owns the relevant type of gun and deposited a large sum the next day serves to raise the probability that John did it and hence that he was at the crime scene when the robbery took place. Similarly, one could hold that each of B and C is supported, in the probabilistic sense, by the other elements of the set. If so, this set is not only coherent in an intuitive sense but also coherent according to Lewis's definition.

Another proposal for how to say something more definite about coherence originates from Laurence BonJour (1985), whose account of coherence is considerably more complex than earlier suggestions. While Ewing and Lewis each proposed to define coherence in terms of one single concept—logical consequence and probability, respectively—BonJour thinks that coherence is a concept with a multitude of different aspects, corresponding to the following *coherence criteria* (ibid.: 97–99):

1. A system of beliefs is coherent only if it is logically consistent.
2. A system of beliefs is coherent in proportion to its degree of probabilistic consistency.
3. The coherence of a system of beliefs is increased by the presence of inferential connections between its component beliefs and increased in proportion to the number and strength of such connections.
4. The coherence of a system of beliefs is diminished to the extent to which

it is divided into subsystems of beliefs which are relatively unconnected to each other by inferential connections.
5. The coherence of a system of beliefs is decreased in proportion to the presence of unexplained anomalies in the believed content of the system.

A difficulty pertaining to theories of coherence that construe coherence as a multifaceted concept is to specify how the different aspects are to be amalgamated into one overall coherence judgment. It could well happen that one system S is more coherent than another system T in one respect, whereas T is more coherent than S in another. Perhaps S contains more inferential connections than T, which is less anomalous than S. If so, which system is more coherent in an overall sense? BonJour's theory remains silent on this important point.

BonJour's account also serves to illustrate another general difficulty. The third criterion stipulates that the degree of coherence increases with the number of inferential connections between different parts of the system. As a system grows larger the probability is increased that there will be relatively many inferentially connected beliefs. For a smaller system, this is less likely. Hence, there will be a positive correlation between system size and the number of inferential connections. Taken literally, BonJour's third criterion implies, therefore, that there will be a positive correlation between system size and degree of coherence. But this is not obviously correct.

The problem, if it is one, can be avoided by dividing the number of inferential connections by the number of elements in the system:

(3') The coherence of a system of beliefs is increased by the presence of inferential connections between its component beliefs and increased in proportion to the number and strength of such connections *divided by the number of elements in the system*.

On the proposal, it is the inferential density rather than the sheer number of inferential connections that is correlated with coherence.

Here is another general challenge for those wishing to give a clear-cut account of coherence. Suppose a number of eye-witnesses are being questioned separately concerning a robbery that has recently taken place. The first two witnesses, Robert and Mary, give exactly the same detailed description of the robber as a red-headed man in his forties of normal height wearing a blue leather jacket and green shoes. The next two witnesses, Steve and Karen, also tell exactly the same story but only succeed in giving a very general description of the robber as a man wearing a blue leather jacket. So here we have two cases of exact agreement. In one case, the agreement concerns something very specific and detailed, while in the other case it concerns a more general proposition. This raises the question of which pair of reports is more coherent. Should we say that agreement on something specific gives rise to a higher degree of coherence, perhaps because such agreement seems more "striking"? Or should we, rather, maintain that the degree of coherence is the same, regardless of the specificity of the thing agreed upon?

To illustrate these points about size and specificity consider the following recently proposed coherence measures:

$$C_1(A_1, \ldots, A_n) = \frac{P(A_1 \wedge \ldots \wedge A_n)}{P(A_1) \times \ldots \times P(A_n)}$$

$$C_2(A_1, \ldots, A_n) = \frac{P(A_1 \wedge \ldots \wedge A_n)}{P(A_1 \vee \ldots \vee A_n)}$$

C_1 was put forward in Shogenji (1999) and is discussed for instance in Olsson (2001). C_2 was tentatively proposed in Olsson (2002) and, independently, in Glass (2002). Following Lewis both measures assign a degree of coherence to a set of propositions in probabilistic terms, but they do it in slightly different ways. I leave it to the reader to verify that C_1 is sensitive to size as well as to specificity, while this is not so for C_2. It has been suggested, therefore, that these two measures actually measure two different things. While C_2 captures the degree of agreement of the proposition in a set, C_1 is more plausible as a measure of how *striking* the agreement is (Olsson 2002; see also Bovens and Olsson (2000) for a discussion of agreement vs. striking agreement). Since these two proposals were made, a large number of other measures have been suggested, many of which are studied in Olsson and Schubert (2007).

3. Coherence and Truth

Let us move on to the question whether the coherence of a belief system implies the truth of its elements. Numerous objections have been leveled against the proposal that the relation between coherence and truth should be of this simple kind, the most important and straightforward of which is based on the observation that a system can be as coherent as you wish without having anything whatsoever to do with reality. This objection is often referred to as the "isolation objection." A dream, for instance, can be extremely coherent without thereby being true. The fact that Dr. Watson dreams that John was at the crime scene at the time of the crime, owns a weapon of the required sort and deposited large sums the day after does not make it true or even probable that all this actually happened. In spite of the coherence among the different parts of the dream we are reluctant, to say the least, to conclude that what was dreamt is really true.

The matter would be radically different had the same information been obtained from different witnesses in a trial; one witness saying that John was at the scene of the crime, the other that he owns the relevant type of gun, and so on. In that case, we would be disposed to accept the contents of the testimonies as true, or at least highly probable. What, then, is it that makes agreement significant in the witness scenario but is missing in the dream scenario? Surely, the difference does not lie in the extent to which the information coheres. If not, where does it lie?

The witness and dream settings are, in fact, disanalogous in two relevant respects. In the witness case we can, absent any reason to think otherwise, take it for granted that each witness is at least to some extent credible. There are, to be sure, witnesses who lie or for other reasons fail to tell the truth, but most witnesses are, after all, reasonably reliable. So, if a witness claims that John was at the crime scene at the relevant point in time, and we have no reasons to question the credibility of that witness, that is a reason for thinking that John was in fact there at that time. It is true, though, that there might not be much more to be said about the witness's degree of credibility, unless we have more information at our disposal, e.g. from a character witness. It would, for example, be naive to think of each witness as being absolutely reliable. At any rate, there is no corresponding reason to suppose that a given episode should become more plausible just because someone dreamt that it took place. For instance, the fact that Dr. Watson dreamt that John was at the crime scene at the relevant point in time is not a reason, however weak, for thinking that John actually was there at that time.

The second relevant disanalogy has to do with independence. When we are querying various witnesses, we may, absent reasons to think otherwise, reasonably assume that they are telling their stories independently. A paradigm case of independence would arise when the witnesses have not agreed beforehand to coordinate their testimonies, say, to the disadvantage of the accused. If they have so agreed, or in other relevant respects influenced each other, their testimonies would not be considered independent. Exactly how the concept of independence is to be understood is a complicated matter the more detailed coverage of which is beyond the scope of this chapter. Again, witness testimonies can usually be assumed to have been delivered independently. The same could not be said of the production of the different parts making up a dream. There is no reason to believe that the various components of Dr. Watson's dream about John were in any interesting sense produced independently. Watson could well have dreamt that John went to the bank to deposit money because he had earlier dreamt that John was at the crime scene. In other words, the dream could very likely have created its own coherence.

We have succeeded in isolating two factors that seem to characterize the conditions under which coherence has a positive effect on the probability that the propositions in a system are true: the sources should be individually partially reliable and collectively independent. The question, though, is whether both these conditions are needed. Perhaps it suffices that one of them holds.

Suppose, then, that the witnesses are partially reliable but that they are not delivering their reports independently. We would have such a situation if one of the witnesses, say Peter, is partially reliable and has, perhaps by threatening the other witnesses, made them give reports that coincide with his report. It is evident that in this case the collective impact of the testimonies does not exceed the singular impact of Peter's testimony. If so, coherence has no confidence-boosting effect.

Suppose, by contrast, that the witnesses are collectively independent but that they are individually completely unreliable. We could for instance imagine a number of independent witnesses who were located too far from the crime scene to get a clear picture of what was actually going on. Suppose that they nevertheless deliver completely agreeing testimonies: the robber was a blond man wearing a T-shirt, say. How would we react to this information? If it is, as we assume, completely clear that the witnesses really could not have seen anything of importance, we would probably judge their agreement as a sheer coincidence. The witnesses just happened to give the same reports. Hence, in this case, too, the high degree of coherence would not affect our assessment of the likelihood of what is being reported.

It should be added that the observation that the witnesses are saying the same thing independently despite the fact that they had been assumed to be completely unreliable would normally be considered an anomalous fact. That observation is, after all, very unlikely given that the witnesses are independent, yet completely unreliable. A sensible reaction would be to reconsider the assumptions that led to the anomaly. For instance, there might be reasons to question earlier information about the witnesses' whereabouts at the time of the crime.

So, the fact that a set is coherent, in the agreement sense, is a reason for thinking that the propositions in the set are likely to be true provided that the sources are partially reliable and independent. Both conditions must be satisfied for coherence to boost confidence (but see Shogenji (2005) for a diverging opinion). To the best of my knowledge, C. I. Lewis was the first to insist that both conditions are needed. The question remains, however, how high the probability gets as the effect of coherence given that these conditions are satisfied. The answer is that a very high probability can be obtained in this way even if the sources are only slightly reliable in themselves. If a sufficient number of such sources report the same thing, this will result in a probability arbitrarily close to 1. This means that the "good reasons" that many hold are necessary for knowledge could very well be of a coherence character: a person's main reasons for claiming knowledge might well be her observation that many sources have reported that thing to be true. This holds so long as we resist, as most contemporary epistemologists do, Descartes' conviction that the reasons required for knowledge must necessitate that which they are reasons for.

It is worth noting that the exact probability that is attained for a system of reports depends on two things. First, it depends on how reliable the sources are individually. If the sources are relatively reliable, relatively few agreeing reports are needed in order to attain a sufficiently high probability. Second, it depends on how probable the thing that is reported was before the reports came in. If what is being reported was already relatively probable, relatively few agreeing reports are needed for a given probability to ensue. There is a complication, though: there are cases where a relatively low initial probability leads to a relatively high probability given that the agreement has been observed (see Olsson 2005a: chapter 3). What is generally true is the following: in order to be in a position to give a more precise probabilistic estimate given the reports, more is needed than just the information that the sources are relatively reliable and independent; what is required is additional information as to how reliable the sources are and how probable the things reported were to begin with. These observations will play a major role as we now proceed to consider anti-skeptical applications of coherence reasoning.

4. Skepticism

The sort of skepticism that shall interest us states that everything we can ever know has the character of *reports* about reality; we can never grasp reality itself. We can, in other words, know only that our senses, memories, and so on *report* that reality is such and such, without ever knowing that reality really *is* such and such. I can know that I seem to see John, that is, that my visual system reports that John is in front of me. I cannot know that John really is there. Similarly, I can know that I seem to remember getting a lot of presents at Christmas when I was a child; not that I really got a lot of presents. By the same token, all I can know is that I have these and these beliefs, that is, that my belief system reports that such and such is the case, not that the contents of my beliefs are really true.

The coherence proposal amounts to granting that no information sources, including our senses, memories, and beliefs, are sufficiently reliable in themselves for knowledge to ensue, while insisting that this does not mean that we cannot know interesting things about reality. We can know that what is reported is true provided that we have many reports whose contents are sufficiently coherent. This proposal goes back to the British idealist tradition. A clear statement can be found in Bertrand Russell's classical book *The Problems of Philosophy* (1912) in which Russell argues that beliefs that are, taken singly, mere probable opinions, can, if they are combined into a system, attain a very high probability on grounds of coherence. A detailed argument for this view was provided by Lewis in his 1946 book. We will return to Lewis's theory in a moment.

To illustrate, suppose you seem to remember not only that you received a lot of Christmas gifts but also that the whole family used to gather at Christmas time. These two memories to some extent cohere: the more relatives, the more gifts a particular child is likely to get (if every relative gives each child a present). Let us, further, assume that many such memories mutually support each other in similar ways. That would, on the coherence proposal, make it highly likely that things happened as you remember them to have.

But here we must be very careful indeed. We concluded, in the previous section, that coherence has a positive effect on the probability of what coheres only if the two conditions of partial reliability and independence are satisfied. In order to conclude that our cohering memories are likely to record what actually happened, we must know in advance—that is, before coherence is invoked—that those memories are individually partially reliable and collectively independent. But whether or not our memories are partially reliable and independent is a substantial empirical question, and according to the skeptic we cannot have any substantial empirical knowledge. We cannot have, therefore, any knowledge regarding the partial reliability and independence of our memories. So, even if we can reliably ascertain that our memories are highly coherent we won't be in a position to tell whether that is a significant fact.

The only way out for the anti-skeptical coherence theorist would seem to be to argue that knowledge about the partial reliability and independence of our memories is not *a posteriori* but *a priori*, the hope being that statements about the partial reliability and independence of our memories belong to the realm of truths that we can grasp just by thinking hard enough about what they mean.

As for partial reliability, reason would, one could hold, break down in its absence. Unless we ascribe a minimum of reliability to our own memory, we would be paralyzed and unable to carry out even the simplest rational activity. So dependent are we on what we remember, or seem to remember, that it is difficult to even imagine what life would be without a firm trust in the credibility of what we clearly recall. This line of thought suggests that the relative reliability of our memory is a *condition for the possibility of rational thought and action*. Arguments that propose to establish that a certain assumption is a condition for the possibility of something else are called, following Kant, transcendental. A transcendental argument along these lines for the partial reliability ("relative unreliability") of our memories was given by Lewis in his 1946 book. It is perhaps more difficult to establish that we, for the same reasons, must assume our memories to be, to a large extent, independent—more difficult but perhaps not impossible.

Yet, even if the anti-skeptic succeeds in carrying out these argumentative feats, two worrisome problems still remain unsolved. As Lewis was well aware, the transcendental argument can establish, at most, that the credibility of our memory is positive; it does not give any hint as to its specific degree. But we said, a moment ago, that in order to be in a position to say something more definite about the probability of the contents of our memories on the basis of coherence, we need to know the initial degree of credibility. Otherwise, we cannot ensure that the resulting probability is high enough for us to rely on the information. Furthermore, we need to have more definite information concerning the prior probability of the data, in this case the contents of our memories, before the coherence was observed. It is unfortunate for the coherentist approach to skepticism that these missing items of knowledge do not seem to be within reach. C. I. Lewis's attempted coherence justification of memory is treated at length in Olsson (2002), Olsson and Shogenji (2004) and Olsson (2005a: chapter 3).

So far we have dealt rather extensively with the possibility of giving a coherence justification of the content of our memories. Philosophers have tried by similar reasoning to justify our beliefs (see, for example, BonJour 1985; Davidson 1986; and, for discussions, Olsson 2005a: chapters 4 and 9) or our trust in the testimonies of others (see, for example, Coady 1992 and, for a discussion, Olsson 2005a: chapter 5). The problems that arise are essentially analogous.

In the light of these remarks, it is severely problematic to hold that the coherence theory provides the long sought-for answer to the problem of skepticism. This is so regardless of whether the skeptical doubts concern our memories, beliefs, or statements of others.

5. Recent Developments

Whether or not coherentism is the right answer to skepticism, the nature of coherence and its link to truth is a matter of independent philosophical interest. Recently, intense efforts have been made to secure a deeper understanding of these subjects. This development was initiated independently by Peter Klein and Ted A. Warfield (1994, 1996) and Michael Huemer (1997). See Cross (1999) for a compelling critique of Klein and Warfield's theory, and for a related reaction Bovens and Olsson (2002). These investigations have led to a large number of formal results couched in probability theory. For instance, what has been said here about the role of partial reliability and independence is easily verified in that manner. At this moment, the probabilistic approach to coherence stands out as the most fertile and productive research program in this area of epistemological research, although this assessment is not unanimously subscribed to. Paul Thagard is a prominent critic of the translation of coherence reasoning into probability calculus (see, for instance, Thagard 2000, 2005 and 2007). For a discussion, see section 9.4 in Olsson (2005a). For other non-probabilistic versions of the coherence theory, see Rescher (1973) and Lehrer (1990) and (2000).

The most spectacular recent results about coherence and probability concern the possibility of finding a measure of coherence that is *truth conducive* in the following sense: if a set of beliefs A is more coherent than another set of beliefs B, then the probability of A is higher than the probability of B. Here it is assumed that the beliefs in question are partially reliable (to the same degree) and that they are independently held. Finding such a measure was first stated as an open problem in Olsson (2002). One would think that it wouldn't be that hard to a find a measure of the required sort given the fortunate circumstances of partial reliability and independence. Alas, it is not only hard to find such a measure; it is impossible. An impossible result to that effect was first proved by Luc Bovens and Stephan Hartmann in their 2003 book. A different impossibility theorem was proved in Olsson (2005a) (see Olsson (2005b) for a detailed discussion of that result, including a comparison with Bovens and Hartmann's theorem).

These impossibility results give rise to a thought-provoking paradox. How can it be that we trust and rely on coherence reasoning, in everyday life and in science, when in fact coherence is not truth conducive? Since the impossibility results were published a number of proposals have been made for how to avoid the anomaly they present us with. As Franz Dietrich and Luca Moretti (2005) prove, coherence in the sense of the C_2-measure is linked to the practice of indirect confirmation of scientific hypotheses. That measure turns out to be, as Moretti (2007) puts it, "confirmation conducive." David H. Glass (2007) argues, similarly, that coherence can provide the key to a precise account of inference to the best explanation, the main idea being to use a coherence measure to rank competing hypotheses in terms of their coherence with a given piece of evidence. In a paper by Stefan Schubert and myself (Olsson and Schubert 2007) we observed that, while coherence falls short of being truth conducive, it can still be "reliability conducive," that is, more coherence, according to some measures, entails a higher probability that the sources are reliable, at least in a paradigmatic case. Staffan Angere (2007, 2008) has argued, based on the results of extensive computer simulations, that the fact that coherence fails to be truth conducive in the sense just referred to does not prevent it from being connected with truth in a weaker, defeasible sense: almost all coherence measures that have an independent standing in the literature satisfy the condition that *most* cases of higher coherence are also cases of higher likelihood. For another reaction, see Huemer (2007). Olsson (2007) and (2008) contain overviews of the impossibility results and some ways of coming to grips with them. Finally, it has been noted that coherence plays an important negative role in our thinking. If our beliefs show signs of incoherence, this is often a good reason for contemplating a revision. See chapter 10 in Olsson (2005a) for an elaboration of this point.

Regardless of how the impossibility results are ultimately dealt with, there is no doubt that the marriage between coherence and probability has led to a tighter connection between the theory of coherence and other areas of philosophy and science in which probability plays a major role. Besides Dietrich and Moretti (2005), several other authors have explored the rather obvious connection to confirmation theory, including Branden Fitelson (2003). For coherence and Bayesian networks, see Bovens and Olsson (2000). Another link to artificial intelligence is described in Glass (2006). The study of coherence, from being a fairly isolated part of epistemology, has developed into an interdisciplinary field of research with fertile connections to philosophy of science, cognitive psychology, artificial intelligence, and philosophy of law.

Acknowledgment

I am indebted to Stefan Schubert for his helpful comments on an earlier version of this chapter.

References

Angere, S. (2007). "The Defeasible Nature of Coherentist Justification," *Synthese* 157 (3): 321–35.
—— (2008). "Coherence as a Heuristic," *Mind* 117 (465): 1–26.
Bender, J. W. (1989). "Coherence, Justification, and Knowledge: The Current Debate," in J. W. Bender (ed.) *The Current State of the Coherence Theory*, Dordrecht: Kluwer, 1–14.
BonJour, L. (1985). *The Structure of Empirical Knowledge*. Cambridge, Mass.: Harvard University Press.
—— (1999). "The Dialectics of Foundationalism and Coherentism," in J. Greco and E. Sosa (eds.) *The Blackwell Guide to Epistemology*, Malden, Mass.: Blackwell, 117–42.
Bovens, L. and Hartmann, S. (2003). *Bayesian Epistemology*, Oxford: Clarendon.
—— and Olsson, E. J. (2000). "Coherentism, Reliability and Bayesian Networks," *Mind* 109: 685–719.
—— (2002). "Believing More, Risking Less: On Coherence, Truth and Non-trivial Extensions," *Erkenntnis* 57: 137–50.

Coady, C. A. J. (1992). *Testimony: A Philosophical Study*, Oxford: Clarendon.
Cross, C. B. (1999). "Coherence and Truth Conducive Justification," *Analysis* 59: 186–93.
Davidson, D. (1986). "A Coherence Theory of Knowledge and Truth," in E. LePore (ed.) *Truth and Interpretation*, Oxford: Blackwell, 307–19.
Dietrich, F. and Moretti, L. (2005). "On Coherent Sets and the Transmission of Confirmation," *Philosophy of Science* 72 (3): 403–24.
Ewing, A. C. (1934). *Idealism: A Critical Survey*, London: Methuen.
Glass, D. H. (2002). "Coherence, Explanation and Bayesian Networks," in M. O'Neill and R. F. E. Sutcliffe et al. (eds.) *Artificial Intelligence and Cognitive Science*, Berlin, Heidelberg, New York: Springer Verlag, Lecture Notes in Artificial Intelligence 2464, 177–82.
—— (2006). "Coherence Measures and Their Relation to Fuzzy Similarity and Inconsistency in Knowledge Bases," *Artificial Intelligence Review* 26 (3): 227–49.
—— (2007). "Coherence Measures and Inference to the Best Explanation," *Synthese* 157 (3): 257–96.
Fitelson, B. (2003). "A Probabilistic Measure of Coherence," *Analysis* 63: 194–99.
Huemer, M. (1997). "Probability and Coherence Justification," *Southern Journal of Philosophy* 35: 463–72.
—— (2007). "Weak Bayesian Coherentism," *Synthese* 157 (3): 337–46.
Klein, P. and Warfield, T. A. (1994). "What Price Coherence?" *Analysis*, 54: 129–32.
—— and —— (1996). "No Help for the Coherentist," *Analysis* 56: 118–21.
Lehrer, K. (1990). *Theory of Knowledge*, First Edition, Boulder: Westview.
—— (1997). "Justification, Coherence and Knowledge," *Erkenntnis* 50, 243–57.
—— (2000). *Theory of Knowledge*, Second Edition, Boulder: Westview.
Lewis, C. I. (1946). *An Analysis of Knowledge and Valuation*, LaSalle: Open Court.
Moretti, L. (2007). "Ways in which Coherence is Confirmation Conducive," *Synthese* 157 (3): 309–19.
Olsson, E. J. (1999). "Cohering with," *Erkenntnis* 50: 273–91.
—— (2001). "Why Coherence is Not Truth-Conducive," *Analysis* 61: 236–41.
—— (2002). "What Is the Problem of Coherence and Truth?," *The Journal of Philosophy* 99: 246–72.
—— (2003). "The Epistemology of Keith Lehrer," in E. J. Olsson (ed.) *The Epistemology of Keith Lehrer*, Dordrecht: Kluwer, 1–20.
—— (2005a). *Against Coherence: Truth, Probability, and Justification*, Oxford University Press.
—— (2005b). "The Impossibility of Coherence," *Erkenntnis* 63 (3): 387–412.
—— (2007). "Guest Editor's Introduction," *Synthese* 157 (3): 267–74.
—— (2008). "The Place of Coherence in Epistemology," in V. F. Hendricks and D. Pritchard (eds.) *New Waves in Epistemology*, New York: Palgrave Macmillan, 192–214.
—— and Schubert, S. (2007). "Reliability Conducive Measures of Coherence," *Synthese* 157 (3): 297–308.
Olsson, E. J. and Shogenji, T. (2004). "Can We Trust Our Memories? C. I. Lewis's Coherence Argument," *Synthese* 142 (1): 21–41.
Quine, W. V. O. and Ullian, J. S. (1970). *The Web of Belief*, New York.
Rescher, N. (1973). *The Coherence Theory of Truth*, Oxford: Oxford University Press.
—— (1979). *Cognitive Systematization*, Oxford: Blackwell.
Russell, B. (1912). *The Problems of Philosophy*, Home University Library, Williams and Norgate.
Shogenji, T. (1999). "Is Coherence Truth-Conducive?," *Analysis* 59: 338–45.
—— (2005). "Justification by Coherence from Scratch," *Philosophical Studies* 125 (3): 305–25.
Thagard, P. (2000). *Coherence in Thought and Action*, Cambridge, Mass.: MIT.
—— (2005). "Testimony, Credibility, and Explanatory Coherence," *Erkenntnis* 63 (3): 295–316.
—— (2007). "Coherence, Truth, and the Development of Scientific Knowledge," *Philosophy of Science* 74 (1): 28–47.

Part IV
KINDS OF KNOWLEDGE

25
INDUCTIVE KNOWLEDGE
Alexander Bird

1. Introduction

In this chapter I take a loose, functional approach to defining induction: Inductive forms of reasoning include those *prima facie* reasonable inference patterns that one finds in science and elsewhere that are not clearly deductive. Inductive inference is often taken to be reasoning from the observed to the unobserved. But that is incorrect, since the premises of inductive inferences can, themselves, be the results of prior inductions. A broader conception of inductive inference regards any ampliative inference as inductive, where an ampliative inference is one where the conclusion 'goes beyond' the premises. 'Goes beyond' can mean: (i) 'not deducible from,' or (ii) 'not entailed by.' Both of these are problematic. Regarding (i), some forms of reasoning might have a claim to be called 'inductive' because of their role in science, yet turn out to be deductive after all—for example, eliminative induction (see below) or Aristotle's 'perfect induction' which is an inference to a generalization from knowledge of *every* one of its instances. Interpretation (ii) requires that the conclusions of scientific reasoning are always contingent propositions, since necessary propositions are entailed by any premises. But there are good reasons from metaphysics for thinking that many general propositions of scientific interest and known by inductive inference (e.g. "all water is H_2O") are necessarily true. Finally, both (i) and (ii) fail to take account of the fact that there are many ampliative forms of inference one would not want to call inductive, such as counter-induction (exemplified by the 'gambler's fallacy' that the longer a roulette wheel has come up red the more likely it is to come up black on the next roll). Brian Skyrms (1999) provides a useful survey of the issues involved in defining what is meant by 'inductive argument'.

Inductive knowledge will be the outcome of a successful inductive inference. But much discussion of induction concerns the theory of confirmation, which seeks to answer the question, "when and to what degree does evidence support an hypothesis?" Usually, this is understood in an *incremental* sense and in a way that relates to the rational credibility of a hypothesis: "When and by how much does e add to the credibility of h?," although 'confirms' is sometimes used in an absolute sense to indicate total support that exceeds some suitably high threshold. Important but largely unanswered questions relate these topics, for example, "does inductive inference correspond to the case of absolute confirmation for some suitable threshold?" I shall discuss inference and confirmation together, though it should be noted that some approaches eschew inference altogether. For example, the Bayesian takes scientific reasoning to be a matter of adjusting credences in propositions in the light of evidence, and says nothing about unqualified belief in a proposition. However, if we are interested in inductive *knowledge* then we must consider inference, since only then do we have a detached proposition that is the possible content of a mental state of knowing.

2. Enumerative Induction

The form of inference discussed above and sometimes called simply 'induction' is a matter of inferring from a sample to the whole of a population. In the paradigm of enumerative induction one argues, as in the examples concerning planetary orbits, as follows:

(E1) all Fs in $P' \subset P$ are Gs
therefore
all Fs in P are Gs.

Where (E1) articulates a rule of inference, the corresponding notion of confirmation is *Nicod's criterion*: an F in P that is also a G confirms the generalization that all Fs in P are Gs. My characterization of enumerative induction, as an inference from a sample to all of a population, is more general than (E1) in order that it should encompass also:

(E2) the proportion of Fs in $P' \subset P$ that are Gs is p
therefore
the proportion of Fs in P that are Gs is p.

(E1) is a special case of (E2) where $p = 1$, but (E2) cannot be considered as a matter of generalizing facts about individual members of P'. Rather, (E2) concerns population level facts.

(E1) is most familiar in the form (E1') 'all known Fs are Gs *therefore* all Fs are Gs.' Another popular way of expressing enumerative induction is (E1'') 'all known Fs are Gs *therefore* the next F to be examined will be G,' which we can gain from (E1) by putting P' = the known Fs, and P = the known Fs plus the next F to be examined. A generalization of (E1'') yields a familiar version of (E2), Reichenbach's 'straight rule' of induction:

(E3) of n known Fs, m are G
therefore
the probability that some unknown F (e.g. the next F to be examined) is G is m/n.

Just as (E2) is a form of enumerative induction, although not a generalization of facts about individuals, we should consider as inductive in this sense various other statistical inferences such as:

(E4) the mean value of parameter L in $P' \subset P$ is μ
therefore
the mean value of parameter L in P is μ.

In general the various techniques of classical statistical inference should be seen as refined instances of enumerative induction; in particular classical statistical inference seeks to correct the defects of (E1), namely, that it (a) does not tell us how large P′ needs to be before we can make the inference concerning all of P, and (b) it does not tell us how confident we should be in the conclusion when we draw it.

The principal weakness of the various forms of enumerative induction is that their scope is severely limited. Note that the conclusions in (E1)–(E4) mention only properties and parameters already mentioned in their premises. Therefore enumerative induction is unable to yield knowledge concerning entities of a kind of which we do not already know. Yet this is a crucial part of science—witness our beliefs in subatomic entities and their properties, or in plate tectonics, or stellar evolution, and so forth.

As Reichenbach's straight rule exemplifies, it is natural to seek to relate confirmation to probability. This thought lies behind Carnap's inductive logic. According to Carnap, inductive logic should be seen as a generalization of deductive logic where the conclusions are drawn only with a certain degree of probability. The degree to which evidence provides absolute confirmation for a hypothesis is the same as the probability of the hypothesis given that evidence: $C(h, e) = P(h\,|\,e)$, where the conception of probability being used is a logical one. The latter operates as follows. Consider a language with predicates denoting properties and names denoting objects. One can construct a complete 'state description,' a maximal description of a way things can be, by saying of each object whether each predicate or its negation holds of it. The simplest approach to logical probability would ascribe to each state description the same probability. The conditional probability $P(h\,|\,e)$ is now fixed and so, therefore, is our confirmation relation. The drawback of this approach is that it does not allow any room for inductive learning. One might have thought that repeated observations of Fs that are Gs (without non-G Fs) would raise the probability that the next F to be examined will be G. But this simple approach to inductive logic does not yield that outcome. Carnap's important move is to concentrate not on state descriptions but on *structure* descriptions. 'Fa∋¬Ga∋¬Fb∋Gb' is a different state description from '¬Fa∋Ga∋Fb∋¬Gb.' But they both have the same structure: 'one thing is F but not G and the other thing is G but not F'. Carnap now distributes probabilities equally among structure descriptions, rather than across state descriptions; then the probability assigned to a structure description is divided equally among the state descriptions with that structure. This distribution of probabilities, m^* yields a confirmation relation c^* that *does* allow for learning from evidence. A central problem for such an approach is to articulate why the distribution m^* is a priori more suitable than some other distribution (e.g. the simple distribution, $m^\dagger$, that gives each state description the same probability). If m^* isn't the a priori right distribution, then in what sense is this account or probability (and confirmation) *logical*?

3. Hypothetico-deductivism

Note that in (E1) the conclusion of the inductive inference entails the premise. In (E2) and (E3) the conclusions make the premises likely (without entailing them). According to (E1)–(E3), inductive support occurs where the inductive conclusion deductively entails the evidence or makes it likely. Hypothetico-deductivism takes this as the central idea in confirmation. Thus:

(HD) *e* confirms *h* iff *h* entails *e*.

Here *h* may be considered to be, for example, the combination of a theory and a set of auxiliary hypotheses. Also plausible, but less frequently discussed is the more general:

(HD′) e confirms h iff h entails that e is likely.

The advantage of hypothetico-deductivism over enumerative induction is that its scope is much wider. Enumerative induction (E1) can be seen as a special case of (HD) for the case where h is a generalization of e; Nicod's criterion is a consequence of (HD). But hypotheses can entail evidence without being generalizations of the evidence. Thus Fresnel's wave theory of light entails that there is a bright spot at the center of the shadow cast by a disk, and is confirmed by the observation of such a spot, even though the wave theory concerns unobservable features of the world and so is no kind of generalization of the observational evidence in question.

This advantage turns out, however, to be a disadvantage, when we see that the deductive relationship allows for too liberal an account of confirmation. The most famous of such problems is the Ravens Paradox. The hypothesis that all ravens are black, combined with the auxiliary hypothesis that object x is not black, entails that x is not a raven. So observing x, a white shoe, provides confirmation for the hypothesis that all ravens are black. Nicod's criterion delivers this conclusion since the white shoe confirms the hypothesis that all non-black items are non-ravens, which is logically equivalent to the hypothesis under test. Many find the conclusion absurd, though others accept it, merely regarding the support as very weak.

There is another problem. Hempel's *special consequence* principle tells us that when e confirms h, then e confirms any consequence of h. This seems reasonable: recall (E1″) 'all known Fs are Gs *therefore* the next F to be examined will be G,' which I claimed to be a special case of (E1), for the population consisting of the known Fs plus the next F to be examined. But strictly (E1)″ follows only if we take the confirmation of the hypothesis that the known Fs plus the next F are all G to entail the confirmation of the proposition deduced from it, that the next F is G. Now assume for the following that h entails e. Therefore h∧p also entails e, for any p. According to (HD) not only is h confirmed by e, but also h′, where h′ is h∧p. The special consequence condition tells us that since e confirms h′, e confirms any consequence of h′, and so, in particular e confirms p. But p was an arbitrary proposition. So any proposition can confirm any other (putting e = h makes that especially clear). It seems obvious that the special consequence principle is at fault. It can only be unrestrictedly true in the case of *absolute* confirmation. However, some restricted version of the special consequence principle would appear to be true for incremental confirmation, if there is ever to be any non-trivial ampliative confirmation—as, for example, in (E1″). One would expect one's theory of confirmation to provide an answer: when evidence confirms an hypothesis, which logical parts of the hypothesis get confirmed and which do not? One response would be to think that while the conjunction h∧p might get confirmed as a whole, this is due just to the confirmation of h whereas p itself gets no confirmation, and this is because p plays no role in deducing e. But now consider p∧(p → h). The proposition e cannot be deduced from the second conjunct alone, so now p does play a deductively essential role—even though p∧(p→ h) is logically equivalent to h∧p. As a theory of confirmation (HD) is thus incomplete; moreover, it does not point towards any obvious satisfactory supplementation.

4. Grue—The New Riddle of Induction

A feature of (E1) and (HD) is that they suggest that inductive confirmation is a *formal* relation. In deductive logic, the relevant relations, such as deducibility hold in virtue of the syntactic form of the relevant propositions. According to hypothetico-deductivism, the same is true of confirmation, because confirmation is held to be the converse of deduction. Likewise enumerative induction holds inductive inference to be licensed on grounds of the formal relation of conclusion to evidence, the latter being just a generalization of the former and generalization being a formal operation.

A major challenge to both these accounts of induction comes from Goodman's (1954) 'New Riddle of Induction,' which shows that confirmation cannot be a formal relation. Define the predicate 'grue$_t$' as holding of x precisely when x is green and is first observed before time t or x is blue and is not first observed before time t. Consider the hypothesis 'all emeralds are green.' Given the auxiliary proposition that emerald a is observed before time t, then we may deduce that a is green. According to (HD), therefore, the observation of a green emerald before t provides confirmation of the hypothesis that all emeralds are grue. But the latter hypothesis has as a consequence the proposition that emeralds first observed after t will be blue. And this surely is *disconfirmed* by the observation of a green emerald before t.

This latter result may be seen as a particular case of the claim made in the preceding section that hypothetico-deductivism makes confirmation of hypotheses too easy. The same goes, however, for the more restrictive enumerative model of induction. Consider (E1) where 'F' = 'emerald,' 'G' = 'grue thing,' P' is the set of emeralds observed to date (which is before t), and P is the set of all emeralds (or is some subset thereof that includes emeralds first observed after t or never observed at all). According to (E1) we are entitled to infer that emeralds first observed after t, or never observed, are grue, and hence, by the definition of 'grue,' are blue.

Neither of these results is acceptable, and so we should conclude that inductive confirmation is not a formal relation. Consequently we should not think that inductive relations are like deductive relations, which can be formalized in an a priori logic. The same applies to Carnap's inductive logic since the probability distribution m^* is relative to a language, with the consequence that that confirmation is also relative to a language. This means that his inductive logic fails to be logical in a key sense. A satisfactory deductive system should have the feature that if two sentences are deductively related in one language, their translations into another language should also be deductively related in the same way. But that does not hold for Carnapian confirmation.

5. Abduction and Inference to the Only Explanation

The hypothetico-deductive model of confirmation is closely related to the deductive-nomological model of explanation, according to which:

(DN)   Laws L and conditions C together explain fact f iff L&C deductively entail f.

Consider (HD). If our hypothesis is that laws L hold and conditions C obtain (i.e. h = L&C), then e confirms this hypothesis precisely when, according to (DN), L&C would explain e. Just as the hypothetico-deductive model of confirmation suffers from problems, so does the deductive-nomological model of explanation. In particular, the relation of explanation is not a formal one, *contra* (DN). From the law that anyone who ingests a pound of arsenic will die within 24 hours, and the fact that Jones had ingested a pound of arsenic, we might deduce the fact that he died within 24 hours. But, in fact, this does not explain his death because he was killed by being hit by a bus before the arsenic could kill him (Achinstein 1983). So background knowledge is required in addition to a deduction in order to work out whether we have an explanation. (Achinstein's case can also be regarded as a counter-instance to (HD). Let us say that we are investigating the hypothesis that a pound of arsenic will kill within 24 hours. The discovery that Jones dies within 24 hours of eating a pound of arsenic confirms that hypothesis as (HD) says it should. However, when we learn that Jones was, in fact, killed by a bus, the fact of his death now lends our hypothesis no support at all. Nonetheless, the death is still deducible from the hypothesis plus the fact of his eating the arsenic. One way to understand this is to consider that the deducibility relation is *monotonic*—if it holds at all, no further addition of information will prevent it from holding. Thus the confirmation relation should also be monotonic. But it is not, as this case shows.)

Even if both (HD) and (DN) are mistaken, what may be correct is the relation between them:

(A) e confirms h iff h would, if true, explain e.

The left to right implication in (A) will not do, however. Incremental confirmation is typically (if not always) transmitted by deduction, whereas explanatory power is not. For example, rising sea levels might be explained by, and confirm the hypothesis of, global warming. From the latter we might be able to deduce that there will be increased droughts, in which case the observation of rising sea levels might confirm that hypothesis that there will be increased droughts. But those future droughts do not explain current increases in sea levels.

The right to left implication in (A) remains plausible, nonetheless. Abductivist (or explanationist) conceptions of confirmation take explanation to be central to inductive confirmation. Note that abductivism does *not* say that e confirms h if h, in fact, explains e, since to know that latter would require already knowing that h is, in fact, true. Rather, abductivism says that the fact that h is a *potential* explanation of e provides confirmation to h.

Abductivism is able to encompass enumerative induction if one thinks that, in the cases where enumerative induction lends confirmation, that is because some relevant fact provides explanatory power. For example, observations of planetary motions confirm Newton's law of gravitation via enumerative induction because the law explains its instances (Armstrong 1983; Foster 1983). In other cases, a common cause explains the known correlation and confirms its extrapolation; we can extrapolate the correlation between a high barometer reading and bad weather, because high pressure is a cause of both. The hypothesis that all emeralds are grue is not confirmed by the observation of green emeralds since background knowledge tells us there is no putative law or causal connection covering all the instances.

Abductivism, the claim that being a potential explanation of some evidence confirms a hypothesis, like (HD), fails to tell us *how much* this explanatory relation supports the hypothesis and, likewise, when we may infer that the hypothesis is true. Inference to the best explanation (IBE) aims to provide a more detailed account of abductivism. IBE employs the intuitive idea that some hypotheses are better potential explanations of the evidence than others, and regards better explanations as more likely to be true. To be more precise, IBE holds that under certain conditions, it is reasonable to infer that the best of a set of competing explanations is the actual explanation and hence is true.

The conditions are: (i) that the best explanation is clearly better than its next best competitor, and (ii) that the best explanation is good enough (it meets some threshold of goodness—if it does not, then we might suspect that the problem of *underconsideration* applies). A key issue for any thorough account of IBE is to explain what explanatory goodness is.

Lipton characterizes IBE as a two-stage process. In the first stage the imaginative capacity of the scientist generates a set of possible explanations of a phenomenon. In the second stage the generated hypotheses are ranked according to their explanatory goodness, and the top ranked is selected.

Three problems face IBE (Lipton 2004: 142–51). The first stage encounters the problem of *underconsideration*. The ranking by goodness at stage two cannot be any guide to truth if the actual (true) explanation is not among those considered by the imaginative power of the scientist at stage one. Even if the actual explanation is among those considered, stage two raises the two remaining problems, which Lipton names *Hungerford's objection* and *Voltaire's objection*. The former notes that beauty is in the eye of the beholder; that is, explanatory goodness is too subjective a quality to be correlated with objective truth. Even if goodness is objective, Voltaire's problem asks why it should be correlated with the truth. Presumably there are possible worlds where explanations that we would judge to be poor explanations are, in fact, very often true. IBE therefore assumes that ours is the best possible world, explanation-wise. Why should we think that this assumption is correct? Lipton notes that if the second-stage ranking is accurate that shows that underconsideration cannot, in fact, be a problem, since ranking is a theory-laden process, and the reliability of the ranking implies the truth of the relevant background theories. In particular, background theories also play a role in setting our standards of loveliness. And so, successful inferential practices will be virtuously reinforcing. (In response to Hungerford's objection, Lipton says that while loveliness might be audience-relative, so also is inference.)

6. Bayesian Confirmation

Bayesian epistemology avoids many of the problems facing other accounts of confirmation, including Hume's problem (see below). It does this by focusing, in its standard subjective form, on rationality of incremental changes to credences. Bayes's theorem:

(B) $$P(h|e) = \frac{P(e|h)P(h)}{P(e)}$$

is derivable from the standard axioms of probability and so is a priori. Subjective Bayesianism tells us that the probabilities in question are subjective degrees of belief (credences) and that if one receives evidence e then one's credence in h should now be made equal to $P(h|e)$ as given by (B), known as Bayesian conditionalization. One's old credence in h is multiplied by $P(e|h)/P(e)$ (where $P(e)$ is one's credence in the evidence, and $P(e|h)$ is one's credence in the evidence, given the hypothesis).

An interesting question concerns the relationship between Bayesianism and other prima facie conceptions of inductive confirmation. Consider, for example, the case where the evidence is deducible from the hypothesis, as in the hypothetico-deductive model of confirmation. Then the old credence will be multiplied by $1/P(e)$, which so long as the evidence proposition is previously unknown, will be greater than one. In this way Bayesianism can encompass (HD) and does better both by giving an account of (HD') and by giving a quantitative measure of incremental confirmation in these cases (the more unexpected the evidence, the better evidence it is). Bas van Fraassen argues that Bayesian confirmation and IBE are in conflict, and that because it can be shown to be irrational to conditionalize in a way that diverges from the Bayesian prescription (thanks to so-called Dutch book arguments), it follows that IBE is in error. Lipton, on the other hand, regards Bayesianism and IBE as compatible. He regards the explanationist considerations that are brought to bear by IBE as heuristics that guide our estimation of $P(e|h)$.

Since Bayesianism deals in the rationality of incremental changes in subjective probabilities, it makes no claim to say what probabilities one's beliefs should have. It tells one only what one's new probabilities should be, once the evidence has been received, given one's old probabilities. Except insofar as those old probabilities were, themselves, based on evidence subject to Bayesian conditionalization, those old are rationally unconstrained. Two people who have the same evidence will find that conditionalization brings their credences closer together. But if they start off with sufficiently divergent distributions of probabilities they will end up with credences that remain very far apart. Since Bayesianism fails to tell one what one should believe nor even how much one should believe certain hypotheses, it is unsuited to giving us an account of inference and so of inductive knowledge. Thus it evades Hume's problem principally by limiting its ambitions. For these reasons, it cannot be that IBE functions *merely* to estimate $P(e|h)$. IBE tells us about inference—what one may believe in the light of the evidence. (For a detailed exposition of Bayesian epistemology, see Chapter 55 in this volume.)

7. Hume's Problem and the Reliabilist Response

The best-known and fundamental problem with any account of the capacity of inductive reasoning to yield knowledge is Hume's problem. What Hume's actual intentions were with this problem are a matter of debate (see Chapter 65 in this volume), but its basic structure is clear. When using some form of reasoning, it seems appropriate to ask whether use of that form of reasoning is justified. Prospects for an a priori justification are poor for those forms of inductive reasoning, the majority, that are ampliative. The very obvious efficacy of inductive reasoning, in science and everyday thought, would seem to be an obvious source of justification. However, the inference from the fact that induction has worked successfully for us on many occasions to its general reliability (we can expect induction to be reliable in current and future applications) is, itself, an inductive inference, an instance of (E1). And so this attempt to justify our inductive practices itself employs an inductive form of inference. As such this justification is circular and so could be thought to fail. Inductive reasoning, thus, seems to be without justification, and so the products of inductive reasoning cannot be knowledge.

One response to Hume's problem is to regard it as decisive. In which case, if one regards science as rational, one must propose a non-inductive basis for scientific reasoning. Sir Karl Popper's falsificationism attempts to do precisely that. Popper (1959) advocated hypothetico-deductivism, but regarded only one special case as admissible, that of absolute disconfirmation: the case where from a hypothesis h one deduces consequence c; one observes that c is false; hence one infers that h is false. Falsificationism is a highly skeptical view: although general hypotheses can be known to be false, they cannot be never known to be true.

Alternatively, in order to avoid skepticism about science, one may seek a diagnosis of Hume's problem that allows us to reject its conclusion. Hume's problem assumes that for S's use of a method M to produce knowledge, it must be the case that M is justified in a manner that is accessible to S. This requirement is a manifestation of epistemological internalism. The *internalist* rejects while the *externalist* accepts the idea that the ability of a process to justify beliefs may depend on some feature of the world that is not accessible to the user of that process (see Chapter 14 in this volume). Goodman's new riddle raises similar problems. It shows that two inductive arguments can have the same syntactic form but differ in their confirmatory power. So confirmation depends on semantic features, such as whether the predicates in question denote natural properties and kinds or not. Those semantic facts are external to the structure of an inductive argument and the truth of its premises. They might be known to the subject, but only as part of background knowledge acquired by science, i.e. by some prior piece of inductive reasoning. Such knowledge will not be a priori.

Reliabilism is one, natural implementation of externalism that offers an explanation of the possibility of inductive knowledge: for a belief to count as knowledge it must be produced by a reliable process or method, one which produced true beliefs in an appropriate range of counterfactual circumstances (Armstrong 1973; Nozick 1981; see Chapter 17 in this volume). If the world is, in fact, non-accidentally regular (e.g. law-governed) in certain respects, then enumerative induction, or certain classes of enumerative inductive inferences at least, might be reliable, and so knowledge generating. Since we are concerned with inductive *inference*, reliability will be a matter of the inferential rule (or pattern) producing true beliefs when given true beliefs as premises. A related reliabilist account might determine when inductively formed beliefs are *justified* (indeed reliabilism is typically seen more as an account of justification).

The reliabilist holds that in order for an inductively inferred belief to be knowledge (or to be justified) it must meet two kinds of condition: (i) an *evidential* condition, that the premises of the inference are suitable, and (ii) a *reliability* condition, that the inference rule employed is a reliable one. As an externalist account, this does not in general require that the subject be aware that the reliability condition holds. Reliabilists, and externalists more generally, hold that for an inductive belief to be justified, it *can* suffice that the reliability condition, in fact, holds (in addition to the evidential condition). Thus Mellor (1991) argues that inductive habits can yield warranted beliefs thanks to natural, contingent, regularities, independently of one's knowing that one has such a warrant. However, one might reasonably ask whether, as a matter of fact, S can have, in addition to her warranted (justified) belief in h, a justified belief in the reliability of R, the rule that led to her belief in h. We do think we have this sort of knowledge and justification. When S's experience in baking leads her to believe a certain technique will lead to a firm crust we believe that her belief is justified. But when S* uses tea-leaves to predict the future, we believe that S*'s resulting beliefs will not be justified. Can our beliefs about the methods of S and S* be justified? And can S herself have a justified belief that her inductively inferred belief (in the future outcome of her baking) is correct?

Let us say that S's rule of enumerative induction, R, is indeed reliable, so that S's belief in h is justified. We may be able to show that R is reliable, for example, by finding that R delivers true beliefs (e.g. predictions about the future that are subsequently verified) in a large number and variety of cases, while delivering no false beliefs (or only a few). If our rule of reasoning in this case is reliable, then by the reliabilist view of justification, our belief that R is reliable is itself justified. And S herself can engage in this reasoning also and acquire the same justified belief. Now let us consider the rule of reasoning, R*, just used to establish the reliability of R. It is clearly a form of enumerative induction. If R is, itself, a general rule of enumerative induction, then R* might be identical to R. Thus we will be using an inductive rule to establish the reliability (and so justify our belief in the reliability) of that very same rule. This would appear to be the very circularity that Hume warns us vitiates any attempt to justify induction.

The standard reliabilist reply draws upon the distinction between *premise-circularity* and *rule-circularity* (Braithwaite 1953: 255–92; see also van Cleve 1984). The former is the kind of circularity in reasoning that is vicious and with which we are familiar—seeking to establish the truth of proposition Q using an argument among whose premises is the proposition Q itself. Rule-circularity, however, is something different, and arises when one employs an argument to establish some proposition concerning a rule R, e.g. that it is reliable, and that argument-form is an instance of that same rule R. The key difference is that in rule-circularity there is no premise asserting the reliability of R, and so the conclusion is *not* among the premises. The Humean critic might object that by employing the rule R we are implicitly assuming the reliability of R, and so, after all, we are assuming what we set out to prove. The reliabilist (and, more generally, externalist) response is that a subject need not have any tacit belief or assumption concerning the reliability of the rules she in fact uses. Normally, it will suffice for knowledge or justification that the rule is reliable. And so while premise-circularity does undermine the epistemic value of the conclusions, rule-circularity does not. Reliabilism itself faces many questions (see Chapter 17 for more details), for example: What degree of reliability is required for justification, and does this differ from the degree of reliability required for knowledge? How do we delineate the rule or belief-forming method that a subject is using? (One and the same particular inference can be considered as an instance of many different inference rules, some of which might be reliable while others are unreliable. Which is *the* rule employed?) Thinking about inductive inferences, is there one general rule 'enumerative induction' that has the form of, for example, (E3), the straight rule of induction? Or are there many rules, methods, and habits that are inductive in character but which are specific to certain subject matters or circumstances? (If so, there might not even be rule-circularity in the reasoning process described above. Note also that the details of the reliability condition required for inductive knowledge will be specific and differ from one inductive practice to another.) These questions are linked, because one might wonder whether one very general rule of induction is likely to be reliable enough to give us inductive knowledge—after all we frequently do get false beliefs from induction; a more specific rule can have better prospects of high reliability.

Hume's problem affects not only enumerative induction but other kinds of ampliative inductive inference such as IBE. The response to the problem of underconsideration and Voltaire's objection, in effect, depends upon it, in fact, being the case that our capacity to generate hypotheses does tend to succeed in including the actual explanation, and it also being the case that our standards of loveliness match the way the world is. If asked to justify those claims, one might suggest that the best explanation of our success in employing IBE is that our hypothesis-generating and loveliness-judging capacities are effective in these respects. But this explanationist argument is just to use IBE in the justification of IBE, exhibiting the very circularity that Hume identified. A reliabilist answer can be given again here. So long as these capacities are indeed effective, IBE will be a reliable way of generating first-order beliefs, which will thus be justified. Furthermore, the second-order argument that IBE is indeed reliable can, for the same reasons, give a justified belief in IBE's reliability. The circularity identified is, again, only rule-circularity, not premise-circularity.

8. Eliminative Induction

One might worry, nonetheless, that IBE is insufficiently reliable to generate inductive *knowledge*. Are our judgments of loveliness so good that the hypotheses judged loveliness are always true? After all, many favored, lovely hypotheses have been found to be false. Note that the ranking process implicitly assumes that the lower ranked hypotheses are still all consistent with the evidence. Perhaps IBE can only justify an ordering of our credences, not an inference that the best is, in fact, true.

A natural extension of this thought would suggest that we can only acquire knowledge of the truth of a hypothesis when inferred from evidence, if that evidence serves to *eliminate* competing hypotheses. *Eliminative induction* goes back at least to Francis Bacon but has been supported by a number of contemporary philosophers (e.g. Earman 1992; Papineau 1993; Kitcher 1993; Bird 2005). Considered as a deductive inference:

(L1)   One of hypotheses $h_1, \ldots, h_i$ is true; hypotheses $h_1, \ldots, h_{i-1}$ are false; *therefore* hypothesis h_i is true.

The capacity of eliminative induction to deliver knowledge of its conclusion depends on our ability to know that the first premise is true, i.e. to know of some suitably limited range of hypotheses, that the true hypothesis is among them. 'Suitably limited' here means sufficiently limited that it is possible to know the second premise; that is, sufficiently limited for us to falsify all but one of the hypotheses referred to in the first premise. Another approach would be to cast eliminative induction as non-deductive:

(L2)   Hypotheses $h_1, \ldots, h_{i-1}$ are false; *therefore* hypothesis h_i is true.

In this case, the inference is reliable when the subject has a reliable disposition to infer the truth of h_i from the falsity of $h_1, \ldots, h_{i-1}$. Here one appeals to reliabilism again: to generate knowledge it might suffice that this inferential disposition is in fact reliable, whether or not the subject knows this. And in this case the disposition might be sufficiently specific that it is indeed sufficiently reliable. Alternatively, one might try to argue that the premises of (L1) can be known in certain cases. For example when the hypotheses are explanatory, it might be possible to know that the possible explanations of some phenomenon are limited to a constrained set of hypotheses:

(L3)   Only hypotheses $h_1, \ldots, h_i$ could explain e; e has some explanation; hypotheses $h_1, \ldots, h_{i-1}$ are false; *therefore* hypothesis h_i is true.

In this way eliminative induction can be seen as a limiting case of IBE, the limiting case where IBE leads to knowledge. Of course, the first premise (and indeed the second and third) will need to be discovered by the methods of scientific investigation that will be broadly inductive in the sense being used here. They might, themselves, be instances of eliminative induction or might depend on enumerative induction. And so the casting of eliminative induction is not intended to solve the problem of induction but, rather, to reveal the structure of an important route to inductive knowledge. Ultimately any attempt to show that our inductive practices, whatever they are, can lead to knowledge will have to appeal to externalist epistemology in some form.

References

Achinstein, P. 1983. *The Nature of Explanation*. Oxford: Oxford University Press.
Armstrong, D. M. 1973. *Belief, Truth, and Knowledge*. Cambridge: Cambridge University Press.
Armstrong, D. M. 1983. *What is a Law of Nature?* Cambridge: Cambridge University Press.
Bird, A. 2005. Abductive knowledge and Holmesian inference. In T. S. Gendler and J. Hawthorne (Eds.), *Oxford Studies in Epistemology*, pp. 1–31. Oxford: Oxford University Press.
Braithwaite, R. B. 1953. *Scientific Explanation*. Cambridge: Cambridge University Press.
Earman, J. 1992. *Bayes or Bust?* Cambridge, MA: Bradford.
Foster, J. 1983. Induction, explanation, and natural necessity. *Proceedings of the Aristotelian Society* 83: 87–101.
Goodman, N. 1954. *Fact, Fiction, and Forecast*. London: Athlone Press.
Kitcher, P. 1993. *The Advancement of Science*. New York: Oxford University Press.
Lipton, P. 2004. *Inference to the Best Explanation* (2nd ed.). London: Routledge.
Mellor, D. H. 1991. The warrant of induction. In *Matters of Metaphysics*. Cambridge: Cambridge University Press.
Nozick, R. 1981. *Philosophical Explanations*. Cambridge, MA: Harvard University Press.
Papineau, D. 1993. *Introduction to Philosophical Naturalism*. Oxford: Blackwell.
Popper, K. 1959. *The Logic of Scientific Discovery*. London: Hutchinson.
Skyrms, B. 1999. *Choice and Chance: An introduction to inductive logic* (4th ed.). Belmont, CA: Wadsworth Publishing.
van Cleve, J. 1984. Reliability, justification, and the problem of induction. *Midwest Studies in Philosophy* 9: 555–67.

26
A PRIORI KNOWLEDGE
Laurence BonJour

As it has been standardly understood, a priori knowledge is knowledge whose *justification* (or warrant) is a priori rather than empirical in character. This assumes that justification is at least a necessary condition for knowledge and that it is the only such condition to which the idea of being a priori meaningfully applies. Thus the focus of this chapter will be a priori justification—which I will take to be the same thing as having an a priori *reason* in support of the proposition or claim in question.

I will begin by explaining and clarifying the distinction between justifications or reasons that are a priori and those that are empirical (a posteriori), also contrasting this distinction with some others with which it is sometimes conflated or confused. Next we will consider some of the main reasons for thinking that a priori justification, so understood, genuinely exists. The rest of the chapter will be concerned with the three main philosophical views that have been held of a priori justification: the *rationalist* view, which defends both the existence of a priori justification and its central significance for the cognitive enterprise; and two versions of *empiricism*, one of which attempts to minimize the importance of a priori justification and the other of which denies its existence altogether.

The Concept of A Priori Justification

As reflected in the historical discussion of this issue, the concept of a priori justification involves two basic elements or aspects, one negative and one positive. Negatively, an instance of a priori justification involves a reason for thinking that a proposition is true whose rational force or cogency does not derive from *experience*, either directly (as in immediate sense perception) or indirectly (as by inference of any sort—deductive, inductive, or explanatory—whose premises, in turn, derive their justification from experience). Here it is important to realize that the sort of independence from experience that is relevant does *not* mean that someone who has undergone no experience of any sort could have such a reason. After all, being justified in accepting any proposition at least requires understanding that proposition, and experience, even experience of some fairly specific sort, might be required for such understanding.

Nor does the idea of an a priori reason, when understood in this way, imply either: (i) that experience-based reasons of some sort could not also count for or against the proposition in question; or (ii) that such experiential reasons could not sometimes override the a priori justification in question; or still less (iii) that an a priori justification renders the proposition certain or infallible, immune to mistake. All of these further claims *might* be true in some cases (though it is doubtful that they are true in all or even most), but they in no way follow from, or are essential to, the basic idea of a priori justification itself.

The obvious question is what counts, for these purposes, as *experience*? The paradigm examples of experience are various kinds of sense experience, including such things as kinesthetic experiences of bodily orientation in addition to those deriving from the five standard senses. But, though this has sometimes been denied in recent discussions, it seems quite clear that *introspective* awareness of one's thoughts, sensations, and other mental states should also count as a variety of experience, and the reasons for belief that such experience provides as empirical rather than a priori. Introspective experience might not depend on clearly identifiable sense organs, but it is still pretty clearly an awareness of temporally located contingent facts that depends on causal relations between those specific facts and the correlative state of awareness; it is thus far more analogous to sense experience than it is to the sort of mental process that is involved in the most paradigmatic cases of allegedly a priori justification (see below). And basically the same thing is true of even the reason for belief in one's own existence that is supplied by the Cartesian *cogito*, since this is based on introspective awareness of the occurrence of specific thoughts and sensations. (For essentially the same reason, such things as clairvoyant or telepathic awarenesses, should they exist, should also count as species of experience.)

But merely ruling out these kinds of experience as relevant to a priori justification obviously does not explain fully how the propositions in question are justified. If their justification does not derive from experience, where then does it come from? What is the nature of the *positive* reason for thinking that such a proposition is true which justification seems to require? Here the traditional view is that such justification results from pure thought or reason or rational reflection: from a direct or immediate insight into the truth, indeed the necessary truth, of the relevant proposition. (A derivative class of a priori reasons, about which little will be said here, would result from similar insights into the derivability of a proposition from one or more premises for which such a priori reasons exist or from a chain of such derivations.) As we will see, while both rationalists and those empiricists who do not simply reject the existence of a priori justification would accept this characterization, they give very different accounts of what such insight involves and, accordingly, of its ultimate cognitive significance.

Thus, summing up, a priori justification is justification that results from rational insight, with no appeal to any sort of experience; while empirical or a posteriori justification is justification that results, at least in part, from experience. (Thus justification that depends on *both* experience *and* insight or reasoning that is in itself a priori in character would count, for the purposes of this classification, as empirical; but this merely taxonomic point should not obscure the fact that such justification is still *partially* a priori.)

There are two other distinctions that are often invoked in the context of discussions of a priori justification. First, there is the *metaphysical* distinction between propositions that are *necessary*, true in all possible worlds, and those that are *contingent*, true in only some possible worlds. (A third category is necessarily false propositions, those that are true in no possible worlds.) Second, there is the logical or structural distinction between propositions that are *analytic* and those that are *synthetic*. Here, as discussed further below in the section on moderate empiricism, there is no one standardly accepted definition of "analytic," but the characterization (due to Frege) of an analytic proposition as one that is either a truth of formal logic or transformable into such a truth of logic by replacing terms with exact synonyms will do as an initial approximation. For the moment, the important point is that each of these distinctions is quite distinct from that between a priori and a posteriori justification, so that none of these concepts should be confused or conflated with each other—as is in fact very frequently done in discussions of the a priori (see, for example, Ayer 1946: 78, where the concept of a synthetic proposition is simply equated with that of an a posteriori or empirical one).

Arguments for the Existence of A Priori Justification

Does a priori justification, as so far characterized, genuinely exist? The rationalist answers this question affirmatively, while one version of empiricism (moderate empiricism), though acknowledging the existence of a priori justification, understands it in a way that drastically limits its scope and significance, and a second (radical empiricism) gives an entirely negative answer to this question. These views will be considered below, but it will be easier to appreciate what is at stake if we first consider the main reasons that have been offered for thinking either that a priori justification does, in fact, exist or, alternatively, that it must exist if severe versions of skepticism are to be avoided.

The Argument from Examples

The most widely discussed reason for thinking that a priori justification exists is that there seem to be many, many examples of propositions for which there are clear and obvious reasons of this sort. Here the most straightforward examples come from mathematics and logic, but there are others of many widely varying kinds. Here is a misleadingly short list, reflecting some of the main types:

1. $2 + 3 = 5$.
2. All cubes have 12 edges.
3. For any propositions P and Q, if it is true that P or Q and it is false that P, then it is true that Q.
4. If object A is larger in a specified dimension (length, area, volume, etc.) than object B and B is, in turn, larger in that same dimension than object C, then A is larger in that dimension than C.
5. No surface can be uniformly red and uniformly blue at the same time.

It is initially very plausible to think that anyone who understands and thinks carefully about each of these propositions will be able to see or grasp immediately that it must be true, that it is true in any possible world or situation—and the same thing also seems to be true of indefinitely many further examples of these sorts and others. From an intuitive standpoint, this sort of seeing or grasping seems to constitute, at least in the absence of further relevant considerations, a good, indeed compelling, justification or reason for thinking that the proposition in question is true, albeit not one that is capable of being stated as a separate proposition. Moreover, while independent experiential reasons might also be found for some or all of these propositions, insights of this basic sort do not seem to depend on experience in any discernible way.

Both rationalists and moderate empiricists claim that examples like these, which could be multiplied more or less without limit, provide compelling evidence for the existence of a priori justification and a priori knowledge. Radical empiricists reject this conclusion and so are obliged to offer some alternative account of our reasons for thinking that such propositions are true, one that makes them dependent on experience after all, or else to simply deny that we have any such reasons. Neither of these alternatives seems initially very plausible.

One other point is worth adding. What is perhaps most misleading about the list of examples just given is that having been chosen for their obviousness, they are far from the most philosophically interesting cases of alleged a priori justification. Rationalists will argue that there are many more interesting, albeit somewhat less obvious, examples as well: propositions about the unlikelihood of complex coincidences of various kinds; certain moral propositions; metaphysical propositions about matters such as the structure of time and space; and many, many others.

Dialectical Arguments for the Existence of A Priori Justification

It is possible to reject such examples as genuine, no matter how intuitively unappealing this may at first seem. But there are also other arguments of a more dialectical character for the existence of a priori justification, arguments that make clear the high skeptical price of rejecting the existence of such justification. (As will be seen later, these arguments also make the moderate empiricist view of the nature of a priori justification more difficult to defend.)

The first such argument is concerned with the relation between experience and certain of the beliefs which it intuitively seems to justify. On any account of the justificatory force of experience, there will be some beliefs whose justification derives from a *direct* relation to experience and others whose relation to experience is less direct, requiring something like an inference from directly experiential premises to further conclusions. Where exactly the line between the beliefs that are directly justified by experience and those that are not actually falls is a difficult issue, which need not be resolved here. But on any view that has ever been seriously advocated, the class of beliefs that are broadly empirical but *not* justified by a direct relation to experience is extremely large, including at least: (i) beliefs about the unobserved past; (ii) beliefs about unobserved situations in the present; (iii) beliefs about the future; (iv) beliefs in laws of nature and similar sorts of generalizations; and (v) beliefs about unobservable entities and processes, such as those described by theoretical science. Taken together, beliefs of these various kinds are obviously fundamental to our picture of the world and our place in it.

But how can experience provide justification for beliefs of these kinds, if not directly? For an inference from directly experiential premises to these further conclusions to be justified seems to require a logically prior justification of some sort for conditional propositions having a conjunction of beliefs for which there are direct experiential reasons as antecedent, and the further belief we are focusing on as consequent—for only this can establish the needed connection between experience and something that it does not justify in the more direct way. Here it will make the issue clearer to suppose that the antecedent of such a conditional is, in fact, a conjunction of *all* the propositions for which there are direct experiential reasons, even though most of these will be irrelevant to any particular consequent.

What sort of reason could we have for thinking that a conditional proposition of the indicated sort is true? If *all* of the things for which there are direct experiential reasons are already contained in the antecedent and if the consequent genuinely goes beyond the content of the antecedent (as only some highly implausible reductionist view could deny for the sorts of propositions in question), then experience can offer no direct reason for thinking that such a conditional proposition is true—and no indirect reason without assuming some other conditional of the very same sort. It apparently follows that the justification for a conditional proposition of this sort, if there is any, can only be a priori in character. In this way, a blanket rejection of the very existence of a priori justification leads to a deep and pervasive version of skepticism, one in which we have no reason for thinking that any of the various seemingly empirical propositions that are not directly justified by experience are true. And this is a result that is difficult to accept.

A further dialectical argument is, in effect, a generalization of the first. It questions whether a view that denies the existence of a priori justification can satisfactorily account for *reasoning* itself. Any reasoned or argumentative transition from a proposition or group of propositions to some further conclusion seems also to rely on there being a good reason for thinking that a conditional proposition is true, in this case one having the conjunction of the premises as its antecedent and the conclusion in question as its consequent. That such a conditional is true (or probably true) is, in general, not the sort of thing that could be directly established by experience, while to say that it is itself arrived at via some further process of reasoning is only to raise the identical issue about that previous step. The suggestion is that if we *never* have a priori justification for thinking that if one proposition or set of propositions is true, some further proposition must be true as well, then there is simply nothing that genuinely cogent reasoning could consist in. In this way, the rejection of a priori justification seems tantamount to intellectual suicide.

Three Main Philosophical Views of A Priori Justification

Rationalism

The view most straightforwardly supported by these arguments is rationalism. According to the rationalist, human beings possess, in addition to the cognitive faculties involved in the various sorts of experience, a fundamental faculty of a priori insight (or a priori intuition) that yields direct and justified apprehensions of necessary truths. Such apprehensions or insights are not regarded by the rationalist as merely brute convictions of truth, on a par with the hunches and fears that might simply strike someone in a psychologically compelling way. On the contrary, these insights at least purport to reveal not just *that* the proposition in question must be true but also, at some level, *why* this is and, indeed, must be so. They are thus, the rationalist claims, putative insights into the essential nature of things or situations of the relevant kind, into the way that reality in the respect in question *must* be. According to rationalism, it is insights or intuitions of this sort that account for the justification of propositions like those enumerated earlier and that also account for justified inferences from directly experiential claims to further broadly empirical conclusions and for successful reasoning in general.

Historical proponents of rationalism have tended to claim that a priori insight is infallible, incapable of being mistaken, though this view is often more taken for granted than explicitly argued for. But, as already mentioned above, such a claim is inessential to the central idea of a priori justification. It is also clear from a wide variety of examples (propositions involved in logical paradoxes, mathematical errors, competing philosophical propositions, etc.), that it could be defended only by insisting that many apparent a priori insights are not genuine, thereby raising the problem of how to distinguish genuine a priori insights from merely apparent ones and thus undercutting the justificatory force of even what seem to be clear cases of such insight. Thus more recent rationalists have repudiated the claim of infallibility, arguing that such a claim is not required for such insights to have substantial justificatory force (see BonJour 1998; and Bealer 1998).

The more moderate sort of rationalist who rejects infallibility can also concede that specific a priori insights can be undermined or even refuted by experience, while insisting at the same time that the connection between experience and any plausible a priori proposition is almost never direct. It follows that the refutation of one a priori proposition by experience will still rely on other a priori insights in the way discussed above—thus providing no real basis for denying that a priori insight is a genuine source of justification.

The rationalist appeal to direct a priori insight as a source of justification has often been alleged to be objectionably "mysterious" or "obscure" (see, for example, Devitt 2005a, 2005b). The idea here seems to be that there is something objectionable, fundamentally irrational or at least a-rational, about a non-experiential source of justification that relies on direct insight and cannot be articulated further by appeal to steps or background principles of some sort. Rationalists will respond that apart from the limited class of propositions that are directly justified by experience, there is in the end simply no other form that a reason for thinking that something is true could possibly take. To be sure, a priori insights can be combined in complicated ways to yield more elaborate arguments, but in the end the various steps in such arguments, together with any premises or principles that they invoke, can only be justified by appeal to the very same sort of a priori insight—if, that is, they are to be justified at all. A rationalist can grant that it would be nice to have a fuller, richer account of a priori insight and how it works. But given both intuitively compelling examples, and an argument showing such insight to be essential to any but the most minimal cognitive functioning, he will argue that the absence of such an account does not yield a serious reason for denying its existence.

One other point about the nature of a priori insights should also be briefly mentioned, though this is one that has been less widely recognized. For a variety of reasons, but most fundamentally because of the role that such insights are supposed to play in deductive inference, it is often, and quite possibly always, a mistake to construe them as *propositional* in form. The problem here is essentially the one pointed out long ago by Lewis Carroll: at least in the most fundamental sorts of cases (think here of *modus ponens*), the application of a propositional insight concerning the cogency of such an inference would require either a further inference of the very sort in question or one equally fundamental, thereby leading to a vicious regress. Instead, it seems, the relevant logical insight must be construed as non-propositional in character, as a direct grasping of the way in which the conclusion is related to the premises and validly flows from them. And once the need for this non-propositional conception of a priori insight is appreciated in the context of deductive inference, it seems plausible to extend it to many other cases as well; in particular, it seems plausible to regard the most fundamental insights pertaining to each of the examples listed in the following section as non-propositional in character. Thus in the red–blue example, the insight is most plausibly viewed as not merely the brute conviction that a certain proposition is true but rather as an insight into the nature and relations of the ingredients of that proposition, mainly the properties of redness and blueness and the relation of incompatibility between them (see further BonJour 2001 [a reply to Boghossian 2001]).

A Priori Justification Without A Priori Insight: Moderate Empiricism

If we set aside the relatively minor issues of infallibility and defeasibility by experience, virtually all serious epistemologists up to the time of Hume and Kant were rationalists in essentially the sense just explained. But since that time, skepticism about a priori justification in general, and rationalism in particular, has become increasingly pervasive. The most prominent position since that time and especially for much of the past century has been a relatively moderate version of empiricism, one that concedes the existence of a priori justification of a sort, but claims that when properly understood, such justification does not have the epistemological and metaphysical significance that is attributed to it by the rationalist. Instead, according to this *moderate empiricist* view, a priori justification, rather than reflecting genuine insights into reality, derives merely from definitions or from conceptual or linguistic conventions.

The basic idea of moderate empiricism is to explain a priori justification in a way that at the same time drastically undercuts its significance. For this purpose, the most standard versions of moderate empiricism appeal to the concept of *analyticity*, holding both (i) that all propositions for which there is genuine a priori justification are analytic, and (ii) that the a priori justification of an analytic proposition does not require the sort of insight into the character of reality advocated by the rationalist, but instead can be explained in a more modest way. It is important to see that each of these claims is equally essential to the view, and thus a successful version of moderate empiricism must advocate one univocal conception of analyticity in relation to which *both* of them can be plausibly defended. In fact, moderate empiricists have put forth not one, but many different and not obviously equivalent conceptions of analyticity, and have often tended to shift illegitimately among them depending on which of these two theses they are defending at any particular moment.

When the various conceptions of analyticity have been sorted out, they fall mostly into two main groups. Some conceptions are *reductive* conceptions: they explain some cases of a priori justification by appeal to other cases, while providing in principle no way to account for the latter cases. Here the most obvious example is the Fregean conception of an analytic proposition already mentioned above. To say that all propositions for which there is genuine a priori justification are, or are transformable into, truths of formal logic obviously does nothing at all to explain how these propositions of formal logic are themselves justified a priori (which they must be if a priori justification is to result from the overall account). And something similar is true of the familiar Kantian conception of an analytic proposition as one whose predicate is included in its subject: this amounts to reducing a priori justified propositions to propositions of approximately the form "all FGH are F," but again without accounting for the a priori justification of those propositions. In addition, there are many propositions that appear to be justified a priori, but which do not seem to fit these reductive accounts—including, in fact, all of the examples cited earlier except (3), which is one of the logical claims whose justification remains unexplained.

Most at least of the moderate empiricist views that are not in this way reductive seem to lose sight of the main epistemological issue altogether by simply equating analyticity with one of the features that a proposition for which there is an immediate a priori justification undeniably has (or at least seems to have) on the rationalist account, not realizing that this fails to yield an independent account of a priori justification itself. The plainest example of this mistake is the view that identifies an analytic proposition with one that is "true by virtue of meaning" or "true by definition" (where these formulations are not further explained in some reductive way). This apparently amounts to nothing more than the view that one who understands such a proposition can see directly or intuitively that it is true—and this is really just a misleading restatement of the rationalist view, not an alternative to it. Obviously a rationalist does not think that one can have rational insight into the truth of a proposition without understanding its meaning; the question is whether such an insight can be entirely reduced to, or accounted for by reference to, that meaning, something that this version of analyticity does nothing to establish. Other would-be versions of moderate empiricism equate analyticity with necessity, again failing to realize that this metaphysical feature fails to account for a priori justification unless supplemented by just the sort of a priori insight into necessity that the rationalist advocates (e.g., Lewis 1946: 57 and Salmon 1967: 30; both seem guilty of this mistake).

Is there any version of moderate empiricism that avoids both of the pitfalls just described? One possibility is a view that holds that a priori justification results from *linguistic convention*. Another, closely related view holds that sentences that express a priori justified propositions (or more plausibly some subset of such sentences) should be viewed as *implicit definitions* of the pivotal terms that they contain, with the suggestion that it is this status as implicitly definitional that accounts for the a priori justification of the propositions in question (see, for example, Boghossian 1996). Unfortunately, however, it is far from clear what these views amount to or how they are supposed to work, and a full consideration of them is impossible here. Both views seem, however, to rely essentially on the idea that a priori justification somehow derives from facts about *language*, and the central problem for such views is that this last claim is very dubious. To say that the justification (or perhaps even the truth) of a priori justified propositions depends on facts about language would apparently mean that alterations in language could make these propositions no longer justified (or perhaps even no longer true)—as opposed to merely changing how they can properly be expressed. In relation to examples of apparent a priori justification like those offered above, such a claim seems fairly obviously mistaken.

One other point worth noticing is that no version of moderate empiricism seems at all likely to be able to account for all of the instances of a priori justification needed to satisfy the dialectical arguments discussed above. In particular, it seems clear that the inferences from directly experiential premises to conclusions that go beyond direct experience cannot plausibly be regarded as merely matters of definition (implicit or otherwise) or linguistic convention or as justified on purely logical or conceptual grounds—at least not if reductive views such as phenomenalism and the even more implausible analogs of phenomenalism that would apply to historical propositions or propositions about seemingly unobservable entities are rejected.

The Rejection of A Priori Justification: Radical Empiricism

A more extreme alternative is to reject the very existence of any sort of a priori justification, a view that has been most prominently advocated by W. V. O. Quine (see Quine 1961). There are two main questions that need to be asked about this more radical version of empiricism. The more obvious one is what the arguments for it, and against the existence of a priori justification, are supposed to be. A second, less obvious question is whether, especially in light of the dialectical reasons in favor of a priori justification discussed above, it is possible for this radical version of empiricism to yield a non-skeptical epistemology.

Quine himself tends to assume that anyone who defends the idea of a priori justification must be a moderate empiricist, and some of his arguments (in particular the famous "circle of terms" argument in Quine 1961) really apply only to that view and are thus ineffective against rationalism. (This argument also makes the mistake, already discussed, of conflating the three main distinctions in the area.)

When these ineffective arguments are set aside, the only very clear Quinean argument that remains is one that appeals to the Duhemian thesis that claims about the world cannot be experimentally tested in isolation from each other but only in larger groups (see Quine 1961). Quine's extreme version of this thesis is the holistic claim that nothing less than "the whole of science" can be meaningfully confronted with experience. From this he infers that any belief in the total "web of belief," including those for which there is allegedly a priori justification, might be "given up" in order to accommodate "recalcitrant experience," and so, apparently, that such a priori justification does not exist after all. But this conclusion does not follow in any clear way, even if the extreme holistic view is accepted. Quine is, in effect, assuming that the *only* reasons relevant to retaining or giving up a belief in the "web of belief" have to do with accommodating experience, but this is just to beg the question against the existence of independent, a priori justification for or against such beliefs by assuming that all justification is empirical. And if this assumption is not made, then a proponent of a priori justification can freely admit that holistic empirical reasons of this sort might count against a proposition for which there is a priori justification, while insisting that the reverse is true as well. Thus the ultimate outcome would depend on the relative weight of these two sorts of reasons in a particular case, with there being no reason to think that a priori justification will always or even very often be overridden—or, still less, that it does not exist at all. And a proponent of a priori justification will also insist (see below) that the very connections among beliefs that result in the holistic web can, in the end, only be understood as a priori in character. (Followers of Quine also sometimes appeal to the alleged "mysteriousness" or "obscurity" of the idea of a priori justification, already discussed above.)

The other main issue concerning radical empiricism is whether it can offer a genuinely non-skeptical epistemology. While the details of Quine's view are themselves quite obscure, it is clear that a belief is supposed to be justified in virtue of being an element of a holistic system of beliefs, some of whose members are appropriately related to experience and which, as a whole, satisfies certain further criteria, such as simplicity, scope, explanatory adequacy, fecundity, and conservatism. Presumably he would say this about beliefs whose content is the apparently a priori justified propositions listed above, and others like them.

While such a claim is very implausible in these cases and many others, the deepest objection to it is more dialectical in character and is, in fact, an application of one of the arguments discussed above. Consider then the conditional proposition (call this Q) that if a proposition is included in a system that satisfies all of the Quinean conditions, whatever exactly they amount to, then it is likely to be true, and ask what reason there is for thinking that this conditional proposition is itself true. Clearly Q cannot be directly justified by experience, and to appeal to *its* inclusion in a holistic system of beliefs satisfying these very conditions seems plainly circular. Thus either there is an a priori reason (whether immediate or resulting from a more extended a priori argument of some sort) for thinking that Q is true, or there is apparently no reason at all. If the latter is the case, then Quine's view fails to yield genuine justification, while if the former is the case, then his rejection of a priori justification must be mistaken. In addition to reiterating the point that a priori justification is indispensable for any justification beyond that yielded by direct experience, this argument also seems to show that a priori justification is at least as well understood as the idea of holistic empirical justification, which turns out, in fact, to depend upon it. Moreover, similar points could be made about the more specific claims that Quine's various criteria are themselves satisfied by a particular holistic system, since none of these can be plausibly construed as being directly justified by experience.

Is there any response to this objection that is available within a broadly Quinean, radical empiricist position? One recent proponent of such a view, Michael Devitt, attempts to argue that circularity apparently involved in justifying Q by appeal to its inclusion in a system satisfying the Quinean conditions is not, in fact, viciously circular (Devitt 2005a, 2005b). Devitt follows R. B. Braithwaite (1953) in distinguishing "premise-circularity" from "rule-circularity," with the suggestion being that while premise-circularity is plainly objectionable, this is not so clearly true of rule-circularity. Thus if we think of Q as a Quinean epistemic rule, the idea is that Q could after all be justified by being included in a system satisfying the Quinean conditions and thus by appeal to Q itself. But this suggestion seems extremely dubious. If the issue is whether accepting beliefs or claims in accordance with Q (in the way that Quine's "holistic empirical" approach sanctions) gives us any reason to think that our results are true and so any justification for the propositions thus accepted, it is obviously no help at all to be told that the claim that those results are likely to be true (or that Q is a good rule) can be arrived at by employing Q itself—the very rule whose truth-conduciveness is in doubt. Such an argument might not beg the question in quite the sense that a premise-circular one does, but it is just as unsatisfactory in relation to the question at issue. Thus the basic objection to a Quinean view still stands: such a view can give no satisfactory account of how the fact that a belief satisfies its requirements constitutes a reason to think that it is true—or indeed of how we can have reason to think that its requirements are indeed satisfied. In this way, radical empiricism, with its rejection of a priori justification, apparently leads only to a deep and pervasive skepticism.

A Summary of Some Main Outstanding Issues

It will be useful to conclude by summarizing the main issues that are reflected in the previous discussion, issues that are still under active debate, adding also some that have not so far been explicitly mentioned.

First, is the rationalist idea of a priori intuition or insight too obscure to be philosophically acceptable or otherwise objectionable on broadly scientific grounds? One issue here, as we have seen, is whether the standard of unacceptable obscurity or the alleged requirement for scientific explanation can themselves be established without an a priori appeal.

Second, a further, related issue is whether the sort of understanding of the content of a claim that the rationalist view seems to require as a basis for a priori intuition or insight or self-evidence can be explained in an acceptable way. Being able to see or grasp in a direct, intuitive way that a claim like "nothing can be red and green all over at the same time" must be true seems to require mental access to the content of this claim, and in particular to the properties of redness and greenness themselves. But many recent accounts of mental content (externalist accounts and those that appeal to a language of thought) have no real room for this sort of direct awareness of content. Is this an objection to the idea of a priori intuition or insight, and so to rationalism (and perhaps also to moderate empiricism), or does it merely show that these accounts of mental content are inadequate (since such a grasp of content is a familiar and undeniable feature of experience)?

Third, is there a viable account of how the non-observational claims that seem from a common-sense standpoint to be justified can be accounted for on a purely empirical basis with no a priori appeal? Does the limitation to empirical sources of justification leave everything that goes beyond direct observation unjustified and arbitrary, as the rationalist argument claims, or is there some way in which a purely empirical epistemology can avoid this result?

Fourth, is there an account of analyticity that can genuinely account for all of the plausible cases of a priori justification? Such an account must avoid presupposing some cases of a priori justification and also must not merely amount to a restatement of the rationalist view in other terms. (See Boghossian 1996 for one effort in this direction.)

Fifth, what is the bearing on this issue of the recently popular idea of *naturalism*? While the idea of naturalism has been elaborated in many different ways, proponents of naturalized epistemology have almost always been hostile to the idea of a priori justification, and some have, in effect, made the rejection of the a priori the defining thesis of naturalized epistemology. But some recent philosophers (see Rey 1998 and Goldman 1999) have argued that when each is properly understood, naturalism and a priori justification can be reconciled.

Sixth, are there viable further alternatives to the three main views discussed above, perhaps alternatives involving a weaker conception of what a priori justification amounts to, but one that still has epistemological value? A number of recent discussions of the a priori (see Boghossian and Peacocke 2000) can be understood as attempts in this direction.

References

Ayer, A. J. (1946) *Language, Truth and Logic*, 2nd ed., London: Gollancz.
Bealer, G. (1998) "Intuition and the Autonomy of Philosophy," in M. DePaul and W. Ramsey (eds.), *Rethinking Intuition: The Psychology of Intuition and Its Role in Philosophical Inquiry*, Lanham, MD: Rowman and Littlefield.
Boghossian, P. (1996) "Analyticity Reconsidered," *Noûs* 30, 360–91.
—— (2001) "Inference and Insight," *Philosophy and Phenomenological Research* 63, 633–40.
—— and Peacocke, Christopher (2000) *New Essays on the A Priori*, Oxford: Oxford University Press.
BonJour, L. (1998) *In Defense of Pure Reason*, Cambridge: Cambridge University Press.
—— (2001) "Replies," *Philosophy and Phenomenological Research* 63, 673–98.
Braithwaite, R. B. (1953) *Scientific Explanation*, Cambridge: Cambridge University Press.
Devitt, M. (2005a) "There is No A Priori," in M. Steup and E. Sosa (eds.), *Contemporary Debates in Epistemology*, Oxford: Blackwell.
—— (2005b) "Reply to BonJour," in M. Steup and E. Sosa (eds.), *Contemporary Debates in Epistemology*, Oxford: Blackwell.
Goldman, Alvin (1999) "A Priori Warrant and Naturalistic Epistemology," in James Tomberlin (ed.), *Philosophical Perspectives*, vol. 13, pp. 1–28.
Lewis, C. I. (1946) *An Analysis of Knowledge and Valuation*, La Salle, IL: Open Court.
Quine, W. V. (1961) "Two Dogmas of Empiricism," in *From a Logical Point of View*, 2nd ed., Cambridge, MA: Harvard University Press.
Rey, Georges (1998) "A Naturalistic A Priori," *Philosophical Studies* 92: 25–43.
Salmon, Wesley (1967) *The Foundations of Scientific Inference*, Pittsburgh: University of Pittsburgh Press.

27
PERCEPTUAL KNOWLEDGE
David Sosa

Introduction

We acquire knowledge through perception. But how? What role does perception play in our knowing things? And what must it be like in order to play that role? These are philosophical issues about perceptual knowledge.

Perceptual experience is a dominant characteristic of consciousness. And it is hard not to feel that experience immediately reveals to us an external reality. That same thought, that experience reveals an external world—a world "beyond" the experience, with its own character—creates a problem, because it opens up the possibility that the world experienced is different from what it appears to be, a possibility that should be closed off, it would seem, if the *revelatory* quality of experience is to be secured.

Securing that quality is not merely a matter of satisfactory self-understanding, not merely a matter of making good philosophically on what our experience appears to us to be (i.e., immediately revelatory): it is in virtue of that revelatory quality that we take ourselves to acquire *knowledge* from perception of the world beyond ourselves. An epistemological issue hangs in the balance. And satisfactory understanding of this way of *connecting* with the world around—by *knowing* it—is pressing for practical reasons too: skepticism is alienating and depressing as much as it is intellectually implausible.

How shall we understand the relationship between perceptual experience and the reality it purports to represent? One way to characterize a deep philosophical tension here is as between (i) the apparent *directness* of perceptual experience—when we see an apple, there doesn't seem to be anything other than (a part of) the apple itself in virtue of seeing which we're seeing the apple—and (ii) an *indirectness* to which we appear to be committed by the intrinsic similarity between veridical experiences on the one hand and illusory and hallucinatory experiences on the other: if an experience can *mis*represent, then how can it be in its nature to represent *directly*? It is this apparent intrinsic indiscriminability between epistemically sound experience and misleading experience, together with the apparent directness of our perceptual contact with external reality, that constitutes the deepest philosophical problem about perceptual knowledge.

Because the issue is complex, touching on questions beyond epistemology in metaphysics and philosophy of mind, there isn't room for a comprehensive survey of all the most important contributions to all the relevant issues. This will be instead a selective, partial, and opinionated review of a small number of the topics and texts that seem especially useful in connection with this deep philosophical issue about the role of perception in knowledge.

Traditionally there are broadly two realist responses to the tension noted above: oppose (i)—deny that perceptual experience is direct in the relevant sense—and thereby embrace "indirect realism," or oppose (ii)—deny that veridical experiences are relevantly similar to illusory or hallucinatory experiences—and thereby embrace "direct realism."

We will look at a representative version of each of direct and indirect realism, considering compelling ways of developing them, in turn. "Sense-datum theory" is an indirect realism whose unpopularity today is perhaps exceeded only by its longevity and tenacity. "Disjunctivism" is a direct realism and of more recent vintage.

For completeness, note that anti-realist positions are also possible, according to which, to take Berkeley's idealism as one example, the world revealed by experience is not, in the relevant sense, "beyond" experience—the character of any world we might engage perceptually is not independent of the character of perceptual experience itself. Although the specifically epistemic motivations for idealism are often insufficiently appreciated, we will simply presuppose realism in our discussion below: idealism and other anti-realisms raise additional, independent metaphysical issues.

Direct Realism: Sense-Datum Theory

In his useful book on our topic, *The Problem of Perception*, A.D. Smith (2002) presents a traditional "Argument from Illusion" in careful detail and a sympathetic light. The argument consists of four steps:

1. Sense experience is subject to illusion: some ordinary objects do not have features they perceptually appear to have.
2. [The "Phenomenal Principle"]: Whenever something perceptually *appears to* have a feature when it *in fact* does not, we are directly aware of something that does actually have that feature.
3. If what we are immediately aware of has a feature the ordinary object does not, we are not in such cases immediately aware of the ordinary object.
4. Even in veridical situations, we are immediately aware of "sense-data," and at best only indirectly aware of normal physical objects.

This argument, in one form or another, has long been a part of the philosophical tradition. In effect, it argues for the existence of a perceptual *intermediary*—a "veil"—between subjects like us and the physical world that we perceive. One version of this view is "sense-datum theory," It's a variety of indirect realism associated with Bertrand Russell among many others.

Characteristic of opposing positions, what we will call "direct realism," is that what gives sensory character to perceptual consciousness is a public quality of some physical object. As we've seen, and as Smith notes, the problem with any such position is that it appears to hold at best only for veridical perceptions.

Smith urges that:

> What the Argument from Illusion attempts primarily to achieve is the recognition that . . . *qualities can be present to consciousness in perception despite the fact*

that they do not characterize the normal physical objects we are said to be perceiving. It then challenges us to make sense of this fact.

(Smith 2002: 36–7)

Objects can appear to us in inaccurate form. The "Phenomenal Principle," expressed in thesis (2) above, embodies one way of making sense of this: the quality is present to consciousness because it is *instantiated* rather by something *else*—a mental particular.

Later, Smith claims that what is essential to direct realism is that "*that which gives sensory character to perceptual consciousness is a public quality of some physical object*" (Smith 2002: 43–4). But how could the public quality of a physical object be what is giving character to experience in cases of illusion or hallucination?

To foreshadow: this question can be given a rather more satisfactory answer than might at first appear. That answer will be, eventually, the key element in opening up new space for the position between direct and indirect realism toward which we will finally move. At this stage, what's important is to appreciate the prima facie difficulty: how can the character of perceptual experience be given by public qualities of ordinary physical objects (as seems to be the case), when experience can have the same character even in cases of illusion, when candidate ordinary physical objects do not have the quality in question, and, in cases of hallucination, when there are no candidate ordinary physical objects?

Before Smith, John Foster had usefully offered a refinement of claims about the directness of perception by distinguishing two sorts of issue about "direct realism" (Foster 2000). One issue concerns specifically *perceptual* mediation in experience. According to direct realism about this issue, once we reach the "origin" of the *in virtue of perceiving* relation as it applies to physical objects (perhaps as a limit), we've reached the origin of the *in virtue of perceiving* relation. Another sort of direct realism insists, rather, that there is no psychological mediation, at all, beyond perceptual relations to physical objects. Once we've reached the origin of the *in virtue of perceiving* relation as it applies to physical objects (perhaps as a limit), we've reached the origin not only of the *in virtue of perceiving* relation but, indeed, of any psychological *in virtue of* relation at all. This stronger direct realism is not supported by the mundane phenomenological evidence mentioned earlier—that the external world appears to be revealed to us in experience and that the constituents of experience seem to be the very physical objects represented, with no other *perception of a physical object* intervening.

Another philosopher, Howard Robinson, was—before Foster—concerned with what he defines as the "intentionality" of perceptual experience, its putting us *in touch* with particular objects in the physical world. Robinson's characterization of Aristotle's views is remarkable in this connection: in sensory experience we are in receipt of *phantasms*, which amounts to our being in receipt of the *form* of the external objects we perceive (Robinson 1994: 4–11). Robinson is doubtful that Aristotle provides any relief for the problems urged for "representationalism" and other conceptions of intentionality that are less restrictive than his: if what constitutes our experience is the form of the object perceived, on a particular conception of *form*, then, according to Robinson, "It is difficult to see how [on Aristotle's view, perception] can constitute an especially good way of being in touch with *that very object*" (Robinson 1994: 9).

But although on the Aristotelian view under consideration, the intentionality of *phantasms* would require the cooperation of *causation*—it would be because *that* phantasm was produced by *that very object* that the phantasm puts you in touch with *it*, this need not rule out the resulting intentionality as the genuine article. Something can possess intrinsic intentionality even if its putting you in touch with particular physical objects requires the satisfaction of conditions external to it.

Qualities of Experience, and the Speckled Hen

Return now to the "Phenomenal Principle," the important premise in the Argument from Illusion above. Gilbert Harman, in his influential paper, "The Intrinsic Quality of Experience," sees the principle as urging that because we can be subject to illusion and hallucination, we must, in experience, actually be *seeing* something internal or mental. According to Harman (1990: 35), this fallacious inference on the part of the "notorious" sense-datum theory of perception arises through failure to keep elementary points straight.

In fact, together with other critics, Harman himself might have done more to maintain important distinctions here, including the one observed earlier between two sorts of direct/indirect realism issue: the sense-datum theorist need not claim that the nature of the awareness we have of the internal items is the same—is, for example, *perceptual*—as the awareness we have of external objects when we see them. Harman seems to be committed to the idea that in hallucination there are some things that we literally *see*: "what Eloise sees before her is a tree, whether or not it is a hallucination" (Harman 1990: 36). And, indeed, with that commitment in place, it might become harder to target the best version of the sort of view Harman seems to want to oppose. The best version of indirect realism does not characterize a subject's relation to sense-data as itself *visual*.

To his credit, Harman does, in effect, take up this issue. He notes that there can seem to be an ambiguity, of the relevant sort, in perceptual verbs. But he thinks it "does not affect the point [he] is trying to make" (Harman 1990: 36). Whether Harman's right about that or not, sense-datum theory faces other difficulties.

The "Speckled Hen" is a compelling example used to create a philosophical problem for a sort of position in epistemology that goes naturally with the acceptance of sense-datum theory (Chisholm 1942). So-called "foundationalist internalism" analyzes the justification of perceptual belief as grounded in a specific relation to perceptual experience. In one version of the position, if one's experience has a certain character, and one, on that basis, forms a belief "to that effect," then that belief is foundationally justified (and further beliefs formed inferentially on the basis of that foundation can be justified in turn).

The problem is that this analysis appears to be insufficient: your experience might be as of a hen with, say, 48 speckles and yet if you were, on that basis, to form a belief that you were having an experience as of a hen before you with 48 speckles, or a belief that there was in fact a hen before you with 48 speckles, such a belief would *not* be adequately justified (no more justified, for example, than the belief that the hen had 47, or 49, speckles—only *withholding* belief seems appropriate). The problem for the postulation of sense-data is that they are of no help, here, in a case like those for which they were designed.

But one might be skeptical, to begin with, about some of the presuppositions involved: it is far from obvious that one's experience could, as in the case described, have a sufficiently determinate character in representing the hen's speckles. Perhaps in the sort of case that would be troubling, what's normally the most plausible description is that the experience is *indeterminate* in various ways.

In order for the counterexample to work, it would have to be that although it would not be justified to form the belief that you're having an experience as of a hen before you with 48 speckles, nevertheless the content of your experience *is* as of a hen with exactly that many speckles—not 47, not 49. The example needs to motivate the thought that the experience is determinate in ways that go beyond your ability to be aware of. But it's not clear this should be maintained.

Two lines of support *would* tend to sustain it: first, we can imagine holding your experience fixed in mind while you, in some sense (and indeed some sense can be given to this, since it is plausible that something like this can be done), take the time to *count* the number of speckles on "the-hen-in-your-experience." If nothing about your experience changes while you perform this count, and if the answer you come up with at the end is 48, then it is plausible that the content of your experience was always as of a hen with that many speckles—was *not* indeterminate in that way. (We can even make sense of your having counted *erroneously*, having *missed* a few of the speckles—again, suggesting that there are a certain number of speckles in some sense there to be counted prior to your noticing them.)

Second, there is a cost to denying that your experience is determinate in the relevant way. For you might it seems be conscious of the hen's having *some* determinate number of speckles (you just don't know how many). So then we appear to be forced to say that although it is determinate that there is some number of speckles the hen has, there is no number of speckles such that it is determinate that the hen has that number of speckles. Or, worse, we might be forced to say that there exists some number of speckles such that it is how many the hen-in-your-experience has and yet it is not the case that the hen has just one, or two, or three . . . for every number.

But there are considerations that go against each of these lines of support. First, while it is more or less plausible that we can hold an experience fixed in mind in such a way that if there were to be an *alteration*, we would notice it, it is less clear that we should notice "changes" in your experience that involve only consistent *specifications* or *determinations*. Indeed, does the defender of the speckled hen objection deny that *any* feature of your experience is indeterminate as envisaged? Suppose not; suppose, for example, that experience simply left open the particular shade of the grass on which the hen was running around. Now you hold the experience fixed and focus on the grass and it resolves into a particular shade of forest green. This resolution process does not present itself as an alteration. But I think it's not implausible to say that although, ultimately, after and because of the process, the grass as experienced is forest green, this was not determinately true of the experience previously.

With respect to the second point, I'm not sure how costly we should find the highlighted consequence: indeed, experiences appear to have precisely the peculiarity to which the critic adverts. They can be such that they're determinately (F or G) and not determinately F and not determinately G. It can be determinate that there exists an n such that $P(n)$ and yet not determinate that $p1$, not determinate that $p2$ . . . and so on without end. It's as if one were to write a (very short!) story that went like this: there was a hen, it had some (number of) speckles, then it passed away. Now, is it determinately true of the hen in the story that it had some number of spots? Apparently so. Is it determinately true that it had one? Two? And so on.

In any case, we can take a different approach again. Grant, for the sake of argument, the speckled hen objection. It relies on a certain distinctive experiential phenomenon; the number of speckles is not *available* in experience in the same way that, say, the number of legs is. This availability might be a matter of degree. But the examples work precisely by focusing on aspects of the experience that are not available in the right way to ground a corresponding belief. Though we would be justified on the basis of our experience in forming a belief that there is a hen there with two legs, we would not be justified in forming a belief that there's a hen there with 48 speckles.

The approach now being considered defines, even if stipulatively, a new sort of psychological category, the "foundational experience," that's just like perceptual experience except that the "unavailable" aspects are left out—it is, by definition, a state all of whose aspects are like the experience of the legs, not of the speckles. And now the justificatory status of perceptual beliefs is determined by their relation to foundational experiences. The resulting position is less substantial than traditional foundationalism. But no speckled hen problems can now arise.

Indirect Realism: Disjunctivism

Whether or not sense-datum theory is viable in the end, a more direct realism might by now have become very tempting, in any case. Is there any way, consistent with the phenomenon of illusion, to avoid the postulation of a perceptual intermediary between the subject and the reality perceived? In his seminal "Criteria, Defeasibility, and Knowledge," John McDowell gives early expression (but see also Hinton 1973 and Snowdon 1981) to a kind of view (that reappears elsewhere in his own work and that has influenced many others), according to which we have "ways of telling how things are" which can subserve our knowledgeable judgments without being "something on which we have a firmer cognitive purchase than we do on the judgment itself" (McDowell 1982: 385).

In an earlier essay McDowell urges us not to interpret away the commonsense thought that one can sometimes literally perceive in another person's facial expression *that he is in pain*. And though he recognizes some difficulties, he thinks ultimately that the opposing view relies on what he calls the "highest common factor" conception of experience and is the product of a problematic "objectifying" tendency in our understanding of human action. In this mode, we do not see human behavior in the right way as *expressive* of our human character; if it is seen as expressive at all, it is as merely the outward manifestation of fundamentally mental goings-on. Objectifying human behavior in this way, according to McDowell, "leads inexorably to the traditional problem of other minds" (McDowell 1982: 393).

Notice how McDowell's dialectic here recapitulates a familiar variety of reaction to the threat of skepticism. McDowell thinks generally that so long as facts themselves are conceived as outside the reach of experience, then skepticism is inevitable. His basic point is that a conception of knowledge in which it can be grounded on what, for all one knows, is consistent with the falsity of what one might know, is inadequate or incoherent (cf. Descartes, and then, much later, Lewis 1996).

McDowell's view is then a species of perceptual "disjunctivism" according to which although veridical experience might be indistinguishable "from the inside" from illusory or hallucinatory experience, that should not lead us to a conception of those experiences on which they are, in relevant respects, *the same*. And disjunctivism is a *direct* realism, in contrast to the *indirect* realism of which sense-datum theory is the most outstanding example. Like sense-datum theory, disjunctivism effectively takes sides on the tension that set the general framework for this discussion, the tension between (i) the apparent *directness* of perceptual experience—when we see an apple, there doesn't seem to be anything other than (a part of) the apple itself in virtue of seeing which we're seeing the apple—and (ii) an *indirectness* to which we appear to be committed by the intrinsic similarity between veridical experiences on the one hand and illusory and hallucinatory experiences on the other. While sense-datum theory takes (ii) to be primary and gives up on the directness of our relation to external reality—it's sense-data that we, primarily, see—disjunctivism takes (i) to be fundamental and gives up on (ii)—the *apparent* similarity between veridical experiences on the one hand and illusory and hallucinatory experiences on the other is merely apparent; it does not reveal any philosophically significant similarity in the nature of those experiences.

Ironically, McDowell, in effect, resists a kind of *epistemological* (rather than perceptual) "disjunctivism." On this analog of the position about perceptual knowledge, there's a deep, in a way *brute*, normative difference between a pair of possible subjects who possess the same *criterion* for belief but only one of whom, because of a mere difference in truth value, *knows*. I think that idea is remarkable because of how it engages McDowell's own defense of a view according to which there's a deep, in a way *brute*, normative difference between those in "phenomenally" indistinguishable states only one of whom, because of nothing more than a causal difference (with, itself, no discernible differential cognitive effect), *perceives*.

McDowell is sensitive to this structural similarity (McDowell 1982: 388–9, and 390) but thinks it is arguable that there are important disanalogies. But consider a pair of cases in both of which someone has experiences of exactly the same "phenomenal type" (experiences they cannot distinguish "from the inside"), but in only one of which the experience is caused in the familiar, normal way. According to McDowell's suggestion, the subject in the latter case can, on the basis of his experience, come by *knowledge*, the subject in the former case cannot. But, we can press, echoing McDowell, the scope of the phenomenal is the same in each case; the fact is outside the reach of the phenomenal, so why should we not conclude that the achievements of the two subjects match? How can a difference in something phenomenally inaccessible to both subjects make it the case that one of them knows while the other does not?

I don't offer this parody in order to defend it. I mean it only to bring out that McDowell's argumentative scheme *could* be applied more broadly. Of course, McDowell has no sympathy for the idea that the *phenomenal* is the limit of the cognitively normative. So the last, rhetorical, question in the preceding paragraph will strike him as badly misguided: "Why shouldn't it?" would likely be his answer. That is, on the other hand, *not* what he would say to the analogous question he himself asks here, "[h]ow can a difference in respect of something conceived as cognitively inaccessible to [two] subjects . . . make it the case that one of them knows . . . while the other does not—rather than leaving them both, strictly speaking, ignorant on the matter?" (McDowell 1982: 373–4). But why not, once one accepts the attractive McDowellian thought about the phenomenal, continue in the same way and find it unproblematic that a difference in respect of something conceived as *cognitively* inaccessible to two subjects might make it the case that one of them knows while the other does not?

Michael Tye nicely lays out a line of thought leading to what he calls "the disjunctivist's insight": that no veridical and hallucinatory experiences share the same representational content. The key element in that insight is that the content of veridical visual experience is *singular*: the objects we perceive are *components* of the contents of our veridical visual experiences. The crucial step in the line of thought is nicely summarized in the following (rhetorical) question: "[H]ow can the object be experienced as being some way unless the object itself figures in the content of the experience?" (Tye 2009: 77).

The thought implicit in that question has a great deal of traction on the contemporary philosophical scene. But from another perspective it can seem bizarre. Why should one think that unless the content of experience is *singular* in the relevant sense, unless the object of an experience partly constitutes its content, then we cannot make sense of the experience's being one in which a particular object is experienced as being some way? A traditional view (whatever its other issues) seems to do perfectly well on this score: so long as an object in the relevant way *causes* an experience with a given content (though it should be no component of the content of the experience it causes), the experience can plausibly be said to be one in which that object is experienced in some way. The object produces (an experience with) a content that is *of* it, precisely because of that causal relation, and *not* because of its figuring in the content: another object could produce an experience with *that same* content.

Disjunctivism promises a direct realism that avoids the veil of perception erected by the sense-datum theory. It too takes sides on the original problem: veridical experiences on the one hand and illusory or hallucinatory experiences on the other are not fundamentally of the same kind. What's true is only that they can't be distinguished. But even aside from the cost of having to take sides on the original issue, disjunctivism is often motivated by a questionable conception of what it takes to have a "singular" thought—a thought that's about a particular object—and indeed by an optional aversion, ironically, to a more general epistemic disjunctivism according to which a mere difference in the truth value of what's believed can mark an important normative distinction between a pair of subjects (one of them *knows*), even when there is no relevant difference in their experiences or in how they're basing their beliefs on those experiences.

An Alternative

But if neither sense-datum theory nor disjunctivism is fully adequate, is there any alternative? I'll close this chapter with a sketch of an alternative view, a view that finds a middle path between direct and indirect realism, a view according to which although the intrinsic character of veridical experiences and their less accurate counterparts might be exactly the same, still, in veridical perceptual experience, the world comes to constitute your experience, so that an external reality is in that sense *revealed* to us (Sosa 2007). The problem of perception, in effect, urges that this combination is incoherent. But that's because one possibility has often been overlooked. (And that even though, in fact, the alternative has well-known historical antecedents: precursors may be found in Brentano and Husserl and even in medieval sources such as Aquinas and maybe Avicenna. For more recent views in the same family, see Bealer (1982), Johnston 2004—which contrasts with Johnston (1996), to which Sosa (1996) was a critique from the perspective developed here; and Forrest (2005).)

There's an important sense in which, whether an experience is illusory or veridical, we "see the same thing." But the problem of perception presses: if in the illusory case we're not seeing the external world, in the veridical case we're not either. Granted, in illusion our experience does not reveal the character of the external world. But we should separate the distal *object* of perception (the pear, or the apple, as the case may be)—what we see, in one sense—and the content of the perception (the shapes and colors, for example, that give character to the experience)—what we see, in another sense.

Already, it might seem, we have erected a veil of perception, a distinction between the immediate elements of experience and the external world. But, and this is our alternative's key distinction: the very same entities that give content to our experience can characterize the object of our experience. The very redness that gives our experience phenomenal character and content can also be exemplified by the apple. There's no additional *particular* object that would need to *be* red (to *instantiate* redness) and whose being red would have to be appreciated by us (and so on—there need be no *intermediary*). There's just the property itself, present—in different *modes*—in the mind of the subject (intentionally) and in the object (by instantiation).

Isn't it right to describe some of our experiences as containing, for example, a red and round apple? If there were a particular that had properties like redness and roundness and whose having those properties mediated our experience of the distal object, then we would have, in effect, sense-datum theory all over again. Preferable is a view on which properties can constitute an experience in a way that accurately represents the part of the world that caused the experience. That will be so, normally, because some object has some properties. So the experience in that way *represents* an object as having a property. That, I think, suffices for us to speak of the experience as containing, for example, an apple. But that is to speak ambiguously: the experience contains the red apple in the sense that the experience is veridical only if an apple is red. But the experience does not contain an apple in the way that it contains redness and the distinctive apple shape and so on. Those properties are essential to the experience and exhaustively characterize it intrinsically.

In both veridical and illusory (and hallucinatory) experiences, we are, in a loose sense, seeing the same "thing." But that sense resolves on analysis. Strictly speaking, in hallucination we are seeing nothing and in illusion we might be seeing something but not just what we are seeing in the veridical case. The sense that we are seeing the same thing in all three cases is given content, on this view, by the claim that all three experiences are constituted by the same properties. But only in the veridical case are all those properties instantiated by the object of the experience. In the hallucination, the limiting case, the experience has no object and in illusion the object lacks some of the properties instantiated.

Again, even if in an ordinary illusion the object does not have the property present in the experience, that need not push us into a view on which, in the veridical case, we do not have any direct engagement with the world around us. In the veridical case, our experience *is* revelatory: the redness we experience is that of the apple. There's no extra category, no new theoretical entity postulated to explain the illusory case (though, admittedly, we must recognize the distinctive intentional mode of presence of the property). Similarly in the illusory case, experience presents itself as revelatory of the world around us. But that is not the way things in fact are, in the sense that the causal circumstances of the relevant part of the physical world do not comport with the content of that experience. The directness of perceptual experience should not be confused with infallibility.

Note that on this alternative to sense-datum theory, some experiences are, after all, *intrinsically* as of a red round object. The link between red round objects and experience with the corresponding character is quite intimate: the very redness and roundness of the object is present, in a different mode, in the experience. We, in a quite literal sense, get *aspects* of the world in mind, even if, of course, physical objects are too bulky to fit.

The initial tension, between (i) perception "reveals" the external world—not some other, internal, thing instead and (ii) illusion and hallucination are just like veridical experience, was supposed to force us to sense-datum theory or disjunctivism (which are indeed partly defined in terms of the position they take on that very tension). But there is room for a middle way: perception reveals the external world directly, not some internal thing instead, because the very properties constituting the experience are instantiated in the external world. In that way the alternative is more like disjunctivism than like sense-datum theory. But on this view hallucination and illusion do have a "highest common factor" with veridical experience: and this "highest common factor" idea is what motivated the sense-datum theorists in the first place and is denied by disjunctivists. Here the alternative is on the side of sense-datum theory.

Importantly, we *can* on this line make robust sense of the appropriateness of forming the belief that there's a red round object before you in the face of that experience. There is now a possible internal relation between the experience and the belief. This relation is internal in two respects: it is typically available to the subject in a distinctive first-person way and it is a relation that is wholly determined by the character of the *relata*—no features of other things matter. The character of the experience determines a class of beliefs that is appropriately based on that experience.

And this takes us back naturally to the specific issues with which we began: how do we acquire knowledge through perception? There is available an attractive conception of the nature of perceptual experience, useful in connection with the problem of perception, that provides a good account of the felt appropriateness of believing a specific way in response to experiences of a given character.

On this view, the veridicality of an experience will be a function of the accuracy of its characterization of its object. What it is for a particular to be the object of an experience has to do with causation: the object of an experience will be, given certain additional conditions, a distinguished part of its external cause. Accordingly, on this view, if the experience is hallucinatory, if the distinctive relation that gives an experience an object simply does not obtain, then the experience literally has no object. We will still want a distinction between the experience's "would-be" object and other things. If Macbeth is not seeing a dagger, then, presumably, his experience is without object; nevertheless, his experience represents a dagger, and not, say, a witch's cauldron. This is familiar philosophical territory: was a fountain of youth the object of Ponce de León's search? "Object" here is a theoretical term. One attractive answer is that his search did not, in fact, have an object. But there are correct and incorrect answers to the question: "What did de León seek?" The distinction some want (and that the alternative here does not directly provide) between the object of (even) a hallucinatory perception and things that are not its object, can be made in another way simply by noting (for example) that Macbeth's experience represents a dagger and not a cauldron.

We began with a purpose: to understand how perception gives a distinctive epistemic status to ordinary empirical belief. In perception we are in receipt of something effectively *given* (contrast with *taken*—we exercise only receptivity, there is no spontaneity). This does not alienate us from our environment: what is given to us in experience is also, often enough, present in the world. In this sense the alternative sketched here is a direct realism. There is no veil of perception, even though there is content to perception in the form of properties that need not be instantiated. Although when a perception is veridical, the properties are instantiated as represented, it's possible that the properties fail to be so instantiated.

The flaw in sense-datum theories was to model our relation to the content of perceptual states on a relation to the external world that is rather *enabled by* our relation to that content. We do perceive the external world in the relevant sense directly, even though illusion is possible. We do so in virtue of having properties as constituents of our experience. When the appropriate cause of our experience instantiates the properties presented, the experience is veridical. Otherwise, it is not. But on this alternative, veridical perception and its less accurate counterparts are states of fundamentally the same kind. They both consist in a specific sort of relation to abstracta. So some of disjunctivism's less attractive features are avoided, too.

On the alternative sketched here, we better understand perception's epistemic role. Because it is in the nature of perception to reveal the world to us, and because the beliefs we form on the basis of perceptual states can bear intimate internal relations with the contents of those perceptions, then perceptual states can differentially justify some of our beliefs. And though the alternative conception of perception does not suffice, by itself, to refute skepticism about our knowledge of the external world, we can better understand how, when all goes well, perception can even yield knowledge.

References

Bealer, G. (1982) *Quality and Concept*, Oxford: Clarendon.
Chisholm, R. (1942) "The Problem of the Speckled Hen," *Mind* 51: 368–73.
Forrest, P. (2005) "Universals as Sense-Data," *Philosophy and Phenomenological Research* 71: 622–31.
Foster, J. (2000) *The Nature of Perception*, Oxford: Clarendon.
Harman, G. (1990) "The Intrinsic Quality of Experience," *Philosophical Perspectives* 4: 31–52.
Hinton, J.M. (1973) *Experiences: An Inquiry Into Some Ambiguities*, Oxford: Clarendon.
Johnston, M. (1996) "Is the External World Invisible?" *Philosophical Issues* 7: 185–98.
—— (2004) "The Obscure Object of Hallucination," *Philosophical Studies* 120: 113–83.
Lewis, D. (1996) "Elusive Knowledge," *Australasian Journal of Philosophy* 74: 549–67.
McDowell, J. (1982) "Criteria, Defeasibility, and Knowledge," in McDowell (1998) *Meaning, Knowledge and Reality*, Cambridge: Harvard University Press. Originally published in *Proceedings of the British Academy* 68: 455–79.
Robinson, H. (1994) *Perception*, London: Routledge.
Smith, A.D. (2002) *The Problem of Perception*, Cambridge: Harvard University Press.
Snowdon, P. (1981) "Perception, Vision and Causation," *Proceedings of the Aristotelian Society* 81: 175–92.
Sosa, D. (1996) "Getting Acquainted With Perception," *Philosophical Issues* 7: 209–14.
—— (2007) "Perceptual Friction," *Philosophical Issues* 17: 245–61.
Tye, M. (2009) *Consciousness Revisited*, Cambridge: MIT.

Further Reading

Anscombe, G.E.M. (1965) "The Intentionality of Sensation: a Grammatical Feature," in R.J. Butler (ed.) *Analytical Philosophy: First Series*, Oxford: Blackwell.
Austin, J.L. (1962) *Sense and Sensibilia*, Oxford: Oxford University Press.
Ayer, A.J. (1940) *The Foundations of Empirical Knowledge*, London: Macmillan.
—— (1967) "Has Austin Refuted the Sense-Datum Theory?" *Synthese* 17: 117–40.
Chisholm, R. (1957) *Perceiving: A Philosophical Study*, Ithaca: Cornell University Press.
Martin, M.G.F. (2002) "The Transparency of Experience," *Mind and Language* 17: 376–425.
Moore, G.E. (1905) "The Refutation of Idealism," in his *Philosophical Studies*, London: Routledge & Kegan Paul.
Price, H.H. (1932) *Perception*, London: Methuen.
Russell, B. (1912) *The Problems of Philosophy*, Oxford: Oxford University Press.
Swartz, R.J. (1965) *Perceiving, Sensing and Knowing*, Los Angeles and Berkeley: University of California Press.

28
SELF-KNOWLEDGE
Sanford Goldberg

Philosophical interest in self-knowledge is long-standing. Socrates cited with approval the Delphic oracle's injunction to "Know Thyself," and he took the fulfillment of this injunction to be a core part of the philosophical life. Descartes regarded a subject's knowledge of the contents of her own mind as providing the foundation for her knowledge of the world more generally. More recently, philosophers have addressed the scope, sources, and nature of one's self-knowledge.

The topic of self-knowledge is also of philosophical interest for the connections it bears to other core issues. In addition to being given center stage in a very traditional (Cartesian and foundational) theory of our knowledge of the world, the sort of self-knowledge that is of interest to philosophers has been alleged to be the distinctive mark of the mental; it has been taken to be intimately related to rational and practical agency, and to our view of ourselves as subjects of experience; it is held to be linked to the nature of the self, as well as to the use and meaning of the first-person pronoun 'I'; it has been connected to the paradoxicality of sentences like, 'It is raining but I don't believe it'; and it has been contrasted with the "problem of other minds."

In what follows we begin in section 1 by charactering the scope of the sort of self-knowledge that is of philosophical interest. In section 2 we examine attempts to provide an epistemological characterization of the judgments involved in this sort of self-knowledge. Our discussion here will raise questions about the sources and nature of self-knowledge; these we examine in section 3, where we will touch on some of the related issues in metaphysics and epistemology.

1. Scope

Is there a sort of knowledge you have of yourself which is different *in principle* from the knowledge another person could have of you? Let us designate the sort of self-knowledge in question as 'Self-Knowledge' (with capital letters). You know such things as your height, your birth name, or what you had for breakfast this morning. But this knowledge isn't distinctive, and so is not Self-Knowledge: in principle others could acquire the same knowledge, and acquire it in the same way, or much the same way, as you did.

When trying to find this special sort of knowledge that you have of yourself, it is tempting to suppose that it can be found in the knowledge you have of your "self," where this "self" is taken to be something to which only you yourself have access. David Hume cast a famous critical eye on this sort of proposal:

> For my part, when I enter most intimately into what I call *myself*, I always stumble on some particular perception or other, of heat or cold, light or shade, love or hatred, pain or pleasure. I never can catch myself at any time without a perception, and never can observe anything but the perception.
>
> (Hume 1888: 252; italics in original)

Hume's point is negative: we should not think of the "self" as a private sort of object to which one oneself, and only one oneself, might (inwardly) direct one's attention. Most contemporary philosophers have accepted this point (for a discussion see Shoemaker 1986).

Might you have a special knowledge of those features that constitute your character? It would seem not. Your character traits are manifested in how you behave under various conditions; those who observe this behavior will be in as good a position as you are to draw conclusions about your character. Indeed, there are even cases where another person—a parent or friend, a partner, a good therapist—knows your character better than you do yourself. To take an example, suppose that Johnny wonders whether he is brave, and on reflecting on the matter concludes that he is. Since being brave is a matter of behaving bravely under adverse conditions, whether Johnny is brave will depend on how he has behaved or would behave under the relevant conditions. On this score his reflections on the matter might well be less reliable than is an objective friend.

Still, many philosophers continue to support the hypothesis that each of us has Self-Knowledge. This hypothesis has been advanced in connection with knowledge of at least three distinct features of oneself. In particular, Self-Knowledge is alleged to involve knowledge of: (i) features of one's own conscious experience (including one's conscious sensory experience, but also one's conscious bodily experiences as well, such as pains, tickles, twinges, and the like); (ii) one's standing beliefs, desires, fears, intentions—in short, what philosophers call one's "propositional attitudes"; and/or (iii) the current relative position of one's own body parts. It is arguable that the items in (i)–(iii) are known by the subject in a special (and an especially authoritative) sort of way—a way that is not available to anyone else who hopes to come to know how the subject stands in these regards. So, for example, while another person can know that you are in pain, only you can acquire such knowledge by feeling the very pain in question. Further, the fact that only you can know that you are in pain by *feeling* the pain seems to account for the especially authoritative nature of the judgments you make regarding your own pains. Analogous things might be said about your beliefs, or about the current position of your body parts: while anyone might acquire knowledge of what you believe, only you can acquire this knowledge through introspection; and while anyone might acquire the knowledge that you are standing with your arms raised above your head, only you can acquire this knowledge through having an inner sense (proprioception) of the relative position of the relevant body parts. Or so many philosophers have argued.

2. Epistemic Principles Regarding First-Person Authority

If the *scope* of Self-Knowledge is delimited by the judgments one makes regarding (i)–(iii), it is natural to think that the *specialness* of Self-Knowledge can be understood in terms of the nature of these judgments. These "first-person judgments," as we will call them, appear to be special in one or both of two ways: first, in that they enjoy a special sort of epistemic authoritativeness ("first-person authority"); and second, in that they appear to be the result of the subject's "privileged access" to the facts in question. We will take up these matters in this and the next section.

What does the authoritativeness of first-person judgments amount to? One of the strongest doctrines in this area is *infallibilism* regarding first-person judgments. According to this doctrine, first-person judgments are guaranteed to be true whenever they are made—or at least whenever they are sincerely made by a subject in good cognitive health. The infallibility of these judgments ensures that they are (as it were) *objectively* authoritative. Arguably, Descartes was an infallibilist regarding a broad swath of first-person judgments. Many contemporary philosophers continue to feel some temptation to hold an infallibilist position regarding more limited domains. For example, we might hold that first-person judgments regarding one's own current pains are infallible: one could not sincerely and in good mind judge that one oneself was in pain when one was not. Those tempted in this way might also be tempted to hold an infallibilist position regarding sensations more generally. And Tyler Burge (1988) has famously held that first-person judgments regarding one's conscious, occurrent thoughts are infallible, because they are self-verifying.

The doctrine of infallibilism should not be confused with its converse, that of *self-intimation*. (Williamson (2000) uses 'luminosity' in place of 'self-intimation' to name the feature in question.) A state of an individual is self-intimating when the following condition holds: whenever the subject is in a state of that type, the subject will judge that she is in that state (so long as she is sane of mind and possesses the relevant concepts).

The combination of infallibility and self-intimation yields the doctrine of *transparency*. A mental state is transparent to its subject when the following holds: the subject is in the mental state in question if and only if she judges that she is in the mental state in question. Transparency rules out errors of commission: it cannot happen that the subject judges that she is in a mental state of this type when she is not. But transparency also rules out errors of omission: it cannot happen that the subject is in a state of this type but fails to judge that she is (even as she attends to the matter). Since transparency involves both infallibility and self-intimation, any doubts about the extent of infallibility and self-intimation are doubts about the extent of transparency.

Another traditional doctrine in this area, weaker than infallibility, is the doctrine of *incorrigibility*. A first-person judgment regarding a mental state is incorrigible just in case it cannot be corrected. Incorrigibility does not entail that these judgments are true; only that they can't be shown false. For this reason, the epistemological significance of incorrigibility—its significance for an account of first-person authority—is not entirely clear. Even so, an incorrigibilist view is natural if one assumes a private mental theater conception of the mental (more on which below); and even philosophers who reject any such conception have endorsed incorrigibility as a feature of some first-person judgments.

It is worth noting that the three doctrines considered so far—infallibility, self-intimation, and incorrigibility—look better in connection with first-person judgments regarding one's sensations, than with those regarding one's standing propositional attitudes. It is difficult (though perhaps not impossible) to imagine rejecting another person's sincere reports of her own sensory experiences. By contrast we can, and sometimes do, reject another person's sincere reports about what she herself believes, hopes, fears, or intends. ("Sure, he *says* that he believes that women are equal to men in the skills needed for this job, but I don't think that he really believes this: he has never hired a woman into this position in his thirty-plus years of hiring.") Such examples strongly suggest that, when it comes to judgments about one's own propositional attitudes, infallibilism and incorrigibility are both false. Counterexamples can be given as well for the hypothesis that standing propositional attitudes are self-intimating. ("Her behavior suggests that she thinks men are incompetent at child-rearing—although she would never admit to as much, even to herself.")

Suppose it is agreed that first-person judgments regarding one's standing propositional attitudes are neither infallible nor incorrigible, and that these judgments do not have a self-intimating subject-matter. Still, it seems that these judgments enjoy *some* (weaker) sort of authoritativeness. Consider your reaction when a friend tells you, "I believe that Mary will come to the party tonight." Normally this settles the matter regarding what your friend believes. In general, we accept another's first-person belief report unless we have positive reasons for rejecting it (in the form of relevant behavioral evidence to the contrary). This gives rise to yet another characterization of first-person authority, in terms of the *positive-presumptiveness* of the relevant judgments. To say that a given judgment is positive-presumptive is to say that it enjoys the benefit of the doubt and so stands by default, where this default is overridden only when there is positive reason to do so. (See Crispin Wright 1989a, 1989b, and 1989c.)

It might well be that first-person authority is to be characterized in different ways, according to the subject matter—(i), (ii), or (iii)—being judged. Thus, where the authoritativeness of one's judgments regarding one's own current pains might amount to infallibility, the authoritativeness of one's judgments regarding what one believes would amount to much less—perhaps to nothing more than positive-presumptiveness.

Of course, it is one thing to *say* that a given first-person judgment is infallible, or positive-presumptive, as the case may be; it is quite another to account for the fact that the judgment has this feature. It is to the latter task that we now turn.

3. On "Privileged Access" and the Nature and Subject-Matter of First-Person Judgments

In the previous section we considered various attempts to articulate what the authoritativeness of first-person judgment comes to. But in virtue of what do these judgments have the authority that they have? Contemporary philosophers have followed one of two familiar strategies in their attempt to account for the authoritativeness of first-person judgments. (As will emerge, the difference between these strategies is a matter of emphasis; they need not be seen as logically exclusive.) A *constructive* account traces the epistemic authoritativeness of first-person judgments to features of the processes that produce these judgments. So, for example, a reliabilist will hold that first-person authority is a matter of the reliability of the processes through which first-person judgments are made; an evidentialist will hold that the processes in question are sensitive to the relevant evidence; and so forth. By contrast, an *ideological* account of first-person authority is one that traces the authoritativeness of first-person judgments to the ineliminable role such judgments play in rational and practical agency. As we will see, both sorts of account can claim virtues, but both face challenges as well. We will conclude by considering the prospects for a 'hybrid' account.

3.1. Constructive Accounts

We begin with constructive accounts. For those who think that mental states are 'private' states to which only the subject herself has direct access, there is a natural constructive account of first-person authority: the 'acquaintance' account. (An early version of the acquaintance account is defended by Russell (1917), from whom the notion of acquaintance is borrowed; more recent versions can be found in Fumerton (1996, 2005, 2009) and Bonjour (2003); and see also Gertler (2001) and Chalmers (2003), where a version of the acquaintance view is defended with respect to one's own occurrent phenomenal states.) According to the acquaintance account of first-person authority, a subject is 'acquainted with' (some subset of) her own mental states, and it is in terms of the features of this relation of acquaintance that we can account for the authoritativeness of first-person judgments. The relation of acquaintance is a relation that holds between a subject and her mental states when the subject enjoys an unmediated access to the state itself. On this view, the unmediated nature of this access accounts for the epistemic security of the subject's first-person judgments: the *access* provided by the subject's acquaintance with her mental states yields a basis on which she forms her first-person judgments regarding those states; and the *unmediated nature* of this access restricts the sorts of errors it would be possible for the subject to make in those judgments. (Whether any errors at all are possible, and if so what sorts, will depend on the details of the correct account of the acquaintance relation and the nature of mental state(s) in question.)

Various questions can be raised regarding acquaintance accounts. For one thing, one might wonder whether the acquaintance account is open to the objections traditionally raised against the privacy conception of the mental: it makes knowledge of other minds—both their existence and their contents—problematic. (This worry will be acute if the acquaintance account is only plausible on the assumption that mental states are private.) In addition, one might question whether the acquaintance account can plausibly be extended to cover the whole range of authoritative first-person judgments we make. For example, while we might think to offer an acquaintance-based account of first-person authority regarding one's own conscious states and/or one's own bodily orientation, it might be doubted that we can do so with respect to one's own propositional attitudes. (Gertler (2001) explicitly mentions this sort of worry as a reason for restricting acquaintance accounts to one's own phenomenal states.)

An alternative constructive account of first-person authority was offered by the mid twentieth-century philosophical behaviorists. Their view of the matter was shaped by their view of mental states (or, more correctly, of sentences involving mental state vocabulary). They held that sentences involving mental state terms can be translated without loss into sentences involving descriptions of the subject's behavior and behavioral dispositions. Consequently, they took first-person judgments to be (equivalent in content to) judgments regarding one's own behavior and behavioral dispositions. Accordingly they thought of first-person judgments as based on (perhaps implicit) inferences from behavioral evidence. So any authoritativeness that these judgments had, they held, derived from one's having a greater amount of relevant evidence, than the evidence others had of one.

The behaviorist account has struck many as surrendering the idea that self-knowledge is special. But this account faces some obvious difficulties. First, it gives up on the idea of "privileged access" altogether: it holds that there is no principled difference between one's knowledge, and another person's knowledge, of one's own mental states. The only differences this view recognizes are those that reflect a mere disparity in the amount of evidence possessed. (The doctrine of privileged access may be false; but its denial ought to be independently established, rather than be a direct implication of one's account of first-person authority.) In addition, it seems implausible to think that first-person judgments, as a class, are always based on behavioral evidence. Often it seems that a subject "just knows" what she herself thinks, fears, senses, and so forth; she doesn't form her judgment on the basis of any evidence, or through any inferential process. (Think about your knowledge of your own occurrent thoughts: it seems strange to think that you acquire this knowledge by observing your behavior.) And even if (contrary to what was just said) this account can handle self-knowledge of one's propositional attitudes, it cannot handle self-knowledge of one's own pains and twitches, or of one's own current body position. One's first-person judgments regarding these are not inferences from observation of one's own behavior.

One lesson from the failure of the philosophical behaviorist account is that first-person judgments should not be seen as epistemically inferential—as depending for their authoritativeness on inferences from e.g. one's behavior. Since any constructive account of first-person authority must have something to say about the processes that eventuate in the formation of first-person judgments, it seems that one who hopes for such an account would do best to regard these processes as non-inferential. What is perhaps the most popular proposal in this regard is to construe the processes in question as processes of a kind of "inner" perception. (See Armstrong 1968 and Lycan 1997; Dretske (1995) speaks of "displaced" perception, but while his is an "internal perception" account, it is somewhat idiosyncratic in that it holds that the first-person judgments themselves are epistemically inferential.)

If the processes that eventuate in first-person judgments are non-inferential, and if "inner perception" is the best model for such a process, then the prospects for a constructive account of first-person authority—one that honors the idea of "privileged access"— will stand or fall with the case to be made for introspection as an inner, perception-like process. The introspection-as-inner-perception proposal has been defended by appeal to two analogies with outer perception. First, it has been argued that, just as in outer perception, where there is a reliable causal connection between the items perceived and the subject's outer-perceptual experience of those items, so too there is such a causal connection between the items of "inner perception" and the subject's inner-perceptual experience of those items. Second, it has been argued that, just as one's outer-perceptual attention might shift from object to object in one's external environment, so too one's inner-perceptual attention might shift from, for example, one's current thought to one's current pain.

The epistemological virtues of the "inner perception" model of introspection are clear. If first-person judgments are formed through a process of inner perception, then the authoritativeness of these judgments can be accounted for in terms of the epistemic features of this process. An analog of one's favored account of perceptual justification and knowledge could then be pressed into service regarding first-person judgments. Reliabilists could hold that first-person authority is a matter of the reliability of the judgments of inner perception. Evidentialists might hold that such authority is a matter of the evidence of inner perception (and then treat the evidence as the inner analog of outer-perceptual experience). Dogmatists about perceptual justification might hold that first-person authority reflects the truth of the principle that, in the absence of countervailing reasons, being in an inner perceptual state as of p suffices to provide justification for endorsing p.

At the same time, "inner perception" accounts of first-person authority face some serious obstacles. First, for at least some first-person judgments, it is unclear that we need anything approaching "inner perception." It is arguable that proprioception and pain perception can be modeled as forms of "inner perception"; but it is much more controversial to suppose that the other items of Self-Knowledge can be so modeled. As Gareth Evans noted, if asked whether you believe that there will be a third world war, typically you address this by looking at the evidence for thinking that there will be a third world war—a matter of looking outward, not inward. Relatedly, it is unclear whether there is any distinctive inner phenomenology associated with the propositional attitudes—in which case an account of introspection in terms of inner perception threatens to be insufficiently general. In addition, one might doubt whether the introspection-as-inner-perception view can do justice to the first-personal nature of the subject-matter. If introspection is really a kind of inner perception, it should be possible—in principle, though presumably not in practice—for one's introspective system to be hooked up to another person's mind/brain, enabling one to introspect the other's mental states. This suggestion has struck many philosophers as nonsensical, suggesting that the inner perception model of first-person authority is wrongheaded from the start.

An additional challenge facing the inner perception model arises from what appears to be an important disanalogy between paradigm instances of outer-perceptual judgments and those of introspection. Suppose that, on the basis of seeing a person you take to be your friend Sam, you form the judgment that Sam is happy. There are two ways in which this judgment might go wrong. First, the person in question might not have the property you ascribed to her—as when she is actually quite sad at the moment. Alternatively, the person you take to be Sam might actually be someone else altogether. Call the latter error one of misidentification. Sydney Shoemaker and Gareth Evans have argued that first-person judgments are immune to errors of misidentification. According to them, this immunity reflects the identification-free nature of the self-reference involved in ordinary uses of the first-person pronoun 'I' (see Shoemaker 1968, 1986, 1994; Evans 1980).

If Shoemaker and Evans are right, then the would-be judgments of inner perception (such as "I am in pain") differ from paradigmatic instances of the judgments of outer perception, in that the former are not susceptible to errors involving misidentification. Is there a way, consistent with acknowledging this point, to salvage the inner perception account of first-person authority? Shoemaker (1994) has identified a challenge facing any attempt of this sort. Since first-person judgments are immune to errors of misidentification, it appears that these judgments do not involve an object-identification component at all. In that case, they should not be modeled as the inner perception *of objects.* So those who seek to retain the inner perception model will have to endorse what Shoemaker (1994) calls the "broad perceptual model." On this model, perception—whether inner or outer—relates a thinker, not to objects, but rather to states of affairs. (As an example consider a judgment like 'It is raining,' made on the basis of observing the weather: such a judgment is perceptual without involving any identification of an object.) But it is hard to see how introspective judgments might be as the broad perceptual model would require.

At issue here is the independence of the subject-matter from the judgments about that subject-matter. Consider a judgment about the weather in Timbuktu. Such a judgment is correct or incorrect, according to how things are weather-wise in Timbuktu. What is more, how things are weather-wise in Timbuktu in no way depends on how any one person *thinks* things are weather-wise in Timbuktu: the weather there is independent of our judgments on the matter. Contrast this with the status of psychological facts. Suppose we want to know what a given person believes about, say, the virtues of playing sports. As we saw in section 2, the person's own judgments on the matter have an all-important role to play here. In the absence of positive evidence to the contrary, her judgments about what she believes are taken to determine the matter: absent behavioral evidence to the contrary, she is taken to believe whatever it is she judges herself to believe. In this way we see that facts about what a given subject believes are *not* independent of her judgments on the matter, in the way that facts about the weather are independent of what she (or anyone else) judges to be the case weather-wise.

The failure of independence between first-person judgments and their subject-matter calls into question the prospects for a constructive account of first-person authority. It is easy to appreciate why this is. The idea behind constructive accounts is that the authoritativeness of first-person judgments has its source in, for example, the reliability of the processes that produce these judgments. But it would now appear that, to the extent that these processes *are* reliable, this is not a matter of their success in tracking the facts, so much as it is a matter of their (defeasibly) *establishing* the very facts at issue. And if this is so, it might lead us to doubt whether Self-Knowledge is actually a cognitive achievement—one whose presence calls for a substantial epistemological account—in the first place. (See Wright 1989b, 1998 and Bar-On 2004 for further discussion.)

3.2. Ideological Accounts

Even so, it is important not to lose sight of the fact that when a person reports on her own state of mind, we assume that her report is correct unless we have positive evidence to doubt its correctness. If a constructive account of the authoritativeness we ascribe to others' first-person judgments is not available, how should we account for it? An *ideological* account of first-person authority holds that the presumption of authority granted to others' self-reports has its source in the preconditions of (rational and practical) agency. On this view, first-person authority has to do with the rationality of first-person judgments in any creature that exhibits rational agency. Ideological accounts can be differentiated both in the precise connections they make between first-person authority and rational agency, and by whether they include some modest constructive component in their overall account of first-person authority.

Davidson (1984, 1987) has argued that authoritative knowledge of one's own thoughts and meanings is a precondition for there being thoughts and linguistic meaning in the first place. The result is that anyone who aims to interpret the speech and thought of another subject must credit that subject with authoritative knowledge of her own thoughts and meanings. Davidson had much less of a positive nature to say on the mechanisms through which subjects have such self-knowledge. What little he did say (see Davidson 1988, 1989) suggests that he would reject the call for any sort of constructive component in an account of first-person authority.

Tyler Burge (1996) appeals to the conditions on being a critical reasoner as part of his account of first-person authority. Burge's idea, roughly, is that one who is a critical reasoner is one who can assess her own beliefs, and the relations between them, in light of the demands of reason. One who believes that it is raining but who looks through the window onto the street and sees no sign of wetness thereby has a reason to give up the belief that it is raining. But in order for this reason to be a reason *for the subject* to give up her belief that it is raining, she must recognize that she believes that it is raining, and recognize as well that she has just acquired evidence that conflicts with this belief.

Burge generalizes the point: one's opinions about the full range of one's own standing propositional attitudes (not just beliefs but also desires, fears, intentions, etc.) enjoy a special entitlement deriving from one's status as a critical reasoner.

As with Davidson's account, we might wonder about the completeness of Burge's account of first-person authority. It is one thing to argue that, as a critical reasoner, one's first-person judgments must be authoritative; it is another to give an account of that authority—to say *how* one's first-person judgments have this authority (Peacocke 1996). On this matter Burge points to what he calls the "non-contingent, rational relation . . . between relevant first-person judgments and their subject-matter or truth" (1996: 98). His claim here appears to be close to the point made above, regarding the lack of independence between first-person judgments and their subject-matter. But even if it is granted to Burge that this sort of consideration establishes that first-person judgments are rational whenever they are made, we might still wonder how these judgments manage to be as reliable as they are. To see why one might still wonder about this, suppose that we grant the non-contingency of the relation between first-person judgments and the facts that are their subject-matter. In particular, suppose that we grant that the judgments themselves serve to defeasibly determine the facts in question. Even so, first-person judgments have two *other* features that make it hard to see how they could be reliable (Wright 1989a, 1989b, 1989c; Goldberg 1999). They are typically formed in a baseless or groundless manner (though see Cassam (forthcoming) for the distinction between epistemic and explanational groundlessness); and yet they are "answerable," after the fashion of dispositions, to the overall behavior of the subject herself (Wright 1989b, 1989c). Thus a question arises: how do a subject's first-personal judgments succeed in squaring as well as they do with her overall behavior, given that she forms these judgments without attending to the relevant behavioral evidence? It is no answer to be told that a subject's first-person judgments stand as correct so long as they cohere with her nonverbal behavior; for what needs explanation is precisely *how* these judgments attain such a high level of coherence with her behavior.

One natural (constructive) suggestion here is that one's first-personal judgments about one's beliefs are generated by the same sort of conditions that give rise to one's forming the very beliefs in question. (For variants on this idea see Wright 1989b, 1989c; Peacocke 1996; Goldberg 2002; and Fernandez 2003.) This constructive suggestion need not be associated with the "inner perception" account of introspection (see e.g. Byrne forthcoming). But it might be used in combination with an ideological account of first-person authority, as part of what we might call a 'hybrid' account. In this respect, the evolving account in Sydney Shoemaker's recent work is of some interest. In broad outline, Shoemaker's account of first-person authority is an ideological one, having developed out of his (1988, 1994) arguments denying the possibility of 'self-blindness'. A self-blind person would be one who has beliefs and desires, possesses the concepts of belief and desire, is fully rational, and yet lacks second-order knowledge of her first-order beliefs and desires. In denying the possibility of self-blindness, Shoemaker is in effect saying that, on pain of irrationality, a creature who possesses the relevant concepts and who attends to the matter will *ipso facto* judge that she has a given propositional attitude whenever she does, in fact, have that attitude. More recently, however, Shoemaker (forthcoming) has proposed something like a mechanism through which such second-order knowledge is acquired. According to this proposal, having an available belief—roughly, having a belief 'come to mind' in a conscious episode—gives one warrant for judging that one has that belief. The warrant in question reflects the claims, first, that full rationality requires that one revise one's beliefs in a way that aims at greater consistency and coherence, and second, that forming such second-order beliefs on the basis of having a belief 'come to mind' satisfies this requirement. Thus Shoemaker's evolving position appears to be something of a hybrid, combining the key feature of an ideological account—first-person authority is understood in terms of its connection to rational agency—with an attempt to provide some modest constructive component—the warrant or authoritativeness of first-person judgments involves the mechanisms through which one's mental states 'come to mind.'

References

Armstrong, D. 1968: *A Materialist Theory of Mind*. (London: Routledge.)
Bar-On, D. 2004: *Speaking My Mind: Expression and Self-Knowledge*. (Oxford: Clarendon Press.)
BonJour, L. 2003: "Reply to Sosa." In BonJour, L. and Sosa, E. *Epistemic Justification: Internalism vs. Externalism, Foundations vs. Virtues*. (Malden: Blackwell.)
Burge, T. 1988: "Individualism and Self-Knowledge." *Journal of Philosophy* 85, 649–63.
Burge, T. 1996: "Our Entitlement to Self-Knowledge." *Proceedings of the Aristotelian Society* 96, 91–116.
Byrne, A. 2005: "Introspection." *Philosophical Topics* 33, 79–104.
Cassam, Q. 2009: "The Basis of Self-Knowledge." *Erkenntnis* 71:1, 35–51.
Chalmers, D. 2003: "The Content and Epistemology of Phenomenal Belief." In Smith, Q. and Jokic, A., eds. *Consciousness: New Philosophical Essays*. (Oxford: Oxford University Press), 220–71.
Davidson, D. 1984: "First Person Authority." *Dialectica* 38, 101–11. Reprinted in Davidson 2001.
Davidson, D. 1987: "Knowing One's Own Mind." *Proceedings and Addresses of the American Philosophical Association*. Reprinted in Davidson 2001.
Davidson, D. 1988: "The Myth of the Subjective." In Benedikt, M. and Berger, R., eds. *Bewusstsein, Sprache und die Kunst* (Vienna: Verlag). Reprinted in Davidson 2001.
Davidson, D. 1989: "What is Present to the Mind?" In Brandl, J. and Gombocz, W. eds., *Grazer Philosophische Studien* 36, Special edition: *The Mind of Donald Davidson* (Amsterdam: Rodopi). Reprinted in Davidson 2001.
Davidson, D. 2001: *Subjective, Intersubjective, Objective*. (Oxford: Oxford University Press.)
Dretske, F. 1995: *Naturalizing the Mind*. (Cambridge: MIT Press.)
Evans, G. 1980: *Varieties of Reference*. (Oxford: Oxford University Press.)
Fernandez, J. 2003: "Privileged Access Naturalized." *The Philosophical Quarterly* 53: 352–72.
Fumerton, R. 1996: *Metaepistemology and Skepticism*. (Lanham, MD: Rowman and Littlefield.)
Fumerton, R. 2005: "Speckled Hens and Objects of Acquaintance." *Philosophical Perspectives* 19: 121–39.
Fumerton, R. 2009: "Luminous Enough for a Cognitive Home." *Philosophical Studies* 142:1, 67–76.
Gertler, B. 2001: "Introspecting Phenomenal States." *Philosophy and Phenomenological Research* 63: 305–28.
Goldberg, S. 1999: "The Psychology and Epistemology of Self-Knowledge." *Synthese* 118:2, 165–99.
Goldberg, S. 2002: "Belief and its Linguistic Expression: Towards a Belief-Box Account of First-Person Authority." *Philosophical Psychology* 15:1, 65–76.
Hume, David, 1888: *Treatise of Human Nature*. Ed. L.A. Selby Bigge. (Oxford: Oxford University Press.)
Lycan, W. 1997: "Consciousness as Internal Monitoring." In Block, N., Flanagan, O., and Güzeldere, G., eds. *The Nature of Consciousness: Philosophical Debates*. (Cambridge: MIT Press.)
Peacocke, C. 1996: "Entitlement, Consciousness, and Conceptual Redeployment." *Proceedings of the Aristotelian Society* 96: 117–58.
Russell, B. 1917: "Knowledge by Acquaintance and Knowledge by Description." In *Mysticism and Logic*. (London: George Allen and Unwin.)
Shoemaker, S. 1968: "Self-Knowledge and Self-Awareness." *Journal of Philosophy* 65:19, 555–67. Reprinted in Shoemaker 1996.
Shoemaker, S. 1986: "Introspection and the Self." *Midwest Studies in Philosophy* 10: 101–20. Reprinted in Shoemaker 1996.
Shoemaker, S. 1988: "On Knowing One's Own Mind." In J. Tomberlin, ed. *Philosophical Perspectives* 2: 183–209. Reprinted in Shoemaker 1996.
Shoemaker, S. 1994: "Self-Knowledge and 'Inner-Sense'." *Philosophy and Phenomenological Research* 54: 249–314. Reprinted in Shoemaker 1996.

Shoemaker, S. 1996: *The First-Person Perspective and Other Essays*. (Cambridge: Cambridge University Press.)
Shoemaker, S. 2009: "Self-Intimation and Second-Order Belief." *Erkenntnis* 71:1, 35–51.
Williamson, T. 2000: *Knowledge and Its Limits*. (Oxford: Oxford University Press.)
Wright, C. 1989a: "Critical Notice: *Wittgenstein on Meaning*." *Mind* 48: 390.
Wright, C. 1989b: "Wittgenstein's Later Philosophy of Mind: Sensation, Privacy, and Intention." *Journal of Philosophy* 86, 622–34.
Wright, C. 1989c: "Wittgenstein's Rule-following Considerations and the Central Project of Theoretical Linguistics." In George, A., ed. *Reflections on Chomsky*. (Oxford: Basil Blackwell.)
Wright, C. 1998: "Self-Knowledge: The Wittgensteinian Legacy." In Wright, Smith, and Macdonald, eds. *Knowing Our Own Minds*. (Oxford: Oxford University Press), pp. 13–46.

29
TESTIMONIAL KNOWLEDGE
Jennifer Lackey

Testimony is responsible, either directly or indirectly, for much of what we know, not only about the world around us but also about who we are. Despite its relative historical neglect, recent work in epistemology has seen a growing recognition of the importance and scope of testimonial knowledge. Most of this work has focused on two central questions, which will be the main topics of this chapter. First, is testimonial knowledge necessarily acquired through transmission from speaker to hearer, or can testimony generate epistemic features in its own right? Second, is justified dependence on testimony fundamentally basic, or is it ultimately reducible to other epistemic sources, such as perception, memory, and reason?

Testimony itself is typically understood quite broadly so as to include a variety of acts of communication that are intended or taken to convey information—such as statements, nods, pointings, and so on. (For a full development of this view, see Lackey 2008.) Knowledge that is distinctively testimonial requires belief that is based or grounded in, not merely caused by, an instance of testimony. For instance, suppose that I sing "I have a soprano voice" in a soprano voice and you come to believe this entirely on the basis of hearing my soprano voice. (This is a variation of an example found in Audi 1997.) While my testimony is certainly causally relevant to the formation of your belief, the resulting knowledge is based on your hearing my soprano voice rather than on what I testified to, thereby rendering it perceptual in nature. What is of import for distinctively testimonial knowledge is that a given belief be formed *on the basis of the content of a speaker's testimony*. This prevents beliefs that are formed entirely on the basis of features *about* a speaker's testimony from qualifying as instances of *testimonial* knowledge.

1. Testimonial Knowledge: Transmission Versus Generation

Much work in the epistemology of testimony centers around the view that knowledge is *transmitted* from speaker to hearer. There are two main theses to this Transmission View (TV) of testimony; one is a necessity claim and the other is a sufficiency claim. In particular:

TV-N: For every speaker, A, and hearer, B, B knows that p on the basis of A's testimony that p only if A knows that p. (See the references for a list of proponents of different versions of this thesis.)

TV-S: For every speaker, A, and hearer, B, if (1) A knows that p, (2) B comes to believe that p on the basis of the content of A's testimony that p, and (3) B has no undefeated defeaters for believing that p, then B knows that p. (See the references for a list of proponents of different versions of this thesis.)

The Transmission View is often supported by a purported analogy between testimony and memory. While memory is said to only preserve knowledge from one time to another, testimony is thought to merely transmit knowledge from one person to another. Thus, neither is a generative epistemic source. For instance, just as I cannot now know that p on the basis of memory unless I non-memorially knew that p at an earlier time, the thought underlying the TV-N is that I cannot know that p on the basis of your testimony unless you know that p. Similarly, just as my knowing that p at an earlier time is sufficient, in the absence of current undefeated defeaters, for me to now know that p on the basis of memory, the TV-S holds that your knowing that p is sufficient, in the absence of undefeated defeaters, for me to know that p on the basis of your testimony.

Now, there are two kinds of defeaters that are standardly taken to be relevant to the satisfaction of condition (3) in TV-S. First, there are what we might call *psychological defeaters*. A psychological defeater is a doubt or belief that is had by S, which indicates that S's belief that p is either false or unreliably formed or sustained. Defeaters in this sense function by virtue of being *had* by S, regardless of their truth-value or epistemic status. (For various views of psychological defeaters, see BonJour 1980, 1985; Nozick 1981; Pollock 1986; Goldman 1986; Plantinga 1993; Lackey 1999, 2006, 2008; Bergmann 1997, 2004; Reed 2006.) Suppose, for instance, that Wally believes that the dog next door is a Siberian Husky but then his wife tells him, and he thereby comes to believe, that it is instead an Alaskan Malamute. In such a case, the justification that Wally had for believing that the neighbor's dog is a Siberian Husky has been defeated by the belief, or psychological defeater, that he acquires via the testimony of his wife. Second, there are what we might call *normative defeaters*. A normative defeater is a doubt or belief that S ought to have, which indicates that S's belief that p is either false or unreliably formed or sustained. Defeaters in this sense function by virtue of being doubts or beliefs that S *should have* (whether or not S does have them) given the presence of certain available evidence. (For various views of normative defeaters, see BonJour 1980, 1985; Goldman 1986; Fricker 1987, 1994; Chisholm 1989; Burge 1993, 1997; McDowell 1994; Audi 1997, 1998; Williams 1999; Lackey 1999, 2006, 2008; BonJour and Sosa 2003; Hawthorne 2004; Reed 2006.) For example, suppose that in the case above, Wally fails to believe his wife when she tells him that the dog next door is an Alaskan Malamute, though he has no good epistemic reason for doing so. Here Wally should believe his wife's testimony, even though he in fact does not, and thus he has a normative defeater for his belief that the dog next door is a Siberian Husky. The thought underlying both psychological and normative defeaters is that certain kinds of doubts and beliefs—either that a subject has or should have—contribute epistemically unacceptable *irrationality* to doxastic systems and, accordingly, defeat the justification possessed by the target beliefs in question.

Moreover, a defeater can itself be either defeated or undefeated. For instance, suppose that after accepting his wife's testimony, Wally consults a handbook on dogs and he discovers that its smaller size indicates that it is in fact a Siberian Husky, thereby providing him with a *defeater-defeater* for his original belief. And, as should be suspected, defeater-defeaters can be defeated by further doubts and beliefs, which, in turn, can be defeated by further doubts and beliefs, and so on. Similar considerations involving reasons, rather than doubts and beliefs, apply in the case of normative defeaters. When one has a defeater for one's belief that p that is not itself defeated, one has what is called an *undefeated defeater* for one's belief that p. It is the presence of undefeated defeaters, not merely of defeaters, that is incompatible with testimonial justification.

While there is much intuitive support for the Transmission View, there are also objections that have been raised to both of its claims. Against the necessity claim, cases have been presented where a speaker fails to believe, and hence know, a proposition to which she is testifying, but she nevertheless reliably conveys the information in question through her testimony. So, for instance, suppose that a devout creationist who does not believe in the truth of evolutionary theory nonetheless researches the topic extensively and, on this basis, constructs extremely reliable lecture notes from which she teaches her 3rd grade students. In such a case, the teacher seems able to reliably teach to her students that *Homo sapiens* evolved from *Homo erectus*, thereby imparting knowledge to her students that she fails to possess herself. Against the sufficiency claim, cases have been presented where a hearer's belief fails to be an instance of knowledge even though the hearer has no relevant undefeated defeaters, the speaker from whom it was acquired has the knowledge in question, and the speaker testifies sincerely. For instance, suppose that a speaker in fact knows that there was a bald eagle in the park this morning because she saw one there, but she is such that she would have reported to her hearer that there was such an eagle even if there hadn't been one. In such a case, the speaker's belief is an instance of knowledge and yet because she is an unreliable testifier, the belief that the hearer forms on the basis of her testimony is not. Both counterexamples show that the Transmission View is false. (Both types of cases are developed in more detail in Lackey 2006, 2008.)

One of the central conclusions that these considerations motivate is the replacement of the TV with conditions focusing on the *statements* of speakers rather than on their states of believing or knowing. More precisely, the TV may be replaced with the following *Statement View* of testimony (SV):

SV: For every speaker, A, and hearer, B, B knows that p on the basis of A's testimony that p only if (1) A's statement that p is reliable or otherwise truth-conducive, (2) B comes to truly believe that p on the basis of the content of A's statement that p, and (3) B has no undefeated defeaters for believing that p. (For a detailed defense of the SV, see Lackey 2006, 2008.)

Further conditions might be needed for a complete view of testimonial knowledge. But regardless of what is added to the SV, such a view avoids the problems afflicting the TV. For instance, despite the fact that the devout creationist in the above case does not possess the knowledge in question, her statement that *Homo sapiens* evolved from *Homo erectus* is reliably connected with the truth via the extensive research that she did on evolutionary theory. So, though she fails the TV-N, she satisfies condition (1) of the SV, thereby enabling her students to acquire the knowledge in question. Conversely, despite the fact that the speaker in the second case above knows that there was a bald eagle in the park this morning, her statement that this is so is not reliably connected with the truth since she would have reported that there was such an eagle even if there hadn't been one. Thus, the hearer cannot acquire knowledge about the bald eagle on the basis of the speaker's testimony. The SV can, therefore, handle both types of counterexamples with ease.

Moreover, the SV reveals that testimony is not merely a transmissive epistemic source, as the TV assumes, but that it can instead generate epistemic features in its own right. In particular, hearers can acquire testimonial knowledge from speakers who do not possess the knowledge in question themselves. In this respect, then, testimony is on an epistemic par with sources traditionally considered more basic, such as sense perception and reason.

2. Testimonial Justification

Another question at the center of work in the epistemology of testimony is how precisely hearers acquire justified beliefs from the testimony of speakers, where justification is here understood as being necessary and, when added to true belief, close to sufficient for knowledge. Traditionally, answers to this question have fallen into one of two camps: *non-reductionism* or *reductionism*. According to non-reductionists—whose historical roots are typically traced to the work of Thomas Reid—testimony is a *basic* source of justification, on an epistemic par with sense perception, memory, inference, and the like. Given this, non-reductionists maintain that, so as long as there are no undefeated defeaters of either the psychological or the normative variety, hearers can be justified in accepting what they are told *merely* on the basis of the testimony of speakers. (See the references for proponents of various versions of non-reductionism.)

In contrast to non-reductionism, reductionists—whose historical roots are standardly traced to the work of David Hume—maintain that, in addition to the absence of undefeated defeaters, hearers must also possess *non-testimonially based positive reasons* in order to be justified in accepting the testimony of speakers. These reasons are typically the result of induction: for instance, hearers observe a general conformity between reports and the corresponding facts and, with the assistance of memory and reason, they inductively infer that certain speakers, contexts, or types of reports are reliable sources of information. In this way, the justification of testimony is *reduced* to the justification for sense perception, memory, and inductive inference. (See the references for proponents of different versions of reductionism.) Broadly speaking, there are two different versions of reductionism. According to *global reductionism*, the justification of *testimony as a source of belief* reduces to the justification for sense perception, memory, and inductive inference. Thus, in order to be justified in accepting the testimony of speakers, hearers must possess non-testimonially based positive reasons for believing that *testimony in general is reliable*. According to local reductionism, which is the more widely accepted of the two versions, the justification for *each instance of testimony* reduces to the justification for instances of sense perception, memory, and inductive inference. So, in order to be justified in accepting the testimony of speakers, hearers must have non-testimonially based positive reasons for accepting *the particular report in question*.

Objections have been raised to both non-reductionism and reductionism. The central problem raised against non-reductionism is that it is said to permit gullibility, epistemic irrationality, and intellectual irresponsibility (see, e.g., Fricker 1987, 1994, 1995; Faulkner 2000, 2002; Lackey 2008). In particular, since hearers can acquire testimonially justified beliefs in the complete absence of any relevant positive reasons on such a view, randomly selected speakers, arbitrarily chosen postings on the internet, and unidentified telemarketers can be trusted, so long as there is no negative evidence against such sources. Yet surely, the opponent of non-reductionism claims, accepting testimony in these kinds of cases is paradigmatic of gullibility, epistemic irrationality, and irresponsibility.

Against reductionism, it is frequently argued that young children clearly acquire a great deal of knowledge from their parents and teachers and yet it is said to be doubtful that they possess—or even could possess—non-testimonially based positive reasons for accepting much of what they are told. (See, for instance, Audi (1997). For a response to this objection, see Lackey 2005, 2008.) For instance, an 18-month-old baby might come to know that the stove is hot from the testimony of her mother, but it is unclear whether she has the cognitive sophistication to have reasons for believing her mother to be a reliable source of information, let alone for believing that testimony is generally reliable. Given this, reductionists—of both the global and the local variety—might have difficulty explaining how such young subjects could acquire all of the testimonial knowledge they at least seem to possess.

There are also objections raised that are specific to each kind of reductionism. Against the global version, it is argued that in order to have non-testimonially based positive reasons that testimony is generally reliable, one would have to be exposed to a wide-ranging sample of reports. But, it is argued, most of us have been exposed only to a very limited range of reports from speakers in our native language in a handful of communities in our native country. This limited sample of reports provides only a fraction of what would be required to legitimately conclude that testimony is *generally* reliable. Moreover, with respect to many reports, such as those involving complex scientific, economic, or mathematical theories, most of us simply lack the conceptual machinery needed to properly check the reports against the facts. Global reductionism, then, is said to ultimately lead to skepticism about testimonial knowledge, at least for most epistemic agents.

Against the local version of reductionism, it is argued that most ordinary cognitive agents do not seem to have enough information to possess relevant positive reasons in all of those cases where testimonial knowledge appears present. For instance, it is argued that most cognitive agents frequently acquire testimonial knowledge from speakers about whom they know very little (see, e.g., Webb 1993; Foley 1994; Strawson 1994; Schmitt 1999. For a response to this objection, see Lackey (2008)). For instance, upon arriving in Chicago for the first time, I might receive accurate directions to Navy Pier from the first passerby I see. Most agree that such a transaction can result in my acquiring testimonial knowledge of Navy Pier's whereabouts, despite the fact that my positive reasons for accepting the directions in question—if indeed I possess any—are scanty at best.

The direction that some recent work on testimony has taken is to avoid the problems afflicting non-reductionism and reductionism by developing qualified or hybrid versions of either of these views (see, e.g., Fricker 1995, 2006b; Faulkner 2000; Goldberg 2006, 2008; Lehrer 2006; Pritchard 2008). For instance, in an effort to avoid the charges of gullibility and epistemic irresponsibility, some non-reductionists emphasize that hearers must be "epistemically entitled" to rely on the testimony of speakers or that they need to "monitor" incoming reports, even though such requirements do not quite amount to the full-blown need for non-testimonially based positive reasons embraced by reductionists (see Goldberg 2006 and 2008, respectively, for these qualifications to a non-reductionist view). And some reductionists, trying to account for the testimonial knowledge of both young children and those hearers who possess very little information about their relevant speakers, argue that positive reasons are not needed during either the "developmental phase" of a person's life—when a subject is acquiring concepts and learning the language, relying in large part on her parents and teachers to guide the formation of her belief system—or when hearers are confronted with "mundane testimony"—about, for instance, a speaker's name, what she had for breakfast, the time of day, and so on (see Fricker 1995 for these modifications to reductionism). On this version of reductionism, then, while positive reasons remain a condition of testimonial justification, such a requirement applies only to hearers in the "mature phase" of their life who are encountering "non-mundane testimony." Such qualified or hybrid versions of both non-reductionism and reductionism often encounter either variations of the very same problems that led to their development, or altogether new objections (see, e.g., Insole 2000; Weiner 2003; Pritchard 2004; Lackey 2008).

Arguably, a more promising strategy for solving the problems afflicting non-reductionism and reductionism should, first, include a necessary condition requiring non-testimonially grounded positive reasons for testimonial justification. This avoids the charges of gullibility, epistemic irrationality, and intellectual irresponsibility facing the non-reductionist's view. Second, the demands of such a condition should be weakened so that merely some positive reasons, even about the type of speaker, or the kind of report, or the sort of context of utterance, are required. This avoids the objections facing the reductionist's position that young children cannot satisfy such a requirement and that beliefs formed on the basis of the testimony of those about whom we know very little cannot be justified. Third, additional conditions should be added for a complete account of testimonial justification, such as the need for the reliability of the speaker's statement found in the SV. This frees the positive reasons requirement from shouldering all of the justificatory burden for testimonial beliefs, thereby enabling the weakening of its content discussed above (for a detailed development of this strategy, see Lackey 2008).

There is, however, an alternative family of views that has been growing in popularity in recent work in the epistemology of testimony, one that provides a radically different answer to the question of how testimonial beliefs are justified. Though there are some points of disagreement among some of the members of this family, they are united in their commitment to at least three central theses. First, and perhaps most important, the *interpersonal relationship* between the two parties in a testimonial exchange should be a central focus of the epistemology of testimony. Second, and closely related, certain features of this interpersonal relationship—such as the speaker *offering her assurance* to the hearer that her testimony is true, or the speaker *inviting the hearer to trust* her—are (at least sometimes) actually *responsible for conferring epistemic value* on the testimonial beliefs acquired. Third, the epistemic justification provided by these features of a testimonial exchange is *non-evidential* in nature. Let us call the general conception of testimony characterized by these theses the *Interpersonal View of Testimony*, or the IVT (proponents of the IVT include Ross 1986; Hinchman 2005; Moran 2006; and Faulkner 2007).

One of the central motivations for the IVT is a perceived failure on the part of existing views of testimony—particularly those that regard a speaker's testimony that p merely as *evidence* for a hearer to believe that p—to adequately account for the import of the interpersonal relationship between the speaker and the hearer in a testimonial exchange. In particular it is argued that a significant aspect of true communication is missing when a speaker is treated as a mere truth gauge, offering nothing more than words. In contrast, proponents of the IVT argue that speakers should be regarded as agents who enter into interpersonal relationships with their hearers. For instance, according to Richard Moran's version of the IVT, a speaker's testimony that p is understood as the speaker giving her *assurance* that p is true. Since assurance can be given only when it is freely presented as such, Moran claims that a speaker freely assumes responsibility for the truth of p when she asserts that p, thereby providing the hearer with an *additional* reason to believe that p, different in kind from anything given by evidence alone.

A central objection facing proponents of the IVT is that the interpersonal features that lie at the heart of their views are not clearly epistemologically relevant. For instance, the mere fact that a speaker offers her assurance to a hearer does not affect the reliability, proper functioning, truth-tracking, evidential relations, or any other relevant truth-conducive feature of the testimony in question. Given this, a speaker can give assurance—and thereby a justified belief—even when she shouldn't be able to, say, because she is a radically unreliable testifier. In an attempt to avoid this sort of problem, some proponents of the IVT add to their view conditions that are distinctively epistemic, such as requiring the reliability of the speaker's testimony or the absence of defeaters on the part of the hearer (see, e.g., Hinchman 2005). The problem with this move is that all of the justificatory work is done by the addition of these new conditions, leaving the interpersonal features epistemologically superfluous. This leads to the following dilemma: either the IVT is genuinely interpersonal but epistemologically impotent, or it is not epistemologically impotent but neither is it genuinely interpersonal (see Lackey 2008 for this objection to the IVT). Either way, the IVT fails to provide a compelling alternative to existing theories in the epistemology of testimony.

References

Audi, R. (1997) "The Place of Testimony in the Fabric of Knowledge and Justification," *American Philosophical Quarterly* 34: 405–22.
——. (1998) *Epistemology: A Contemporary Introduction to the Theory of Knowledge*, London: Routledge.
Bergmann, M. (1997) "Internalism, Externalism and the No-Defeater Condition," *Synthese* 110: 399–417.
——. (2004) "Epistemic Circularity: Malignant and Benign," *Philosophy and Phenomenological Research* 69: 709–27.
BonJour, L. (1980) "Externalist Theories of Epistemic Justification," *Midwest Studies in Philosophy* 5: 53–73.
——. (1985) *The Structure of Empirical Knowledge*, Cambridge, MA: Harvard University Press.
—— and E. Sosa. (2003) *Epistemic Justification: Internalism vs. Externalism, Foundations vs. Virtues*, Oxford: Blackwell Publishing.
Burge, T. (1993) "Content Preservation," *The Philosophical Review* 102: 457–88.
——. (1997) "Interlocution, Perception, and Memory," *Philosophical Studies* 86: 21–47.
Chisholm, R. (1989) *Theory of Knowledge*, 3rd edn, Englewood Cliffs, NJ: Prentice-Hall.
Faulkner, P. (2000) "The Social Character of Testimonial Knowledge," *The Journal of Philosophy* 97: 581–601.
——. (2002) "On the Rationality of our Response to Testimony," *Synthese* 131: 353–70.
——. (2007) "What Is Wrong with Lying?" *Philosophy and Phenomenological Research* 75: 535–57.
Foley, R. (1994) "Egoism in Epistemology," in F. Schmitt (ed.) *Socializing Epistemology: The Social Dimensions of Knowledge*, Lanham, MD: Rowman and Littlefield: 53–73.
Fricker, E. (1987) "The Epistemology of Testimony," *Proceedings of the Aristotelian Society*, supp. vol. 61: 57–83.
——. (1994) "Against Gullibility," in B. Matilal and A. Chakrabarti (eds.) *Knowing from Words*, Dordrecht: Kluwer Academic Publishers: 125–61.
——. (1995) "Telling and Trusting: Reductionism and Anti-Reductionism in the Epistemology of Testimony," *Mind* 104: 393–411.
——. (2006b) "Knowledge from Trust in Testimony is Second-Hand Knowledge," *Philosophy and Phenomenological Research* 73: 592–618.
Goldberg, S. (2006) "Reductionism and the Distinctiveness of Testimonial Knowledge," in J. Lackey and E. Sosa (eds.) *The Epistemology of Testimony*, Oxford: Oxford University Press: 127–44.
——. (2008) "Testimonial Knowledge in Early Childhood, Revisited," *Philosophy and Phenomenological Research* 76: 1–36.
Goldman, A. (1986) *Epistemology and Cognition*, Cambridge, MA: Harvard University Press.
Hawthorne, J. (2004) *Knowledge and Lotteries*, Oxford: Oxford University Press.

Hinchman, E. (2005) "Telling as Inviting to Trust," *Philosophy and Phenomenological Research* 70: 562–87.
Insole, C. (2000) "Seeing Off the Local Threat to Irreducible Knowledge by Testimony," *The Philosophical Quarterly* 50: 44–56.
Lackey, J. (1999) "Testimonial Knowledge and Transmission," *The Philosophical Quarterly* 49: 471–90.
——. (2005) "Testimony and the Infant/Child Objection," *Philosophical Studies* 126: 163–90.
——. (2006) "Learning from Words," *Philosophy and Phenomenological Research* 73: 77–101.
——. (2008) *Learning from Words: Testimony as a Source of Knowledge*, Oxford: Oxford University Press.
Lehrer, K. (2006) "Testimony and Trustworthiness," in J. Lackey and E. Sosa (eds.) *The Epistemology of Testimony*, Oxford: Oxford University Press: 145–59.
McDowell, J. (1994) "Knowledge by Hearsay," in B. Matilal and A. Chakrabarti (eds.) *Knowing from Words*, Dordrecht: Kluwer Academic Publishers: 195–224.
Moran, R. (2006) "Getting Told and Being Believed," in J. Lackey and E. Sosa (eds.) *The Epistemology of Testimony*, Oxford: Oxford University Press: 272–306.
Nozick, R. (1981) *Philosophical Explanations*, Cambridge, MA: The Belknap Press.
Plantinga, A. (1993) *Warrant and Proper Function*, Oxford: Oxford University Press.
Pollock, J. (1986) *Contemporary Theories of Knowledge*, Totowa, NJ: Rowman and Littlefield.
Pritchard, D.H. (2004) "The Epistemology of Testimony," *Philosophical Issues* 14: 326–48.
——. (2008) "A Defence of Quasi-Reductionism in the Epistemology of Testimony," *Philosophica* 78: 13–28.
Reed, B. (2006) "Epistemic Circularity Squared? Skepticism about Common Sense." *Philosophy and Phenomenological Research* 73: 186–97.
Ross, A. (1986) "Why Do We Believe What We Are Told?" *Ratio* 28: 69–88.
Schmitt, F. (1999) "Social Epistemology," in J. Greco and E. Sosa (eds.) *The Blackwell Guide to Epistemology*, Oxford: Blackwell Publishers: 354–82.
Strawson, P.F. (1994) "Knowing From Words," in B. Matilal and A. Chakrabarti (eds.) *Knowing from Words*, Dordrecht: Kluwer Academic Publishers: 23–27.
Webb, M. (1993) "Why I Know About As Much As You: A Reply to Hardwig," *The Journal of Philosophy* 110: 260–70.
Weiner, M. (2003) "Accepting Testimony," *The Philosophical Quarterly* 53: 256–64.
Williams, M. (1999) *Groundless Belief: An Essay on the Possibility of Epistemology*, 2nd edn, Princeton, NJ: Princeton University Press.

For endorsements of the TV-N, see:

Audi, R. (1997) "The Place of Testimony in the Fabric of Knowledge and Justification," *American Philosophical Quarterly* 34: 405–22.
——. (1998) *Epistemology: A Contemporary Introduction to the Theory of Knowledge*, London: Routledge.
——. (2006) "Testimony, Credulity, and Veracity," in J. Lackey and E. Sosa (eds.) *The Epistemology of Testimony*, Oxford: Oxford University Press: 25–49.
Burge, T. (1993) "Content Preservation," *The Philosophical Review* 102: 457–88.
——. (1997) "Interlocution, Perception, and Memory," *Philosophical Studies* 86: 21–47.
Faulkner, P. (2006) "On Dreaming and Being Lied To," *Episteme* 3: 149–59.
Hardwig, J. (1985) "Epistemic Dependence," *The Journal of Philosophy* 82: 335–49.
——. (1991) "The Role of Trust in Knowledge," *The Journal of Philosophy* 88: 693–708.
McDowell, J. (1994) "Knowledge by Hearsay," in B. Matilal and A. Chakrabarti (eds.) *Knowing from Words*, Dordrecht: Kluwer Academic Publishers: 195–224.
Owens, D. (2000) *Reason without Freedom: The Problem of Epistemic Normativity*, London: Routledge.
——. (2006) "Testimony and Assertion," *Philosophical Studies* 130: 105–29.
Plantinga, A. (1993) *Warrant and Proper Function*, Oxford: Oxford University Press.
Reynolds, S. (2002) "Testimony, Knowledge, and Epistemic Goals," *Philosophical Studies* 110: 139–61.
Ross, A. (1986) "Why Do We Believe What We Are Told?" *Ratio* 28: 69–88.
Schmitt, F. (2006) "Testimonial Justification and Transindividual Reasons," in J. Lackey and E. Sosa (eds.) *The Epistemology of Testimony*, Oxford: Oxford University Press: 193–224.
Welbourne, M. (1979) "The Transmission of Knowledge," *The Philosophical Quarterly* 29: 1–9.
——. (1981) "The Community of Knowledge," *The Philosophical Quarterly* 31: 302–14.
——. (1986) *The Community of Knowledge*, Aberdeen: Aberdeen University Press.
——. (1994) "Testimony, Knowledge and Belief," in B. Matilal and A. Chakrabarti (eds.) *Knowing from Words*, Dordrecht: Kluwer Academic Publishers: 297–313.

Williamson, T. (1996) "Knowing and Asserting," *The Philosophical Review* 105: 489–523.
——. (2000) *Knowledge and its Limits*, Oxford: Oxford University Press.

For endorsements of the TV-S, see:

Adler, J. (1994) "Testimony, Trust, Knowing," *The Journal of Philosophy* 91: 264–75.
——. (2002) *Belief's Own Ethics*, Cambridge, MA: The MIT Press.
Audi, R. (1997) "The Place of Testimony in the Fabric of Knowledge and Justification," *American Philosophical Quarterly* 34: 405–22.
Austin, J.L. (1979) "Other Minds," in his *Philosophical Papers*, 3rd edn, Oxford: Oxford University Press.
Burge, T. (1993) "Content Preservation," *The Philosophical Review* 102: 457–88.
Coady, C.A.J. (1992) *Testimony: A Philosophical Study*, Oxford: Clarendon Press.
Evans, G. (1982) *The Varieties of Reference*, Oxford: Clarendon Press.
Fricker, E. (1987) "The Epistemology of Testimony," *Proceedings of the Aristotelian Society*, supp. vol. 61: 57–83.
McDowell, J. (1994) "Knowledge by Hearsay," in B. Matilal and A. Chakrabarti (eds.) *Knowing from Words*, Dordrecht: Kluwer Academic Publishers: 195–224.
Owens, D. (2000) *Reason Without Freedom: The Problem of Epistemic Normativity*, London: Routledge.
——. (2006) "Testimony and Assertion," *Philosophical Studies* 130: 105–29.
Welbourne, M. (1979) "The Transmission of Knowledge," *The Philosophical Quarterly* 29: 1–9.
——. (1981) "The Community of Knowledge," *The Philosophical Quarterly* 31: 302–14.
——. (1986) *The Community of Knowledge*, Aberdeen: Aberdeen University Press.
——. (1994) "Testimony, Knowledge and Belief," in B. Matilal and A. Chakrabarti (eds.) *Knowing from Words*, Dordrecht: Kluwer Academic Publishers: 297–313.
Williamson, T. (1996) "Knowing and Asserting," *The Philosophical Review* 105: 489–523.
——. (2000) *Knowledge and its Limits*, Oxford: Oxford University Press.

For endorsements of non-reductionism, see:

Audi, R. (1997) "The Place of Testimony in the Fabric of Knowledge and Justification," *American Philosophical Quarterly* 34: 405–22.
——. (1998) *Epistemology: A Contemporary Introduction to the Theory of Knowledge*, London: Routledge.
——. (2006) "Testimony, Credulity, and Veracity," in J. Lackey and E. Sosa (eds.) *The Epistemology of Testimony*, Oxford: Oxford University Press: 25–49.
Austin, J.L. (1979) "Other Minds," in his *Philosophical Papers*, 3rd edn, Oxford: Oxford University Press.
Burge, T. (1993) "Content Preservation," *The Philosophical Review* 102: 457–88.
——. (1997) "Interlocution, Perception, and Memory," *Philosophical Studies* 86: 21–47.
Coady, C.A.J. (1992) *Testimony: A Philosophical Study*, Oxford: Clarendon Press.
——. (1994) "Testimony, Observation and 'Autonomous Knowledge'," in B. Matilal and A. Chakrabarti (eds.) *Knowing from Words*, Dordrecht: Kluwer Academic Publishers: 225–50.
Dummett, M. (1994) "Testimony and Memory," in B. Matilal and A. Chakrabarti (eds.) *Knowing from Words*, Dordrecht: Kluwer Academic Publishers: 251–72.
Evans, G. (1982) *The Varieties of Reference*, Oxford: Clarendon Press.
Foley, R. (1994) "Egoism in Epistemology," in F. Schmitt (ed.) *Socializing Epistemology: The Social Dimensions of Knowledge*, Lanham, MD: Rowman and Littlefield: 53–73.
Goldberg, S. (2006) "Reductionism and the Distinctiveness of Testimonial Knowledge," in J. Lackey and E. Sosa (eds.) *The Epistemology of Testimony*, Oxford: Oxford University Press: 127–44.
Goldman, A. (1999) *Knowledge in a Social World*, Oxford: Clarendon Press.
Graham, Peter J. (2006) "Liberal Fundamentalism and Its Rivals," in J. Lackey and E. Sosa (eds.) *The Epistemology of Testimony*, Oxford: Oxford University Press: 93–115.
Hardwig, J. (1985) "Epistemic Dependence," *The Journal of Philosophy* 82: 335–49.
——. (1991) "The Role of Trust in Knowledge," *The Journal of Philosophy* 88: 693–708.
Insole, C. (2000) "Seeing Off the Local Threat to Irreducible Knowledge by Testimony," *The Philosophical Quarterly* 50: 44–56.
McDowell, J. (1994) "Knowledge by Hearsay," in B. Matilal and A. Chakrabarti (eds.) *Knowing from Words*, Dordrecht: Kluwer Academic Publishers: 195–224.
Millgram, E. (1997) *Practical Induction*, Cambridge, MA: Harvard University Press.
Owens, D. (2000) *Reason Without Freedom: The Problem of Epistemic Normativity*, London: Routledge.

——. (2006) "Testimony and Assertion," *Philosophical Studies* 130: 105–29.
Plantinga, A. (1993) *Warrant and Proper Function*, Oxford: Oxford University Press.
Reid, T. (1983) *Essay on the Intellectual Powers of Man*, in R. Beanblossom and K. Lehrer (eds.) *Thomas Reid's Inquiry and Essays*, Indianapolis: Hackett.
Ross, A. (1986) "Why Do We Believe What We Are Told?" *Ratio* 28: 69–88.
Rysiew, P. (2002) "Testimony, Simulation, and the Limits of Inductivism," *Australasian Journal of Philosophy* 78: 269–74.
Schmitt, F. (1999) "Social Epistemology," in J. Greco and E. Sosa (eds.) *The Blackwell Guide to Epistemology*, Oxford: Blackwell Publishers: 354–82.
Sosa, E. (2006) "Knowledge: Instrumental and Testimonial," in J. Lackey and E. Sosa (eds.) *The Epistemology of Testimony*, Oxford: Oxford University Press: 116–23.
Strawson, P.F. (1994) "Knowing From Words," in B. Matilal and A. Chakrabarti (eds.) *Knowing from Words*, Dordrecht: Kluwer Academic Publishers: 23–27.
Webb, M. (1993) "Why I Know About As Much As You: A Reply to Hardwig," *The Journal of Philosophy* 110: 260–70.
Weiner, M. (2003) "Accepting Testimony," *The Philosophical Quarterly* 53: 256–64.
Welbourne, M. (1979) "The Transmission of Knowledge," *The Philosophical Quarterly* 29: 1–9.
——. (1981) "The Community of Knowledge," *The Philosophical Quarterly* 31: 302–14.
——. (1986) *The Community of Knowledge*, Aberdeen: Aberdeen University Press.
——. (1994) "Testimony, Knowledge and Belief," in B. Matilal and A. Chakrabarti (eds.) *Knowing from Words*, Dordrecht: Kluwer Academic Publishers: 297–313.
Williamson, T. (1996) "Knowing and Asserting," *The Philosophical Review* 105: 489–523.
——. (2000) *Knowledge and its Limits*, Oxford: Oxford University Press.

For endorsements of reductionism, see:

Adler, J. (1994) "Testimony, Trust, Knowing," *The Journal of Philosophy* 91: 264–75.
——. (2002) *Belief's Own Ethics*, Cambridge, MA: The MIT Press.
Fricker, E. (1987) "The Epistemology of Testimony," *Proceedings of the Aristotelian Society*, supp. vol. 61: 57–83.
——. (1994) "Against Gullibility," in B. Matilal and A. Chakrabarti (eds.) *Knowing from Words*, Dordrecht: Kluwer Academic Publishers: 125–61.
——. (1995) "Telling and Trusting: Reductionism and Anti-Reductionism in the Epistemology of Testimony," *Mind* 104: 393–411.
——. (2006a) "Testimony and Epistemic Autonomy," in J. Lackey and E. Sosa (eds.) *The Epistemology of Testimony*, Oxford: Oxford University Press: 225–50.
——. (2006b) "Knowledge from Trust in Testimony is Second-Hand Knowledge," *Philosophy and Phenomenological Research* 73: 592–618.
Hume, D. (1977) *An Enquiry Concerning Human Understanding*, Eric Steinberg (ed.) Indianapolis: Hackett.
Lehrer, K. (2006) "Testimony and Trustworthiness," in J. Lackey and E. Sosa (eds.) *The Epistemology of Testimony*, Oxford: Oxford University Press: 145–59.
Lipton, P. (1998) "The Epistemology of Testimony," *Studies in History and Philosophy of Science* 29: 1–31.
Lyons, J. (1997) "Testimony, Induction and Folk Psychology," *Australasian Journal of Philosophy* 75: 163–78.
Pritchard, D. (2008) "A Defence of Quasi-Reductionism in the Epistemology of Testimony," *Philosophica* 78: 13–28.
Van Cleve, J. (2006) "Reid on the Credit of Human Testimony," in J. Lackey and E. Sosa (eds.) *The Epistemology of Testimony*, Oxford: Oxford University Press: 50–74.

30
MEMORY KNOWLEDGE
Sven Bernecker

Introduction

Knowledge can be subdivided according to the sources from which it arises. Among the basic sources of knowledge and justification are perception, testimony, reason, and inference. Whether memory is a basic source of knowledge is a controversial issue. Some philosophers maintain that memory only retains or preserves knowledge but doesn't generate new knowledge. Others insist that there are cases where a person first comes to know by remembering.

Section 1 explains the distinction between direct and representative realism about memory. Section 2 concerns the question of whether memory implies knowledge. Section 3 examines whether memory is merely a preservative source of justification and knowledge or whether it can also function as a generative source. Finally, section 4 discusses responses to skepticism about memory knowledge.

1. The Objects of Memory

Traditionally philosophers were concerned with the debate between representative (or indirect) and direct realism about memory. The discussion of memory closely followed the discussion of perception. Just as philosophers have debated the question whether perception is a direct awareness of objects or an inferential procedure, so it has been debated whether memory provides mediate or immediate awareness of the past.

Representative realism about memory claims that, though there is a past that causes us to have memory experiences, we are not directly or immediately aware of the past. What we are directly aware of are the effects the past has on us—representations or sense-data of things past. We remember something not by way of being directly aware of that thing, but rather a mediating representation of that thing. To remember is to undergo a certain sort of mental experience; it is to experience a mental representation which reproduces some past sense-experience. Among the advocates of the representative theory are Hume (1978: 8–10), James (1890: i. ch. 16), Locke (1975: 149–55), and Russell (1995a: ch. 9).

What speaks in favor of representative realism is the fact that, phenomenologically speaking, there might be no difference between veridical and illusory rememberings. There doesn't seem to be a subjective mark whereby we can distinguish between those rememberings in which the object as presently visualized is identical with the object as originally seen and those in which it is not. Why not, therefore, say that what is directly remembered in either case is something internal to us—a representation or sense-datum? The representative realists claim that even in cases of veridical remembering the primary object of awareness is a representation of the past thing rather than the thing itself.

The most widely canvassed objection to representative realism about memory is that it makes the past unknowable. If all we are directly aware of are our representations about the past, how can we know that there is a past at all, much less that the past is the cause of our present representations? How can we discriminate memory representations from other representational states such as figments of the imagination? The need to discern memory representations from other kinds of representations is particularly pressing if one wants to base knowledge on ostensible memories. It seems that to come to know about the past on the basis of one's ostensible memories one would have to first establish what the past was like and then check one's ostensible memories against the past facts. But how can one do this if, as the representative realist insists, the direct objects of memory are internal representations? To discover whether something is a genuine memory representation, one would have to inspect it from an external point of view, but, according to the representative theory, the only way of finding out what happened in the past is via one's representations of the past. Thus the representative theorist finds himself imprisoned within his representations, with no way of confirming that the ostensible memory representations do, in fact, reveal the past, as they have to if he is to have memory knowledge.

Some advocates of representative realism have responded to this problem by maintaining that one can indeed tell, by reflection alone, whether a particular representation one is having stems from memory or one of the other faculties of the mind, such as perception or imagination. The feature of memory representations that distinguishes them from other kinds of representational states and that stamps them as authentic is the *memory marker*. Memory markers are defined as a priori knowable features of memory representations on the basis of which they can be distinguished from other mental phenomena. Memory markers have been described by representative realists in a number of ways, as the feeling of warmth and intimacy (James 1890: i. 650), the feeling of familiarity and pastness (Russell 1995a: 163), or as the force and vivacity of memory representations (Hume 1978: 9–10, 85–6).

The problem all the various proposals of memory markers have in common is that they don't offer a reliable mark. There are cases in which these alleged memory markers are present, but in which there is no inclination to speak of memory, and there are instances where memories lack these alleged markers. What is more, the features identified as memory markers don't bear their own explanation upon their face. The mere fact, if it is one, that we are inclined to associate representations that strike us as familiar with memory, doesn't imply that we are justified to make this association. The required justification could, of course, come from some independent evidence suggesting that memories appear familiar more often than fantasies. Yet if such evidence exists at all, it isn't available by reflection alone. Alternatively the required justification could be the result of a general principle whereby it is reasonable to trust our cognitive faculties (including our memories) even though we lack a non-question-begging assurance of their reliability. But if we are entitled to trust our cognitive faculties, including our memory, then memory markers are superfluous (cf. Bernecker 2008: chs. 5–6).

According to *direct realism*, we don't remember the past by virtue of being aware of a representation presenting the past to us, rather, our awareness of the past is direct. Although remembering something requires the having of representations and although these representations determine the way the thing appears to us, there is no reason to suppose we are aware of these representations themselves. We are aware of the past thing by internally representing the thing, not by being aware of the internal representation of the thing. Representations, according to the direct realist, don't function as the objects of memory, but are merely the vehicle of memory. Direct realism about memory is defended by, among others, Laird (1920: 56), Reid (1997: essay 3), and Russell (1997: 114–15).

Direct realism derives some of its plausibility from the fact that when we remember something, what we are aware of is just that thing, and nothing further. As Reid (1997: 28) remarks, "upon the strictest examination, memory appears to me to have things that are past, and not present ideas, for its object." Since, on the realist view, what we are directly aware of in memory is the past event in *propria persona*, and not some representation of it, one of the difficulties of representative realism about memory disappears: the difficulty of explaining how we can be justified in inferring the occurrence of a past thing from a present memory representation. If what we are directly aware of is the past event itself, and not just a representation thereof, no such inference is required.

Though direct realism makes some problems disappear, it gives rise to others. One of the problems of direct realism is to explain our direct acquaintance with, or experience of past things. Another worry is that direct realism is incompatible with the highly intuitive causal theory of memory, that is, the view that for someone to remember something his representation of that thing must be suitably causally connected to his past representation of that same thing. Hume famously held that the relation between cause and effect is a metaphysical rather than a logical relation and that, therefore, causal relations cannot be known a priori. The only way in which a particular effect can be inferred from a given cause is on the basis of experience, in particular by observation of a regularity between events of the same type. Now, there is the worry that direct realism about memory is incompatible with the causal theory of memory because it violates the Humean requirement whereby a cause and its effect must be "independent existences" (1978: 79–80). For, given direct realism, if the effect is characterized as "S's having a memory representation of X," then it *is* possible to tell a priori that X occurred.

The Humean worry that if there is a logical relation between two events that supports an a priori inference from one to the other, then there is no room left for causal efficacy among them is misguided. We can always re-describe the effect in a way as to make it an entailment of the cause. But from this it doesn't follow that causation is a myth. For even if we chose to describe the effect-event in a different manner it would still follow the cause with the same regularity as before. Causation is a relation between events. Logical relations, however, hold between propositions and linguistic entities. And just because there is a logical relation between the descriptions of two events doesn't preclude that the events themselves stand in a causal relation. Thus there is no reason to suppose that direct realism conflicts with the causal theory of memory.

2. Memory and Knowledge

According to received wisdom in epistemology, remembering that p implies knowing that p. Propositional memory is thought to be long-standing or continuing knowledge. Audi (2003: 69), for example, says that "if you remember that we met, you know that we did. Similarly, if you remember me, you know me." Malcolm (1963: 223) defines propositional memory thus: "A person B remembers that p if and only if B knows that p because he knew that p." And Margalit (2002: 14) writes: "To remember now is to know now what you knew in the past, without learning in-between what you know now. And to know is to believe something to be true. Memory, then, is knowing from the past."

Most philosophers hold that the concept of propositional knowledge has three necessary conditions: belief, truth, and justification (however construed). (I use the term "justification" to refer to any factor that transforms a true belief into knowledge.) Given that memory implies knowledge and given the transitivity of implication, memory implies belief, truth, and justification. Now it is beyond doubt that both knowledge and memory imply truth. Just as you can know that p only if p is true, so you can remember that p only if p is true. If not-p, then you might think you remember that p, but cannot actually remember that p. Truth is a component of both knowledge and memory. The task of evaluating the view whereupon memory is a form of knowledge is thus a matter of determining the tenability of the belief constraint and the justification constraint.

To see that one can remember that p without believing that p consider the following example adapted from Malcolm (1963: 213–14): S suddenly finds himself with the thought that he has been kidnapped when he was a small boy. The idea that he has been kidnapped just pops into his head; it seems to come "out of the blue." S can't make sense of this idea and takes it to be merely imaginary; after all the likelihood of being kidnapped is low. What is more, the idea in question is inferentially isolated from the large body of inferentially integrated beliefs to which S has access. Nothing of what S knows or believes about his past connects with the idea that he has been kidnapped. But now suppose that, unbeknown to S, it is in fact the case that he has been kidnapped. The flashbulb thought is an instance of propositional memory.

Believing that p involves holding p true yet it doesn't involve actively reflecting on p or an especially high degree of confidence with respect to p. Given that acceptance is a central component of both occurrent and dispositional belief, it would be wrong to say that S *believes* that he was kidnapped when he was a small boy. For only after he is presented with the police record and newspaper clippings about his kidnapping does he reluctantly consent to the thesis according to which the thought in question springs from his memory rather than his imagination. And when he finally accepts this thesis he acquires a novel belief rather than reviving a dormant one. Thus S not only remembers that p without believing that he remembers that p, but he remembers that p without believing that which he remembers, namely p. (Obviously, if knowledge didn't imply belief, as some argue, cases of memory without belief wouldn't count against the thesis that to remember that p is to know that p.)

The most compelling cases of memory without justification are ones where the subject remembers that p but where there is some defeating information such that, if he became aware of it, he would no longer be justified in believing p. Despite the dazzling number of different conceptions of epistemic justification, philosophers on both sides of the internalism/externalism divide sign up to the idea that justification is incompatible with undefeated defeaters. In the case of epistemic internalism, it is obvious that the presence of undefeated defeaters undermines justification. Given that what justifies a belief is a mentally accessible item (something that one can come to know whether it obtains just by reflecting on one's mental states), being justified in believing p excludes a person's having sufficient reasons for supposing either that p is false or that the belief that p is not grounded or produced in a way that is sufficiently truth-indicating. Moreover, the majority of externalists hold that although a subject need not be aware of the factors that justify his belief, he might not be aware of evidence that undermines his belief. In addition to the reliabilist justification condition they adopt a no-defeater condition that ensures that a justified belief is not incoherent with the background information the subject possesses.

Consider the following case of memory without justification. In the past S learned that John F. Kennedy was assassinated in 1963. He came to know this fact. Today S's friends play a practical joke on him. They tell him that Kennedy wasn't assassinated until 1964 and present him with plausible yet misleading evidence to this effect. Given the incompatibility of justification with the presence of undefeated defeaters, S doesn't know anymore that Kennedy was assassinated in 1963, for he is unable to rule out the relevant alternative that he was not assassinated until 1964. He fails to know that Kennedy was assassinated in 1963, despite the fact that he still remembers this fact. This example is meant to show that one can know at t_1 that p, remember at t_2 everything one knew at t_1, and yet fail to know at t_2 that p—even though one continues to truly believe that p—for the reason that one isn't anymore justified in believing that p. The upshot is that memory doesn't imply knowledge since it implies neither belief nor justification. Not only is it possible to remember something one doesn't believe but also one might acquire some plausible yet misleading evidence that destroys the status as justified belief of the once-genuine justified belief that one still remembers (cf. Bernecker 2010: 65–94).

3. Memory and Justification

Even if memory doesn't imply justification and knowledge, memory beliefs can, of course, be justified and qualify as knowledge. And so the question arises whether memory is merely a preservative source of justification and knowledge or whether it can also function as a generative source.

The standard view, which may be called *preservationism*, has it that memory is nothing but a preservative source of justification and knowledge. Just as testimony is said to transmit knowledge from one person to another, memory is said to preserve knowledge from one time to another. Both in the case of memory knowledge and testimonial knowledge the proposition in question must have been known when it was originally acquired and a source other than memory or testimony, respectively, must have been responsible for its original acquisition (Plantinga 1993: 61n). If one justifiably believes that p on the basis of memory, then one must have acquired this justification in a nonmemorial way at some earlier time. Memory cannot improve the epistemic status a belief has at the time of recall vis-à-vis the epistemic status it had at the time it was originally acquired. Memory is incapable of making an unknown proposition known, an unjustified belief justified, or an irrational belief rational—it can only preserve what is already known, justified, or rational.

How does memory preserve the positive epistemic status of the original belief? According to some preservationists (e.g., Conee and Feldman 2004: 60–1), epistemic justification is a matter of internal or conscious justifying factors. The obvious problem with internalist preservationism is that there are numerous justified memory beliefs for which there are no internal or conscious justifying factors because they are (irretrievably) forgotten. This is how Williamson (2007: 110–11) states the problem:

> Many of our factual memories come without any particular supporting phenomenology of memory images or feelings of familiarity. We cannot remember

how we acquired the information, and it may be relatively isolated, but we still use it when the need arises. Although few if any memories stand in total isolation from the rest of our conscious lives, very many memories are too isolated to receive impressive justification from other internal elements.

Internalists seem to be stuck with the implausible result that retained beliefs are unjustified unless the past evidence is also recalled. In response to the problem of forgotten evidence, virtually all proponents of preservationism adopt the *principle of continuous justification*: at t_2, S's belief from t_1 that p is continuously justified if S continues to believe at t_2 that p—even if he lost his original knowledge-producing justification and has acquired no new justification in the meantime (Shoemaker 1967: 271–2). According to some preservationists (e.g., Pappas 1980), continuous justification is a kind of basic or foundational justification. According to others (Burge 1993: 458–9; Owens 2000: 153), the reason we are continuously justified in holding our memory beliefs is that we are entitled to believe what memory "serves up," in the absence of defeaters.

According to *generativism*, a memory belief can not only be *less* but also *more* justified than the original belief. A memory belief might be justified even if the original belief wasn't justified. How does memory generate justification? According to Audi (1995: 37) and Pollock (1974: 193), it is the phenomenology of recalling that generates justification for memory beliefs. They draw a parallel between memory and perception. In a standard case of perceptual belief, one is "appeared to" in a certain way and, on the basis of this appearance, comes to justifiably believe something about the perceptual surroundings. Similarly, when one remembers something one has a recollection and, on the basis of this phenomenal state, comes to justifiably believe something about the past. The idea is that if one bases one's belief that p on one's state of seeming to remember that p, and p is undefeated, then one is at least prima facie justified in believing p.

Even if we grant that there is a distinctive phenomenology that attends all the memory beliefs we are justified in holding and even if we grant that the experiential features of memory beliefs can do the epistemic work that Pollock and Audi assign to them, this version of generativism runs into problems. In the absence of defeating conditions, the epistemic status of a belief is said to improve simply in virtue of the belief being recalled. Every time a belief is retrieved from memory it receives an extra epistemic boost. But is it plausible to suppose that, everything else being equal, a belief that is retrieved often enjoys a better epistemic status than a belief that is retrieved infrequently? There doesn't seem to be a neat correlation between the positive epistemic status a belief has and the number of times it has been retrieved from memory. Following McGrath (2007: 19–22), we can call this the *epistemic boost problem*.

According to Audi's and Pollock's *radical generativism*, memory can generate new justificatory factors, new evidence. If, for instance, I came to justifiably believe at t_1 that p and if I remember at t_2 that p, then the memory belief inherits (some of) the justification the original belief had and there will be an additional justificatory element due to the process of remembering. The justification of the memory belief has two parts: there is a preserved component and a new component due to the act of recalling. *Moderate generativism* (cf. Bernecker 2010: 96–103; Lackey 2005: 640–4), by contrast, agrees with preservationism in that the memory process generates no new elements of justification or evidence. Memory cannot make justification and knowledge from nothing. Instead, the only way for memory to function as a generative source of justification is by removing defeaters and thereby unleashing the justificatory potential that was already present at the time the belief was initially entertained. All the elements required for a memory belief to be justified must already have been present when the belief was encoded. If the original belief had no justificatory potential, then memory cannot turn it into a justified belief. Memory can generate justification only by lifting justificatory elements that were previously rebutted or undermined by defeating evidence.

4. Skepticism about Memory Knowledge

"S remembers that p" implies that p is the case. Though memory entails truth, we are frequently mistaken in thinking that we remember something. Memories are not transparent to the mind in the sense that we can identify them and discriminate them from other states in any possible situation. Whether we genuinely or ostensibly remember that p we cannot tell just by reflection. But we all trust our ostensible memories to a greater or lesser degree. What reasons, if any, do we have for believing that events we seem to remember actually happened? What kind of justification do we have for accepting (at least some of) our ostensible memories as reliable information about the past? Do we, for example, have any way of ruling out Russell's (1995a: 159) hypothesis whereupon the world sprang into being five minutes ago, exactly as it then was, with a population that seemed to remember a wholly unreal past?

As was shown above (section 1) there are no intrinsic features of memory experiences from which it can be read off that they are memory experiences rather than imaginary experiences. Given that there are no memory markers, is it possible to validate ostensible memories by checking them against the past events they are (purportedly) about? This isn't possible because the past events have ceased to exist and hence are not available for comparison. Could we then validate ostensible memories by means of diaries, photographs, testimony, and the like? The problem with this proposal is that it begs the question at issue: the employment of this kind of evidence assumes the trustworthiness of some ostensible memories (one's own or someone else's). Any inductive argument to the effect that ostensible memories are, in general, reliable depends on other memories. And however great the probability of an inductive generalization might be, its probability is based on (what we take to be) past observations; and we have only memory to confirm those past observations. But how else, then, should we validate our ostensible memories?

Lewis (1949: ch. 11) suggests that we can validate our ostensible memories by examining the degree to which they cohere. Such coherence (he calls it *congruence*) is said to raise the probability of what is remembered to the level of practical certainty in a way analogous to that in which agreement of independently given testimonies can convince us that what is being testified is true. The idea is that the degree of coherence of our ostensible memories is sufficiently high for rational and practical reliance. But coherence can play this amplifying role only if the states of ostensible memory have some positive degree of initial credibility. And one might think that our ostensible memories lack the required initial credibility due to systematic delusion or general unreliability. Lewis argues that these prima facie possibilities are not genuine possibilities since they are either incoherent or contradict our experience. However, the argument against the possibility of systematic delusion depends on the contentious verifiability criterion of meaning (whereby a statement is meaningful if and only if it is either analytic or empirically verifiable). And even if the verifiability criterion of meaning is conceded, Lewis seems to overestimate the power of coherence to amplify probability.

Malcolm (1963: 193–6) and Shoemaker (1963: 229–34) take a very different approach to the task of validating our ostensible memories. They argue that the general reliability of ostensible memories is an analytic truth. There are two main arguments to the effect that ostensible memories are necessarily reliable. According to the first argument, if someone were to consistently make wildly inaccurate claims about the past and seemed to remember things that never happened, we would have to say not that he was misremembering, but that he has lost his understanding of "to remember." The problem with this argument is that habitual mistakes about memory claims need not be mistakes of meaning rather than fact. Even if someone's memory claims were consistently wrong, he could still have a correct understanding of the verb "to remember." That he correctly understands the verb "to remember" could be established by the fact that he uses it to talk only about things that he believes did happen and not about things that he believes he imagined. The second argument to the effect that ostensible memory is necessarily reliable rests on the observation that one cannot help thinking that one's confident memory beliefs constitute knowledge. However, just because one cannot question one's own confident memory beliefs doesn't mean that one cannot question someone else's claim concerning his confident memory beliefs. Moreover, even if it is incoherent to question one's confident memory beliefs, this doesn't mean that one couldn't be consistently false. The skeptical problem actually gets worse because not only is it possible that one's memory beliefs are consistently false but also one might be incapable of coherently entertaining this possibility.

In the end, none of the strategies for validating ostensible memories seem to work. We don't seem to be able to put our reliance on memories in question and then demonstrate the reliability of a given ostensible memory. As Russell (1995b: 154) remarks, "no memory proposition is, strictly speaking, verifiable, since nothing in the present or future makes any proposition about the past necessary." At the same time, we cannot secure a connection with epistemic rationality unless we trust at least some of our ostensible memories. This has led some philosophers (e.g., Burge 1993) to work out a transcendental argument to the effect that we have an a priori entitlement to trust our ostensible memories, unless there are stronger reasons not to do so.

References

Audi, R. (1995). "Memorial Justification," *Philosophical Topics* 23: 31–45.
Audi, R. (2003). *Epistemology: A Contemporary Introduction to the Theory of Knowledge*. 2nd edn. London: Routledge.
Bernecker, S. (2008). *The Metaphysics of Memory*. Dordrecht: Springer.
Bernecker, S. (2010). *Memory: A Philosophical Study*. Oxford: Oxford University Press.
Burge, T. (1993). "Content Preservation," *The Philosophical Review* 102: 457–88.
Conee, E. and Feldman, R. (2004). *Evidentialism: Essays in Epistemology*. Oxford: Clarendon.
Hume, D. (1978). *A Treatise of Human Nature*, ed. L.A. Selby-Bigge. 2nd edn. rev. P.H. Nidditch, Oxford: Oxford University Press.
James, W. (1890). *The Principles of Psychology*. 2 vols. London: Macmillan.
Lackey, J. (2005). "Memory as a Generative Epistemic Source," *Philosophy and Phenomenological Research* 70: 636–58.
Laird, J. (1920). *A Study in Realism*. Cambridge: Cambridge University Press.
Lewis, C.I. (1949). *An Analysis of Knowledge and Valuation*. La Salle: Open Court.
Locke, J. (1975). *An Essay Concerning Human Understanding*, ed. P.H. Nidditch. 2nd edn. Oxford: Clarendon.
Malcolm, N. (1963). *Knowledge and Certainty*. Ithaca, NY: Cornell University Press.
Margalit, A. (2002). *The Ethics of Memory*. Cambridge, MA: Harvard University Press.

McGrath, M. (2007). "Memory and Epistemic Conservatism," *Synthese* 157: 1–24.
Owens, D. (2000). *Reason Without Freedom*. London: Routledge.
Pappas, G. (1980). "Lost Justification," *Midwest Studies in Philosophy* 5: 127–34.
Plantinga, A. (1993). *Warrant and Proper Function*. New York: Oxford University Press.
Pollock, J.L. (1974). *Knowledge and Justification*. Princeton, NJ: Princeton University Press.
Reid, T. (1997). *An Inquiry into the Human Mind*, ed. D.R. Brookes. Edinburgh: University of Edinburgh Press.
Russell, B. (1995a). *The Analysis of Mind*, intro. T. Baldwin. London: Routledge.
Russell, B. (1995b). *An Inquiry into Meaning and Truth*, intro. T. Baldwin. London: Routledge.
Russell, B. (1997). *The Problems of Philosophy*. New York: Oxford University Press.
Shoemaker, S. (1963). *Self-Knowledge and Self-Identity*. Ithaca, NY: Cornell University Press.
Shoemaker, S. (1967). "Memory," in P. Edwards (ed.), *The Encyclopedia of Philosophy*. New York: Macmillan, vol. 5, 265–74.
Williamson, T. (2007). "On Being Justified in One's Head," in M. Timmons, J. Greco, and A.R. Mele (eds.), *Rationality and the Good: Critical Essays on the Ethics and Epistemology of Robert Audi*. Oxford: Oxford University Press, 106–22.

Further Reading

Dretske, F. and Yourgrau, P. (1983). "Lost Knowledge," *Journal of Philosophy* 80: 356–67.
Huemer, M. (1999). "The Problem of Memory Knowledge," *Pacific Philosophical Quarterly* 80: 346–57.
Locke, D. (1971). *Memory*. London: Macmillan.
Martin, C.B. and Deutscher, M. (1966). "Remembering," *The Philosophical Review* 75, 161–96.
Naylor, A. (1971). "B Remembers that P from Time T," *Journal of Philosophy* 68: 29–41.
Senor, T. (1993). "Internalistic Foundationalism and the Justification of Memory Belief," *Synthese* 94: 453–76.
Urmson, J.O. (1967). "Memory and Imagination," *Mind* 76: 83–91.

31
SEMANTIC KNOWLEDGE
Peter Ludlow

We often talk about people knowing the meanings of expressions and sentences (or utterances thereof), but this kind of knowledge is probably more extensive than we realize. In the first place, our semantic knowledge appears to be unbounded—for an unlimited number of expressions (up to memory and processing limitations) we know what those expressions can (and cannot) mean. For example, despite having never encountered the sentence before, we all appear to know the meaning of 'I want to adopt a cat that chased a mouse that stole some cheese from the bedroom of the oldest daughter of the 43rd President of the United States.'

Our semantic knowledge is also very broad, in that it covers a wide range of linguistic phenomena and intersects with a broad range of other linguistic abilities. For example, we appear to have syntactic knowledge that 'Who did John kiss?' is a correct way to form a question in English and that 'John kissed who?' is not, unless we stress the 'who' as in 'John kissed WHO?', and we know the natural interpretation of the sentence with a stressed 'who' is as a kind of "echo question"—we are not really asking who John kissed but, rather, we are asking the interlocutor to repeat herself because we did not hear or because we found the information so surprising on the first pass.

Some would say that we not only know the meanings of expressions, but we also know the rules by which we compute these meanings. And of course much of this knowledge (whether of sentence meanings or rules) appears to be tacit knowledge.

This semantic knowledge is not only very broad but it also has played a critical role both in syntactic theorizing in linguistics and in numerous philosophical arguments made during the past one hundred and twenty years. We might not recognize that many of the premises of our arguments in analytic philosophy rest upon our semantic knowledge, but, as we will see, they do.

In this chapter I explore some of the richness and complexity of our semantic knowledge, as well as some of the puzzles that arise when we begin to reflect on the nature of such knowledge. I'll begin in part 1 with a sample of some of the myriad semantic facts that we appear to have knowledge of, and point out some of the places where this semantic knowledge has been exploited in syntax and in analytic philosophy. I'll also take a look at the feasibility of our having knowledge of the underlying semantic rules. In part 2 I'll discuss the nature of this semantic knowledge: does it involve knowledge of the external world, or, as some have argued, is it "internal" knowledge? In part 3 I'll take up the question of our access to this knowledge—typically through linguistic intuitions or judgments—and discuss some of the worries about this form of access. Finally, in part 4, I'll address skeptical worries that have been raised by philosophers such as Kripke.

KINDS OF KNOWLEDGE

1. The Richness of Our Semantic Knowledge

Even the most mundane (utterances of) sentences belie a considerable amount of semantic knowledge. Consider the oft-used example 'The cat is on the mat.' We know that if this sentence is to be uttered intelligibly and truly there should be exactly one salient cat and exactly one salient mat (or that one of each can be made salient by our utterance and other contextual clues, like pointing, that we provide). We also know what kinds of things 'cat' is true of and we know what kinds of things 'mat' is true of, although our knowledge of the extensions of these terms might be incomplete or underdetermined—for example, there are things we know to be mats and things we are not so sure about (is that a mat or a discarded piece of cardboard on the floor?). To this end we know that whether something falls in the extension of 'mat' depends on human intentions in a way that falling in the extension of 'cat' does not. Further, as Higginbotham (1989b) has stressed, our knowledge of the meanings of expressions such as 'cat' and 'mat' are *partial*, but can also be expanded by learning how experts use the term 'cat' or by learning about ways people use the term 'mat' in new contexts (for example, in a gym or an art class). There might even be expectations about how much of the meaning we are expected to know.

Our semantic knowledge also extends to knowledge we have of secondary and tertiary ways expressions can be used truly. We know that one way for 'The cat is on the mat' to be true is for the cat to be on top of the mat, but not floating above the mat—the cat must be in physical contact with the mat. But we also know there are other ways an utterance of the sentence could be true. For example, we know that if we nail the doormat to the wall and the cat leaps up and clings to the mat with its claws, 'The cat is on the mat' is arguably true in this case too.

Although we might not express our knowledge in these terms, we know that 'cat' and 'mat' are count nouns (unlike mass nouns like 'water'), and that being 'on the mat' is a "stage level predicate" not an "individual level predicate" (unlike the predicates 'four legged' and 'calico'). That is, we know it is the sort of predicate that is likely only true of the cat temporarily. We also know that the sentence is in the present tense and hence that for it to be true the cat must be on the mat now.

Our semantic knowledge extends to inferential knowledge involving this simple case. If I know 'the cat is on the mat is true' then I know it will be true that 'the cat was on the mat', that 'something was on the mat' will be true etc.

There are many more bits of semantic knowledge that we have about simple sentences like 'The cat is on the mat', but our semantic knowledge extends to much more complex constructions as well. For example, we know that the following sentences are ambiguous.

(1) John went to the bank.
(2) Flying planes can be dangerous.
(3) Every man loves some woman.

Our knowledge also extends to subtle facts about the interpretation of pronouns and reflexives. For example, one fact that plays an important rule in binding theory in linguistics is that in (4) 'himself' can be associated with 'Bill' but not 'John' (unless, for some reason, John does not realize he is Bill).

(4) John said Bill likes himself.

SEMANTIC KNOWLEDGE

There are many more things we know about binding facts. Geach (1962) and many subsequent philosophers and linguists working in discourse representation theory have appealed to our knowledge that in a "donkey sentence" such as (5), the pronoun 'it' can be associated with 'a donkey,' but the pronoun cannot be associated with 'no donkey' in (6) (contrast with 'No donkey thinks someone should own it').

(5) Everyone who owns a donkey beats it.
(6) Everyone one who owns no donkey beats it.

Another piece of semantic knowledge relating to binding facts can be found in Chomsky (1986), who makes the case for innate linguistic structures involving binding theory by appealing to our knowledge that even though (7) is unambiguous, (8) is ambiguous between: (i) a reading in which we are asking what letter John filed without doing his daily reading and (ii) what letter John filed without reading it (the filed letter).

(7) John filed every letter without reading it.
(8) What letter did John file without reading?

We also have knowledge about facts that mix scope and binding facts, and this knowledge has been deployed in linguistic theorizing. For example, May (1977) made the case for a linguistic level of representation LF, by appealing to our knowledge that in (9), 'every city' can bind 'it', but only if it also takes scope over 'someone.'

(9) Someone from every city hates it.

Our knowledge also appears to extend to the interpretation of implicit linguistic elements. In Ludlow (1989) I made the case for implicit comparison classes being represented by appealing to our knowledge that the preferred comparison class in (10) is glasses of orange juice, but the preferred comparison class in (11) is just glasses.

(10) That glass of orange juice is large.
(11) That glass with orange juice in it is large.

As noted earlier, our semantic knowledge also includes knowledge about entailment relations. For example, philosophers and linguists working on generalized quantifier theory (e.g., Barwise and Cooper 1981; Higginbotham and May 1981) have relied upon the fact that if collies are dogs then we know that (12) entails (13) but not (14).

(13) Every dog barked.
(14) Every collie barked.
(15) Every animal barked.

Another case where our knowledge of entailment relations plays a role in analytic philosophy is in Davidson's (1967) case for events. Davidson's argument relied upon our knowledge that (16) entails (17).

(16) John buttered the toast with a knife.
(17) John buttered the toast.

And, of course, philosophical appeal to our knowledge of entailment relations goes back at least as far as Frege (1892), who famously made the case for senses by appealing to our knowledge that (18) does not entail (19).

(18) John believes the morning star is visible in the morning.
(19) John believes the evening star is visible in the evening.

The list goes on. I would argue that nearly every paper in analytic philosophy relies upon semantic knowledge in some crucial way. Of course, most papers do not put the matter this way. Typically they will talk about our "intuition" that (16) entails (17) or perhaps our "judgment" that this is the case, but this is false modesty. Clearly we do know that (16) entails (17), even if that knowledge is defeasible. Indeed part of the strength of these philosophical arguments is that they rest upon our semantic knowledge. Of course, there are many example sentences in philosophy papers that are less clear and that are disputed, but this does not mean that other semantic facts are not known to us, and good thing too, because those facts anchor some of our best and most important philosophical theories.

Clearly some of the semantic knowledge that I have just discussed would count as "tacit knowledge." Perhaps we never before thought about the possible interpretations of 'John filed every letter without reading' (indeed, Chomsky's argument crucially relies upon the assumption that we haven't). So we need to allow for the possibility of knowing that P in the case where we are not entertaining P, but if called upon to judge whether or not P is the case we would be in a position to truthfully and justifiably assert P, we would judge that P, and whatever other conditions we think normally apply to knowledge. This isn't the place to discuss tacit knowledge (see Evans (1981), Davies (1987), Wright (1986) for a discussion of tacit semantic knowledge), but I do want to note that most of our semantic knowledge would count as tacit in this rough and ready sense.

Some philosophers and linguists have contended that we not only have (tacit) knowledge of the semantic facts listed above, but also that we have knowledge of the rules that underwrite those facts. So, for example, we might think that there are rules that explain why 'himself' can be linked with 'Bill' and not 'John' in English (in Swedish such long-distance binding would be possible) and we might therefore think that we (tacitly) know those rules.

Chomsky himself seems ambivalent about whether we have knowledge of linguistic rules, shifting between talk about "knowing rules" and "cognizing rules." There is certainly some reason to avoid using the term 'knowledge' in this context. With the exception of the simplest lexical axioms, such rules are discovered by intensive and subtle theoretical study, and are typically offered tentatively as part of inferences to the best exploration of our linguistic competence. We don't have first-person access to such rules, and we can't produce them on request as we can with standard examples of tacit knowledge. At best, only theoretical linguists know what those rules are, and this knowledge seems to be a species of scientific or theoretical knowledge that is not in any interesting sense semantic knowledge.

In Ludlow (2010) I suggested that we can put the matter this way: we *know* semantic facts (and perhaps some simple lexical rules), and we *have* semantic rules. Presumably, the fact that we have the semantic rules that we do *explains* why we have the semantic knowledge that we do. Intuitions or judgments come into the picture in that they provide *evidence for* the semantic facts. The picture is something like the following.

(we have)   (we know)
Semantic Rules → explain/predict → **Semantic Facts** ← evidence for ← **Semantic Judgments**
                      ← are evidence for ←

Of course, if we are to have knowledge of semantic facts everything turns on whether our semantic judgments are reliable. I will turn to this question in section 3. First, however, it will be useful to say a bit more about the nature of semantic knowledge (assuming for now that we have it).

2. The Nature of Our Semantic Knowledge

Some philosophers and linguists have supposed that if we talk about knowledge of meaning then we must ipso facto be talking about knowledge of some kind of internal mental state—knowledge of meaning entails that meanings must be in the head.

I don't wish to bring up the debate about externalism about content and the idea that "meanings ain't in the head" (cf. Putnam 1975), but I do want to stress that when we talk about knowing the meaning of an expression or knowing what an expression refers to we are not committed to this knowledge being Cartesian. To the contrary, it is completely plausible to invoke an anti-Cartesian conception of knowledge and contend that we have knowledge of semantic facts like the following.

(20) 'water' refers to water

The idea is that our knowledge of this fact straddles language and the external world. It tells us that (to a first approximation) the word spelled w-a-t-e-r refers to (is used to refer to) the substance water.[1]

Two confusions must now be avoided. First, nothing about the possibility of such knowledge tells against a Cartesian picture about the syntax of natural language. As I argued in Ludlow (2003) we could quite easily wed an externalist picture about semantics to a Chomskyan internalist picture about syntax. The latter would be a theory of language as a chapter of narrow psychology, and semantics would be a story about our knowledge of the relations between those narrow representations and the external world.

The second confusion would be in supposing that externalism about semantics implies that semantics (and our knowledge of semantics) could not be a chapter in cognitive psychology. To the contrary, such a theory could be a chapter in cognitive psychology provided that we follow Burge (1986) in understanding cognitive psychology in an appropriately anti-Cartesian way. Psychology need not be construed as "methodologically solipsistic" in the sense of Fodor (1980).

This point holds even if we wish to talk about knowing semantic rules and not just semantic facts. There is no reason why the rules of a semantic theory cannot, as it were, straddle language and the world. Indeed, we might take (20) as a rule or axiom in our semantic theory; nothing in that would tell against the idea that a semantic theory (or a theory of our knowledge of semantic rules) could not be part of cognitive psychology.

There is perhaps a subsidiary confusion that needs to be avoided here. If we introduce (20) into our semantic theory as a basic lexical axiom, and if we say that an agent knows the rule, and if we say that our theory of the agent's knowledge is a chapter in cognitive psychology, this is not to say that the rule is in the agent's head. To the contrary, we might say that the rule is *represented* internally, but that the represented rule itself is an abstract object (linking language and the world) that is the object of our knowledge.

3. Concerns about Our Semantic Knowledge

As I noted earlier, we can think of semantic facts being things that we know, but how do we come to know these facts? For the most part we rely upon our first-person judgments, and this naturally tends to be a source of concern. Judgments, after all, can be mistaken. We might misjudge the meaning of an expression and we might misjudge an inferential relation as holding when it does not. Indeed, examples of such misjudgment are all too common. Because of the possibility of error in cases such as these, a number of philosophers and linguists have opted for talking about semantic intuitions in place of judgments.

Following Williamson (2004), discussing philosophical "intuitions" more generally, I think we should resist the move to talk of intuitions. Williams puts the case for resistance in the following way.

> what are called "intuitions" . . . are just applications of our ordinary capacities for judgement. We think of them as intuitions when a special kind of scepticism about those capacities is salient. Like scepticism about perception, scepticism about judgement pressures us into conceiving our evidence as facts about our internal psychological states: here, facts about our conscious inclinations to make judgements about some topic rather than facts about the topic itself. But the pressure should be resisted, for it rests on bad epistemology: specifically, on an impossible ideal of unproblematically identifiable evidence.

Of course the mere fact that we swap talk of intuitions for talk of judgments does not ameliorate worries about the character of our semantic judgments. And to be sure, linguists have expressed a number of concerns about the reliability of our judgments in semantics (and linguistics more generally).

Linguistics papers and philosophy papers are full of semantic judgments that are disputed, but this does not tell against semantic knowledge. It rather suggests that in arguing for one theory over another we are often forced to seek out more subtle examples, and some of these judgments are tentative. Undisputed cases don't appear in papers because they are already incorporated into the available candidate semantic theories. A theory that predicts 'The cat is on the mat' to mean that every dog is smoking orange peels will not be in the discussion.

Still, even for simple cases such as 'the cat is on the mat' one might press on why we should think that semantic judgments are sufficient to support semantic knowledge. There are two routes one can go here. The first, taken by Stich (1972) is to divorce the judgments from the objects of judgment (in this case semantic facts). The second route is to argue that we have good independent evidence to believe in the reliability of our semantic judgments. Let's start with Stich's approach.

According to Stich (1972) linguistic theory is fundamentally an attempt to account for our faculty of judgment or linguistic intuitions by systematizing or axiomatizing our intuitions. Linguistic theory, then, would be a theory of our linguistic judgments. Semantic theory, would simply be a theory of judged entailment relations without regard to whether those relations tracked actual logical relations.

There might be some interest in such a project, but at a minimum it does not seem to me to be the project that linguists are engaged in. For linguists, intuitions or judgments are data that support linguistic facts. Chomsky (1982), for example, is pretty explicit about this point: "To say that linguistics is the study of introspective judgments would be like saying that physics is the study of meter readings, photographs, and so on, but nobody says that" (pp. 33–34). Likewise, semantic knowledge would not have much philosophical interest if it were simply knowledge of the meaning judgments and entailment relations we happen to make. Stich rescues judgments, but the Cartesianism returns in that the external object of those judgments is lost.

If we allow that there are semantic facts is there some way we can show that semantic judgments are reliable? There are a number of answers here. In the first place we can find widespread agreement on these judgments at least within our linguistic communities. We might not agree on all cases, but the mere fact that we successfully communicate at all suggests that we agree on many semantic facts.

It is also incorrect to think that semantic judgments are our only route to semantic facts. Inferential facts are a case in point. Getting logical inferences wrong can have fatal consequences, and we have, of course, developed logical models that can be used to evaluate the reliability of our entailment judgments.

Furthermore, analysis of corpora data can give the lie to claims about the possibility or impossibility of certain uses of language and interpretations of linguistic expressions. Like our semantic judgments corpora data might contain error, but this does not mean that it cannot be a source of semantic knowledge or that it cannot be used to calibrate and test our semantic knowledge.

Of course most of the semantic knowledge we have is not checked against a corpus or formalized and checked for logical coherence. We rely upon our judgments themselves, and we presumably have no idea *how* those judgments were formed and few of us might be in a position to explain *why* those judgments are reliable. This suggests that to a first approximation any account of semantic knowledge is going to be reliabilist. That is, our semantic knowledge is underwritten by the fact that it is the product of reliable processes, much like some people have claimed for perceptual knowledge. We need not know what those processes are (just like in the case of perception most of us simply don't know); what entitles us to semantic and perceptual knowledge is that the relevant processes are in fact reliable.

4. Skepticism about Semantic knowledge

In the previous section we canvassed a number of worries about the reliability of our semantic judgments and, by extension, about the extent of our semantic knowledge, but some philosophers (notably Quine, Kripke, and Wittgenstein) have offered full-on skeptical arguments that, when applied to semantic knowledge, appear to go to the heart of whether semantic knowledge is even possible. Let's focus on Kripke's argument, which he offers as a possible interpretation of Wittgenstein's argument.

Kripke's Version of Wittgenstein's Skeptical Argument

What fact can one appeal to in order to justify saying that a particular rule used in the past is identical to the rule being used now? Take Kripke's (1982) example of someone (let's say Jones) who determines that '68 plus 57 = 125' is true. The skeptic then asks Jones how she knows that the rule meant by 'plus' right now is the same rule she meant by 'plus' in the past. Suppose that Jones has never before added two numbers totaling greater than 57. Is it not possible that in the past Jones was using 'plus' to refer to another rule altogether, perhaps one which we might call 'quus,' which is like plus in all respects except that when two numbers totaling greater than 57 are quused, the answer is 5, not 125? Jones would surely be right in saying that the skeptic is crazy. But what fact about Jones (or the world) could we point to show that she was in fact using the rule plus before? Of course if we cannot succeed, then there is not merely a problem for past uses of 'plus' but for current one's as well. When we say that we are using an expression to denote a particular rule, what fact backs up our assertion? As Kripke puts the problem:

> Since the sceptic who supposes that I meant quus cannot be answered, there is no fact about me that distinguishes my meaning plus and my meaning quus. Indeed there is no fact that distinguishes my meaning a definite function by 'plus' (which determines my responses in new cases) and my meaning nothing at all.
>
> (Kripke 1982: 21)

It is natural to think we can get around the skeptical argument by saying that the addition function is, in turn, defined by the rule for counting, and the quus rule violates the counting rule at a more basic level. But here the Kripkean skeptic can reply that there will be a non-standard interpretation of the rule denoted by 'count.' Perhaps Jones is really using the rule quount.

There is a temptation to say the skeptical argument is nothing more than Goodman's puzzle about grue. Recall, that given a predicate 'grue,' which is true of objects that are green before the year 2100, and blue thereafter, any evidence we find which confirms that all emeralds are green will also confirm all emeralds are grue. Applied to the case of Jones, we could say the following. Until she begins to add numbers greater than 57, any evidence that confirms that Jones is following the rule addition, will also confirm that she is using the rule quaddition.

Kripke thinks there is an important difference in these cases. According to Kripke, Goodman's argument presupposes the stability of our semantic knowledge—in particular he presupposes the extensions of 'grue' and 'green' to be understood. In effect, one has to assume semantic knowledge to even get the grue puzzle off the ground.

There is a great deal of literature on Kripke's version of the skeptical argument, but if we focus on the narrow question of whether the argument really undermines our semantical knowledge I think that Soames (1998) provides the best answer to the core part of the argument (other aspects of the argument are not directly engaged by Soames). According to Soames, Kripke's skeptical argument incorporates two different notions of determination (as in what it is that *determines* that I meant plus instead of quus). The first is an epistemological notion of determination and the second is a notion of determination that is grounded in metaphysical necessity.

On the question of epistemological determination, Soames concedes that if meaning statements are grounded in non-intentional facts we wouldn't be in a position to know how they are grounded or to demonstrate the truth of the intentional claims, but why should we expect to know this? Wasn't this the whole point of Kripke's case for necessary a posteriori truths?

> [the skeptics] try to establish that no collection of nonintentional truths will allow us to *demonstrate* the truth of the relevant intentional claims. This, I have suggested, is tantamount to an attempt to convince us that claims about meaning (and propositional attitudes) are not a priori consequences of any set of nonintentional truths.
>
> On this point it must be admitted that the skeptic has a strong case. . . . I don't know how to give such a derivation and I am not sure that any is possible . . .
>
> If it were clear that any necessary consequence of a set of claims P was also an a priori consequence of P, this admission would provide the skeptic with just what he needs; for then he could force me to admit that claims about meaning may not be necessary consequences of nonintentional truths. That would conflict with my conviction that meaning facts must supervene on nonintentional facts, and so would threaten my pretheoretic commitment to meaning facts. However, this argumentative strategy fails. Thanks to the work of Kripke and others, it has become clear that many necessary consequences of propositions are not apriori consequences of them. Consequently my admission that claims about meanings may not be apriori consequences of nonintentional truths need not undermine my belief that they are necessary consequences of those truths.
>
> (Soames 1998: 230–231)

In effect, if there are some nonintentional facts that necessarily determine the rule I am following, it does not follow that I should be in a position to know these facts (as we are taught by Kripke 1980). A remarkable error for Kripke, of all people, to have made.

With respect to the notion of metaphysical determination, Soames argues that however we broaden the relevant class of non-intensional facts, there is no reason for us to reject the metaphysical determination—the idea that meaning facts are necessarily determined by nonintensional facts.

> Would the result change if we enlarged the set of potential meaning-determining truths still further to include not only all truths about my dispositions to verbal behavior, but also all truths about (i) the internal physical states of my brain, (ii) my causal and historical relationships to things in my environment, (iii) my (nonintentionally characterized) interactions with other members of my linguistic community, (iv) their dispositions to verbal behavior, and so on? Is there a possible world in which someone conforms to all those facts—precisely the facts that characterize me in the actual world—and yet that person does not mean anything by '+'?
>
> I think not. Given my conviction that in the past I did mean addition by '+', and given also my conviction that if there are intentional facts, then they don't float free of everything else, I am confident that there is no such world. Although I cannot identify the smallest set of nonintensional facts about me in the actual world on which mean facts supervene, I am confident that they do supervene. Why shouldn't I be?
>
> (Soames 1998: 229)

In sum, Soames is arguing for a stable philosophical fixed point in which we hold that meanings are necessarily determined by a broad range of nonintensional facts, but in which we are not in a position to know *how* they are determined. But lacking knowledge of how the meanings are determined does not undermine the semantic knowledge itself.

Conclusion

Our semantic knowledge is not only extensive, but also lies at the foundation of many of our philosophical and linguistic theories—indeed, if Kripke is right, even many skeptical arguments (such as the grue puzzle) presuppose that our semantic knowledge is intact. Concerns about the status of semantic knowledge and skepticism about semantic knowledge are, therefore, daggers aimed at the heart of analytic philosophy. In the face of this we need to ask: Are we entitled to claims of semantic knowledge? Extant skeptical arguments about semantic knowledge appear to fall short, but there remain concerns about particular claims of fact and the veracity of the semantic judgments that support those claims. Fortunately we have ways of corroborating semantic judgments with other sources of evidence. This opens the door to a reliabilist story on which we are entitled to our semantic knowledge because of the reliability of our semantic judgments. Of course, the reliability of semantic judgments (like all linguistic judgments) has been a point of controversy, to say the least.

Note

1 Obviously, as Chomsky (2003) has stressed, our knowledge of the meaning of 'water' is much more robust than this, but (20) at least reflects some of what we know. In the terminology of Dummett (1975) (20) is not a "robust" description of what we know but a "modest" one. See also Higginbotham (1989a) on this point.

Bibliography

Barwise, J., and R. Cooper. 1981. "Generalized Quantifiers and Natural Language." *Linguistics and Philosophy* 4, 159–219.
Burge, T. 1986. "Individualism and Psychology." *The Philosophical Review* 95, 3–45.
Chomsky, N. 1982. *The Generative Enterprise: A Discussion with Riny Huybregts and Henk van Riemsdijk*. Dordrecht: Foris.
Chomsky, N. 1986. *Knowledge of Language*. New York: Praeger.
Chomsky, N. 2003. "Reply to Ludlow." In N. Hornstein and L. Antony (eds.), *Chomsky and His Critics*. Oxford: Blackwell Publishers, 287–295.
Davidson, D. 1967. "The Logical Form of Action Sentences." In *Essays on Actions and Events*. Oxford: Oxford University Press, 1980.
Davies, M. 1987. "Tacit Knowledge and Semantic Theory: Can a Five Per Cent Difference Matter?" *Mind* 96, 441–462.
Dummett, M. 1975. "What is a Theory of Meaning?" In S. Guttenplan (ed.) *Mind and Language*. Oxford: Oxford University Press, 97–138.
Evans, Gareth. 1981. "Semantic Theory and Tacit Knowledge." In S. Holtzman and C. Leich (eds.) *Wittgenstein: To Follow a Rule*. London: Routledge and Kegan Paul.
Fodor, J. 1980. "Methodological Solipsism Considered as a Research Strategy in Cognitive Psychology." *Behavioral and Brain Sciences* 3, 63–73.
Frege, G. 1892, "Sinn und Bedeutung," *Zeitschrift fur Philosophie und philosophische Kritik*, 100, 25–50 (published as "Sense and Reference," in P. Geach and M. Black (eds.), *Translations from the Philosophical Writings of Gottlob Frege*. Oxford: Blackwell, 1952.
Geach, Peter. 1962. *Reference and Generality*. Ithaca: Cornell University Press.
Higginbotham, J. 1989a. "Elucidations of Meaning." *Linguistics and Philosophy* 12, 465–517.

Higginbotham, J. 1989b. "Knowledge of Reference." In Alexander George (ed.), *Reflections on Chomsky*. Oxford: Blackwell, 153–174.

Higginbotham, J. and R. May. 1981. "Questions, Quantifiers, and Crossing." *Linguistic Review* 1, 41–79.

Kripke, S. 1980. *Naming and Necessity*. Cambridge, MA: Harvard University Press.

Kripke, S. 1982. *Wittgenstein on Rules and Private Language*. Cambridge, MA: Harvard University Press.

Ludlow, P. 1989. "Implicit Comparison Classes." *Linguistics and Philosophy* 12, 519–533.

Ludlow, P. 2003. "Referential Semantics for I-Languages?" In N. Hornstein and L. Antony (eds.), *Chomsky and His Critics*. Oxford: Blackwell Publishers, 140–161.

Ludlow, P. 2010. *The Philosophy of Generative Linguistics*. Oxford: Oxford University Press.

May, R. 1977. *The Grammar of Quantification*. Unpublished Ph.D. dissertation, MIT.

Putnam, H. 1975. "The Meaning of 'Meaning'." In K. Gunderson (ed.), *Language, Mind and Knowledge. Vol. 7, Minnesota Studies in the Philosophy of Science*. Minneapolis: University of Minnesota Press.

Soames, S. 1998. "Skepticism about Meaning: Indeterminacy, Normativity, and the Rule-Following Paradox." In A. Kazmi (ed.), *Meaning and Reference. The Canadian Journal of Philosophy*, Supplementary Volume 23.

Stich, S. 1972. "Grammar, Psychology, and Indeterminacy." *Journal of Philosophy* 69, 799–818.

Williamson, T. 2004. "Philosophical 'Intuitions' and Scepticism about Judgement." *Dialectica* 58, 109–153.

Wright, C. 1986. "Theories of Meaning and Speakers' Knowledge." In S.G. Shanker (ed.), *Philosophy in Britain Today*. Albany: SUNY Press, 267–307.

32
SCIENTIFIC KNOWLEDGE
Peter Achinstein

The claim is often made that scientific inquiry is superior to other forms of inquiry because it is capable of supplying knowledge of the world, and, of all forms of inquiry, it is the most likely to do so. Many of those who make this claim subscribe to the following Principal Theses:

1. Science aims at and can achieve knowledge of the world.
2. Knowledge in science requires proof, the standards for which are universal for all the sciences, and can be formulated in a set of rules called the "scientific method."
3. Although unproved propositions (sometimes called "hypotheses") are introduced into science for purposes of investigation, scientists are not justified in believing them until they are proved in accordance with the standards set by the "scientific method."

In what follows, three prominent but very different historical views about scientific knowledge will be discussed, each of which subscribes to the three Principal Theses. Afterwards various more contemporary positions will be examined that contradict one or more of these three ideas.

Part I. Views Defending the Three Principal Theses

1. *Cartesian Rationalism* René Descartes (1988), in his *Rules for the Direction of the Mind*, written between 1619 and 1628, and published posthumously in 1701, offers 21 rules for how to gain scientific knowledge. The view is a form of Rationalism according to which, although experience can suggest ideas to the scientist, whether these ideas are true can be known only by pure thought of a sort characteristic of mathematics. Rule 1 states that the aim of science is not just truth, but justified truth. Rule 2 states that the only kind of legitimate justification in science is that which leads to certainty, and not mere probability. By "certainty" Descartes does not mean "beyond reasonable doubt" (by analogy with a criminal legal standard), but "beyond any possible doubt" (as he envisages being the case in mathematics). Rule 3, the most important one for our purposes, is that the only way to obtain truth that is justified beyond any possible doubt is to employ what he calls "intuition" and "deduction." The former he characterizes as "the indubitable conception of a clear and attentive mind which proceeds from the light of reason." His examples include one's thought that one exists, that one is thinking, that a triangle has three sides, and that 2 + 2 = 4. Their truth is immediately evident to us

just by thinking them. By "deduction," Descartes means a continuous, uninterrupted train of reasoning to some proposition that follows necessarily from other propositions known with certainty. Example: an inference from $2 + 2 = 4$ and $3 + 1 = 4$ to $2 + 2 = 3 + 1$. In rules 5–8, Descartes advocates solving scientific problems by raising a series of more and more basic questions that will lead eventually to a set of "intuitions" from which "deductions" can be made to propositions that will solve the problems. Descartes makes it clear in rule 12 that although sense experience might suggest ideas about the world (e.g., that two points determine a line, or that a force is required to change a moving body's direction), the truth of these ideas is established scientifically only by an "intuition" of the facts they represent or by a "deduction" of these facts from others similarly established.

Descartes intends these rules to be applicable to the sciences generally, not just to mathematics. One of the best places to see this in his work is in his derivations in physics of what he takes to be the laws governing bodies in motion (in his work *Principles of Philosophy* (1971)). From "intuitions" about motions of bodies (including that the "quantity of motion" of a body is its volume times its speed), and from "intuitions" concerning God (in particular that God exists and is the "efficient cause of all things," including motion, and that God is immutable), Descartes "deduces" a fundamental principle in his physics: God sustains the total quantity of motion in the universe, which is therefore conserved, even if the motions of individual bodies vary. The latter is an early formulation of what came to be known as the principle of conservation of momentum, in which "momentum" is understood as mass (not Cartesian volume) times velocity (which contains not only the Cartesian idea of speed but direction as well). From his conservation of motion principle Descartes deduces three "laws of nature," the first two of which yield what came to be known as the law of inertia—that moving bodies if left to themselves tend to continue to move in straight lines. With this idea Descartes provides a revolutionary answer to the age-old question of why projectiles continue in motion after they are launched: they do so because they are already in motion and there is no force acting to change that motion.

Descartes subscribes to the three Principal Theses: science aims at and can achieve knowledge of the world. This requires proof beyond all possible doubt, which can be achieved via the method of "intuitions" and "deductions," satisfying standards universal for all the sciences. While unproved propositions (e.g., ones suggested by sense experience) can be introduced for purposes of investigation, scientists are not justified in believing them until they are proved in the Cartesian way; otherwise their truth can be doubted.

2. *Inductivism: Newton and Mill* Descartes' rationalist views about science were completely rejected by Empiricists, who hold that knowledge about the physical world is possible only through observation and experiment, not through Cartesian intuitions, which are notoriously unreliable, nor from Cartesian deductions from these. One of the most prominent forms of empiricism in science, Inductivism, was defended in the late seventeenth and early eighteenth centuries by Isaac Newton (1999) in his great scientific work *Mathematical Principles of Natural Philosophy* (usually called the *Principia*), and in the mid-nineteenth century by John Stuart Mill (1872) in his philosophical work *A System of Logic*.

Book 3 of Newton's *Principia*, in which he derives his law of universal gravitation, begins with four "rules for the study of natural philosophy." Although following these rules does not guarantee scientific knowledge of the physical world, it is the best way to proceed to gain such knowledge. The first two rules pertain to inferences to causes of phenomena from observed effects:

(RULE 1): If one cause will suffice to explain phenomena, more causes should not be inferred.
(RULE 2): From effects of the same kind, the same kind of cause should be inferred.

So, to use Newton's own examples, if one universal force of gravity suffices to explain the motions of all the planets in our solar system, one should not infer a different force of gravity for each planet; and if stones in Europe and America fall in the same way, then one should infer that they have the same cause.

The third and fourth rules express ideas about inductive reasoning in which generalizations are inferred from observations and experiments on bodies:

(RULE 3): Properties that belong to all bodies on which experiments can be made should be inferred to belong to all bodies universally.
(RULE 4): One should consider such inductive generalizations to be true, or approximately true, until new phenomena are discovered that show that the generalizations need to be revised.

Newton provides some simple examples:

> The extension of bodies is known to us only through our senses, and yet there are bodies beyond the range of these senses; but because extension is found in all sensible bodies, it is ascribed to all bodies universally. . . . That all bodies are movable and persevere in motion or in rest by means of certain forces (which we call forces of inertia) we infer from finding these properties in the bodies that we have seen.

These two examples are of special interest because they are examples cited by the rationalist Descartes as examples of propositions that can be known only by pure reason. (For Descartes we can "intuit" that bodies are extended in space; and we can "deduce" that they persevere in their motion, as Descartes' first and second laws of motion state.) By contrast, Newton is claiming that such generalizations can be known to be true only by observations of extended and moving bodies, not by pure thought. Newton goes on to show how each of his four methodological rules for the study of natural philosophy is actually used in the derivation of his law of gravity from observed phenomena involving the motions of the known planets and their moons.

John Stuart Mill (1872) offers a formulation of scientific inductivism that is more philosophically developed than Newton's, though without Newton's applications to sophisticated scientific examples. He defines induction as "the process by which we conclude that what is true of certain individuals of a class is true of the whole class, or that what is true at certain times will be true in similar circumstances at all times." So if all the As examined are Bs, and we make an inference to the proposition that all As are Bs, this is what Mill calls an induction. Not all inductions are justified; it depends on the number and variety of the As examined and found to be B, on the sorts of properties A and B are, and on additional knowledge we have about these and related properties.

Among the most important general propositions of concern to scientists are laws causally relating properties, e.g., "forces produce accelerations." Mill presents four "methods of experimental inquiry" for determining whether a generalization inferred inductively is truly causal. This involves not just observing As and Bs but performing experiments on them. Suppose that bodies on which forces are exerted always accelerate. To determine whether this is a causal relationship Mill's first method (the "method of agreement") tells us to exert forces on a variety of different types of bodies (e.g., ones with different masses, sizes, shapes, and positions) such that the only relevant property in common is that all these bodies were subjected to a force. If all such bodies accelerate then we can infer not only that forces and accelerations are constantly conjoined, but that forces cause accelerations. Another method, the "method of difference," asserts that we can test for causation by examining two groups of bodies in which the only relevant difference is that in one group forces are exerted while in the other they are not. If bodies in the first group accelerate but not those in the second, we can infer that forces cause accelerations.

In the theoretical sciences, effects are often explained by reference to multiple causes. For such purposes Mill introduces his "deductive method," which requires three steps in order to infer the truth of a theoretical system: causal-inductive generalizations from experiments and observations to a set of causal laws comprising the system; "ratiocination," which involves deductive inferences showing how this set, if true, can explain and predict various observable effects; and verification of the new effects predicted. If and only if these three steps are appropriately followed, we can infer the truth of the theoretical system.

Both Newton and Mill subscribe to the three Principal Theses about scientific knowledge. They agree that science aims at and can achieve knowledge of the world; that such knowledge requires proof (indeed Mill, in his initial definition of "induction," defines it as "the operation of discovering and proving general propositions"); and that the standards of proof are universal. However, their concept of proof in the sciences is very different from Descartes'. For them, it is proof "beyond reasonable doubt," not "beyond any possible doubt." A proof can be overturned by new experiments and observations not previously available to the scientific community. However, if the standards of proof advocated by Newton and Mill are satisfied by scientists—i.e., if the "scientific methods" advocated by Newton and Mill are appropriately applied—then the scientists are justified in believing the propositions "proved." Finally, although Newton in his writings introduces unproved propositions, and Mill allows them to be introduced for purposes of investigation, neither of these inductivists permits inferences to their truth. Their claim is that scientists are not justified in believing them until they are proved in accordance with the standards of the scientific method they propose.

3. *Inference to the Best Explanation: William Whewell* In the mid-nineteenth century, the British scientist, philosopher, and historian of science, William Whewell (1840), formulated a scientific method that, although empirical, he regarded as very different from, and far superior to, the inductivism of Newton and Mill. (In fact the contemporaries Mill and Whewell debated each other in print.) Whewell believed that the methods of Newton and Mill would allow scientists to infer the truth of theories postulating unobserved causes only if the latter were of a type previously observed. But, Whewell claimed, it is possible to have knowledge of the truth of theories postulating unobserved

causes of a sort very different from any previously observed. One of his favorite examples was the wave theory of light that postulates unobservable transverse waves undulating in an unobservable ether.

Whewell's method contains two stages, the first of which is the discovery not of the truth of a hypothesis, but of the idea of the hypothesis. His example is that of Kepler discovering the idea that the planet Mars travels in an elliptical orbit about the sun. This involves two things: observations of the phenomena (in this case observations, made by the astronomer Tycho Brahe, of the position of Mars at different times of the year); and the introduction of "some general conception, which is given, not by the phenomena, but by the mind" (in Kepler's case, an idea that connects Tycho's observations, namely, that the observed points lie on an ellipse). Whewell calls the observations plus the mental conception a "colligation" of the facts, which involves a "conjecture," not an inference to its truth. The conjecture needs to be tested, which is the second stage of Whewell's method.

In the testing stage Whewell imposes various conditions, the satisfaction of which will allow one to conclude with certainty that the hypothesis is true. First, the hypothesis should not only explain phenomena that have been observed but also predict ones not yet observed. Second, it should explain and predict phenomena "of a kind different from those which were contemplated in the formation of our hypothesis." Whewell speaks of this as the "consilience of inductions." In the third condition Whewell introduces the idea that a hypothesis is usually part of a system or theory whose members are not framed all at once, but are introduced, added to, and altered over time, as a result of discoveries of new phenomena. If in this process the theory becomes simpler, more unified, and more coherent, then one can infer with the highest certainty that it is true; if it becomes more complex, less unified, and less coherent, then one can infer that it is false. On the basis of these three criteria Whewell proclaimed that, given the optical phenomena that had been observed by the mid-nineteenth century, one could confidently infer the truth of the wave theory of light and the falsity of the competing particle theory.

Whewell's scientific method is most akin to what contemporary writers such as Gilbert Harman (1965) and Peter Lipton (2004) have called "inference to the best explanation." The idea is holistic, since one most confidently infers the truth not of an isolated hypothesis, but of a system of hypotheses; and one does so if that system provides the best—the simplest, most unifying, most coherent—explanation of all the data. Whewell regards such inferences as providing a proof of the system and therefore knowledge of its truth, which is what science aims at. Accordingly, like the other methodologists discussed above, he subscribes to the three Principal Theses.

In his critical discussion of Whewell, Mill notes that one of the most important differences between them can be seen in the context of Mill's "deductive method," which also involves a theoretical system of hypotheses. For Whewell what is required to infer the truth of the system is given in Mill's "ratiocination" (explaining and predicting various phenomena) and his "verification" (determining by observation and experiment whether predictions are correct). But, Mill complains, Whewell has omitted the first "inductive" step, which requires causal-inductive reasoning to the set of hypotheses considered in "ratiocination." Otherwise, Mill says, different conflicting theories could all be inferred using Whewell's criteria. (For a discussion of this issue and others in the Mill–Whewell debate, see Achinstein 1991.)

Part II. Views Attacking the Principal Theses

Various more recent views will be considered, each of which rejects one or more of the Principal Theses.

1. *"Science Does Not Aim at and Cannot Achieve Knowledge of the World"* One of the strongest forms of this view is the "Falsificationist" position of Karl Popper (1959) in the twentieth century. Following Hume's discussion of the justification of induction in the eighteenth century, Popper regards any inference to the truth of a general scientific hypothesis or theory from particular observations and experiments to be unjustified. Such inferences cannot be shown to be valid a priori by deductive reasoning; nor can they be justified empirically by their past success, since that would be using this form of reasoning to justify itself.

Popper's view is that the aim of science is not to prove that theories are true, but to eliminate false ones. For this purpose he formulates a falsificationist version of a scientific method called "hypothetico-deductivism" or "the method of hypothesis."

On his version science begins with observations and questions about them. To answer these questions the scientist introduces a set of hypotheses, which are to be treated as guesses or conjectures, rather than as inferences from the observations. From the hypotheses conclusions are to be inferred deductively. If any of these conclusions can be shown to be false by observation and experiment, then the set of hypotheses must be revised or replaced. If all the observational conclusions turn out to be true, then, because of Popper's rejection of non-deductive reasoning, we cannot infer that the hypotheses are true or even probable. All we can say is: "So far so good; the hypotheses have not been shown to be false." The best procedure for the scientist, in response to a set of observations and questions about them, is to propose the strongest, most general hypotheses that have not yet been refuted by experiment and observation, and try to refute them by severely testing their observational consequences. Although we cannot have knowledge of their truth, we can and should proceed to root out error. Popper believes that this is how the best scientists in fact operate.

A less extreme view is held by a group of scientists and philosophers under the general category "anti-realism" or "instrumentalism." It begins by distinguishing the "observable" part of the world from the "unobservable." Take, for example, the electron theory designed to explain cathode rays produced by an electrical discharge in a highly evacuated cathode tube. The observable part of the world would include the scintillations produced by the rays on the glass of the tube; the unobservable part would include the negatively charged electrons postulated by J.J. Thomson in 1897 to explain these scintillations. What the anti-realist says is that scientists can have knowledge of truth of claims about the observable part of the world, but not the unobservable.

The basic idea is that science is empirical, and hence can only sanction inferences to what is observable in nature, not what is unobservable. For example, Pierre Duhem (1954), a French physicist who also wrote works in the history and philosophy of science, says this:

> Now these two questions—Does there exist a material reality distinct from sensible appearances? And What is the nature of this reality?—do not have their source in experimental method, which is acquainted only with sensible appearances and can discover nothing beyond them. The resolution of these questions transcends the methods used by physics; it is the object of metaphysics.

And the contemporary philosopher of science Bas van Fraassen (1980) similarly writes: "I explicate the general limits [of experience] as follows: *Experience can give us information only about what is both observable and actual.*" For such anti-realists empirical science cannot give us knowledge of the unobservable world. What it can do is give us theories that are, in van Fraassen's words, "empirically adequate," that is, theories whose claims about the observable part of the world are true. Such theories might make claims about unobservables such as electrons, but these theories are to be judged not on the grounds of their truth about electrons but on the grounds of whether what they entail about observable "electron effects" is true. If a theory postulates unobservables, then at best we are justified in believing only that the theory is empirically adequate, not that the theory is true.

Responses

At the heart of many responses to Popper's falsificationism is a rejection of two of his main claims: (i) that, by contrast to deduction, inductive reasoning is invalid; (ii) that induction is not in fact employed by good scientists. The second claim is addressed by pointing to many actual uses of inductive reasoning in the sciences, even explicit ones, as in Newton's derivation of his law of universal gravitation. The first claim, the most controversial one, can be addressed, in part at least, by asking why Popper believes that deductive reasoning is valid. If he says that deductive reasoning always leads from truths to truths, then that claim depends on the assumption that he means "valid" deductive reasoning. (There are fallacious deductive arguments in which truths do not always lead to truths.) But then an analogous claim can be made for inductive reasoning: "valid" inductive reasoning leads from truths to *probable* truths. If the claim is that *some* inductive arguments are invalid, then that is something with which inductivists can agree. But this hardly establishes the invalidity of induction in general. (The topic of the justification of induction is a large and complex one; for discussions of various issues, see the anthology of Swinburne (1974)).

At the heart of responses to "anti-realism" lies the question of why anti-realists such as Duhem and van Fraassen assume that scientists can make inferences only about what is observable, not what is unobservable. These writers offer no argument whatever for this claim: *they simply make this a fundamental assumption*. Yet scientists do in fact make causal-inductive inferences from observed effects to unobservable entities, forces, and properties—as Newton did to the universal force of gravity, and Thomson did to the existence of electrons. What anti-realists fail to show is why such inferences can be made from observed effects to unobserved, but observable causes cannot be made from observed effects to unobservable causes. Why does the unobservability of the entities inferred make an inference of this sort invalid? (For a discussion of *possible* anti-realist arguments, and realist replies, see Achinstein 2002.)

2. "*There is no Universal Standard of Proof, or Scientific Method, that Must Be Followed for All Times, and For All the Sciences*" The strongest version of this claim is that of the philosopher of science Paul Feyerabend (1970), who defends a view he calls an "anarchistic theory of knowledge," or "anything goes." In actual scientific practice, he asserts, "there is not a single [methodological] rule, however plausible, and however firmly grounded in epistemology, that is not violated at some time or other." According to Feyerabend, such violation is not a bad thing but a good one, since only in this way can scientists discover errors in accepted theories and only in this way can new, interesting theories be

developed. The sole methodological principle to which Feyerabend subscribes is what he calls the "principle of proliferation"—the idea that scientists should introduce and elaborate "hypotheses which are inconsistent either with well-established theories or with well-established facts." But there are no general rules to be followed in "proliferation" other than "Anything goes."

The historian and philosopher of science Thomas Kuhn (1970) developed a somewhat more moderate view in the "Postscript" to his classic work *The Structure of Scientific Revolutions*. There are, he claims, values shared by scientific communities generally. He mentions predictive accuracy, consistency, and simplicity. But, he insists, these values do not function as rules that uniquely determine what theory to believe, since values can be applied differently by different scientists even in the same community. Two scientists might agree on the importance of simplicity as a criterion for believing a theory, yet they might apply the concept of simplicity differently, depending on subjective considerations involving training and personality.

Finally, John Norton (2005), in defending what he calls a "material theory of induction," claims that the reason there have been many conflicting accounts of scientific inference, including those presented in section 1, is that those who formulate them "have sought formal theories of induction based on universal inference schemas." But, he claims, "our inductions are not susceptible to full systematization by a formal theory . . . [since] the warrant for an induction is not ultimately supplied by a universal template; the warrant is supplied by a matter of fact." What warrants an inference from "these samples of copper melt at 1083 degrees Centigrade" to "all copper melts at that temperature" is that copper is a metal, and metals are generally uniform in their melting points—not some formal principle of induction telling us to infer all As are Bs from the fact that all observed As are Bs. And what fails to warrant an inference from the fact that all 100 voters sampled in Maryland vote Democratic to the claim that all voters in Maryland do is not that it fails to satisfy such a principle of induction, but the fact that the sample is too small, that voters in all states are not uniform in their voting habits, etc. General methodological rules—e.g., Newton's four rules—are mere window dressing. What is doing the work in the causal-inductive inferences Newton makes to his law of gravity is not Newton's "general template" urging scientists to infer the same cause from effects of the same kind, but the fact that accelerations are produced by forces and that the accelerations of the planets all satisfy an inverse square force law.

Responses

In response to Feyerabend, defenders of universal scientific methods can say that his "principle of proliferation" is not at all incompatible with universal methods. His principle does not tell us to infer or to believe a theory that is inconsistent with one accepted on the basis of a scientific method. It tells us only to consider such a theory. Scientists defending a theory on the basis of a universal method do this a good deal of the time. For example, Newton, in giving some arguments in favor of his particle theory of light, considers the incompatible wave theory, and notes empirical problems with it. If Feyerabend means that one should *infer* or *believe* a theory incompatible with the well-established one simply because it is a conflicting theory, then indeed his view would and should have few if any followers.

Feyerabend also claims that although generally it is "good policy" to act in accordance with rules of reasoning such as Newton's four rules, they should not be universally followed. There are numerous important occasions on which they are, and should be, violated or ignored. In response, we need to draw a distinction between, on the one hand, violating or ignoring a rule, and, on the other, knowing when it is supposed to be applied and when not. One might refuse to use inductive generalization when one has very few instances, or when they are all of the same narrow type, or when other information exists that makes the generalization implausible. But this is not violating or ignoring the rule; it is simply realizing that it is not applicable in such situations. If this is all Feyerabend means, then those he is criticizing would agree. Is Feyerabend suggesting that even when inductive generalizations are perfectly justified (say, because they are based on numerous and varied instances, the properties involved are of the right sort, etc.), there are numerous important occasions on which the inductive conclusions should not be drawn, or on which some conflicting conclusions should be drawn? Unless some reason can be given for this (other than "the inductive conclusion might be false"), those he is criticizing should be unmoved.

In response to Kuhn's subjective aspects of "shared values," a defender of objective scientific standards can reply by making some distinctions. First, there is the idea that different scientists, confronted with the same data and the same background theories, do indeed sometimes come to different conclusions about whether, or to what extent, the data confirm or support a conclusion. That is perfectly compatible with the scientific standards being objective, even though there are differences between scientists in their beliefs about whether the data conform to those standards. Second, there is the idea that even though whether, or to what extent, the data support a hypothesis is an objective matter, whether it is reasonable to take certain actions with respect to that hypothesis (e.g., to test it by designing and building expensive equipment) is at least in part subjective. Finally, there is the idea that the data might be such that, in conformity with the objective standards, they do not clearly point to any particular conclusion, or if they do, how strongly they support that conclusion is not clear. (The analogy here is with a medical test coming back "inconclusive.") None of these possibilities, however, suffices to make the standards or "shared values" in any way subjective.

In response to Norton, the empiricists Newton, Mill, and Whewell will deny that they are providing general formal templates for valid scientific inferences which are such that any inferences having these forms will be valid. For example, Mill explicitly says that some inductions of the form "all observed As are Bs; therefore all As are Bs" are valid, and some are fallacious. The validity of an inference of this form depends on various empirical factors in addition to the fact that all observed As are Bs. Unlike formal deductive logic, to determine the validity of an inductive inference of the form noted, you can't just look at its form. This view is also implicit in the works of Newton and Whewell. What these writers are saying is that in order to obtain scientific knowledge of the world via "proofs" one needs to produce arguments that have a certain structure (e.g., that infer similar causes from similar effects; that generalize from observed samples to populations). They are not claiming that these arguments are valid simply in virtue of their structure.

3. *"Scientists Can Be, and Frequently Are, Justified in Believing Unproved Propositions"*
This claim runs counter to the last (and arguably the most vulnerable) of the three Principal Theses, according to which scientists are justified in believing propositions only if they are proved in accordance with the standards set by the "scientific method." One of the best defenses (and illustrations) of this claim was offered in 1875 by the great

British theoretical physicist James Clerk Maxwell (1875). He introduced what he called a "method of physical speculation" for developing and defending a theory you cannot at the moment experimentally prove, and doing so in a way that can make it possible to be justified in believing the theory to be true. The particular theory he was concerned with was the kinetic-molecular theory of gases and liquids which postulates molecules that cannot be observed, and makes claims about their motions that at the time could not be demonstrated to be true by observation and experiment. Maxwell contrasts his "method of physical speculation" with two others: Newtonian inductivism, which is meant to provide proof "beyond reasonable doubt," and "the method of hypothesis," in which an hypothesis is assumed without proof or any argument and its consequences tested. Maxwell's method is weaker than the former, but stronger than the latter, which at best yields "instance confirmation," but not justified belief.

Maxwell's method (which can be gleaned more from his actual use of it than from his pronouncements about it) is to be employed when developing and defending a theory about unobservables when whatever experimental evidence exists does not suffice to establish the theory. It is particularly appropriate for theories in which the unobservables comprise a micro-system of which some observable macro-system is claimed to be composed, and in which the behavior of the micro-system is supposed to determine that of the macro-system. There are four components.

i. *Independent Warrant.* Whatever reasons one can offer should be given for the existence of the unobservables and in favor of supposing that the principles used are applicable to these unobservables. These reasons might include appeal to experiments that provide some indirect but not conclusive support for supposing that some type of unobservables comprise the macro-system and produce observed behavior of the macro-system. (For example, Maxwell mentions friction experiments suggesting that heat is not a fluid but a motion of bodies too small to see.) The independent warrant might include an inductively based appeal to the success of the principles in other domains. (For example, in applying the laws of classical dynamics to molecules, Maxwell argues that such laws have been successful in astronomy and in electrical science.) The independent warrant can also appeal to methodological ideas such as simplicity or unification. (Maxwell argues that his molecular theory satisfies these criteria by explaining macro-systems composed of bodies in terms of micro-systems composed of bodies, and so introduces no new ontological category.) The strength of this independent warrant can vary, depending on the arguments given. It does not yield proof, but it is a good deal more than saying simply "let's make these assumptions without argument, and see what consequences follow."

ii. *Explanations.* The second component of Maxwell's method consists in giving explanations of known properties, laws, and experimentally established deviations from these laws, from assumptions made about the unobservable micro-system. (Maxwell shows how to derive Boyle's law for gases from his molecular assumptions, and how to derive known deviations from this law from a virial equation for certain macro-systems when that equation is applied to the molecular system he postulates.)

iii. *Theoretical Development.* The postulation of unobservables satisfying the properties and principles introduced will suggest a range of questions about what properties and principles in addition to those introduced in components 1 and 2 these unobservables satisfy. To the extent possible, the theorist should attempt to develop the theory further by answering these questions. This usually requires the introduction of new theoretical assumptions about the unobservables for which there might be no independent warrant, and derivations of new results that might or might not be testable by known means. (Maxwell formulates a series of questions about the motions of molecules, their mean-free paths, the distribution of molecular velocities, etc. To answer them he introduces various new assumptions, which he had no way of experimentally verifying, and draws new conclusions, including his famous distribution law for molecular velocities, which he had no way of testing.)

iv. *Unsolved Problems*. These can include a reference to known laws and properties of the macro-system not yet explained, as well as experimental results that are not in accord with certain consequences of the theory. (From his theory Maxwell derived information about specific heats of gases that are not in accord with observed values; and he notes various properties of gases, including electrical ones, the theory does not explain.) This, of course, is not a way of defending the theory, only the "theorist" by showing that he is aware of difficulties and knows aspects of the theory that need further development.

Maxwell's method offers a defense of a theory that is of two sorts: epistemic and non-epistemic. First, the independent warrant cited for assumptions introduced might provide enough epistemic warrant to make one justified in believing them, even though they have no experimental proof; and if from those assumptions one can derive known laws and deviations, then one might be justified in believing them on the basis of a range of known phenomena. Second, an important way of defending a theory is by showing that it can, and how it can, be developed theoretically, even when that theoretical development involves postulating or deriving new theoretical propositions for which there is no experimental proof or even independent warrant. What such theoretical development adds is "completeness"—a non-epistemic value Maxwell regards as valuable for its own sake. Without it, he claims, the basic assumptions of the theory are "vague" in the sense of being underdeveloped and imprecise. From the use of his method in developing his kinetic-molecular theory the way he did, Maxwell concluded that he was epistemically justified in believing the basic assumptions of his theory, and non-epistemically justified in continuing to pursue this theory—even though neither he nor others had provided experimental proof.

On the Maxwellian view, then, you can accept the first two Principal Theses (which Maxwell in fact does) without accepting the third. Even if scientific knowledge requires proof satisfying some preferred "scientific method," scientists can be justified in believing and pursuing a theory they are not yet able to prove and claim to be scientific knowledge (see Achinstein 2010).

Conclusion

Despite the fact that there is no general agreement about scientific methodology among the influential historical writers cited, there is agreement among them about the three Principal Theses governing scientific knowledge. More contemporary writers have enlivened the discussion by challenging one or more of even these common theses. It has been claimed by some that no scientific knowledge is possible at all, or that it is possible only with respect to the observable world, or that standards of proof required for scientific knowledge are not universal but theory-specific, or that scientists can be justified in believing hypotheses without proof. As is the case with philosophical arguments generally, these more recent discussions yield no universally accepted position. But they do furnish a very valuable stimulus for thinking about the nature of scientific inquiry, and about whether, and to what extent, such inquiry can, or needs to, supply knowledge of the world.

References

Achinstein, Peter (1991) *Particles and Waves*, New York: Oxford University Press.
—— (2002) "Is there a Valid Experimental Argument for Scientific Realism?" *Journal of Philosophy* 99, 470–95.
—— (2010) "What to Do if You Want to Defend a Theory You Cannot Prove: A Method of 'Physical Speculation'," *Journal of Philosophy* 107, 35–56.
Descartes, René (1971) *Descartes: Philosophical Writings*, trans. and ed. Elizabeth Anscombe and Peter Thomas Geach, Indianapolis: Bobbs-Merrill.
—— (1988) *Descartes: Selected Writings*, trans. John Cottingham, Robert Stoothoff, and Dugald Murdoch, Cambridge: Cambridge University Press.
Duhem, Pierre (1954) *The Aim and Structure of Physical Theory*, trans. Philip P. Wiener, Princeton: Princeton University Press.
Feyerabend, Paul (1970) "Against Method: Outline of an Anarchistic Theory of Knowledge," *Analyses of Theories and Methods of Physics and Psychology*, ed. Michael Radner and Stephen Winokur, vol. 4 of *Minnesota Studies in the Philosophy of Science*, Minneapolis: University of Minnesota Press.
Harman, Gilbert (1965) "Inference to the Best Explanation," *The Philosophical Review* 74, 88–95.
Kuhn, Thomas (1970) *The Structure of Scientific Revolutions*, 2nd ed., Chicago: University of Chicago Press.
Lipton, Peter (2004) *Inference to the Best Explanation*, 2nd ed., London: Routledge.
Maxwell, James Clerk (1875) "On the Dynamical Evidence of the Molecular Constitution of Bodies," *The Scientific Papers of James Clerk Maxwell*, ed. W.D. Niven, New York: Dover, 1965.
Mill, John Stuart (1872) *A System of Logic, Ratiocinative and Inductive*, 8th ed. London: Longmans (new impression 1959).
Newton, Isaac (1999) *The Principia: Mathematical Principles of Natural Philosophy*, trans. I. Bernard Cohen and Anne Whitman. Berkeley: University of California Press.
Norton, John (2005) "A Little Survey of Induction," in Peter Achinstein, ed. *Scientific Evidence: Philosophical Theories and Applications*, Baltimore: Johns Hopkins University Press, 9–34.
Popper, Karl (1959) *The Logic of Scientific Discovery*, New York: Basic Books.
Swinburne, Richard (1974) *The Justification of Induction*, Oxford: Oxford University Press.
Van Fraassen, Bas (1980) *The Scientific Image*, Oxford: Clarendon Press.
Whewell, William (1840) *The Philosophy of the Inductive Sciences, Founded upon their History*, 2 volumes, London: John W. Parker; reprinted London: Routledge/Thoemmes Press, 1996.

Further Reading

Selections from many of the writers discussed in this article, together with critical discussions, can be found in the present author's *Science Rules: A Historical Introduction to Scientific Methods*, Baltimore: Johns Hopkins University Press, 2004. Some of the material in this chapter is derived from that work.

33
LOGICAL AND MATHEMATICAL KNOWLEDGE

Otávio Bueno

Introduction

What is mathematical and logical knowledge? And how are such kinds of knowledge obtained? In order to answer these questions, we need to determine, first, what mathematics and logic are about. But any such answers presuppose certain philosophical conceptions of mathematics and logic, and depending on the conception that is adopted, different answers are advanced.

For example, according to a Platonist account of mathematics, mathematical objects exist independently of us. These objects are not mind-dependent (their existence is not the result of our mental processes and linguistic practices), and they are abstract (that is, mathematical objects are causally inert and are not located in space-time). On a Platonist view, mathematics is ultimately about mathematical objects and their relations, the structures they determine and the concepts that are introduced in order to describe them. But how can we form even reliable beliefs, let alone knowledge, of such an abstract realm? This is the epistemological problem faced by Platonism. In what follows, I will discuss some strategies that Platonists have developed in order to address this problem. As will become clear, these strategies rely, in more or less direct ways, on the use of logic, and so they presuppose some logical knowledge (knowledge of what follows from what).

According to nominalists, mathematical objects do not exist or, at least, need not be taken to exist to make sense of mathematics. Clearly, if these objects do not exist, we do not—in fact, we cannot—have knowledge of them as objects that exist independently of their descriptions. In this guise, there is not much we can know about them of mathematical interest. Presumably, we can know things such as that they can be thought of by us, that Platonists believe that they exist, and so on. But these are not mathematically significant properties. In the end, the epistemological problem of mathematics is ultimately dissolved. However, another problem emerges. How can we distinguish a mathematician from a non-mathematician with respect to their mathematical beliefs? In outline, what distinguishes them is their logical knowledge (Field 1989). A mathematician has significantly more logical knowledge involving mathematical principles than a non-mathematician does. She knows what follows or not, given a logic, from various mathematical principles, whereas a non-mathematician lacks, in many cases, that sort of knowledge.

So, both Platonists and nominalists about mathematics ultimately rely on logical knowledge. After critically discussing some of the main Platonist strategies to accommodate mathematical knowledge, I will examine a non-Platonist strategy that re-conceptualizes the whole issue, suggesting that it also offers an account of logical knowledge that even Platonists can adopt.

Mathematical Knowledge Via Abstraction

The first approach to mathematical knowledge I will consider emphasizes the importance of having a suitable conception of mathematical ontology. In fact, the idea is that once the ontology of mathematics is properly worked out, mathematical epistemology will turn out to be much less troublesome than it might initially seem to be.

This strategy was most thoroughly developed by the Fregean Platonists (Frege 1974: Hale and Wright 2001). On this approach, the abstract character of mathematical objects emerges from the kind of thing these objects are: objects that fall under certain concepts. Given that Fregean concepts are abstract, mind-independent things, numbers and other mathematical objects inherit the same abstract character from the concepts they fall under. The Fregean Platonist has no difficulty in making sense of the objectivity of mathematics, given the mind-independence of the concepts involved in their characterization. Frege's own motivation to develop his proposal, which was initially developed to make sense of arithmetic, emerged from the need to provide a formulation of arithmetic in terms of logic. Frege had developed the first formal system of symbolic logic (in fact, it was a version of second-order logic), and his goal was to show that arithmetical concepts could be reduced to logical concepts (such as identity, predication, negation, and conjunction) plus some definitions. Frege was, thus, what we now call a *logicist* about arithmetic. For instance, the number 0 was characterized in terms of the concepts of negation, identity, and predication: 0 is the number of objects that fall under the concept *not identical to itself* (since no objects fall under that concept, the characterization seems quite right).

Crucial to Frege's approach was the use of what is now called Hume's Principle: two concepts are equinumerous if, and only if, there is a one-to-one correspondence between them. Hume's Principle was used at various crucial points. For instance, it was invoked to show that the number 0 is different from the number 1. As just noted, the concept 0 is characterized in terms of the number of objects that fall under the concept *not identical to itself*. The concept 1, in turn, is characterized in terms of the concept *identical to 0*. Now, given that nothing falls under the concept *not identical to itself*, and only one object falls under the concept *identical to 0*, by Hume's Principle, these two concepts are not equinumerous. As a result, 0 is distinct from 1.

How can one establish that Hume's Principle is true? Frege thought he could derive Hume's Principle from a basic logical law (called Basic Law V). According to this law, the extension of the concept F is the same as the extension of the concept G if, and only if, the same objects fall under the concepts F and G. Basic Law V seemed to be a fundamental logical law, dealing with concepts, their extensions, and their identity. It seemed to have the right sort of generality and analytic character that was needed for a logicist foundation of arithmetic.

But here is the problem: Basic Law V is inconsistent. It immediately raises Russell's paradox once we consider the set of all sets that are not members of themselves (Boolos

1998). However, not everything was lost. Although Frege acknowledged the problem, and tried to fix it by introducing a new, consistent principle, his solution ultimately did not work. The principle that Frege introduced as a replacement for Basic Law V, although logically consistent, was inconsistent with the claim that there are at least two distinct numbers. Since the latter claim was true in Frege's system, the proposed principle was unacceptable (Boolos 1998).

There was, however, a different solution available to Frege. He could have jettisoned the inconsistent Basic Law V, and adopted Hume's Principle as his basic principle instead. Given that the only use that Frege made of Basic Law V was to derive Hume's Principle, if the latter were assumed as basic, one could then run, in a perfectly consistent manner, Frege's reconstruction of arithmetic. In fact, we could then credit Frege with the theorem to the effect that arithmetic can be derived in a system like Frege's from Hume's Principle alone. Frege's approach could then be extended to other branches of mathematics. To implement a program along these lines is one of the central features of the neo-Fregean approach to the philosophy of mathematics (Hale and Wright 2001; for a critical discussion, see Boolos 1998).

But in order to carry out this program, at least within Fregean lines, it is crucial that Hume's Principle be analytic. However, as Boolos (1998) argued, how can something that entails the existence of infinitely many objects (infinitely many natural numbers) be considered analytic? This is a challenge that neo-Fregeans have tried to address (Hale and Wright 2001).

Part of the motivation for Frege's logicism was epistemological. The logicist approach can offer a suitable account of our knowledge of arithmetic, and of other branches of mathematics, if suitable abstraction principles (similar to Hume's Principle) are identified for other areas of mathematics, such as analysis, algebra, and set theory. The central epistemological move is that with the introduction of suitable abstraction principles, the relevant properties of the objects under consideration can be adequately captured in terms of only logic and definitions. The Fregean is then in a position to make sense of mathematical knowledge.

This strategy faces considerable challenges. It is unclear even which abstraction principles are acceptable (Linnebo and Uzquiano 2009). Moreover, given the logicist setting, there are significant constraints on the allowable concepts and constructions. To account for mathematical knowledge, the Fregean introduces a parallel discourse to mathematical practice—a discourse that often has no counterpart in actual mathematical practice. As a result, the account is unable to explain mathematical knowledge as the latter is actually obtained by mathematicians.

Mathematical Knowledge Via Intuition

Kurt Gödel approached mathematical knowledge very differently. On his view, the truth of basic mathematical axioms can be obtained directly by intuition (Gödel 1964; Maddy 1990). Frege thought that intuition played a role in how we come to know the truth of geometrical principles (which, for him, following Kant, were synthetic a priori); but arithmetic, being derivable from logic and definitions, was analytic. For Gödel, however, not only the principles of arithmetic, but also the axioms of set theory can be apprehended directly by intuition. We have, Gödel claims, "something like a perception of the objects of set theory" (1964: 485). That is, we are able to "perceive" these objects as having certain properties and lacking others, in a similar way that we perceive physical objects around us. That we have such a perception of set-theoretic objects is supposed to be "seen from the fact that the axioms [of set theory] force themselves upon us as being true" (Gödel 1964: 485).

The issue then arises: how exactly does the fact that the axioms of set theory "force themselves upon us as being true" support the claim that we "perceive" the objects of set theory? Gödel seemed to have a broad conception of perception, and when he referred to the objects of set theory, he thought that we "perceived" the concepts involved in the characterization of these objects as well. The point might seem to be strange at first. After all, how exactly are we supposed to "perceive" abstract objects? With further reflection, however, and an extra bit of clarification, the point is not unreasonable. In fact, an analogous move can be made in the case of the perception of physical objects. For example, in order for me to perceive a tennis ball, and recognize it *as* a tennis ball, I need to have the concept of *tennis ball*. Without the latter concept, at best I will perceive a round yellow thing—assuming I have *these* concepts. Similarly, I would not be able to recognize certain mathematical objects *as* objects of set theory unless I had the relevant concepts. The objects could not be "perceived" to be set-theoretic except if the relevant concepts were in place.

But to be able to justify the "perception" of set-theoretic objects from the fact that the axioms of set theory are forced upon us as being true, Gödel needs to articulate a certain conception of rational evidence (Parsons 2008: 146–148). Minimally, we have rational evidence for a proposition—such as an axiom of set theory—only if we make sense of the concepts that occur in that proposition and, in making sense of them, we realize that what is stated in that proposition is true. When we make sense of these concepts, we "perceive" them. Mathematical concepts are robust in their characterization, in the sense that what they stand for is not of our own making. Our perception of physical objects is similarly robust. If there is no pink elephant in front of me right now, I cannot perceive one. And you cannot fail to perceive the letters of this sentence as you read it, even though you might not be thinking about the letters as you read the sentence, but what the latter stands for. The analogy between sense perception and the "perception" of concepts is grounded on the robustness of both.

The robustness requires that I perceive what is the case, although I can, of course, be mistaken in my perception. For instance, as I walk on the street, I see a bird by a tree. I find it initially strange that the bird does not move as I get closer to the tree; just to find out, when I get close enough, that there was no bird there, but a colorful piece of paper. I thought I had perceived a bird, when in fact I perceived something else. The perception, although robust—something was perceived, after all—is fallible. But I still perceived what was the case: a piece of paper in the shape of a bird. I just mistook that for a bird, something I corrected later.

Similarly, the robustness of our "perception" of the concepts involved in an axiom of set theory is part of the account of how that axiom can force itself upon us as being true. By making sense of the relevant set-theoretic concepts, we "perceive" the latter and the connections among them. In this way, we "perceive" what is the case among the sets involved. Of course, similarly to the case of sense perception, we might be mistaken about what we think we perceive—that is part of the fallibility of the proposal. But the "perception" is, nevertheless, robust. We "perceive" something that is true.

This account of "perception" of mathematical concepts and objects is, in fact, an account of mathematical intuition. Following Charles Parsons (2008: 138–143), we should note that we have intuition of two sorts of things. We have intuition of objects (e.g., the intuition of the objects of arithmetic), and we have intuition that some proposition is true (e.g., the intuition that "the successor of a natural number is also a natural number" is true). The former can be called "intuition *of*," and the latter "intuition *that*." In the passage quoted in the first paragraph of this section, Gödel seems to be using the intuition *that* the axioms of set theory force themselves upon us to support the corresponding intuition *of* the objects of set theory. The robustness of both intuitions involved here is a central feature of the account.

The fallibilism that underlies this account of mathematical intuition contributes to making it more plausible. We might be wrong, after all, about which mathematical entity we think we have an intuition of, and we might be wrong in the intuition that a certain axiom is true. However, once these possibilities are acknowledged, it becomes clear that we need an account of the reliability of these mathematical intuitions. Otherwise, what prevent us from thinking that we are having an intuition of certain numbers, when we are in fact having an intuition of certain sets? And given that numbers, in general, are different from sets, the intuition in question could be misleading. Similarly, we might have an intuition that a certain axiom is true when unbeknown to us the axiom in question is inconsistent. Think about Frege having the intuition that Basic Law V was true. Accounts of mathematical intuition within a Platonist setting invite concerns along these lines, since they need to ensure that the intuitions involved are about the right sort of objects, and that they offer reliable information regarding the appropriate relations among the objects in question.

Mathematical Knowledge as Continuous with Empirical Knowledge

There are dramatic ways in which considerations regarding empirical matters can shape an epistemology of mathematics. In the hands of the Quinean Platonist, there is a close connection between mathematics and the empirical sciences. Suppose you have a strong nominalistic tendency, but find out that, in the end, you cannot avoid being committed to the existence of mathematical objects when you try to make sense of the best theories of the world. In this case, you probably are a Quinean Platonist. W.V. Quine himself was such a Platonist (Quine 1960). Even when he acknowledged the indispensable role that reference to mathematical objects plays in the formulation of our best theories of the world, Quine insisted that he was only committed to one kind of mathematical object: classes. All the other mathematical objects that he needed, such as numbers, functions, and geometrical spaces, could be obtained from classes.

For the Quinean, Platonism is a matter of ontological honesty. Suppose you are a scientific realist about science, that is, you take scientific theories to be true (or, at least, approximately true), and you think that the terms in these theories refer. So, for example, in quantum mechanics, you acknowledge that it is crucial to refer to things like electrons, protons, photons, and quarks. These posits are an integral part of the theory, and positing their existence is crucial to the explanation of the behavior of the observable phenomena. These explanations include making successful predictions and applying quantum theory in various contexts. Now, in the formulation of quantum mechanics, it is indispensable to refer not only to electrons and other quantum particles, but also to mathematical objects. After all, it is in terms of the latter that we can characterize the former. For instance, there is no way to characterize an electron but in terms of a certain group of invariants. These invariants are particular mathematical functions (particular mappings). So, to acknowledge commitment to the existence of electrons but deny the existence of the corresponding mathematical functions is to take back what has to be assumed in order to express what such a physical object is. To engage in this, Quine insists, is to indulge in double thinking, in ontological dishonesty.

Quine's indispensability argument is an attempt to get us straight—particularly the scientific realists among us. According to this argument (Quine 1960; Putnam 1971; Colyvan 2001):

(P1)   We ought to be ontologically committed to all and only those entities that are indispensable to our best theories of the world.
(P2)   Mathematical entities are indispensable to our best theories of the world.
Therefore We ought be to be ontologically committed to mathematical entities.

The point of the indispensability argument is to ensure that mathematical and physical posits be treated in the same way. In fact, on the Quinean picture, there is no sharp divide between mathematics and empirical science. Both are part of the same continuum and ultimately depend on experience. There is only a difference in degree between them. Certain mathematical theories are presupposed and used in various branches of science but, typically, the results of scientific theories are not presupposed in the construction of mathematical theories. In this sense, the theories in mathematics are taken to be more general than the theories in science. Mathematics also plays a fundamentally instrumental role in science, helping the formulation of scientific theories and the expression of suitable relations among physical entities.

Of course, not every mathematical theory has indispensable applications in science. For example, theories about inaccessible cardinals in set theory do not seem to have found such applications. For Quine, such theories constitute mathematical recreations, and do not demand ontological commitment, that is, commitment to the existence of the entities they posit. The situation is entirely different, however, when we consider those mathematical theories that are used in science. Given that we cannot even formulate the corresponding scientific theories without using (and quantifying over) mathematical objects—such as functions, numbers, and geometrical spaces—the existence of the latter is required as much as the existence of physical posits—such as neutrons, protons, and positrons. Platonism then becomes the outcome of an honest understanding of the ontology of science.

To the extent that we want to describe mathematical knowledge as knowledge about mathematical objects, relations, and structures, the indispensability argument indicates which objects, relations, and structures we should be ontologically committed to (namely, those that are indispensable to our best theories of the world). From this point of view, mathematical knowledge ultimately emerges from, and is continuous with, empirical knowledge. We have good reason to posit some mathematical objects to the extent that such a positing is indispensable to our best theories of the world (theories that are simple, explanatory, heuristically fruitful, and empirically successful). There is no need to reconstruct these objects within a logicist setting or to have suitable mathematical intuitions about them (the reduction that Quine favors is to set theory, not to logic). Positing the objects as part of the theories is all that is needed.

It is not clear, however, that this account accommodates mathematical knowledge in general. It is often the case that what eventually becomes applied mathematics is first developed independently of any application context. It is only later that the mathematical theories in question are eventually applied. So an account is still needed of how something that is merely a form of mathematical recreation suddenly raises to the level of serious ontological commitment upon successful application. Even if this proposal offered an adequate picture of applied mathematics, an account of mathematical knowledge in pure mathematics is still needed. Simply describing pure mathematics as a form of mathematical recreation does not illuminate the central role it plays in the development of applied mathematics.

Mathematical Knowledge Via Structure Identification

Perhaps we should not think of the basic focus of mathematical investigation as the study of objects; rather, we should conceptualize mathematics as the study of structures. Mathematical knowledge is then not knowledge of mathematical objects, but of mathematical structures. This is the key point of mathematical structuralism. Different forms of structuralism provide different accounts of structure (Resnik 1997; Shapiro 1997). But, crucially for the structuralist, it does not matter which mathematical objects one considers; as long as they satisfy the relevant structure it will be sufficient to explain the possibility of mathematical knowledge.

This move is clearly found in Michael Resnik's defense of structuralism. To explain the possibility of mathematical knowledge, Resnik introduces the notion of a *template*, which is a concrete entity—including things such as drawings, models, blueprints—and is meant to link the concrete aspects of our experience with abstract *patterns* (Resnik's term for structure). The crucial idea is that there are structural relations (such as isomorphisms) between templates and patterns that allow us to represent the latter via the former. In particular, it is because there are such structural relations between patterns and templates that mathematicians can use proofs—the process of creating and manipulating concrete templates via certain operations—to generate information about abstract patterns (Resnik 1997: 229–235). And given that mathematicians only have access to templates, no direct access to positions in patterns—that is, no direct access to mathematical objects—is presupposed in Resnik's picture.

Patterns have a significant feature according to Resnik: the positions in such patterns are incomplete. This means that there is no fact of the matter as to whether these positions have certain properties or not. Consider, for example, the third position in the natural number pattern (for simplicity, call that position "the number 3"). It is not clear that there is a fact of the matter as to whether this position—the number 3—is the same as the corresponding position in the real number pattern. In other words, it is not clear that there is a fact of the matter as to whether the number 3 in the natural number pattern is the same as the number 3 in the real number structure. After all, the properties that a position in a pattern has depend on the pattern to which it belongs. In the natural number pattern, the number 3 has the fourth position in the pattern—that is, the number 4—as its immediate successor. But this is not the case in the context of the real number pattern. Of course, in the real number pattern, the immediate successor of the number 3 *that is also a natural number* is the number 4. But to say that this is the same property as the one in the natural number pattern is already to assume that the corresponding numbers are the same, which is the point in question. It is then not obvious how issues such as these can be decided.

According to Resnik, rather than a problem, this incompleteness of the positions in a pattern (or structure) is a significant feature of mathematics. Ultimately, we will not be able to decide several issues about the identity of the positions in a structure. We can decide, however, issues about the mathematical structures themselves, where such incompleteness typically does not emerge. That is expected on a structuralist account. After all, what we get to know when we know mathematics does not have to do with the nature of mathematical objects, but rather the structures (or patterns) they are part of.

One significant benefit of mathematical structuralism, at least on Resnik's view, is that mathematical objects drop out of the picture entirely. This simplifies significantly the epistemology of mathematics. After all, the mathematical structuralist does not require any logicist formulation of mathematical objects via abstraction principles. Moreover, no access to mathematical objects via mathematical intuition is presupposed, nor is a problematic distinction between mathematical recreation and ontologically committing mathematics ever made.

The epistemological difficulties emerge, not surprisingly, at the level of mathematical structures. What reasons do we have to believe that by manipulating concrete templates we successfully describe abstract mathematical patterns? How can we know that there is an isomorphism between a certain concrete template (to which we do have access) and an abstract pattern (to which we have none)? Clearly, we cannot simply stipulate that once a given template is formulated—even if it is a consistent or a coherent template—there is an isomorphic abstract pattern that corresponds to it. After all, it is still possible that no mathematical structures exist, or that only some such structures exist, and hence some templates correspond to no abstract patterns. What is needed here is the development of a strategy that guarantees the alleged connection between templates and patterns. It is unclear, however, how such a strategy can be implemented without presupposing any access to patterns.

Mathematical "Knowledge" Via Logical Knowledge

The epistemological difficulties faced by the Platonist views discussed so far motivate the need for a different approach to mathematical knowledge. The difficulties emerged because of the assumption that a domain of abstract objects (or structures) exists independently of us, and that domain needs to be described. If we drop this assumption, the difficulties will also vanish. For such difficulties challenged the way in which each Platonist strategy tried to forge a connection between mathematical objects (or structures) and particular mechanisms of belief generation about them. But if mathematical objects or structures do not exist, or are not taken to exist, is there any sense in which there is mathematical knowledge? What is such knowledge about?

Nominalist views in the philosophy of mathematics, we noted, either deny the existence of mathematical objects (Field 1989; Azzouni 2004) or do not require the existence of these objects to make sense of mathematics (Bueno 2008). The latter form of nominalism offers an agnostic position, according to which the issue of the existence of mathematical objects (or relations) is left open.

But if mathematical objects (and relations or structures) do not exist, or are not taken to exist as part of an account of mathematics, what kind of knowledge do we have of mathematics? Clearly, we cannot have knowledge of mathematical objects (relations or structures) if they do not exist. In this case, mathematical "knowledge" becomes knowledge of what follows from certain mathematical principles: logical knowledge (Field 1989). Whether mathematical objects exist or not, once certain mathematical principles are introduced and a given logic is adopted, the issue arises as to what follows from such principles. This is the scope of mathematical "knowledge" on a nominalist setting.

Are there any constraints on what counts as an acceptable mathematical principle? As opposed to the neo-Fregean strategy that requires very specific types of abstraction principles (due to the logicist demands on the program), no similar constraints are found here. From a mathematical point of view, there are no real constraints on allowable principles. The only significant requirement is that these principles produce interesting mathematics, that is, the principles are computationally tractable (so some results can be derived from them), and the results are unexpected, compelling, and illuminating.

Although typically mathematical principles are taken to be consistent, they need not be and, in some instances, they are not. In that case, assuming that the principles are not revised, the underlying logic cannot be classical, otherwise the resulting theory becomes trivial, that is, every statement follows from the principles in question. To prevent such triviality in the presence of inconsistent principles, it would be better if the underlying logic were paraconsistent. This logic tames inconsistency by not allowing everything to follow from the latter (da Costa et al. 2007).

On this approach to mathematical "knowledge," the existence of mathematical objects, relations, or structures plays no role. What matters is what can be derived from the relevant principles, assuming a given logic. Note that once some mathematical principles are introduced and a particular logic is adopted, it is not up to us what follows (or not) from such principles. In this sense, mathematics is objective—independently of the existence of mathematical objects.

As an illustration of the account, let us consider the concept of a metric. To operate mathematically with this concept, we need first to specify which conditions the concept satisfies. These conditions are formulated in the relevant mathematical principles. Let us assume that real numbers have been introduced via suitable mathematical principles in the usual way. We can then specify a metric d as a two-place function defined on the Cartesian product of a non-empty set S with values in the set of real numbers, as follows: d is always positive ($d(x, y) \geq 0$, for every x and y in S); d has value 0 precisely when its arguments are the same ($d(x, y) = 0$ if, and only if, $x = y$), and d satisfies the properties of symmetry ($d(x, y) = d(y, x)$, for every x and y in S), and triangle inequality ($d(x, z) + d(z, y) \geq d(x, y)$, for every x, y and z in S). A metric space is then a pair (S, d), where S is a non-empty set and d is a metric.

What follows from these principles? Suppose that we now introduce the concepts of a sequence $\{x_k\}$ in S, and that we say that the sequence $\{x_k\}$ converges to x in S (with respect to the metric d) as long as $\lim_k d(x_k, x) = 0$. We can then prove that if a sequence in a metric space converges, it converges to a unique point; that is, if $\lim x_k = x$ and $\lim x_k = y$, then $x = y$. After all, given that the metric satisfies the triangle inequality, $d(x, x_k) + d(x_k, y) \geq d(x, y)$, for all k, it follows that $d(x, y) = 0$. Thus, since $d(x, y) = 0$ if, and only if, $x = y$, we obtain the result.

Clearly, this is a simple fact about sequences in a metric space. And it might be very tempting to think of it as a fact about objects, such as sequences and metric spaces. There is nothing wrong with that as long as we do not reify the objects, and suddenly start thinking that they exist. The mathematical principles referred to above allow us to describe these objects (sequences, metric spaces), but the existence of the latter plays no role in the account. What matters is how the objects have been characterized and which results can be derived. The facts in question are facts about what follows from the principles involved, not about the existence of mathematical objects.

Logical Knowledge

The account just sketched relies on the adoption of a particular logic to obtain derivations from the relevant mathematical principles. Clearly, depending on the logic that is adopted, different results can be derived from the same mathematical principles. For instance, as noted, if the principles are inconsistent and the logic is classical, everything follows from the principles. This is not the case, however, if the logic is paraconsistent. There is, of course, a plurality of logics besides the classical one, such as intuitionistic logic, quantum logic, deontic logic, and relevant logic, among many others. Which of these logics (if any) is the right one?

The answer depends on the stance one adopts regarding logic. For the logical monist, there is only one such logic (Quine 1986; Priest 2006); for the logical pluralist, there are several (Beall and Restall 2006; Bueno and Shalkowski 2009). The monist needs to explain: (i) why there is only one logic, despite the apparent plurality of logics, and (ii) why the logic he or she defends is indeed the right one. Note that logical monists need not take classical logic as the correct one, since the right logic might well be non-classical, or even just a fragment of some logics (Priest 2006). The pluralist, in turn, needs to explain: (i) why the plurality of logics is a genuine fact, and (ii) why despite that plurality, we do not get logical anarchy (a situation in which anything goes as far as logical derivation).

But what does it mean to say that a logic is the right one? The right logic is the one that provides, to borrow Stephen Read's useful phrase, "the correct description of the basis of inference" (Read 1988: 2). When we are given a logic, we are given certain inferences that are sanctioned as valid. A correct description of these inferences is one that sanctions as valid those inferences that intuitively seem to be so, and does not sanction as valid those inferences that intuitively do not seem to be so. The logical pluralist insists that there are many correct descriptions of the basis of inference, whereas the monist denies that this is the case. The determination of which inferences are correct (or not) is a matter of a conceptual evaluation—of comparison of which inferences are sanctioned as valid by a given logic and which inferences seem to be intuitively so. This presupposes that there is a primitive modal concept of consistency that is being used in the assessment. In fact, on this view, a statement A intuitively follows from a statement B if the negation of A is inconsistent with B (Bueno and Shalkowski 2009).

Some monists insist that any departure from classical logic simply amounts to a change of subject matter. Classical negation is negation; any change in the properties that negation might satisfy entails that we are no longer considering negation—we are talking about something else (Quine 1986). But clearly this argument assumes the point in question, namely, that we already know what the right logic is (namely, classical logic), and that there is only one such correct logic. Logical monism is simply assumed.

The logical pluralist, in turn, argues that different logics are right (or adequate) for different domains: intuitionist logic is adequate to capture constructive features of mathematical reasoning, whereas paraconsistent logic succeeds in dealing with inconsistent bits of information without triviality (da Costa et al. 2007; Bueno and Shalkowski 2009). Some logics, however, are simply inadequate for certain domains. For example, due to explosion—the fact that, in classical logic, everything follows from a contradiction—classical logic is unable to deal with inconsistency without simply rejecting some of the offending contradictory principles. Given that some logics are adequate for some domains, and inadequate for others, despite the pluralism, we do not obtain logical anarchy. Not everything goes with regard to logical derivation (Bueno and Shalkowski 2009).

Note that the account of logical knowledge sketched here, despite not presupposing the existence of abstract entities, is one that the Platonist about mathematics, in principle, can also adopt. The account highlights the importance of logic selection on the basis of the connection between the validity of certain inferences given a logic and what is intuitively taken to be valid given a primitive concept of consistency. Nothing in this account rules out Platonism. In this way, the epistemology of logic is an area that Platonists and anti-Platonists can fruitfully explore together.

References

Azzouni, J. (2004) *Deflating Existential Consequence*, New York: Oxford University Press.
Beall, J.C. and Restall, G. (2006) *Logical Puralism*, Oxford: Clarendon Press.
Benacerraf, P. and Putnam, H. (eds.) (1983) *Philosophy of Mathematics: Selected Readings* (2nd edition), Cambridge: Cambridge University Press.
Boolos, G. (1998) *Logic, Logic, and Logic*, Cambridge, MA: Harvard University Press.
Bueno, O. (2008) "Nominalism and Mathematical Intuition," *Protosociology* 25: 89–107.
Bueno, O. and Shalkowski, S. (2009) "Modalism and Logical Pluralism," *Mind* 118: 295–321.
Colyvan, M. (2001) *The Indispensability of Mathematics*, New York: Oxford University Press.
da Costa, N.C.A., Krause, D., and Bueno, O. (2007) "Paraconsistent Logics and Paraconsistency," in Jacquette (ed.) (2007): 791–911.
Field, H. (1989) *Realism, Mathematics and Modality*, Oxford: Basil Blackwell.
Frege, G. (1974) *Foundations of Arithmetic* (translated by J.L. Austin), Oxford: Basil Blackwell.
Gödel, K. (1964) "What is Cantor's Continuum Problem?," in Benacerraf and Putnam (eds.) (1983): 470–485.
Hale, B. and Wright, C. (2001) *The Reason's Proper Study*, Oxford: Oxford University Press.
Jacquette, D. (ed.) (2007) *Philosophy of Logic*, Amsterdam: North-Holland.
Linnebo, Ø, and Uzquiano, G. (2009) "Which Abstraction Principles Are Acceptable? Some Limitative Results," *British Journal for the Philosophy of Science* 60: 239–252.
Maddy, P. (1990) *Realism in Mathematics*, Oxford: Clarendon Press.
Parsons, C. (2008) *Mathematical Thought and its Objects*, Cambridge: Cambridge University Press.
Priest, G. (2006) *Doubt Truth to Be a Liar*, Oxford: Clarendon Press.
Putnam, H. (1971) *Philosophy of Logic*, New York: Harper and Row. (Reprinted in Putnam 1979: 323–357.)
Putnam, H. (1979) *Mathematics, Matter and Method* (2nd edition), Cambridge: Cambridge University Press.
Quine, W.V. (1960) *Word and Object*, Cambridge, MA: The MIT Press.
Quine, W.V. (1986) *Philosophy of Logic* (2nd edition), Cambridge, MA: Harvard University Press.
Read, S. (1988) *Relevant Logic*, Oxford: Blackwell.
Resnik, M. (1997) *Mathematics as a Science of Patterns*, Oxford: Clarendon Press.
Shapiro, S. (1997) *Philosophy of Mathematics: Structure and Ontology*, New York: Oxford University Press.

34
AESTHETIC KNOWLEDGE
Matthew Kieran

Why Aesthetic Knowledge?

Creating and appreciating art is a rational activity. Our descriptions, responses, and evaluations are not only informed by thought but are constrained and guided by various criteria. Look at a music review and it will contain characterizations of the music, what it appears to be doing, and why, as well as judgments as to why the overall effect is good, bad, or indifferent. Alternatively consider what often happens after seeing a movie with friends. We talk about why we enjoyed it (or didn't), how good it was, and strive to justify our judgments where we disagree. Furthermore, we often change our minds in light of considerations raised by others and defer to the expertise of others. Thus underlying our ordinary aesthetic practices is the presumption that at least some disputes are rationally resolvable and some people do know more about certain aspects of the aesthetic realm than others, whether it be indie rock, film noir, or contemporary literature. Aesthetic appreciation is also an activity that is valued highly. We enjoy aesthetic appreciation for its own sake and tend to think that engaging with art cultivates our minds in ways that add to our understanding of the world. The bewitching elegance of a painting or design can not only be absorbing in its own right but the ways in which a work is expressive, profound, or insightful can enhance our understanding. Shakespeare's plays would surely be less significant if they did not express and explore fundamental aspects of human nature in the ways they do. Why be interested in aesthetic epistemology? First, it is worth understanding when, where, and why we can legitimately make art critical judgments or claims. Second, it may prove fruitful to consider what the differences and similarities in the aesthetic case are as contrasted with other areas.

Aesthetic Concepts

When considering the epistemology of aesthetic judgment we need to know which features of an object are aesthetically relevant, how they relate to others and how we can come to our knowledge of them. Sibley (1959, 1965) distinguishes aesthetic knowledge from other kinds of knowledge (such as interpretative or historical knowledge). Aesthetic judgment involves the attribution of aesthetic properties and Sibley starts from considering paradigmatic aesthetic attributions such as "unified, balanced, integrated, lifeless, serene, somber, dynamic, powerful, vivid, delicate, moving, trite, sentimental, tragic" (1959: 421). The list ranges from formal aesthetic concepts to reactive and emotional ones and we should be careful to distinguish between the use of such terms in aesthetic and non-aesthetic ways. Now, according to Sibley, successfully picking out aesthetic features requires perception and taste. We have to apprehend the relevant features of the work *as* balanced or dynamic. It is one thing to see that Picasso's *Weeping Woman* has thick marks of black paint across a depicted woman's face. Any standard viewer can see that. It is, however, quite another matter to be able to see the slashing angularity of the painted marks as conveying a discomforting sense of fingers viciously clawing away.

According to Sibley, while the attribution of aesthetic concepts depends on non-aesthetic features, the aesthetic character of a work can never be inferred from its non-aesthetic character. This is not to say that we can't make any inferences at all since we might be able to rule certain aesthetic attributions out (this is what Sibley means by stating that aesthetic concepts are negatively condition governed). It is hard, for example, to conceive of how a canvas evenly painted grey all over in thinly applied water-color could be gauche. Now, contra Sibley, at least some aesthetic concepts do seem positively condition governed. If a piece of music exemplifies a certain kind of contrapuntal composition then we will know that it is a fugue and possesses a certain kind of unity (Kivy 1973: 38–9, 1979). Nonetheless, the spirit of Sibley's claim is that no amount of information about a work's non-aesthetic features could rationally compel us to judge that the work possessed particular aesthetic attributes where, crucially, the attributions have at least partly evaluative components. An accurate non-aesthetic description of a song or movie will never be enough to tell you whether or not it really is elegant, vital, or moving as opposed to say prosaic, banal, or lifeless. It is the job of the critic to show others how to perceive what she does, using a range of methods devoted towards orientating and promoting the appropriate perception.

If aesthetic features are those picked out by taste and taste is the capacity to pick out aesthetic features, then worries about circularity arise. We might also wonder just what this seemingly mysterious faculty of taste is (Cohen 1973). One way of understanding the claim renders it trivial. Taste could just be the capacity that all of us possess to apply aesthetic terms and, as with other concepts, we need education to learn how to apply them appropriately. What it is to have taste just is to be able to attribute aesthetic concepts. This is something we do all the time, from appraising the elegance of a football pass or new outfit to judging the aesthetic character of art works. If the claim is that taste somehow goes beyond the capacity of most normal people then it either looks false or at best uninformative.

Let us assume that taste just is the ability to apprehend how aesthetic concepts apply in our experience with a work. Now none of this is to deny that there aren't better or worse aesthetic appreciators. Hume famously discusses a case from *Don Quixote* where Sancho's kinsmen pronounce a village's wine to be marred for different reasons, in particular a hint of leather and iron, respectively (Hume 1993). The villagers mock them and enjoy the wine, yet when the bottom of the barrel is reached a rusty key attached to a leather thong is found. As with wine so, too, with art, since the refinement of certain capacities we all share is required in order to be able to grasp more completely the aesthetic character of a work. Indeed Hume goes on to characterize ideal critics as requiring not only a wealth of comparative experience but also delicacy of imagination, sympathy, and freedom from prejudice or fashion. Now two questions arise. First, what knowledge is relevant to apprehending the aesthetic character of a work? Second, what role does the notion of an ideal critic play?

Art seems disanalogous from wine in at least one crucial respect. Artistic appreciation might be sensuously mediated but the aesthetic character of a work doesn't seem straightforwardly identifiable with its directly perceivable sensuous character. The model of perceptual taste looks ill fitted to the case of literature and, furthermore, even in perceptual artistic media the application of aesthetic concepts often depends on relational features. What it is for a work to belong to a certain category, have a particular style or possess particular aesthetic, expressive or cognitive features often depends on its relation to other works (Walton 1970). Consider Mondrian's mid to late phase where the geometric lines and colored blocks have a rigid, austere quality. Given this it is appropriate to see Mondrian's *Boogie Woogie* as a riot of color with a free, dynamic vibrancy concomitant with the title's allusion to jazz. The same design produced by Miro would have been rigid and austere when compared with his typical penchant for organic squiggles squirming amid brightly colored canvases. Relational knowledge plays a huge role in fixing a work's aesthetically relevant features and how we should appreciate them. This is compounded by the role that creative originality plays in art. Two works might be perceptually indiscernible and yet where one was created years before the other we should appreciate and value them differently, for example the later work might be derivative, a pastiche, or forgery depending on the intention under which it was produced (Davies 2004; Kieran 2005: 6–46).

What role does the ideal critic play? One Humean-influenced idea is that we should idealize the notion of a good critic in order to track (or even constitute) what a work's aesthetic features are, their inter-relations and thereby what a work's value is. Ideal critics possess standard human nature but, in addition, have honed the aspects of such required for full aesthetic appreciation. One way of attempting to fix just what these are is by identifying the capacities, skills, knowledge, and attitudes required to appreciate the great works of the past. The recommendations of an ideal critic are likely to point us toward works that yield greater satisfaction than those we are likely to make for ourselves in our non-idealized situation (Levinson 2002). However, matters are not quite so straightforward. Even setting aside worries about the convergence of judgment of all ideal critics, there is reason to worry about idealization in the intrapersonal case. The notion of an ideal critic stripped away from personal contingencies and history looks worrying given that much of the best criticism is personal. If the notion of an idealized counterpart to ourselves is that of a hypothetical ranker able to take on different dispositional sets and run through them evaluating works accordingly then it is far from clear how the resultant idealizing pronouncements are epistemically authoritative for us (Kieran 2008). Indeed, how could we even be in a position to know what such an ideal critic would recommend for us to appreciate? It might be much more fruitful to think in terms of a general point of view, according to which the best epistemic guide is what emerges from the pronouncements and verdicts of different actual critics across time and cultures (Sayre-McCord 1994). Good actual critics possess greater refinement and knowledge than most while nonetheless responding to works in ways shaped by their own psychological individualization. What emerges across the verdicts of such is the sum of different perspectives or takes on a work. The more robust a work is in the face of such differences, the greater the indication of its worth.

Aesthetic Particularism, Principles, and Reasons

Are there general reasons or principles that might guide and justify aesthetic judgment? Many are tempted by the thought that aesthetic thought, as contrasted with ethics, is necessarily particularist either because critical reasoning aims at perceptual apprehension, which cannot be compelled by rational justification (Hampshire 1954; Isenberg 1949; Mothersill 1984: 143), or on the grounds that aesthetically relevant features and concepts change valence across particular cases (Goldman 2006).

While fine brushwork is often a good making feature of a painting nonetheless in a late Titian it might undermine a work's expressivity. Consider many aesthetic concepts that have both a descriptive and evaluative aspect and it seems that the valence can change due to the particulars of the case. Terms such as gaudy, brash, and vulgar are typically negatively valenced but they can sometimes be applied in ways that connote praise. It makes sense to praise scenes in Shakespeare and Chaucer's *The Wife of Bath's Tale* for their riotous vulgarity or appreciate the gaudy, non-naturalistic colors distinctive of Fauvism. Obscenity might typically be a bad making feature in works, yet in passages from Joyce's *Ulysses*, Philip Larkin's poetry, or the art of Jake and Dinos Chapman it is often playful. Thus the typical evaluative valence of aesthetically thick concepts can sometimes be undermined, enhanced, neutralized, or even inverted. No amount of argument can compel us to the conclusion that this is so in any particular case; rather, it is a matter of coming to see how and why this is so as worked through in the context of the particular work in question.

What might explain how and why this is so? The complex inter-relationality of aesthetic features suggests aesthetic holism. If aesthetic holism is right, then justifying reasons seem to be variable in the sense that being a reason of a certain kind (e.g., 'because it is gaudy') will not necessarily underwrite one and the same justification (e.g., insofar as something is gaudy it is aesthetically disvaluable). If principles are taken to be highly general and codifiable articulations of the connection between a justifying reason and the judgment it is a reason for, then aesthetic holism seems to present a problem for the idea that there are aesthetic principles.

Despite such considerations there are those who have argued that there are general aesthetic reasons (Beardsley 1962; Sibley 1983; Shelley 2007) or principles (Conolly and Haydar 2003; Dickie 1988, 2006). How might an argument for such claims proceed? One place to start from is the intuition that any aesthetic reason requires a normative basis to explain it. If this were not the case then it is hard to see what, if anything, could serve to rescue aesthetic justification from being a random and arbitrary matter. Furthermore, aesthetic reasons do seem at the very least to be implicitly general in form. While it is true that any adequate critical appreciation must attend to the particular ways a work realizes its aesthetic features, nonetheless reasoned justification of evaluations has an apparently general structure. What is it that makes Balzac, Dickens, or Tolstoy great writers? Part of the explanation lies in the richness of the imagery as well as their truth to life: the rich metaphorical characterization that draws out the nature of, and inter-actions among, human emotions, character, and social milieu. How they do so differs markedly in particulars, yet this should not detract from the recognition that part of what explains why they are valued so highly are reasons that are general in form and holds across the differences between them. This is not itself sufficient to show that there must be aesthetic principles. What is further required is an argument to suggest either that: (a) principles can be arrived at from generalizations arrived at on the basis of actual experience and thought experiment (Dickie 1988, 2006), or, more strongly, (b) that the normative basis of aesthetic reasons depends upon the existence of aesthetic principles (Conolly and Haydar 2003). After all, someone might think, where else could the normative force come from?

Now one thing to bear in mind here is that we are primarily interested in the epistemic thesis. Even if there are general aesthetic reasons or principles it does not thereby automatically follow that we must use them in order to justify aesthetic judgments. Work in linguistics, the science of perception, neuroscience, and cognitive science suggests there might be underlying principled naturalistic explanations as to why we appreciate works as we do. There is evidence to suggest that certain literary techniques involving heightened processing costs function in particular ways that enhance patterning effects or salience (Sperber and Wilson 1995) and in the visual arts it has been argued that studying perceptual processing yields principles that explain how and why we take pleasure in certain visual structures (Ramachandran and Hirstein 1999; Kawabata and Zeki 2004). Yet even if such approaches are genuinely explanatory it does not automatically follow that the resultant reasons or principles are of the right kind to feature as justifications for aesthetic evaluations. After all, it is not obvious that such principles are the right kind to feature in art critical appreciation and evaluation, since any straightforward causal story cannot make room for the normative aspect of aesthetic judgment. What is required to make progress here is both conceptual work on the nature of our aesthetic intuitions and the disentangling of the multiple factors that underlie and contribute to aesthetic appreciation. Furthermore, many factors that figure in appreciation concern the intentional content of the prescribed propositional attitudes. What justifies or merits many of our cognitive-affective responses to works depends upon both the artistic conventions involved and the criteria that govern the relevant emotional or, more broadly, propositional attitudes concerned. Pity, for example, might be diminished to the extent it is judged undeserved, or naive sentimentality in a work might undermine judgments about its emotional depth or truth to life.

Insofar as reasons underwrite our aesthetic judgments it would seem that, contra Beardsley, they can be both general and context-sensitive, where the reasons are taken to be defeasible ones—i.e., prima facie or pro tanto (Bender 1995). This is perfectly consistent with the recognition that inter-relations to other features means that the prima facie goodness or badness of some feature can be overridden, trumped, or undermined given its context. The technical mastery of painting and compositional structure might well be prima facie good making features of a painting, and yet the sentimentality as expressed in some particular work might be strong enough to render the work mediocre and banal. Furthermore, it could be argued, wherever there are valence switches this must be for a principled reason on pain of arbitrariness. Thus, for example, fine brushwork might be a prima facie good making feature in painting but in a late Van Gogh, late Titian, or Jackson Pollock it would cut against a work's expressiveness. Valence variability or change in particular contexts can be explained in a way that does not undermine the applicability of general reasons. Thus the generality of critical reasons looks secure and might yet provide a basis from which to argue for aesthetic principles. After all, the less descriptively fine-grained the relevant thick concept is and the more general the applicability of the justifying reason, the more it might begin to look as if we are nearing something close to an aesthetic principle (e.g., 'insofar as something is sentimental its value as a work of art is lessened'). Nonetheless, even if this were the case, it would not follow that there is a unique lexically ordered set of principles. After all, even if aesthetic principles could be secured further argument would be required to show that there are any higher-order principles which determine how they inter-relate—a Herculean looking task, especially if there are permissible differences in the prioritization of distinct aesthetic sensibilities or values. Alternatively, there might be some reason to think that a mixed view holds, namely that while there might be some aesthetic principles, not all justifying reasons advert to or depend on such.

Aesthetic Testimony and Skepticism about Aesthetic Knowledge

It has seemed to many that we cannot gain aesthetic justification or knowledge from anything other than our own experience. This can't be true for all aesthetic judgments. After all, we can make description-based warranted attributions without experiencing a work. If we read the Cliffs notes on a particular novel we can gain warrant for making all sorts of claims, for example, who created a work, when, what style it is in, its structure and themes. The interesting claim is that we cannot judge the good making features of a work without experiencing it. This amounts to "a well-entrenched principle in aesthetics, which may be called the Acquaintance Principle, and which insists that judgments of aesthetic value, unlike judgments of moral knowledge, must be based on first-hand experience of their objects and are not, except within very narrow limits, transmissible from one person to another" (Wollheim 1980: 233).

Now for some, such as Kant, there are no limits within which aesthetic testimony can be transmissible (Kant 1952: S. 33). Yet, as has been pointed out (Budd 2003), this is just because Kant defined aesthetic judgment as being necessarily based on a hedonic response to the object judged. Thus while we cannot aesthetically judge (construed in Kant's terms) an object without experiencing it, this does not preclude aesthetic knowledge about an object's value from being transmissible. It has been argued that in the aesthetic case, unlike other areas, we do not have a priori reason to take warrant to be transmitted via testimony but, nonetheless, testimony can provide an evidential basis for justification (Hopkins 2000). The basic idea is that if someone says that they witnessed a certain event yesterday or was morally outraged, we should believe them unless other countervailing considerations emerge. If someone says that a film was good, who knows? Unless, that is, we have additional reason to believe the testifier. One reason for holding that aesthetic testimony is weaker as contrasted with other realms arises from the assumption that there are different aesthetic sensibilities. This cannot be Kant's position. Kant famously held that aesthetic judgment proper depended upon the operations of the faculties of imagination and understanding, ones we all must share as rational embodied agents. Nonetheless perhaps what explains the weakness of aesthetic testimony involves the indexing of aesthetic judgment to distinct aesthetic sensibilities. Yet simplistic relativism about the aesthetic is problematic and it is unclear why sophisticated expressivism or anti-realism about aesthetics would explain what is supposed to be distinctively problematic about aesthetic testimony (Meskin 2007). Furthermore, even granting relativism, it is unclear why testimony could not transmit justification at least relative to whatever the relevant framework or sensibility implicitly invoked is. It has been argued that aesthetic testimony is variegated and, in some areas, more unreliable than elsewhere due to folks' presumption of relativism as often expressed by the phrase 'beauty is in the eye of the beholder' (Meskin 2004). Indeed, the unreliability of such might be alternatively explained or compounded by a range of other factors ranging from the amount of relevant relational knowledge required and aesthetic expertise, to the easy conflation of what we like with what is aesthetically good (Meskin 2004, 2007). One interesting parallel between ethics and aesthetics when it comes to testimony is that there seems to be something importantly lacking about an agent who gains his ethical/aesthetical knowledge (assuming there is such a thing) via testimony. Instead, these are things which, intuitively, one should (ultimately at least) ascertain for oneself. One possible explanation for this is that what we seek in these domains is not merely knowledge but understanding. Understanding, however, cannot be gained passively through the testimony of experts.

It has been argued that the aesthetic is particularly susceptible to snobbery due to a range of factors including some of those cited above (Kieran 2010). To take just one consideration, where pleasure is taken in engaging with a work, we have strong defeasible reason to value it and thus to judge that it is good. Given standard appreciators and conditions, defeasibility arises due to two considerations: (a) whether an appreciator is suitably informed and discriminating, and (b) whether an appreciator identifies and responds appropriately to the aesthetically relevant features. However, we are often terrible at identifying in aesthetic appreciation when, where, and why our pleasure is, or may be, a result of aesthetically irrelevant bias. Empirical studies suggest that factors we are unconscious of, ranging from familiarity to status cues, influence the pleasure taken in appreciation. Frederic Brochet's infamous wine tasting experiments bring this out nicely. In one experiment Brochet used the same middling Bordeaux wine and decanted it into two different bottles. One bottle bore all the marks of an ordinary vin de table while the other was a smart grand cru bottle. Out of a sample of 56 oeneology students only 12 judged the wine from the cheap bottle to be worth drinking while 40 judged the wine in the more expensive looking bottle to be worth drinking. It was the same wine. This simply reflects the extent to which expectations can be cued up and influenced by aesthetically irrelevant factors we are wholly unaware of. It is no surprise that multinational corporations spend huge amounts of money on marketing and brand placement for precisely this reason. Intuitively it seems that if we are judging or responding snobbishly then we lack internal justification for aesthetic claims and we are not in a legitimate position to claim aesthetic knowledge. (Is this true though? Won't it seem to us that X is better than Y, and won't it seem to us that we are good at making these judgments? In a purely internal sense, then, one could argue that any beliefs so formed are very reasonable, even despite their unreliable basis.) We are judging a work to be good or making critical claims about a work for the wrong sorts of reasons (i.e., because doing so marks us out as superior in some way relative to some group). Whatever else is true, any adequate account of aesthetic appreciation ought to preclude the idea that something is aesthetically good just in virtue of a certain class or group's perceived social status. Given the pervasiveness of snobbery and the difficulty of knowing whether or not someone is being snobbish we get a skeptical problem—how can we know whether or not any particular aesthetic response or judgment really is justified?

One way of answering the challenge appeals to reliability. What matters is the reliability of the faculties and processes involved in arriving at aesthetic judgments. Snobbish judgment might tend toward error but it is not necessarily mistaken and snobs can acquire justification. Tracking the judgments of acknowledged critics and working at aesthetic appreciation might put the snob in a position to make, reliably, the right sorts of aesthetic judgments and claims. An alternative virtue-theoretic approach emphasizes the ways in which snobbish motivation constitutes an appreciative vice which thereby undermines the epistemic status of the snob's beliefs (Kieran 2010). Even where snobbery reliably arrives at the right judgments this will be so for the wrong sort of reasons. Hence a snob's achievement is not epistemically praiseworthy in the way in which the judgment of a true appreciator is. Furthermore, the true appreciator's knowledge connects up to appreciation in the right sort of way. Aesthetic knowledge matters primarily for the ways in which it inflects and feeds back into our appreciation.

Aesthetic Cognitivism

Aesthetic epistemology is not just concerned with knowledge about aesthetics and art but the ways in which we can gain knowledge through our experiences with art. Plato famously thought that art could afford no knowledge whatsoever. In part the claim arose as a function of Plato's metaphysics, according to which works are only imperfect imitations of actual objects, which themselves are only imperfect instantiations of abstract forms. Art, for Plato, is two removes from, and thus doubly distortive of, reality. Nonetheless, Plato's skeptical worry can be articulated without adverting to his distinctive metaphysics.

When engaging with art works we entertain imaginings about make-believe worlds. The artistic techniques and conventions deployed prompt particular imaginings and thereby shape our responses. Artists need not have any great knowledge about what they represent, nor need appreciators be interested in what is true or false. When responding to *Dracula* or a painterly landscape it is beside the point to complain that such an entity could not exist or that the landscape never existed as it was painted. Games of make-believe need not aim at, or fix on to, reality. To the extent we are impressed by this line of reasoning it might be thought that art can only have at best an accidental relation to knowledge. Furthermore, to the extent that art is accidentally related to knowledge, what it does reveal can only be trivial commonplaces. Nash's *We Are Making a New World* conveys desolation at the horrific waste of human life in WWI and Balzac's novels convey the cynicism of people preoccupied by social calculation, but do we really acquire any worthwhile knowledge from them? The propositions that vast loss of life in war is tragic or that preoccupation with social esteem lends itself to cynicism are hardly enlightening in any deep sense. The propositions involved are either truisms or we are prepared to assent to them only to the extent to which we are already inclined to believe them independently of, and prior to, experiencing the works in question (Stolnitz 1992; Gibson 2003).

A quick response to this challenge is to point out that many art works are epistemically constrained with respect to truth (Friend 2007). It is integral to certain kinds of literary essays, non-fiction novels, still life painting, and portraiture that they are constrained by, and aim to inform us about, how things actually are. Hence the scandal when Misha Defonseca's Holocaust memoirs (1997) and James Frey's autobiographical novel (2003) turned out to be fraudulent. Daniel Mendelsohn's *The Lost* (2006) can tell us what happened to six relatives during the Holocaust and much about his attempt to uncover their story, which in turn suggests much about the nature of memory and our relations to the past. Photographers such as Martin Parr can show us what life was like for dying industrial communities in northern England at the turn of the last century or what life is like for the internationally wealthy at the start of the twenty-first century. Nonetheless, such a move leaves the charge unanswered as applied to fictional works.

What if anything can we learn from fictional works? One option is to concede that while we cannot gain knowledge from fiction, nonetheless art works can get us to care about the truths they concern. It is one thing to know in the abstract that racism is bad, it is quite another to read *To Kill a Mockingbird* and be moved to care about its perniciousness. Another option emphasizes the extent to which fictional works might afford practical knowledge, phenomenal knowledge, or even knowledge of ways of apprehending others, that are not wholly reducible to straightforward propositions. Literary narratives, for example, might be particularly well suited to showing us how to apprehend morally relevant features of particular situations (Nussbaum 1990). A more direct approach argues that fictional works can and do afford propositional knowledge (Carroll 1998, 2002; Gaut 2006, 2007; Kieran 2005; Stock 2007). A modest version of the strategy holds that artistic narratives can clarify the nature and inter-relations of our beliefs and presumptions that we hold. We might all recognize that desire for social esteem does not necessarily lead to happiness, but reading *Anna Karenina* might show how it is that the desire for social esteem can lead people to act in ways that are self-deceived, that this in turn can undermine the capacity to be true to one's self, and hence how valuing social esteem can lead away from, rather than towards, true happiness. A stronger version of this strategy holds that in addition to clarification more radical cognitive revisions are possible, on the grounds that works are capable of revealing genuine insights to us that might cut against the grain of our prior beliefs through utilizing strategies such as imaginative identification.

It is worth pointing out that we can learn straightforwardly from works how some actual people (e.g., artists) experience, conceive of, and respond to the world, or how some possible people could do so (e.g., where a work's narrator is not to be straightforwardly identified with its creator). At least to the extent that we are impressed by the thought that writers and artists are often more perceptually or emotionally discriminating than most, this looks as if it should be enough to render art cognitively significant. Furthermore, given that we learn from experience there is reason to hold that we can also learn from imaginative experience (Currie 1995; Kieran 1996; Gaut 2007). A standard way of trying to find out how one would feel in a certain kind of situation is by imagining oneself to be in such a scenario. If that is right, then works can provide particularly complex and rich ways of exercising our imaginations in epistemically significant ways, or even finding out about one's actual or possible desires and dispositions. None of this is to claim that there is a straightforward relationship between what we can imagine, conceivability, and knowledge (Stokes 2007). Yet at least to the extent that we hold there is some such relationship, then that will be the extent to which we can hold that what works can get us to imagine might show us something about how things could be or, indeed, are.

Thus far we have focused primarily upon the contents of beliefs we can glean from works and worries about the justification of such. A rather different strategy looks elsewhere for art's cognitive significance. One route involves emphasizing the extent to which the cognitive significance of works is not reducible to knowledge but is closely related to understanding. Works might draw out how our beliefs relate to human activity, practices and the ways in which such things have significance for us (Gibson 2007) or cultivate our imaginative understanding of the significance of certain beliefs (Kieran 1996). Another route stresses the exercise of a range of cognitive capacities and virtues involved in art appreciation (Kieran 2005; Lopes 2005). Attending to Monet's Rouen cathedral painting series, where each picture depicts the cathedral from distinct viewpoints with markedly different lighting effects, might cultivate the capacity to perceive small visual differences and grasp how they can have striking effects upon the overall impression. This kind of account can be broadened out with respect to all art forms. Reading Sappho's poetry alongside Catullus's transliterations can cultivate greater discrimination with respect to minute differences in literary form, allusion, and thus language in general. Indeed engaging with works might develop not just our discriminative capacities but broader intellectual virtues ranging from the patience, self-discipline, and humility to the imaginativeness required to do justice to, and appreciate, a work.

References

Beardsley, M. (1962) "On the Generality of Critical Reasons," *Journal of Philosophy* 59: 477–86.
Bender, J. W. (1995) "General but Defeasible Reasons in Aesthetic Evaluation," *Journal of Aesthetics and Art Criticism* 53: 379–92.
Budd, M. (2003) "The Acquaintance Principle," *British Journal of Aesthetics* 43: 386–92.
Carroll, N. (1998) "Art, Narrative and Moral Understanding," in J. Levinson (ed.) *Aesthetics and Ethics: Essay at the Intersection*, Cambridge: Cambridge University Press.
—— (2002) "The Wheel of Virtue: Art, Literature and Moral Knowledge," *Journal of Aesthetics and Art Criticism* 60: 3–26.
Cohen, T. (1973) "Aesthetic/Non-aesthetic and the Concept of Taste," *Theoria* 39: 113–52.
Currie, G. (1995) "The Moral Psychology of Fiction," *Australasian Journal of Philosophy* 73: 250–9.
Conolly, O. and B. Haydar (2003) "Aesthetic Principles," *British Journal of Aesthetics* 43: 114–25.
Davies, D. (2004) *Art as Performance*, Oxford: Blackwell.
Defonseca, M. (1997) *A Memoire of the Holocaust Years*, Gloucester, MA: Ivy Press.
Dickie, G. (1988) *Evaluating Art*, Philadelphia: Temple University Press.
—— (2006) "Iron, Leather and Critical Principles," in M. Kieran (ed.) *Contemporary Debates in Aesthetics and the Philosophy of Art*, Oxford: Blackwell.
Frey, J. (2003) *A Million Little Pieces*, New York: Doubleday Books.
Friend, S. (2007) "Narrating the Truth (More or Less)," in M. Kieran and D. Lopes (eds.) *Knowing Art: Essays in Aesthetics and Epistemology*, Dordrecht: Springer.
Gaut, B. (2006) "Art and Cognition," in M. Kieran (ed.) *Contemporary Debates in Aesthetics and the Philosophy of Art*, Oxford: Blackwell.
—— (2007) *Art, Emotion and Ethics*, Oxford: Oxford University Press.
Gibson, J. (2003) "Between Truth and Triviality," *British Journal of Aesthetics* 43: 224–37.
—— (2007) *Fiction and the Weave of Life*, Oxford: Oxford University Press.
Goldman, A. (2006) "There are No Aesthetic Principles," in M. Kieran (ed.) *Contemporary Debates in Aesthetics and the Philosophy of Art*, Oxford: Blackwell.
Hampshire, S. (1954) "Logic and Appreciation," in W. Elton (ed.) *Aesthetics and Language*, Oxford: Blackwell.
Hopkins, R. (2000) "Beauty and Testimony," in A. O'Hear (ed.) *Philosophy, the Good, the True, and the Beautiful*, Cambridge: Cambridge University Press.
Hume, D. (1993) "Of the Standard of Taste," in S. Copley and A. Edgar (eds.) *Hume: Selected Essays*, Oxford: Oxford University Press.
Isenberg, A. (1949) "Critical Communication," *The Philosophical Review* 58: 330–44.
Kant, I. (1952) *Critique of Judgement*, Oxford: Oxford University Press [orig. 1790].
Kawabata, H. and S. Zeki (2004) "Neural Correlates of Beauty," *Neurophysiology* 91: 1699–705.
Kieran, M. (1996) "Art, Imagination and the Cultivation of Morals," *Journal of Aesthetics and Art Criticism* 54: 337–51.
—— (2005) *Revealing Art*, London: Routledge.
—— (2008) "Why Ideal Critics are not Ideal: Aesthetic Character, Motivation and Value," *British Journal of Aesthetics* 48: 278–94.
—— (2010) "The Vice of Snobbery: Aesthetic Knowledge, Justification and Virtue in Art Appreciation," *Philosophical Quarterly* 60(239): 243–63.
Kivy, P. (1973) *Speaking of Art*, The Hague: Martinus Nijhoff.
—— (1979) "Aesthetic Concepts: Some Fresh Considerations," *Journal of Aesthetics and Art Criticism* 37: 423–32.
Levinson, J. (2002) "Hume's Standard of Taste: The Real Problem," *Journal of Aesthetics and Art Criticism* 60: 227–38.
Lopes, D. (2005) *Sight and Sensibility*, Oxford: Clarendon Press.
Mendelsohn, D. (2006) *The Lost: A Search for Six of the Six Million*, New York: HarperCollins.
Meskin, A. (2004) "Aesthetic Testimony: What Can We Learn from Others about Beauty and Art?," *Philosophy and Phenomenological Research* LXIX: 66–91.
—— (2007) "Solving the Puzzle of Aesthetic Testimony," in M. Kieran and D. Lopes (eds.) *Knowing Art: Essays in Aesthetics and Epistemology*, Dordrecht: Springer.
Mothersill, M. (1984) *Beauty Restored*, Oxford: Oxford University Press.
Nussbaum, M. (1990) *Love's Knowledge*, New York: Oxford University Press.
Plato (1974) *The Republic*, 2nd ed., Harmondsworth: Penguin [orig. approx. 375 BC].

Ramachandran, V. S. and W. Hirstein (1999) "The Science of Art: A Neurological Theory of Aesthetic Experience," *Journal of Consciousness Studies* 6: 15–51.
Sayre-McCord, G. (1994) "On Why Hume's 'General Point of View' Isn't Ideal—And Shouldn't Be," *Social Philosophy and Policy* 11: 202–28.
Shelley, J. (2007) "Critical Compatibilism," in M. Kieran and D. Lopes (eds.) *Knowing Art: Essays in Aesthetics and Epistemology*, Dordrecht: Springer.
Sibley, F. (1959) "Aesthetic Concepts," *The Philosophical Review* 68: 421–50.
—— (1965) "Aesthetic and Nonaesthetic," *The Philosophical Review* 74: 135–59.
—— (1983) "General Criteria and Reasons in Aesthetics," in J. Fisher (ed.) *Essays on Aesthetics*, Philadephia: Temple University Press.
Sperber, D. and D. Wilson (1995) *Relevance: Communication and Cognition*, Oxford: Blackwell.
Stock, K. (2007) "Fiction and Psychological Insight," in M. Kieran and D. Lopes (eds.) *Knowing Art: Essays in Aesthetics and Epistemology*, Dordrecht: Springer.
Stokes, D (2007) "Art and Modal Knowledge," in M. Kieran and D. Lopes (eds.) *Knowing Art: Essays in Aesthetics and Epistemology*, Dordrecht: Springer.
Stolnitz, J. (1992) "The Cognitive Triviality of Art," *British Journal of Aesthetics*, 32: 191–200.
Walton, K. (1970) "Categories of Art," *The Philosophical Review* 79: 334–67.
Wollheim, R. (1980) *Art and its Objects*, 2nd ed., Cambridge: Cambridge University Press.

35
MORAL KNOWLEDGE
Robert Audi

Common parlance seems to presuppose that there is genuine moral knowledge. We hear people say that someone knew full well that he was doing wrong and did it anyway, or that someone knew a friend had been immoral but would not acknowledge this, or that some people pretend not to know their moral responsibilities. Indeed, mere sanity is supposed to imply ability to "know the difference between right and wrong." But there are skeptics about moral knowledge, as about other kinds of knowledge; and the former include people not skeptical about other domains, such as natural science (see Sinnott-Armstrong 2006 for a full-scale treatment of the nature and varieties of moral skepticism). Two kinds of skepticism should be distinguished. One denies that there is moral knowledge but not that there is *justification* for moral claims. The other denies that there is either moral justification or moral knowledge. We must consider both possibilities, but the prior question is whether there are even moral propositions to be known.

I. The Cognitivity of Moral Discourse

On one view of moral discourse, there *cannot* be moral knowledge or moral justification, owing to lack of the right raw material. I refer to *noncognitivism*. In a generic form, this is the view that moral claims, such as that lying is wrong, are not "cognitive," i.e., do not express propositions or anything capable of truth or falsity (of being "cognized" in one sense of that term). Originally, noncognitivism took the form of emotivism, for which moral claims express emotion but not propositions (Ayer 1936). A later version is *prescriptivism*, which made their prescriptive—especially, action-guiding—content, as opposed to any descriptive content they have, central (Hare 1952). More recent versions are often called *expressivism*, since they take moral claims to express attitudes or commitments but not to assert propositions (Gibbard 1990). All of these views are antirealist: they assert or presuppose that there are no moral properties to be truly *or* falsely ascribed to actions or persons and, correspondingly, no facts about any moral reality for declarative moral sentences to express.

Why might one hold noncognitivism? Once this is understood, we can see whether the major alternatives in moral epistemology can solve the problems that motivate noncognitivism. Let us begin with an influential metaphysical perspective.

Suppose that, like a great many philosophers, one holds a kind of naturalism that, at least since David Hume, has gained strength in the Anglo-American intellectual world and elsewhere. In broad terms, this kind of naturalism is the view that nature—roughly, the physical universe—is all there is and that the only basic truths are truths of nature (for an examination of the varieties and some difficulties of naturalism, see Audi 2000).

Then, any genuine properties will be physical—the kind central in explanations and predictions in physics, chemistry, and other natural sciences. If there are moral properties, then, they must be reducible to physical properties. Noncognitivists, however, deny that moral terms express anything for which such reducibility is possible. For them, to say that an act is wrong, for instance, is not to attribute a property to it, such as causing suffering. It is to express a certain kind of negative attitude toward the act, as opposed to ascribing a property to it.

*On the epistemological side, it is not unnatural to think that if a claim represents knowledge, it should be appraisable on the basis of *experience or reason*: roughly, on the basis of sense experience or a priori reflection (the kind appropriate to logic and pure mathematics). But many skeptics and some non-skeptical naturalists deny that either experience or a priori reflection can yield moral knowledge. They hold that perception cannot ground it; moral terms do not, for instance, express observable properties. Moral terms are not even empirical in the way psychological ones are: not, for example, names of emotions or attitudes. But moral terms are also not the kind central in logic or mathematics, where self-evidence and rigorous proof can ground knowledge.

Some thinkers endorse noncognitivism for a different kind of reason. Many follow Hume in maintaining that moral judgments are, on their own, motivating for those who hold them, whereas "factual" judgments (roughly, descriptive judgments) are not. This view goes with the idea that actions—including omissions—speak louder than words: when (without special circumstances) people do not act on their declared moral judgments, we do not believe they really hold those judgments. We also tend to be motivated to act on our own moral judgments, and they often "feel" motivating. To be sure, we are also motivated by discovering such plain facts as that a hailstorm is approaching; but noncognitivists tend to hold that this is because we are motivated by an independent aversion to being hit by hail, not just by judging that there is in fact a hailstorm approaching. Moral judgments, by contrast, are considered *intrinsically* motivating, needing no support from independent desires (for detailed accounts of the relation of moral cognitions to motivation, see Audi 1997; cf. Smith 1993 and Parfit 1997).

One might think that, for noncognitivists, ordinary moral discourse cannot be seen as rational. But noncognitivism does not imply that. Attitudes, after all, and not just propositions, might be supported by good reasons and might be rational. To say, for instance, that only one of two assailants did wrong in beating an old man for his wallet, though they differed only in skin color, would be inadmissible: incapable of expressing a rational attitude. Morality can impose constraints on rational attitudes just as, on cognitivist views, it can impose them on believing propositions. Even a kind of objectivity seems possible: rational moral attitudes must be based not on prejudice but on relevant facts, such as facts about what causes suffering or promotes social harmony.

Many objections have been brought against noncognitivism (for criticism of Gibbard see Sinnott-Armstrong 1993 and Dreier 1999, which shows how a plausible generalization of the view tends to undermine its claim to expressivist as opposed to cognitivist status; and, on the Frege-Geach problem, van Roojen 1996, which is also a critique of Simon Blackburn). This is not the place to discuss these objections. It is better in a short sketch in moral epistemology to indicate what kinds of considerations support the alternative, moral realist views. If moral realism is sound, then there really are at least moral propositions to be candidates for knowledge, and there is less reason to deny cognitivity to moral claims that, in form and important functions, seem to ascribe genuine properties to acts and to have truth value.

II. Reductive Realism

Some philosophers hold reductivist views that challenge the metaphysical anti-realism common to noncognitivists. For reductivists, we *can* show something noncognitivists deny: that moral terms express natural properties, in a sense implying that moral properties are reducible to (hence really are) natural ones and thus are real.

John Stuart Mill appears to have held a realist ethical naturalism. At least three degrees of ethical naturalism should be distinguished. First, one might hold that moral properties are equivalent to certain natural ones. For instance, the property of being obligatory might be considered *equivalent* to the property of producing at least as favorable a contribution to the proportion of happiness to unhappiness (in some specified population) as any alternative the agent has. Second, one might hold that moral properties are *identical* with certain natural ones. The same example will serve: this intermediate naturalistic reductivism would simply interpret the equivalence as representing an identity rather than just a necessary correspondence: to be a moral property *is* to be a causal-hedonic property of the kind just illustrated. Third, a strong moral naturalism would take this identity claim to be conceptually true, in the sense entailing knowability on the basis of analysis of the constituent concepts.

Mill apparently held not only that moral properties are equivalent to certain natural ones but also (for at least some normative terms) the strong naturalistic view. He said, for instance, "that to think of an object as desirable (unless for the sake of its consequences), and to think of it as pleasant [where pleasantness is a natural, psychological property], are one and the same thing" (1861/1979, p. 38). Mill did not make all the distinctions just presented, but this statement (in which 'desirable' means roughly 'intrinsically good') at least illustrates one thesis of analytical naturalism even if, for deontic terms (e.g. 'ought', 'obligatory', and 'wrong'), he held only the intermediate view.

This intermediate naturalism is held by some who reject strong naturalism. On the theoretical reductivist view (sometimes called Cornell Realism), moral properties are like certain theoretical properties of a kind important in scientific theories. They are not observable, as are colors and shapes; but they are natural, causally efficacious, and understandable in a complex network of explanatory and descriptive relations to other natural properties (Boyd 1988; Sturgeon 1985).

On any of these reductivist views, moral knowledge is possible on the basis of the "descriptive" natural knowledge grounding it. For a very strong naturalism, to know that an action has a certain moral property is equivalent to knowing that it has the identical natural one, such as optimally conducing to the proportion of happiness to unhappiness in a certain population. For the theoretical and even the weak reductivist views, provided one knows to what natural property a moral property is identical (say by knowing a "bridge principle" linking them), one can have as good grounds for knowing that something has the moral property as for knowing it has the natural property with which that moral property is identical.

III. Non-reductive Realism

Moral realism and an associated moral epistemology need not be reductive, and philosophers tend to resist the strong theses constituted by reductive identifications. G. E. Moore, for instance, famously argued against naturalism about the good (he also said that all propositions about the good are synthetic; see 1903, p. 7). He did not, to be sure, consider theoretical naturalism, but he probably would have rejected the idea that identity of properties could be theoretical yet not conceptual. This is evidenced by his conceptually identifying *being right* with *being maximally contributory toward the (intrinsically) good*. That identification would make him a reductivist about the right—a "definist" in one terminology—but not a naturalist about the right, since he regarded the property of being intrinsically good as non-natural. In any case, he thought we have, through rational intuition, two kinds of general moral knowledge: conceptual knowledge about what kinds of acts are right (a kind of moral knowledge); and metaphysical knowledge indicating what kinds of things are intrinsically good. Since some kinds of goodness are non-moral, and since he might have considered moral goodness derivative from non-moral goodness, we might call knowledge of the good, for him, *ethical* rather than moral.

It is important to see, however, that Moore accommodated the possibility of moral knowledge of particular propositions, such as that a specific killing was wrong. For him, we can know such a proposition if we know that the action failed to conduce at least as favorably to the good as any alternative the agent had. Granted, one could be skeptical here, but many would think that we *can* know, or at least justifiedly believe, that, say, the gratuitous killing of a philanthropist satisfies that description.

If Moore is an *anti-reductivist* intuitionist, an intuitionist as such might simply be a *metaphysical neutralist*: a neutralist intuitionism leaves open whether moral properties are natural but asserts that we can sometimes have non-inferential intuitive knowledge of moral truths involving them (Audi 2004). Broadly interpreted, W. D. Ross's view might be understood so, though his philosophical judgment was apparently non-naturalist. Ross certainly did not agree with Moore in taking propositions about the right to be equivalent to any set of propositions about the good; but he did hold, with Moore and others, that moral properties are *consequential* on non-moral ones: i.e., moral properties, say wrongness, are possessed *in virtue of* some natural property, such as killing. (See Ross 1930, p. 28, on parti- vs. toti-resultant attributes.) Consequentiality is not a reductive relation. Being wrong might be consequential on being a killing, but is not reducible to that property. Still, the consequentiality of a property on properties of another kind does not preclude its reducibility to *some* set of properties of the kind representing its basis. When a thing has a moral property, such as being wrong, in virtue of possessing a natural property, say being a killing, the former is not even equivalent to the latter; but it does not follow that being wrong is irreducible to *any* set of properties, including a set of the kind—for instance, natural properties—of the property on which it is consequential.

In epistemology, Ross was a rationalist: he held (against Hume, Mill, and other empiricists) that we can know substantive propositions (as opposed, say, to truths of formal logic) a priori, hence without relying on perceptual evidence. Ross, indeed, held that it is *self-evident* that given an act's having certain properties (a kind one might consider natural), it also has the moral property of being a "prima facie duty." By this he meant roughly being morally supported by a consideration (say, being promised) that, if not opposed by an at least equally strong consideration (say, causing harm), indicates what one ought, all things considered, to do. Now the self-evident is knowable a priori, so such principles as that lying is prima facie wrong represent a kind of general moral knowledge accessible to us. Ross emphasized that propositions about *final* duty—duty all things considered—such as what I am *overall* obligated to do for a distressed friend, are never self-evident and that even propositions that are self-evident might not be knowable without a certain "mental maturity" (Ross 1930, p. 29). Unfortunately, however, he compared the self-evident moral truths in question with *obvious* truths, such as those of elementary arithmetic (pp. 29–30). This comparison opens the way to a skepticism that is arguably not justified against his main view.

If intuitionists are to claim self-evidence for the moral principles they consider basic, they need an account of the self-evident that accommodates the intuitive idea of knowability without dependence on premises (an idea implicit in a proposition's being evident in *itself*), but does not invite an expectation of obviousness or even incontestability. Here is the core of my account: Self-evident propositions are truths such that (a) adequately understanding them is sufficient for justification for believing them (which does not entail that adequately understanding them *entails* believing them), and (b) believing them on the basis of adequately understanding them entails knowing them. We might also speak of a *full* understanding to avoid the suggestion that an adequate understanding is simply one sufficient for knowledge of the self-evident; neither term is ideal, but 'full' has the disadvantage of suggesting maximality. On this conception of self-evident propositions, they need not be obvious or even readily understandable. (For a detailed account of self-evidence, see my 1999; my 2008 makes some extensions.)

It is also important for understanding self-evidence to see that being justified *in* believing does not entail actually believing. Think of parents who have excellent evidence of their children's wrong-doing, but cannot believe them guilty. The proposed account of self-evidence thus allows for rejection of a self-evident proposition by people holding competing ethical theories or by skeptical philosophers who might not believe even what non-skeptics find obvious. A utilitarian, for instance, might hold that in certain terminal illnesses, voluntary euthanasia would not be even prima facie wrong. Even lengthy and thoughtful discussion between the opposing theorists on this issue might not yield consensus.

One might now think that if self-evidence allows for such persisting disagreements between rational moral philosophers, then even the self-evidence of certain moral propositions does not guarantee their knowability, at least by a normal person. This view is defensible, but has been challenged (Audi 2008; Kelly 2005). It cannot be appraised here, but two points will help to put it in perspective. First, if disagreements of this sort preclude anyone's knowing the disputed proposition (or its negation), then a similar skepticism besets claims to scientific knowledge and perhaps even to mathematical knowledge, at least where incontestable proofs are unobtainable. Second, and perhaps more important, the possibility of such disagreements does not imply that neither party can be *justified*. Since justification for believing a proposition, unlike knowing it, does not entail its truth, two people can be justified in believing mutually incompatible propositions. If knowledge is unobtainable, then, justification might not be. Justification is an important epistemic status. Achieving it implies both that one is intellectually responsible regarding the proposition in question and, often, that where one's belief is true, it constitutes knowledge.

If intuition, conceived as a kind of rational cognition, can yield moral knowledge, one might wonder whether a theorist who thinks there is intuitive moral knowledge can account for the epistemological role of reflective equilibrium. Consider a case of such equilibrium: a kind of balance among one's intuitions and other cognitions concerning a judgment of what, in a case of conflicting prima facie obligations, one ought, all things considered, to do. (Rawls 1971/1999 is a major source of discussion of reflective equilibrium, which he calls "a mutual adjustment of principles and considered judgments" (p. 18 n7); see also 17–19 and 42–44.) Suppose that as a physician you promise a man to keep confidential that you are treating him for AIDS. Now imagine that his estranged wife becomes your patient and tells you she plans to return to him soon. She has discovered he is your patient and asks you whether he is infected. You can say you never discuss one patient with another without the prior consent of the former, but you might know that he will not give his consent and cannot be reached in time. This kind of case is one in which you might have no intuition as to what to do and should consider all the facts and select the most plausible option. You might, to be sure, have an intuitive sense that answering her question directly would be wrong: you would either break a promise or lie. The thought of either puts you in disequilibrium. In seeking a solution that achieves equilibrium, you might see that you can say that your policy is to urge anyone who has the least doubt in such cases to exercise great caution. The thought that this might reveal the confidential information could now be a discordant note, but that might be neutralized by the realization that you would be making a policy statement. Might you *know* the truth of your moral judgment arrived at by achieving such equilibrium? There is no reason to rule this out, but there is also no guarantee that reaching reflective equilibrium on a moral question implies knowledge or even justification.

We should also ask whether a *failure* to achieve reflective equilibrium regarding a moral question implies that one does *not* know its answer. This is doubtful; still, such a failure can be *disconfirmatory* and might indicate that one at least lacks justification. The search for reflective equilibrium, then, can yield confirmation *or* disconfirmation. But its value in this does not imply that moral knowledge never comes without it. In one kind of case, however, it is commonly essential: in seeking to frame a generalization, say for dealing with conflicts like the one just considered. Here we should achieve an outlook in which any principle we endorse is consistent with cases—real and hypothetical—of the kind it bears on. As Ross apparently saw, a lesson of such efforts is that holding unqualified generalizations, such as 'Never break a promise'—by contrast with 'There is always a prima facie *reason* to keep promises'—is unlikely to allow maintaining equilibrium in difficult cases. On a modest moral epistemology, then, such unqualified generalizations are not taken to represent knowledge.

What we have seen so far brings out both the epistemic resources of moral realism, especially as supported by intuition, to provide for moral knowledge and justification. But we have also seen reason to think that skepticism about moral justification is less plausible than skepticism about moral knowledge—which is not to say just how plausible either is.

One further point of clarification should help. Our topic has been normative: mainly knowledge or justification regarding propositions *of morality*. These are chiefly (1) attributions of moral properties to specific actions or particular persons or (2) generalizations, such as Ross's prima facie duty principles or Mill's Principle of Utility, which can support such attributions when the relevant act is subsumable under them. Our concern has not been propositions *about morality*, the kind belonging to metaethics, such as the thesis that there are irreducible moral properties. One can certainly be skeptical regarding them as well, but the two kinds of skepticism are independent.

IV. Moral Knowledge and Reasons for Action

For Ross and, indeed, for any moral non-skeptic, one kind of moral knowledge is to the effect that there is a moral reason for action. A Rossian intuitionist should hold that knowledge of the obtaining of any of the a priori grounds of duty, for instance a promise, is sufficient for knowledge of a prima facie moral reason. More is required for knowledge of an *overall* reason. Other moral theorists can make the same distinction. At least typically, we need better grounds for knowledge that an act is supported by overall moral reason (hence is a final obligation) than for knowledge that it is supported by a prima facie reason. The same holds for justification in ascribing reasons.

So far, I have left open whether having knowledge or justification regarding moral reasons implies seeing the element in question, say promising, *as* a reason. It does not. Knowledge of an element that *is* a reason does not entail knowledge of its *being* a reason. Children, even before acquiring the concept of a reason, acquire some concepts, such as that of hurting someone or of lying, whose referents (hurting and lying) *constitute* reasons. A child can, then, believe that hitting baby sister would hurt her before the child can see this as a reason not to hit her.

Even where we know there is a moral reason to A, moreover, we might not know its *weight*—how strong a reason it is—either in absolute terms or in relation to some competing reason. This suffices to explain why resolving conflicts of prima facie obligation can be so difficult. Is the obligation not to harm others so strong that, to protect someone from harm, one should always be ready to violate the obligation not to lie? Ross addressed this kind of question and held that there is no general principle for resolving such conflicts (1930, pp. 30–32). Mill recognized such conflicts too, but considered his Principle of Utility sufficient for resolving them (1861/1979, p. 25). This position does not commit Mill to holding that we can in general *know* the exact weight of a moral reason or can always in practice know even which of two conflicting sets of obligations is stronger. But his utilitarianism does appear to commit him to maintaining that the strength of a moral reason is "proportional" to the extent to which the consequences of performing it yield a favorable ratio of the good to the bad as compared with available alternatives. (The kind of measurement of happiness and suffering to which Mill is committed is not ratio measurement; and, for decision problems, his qualitative factor, as where one pleasure is better than another, can be represented in terms of quantity, say, by simply assigning much higher numerical value to the higher-quality pleasure as against the competing lower-quality one.)

For utilitarian and certain other consequentialist theories, then, a kind of commensurability of different moral reasons is posited, and their relative strength can be taken to be, in principle, knowable. One might think that, insofar as we can weight certain elements in life, such as hurting people and lying to them or, on the positive side, aiding others and improving one's own capacities, we can place acts in a hierarchy depending on the net value of their consequences. But if this should be so, it would be at best a contingent truth. Some lies might have good consequences overall; some beneficent deeds might have bad consequences overall. Commensurability of the imperfectly quantitative kind Mill is committed to implies at most that we can know, in individual cases, which of two conflicting sets of obligations is stronger. It does not imply that we can typically know such generalizations as that hurting someone is invariably worse than lying.

Intuitionists have tended to deny that there is any a priori hierarchy among the prima facie obligations; and although many of them would hold that by and large the obligation not to harm is stronger than the obligation of beneficence, no plausible intuitionism implies the a priori knowability of such overriding for any particular conflict between prima facie obligations. Here, however, the reason for the restriction is not the difficulty of calculation, as with total "utility"; it is that overall obligation is not an additive matter in the first place. Intuitionists might point out that an act could be seen to have complex relations of *fittingness* (a non-additive notion) that bear on whether it is morally permissible. Thus, criticizing a student in detail for a careless paper, though a prima facie teaching obligation, might ill-befit the student's vulnerability. There might be overall moral reason to abstain from the action even if its long-run consequences have positive value exceeding the negative value of the suffering one would cause.

Kant also deserves discussion in relation to the possibility of moral knowledge in the common cases of conflicting prima facie obligations. Interpreting his ethics in an overall way is impossible here, but perhaps we might assume that he took us to have a priori knowledge of the categorical imperative, say of the truth of the principle (which is a reading of one of his formulations of the imperative) that an act is right if and only if it treats no one concerned "merely as a means" and everyone concerned "as an end." He might have held that we can also know a priori the kinds of principles and applications of them that we find in relation to his four famous examples (Kant 1948, secs 429–430).

Kant was not committed to claiming the possibility of a priori moral knowledge regarding specific actions. He seems to have held, however, that one could know what one ought to do by pursuing the question in the light of the categorical imperative (presumably in any formulation, but certainly using two or more formulations for the clarity one can thereby gain). Did Kant think that we could be assisted in achieving moral knowledge by appeal to an a priori hierarchy among the prima facie obligations? He apparently held (in some passages) that where perfect and imperfect obligations conflict, for instance obligations not to lie with obligations to protect the innocent, the former have priority. But this view is not required by the categorical imperative: situations of conflict can be referred to that master principle *regardless* of the kinds of obligations involved. Once a resolution is reached by using the imperative, one can claim knowledge or justification of the judgment thus formed; but the procedure is complex enough to allow skeptics to raise doubts. Nonetheless, the categorical imperative framework surely adds to our resources for justifying moral claims. It is also important to see that often a judgment based on a proper appeal to the categorical imperative is also supported by intuition.

Particularly in interpreting Kant, we should distinguish between knowledge of moral obligation and knowledge of "moral worth," roughly moral creditworthiness. He saw that we can do what we ought to do, but do it for the wrong reason, or at least for a reason that is of the wrong sort to give the action based on it moral worth. If Kant was not a skeptic about our knowledge of the obligatory, he was perhaps skeptical about presumptive knowledge of moral worth in certain cases (this issue is discussed in detail in chapter 3 of my 2006, which addresses both actions supported by more than one piece of practical reasoning and actions performed for two or more reasons). If I cannot know that I am keeping a promise for a moral reason rather than from self-interest, I cannot know that my doing it has moral worth. Knowledge that I *have* a moral reason and have acted in accord with it—have done the deed it calls for—does not imply knowledge that I have acted *for* that reason. Similarly, knowledge that a person acts virtuously does not imply knowledge (or even necessarily a basis for knowledge) that the person is virtuous. Prudence can effectively mimic virtue.

The upshot of these considerations about moral worth is that one kind of moral knowledge depends on knowledge of why people do certain deeds and not just of why they *should* do them or of whether, on a given occasion, they have done what they should.

But it is sometimes enormously difficult to know why people do what they do. Even in our own case, we can easily be mistaken. None of these points commits us to wholesale skepticism about knowledge of moral worth. But that knowledge is difficult to attain in some cases, and achieving it might require considerable psychological insight.

V. Moral Knowledge and Ethical Relativism

Our discussion has presupposed that if moral claims are truth-valued, they are in some sense universally true or universally false, in the same way that ordinary descriptive factual propositions, say common-sense observational statements, are true or false. Is there, however, a way their truth might be relative, in which case knowledge of them would be correspondingly so? There are many varieties of ethical relativism, but it might suffice for our purposes to consider three kinds.

The first case is the thesis that moral obligation (hence at least one kind of moral truth) is relative to circumstances. Consider the prohibition of killing. It is not generally thought that killing is wrong *when* required for self-defense. We might call this view *circumstantial relativism* or *relativizationism*. It is compatible with standard ethical views so long as they are taken to ascribe overall moral obligations to persons in the light of their circumstances. This is how standard views are best interpreted, so the idea that moral obligation is relative to circumstances is not incompatible with such universalistic theories as those of Aristotle, Kant, Mill, and Ross (cf. Aristotle's point, in *Nicomachean Ethics* 1106b–1107a, that "virtue . . . is a state involving a rational choice, consisting of a mean *relative to us* and determined by reason" (emphasis added)).

The second kind of relativism is less easily characterized: it is the view that moral standards are relative to culture or other contingencies of human life in such a way that there are no universally valid moral standards or even universally valid ways to justify moral claims. The force of such a view is, in part, to contrast ethics with science, for which both kinds of standards are widely believed to exist. For this kind of relativism—call it *status relativism*, since it concerns the ontological and epistemic status of moral claims—moral knowledge is knowledge of (or in some sense within) a particular culture's or group's standards of behavior. One could know that, for instance, incest is wrong-in-America, but not that it is wrong simpliciter. Exactly what this contrast comes to is not altogether clear, but a way to interpret it can be seen in relation to the third kind of relativism.

Suppose that, instead of speaking of morality simpliciter, we speak of *a* morality relative to a culture (or other suitably cohesive group) and conceive a morality as a set of standards for regulating behavior in a group such that the standards (1) have as their main purpose to preserve social coordination and promote some kind of human welfare and (2) are internalized in most group members in such a way that their violation tends to evoke strong principled disapproval and conformity to them tends to be encouraged and to evoke approval. We can now speak of a *pluralistic relativism*: the view that there is more than one (actual) morality, and no one set of moral standards that can be properly considered the one true morality (this kind of relativistic view is expressed by Wong (2006), e.g. pp. 68–70; but note the axiology, for instance in the relation to "worthwhile lives" (pp. 69 and 72), where one senses a commitment to a kind of objective value). Notice, however, that this view allows that all the moralities that can play the indicated role for human groups might share *some* standards. It is also left open that justification of moral claims within a group might be *objective*, even scientific.

Pluralistic relativism, then, though it denies that there is *one* true morality, leaves open that there might be only a limited number of overlapping moralities that can serve the social function of a morality. It also leaves open that the differences might be, from the point of view of the standard ethical theories, minor. Certain elements in what is commonly called 'sexual morality' (say, standards prohibiting extra-marital sex) might exemplify standards that can vary among societies across which there is almost complete agreement on, say human rights. In any case, pluralistic relativism would provide a basis for both *intragroup moral knowledge*—knowledge of what kinds of acts are, under the group's standards, obligatory—and also some *intergroup moral knowledge*—knowledge of what is obligatory under the standards common to the groups in question. Like the other forms of relativism, then, this one does not entail the impossibility of moral knowledge or, especially, of justification for moral claims.

VI. The Possibility of Cognitivity without Realism

We began by considering the view that moral claims lack cognitive content and hence are not even candidates for objects of knowledge or justified belief. We saw how a commitment to naturalism, together with certain other views, motivates noncognitivism. Without implying that noncognitivism is indefensible, we proceeded to consider realist cognitivist views that seem sufficiently plausible to warrant considering noncognitivism both theoretically avoidable and a departure from common sense. But the views we contrasted with it, including the relativist positions, are all realist. They differ about the nature of moral properties but each countenances them. Might one preserve cognitivity without endorsing realism?

In part, this is what at least some ethical constructivists attempt to do. Consider how John Rawls views Kant. He contrasts Kant with ethical intuitionists, for whom Rawls thinks "moral first principles and judgments, when correct, are true statements about an independent order of moral values" (Rawls 1993, p. 91); for Kant, "the order of moral and political values must be made, or itself constituted, by the principles and conceptions of practical reason" (p. 99). This view goes with the point that "Kant is the historical source of the idea that reason, both theoretical and practical, is self-originating and self-authenticating" (p. 100). Rawls does not explain how anything can originate or even authenticate itself. Both ideas are unclear, and whether Kant himself is committed to relying on them cannot be pursued here.

For our purposes, it might suffice to distinguish three things that, consistently with what Rawls says above, might be meant by 'moral constructivism' and to connect them with the possibility of moral knowledge.

A *genetic construction* (in ethics) is a procedure for arriving at (roughly, formulating and accepting) moral principles or moral judgments, as where one must make a decision on what to do. *Genetic constructivism*, then, would be the associated view that moral principles and judgments are arrived at by (or might evolve from) some procedure, such as applying the categorical imperative.

By contrast, an *epistemic construction* is a procedure, potentially but not necessarily combinable with a genetic construction, for coming to know or acquire justification for moral judgments or principles. *Epistemological constructivism* would be the view that such knowledge or justification—where "justification is addressed to others" (p. 100)—must be acquired, or at least validatable, in the prescribed way. Again, the categorical imperative might serve as the core of a framework for constructing a justification of a moral judgment.

Thirdly, a *metaphysical construction* is a way of *creating* a grounding basis for one or more sound moral judgments or principles, as where, in accord with practical reason, one creates valid moral principles or just laws, which in turn create obligations. Rawls's terminology of self-authentication suggests that he takes Kant to be a metaphysical constructivist, one who regards the moral soundness of a judgment as *created* by, or in any case grounded in, its emergence from a proper construction, such as a correct application of the categorical imperative. That lying is wrong, for instance, is not true because, owing to "an independent order of moral values," the property of being a lie grounds the property of wrongness; it is true because (for one thing) we can construct a valid veracity standard from the categorical imperative and cannot rationally universalize principles that generally allow lying.

How one might succeed in either epistemic or metaphysical constructions without *some* "independent" standards to guide one, such as the idea that human beings have value and hence cannot be treated merely as means, is puzzling. It is not clear, moreover, that Kantian ethics is committed to affirming this possibility. In the *Groundwork* Kant posits "something *whose existence* has *in itself* absolute value," such that "in it alone, would there be the ground of a possible categorical imperative" (1948, sec. 428, p. 95). The reference to a ground suggests an antecedent basis for the soundness of the imperative. This suggestion is combinable with the view that hedonic value and promissory obligation may be as plainly real as the experiences and interpersonal relations on which they are grounded.

The important point here is that despite the terminology of construction, none of the positions just described is necessarily anti-realist. Even metaphysical constructivism presupposes using some raw materials and can be taken to describe a method for discovering a principle true to the moral facts or at least the axiological facts, for instance the fact that rational beings have a kind of absolute value. Obligatoriness, for example, would be conceived as the property of being endorsable on the basis of a certain kind of constructive procedure: to be obligated to keep a promise would be to have the property of being such that, if we correctly viewed the facts of one's case in relation to the categorical imperative, we would frame a principle of action requiring promise-keeping in the circumstances one is in. The obligation is, to be sure, a highly complex property and can be viewed as a construct from a sound reasoning process; but (a) the property of undergoing such a process and (b) the resultant moral property an act might have of being required by the conclusion of that process are real properties. Given that they essentially involve *our* reasoning, they need not be conceived as part of an "independent order"; but other theorists might note that in this sense of 'independent', our pleasures and pains are not part of such an order either: they are intrapersonal and depend on our experiences. If there were no experiences, there would be no hedonic value. Similarly, if there were no interpersonal relations, there would be no promissory obligations.

* * *

If we distinguish moral knowledge from knowledge of morality, and if we take moral discourse to be cognitive, then apart from strong skepticism (which is set aside in this chapter), there are many plausible ethical theories that provide a basis for the view that we know both some moral principles and some singular moral judgments. Moreover, since, in the contexts that concern us, knowledge requires stronger grounding than justification, whatever the case for our having moral knowledge, the case for our having moral justification with the same content is stronger. Similarly, whatever the case for knowledge or justification regarding overall judgments of moral obligation, there is a stronger case for prima facie judgments favoring the same act.

Parallel points hold for knowledge and justification regarding moral reasons for action. Those reasons, like moral judgments based on them, divide into the prima facie and the overall, and knowledge and justification concerning the latter are more difficult to achieve than concerning the former. One could thus be a skeptic about judgments of overall obligation even if one countenances knowledge of prima facie obligations. It is important to see, however, that even positing variable degrees of justification that one considers insufficient for knowledge might allow for objectivity in holding moral judgments and provide for the possibility of rational resolution of moral disagreements. Natural facts might be an anchor for moral judgments even if the former do not dictate the latter and allow for disagreements within the range that the anchoring permits.

The case of knowledge of moral worth, however, is different from all those just recalled. The moral worth of an action or person depends essentially on operative motivation—on the motivational explanation of the action or the motivational nature of the person—and these can be very difficult to know, even in our own case. We do seem sometimes to know that we have acted *for* a moral reason, or that a person is predominantly motivated by morally acceptable desires; but here skepticism is more plausible than regarding moral obligation. Skepticism is, in any event, a powerful view and, at best, difficult to refute. Whether some degree of it is warranted in moral matters is a perennial issue, but we have seen no reason to consider wholesale skepticism unavoidable or even to think that on this point ethics is necessarily more vulnerable than other domains of inquiry.

Acknowledgment

For helpful comments on earlier versions of this chapter I thank an anonymous reader, Michael Quante, and audiences at the Universities of Cologne and Notre Dame.

References

Aristotle. 2000. *Nicomachean Ethics*. Roger Crisp trans. Cambridge: Cambridge University Press.
Audi, R. 1997. Moral Judgment and Reasons for Action, in Garrett Cullity and Berys Gaut, eds., *Ethics and Practical Reason*, Oxford: Oxford University Press, 125–159.
Audi, R. 1999. Self-Evidence. *Philosophical Perspectives* 13, 205–228.
Audi, R. 2000. Philosophical Naturalism at the Turn of the Century. *Journal of Philosophical Research* 25, 27–45.
Audi, R. 2004. *The Good in the Right: A Theory of Intuition and Intrinsic Value*. Princeton: Princeton University Press.
Audi, R. 2006. *Practical Reasoning and Ethical Decision*. London: Routledge.
Audi, R. 2008. Intuition, Inference, and Rational Disagreement in Ethics. *Ethical Theory and Moral Practice* 11, 475–492.
Ayer, A. J. 1936. *Language, Truth and Logic*. London: Gollancz.
Boyd, R. 1988. How To Be a Moral Realist. In Geoffrey Sayre-McCord, ed. *Essays on Moral Realism*. Ithaca: Cornell University Press.
Dreier, J. 1999. Transforming Expressivism. *Nous* 33, 4, 558–572.
Gibbard, A. 1990. *Wise Choices, Apt Feelings*. Cambridge, MA: Harvard University Press.
Hare, R. M. 1952. *The Language of Morals*. Oxford: Oxford University Press.
Kant, I. 1948. *Groundwork of the Metaphysics of Morals*. H. J. Paton trans. London: Hutchinson.

Kelly, T. 2005. The Epistemic Significance of Disagreement. *Oxford Studies in Epistemology*. Oxford: Oxford University Press, 167–196.
Mill, J. S. 1861/1979. *Utilitarianism*. Indianapolis: Hackett.
Moore, G. E. 1903. *Principia Ethica*. Cambridge: Cambridge University Press.
Parfit, D. 1997. Reason and Motivation. *Proceedings of the Aristotelian Society*, supp. vol. 71, 99–130.
Rawls, J. 1971/1999. *A Theory of Justice*. Cambridge, MA: Harvard University Press.
Rawls, J. 1993. *Political Liberalism*. New York: Columbia University Press.
Ross, W. D. 1930. *The Right and the Good*. Oxford: Oxford University Press.
Sinnott-Armstrong, W. 2006. *Moral Skepticisms*. Oxford: Oxford University Press.
Sinnott-Armstrong, W. 1993. Some Problems for Gibbard's Norm Expressivism. *Philosophical Studies* 69, 297–313.
Smith, M. 1993. *The Moral Problem*. Oxford: Blackwell.
Sturgeon, N. 1985. Moral Explanations. In David Copp and David Zimmerman, eds., *Morality, Reason, and Truth*. Totowa, NJ: Roman and Allanheld.
Van Roojen, M. 1996. Expressivism and Irrationality. *The Philosophical Review* 105, 311–333.
Wong, D. 2006. *Natural Moralities*. Oxford: Oxford University Press.

36
RELIGIOUS KNOWLEDGE
Linda Zagzebski

I. Introduction

Religion is a complex human practice that includes distinctive emotions, beliefs, acts, and artistic and musical creations that express and foster a sense of the sacred. People who belong to a particular faith tradition generally think that they have religious knowledge acquired through the practice of their religion, but their religious beliefs form only one part of the practice. Beliefs have a more central role for some people than for others, and beliefs are much more important in some religions than in others. Christianity and Islam are doctrinal religions the practice of which makes certain beliefs crucial, whereas Buddhism is much less focused on requiring belief as part of the practice. Nonetheless, an important way we distinguish one religion from another religion is in the beliefs that are characteristic of the different religious traditions. There might also be beliefs that distinguish those who practice religion from those who practice none, but that difference is harder to identify.

Philosophers care about whether the teachings of any religion are true because many religions offer answers to questions philosophers ask: What is the origin of the material world? What is the nature of the human person? Is there a God? Where did good and evil come from? Is there an afterlife? Philosophers ask these questions from outside the practice of any religion and without assuming that one or more religions offer true answers to these questions. Philosophy is a practice also, and while the rules of philosophy are themselves a topic for philosophical debate, it is fair to say that philosophers have always had especially strong standards for what counts as good answers to questions like those given above, and especially strong standards for evaluating answers that are proposed by others. To the extent that the beliefs of one religious practice compete with the beliefs of another practice on issues philosophers raise, philosophy attempts to adjudicate the dispute.

Philosophers make more distinctions than those commonly made outside the practice of philosophy. An important one for the topic of this essay is the distinction between knowledge and reasonable belief. Philosophers almost always agree that you cannot know something unless it is true, but you can be reasonable in believing something even when it is false. For instance, you can be perfectly reasonable in believing that high blood cholesterol increases your chances of getting heart disease, but if it turns out that the belief is false, you do not know it. So believing reasonably does not guarantee that you get the truth, and so it does not guarantee knowledge. It is also possible that you get the truth without believing reasonably. You can be unreasonable but lucky. So maybe you believe that drinking green tea increases longevity because you read it in an advertisement for green tea. But even if it's true that green tea will make you live longer, you do not know it if your source is an ad. You do not know it because the belief is unreasonable in your circumstances. So knowledge seems to require some combination of believing the truth and believing reasonably.

The way in which truth and reasonable belief come apart makes it tempting to think that philosophers should undertake a discussion of the reasonableness of religious belief independently of an investigation of religious truth. In other words, truth is one thing, reasonableness is another, and knowledge is some combination of the two. If so, religious truth is one thing, reasonableness in religious belief is another, and religious knowledge is some combination of the two. This seems to me to be basically correct as far as it goes, and for most of this essay I will concentrate on the reasonableness of religious belief rather than its truth. In a later section we will briefly look at an influential theory of religious knowledge that rejects the independence of truth and reasonableness in the case of Christian belief.

II. Religious Belief and the Guiding Principles of Enlightenment Philosophy

We have undertaken an investigation of the topic of religious knowledge by starting from philosophy, not religion, but it is not obvious that this is the right way to proceed. If we think that we should begin with a treatment of knowledge outside of the domain of religion, and then apply that treatment to the question of what religious knowledge is and whether it is possible, we might end up with a distorted view of the nature of religious knowledge. That is because philosophers generally begin with certain paradigm cases of knowledge, and that limits the way the concept of knowledge is applied outside the domain of the paradigms. Typically, the paradigms consist of simple cases of perceptual knowledge, knowledge based on memory, and uncontroversial cases of scientific knowledge. This method creates problems for understanding many kinds of knowledge, particularly moral knowledge, knowledge that depends upon skill, and knowledge that depends upon special experience or wisdom. If there is knowledge that derives from the wisdom of a few exceptional persons or traditions, or which depends upon experiences that not every human being has, religious knowledge would undoubtedly be in that category. But it is hard to account for this kind of knowledge if we permit the standard paradigms of knowledge to dictate the way we understand religious knowledge.

There are reasons why modern philosophers have the paradigms that we have. We have inherited attitudes and principles that severely limit the sources of knowledge that we trust, and which set norms for the proper relation among the beliefs we accept as reasonable. Most of these attitudes arose during the Enlightenment. Some of them are well known and often debated, but some of them have been so completely assimilated that they are not even noticed. For instance, students of Descartes are well aware that Descartes was a foundationalist. He thought that our beliefs have a structure like an inverted pyramid, with a few beliefs at the bottom supporting the entire edifice of our beliefs. To have the most reasonable and secure structure, the foundational beliefs ought to be indubitable—absolutely certain. Descartes' endowment included a widely discussed proclivity to foundationalism, but he also left us something else: a suspicion of epistemic authority and a lack of trust in the wisdom of traditions and other individuals. Descartes begins his *Meditations* with a lament that people and institutions he had previously trusted epistemically let him down. And his own senses had let him down. So his search for a new method of getting knowledge was based on a loss of epistemic trust in others and a partial loss of trust in himself. Experiences of loss of trust in authority and traditions were widespread in the early modern period. The result is that suspicion of authority of all kinds is deeply ingrained in modern culture.

We have inherited another idea from the Enlightenment that affects the way we approach religious knowledge: intellectual egalitarianism. It is commonly assumed that we are all roughly equal in our epistemic capacities. Any experience that grounds belief must be an experience anybody can have. Furthermore, it is assumed that either nobody is especially wise, or if there are wise persons, we cannot identify them in a way that would be useful to ourselves. So if there are epistemic communities, they have no authority structure, no trustworthy traditions, and there are no persons to whom the rest of us should defer for their insights. Both egalitarianism and the modern suspicion of authority are important components of political liberalism. So the suspicion of epistemic authority and intellectual egalitarianism has roots in modern political theory as well as in epistemology. These aspects of philosophical practice are generally not debated because they are taken for granted.

There are many different ways in which these principles and attitudes affect the way philosophers approach the reasonableness of religious belief and the possibility of religious knowledge. For instance, it is not generally noticed that discussions of the justification of religious belief, at least since Hume, assume two different forms of foundationalism. First, it is assumed that theistic belief is the foundation for all other religious beliefs. Second, it is assumed that beliefs are the foundation of religion. Religion is a practice in which beliefs come first and the rest of the practice, including religious emotions, acts, and rituals derive their justification from the independent justification of religious beliefs.

These two forms of foundationalism, together with intellectual egalitarianism and the suspicion of authority, explain a line of thought about religion that has persisted since the Enlightenment. This line of thought leads to a general doubt about the reasonableness of religious belief. It goes as follows:

(1) The justification of the practice of religion depends upon the justification of religious beliefs.
(2) The justification of religious beliefs depends upon the justification of theism.
(3) The justification of theism depends upon the success of arguments the premises of which must be accessible to any ordinary intelligent person. No special experience can be assumed, and no reliance on authority can be made.

These assumptions lead to skepticism about religion if we add one more claim:

(4) There is no sound argument for theism that begins with premises accessible to any ordinary intelligent person without reference to special experience or to authority.

In my judgment none of the claims (1)–(3) has been established. In fact, I believe that they are all false. It would take a much more elaborate theory of the human person than epistemologists agree upon to establish (1). Why should we think that emotions must be justified by a prior and independent justification of beliefs? Of course, some emotions do need to be justified by beliefs. For example, my fear of the object in my backyard needs to be justified by my belief that it is a large snake. But some emotions might be more basic than any belief and the emotion can serve to justify the belief, not vice versa. I think that there are emotions that ground moral beliefs in this way. We feel repugnance at a display of arrogance, admiration of an act of courage, and indignation at acts of injustice. If we are adept at moral philosophy we might be able to explain what is good about courage and how this is an act of courage, and what is bad about arrogance and injustice and why these particular acts qualify as acts of arrogance or injustice, but it is highly doubtful that we would engage in moral theorizing of this kind were it not for the more fundamental insight into the value or disvalue of particular acts that we detect through emotions (see, for example, Nussbaum 2001, esp. chap. 1; Solomon 2007, esp. chap 18; Zagzebski 2004, esp. chap. 2). Similarly, it seems to me that there is a range of religious emotions, including reverence, awe, and compunction that serve a parallel role in revealing religious value to us. In any case, the possibility that religious emotions play a fundamental role in the justification of religious practice has not been ruled out.

The truth of claim (2) has not been established either. Sandra Menssen and Thomas D. Sullivan (2002) have argued that it is not always reasonable to establish the existence of a person before establishing that that person has communicated with you. They give the example of the SETI research program (Search for Extra-Terrestrial Intelligence) which monitors huge numbers of radio signals from space in an attempt to discover if any of them would probably be sent by intelligent beings elsewhere in the universe. Suppose that the researchers discover a 1126-bit sequence corresponding to the prime numbers from 2 to 101. They would be justified in believing, "Some highly intelligent being has sent this signal," and that in turn would justify them in inferring, "Some highly intelligent form of life exists (or existed) elsewhere in the universe." Menssen and Sullivan use this example to argue for the falsehood of the following common view on the relation between belief in revelatory claims and belief in theism:

> One cannot obtain a convincing philosophical case for a revelatory claim without first obtaining a highly plausible case for the existence of God.

But if Menssen and Sullivan are right that that view is false, so is assumption (2). Although it is often taken for granted that it is not reasonable to adopt the beliefs of a theistic religion without first justifying belief in God, that might not be the way a reasonable person operates. A belief such as "I have been forgiven by God" logically presupposes that God exists, but it does not follow that I cannot be justified in believing the former without first being justified in believing the latter. In some cases it might be the reverse.

Claim (3) has been more frequently discussed than the other two, and it has many detractors. Some philosophers object to the fact that it rules out arguments for theism that are based on religious experience. William Alston (1993) has proposed that religious experience can justify religious belief for the persons who have those experiences, in a way that parallels the justification of beliefs about the physical world based on sense experience. This approach to religious knowledge is particularly attractive to empiricists since they maintain that individual experience is the ultimate source of knowledge. But it requires the rejection of a strong form of intellectual egalitarianism.

There are other reasons to reject claim (3). Religion is a communal practice. Of course, individual persons can be religious without participating in a religious community, but the main reason most religious persons think they have religious knowledge is that they have acquired it through participation in a religious community with authoritative teaching. The authority might derive from a sacred text or from tradition or from some combination of the two, but it is very doubtful that most people think their religious knowledge derives from their personal experience and the use of their own reason. Nor do they think that their beliefs are based on testimony from their community, the trustworthiness of which is something they can demonstrate by the use of their reason unaided by participants in that same community. What account of knowledge and reasonable belief would explain this?

My position is that trust in ourselves is the bottom line, but self-trust leads us to trust certain others more than ourselves in some respects. Self-trust supports trust in authority and in the wisdom of certain individuals. One way to see this is that there is a natural desire for truth, and there is a natural belief that the natural desire for truth is satisfiable. Trusting that natural belief requires us to have a basic trust that our natural faculties and dispositions to form beliefs put us in a good position to get the truth. But we do not trust ourselves equally all of the time, and we trust ourselves in particular when we have the disciplined love of truth I call epistemic conscientiousness. We are epistemically conscientious when we exercise our belief-forming faculties to the best of our ability. When we are epistemically conscientious we conscientiously come to believe that there are other people who are more trustworthy than ourselves, and since we trust the way we come to have such a belief, we trust the belief. There are individuals who have qualities we trust in ourselves in a greater degree than we have ourselves—epistemic conscientiousness, the ability to evaluate evidence, good practical judgment, and many other qualities that a conscientious person trusts in her search for truth. In many cases deferring to the judgment of such a person follows from consistent self-trust.

Trust in ourselves leads us to trust certain others more than ourselves in another way. There are emotions that most of us trust and emotions that most of us do not trust. An emotion that I think we trust when we are conscientious is the emotion of admiration. When we trust our emotion of admiration, we trust that the person we admire is admirable, deserving of admiration. Sometimes we epistemically admire another person and trust that emotion. We then trust that the person we epistemically admire is epistemically admirable. If that person believes something in the domain of her admirability, that gives us a reason to believe it too. Of course, that reason can be defeated by other things we trust more, but many times there is nothing we trust more.

Wisdom is often imbedded in communities rather than in individuals. This is especially true when the community exists to pass on the wisdom of an individual whose exceptional wisdom occurs only once in a millennium, or once in ten millennia. A person might belong to such a community and trust it in a way that is similar to his trust in himself. He might admire the quality of wisdom that he perceives in the community and might trust that admiration. I think that trust in wise persons and the wisdom of communities is the basis of epistemic authority. Authority rests upon trust, and trust in authority is justified by self-trust.

Trust in authority can lead to knowledge. One way is through testimony of those in authority, and knowledge through testimony can be justified by conscientious trust. I see no reason that there cannot be religious knowledge acquired through testimony in this way. But we acquire knowledge from trusted others in ways other than testimony. My position is that we acquire many kinds of knowledge, including religious knowledge, by imitating those who have it, the people whose wisdom we admire. A conscientious person imitates the intellectual habits and ways of knowing of those she epistemically admires. This is the way we learn a specialized field of learning or a skill. We imitate those who have mastered the field. There are methods developed by the best practitioners of each field that are transmitted to the next generation during the course of the practice of the field. The same point applies to methods of meditation and contemplation developed over many centuries by spiritually wise mentors in religious communities. With luck, imitating an exemplar of spiritual wisdom can result in acquiring some of the most important truths a human being can learn.

This approach to religious knowledge runs counter to the modern value of intellectual egalitarianism and the dis-valuing of authority. We live in an age that has sometimes been called "the age of suspicion" because so many intellectual trends undermine trust—trust in political, religious, and epistemic authority, and trust in traditions of wisdom. At the epistemic extreme, it undermines trust in testimony as a source of knowledge. Since testimony, authority, and the existence of wise persons are crucial to the transmission of religious knowledge as understood within most of the major religious traditions, the suspicion of the age undermines religion more directly than it undermines human practices that do not rely upon wisdom or authority, such as modern science. But all human practices require trust among the participants in the practice, and all human beings need to trust themselves when they are being conscientious. I find it doubtful that our age can undermine trust in authority and wisdom so thoroughly without also undermining the trust that no one wants to give up.

III. Connecting the Truth of Religion with Reasonable Belief: Alvin Plantinga

Alvin Plantinga is well known for his sustained attack on (3). Plantinga does not critique the features of (3) we have mentioned, and he does not attack foundationalism. Plantinga accepts a form of foundationalism himself, but argues that belief in the existence of God can be in the foundation (Plantinga 1983, 1993). Recently, he has argued that Christian belief can be in the foundation as well (Plantinga 2000). Belief in Christian doctrines can be the result of the instigation of the Holy Spirit on the occasion of a person's coming in contact with the doctrine, for instance, when hearing the Gospel proclaimed. If this process of acquiring belief is in accordance with the divine design plan for human beings after the Fall, these beliefs are produced by a reliable process for getting truth, one that results from epistemic faculties working properly as God intended. If this assumption is true, beliefs acquired in this way are rational in several different senses of rational, and constitute knowledge. They are foundational or properly basic beliefs.

What makes Christian belief reasonable on this approach cannot be separated from its truth. In section I we saw that philosophers almost always separate rationality or reasonableness from the truth of a belief. What makes a belief reasonable is one thing; what makes it true is something else. A belief can be reasonable but false, or true and unreasonable. Plantinga does not reject the separation of truth and reasonableness in general, but he defends a way of thinking about Christian belief that ties its reasonableness to its truth. Plantinga argues that provided that the world is a certain way and human beings are a certain way, it is reasonable to believe certain things that Christianity teaches, and we have knowledge of those things. If the world is a different way, then it is not reasonable to believe those things, and we do not know them.

The argument depends upon the idea that one of the tenets of Christianity is a teaching about the way in which Christians come to believe in the tenets of Christianity. Christianity not only explains *what* the religious truth is, but *how* it is that we come to believe those truths in a way that is reasonable. So among the core Christian doctrines such as the doctrine that Jesus Christ is the Son of God, there is a doctrine that says that Christians come to believe those doctrines by the power of the Holy Spirit according to a design plan that is aimed at truth in the same way that our other faculties, such as sensation, memory, and reasoning, are aimed at truth. It follows that if the core set of Christian doctrines is true, belief in it in the way described by one of the doctrines in the set is reasonable. The truth of Christianity guarantees its reasonableness, so reasonableness comes for free. And if it is true, it also has the combination of truth and reasonableness needed for knowledge. So if Christianity is true, belief in it is reasonable and Christians have knowledge of the tenets of Christianity (Plantinga 2000: chaps 6 and 8).

I think that Plantinga has succeeded in demonstrating the conditional thesis that *if* Christianity is true and includes among its doctrines a crucial claim about the way in which Christians get Christian beliefs, then believing those doctrines is rational for those who believe in the way described by that doctrine. The question is what has been accomplished for those of us who want to know if Christian belief is rational. To be told that it is rational if true is not very helpful for those who think that its truth is undetermined. Even people who are Christians and hence believe Christian doctrines are true might want something else when they ask whether Christian belief satisfies standards of rationality. To explain what I think that is, I want to identify a principle of rationality that I think explains what is worrisome about Plantinga's position, and why the issue of religious knowledge and reasonable belief is an appropriate topic for a handbook in epistemology.

I assume that rationality is an intrinsic part of human nature, perhaps even the part that most clearly defines it. I do not insist that no non-human animals are rational, but I do insist that all normal humans are rational; in fact, it is part of what we *mean* by rationality that it is connected with our humanity. Rationality, therefore, transcends both individual differences and cultural differences, as well as differences between one religious tradition and another. To be rational is to be able to talk to other persons and to make oneself understood, no matter who those other persons are. It is what permits us to form a human community, one that transcends the individual human communities that we inhabit, including religious communities. The fact that rationality is an intrinsic part of our humanity has a corollary, and this is the principle of rationality I wish to propose. I call it the *Rational Recognition Principle*:

> If a belief is rational, its rationality is recognizable, in principle, by rational persons in other cultures.

This principle obviously needs to be nuanced and much has to be packed into the qualification "in principle." I am not suggesting that every human everywhere is capable of grasping the rationality of every rational human belief. But I am suggesting that our common humanity means at least that the most rational persons—the wisest persons—in all cultures can comprehend the rationality of the beliefs of rational persons in other cultures. It is this property that explains why philosophy exists as a cross-cultural discipline, and why the issue of religious knowledge is a topic that philosophers can discuss whether or not they adhere to any religious tradition.

It seems to me that Plantinga's strategy violates the Rational Recognition Principle. It does not permit a rational observer outside the community of believers to distinguish between the rationality of Christianity as defended by Plantinga and the beliefs of any group, no matter how irrational and bizarre—sun-worshipers, cult-followers, devotees of the Greek gods . . .—assuming that they are clever enough to build their own epistemic doctrines into their models the way Plantinga does. So a clever believer in Zeus might also believe that Zeus struck him with a bolt of lightning that has the effect of giving him true beliefs, including the belief that Zeus exists and struck him with a bolt of lightning. But don't we think that the Zeus believer is not rational, even though he and the members of his cult are able to produce an argument exactly parallel to Plantinga's? If so, the rationality of religious beliefs must depend upon something other than their truth. That something else, I submit, must be such that its rationality is understandable to any rational person, if not to every rational person everywhere, then at least to the most rational persons anywhere.

So what does a conscientious person do? The question answers itself. She is conscientious. Nobody can expect more of her, but they should not expect less. The Enlightenment strictures on religious belief with which we began are much too demanding. They do not permit a reasonable person to trust what she trusts when she is conscientious. But it seems to me that Plantinga's strictures are not demanding enough. A conscientious person pays attention to other conscientious persons, and she pays special attention to those she regards as wise, whether or not they are members of her own tradition. This is not to suggest that she must be egalitarian and trust the persons of other communities as much as she trusts the members of her own, but her recognition of the rationality common to all human beings and which is present in an exemplary form in some human beings should lead her to treat other persons, even those outside her community as checks on her beliefs.

Religious knowledge in some ways is a special kind of knowledge because it depends so heavily on trust in authorities and exemplars of wisdom. But in other ways religious knowledge is just like any other knowledge. It is getting the truth in a way that is epistemically conscientious.

References

Alston, William P. 1993. *Perceiving God: The Epistemology of Religious Experience*. Ithaca: Cornell University Press.
Menssen, Sandra and Sullivan, Thomas D. 2002. "The existence of God and the existence of Homer: rethinking theism and revelatory claims." *Faith and Philosophy* 19, 331–47.
Nussbaum, Martha Craven. 2001. *Upheavals of Thought: The Intelligence of Emotions*. Cambridge: Cambridge University Press.
Plantinga, Alvin. 1983. "Reason and Belief in God," in *Faith and Rationality: Reason and Belief in God*, ed. A. Plantinga and N. Wolterstorff. Notre Dame: University of Notre Dame Press.
———. 1993. *Warrant and Proper Function*. New York: Oxford University Press.
———. 2000. *Warranted Christian Belief*. New York: Oxford University Press.
Solomon, Robert C. 2007. *True to Our Feelings: What Our Emotions Are Really Telling Us*. New York: Oxford University Press.
Zagzebski, Linda Trinkaus. 2004. *Divine Motivation Theory*. Cambridge: Cambridge University Press.

Part V
SKEPTICISM

37
PYRRHONIAN SKEPTICISM
Richard Bett

Pyrrhonian skepticism takes its name from the shadowy figure of Pyrrho of Elis (ca. 360–270 BCE). It is debatable to what extent Pyrrho was concerned with questions that we would call epistemological (for a brief survey of the main options see Bett 2006), or to what extent he would have satisfied any reasonable definition of a skeptic. Beyond a few immediate followers, he appears to have been all but forgotten until early in the first century BCE, when another somewhat shadowy figure, Aenesidemus of Cnossos, appealed to Pyrrho as a key inspiration for a new form of skeptical thinking. Aenesidemus' writings have not survived, but we do have a summary of his central work *Pyrrhonist Discourses* (*Purrôneioi Logoi*) by Photius, the ninth-century Patriarch of Constantinople (*Bibl.* 169b18–171a4—in Greek and in English, except for brief critical remarks by Photius himself, in Long and Sedley (1987), passages 71C and 72L). And it is the movement begun by Aenesidemus that is now known as Pyrrhonian skepticism; indeed, it is from this movement that the term *skeptikos*, on which more below, actually originated. By far the most important representative of this movement, at least from our perspective, is Sextus Empiricus (probably second century CE), the one Pyrrhonist of whom we have extensive surviving writings. Another important source is Diogenes Laertius' *Life of Pyrrho* (9.61–108), parts of which consist of summaries of what are clearly later Pyrrhonist ideas, rather than anything traceable to Pyrrho himself. For the most part, however, I will confine myself to Pyrrhonism as represented by Sextus.

What is a Pyrrhonian Skeptic?

Pyrrhonian skepticism differs in multiple ways from Cartesian skepticism. (For an excellent account of the differences, see Williams 2010.) One of the most obvious differences is that for Descartes, skepticism is a threat to be warded off, whereas for the Pyrrhonists it is an outlook to be embraced. Another is that for the Pyrrhonists, skepticism is not specially about epistemology. Sextus treats what we call epistemology as just one subject among others, on a par with them and to be examined by the same methods; I return to this point below. In addition, in as much as skepticism on the Cartesian understanding is a *thesis* (an epistemological thesis—but for the present point, the subject-matter would make no difference), the Pyrrhonian skeptic would consider it just as much deserving of suspicion as its negation.

Sextus' best-known work, *Outlines of Pyrrhonism* (usually known by the abbreviation *PH*, the initials of the title in Greek) actually begins by making this very point. Sextus distinguishes three possible positions or attitudes: some people think that they have discovered the truth, some people think that the truth cannot be apprehended, and some people are still searching. It is the second position—one that Sextus, rightly or wrongly, associates with certain of the Academics—that is evidently closest to what in modern times has been understood as skepticism. But it is the third stance, not the second, that Sextus describes as the skeptic's. In fact the Greek word *skeptikos* means "inquirer"; the skeptic is actually defined as someone who keeps on searching, as opposed to someone who has come to a definite position—including a definite position to the effect that knowledge is impossible. The latter kind of position is just as subject to Sextus' criticism as a form of "dogmatism"—his favorite term for a non-skeptical outlook—as are positive views about the nature of things. (Modern scholars tend to refer to such positions as "negative dogmatism," although this is not a term Sextus actually uses.)

There is, however, room for dispute about how far Sextus really maintains the stance of an open-minded "inquirer." On the one hand, there do seem to be places where Sextus is opting for certain definite positions. I return to this point below. On the other hand, his most general account of what skepticism is, together with much of his actual practice, seems not to fit the pose of an "inquirer"—despite being in accord with it on the avoidance of definite positions, at least if by "positions" one means "theses asserted."

That account, in one of the most important surviving sentences in all of Sextus, is as follows:

> The skeptical ability is one that produces oppositions among things that appear and things that are thought in any way whatsoever, one from which, because of the equal strength in the opposing objects and accounts, we come first to suspension of judgement, and after that to tranquility.
>
> (PH 1.8)

Sextus refers to skepticism as an ability; as we have been led to expect, then, it is not any kind of doctrine or theory, but a certain way of doing things. But the notion of continuing inquiry, at least in any usual sense of "inquiry," seems somewhat remote from the procedure described here. The procedure seems, rather, to consist in the assembling of opposing arguments, ideas or impressions, in such a way that both (or all) sides of the opposition are equally powerful and thereby together induce suspension of judgment. And the skeptic, as someone accomplished in this procedure, looks not like an open-minded inquirer, for whom eventual discovery of the truth is still a live possibility, but like a person who has decided that tranquility is what he wants, and that suspension of judgment is the surest way to it—and therefore concentrates on producing and maintaining suspension of judgment.

This does not require assent to the definite claim that tranquility is a good thing, or that suspension of judgment is the rationally required reaction to the situation of "equal strength" among the oppositions; nor does the notion of "equal strength" itself have to be understood in terms of equal rational justification. "Equal strength" can very well be seen as a psychological notion—one simply (if the skeptic's "ability" is accomplished enough) finds oneself experiencing each pole of the opposition as equally persuasive. Suspension of judgment, too, might simply be a result one finds oneself experiencing, rather than deciding upon as the *appropriate* reaction. And finally, the skeptic's orientation towards tranquility might simply be a brute fact about his motivations, rather than anything for which he would be interested in giving a defense. Sextus does not, then, need to be seen as having fallen into one of the two stances that he opened the book by repudiating (the belief that one has discovered the truth or the belief that this is impossible). But there is at least a certain kind of pre-arranged system of skeptical activity—an activity that much of his surviving work appears to exemplify—that does not seem to fit well with the picture of the skeptic as someone still searching. (For an interpretation that finds more credibility in the picture of the skeptic as an inquirer, see Perin 2006.)

Sextus' account of how someone comes to be a skeptic sheds some further light upon this, but does not eliminate the tension just referred to. He says that the skeptic starts out as just a normal philosopher—that is, someone seeking tranquility by means of discovering the truth (*PH* 1.12, 26). The attempt fails; instead of reaching a secure understanding of things, one finds equally powerful positions on opposite sides of any given issue, which results, as we have seen, in suspension of judgment. And then, as it turns out, this very suspension of judgment produces the tranquility that one had originally been hoping for (*PH* 1.26). Now, from the description of the original, pre-skeptical position, it sounded as if the worry from which one was seeking release was a worry associated with not knowing what to believe; and so one might expect that the tranquility one eventually gets derives from a radical change of attitude in which knowledge of how things are ceases to seem important. In fact, though, the way Sextus describes it is rather different; whenever he explicitly discusses why suspension of judgment yields tranquility (*PH* 1.27–30, 3.235–8, *Against the Ethicists* 110–67), the focus is on freedom from beliefs specifically about good and bad. If one is a dogmatist (or an ordinary non-philosophical person), one believes certain things to be really good and others to be really bad, and so one cares desperately about getting or keeping the good things and avoiding the bad things; for the skeptic, who has shed all such beliefs, nothing matters to anything like the same extent.

One question this raises is why (as Sextus makes quite clear) skepticism includes suspension of judgment on *all* topics, rather than just on goodness and badness. Another is how the search for the truth, and its abandonment, is even relevant; for it now sounds as if beliefs to the effect that things are really good or bad are worrisome simply in virtue of their content—whether or not they are true, or even known to be true, seems unimportant. There is, then, some difficulty in seeing just how the relation between suspension of judgment and tranquility is supposed to work. A third question is how this account of the origin of skepticism fits with Sextus' picture of the activity of a settled skeptic. For in the account of the origin, the equal strength of the opposing positions appears to be a brute fact with which one is presented, generating suspension of judgment as an unexpected consequence. In his characterization of the skeptic's "ability," however, Sextus makes it sound as if the equal strength is a product of the skeptic's deliberate artifice in assembling the oppositions. (This could, of course, invite charges of subterfuge or intellectual dishonesty—to which the skeptic's reply would surely be that such charges presuppose norms of rationality, logical validity, etc. to which a skeptic does not subscribe.) It would at least have been helpful if Sextus had provided some account of the transition between the moment of first reaching tranquility via suspension of judgment and the condition of a settled skeptic who habitually exercises his or her developed "ability" to produce oppositions. Finally, as already noted, the account of the origin of skepticism does not help to justify the notion of the skeptic as an inquirer. The person who becomes a skeptic does, to be sure, start out as an inquirer; but it sounds as if the moment of becoming a skeptic is precisely when one gives up on inquiry and focuses instead on pondering the equal strength of opposing arguments and impressions.

The Limited Role of Epistemology

However we try to resolve these problems, it is clear—to pick up another point already touched on—that Pyrrhonian skepticism is not an exclusively epistemological outlook. For one thing, there is the ethical or practical component having to do with tranquility; Pyrrhonian skepticism is a *way of life*, one that its adherents actively recommend. Sextus is well aware of the objection, standardly leveled against skeptics in antiquity, that a life without definite beliefs is simply impossible. He responds by saying that it is quite possible to act in light of how things strike one, without taking any stand as to whether they really are as they appear (*PH* 1.21-4). One eats when one feels hungry; one follows the customs of one's native land; and so on. There is a difficult question here as to the scope of the skeptic's suspension of judgment. Does it cover only issues concerning the real, underlying *natures* of things—the kinds of questions addressed in various theoretical disciplines—leaving all or most everyday beliefs intact; or are beliefs such as that I am now sitting in my office, that there is a table in front of me, etc., also supposed to be matters about which a skeptic suspends judgment—leaving him with no more than the ability to register the character of his current phenomenal experience? The general tenor of most of Sextus' surviving writings—where it is the dogmatists who are under scrutiny, whether in philosophical matters or in other theoretical disciplines such as grammar, mathematics or astrology—seems to support the first option, as does his periodic insistence that he is "on the side of ordinary life," as against the rarefied abstractions of the dogmatists. But it is not clear that this posture is consistently sustained. One question might be whether everyday beliefs such as those just mentioned are taken to *commit* one to more fundamental beliefs such as that there is a criterion of truth, or that a coherent account can be given of concepts such as time and place—all topics that come under Sextus' skeptical scrutiny. (On this general issue see the essays collected in Burnyeat and Frede 1997; also Brennan 2000.) Clearly how one resolves this issue affects the plausibility of Sextus' claim to be able to live a skeptical life. But in any case, Sextus does take skepticism to have an effect on one's life (a beneficial effect) beyond the purely theoretical domain, and in that respect he conspicuously differs from Descartes and most philosophers since.

Another way in which Pyrrhonian skepticism is not exclusively epistemological is that, as mentioned earlier, the issues addressed range far beyond epistemology. (This is true even if we accept the narrower, purely theoretical interpretation of the scope of suspension of judgment.) Following the general exposition of skepticism in *PH* 1, Sextus devotes the remaining two books of the work to the three main areas of philosophy, as recognized in later antiquity: logic, physics and ethics. The same is true of the much longer work that seems to have followed the same general plan as *PH*; from this (only partially surviving) work we have two books *Against the Logicians*, two *Against the Physicists*, and one *Against the Ethicists*. In addition, a third surviving work of Sextus treats a variety of specialized sciences. In general Sextus' goal is the one we have been led to expect; he seeks to generate suspension of judgment about the existence of the things the dogmatists discuss in these various fields, or about the truth of any particular theory of the nature of these things as opposed to any other theory, by devising sets of opposing arguments. In many cases the arguments on the negative side of the question—the question, say, whether there are causes—will be arguments devised by the Pyrrhonists themselves; and so it can sometimes look as if Sextus is aiming to *refute* the dogmatists on the subject in question. But he repeatedly indicates that this is not so: he is simply supplying an opposing argument of equal strength, with a view to producing suspension of judgment. (He also points out that this might often require a more extensive body of argument on the negative side, given the weight of the standard presumption in favor of such things as the existence of causes; see, e.g., Against the Logicians 1.443.)

Now, among the subjects he considers are several that we would classify under epistemology; in the ancient taxonomy, they belong under logic. So, he addresses at length in the logical portions of his work the question whether there is a criterion of truth—that is, whether there is any kind of impression or thought whose content is in some way guaranteed to be true—and also whether there are such things as signs or demonstrations—both of these being thought of as means by which to establish truths about what is not apparent on the basis of truths about the apparent. But these are of no more inherent importance to him than questions about causes, or motion, or God (all of which for him belong under physics), about the good and the bad (which belong under ethics), or about geometry, astrology or other fields of specialized study. It is true that Sextus' arguments very frequently have an epistemological dimension; one of his most common approaches is to try to challenge or undermine the justification for holding some particular position, and so questions concerning the nature of justification are rarely out of sight for long. But these questions arise regardless of subject-matter; they are no more prevalent when the topic under discussion is epistemological than when it is physical or ethical. They are an aid to producing the desired situation of "equal strength" among the alternatives, and are not in general the main focus of attention in their own right. Finally, to repeat, even within the epistemological domain, Sextus' aim is not to show that we do not or cannot have certain kinds of knowledge (or, for that matter, justified or reasonable belief). *Those* claims, too, are ones about which he aims to suspend judgment, just as much as about positions claiming that we do have knowledge. Pyrrhonian skepticism (again, in this particular area, which is just one among many) is *about* epistemology; it is not a position *within* epistemology.

The Modes, and the Adoption of Definite Positions

This, at least, is the dominant state of affairs in Sextus, and the one to which his official presentation of Pyrrhonism seems to commit him. But, as noted earlier, there are places where Sextus does seem to be arguing on his own behalf for definite conclusions, and where it is not so easy to understand this as just one side of an opposition. Perhaps the most prominent of these, and certainly the one most relevant to our purposes, is the section of PH 1 devoted to the Pyrrhonian Modes, or standardized forms of skeptical argumentation (31–186). Sextus presents these as means to suspension of judgment—either, we may presume, for non-skeptics who have not yet been converted, or for skeptics who feel in danger of lapsing into dogmatism. But the Modes, taken by themselves, are most easily read as arguments to the effect that we *must* suspend judgment—where the necessity is hard not to read as logical or rational rather than merely psychological—because there are insuperable challenges to the adequate justification of any position, or because we are not in a position to know the real nature of things.

Sextus lays out several sets of Modes, of which the most important are the Ten and the Five. (For a fine recent treatment of the Modes, see Woodruff 2010. Valuable longer treatments are Annas and Barnes (1985) for the Ten Modes and Barnes (1990) for the Five.) The Ten Modes present a great variety of opposing impressions. Other animals perceive things differently from humans; one human perceives things differently from another; even in a single human, the deliverances of different senses are often in opposition to one another; and even in the case of a single sense, different circumstances (such as being healthy or sick, young or old) lead to opposing impressions. These are the first four. The rest do not maintain the same sense of a natural and deliberate sequence, and Sextus says some confusing things about how they relate to one another (*PH* 1.38–9); but the general effect is to generate multiple sets of oppositions, and the first four are as good an illustration of this as any.

The Five Modes are much more general in scope, and together amount to an argument-scheme that purports to undermine any attempt at justification whatever. In the order in which Sextus first introduces them (*PH* 1.165–9), they are: Undecidable Dispute, Infinite Regress, Relativity, Hypothesis, and Circularity. The Mode of Undecidable Dispute simply asserts that there is undecidable dispute about the matter under discussion. By itself, of course, this hardly carries much weight; the skeptic will have to fill out the claim with a specific illustration of the existence of undecidable dispute in any given case. But that is precisely what the skeptical "ability" of which Sextus spoke earlier is designed to do. Suppose, however, that the skeptic's opponent claims that the matter *is* decidable in some particular way. In that case the skeptic will demand justification for the position the opponent adopts; if justification is given, he will demand that the justifying claim, too, be justified; and so on. And, Sextus argues (*PH* 1.171–4), only three eventual outcomes to this process are possible. Either (1) the chain of justification never ends—in which case we have the Mode of Infinite Regress. Or (2) the opponent comes to a proposition that is claimed not to need any justification beyond itself; this Sextus interprets as arbitrarily plumping for that proposition, when one might as well have plumped for many others—in which case we have the Mode of Hypothesis. Or (3) the process of justification eventually relies on a proposition that was already employed earlier on—in which case we have the Mode of Circularity. Of course, this is just the beginning of an argument; many, in the ancient world and since, would contest the notion that these are the only three possibilities. Aristotle, for example, who is already aware of patterns of argument foreshadowing several of the Five Modes (*Posterior Analytics* I.3), would dispute the idea that positing argumentative starting-points that do not need justification beyond themselves is merely opting for arbitrary "hypotheses." Still, there is no doubt that these Modes taken together constitute a serious challenge to any justificatory project.

The Mode of Relativity is hard to relate to the other four, and Sextus tacks it on to the above schema as no more than an afterthought (*PH* 1.175). In describing it he simply says that the object under consideration appears a certain way in relation to the person judging it and in relation to the things observed along with it, but "as for how it is in its nature, we suspend judgment" (*PH* 1.167). As Sextus remarks, this consideration already came up in the Ten Modes; one of the Ten is actually a very similar general Mode of Relativity—a further anomaly in itself—but this form of argument involving relativity occurs a number of other times in the Ten Modes. I shall suggest below that this represents a survival of a separate, pre-Sextan variety of Pyrrhonism. For now, it is enough to observe that the Mode of Relativity sits awkwardly among the Five; the other four seem to fit together much better by themselves.

The Five Modes, as noted earlier, look like a knock-down argument (or a sketch of one) to the effect that rational justification is impossible. Sextus concludes by saying that "it is absolutely necessary to suspend judgment about the matter put before us" (PH 1.177), and that accurately represents the tone of what has preceded; suspension of judgment is "absolutely necessary" because the schema developed permits no escape. It would be possible to use one or more of the Five Modes as part of an argument for one side of a pair of opposing arguments; in his examination of specific topics, Sextus frequently does so. But in his exposition of the Five Modes themselves, he makes them smack far more of negative dogmatism. To return to a formulation used above, they differ from Sextus' usual method by being a position within epistemology—a position that, in the modern usage, would be classified as skepticism, but which, as we have seen, is not what Sextus himself generally understands by skepticism.

The same impression is given by the Ten Modes (which have far less importance in Sextus' work as a whole than do the Five). One reason for saying this is that the opposing impressions with which the Ten Modes deal are often not ones with which an individual subject could be simultaneously presented. (For appreciation of the importance of this point I am indebted to Williams (2010).) In the case of the first two Modes, on the contrast between human and animal perceptions and between the perceptions of different humans, the same subject cannot experience both poles of the opposition at all; in the case of the first, there actually has to be an elaborate argument, of seemingly dogmatic character, for the conclusion that animals do indeed experience things differently from humans (PH 1.41–58). In the case of the fourth, the same person can, of course, be sick and healthy, or young and old, but not at the same time. So much of the time, at any rate, Sextus cannot be read as saying, "Feel the equal strength of these opposing impressions with which I am presenting you, and find yourself suspending judgment between them." Rather, he has to be read as saying, "*There are* these opposing impressions; there is no way to decide between them in terms of truth; so you have no choice but to suspend judgment between them"; and the supposed necessity here is difficult not to see as one imposed by the force of argument.

This point is reinforced by the fact that the Ten Modes, in Sextus' presentation of them, frequently employ considerations borrowed from the Five Modes. This cannot have been what they looked like in their original formulation. Sextus tells us that the Ten Modes are earlier than the Five; elsewhere (*Against the Logicians* 1.345) he attributes them to Aenesidemus, so the Five must have been developed at some point in the two centuries or more between Aenesidemus and Sextus himself. (Diogenes Laertius, 9.88, attributes the Five to someone called Agrippa, but we know nothing else about this person.) So Sextus' version of the Ten Modes is a revision of the original Ten Modes, incorporating elements that did not at first belong there. Aside, though, from this historical issue, the appearance of the Five within the Ten makes the Ten all the more likely to come across as dogmatic; for as we saw, that is the impression left by the Five themselves.

A third point is that, when the Five are not brought in, the Ten often employ the form of argument mentioned a little earlier, in connection with the Relativity Mode. Several of the Ten Modes end by saying that we are not in a position to say how things are in their real nature; we can only say how they are (or, more often, how they appear) in some given set of conditions, where the appearance varies with the conditions. The idea seems to be that for something to be a certain way *by nature*, it would have to strike us *invariably* as being that way; the nature of a thing is something fixed, and the only way for us to apprehend that fixed nature would be if its effects on us were also fixed. Since, as the oppositions drawn to our attention by the Mode in question illustrate, this is not the case (at least in the respect drawn attention to), the prospects are closed off for any attempt to determine the thing's nature (again, in that respect—but then, if it always turns out like this, as the Modes collectively seem designed to show, the conclusion can, presumably, be generalized).

Now this too, by the standards Sextus sets up at the outset of *PH*, is a dogmatic conclusion. Sextus repeatedly claims, after cataloging some set of relativities, that we *cannot say* how things are in their real nature. The argument depends upon a particular conception of what a thing's nature would be like, and a particular view of how one might grasp that nature. Relativity had no role in Sextus' initial characterization of skepticism; besides being dogmatic according to the terms of that characterization, this other style of argument seems to appeal to quite different kinds of considerations.

I mentioned that Sextus ascribes the Ten Modes to Aenesidemus. And there is reason to believe that the position just sketched was *the* Pyrrhonist position in an earlier phase of its history than that represented for us by most of Sextus' own work. (For a more detailed account of this line of interpretation, see Bett 2000, chapter 4.) The most extensive surviving instance of this position actually appears in Sextus himself. In *Against the Ethicists*, Sextus argues that nothing is either good or bad by nature. The argument depends on the fact that there is nothing which strikes everyone uniformly as good or as bad. Hence I can speak about what strikes me as good in a certain set of circumstances, but not in others; and we can speak about what strikes some one person as good, but not other people. However, we cannot say, of any of these merely relative goods, that their goodness belongs to the real nature of the things in question. Indeed, since nothing comes across to us as good (or bad) other than in this merely relative manner, we can say that *nothing* is good (or bad) in its real nature. This seems to go beyond the pattern of thought represented in the Ten Modes, in that it assumes that, were anything to be fixedly and invariably good or bad, we would recognize it as such; the Modes would conclude only that we cannot determine the real nature of things as far as goodness or badness is concerned. (In fact, this is just what the Tenth Mode, having to do with ethical variation, does conclude, PH 1.163.) But *Against the Ethicists* is in step with the Modes in refusing any attempt to offer a positive characterization of anything's nature; shared, uniform impressions—which are precisely what we do not find—would be necessary for that.

In this particular book, then, Sextus seems to exemplify this distinct form of Pyrrhonism centered around relativity. The case for regarding it as earlier than Sextus' usual Pyrrhonist stance, and for connecting it with Aenesidemus, comes not just from its appearance in the Ten Modes of Aenesidemus. Photius' summary of Aenesidemus' *Pyrrhonist Discourses*, which I mentioned at the beginning, seems to describe the same sort of view. Again we have an emphasis on the Pyrrhonist's self-limitation to relativized assertions, coupled with assertions that certain things (in their real nature, we may presume) are beyond our cognitive grasp. There are also traces of it in the summary of Pyrrhonism given in Diogenes Laertius' *Life of Pyrrho* (also mentioned at the outset), which appears to be independent of Sextus, even though Sextus and Diogenes are at times clearly drawing on the same (now unknown) source.

The position just described might strike us as unintuitive and even naive. But the idea that variability in our impressions of things closes us off from discerning the real natures of things—or even allows us to assert that they *have no* real nature—has a long history in Greek philosophy. It is just such variability that makes Plato portray the world shown us by the senses as, on the one hand, not a possible object of knowledge (at least, if unchanging Forms are not there to help), and on the other, not genuine *beings* at all (see especially the end of *Republic* V). The Stoics, too, appeal to a similar line of thinking about variability in arguing that nothing is genuinely good or bad except virtue and vice, respectively. The Pyrrhonists, then, are by no means alone in appealing to these considerations concerning relativity. But this just underscores the fact with which I began this historical digression. This earlier Pyrrhonist position is, by Sextus' usual standards, a form of dogmatism; hence its periodic appearance in the Ten Modes only adds to their dogmatic character.

Both the Five and the Ten Modes, then, seem to amount to arguments for a definite epistemological position—that the nature of things is unknowable. Michael Williams has tried to explain this by suggesting that the Modes are themselves only one side of an opposition, the other side being the dogmatic positive epistemologies of non-skeptical philosophers (see Williams 2010, also Williams 1988). In this case the Modes would be an application, within the area of epistemology, of the normal Pyrrhonist method of assembling oppositions. Now, I do not think this can be made to fit the text; Sextus seems to be quite clear in saying that the Modes, taken all by themselves, are means for the producing or maintaining of skeptical suspension of judgment. But we might very well agree that this would be a better—or at any rate, more consistent—use of the Modes than the use for which he in fact seems to employ them; we might also agree that, elsewhere, he does in fact make use of the Modes, especially the Five, in negative arguments that clearly are designed to be juxtaposed with positive arguments of the dogmatists. So Williams' proposal is certainly in the spirit of Sextus' usual Pyrrhonist practice.

Contemporary Echoes of Pyrrhonism

The epistemological focus of the Modes—something that, as we saw, is not characteristic of Pyrrhonism as a whole—and also, perhaps, their somewhat doctrinal character explain why they are the aspect of ancient Pyrrhonism that has most attracted the attention of contemporary epistemologists. Specifically, in recent years the term "Agrippan trilemma" has become widespread, referring to the Modes of Infinite Regress, Hypothesis, and Circularity from the Five Modes (of Agrippa)—the three that, as we saw, together purport to undermine any attempt at resolving "undecidable dispute" in any particular direction, and hence together constitute a global challenge to any project of justification. This has often affected the way fundamental issues in epistemology are framed; it has also led to a recognition of the longevity of the considerations with which any positive epistemology has to deal. But it is not clear that it has had much effect on the subject beyond that (see, for example, Sosa 2007: Lecture 6, which elegantly employs the Agrippan trilemma—what Sosa calls the "Pyrrhonian Problematic"—to explore issues concerning skepticism and foundationalism that were already central in contemporary epistemology).

An exception is, perhaps, Robert Fogelin, who has called himself a neo-Pyrrhonist. This involves arguing that "no justificatory program seems to show any prospect of solving the Agrippa problem" (Fogelin 1994: 193). But Fogelin also distinguishes "philosophical skepticism"—that is, "skepticism that arises from philosophical reasoning," of which he takes the Agrippan trilemma to be a specimen—from "skepticism *about* philosophy," which he sees as the outcome of a confrontation between the Agrippan trilemma and various leading theories of justification (Fogelin 1994: 3). He also takes himself to be following Sextus in this respect; his understanding of the function of the Agrippan Modes in Sextus is thus similar to Williams' (see the end of the previous section). Again, this is open to challenge on historical grounds, but perhaps represents what Sextus *should have* done (or does only at his best) in presenting the Modes. There is, however, some question why, by Fogelin's own argument, the Agrippan trilemma does not *defeat* these theories of justification, rather than inducing suspension of judgment about them—in which case we have a particular, negative result *within* philosophy rather than Pyrrhonian suspension of judgment *about* it. These and other questions about Fogelin's Pyrrhonism have been examined, and refinements of it proposed, by philosophers and historians of philosophy in Sinnott-Armstrong (2004b). But Fogelin can reasonably be seen as developing an updated Pyrrhonism.

Sinnott-Armstrong himself argues for what he calls "Classy Pyrrhonism," in which epistemic claims are understood as justified, or not, in relation to different contrast classes, but the *appropriateness* of any given contrast class is never unequivocally endorsed. In this way everyday knowledge-claims can be taken as perfectly acceptable (given everyday standards of justification), and skeptical challenges (which depend on much more stringent standards) also given their place (see Sinnott-Armstrong 2004a, also Sinnott-Armstrong 2006, which applies this framework to the epistemology of moral claims). The key Pyrrhonist element here is the avoidance of "normative epistemology." Nonetheless, it is clearly an epistemological project, and one with rather more definite commitments than either Sextus, most of the time, or Fogelin would probably welcome.

Fogelin also detects a Pyrrhonist strand in Wittgenstein (Fogelin 1994: Appendix B). The Wittgensteinian themes of philosophy as therapy, and philosophy as needing to come to an end, certainly have a family resemblance to Sextus' approach. But Fogelin acknowledges that the parallel goes only so far, and others (Sluga 2004; Stern 2004) have questioned how useful it really is to look at Wittgenstein in Pyrrhonian terms.

References

Annas, J. and Barnes, J. (1985) *The Modes of Scepticism*, Cambridge: Cambridge University Press.
Barnes, J. (1990) *The Toils of Scepticism*, Cambridge: Cambridge University Press.
Bett, R. (2000) *Pyrrho, his Antecedents and his Legacy*, Oxford: Oxford University Press.
Bett, R. (2006) "Pyrrho," in E. Zalta (ed.) *The Stanford Encyclopedia of Philosophy*, online, http://plato.stanford.edu/entries/pyrrho/.
Brennan, T. (2000) "Criterion and Appearance in Sextus Empiricus," in J. Sihvola (ed.) *Ancient Scepticism and the Sceptical Tradition*, Acta Philosophica Fennica 66: 63–92.
Burnyeat, M. and Frede, M. (eds.) (1997) *The Original Skeptics: A Controversy*, Indianapolis: Hackett.
Fogelin, R. (1994) *Pyrrhonian Reflections on Knowledge and Justification*, New York: Oxford University Press.
Long, A. and Sedley, D. (1987) *The Hellenistic Philosophers* (2 vols.), Cambridge: Cambridge University Press.
Perin, C. (2006) "Pyrrhonian Scepticism and the Search for Truth," *Oxford Studies in Ancient Philosophy* 30: 337–60.
Sinnott-Armstrong, W. (2004a) "Classy Pyrrhonism," in Sinnott-Armstrong 2004b.
Sinnott-Armstrong, W. (ed.) (2004b) *Pyrrhonian Skepticism*, New York: Oxford University Press.
Sinnott-Armstrong, W. (2006) *Moral Skepticisms*, New York: Oxford University Press.
Sluga, H. (2004) "Wittgenstein and Pyrrhonism," in Sinnott-Armstrong 2004b: 99–117.
Sosa, E. (2007) *A Virtue Epistemology: Apt Belief and Reflective Knowledge, Volume I*, Oxford: Oxford University Press.

Stern, D. (2004) *Wittgenstein's Philosophical Investigations: An Introduction*, Cambridge: Cambridge University Press.
Williams, M. (1988) "Scepticism Without Theory," *Review of Metaphysics* 41: 547–88.
Williams, M. (2010) "Descartes' Transformation of the Skeptical Tradition," in R. Bett (ed.) *The Cambridge Companion to Ancient Scepticism*, Cambridge: Cambridge University Press.
Woodruff, P. (2010) "The Pyrrhonian Modes," in R. Bett (ed.) *The Cambridge Companion to Ancient Scepticism*, Cambridge: Cambridge University Press.

Further Reading

Sextus Empiricus (1994, 2nd ed. 2000) *Outlines of Scepticism*, tr. J. Annas and J. Barnes, Cambridge: Cambridge University Press. (English translation of *PH*, with Introduction and Notes.)
Sextus Empiricus (2005) *Against the Logicians*, tr. R. Bett, Cambridge: Cambridge University Press. (English translation with Introduction and Notes.)

38
CARTESIAN SKEPTICISM
Steven Luper

It seems to me that I am typing right now. To you, presumably, it appears that you are now reading. But what if you and I are dreaming, you of reading and me of typing? Possibilities like this seem to threaten our claim to know things about the world. Let us say that a hypothesis, SK, is a *skeptical hypothesis* relative to subject S just in case (a) SK says that S is in situation or possible world W, (b) S's being in W is inconsistent with S's own beliefs about S's situation, and yet (c) S's experiences in W are indistinguishable from the experiences S has in the actual world. The hypothesis that I am merely dreaming of typing this essay is a skeptical hypothesis for me, since the world it says I am in is experientially indistinguishable from the actual world: it would seem as if I were typing my essay even if I were merely dreaming that I was typing it.

According to a view which I will call *Cartesian skepticism*, no one can know anything about the world because doing so requires knowledge of skeptical hypotheses which is unavailable. Cartesian skeptics argue as follows. Take any contingent proposition about the world (not about one's own mind), PW. We can easily find a skeptical hypothesis SK such that we can know PW only if we can also know not-SK. Hence the following principle is true:

SP: Where PW is any contingent proposition about the world, and S is any subject, there is a skeptical hypothesis SK such that S can know PW only if S can know not-SK.

However (the argument continues) it is impossible to know that skeptical hypotheses are false, since they are consistent with all of our experiences. Hence we cannot know PW. Thus the argument, in its simplest form, is this:

The Cartesian Skeptic's Argument:

1. SP.
2. No one can know that skeptical hypotheses are false.
3. So no one can know anything about the world.

In what follows I examine some ways to support Cartesian skepticism, and some ways to criticize it. First I will distinguish it from some other forms of skepticism.

Other Forms of Skepticism

What we know depends, of course, on what is required for knowledge. Given sufficiently demanding requirements, knowledge will be impossible. For example, it will be impossible on the assumption that nothing is known unless it is established without taking anything whatever for granted. If we take nothing for granted, we will be unable to presume that we understand our own thoughts and language, and unable to trust reason (Hume 1975; Wittgenstein 1969). We will therefore have no way to think our way into knowledge. We cannot even doubt a claim, even the claim that we lack knowledge, without presupposing that various things are true (Pierce 1877).

Skepticism can arise even on weaker requirements. Suppose that a belief counts as knowledge only if adequately justified. Now consider the following claims about adequate justification, all of which arise in the literature on Pyrrhonian skepticism (see Sextus 1967):

> It cannot be circular.
> It cannot rely on mere assumptions.
> It cannot be an infinite regress (because we cannot grasp such a justification).
> It cannot rely on a proposition that is in dispute.

According to regress skepticism, knowledge is impossible since it requires justification that meets the first three conditions, and any finite, noncircular justification must begin with a premise that is not based on any further claim, which makes that premise a mere assumption.

There are ways to resist this route into skepticism. One way is to deny that knowledge requires justification. According to externalists (such as Frank Ramsey (1929); Alvin Goldman (1967); Fred Dretske (1970, 2003); and David Armstrong (1973)) we can know at least some things by arriving at beliefs via sufficiently reliable methods even if we are not justified in thinking that our beliefs have been arrived at this way. Since knowledge need not involve justification, regress skepticism is not a threat.

Instead of resisting skepticism by appealing to externalism, we could try to demonstrate the possibility of beliefs that are justified but not by other beliefs, or we could deny that adequate justification must meet all of the first three conditions (e.g., by embracing the legitimacy of circular coherentist justification). However, skepticism remains a threat if we accept the last adequacy condition. If knowledge requires justification that avoids disputed propositions, skepticism itself destroys knowledge. Suppose you claim to know you have hands because your experiences are best explained by your having hands, and I claim that you do not know this since knowledge requires certainty. Neither of us has adequately justified his claim if this means defending it solely on undisputed grounds. Nevertheless, you do not know you have hands, for your claim is plausible only if knowledge does not entail certainty, and I take the view that knowledge does entail certainty.

Accepting the last adequacy condition not only permits skeptics to destroy knowledge, it also makes it impossible to regain knowledge by rejecting conditions that force us into skepticism, for we cannot reject these without placing ourselves in dispute with skeptics. Skeptics will not agree that a condition is objectionable just because it forces us into skepticism.

Of course, we can, and should, reject the last adequacy condition. It is absurd to say that we are not justified in believing things whose defense appeals to claims that others dispute. Your belief that you exist does not become irrational just because I opt to defend solipsism. Similarly, criticisms of skepticism can be reasonable even if, as they must, they rely on disputed claims.

A final point about the various forms of skepticism: theorists responding to one form of skepticism are sometimes criticized for failing to disprove other forms. But we need not take on all forms of skepticism at once. In particular, a telling criticism of Cartesian skepticism might not speak to regress skepticism at all.

Let us turn to Cartesian skepticism now. We can begin with a few words about René Descartes.

Descartes and Skepticism

Descartes himself was not a Cartesian skeptic. He was an antiskeptic. Nevertheless, there is good reason to speak of 'Cartesian skepticism,' since Descartes clarified and struggled against the stance we have called 'Cartesian skepticism,' and because he was committed to SP: he thought that we can know things about the world only if we can know that certain skeptical hypotheses are false. In accepting SP, he conceded quite a bit to the skeptic, but he thought the damage could be contained since we can know, with certainty, that skeptical hypotheses are false.

Usually certainty is understood as *immunity to error*, roughly as follows: subject S is certain that P iff either S's belief P cannot possibly be mistaken, or S has eliminated the ways in which it might be mistaken. Let M be a way in which S's belief P might be mistaken; S eliminates M by deducing not-M from beliefs S has that cannot be mistaken. Descartes himself understood certainty in terms of indubitability, or *immunity to doubt*. How he understood indubitability itself is a controversial matter, but given the way he argues (in Meditation II) for the indubitability of the proposition that he exists, namely by noting that he must exist to be deceived, it is reasonable to accept the following interpretation: S's belief P is indubitable for S, or immune to skeptical doubts, iff S believes, correctly, that if any proposition that is a skeptical hypothesis for S holds, then P also holds. For example, in any skeptical scenario, S exists, so the corresponding belief is indubitable for S. Supposing that S has experiences E, the proposition that S has E is indubitable for S, since it is true in any situation sketched by the skeptic. Descartes analyzed knowledge in terms of indubitable beliefs and their consequences, as follows: S knows P with certainty just in case (a) S's belief P is indubitable for S or (b) S sees that her belief P follows from things that meet condition (a) or (b).

If knowledge entails either form of certainty, SP is true. Consider a proposition about the world, PW. I would be mistaken about PW if various skeptical hypotheses SK were true. So my belief PW can be immune to error only if I eliminate SK, and thus am certain of not-SK, as SP asserts. Moreover, if my belief PW is immune to doubt, then, by (b), I can know not-SK by deducing it from PW. So SP is true on Descartes' analysis as well.

After equating knowledge with certainty, Descartes set out, in his *Meditations* (1641; page references are to the Cottingham edition), to explain how we can know things about the world. He said (p. 61) that we can identify "all the errors" to which our nature is liable, and we can "correct or avoid them without difficulty." This is because we know God exists and he would ensure that we have ways to do these things. However, Descartes does not make it clear what these ways are (his explanations are filled with qualifications that are inconsistent with the guarantee of certainty; e.g., he says (p. 61) that the senses "report the truth *much more frequently than not*," and we "can *almost always* make use of more than one sense to investigate the same thing"), and his case for God's existence is notoriously unconvincing.

Let us now put Descartes' own efforts aside, and consider Cartesian skepticism anew.

Defense of Cartesian Skepticism

Recall that the skeptic's argument is this:

1. SP.
2. No one can know that skeptical hypotheses are false.
3. So no one can know anything about the world.

As formulated, the first two premises are undefended. That is easy to correct if, like Descartes, we equate knowledge with certainty.

We have already seen that the first premise, SP, is true if knowledge is certainty. Now consider the second premise. Presently, I believe that every skeptical hypothesis I can think of is false. In particular, I believe that I am not dreaming, and hence that skeptical hypotheses that say I am are false. However, my belief might well be mistaken. If my experiences were the product of a dream, or produced in some other skeptical scenario, I would still believe, mistakenly, that nothing of the sort is occurring. Hence the second premise is true if knowledge entails certainty. But if both the first and second premises of the skeptic's argument are correct, Cartesian skepticism is irresistible.

Let us add that principles that are considerably stronger than SP are true if knowledge is certainty. Whatever positions me to know P would have to position me to know that various skeptical hypotheses were false; at a minimum these would include ones that are incompatible with P. So the following principle would be true:

SPC: Where PW is any proposition about the world and SK is any skeptical hypothesis, if PW entails not-SK then S knows PW only if S is in a position to know not-SK.

In fact, anyone who equates knowledge with certainty must accept a principle that is even stronger than SPC, namely, the principle that knowledge is closed under entailment, at least in the following qualified sense:

GK: If, while knowing various propositions, subject S believes P because S knows that they entail P, then S knows P.

For we can be certain about the things entailed by things we know with certainty.

This way of defending Cartesian skepticism fails if knowledge is not certainty. Hence it might seem easy to reject skepticism: we can deny that knowledge is certainty, say, because the equation of knowledge with certainty makes nonsense of our ordinary ways of using the term 'knowledge' and its cognates. After all, we say we know all sorts of things about the world; we would not speak this way if we thought knowledge required certainty. This argument is plausible, but it has been questioned. Peter Unger (1971, 1975) argues that 'certain' is one of several adjectives, such as 'flat' or 'useless,' that seem "absolute" in the sense that they denote a "limiting state or situation to which things may approximate more or less closely." Nothing is absolutely flat; things only approximate the limiting state of flatness. Despite this, we still use 'flat'; we settle for high degrees of flatness. In some contexts we are more stringent about degree of flatness than in others. But we must acknowledge that nothing is ever wholly flat. All this is true of "certainty" as well: in some contexts we are more stringent about doubtfulness than in others, but "if someone is certain of something, then that thing is not at all doubtful so far as he is concerned."

We have considered the main route into Cartesian skepticism: the equation of knowledge with certainty. Now let us consider some reasons for rejecting Cartesian skepticism.

Responses to Cartesian Skepticism

There are three main ways to respond to Cartesian skepticism. We might argue that skeptical hypotheses are self-refuting and hence not really possible, or that, while possible, their falsity is harmlessly unknowable, or knowable, so they constitute no threat to our ordinary knowledge claims.

Self-Refuting

Hilary Putnam (1981) argued that the hypothesis that we are brains in vats is, with certain qualifications, self-refuting. It is falsified by the very nature of language or thought. He describes a world he calls Twin Earth that is like Earth except that it lacks water; instead, it has a substance called XYZ that looks and feels like H_2O but has a different chemical composition. On Twin Earth people even use the term 'water.' But, according to Putnam, their term does not refer to the same thing as ours. Our term 'water' refers to H_2O; theirs refers to XYZ. On the basis of thought experiments like this, Putnam concludes that the meaning of our words and the contents of our thoughts is determined by causal relationships between us and things in the world. Because we interact with H_2O, our term 'water' refers to H_2O, while on Twin Earth they interact with XYZ, so their term 'water' refers to XYZ. This causal view of the meanings of terms has interesting implications for skepticism. Suppose that we are right to think that we are not really brains in vats. Still, there is a possible world in which everyone is, and has always been, brains in vats, and in which their perceptual input is qualitatively just like ours. Just imagine a world in which the entire human race spends its entire existence as brains in vats maintained by sophisticated aliens. Putnam claims that, in this Vat World, when people say "I'm a brain in a vat," their words would not mean what ours do when *we* say "I'm a brain in a vat." This is because the referent of a word is determined by certain causal relationships between the people who use that word and the things they interact with, and whereas we interact with vats, people in the Vat World do not. What they interact with is some sort of elaborate ersatz sensory input controlled by the computers used by the aliens. Their term "vat" refers to something in the sensory input provided by the aliens. Hence the skeptical hypothesis "We are brains in vats" is self-refuting: whether they utter the words "We are brains in vats," or we do, what is said is false.

Putnam's proposal is that our words come to refer to things in our environment with which we interact in certain ways. A similar proposal is that the contents of our thoughts are determined in a similar way: our thoughts are about the things with which we interact. On this view, we could imagine a Vat World peopled by brains in vats whose mental lives are qualitatively identical to ours yet whose thoughts are very different from ours. When they are in a state of mind that is qualitatively identical to the state *we* are in when we wonder, "is this stuff water?," *they* are not thinking about water at all. They are

thinking about something with which they are in causal contact, call it *schmater*. If our environment really does determine the referents of our words and the contents of our thoughts, perhaps we can use this against the skeptic, by arguing as follows:
The Causal Theorist's Argument:

1. I know I am thinking about water (and that my word 'water' refers to water).
2. I would be thinking about schmater, not water, if I were a brain in a vat.
3. So I know I am not a brain in a vat.

Unfortunately, neither Putnam's contention nor the Causal Theorist's Argument is much help against Cartesian skepticism.

First, Putnam's strategy cannot be extended to all skeptical hypotheses. Consider the hypothesis that all of us were seized yesterday by aliens, who removed our brains, put them into vats, and began giving us illusory sensory data. As the victims of these aliens, our words would have their familiar meanings, and our thoughts their familiar contents; 'vats,' for example, would refer to vats, and if we were to say or think, "We are brains in vats," we would indeed be saying or thinking something true. The causal account of reference and mental content is entirely consistent with the possibility that this skeptical hypothesis is true.

Second, it is not clear that the Causal Theorist's Argument is plausible. As Anthony Brueckner (2003) has noted, it seems possible for skeptics to respond as follows: from the inside, thinking about water is qualitatively identical to thinking about schmater. So I do not know I am thinking about water rather than schmater, and hence am in no position to rule out the possibility that I am a brain in a vat. Moreover, knowing that I am thinking about water does not rule out the possibility that I am a brain in a vat. Knowing this is compatible with the possibility that I am a brain in a vat, so long as I am *actually* a brain in a vat! If I am, then my knowing I am thinking about water will turn out to *be* my knowing I am thinking about the brain-in-vat counterpart of water.

Harmlessly Unknowable

Our inability to know that skeptical hypotheses are false would be harmless if it did not threaten our commonsense knowledge claims. Perhaps we can resist Cartesian skepticism by arguing that, while we cannot know we are not deceived by demons or superscientists, this does not stop us from knowing that we are reading or writing articles and so forth.

For this strategy to succeed, we will need some way to stop our inability to know whether skeptical hypotheses are true from undermining our commonsense knowledge claims. When skeptics deny these claims, they tend to rely on principles such as SP, SPC and GK. If such principles are false, we can insist on our commonsense knowledge claims yet admit that we do not know that skeptical hypotheses are false.

Of course, the strategy we are considering will also force us to deny that knowledge is the same thing as certainty, since, as we have seen, this equation forces us to accept SP, SPC and GK. Moreover, if knowledge required certainty, the discriminatory powers we would need in order to know things about the world would be great indeed. We would need to be able to discriminate between actually reading an essay, on one hand, and undergoing the experiential equivalent while dreaming or being deceived by Descartes' demon. Denying that knowledge is certainty allows us to say that the discriminatory powers we need to know things about the world will vary depending on our circumstances and the challenges arising in them (Luper 1987). On this view, which we can call the *variation thesis*, ordinary discriminatory powers suffice in ordinary circumstances, in which, for example, we are able to distinguish between being confronted with a bird and being confronted with a friend who is bird hunting with us, but much greater power is necessary when things that are hard to detect are close possibilities. If, for example, the planet were invaded by aliens capable of disguising themselves as birds we would not know, just by looking, whether the creature in front of us is a bird or an alien. We would need a better way to discriminate between the two. On the variation thesis, skeptical possibilities do not preclude our knowing things in ordinary circumstances.

Various ways of understanding knowledge are consistent with the variation thesis. One such analysis is the tracking account defended by Fred Dretske (1970, 1971, 2003) and Robert Nozick (1981). Very roughly, it says that a subject S knows that a proposition P is true just when S *tracks P's truth*, and that S tracks P's truth just when S has an experience E such that

(1) S's belief P is based on S's having E, and
(2) Not-P → not-(S has E).

Condition (2) is expressed as a subjunctive conditional; read a conditional of the form P → Q as "if P held, Q would hold" (for further clarification see Lewis 1973). It says that in the closest worlds to the actual world in which P holds, Q does too.

Dretske and Nozick note that the tracking analysis is plausible in a wide range of cases. For example, it says that I know that there is a bird in front of me because I can distinguish it from other things that I might encounter in my circumstances, such as tables, fishes, and tractors. In the closest worlds to the actual world in which there were not a bird before me, I would not have the experiences I have now—I would not be 'appeared to birdly.' It is true that if the bird-simulating aliens came I might be appeared to in a birdlike way even though no bird is in front of me. But the mere possibility of such aliens does not preclude my knowing I see a bird.

The tracking account has another important attribute: if it is correct, then principles such as GK are false. This we can verify using some examples. As we said earlier, I know that the creature in front of me is a bird, since, were it not, I would not be appeared to birdly. However, I do not know that the creature in front of me is not an alien simulating a bird. I do not know this, according to the tracking analysis, since I would still be appeared to birdly if a bird-simulating alien were before me. However, the proposition that the creature in front of me is a bird entails that it is false that the creature is a bird-simulating alien. Hence GK must be false: you know the creature is a bird, and that this entails it is not a bird-simulating alien; according to GK, then, knowing it is a bird positions you to know it is not a bird-simulating alien. Yet you do not track, and hence do not know, it is not a bird-simulating alien. Similar reasoning shows that while you track and hence know you have hands, you do not know that aliens have not removed your brain, placed it into a vat, destroyed your body, and are presently making it appear as if your body is intact. Once again, GK must be false. The same examples illustrate the falsity of SPC. SP cannot be proven false in this way, but it is false if, given the tracking account (as stated), we cannot track the truth of any skeptical hypothesis.

Nozick and Dretske are not the only proponents of the view that skeptical hypotheses are harmlessly unknowable. In recent work, Gilbert Harman, writing with Brett

Sherman, defends this view as well. According to Harman, "one knows only if one believes as one does because of something that settles the truth of that belief" (Harman and Sherman 2004, p. 498). He also says that we make various assumptions, perhaps tacitly, in the course of coming to know things. For example, in ordinary situations, you might come to know you have hands just by having certain experiences: having them settles the truth of your belief. However, in believing in your hands on these grounds, you assume that you are not merely dreaming that you have hands, and you are not a brain in a vat. But you do not know that the assumptions hold, since you lack grounds that settle their truth. According to Harman, the upshot is that it is possible to know things that entail other things which we assume but are in no position to know, so we should reject "strong closure principles" such as GK.

Although some theorists deny closure principles in order to support the claim that skeptical hypotheses are harmlessly unknowable, this strategy has received heavy criticism. Most of the critics say that GK (and the weaker principles which it entails) is extremely plausible, and should be rejected only if there are very compelling reasons for doing so. Admittedly, if holding onto GK commits us to skepticism, there might well be compelling grounds for rejecting GK. However, there seem to be defensible ways to reject Cartesian skepticism without abandoning GK.

One way has been offered by (speaker-centered) contextualists (e.g., Lewis 1996), who say that whether it is proper for a speaker to attribute knowledge to a subject depends on the context of the speaker, and in some contexts, say while doing epistemology, it is proper to attribute knowledge only to subjects who meet elevated standards, such as certainty. In such contexts people cannot properly be said to know things about the world. But in ordinary contexts, such as while driving to work, the standards for knowledge attributions are more relaxed, and people can properly be said to know a great deal about the world. GK is true in any context. But it cannot be used to show that people who know things about the world are in a position to know that skeptical hypotheses are false, because there is a shift in context anytime the issue of skeptical possibilities arises; if someone considers whether he is a brain in a vat, he is thereby placed in a context with elevated standards, and can be said to know neither that he is not a brain in a vat nor anything about the world that implies that he is not a brain in a vat. Thus for contextualists skeptical possibilities are harmlessly unknowable—as long as we ignore them.

Knowable

Next let us ask whether there are good reasons for saying we know that (at least some) skeptical hypotheses are false.

Famously, G.E. Moore (1962) argued that we can know *with certainty* that (at least some) skeptical hypotheses are false. He defended this claim by turning the skeptic's argument on its head. Moore assumed, as the skeptic does, that he could know things about the world, such as that he had hands, only if he could know he was not dreaming. But Moore used this assumption against the skeptic, as follows:

1. S can know something about the (mind-independent) world only if S can know she is not dreaming.
2. S knows various things about the world, such as that she has hands.
3. So S can know that S is not dreaming.

The conclusion of this argument entails that many skeptical hypotheses are false, namely any of them that entail that S is dreaming. So according to Moore, we can know that all such skeptical hypotheses, as pertain to us, are false. Moreover, we can know this with certainty, as we are certain we have hands. Furthermore, if 1 is correct, presumably related claims are too, such as these: S can know he has hands only if S can know her experiences are not the product of superscientists, or demons, and so on. On Moore's view we can know, with certainty, that no skeptical hypotheses are true that involve our having ersatz experiences.

Moore's argument faces a glaring objection, however: it seems false that we are certain that we have hands. Moore was not clear about the nature of 'certainty.' However, if certainty entails immunity to error, then we are not certain we have hands. Our belief would be false if we were merely brains in vats being deceived by superscientists, and we cannot eliminate this possibility on the basis of other things about which we cannot be mistaken.

Moore's argument is more plausible if we reject the equation of knowledge with certainty. Moreover, even if we reject this equation, we can learn something from his discussion, namely this: if we know things about the world, surely we will also know that many, if not all, skeptical hypotheses are false. For GK (and SPC, which GK entails) seems extremely plausible. So if we know we have hands, then we can know that any skeptical hypothesis that is inconsistent with our having hands is false.

Still, the antiskeptical strategy of citing GK and the assumption that we know we have hands seems no better than the skeptical strategy of citing GK and the assumption that we cannot know that skeptical hypotheses are false. A better antiskeptical strategy is to supply an account of knowledge that supports both GK and the variation thesis. This we can accomplish by replacing the tracking account with the *safe indication* view (Luper 1984; Sosa 2003; Pritchard 2005; and others), which holds, roughly, that S knows P just when S believes P on the basis of an experience E that safely indicates P's truth; that is,

(1) S's belief P is based on S's having experience E, and
(2) S has E $\rightarrow$ P.

The safe indication analysis is closely related to the tracking account; the second condition of the one is the contraposition of the second condition of the other. And like the tracking account, the safe indication view has plausible implications across a wide range of cases. For example, it implies that you know you have hands. Presumably, your belief that you have hands is based on your seemingly experiencing your hands; in the closest worlds to the actual world in which you had such experiences, you would indeed have hands. However, safe indication differs strikingly from tracking in two ways. First, what safely indicates the truth of some proposition (or propositions) P also safely indicates the truth of the things that P entails, so GK is true given the safety account. Second, our experiences safely indicate that various skeptical hypotheses are false. In the closest worlds to the actual world in which you seem to have hands, you are not a brain in a vat, and not having a dream that creates experiences that exactly match those you actually have. Hence on the safe indication account you know that these skeptical hypotheses are false. It is true that you would not know you were not vatted if you *were* vatted, or if in your circumstances people often found themselves vatted. It is also true that your experiences would be just like they are now if you were vatted. Hence the plausibility of the claim that you know that you are not a brain in a vat hinges on the variation thesis.

There are other ways to defend the claim that we know that skeptical hypotheses are false. Many theorists (e.g., Harman 1968; Vogel 1990) criticize skeptical hypotheses on the grounds that such hypotheses are not the best explanations of a person's experiences. Skeptical hypotheses are consistent with my having the experiences I have, but a better explanation of my experiences and their features is the commonsense view that there is an array of physical objects, including my body, and some of these objects act upon my body in such a fashion as to cause the experiences I have. Coherentists (e.g., Lehrer 1974, 2003; BonJour 1985) criticize skeptical hypotheses on these grounds. They say that a set of beliefs is justified (as a whole) to the extent that it is coherent, and that the coherence of our beliefs is boosted to the extent that some of them support others, and reduced to the extent that such support does not exist. Given their explanatory impotence, skeptical hypotheses are not well supported; our scheme of beliefs is more coherent without them. Coherentists also reject skeptical hypotheses on the grounds that they are inconsistent with wide swatches of our beliefs and these beliefs are themselves mutually supporting.

Of course, even if skeptical hypotheses are not the best explanations of my experiences, it does not follow that I know that skeptical hypotheses are false. What follows is that I am justified in believing that skeptical hypotheses are false, and it is well known that justified true belief does not constitute knowledge. But there are accounts of knowledge that dovetail well with the coherentist account of justification, and according to some such combinations it is possible to know that skeptical hypotheses are false. Consider, for example, the defeasibility account of knowledge (defended by Klein (1971), among others). According to (one version of) this analysis, a subject S knows P iff

1. P is adequately justified for S on the basis of grounds G, and
2. G are undefeated for S by any proposition D that is not misleading, where:
   (a) D *defeats* G iff D is true and P is not justified for S on the basis of the conjunction of G and D, and
   (b) D is *misleading* iff D justifies S in believing something false.

Given defeasibilism, I know things about the world as long as I have adequate and undefeated justification for my beliefs. In view of its demand that known propositions be undefeated, defeasibilism is an externalist account of knowledge, and it is committed to the variation thesis, since my circumstances determine which propositions would defeat my evidence. Moreover, if I am justified in believing that a skeptical hypothesis SK is false on the grounds that it is not the best explanation of my experiences, nothing stands in the way of my knowing not-SK. But of course if SK is true, it will defeat my justification for believing not-SK.

References

Armstrong, David, 1973, *Belief, Truth and Knowledge*, London: Cambridge University Press.
BonJour, Lawrence, 1985, *The Structure of Empirical Knowledge*, Cambridge, MA: Harvard University Press.
Brueckner, Anthony, 2003, "Trees, Computer Program Features and Skeptical Hypotheses," in Luper 2003, pp. 217–227.

SKEPTICISM

Descartes, René, 1641, *Meditations on First Philosophy*, in Cottingham et al. 1984, *The Philosophical Writings of Descartes*, Cambridge: Cambridge University Press.

Dretske, Fred, 1970, "Epistemic Operators," *Journal of Philosophy* 67: 1007–23.

——, 1971, "Conclusive Reasons," *Australasian Journal of Philosophy* 49: 1–22.

——, 2003, "Skepticism: What Perception Teaches," in Luper 2003, pp. 105–19.

Goldman, Alvin, 1967, "A Causal Theory of Knowing," *Journal of Philosophy* 64.12: 357–72.

Harman, Gilbert, 1968, "Knowledge, Inference and Explanation," *American Philosophical Quarterly* 5: 164–73.

—— and Sherman, Brett, 2004, "Knowledge, Assumptions, Lotteries," *Philosophical Issues*, 14, Epistemology: 492–500.

Hume, David, 1975, *Enquiry Concerning Human Understanding*, in *Enquiries Concerning Human Understanding and Concerning the Principles of Morals*, edited by L. A. Selby-Bigge, 3rd edition revised by P. H. Nidditch, Oxford: Clarendon Press.

Klein, Peter, 1971, "A Proposed Definition of Propositional Knowledge," *Journal of Philosophy* 67.16: 47–82.

Lehrer, Keith, 1974, *Knowledge*, Oxford: Oxford University Press.

——, 2003, "Skepticism, Fallibility and Circularity," in Luper 2003, pp. 95–105.

Lewis, David, 1973, *Counterfactuals*, Cambridge, MA: Harvard University Press.

——, 1996, "Elusive Knowledge," *Australasian Journal of Philosophy* 74.4: 549–67.

Luper, Steven, 1984, "The Epistemic Predicament," *Australasian Journal of Philosophy* 62: 26–48.

——, 1987, "The Causal Indicator Analysis of Knowledge," *Philosophy and Phenomenological Research* 47: 563–89.

——, ed., 2003, *The Skeptics*, Aldershot: Ashgate Publishing, Limited.

Moore, G. E., 1962, "Certainty," in *Philosophical Papers*, London: George Allen and Unwin.

Nozick, Robert, 1981, *Philosophical Explanations*, Cambridge, MA: Harvard University Press.

Pierce, Charles, 1877, "The Fixation of Belief," *Popular Science Monthly* 12 (November 1877), 1–15.

Pritchard, Duncan, 2005, *Epistemic Luck*, Oxford University Press.

Putnam, Hilary, 1981, "Brains in a Vat," in *Reason, Truth and History*, Cambridge: Cambridge University Press.

Ramsey, Frank, 1929, "Knowledge," in D. H. Mellor, ed., *Philosophical Papers*, Cambridge: Cambridge University Press, 1990.

Sextus Empiricus, *Outlines of Pyrrhonism*, trans. R. G. Bury, 1967, Cambridge, MA: Harvard University Press.

Sosa, Ernest, 2003, "Neither Contextualism nor Skepticism," in Luper 2003, pp. 165–83.

Unger, Peter, 1971, "A Defense of Skepticism," *The Philosophical Review* 80: 198–219.

——, 1975, *Ignorance: A Case for Skepticism*, Oxford: Oxford University Press.

Vogel, Jonathan, 1990, "Cartesian Skepticism and Inference to the Best Explanation," *Journal of Philosophy* 87.11: 658–66.

Wittgenstein, 1969, *On Certainty*, New York: Harper Torchbooks.

39
SKEPTICAL DOUBTS ABOUT SELF-KNOWLEDGE
Fred Dretske

Valid arguments – even those with true premises—don't take you very far if you don't know whether the premises are true. The fact that I'm in Heidelberg doesn't give me a reason to believe I'm in Germany unless I know (or at least have reason to believe) I'm in Heidelberg. So why does everyone believe the *Cogito*—I think, therefore I am—is such an impressive argument? Because, I suppose, everyone thinks he knows the premise is true. Everyone who thinks he thinks, thinks he *knows* he thinks. So everyone thinks his existence as a thinking being is the conclusion of an irresistible argument.

The Cartesian inference is certainly valid, no doubt about that. And the premise is clearly true—at least it is for everyone who thinks it is true. I'm not questioning either of these claims. I do, however, think it worth pondering the question of whether—and if so, how—one knows that the premise is true. What reason do thinkers have for thinking they think? Is it simply the fact that they think?

1. Self-Verifying Thoughts

Clyde has cancer, but the fact that he has cancer doesn't give him a reason to believe he has cancer. Why, then, should the fact that he thinks give him a reason to think he thinks? There might be something about thinking as opposed to having cancer that—automatically, as it were—provides one with a reason for thinking one is doing it, but if so, we need to know what that is.

Is it, perhaps, because one can think one has cancer and be wrong, but one can't think one thinks and be wrong? Is it, in other words, because thinking one thinks is, as philosophers like to put it (though Descartes put it differently), a self-verifying thought? Unlike the thought that one has cancer or a thought about almost any other topic, the thought that one thinks has to be true.

The thought that one thinks is self-verifying—no doubt about that—but having a self-verifying thought doesn't mean one has a reason to think one thinks—not unless one has reason to think one has this self-verifying thought. We are, then, back to where we started—maybe, even, a little *behind* where we started. Remember, our question is: what reason does one have for thinking one thinks? It is no answer to say that *if* one thinks one thinks, one can't be wrong. That just leaves the question: what reason does one have for thinking one thinks one thinks?

According to extreme versions of reliability theory (I don't know whether anyone actually holds this extreme view), the fact that this thought (the thought that one thinks) is self-verifying means that one *knows* one thinks merely by believing one thinks. Beliefs that are perfectly reliable qualify as knowledge. There is, however, nothing in such theories that provides help in the current project. There is nothing in such theories that reveals what *reasons* one has for thinking one thinks. On the contrary, according to such austere theories of knowledge, one can know that p is true while having absolutely no reasons for thinking p is true—while, in fact, having reasons to think p is false. What we are looking for here is something a little more satisfying, something a thinker has access to that would justify his or her confidence that he or she is a thinking being. We are, that is, looking for reasons whether or not such reasons are deemed necessary for knowledge according to certain frugal conceptions of knowledge.

We do enjoy a special kind of authority about *what* we think, but that should not be confused with an authority about the fact that we think it. Several philosophers (e.g., Heil 1988; Burge 1988) have argued—persuasively to my mind—that with respect to a certain limited class of thoughts (conscious current thoughts), one thinks whatever one thinks one thinks. We enjoy a kind of infallibility about what we think, and, therefore, an authority that comes with such infallibility. This is so because in thinking (at the second level, so to speak) that we think (at the first level) that so-and-so, we thereby think that so-and-so. In thinking that I am thinking there is water in the glass I thereby think there is water in the glass. It is like an exasperated mother saying to her misbehaving son, "I'm telling you, Billy, stop pestering your sister." If we ignore the possible performative character of her utterance (in which case what Mother says is neither true nor false) Mother can't really be wrong in what she says to Billy. She tells him whatever she says she tells him. Even if the words she utters ("Stop pestering your sister") mean by prior agreement between Mother and Son that he should get ready for bed, Mother is still correct in using the words, "Stop pestering your sister" to say what she is telling her son to do. She *is*, as she says she is, telling him to get ready for bed. So she can't be wrong no matter what the words she uses mean. The same is true for thought. One uses the content of the 1st order thought to think, at the 2nd level, what one is thinking at the first level. There is no room for mistake no matter what one (at the 1st level) happens to be thinking or how (with what "words" in the language of thought) one thinks it.

If this is the way thought about (current conscious) thoughts work, then we all enjoy a kind of infallibility in our thoughts about our currently conscious thoughts. But even if things do work this way, it doesn't help us understand what reasons we have for thinking we have thoughts, much less such infallible thoughts. If I think I am thinking it is hot out, then if Burge and Heil are right, that must be what I am thinking. And if I think that I am thinking, that too must be what I am thinking. But what tells me, what reason do I have to think, I actually have these foolproof thoughts about what I am now thinking? The answer to that question is not answered by the infallible nature of higher-order thoughts about what one is thinking. Mother does not have a reason to think she is telling her son to do X just because she knows that *if* she is saying "I'm telling you to do X," then she can't be wrong. She *is* telling him to do X. But what reason does she have for thinking she is saying this? Infallibility about what you think you are thinking and about what you say you are saying doesn't give you a reason to think you are thinking or saying anything. If you have such a reason, it must come from elsewhere.

I will return in a moment to this important difference between knowing what you think and knowing you think it, but, first, a reminder of just what we are looking for. We are looking for reasons S has for thinking S thinks that are not available to others. We are looking for facts that S has exclusive, and therefore privileged, access to that in some way indicate or constitute evidence that S thinks. If S is a normal human being, of course, we *all* have reasons to think he thinks. He has a Ph.D. in physics, forty-three publications, and he runs rings around us at the bridge table. Of course he thinks—probably better than we do—and there is no shortage of reasons for believing this to be so. And if we have such reasons, so too does S. Anything *we* can point to as accomplishments symptomatic of S's mental prowess are also available to S. If we have reasons for thinking S thinks—and we clearly do—so does S: exactly the same facts we have.

This is not in question. Of course we, and therefore S, have reasons to think S is a thinking being. What is in question is whether there are any facts that indicate this to be so that S has *exclusive* access to, facts or conditions that S is aware of that we can't be aware of—at least not in the direct and authoritative way that S is. Is there anything S is aware of that others can't be aware of that give S an evidential edge on questions about whether S has thoughts?

One way to proceed in an investigation of this sort is to look at how we learned we think. We all think before we ever discover what thinking is. Before we think we think. So at some point in time, or during some phase of childhood, we learned we think. How did we learn this? Who taught us? Parents? Did we take their word for it? Were we already aware of our own thoughts as we were of lamps and television sets and merely had to learn (as we did with ordinary objects) what to call them? Before pursuing this line of inquiry, though, a few words about terminology.

2. Terminological Matters

What is to count as a thought? Like Descartes, I intend to be pretty inclusive. Any description of S whose truth requires S to think or be *able* to think, in the everyday sense of the word "think," will be considered a description of S as thinking. This includes not only thinking in the everyday sense (I think someone is following me, he thinks she is home), but all the so-called propositional attitudes insofar as the verbs are understood as taking a factive complement: believing, judging, knowing, perceiving (i.e., seeing, hearing, feeling, tasting), doubting, remembering, regretting, being sorry, hoping, intending, wanting, and imagining that so-and-so. Even wondering whether something is so or pretending that something is so (that a banana is a telephone, for instance) will count as thinking on this generous construal of thought. One doesn't, of course, have to think (in the narrower sense) that something is so in order to wonder whether it is so or pretend that it is so, but one cannot wonder or pretend without being *able* to think that it is so—without, that is, having the capacity for thinking it is so. In this broad inclusive sense, then, thinking is doing something that creatures that cannot think (in the narrower everyday sense) can't do. Sensations (pains, itches, tickles, hunger, thirst), emotions (anger, fear), and moods (elation, depression) do not qualify as thoughts although these feelings, moods, and emotions might well combine with thoughts to yield composite states that qualify as thoughts—e.g., anger that she left, fear that he will fall, and relief that she got home safe. I continue to speak of one's reasons for thinking one thinks, but given this inclusive and broad understanding of what a thought is, our query could be put: what reasons (to which one has exclusive access) does one have for thinking one *can* think in the narrower everyday sense of this word.

One final terminological note. In speaking of thoughts (fears, perceptions, etc.) one can be speaking of either (1) what one thinks, the *content* of the thought, or (2) what is often called the *act* of thinking, that which distinguishes my thought that today is Friday from your thought that today is Friday. When we speak of a person's belief (fear, hope), for instance, it is sometimes unclear whether we mean to be speaking of content, *what* the person believes (fears, hopes), or their *believing* (fearing, hoping) it, a mental action. I will always try to make it clear which I intend to be referring to when there is any chance of misunderstanding.

3. Acquaintance with Content

So much for sharpening tools. It is time to use them. Imagine, then, a normal three-year-old, Sarah, who thinks but hasn't yet learned she thinks. That one thinks is something psychologists tell us (I rely here on Astington 1993; Bartsch and Wellman 1995; Carpendale and Lewis 2006; Flavell 2003; Gopnik 1993) that children only come to fully understand around the age of three or four years. Sarah, a typical three-year-old, isn't quite there. She thinks Daddy is home. That is what she tells Mommy. That is why she runs to open the door when she hears an automobile pull in the driveway. What Sarah tells Mommy is (what else?) what she thinks (knows, hears): that her father is home. She does not, however, realize that she thinks it. She might use the word "think," ("know" or "hear") in describing herself, but if she does, she doesn't yet fully understand that what she is giving expression to is a fact about herself, a subjective condition having a content (what she thinks) that might not be true. She will, however, soon acquire this knowledge. How and from whom? No doubt from parents, teachers, older siblings and friends. If one doesn't actually teach children this, if they merely absorb it the way children acquire their native language, it is nonetheless from others, or at least with the help of others, that Sarah will learn that what she has been telling them is what she has been thinking, what she believes, what she (sometimes) even knows. It is from (or with the help of) other people (and, perhaps, a few disappointed expectations) that she will learn that she has thoughts that usually correspond to the way things actually are, but that sometimes fail to match the facts. In the process she will learn that her behavior and, of course, the behavior of others can be explained not only by the fact that her father is home (Sarah already understands this), but also by her *thinking* he is home—something (Sarah will learn) that can be true of her, and can explain her excited rush to the door, without her father actually being home. As Jonathan Bennett (1991: 97) once put it in describing what psychologists have learned about child development, a two-year-old predicts and explains another person's behavior on the basis of what she, *the child*, thinks is true; a four-year-old does so on the basis of what *the other* person thinks is true (or at least what the child thinks the other person thinks is true). To reach this level of sophistication one has to understand, as two-year-olds do not, what it means to think something is true. That is why normal two-year-olds do not understand the behavior of someone who goes to the door when no one is there. A four-year-old will understand this: the person went to the door because *the person* (but maybe not the four-year-old) *thought* there was someone at the door.

To understand what kind of access we, those of us who think we have thoughts, have to our own thoughts, and thus what kind of reasons we have for thinking we have them, it is instructive to consider the kind of access Sarah, a person who doesn't think she has them (she doesn't think she doesn't have them either), has to her thoughts. I said above that Sarah told her mother that her father was home and rushed to open the door because she *thought* he was home. It might not have been her father she heard pulling into the driveway, of course, but Sarah thought it was, and the fact that she thought so explains why she behaved that way. If she had thought, instead, that it was the mailman she wouldn't have told her mother that her father was home and she wouldn't have rushed to open the door. Sarah's thoughts and desires explain her behavior in exactly the same way our thoughts and desires explain ours. The only difference is that Sarah does not yet understand that her behavior can be explained by the fact that (whether or not her father is home) she *thinks* he is home. We do.

If Sarah's behavior is to be explained by what she thinks even when she does not realize she thinks it, and the behavior in question is a deliberate, purposeful act (Sarah has and is prepared to give *reasons* for what she does, and these reasons are, in part, what she thinks), there must be a sense in which Sarah is aware of what she thinks—that her father is home—without being aware that this is something she thinks. Call this form of awareness *acquaintance*. Sarah is acquainted with what she thinks. Although this word has a troubled philosophical history, I use it in its ordinary sense, the sense in which one can be acquainted with—in fact, good friends with—a philosopher and not know he is a philosopher. It is in this epistemically uncommitted sense of awareness that Sarah is acquainted with what she thinks: she is aware (conscious) of what she is thinking in a way that doesn't require her to know (or even think) it is something she is thinking in order to be aware of it. If she had thought, instead, that it was the mailman, she would have been acquainted with, aware of, something different. Something different would have been going through her mind—her *conscious* mind—at the time she spoke to her mother. She would, therefore, have behaved differently.

What is it that Sarah is acquainted with (aware of) when she thinks her father is home? We cannot say it is (the fact) that her father is home because her father needn't be home for her to think he is home and to behave (and to give the same reasons for behaving) in exactly the same way. Whatever she is acquainted with when she thinks he is home must, therefore, be (logically) independent of her father's actual whereabouts in the same way her thought that he is home is (logically) independent of his actual whereabouts. So it can't be the *fact* that her father is home. There might be no such fact. Nor can we say that what Sarah is acquainted with when she thinks her father is home is the fact that *she thinks* her father is home because although this (unlike her father's being home) must be a fact, it is not a fact that Sarah, lacking the concept of thought, can be aware of. What, then, if it isn't a fact, is Sarah aware of when she thinks her father is home? Well, *propositions* have traditionally played this epistemological/semantic role. They are the objects of thought. In thinking that her father is home, Sarah is acquainted with a proposition, the proposition that her father is home. Propositions are the meanings of declarative sentences—those sentences we use to express what one thinks. They can be either true or false. So what Sarah is acquainted with when she thinks her father is home is a proposition that might be false. And given the way we are understanding acquaintance, Sarah can be acquainted with this proposition without knowing it is a proposition. If this (acquaintance with propositions) sounds a bit strange, one has to remember that it is merely our way of saying that one can be aware of what one thinks in the same way *we* (who know we think) can be aware of it *without* knowing it is something one thinks. Indeed, one way to describe the conceptual development of children is to say that what they learn at around the age of four is that what they had been taking to be (what we call) facts about the world are really (what we call) propositions—entities that (unlike facts) can be false. Awareness of the proposition that her father is home does not mean, of course, that Sarah cannot (also) be aware of the fact that he is home, but awareness of the fact requires more than awareness of the proposition that he is home. It requires, in addition, awareness that this proposition is true.

4. Awareness of What One Thinks

So there is a sense, a perfectly straightforward sense, in which one has a privileged awareness of one's own present conscious thoughts even *before* one knows one has them. If we want to find out what Sarah thinks, we have to ask *her*. She is the authority on what she thinks *despite* not knowing she thinks it. We cannot, to be sure, find out what Sarah thinks by asking her what she thinks. She won't understand what we are talking about. But there are indirect ways of getting the answer to this question. Given a cooperative child, we can ask Sarah whether her father is home. Or why she is rushing to open the door. The answers will reveal, quite unerringly, what Sarah thinks. If Sarah wasn't aware of what she thinks, how could she know how to answer these questions?

What this tells us is that our point of contact with our own thoughts is through their content: *what* it is we are thinking. We have a privileged and exclusive access to our own thoughts through acquaintance with their propositional content. This mode of access gives our own acts of thought their peculiar diaphanous quality: the *acts* of thought are absolutely invisible to the person whose thoughts they are. All one is aware of (at least up to the age of three or four) is their content. Later (after three or four) one becomes aware of the fact that this is the content of one's own thought. Something of this puzzling nature can, perhaps, be brought out by comparing thoughts (one's own thoughts) to verbal representations. People say things and they think things. One's access to what a person (including oneself) says is through the person's act of saying it—an acoustic or observable event of some sort. We hear the person *say* he has a dental appointment, and then, if we understand the language, we come to know, become aware of, what that person said, the proposition expressed. We go from the saying to what-is-said, from *act* to *content*. In the case of thought, however, the route of access is reversed. Our only point of contact with our own thoughts is through their content. Sarah thinks Daddy is home, that it is raining, and that the dog is barking. Despite no awareness that she thinks these things, and no awareness of her own *acts* of thought, she is, nonetheless, fully aware of (that is, acquainted with) what it is she thinks—the content of these assorted thoughts. Sarah will eventually learn that there is something about (in?) her—something very personal (everyone has their own thoughts) and private (one can keep one's thoughts to oneself)—to which this content is somehow attached. She first becomes aware of what she thinks—the proposition that her father is home—and later learns that this fact (or what she took to be a fact) was, so to speak, attached to *her* thoughts but perhaps to no one else's thoughts. Nor does it depend in any essential way on Daddy's whereabouts. Unlike a person saying, "Daddy is home," a verbal action one can become fully aware of without understanding what is being said (the proposition that is being expressed), one can be (and at two years, one *is*) acquainted with what one is thinking (this proposition) while having absolutely no awareness or understanding of the act of thought itself. The mode of access is completely reversed.

This mode of access to one's own thoughts continues, of course, *after* one finds out one thinks. One learns, around the age of four, that people, including oneself, have these privately accessible thoughts. One becomes aware *that* one thinks, but in learning this one doesn't become aware *of* one's own thoughts in any way other than the way one was aware of them before one learned this. The access is still via their content. One doesn't suddenly, at the age of four, become aware of one's own *acts* of thought. One simply becomes aware, learns, comes to believe, that such acts of thought must exist somewhere inside each thinker for a thinker to have the thoughts (the thought-contents) she has, thought-contents to which each thinker has privileged and authoritative access (i.e., acquaintance with).

5. Skeptical Conclusions

Well, if this is our mode of access to our own thoughts, doesn't this provide us with an answer to the skeptic's question—the question of what reason we have for thinking we think? Everyone who thinks has a reason to believe he thinks because he is acquainted with the propositions that are the content of his own thoughts and which indicate the presence of the thoughts for which they are the content.

Unfortunately, this doesn't work. When you think, there is nothing you are aware of that indicates you are thinking. What you are aware of (or acquainted with) is a proposition and propositions do not indicate anything. They are not reasons to believe that anything is so. Unlike facts (conditions, states of affairs), propositions can be either true or false, and a proposition with indeterminate truth-value does not increase the probability that anything else is true. Propositions are a dime a dozen. They are epistemologically worthless. The proposition that pigs have wings is a perfectly respectable proposition—something a person might actually think—but has absolutely no probative value. It certainly isn't a reason to think pigs can fly. If it were a reason, we would all have a reason to think that pigs can fly. What would be a reason to think pigs can fly is if it were *true* that pigs have wings, if it were a *fact* that pigs have wings, if pigs actually had wings. The proposition that pigs have wings, though, doesn't require pigs to have wings. So a person's awareness of what he thinks when he thinks pigs have wings—the proposition that pigs have wings—doesn't give him a reason to believe that pigs can fly. It doesn't give him a reason to believe anything. It doesn't, in particular, give him a reason to think that he is *thinking* pigs have wings. This is true even when *what* a person thinks is that he is presently thinking that pigs have wings. The person needs a reason to think that this proposition (that he is thinking that pigs have wings) is true in order to have a reason to think that he thinks, and we are back to where we started: looking for reasons to think one thinks.

What this means is that there is nothing we are aware of when we think that indicates we are thinking. We are aware of what we think, a proposition, and we enjoy a privileged and authoritative form of awareness of this content, yes, but thought content is evidentially worthless. Privileged awareness of it makes one an authority on *what* one thinks in the same way Sarah (who doesn't know she thinks) is an authority on what she thinks, but it doesn't give one a reason, much less make one an authority, on whether or not one is thinking it.

What, then, is one's reason, one's evidence, for thinking one thinks? If our mode of contact with our own thoughts doesn't give us a reason to think we are having these thoughts, what does? I haven't found anything—at least nothing one has privileged access to, nothing one's neighbors and friends don't have equal access to. If this is, indeed, so, then there is a genuine problem of self-knowledge. It turns out to be pretty much the same problem as the problem of *other* minds.

References

Astington, J. W. 1993. *The Child's Discovery of the Mind*. Cambridge, MA: Harvard University Press.
Bartsch, K. and H. M. Wellman. 1995. *Children Talk About the Mind*. Oxford: Oxford University Press.
Bennett, J. 1991. How to Read Minds in Behavior: A Suggestion from a Philosopher. In A. Whiten (ed.) *Natural Theories of Mind* (pp. 97–108). Oxford: Basil Blackwell.
Burge, T. 1988. Individualism and Self-Knowledge. *Journal of Philosophy*, 85: 649–93.
Carpendale, J. and C. Lewis. 2006. *How Children Develop Social Understanding*. Malden, MA: Blackwell Publishing.
Flavell, J. H. 2003. *Development of Children's Knowledge About the Mind: The Heinz Werner Lectures*. Worcester, MA: Clark University Press.
Gopnik, A. 1993. How We Know Our Minds: The Illusion of First Person Knowledge of Intentionality. *Behavioral and Brain Sciences*, 16, 1–14.
Heil, J. 1988. Privileged Access. *Mind*, 47: 238–51.

40
SKEPTICISM ABOUT KNOWLEDGE OF OTHER MINDS
Anita Avramides

The philosophical issue of skepticism is one that can be located within epistemology—although epistemologists dispute the significance and centrality of this issue. The problem of other minds is often taken to be a skeptical problem. Skeptical questions have a long history; the history of questions concerning the minds of others has a shorter, somewhat less clear, history. This observation alone should lead one to approach the topic of "skepticism and other minds" with a degree of caution. Although I shall discuss the intersection of these issues, I shall not feel constrained to see all questions arising in connection with the latter as falling into a subclass of questions arising in connection with the former. Insofar as it is meaningful to talk of two traditions in philosophy, what follows is firmly rooted in the analytic tradition; there is still a rich seam to be mined in the continental/phenomenological tradition.

Some Ancient History

Skepticism is a philosophical problem whose roots can be traced back to ancient times and to two main schools of skeptical thought: the Academic and the Pyrrhonian. Myles Burnyeat (1982) and Bernard Williams (1981) argue that the skepticism of these early philosophers is prefaced on an assumption that an experiencing subject acts in a world, with a focus on questions concerning how we can know truths about this world. They argue that the skeptic of ancient times is a realist who does not question the existence of the world, but only its state or condition. Avramides (2001) observes that skepticism concerning the existence of other minds also appears to have no place here. These early skeptics assume the existence of others in order to raise doubts about dogmatic claims concerning the nature of the world.

A group of lesser-known skeptics in ancient times, the Cyrenaics, are reported by the second-century skeptic Sextus Empiricus (AD 160–210 [2000]: 195–198) to have made the following observation about experience:

> For each person is aware of his own private *pathos* [affections], but whether this *pathos* occurs in him and his neighbour from a white object neither can he himself tell, since he is not submitting to the *pathos* of his neighbor.... And since

no *pathos* is common to us all, it is hasty to declare that what appears to me of a certain kind appears of this same kind to my neighbour as well.

The question raised here is on a par with the kind of question about the world that one finds throughout the ancient skeptical literature: given that each person is aware of his own affections, and given that he cannot "submit" to the affections of another, we cannot know whether what appears to me is of the same kind as what appears to another. We might label this the *knowledge what* question: 'How do I know *what* another is thinking or feeling?' We can think of this as a restricted skeptical question because, in raising it, there is an assumption that the other does have a mind.

Modern Skepticism

Descartes and the Seeds of a Problem

The skepticism of modern philosophy traces its roots back to Descartes' *Meditations*. Descartes was familiar with the work of Sextus and developed his skepticism against this background. Descartes considers the arguments of the earlier skeptics—the possibility of illusion, of hallucination, and of dreaming—and to these he adds another: the possibility that we are being deceived by an evil demon. The importance of this consideration is that it allows us to question, not just how things are beyond my thought, but whether there is anything that corresponds to my thought. Once this question is raised we can ask a much more radical skeptical question, both about the world of objects and about the minds of others. We might label this the knowledge *that* question: 'How do I know *that* others have minds?' Another way of formulating the question is to start by reflecting on one's own experience and ask how I know that I am not the only mind. It is modern, Cartesian, skepticism that Simon Blackburn characterizes when he writes: "Classically, skepticism springs from the observation that the best methods in some area seem to fall short of giving us contact with the truth (there is a gap between appearance and reality)" (Blackburn 1994: 340). In the case of another mind the gap might be said to be between the body and the mind of the other. Fitting together radical skepticism about the world of bodies with that concerning another mind, Donald Davidson once observed: "If there is a logical or epistemic barrier between the mind and nature, it not only prevents us from seeing out; it also blocks a view from the outside in" (Davidson 1991: 154). It is a blocked view "from the outside in" that gives rise both to the radical and the restricted skeptical problem of other minds.

Descartes raises a radical skeptical question concerning the world of bodies, but there is no acknowledgment in his work of a problem concerning the mind of another. Nevertheless, when Descartes wants to convince the reader that, contrary to the usual way of thinking, we know mind better than body, he writes: "But then if I look out of a window and see men crossing the square . . . I normally say that I see men themselves . . . Yet do I see more than hats and coats which could conceal automatic machines?" (Descartes 1984 [1641]: 21).

Philosophers have found in this passage the seeds of a radical skeptical problem: 'How can I distinguish between a man/person/being with a mind and an automated machine/ zombie/body without a mind?'

Malebranche's Two Ways of Knowing Mind

Nicolas Malebranche (1674–1675) delineated four distinct ways of knowing, two of which are connected with mind: knowledge of one's own mind is through consciousness or inner sensation; knowledge of another's mind is "by conjecture." The need for conjecture in the case of others follows from the following observations. Firstly, we cannot know another mind in the way we know bodies, since "our soul . . . not being corporeal, cannot be represented to the mind by corporeal images" (Malebranche 1997 [1674–1675]: 62–63). And secondly "we cannot compare our mind with other minds in order to discover clearly some relation between them" (Ibid.: Elucidation 11). Malebranche differentiates between knowledge of another's sensations and knowledge that another knows certain truths (e.g. twice two is four, or it is better to be just than rich). This difference reflects the fact that the body plays a role in the experience of sensations, but not in the knowledge of truths. Where the body plays a role, Malebranche holds that "I am almost always mistaken in judging others by myself" (Ibid.: 239). This is because, if we recognize the difference between a sensation and its cause, then we must also recognize that:

> it can happen that similar motions in the interior fibers of the optic nerve do not produce the same sensation for different people . . . and it might happen that motion that will cause the sensation of blue in one person will cause that of green or grey in another, or even a novel sensation that no one has ever had.
>
> (Ibid.: 63)

Malebranche further considers that, even if we were to think that God *has* arranged things so that the same sensations are conjoined to the same motions of the brain, "there is no reason to suppose a perfect resemblance in the optic nerve of all men" (Ibid.: 66).

Malebranche makes observations (where Descartes does not) concerning knowledge of other minds. Interestingly, he appears *not* to raise the radical skeptical question. Our conjectures appear to presuppose that others do have minds; they concern the knowledge *what* question, raising only a restricted skeptical problem.

Berkeley and Reasoning to the Probability of Another (Finite) Mind

When we read the works of George Berkeley (1975 [1710], 1975 [1713]) we find that he, like Malebranche, emphasizes a difference in the way we know our own and other minds. Unlike Malebranche, however, Berkeley does raise a radical skeptical problem. When considering knowledge of his own mind Berkeley makes the following observation: "I know what I mean by the terms *I* and *myself*; and I know this immediately, or intuitively, though I do not perceive it as I perceive a triangle, a colour, or a sound" ([1713]: 231). When considering knowledge of another (finite) mind, Berkeley believes we can do no better than to employ a form of reasoning. He explains why this is so when he writes:

> A human spirit or person is not perceived by sense, as not being an idea. . . . It is plain, we do not see a man—if by *man* is meant that which lives, moves, perceives and thinks as we do: but only such a certain collection of ideas, as

directs us to think there is a distinct principle of thought and motion like unto ourselves, accompanying and represented by it.

([1710]: 124)

Berkeley further points out that, while our knowledge of our own mind is through intuition and therefore secure, our knowledge of the mind of another is only probable ([1713]: 185).

Malebranche and Berkeley make several interesting observations about mind, among them: (i) there is a notable difference in the way in which we know our own and another mind; and (ii) the way in which we know another mind is very different from the way in which we know body. Berkeley puts this point by saying that we do not *perceive* another mind. This is an idea that has interested philosophers of recent times, with some proposing that we do in fact perceive other minds (see below). On the whole, however, philosophers have tended to agree with Berkeley. The idea that we do not perceive other minds goes along with another: that the behavior of another is the outward trapping of the other's mind. Despite these similarities, Malebranche appears to raise only a restricted skeptical question concerning the mind of others, while Berkeley raises both a restricted and a radical skeptical question. It is important that Berkeley is able to explain how it is that we (successfully) reason to the existence of other minds, for without such reasoning his philosophy would be mired in solipsism.

Reid: First Principles vs. Reason

Malebranche and Berkeley both inherited their philosophical framework from Descartes, although both were concerned to correct what they saw as defects in it. One philosopher to raise questions about the Cartesian framework that would lead him to a rejection of it, is Thomas Reid. Reid was bothered by what he saw as the inevitable outcome of Descartes' philosophy: skepticism with respect to other intelligent beings. This is a skepticism that he finds in Berkeley's philosophy, which he takes to be mired in solipsism. Whether Reid is correct or not depends upon one's assessment of Berkeley's proposals for how it is that we know that another has a mind. Reid, however, does not review Berkeley's arguments. What Reid claims is that *all* methods of reasoning—such as by analogy or conjecture—yield insecure foundations for knowledge. According to Reid, reasoning must be grounded on *first principles*. This commitment to first principles is something that marks Reid out as a philosopher of common sense, and as a profoundly anti-Cartesian philosopher. Among the first principles of contingent truths that Reid believes form the foundation of all reasoning are these:

There is life and intelligence in our fellow men with whom we converse.

Certain features of the countenance, sounds of the voice and gestures of the body, indicate certain thoughts and dispositions of mind.

There is much to be said both for and against the operation of first principles in philosophy. For our purposes, it is sufficient to note how Reid's use of these first principles is designed to provide a secure foundation for our knowledge of other minds.

What is important for Reid is that one's relation to others is built on a secure foundation. Reid does not say that we perceive the minds of others. Rather, he holds that one of the foundations of all our reasoning is that there are other intelligent beings. This is an important and profoundly anti-Cartesian observation. It is not designed as a way of combating skepticism but as eliminating the framework within which skepticism arises. According to Reid the skeptical framework is the Cartesian one, and what should replace it are first principles of contingent truths.

John Stuart Mill and Proof of the Real Externality of Another Mind

Reid's philosophy is the subject of much discussion by the nineteenth-century philosopher Sir William Hamilton, and the writings of Hamilton are the subject of an important work by John Stuart Mill (1872). Mill characterizes Reid's philosophy as one that holds that the existence of the external world and other minds is something we are compelled to believe in by our mental constitution. What we are compelled to believe in is what is captured in Reid's first principles of contingent truths. In the place of this Mill proposes that all truths are known in one of two ways: either directly through the authority of consciousness, or indirectly by inference from truths known directly. Mill's psychological theory (or phenomenalism) is intended to account for our belief in matter and in mind. It is important to note that the development of Mill's theory marks a return to and an acceptance of the Cartesian framework. It is a framework that—despite much talk of its overthrow—still dominates philosophical thinking about mind today.

Mill believes there is an asymmetry between our belief in objects external to ourselves and our belief in intelligent beings other than ourselves: while the former is a construction out of groups of possible sensations, the latter corresponds to the existence of other, quite separate, minds. Indeed, Mill goes so far as to write that, "I do not believe that the real externality to us of anything, except other minds, is capable of proof" (Mill 1872: 238–239). Indeed, Mill's "proof" has come to be taken as the *locus classicus* of one of the more popular forms of reasoning to the existence of other minds, the argument from analogy:

> I conclude that other human beings have feelings like me, because, first, they have bodies like me, which I know, in my own case, to be the antecedent conditions of feelings; and because, secondly, they exhibit the acts and other outward signs, which in my own case I know by experience to be caused by feelings.
>
> (Mill 1872: 243)

While all the material for an argument by analogy is present in Mill's work, Mill claims that he is offering a good inductive argument to the desired conclusion. He writes: "If the evidence stopped here [in a conclusion drawn from analogy], the inference would be but an hypothesis; reaching only to the inferior degree of inductive evidence called Analogy" (Mill 1872: 260). Mill believes the evidence is stronger than that:

> I find that my subsequent consciousness presents those very sensations, of speech heard, of movements and other outward demeanor seen . . . which, being the effects or consequents of actual feelings in my own case, I should expect to follow upon those other hypothetical feelings if they really exist: and thus the hypothesis is verified. It is thus proved inductively that there is a sphere beyond my consciousness.
>
> (Mill 1872: 260)

A similar point was made by A.J. Ayer over half a century later (Ayer 1956).

It is worth pausing to note that Mill's inductive proof yields a conclusion stronger than that yielded by the argument from analogy, yet still falls short of the secure foundations for which Reid was searching. Of course our hypothesis here would be well confirmed, but it is arguable that this still misses the point. Just what point it misses is not easy to explain. A contemporary critic of Mill's, H. F. O'Hanlon, attempted to explain Mill's mistake by pointing out that Mill simply assumes that we can extend the principles of inductive inference beyond our own sphere of consciousness, whereas the existence of another sphere of consciousness is precisely what wants proving. Mill was quick with a rejoinder: "There is nothing in the nature of the inductive principle that confines it within the limits of my own consciousness, when it exceptionally happens that an inference surpassing the limits of my consciousness can conform to inductive conditions" (Mill 1872: 259). Who is correct here is a matter of some consequence.

The Appearance–Reality Distinction

Descartes' Distinction and the Cartesian Question

Descartes constructs his entire *Meditation* from the first-person point of view and aims to question everything beyond this. In particular, his skeptical considerations are founded on a distinction between the world as it appears to a mind and as it is apart from any mind. Let us call this appearance–reality distinction "Descartes' distinction," and the question it gives rise to "the Cartesian question." Both the distinction and the question are the result of what Descartes took to be our capacity to doubt the existence of bodies while remaining steadfastly unable to doubt the existence of mind. Once Descartes' distinction is in place, it is possible to see that it gives rise to further distinctions and questions, this time concerning minds other than one's own. When I contemplate another's mind, the appearance–reality distinction is in its mirror image, so to speak. While it is the other's body that appears to me, it is the reality of the other's mind that is in question. And this question remains even after the existence of bodies has been proved. As Davidson so aptly observed (above), the problem now is that our view is blocked "from the outside in."

If we accept that this appearance–reality distinction gives rise to both a radical and a restricted skeptical problem about other minds, we must also remember that these problems do not attach to *all* minds. My mind is exempt from such doubts. There is also an interesting difference between the appearance of a body and the appearance of a mind: in the case of the external world what appears to the subject is *a body*; in the case of another mind what appears to a subject is also *a body*, while what we take this to be an appearance *of* is another mind.

Reasoning Across the Gap

Thus the gap between my mind and the world of bodies opens up another gap between my mind and all other minds, and these gaps give rise to skeptical questions, both radical and restricted. Philosophers since the time of Descartes have suggested various methods of reasoning to the conclusion that other minds do exist and experience the world roughly along the same lines as I do. As indicated above, Berkeley explicitly acknowledges that the conclusion of any such reasoning can only be probable, while Reid insists we must resist this conclusion. What Reid points to is the fundamental nature and importance of the relation between one's own and other minds. "When a child asks a question of his nurse, this act supposes . . . a conviction that the nurse is an intelligent being, to whom he can communicate his thoughts, and who can communicate her thoughts to him" (1969 [1785]: 72). The importance of this conviction and the security of this relation led Reid to reject the Cartesian framework that requires that we reason to the existence of other minds.

John Stuart Mill returned philosophy to its Cartesian roots, and since his time many philosophers have been content to discuss different methods of reasoning to the existence of other minds. Questions about a more secure foundation tend to be lost after Reid (although I mention an important exception below). The argument from analogy and the argument from induction are two popular responses, both in the history of philosophy and today. Although the argument from analogy has tended to find less favor since the middle of the twentieth century, it has had a rigorous defense in the past few decades from some Australian philosophers (Hyslop and Jackson 1972; Hyslop 1995). More popular has been an argument from best explanation (Pargetter 1984; cf. Putnam 1975; Ayer 1973). In his defense of the argument from analogy we find that Hyslop, in effect, takes the side of Mill against O'Hanlon. Hyslop sees little problem in extending one's inductive argument outside the sphere of one's consciousness, and he believes that we should rest content with the weak inductive argument that is the argument from analogy. Pargetter, on the other hand, insists that we can bypass this—and other—problems with the argument from analogy by moving to an argument from best explanation. Here all that matters is the explanatory power of the conclusion. Pargetter is clear that, on his account, "my reason for believing in the existence of other minds similar to my own is in all important respects the same as the scientific realist's reason for believing in the existence of sub-atomic particles" (Pargetter 1984: 159). Insofar as Pargetter's form of reasoning bypasses O'Hanlon's problem, it is to be preferred to Hyslop's. It does, however, raise a new question: Is it correct to think that my reason for believing in the existence of other minds *is* in all important respects the same as the scientific realist's reason for believing in sub-atomic particles?

It is worth remembering that in all these cases of reasoning, the conclusion that others have minds is only probable. Of course, the conclusion is *highly* probably, or can be considered to be a *well confirmed* hypothesis. But it is not a conclusion that could be said to be 'skeptic proof' in the way that Reid thought it must be.

What Is Mind?

Each of the arguments mentioned above is designed to take us from something we perceive (the body of another) to something we do not perceive (the mind of another). We must, however, be careful about the conclusion of our reasoning here. It is one thing to reason that another mind exists, and yet another to understand the nature of that existence. If we return to Berkeley we find that he is very clear that he does not think it a contingent fact that I do not *perceive* a mind. He does not take it that the mind lies hidden behind or inside the body that we do perceive. He does not believe that, could we but peer around the body, we *would* perceive the mind of another.

> We may infer . . . that . . . it is not more reasonable to think our faculties defective, in that they do not furnish us with an idea of spirit or active

thinking substance, than it would be if we should blame them for not being able to comprehend a *round square*.

(1975 [1710]: 120)

If Berkeley is right—if a mind is not the sort of 'thing' that is capable of being perceived—then what appears in the case of a mind would necessarily be something else. But if we think about this a little more, it can come to seem odd that there should be *any* sort of 'appearance' of such a 'reality.' It may be that in the case of mind there is no appearance–reality distinction.

If Berkeley is right this leaves us with the question, 'How are we to understand the reality or the nature of mind?' It might also give us pause when considering whether reasoning from the body of another to the mind of another—be it by employing an argument from analogy, induction or best explanation—is the correct way to understand our knowledge of another mind. We might wonder whether there is any better way of dealing with a skeptic concerning the mind of another than telling him that it is highly likely that the body I observe moving in various ways is backed by a mind.

Ignoring the Skeptic

The Cartesian tradition accepts that skeptical questions lie at the heart of epistemology and takes it that philosophers must in some way engage with them. Some epistemologists of more recent times have held that we can have knowledge *without* having to engage with the skeptic. These epistemologists have come to be known as knowledge externalists, and their more traditional opponents as knowledge internalists. These externalists do not have a response to skepticism, but insist that epistemology can proceed without one. Thus there has been a succession of externalists who hold that the skeptical possibility is "idle" (Goldman 1976: 775), or irrelevant (Dretske 1970), or that the skeptic's question concerns a possible world too distant to bother us (Nozick 1981). According to these externalists it is possible to know, for example, that another is in pain without knowing that the other is not an automaton.

If one looks at Nozick's counterfactual analysis it is clear why knowledge that, for example, one's daughter is in pain can be achieved while knowledge that she is not an automaton is not forthcoming. According to Nozick's analysis, knowledge is a true belief that tracks the truth, and tracking involves, among other conditions, the following: if a proposition p were not true, subject S would not believe that p. If my daughter is writhing in pain as the result of a boulder falling on her foot, my belief that she is in pain tracks the fact that she is: if she were not in pain she would not be behaving like that, so I wouldn't believe that she was in pain. If, however, my daughter were an automaton she might still behave in this fashion and I might still believe that she was in pain, so this tracking condition would not be fulfilled. Nozick concludes that I do *not* know that my daughter is not an automaton (Nozick 1981: 218). The radical skeptical possibility concerning the mind of others is left in place on this and other knowledge externalist accounts of knowledge.

We could say that these externalists side-step the radical skeptical problem while offering a reply only to a restricted skeptical question. I know that my daughter is in pain because (on one view) I can track her pain. It is not clear that this would have satisfied Reid. While contemporary knowledge externalists put the skeptic to one side and get on with the business of saying how we can have knowledge, Reid attempts to engage with—and reject—the Cartesian framework that he believes leads to the radical problem.

Perception and Other Minds

Quassim Cassam (2007) has recently defended a perceptual model of our knowledge of another mind, which he contrasts with inferential models of the sort considered above. Cassam's defense of the perceptual model takes the form of removing obstacles that stand in the way of our accepting it. What Cassam wants to be able to say is that I *see*, for example, that another *is angry*. The sense in which I see this is that: (i) I see the other; (ii) the other is angry; (iii) the conditions are such that the other wouldn't look the way he looks now unless he was angry; and (iv) believing that the conditions are like this I take the other to be angry. Cassam emphasizes that "I *have* in the way the [other] looks a reason for believing that he is angry" (Cassam 2007: 164), and he notes that there is an important difference between having a reason and concluding as the result of some process of reasoning. Cassam calls this a case of "primary epistemic seeing," and models it on an idea of Dretske's. Dretske introduces the idea in connection with seeing that a piece of metal is hot. He suggests that I can see that the metal is hot (a case of primary epistemic seeing) just so long as I see that it is hot by seeing it glow "in the way characteristic of hot metal" and *not* by seeing how another object—say a temperature gauge—behaves (cf. Dretske 1969). Cassam defends the perceptual model in a way that might be thought not to conflict with the Berkelian observation that we do not perceive another's mind. Cassam points out that, in the case of the metal, we do not actually see its heat (heat can be felt but not seen); nevertheless, I can see that the metal is hot. So I can see that another is angry without seeing his anger.

Although Cassam's work here follows Dretske's, it also departs from it in important ways. Dretske, like Nozick, holds that I can know, for example, that my daughter is in pain, but not that she is not an automaton. Cassam disagrees. He holds that I can know both that another is in pain and that she is not an automaton. If one can see that one's daughter is in pain then she cannot be an automaton. Cassam suggests that one's knowledge that one's daughter is not an automaton "owes its credentials to the fact that [one] can see" that she is in pain (2007: 165). This difference between Cassam and Dretske reflects another. Dretske appears to accept the following relationship between skepticism and knowledge: we must be in a position to rule out the skeptical possibility *in advance and in independence of* our claim to know. As Dretske believes this cannot be done, he proposes instead that epistemology can proceed without answering the skeptic. Cassam does not accept that we must respond to the skeptic *in advance and in independence of* our claim to know. Thus he is able to say that I can see that my daughter is in pain, something that wouldn't be possible if she were an automaton. Like G.E. Moore before him, Cassam holds that our commitment to the external world and the mind of another is stronger than our commitment to any skeptical possibility (Moore 1953).

A Secure Foundation

When Reid rejects the Cartesian framework that he believes leads to radical skepticism, he puts in its place a series of first principles with the aim of setting our relations to others on a more secure foundation. It seems fair to say that philosophers who offer one or another of a form of reasoning from the body of another to the mind of another are adhering to that Cartesian framework. The externalist rejects the Cartesian legacy in epistemology, arguing that the skeptic should not be taken to stand in the way of knowledge, but this is a rejection of only a part of that legacy. It is not as radical a rejection of Descartes' work as it needs to be to achieve the secure foundation that Reid was after. Like the internalist, the externalist still accepts the radical skeptical question; he just thinks we can ignore it. Reid does not just ignore the skeptic, but aims to take away the very structure within which he works. In this way Reid is more radical in his rejection of the Cartesian legacy. Reid is also arguably more radical than Cassam. Cassam claims that his perceptual model can do better than an argument from best explanation because the latter can only lead us to the conclusion that it is highly unlikely that another is not an automaton and "highly unlikely isn't good enough" (2007: 166–167). But Cassam's perceptual model depends crucially on the idea of commitment, and he does not say enough about this idea to convince that his model can do better. Cassam allows for the skeptic's question and believes he can show how knowledge is possible. The security that Reid was after leaves no room for the skeptic. As Reid sees it, our commitment to others runs deep.

From Reid to Wittgenstein

A philosopher who can be taken to react to skepticism in a way not dissimilar to Reid is Ludwig Wittgenstein. Wittgenstein, too, is concerned with the Cartesian framework which gives rise to the skeptic's questions. And, like Reid, Wittgenstein takes our relationship to the world and to others as an important starting point in his philosophy. But in the place of first principles, Wittgenstein carefully examines the nature and development of our use of language to see what we can learn about ourselves in relation to others.

What Wittgenstein struggles to understand is the asymmetry between the first- and third-person uses of our talk about sensations. He also identifies a certain mistake in the way philosophers proceed here: they notice an asymmetry between what I feel in my own case and what I observe (behavior) in the case of the other, and they attempt to account for this difference by assuming that the observed behavior shields the other's experience from us. Philosophers, then, resort to reasoning by analogy, induction or the like in order to obtain knowledge of the other's mind. He writes: "I wished to say that talking about his toothache at all was based upon a supposition, a supposition which by its very essence could not be verified." He quickly continues: "But if you look closer you will see that this is an entire misrepresentation of the use of the word 'toothache'" (Wittgenstein 1968: 281). Much of Wittgenstein's work (including the private language argument) is directed at trying to identify the nature of this misrepresentation and at explaining how better to think about sensations and thoughts in oneself and in others. Many nowadays (see Chihara and Fodor 1966: 390) are inclined to dismiss these thoughts on the grounds that is mired in verificationism (which they believe can be shown to be mistaken). But many others find in Wittgenstein's work, scattered as it is across many published and unpublished volumes, a rich source when thinking about one's own and other minds. Wittgensteinian ideas are also standardly invoked in critiques of the argument from analogy, and other such forms of reasoning (see Bilgrami 1992).

Learning from Wittgenstein

Because of the extent and complexity of Wittgenstein's work I can only gesture at a possible lesson that can be learned from it, which is this: the radical skeptical problem that philosophers have struggled with under the heading 'the problem of other minds' is only a problem if one misunderstands what Wittgenstein calls "the grammar" of our language. In the place of radical skeptical questions here, Wittgenstein urges that we look at the way we use words connected with mind—words such as 'pain,' 'anger,' 'belief,' and the like—and thereby come to understand what our concepts of these 'states,' 'events,' 'conditions,' etc. are. Insofar as there is a problem here, it is conceptual, not epistemological. Wittgenstein writes in one place: "My attitude is an attitude towards a soul; I am not of the *opinion* that he has a soul" (Wittgenstein 1958: 178e). This remark and others in a similar vein seem designed to turn us away from the idea that what we have here is any kind of epistemological relation, that *knowing* that another has a mind is not the right way to think of our fundamental relations to others. Like Reid before him, Wittgenstein appreciates that the security of our relationship to others is not adequately captured in such an epistemology. Wittgenstein hints at another way when he writes that the child acts first and then can be said to know (Wittgenstein 1969: 71e). Perhaps the key to understanding the secure foundation of our relations to others lies in exploring the difference between knowing the world and acting in it with others. Wittgenstein is careful to tease out the radical skeptical question, 'How do I know that another has a mind?', and helps us to see something odd about it. Understood aright, our concepts here are such that they leave no room for this question.

If this is right, then the "problem of other minds" needs to shift away from its association with radical skepticism. Of course this still leaves the restricted question, and we may still speak, for example, of "our knowledge that another is in pain." But we need not fear that this restricted question will precipitate the more radical one. The issue of solipsism should no longer plague philosophy.

References

Avramides, A. (2001) *Other Minds*, London and New York: Routledge.
Ayer, A.J. (1956) *The Problem of Knowledge*, Harmondsworth: Penguin Books Ltd.
Ayer, A.J. (1973) *The Central Questions of Philosophy*, Harmondsworth: Penguin Books Ltd.
Berkeley, G. (1975 [1710]) *A Treatise Concerning the Principles of Knowledge*, in M. Ayers (ed.) *The Philosophical Works*, London: Dent.
Berkeley, G. (1975 [1713]) *Three Dialogues between Hylas and Philonous*, in M. Ayers (ed.) *The Philosophical Works*, London: Dent.
Bilgrami, A. (1992) "Other Minds," in J. Dancy and E. Sosa (eds.) *A Companion to Epistemology*, Oxford: Blackwell.
Blackburn, S. (1994) *The Oxford Dictionary of Philosophy*, Oxford: Oxford University Press.
Burnyeat, M. (1982) "Idealism and Greek Philosophy: What Descartes Saw and Berkeley Missed," in G. Vesey (ed.) *Royal Institute of Philosophy Lectures*, 13: 19–50.
Cassam, Q. (2007) *The Possibility of Knowledge*, Oxford: Oxford University Press.
Chihara, C.S. and Fodor, J.A. (1966) "Operationalism and Ordinary Language: A Critique of Wittgenstein," in G. Pitcher (ed.) *Wittgenstein: The Philosophical Investigations*, London: Macmillan.
Davidson, D. (1991) "Three Varieties of Knowledge," in A.P. Griffiths (ed.) *A.J. Ayer Memorial Essays*, Cambridge: Cambridge University Press.
Descartes, R. (1984 [1641]) *Meditations on First Philosophy* (trans. J. Cottingham, R. Stoothhoff and D. Murdock), in *The Philosophical Works of Descartes*, Vol. I, Cambridge: Cambridge University Press.
Dretske, F. (1969) *Seeing and Knowing*, London: Routledge & Kegan Paul.
Dretske, F. (1970) "Epistemic Operators," *Journal of Philosophy* 67, 1007–1023.

Goldman, A. (1976) "Discrimination and Perceptual Knowledge," *The Journal of Philosophy*, 73: 771–791.
Hyslop, A. (1995) *Other Minds*, Dordrecht/Boston/London: Kluwer Academic Publishers.
Hyslop, A. and Jackson, F. (1972) "The Analogical Inference to Other Minds," *American Philosophical Quarterly*, 9(2): 168–176.
Malebranche, N. (1997 [1674–1675]) *The Search After Truth*, (trans. & ed. T.M. Lennon & P.J. Olsen), Cambridge: Cambridge University Press.
Mill, J.S. (1872) *An Examination of Sir William Hamilton's Philosophy* (4th edition), London: Longman, Green, and Dyer.
Moore, G.E. (1953) *Some Main Problems of Philosophy*, London: Allen & Unwin.
Nozick, R. (1981) *Philosophical Explanations*, Oxford: Clarendon Press.
Pargetter, R. (1984) "The Scientific Inference to Other Minds," *Australasian Journal of Philosophy*, 62(2): 158–163.
Putnam, H. (1975) "Other Minds," in *Mind, Language and Reality*, Philosophical Papers Volume 2, Cambridge: Cambridge University Press.
Reid, T. (1969 [1785]) *Essays on the Intellectual Powers of Man*, introduction by B.A. Brody, Cambridge, MA: MIT Press.
Sextus Empiricus (AD 160–210 [2000]) *Against the Professors* (M) VII. (trans. R.G. Bury), Cambridge: Harvard University Press.
Williams, B. (1981) "The Legacy of Greek Philosophy," in I. Finley (ed.) *The Legacy of Greek Philosophy: A New Appraisal*, Oxford: Oxford University Press.
Wittgenstein, L. (1958) *Philosophical Investigations* (3rd edition) (trans. G.E.M. Anscombe), Oxford: Oxford University Press.
Wittgenstein, L. (1968) "Notes for Lectures on 'Private Experience' and 'Sense Data'," *The Philosophical Review*, 77(3): 275–320.
Wittgenstein, L. (1969) *On Certainty* (ed. G.E.M. Anscombe & G.H. Wright), New York: Harper & Row.

41
SKEPTICISM ABOUT INDUCTIVE KNOWLEDGE
Joe Morrison

Introduction

Hume's argument against inductive knowledge is perhaps one of the most endearing and enduring arguments in philosophy. It is relatively simple and direct, but even after close examination it loses none of its beguiling power. Inductive inference is ampliative—the propositions that an agent knows are used to infer new propositions, and these new propositions go beyond what was already known (see "Inductive Knowledge," Chapter 25 in this volume). Inductive inferences are the means by which agents reason from specific claims to general claims; from claims about past instances to future instances; and from observed states of affairs to unobserved and perhaps unobservable states of affairs. The Humean problem for induction is as follows. Some of our beliefs are formed by inductive inference, and since we want reason to think that those beliefs are justified we should provide some grounds for thinking that inductive inference itself is justified. Induction cannot be defended by a deductive argument; inductive inferences are not deductively valid, since deductive inference is non-ampliative. Any attempt to give a deductive argument for an ampliative conclusion would have to include among its premises a claim to the effect that current knowledge can be extended to new instances. Such a claim involves an inductive inference, and will need further defense. And any attempt to give an inductive justification of induction will be viciously circular. So inductive inference is not justified. The result is that beliefs formed by inductive inference are not formed by a justified method, so they are not justified, and so cannot qualify as knowledge.

This attack on the possibility of inductive knowledge can be used to generate a second skeptical problem, the underdetermination thesis, which illustrates a general relationship between inductive inference and skeptical arguments. An inductive inference attempts to secure a conclusion which goes beyond the content of the premises: we have seen two hundred white swans, so we infer that the two-hundred-and-first swan will be white. Compare this with a slightly different induction, where from the same premises we infer that the two-hundred-and-first swan will be white and majestic. Hume's argument tells us that neither inference is justified. And an inference to the conclusion that the two-hundred-and-first swan will be white and not-majestic is similarly unjustified. If all inductive inferences are unjustified, then one induction is just as good as another: they're all no good at all. Worse than that, these same premises are compatible with a set of conclusions that is logically inconsistent. Since we have no reason for favoring one conclusion over any of the others on the strength of the premises alone, and since the conclusions are mutually exclusive, we shouldn't believe any of them. Any inductive attempt to go beyond our premises is thus faced with a problem of underdetermination, whereby many competing candidate conclusions have equivalent epistemic standings. Samir Okasha has argued that a similar argumentative form can be found in all skeptical arguments (Okasha 2003). Take the familiar 'brain-in-a-vat' scenario: all of your current experiences no more determine that you're an embodied human being reading this text than that you're a disembodied brain in a vat being fed experiences as such. Since you've no more reason to believe that you're an embodied human being than a disembodied brain, you cannot know either. The primary difference between inductive skepticism and this global skepticism is that the conclusions of inductive inferences are underdetermined by whatever the actual premises might happen to be, while global skepticism suggests that knowledge claims are underdetermined by all possible evidence.

So there are at least two projects for responding to skepticism about inductive knowledge. One is to argue against Hume's problem: to try to spell out why and how inductive inferences are justified. Such strategies might involve any of the following: arguing that deductive defenses of induction are possible; that inductive arguments for induction are not viciously circular—after all, deduction seems to be justified deductively; that there are justifications of induction which are neither deductive nor inductive; that induction needs no justification—perhaps by arguing that inductive inference is epistemically basic, or that it is analytic that inductive inferences are justified. The second project is to argue against the underdetermination thesis which claims that for any inductively inferred conclusion there is an epistemically equivalent rival. Such projects will attempt to explain why some inductive inferences are better or worse than others, even if we cannot give a general account of why inductive inferences are justified. This latter project is comparable to the attempt to give accounts of justification which do not attempt to defeat global skepticism. Such accounts might concede that the reasons which support my belief that the bank is open might not be sufficient to defeat evil-demon or brain-in-vat-type hypotheses, but nevertheless those reasons are still sufficient to justify the belief that the bank is open, and do not justify the belief that the bank is shut.

These two projects are independent. A satisfactory resolution to the problem of underdetermination will not secure the conclusion that induction is justified in the global sense: we might be able to explain why one inductive inference is preferable to another, without thereby explaining why any inductive inference is justified at all. Indeed, most philosophers working in confirmation theory are not attempting to defend induction in general; success in the second project will not secure success in the first. Perhaps more importantly, there are specific, non-Humean arguments for the underdetermination thesis that for any inductively inferred conclusion there is an epistemically equivalent rival. This means that even if it could be shown that Hume's problem can be defused, the problem of underdetermination might still persist: success in the first project might not secure success in the second. In what follows, I will focus on attempts to complete the second project. I will introduce a pervasive argument for thinking that the problem of underdetermination is a genuine threat: the argument from holism. The final sections will consider responses to holism and underdetermination problems.

The Method of Hypothesis

We can be aware of the Humean problem but still acknowledge that inductive inference seems to work, and that clarifying what distinguishes good inductive inferences from bad inductive inferences is a productive activity. Such was the project of the logical empiricists. Hans Reichenbach attempted to do it using a frequency interpretation of probability (Reichenbach 1961). In a related vein, Rudolph Carnap developed a probabilistic *logic* of induction (Carnap 1936). Bayesianism also uses the probability calculus to establish norms of inductive reasoning, which can be used to assess and quantify the empirical justification our evidence has on our inductively inferred conclusions. One natural intuition is that the greater the body of known propositions (let's call them the evidence), the greater the amount of inductive support they pass on to the conclusion of an inductive inference, and thus the better supported is the conclusion. But there are other natural intuitions available about the nature of inductive support. Hempel was keen to try to articulate all of these intuitions and thereby give an analysis of inductive support, or confirmation (Hempel 1965). Such an analysis should allow us to identify when one inductive inference is better than another, and when one body of evidence favors one conclusion over another, thereby avoiding problems of underdetermination.

Current knowledge is not the only source of support for an inductively inferred conclusion. Suppose, hypothetically, that the conclusion is true. It seems a plausible intuition that any deductive consequence of that conclusion will count as evidence for the conclusion. Hypothetico-deductivism made this a central tenet of its analysis of inductive support; a crude version of this principle maintains that for α to support β it suffices for α to be deductively derivable from β (for examples, see Braithwaite 1959; Grimes 1990). Working out what propositions would follow from an hypothetical conclusion if it were true, and then attempting to determine the truth of those propositions is thus a method of gathering support for the conclusion. Problems of underdetermination can be tackled insofar as competing conclusions will yield different predictions, and so a notion of selective support can be achieved: the evidence will favor one hypothesis over another just in case it makes more correct predictions than the other.

Karl Popper also employed this hypothetical method, but in a different fashion. Popper claimed to have solved the Humean problem (Popper 1963: 55), but later acknowledged that he had merely avoided it (1992: 56). Rather than deal with the Humean problem of justifying inductive inferences, Popper maintained that no such inferences ever occur. He thought that a proper study of actual scientific method would reveal that apparently inductive inferences, which seem to proceed from known claims and past evidence to new propositions, actually involve a method of conjecture and refutation. Rather than rely solely upon current knowledge in making ampliative inferences, what actually happens is that current knowledge informs a selection of an ampliative hypothesis, and then that hypothesis is tested. First of all the epistemic agent comes up with a new hypothesis which seems to follow, in some sense, from past observations (their current evidence). This hypothesis will go beyond the propositions currently known: it might make a claim with a wider extension than is currently known, or concern future, unobserved or unobservable things. The second step is where the agent attempts to derive some testable propositions from the hypothesis, or conjecture. Finally, she sets about carrying out those tests, by making new observations. So far this doesn't sound too different from hypothetico-deductivism. The principal difference is that instead of deriving predictions which, if true, would support the hypothesis, Popper thinks that we should attempt to derive predictions which, if false, would show the hypothesis to be false. Rather than try to show how we are justified in holding on to these hypotheses because they are supported or confirmed by the evidence, Popper argues that we are justified in holding on to our conclusions on the grounds of their having been tested. "So long as a theory stands up to the severest tests we can design, it is accepted; if it does not, it is rejected" (1963: 54). Our observations will justify our accepting an ampliative hypothesis just in case they provide testimony to the resilience of that hypothesis in the face of attempted falsification.

Popper wanted to preserve the idea that there is a deductive relationship between observations and the ampliative conclusion of a putatively inductive inference; as a result, he repudiated the notion of inductive support or confirmation. Rather than inductively support the conclusion, the evidence is only able to refute it: "Only the falsity of the theory can be inferred from empirical evidence, and this inference is a purely deductive one" (Popper 1963: 55). Willard V. O. Quine openly endorses this picture of the relation:

> Traditional epistemology sought grounds in sensory experience capable of implying our theories about the world, or at least of endowing those theories with some increment of probability. Sir Karl Popper has long stressed, to the contrary, that observation serves only to refute theory and not to support it.
> (Quine 1990: 12)

Where the logical empiricists attempted to formalize and explicate an independent notion of inductive support or confirmation, Quine and Popper think that we should stick with deductive relations between evidence and hypotheses in the form of falsification. However, the two strategies also share some things in common. Both positions involve a method of hypothesis, where predictions are derived from the ampliative conclusion and then tested. Both make pragmatic appeals in favor of accepting those hypotheses. Logical empiricists thought that we are justified in accepting hypotheses on the basis that they work—they make correct predictions; falsificationists think we are justified in accepting hypotheses just so long as they continue to work—only if those hypotheses do not make false predictions. We could summarize both approaches under Quine's slogan that "nothing succeeds like success" (1969: 128), so long as we did not ignore the important philosophical differences. For the logical empiricists, the success of our hypotheses' predictions is counted as support for those hypotheses; while for the falsificationists, the success of our hypotheses (their continued ability to prevail in the face of attempted falsifications) is counted simply as a reason not to reject them. Popper's falsificationism similarly attempts to deal with the underdetermination problems by the method of hypothesis. Two logically inconsistent hypotheses will yield inconsistent predictions—identifying which prediction is wrong will falsify that hypothesis.

Probabilistic theories of confirmation offer a rival account of the nature of prediction and its relation to confirmation and falsification. When logical empiricists started to equate epistemic support with the mathematical apparatus of probability, a formula devised by Thomas Bayes came to be used to calculate and express the quantitative relations between hypotheses and evidence. The probabilistic framework in use centers on the idea that the epistemic status of a proposition can be expressed as a quantitative value. These values, or probabilities, are used to represent our confidence in the truth of the proposition, or the extent to which we would take risks about their truth, where 0 represents no confidence and 1 represents certainty. Using the axioms of the probability calculus we can construct Bayes' formula, which can be used to calculate what *degree* of support one proposition confers upon another. Underdetermination problems for Bayesians will be more nuanced—it's not sufficient for two hypotheses just to predict all the same evidence; they also need to imply the evidence to the same degree, and the hypotheses need to have identical prior probabilities.

Underdetermination and Holism

Both hypothetico-deductivism and falsificationism construe prediction as a deductive relation: a hypothesis h predicts e just in case h entails e. The problem of underdetermination is where evidence can equally support a variety of conflicting hypotheses: the evidence fails to uniquely determine or selectively support a specific hypothesis. If both h_1 and h_2 entail e, then e supports them both to the same extent; or alternatively, e fails to falsify both of them, putting both h_1 and h_2 on a par, epistemically speaking. Assuming that h_1 and h_2 are inconsistent, our epistemic agent cannot be justified in believing h_1 on the grounds of e. As such, demonstrating that for any hypothesis there is a possible predictively equivalent alternative is a direct way to argue for the underdetermination thesis.

(One concern we might have here is as follows: if two hypotheses are entirely predictively equivalent—if they entail all and only the same predictions—then in what sense are they in tension? For example, the verificationists' principle stated that the meaning of a sentence is exhausted by its 'empirical significance'—the collection of observations that it would entail if it were true. For verificationists, two entirely predictively equivalent hypotheses would have precisely the same meaning; they could not be in tension, for any putative disagreement between them results in no difference in predictions, and is therefore meaningless. However, this verificationist principle is no longer recognized as a plausible account of meaning, partly due to the problems below.)

Why think that for any hypothesis there will always be a predictively equivalent alternative hypothesis? The simple example of 'tacking problems' for hypothetico-deductivism will serve to illuminate the general idea. If h entails e, then so does $(h\&f)$, where f is a logically independent proposition. So, by the hypothetico-deductive principle we saw above, e confirms h, and it also confirms $(h\&f)$. But if f is logically independent from h, then so is its negation. So because both $(h\&f)$ and $(h\&\sim f)$ entail e, it follows that e equally supports $(h\&f)$ and $(h\&\sim f)$, which are inconsistent (see Chapter 25: §3).

Perhaps the fact that e follows from h regardless of whether f is true or false is a reason for thinking that f has nothing to do with predicting e, and thus by giving such an independence proof we can say with confidence that e supports h alone in this case. Such a strategy was favored by Popper (1963: 239). But the case for the possibility of predictively equivalent hypotheses can be made more complicated, so that independence proofs aren't obviously available.

The argument relies on a claim most often associated with Quine and Pierre Duhem which says that prediction is holistic. Most hypotheses, taken by themselves, do not tell us what to infer: it is not obvious what evidence statements are entailed by individual hypotheses.

> [I]n order to deduce from this proposition the prediction of a phenomenon and institute the experiment which is to show whether this phenomenon is or is

not produced . . . [the scientist] does not confine himself to making use of the proposition in question; he makes use also of a whole group of theories accepted by him as beyond dispute.

(Duhem 1954: chapter 6, §2)

[An individual theoretical sentence] will not have its separable bundle of observable or testable consequences. A reasonably inclusive body of scientific theory, taken as a whole, will indeed have such consequences . . . as Duhem has emphasized, these observation conditionals are implied only by the theory as a whole.

(Quine 1981: 70–71)

This holistic prediction thesis states that for most hypotheses, individual hypotheses do not entail some e; rather, a conjunction of the hypothesis with some additional claims will entail some e. As it is presented by Duhem above, this prediction thesis appears to be an empirical claim about the practices of working scientists, or at the very least it is an appeal to an intuitively plausible account about what they do. Quine's motivation for the prediction thesis is intimately tied up with his theories concerning 'observation-sentences' and 'observation-categoricals' (Quine 1990: 9–10). Another motivation for the thesis follows from the theory-laden nature of evidence (Morrison 2010). If correct, the prediction thesis suggests that independence proofs are not straightforwardly available—the sum (of hypothesis with additional claims) is predictively greater than its parts. This problem for independence proofs is illustrated by considering predictions that are the consequence of the conjunction of more than one hypothesis, neither of which taken independently yields any predictions.

Similarly, Bayesian accounts of prediction and confirmation will have to modify their models in line with the prediction thesis such that the degree to which some individual h makes e probable is 0, and only non-zero when h is conjoined with some other set of statements. In addition, it might no longer be possible to talk about the prior probability of some h taken individually—the prediction thesis could be taken to suggest that such values don't exist.

The contrapositive of the prediction thesis is the falsification thesis. If, for the most part, the prediction of evidence statements only follows from conjunctions of hypotheses and auxiliary assumptions, then a false prediction entails that the conjunction is false.

> The [scientist] can never subject an isolated hypothesis to experimental test, but only a whole group of hypotheses; when the experiment is in disagreement with his predictions, what he learns is that at least one of the hypotheses constituting this group is unacceptable and ought to be modified; but the experiment does not designate which one should be changed.
>
> (Duhem 1954: chap. 6, §2)

If the conjunction (h&a) predicts e, and we discover that not-e, it follows that (h&a) is falsified, but we are unsure as to how to distribute the blame. What has gone wrong? The hypothesis, or one of the auxiliary assumptions? Such a test does give us some useful epistemological information: it tells us that we're not justified in relying upon the conjunction of that hypothesis with that set of auxiliary assumptions. But we are faced with a type of underdetermination problem in which the evidence underdetermines what has gone wrong. Indeed, we might be unable to identify whether a particular hypothesis has been tested at all. So it seems plausible that two competing hypotheses could be predictively equivalent as a consequence of the company of auxiliary assumptions that they keep, and our evidence won't allow us to reject one and retain the other, since it fails to specify which parts are letting the side down.

Relevance

The issue at stake concerns identifying grounds for specifying why *e* is relevant to H in particular: why *e* supports *h* in particular (rather than a host of things which may be 'tacked on' to *h*), and why not-*e* falsifies *h* in particular. So a solution to the skeptical problem of underdetermination will be to come up with an account of evidential relevance, while negotiating the added complication that is holism.

Popper's response was to invoke independence proofs, but the details do not clearly engage with the spirit of the prediction thesis. He also suggested that in some cases it is a matter of "sheer guesswork which [. . .] ingredients should be held responsible for any falsification" (1963: 239), but that the "temporary successes of our theories [allow us to be] reasonably successful in attributing our refutations to definite portions of the theoretical maze" (p. 243). The guesswork in resolving the underdetermination of falsification is supposed to be informed by background knowledge about which of our hypotheses is working well. It is a matter of some debate whether this notion of "temporary successes" that Popper called 'corroboration' is an epistemic quantity that is distinct from confirmation (see Putnam 1991 for discussion). In a comparable vein, Clark Glymour attempted to provide an account of evidential relevance for theories of confirmation in which background knowledge determines which claims have been confirmed (Glymour 1975, 1980). The method is called 'bootstrapping'—the image is that someone lifts themselves up by pulling on their own bootstraps, and analogously that matters of evidential relevance are determined within a system of hypotheses and background knowledge, and not externally by some general criterion. The net result of bootstrapping is that evidence claims do not confirm hypotheses simpliciter but, rather, that inductive support is relative to particular theories (systems of hypotheses, evidence and background knowledge).

Kenneth Gemes has given accounts of how to axiomatize theories in order to give a theory of content, whereby we can begin to work out the significance of parts of theories. Such a strategy confronts the problem of relevance straight on—it allows us to distinguish which parts of a theory are relevant or irrelevant to the prediction of some evidence claim (Gemes 1993, 1998a, 1998b).

Various methods have been suggested for modifying the Bayesian formula to take on board the insights of holism (Dorling 1979; Earman 1992; Howson and Urbach 1993: §7.h; Strevens 2001; but see also Fitelson 1999; Fitelson and Waterman 2005, 2007; Strevens 2005). But it might be that holism has some commitments that rule out using various Bayesian measures. For example, the Bayesian formula requires that we give a value for the likelihood of the evidence, $P(e,h)$, which is the probability that the evidence will occur assuming that the hypothesis is true, prior to observing it. Likelihood theorists use a confirmation measure that consists of contrasting two such values for two different hypotheses (Royall 1997; Sober 1995). As such, it is important that a value can be given—particularly if we wish to contrast two seemingly predictively equivalent hypotheses to enable further evidence to decide between them. However, at first glance, it seems as though the prediction thesis says that no such value can be given: that it does not make sense to talk about the likelihood of the observation given an individual hypothesis, since individual hypotheses have no observable consequences.

The standard response is to calculate the likelihood as being a value that is expressed relative to our background theory or knowledge: $P(e,h|k)$. Indeed, the whole Bayesian formula can be written with a 'given k' added in at each relevant place—most expressions leave it out simply for expediency. But one issue with doing so that is potentially worrying is that our background theory (k) might include information affecting the value that we might give to $P(e,h)$—information which does not directly concern h, indeed, which we might think is *irrelevant* to the likelihood of e but which will affect it regardless.

This concern should not be considered as fatal to the possibility that Bayesianism and holism be compatible, since it will depend on how we choose to represent the claim that some irrelevant part of k affects $P(e,h)$, on how we think that prior probabilities are fixed, and which measure of confirmation we use. It might be that holism *constrains* our story about priors (Christensen 1992: 556), or our choice of measure.

What each of these responses has in common is the attempt to generate some sort of generalizable schema by which the relevance of some evidence can be attached directly to a particular hypothesis, thereby attempting to cripple the first steps of an argument for underdetermination. John Norton has argued that there are no universal rules of induction (Norton 2003, 2005). Rather, he argues that particular facts, local to the domain in which the inductive inference is being made, help to determine the nature of the epistemic support.

> We can be quite sure of a result in science as long as we look at the particulars of the result and the evidence that supports it, but we often end up struggling to explain by means of standard inductive inference schemas how the evidence can yield that strength of support.
>
> (Norton 2003: 669)

It will be interesting to see how further examination of his 'material theory of induction' manages to explain away apparent problems of underdetermination, although it seems a likely supposition that such problems will be described as a consequence of the mistaken attempt to give universal or generalized accounts of inductive inference. In addition, Norton argues that his material theory of induction is not exposed to Hume's problem concerning the justification of inductive inferences, so is seemingly able to take on both of the skeptical challenges presented in the introduction.

References

Braithwaite, R. B. (1959) *Scientific Explanation*, Cambridge: Cambridge University Press.
Carnap, R. (1936) "Testability and Meaning," *Philosophy of Science*, 3(4): 419–471.
Christensen, D. (1992) "Confirmational Holism and Bayesian Epistemology," *Philosophy of Science*, 59: 540–557.
Dorling, J. (1979) "Bayesian Personalism, the Methodology of Scientific Research Programmes, and Duhem's Problem," *Studies in History and Philosophy of Science*, 10: 177–187.
Duhem, P. (1954) *The Aim and Structure of Physical Theory*, Princeton: Princeton University Press.
Earman, J. (1992) *Bayes or Bust*, Cambridge, MA: The MIT Press.
Fitelson, B. (1999) "The Plurality of Bayesian Measures of Confirmation and the Problem of Measure Sensitivity," *Philosophy of Science*, 66: 362–378.

Fitelson, B. and Waterman, A. (2005) "Bayesian Confirmation and Auxiliary Hypotheses Revisited: A Reply to Strevens," *British Journal for the Philosophy of Science*, 56: 293–302.

—— and Waterman, A. (2007) "Comparative Bayesian Confirmation and the Quine-Duhem Problem: A Rejoinder to Strevens," *British Journal for the Philosophy of Science*, 58(2): 333–338.

Gemes, K. (1993) "Hypothetico-Deductivism, Content & the Natural Axiomatization of Theories," *Philosophy of Science*, 60: 477–487.

—— (1998a) "Hypothetico-Deductivism: The Current State of Play; The Criterion of Empirical Significance: Endgame," *Erkenntnis*, 49(1): 1–20.

—— (1998b) "Logical Content and Empirical Significance," in P. Weingartner, G. Schurz and G. Dorn (eds.), *The Role of Pragmatics in Contemporary Philosophy: Proceedings of the 20th International Wittgenstein Symposium*, Vienna: Hölder-Pichler-Tempsky.

Glymour, C. (1975) "Relevant Evidence," *Journal of Philosophy*, 72(14): 403–426.

—— (1980) *Theory and Evidence*, Princeton, NJ: Princeton University Press.

Grimes, T. R. (1990) "Truth, Content, and the Hypothetico-Deductive Method," *Philosophy of Science*, 57: 514–522.

Hempel, C. (1965) *Aspects of Scientific Explanation*, New York: Free Press.

Howson, C. and Urbach, P. (1993) *Scientific Reasoning: The Bayesian Approach* (2nd ed.), Chicago: Open Court.

Morrison, J. (2010) "Just How Controversial Is Evidential Holism?" *Synthese*, 173: 335–352.

Norton, J. D. (2003) "A Material Theory of Induction," *Philosophy of Science*, 70: 647–670.

—— (2005) "A Little Survey of Induction," in P. Achinstein (ed.), *Scientific Evidence: Philosophical Theories and Applications*, Baltimore, MD: Johns Hopkins University Press.

Okasha, S. (2003) "Scepticism and its Sources," *Philosophy and Phenomenological Research*, 67(3): 610–623.

Popper, K. (1963) *Conjectures and Refutations—The Growth of Scientific Knowledge*, London: Routledge & Kegan Paul.

Putnam, H. (1991) "The 'Corroboration' of Theories," in R. Boyd, P. Gasper and J. D. Trout (eds.), *The Philosophy of Science*, Cambridge, MA: MIT Press.

Quine, W. V. (1969) "Natural Kinds," in Quine (ed.), *Ontological Relativity and Other Essays*, New York: Columbia Press.

—— (1981) "Five Milestones of Empiricism," in Quine (ed.), *Theories and Things*, Cambridge, MA: Harvard University Press.

—— (1990) *Pursuit of Truth*, Cambridge, MA: MIT Press.

Reichenbach, H. (1961) *Experience and Prediction*, Chicago: University of Chicago Press.

Royall, R. (1997) *Statistical Evidence: A Likelihood Paradigm*, London: Chapman and Hall.

Sober, E. (1995) "Contrastive Empiricism," in Sober (ed.), *From a Biological Point of View*, New York: Cambridge University Press.

Strevens, M. (2001) "The Bayesian Treatment of Auxiliary Hypotheses," *British Journal for the Philosophy of Science*, 52: 515–537.

—— (2005) "The Bayesian Treatment of Auxiliary Hypotheses: A Reply to Fitelson and Waterman," *British Journal for the Philosophy of Science*, 56: 913–918.

42
RULE-FOLLOWING SKEPTICISM
Alexander Miller

1. Rules, Rule-Following and Meaning

Suppose that you intend to follow the rule "Add 4" in continuing the arithmetical series: 0, 4, 8, ... Intuitively, you can continue the series in ways that *accord* or *fail to accord* with the dictates of the rule. For example, the continuation 16, 20, 24, . . . would accord with the rule, while 17, 20, 23, . . . would fail to accord with the rule. In other words, the first continuation would be *correct* according to the rule, while the second continuation would be *incorrect* according to the rule. In this way we can think of the rule as providing a *normative standard*, according to which particular continuations of the series count as correct or incorrect. The notion of rule-following is important in the philosophy of language because intending to follow a rule such as "Add 4" is analogous to meaning something by a linguistic expression. The meaning of a linguistic expression provides a normative standard according to which particular uses of that expression count as correct (or incorrect), as according with (or failing to accord with) that meaning. For example, given that as a matter of mathematical fact the result of adding the numbers 68 and 57 is 125, and given the normal meanings of "68," "57," "+" etc., the answer "125" to the query "What is 68 + 57?" will be correct, while the answer "5" will be incorrect.

To return to our first example, suppose that Smith has continued the series 0, 4, 8 . . . up to 992, 996, 1000. Is there a fact of the matter concerning which (if any) rule Smith has been following in doing so? It is certainly *possible* that Smith has chosen those numbers entirely by accident so that there simply is no rule that he's been following, but that would be unusual, and ordinarily we'd be inclined to say that there is a fact of the matter: in all likelihood, Smith has been following the rule "Add 4" (and not, say, the rule "Add 4 up to 1000 and then add 8 thereafter," or not following any rule at all but simply writing down numerals arbitrarily).

The discussions of rule-following in Ludwig Wittgenstein's *Philosophical Investigations* (Wittgenstein 1953) and *Remarks on the Foundations of Mathematics* (Wittgenstein 1974) have inspired a number of leading philosophers—principally Saul Kripke and Crispin Wright—to consider arguments that challenge the idea that there can be a fact of the matter as to which if any rule we are following in writing out a series like the one above, or a fact of the matter as to what a speaker means by linguistic expressions (Kripke 1982; Wright 1980: chapters 2 and 12). Kripke and Wright initially developed their discussions of rule-following independently, and a full discussion of rule-following skepticism would have to consider both. Here we'll concentrate on the discussion in (Kripke 1982). (Note that Wright's more recent discussions of rule-following, collected in Wright (2001), focus more on whether there can be *objective* facts about rule-following and meaning.)

Kripke's discussion of rule-following skepticism "should be thought of as expounding neither 'Wittgenstein's' argument nor 'Kripke's': rather Wittgenstein's argument as it struck Kripke, as it presented a problem for him" (Kripke 1982: 5). In what follows "Kripke's Wittgenstein" (or "KW" for short) refers to the purveyor of "Wittgenstein's argument as it struck Kripke." According to KW, the idea that there can be a fact of the matter as to what rule Smith has been following is an illusion, and the idea that there can be a fact of the matter as to what meaning a speaker associates with, for example, the "+" sign is also illusory: there can be no fact of the matter as to what Smith means by "+," and indeed no fact of the matter as to whether the "+" sign as used by Smith means anything all.

2. Ontological and Epistemological Skepticism

An *epistemological skeptic* about a region of thought attempts to undermine the knowledge-claims that we typically make within it. For example, an epistemological skeptic about the external world might argue that I am not entitled to claim that I know that at 9.42 a.m. on September 8, 2008 I am wide awake and sitting in my room in Birmingham (perhaps, as with the skeptic who figures in Descartes' *Meditations*, because for all I know I might be having an especially vivid and unusually coherent dream). The epistemological skeptic is prepared to concede that there is a fact of the matter as to whether I'm currently awake or having an especially vivid and unusually coherent dream; he questions only whether I'm entitled to say that I know which of the two possibilities actually obtains. Rule-following skepticism, as considered here, is first and foremost a form of *ontological skepticism*. KW argues not just that we don't *know* whether we mean, for example, addition by "+" or intend to follow the rule "Add 4" but, more strongly, that in these cases there simply can *be* no fact of the matter for us *to* know: there can be no fact of the matter as to which rule we intend to follow in tracing out the series or as to what the "+" sign means. So KW is first and foremost an *ontological skeptic* who denies that there can be facts about rule-following and meaning (although as we'll presently see, KW's argument for ontological skepticism goes via an epistemological route).

3. The Skeptical Argument

Suppose that the largest number Smith has reached previously in (apparently) tracing out an arithmetical series has been 996 and that the largest number he has encountered in prior attempts to answer arithmetical queries has been 57 (these assumptions import no loss of generality into the argument to follow: since Smith is a finite creature, we can always find numbers to play the roles of 996 and 57). If there could be a fact about the rule Smith intends to follow, or a fact about what he means by the "+" sign, there would be a fact about how he ought to expand the arithmetical series (in order to accord with the relevant rule), and a fact about how he ought to answer the query "68 + 57 = ?" (in order to accord with the relevant meaning and—given the mathematical facts—his intention to speak the truth).

KW argues that there can be no fact about how Smith ought to expand the number series, and no fact about how he ought to answer the query "68 + 57 = ?" Perhaps—KW suggests—Smith intends to follow the rule "Gradd 4," where gradding 4 is the same as adding 4 to numbers smaller than 1000 but the same as adding 8 to numbers greater than or equal to 1000. If Smith is a gradder rather than an adder he ought to continue the series 992, 996, 1000, 1008, 1016, . . . and not as one might expect 996, 1000, 1004, 1008, 1012 . . . and so on. Likewise, KW suggests that perhaps Smith doesn't mean addition by "+" but rather *quaddition*, where *quadding* two numbers is a matter of adding them if they are both less than 57, but giving the answer "5" if either of them is greater than or equal to 57. Since 68 quus 57 is 5, if Smith meant quaddition by "+," he ought to answer "5" to the query "68 + 57 =?," and not (as we might think), "125."

As we noted above, KW's argument for ontological rule-following skepticism goes via an epistemological route. KW allows us *unlimited epistemic access* to two types of fact about Smith—facts about his previous behavior and behavioral dispositions, and facts about his mental history and mental states—and argues that even given omniscient and unlimited access to these two types of fact we cannot find any fact that might constitute Smith's intending to gradd rather than add in expanding the series or his meaning addition rather than quaddition by "+." Given the (plausible) assumption that facts about rule-following and meaning would have to be found in these areas if they are to be found anywhere, it follows that if unlimited epistemic access to *them* fails to yield a fact that might constitute Smith's intending to follow "Add 4" rather than "Gradd 4," or a fact that might constitute his meaning addition rather than quaddition, there simply *are* no such facts to be found.

Facts about how Smith has behaved in the past aren't capable of making it the case that he means addition by "+" or following the rule "Add 4" in extending the series, since everything that he has done previously is consistent with his meaning quaddition by "+" or intending to follow the "Gradd 4" rule: ex hypothesi, he had never previously dealt with cases where the numbers in play were large enough for "Add 4" and "Gradd 4," or meaning addition and quaddition, to require different extensions of the series or different answers to arithmetical queries (Kripke 1982: 7–15). KW next considers facts about how Smith is *disposed* to extend the series, or answer arithmetical queries, and finds these unsuitable to constitute facts about rule-following and meaning. For one thing, Smith's dispositions (like his past actual behavior with the "+" sign) are finite, so facts about his dispositions will be unable to distinguish between his meaning addition and his meaning, for example, *skaddition*, where the result of skadding two numbers x and y is the same as adding them, except for cases where the numbers involved are so large that Smith will die before he is able to respond to the arithmetical query, in which case, the result is 5: KW argues that Smith's actual dispositions are consistent both with his meaning addition by "+" and with his meaning skaddition by "+." Furthermore, even supposing it was true that *if* Smith had reached 1000, he *would* have continued 1004, 1008, and so on, or true that *if* he'd been asked "68 + 57 =?" he *would* have replied with "125" rather than "5," in neither case could *these* facts be regarded as constituting his intending to follow the rule "Gradd 4," or meaning addition by "+." Facts about the rule he intended to follow, or what he meant by "+," are *normative* facts; facts concerning how he *ought* to expand the series of numbers or reply to arithmetical queries. But the facts about Smith's behavioral dispositions tell us at most what he *would* do in certain circumstances, as opposed to telling us what he *ought* to do in those circumstances (Kripke 1982: 22–38). In a passage that has been widely quoted, Kripke writes:

> Suppose I do mean addition by "+." What is the relation of this supposition to the question how I will respond to the problem "68+57"? The dispositionalist gives a *descriptive* account of this relation: if "+" meant addition, then I will answer "125." But this is not the proper account of the relation, which is *normative*, not descriptive. The point is *not* that, if I meant addition by "+", I *will* answer "125", but rather that, if I intend to accord with my past meaning of "+", I *should* answer "125." Computational error, finiteness of my capacity, and other disturbing factors may lead me not to be *disposed* to respond as I *should*, but if so, I have not acted in accordance with my intentions. The relation of meaning and intention to future action is *normative*, not *descriptive*.
>
> (1982: 37)

KW then argues that none of the following kinds of fact can be what constitutes meaning addition by "+," because they fail to pin down a determinate meaning, or fail to capture meaning's normative character (similar arguments apply in the case of following a rule governing the expansion of an arithmetical series): the alleged fact that Smith's use of "+" is governed by the *counting* rule or by his grasp of *general thoughts* or *instructions* (Kripke 1982: 15–17); the fact that "+" as used by Smith figures in various arithmetical laws that are definitive of addition (1982: 16–17); the totality of facts about Smith's past mental history, construed in terms of *occurrent* mental states (1982: 17–22; see also 43–51); the fact that Smith embodies "a kind of machine, whose potential actions embody the [addition] function" (1982: 32–35); the fact that the hypothesis that Smith meant addition by "+" is the *simplest* of the hypotheses consistent with how he behaves (1982: 37–39); the alleged fact that (when Smith uses "+") he has "an irreducible experience, with its own special *quale*, known directly . . . by introspection" (1982: 43–51); the alleged fact that Smith is in "a primitive state, not to be assimilated to sensations or headaches or any 'qualitative' states, nor to be assimilated to dispositions, but a state of a unique kind of its own" (1982: 51–53); the alleged fact that Smith grasps an objective and abstract entity—the sense of "+"—and that this abstract entity singles out the addition function as the referent of "+" as used by Smith (1982: 53–54).

There are thus no facts about rule-following and meaning, according to KW's argument, so "it seems that the entire idea of meaning [and rule-following] vanishes into thin air" (1982: 22).

4. The Skeptical Solution

There are thus no facts in virtue of which claims such as "Smith means addition by '+'" or "Smith intends to follow the rule 'Add 4'" are true or false: there is simply no fact of the matter either way. Kripke describes this result as a "skeptical paradox" (1982: 68), and suggests that it threatens us with the conclusion that "all language is meaningless" (1982: 71), a conclusion that he describes as "incredible and self-defeating" (ibid.) and "insane and intolerable" (1982: 60). He then suggests that KW offers us a radical way of avoiding the insane and intolerable conclusion.

Using Hume's discussion of judgments about causation as his model (Hume 1748), Kripke distinguishes between two different sorts of response to a skeptical philosophical problem:

> [A] proposed solution to a skeptical philosophical problem [is] a *straight* solution if it shows that on closer examination the skepticism proves to be

unwarranted. A skeptical solution of a skeptical problem begins on the contrary by conceding that the skeptic's negative assertions are unanswerable.

(1982: 66)

Whereas a straight solution would attempt to find a fact in virtue of which, for example, "Smith means addition by '+'" might be true—perhaps by arguing that contra KW dispositional facts can both pin down determinate meanings and capture the normativity of meaning—a skeptical solution concedes up front that there can be no such facts: "Wittgenstein holds, with the skeptic, that there is no fact as to whether I mean plus or quus" (1982: 71).

The main idea of the Skeptical Solution is that the "insane and intolerable" paradox can be avoided by arguing that ascriptions of meaning and rule-following have a *non fact-stating* function. An analogy with an emotivist view of ethical judgment might help explain the idea (McGinn 1984: 65). Suppose that for one reason or another you have reached the conclusion that there are no such things as moral facts, so no facts in virtue of which claims such as "Stealing is wrong" can be true or false. Then, you might worry that moral thought and talk is liable to be convicted of a massive and systematic error: since moral claims purport to describe moral facts, and there are no such facts, the conclusion that all (positive, atomic) moral judgments are false appears to follow, threatening us with a form of moral nihilism according to which the notions of right and wrong "vanish into thin air." An emotivist view of ethical judgment attempts to avoid the spiral into moral nihilism by denying that the *function* of ethical claims is to state facts: according to the emotivist, moral claims do not purport to describe moral facts, since they have a non fact-stating function, the expression of emotion. A. J. Ayer proposed a famous example of such a view:

> If I say to someone, "You acted wrongly in stealing that money", I am not stating anything more than if I had simply said, "You stole that money." In adding that this action is wrong, I am not making any further statement about it. I am simply evincing my moral disapproval about it. It is as if I had said, "You stole that money", in a peculiar tone of horror, or written with the addition of some special exclamation marks. The tone, or the exclamation marks, adds nothing to the literal meaning of the sentence. It merely serves to show that the expression of it is attended by certain feelings in the speaker. . . . If I now generalise my previous statement and say, "Stealing money is wrong", I produce a sentence which has no factual meaning—that is, expresses no proposition that can be either true or false.
>
> (Ayer 1946: 107)

The Skeptical Solution proposed by KW suggests that judgments about rule-following and ascriptions of meaning can be viewed as possessing a non fact-stating role. Although it would be implausible to suggest that "Smith means addition by '+'" has the function of expressing an emotion or a feeling, KW's idea seems to be that it can be viewed as expressing our confidence that Smith's use of "+" will agree with that of our speech-community, or perhaps as marking our acceptance of Smith as a member of that community (Kripke 1982: 92). It follows—according to KW—that our practices of ascribing rule-following and meaning avoid the spiral into nihilism threatened by the skeptical paradox. Kripke argues further that in spelling out the detail of the skeptical solution KW reaches the view that the notions of rule-following and meaning only make sense relative to a *community* of rule-followers or speakers and that consequently "solitary" language and rule-following is impossible (1982: 96). (Note that the interpretation of KW as advocating a form of non-factualism is challenged in Wilson 1994. For a reply to Wilson, see Miller 2009.)

5. How Plausible is the Skeptical Solution?

The ascription of a non fact-stating function to a type of statement still presupposes that there is a distinction between correct and incorrect uses of statements of that type. For example, suppose that statements of the form "X is bad" have the function of expressing moral disapproval of X, while statements of the form "X is yummy" have the function of expressing a desire to eat X. Suppose that I intend to express moral disapproval of George Bush, and I utter, "George Bush is yummy." Then we can say that this use of the sentence is incorrect, unlike "George Bush is bad," which, modulo my intention, would have been correct. In other words, a serious non-factualist account of the semantic function of a type of statement requires a distinction between correct and incorrect uses of statements of that type, on pain of collapsing into a form of nihilism about the type of statement in question (according to which utterances of statements of that type would be *mere noise* or mere "sounding off," and hence not assessable in terms of correctness and incorrectness).

This suggests that whatever may be the case with non-factualism in other areas, such as ethics, a non-factualist response to Kripke's skeptical paradox about meaning will not be sufficient to avoid the "insane and intolerable" conclusion that all language is meaningless. *This is because the skeptical argument rehearsed in §3 applies to expressions with non-descriptive semantic functions as well as statements with descriptive semantic functions.* And this is so because even in the case of statements with non-descriptive semantic functions, there are requirements in the light of which uses of those statements can be assessed as either correct or incorrect.

To put it another way, the skeptical argument targets the notion of a rule per se, not just the notion of a rule governing the use of expressions with descriptive semantic functions: even non fact-stating language is rule-governed, and hence susceptible to the argument of the rule-following skeptic.

We can illustrate how the rule-following skeptic's argument can be extended even to non-factualist language as follows. Suppose for the sake of argument that we hold an emotivist account of judgments about goodness according to which the semantic function of "X is good" is to express moral approval of X. Suppose at time t I intend to express moral approval of Fidel. Then, it seems, I ought to utter "Fidel is good." However, according to the rule-following skeptic, I should not utter "Fidel is good" because the rule governing "good" is not

R1: Utter "X is good" if and only if you intend to express moral approval of X

but, rather,

R2: Utter "X is good" if and only if (a) it is time $t^* < t$ and you intend to express moral approval of X or (b) it is time $t^{**} \geq t$ and you intend to express moral disapproval of X.

If R1 is the rule governing my use of "good" then my utterance of "Fidel is good" at time t is correct, while if R2 is the condition governing my use of "good" then my utterance of "Fidel is good" at time t is incorrect (since I do not at that time intend to express moral disapproval of Fidel). Putting it fancifully, one might say: according to R1, "good" expresses moral approval, whereas according to R2, "good" expresses moral *schmapproval* . . . .

Now, just as earlier the skeptic allowed me omniscient access to facts about my behavioral dispositions, mental life and so on and challenged me to find a fact in virtue of which "+" as I use it means addition rather than quaddition, the skeptic now challenges me to justify the claim that "good" as I use it is governed by rule R1 rather than rule R2. As before, the skeptic's claim is that we can find no such fact. (Note that for the emotivist, "correctness" as applied to uses of "Fidel is good" is not to be identified with truth. So in setting up the skeptic's argument as above we are not guilty of conflating emotivism with a form of cognitivist subjectivism, according to which facts about our intentions are written into a truth-condition for "Fidel is good.")

The considerations above suggest that any form of non-factualism that is more sophisticated than, for example, a very crude form of emotivism that views moral judgments as mere "sounding off," presupposes determinate facts about the semantic functions of linguistic expressions, or the rules governing their correct use, irrespective of whether those functions are conceived to be descriptive or non-descriptive or whether the rules govern description or some non-descriptive linguistic practice. A generalized version of KW's argument establishes that there are no such facts. So the strategy of the Skeptical Solution—conceding that there are no facts about meaning but attempting to prevent this from spiraling into a form of nihilism about meaning via the adoption of non-factualism about ascriptions of meaning—is ultimately self-defeating. Any form of non-factualist account of a region of discourse presupposes that there are normative standards governing the correct and incorrect use of expressions belonging to it, so non-factualism about meaning—which denies that there are any such normative standards—is ultimately self-contradictory.

(It is perhaps worth pausing briefly to note in more detail how the skeptical argument generalizes beyond the descriptive cases. In the case of a descriptive expression such as "+," whatever fact that is proposed as making it the case that "+" means the addition function must be inconsistent with the hypothesis that "+" means some other function, such as quaddition. In the generalized version of the argument, which applies to both descriptive and non-descriptive language, this becomes: whatever fact that is proposed as making it the case that rule R_a is the rule governing Smith's use of expression E must be inconsistent with the hypothesis that the rule governing his use of E is R_b, where R_a and R_b are such that for some possible use Δ of E, Δ is correct according to R_a but incorrect according to R_b.)

We can reiterate the point by considering what would happen if KW's Skeptical Solution were construed as characterizing ascriptions of meaning as, for example, disguised orders or commands, i.e. if we attempt to view utterances of ascriptions of meaning as performing speech-acts such as ordering or commanding.

To see how, suppose I intend to get Jones to open the window at time t. So I utter "Open the window!" Intuitively, this utterance is correct, modulo my intention to get Jones to open the window. But the skeptic can argue that it is incorrect, since actually "window," as I use it, means windows before time t but doors at time t and thereafter. (In fact, "window" actually means *qwindow* . . . .) Thus, despite the fact that "Open the window!" is an imperative rather than a description, it presupposes facts about the meanings of its constituent expressions. So, any form of non-factualism about a kind of statement presupposes facts about the meanings of the various expressions that figure in those statements. So, the strategy of the Skeptical Solution—conceding that there are no such facts but attempting to stem the paradoxical consequences of this via a non-factualist account of ascriptions of meaning—is again seen to be ultimately self-defeating.

Anandi Hattiangadi develops an argument (2007) which is superficially similar to that just rehearsed, so it is perhaps worthwhile to point out that Hattiangadi's argument, unlike the argument above, actually misconstrues the nature of the Skeptical Solution. Hattiangadi writes:

> The skeptic might say that meaning ascriptions are neither true nor false because they are only masquerading as judgements when they are really something else. The judgements that Jones means *addition* by "plus" and that Jones's uses agree with our own are both expressions of approval. When we see Jones adding, if he does so in a way that we like, we might say "fantastic!", "wonderful!", "well done!", or we might say "Jones means *addition* by 'plus'." The latter takes the form of a declarative sentence, but it is just another way of expressing our approval of what Jones does. One expression of approval (a.k.a. the "judgement" that Jones's uses of "plus" agree with our own) could then be said to legitimate another expression of approval (a.k.a. the "assertion" that Jones means *addition* by "plus").
>
> Unfortunately, this too presupposes meaning. The skeptical argument is particularly lethal; its conclusion is not just that sentences and beliefs have no truth conditions, but more importantly, that words and concepts have no correctness conditions. Thus it is not just meaning and belief ascriptions that are bereft of content, but any word or sentence whatsoever—including sentences that putatively express approval or disapproval. If the sentence, "Jones's uses of 'plus' agree with mine" is to express approval, it must be meaningful. If "Jones" does not refer to Jones, then it cannot be used to express approval of what *Jones* does, as opposed to Smith or Baker. If the phrase "uses of 'plus'" has no meaning, it cannot be used to express approval of Jones's *uses of "plus"*, as opposed to her gestures or her taste in music. Once again, we need to suppose that some words have meanings in order to legitimate meaning ascriptions. Yet, meaning non-factualism makes such appeal to meanings illicit.
>
> (Hattiangadi 2007: 89–90)

Hattiangadi here appears to attribute to KW the "insane and intolerable" view that all language is meaningless, when in fact KW's non-factualism is, in intention at least, supposed to provide a way of avoiding that "incredible and self-defeating" conclusion. In other words, Hattiangadi assumes that KW's Skeptical Solution *explicitly embraces* a view that it is intended to avoid. The Skeptical Solution does not *concede* that all language is meaningless: KW after all castigates that claim as "insane and intolerable" and "incredible and self-defeating" and proposes the Skeptical Solution as affording us a way of avoiding it.

In contrast, the point of our argument is not that the words used in non-descriptive sentences need to be meaningful in order for the sentences to carry out the non-descriptive function we are assuming them to have (although clearly they do) but, rather, that even if KW, in propounding the Skeptical Solution, is explicitly committed to avoiding an insane and intolerable form of meaning nihilism, a *generalized* version of the skeptical argument as applied to descriptive expressions can be re-employed to show that even non-descriptive sentences have no determinate semantic function and are governed by no determinate rule. The upshot of which is that KW is forced, by the generalized version of the argument he accepts as directed against descriptive expressions, to embrace the "insane and intolerable" form of nihilism that he intends his Skeptical Solution to avoid.

The upshot of these considerations is thus that the "insane and intolerable" meaning nihilism threatened by the skeptical argument cannot be avoided by embracing a skeptical solution or a form of non-factualism about ascriptions of meaning. In Crispin Wright's words:

> The Skeptical Solution seems to me, therefore, to be a failure. More: to sustain the Skeptical Argument is to uncage a tiger whose depredations there is then no hope of containing.
>
> (Wright 1984: 106)

If meaning nihilism is to be avoided, a straight solution—an account of the facts that render ascriptions of meaning true or false—would thus appear to be mandatory.

Acknowledgments

For comments and discussion, I am grateful to Paul Broadbent, Wilson Cooper, Kirk Surgener, Daniel Whiting, Crispin Wright, and seminar audiences at the Universities of Turku, Aberdeen and Szczecin.

References

Ayer, A. J. (1946) *Language, Truth and Logic*, 2nd Edition, London: Gollanz.
Hattiangadi, A. (2007) *Oughts and Thoughts: Skepticism and the Normativity of Content*, Oxford: Oxford University Press.
Hume, D. (1748) *An Enquiry Concerning Human Understanding*, eds. L. A. Selby-Bigge and P. H. Nidditch, Oxford: Clarendon Press 1975.
Kripke, S. (1982) *Wittgenstein on Rules and Private Language*, Oxford: Blackwell.
McGinn, C. (1984) *Wittgenstein on Meaning*, Oxford: Blackwell.
Miller, A. (2009) "Kripke's Wittgenstein, Factualism and Meaning," in D. Whiting (ed.) (2010) *The Later Wittgenstein on Language*, Basingstoke: Palgrave, pp. 167–190.
Wilson, G. (1994) "Kripke on Wittgenstein on Normativity," reprinted in Miller and Wright (eds.) *Rule-Following and Meaning*, Chesham: Acumen.
Wittgenstein, L. (1953) *Philosophical Investigations*, Oxford: Blackwell.
Wittgenstein, L. (1974) *Remarks on the Foundations of Mathematics*, Oxford: Blackwell.
Wright, C. (1980) *Wittgenstein on the Foundations of Mathematics*, London: Duckworth.
Wright, C. (1984) "Kripke's Account of the Argument against Private Language," reprinted in his *Rails to Infinity* (2001).
Wright, C. (2001) *Rails to Infinity*, Cambridge, MA: Harvard University Press.

Further Reading

Miller, A. and Wright, C. (eds.) (2002) *Rule-Following and Meaning*, Chesham: Acumen. (A collection of some of the most important reactions to KW's arguments, including contributions by Blackburn, Boghossian, McDowell, McGinn, Pettit and Wright.)

Miller, A. (2007) *Philosophy of Language* (revised and expanded 2nd edition), London: Routledge. (Chapters 5 and 6 give an overview of the literature inspired by Kripke's discussion of rule-following skepticism. Chapter 4 gives an overview of W. V. O. Quine's approach to skepticism about meaning.)

43
MORAL SKEPTICISM
Geoffrey Sayre-McCord

Introduction

All the standard arguments for global skepticism apply mutatis mutandis to moral skepticism. Whatever reason there is to doubt we know anything, is reason to doubt that we have moral knowledge. Yet our moral views invite skepticism even if global skepticism is false. One doesn't need to be a skeptic about everything to have serious doubts about moral knowledge.

The grounds of moral skepticism are legion. They are found in the evidently irreconcilable moral disagreements that are a familiar fact of life. They are found in the difficulty people often have in articulating, let alone explaining in any precise way, what they mean when they say that something is morally wrong or a moral duty. They are found in the fact that, as it seems, people might have all the same non-moral beliefs about (say) some course of action, about the alternatives, and about their effects, and yet still intelligibly disagree about whether so acting is morally permissible. They are found in the recognition that moral arguments are not something that might even conceivably be settled by empirical investigation. They are found in the striking extent to which an appeal to intuitions or gut feelings (that not everyone shares) are the only "argument" people have for the moral views they embrace. And they are found in the ways in which peoples' moral views look to be more a reflection of private interest or cultural practice or even biological forces, than a recognition of independent moral facts.

These familiar observations offer significant grounds for skepticism, notwithstanding the strength of peoples' moral convictions and their readiness to sacrifice in the name of those convictions. There is a long history of moral skeptics appealing, in different ways, to these observations. Along the way, a remarkable variety of positions have emerged.

One way to understand the variety of views that count as versions of moral skepticism is to relate them to a standard account of the nature of knowledge, moral and otherwise. According to this account, knowledge is justified, true, belief. The idea is that a person will not count as knowing something in particular if she does not believe it; or if, though she believes it, it isn't true; or if, though she believes it, and it is true, she is not justified in believing it. This is regularly offered as a general account of knowledge and is not supposed to be specific to moral knowledge. Nonetheless, specific versions of moral skepticism can be sorted according to whether they deny (i) that people have moral *beliefs*; or, granting moral beliefs, (ii) that such beliefs are *true*; or, granting that people might have moral beliefs, and that some of them might be true, (iii) that people ever have an appropriate *justification* for those beliefs.

In what follows, I will canvass the arguments people have offered for thinking that we don't have moral beliefs; that if we do, none of them are true; and that, even if some might be true, we are never justified in thinking of any of them (or, at least, any that are substantive) that they are true.

Do People Have Any Moral Beliefs?

The suggestion that people do not have moral beliefs might seem difficult to take seriously. It seems clear that people do sometimes sincerely believe that, for instance, racism is morally wrong, or that justice demands that we treat others as equals. These claims and others seem to express moral beliefs that at least some people genuinely have. In fact, such beliefs sometimes seem to be among people's strongest commitments.

Still, a powerful strain of moral skepticism has its roots in denying that people have moral beliefs. These moral skeptics grant that people sometimes genuinely accept the positions they advocate. Their distinctive claim is that moral convictions, no matter how strongly held, are not *beliefs*. Instead, these skeptics argue, peoples' moral views are a reflection of their affective, and not their cognitive, attitudes. To hold a moral view, they argue, is a matter of looking at some things with approval and others with disapproval, or of being motivated to do some things and not others, or of hoping others will behave in one way rather than another. It is not a matter of having a belief with a distinctively moral content.

According to these "non-cognitivists" (as they are usually called), once we distinguish a person's beliefs from her other (non-belief) attitudes, and, specifically, once we recognize the distinctive role of her preferences, of her desires and aversions, and of her approvals and disapprovals, none of which are themselves beliefs, we'll see (they argue) that a person's moral convictions are among these non-belief attitudes. Having a moral view is not a matter of having a belief.

The apparently necessary connection between a person's moral commitments and what she is motivated to do is the most influential argument for thinking that moral attitudes are not *beliefs*.

The argument goes back at least to David Hume who emphasized the distinctively practical role of moral thought (see Hume 1978). It starts with the observation that if a person is utterly unmotivated to pursue, promote, or protect what she claims to be good or right (or to oppose and work against what she claims to be bad or wrong) her claims will have been shown not to express her genuine views.

The argument goes on to claim that beliefs are all, in themselves, motivationally inert. Simply knowing which belief a person might have doesn't by itself (the argument goes) tell us how the person will be motivated. To know how someone might be motivated we need to know what preferences she has. This marks a sharp contrast, the argument goes on, between a person's moral views, on the one hand, and her beliefs, on the other, since in knowing a person's moral views we do know that she will be motivated in certain ways. This contrast shows, the argument concludes, that a person's moral views are not among her beliefs.

There are various ways one might push against this argument. For instance, one might deny that in holding a moral view, one is, ipso facto, motivated at all one way or the other. Even if normally coming to hold that something is good or right has a motivational impact, there certainly seem to be cases where a person sincerely recognizes that something is morally right and yet shows no motivation to do it. Or one might argue

465

that the motivational impact of our moral views actually establishes that, at least in some cases, knowing a person's beliefs does tell us about that person's motivations.

A different argument for thinking people lack moral beliefs highlights the difficulty people have in identifying and articulating just what they mean in saying that something is right or good or wrong or bad.

Following G. E. Moore, many philosophers argue that any attempt to define moral terms is bound to fail (Moore 1903). They note that for any proposed definition (say, of 'good' as 'pleasant' or 'the object of desire' or 'conventionally accepted,' or of 'right' as 'conducive to happiness' or 'approved by God' or 'consistent with society's rules') one can intelligibly ask, of whatever met one's preferred definition, whether it really was good or right. That these are intelligible questions seems to show that (i) thinking something satisfies the proposed definition and (ii) thinking that thing is good or right involves thinking two different things. Yet if the definitions were successful, the argument supposes, the thoughts would be one and the same (just as thinking something is a triangle is one and the same as thinking that it is a three-sided plane figure).

The worry is not about any particular proposed definition. Rather, it seems, any attempt to define moral terms by appeal to events or properties that are testable or in other ways cognitively tractable, will leave open an important question: are things that satisfy the definitions actually good or right? Even if we end up answering "yes," our being able intelligibly to raise the question seems to establish that the proposed definitions fail as definitions. They each fail to capture a distinctive and important element of what we are doing in making moral claims.

What, though, is this missing important element? Non-cognitivists hold that it is not some additional cognitive component, over and above what is captured by some definition. Instead, they maintain, the extra element is some non-cognitive attitude that we are expressing in making a moral judgment.

This suggestion fits naturally with the motivation argument, since it returns us to the view that sincere moral judgments are tied to some non-cognitive attitude (that many have argued is a motivating attitude). The two arguments fit together so well that their coincidence is reasonably taken as an additional consideration in favor of both.

Importantly, while non-cognitivists reject the idea that we have moral beliefs, and so (on the assumption that knowledge entails belief) reject the idea that we have moral knowledge, they can and often do offer an account of what we are doing in saying of someone that she has moral knowledge: we are expressing our approval of her moral commitments. Just as our moral thought and talk is used to express our attitudes, so too (on this view) is our thought and talk about knowledge and justification. In counting someone as knowing something, or in characterizing her as being justified, we are, on this view, not reporting a fact or expressing a belief, but instead we are expressing some non-cognitive attitude of our own concerning her (Blackburn 1993; Gibbard 1990).

Do People Have Any True Moral Beliefs?

Without denying that it might be impossible to define moral terms in any way other than by appeal to other moral terms, many hold that we are nonetheless expressing beliefs, and purporting to report facts, when we make moral judgments. We are not simply expressing our likes (and dislikes), we are claiming that those things are right, or good (or wrong, or bad, and these claims are properly evaluated as true or false in light of the way the world actually is. On this cognitivist view, liking (or disliking) something shouldn't be mistaken for thinking it good (or bad). The latter involves forming a belief about the thing, perhaps a belief that justifies our liking (or disliking) it, but in any case a belief that is distinct from, and something over and above, the feelings in question.

Thinking that people have moral beliefs, though, is compatible with thinking all the beliefs are false. As a result, one might embrace cognitivism and yet advance an error theory, according to which no moral beliefs are true. Error theorists grant that we do have moral beliefs and that, in making moral claims, we are purporting to report facts about how the world is, morally. In that respect, it is less radical than non-cognitivism. In another respect, however, it is much more radical, since error theorists hold that our moral thought is fundamentally mistaken, whereas the non-cognitivists challenge our understanding of what we are doing in making moral claims, but might leave our making those claims utterly unchallenged (Mackie 1977).

A useful parallel here is found in the modern view of the Greek Gods. In ancient Greece, people had beliefs about Zeus and the other Olympian Deities, beliefs that were strongly held and tremendously influential Yet we now see those beliefs as fundamentally mistaken, no matter how sincerely held and no matter how salutary in their effects. Other useful parallels are found in, for instance, current scientists' rejection of beliefs concerning phlogiston, and the now common rejection of the idea that there are witches with occult powers. As we see things, particular claims about Zeus' desires, or phlogiston's effects, or the magical impact of a witch's incantation, are false because they presuppose the existence of things that don't actually exist—Zeus, phlogiston, occult powers, respectively.

Similarly, error theorists about morality argue that particular moral claims, which they grant often express sincerely held beliefs, are all false because they presuppose the existence of things that don't exist. Different error theorists trace the mistake to different specific presuppositions that, they argue, are part and parcel of holding a moral view. But they all maintain that our moral thought and talk presupposes the presence of something that, simply put, does not exist.

According to some, in holding a moral belief we are presupposing authoritative standards for human behavior. And, they go on to argue, there are no such standards, so we should reject all the beliefs (i.e. all moral beliefs) that commit us otherwise.

According to others, we are presupposing desire-independent reasons for acting in certain ways, such that people have reason to act in certain ways, regardless of their desires. And, they go on to argue, there are no such reasons, so we should reject all the beliefs (i.e. all moral beliefs) that commit us otherwise.

According to still others, we are presupposing the existence of an all powerful and loving creator who sets the standards for our behavior, or establishes reasons for us to act, or in some other way provides what has to be in place for any moral claims to be true. And, they go on to argue, there is no such creator, so we should reject all the beliefs (i.e. all moral beliefs) that commit us otherwise.

In whichever way the details are worked out, error theorists maintain that we should reject all moral beliefs as being false on the grounds that, in holding them, we are committed to something that does not exist.

Clearly, the error theorist's position is only as strong as her grounds for thinking (i) that the presuppositions she identifies are ones to which we are committed in holding a moral belief, and (ii) that the relevant presupposition is false. Predictably, cognitivists who reject the error theory regularly argue either (i') that the claims about what moral beliefs presuppose get things wrong or (ii') that, while they are right, the presupposition is satisfied. In taking the first line, the argument is that error theorists saddle those with moral beliefs with commitments that are not theirs to bear. In taking the second line, the argument is that the relevant commitments are, contra the error theorists, commitments for which we have, on balance, grounds for thinking they are satisfied.

Working through these issues is nicely complicated and involves weighing evidence that certain presuppositions are in play, evidence that the presuppositions are not satisfied, and evidence that people might have gone so far wrong. All of this gets balanced, in the process, against the evidence that some things really are right or wrong, good or bad.

But this last bit of evidence needs to be handled carefully. The error theorists are challenging the claim that anything is right or wrong or good or bad. So, to the extent contrary evidence presupposes what is at stake (as presumably most of our moral evidence in favor of particular moral claims, does) there is a pressing worry about begging the question. Of course, error theorists acknowledge, if cruelty is always wrong, then evidence that someone has done something wrong is found in their having been cruel. But the claim that cruelty is always wrong, no less than the claim that a particular person did something wrong, presupposes, they will argue, just what is in question.

However, the conviction that some things are genuinely right or wrong, good or bad, provides impetus for showing either that the purported presuppositions are not actually being made, or that they can be vindicated. That fact understandably structures how people set about defending their moral beliefs as not actually undermined by the error theorist's challenge.

In the process, error theorists and their opponents, alike, work to figure out what people are claiming in saying that something is right or wrong, good or bad, since arguments for or against certain candidate presuppositions turn on what is involved in these claims. These debates introduce discussion of whether the putative moral facts would have to be something supernatural, or whether they might properly be identified with, or constituted by, natural entities or properties. And these debates force a discussion as well about what might constitute successful definitions of our moral terms, about whether such definitions are necessary or desirable, and about how it is that our language and our thoughts might come to be about various things in the way they apparently are.

In the context of a discussion of skepticism, the important point is that if the error theorists are right, we lack moral knowledge (assuming that knowledge entails justified true belief) because none of our moral beliefs are true. Importantly, in making their argument, error theorists are not claiming that no one has, or has ever had, justified moral beliefs. Error theorists argue that *we* have grounds for rejecting all moral beliefs as false, on the grounds we have for thinking that they all have false presuppositions. Yet their position is consistent with holding that people who lack the evidence we have, or have different evidence, might well be perfectly justified in holding the moral beliefs they do. Their point is that, justified or not, we have reason to think such beliefs are actually false.

Are Any Moral Beliefs Justified?

But what would it take for someone's moral beliefs to be justified?

An attractive answer to this question, provided by "foundationalism," starts with the idea that a belief is justified if but only if (i) there is evidence for it, or (ii) it is, in some way, self-evident (or not in need of evidence, though able to provide evidence for other beliefs, or, at least, not such that there could be any good evidence against it). And the answer continues with the thought that beliefs that fall into (i) do so thanks to being properly related to those that fall into (ii). (Foundationalism doesn't require that the foundational beliefs be dubitable, corrigible, or even true. They simply need to be able to justify other beliefs without having to secure support from other beliefs.)

Foundationalism brings two questions to the fore. Which beliefs are of type (ii)? (Here, talk of self-evidence, certainty, indubitability, etc. looms large.) And: What does it take for a belief to count as being "properly related" to those beliefs? (Here, talk of entailment, evidential relations, explanations, and inductive support, looms large.) Among foundationalists, there is a great deal of disagreement as to how to answer these two questions.

In thinking specifically about moral beliefs, explanatory relations have become especially salient (see Harman 1977 and Sayre-McCord 1988). The problem is that the truth of our moral beliefs seems not to play any explanatory role in our understanding of our own experiences, nor of what happens in the world, nor why. Even when evil people do horrible things to virtuous people, we can have (in principle) a full explanation of what the evil people have done and why, and what happens to the virtuous people, and how they suffer, all without having to appeal to our moral beliefs at all. Psychology, sociology, biology, and physics, in some combination, provide the explanation. While adding talk of evil and virtue might let us categorize those involved, it seems not to help us explain what has happened. Similarly, we might find ourselves repulsed by the behavior of the evil person and indignant at the treatment the virtuous person has suffered. While we might be tempted to say that our being repulsed is explained by the person's evil nature and our indignation is explained by undeserved suffering, our reactions are fully explained by appeal to our having the moral beliefs we do, without having to suppose those beliefs are true. We would have been repulsed and indignant, having believed the person evil and the sufferer virtuous, even if, as a matter of fact, our beliefs were false. According to many moral skeptics, this point holds generally and shows that our moral beliefs are explanatorily impotent.

This is going just a bit fast. After all, the truth of our moral beliefs would, it seems, explain the truth of other moral beliefs. The wrongness of cruelty explains why a person who is cruel is evil, and the virtue of a victim explains why that person's suffering is undeserved. Perhaps. Yet, the skeptics point out, all of our moral beliefs are being called into question. So these explanatory relations *among* our moral beliefs are of no justificatory value unless some of our moral beliefs are independently justified. Our moral beliefs could be justified, they insist, only if either they bear some other relation to privileged beliefs, or they themselves fall into the privileged class. But, according to the skeptics, neither is plausible.

So, for instance, our moral beliefs would bear an appropriate relation to privileged beliefs if they were entailed by those beliefs. Thus, if the fact that something was pleasant entailed that it was morally good, or if the fact that some course of action maximized happiness entailed that it was morally right, then as long as we were justified in believing certain things were pleasant or certain courses of action maximized happiness, our beliefs concerning what was morally good or right could be justified.

Yet Moore's observation that there is always an open question when it comes to whether something that satisfies a non-moral description (as, for instance, being pleasant) satisfies as well a moral description (as, for instance, being morally good), renders contentious (to say the least) the claim that there are entailment relations between the content of non-moral beliefs and the content of moral beliefs (Moore 1903; Sayre-McCord 1997).

Inductive relations seem no better placed to provide justifications for our moral beliefs. After all, inductive relations supporting particular moral beliefs require already having on hand, as justified, some moral beliefs that we can use as the basis for the induction. That simply shifts back to those beliefs, leaving us unable to make a legitimate induction on their basis unless they are themselves justified.

If, as it appears, explanatory, entailment, and inductive relations exhaust the relevant possibilities, there seems no hope for the justification of our moral beliefs unless some moral beliefs count as epistemically privileged—as self-evident, or indubitable, or in some other way such that we are both justified in holding them and able to rely on them in justifying other moral beliefs. Indeed, virtually all foundationalists end up taking this view. (The skeptics, of course, deny that any moral beliefs qualify, while the non-skeptics maintain that some do.) The challenge facing non-skeptics, at least those who accept foundationalism, is to show that some moral beliefs qualify as epistemically privileged.

Some moral beliefs might immediately come to mind as not possibly false—for instance, that committing a murder is morally wrong. But what seems to guarantee this truth—its being an analytic that murder is wrong—seems to guarantee as well its triviality. For such beliefs to justify other moral beliefs, we need another substantive belief, for instance, that a certain act was a murder (and not a justified killing). But the justification of these beliefs is just what is at issue, and the (trivial) truth of various analytic claims seems to be of no help with them.

One might argue that the available analytic truths are much more surprising and complicated than this example suggests. One might hold too that discovering their truth is a kind of revelation even to those who are sophisticated in their moral thinking. Yet, surprising or not, complicated or not, a revelation or not, analytic moral truths, considered alone, still apparently leave us with no justification for specific substantive moral beliefs. For this reason, the ambition of those who ground moral epistemology in analytic truths involves finding successful analyses that trade in epistemically unproblematic non-moral terms. Only then, relying on the analyses, and relevant, and justified, non-moral beliefs, might the moral beliefs in question inherit epistemic credentials.

If, for instance, a correct analysis reveals that something is morally wrong if in doing it one is acting contrary to the recommendation of one's ideal advisor, and if we can have a justified view of what one's ideal advisor would recommend, then we could have a justified belief about what is wrong. The challenge, the skeptic will press, is to show that the terms of the analysis themselves have the required epistemic credentials.

Alternatively, putting putative analytic truths aside, one might defend some substantive moral beliefs a priori, even if not analytic. Thus, for instance, one might maintain, as an a priori truth, that an action is wrong if and only if the agent could not consistently will that everyone act on the same grounds she is taking as sufficient for her.

Against such views, a moral skeptic presses two challenges. The first challenge is to show that the claim is, in fact, an a priori truth. The second is to show that our beliefs concerning what an agent might consistently will are on a better footing, epistemically, than the moral claims concerning the wrongness of an action seem to be. Predictably, bearing each of these burdens is a real challenge.

Hoping to meet both burdens, moral intuitionists argue that there are some substantive moral claims that all who are morally competent, clear-headed, and unbiased, can be brought to recognize as true. Moreover, they maintain, the credentials of these claims are comfortably on a par, epistemically, with the rules of logic and the axioms of mathematics. As the intuitionists emphasize, the rules of logic and the axioms of mathematics admit of no more proof, nor do people think they need more proof, than is found in the fact that those who are logically or mathematically competent, clear-headed, and unbiased, can "see" their truth. The reflective faculties of humans, no less than their sensorial faculties, are, when properly used, sources of information about the world (Ross 1930).

Thus, for instance, they suggest that we are justified in believing that, other things being equal, promises ought to be kept, and that (again) other things being equal, if possible, we ought to help those in need. We are justified in believing these things not because they help us explain our experiences, nor because they are analytic truths, but because, on reflection, those who are morally competent, clear-headed, and unbiased, see their truth. Once such claims are on hand, the intuitionists note, we can justify other moral beliefs by appeal to them. So while most of our moral beliefs are not themselves directly intuitive—our moral world is far too complex for that—moral intuition provides the fundamental truths that we can use to justify our other moral beliefs.

Moral skeptics, though, highlight that what strikes people as intuitive, when it comes to morality, so regularly reflects how they happen to have been raised, and what their interests are, that there is a persistent, and seemingly well-grounded, suspicion that what gets valorized as intuitive is really simply what one is unwilling to reject.

More generally, moral skeptics press, there are no substantive moral claims that are unchallengeable and so none that are not in need of some evidence or support. Yet that suggests, they hold, that no moral beliefs are properly seen as epistemically privileged in a way that would allow them to serve as a foundation for our other moral beliefs. And if no moral beliefs are foundational (i.e. appropriately epistemically privileged), and no set of exclusively non-moral beliefs can alone provide a justification for our moral beliefs, then no moral beliefs are justified at all. This argument holds even if some of our moral beliefs are, in fact, true. The problem here is not that there are no moral truths, but that even if there are such truths, we apparently have no reason whatsoever to think that we have got them right.

Putting things this way brings us back to the explanatory challenge. Unless the truth of our moral beliefs figures, at the very least, in an explanation of why we hold the beliefs we do—unless we have grounds for thinking that our moral beliefs have been, and are, responsive to the (moral) truth—we have reason to worry that our moral views simply free-float from the moral facts (assuming there are such facts).

This worry is amplified by the extent to which psychology, sociology, political science, and evolution, with appeals to self-interest, false consciousness, political influence, and genetic advantage, seem in some combination to offer compelling explanations of our moral beliefs; all, it seems, without ever giving us reason to think any of them are true.

In order to establish that our moral beliefs are responsive to the moral facts we must justify our view that the facts are one way rather than another. Eschewing an appeal to intuitions, and the claim that some substantive moral claims are epistemically privileged in the way foundationalists demand, those who reject skepticism offer a variety of arguments in favor of some substantive position or another. Thus, for instance, Kant offers a transcendental argument for the categorical imperative, while Mill defends hedonism on the grounds that our view of the desirability of our own pleasure commits us to acknowledging anyone else's like pleasure as equally desirable (even if it is not equally desired). Others appeal to our capacity to engage in practical reason, or to some inescapable feature of our nature, arguing that it commits us to accepting some principle or other (Korsgaard 1996). Still others find arguments for substantive moral claims in our need for shared standards for cooperation, or our commitment to mutual respect, or in the capacity of certain standards to explain and justify our more particular moral judgments (Gauthier 1986; Scanlon 1998; Rawls 1971).

Of course, in offering such arguments (in the attempt to show that our beliefs are responsive to the truth), we are supposing that they are themselves sensitive to the truth. A skeptic will charge that, in doing so, these defenses all assume, illegitimately, that some of our beliefs are right.

Interestingly, according to many, moral beliefs are not the only ones that suffer this problem. In fact, it seems attempts to establish that any contingently true beliefs are appropriately sensitive to the facts they concern will implicitly or explicitly appeal to other beliefs about those very facts. After all, it is only if we have those facts right that we can show that our beliefs are appropriately sensitive to the facts. But we are then presupposing that (some of) our beliefs are appropriately sensitive to the facts when we try to establish that they are.

Those who embrace global skepticism often press this point and rely on it in arguing that virtually all of our beliefs are unjustified, with the result that we lack knowledge not simply of morality but of the external world, of other minds, even of our own experiences. At the same time, many who reject global skepticism embrace this point too, and then take it as grounds for thinking that in some way or other the foundationalist has misunderstood what is required for justification. In particular, they reject the idea that a belief can be justified only if it is either self-evident (or otherwise epistemically privileged) or justified by appeal, ultimately, to such beliefs. Instead, they maintain, we can succeed in justifying a particular belief by appeal to another, without supposing we can get a perspective on our beliefs that allows us, from outside (so to speak), to show that our beliefs are responsive to the facts. Such a perspective is, in principle, unavailable, they argue, so if there is justification at all, ever, it must not require our having succeeded in taking this perspective.

With this in mind, coherentists about justification argue that how justified our beliefs are—moral beliefs, no less than beliefs about the taste of coffee or the effects of penicillin or the fuel economy of a car, or whatever—is dependent on, and a reflection of, how they are related to the other things we believe, with there being no need for any of the beliefs to be epistemically privileged in the way a foundationalist requires.

This suggestion meets with a familiar objection that is right in the point it makes, but which, in the process, reveals a common misunderstanding of what the coherentist holds. The objection is that the extent to which beliefs happen to hold together is no evidence that they are true. Indeed, for any set of coherent beliefs, it seems easy to imagine an alternative set that is just as coherent, yet incompatible. A piece of fiction need be no less coherent than a historical treatise. That means that one cannot reasonably offer, as evidence of the truth of one's beliefs, that they are coherent. Coherence is not evidence of truth. The misunderstanding here is in thinking that a coherentist offers coherence as evidence of truth. She doesn't, or at least shouldn't. The coherentist's proposal is, or should be, that while (relative) coherence is not evidence of truth, it is a measure of the strength of the evidence the person has. The idea is that each person's evidence for whatever she might be considering is found in the contents of her other beliefs. The more the contents of her beliefs support some claim, the more coherent the claim is with her beliefs and the more justified she is in believing it (Sayre-McCord 1996).

Coherentism takes as given, but not as privileged, whatever beliefs we find ourselves with. It then sees the process of testing, refining, and justifying our beliefs as a matter of seeing how the various things we believe hang together, putting ourselves in place to gather more information (which becomes available as we form new beliefs), and refining and rejecting various claims in light of our evidence. As the skeptic has pointed out, none of the beliefs count as unchallengeable. Yet, contrary to the skeptic's claim, in the face of challenges, a person is justified in appealing to, and indeed has no recourse but to appeal to, whatever she does believe.

This of course leaves open the possibility that a person's justified beliefs, even those that are extremely well justified, might turn out to be false. Justification is no guarantee of truth on the coherentist's view. But that does not mean that a person had no reason to think of her justified beliefs that they are true—she has all the reason provided by her other beliefs. Each of these beliefs can be challenged, but each is also in principle something that might meet the challenge.

While the coherence theory of justification is meant to account for how our scientific theories and our common-sense beliefs about the world might be justified, even though they are neither self-evident (nor otherwise epistemically privileged) nor supported by beliefs that are, the account applies directly to moral beliefs as well. To say that is not, of course, to say that our moral beliefs will, on the coherentist account, turn out to be justified. That cannot be determined ex ante and depends on seeing whether, and how, our moral (and other) beliefs hang together, putting ourselves in a position to gather more information, and refining and rejecting various claims in light of our evidence. Coherentism makes sense of how we might intelligibly discover that our moral beliefs are appropriately responsive to the facts, without thereby ensuring that they are. Far from it.

Part of what makes moral skepticism a serious challenge is that, as we consider the full range of what we take ourselves to know—about how moral convictions are shaped and changed, about how the world operates more generally, and about how we might gather information effectively—we find grounds for suspecting that our moral beliefs do not cohere well with our other beliefs. At the same time, our moral convictions are so central to our understanding of ourselves and others that coming to grips with them, either as justified beliefs, or as unjustified beliefs, or as convictions not properly seen as beliefs at all, is a challenge we cannot reasonably ignore.

References

Blackburn, S. (1993) *Essays in Quasi-Realism*, Oxford: Oxford University Press.
Gauthier, D. (1986) *Morals by Agreement*, Oxford: Oxford University Press.
Gibbard, A. (1990) *Wise Choices, Apt Feelings*, Cambridge, MA: Harvard University Press.
Harman, G. (1977) *The Nature of Morality*, New York: Oxford University Press.
Hume, D. (1978) *A Treatise of Human Nature*, Oxford: Oxford University Press. Originally published in 1739–40.
Korsgaard, C. (1996) *Sources of Normativity*, New York: Cambridge University Press.
Mackie, J. L. (1977) *Ethics: Inventing Right and Wrong*, London: Penguin Books.
Moore, G. E. (1903) *Principia Ethica*, Cambridge: Cambridge University Press.

Rawls, J. (1971) *A Theory of Justice*, Cambridge, MA: Harvard University Press.
Ross, W. D. (1930) *The Right and the Good*, Oxford: Oxford University Press.
Sayre-McCord, G. (1988) "Moral Theory and Explanatory Impotence," *Midwest Studies in Philosophy*, Vol. XII, Morris: University of Minnesota Press, 433–457.
—— (1996) "Coherentist Epistemology and Moral Theory," in W. Sinnott-Armstrong and M. Timmons (eds.) *Moral Knowledge?* Oxford: Oxford University Press, 137–189.
—— (1997) "'Good' on Twin Earth," *Philosophical Issues*, 8, 267–292.
Scanlon, T. *What We Owe to Each Other*, Cambridge, MA: Harvard University Press.

Part VI
RESPONSES TO SKEPTICISM

44
SKEPTICISM AND ANTI-REALISM
Richard Schantz

I. Realism and Anti-Realism

To gain an understanding of the dialectical relationship between skepticism and anti-realism, we must begin with a characterization of realism. After all, it is realism that seems to pave the way to skepticism or at least to contain a certain skeptical potential. Anti-realism, then, deems itself as faced with the task of trying to give a satisfactory theoretical answer to the skeptical challenge. This is the typical argumentative pattern of the debate.

The basic idea of realism about a particular domain can be roughly expressed as a conjunction of two theses, an existence thesis and an independence thesis: firstly the kinds of thing distinctive of that domain exist, and secondly their existence and nature are objective and independent of us, of our perceptions, thoughts, and language. The things within the domain must be out there to be discovered rather than constructed or constituted by our minds or our conceptual schemes. Anti-realism rejects this conjunction of theses. Some forms of anti-realism attack the existence thesis by flatly denying that entities of the relevant kind really exist, while according to other forms entities of the relevant kind do exist but are not objective or have no independent status in reality.

Realism and anti-realism are domain-specific positions. There are distinct categories of entities one can be realist or anti-realist about: physical objects, universals, mental states, space, time, moral values, God, numbers, meaning, and so on. Most philosophers are neither global realists nor global anti-realists. Rather, most of them are pickers and choosers, local realists about some kind of entities, and local anti-realists about others.

I shall be concerned here only with the traditional debate between realism and anti-realism about the external, physical world, that is, with the debate about whether physical objects and events exist independently of the mental. Realists maintain that there really are mountains, rivers, and stars, and that their existence and nature, what they are like, are constitutively independent of what anyone happens to believe or say about the matter. Usually anti-realists do not dispute that there are such things. Quite the contrary, they maintain that, of course, everyday macroscopic objects do indeed exist, but, so they typically add, not objectively, not independently of us—not "without the mind."

Realism and anti-realism, as so far characterized, are ontological or metaphysical theses. It is often suggested, however, that this characterization should be supplemented to include an epistemological thesis. Two proposals, not incompatible but highlighting different aspects of our epistemic situation, can be distinguished. Some realists, the epistemological optimists, claim that we are mostly capable of acquiring knowledge about the objective world; they are persuaded that, difficult as it might be, the world is principally epistemically accessible to us (Davidson 1986; Devitt 1984; McDowell 1994). Other realists, however, the epistemological pessimists, are a bit more cautious in this regard (Nagel 1986; Stroud 1984; Williams 1978). They tend to stress the ever-present possibility of error and ignorance. There is no guarantee that our beliefs about the world, even if they are maximally supported by evidence, are true. Truth about the world, so they characteristically contend, is always potentially evidence-transcendent or verification-transcendent.

The crucial point is that, according to realism, there is a logical gap between our beliefs about the world, or our sensory experiences of it, and the way the world is in itself. The totality of our beliefs about the world is one thing, the objective world quite another; obviously, our believing something to be so-and-so, does not make it so. This basic realist conviction, apparently a platitude acknowledged by both naive and reflective common sense, is the main reason why many philosophers think that realism is threatened by a deep internal tension: if the world is constitutively independent of our experiences and beliefs, then how can we be confident of gaining any knowledge about it?

While the camp of the so-called epistemological realists seeks to combine its ontological thesis of the mind-independence of the world with the epistemological thesis that it is nevertheless humanly possible to gain knowledge about it, epistemological skeptics resolve the apparent tension in realism in a quite different way: they assert that it is impossible to know anything about the external, objective world at all; we can attain knowledge, at most, only of our minds and its ideas or representations. This is the standpoint of skepticism about the external world. We can know neither that there is an external world nor, should there be one, what it is like.

In this dialectical situation anti-realists—idealists, verificationists, phenomenalists, Kantians, social constructivists, etc.—enter the stage. Deeply convinced that metaphysical realism opens the door to skepticism, anti-realists argue that the realist conception of an independent world behind the appearances, beyond the world as we perceive it and believe it to be, is wrong or even incoherent. They often urge that there are significant connections between understanding and verification, which the skeptic simply ignores. The only world there is, the only world we can find out about, is the world our senses present to us. A hypothesis with no connection to experience is regarded as spurious; after all, it could never be verified or falsified. So anti-realists tend to assert that we cannot even understand the skeptic's speculations about the wildly different ways the world might really be, even though all our experiences remain unaltered. According to anti-realism, there is indeed an ordinary perceptible world, a world of trees, tables, and stars, but this world is, in a philosophically significant sense, dependent on, or constituted by, our epistemic activities. So what the anti-realists are willing to abandon is the distinctive realist conception of the world as what is there anyway, the alleged objectivity and autonomy of the world. To block skepticism, they offer us a revisionary ontology, which marks a considerable departure from the deeply entrenched metaphysics of common sense.

The skeptic, on the other hand, need not deny the existence of an independent world. She is an agnostic, who merely claims that we do not know whether or not such an objective world, a world as the realist conceives it, really exists. To achieve her aim, it is enough to raise reasonable doubts about our beliefs concerning the external world, thereby seeking to show that we are not justified in holding these beliefs, and so do not know that they are true. Anti-realism is a drastic reaction to skepticism; it is a radical form of anti-skepticism. Our knowledge of the world is unproblematic and secure because it seems to be not very difficult to know what is going on in our own minds—in our subjective or internal world.

II. Radical Skepticism

The classic work on the philosophical problem of our knowledge of the external world is Descartes' *Meditations* in which he places all the beliefs he had formerly accepted in doubt in order to put his whole system of beliefs on a secure foundation and to build a reliable edifice of knowledge. His ambitious project is to make a general examination of everything he believes or takes to be true, with the aim of conclusively eliminating all error. To this purpose, he employs his famous "method of doubt": he decides to tentatively reject any belief or principle that is not absolutely certain, any for which some reason for doubt can be found, some possible way in which the belief might be false.

The major part of our beliefs and our knowledge of the physical world is based on, or grounded in, sensory experience. No wonder, then, that empiricism—the view that most, or even all, of our knowledge comes to us from the evidence of the senses—once clearly dominated the epistemological scene. So it is reasonable for Descartes to begin by casting doubts on the reliability of the senses as a source of knowledge. He points out first that the senses sometimes deceive us. Sometimes things appear different from the way they really are, so our judgments about how they really are, if based on the ways they appear, can be wrong. One might be tempted to conclude that as a general source of knowledge the senses should never again be trusted. But, plainly, such a simple version of the argument from illusion would not be sound. From the fact that something is sometimes deceptive it does not follow that it is always deceptive. Fallibility does not entail general skepticism. However, Descartes regards the argument from illusion as only the first stage in the over-all structure of his skeptical argument. He himself recognizes that the senses might be reliable in circumstances that we would ordinarily regard as favorable.

At this point, he introduces his famous "dreaming argument" as an adequate reason for doubting all of his sense-based beliefs. He reminds us of the fact that we sometimes sleep and therein dream. Dreams are contentful conscious experiences whose content does not correspond in any reliable way to events in our surroundings, and therefore they do not yield knowledge of what is going on in the world around us. Descartes claims that the impossibility of distinguishing being awake from being asleep by certain marks provides reason for doubting even those sense-based beliefs that are formed under the best possible circumstances. Thus, we cannot rule out the possibility that we are presently dreaming. For all we know, we might even be dreaming all the time. And if we cannot know that we are not dreaming, we can know nothing about the real extramental world. A necessary condition for our knowledge of the world around us cannot be fulfilled.

Finally, Descartes introduces his most radical doubt-inducing argument: the hypothesis of an evil demon. Suppose there is an omnipotent being bent on universal deception. Such a being would be capable of artificially producing in my mind all my sensory experiences of the world without these being related to objects and events in the external world. Hence the real world could be very different from the way it appears to be. Perhaps there even exists no real external world at all.

An updated variant of Descartes' thought experiment is the renowned science fiction scenario of a "brain in a vat" (Putnam 1981). Imagine that evil scientists have removed your brain from your body and placed it in a vat of nutrient fluids that keep the brain alive and functioning. They have also inserted lots of electrodes into your brain and in all the relevant nerve fibers in order to be capable of delivering inputs to the normal neural information channels. The electrodes are controlled by a sophisticated supercomputer that contains a complete model of the physical world and does the calculations necessary to produce the same pattern of neural stimulation as a normal brain in a human body receives. As a result, you enjoy the same sort of experiences and thoughts as you would enjoy if you were a normal, embodied human being. The scientists have put you in a virtual reality that, for you, is qualitatively indistinguishable from the real world you think you live in.

The skeptical question now is: how do you know that you are not a brain in a vat? You might reply that there is no evidence to suggest that you are a brain in a vat. This is surely right. The crucial point, however, is that if you were a brain in a vat, you would not possess any evidence for this hypothesis either. According to the brain-in-a-vat scenario, you would have the same kinds of sensory experiences as you are having when you perceive external objects in the normal way. Moreover, your sensory experience is ultimately all the evidence you have to go on. All your beliefs about the external world depend in the end on your sensory experiences. Therefore, you have no evidence that the skeptical scenario is not true, and, therefore, you cannot know that you are not a brain in a vat. From this, the skeptic infers that you do not know anything about the external world at all.

The various thought experiments we have considered seem to support radical skepticism about the external world. This position differs from other, less radical forms of skepticism by aiming primarily at justification simpliciter, not at some demanding conception of knowledge, which requires certainty or indefeasible justification or at least a high degree of justification. For Descartes and his numerous followers, certainty was an essential feature of knowledge. Our modern conception of knowledge, however, is fallibilist. We have learned to recognize that the logical possibility of error can never be ruled out entirely. Every one of our empirical beliefs might turn out to be false. Hence radical skepticism should not be confused with the quite plausible fallibilist standpoint that our beliefs always fall short of being certain. Rather, the main thesis of radical skepticism is the dramatic thesis that the justification condition for knowledge cannot be fulfilled. Our actual system of beliefs is not justified at all because there are many empirically equivalent alternatives, which are logically no less coherent. In contrast, non-radical forms of skepticism typically concede the possibility of justification, even of strong justification, but deny the possibility of knowledge. Its advocates merely maintain that, while we might have all sorts of good reasons for our beliefs, we cannot be absolutely certain, or strongly enough justified, to believe that they are really true because there is some error possibility, however remote, which we cannot exclude.

III. The Problem of Our Knowledge of the External World

We seem to have lost the world (Stroud 1984: 1–38). We know how things appear to us but we do not know how they really are. We know the contents of our conscious experiences but we cannot dismiss the possibility that they are totally disconnected from the objective world. The Cartesian problem of our knowledge of the external world is the problem of how we can attain knowledge of the world around us if the information the senses deliver is compatible with many different ways the world might be. The skeptical arguments seem to have shown that direct realism is not a tenable position. According to direct realism, we are directly aware of real physical objects and events in perception and thereby often, indeed typically, acquire direct or immediate knowledge of them. If the skeptical arguments are correct, direct realism must be wrong because the most important consequence of those arguments is that we are never perceptually directly aware of the physical objects in the external world. The direct objects of perception or sensory experience are a special kind of mental or subjective objects instead—objects that are usually called "sense-data," "sense," or "appearances." It is characteristic of these entities that their existence and properties are dependent on our awareness of them.

The problem of our knowledge of the external world can now be formulated as the problem of whether, and if so, how, beliefs about external objects can be justified on the basis of the direct perception of sense-data. If the skeptical conclusion is accepted, direct realism is a non-starter. But there is another realist option: representative or indirect realism. Historically, John Locke was surely its most prominent advocate; a judicious modern proponent of it is Frank Jackson (Jackson 1977). This theory holds that there really are external objects with which we causally interact in perception and about which we thereby acquire knowledge, indirect knowledge based on the more direct knowledge of the directly perceived sense-data, which represent and are caused in us by objects in our surroundings. So, according to this theory, beliefs about the external world are inferable from beliefs about sense-data by some cogent inductive argument. Surely, it is prima facie a plausible idea that a causal inference could lead us from the effects, the directly perceived sense-data, to their causes, the external objects and events.

But this simple type of induction is of no help. As David Hume, the eminent skeptic, has argued, causal relations can be known only by observing the regular sequence of cause and effect—in particular, by observing the cause being followed by the effect on a number of occasions. Establishing causal relations requires independent access to the objects or events to be correlated; we have to experience both sides of the causal relation. Thus it is impossible to establish any correlations between objects existing outside sensory experience and sensory experience itself. Since by hypothesis we have no independent access to physical objects, we cannot observe the presence of such objects causing our sense-data. Therefore, Hume concludes, the assertion that such a causal relation exists can never be known or justified.

Some advocates of representative realism invoke a more sophisticated form of inductive inference, hypothetical induction or abduction, to help to justify their belief in the external world. This is a method of reasoning in which a hypothesis is inferred as the best, or most likely, explanation of certain phenomena. Accordingly, it is claimed that the hypothesis or theory that there is an external world of persistent physical objects behaving in regular law-governed ways with which we are causally interacting offers the best explanation of the course of our sensory history, of why and how our various sensory experiences with their characteristic regularity and order, their "constancy and coherence," as Hume called it, arise.

Plainly, the radical skeptic is not impressed by the realist's appeal to hypothetical induction. In fact, this version of representative realism seems to be an easy target for his typical skeptical assaults. He will simply ask how we are supposed to know that sense-data represent or correspond to real physical objects if we are always presented with sense-data and never with physical objects themselves. The standard objection to representative realism is that it is a veil-of-perception doctrine. If we can directly perceive only sense-data, then these mind-dependent entities form a veil, or a barrier, preventing us from ever acquiring any knowledge about external objects. If we can never break out of the circle of sense-data, how can we know what properties the external objects possess, indeed, how can we even know that there are such objects? After all, we cannot draw the veil aside, to look whether there is something behind it. Hence, the skeptic concludes, the hypothesis that there is an external, objective reality is massively underdetermined by all the evidence we will ever have to go on.

IV. Phenomenalism

Ontological phenomenalism is a direct and sharp response to the serious epistemological difficulties raised by representative realism. Its defenders are prepared to reject realism completely. In the history of philosophy, George Berkeley was doubtlessly its most illustrious champion. Deeply convinced that Locke's representative realism unavoidably leads to skepticism, Berkeley offered a strikingly simple solution. He made the drastic proposal to solve the problem of skepticism by an ontological reduction. If the root of skepticism is the distinction between sense-data and physical objects, then to undermine skepticism we apparently need only to identify physical objects with sense-data. Thus phenomenalism's central claim is that physical objects are nothing but complexes or groups of sense-data. This claim implies that to be real is to be perceived. Phenomenalism is a form of idealism, of the doctrine that the natural objects making up the external world are in some way mind-correlative.

If a physical object is identical with a complex of sense-data, then the relation between the perception of a certain set of sense-data and the perception of a physical object is not contingent, as in representative realism, but necessary. Our claims to perceive physical objects can be justified by logical means, by deductively deriving them from premises about sense-data. The logical gap between appearance and objective reality seems to be closed. Thus, the theory seems to have clear epistemological advantages over representative realism. But the pressing question naturally arises of whether these advantages have not been purchased at too high a price, namely implausible ontological consequences. After all, phenomenalism's novel conception of a physical object diverges massively from the standpoint of common sense.

Perhaps the best-known objection to ontological phenomenalism is that it has the absurd consequence that physical objects exist discontinuously, that they constantly jump into and out of existence. Sense-data are short-lived entities; they exist only when and only as long as they are being perceived. Hence, since a physical object is nothing but a complex of sense-data, it follows that it ceases to exist when nobody perceives it, and begins to exist anew when somebody perceives it again at a later time. But surely this is an extremely implausible result, for physical objects exist continuously while they are not being perceived by anybody. Berkeley anticipated this objection and replied that the groups of sense-data that are identical with physical objects exist continuously even when not being perceived by a finite being because there is an infinite being, namely God, who preserves them in existence by, according to his official view, having ideas of them in His mind.

It remained to John Stuart Mill to present a version of ontological phenomenalism that is independent of any assumptions about the existence of God (Mill 1865). His essential innovation was the introduction of the concept of a possible sense-datum. A possible sense-datum is simply one that could be obtained under certain specifiable conditions. So, according to Mill's version of phenomenalism, a physical object is identical with a complex of actual and possible sense-data—physical objects, in his own words, are "permanent possibilities of sensation." The possible sense-data take over the function of Berkeley's deus ex machina as guarantors of the existence of unperceived objects. For even if no actual sense-data of a given physical object exist at this moment—because nobody is perceiving it—we can still say, according to Mill, that if anybody were to look at it, he would perceive sense-data belonging to it. But a physical object, during intervals of time when nobody is perceiving it, consists of possible sense-data and nothing else. Mill's theory thus seems to deprive physical objects of their categorical status and to concede to them a merely hypothetical status as unfulfilled possibilities. But, since merely possible existence is a mode of non-existence, this theory embodies a bizarre conception of objective physical reality. It implies, among other things, that an existent physical object can consist of non-existent components, and that whenever a certain event is being perceived, without its cause also being perceived, a mere possibility gives rise to an actual effect.

The ensuing development of phenomenalism can be understood as a succession of heroic attempts to preserve its epistemological advantages while avoiding its manifest metaphysical absurdities. A milestone in this development was an influential study by A. J. Ayer, which initiated a new phase of the phenomenalistic movement: analytical phenomenalism (Ayer 1940). Its main difference from ontological phenomenalism lies in its linguistic orientation. According to analytical phenomenalism, physical objects do not literally consist of sense-data, but are "logical constructions" out of them. In his explication of this puzzling assertion, Ayer formulates the central thesis of analytical phenomenalism: propositions which are usually expressed by sentences referring to physical objects could also be expressed by, reduced to, or translated into statements referring exclusively to sense-data.

In the wake of Ayer's discussion, the claim that statements about physical objects can be reduced to statements about sense-data came to be understood as the claim that the relationship between these two classes of statements is a relationship of logical or analytical equivalence. So, according to analytical phenomenalism, propositions about the physical world are logically equivalent to logically complex propositions about the appropriate sorts of sensory experiences we do, or in a variety of conditions, would have. To assert that a certain physical object exists is just to assert that certain sense-data have been perceived, are being perceived, or would be perceived under certain specifiable circumstances. To solve the problem of the unperceived existence of physical objects the phenomenalist employs the conceptual machinery of subjunctive conditionals, including, of course, counterfactuals. The proposal is that claims about actually unperceived objects are nothing more than useful abbreviations for claims about what experiences or sequences of experience a person would enjoy if certain conditions were fulfilled. The use of subjunctive conditionals, however, presupposes the existence of lawful regularities between patterns of sense-data. Since the phenomenalist program is to fully reduce talk about the physical world to talk about experience, pure laws of experience are needed; laws whose antecedents and consequents must be specifiable solely in terms of sense-data, without reference to any physical objects or processes.

A severe objection to phenomenalism denies that there are such regularities between patterns of sense-data. Surely, the stream of our sensory episodes is not chaotic. We can indeed discover complex uniformities in our sensory histories, but discovering them depends on the conceptual framework of physical things in space and time, which includes a conception of ourselves as persons having a body. The regularities we notice reflect the fact that we live in an environment consisting of such and such physical objects. We have no idea of how to find lawful regularities without relying upon our knowledge of the particular physical and physiological conditions in which our perceptions occur. So what the phenomenalist discovers are object-dependent uniformities, but what he needs are object-independent uniformities. The snag is that the reference to external and internal physical conditions is essential and ineliminable. The sphere of sensory experience does not exhibit an intrinsic order of its own. That is why the grand project of translating sentences about physical objects into sets of sentences about sense-data is doomed to failure. In the end, phenomenalism comes to grief because of its commitment to epistemological atomism. There is no avoiding the basic insight of epistemological holism: single statements about physical objects have no fund of experiential consequences they can call their own. It is only as members of more or less comprehensive systems of statements that they have definite experiential consequences.

V. Epistemic Conceptions of Truth

The fundamental realist conviction that the facts of the world are not bound to be what we take them to be is often expressed as a thesis about the relation between truth and justification: our beliefs about the objective world, even if they were maximally supported by evidence, might still be false. Truth, for the realist, is a radically non-epistemic notion (Putnam 1978: 125), and so the truth of our beliefs about the world is always potentially evidence-transcendent. Truth is one thing, justification another.

Some realists think that the best way to explicate their conception of truth is to embrace a version of the correspondence theory of truth, according to which the truth of a proposition has to be explained in terms of a referential relation to the world. The basic intuition is that a proposition is true just in case there is a fact to which it corresponds, and false just in case it does not correspond to a fact. Advocates of a full-blooded correspondence theory are confronted with the difficult task of spelling out explicitly the relation between the proposition that p and the fact that p by virtue of which the former is made true by the latter.

But, actually, realists need not espouse a detailed form of the correspondence theory of truth. It is also open to them to adopt a version of the so-called deflationary conception of truth, and many contemporary realists do so. The central claim of deflationism is that the various attempts of traditional philosophers to analyze the inner nature of truth were misguided, and thus must be deflated. Truth, on the deflationary account, has no nature. Hence the concept of truth is not a philosophically contentious concept, not a concept that stands for a substantial or robust property. Rather, propositions expressed by sentences of the form "The proposition that p is true" are logically equivalent to the proposition expressed by p itself. Consequently, the whole content of the truth-predicate is given by the totality of appropriate instances of the conceptually fundamental equivalence schema "The proposition that p is true if and only if p."

The important point, for the realist, is that the deflationary perspective shares the idea that the truth of a belief about the world depends on the way the world is, and thus is, in at least a minimal sense, a matter of correspondence or fitting the facts. Truth is, both for the authentic correspondence theorist and for the deflationist, a radically non-epistemic concept, a concept without any conceptual connections to verification, justification, or other epistemic notions. Anti-realists tend to overlook the option of connecting realism with a deflationary account of truth. Commonly, the target of their assaults is the traditional combination of realism with a robust correspondence theory of truth.

The central realist idea, however, that truth is an epistemically unconstrained concept, has quite often been regarded as an entering wedge for a variant of the skeptical challenge. The objection is often raised that if the truth of a belief does not in any way depend on an internal trait of it, such as its epistemic status, but on a relation to something external, on a transcendent fact in the objective world, then the tie between justification and truth is severed. On the realist view, so it is often argued, the criterion of truth and the nature of truth seem to be torn apart, with the disastrous consequence that it becomes impossible to determine whether our beliefs are true. This is supposed to be so because in order to determine whether a belief is true we would have to determine whether it corresponds to a fact. But we cannot compare a belief with reality because there is no direct, conceptually unmediated grasp of facts or objects which we are simply given to our consciousness. All our epistemic states are conceptually structured and have a propositional content. Thus, in attempting to apprehend the external side of the correspondence relation, we find ourselves with just another belief and so end up comparing a belief with a different belief—even if it is a perceptual belief. We can never get outside the circle of our beliefs to inspect the independent facts that are supposed to make our beliefs true. Hence the principal assumption of epistemological foundationalism, that there is such a thing as verification by confrontation, must be thrown overboard. There are no epistemologically basic beliefs that require no justification or justify themselves.

For many philosophers, an argument along these lines has been the main motive for espousing the coherence theory of justification, according to which justification is solely a matter of internal relations among beliefs. Only beliefs can contribute to the determination of what one can be justified in believing. But a coherence theory of justification alone is not capable of meeting the skeptical challenge. On the contrary, if justification consists in supporting beliefs by other beliefs, whereas truth depends on relations between beliefs and the external world, then the skeptic can ask one of his characteristic questions, namely the question of why even an ideally coherent and comprehensive system of beliefs might not be false about the real world. To establish the required connection between coherence and truth and thereby to avoid skepticism, many philosophers of a verificationist frame of mind—interestingly enough, both logical positivists such as Otto Neurath and Carl G. Hempel and neo-Hegelian absolute idealists such as H. H. Joachim, F. H. Bradley and Brand Blanshard—have combined their coherence theory of justification with the coherence theory of truth (Neurath 1932–33; Hempel 1935; Joachim 1906; Bradley 1914; Blanshard 1939). According to the latter, a belief is true if and only if it is an element of a maximally coherent and maximally comprehensive system of beliefs. In explaining truth in terms of internal coherence, this theory puts forward an epistemic analysis of truth. Any such theory has immense metaphysical consequences. Since the truth-value of a belief is not something that it possesses independently of our capacity to find it out, reality is no longer conceived of as independent of what we may think about it. Rather, reality itself is determined by the coherent system of beliefs.

Many philosophers have proposed epistemic analyses of truth, analyses that attempt to define truth by verifiability, by rational assertibility, by permanent credibility, by superassertibility, or by justifiability under ideal conditions. Obviously, truth cannot simply be identified with justification simpliciter. There are countless beliefs that were once justified for certain persons at certain times, but which later turned out to be false. Justification is tensed and so can be lost. But truth is a stable or permanent property, a property that cannot be lost. So advocates of epistemic accounts had to refine their position. Aware of our fallibility, testified by the enormous changes that have happened in the history of human thought, they came to believe that truth should not be bound to what is justified by present standards. Our present epistemic situation might be imperfect; it might not include all the relevant evidence. Rather, so the improved suggestion goes, truth consists in coherence with the system of beliefs that human investigators will hold at the final stage of inquiry, in the limit of an ideal science which has all relevant evidence at its disposal. So C. S. Peirce famously claimed: "The opinion which is fated to be ultimately agreed to by all who investigate, is what we mean by the truth" (Peirce 1934: 5.407). More recently, Hilary Putnam, during his interim internal realist phase, maintained that truth is an idealization of rational acceptability (Putnam 1981: 55). It should be mentioned, however, that he later abjured any attempt to define truth in epistemic terms (Putnam 1988: 115).

Critics have raised the objection that the ideal justifiability account of truth is circular since its main concept of an epistemically ideal situation ultimately cannot adequately be defined without reference to the concept of truth (Alston 1996: 188–230). Proponents of the epistemic approach to truth have wisely abstained from making any serious attempt to specify what ideal epistemic conditions for a given belief involve, thus preventing the construction of counterexamples in which someone might be ideally justified in holding a false belief. One thing is clear, however: the possibility of error must be ruled out definitely. Hence one might suggest characterizing ideal conditions as conditions in which all relevant sources of error have been identified. But it seems hardly possible to understand this suggestion without a prior grasp of the concept of truth.

Moreover, numerous philosophers hold that there is even a conceptual connection between the very concept of epistemic justification and the concept of truth (Schantz 2007). After all, it is constitutive of justification that it leads to the truth. These philosophers share the view that it is an essential element of the concept of epistemic justification that it is truth conducive. This means that the conditions of justification must be such that satisfying them can guarantee that it is very probable that a particular belief is true. Certainly, manifold attempts have been made to characterize epistemic justification without referring to the concept of truth in any way at all. The decisive point, however, is that those who advocate equating truth and justification under epistemically ideal conditions cannot find support in such attempts to sever the conceptual connection between justification and truth, because their entire argument that truth is nothing other than epistemically ideal justification fails if the concept of justification does not involve truth conducivity. For if the concept of justification does not even include a guarantee of the probability that a statement is true, it is obvious that a belief, regardless of how ideally justified it might be, can nonetheless be false.

VI. Final Remarks

Neither the various foundationalist and reductionist enterprises of phenomenalism nor the attempts, rooted in the coherence theory of truth, to refashion the concept of truth in epistemic terms provide us with really persuasive responses to the threat of skepticism. The serious problem with anti-realist positions is that they are prepared to make too large concessions to skepticism. After all, they agree with the skeptic that our ordinary conception of knowledge of an objective world must be given up. The knowledge they rescue is no longer knowledge of genuine worldly facts but, ultimately, merely knowledge of subjective or internal facts.

Natural realism with its central assumption that the world is independent of the existence of sentient beings is hard to shake. There were stars long before there were people having thoughts about them, there would have been stars even if no intelligent beings had ever evolved, and there will be stars long after we have disappeared from the scene. Such facts do not seem to depend on what anyone believes or under certain circumstances would believe. On the other hand, realism seems to open the door to skepticism. But is this really true? We must guard against an influential confusion, the confusion of the omnipresent possibility of error with the threat of radical skepticism. Clearly, human beings are prone to error in their judgments about what is the case. Even our most successful scientific theories had to be abandoned in the light of new discoveries. Hence we ought to appreciate the basic insight of fallibilism that the possibility of error can never be ruled out entirely. We have to make allowance for corrigibility. But fallibilism must be sharply distinguished from radical skepticism. It is one thing to hold that any of our beliefs might involve error; it is another to hold that none of our beliefs is justified at all.

References

Alston, W. (1996) *A Realist Conception of Truth*, Ithaca: Cornell University Press
Ayer, A. (1940) *The Foundations of Empirical Knowledge*, London: Macmillan
Blanshard, B. (1939) *The Nature of Thought*, 2 vols., London: Allen & Unwin
Bradley, F. H. (1914) *Essays on Truth and Reality*, Oxford: Oxford University Press
Davidson, D. (1986) "A Coherence Theory of Truth and Knowledge," in E. LePore (ed.) *Truth and Interpretation. Perspectives on the Philosophy of Donald Davidson*, Oxford: Blackwell, 307–319
Devitt, M. (1984) *Realism and Truth*, Oxford: Blackwell
Hempel, C. G. (1935) "On the Logical Positivists' Theory of Truth," *Analysis* 2, 50–59
Jackson, F. (1977) *Perception. A Representative Theory*, Cambridge: Cambridge University Press
Joachim, H. H. (1906) *The Nature of Truth*, Oxford: Oxford University Press
McDowell, J. (1994) *Mind and World*, Cambridge, MA: Harvard University Press
Mill, J. S. (1865) *An Examination of Sir William Hamilton's Philosophy*, London: Longmans et al.
Nagel. T. (1986) *The View from Nowhere*, Oxford: Oxford University Press
Neurath, O. (1932–3) "Protocol Sentences," *Erkenntnis* 3, 204–214
Peirce, C. S. (1934) *Collected Papers* vol. 5, Cambridge, MA: Harvard University Press, 1958
Putnam, H. (1978) *Meaning and the Moral Sciences*, London: Routledge
—— (1981) *Reason, Truth, and History*, Cambridge: Cambridge University Press
—— (1988) *Representation and Reality*, Cambridge, MA: Harvard University Press
Schantz, R. (2007) "Why Truth is not an Epistemic Concept," in D. Greimann and G. Siegwart (eds.), *Truth and Speech Acts*, London: Routledge, 307–320
Stroud, B. (1984) *The Significance of Philosophical Scepticism*, Oxford: Oxford University Press
Williams, B. (1978) *Descartes: The Project of Pure Enquiry*, Harmondsworth: Pelican

45
SKEPTICISM AND EPISTEMIC EXTERNALISM
Richard Fumerton

The internalism/externalism debate occupies center stage in contemporary epistemology. While externalists offer a number of different arguments in support of their approach to understanding epistemic concepts, an important advantage they often claim for their views is that they can avoid classical arguments for skepticism. In what follows, I will not be primarily concerned with evaluating the general plausibility of externalism. Instead, I will examine how, if at all, externalists can occupy a high ground in the battle against the skeptic.

Kinds of Skepticism

Let us begin by distinguishing different kinds of skepticism. In the first place we should distinguish skepticism concerning *knowledge* from skepticism concerning *justification*. We should also distinguish *global* skepticism from what we might call *local* skepticisms. The global skeptic concerning knowledge asserts that we don't (some would say can't) know anything. Local skeptics concerning knowledge claim only that we don't or can't have knowledge concerning certain classes of propositions, such as propositions describing the past. The global skeptic concerning knowledge is committed to the slightly awkward view that we don't or can't know even that global skepticism is true, but that skeptic can consistently claim to have good reason to believe that the view is true.

The *global* skeptic concerning justified belief claims that we have no *epistemic* justification for believing anything. (There might be reasons other than epistemic reasons, such as practical reasons, but unless I indicate otherwise you should always construe the reasons or justification I describe as epistemic.) The *local* skeptic concerning justified belief claims that we have no justification for believing certain classes of proposition. There have been very few global skeptics concerning justification. Such skeptics would be committed to the very odd view that they have no justification at all for believing that their view is true, and one would surely wonder why, realizing that, they bother to assert it.

It would, however, be a mistake to dismiss for this reason the philosophical interest of arguments for global skepticism concerning justified belief. The skeptic's target might be in the equally awkward position of *believing* the premises of a deductively valid argument for global skepticism. And the fact that the conclusion of the argument entails that we don't have any reason to believe those premises still leaves the proponent of commonsense in a quandary. Put another way (as Duncan Pritchard once suggested to me), an argument for global skepticism could still be interesting by presenting us with a paradox. When Zeno presents an argument for the conclusion that we can't move through space, philosophers often find the argument interesting and important despite the fact that they don't, of course, believe the conclusion. Rejecting the conclusion doesn't tell them which premises or reasoning to reject, and until we figure that out we are philosophically unsatisfied. Still, I do think that there are very few global skeptics concerning the possibility of justified belief. There are, however, many very interesting versions of *local* skepticism concerning justified belief, some of which present a formidable challenge to commonsense.

In what follows I focus on local skepticism concerning justification for believing various propositions endorsed by commonsense. It is here, I think, that paradigmatic externalists are best positioned to argue that they have a dialectical advantage over traditional internalists in turning back the skeptical challenge. Many skeptical arguments against the possibility of knowledge threaten externalists just as much as they threaten internalists. The reason is that many of those arguments employ closure principles to argue for incredibly high standards of justification for knowledge. We claim to know some commonsense proposition P, but are uncomfortable claiming to know some other proposition Q that is entailed by P. I claim to know, for example, that I will be in France this summer, but feel uncomfortable claiming to know that I won't die in a car accident this spring. But if I know that P entails Q and acknowledge that I don't know that Q, then I should feel uncomfortable, the argument goes, in claiming to know that P. There are all sorts of moves and countermoves made in response to these sorts of arguments, but many of them cut across the internalism/externalism divide. A reliabilist endorsing the view that knowledge requires justified belief, but who allows that the justification in question need not guarantee the truth of what is believed can probably join forces with traditional internalists in trying to figure out how to respond to closure arguments against the possibility of knowledge. In any event, I have always thought that the concept of justification is of far more interest to epistemology. On one (to be sure controversial) view, the factors that turn justified belief into knowledge are matters beyond our epistemic control. Knowledge requires the world to co-operate in various ways. The best we can do is make sure that our beliefs are epistemically rational. If other factors conspire to deprive us of knowledge, then we are simply unlucky.

The Structure of Skeptical Arguments

As Ayer (1956) pointed out, many skeptical arguments for local justification skepticism have a common structure. The skeptic's first step is typically to convince us that the beliefs under skeptical attack are not noninferentially justified. The next step is to drive a logical wedge between the best possible evidence we can have for believing the propositions under attack and the truth of those propositions. Put another way, the skeptic argues that we cannot deduce the relevant propositions from the best available evidence. The skeptic then claims that there are no plausible nondeductive principles of reasoning that will sanction the relevant inference. So consider the following skeptical argument against the possibility of having justified belief about past experience (and to avoid raising the problem of perception, suppose we restrict the content of the memory belief to past subjective experience):

1m) Beliefs about past experience are not noninferentially justified.
2m) The best evidence I can have for believing that I had some experience this morning is that I seem to remember having had the experience, and to justifiably believe that I did have the experience I must be in a position to justifiably *infer* that proposition from what I seem to remember.
3m) To justifiably infer some proposition P from another proposition E, I must be in a position to see that E makes probable P (where E's entailing P can be viewed as the upper limit of E's making probable P).
4m) I know that what I seem to remember doesn't entail any proposition about the past.
5m) I can't inductively establish that apparent memory is a reliable indicator of past events—I would have to rely on memory to establish the relevant correlations.
6m) There is no other way to establish the reliability of apparent memory as an indicator of past events.

Therefore,

7m) I have no justification for believing any proposition about past experience.

Or consider the following familiar argument for skepticism with respect to justified belief about the external world:

1e) I am never noninferentially justified in believing any contingent proposition describing the existence of a physical object.
2e) The best evidence I can possibly have for the existence of anything physical are truths describing my sensations (what I seem to see, feel, hear, smell, and taste), and to justifiably believe that there is, for example, a table before me now, I must be in a position to justifiably infer that proposition from what I seem to perceive.
3e) To justifiably infer some proposition P from another E, I must be in a position to see that E makes probable P (where E's entailing P can be viewed as the upper limit of E's making probable P).
4e) I know that no proposition that describes only subjective experience entails the truth of any proposition asserting the existence of a physical object.
5e) I can't inductively establish that my sensations are a reliable indicator of the presence of physical objects—while I can correlate sensations with sensations perhaps, I can't correlate sensations with physical objects.
6e) There is no other way to establish that sensation is a reliable indicator of physical reality.

Therefore,

7e) I have no justification for believing any propositions describing physical reality.

Each of the premises can, of course, be challenged. As we shall see below, premises (1), (2), (3), (5), and (6) of both arguments might well be challenged by most contemporary versions of externalism.

The Internalism/Externalism Debate

Before we examine externalist responses to traditional skeptical arguments we should pause to say a few words about the internalism/externalism controversy (cf. Fumerton 1995: Chapter 3). There is, unfortunately, no one way that the controversy has been understood by contemporary epistemologists. We can distinguish all of the following versions of internalism and define corresponding versions of externalism in terms of their rejections of the relevant internalist thesis.

Internal State Internalism

The very label "internalism" suggests what is, perhaps, the most natural way of understanding the internalist's thesis. The *internal state internalist* claims that the justification one has for believing a given proposition is fully determined by the internal states of the believer. The strongest, and most common, way of understanding this claim is that in all possible worlds your internal twins have precisely the same justification you have for believing, disbelieving, and withholding belief in various propositions. In its most plausible form, I believe, the claim should be restricted to the propositional justification there is for someone to believe a given proposition (in contrast to a claim about what the person justifiably believes, where the latter might involve basing one's belief on the appropriate justification available, a relation that, in turn, might involve a belief's having the appropriate causal origin). The externalist who rejects internal state internalism is convinced that we must look beyond the internal states of a believer to find the source of justification, if any, enjoyed by a given belief. The causal history of a belief, for example, is often thought by externalists to be critical.

While the view might seem relatively straightforward, it is no small feat to define clearly the relevant concept of an internal state. So, for example, if properties are universals and one can be acquainted in thought with a universal, shall we understand being acquainted with a universal as an internal state? If we presuppose an understanding of self or mind, we might, for present purposes, construe internal states as nonrelational properties of the self along with introspective awareness of such properties and also, if there is such a thing, acquaintance "in thought" with abstract entities such as universals, numbers, logical relations, and the like.

Access Internalisms

Perhaps because there has been a long tradition associating states of mind with states to which we have a privileged introspective access, a great many self-proclaimed internalists explain their internalism in terms of access requirements for justification. We can distinguish among others the following views. *Actual Access Internalism* advances the very strong thesis that a condition J constitutes S's justification for believing P only if S has direct access to the fact that J obtains and is justification for S to believe P. *Potential Access Internalism* requires only that S be able to (when possessing requisite concepts) access directly the fact that J obtains and is justification for believing P. The ability in question can be understood in different ways, as can the access. Where J is a mental state, the access in question is typically taken to be introspective and its status as justifier is taken to be knowable a priori.

I have argued elsewhere (Fumerton 1995) that one should be very careful before accepting access requirements on justification, even if one is an internal state internalist.

Problematic regress is extremely difficult to avoid on most versions of access internalism—even those that insist only on potential access.

Inferential Internalism

Of special interest to us here is a view that I have called inferential internalism. The inferential internalist insists on the following principle governing inferential justification:

(PIJ) There is justification for S to believe one proposition P on the basis of another proposition E only if (1) there is justification for S to believe E, and (2) there is justification for S to believe that E makes probable P (where entailment can be viewed as the upper limit of making probable).

Almost all foundationalists, internalist and externalist alike, accept the first clause of the principle, but externalists of all stripes will typically deny the second. As the skeptical arguments presented above suggest, the skeptic traditionally presupposed both clauses of (PIJ), and the externalist's rejection of the second clause helps enormously in the fight to deflect the force of the skeptic's challenge.

Externalist Responses to Traditional Skeptical Arguments

I suggested earlier that externalists will often claim that it is an advantage of their view that they can respond effectively to the skeptical challenge. And certainly on the face of it this claim is plausible. It's a bit difficult to discuss the issue, however, given that there are a number of quite different versions of externalism. Let's proceed by looking at a sampling of externalist responses to each of the controversial premises of the skeptical arguments sketched above.

Premises (1m) and (1e) deny that we have noninferential justification for believing propositions describing past experiences and the external world, respectively. Arguments for this position typically presuppose some version of internalism. So on the view I find plausible, for example, one has noninferential justification for believing some proposition P when one is directly acquainted with the truthmaker for P while one is directly acquainted with the correspondence between one's thought that P and that truthmaker. I have also argued that one might be able to gain noninferential justification for believing falsely that P when one is directly acquainted with a fact *very* similar to the truthmaker for P. On such a view one can establish that one lacks noninferential justification for believing truths about the past or truths about the external world if one can establish that one is never directly acquainted with the relevant truthmakers for such truths. And the following arguments seem persuasive to the acquaintance theorist:

1) In nonveridical memory, we can seem to remember having had an experience in such a way that we possess the very same justification for believing that truth about the past that we would have had were we veridically remembering that experience.
2) The justification we have in the nonveridical case is obviously not direct acquaintance with a past experience—by hypothesis the past experience didn't occur.

Therefore,

3) The justification we have in the veridical case (the same *kind* of justification) is not direct acquaintance with past experience either.

The familiar argument against epistemological direct realism is run the same way:

1) In nonveridical experience, we can seem to experience a physical object in such a way that the relevant appearance gives us the very same justification we would have had were we veridically seeing a physical object.
2) The justification we have in the nonveridical case is obviously not direct acquaintance with a physical object—by hypothesis the physical object doesn't exist.

Therefore,

3) The justification we have in the veridical case (the same kind of justification) is not direct acquaintance with a physical object either.

Both arguments have enormous appeal, at least for the philosopher who endorses the relevant account of noninferential justification. To be sure one can still advance the so-called disjunctivist hypothesis that the justificatory states in the "good" and the "bad" cases should receive a quite different ontological analysis, but the phenomenological indistinguishability of the "good" and the "bad" cases puts enormous pressure on the plausibility of such a view. But at least some externalists needn't go the disjunctivist route.

Consider, for example, standard process reliabilism. And let's use as our model the original formulation of the view suggested by Goldman (1979). According to Goldman a belief is noninferentially justified when it is produced by a belief-independent, unconditionally reliable belief-producing process. A belief-producing process is belief-independent when it takes as its input something other than another belief. (To accommodate noninferential introspective knowledge of what one believes, one should modify this to allow a belief-independent process to take as input a belief when the justificatory status of the belief is irrelevant to the output belief—in this case a metabelief). A process is unconditionally reliable in virtue of the fact that its output beliefs are usually true (we don't have to make the reliability that defines justification a reliability that is conditional on the truth of input beliefs). To avoid obvious counterexamples, reliabilists will almost always turn from actual frequency to something like counterfactual frequencies in defining reliability.

Despite the fact that we sometimes misremember and misperceive, it seems obvious that we *could* live in a world in which both beliefs about experience relying on apparent memory about past experience and perceptually based beliefs result from unconditionally, generally reliable processes. And if they do then premises (1m) and (1e) of the skeptic's argument will be false. A great deal depends, of course, on how the reliabilist handles the well-known generality problem for reliabilism. Painting with a broad stroke, the problem is just this. It seems that we can characterize relevant belief-producing processes in any number of different ways. Moreover, the reliabilist will probably want to relativize the relevant reliability that defines the epistemic status of a belief to a given kind of environment, and the relevant kind of environment can be characterized in any number of different ways. So when I reach the conclusion that there is a dog in front of me, I can characterize the belief as resulting from visual experience, resulting from visual experience under ideal conditions of perception, resulting from visual experience when I am completely inebriated, resulting from visual experience with background familiarity with various sorts of dogs, and so on. Still, however we characterize the relevant belief-producing process in trying to solve the generality problem, there seems to be no a priori objection to the possibility of the process being both belief-independent and unconditionally reliable (though there might be good empirical reason to reject the supposition that the process really is belief-independent).

Of course, the reliabilist hasn't yet given us a reason to believe that the relevant premises of the skeptical argument are false, but we are in a position to reject the traditional foundationalist's argument *for* the truth of the premises. That argument presupposed that the truthmaker for a noninferentially justified belief, or at least something very close to the truthmaker for a noninferentially justified belief would enter any plausible story about what makes the belief noninferentially justified. And our reliabilist (like some other internalists—for example, philosophers who take mere belief or seeming to have evidential weight) is straightforwardly rejecting that presupposition. Noninferentially justified beliefs on a reliabilist's view can be just barely more likely to be true than false.

While a reliabilist is in a position to reject premises (1m) and (1e) of the skeptical arguments, other externalists hold views that are similarly positioned to reject the critical premises, but for different reasons. The arguments against the existence of noninferential justification for believing propositions about the past and the external world both critically claim that we have the *same* justification for believing such propositions in the veridical cases that we have in the phenomenologically indistinguishable nonveridical counterparts. As we saw above, the reliabilist can grant that claim but argue that it is compatible with our having noninferential justification in both the "good" and the "bad" cases. Other externalists will allow that the justification is importantly different but that it is, nevertheless, noninferential in the "good" case. Consider, for example, an externalist who gives a causal account of direct (noninferential) knowledge (and with that knowledge, justified belief). The crudest of such views will allow that one has direct knowledge of P when the fact that P is causally responsible for the belief that P, where the causal chain leading from the fact that P to the belief that P contains no belief states as intermediate links. In veridical memory, the belief P about the past is, arguably, caused in this way by the fact that P. The apparent memory and the belief it induces obviously aren't caused in this way by the fact that P. So this externalist will claim noninferential status for the belief that P in the veridical case and deny it in the nonveridical case. And, of course, exactly the same sort of move can be made for perception.

Timothy Williamson (2000) is another philosopher who will deny the claim that we have the same justification in both "good" and "bad" cases. While much of the tradition has tried to explain knowledge in terms of allegedly more fundamental epistemic concepts such as justification and evidence, Williamson suggests a dramatic alternative to this way of thinking. His idea is that we should explain evidence in terms of what he takes to be the more fundamental concept of knowledge. He suggests, in effect, that we should *identify* our evidence with those propositions we know to be true. We can then talk about justified belief that falls short of knowledge in terms of the probability various propositions have for us relative to the evidence we possess. Famously, Williamson refuses to provide an analysis of knowledge (though he is willing to identify various conditions that are necessary for one to know a given proposition). In any event, Williamson will claim that (veridically) remembering that P just is a *species* of knowledge, and that seeing that P is another species of knowledge. In veridical memory and perception our evidence base includes the truths remembered and perceived. There is no corresponding truth in the case of what I have been calling apparent memory and apparent perception, so, trivially, we don't have the same evidence in the veridical and the nonveridical cases. Williamson's view is clearly a version of epistemic externalism. The conditions that constitute one's having a justified belief include the conditions that constitute knowledge. Knowledge requires the truth of what is believed and since he thinks that we know truths about the past and the external world, it is at least sometimes true that the factors that make a given belief justified include facts that lie outside of us.

There is no real distinction between inferential and noninferential knowledge on Williamson's view. The "foundation" relative to which we assess various probabilities is the entirety of what we know. So, like the causal theorist, Williamson will deny that we have the same justification in the good and bad cases, and, as we have seen, he is in a position to deny premises (2m) and (2e) of the skeptic's argument. He will reject the skeptic's retreat to apparent memory and appearance as more secure foundational truths from which we must infer truths about the past and the external world, respectively. Given that he thinks we know that the past experience occurred in the case of veridical memory or that the external object exists in the case of veridical perception—indeed that actually remembering that and actually perceiving that are just species of knowledge, the probability of these respective propositions known relative to our evidence is, trivially, 1. In the nonveridical case the probability of those same propositions is far less than 1—it is whatever such probabilities are relative to known propositions about apparent memory and mere appearance. Of course, given that some of the propositions Williamson claims we know seem obviously more (epistemically) certain than others, one might well take this consequence of Williamson's view to be a reductio of it. Traditional foundationalists have a much more narrow conception of foundational knowledge. They are positioned to claim that probability is always probability relative to *foundational* knowledge.

The externalists we discussed above might feel no need to proceed to an examination of premises (3m) and (3e) of our sample skeptical arguments since they might reject the premise that we lack noninferential justification for believing the propositions under skeptical attack. Indeed, I have argued elsewhere that most externalists are committed to the view that there is no a priori restriction on the range of propositions for which we have noninferential justification. To the chagrin of many externalists, Plantinga (2000) is quite correct in suggesting that there is nothing internally inconsistent in the supposition that we have noninferential justification for believing that God exists. Still, it is worth remembering that there is also nothing in the externalist's account of justification that *requires* them to view the propositions under skeptical attack as noninferentially justified. Indeed, in the case of perceptually produced beliefs it seems to me that it is almost bizarre to suppose that the belief-producing process is belief-independent. If anything seems obvious to me it is that commonplace beliefs about our physical surroundings carry with them a host of (causally operative) background assumptions about conditions of perception—some of them extremely complicated. To be sure these background beliefs might not rise to the level of occurrent beliefs of which we are conscious, but there is no reason to reject the possibility of dispositional beliefs being processed as input where that processing results in a torrential output of beliefs about our environment. So it is still worth looking at how an externalist would respond to premises (3m) and (3e) through (6m) and (6e) of the skeptic's argument.

The first thing to note is that premises (3m) and (3e) of our sample skeptic's argument will be rejected by all of those externalists (and internalists, for that matter) who reject the second clause of the principle of inferential justification. And virtually all externalists reject the principle. As I suggested earlier, I think that all of the historically important skeptics just took the principle for granted. Unless you "see" the connection between your evidence and that which you infer from your evidence, you are hardly in a position to gain justification through the inference. At least this is true for *ideal* justification—the kind of justification that the philosopher seeks in order to gain assurance of the truth. To be sure, we might allow that there is something good about a belief that is caused by justified beliefs in propositions that do in fact support a given conclusion, and I have argued elsewhere (Fumerton 2004a) that one might well allow for derivate concepts of degenerate justification. But even in the case of deductively valid inference it doesn't take a whole lot of argument to convince many that one is in a better position vis à vis believing in an epistemically ideal way the conclusion of the argument if one sees that the premises do entail the conclusion (Fumerton 2004b). In any event, paradigmatic externalists will quite unapologetically reject any view about inferential justification that requires for inferential justification anything as strong as the conditions laid down by the inferential internalist. It is enough, the reliabilist will argue, that the inferential process resulting in belief be appropriately conditionally reliable. It is enough the causal theorist might argue that belief in the proposition inferred be caused by a chain of reasoning that leads all of the way from the truthmaker for the belief to the belief (though the causal theorists will have their hands full dealing with counterexamples involving so-called deviant causal chains). It is enough for justified belief that P, Williamson might argue, that the conditional probability of P on your evidence E is high. Premises (4m) through (6m), and (4e) through (6e) could be true in our sample skeptical arguments, but their truth doesn't prevent you from possessing inferential justification even on the assumption that the justification in question is inferential.

Moving Up a Level

Even if the externalists were right in arguing that the truth of their metaepistemological account involves rejecting the skeptic's demands on both noninferential justification and inferential justification, many wonder if skeptical problems won't simply reappear at another level. Perhaps, the argument goes, we have justified beliefs as the externalist understands justification, but without good reason to believe that our beliefs are justified, won't we be in the unsatisfying position of having to admit that we should be silent on the question of whether or not our beliefs are justified (assuming that a minimal norm for acceptable assertion in this sort of context is that one have good reason to believe what one asserts)? And externalists seem to be anything but silent on that question. They seem to assert with an odd sort of subjective certainty that most of the commonsense beliefs we find ourselves inclined to form are indeed justified. Externalists often accuse internalists of confusing conditions necessary for having second-level justification that we have justified beliefs with conditions necessary for having first-level justified beliefs. But again, even if that were true, the philosophically inclined will surely want some reason to believe that we have justified beliefs.

As it turns out, on most externalist analyses it won't be much more difficult to get metajustification than it will be to get justification. Consider again the reliabilist's account of justification. And assume for this discussion that our reliabilist has conceded that there is such a thing as apparent memory and that there is a belief-producing process that takes as input these apparent memories and generates beliefs about past experience. What could get me justification for believing that I have justification for believing various propositions about the past? Well, according to the reliabilist, for beliefs about the past to be justified the process that yields them needs to be reliable. For a belief that these beliefs are justified to be justified there must be some reliable way of reaching the conclusion that the relevant beliefs are reliably produced. Now *if* memory is reliable and induction is reliable, then we are in business with what some call a track record argument. I seem to remember seeming to remember P while I also seem to remember P. Relying on apparent memory I conclude that I seemed to remember P when P. I seem to remember seeming to remember Q while I also seem to remember Q. Relying on apparent memory again, I infer that I seemed to remember Q when Q. I do this again and again with different memories, and eventually conclude on the basis of massive success in relying on memory to reach true conclusions about the past that memory is indeed reliable. That wasn't hard! While we are at it, we might as well use memory, induction, and perception to justify our belief that beliefs resulting from sense experience are reliably produced. I seem to see a table and conclude that there is a table there. I seem to see a tree and conclude that there is a tree there. I seem to see a dog and conclude that there is a dog there. I seem to remember all these successful beliefs produced by sense experience, and conclude that experientially produced beliefs are usually true. That wasn't hard either!

Indeed on the reliabilist's view, it isn't hard to get second-level justification for believing that one has first-level justified beliefs *provided that* we have the first-level justification the reliabilist thinks we have. Things can, of course, not go well. As memory begins to fade, I might find myself seeming to remember many occasions on which I reached false conclusions relying on memory. But absent the kind of situation in which a faculty turns on itself, getting justification for believing that the faculty is reliable is easy. So easy that many philosophers get a bit nervous. I have argued elsewhere (Fumerton 1995: Chapter 6) that the reliabilists' commitment to the legitimacy of track record arguments of this kind for the reliability of belief-producing process is, in effect, a reductio of their account of justified beliefs. Can we really rely on memory to justify our belief that memory is reliable? Can we rely on perception to justify our belief that perception is reliable? We would find it comical if an astrologer tried to assure us of the legitimacy of astrological reasoning by claiming to read in the stars that astrology is legitimate. We would find it comical if a tea leaf reader relied on tea leaf reading to assure us that tea leaf reading is a reliable way of making predictions. Isn't there something equally problematic about our reliabilist using the very process the reliability of which we are trying to establish in order to get philosophically respectable justification that the process is reliable?

Peter Markie (2005) has argued that we can alleviate at least some of the initial concern we might have with what Cohen (2002) has called the problem of easy knowledge, by making a distinction between what will get us justification and what we can permissibly do in the context of arguing. There are rules, Markie argues, governing the practice of argument. One of those rules is that one can't beg the question against one's opponent. One begs the question when one "too obviously" presupposes the truth of one's conclusion or the legitimacy of one's reasoning when that is the very topic under dispute. The skeptic who denies the legitimacy of reliance on memory will quite correctly characterize as objectionably question-begging any argument that presupposes the reliability of memory. But even if that were true, Markie argues, it doesn't prevent us from acquiring the metalevel justification in the way described above.

While Markie's suggestion is intriguing, one can't help but wonder if the distinction doesn't collapse at least in the context of philosophical reflection. As epistemologists, when we think about the question of whether a given way of forming belief is epistemically legitimate, we want to convince ourselves of the truth—we want to gain philosophical assurance. And in that context it is hard to see how we can gain the assurance we want with an argument that presupposes the very truth of that about which we were intellectually curious.

I focused above on how the reliabilist might appeal to track record reasoning to secure justified belief that we have justified belief. Other externalists might proceed differently. But by and large the story will be similar. One exception might be Williamson. It's hard to know how he would think of justified belief about justified belief. On his view what we are justified in believing is always a function of what is probable relative to our evidence. And that is defined in terms of probability relative to what we know. Because we don't get an analysis of knowledge it's hard for me to tell how he figures out when we know and when we don't know. Despite the fact that he doesn't embrace a causal theory of knowing, he seems to me only really comfortable ascribing knowledge to people when there is a causal link between the truthmaker for a belief and the belief. I'm not sure, therefore, whether he thinks we can get knowledge of general truths when our only means of discovering them is enumerative induction. Still I'm quite confident that he thinks we can know propositions about the past and that we can have introspective knowledge that we seemed to remember many of these truths about the past. So we would still have available as evidence premises we could use in an inductive justification for the proposition that memory is reliable. Put another way, the proposition would presumably be probable relative to what we know, and we could presumably know that it is probable relative to what we know as long as we could know the relevant principle of probability. As I said, I don't really know how Williamson decides what we do and don't know, but I imagine he thinks that the relevant truths about relative probability are among the things we know.

Summary

The majority of epistemologists agree with Chisholm's (1966: Chapter 4) suggestion that we must choose at the outset whether or not to take skepticism seriously. The implication of Chisholm's view is that we should simply make whatever adjustments are necessary to our epistemology in order to avoid skepticism with respect to ordinary, commonplace claims about the world around us. Externalism clearly has advantages in allowing for the possibility of justified belief.

It has always seemed to me that philosophers show a bit of hubris in assuming that their desire for intellectually satisfying justification will be met. And one can't help but wonder if the externalists haven't simply changed the subject matter of epistemology in their zeal to avoid the skeptic's arguments. Earlier, I argued that if paradigmatic externalist analyses of epistemic concepts were correct, it wouldn't be much more difficult to get metajustification for believing that one has justified beliefs than it would be to have first-level justification. But even many externalists will sometimes betray uneasiness about this implication of their views when they retreat to more modest characterizations of their positions. For example, it is so very tempting for the reliabilist to claim only that *if* various belief-producing processes are reliable then our commonsense beliefs are justified. And *if* those same belief-producing processes are reliable then we will have metajustification for believing that we have justified beliefs. But as philosophers, of course, we want justification for believing more than the conditional statement. When the externalists trot out something like a track record argument to justify their belief that we have all sorts of justified beliefs, many of us can't help but ask again how we can tell that the relevant processes are, in fact, reliable. We'll probably just get another track record argument that will net us meta-metajustification, but we won't feel that we are getting any closer to the kind of philosophical assurance we sought when we asked the question about metajustification, or, for that matter, when we sought first-level justification.

It therefore strikes many internalists that the externalist is content to rely on a kind of faith in the reliability of at least our most basic ways of forming beliefs. And the most plausible definition of faith is belief without justification.

References

Ayer, A. J. 1956. *The Problem of Knowledge*. Edinburgh: Penguin.
Chisholm, Roderick. 1966. *The Problem of Knowledge*. Englewood Cliffs, NJ: Prentice Hall.
Cohen, Stewart. 2002. "Basic Knowledge and the Problem of Easy Knowledge," *Philosophy and Phenomenological Research*, 65: 309–29.
Fumerton, Richard. 1995. *Metaepistemology and Skepticism*. Totowa, NJ: Rowman and Littlefield.
—— 2004a "Achieving Epistemic Ascent," in *Sosa and his Critics*, Blackwell, 2004, 72–85.
——2004b "Epistemic Probability," *Philosophical Issues*, 14: 149–64.
Goldman, Alvin (1979). "What is Justified Belief?" in *Justification and Knowledge*, ed. George Pappas. Dordrecht.
Markie, Peter. 2005. "Easy Knowledge," *Philosophy and Phenomenological Research*, 70: 406–16.
Plantinga, Alvin. 2000. *Warranted Christian Belief*. Oxford: Oxford University Press.
Williamson, Timothy. 2000. *Knowledge and Its Limits*. Oxford: Oxford University Press.

46
SKEPTICISM AND SEMANTIC EXTERNALISM
Anthony Brueckner

The Cartesian Skeptical Argument

In Meditation I, Descartes had us consider a world in which my mind exists just as it actually is and yet no physical things exist. In this world, another mind, God-like in its power, causes me to have my experiences: this is the *malin genie*, the Evil Genius. Let us consider an updated version of the skeptical concerns that Descartes raised via the Evil Genius (Descartes 1996). Imagine a living brain floating in a vat of nutrient fluids while attached to a supercomputer. The computer is programmed to provide electrical stimuli to the brain that are just like those a normal brain receives due to input to the sense-organs connected to the normal brain. As a result, the brain in a vat is caused to have experiences just like those of a normal human. The brain in a vat, we are to imagine, is the subject of conscious mental life just like that of a normal human: experience, thought, belief, desire, intention, and so on. Upon having various experiences, the brain in a vat thinks, "The waves are breaking nicely here on Sands Beach in Santa Barbara." Imagine that the brain in a vat is a mental twin of you: whenever you have an experience of seeing sand and surf, the brain in a vat has an exactly similar experience. When you think, "The sand is hot, and the surf is big," the brain thinks, "The sand is hot, and the surf is big." According to the Cartesian philosopher, the brain in a vat is massively mistaken about his world. He believes that he is sitting on a beach, for example, even though he is not. He cannot *sit* anywhere.

You might ask: in the imagined vat scenario, what is the explanation for the envatted brain's predicament? On one version of the thought experiment, we are to imagine a normal human who is kidnapped by evil neuroscientists who relieve him of his brain in order to test the deceptive powers of their supercomputer's brain-manipulating program. (This is similar to the situation depicted in the movie *The Matrix*.) On a different version of the thought experiment (due to Hilary Putnam), we are to imagine that the brain has always been envatted; there are no evil neuroscientists; there are no trees or beaches in the vat world; there is nothing but the brain in its vat in a room with the supercomputer; and this arrangement has come about as a result of some cosmic accident (Putnam 1981). We will call this special Putnamian brain in a vat a BIV. The immaterial Evil Genius, as the cause of my experiences, plays a role in Descartes' thought experiment that parallels that of the supercomputer in the BIV scenario. From now on, let SK stand for the proposition that I am a BIV.

After having sketched the BIV hypothesis SK, the skeptic issues a challenge: can I rule out the possibility described in the hypothesis? Do I know that the hypothesis SK is false? The skeptic now argues as follows. Choose any target proposition P concerning the external world which I think I know to be true (for example, the proposition that I am sitting at a computer). Here is the now-standard formulation of the Cartesian skeptical argument:

(1) If I know that P, then I know that ~SK.
(2) I do not know that ~SK.

So,

(3) I do not know that P.

Premise (1) is backed by the principle that *knowledge is closed under known entailment*:

(CL) For all S,α,β: If S knows that α, and S knows that α entails β, then S knows that β.

Since I know that P entails that ~SK, by (CL) I know that P only if I know its entailed consequence: ~SK. Premise (2) is backed by the consideration that my experiences do not allow me to discriminate between the hypothesis that ~SK (I am *not* a BIV but, rather, a normal human) and the hypothesis that SK (I *am* a BIV). My experience would be the same regardless of which hypothesis were true. So I do not know that ~SK.

Putnam's Semantic Externalism

Let us now consider a response to the skeptical argument that employs some ideas that derive from the work of Putnam (Putnam 1981; Brueckner 1986, 1992, 2003). Imagine that a Martian looks at a paint blob that causes him to form a mental image that exactly resembles my mental image of a palm tree. Imagine that the Martian has had no causal contact with trees and no causal contact with anyone who has had causal contact with trees. My image is an image *of* a palm tree; it *represents* and *refers to* palm trees. But even though the Martian's image exactly resembles mine, his image does not have the foregoing *semantic* features of aboutness, representation, and reference. Putnam's intuition is that there is a causal constraint on such semantic features that is not satisfied by the Martian's image.

We are assuming that the BIV has a language that he uses in thinking, believing, wondering, and so on. The BIV never speaks or writes, of course, but he has a rich mental life that involves use of his language. The BIV's language is superficially just like English (recall that we imagined him to be my mental twin, though, as we will shortly see, this cannot be quite right). For example, whenever I think a thought using the sentence "That is a palm tree," my BIV twin thinks a thought using that sentence. But what do the BIV's words "palm tree" refer to? Given the foregoing considerations concerning the Martian's image, Putnam maintains that the BIV's "palm tree" does not refer to palm trees, just as the Martian's image does not refer to or represent palm trees. This is because the causal constraint on reference is not satisfied by the BIV's words "palm tree" and palm trees. That is, there are no palm trees in the vat world to serve as referents for his words "palm tree"; the BIV never has any causal contact—direct or indirect—with palm trees, and thus his words do not refer to palm trees. What do those words refer to, then? One answer that is suggested by Putnam is as follows. Find the entities in the vat world that play a causal role vis à vis the BIV's uses of "palm tree" that is analogous to the causal role that palm trees play vis à vis a normal English speaker's uses of "palm tree." The best candidates for such entities are the recurring computer program features that cause electrical stimuli in the brain, which stimuli, in turn, produce experiences just like those that are produced in normal humans as a result of seeing palm trees. Call these *PT program features*.

So, on this view, the BIV's words "palm tree" differ in their reference from a normal human's words "palm tree." So there must also be a difference in meaning between the BIV's words and a normal human's words, given that the meaning of a term determines its reference. These semantic differences will also induce a difference between the truth conditions of a BIV's sentence "A palm tree is near" and those of a normal human's corresponding sentence. The normal human's sentence "A palm tree is near" is true if and only if a palm tree is near to the human, whereas the BIV's sentence "A palm tree is near" is true if and only if PT program features are running. The semantic differences between the BIV's language (call it *vat-English*) and that of a normal human are ultimately induced by the differences between the two creatures' external, causal environments. Let us call this Putnamian view *semantic externalism*.

Semantic externalism engenders some interesting results concerning the mental states of the BIV. Since the BIV's words "palm tree" do not refer to palm trees and differ in meaning from a normal human's corresponding words, and since his sentence "A palm tree is near" does not have the same truth conditions as a normal human's corresponding sentence, we cannot say that when the BIV thinks a thought using that sentence, he is thinking a thought with the *same content* as a normal human's thought *that a palm tree is near*. The semantic differences between languages that we have noted induce differences in the contents of the mental states had by the BIV and a normal human. The BIV cannot think that a palm tree is near, nor can he think that there are big waves at Sands Beach. The BIV's corresponding thoughts are about the entities in his external, causal environment which systematically produce his experiences, namely, recurring computer program features such as the PT program features. So the contents of the BIV's thoughts, beliefs, desires, and wonderings depend upon his external, causal environment. This view is known as *content externalism*, and it is really a form of semantic externalism, insofar as the content-properties of intentional states of mind are plausibly considered *semantic* properties of the states.

Now we see that the BIV cannot be the mental twin of a normal human. If God were to somehow "look inside" the minds of the BIV and his normal human counterpart, then he could not distinguish the two creatures' mental states purely on the basis of their inner phenomenology. But the states would nevertheless differ in content in virtue of the differences between the creatures' external, causal environments. Now we also see that one of our key initial Cartesian claims about the BIV thought experiment was not correct. That is, we characterized the BIV as being massively mistaken about his world. But that claim presupposed that when the BIV has a belief that he expresses via his sentence "A palm tree is near," the content of the belief in question is *that a palm tree is near*. If the BIV had that belief, then he would be mistaken, since no palm tree is near to him. But according to semantic externalism, the BIV has no such belief. Instead, he has a belief about computer program features—a belief that is *not* mistaken, given that the appropriate program features are running, producing "treeish" experience. According to the content externalist, the Cartesian philosopher is mistaken in the following assumption: in the BIV thought experiment, we can *hold fixed* the mental life of a normal human while varying, in thought, his external environment (normal world to vat world), with the result that the BIV's beliefs are those of a normal human and hence massively mistaken.

Putnamian Responses to Skepticism

Let us now return to the Cartesian skeptical argument formulated earlier. Its second premise is

(2)   I do not know that ~SK.

In other words, I do not know that I am not a BIV. We will now construct an argument for the conclusion that ~SK—that I am not a BIV. If the argument is successful, then I can claim to *know* ~SK on the basis of knowing the premises of the argument and knowing that they logically imply the conclusion, ~SK. By this method, we will block the Cartesian skeptical argument by showing that its premise (2) is false. In order for this strategy to work, we must make a case for the claim that my knowledge of the constructed anti-skeptical argument's premises does not somehow rest upon or presuppose knowledge of propositions about the external world. As we will see, it is a rather delicate matter to decide whether our constructed argument satisfies this criterion of adequacy. We are trying to construct a sort of *transcendental argument* for ~SK: an argument whose premises are (i) thin enough to be allowed in play by the skeptic (since they do not somehow presuppose knowledge about the external world), but, at the same time, (ii) strong enough to establish the conclusion ~SK.

The Disjunctive Argument

Let "brain*" refer to the computer program feature that causes experiences in the BIV that are qualitatively indistinguishable from normal experiences that represent brains, and let "vat*" refer to the computer program feature that causes experiences that are qualitatively indistinguishable from normal experiences that represent vats. A BIV, then, is not a brain* in a vat*: a BIV is not a certain computer program feature located in a certain other computer program feature. Here is the *Disjunctive Argument* that is suggested by Putnam's text (hereafter *DA*):

(a)   Either I am a BIV (speaking vat-English) or I am a non-BIV (speaking English).
(b)   If I am a BIV (speaking vat-English), then my utterances of "I am a BIV" are true iff I am a brain* in a vat*.
(c)   If I am a BIV (speaking vat-English), then I am not a brain* in a vat*.
(d)   If I am a BIV (speaking vat-English), then my utterances of "I am a BIV" are false. [(b),(c)]
(e)   If I am a non-BIV (speaking English), then my utterances of "I am a BIV" are true iff I am a BIV.
(f)   If I am a non-BIV (speaking English), then my utterances of "I am a BIV" are false. [(e)]
(g)   My utterances of 'I am a BIV' are false. [(a),(d),(f)]

DA stops short of delivering the desired result, namely a proof of

>   (~SK) I am not a BIV.

To establish ~SK we need to add a couple of further steps:

(h) My utterances of "I am not a BIV" are true.
(T) My utterances of "I am not a BIV" are true iff I am not a BIV.

~SK follows from (h) and (T). Step (h) itself follows from (g) on natural assumptions about negation, truth, and quotation, but (T) is problematic in the current anti-skeptical context. The assumption of (T) seems to beg the question against the skeptic. Putnam's semantic externalist picture is this: if I am a non-BIV (speaking English), then (T) is the correct statement of the truth conditions of my sentence "I am a BIV," using the device of disquotation; but if instead I am a BIV (speaking vat-English), then the correct statement of my sentence's truth conditions is the strange one given in (b) of DA, *not* using the device of disquotation. So in order to know that (T) is the correct statement of my sentence's truth conditions, I need to know that I am a non-BIV (speaking English). But *that* is what the anti-skeptical argument was supposed to *prove*. According to this objection, *Supplemented DA* (DA plus (h) and (T)) is *epistemically circular*, in William Alston's sense: knowledge of one of its premises—(T)—requires knowledge of its conclusion (Alston 1989).

The Simple Arguments

Let us consider two other reconstructions of Putnam's thinking regarding BIVs. Here is *Simple Argument 1 (SA1)*:

(A) If I am a BIV, then my word "tree" does not refer to trees.
(B) My word "tree" refers to trees.
(C) I am not a BIV. [(A),(B)]

We will discuss (B) below. Premise (A) comes from Putnam's semantic externalism, as seen above. DA's claims about the BIV's sentences' truth conditions are grounded in claims about reference such as (A): since the BIV's words differ in their referents from the corresponding words of a normal speaker, the BIV's sentences accordingly differ in their truth conditions from the corresponding sentences of a normal speaker.

The semantic differences just mentioned induce differences at the level of thought content that are exploited in the following *Simple Argument 2 (SA2)*:

(D) If I am a BIV, then I am not thinking that trees are green.
(E) I am thinking that trees are green.
(F) I am not a BIV. [(D),(E)]

We will discuss (E) below. Regarding (D): since the BIV's word "tree" does not refer to trees when he uses the sentence "Trees are green" as a vehicle for thinking a thought, his thought does not have the content *that trees are green*. Rather, it has some content concerning tree*s, that is, computer program features that cause in the BIV experiences that are qualitatively indistinguishable from normal experiences that represent trees. Perhaps the content is something like this: the program feature that causes "treeish" experience is associated with a program feature that causes experiences that are qualitatively indistinguishable from normal experiences that represent objects as being green.

SA2 highlights the connection between semantic externalism and the mind. Not only do meaning, reference, and truth conditions depend upon one's external environment in the ways we have discussed; further, the representational contents of one's thoughts, beliefs, desires, and other propositional attitudes also depend upon circumstances external to one's mind.

The simple arguments are obviously simpler than DA. Further, they do not commit the anti-skeptic to a specification of the referents of the BIV's words and the contents of its thoughts. The arguments rest only upon the claim that the referents and contents in question *differ from* my referents and contents. Another advantage of the Simple Arguments is that they do not, on the face of it, seem to beg the question against the skeptic, as did Supplemented DA.

Objections to the Simple Arguments and Responses

Let us now turn to an objection to SA1. Though the argument does not obviously require knowledge that I am a non-BIV (speaking English), as Supplemented DA seemed to, its premise (B) does seem upon reflection to be question begging. On a natural understanding of (B), the truth of this premise requires the existence of trees as referents for my word "tree." So to know that (B) is true, I would need to know that I am a non-BIV in a world containing trees, rather than a BIV in a treeless vat world. This problem infects SA2 as well, since my ground for holding that I *can* think tree-thoughts while the BIV *cannot* is ultimately the claim that the words we use to express our respective thoughts differ in reference (trees versus things that are not trees, such as tree*s).

SA1 can be modified so as to avoid this objection:

(A*)   If I am a BIV, then it is not the case that if my word "tree" refers, then it refers to trees.
(B*)   If my word "tree" refers, then it refers to trees.
(C)   I am not a BIV. [(A*),(B*)]

Premise (A*) comes from semantic externalism. Re premise (B*): knowledge that there are trees in my world is not required in order to justify this premise. But a problem still remains. In order to know (B*), don't I need to know that I am a non-BIV (speaking English), so that I can use the device of disquotation in stating the referents of my words (if they do have referents at all)?

A similar worry can be laid at the door of SA2. In order to know its second premise, (E), I need to know what I am now thinking. But if I am a BIV, then I use the sentence "Trees are green" to express some thought concerning tree*s. So in order to know what I am now thinking (in order to know that I am thinking that trees *are green*), it seems that I need to know that I am not a BIV thinking a thought with a strange content.

A reasonable response to the foregoing objection to Modified SA1 is as follows. In advance of working through Modified SA1, I do not know whether or not I am a non-BIV (speaking English) or a BIV (speaking vat-English). But I do know certain things about my own language (whatever it is and wherever I am speaking it). By virtue of knowing the meaning of "refers" and the meaning of quotation marks, I know that disquotation can be correctly applied to any successfully referring term of my language, in the way that (B*) indicates for my word "tree." This is a priori knowledge of semantic features of my own language (whatever it is—English or vat-English). I know (A*) in virtue of my a priori, philosophical knowledge of the theory of semantic externalism and of how it applies to the case of the BIV. Knowing (A*) and (B*), I can then knowledgeably deduce that I am not a BIV.

A similar response to the foregoing objection to SA2 is that I have knowledge of my own mind that is not experientially based. I can gain the knowledge that I am now thinking that trees are green via introspection. Putting this self-knowledge together with my a priori, philosophical knowledge of SA2's first premise, (D), (knowledge based upon my understanding of semantic externalism), I can then knowledgeably deduce that I am not a BIV. A problem for this response has been raised by various philosophers. It has been suggested that semantic externalism engenders severe limits on self-knowledge: if I do not know that I am not a BIV, then I do not know which contents my thoughts possess: the normal ones that I think that they possess, or the strange ones that they possess if I am a BIV. So the response we have considered might be in trouble if semantic externalism gives rise to such skepticism about knowledge of content (Ludlow and Martin 1998; Nuccetelli 2003).

A final objection to the semantic arguments is hard to dispute. The problem is the narrow scope of the arguments. They cannot prove that I am not a recently disembodied brain in a vat (as opposed to a Putnamian BIV). If I have been speaking English up until my recent envatment, then my words will retain their English referents (to trees and so on) and my thoughts will retain their normal contents (about trees and so on). Thus, the Putnamian semantic externalist considerations will find no purchase against the skeptical hypothesis that I am a fledgling brain in a vat. On the recent envatment hypothesis, I am not massively mistaken about my world in the way I would be if I were a BIV or a victim of Evil Genius deception. Depending on the details of the skeptical hypothesis, I might well have a very large body of correct views about my world. In order to accommodate this point, the skeptic could proceed in a piecemeal fashion, constructing a different 'recent envatment' hypothesis for each of my beliefs (I believe that I ran yesterday—but I could have been envatted the day before yesterday and so not have done any running yesterday . . .) (Brueckner and Altschul 2010).

Another more radical brain-in-a-vat hypothesis that is left unscathed by semantic externalism is that I am a brain in a vat whose experiences are randomly caused by a supercomputer: there are no systematic causal connections, for example, between the computer program features and my recurring "treeish" experiences. The semantic externalist would say that in such a vat world, my words fail to refer to things in my world, and no truth conditions can be properly assigned to my sentences. These sentences accordingly fail to express contentful thoughts. On this radical brain-in-a-vat hypothesis, I am asked, then, to countenance the (alleged) possibility that I am not thinking contentful thoughts via meaningful sentences with reference and truth conditions. But if this 'possibility' is actual, then there is no such thing as a *skeptical argument* upon which I am reflecting. Thus, this radical skeptical hypothesis might well in the end undermine itself.

Davidson, Radical Interpretation, and Charity

Let us now discuss some anti-skeptical considerations that flow from Donald Davidson's semantic externalist account of *radical interpretation*, in which I am trying to understand a speaker whose language is utterly foreign to me (Davidson 1984, 1986). My task in radical interpretation is to simultaneously solve for two unknowns: What do the speaker's sentences mean? Which beliefs do his (sincere) utterances express? Using Quine's famous example, imagine that my foreign informant utters the sentence "Gavagai" only in the presence of rabbits. What do *I* believe when confronted by a rabbit? Which English sentence do *I* use to express my occasioned belief, i.e., to which English sentence do I assent when prompted by the rabbit stimulus? I believe that a rabbit is present, and I use "A rabbit is present" to express that belief. How should I interpret my informant when he utters "Gavagai"? Should I attribute to him the belief that a large hadron collider is present and translate his sentence accordingly? Obviously not. I should reason that the presence of the rabbit in front of us causes in him the same belief that it causes in me, and I should translate "Gavagai" accordingly.

These remarks suggest the following principle:

> In radical interpretation, assign beliefs by reference to their causes, and translate the foreigner's belief-expressing sentences accordingly.

Davidson calls this method of assigning meanings and beliefs *triangulation* (Davidson 2001). The method of triangulation goes hand in hand with Davidson's Quine-inspired *Principle of Charity*:

> In radical interpretation, maximize agreement in belief between you and the subject of interpretation.

In the presence of the rabbit, *I* am not caused to believe that a large hadron collider is present, and the rabbit does not prompt my assent to "A large hadron collider is present." So in interpreting my foreign informant, I should *bring him into agreement with me* by attributing to him the belief that is caused in me by the rabbit.

Triangulation embodies a semantic externalist approach to radical interpretation. According to Davidson's method, the correct attribution of meanings and beliefs is constrained by the interpretee's causal environment. Charity is entrained by this constraint.

Davidson has a famous anti-skeptical argument that proceeds from the foregoing views (Davidson 1986). The argument starts with the observation that given Charity, I cannot encounter another language user who is correctly interpreted as holding beliefs which do *not* substantially overlap my own. Massive disagreement between me and the interpretee is not possible. The point holds mutatis mutandis for the case in which I am the interpretee undergoing scrutiny by an interpreter: massive disagreement between us is not possible, given Charity.

How is this relevant to skepticism? Both interpreter and interpretee might well be massively mistaken about their world even given their substantial agreement in belief. For all that has been said, I must take seriously the skeptic's suggestion that *I* might be massively mistaken about *my* world, as I would be were I a brain in a vat. A related worry is expressed by Michael Williams. Isn't the Davidsonian appeal to constraints on radical interpretation question begging in the context of discussion of skepticism? Doesn't this appeal presuppose that an interpreter can come to *know* what another's meanings and beliefs are by coming to know facts about the stimuli which prompt the informant's utterances (Williams 1996; Brueckner 1999)? Davidson is well aware of this limitation on the anti-skeptical force of Charity. This is why he invokes the possibility of an *omniscient interpreter* (hereafter an OI).

Davidson maintains that the following situation is possible: an omniscient being, believing all and only true propositions, attributes meanings to my sentences and correlative beliefs to me. The OI is just as much subject to the constraints of Charity as any interpreter. In such a situation, Charity dictates that the OI maximize agreement in belief between him and me, regarding the subject matters about which we both form opinions; the OI has many recondite beliefs that I do not share. (NB. We are not to suppose that the OI starts in ignorance of my meanings and beliefs and ends by forming beliefs about me on the basis of evidence that he gleans from observing my linguistic behavior in the presence of various environmental stimuli. Instead, the OI has thoroughly correct and exhaustive beliefs about my meanings and beliefs that *conform to* the method of triangulation and respect Charity. On Davidson's view of meaning and belief, meanings and beliefs are just *what would be attributed to me by an interpreter guided by the constraining principles of radical interpretation*.)

Since the OI's beliefs are true without exception, and those beliefs which he attributes to me match his own as much as possible, the result is that the beliefs which he attributes to me are mostly true. If we suppose, finally, that the OI's interpretation of me is correct (which it must be given his omniscience), then it follows that, in the envisaged possible situation, most of my beliefs are true. In the possible situation we are considering, then, the skeptic's suggestion that I might be massively mistaken is simply a nonstarter.

Richard Foley and Richard Fumerton pointed out that unless Davidson is a theist who holds that we are in fact in the company of an OI, the OI considerations are compatible with my *actually* being massively mistaken (Foley and Fumerton 1985). Foley and Fumerton in effect consider a Davidsonian reply along the following lines.

> Surely an OI is at least a *possible* being. Consider, again, a possible world W containing an OI along with me. Assume that (1) my beliefs in W are just those which I actually have, and (2) the states of affairs relevant to the truth and falsity of those beliefs are just those which actually obtain. Since my beliefs in W substantially overlap those of the OI, my beliefs in W will not be massively mistaken about W. Given assumptions (1) and (2), it then follows that my beliefs about the actual world are not massively mistaken about the actual world.

Foley and Fumerton in effect reply as follows.

> I grant that there are worlds containing me and an OI—which are worlds in which I am perforce massively right about my world. But why should I grant that there is a possible world such as W, containing me and an OI *and* satisfying assumptions (1) and (2)? If I am in fact massively mistaken, then there is no world containing me and an OI *and* satisfying (1) and (2), though there are worlds containing me and an OI which differ from the actual world in respect of what I believe and in respect of the states of affairs relevant to the truth of my beliefs. Nothing about my *actual* freedom from error follows from the bare assumption that there is a world containing me and an OI. The stronger assumption regarding conditions (1) and (2) is unwarranted since question begging.

Let us consider an alternative assumption about possibility (Brueckner 1991). Grant for the moment that there is a possible world containing a being who is modeled on a Leibnizian god who possesses perfect modal knowledge (knowledge which, were he a creator, the god could employ in a choice regarding which of all the possible worlds is the one to be made actual):

(L) Some possible world W* contains an OI who has perfect knowledge about all possible worlds, including the actual world; thus the OI believes, among other things, all and only true propositions about the actual world.

(NB. There is no commitment here to Lewisian modal realism. (L) could be paraphrased along the lines of: There might have been an OI with perfect modal knowledge ... The truth-maker of such modal talk could be held to be an actually existing abstract entity, rather than a non-actual, concrete, existent, Lewisian possible world.)

For all that has been assumed in (L), W* is not the actual world and does not contain me. So the foregoing criticisms from Foley and Fumerton do not apply to (L).

Given (L) and Charity, we can show that I am not massively mistaken in my actual beliefs about the actual world, as follows. The OI contained in W* has beliefs about the meanings of the sentences to which I actually assent and about what beliefs those sentences express as I actually use them. He arrives at these beliefs through radical interpretation that is constrained by Charity. Thus, he maximizes agreement in belief between him and me. In particular, he attributes to me beliefs about my world (the actual world) which are in agreement with *his* beliefs about my world. His beliefs about my world, the actual world (which are of the form "Proposition P is true at W_1," where "W_1" denotes the actual world) are all true. Thus my beliefs about my world (the actual world) are at least mostly true. Thus I am not actually massively mistaken about my world.

The simplest way of responding to this twist on Davidson's omniscient interpreter anti-skeptical strategy is to deny the possibility of a Leibnizian OI with perfect modal knowledge. Just as one might have qualms about the possibility of a necessary being (in light of the Leibnizian ontological argument), one might also have qualms about the possibility of a Leibnizian OI: given Charity, such a being's mere possibility delivers the result that I am mostly right about my world.

Conclusion

We have looked at two ways of using semantic externalist ideas against Cartesian skepticism. Both sorts of anti-skeptical argument could be seen as a transcendental argument in the grand Kantian mold, in which some sort of mind-to-world connection is discerned—a connection that would enable us to argue from unproblematically knowable facts about mind and language to a substantial, surprising anti-skeptical conclusion. Let the reader be the judge of the success of these anti-skeptical strategies.

References

Alston, W. (1989) "Epistemic Circularity," in *Epistemic Justification: Essays in the Theory of Knowledge*, Ithaca: Cornell University Press.
Brueckner, A. (1986) "Brains in a Vat," *Journal of Philosophy* 83: 148–67.
—— (1991) "The Omniscient Interpreter Rides Again," *Analysis* 51: 199–205.
—— (1992) "Semantic Answers to Skepticism," *Pacific Philosophical Quarterly* 73: 200–19.

—— (1999) "Transcendental Arguments from Content Externalism," in R. Stern (ed.) *Transcendental Arguments: Problems and Prospects*, Oxford: Oxford University Press.
—— (2003) "Trees, Computer Program Features, and Skeptical Hypotheses," in S. Luper (ed.) *The Skeptics: Contemporary Essays*, Aldershot: Ashgate.
—— and Altschul, J. (2010) "Terms of Envatment," in *Essays on Skepticism*, Oxford: Oxford University Press.
Davidson, D. (1984) "A Radical Interpretation," in *Inquiries into Truth and Interpretation*, Oxford: Oxford University Press.
—— (1986) "A Coherence Theory of Truth and Knowledge," in E. Lepore (ed.) *Truth and Interpretation: Essays on the Philosophy of Donald Davidson*, Oxford: Blackwell.
—— (1996) "Three Varieties of Knowledge," in *Subjective, Intersubjective, Objective*, Oxford: Oxford University Press.
—— (2001) "Radical Interpretation," in *Inquiries into Truth and Interpretation*, Oxford: Oxford University Press.
Foley, R. and Fumerton, R. (1985) "Davidson's Theism?," *Philosophical Studies* 45: 83–9.
Ludlow, P. and Martin, N. (ed.) (1998) *Externalism and Self-Knowledge*, Stanford: CSLI Press.
Nuccetelli, S. (ed.) (2003) *New Essays on Semantic Externalism and Self-Knowledge*, Cambridge: MIT Press.
Putnam, H. (1981) *Reason, Truth and History*, Cambridge: Cambridge University Press.
Williams, M. (1996) *Unnatural Doubts: Epistemological Realism and the Basis of Scepticism*, Princeton: Princeton University Press.

Part VII

KNOWLEDGE AND KNOWLEDGE ATTRIBUTIONS

47
CONTRASTIVISM
Adam Morton

We often backtrack in ascriptions of knowledge. "Well, I'm not *that* sure," "That's what I *think*, at any rate," "She knows as well as a ten year old could." Elsewhere, backtracking can mean shift of parameter. "Well, it's left from your point of view," "Always in the past year, at any rate," "Big for a mouse, I meant." This insinuates a tempting idea. Perhaps some disputes about knowledge are hollow, because we ignore factors to which a meaningful ascription of knowledge is relative. Several developments in epistemology can be taken as ways of working out this idea. There is Peter Unger's (1975) suggestion that "know" is like "flat," requiring comparison to some standard or purpose. There is epistemic contextualism, entailing that a person knows that they have toenails when discussing how to trim them, but does not when engrossed in a discussion of Cartesian skepticism. And then there are "rather than" positions, which say that a person typically knows that she has ten toenails rather than thirty-six, but does not typically know that she has ten toenails rather than a number that flummoxes human counting routines. This chapter is about "rather than" positions. I shall be concerned with contrastivism about knowledge, the idea that "knows that p rather than that q" has advantages over simple "knows."

Philosophers have often made suggestions that can be interpreted in the "rather than" idiom. Fred Dretske's ideas are particularly important. And in the past few years, several philosophers have explicitly suggested that "s knows that p" can profitably be expanded to "s knows that p rather than q" (Dretske 1972; Johnsen 2001; Karjalainen and Morton 2003; Schaffer 2004, 2005). The claim might be that when we say that a person knows something the ascription is always implicitly relative to some alternative proposition. Or the claim might be that although this is not what we normally mean when we ascribe knowledge, philosophical and other purposes would be better served if we did always provide a contrast. Or it might be simply that we do have the contrastive form of knowledge-ascription, and that it is in some ways important. I compare these claims at the end of this chapter. I must begin, though, with a less impressionistic explanation of what the core ideas are.

The Dretske Phenomenon

By this I mean the phenomenon of partial Gettierization, first described in Dretske (1970). A person can have a belief that involves the combination of several items of information. Sylvia might believe that the man in front of her is drunk. This combines three pieces of information: that it is in front of her, that it is a man, and that it is drunk. One way of attributing the belief to her would be to point to the person swaying before her and say "Sylvia thinks he is drunk." Suppose that it is a man (no cross-dressing) and is before her (no mirrors) and is drunk (not ill, not exhausted), and suppose that Silvia has evidence for all three. But suppose there are hidden problems with two of the three. The man has just come from a party of cross-dressers around the corner; there is a mirror in the line of sight. But the drunk part is uncomplicated. We would say "Silvia knows he is drunk." The "he" form has the advantage of focussing us on the information that is most likely to be of importance to Sylvia, that the person is drunk. She knows *that*, even though there is something incomplete or imperfect about her knowledge. We can describe the gaps in her knowledge by saying that she does not know that the man is in front of her, and that she does not know that he is a man. But to describe the part that is not flawed, we cannot say "Sylvia knows that the man in front of her is drunk," since that could be taken to include the parts that are flawed.

Sylvia knows that the man is drunk *rather than* sober, ill or exhausted. We might suggest this in conversation with verbal stress "Sylvia knows that he is *drunk*." Even this is not quite explicit enough; we have to read into it the assertion that the indicated contrasts are the only ones that we are claiming Sylvia's information satisfies. So for greater accuracy we should say "Sylvia knows the man in front of her is drunk rather than sober (etc.), but she does not know that he is a man rather than a woman or a robot, or that he is in front of her rather than seen through a mirror (etc.)." Saying this is compatible with the information that it is a man and that he is in front of her being true, and even well-supported by evidence. It is with respect to status as knowledge that the failures of contrast are relevant.

Now many examples come to mind. There are examples based on accuracy. Sylvia might know that the man is roughly five meters away. Suppose her knowledge is accurate to within a meter. So she knows that he is five meters away rather than six or four meters, but she does not know that he is five meters away rather than 4.8 or 5.2. There are examples based on conceptual repertoire. Sylvia might never have heard of tardive diskenesia, which can present symptoms similar to those of drunkenness. So it might be helpful to say that Sylvia knows that the man is drunk rather than sober, and knows that he is drunk rather than exhausted or fevered, but that she does not know that he is drunk rather than suffering from tardive diskenesia. There are also examples based on the limited discriminatory power of evidence. Sylvia might know that the man is a man rather than a woman, because she is very sensitive to normal gender differences. But nothing her eyes tell her might be relevant to the question of the person's chromosome pattern. So she does not know that the person is an XY man rather than a transgendered person. There are many examples along these lines involving scientific theories and the limited power of evidence to choose between them.

In saying that someone knows that p rather than that q we might be making a trivial or a stringent contrast. Saying that Sylvia knows that there is a drunk in front of her rather than that there is not a drunk in front of her, does not give more information than saying that she knows that there is a drunk in front of her. Saying that she knows that the man in front of her is drunk rather than not drunk, is more informative: it focuses specifically on drunkenness. Saying that Sylvia knows that the man is drunk rather than sober, but does not know that he is drunk rather than suffering from tardive diskenesia, gives yet more information. If we identify a person's knowledge with the range of her beliefs which are known relative to very wide contrasts then we might find that there is little difference between knowledge and true belief supported by evidence. If we identify knowledge with beliefs known relative to very narrow contrasts then we might find that people have almost no knowledge. But we do not need to make either identification. We can just describe people's epistemic situation in terms of what they do and do not know relative to different contrasts.

Giving the details of a person's epistemic situation is usually more complex than might be predicted from a very simple contrastivism. Sylvia knows that the man is 5 meters away and drunk rather than 4 meters away and exhausted; she does not know that he is 5 meters away and drunk rather than 4.8 meters away and suffering from tardive diskenesia. She also knows that he is 5 meters away and drunk rather than 12 meters away and suffering from epilepsy; and does not know that he is 5 meters away and drunk rather than 5.2 meters away and suffering from Sydenham's Chorea. The full contrastive story will require many, perhaps infinitely many, detailed contrastive attributions.

Discriminatory Capacities

Our knowledge is in part based on our capacity to tell things apart. Most people can tell dogs from frogs. But there are individuals and kinds that we cannot discriminate. Marbles can be pretty hard to distinguish. Imagine that you have been taught how to tell Astogmatic marbles from Blosphemious ones. You have a list of crude criteria and also you've just been trained with examples: we rap your knuckles or feed you cookies until you can answer correctly. We have a big bucket of a million marbles, and they're all Astogmatic or Blosphemious: all that is except for two or three Croduloid ones somewhere in there. The Croduloids can look like Astogmatics or Blosphemiouses, except for very subtle magnetic characteristics that it takes years to understand. You draw a marble from the bucket and you are sure that it is an Astogmatic one: indeed given that you are 100 percent accurate when it's just As versus Bs, and that the probability of this being one of the two or three Cs is minimal, your confidence is justified.

Suppose that the marble is in fact Astogmatic. Is your belief, that it is, knowledge? You have more evidence for it than you do for many things that we routinely credit as knowledge. But for all you know it might turn out to be a Croduloid. You have the capacity to know when things, marbles at any rate, are Astogmatic rather than Blosphemious, but you do not have the capacity to know when things are Astogmatic rather than Croduloid. This natural description of your capacities can apply equally well to the result of using them: you know that the marble is Astogmatic rather than Blosphemious, and you do not know that it is Astogmatic rather than Croduloid.

A variation on the example evokes stronger intuitions. Suppose that the bucket of marbles is chosen at random from a whole warehouse of such buckets. Out of a million buckets all but two or three are composed of Astogmatics and Blosphemiouses, and these two or three have a small proportion of Croduloids. You choose a marble from the bucket picked at random from the warehouse. You conclude correctly that it is Astogmatic. In so doing you are presupposing that the extremely unlikely choice of a Croduloid-containing bucket has not occurred. So in knowing that the marble is Astogmatic rather than Blosphemious you are remaining ignorant whether it is Astogmatic rather than Croduloid. You are in no position to eliminate unlikely possibilities about the choice of bucket, but your training and vision suffice to eliminate possibilities about the marble taken from whatever bucket was chosen.

The limits of a person's discriminatory capacities are like margins of error in measurements. Measurements show that a star is 7 light years away plus or minus 0.01 light years. So it is determined not to be more than 7.01 light years away and not to be less than 6.99 light years away. If these measurements are accurate and we trust them, then we know that the star is 7 light years away rather than 8, but do not know that it is 7 light years away rather than 7.005 light years away. Ascribing contrastive knowledge to a person is like describing them as having a degree of accuracy in one dimension of their representation of the world (see Morton and Karjalainen 2008).

Assumptions: Knowledge Modulo Q

Often we cannot settle whether or not something is true, though we are pretty sure that it is. Whether the bucket is Croduloid-free, or whether the universe is a law-governed place. One solution is just to take it for granted and get on with science and action. Philosophers have sometimes resisted the idea that beliefs further down the line from such an assumption can count as knowledge. But the number of unjustified assumptions scattered around our systems of belief is then very worrying, especially when one considers not only completely arbitrary assumptions but also assumptions for which there is serious but not overwhelming support. There is a natural contrastive solution. When some aspects of a belief are not known, then the whole belief itself is known in a way that is relative to those aspects. The belief is known modulo the assumptions, as a mathematician might say: it is known as a representative of a class of beliefs, ultimate choice between which is not possible.

When p is known modulo an assumption then the knower knows p rather than other possibilities that depend on the same assumption, but does not know p rather than other possibilities that depend on alternatives to it. What "depend on" and "alternatives" exactly amount to will depend on one's theory of knowledge. Contrastivist vocabulary allows an epistemology to hold that a person can know that the marble is Astogmatic modulo the assumption that it is not Croduloid. Or that Sylvia knows that there is a drunk before her, modulo the assumption that the apparition is human. Or that an astronomer knows that a star is 7 light years away modulo the assumption that certain equipment is working properly within a certain margin of error.

Knowledge can be modulo an assumption in very ordinary circumstances. Sylvia is walking in the woods in fading light. She sees a large black animal on a branch and assumes unreflectively that it is a bird. It is a bird but it is also true that the neighbor's cat likes to sit on branches. She concludes that it is a raven, because of its size and color. She knows, modulo the bird assumption, that it is a raven rather than a crow (size) and that it is a raven rather than an eagle (color). She does not know that it is a raven rather than a cat, or that it is a bird rather than a mammal. Does she know that it is an animal, or that it is a black animal? She knows, modulo the arbitrary bird assumption. It is harder to put this as a single contrastive statement. She knows that it is an animal—bird or mammal—rather than an eagle, and that it is an animal rather than a stone, but she does not know that it is an animal rather than a bird in particular. It is misleading here to give the positive contrasts without also giving the negative ("does not know") ones.

The fact that a person has assumed or presupposed that p, or just ignored the possibility that not p, does not have to show that she does not know that p rather than q, or that she does not know that r rather than s, where r would be false if p was. For p might be something that she can ignore, without affecting her attitude to r. If Sylvia doesn't pay any attention to the possibility that the thing in the tree is the last surviving pterodactyl, that really makes no difference to whether she knows that it is a bird rather than some other animal. There are many possible positions here. On a very demanding view, the failure to have evidence that p rather than q, or to be sensitive to the contrast between p and q, will result in the person's failing to have a wide range of contrastive knowledge. On a more tolerant view, the impact will be minimal. This is an important issue if one takes our beliefs to be riddled with more or less arbitrary assumptions.

The New Skepticism

The tug of intuitions between Moorean confidence and Cartesian doubt is a dramatic version of conflicts that arise in everyday epistemic life (see DeRose 1995). Some of these can be arranged in patterns that invite contrastivity. There are cases that turn on accuracy. It seems obvious that Sylvia knows she is larger than her sister, but her sense of her and others' features might be systematically distorted. There are cases that turn on conceptual repertoire. It seems obvious that Sylvia knows that she is a woman. But she might not distinguish between various natural kinds that "woman" labels. There are cases that turn on the limits of the power of evidence to discriminate. It seems obvious that Sylvia knows that her college graduation is a unique event. But it is possible that after the universe collapses into a singularity it will re-expand into a universe identical to the present one, repeating her graduation in every detail.

These can be described as traditional skeptical possibilities, in which what a person takes to be knowledge is in fact false. But post-Gettier epistemology makes another kind of skepticism possible. We can have large-scale knowledge failure even though most of our beliefs are true and supported by evidence, if they fail to meet additional conditions for knowledge. (A little-remarked-on development: epistemologists now generally share a fallibilist attitude that makes traditional skepticism less attractive, but they also share attitudes that make the new skepticism more threatening.) We need only a change of emphasis. The skeptical possibility is now presented as an alternative to the person's beliefs which, unless she can eliminate it, disqualifies them as knowledge. One influential version of the new epistemology requires that in order to have knowledge one must be able to eliminate relevant alternatives to the beliefs in question (Dretske 1970; Lewis 1996). (Rival accounts will impose alternative conditions which for present purposes amount to much the same.) A link with contrastive knowledge emerges here via the Dretske phenomenon.

Consider again Sylvia's belief that the man in front of her is drunk. She is unlikely to have considered and eliminated all the alternatives to his being a man, to his being in front of her, and to his being drunk. Some of these are relevant in many circumstances, and in most circumstances many of them will be, so that it might be fairly rare that a person's belief is knowledge-worthy throughout its content. On the very plausible assumption that we do not in fact normally exclude all the alternatives relevant to the total content of many of our beliefs, we get the conclusion that we rarely know the whole content of many of our beliefs.

This is a skeptical conclusion. But I think it is a true one, and one that we can live with. Sylvia probably does not know that there is a male human being directly before her and between three and ten meters away who is suffering the effects of excessive ingestion of CH_3CH_2OH. But she might well know that the guy before her is drunk rather than sober. Or that it is a man rather than a woman who is before her and showing symptoms of drunkenness. Or that the apparently male person acting drunk nearby is directly in front of her rather than more than 5 degrees from her line of sight. Which contrasts apply will depend on what she has been considering and paying attention to, and which aspects of the environment she is sensitive to. And it might be very hard for her or anyone to tell which contrasts apply and which do not. It might be hard to determine which of her assumptions are arbitrary in ways that block which contrasts. So of all the things Sylvia truly believes, a scattered subset fail to be knowledge with respect to the contrasts that she might expect, and some fail to be knowledge with respect to any contrast. Knowledge of how non-knowledge is scattered among one's beliefs is rare and difficult.

We can apply this point of view to classic cases. Take Sylvia sitting in a philosophy seminar making a Moorean point. She waggles her appendages with conviction. She stresses that she sees and feels her hands and that there are two of them. What more could anyone want? Well, since it is a philosophy seminar she is thinking of irrefutable and probably irrelevant blockbuster possibilities. But she has not gone through a lot of nearer-to-home scenarios. Supposing there are two of these things, what claim does she have on them *as hers*? Might she have sold them to someone last night in the pub? The chances are that she has not even given the matter any thought. Might they be not hands but grafts of giant axolotl paws, which look a lot like human hands (Cortázar 1952)? So she might know that she is linked to two hands rather than to none, but not know that she possesses two human hands rather than none. The differences between these contrasts have probably not occurred to her. Might she be suffering a failure of motor control and proprioception, analogous to the well-known tendency of people who have limited neural contact with their limbs to disown them, so that she thinks that hands that are actually attached to someone else are her own? There are many such possibilities, and she can only eliminate a few of them. Some will be more relevant to her situation than others, but she might well not have any rebuttal for some of the more relevant of them. So Sylvia's claim to knowledge that she has *two* hands rather than none or three is more robust here than her claim to know that she *has* two human hands of her own. But in other situations the balance will fall differently. Or, to put the point more carefully, allowing the inevitable vagueness of "know," Sylvia's claim to know that she has two hands rather than none is stronger than her claim to know that she has two hands rather than being in contact with two appendages that are not her own home-grown hands. But the relative strength of these claims, and the factors that affect their strength, depend on her circumstances in ways that it is hard for her to assess.

Contrastive knowledge is not skeptic-proof. The claim is comparative: contrastive knowledge survives more challenges. It is an important claim when combined with the new skepticism. The result is the suggestion that if we do not concede that many knowledge claims are contrastive then we can sustain our pretensions to know a lot only by having low epistemic standards.

Lotteries

People usually refuse to ascribe knowledge that individual lottery tickets will lose, even when the probability of losing is higher than that of many propositions they do believe. They do, however, have beliefs from which it follows that individual tickets will lose, and will describe these as knowledge. Someone might claim to know that he will still be living in his cheap apartment in a year's time, in spite of the million dollar lottery ticket on his desk. John Hawthorne (2004) has argued persuasively that ubiquitous situations with these general features have a lot in common with skeptical hypotheses. There are claims to knowledge here which it seems outrageous to deny, but which seem to be undermined by the fact that we cannot be sure that some very unlikely but inconsistent event will not occur.

One person knows that he will be in his apartment rather than in a mansion, but does not know that he will be in his apartment after failing to win the lottery rather than in a mansion as a result of winning. Someone else knows that she will be delighted when her daughter gets her medical degree, rather than disappointed, but does not know that she will be delighted having escaped death by car crash, lightning strike, epidemic, or political violence, rather than dead from some such cause. Or so a contrastive epistemologist would naturally say. The contrastive idiom seems naturally suited to express the way that we both have knowledge and—seen from a different perspective—fail to have it, of these everyday expectations.

One rationale is the modulo phenomenon already described. Assume that people normally suspend judgment on whether an individual lottery ticket will win or lose. Then they can proceed to form other beliefs, carefully skipping around the gaps in conceptual space left by this agnosticism. They will do this largely by making a scattered set of arbitrary assumptions. Our ticket-holder will assume that he will still be in his apartment in a year's time, that his relatives will continue to be as inattentive to him as they now are, and that generally his life will go on its present course. The mother of the medical student will make similar assumptions about the persistence of the familiar. They will not assume that particular persistence-disturbing events—lottery wins, car accidents—will not occur. These things are not ruled out, though some events closely linked to them or their non-occurrence are explicitly ruled in. The result is a rather messy patchwork of beliefs, providing the assurance about the future needed for normal planning while not excluding developments that the person knows just might occur. And, modulo the suspended judgment and the resulting patchwork, the person has a good deal of contrastive knowledge.

Systematic Contrasts: Kant Without Tears

Most of the contrastivity so far discussed comes from the way individual people eliminate possibilities in the course of their belief-formation. There are also grounds for supposing that human knowledge is in general attuned to certain dimensions of contrast, so that humans can hope to know things of one kind rather than another, but not rather than some third kind. For example, there is *Kantian contrastivism*, which counts as epistemically distinct possibilities those descriptions of the world that differ in the distribution of things in space and time and the causal relations between them, and which discounts, as epistemically insignificant, many differences between descriptions that cannot be expressed in these terms. Thus a Kantian agent can know that the tides are the result of the gravitational force of the moon rather than the rotation of the earth, but cannot know that the tides are the result of the gravitational force of the moon rather than the result of a pre-established harmony between them and the moon's movements (see especially Kant 1787: A278/B334).

Kantian contrastivism is different from its descendant *positivist contrastivism*, which counts as epistemically distinct possibilities only those descriptions that could be discriminated by possible empirical evidence. A positivist agent can know that objects near the surface of the earth accelerate towards its center at $980 \, cm/sec^2$ rather than

700 cm/sec^2, but cannot know that objects accelerate down because of gravity rather than accelerating down because of Newtonian gremlins.

Both Kantian and positivist contrastivism are different from *reliabilist contrastivism*, which distinguishes beliefs epistemically when the process that produces them is sensitive to the differences in their truth conditions. A reliabilist agent can know that a ball is accelerating downwards at about 900 cm/sec^2 rather than 450 cm/sec^2—she has enough accuracy to catch it—but not that it is accelerating downwards at 900 cm/sec^2 rather than 905 cm/sec^2. Reliabilist contrastivism provides a simple way of describing the knowledge of non-human species. Salmon know that their target stream is this one rather than that one; they do not know that it is a stream rather than a sluice; they do not know that they are going up it to mate rather than to feed (Kornblith 2002: ch 2). The salmon example shows how hard it is to find exactly the right set of contrasts to capture a non-human set of sensitivities. It would be surprising if they could always be characterized in common-sense terms. So the best way is to specify the contrastivity—what kinds of facts the animal can respond to differently from what other kinds—as an object in itself, without trying to find human words for the conceptual repertoire involved.

Given that there are physical properties to which members of any species are not sensitive, it would be amazing if the same were not true of human beings. Sensitivity includes inferential and hypothesizing capacities, so the suggestion is that there are aspects of the universe we do not register at all. Or, more carefully, that there are distinct sets of possible worlds such that no human being can know that the actual world is a member of one set rather than the other. Call this *hyper-realist contrastivism*. My purpose now is not to defend it, but to point out a natural way of stating the position, in terms of contrast spaces underlying our knowledge.

Many big pictures of human knowledge combine a knowledge-affirming and a knowledge-denying side in ways that suggest a contrastive formulation. Besides Kant's transcendental realism, a similar interpretation could be put on Hilary Putnam's internal realism, on van Fraassen's constructive empiricism, and on structural realism in contemporary philosophy of science (Ladyman 1998; van Fraassen 2006). Structural realism holds that we can know that the laws of nature have one form rather than another, but cannot know that the objects satisfying them are of one kind rather than another. Some contrasts are out of bounds.

Which Contrastivism?

I end with a very basic question that has been with us from the beginning. What really is the claim that knowledge is contrastive? Is it (a) that when people naively ascribe dyadic knowledge to others they are really describing a triadic relation between person, target proposition, and contrast proposition? Is it (b) that the triadic form is a variant that is available to us in common sense, as a fall-back from full dyadic knowledge and that has interesting philosophical uses? Is it (c) that the triadic form is an option with a loose resemblance to our everyday use of "know" that has a philosophical payoff as an extension of it? Is it (d) that the triadic form is a philosophical invention, a creature of theory that should be used to replace the confused or confusing ordinary concept?

(a) and (d) are the strongest positions. (a) suggests that the hidden form of "know" has an extra argument place, which is usually left implicit. If this were true we would expect that whenever we make an intelligible ascription of knowledge it will be possible to extract enough information from the context to fill in the missing contrast proposition. Jonathan Schaffer (2007) has suggested something stronger, that the linguistic structure of "know" is triadic. In fact, Schaffer believes that (a) can only be true if this is the case. Some form of (a) might be true, though, even if the facts about "know" are not coded linguistically. Compare "to the right of." When a is to the right of b we have to take account of a direction—the red buoys to port when entering a European harbor are to starboard when leaving it—and also of which direction is up—entry signs in space will need to have arrows as well as colors. But there is no evidence that the lexical item "to the left of" is anything but a two place relation. So I shall take it that we can defend some version of (a) by claiming that the facts that make a knowledge claim true or false are contrastive, and that awareness of these facts guides us in ascribing knowledge to one another.

I take it that (d), the other extreme position, is not very attractive. It is a position of last resort. In effect it says "we can't make much sense of knowledge, so if we are to have something to mark our epistemic achievements, it has to be something rather different from what we have taken to be the target." That is a skeptical position that, unlike the skeptical positions sketched above, is not balanced by a corresponding affirmation of knowledge. So in that respect it undermines the aim of admitting the force of skepticism while relativizing in a way that allows it to be consistent with an equally definite affirmation. It also undermines the aim of reacting to the Dretske phenomenon by letting a belief be both known and not known relative to different aspects of its content. On a (d)-type position a partially Gettierized proposition is not known—in the standard meaning of "know"—in any respect.

But in all of (a)–(d) the formulation in terms of a triadic propositional attitude is misleading. For, as we have seen, the full content of a contrastive knowledge-ascription is not given by a single contrast proposition. One needs a more complex list of which contrasts the person manages with respect to the fact in question, and which not. So in saying that a person knows p rather than q we are not describing their full epistemic situation with respect to p, just as we are not when we say simply that they know that p. Saying that the person knows that p rather than q better than they know r rather than s—that they can discriminate p-possibilities from q-possibilities more reliably than they can discriminate r-possibilities from s-possibilities—gives more information than either (Hetherington 2001). But, still, for the reasons just given this too does not give a complete report on the person's epistemic relation to p.

And that is the answer to the original question. None of (a)–(d) are completely satisfactory, though each has some truth to it. A person in a situation has an epistemic situation with respect to a possibility or fact. It is this situation that makes knowledge attributions true or false, when they have definite truth values. We make knowledge attributions on the basis of partial information about it. Contrastive idioms capture more of the epistemic situation, so that when people make non-contrastive attributions some of the information they are using can be helpfully expressed in contrastive terms. To that extent (a) is correct. Some, not all, of the tangles we get into when trying to sum up our individual and species-wide epistemic situations can be resolved by using a richer vocabulary. To that extent (b) is correct. The more of the structure of epistemic situations we want to capture the further we have to move from the very simple things we say in everyday life. To that extent (c) is correct. There are some aspects of some epistemic situations that are almost impossible to describe unconfusingly in non-contrastive terms. To that extent (d) is correct.

The upshot is that a systematic use of everyday idioms of contrastive knowledge, directed deliberately towards aspects of our epistemic situation that are hard to describe in non-contrastive terms, is a valuable tool. We should not neglect it.

References

Cortázar, Julio (1952/1996) "Axolotl," in *La autopista del sur y otras cuentas*, Penguin Books.
DeRose, K. (1995) "Solving the Skeptical Problem," *The Philosophical Review* 104, 1–52.
Dretske, F. (1970) "Epistemic Operators," *The Journal of Philosophy* 67, 1007–1023.
Dretske, F. (1972) "Contrastive Statements," *The Philosophical Review* 81, 411–437.
Hetherington, Stephen (2001) *Good Knowledge, Bad Knowledge*. Oxford University Press.
Hawthorne, John (2004) *Knowledge and Lotteries*. Oxford University Press.
Johnsen, Bredo (2001) "Contextualist Swords, Skeptical Plowshares," *Philosophy and Phenomenological Research* 62: 385–406.
Kant, Immanuel (1787) *Kritik der reinen Vernuft* (Critique of Pure Reason). For a clear contemporary translation, by Jonathan Bennett, see http://www.earlymoderntexts.com/kcpr1.html, and http://www.earlymoderntexts.com/kcpr2.html.
Karjalainen, Antti and Adam Morton (2003) "Contrastive Knowledge," *Philosophical Explorations* 6: 74–89.
Kornblith, Hilary (2002) *Knowledge and its Place in Nature*. Oxford University Press.
Ladyman, J. (1998) "What is Structural Realism?" *Studies in History and Philosophy of Science* 29: 409–424.
Lewis, David (1996) "Elusive Knowledge," *Australasian Journal of Philosophy* 74: 549–567.
Morton, Adam and Antti Karjalainen (2008) "Contrastivity and Indistinguishability," *Social Epistemology* 22: 271–280.
Schaffer, Jonathan (2004) "From Contextualism to Contrastivism," *Philosophical Studies* 119: 73–103.
Schaffer, Jonathan (2005) "Contrastive knowledge." In: *Oxford Studies in Epistemology 1*, edited by T. Gendler and J. Hawthorne. Oxford: Oxford University Press.
Schaffer, Jonathan (2007) "Closure, Contrast, and Answer," *Philosophical Studies* 133: 233–255.
Unger, Peter (1975) *Ignorance: A Case For Skepticism*. Oxford University Press.
Van Fraassen, B. C. (2006) "Structure: Its Shadow and Substance," *The British Journal for the Philosophy of Science* 57: 275–307.

48
CONTEXTUALISM
Patrick Rysiew

1. Introduction: What Contextualism Is (And Isn't)

Whether you know that *p* depends on many features of you and your situation. Epistemologists disagree over which such features are important—whether knowing depends on what else you believe, on objective features of your situation beyond whether *p* is true, on certain counterfactuals holding of you, on your evidence for (/against) *p*, on the etiology of your belief, and so on. The natural thought, though, is that the *meaning* of 'S knows that *p*,' for example, is insensitive to shifts in factors such as these, and that once such factors are fixed the proposition expressed by such a sentence is either true or false.

Hence the significance of epistemic contextualism (EC). For contextualists deny the 'invariantist' (Unger 1984) thinking just articulated. In the words of one leading contextualist, EC is the view that "the truth conditions of sentences of the form 'S knows that *p*' or 'S does not know that *p*' vary in interesting ways depending on the context in which they are uttered" (DeRose 1992: 914), and 'context' here means none other than such things as the interests, expectations, and so forth of knowledge attributors (e.g., DeRose 1999: 189–190; Cohen 1999: 57). Put slightly differently, EC is the view that the proposition expressed by a given tokened knowledge sentence depends upon features of the knowledge attributor(s)' psychology and/or conversational-practical situation. As a result of such context-dependence, it's said, utterances of a given such sentence, made in different contexts, might differ in truth value.

Before proceeding further, and by way of further clarifying EC, we should pause to fend off a pair of possible confusions.

The first stems from the fact that different views have been termed 'contextualist'. Again: EC as we're discussing it here concerns the *truth conditions* of knowledge sentences, or the propositions expressed by utterances thereof. The thesis is that it is only relative to a contextually determined standard that a knowledge sentence expresses a complete proposition; further, change the standard, and you change what the sentence expresses. This view differs significantly from 'contextualism' of the sort defended by David Annis (1978) and Michael Williams (1991), which is an attempt to clarify the nature of knowledge and/or justified belief itself. At the same time, in its linguistic orientation EC naturally *comports* with another bearer of the 'contextualism' label: namely, the general semantical-linguistic approach that sees 'context' as central to certain fundamental semantic issues, including meaning itself. (See, e.g., Recanati 1989; Travis 2005.) Still, EC should not be confused with this general philosophy of language view.

The second possible confusion to guard against concerns just wherein the relevant context-sensitivity resides, if EC is true. Here, it's useful to consider utterances involving uncontroversially context-sensitive terms. For instance, just what proposition is expressed by an utterance of

(1) 'It's raining,'
(2) 'I'm hungry,' or
(3) 'That's red,'

depends in obvious ways upon such facts as the location (1) or identity (2) of the speaker, and/or the referent of the demonstrative (3). Similarly, it is plausible that attributions of tallness or flatness are context-sensitive, insofar as there are varying standards that one might have in mind in applying either predicate and which affect just what is said in doing so.

Note, though, that insofar as the truth *value* of such utterances "depends on context," that is because their truth *conditions*—or, the proposition expressed thereby—are so dependent: it is not as though (1)–(3) each has fixed truth-evaluable contents, the truth *values* of which happen to depend on context, perhaps because there are context-variable standards for *their* assessment. So too for EC: though the thesis is sometimes put in terms of the context-variability of knowledge sentences' truth *values* (e.g., Rieber 1998: 190; Cohen 1998: 289; 2005: 57), or variable "standards" for knowing or for what "counts as" knowing (DeRose 1995), this is misleading (Bach 2005: §I): those truth values shift only because, according to EC, *different propositions are expressed in different contexts*.

Likewise, just because EC is a thesis about knowledge sentences' truth conditions it is not a thesis about knowledge itself. So it is misleading too when EC is described, as it sometimes is, as the view that *whether one knows* depends upon context (Feldman 2004: 24; Bach 2005: 54–55). EC is an *epistemological* theory only in the sense that it concerns sentences used in attributing (/denying) "knowledge," as opposed to those employing some non-epistemological term(s).

But while it does not concern knowledge (/justified belief) in the way that traditional epistemological theories do, EC's departure from the traditional epistemological assumption of 'invariantism' is claimed to allow an attractive solution to certain long-standing puzzles about knowledge, as well as to best comport with our everyday knowledge-attributing practices. As we'll see, there is good reason to doubt whether EC delivers on all it promises, and indeed whether it is really well supported. But first, a brief review of the sort of considerations used to motivate EC is in order.

2. Theoretical Motivations

Although EC is not itself a theory of knowledge (or other epistemic matters), it has been said to afford a resolution of certain epistemological puzzles, both ordinary and extra-ordinary. Most notably, EC is said to give us a way of responding to certain cases in which we have apparently inconsistent knowledge claims, each of which enjoys some real plausibility. Though these puzzles are not exclusively skeptical, it is EC's offering a solution to skeptical problems that figures most prominently in recent discussions. So that is the natural place to start.

CONTEXTUALISM

2.1. A Skeptical Puzzle

Consider one particular form of skeptical argument upon which leading contextualists have focused (e.g., Cohen 1986, 1988, 2005; DeRose 1995; Neta 2003a & b). We'll call it 'SA', for 'skeptical argument':

P1. I don't know that not-*h* [*h* = some skeptical 'hypothesis'; e.g., that I'm a bodiless brain in a vat, being stimulated to have just those experiences I would be having if I weren't a brain in a vat ('BIV')].

P2. If I don't know that not-*h*, then I don't know that *p* [*p* = some mundane proposition which we commonly take ourselves to know; e.g., that I have hands].

C. So, I don't know that *p*.

SA constitutes a puzzle because (a) each of the premises enjoys some plausibility. As to P1, how, after all, could I know that I'm not a bodiless brain in a vat? By waving my arms around? As to P2, it is just an instance of the closure principle for knowledge—i.e., the principle that if *S* knows that *p* and that *p* entails *q*, then *S* knows that *q* (a rough statement, but good enough here); and many, including leading contextualists, are inclined to regard this principle as axiomatic. But (b) given our intuitive anti-skepticism, C seems immensely *im*plausible, even though (c) the argument appears to be formally valid.

On the face of it, we have a paradox—a set of independently plausible but seemingly mutually inconsistent propositions. Because *that* is the problem, a complete solution to SA will have to explain both which of the assumptions lying behind the generation of the paradox should be rejected and why, and why the assumption singled out for rejection struck us as plausible in the first place (DeRose 1995).

At first blush, it might seem that there are just three possible responses to SA:

i. we can capitulate to skepticism;
ii. we can reject P2 and the closure principle on which it depends; or
iii. we can reject P1 (the 'Moorean' response, as it's sometimes called).

Essential to EC is the idea that these three options do not exhaust the possible responses to SA. Stephen Schiffer (1996, 2004) agrees, but his recommendation is that we admit (iv) that our concept of knowledge is incoherent, and that epistemological paradoxes such as SA are irresolvable. For most, this is no more satisfactory than embracing skepticism.

Enter the contextualist alternative: (v) we deny that SA's conclusion really does threaten our intuitive anti-skepticism. According to EC, recall, the proposition expressed by a given knowledge utterance crucially depends upon 'context.' If a token of '*S* knows that *p*' is true just in case the subject has a true belief and is in a strong epistemic position vis-à-vis *p*, there might be variable standards governing just *how* strong the subject's epistemic position must be in order for the tokened sentence to express a truth. While different contextualist theories differ in their details (see Rysiew 2007a: §3.3), the basic contextualist solution to SA involves claiming that it involves a dramatic upwards shift in the operative standards. Those standards are not epistemic in the strict sense, of course, since they do not concern knowledge per se; but they do affect whether a given tokening of 'S knows that p' expresses a truth; for they affect just what it expresses.

Thus an utterance of P1, such as occurs in SA, might express a truth only because, owing to the introduction of a high-standards context, what it expresses is that the subject does not stand in an *extraordinarily strong* epistemic position with regard to the proposition that he has hands. But that, of course, is compatible with his meeting the lower standards ordinarily in play.

Of course, we still need an explanation of why we *thought* that the skeptic's claims threatened our ordinary claims to know. The contextualist seeks to explain this—more generally, why we might think that what is said in a given 'high-stakes' case is incompatible with what is said in its 'low-stakes' counterpart—by adopting an *error theory*: "competent speakers can fail to be aware of [. . .] context-sensitive standards, at least explicitly, and so fail to distinguish between the standards that apply in skeptical contexts, and the standards that apply in everyday contexts" (Cohen 1999: 77; 2005: 60; DeRose 1995: 40–41; 1999: 194; 2004: 37).

2.2 Everyday Cases

While a major selling point of EC is supposed to be its resolution of skeptical puzzles, contextualists also emphasize EC's (alleged) consonance with our ordinary knowledge-attributing practices. There too, they say, we find evidence of the same sort of context-sensitivity that SA exploits.

For a couple of reasons, it's very important not to overlook this appeal to everyday cases. First, as we will see, a number of philosophers have questioned just how effective EC is in its response to skepticism; and if they are right, then it matters greatly that the effectiveness of that response is not EC's sole basis. Second, as Keith DeRose says, "the contextualist's appeal to varying standards for knowledge in his solution to skepticism would rightly seem unmotivated and ad hoc if we didn't have independent reason from non-philosophical talk to think such shifts in the content of knowledge attributions occur" (2002: 169). But in fact, DeRose says, "The best grounds for accepting contextualism concerning knowledge attributions come from how knowledge-attributing (and knowledge-denying) sentences are used in ordinary, non-philosophical talk: What ordinary speakers will count as 'knowledge' in some non-philosophical contexts they will deny is such in others" (2005: 172; 2006: 316). Likewise, as with DeRose (1992) and his well-known Bank Case, Stewart Cohen claims that examples such as the following "strongly [suggest] that ascriptions of knowledge are context-sensitive" (1999: 59):

> Mary and John are at the L.A. airport contemplating taking a certain flight to New York. They want to know whether the flight has a layover in Chicago. They overhear someone ask a passenger Smith if he knows whether the flight stops in Chicago. Smith looks at the flight itinerary he got from the travel agent and responds, "Yes I know—it does stop in Chicago." It turns out that Mary and John have a very important business contact they have to make at the Chicago airport. Mary says, "How reliable is that itinerary? It could contain a misprint. They could have changed the schedule at the last minute." Mary and John agree that Smith doesn't really *know* that the plane will stop in Chicago. They decide to check with the airline agent.
>
> (Ibid.: 58)

Here too, contextualists claim that regarding the relevant sentences' truth conditions as context-dependent makes best sense of the flexibility in knowledge-attributing behavior. Thus, contextualists tend to agree that in *everyday* cases, such as that just described, the practical importance of the subjects' 'getting it right' tends to raise the standards for the truth of a sentence of the form 'S knows that p'. (Remember: what changes here is what an utterance of such a sentence expresses; we do not have a fixed such proposition, with different standards for *its* truth applying in the more demanding context.) So here too, the sentences used by someone in a 'high-stakes' context (John and Mary) and their 'low stakes' counterpart (Smith) can both be true, since the propositions they express are not really conflicting after all. (For discussion of when such a claim should/shouldn't be made, see DeRose 2006: §1; 2005: §§3–4.)

In general, then, EC posits a neat symmetry between the flexibility in our (alleged) judgments as to the truth of a given knowledge claim/denial, and a parallel plasticity in the truth conditions (and, as a result, truth *values*) of the knowledge-attributing sentences we utter. And if speakers realize, however tacitly, that what is expressed by such utterances is a context-sensitive matter, that can be used to explain the observed tendency to attribute/deny knowledge in a way that depends on such things as "the purposes, intentions, expectations, presuppositions, etc., of the speakers who utter these sentences" (Cohen 1999: 57).

2.3 Other Allegedly Pro-Contextualist Considerations

In addition to the foregoing, some contextualists (e.g., Cohen 1988, 1998; Lewis 1996; Rieber 1998; Neta 2002) have suggested that EC enables an attractive solution to 'the lottery problem.' So too, David Lewis (1996) has proposed extending EC to the Gettier problem; but this is a much more controversial idea among EC's proponents. Controversial too is whether *concessive knowledge attributions* (Rysiew 2001)—i.e., sentences of the form 'S knows that p, but it is possible that q' (where q entails not-p)—motivate EC. (Lewis (1996) thinks so; both Stanley (2005a) and Dougherty and Rysiew (2009) disagree, though for rather different reasons.) Finally, DeRose (2002) has argued that 'the knowledge account of assertion' (Williamson 2000)—the idea that one should assert only what one knows—favors EC. But whether the knowledge account is correct is highly contentious (e.g., Weiner 2005); and several people have pointed out that there is no direct path from it to EC anyway (e.g., Blackson 2004; Leite 2007).

In any case, it is fair to say that the consideration that has figured most prominently in arguments for EC is the fact that there are some cases, skeptical and otherwise, about which both a knowledge claim and a surface-incompatible knowledge-denial have some appeal. The primary virtue of EC is supposed to be that it gives us a straightforward way of accommodating this: the claims can both be true because they don't express contrary propositions after all.

3. Objections to Contextualism

In spite of its promising a neat solution to certain problems involving knowledge attributions, EC remains very controversial, with critics pointing out several serious difficulties it faces. Here, three are discussed.

3.1. Is EC Linguistically Plausible?

According to EC, 'know(s)' is a context-sensitive term. However, it's not clear that the linguistic data surrounding 'know(s)' is what one would expect were it genuinely context-sensitive. For example, Jason Stanley (2004) argues that, unlike 'flat' and 'tall,' for example, 'knows' is not clearly gradable. (It makes sense to describe someone as "very tall," but while I might say that someone knows something "very well," 'very' does not seem here to function as a degree modifier.) And while '(is) justified' is obviously gradable, even if gradability were sufficient for context-sensitivity, from the fact that knowledge requires justification it would not follow that 'knows' is context-sensitive as well (*pace* Cohen 1999: 60). Nor, Stanley argues, does 'know(s)' behave like indexicals ('I,' 'here') or relational terms (such as 'enemy').

In a related argument, Herman Cappelen and Ernie Lepore (2003) contend that, according to certain tests for the genuine context-sensitivity of a term, 'know(s)' just does not pass muster.

Finally, John Hawthorne points out that with uncontroversially context-dependent terms, we find it very natural to employ "the clarification technique." For instance: I balk at your claim that Kansas is flat, pointing out that there is a small rise just ahead of us. You clarify: "Well, what I meant was that there are very few mountains." Hawthorne's point is that we have very few techniques of clarification in the case of 'know(s)'; whereas, it "is through the clarification technique that sensitivity to context-dependence is manifested" (2004: 104–106).

Responses on behalf of EC to such arguments vary. Commenting on Stanley, Barbara Partee (2004) agrees that 'know(s)' is unlike expressions such as 'tall', but that perhaps better models are available. Nikola Kompa (2002) suggests that the context-sensitivity of 'know(s)' is best understood as deriving from a sui generis sort of "unspecificity." And Rob Stainton (2010) argues that if there are pragmatic determinants of what is stated/asserted/claimed, then what is stated (/etc.) in different uses of "knowledge" sentences can vary in truth conditions, even if 'know(s)' itself is not context-sensitive. (Here, we see a connection between EC and its philosophy-of-language namesake mentioned above; a similar connection is evident in Travis (2005).)

Ceding less ground, Peter Ludlow (2005) argues that questions about gradability are too crude a standard by which to judge whether 'know(s)' is context-sensitive. Ludlow disagrees with Hawthorne about the prevalence of clarificatory devices for 'know(s)' and argues that there is good reason to think its semantics includes some placeholder(s) for the variable standards that EC posits. Like DeRose (2005), Ludlow casts EC as a piece of 'ordinary language' philosophy, and he presents the results of Google searches in which clauses like, ". . . by objective standards," ". . . by academic standards," ". . . with some certainty," ". . . doggone well . . .," and so on, accompany uses of 'know(s).'

It's not clear what to make of such data. In general, from the fact that different qualifying phrases are used in making some evaluative judgments (whether x is/isn't F, whether S does/doesn't A) in different domains, it does not immediately follow that a contextualist semantics for the relevant terms ('F-ness,' '(to) A') is correct (cf. Conee 2005: 50–51). Such devices might be semantically revealing—as they arguably are with, for instance, "He's pretty tall for a jockey"; but they might be grammatically misleading—as they would be with, for example, "She spoke with confidence," or "By anyone's reckoning, Albert lied." In the latter cases, the extra information involves, not the making explicit of context-variable standards (for "speaking" or "lying"), but the featuring of information over and above that encoded in the relevant verb (the manner of speaking, the obviousness of the deceit). In the same fashion, the qualifying phrases in Ludlow's examples *might* be overt references to standards for knowing per se; but they might be serving merely to indicate such things as the nature or quality of the subject S's evidence, just who has judged S to be a knower, S's exact degree of confidence, the uncontroversial character of S's knowing or of what S knows, and so on.

3.2. Does EC Really Help with Skepticism?

Recall (§1) that EC is a semantic or linguistic thesis—it doesn't concern knowledge itself, but rather the context-variable nature of the propositions expressed by utterances of 'knowledge'-attributing/-denying sentences. Just because this is so, one can wonder whether EC successfully engages skepticism. Various versions of this objection have been lodged (e.g., Feldman 1999, 2001, 2004; Klein 2000; Kornblith 2000; Sosa 2000; Bach 2005). On one version, (e.g., Conee 2005; Feldman 2001), it's noted that EC per se does not generate the results essential to the contextualist resolution of SA, for example, since EC alone does not ensure that the propositions expressed by utterances of knowledge sentences in ordinary contexts are true.

On another version, the objection is that EC does not correctly characterize the skeptical problem. As we have seen, EC has it that skeptical claims express truths only relative to extraordinarily high epistemic standards. But, the objection runs, what's at issue between skeptics and non-skeptics is whether we satisfy even our ordinary epistemic standards (Kornblith 2000; Feldman 2004). As Ernest Sosa (2000) puts it, the antiskeptical "Moorean stance" is not the thesis that folks in ordinary situations who claim to "know" things often express truths. Rather, it "is a stance, adopted in a philosophical context, about what one then knows and, by extension, what people ordinarily know" (Sosa 2004: 281).

Of course, the contextualist might counter that this Moorean view presumes falsely that there is some 'knowledge' proposition which is both true and expressible acontextually: perhaps the Moorean view itself manifests a failure to be aware of the context-sensitivity of the expressions in question (§2.1). But both that error theory and the contextualist's appealing to it have been the target of strong objections. So, while other grounds for dissatisfaction with an EC-based response to skepticism have been cited—for example, that it's not well-positioned to explain the plausibility of certain anti-skeptical claims (e.g., Sosa 2000: 15), that it's not obviously applicable to forms of skeptical argument beyond SA (e.g., Feldman 2001: 78ff.), or that it makes certain true "knowledge" propositions inexpressible (e.g., Brady and Pritchard 2005)—we will leave those aside, and turn instead to worries about EC's error theory.

3.3. Is the Contextualist's Error Theory Problematic?

As we've seen, one of the major attractions of EC is said to be that it allows us to resolve certain apparent conflicts among sets of individually plausible claims without forcing us to reject any of the members thereof as false. However, as we've also seen (§2.1), contextualists are committed to the claim that we fail to fully appreciate the contextualist semantics and/or to faithfully track shifts in context.

This gives rise to another oft-voiced objection to EC (e.g., Schiffer 1996; Hofweber 1999; Rysiew 2001; Hawthorne 2004; Conee 2005; Williamson 2005). As formulated by Stephen Schiffer, the objection is simply that it is implausible that we would get "bamboozled by our own words" (1996: 329) in the way the contextualist alleges, since "speakers would know what they were saying if knowledge sentences were indexical in the way the Contextualist requires" (ibid.: 328).

This complaint might seem not to have much weight. With respect to SA above, for example, the two premises are (suppose) individually quite plausible, the argument appears valid, yet the conclusion seems very *im*plausible. So "something plausible has to go" (DeRose 1995: 2)—we're going to end up being confused (mistaken) about *something*. This is one of the ways in which Cohen has recently responded to concerns about contextualism's error theory (Cohen 2005: 70). And DeRose (2006) has replied along similar lines: if you present a group of subjects with SA, for instance, and ask them whether the conclusion contradicts an ordinary claim to know, some will say 'yes,' and some will say 'no.' If contextualism turns out to be true, then many are blind to *that*, and so on. So, whoever's right, a substantial portion of ordinary speakers are afflicted by "semantic blindness" (Hawthorne 2004: 107). 'Bamboozlement' is something we're stuck with either way.

In assessing this type of response to the objection under consideration, it is useful to separate out two questions: First, whether, considered on its own, the contextualist's error theory is plausible. Second, whether that theory raises any problems internal to the contextualist view.

As to the first question, there *are* precedents for the type of error that the contextualist says is going on in the case of knowledge attributions. For example, by implicitly raising the standards—drawing attention to previously disregarded bumps, etc.—you can get a competent speaker to take seriously 'flatness skepticism,' the view that nothing's really flat (Cohen 1999: 78–9; 2001: 91; 2004: 193; 2005: 60, 70).

However, such cases are conspicuous in manifesting a *disappearance effect*: when an apparent incompatibility between certain uttered sentences is due to their expressing different propositions, once this is pointed out, any appearance that they are incompatible tends to go away. Thus, we might 'disagree' over whether Kansas is flat, but once it is made clear that you mean *relatively un-mountainous* and I mean *devoid of any hills at all*, we quickly agree that we were both right. But for many, no such effect attends the consideration of EC (Feldman 2001: 73, 77–78; Rysiew 2001: 484–485; Conee 2005: 55, 66). Thus, using subscripts to denote the context-sensitivity that the contextualist alleges is at work in the airport case (§2.2), we can make explicit the (alleged) truth-conditional content of the two uttered sentences as follows:

(SMITH) 'S has a true belief and is in a strong$_{C1}$ epistemic position,' and
(MARY) 'It is not the case that (S has a true belief and is in a strong$_{C2}$ epistemic position)'

(Rysiew 2007b: 652–653; cf. Bach 2005: §1)

To many, however, such renderings of the relevant claims don't bring to light a context-sensitivity that's immediately obvious upon being brought to our attention; they serve only to highlight the controversial character of EC.

Acknowledging this fact, Cohen notes that there are "varying degrees to which competent speakers are blind to the context-sensitivity in the language" (2005: 61). That of indexicals ('I,' 'now') is easy to spot, that of 'flat' somewhat harder. For 'knows,' "it may be very difficult even after some amount of reflection for competent speakers to accept context-sensitivity. It may take subtle philosophical considerations concerning the best way to resolve a paradox in order to 'see' the context-sensitivity of 'knows'" (ibid.).

This type of response to the worry at hand brings into focus the second sort of concern noted above: that the contextualist's error theory raises problems internal to the contextualist view itself. For, to the extent that the context-sensitivity of the relevant expressions can remain deeply hidden, even after careful reflection, it becomes even less clear than it already was that in the cases of concern (SA, the airport example, etc.) what's driving our judgments as to whether what speakers say is correct is, as the contextualist says, precisely an *awareness* of that context-sensitivity.

More has been said concerning the plausibility of EC's error theory (for which, see Rysiew 2001: §3 and §10; 2007a: §4.3). But it's clear that we've moved beyond considerations merely of the contextualist's imputation of linguistic error to ordinary speakers: in spite of how it is sometimes presented, both by critics of EC (e.g., Schiffer 1996; Hawthorne 2004) and by its defenders (e.g., DeRose 2006), the issue does not concern semantic 'blindness' or 'bamboozlement' per se. Rather, it has to do with the unsatisfactory or troubling nature of the contextualist's appeal to such a thing in particular.

Still other criticisms of EC have been made as well (see Rysiew 2007a: §4.5). Of course, if EC were the only solution to the data that inspire it, we'd have good reason to at least hope that all the various problems facing EC could be overcome. However, several alternative treatments of the relevant data have been proposed.

4. Alternative, Non-Contextualist Accounts

Among critics of EC, at least three such alternative explanations have emerged. Since each is intended to preserve the thought that we do ordinarily know many things, the granting of knowledge in the relevant 'low standards' case is taken to express a truth. What needs explaining, then, is why denying knowledge of the same subject can seem correct once the standards are raised, even though nothing in the subject's situation changes. Though they are not obviously competing, each attempt to explain this in non-contextualist terms keys on different factors. Framed in terms of the airport example described above (§2.2), and in broad outline only, these sample non-contextualist proposals are as follows.

4.1. Salience, Conflicting Arguments, and Focusing Effects

When we find people seeming to disagree about some matter, often that's because there is a genuine conflict of evidence—arguments and considerations on either side of the issue, none of which can be easily dismissed. And which of these one focuses on can affect one's view as to the truth of the proposition in question. So, for instance, if Mary and John focus on the various ways in which Smith might be mistaken (e.g., because of a misprint in the itinerary), this can get them thinking that he does not know what he claims to know, especially if focusing on a possibility tends to make one over-rate its probability. (See especially Feldman 2001: 74–78. For similar ideas, see Williamson 2005: 112; Conee 2005: 63–66; and Rysiew 2001: 503–505.)

4.2. Psychological Presuppositions of Attributing Knowledge

Kent Bach (2005: 76–77) points out that if Mary is not sure that Smith's itinerary is reliable, she won't be confident enough herself to believe that the plane will stop in

Chicago, in which case she cannot coherently attribute *knowledge* of that fact to Smith. Indeed, Mary will have to deny that she knows it, "since she thinks that it is not yet established. And, since Smith has no evidence that she doesn't have, she must deny that he knows it [too]." In a similar spirit, Jonathan Adler (2006) suggests that such cases are best explained in terms of the subject's diminished confidence as to p, where the latter does not imply a lack of belief.

4.3. Pragmatic Factors

According to some (e.g., Blaauw 2003; Black 2005; Brown 2006; Pritchard 2010; Rysiew 2001, 2005, 2007b), pragmatic factors explain the relevant knowledge-attributing behavior. (There are differences among these views; here, one sample elaboration is sketched.) In the airport case, it is mutually obvious to John and Mary that they want to ensure that their epistemic position with respect to the flight plan is *very* strong—strong enough to rule out the possibility of a misprint, for example, being in an epistemic position of such strength might or might not be required for knowing. Hence, whether Smith does know—whether the proposition literally expressed by "Smith knows . . ." is true—might or might not be relevant to John and Mary's concerns. Either way, 'S knows that p' entails that S is in a good epistemic position—this is why granting someone knowledge involves representing them as entitled to their belief. But it would be odd of Mary and John to grant Smith such an entitlement (by saying 'he knows') and represent him as being in a good epistemic position if they thought that his evidence wasn't so good as to put their concerns to rest. Whereas, by denying knowledge to Smith, they are able to express the thought, which seems not just relevant but true, that his epistemic position is not so good that they do not need to check further. And if they (we) read what is conveyed by the relevant utterance onto the sentence uttered, the knowledge denial will strike them (us) as expressing a truth.

Of course, the contextualist can deny that pragmatic factors play any real role in the relevant cases. Suppose that's so—i.e., suppose that the information that each of the speakers in the airport example (e.g.) is concerned to communicate, and to which our intuitions about their utterances are responsive, is nothing more or less than that which is, according to EC, what the sentence he/she utters semantically expresses. In that case, we should expect that our laying bare those contents—as we did with (Smith) and (Mary), the explicit relativizations in §3.3—will generate the very same response as did their inexplicit counterparts. But of course they don't: the airport case, or SA, presents a puzzle only because the relevant claims strike us as incompatible; but (Smith) and (Mary) are obviously compatible—and not just with each other, but with a non-contextualist view of the truth conditions of knowledge sentences (Rysiew 2007b: 652–653)! In response, the contextualist could once again resort to his/her error theory; but at this point such a move should appear rather strained.

4.4. Other Alternative Views

Each of the preceding alternative treatments of the data can be made to fit with standard epistemological thinking about knowledge (and 'knows'). But EC faces other recent and less orthodox competitors, including those treated in other essays in this volume—contrastivism (e.g., Karjalainen and Morton 2003; Schaffer 2004); 'subject sensitive invariantism' (e.g., Fantl and McGrath 2002; Hawthorne 2004; Stanley 2005b); and relativism (e.g., MacFarlane 2005). As the field of available views expands, the case for EC's providing a uniquely viable treatment of the data that inspires it is further weakened.

5. Conclusion

EC has garnered a lot of attention in recent years, and rightly so. It poses a challenge to standard, invariantist thinking. Just as importantly, it has forced epistemologists to pay closer attention to our actual knowledge-attributing practices. However, whether it provides the best account of the latter, and the best resolution of certain long-standing philosophical problems, is far from clear.

References

Adler, J., 2006, "Withdrawal and Contextualism," *Analysis*, 66(4): 280–285.
Annis, D. B., 1978, "A Contextualist Theory of Epistemic Justification," *American Philosophical Quarterly*, 15(3): 213–219.
Bach, K., 2005, "The Emperor's New 'Knows'," in G. Preyer and G. Peter, eds., *Contextualism in Philosophy: Knowledge, Meaning, and Truth*, Oxford: Clarendon, pp. 51–89.
Blaauw, M., 2003, "WAMing Away at Contextualism," *Nordic Journal of Philosophy*, 4(1): 88–97.
Black, T., 2005, "Classic Invariantism, Relevance, and Warranted Assertability Manœuvers," *Philosophical Quarterly*, 55(219): 328–336.
Blackson, T., 2004, "An Invalid Argument for Contextualism," *Philosophy and Phenomenological Research*, 68(2): 344–345.
Brady, M. and D. H. Pritchard, 2005, "Epistemological Contextualism: Problems and Prospects," *Philosophical Quarterly* 55(219): 161–171.
Brown, J., 2006, "Contextualism and Warranted Assertibility Manoeuvres," *Philosophical Studies*, 130: 407–435.
Cappelen, H. and E. Lepore, 2003, "Context Shifting Arguments," *Philosophical Perspectives 17: Language and Philosophical Linguistics*: 25–50.
Cohen, S., 1986, "Knowledge and Context," *Journal of Philosophy*, 83: 574–583.
——, 1988, "How to be a Fallibilist," *Philosophical Perspectives, 2: Epistemology*: 91–123.
——, 1998, "Contextualist Solutions to Epistemological Problems: Skepticism, Gettier, and the Lottery," *Australasian Journal of Philosophy*, 76(2): 289–306.
——, 1999, "Contextualism, Skepticism, and the Structure of Reasons," *Philosophical Perspectives 13: Epistemology*: 57–89.
——, 2001, "Contextualism Defended: Comments on Richard Feldman's 'Skeptical Problems, Contextualist Solutions'," *Philosophical Studies*, 103: 87–98.
——, 2005, "Contextualism Defended" and "Contextualism Defended Some More," in M. Steup and E. Sosa, eds., *Contemporary Debates in Epistemology*, Malden MA: Blackwell, pp. 56–62, 67–71.
Conee, E., 2005, "Contextualism Contested" and "Contextualism Contested Some More," in M. Steup and E. Sosa, eds., *Contemporary Debates in Epistemology*, Malden MA: Blackwell, pp. 47–56, 62–66.
DeRose, K., 1992, "Contextualism and Knowledge Attributions," *Philosophy and Phenomenological Research*, 52(4): 913–929.
——, 1995, "Solving the Skeptical Problem," *The Philosophical Review*, 104(1), 1–52.
——, 1999, "Contextualism: An Explanation and Defense," in J. Greco and E. Sosa, eds., *The Blackwell Guide to Epistemology*, Malden, MA: Blackwell, pp. 185–203.
——, 2002, "Assertion, Knowledge and Context," *The Philosophical Review*, 111(2): 167–203.
——, 2004, "Sosa, Safety, Sensitivity, and Skeptical Hypotheses," in J. Greco, ed., *Ernest Sosa and His Critics*, Cambridge, MA: Blackwell, pp. 22–41.
——, 2005, "The Ordinary Language Basis for Contextualism and the New Invariantism," *Philosophical Quarterly*, 55(219): 172–198.
——, 2006, "'Bamboozled by Our Own Words': Semantic Blindness and Some Arguments Against Contextualism," *Philosophy and Phenomenological Research*, 73(2): 316–338.

Dougherty, T. and P. Rysiew, 2009, "Fallibilism, Epistemic Possibility, and Concessive Knowledge Attributions," *Philosophy and Phenomenological Research*, 78(1): 123–132.
Fantl, J. and M. McGrath, 2002, "Evidence, Pragmatics, and Justification," *The Philosophical Review*, 111: 67–94.
Feldman, R., 1999, "Contextualism and Skepticism," *Philosophical Perspectives 13: Epistemology*: 91–114.
——, 2001, "Skeptical Problems, Contextualist Solutions," *Philosophical Studies*, 103: 61–85. (A revised version of Feldman 1999.)
——, 2004, "Comments on DeRose's 'Single Scoreboard Semantics'," *Philosophical Studies*, 119(1–2): 23–33.
Hawthorne, J., 2004, *Knowledge and Lotteries*, Oxford: Oxford University Press.
Hofweber, T., 1999, "Contextualism and the Meaning-Intention Problem," in K. Korta, E. Sosa, and X. Arrazola, eds., *Cognition, Agency and Rationality*, Dordrecht: Kluwer, pp. 93–104.
Karjalainen, A. and A. Morton, 2003, "Contrastive Knowledge," *Philosophical Explorations*, 6(2): 74–89.
Klein, P., 2000, "Contextualism and the Real Nature of Academic Skepticism," *Philosophical Issues*, 10: 108–116.
Kompa, N., 2002, "The Context Sensitivity of Knowledge Ascriptions," *Grazer Philosophische Studien*, 64: 11–18.
Kornblith, H., 2000, "The Contextualist Evasion of Epistemology," *Philosophical Issues*, 10: 24–32.
Leite, A., 2007, "How to Link Assertion and Knowledge Without Going Contextualist: A Reply to DeRose's 'Assertion, Knowledge, and Context'," *Philosophical Studies*, 134: 111–129.
Lewis, D., 1996, "Elusive Knowledge," *Australasian Journal of Philosophy*, 74(4): 549–567.
Ludlow, P., 2005, "Contextualism and the New Linguistic Turn in Epistemology," in G. Preyer and G. Peter, eds., *Contextualism in Philosophy: Knowledge, Meaning, and Truth*, Oxford: Clarendon, pp. 11–50.
MacFarlane, J., 2005, "The Assessment Sensitivity of Knowledge Attributions," in T. S. Gendler and J. Hawthorne, eds., *Oxford Studies in Epistemology 1*, Oxford: Oxford University Press, pp. 197–233.
Neta, R., 2002, "S knows that P," *Noûs*, 36(4): 663–681.
——, 2003a, "Skepticism, Contextualism, and Semantic Self-Knowledge," *Philosophy and Phenomenological Research*, 67(2): 397–411.
——, 2003b, "Contextualism and the Problem of the External World," *Philosophy and Phenomenological Research*, 66(1): 1–31.
Partee, B., 2004, "Comments on Jason Stanley's 'On the Linguistic Basis for Contextualism'," *Philosophical Studies*, 119(1–2): 147–159.
Pritchard, D. H., 2010, "Contextualism, Skepticism, and Warranted Assertibility Manoeuvres," in J. K. Campbell, M. O'Rourke and H. S. Silverstein, eds., *Knowledge and Skepticism*, Cambridge, MA: MIT Press, pp. 85–103.
Recanati, F., 1989, "The Pragmatics of What is Said," *Mind & Language*, 4(4): 295–329.
Rieber, S., 1998, "Skepticism and Contrastive Explanation," *Noûs*, 32(2): 189–204.
Rysiew, P., 2001, "The Context-Sensitivity of Knowledge Attributions," *Noûs*, 35(4): 477–514.
——, 2005, "Contesting Contextualism," *Grazer Philosophische Studien*, 69: 51–70.
——, 2007a, "Epistemic Contextualism," in E. Zalta, (ed.), *The Stanford Encyclopedia of Philosophy*. URL = http://plato.stanford.edu/archives/fall2007/entries/contextualism-epistemology/.
——, 2007b, "Speaking of Knowing," *Noûs*, 41(4): 627–662.
Schaffer, J., 2004, "From Contextualism to Contrastivism," *Philosophical Studies*, 119(1–2): 73–103.
Schiffer, S., 1996, "Contextualist Solutions to Skepticism," *Proceedings of the Aristotelian Society*, 96: 317–333.
——, 2004, "Skepticism and the Vagaries of Justified Belief," *Philosophical Studies*, 103: 161–184.
Sosa, E., 2000, "Skepticism and Contextualism," *Philosophical Issues*, 10: 1–18.
——, 2004, "Replies," in J. Greco, ed., *Ernest Sosa and His Critics*, Cambridge, MA: Blackwell, pp. 275–325.
Stainton, R., 2010, "Contextualism in Epistemology and the Context-Sensitivity of 'Knows'," in J. K. Campbell, M. O'Rourke and H. S. Silverstein, eds., *Knowledge and Skepticism*, Cambridge, MA: MIT Press, pp. 137–163.
Stanley, J., 2004, "On the Linguistic Basis for Contextualism," *Philosophical Studies*, 119(1–2): 119–146.
——, 2005a, "Fallibilism and Concessive Knowledge Attributions," *Analysis*, 65(2): 126–131.
——, 2005b, *Knowledge and Practical Interests*, Oxford: Oxford University Press.
Travis, C., 2005, "A Sense of Occasion," *Philosophical Quarterly*, 55(219): 286–314.
Unger, P., 1984, *Philosophical Relativity*, Minneapolis: University of Minnesota Press.

Weiner, M., 2005, "Must We Know What We Say?," *The Philosophical Review*, 114(2): 227–251.
Williams, M., 1991, *Unnatural Doubts: Epistemological Realism and the Basis of Skepticism*, Cambridge, MA: Blackwell.
Williamson, T., 2000, *Knowledge and its Limits*, Oxford: Oxford University Press.
—— 2005, "Knowledge, Context, and the Agent's Point of View," in G. Preyer and G. Peter, eds., *Contextualism in Philosophy: Knowledge, Meaning, and Truth*, Oxford: Clarendon, pp. 91–114.

49
RELATIVISM AND KNOWLEDGE ATTRIBUTIONS
John MacFarlane

Relativism, in the sense at issue here, is a view about the meaning of knowledge attributions—statements of the form "*S* knows that *p*." Like contextualism, it holds that the truth of knowledge claims is sensitive to contextual factors, such as which alternatives are relevant at the context, or how high the stakes are. For the relativist, however, the relevant context is the context from which the knowledge claim is being *assessed*, not the context at which it was *made*.

The Relativist's Position

One kind of relativist position can be defined by its acceptance of the following four theses:

Local Invariantism:
The relation expressed by "know" does not vary with context.

Dyadic Relation:
This relation is a two-place relation; it does not have implicit argument places that must be filled through hidden variables in the logical form or "free enrichment."

Fancy Intensions:
Although "know" invariantly expresses the knowledge relation, this relation does not have an intension of the familiar sort—a function from possible worlds and times to truth values. That is, its extension is not determined by the state of the world at a time, but depends on something else in addition, which we will call an *epistemic standard*.

Assessment Sensitivity:
The accuracy of an assertion or belief depends on the epistemic standard that is relevant at the context of assessment. Thus, there is no "absolute" answer to the question whether such an assertion or belief is accurate; accuracy is an assessment-sensitive matter.

A few words of explanation are in order.

Local Invariantism is rejected by philosophers who take "know" to be an *indexical*. An indexical is a word whose content (its contribution to the propositions expressed by sentences of which it is a part) is determined in part by features of the context. A paradigm is "today," which denotes the day on which it is uttered. Some epistemic contextualists (Cohen 1988: 97; DeRose 1996: 194 n.4) hold that "know" is indexical, meaning that there are many different knowledge relations, and the particular relation expressed by "know" on an occasion of use depends on contextual factors such as relevant alternatives or practical stakes.

One might accept Local Invariantism, however, while still holding that the contents of sentences of the form "S knows that p" depend on contextual factors of this kind. For one might reject Dyadic Relation and hold that "know" invariantly expresses a *three*-place relation between a person, a proposition, and something else—perhaps an epistemic standard, a set of alternatives, or a "question" (Schaffer 2004b). Although no part of the English sentence explicitly denotes the third relatum, it might be denoted by an "aphonic" element in the deep syntax, or the speaker might simply expect hearers to be able to fill in the blank using contextual cues. Let us call views with this shape *relational contextualism*.

Views that accept both Local Invariantism and Dyadic Relation take knowledge-attributing sentences not containing other indexical or demonstrative elements to have contents that are invariant over contexts of use. All such views, then, can be characterized as forms of invariantism. We can distinguish, however, between *standard invariantism*, which rejects both Fancy Intensions and Assessment Sensitivity; *nonindexical contextualism*, which accepts Fancy Intensions and rejects Assessment Sensitivity; and *truth relativism*, which accepts both Fancy Intensions and Assessment Sensitivity.

According to standard invariantism, "know" invariantly expresses a two-place relation between persons and propositions—the relation of knowing—and this relation has an intension of the standard sort: a function from worlds and times to extensions. There is still a lot of room for arguing about what that intension looks like. *Skeptical invariantists* say that x stands in the knowing relation to p at a world w and time t just in case x's evidence for p at w and t is strong enough to rule out any possibility that p is false, while *dogmatic invariantists* propose a more relaxed condition, and *subject-sensitive invariantists* hold that the strength of evidence required for x to stand in the knowing relation to p at w and t depends on aspects of x's practical situation at w and t (Hawthorne 2004: chs. 3–4). But although these different invariantist positions disagree about which worldly states of affairs suffice for a person to stand in the knowing relation to a proposition, they all assume that there is a definite, context-independent, answer to this question. That assumption is precisely what relativists and nonindexical contextualists deny in accepting Fancy Intensions.

According to Fancy Intensions, there is no answer to the question at issue between dogmatic, skeptical, and subject-sensitive invariantists, because the knowing relation does not have any particular extension at a world and a time. In order to get an extension, one must specify not just a world and a time, but also an *epistemic standard*, which determines how well placed a subject must be in order to stand in the knowing relation to a proposition. We can be neutral here about what an epistemic standard consists in. On some views, it will be defined by a threshold strength of evidence required for knowledge; on others, by a set of relevant alternatives that must be excluded if the subject is to have knowledge. In what follows we will talk of standards being "low" and "high," but we do not mean to imply that standards must be linearly ordered. Sets of relevant alternatives, for example, are only partially ordered.

In order to explain Assessment Sensitivity, which separates relativists from non-indexical contextualists, we must say a few words about what is meant here by "accuracy." It is standard in semantics to think of contents as having their extensions relative to possible worlds, or in some cases worlds and times (see King 2003 for a nice discussion of some of the issues relevant to choosing between these two options). That means that propositions have truth values relative to worlds (or worlds and times). But in these frameworks, whether a speaker has gotten it right—whether her assertion is accurate—depends only on the truth value of the asserted content relative to the world and time of the context of use. Thus, even though the content of an assertion is something that has different truth values relative to different worlds (and perhaps times), whether a particular assertion is accurate is, in standard frameworks, an absolute matter.

The point is perhaps easiest to see if we work with "tensed" propositions, which have different truth values relative to different times. According to temporalists, in saying "Socrates is sitting," one expresses the tensed proposition that Socrates is sitting—a proposition that is true relative to some times (noon) and false relative to others (midnight). ("Eternalists," by contrast, hold that this sentence expresses different eternal propositions when used at different times.) Suppose Jake asserts this proposition at noon, when Socrates is sitting on a bench at the agora, and Sally asserts it at midnight, when Socrates is lying down at the symposium. Then, as both parties can recognize, Jake's assertion is accurate, while Sally's is not. Even though the truth of the proposition asserted is time-relative, the accuracy of an assertion of it is not; the accuracy of an assertion depends on the truth value of its content at the time the assertion was made.

The point can also be made with standard "eternalist" propositions. Suppose we are considering an assertion, in a possible world where diamonds can be found just about everywhere, of the proposition that diamonds are rare. Although this would be an assertion of a proposition that is true in the actual world, it would nonetheless be inaccurate, since diamonds are not rare in the world at which the assertion is made. Accuracy hangs on truth in the world in which the assertion is made.

But what about the new coordinate that Fancy Intensions adds to intensions—the epistemic standard? Which epistemic standard do we look at in determining whether a particular assertion or belief that p is accurate? A natural view is that, just as accuracy depends on the world and time of the context of use, so it depends on the epistemic standard that is relevant at the context of use. This view would resemble indexical contextualism in taking the extension of "know" (as used at a particular context) to depend not just on the worldly state of affairs but on a contextually relevant epistemic standard. It would depart from it, however, in denying that the *content* of "know" varies with the contextually relevant epistemic standard. MacFarlane (2005b, 2007a, 2007b, 2009) has dubbed such views forms of *nonindexical contextualism*. (Nonindexical contextualist accounts of "know" are defended by Kompa (2002) and Brogaard (2008).)

But this decision about how to treat the epistemic standard coordinate when evaluating uses of propositions is not the only possible one. One could, alternatively, take the accuracy of an assertion or belief that p to depend on the truth of p at the world and time of the context of use and the epistemic standard that is relevant at the context of *assessment*. On this view, there are no absolute facts about accuracy; a particular assertion or belief might be accurate as assessed from one context and inaccurate as assessed from another, if different epistemic standards are relevant at the two contexts. It is this move—relativizing accuracy—that raises the philosophical questions that have traditionally been associated with "relative truth." So this view deserves the label *truth relativism*. (Relativist accounts of "know" are defended by Richard (2004) and MacFarlane (2005a).)

Instead of relativizing truth, one might take the *contents* of knowledge attributions to be assessment-sensitive. According to *content relativism*, there is no assessment-independent fact of the matter about what proposition is asserted by an utterance of a knowledge-attributing sentence. This view accepts Assessment Sensitivity, because the accuracy of an assertion depends in part on what its content is, and according to content relativism, this depends on the context of assessment. It parts company with truth relativism, however, in rejecting Fancy Intensions and either Local Invariantism or Dyadic Relation. *Indexical content relativism* resembles indexical contextualism in rejecting Local Invariantism, while *relational content relativism* resembles relational contextualism in rejecting Dyadic Relation. (For a defense of a form of content relativism, see Cappelen 2008.)

We can categorize the positions we have discussed by looking at which of the four principles they accept (Table 49.1).

The Case for Relativism

Relativism about knowledge attributions can be seen as a kind of synthesis of contextualism and invariantism. Like the contextualist, the relativist holds that the truth of knowledge attributions is relative to contextual epistemic standards. And like the invariantist, the relativist holds that "know" expresses the same relation at every context of use. So a case for relativism can be made by cobbling together the best of the invariantists' arguments against contextualism and the best of the contextualists' arguments against invariantism. Relativism promises to retain what is right about both contextualism and invariantism while avoiding their flaws.

Against Contextualism

The literature contains quite a few different arguments against contextualism. Some of these apply only to indexical contextualism, while others apply also to relationalism and/or nonindexical contextualism.

Table 49.1

	Local Invariantism	Dyadic Relation	Fancy Intensions	Assessment Sensitivity
Indexical contextualism		✓		
Relational contextualism	✓			
Invariantism	✓	✓		
Nonindexical contextualism	✓	✓	✓	
Truth relativism	✓	✓	✓	✓
Indexical content relativism		✓		✓
Relational content relativism	✓			✓

One argument against indexical contextualism and relationalism is that competent speakers ought to know whether the contents of their knowledge claims are contextually sensitive. Yet, as Schiffer (1996: 326–7) observes, "no ordinary person who utters 'I know that p,' however articulate, would dream of telling you that what he meant and was implicitly stating was that he knew that p relative to such-and-such standard" (see also Feldman 2001: 74, 78–9; Hawthorne 2004: §2.7). (For a defense of the contextualist's imputation of "semantic blindness" here, see DeRose 2006.)

Another argument (Hawthorne 2004: §2.7) is that "know" does not behave like paradigm context-sensitive terms inside attitude reports. If Joe, in a high-stakes context, says "I don't know whether the bank will be open tomorrow," Sarah can say the next day, in a low-stakes context, "Joe said he didn't know whether the bank would be open today." Sarah uses "today" instead of "tomorrow" in reporting the content of Joe's claim, because "tomorrow" is indexical and would not have the same content if she were to use it that it did when Joe used it. But she does not find another word to replace "know," and this suggests that she takes "know" as she uses it to express the same relation that it expressed when Joe used it the day before. However, this argument does not have any force against nonindexical contextualism, which holds that the *content* of "know" remains invariant between contexts. Nor does it rule out relationalist accounts of "know," which allow that the reporter can "fill in" the implicit argument place in the same way as the original speaker did.

A third argument, which counts against all three forms of contextualism, is that contextualist views make faulty predictions about agreement and disagreement, and about proprieties for correction and retraction of assertions (Feldman 2001: 77; Rosenberg 2002: 164; Hawthorne 2004: 163; Richard 2004: 216–17; MacFarlane 2005a: §2.3; Stanley 2005: 52–6). Here there seems to be a real contrast between "know" and context-sensitive words like "tall." If Joe says that Chiara is tall (meaning tall *for a fifth-grader*) and Sarah says that she is not tall (meaning tall *for an American female*), they have not disagreed, and (barring misunderstanding) Joe will not take Sarah's claim to be any kind of challenge to his own. It would be positively bizarre for Joe to say to Sarah, "Yes, you're right, she *isn't* tall after all; I take back what I said." Things are otherwise with "know." If Joe (in a low-standards situation) says, "I know that the bank is open on Saturday," and Sarah later says (in a high-standards situation), "You didn't know that the bank was open," Joe will naturally take Sarah's claim as a challenge to his own, and either defend his claim or withdraw it. We do not expect him to say (as the contextualist account would suggest he should): "Yes, you're right, I didn't know. Still, what I said was true, and I stick by it. I only meant that I knew-by-low-standards." Similarly, the skeptic regards himself as disagreeing with ordinary knowledge claims, but if the contextualist is right, this is just a confusion.

Thus the contextualist seems forced to say that ordinary speakers are *mistakenly* taking themselves to disagree (or to agree). But attributing this kind of error tends to undermine the positive case for contextualism, which rests largely on observations about speakers' propensities to use "know" in various contexts. The more semantic and substantive error we attribute to speakers, the less their usage can tell us about the meanings of their words.

Against Invariantism

Invariantists have an easy time explaining speakers' perceptions of agreement and disagreement, since they take them to be veridical. But they have a hard time explaining the basic data that motivate contextualism. There *does* seem to be some variation in the strength of the epistemic position one must be in if one is to count as "knowing." Contextualists explain that by saying that the extension of "know" is sensitive to contextual factors. How can invariantists explain it?

One strategy would be to attribute this variation to speaker error. Perhaps speakers systematically misjudge the strength of subjects' epistemic positions, and that explains why they are readier to count someone as "knowing" in some situations than in others. Speakers certainly do make mistakes of this kind. However, this strategy is committed to positing a source of *systematic* error that precisely mirrors the contextual variation we see in the usage of "know." This is a tall order.

A second strategy is to appeal to loose use or figurative uses of language. Perhaps knowledge demands a very high standard of evidence—so high that we rarely if ever meet it. If we wish to speak literal truth, then, we should not say that we know, but describe our evidence more precisely, acknowledging its limitations. In practice, though, this would often be pedantic and pointless. Just as it serves our purposes to say that it's noon, when in fact it is one minute past noon, so it might serve our purposes to say that we know, when in fact we only approximate the epistemic position required for knowledge (Schaffer 2004a; Davis 2007). This strategy concedes that the skeptic is correct that, strictly speaking, knowledge is rare, and holds that our knowledge claims can be explained as loose use.

One problem with the loose use strategy is that speakers are normally conscious of their loose use. We might ask: "Strictly speaking, is it noon, or one minute past noon?" And the loose talker will say (with an exasperated grumble): "Okay, if you want to be precise, it's not noon, it's one minute past." So the loose use strategy requires that speakers are normally aware that their knowledge claims are not strictly true. If that were so, however, skepticism would be universally accepted as true but uninteresting. And it isn't.

A loose use theorist might hold, alternatively, that standards for knowledge are invariant but moderate, so that the skeptic's denials of knowledge are false. Uses of "know" that seem to assume a stricter standard could perhaps be explained by appeal to implicatures (Rysiew 2001). One would also like some explanation, however, of why the standard for knowledge is what it is, and not something stricter or laxer.

A third invariantist strategy for explaining the apparent variation in standards for knowing is subject-sensitive invariantism (SSI) (Hawthorne 2004; Stanley 2005). According to SSI, the standard a subject must meet in order to stand in the knowledge relation to a proposition (at a particular possible world and time) depends on the subject's practical situation (at that world and time). This is not a contextualist position, because the relevant epistemic standard is fixed by the *subject's* situation, not the speaker's. Nor does it require "fancy intensions": since the world and time of evaluation fix a relevant standard for the subject, the intension of "know" does not need to be separately relativized to a standard.

SSI yields the same predictions as contextualism about present-tense, first-person knowledge attributions ("I know that *p*"), since for these the speaker's context and the subject's circumstances coincide. To distinguish the two views, we must look at third-person or past-tense knowledge attributions. Contextualism predicts that the accuracy of assertions of "Joe knew last Friday that the bank would be open on Saturday" can depend on aspects of the speaker's current situation (for example, whether the stakes are high, or whether a given possibility is contextually salient), while SSI predicts that it will depend only on Joe's situation last Friday. There is considerable disagreement about which of these predictions is better supported (see Hawthorne 2004; Stanley 2005; DeRose 2004, 2005). DeRose (2005: 189) notes that the contextualist can accommodate many cases that might seem to support SSI, because "sometimes speakers' own conversational purposes call for employing standards that are appropriate to the practical situation of the far-away subjects they are discussing." But, he observes, it is hard to see how SSI could accommodate the cases that seem to support contextualism.

Relatedly, SSI predicts that when the subject's circumstances are shifted by a temporal or modal embedding, there should be a corresponding shift in the standards the subject must meet in order to count as knowing. Thus, it predicts that sentences such as the following should come out true:

(1) Joe doesn't know that the bank is open on Saturdays, but five minutes ago, before he learned that he would have to pay for emergency surgery on Sunday, he did know that it is open on Saturdays.
(2) I don't know whether the bank is open on Saturdays, but if I didn't really need the money on Sunday I would know.

Even proponents of SSI are embarrassed by these predictions, and try to explain them away. Hawthorne (2004: 162–5) invokes a kind of error theory, arguing that we tend to "project" our current standards to other knowers, times, and circumstances (for criticism, see MacFarlane (2005a: §3.2.2)). Stanley (2005: ch. 6) argues that contextualist views have similar bad consequences for modal embeddings, and that SSI can handle temporal embeddings (for criticism, see Blome-Tillman 2009). In the end, Hawthorne and Stanley concede that temporal and modal embeddings are problematic for SSI, but that SSI should be accepted anyway because the problems facing contextualism and standard invariantism are worse. But this argument is weaker if there is a genuine relativist alternative that avoids both the embedding problem and the standard problems with contextualism.

Relativism as Synthesis

Many people find something compelling in both the arguments against contextualism and the arguments against invariantism. The relativist account provides a third option, removing the need to choose between two unpalatable alternatives.

As we have seen, invariantism faces difficulties accounting for the apparent contextual variation in the standards one must meet to be counted as "knowing." Relativism accounts for this variation straightforwardly, since it takes the epistemic standard relevant for evaluating instances of "know" to be fixed contextually. But, unlike contextualism, it takes this standard to be fixed by features of the context of assessment, rather than the context of use. Because of this, it avoids the problem of "lost disagreement" faced by all forms of contextualism. Suppose Joe says "Moore knows that he has hands," and René says "No, Moore doesn't know that he has hands." If, as the relativist holds, the accuracy of these assertions depends on the standards relevant at the context of assessment, then, although *which* of them is accurate might vary from one perspective to another, from *no* perspective will it be possible for *both* assertions to be accurate. This helps explain why we take these assertions to express a disagreement, even when they are made in very different contexts.

From the relativist's point of view, invariantism and contextualism each capture part of the truth about knowledge attributions. Invariantism is right that there is a single knowledge relation, and that the accuracy of knowledge ascriptions does not depend on which epistemic standard is relevant at the context of *use*. But contextualism is right that the accuracy of such ascriptions depends somehow on contextually relevant standards. Relativism seeks to synthesize these insights into a more satisfactory picture.

Questions for the Relativist

Although relativism does not share the problems of invariantism and contextualism, it faces philosophical difficulties of its own. Here are some questions the relativist needs to answer. (Answers are not attempted here.)

(1) It would be odd if "know" were the only expression for which a relativist semantics was appropriate. Indeed, the relativist semantics would appear ad hoc if "know" were its only target. Are there other expressions for which a relativist treatment is needed? How does "know" relate to them? (See MacFarlane 2003; Richard 2004; Lasersohn 2005; MacFarlane forthcoming.)

(2) Assuming "know" has a relativist semantics, can anything be said about *why* an expression with the role of "know" should work this way, or is this just a brute fact?

(3) Can the relativist really vindicate the intuitions of disagreement that proved difficult for the contextualist (and even the nonindexical contextualist)? What is required for disagreement, in general? (See MacFarlane 2007a.)

(4) Are there any operators that shift the epistemic standards coordinate of circumstances of evaluation, as modal operators bind the world parameter? If not, how can we motivate positing this coordinate? (See Stanley 2005: ch. 7; MacFarlane 2009: §6.)

(5) Can we really make sense of the idea that there is no absolute answer to the question whether a particular assertion is accurate, but only a perspective-relative one? (See MacFarlane 2005b.) Even if we can make sense of a relativist linguistic practice, could it be rational to engage in such a practice? (See Zimmerman 2007.)

Whether the relativist synthesis is really an improvement on invariantist and contextualist views will depend on whether these (and other) questions can be answered adequately.

References

Blome-Tillman, M. (2009) "Contextualism, Subject-Sensitive Invariantism, and the Interaction of 'Knowledge'-Ascriptions with Modal and Temporal Operators," *Philosophy and Phenomenological Research* 79: 315–31.

Brogaard, B. (2008) "In Defence of a Perspectival Semantics for 'Know'," *Australasian Journal of Philosophy* 86: 439–59.

Cappelen, H. (2008) "Content Relativism and Semantic Blindness," in M. García-Carpintero and M. Kölbel (eds.), *Relative Truth*, Oxford: Oxford University Press, ch. 12, 265–86.

Cohen, S. (1988) "How To Be a Fallibilist," *Philosophical Perspectives* 2: 91–123.

Davis, W. (2007) "Knowledge Claims and Context: Loose Use," *Philosophical Studies* 132: 395–438.

DeRose, K. (1996) "Relevant Alternatives and the Content of Knowledge Attributions," *Philosophy and Phenomenological Research* 56: 193–197.

DeRose, K. (2004) "The Problem with Subject-Sensitive Invariantism," *Philosophy and Phenomenological Research* 68: 346–50.
DeRose, K. (2005) "The Ordinary Language Basis for Contextualism and the New Invariantism," *Philosophical Quarterly* 55: 172–98.
DeRose, K. (2006) "'Bamboozled by Our Own Words': Semantic Blindness and Some Arguments Against Contextualism," *Philosophy and Phenomenological Research* 73: 316–38.
Feldman, R. (2001) "Skeptical Problems, Contextualist Solutions," *Philosophical Studies* 103: 61–85.
Hawthorne, J. (2004) *Knowledge and Lotteries*, Oxford: Oxford University Press.
King, J. (2003) "Tense, Modality, and Semantic Values," *Philosophical Perspectives* 17: 195–247.
Kompa, N. (2002) "The Context Sensitivity of Knowledge Ascriptions," *Grazer-Philosophische Studien* 64: 1–18.
Lasersohn, P. (2005) "Context Dependence, Disagreement, and Predicates of Personal Taste," *Linguistics and Philosophy* 28: 643–86.
MacFarlane, J. (2003) "Future Contingents and Relative Truth," *Philosophical Quarterly* 53: 321–36.
MacFarlane, J. (2005a) "The Assessment Sensitivity of Knowledge Attributions," in T. Szabó Gendler and J. Hawthorne (eds.), *Oxford Studies in Epistemology* 1: 197–233. Reprinted in E. Sosa, J. Kim, J. Fantl, and M. McGrath (eds.), *Epistemology: An Anthology*, second edition, Oxford: Blackwell, 2008.
MacFarlane, J. (2005b), "Making Sense of Relative Truth," *Proceedings of the Aristotelian Society* 105: 321–39.
MacFarlane, J. (2007a) "Relativism and Disagreement," *Philosophical Studies* 132: 17–31.
MacFarlane, J. (2007b) "Semantic Minimalism and Nonindexical Contextualism," in G. Preyer and G. Peter (eds.), *Context-Sensitivity and Semantic Minimalism: New Essays on Semantics and Pragmatics*, Oxford: Oxford University Press, 2007, 240–50.
MacFarlane, J. (2009) "Nonindexical Contextualism," *Synthese* 166: 231–50.
MacFarlane, J. (forthcoming) "Epistemic Modals are Assessment Sensitive," in E. Egan and B. Weatherson (eds.), *Epistemic Modality*, Oxford: Oxford University Press.
Richard, M. (2004) "Contextualism and Relativism," *Philosophical Studies* 119: 215–42.
Rosenberg, J. F. (2002) *Thinking About Knowing*, Oxford: Oxford University Press.
Rysiew, P. (2001) "The Context-Sensitivity of Knowledge Attributions," *Noûs* 35: 477–514.
Schaffer, J. (2004a) "Skepticism, Contextualism, and Discrimination," *Philosophy and Phenomenological Research* 69: 138–55.
Schaffer, J. (2004b) "From Contextualism to Contrastivism," *Philosophical Studies* 119: 73–103.
Schiffer, S. (1996) "Contextualist Solutions to Scepticism," *Proceedings of the Aristotelian Society* 96: 317–33.
Stanley, J. (2004) "On the Linguistic Basis for Contextualism," *Philosophical Studies* 119: 119–46.
Stanley, J. (2005) *Knowledge and Practical Interests*, Oxford: Oxford University Press.
Zimmerman, A. (2007) "Against Relativism," *Philosophical Studies* 133: 313–348.

50
EPISTEMIC MODALS
Josh Dever

1. Initial Scene-Setting

Let's begin with some truisms. First truism: one of the many things that philosophers want is a theory of epistemology, laying out generalizations regarding epistemological notions such as knowledge, justification, and evidence, and predicting (for example) under what conditions various agents will know various things. Second truism: philosophers want not just any theory of epistemology, but the right theory. That means we need a method of selecting among the vast array of possible epistemological theories. Such a method might deploy any number of considerations, such as theoretical elegance and integration with neighboring areas of philosophy, but surely (third truism) a central feature of any plausible method is conformity to epistemological data, in the form of facts of the form *so-and-so knows/doesn't know such-and-such under these circumstances*, or *so-and-so has/doesn't have good reason for believing such-and-such under these circumstances*.

Epistemologically minded philosophers thus have reason to collect epistemological data. There are many ways to gain such data, but one central method is via judgments about sentences that contain epistemological vocabulary. So, in the ideal (or, perhaps, oversimplified) case, a piece of epistemological theorizing might proceed through the following stages:

1. The sentence "Jones knows that the cat is on the mat" is true.
2. Therefore, Jones knows that the cat is on the mat.
3. Epistemological theory T entails that Jones does not know that the cat is on the mat.
4. Therefore, T is not the right epistemological theory.

Hence, a fourth and final truism: those interested in epistemology have reason to be interested in the linguistic devices for reporting epistemological facts.

The four truisms present a pretty picture of (a certain aspect of) epistemological theorizing, but in the real philosophical world, things inevitably become more complicated. Here are two complicating factors. First, not all epistemological vocabulary is transparently epistemological. No one will miss the fact that constructions of the form "A knows that p" or "That p is a reason to believe that q" are important sources of data for epistemological theorizing, but other constructions might only with some coaxing reveal their epistemological relevance. Indicative conditionals, for example, are often taken to depend on the evidential state of speakers—consider a view on which the truth (or assertability) of "If p, then q" requires that the conditional probability of q given p exceed some threshold. So—moving on from mere truisms to the more exalted realm of morals—we observe:

> **First Linguistic Moral**: Philosophers interested in epistemology have a derivative reason to be interested in the philosophy of language—detailed semantic theory construction may reveal unexpected epistemological aspects to the semantic values of expressions or constructions.

Second, not all epistemological vocabulary is semantically transparent. It would be nice if we could move directly from the truth of the sentence "Jones knows that the cat is on the mat" to the fact that Jones knows that the cat is on the mat, but it might turn out that such movement is too simple-minded. Suppose, for example, that knowledge attributions have a contextual element—perhaps an utterance U of "A knows that p" made in context C expresses the claim that A's p-favoring evidence is strong enough to defeat all alternatives to p salient in C. Contextually sensitive claims cannot be straightforwardly transported from one context to another—if I know that "It's hot here" has been truthfully uttered in one context (in location L_1), I cannot conclude (in my different context, in location L_2) that it's hot here. Similarly, given a contextualist component to epistemological vocabulary, an epistemologist situated in a different context C_0 who moves from the truth of U (made in C) to the fact that A knows that p errs, since that fact, as expressed in context C_0, is the fact that A's evidence suffices to defeat alternatives salient in C_0, not C. If there are alternatives salient in C_0 but not in C, the truth of U will not in fact justify the conclusion the epistemologist reaches. Possible lack of semantic transparency leads to:

> **Second Linguistic Moral**: Philosophers interested in epistemology have a(nother) derivative reason to be interested in the philosophy of language—detailed semantic theory construction may reveal unexpected semantic complexities to expressions or constructions with an epistemological aspect to their semantics, and these complexities may shape the proper use of linguistic data in epistemological theorizing.

In short, more data and better understanding of data are both good things, and both of these good things give those interested in epistemology reason also to be interested in some parts of philosophy of language and formal semantics.

2. Modals

So much for initial scene-setting. We turn now to examining the way in which these morals play out in one particular case: that of modal vocabulary. Consider the words "might" and "must." It is a standard observation (at least since Kratzer (1977)) that these modal terms admit a variety of readings:

1. **Metaphysical**: My yacht might have been longer than it is.
2. **Deontic**: Tax returns must be filed by April 15.
3. **Preferential**: We might order Thai take-out for dinner.
4. **Dispositional**: Conference participants who must cough repeatedly are encouraged to step outside.

Among these various readings is typically taken to be an epistemic reading. Thus a speaker can utter:

(1) The black marble must be in the first box.
(2) The red marble might be in the second box.

to convey (respectively) that the black marble's being in the first box is something she knows, and that the red marble's being in the second box isn't something she can rule out, given what she knows.

There are two reasons for taking the modals in these sentences to be epistemic. First, our immediate grasp of the truth conditions is epistemic—such utterances just seem to depend on matters of what's known and unknown. (There is, for example, no metaphysical or deontic necessity to the black marble being in the first box.) Second, we judge that agents can differ in what modalized statements they can truthfully make, in cases in which differences in the epistemic states of the agents seem most prominent. Thus suppose both Alice and Barbara know that exactly one of the two boxes contains a black marble, but Alice (and not Barbara) has looked in the second box, and seen it to be empty. Then both of the following utterances look true:

(3) (Uttered by Alice) The black marble must be in the first box.
(4) (Uttered by Barbara) The black marble might not be in the first box.

On the plausible assumption that "must" and "might" are duals:

Duality: "Must p" is equivalent to "Not might not p."

Alice's utterance and Barbara's utterances are, syntactically, contradictories. Their simultaneous truth is then explained by hypothesizing that Alice's modal depends on her epistemic situation, while Barbara's modal depends on hers.

"Must" and "might" are not the only modals with epistemic readings—others include "can"/"could," "probably," and "certainly"—but these two will be used as the paradigm cases in this discussion. Many of these other epistemic modals introduce interesting complications that lie beyond the scope of this piece.

Here is a tempting first-draft semantics for epistemic "must" and "might." Given an agent A, let KA be the set of all propositions known by A. Given a proposition p, let $[[p]]$ be the set of possible worlds at which p is true. Then $EA = \cap_{p \square KA} [[p]]$ is the set of possible worlds consistent with what A knows. (Given the facticity of knowledge, the actual world is always an element of EA.) Given a context C, let CS be the speaker in the context. Then:

1. An utterance of "It must be that p" in context C is true iff ECS is a subset of $[[p]]$.
2. An utterance of "It might be that p" in context C is true iff $ECS \cap [[p]] \neq \emptyset$.

Informally: a must claim is true if every world epistemically open to the speaker supports the prejacent; a might claim is true if some world epistemically open to the speaker supports the prejacent. The difficulties that this first-draft theory encounters provide the point of entry to the philosophical interest of epistemic modals.

3. Whose Knowledge?

Consider the following case:

> **Case 1**: Alice and Barbara are engaged in a cooperative attempt to determine the location of a red marble. There are four marbles—black, red, yellow, and green—and four boxes, with exactly one marble in each box. Alice has looked in the first box, and seen a yellow marble in it. Barbara has looked at a pair of rules governing the placement of marbles, one of which is "If the first box contains a yellow marble, the third box contains a blue marble" and the other of which is "If the first box does not contain a yellow marble, the fourth box contains a red marble." Prior to combining their information, they have the following exchange:
>
> ALICE: I wonder if the red marble might be in the second box.
> BARBARA: I don't know—that depends on what you saw in the first box. Did it contain a yellow marble?
> ALICE: Yes, it did.
> BARBARA: In that case, the red marble might indeed be in the second box.

Alice and Barbara's discourse in Case 1 seems fine—they both speak reasonably and truly. But it provides a challenge to the first-draft semantics. According to this semantics, when Alice wonders if the red marble might be in the second box, she is wondering whether it is compatible with what she knows that the red marble be there. But this would be odd—surely she knows that it is compatible with what *she* knows that it be there. And Barbara's response is also puzzling, both because it would seem too obvious to be worth mentioning that *she* does not know what is compatible with *Alice's* knowledge (including undisclosed knowledge about the contents of the first box), and because her follow-up question would seem irrelevant to the target "might" claim.

Case 1 thus suggests that epistemic modals sometimes run not on the egocentric epistemic state of the speaker, but on the total knowledge of the conversational participants. Given a group G of individuals, let the *distributive epistemic state* of G, or E^D_G, be $\cap_{g \in G} E_g$. The moral of Case 1 is that we must consider the semantic rules:

1. An utterance of "It must be that p" in context C is true iff $E^D_{C_G}$ is a subset of $[\![p]\!]$, where C_G is the group of discourse participants in C.
2. An utterance of "It might be that p" in context C is true iff $E^D_{C_G} \cap [\![p]\!] \neq \emptyset$.

Whether these semantic rules represent a competing analysis to the first-draft rules, or merely another possible meaning of epistemic modals, remains to be determined.

Distributive readings of epistemic modals broaden the sphere of epistemic interest beyond the individual to a larger group. Similar cases show that the relevant group needn't be limited to the discourse participants:

> **Case 2**: Charles and Daniel are discussing the financial forecast for their Silicon Valley startup. Having determined that losses are inevitable in the second quarter, they move on to later in the year.
>
> CHARLES: Might we make a profit in the third quarter?

DANIEL: I don't know. I've got the sales projections here with me, but my assistant has the expense projections, and without both, I can't say whether a profit is possible.

Similar cases can be constructed in which the relevant group contains only some of the discourse participants.

Other cases show that the epistemic reach of modals can, rather than broaden from the egocentric to the communal, instead displace from one individual to another. One such style of exocentric reading is available in deferential cases:

Case 3: Ethan and Francine are running an experiment in which an electron has been fired into a chamber. A discussion ensues regarding the possible location of the electron.

ETHAN: Might the electron be in the top half of the chamber?
FRANCINE: I don't know—I forgot to note the orientation of the electron gun. But Gretchen would know if it might be there—she set the gun orientation before she left this morning.

In Case 3 (which shares the same form as the Cancer Test Cases of DeRose (1991)), it is the epistemic state of Gretchen, not a conversational participant, that determines the truth conditions for the "might" claim. Other exocentric cases shift the epistemic modal onto the epistemic state of an agent other than the speaker for nondeferential reasons, as in:

Case 4: Gerald the geography teacher is watching his student Harold label a map of Brazil. As Harold labels one city Uberlândia:

GERALD: If a city of population at least 600,000 lies on the north-south line between São Paolo and Brasilia, must it be Uberlândia?

As Harold labels a river:

GERALD: Not so fast—that might be Paranapanema River.

In fact, Uberlândia is the only city of that size between São Paolo and Brasilia, and the river Harold is labeling is, as Harold has labeled it, the Paraná River. But Harold's grasp of the facts is weak—he doesn't know the exact population of Ribeirão Preto, and was only guessing at the relative locations of the Paraná and Paranapanema Rivers. Gerald, though, is fully aware of the geographic facts. Nevertheless, it seems that Gerald's question to Harold was a reasonable and relevant one, and that his comment was correct. Such judgments suggest that Gerald is using the epistemic modals exocentrically to depend on Harold's epistemic state (despite the inferiority of that state), as part of a pedagogical practice.

In addition to shifting the epistemic burden from the speaker (partially or wholly) to other agents, we can also find uses of epistemic modals in which the space of worlds over which "might" and "must" range is constrained by information not possessed by any agent. Such cases were first discussed in Hacking (1967); a case with the same flavor is:

Case 5: Irene is an emergency room physician, and is treating John, who is complaining of chest pain and shortness of breath. Irene hastily announces to John:

IRENE: You might be having a heart attack.

She then sends him for bypass surgery. The surgery, however, finds no arterial blockage or signs of cardiac damage, and the surgeon Katherine concludes that John was merely suffering from indigestion. Irate, Katherine chastizes Irene:

KATHERINE: You put the patient through a dangerous procedure for no good reason.
IRENE: But I had a good reason—I thought he might be having a heart attack.
KATHERINE: Look, a simple EEG test could have been used to check your diagnosis. Five minutes of checking would have shown that you were wrong, and that there was no chance he was having a heart attack.

In Case 5, Katherine's assertion that Irene's original "might" claim was incorrect seems true, even though nothing that Irene, or anyone else, knew at the time ruled out the possibility that John was having a heart attack. The case thus suggests that the evidence relevant to epistemic modals can extend beyond what is actually known to include that which could easily have been ascertained. (Note that if Irene had done an EEG test, and taken other standard diagnostic precautions, but John had been suffering from a rare condition which mimics the symptoms of a heart attack and can only be differentiated with unusual and hazardous tests, it would seem unreasonable to object to her claim that John might be having a heart attack.)

Finally, in addition to shifting the appropriate source of information, we can also shift the *type* of information to which the epistemic modals are sensitive. (The distinction here is ultimately artificial, but helpful.) Thus consider:

Case 6: Leonard is attempting to prove that when P is a point on the circumcircle of triangle ABC, the feet A_1, B_1, and C_1 of the perpendiculars from P to the sides of ABC are collinear. After studying a diagram extensively and tracking out various angle identities, Leonard announces in triumph:

LEONARD: Aha! AC_1PB_1 is a cyclic quadrilateral. So angles C_1PA and C_1B_1A subtend the same arc, and are identical. That gives me that angle A_1B_1C equals angle C_1B_1A, and hence A_1, B_1, and C_1 must all lie on a line.

The striking phenomenon here is that Leonard could not, prior to completing his proof, correctly make his "must" claim—even if he already knew, perhaps because his geometry teacher told him so (without proof), that the points were collinear. In this use of the epistemic modal, what is required is that the prejacent claim be entailed by the information that Leonard has on pure "compass and straight-edge" grounds.

Such cases show that one major project in investigating the semantics of an epistemic modal is properly delimiting the space of worlds over which the modal ranges (or, equivalently, the set of evidence used in generating that space)—call this space of worlds, following Kratzer (1981), the modal base for that (use of the) modal. There are at least three different approaches that can be pursued here:

1. **Ambiguity**: We already distinguish epistemic, metaphysical, deontic, preferential, dispositional, circumstantial, and other readings of modals. The above cases could be accommodating by hypothesizing further readings: egocentric, group distributive, deferential exocentric, and so on.
2. **Naive Unificationism**: We can seek a general formula for carving out the right modal base, one which yields the correct prediction in each of the above cases. For example, Teller (1972: 310–311) suggests that:
   It is possible that p if and only if

   (a) p is not known to be false by any member of community C
   (b) Nor is there a member, t, of community C, such that if t were to know all the propositions known to community C, then he could, on the strength of his knowledge of these propositions as basis, data, or evidence, come to know that p is false.

3. **Sophisticated Unificationism**: Seeking to preserve elements of both **Ambiguity** and **Naive Unificationism**, we can pursue a contextually sensitive general formula for selecting the modal base—one which, in the manner of DeRose (1991), appeals to notions such as contextually relevant communities of agents and sources of information.

4. A Methodological Worry

Selecting among, or further refining, these three options lies beyond the scope of this overview. Instead, we turn now to a concern about the data driving the search for a proper specification of the bounds of epistemic space. The cases presented above present two types of evidence:

1. Judgments (by the theorist, situated in a neutral theoretical context) of the truth or falsity of claims made (in a different context) involving epistemic modals.
2. Expressions of agreement or disagreement with, or correction of, epistemically modalized claims, made by agents in the context under consideration.

Both of these evidence types, however, are problematic.

Expressions of agreement and disagreement typically take one of two forms. Sometimes there is a repetition, inside a "that"-clause, of the claim which is being (dis)agreed with—I disagree that it might be raining. In other cases, devices of propositional anaphora are used to refer back to what was claimed before—I agree with that/what you said. If, however, an expression contains any context-sensitive elements, its repetition in a (dis)agreement might not express the same proposition as the original use, and the (dis)agreement can then be used as a source of data only with much caution. (See, for example, the discussion in chapters 2 and 3 of Cappelen and Hawthorne (2009) on the difficulties context-sensitivity can create in this type of data use.) If the semantics of "might" and "must" include any contextual element in the selection of the modal base, then repetition-style expressions of (dis)agreement might fail to express exactly the same propositional content (in the theoretical sense relevant to construction of a formal semantic theory) as the original use.

In an attempt to avoid these difficulties, anaphoric data is often employed. If Alice makes an utterance with a context-sensitive element:

(5) **Alice**: I am a linguist.

Barbara can engage with Alice by using expressions anaphoric on Alice's utterance:

(6) **Barbara**: I agree with that/what Alice said.

In this way, the indexical "I" does not shift its interpretation to that determined by Barbara's context. However, propositional anaphora is a notoriously complicated matter (see Asher 1993 for numerous examples), and it is far from clear that all of the pitfalls of context-sensitivity can be safely avoided using anaphoric mechanisms. (Consider the acceptability of the following discourse:

(7) **Alice**: I'm so bored with this lecture.
(8) **Barbara**: I couldn't agree more with that. Let's leave.

Despite the anaphoric "that," the interpretation of "I" needs to shift to Barbara.)

These difficulties caused by the interaction of context-sensitivity and agreement/disagreement data are broad ones impacting discussions throughout philosophy of language. The assessments of truth and falsity of epistemically modalized claims, however, display a more local problem. This local difficulty derives from a phenomenon of *trumping*. Hawthorne (2004) observes that "ordinary people evaluate present tense claims of epistemic modality as true or false by testing the claim against their own perspective" (27). This is a good first approximation, but the phenomenon is slightly more subtle—an agent will prefer his own perspective only when he is confident that his evidential state is superior to that of the agent making the original epistemically modalized claim. Thus in the following situation:

(9) **Michelle**: I just spoke to Oscar, and given what he told me, he must be in Paris by now.
(10) **Nathan**: That can't be right—I have no idea where Oscar is.

Nathan's assessment of Michelle's claim is highly unnatural, despite the fact that it reflects his own evidential perspective, because he knows his perspective is evidentially inferior to Michelle's. The more precise description of the phenomenon is thus:

> **Trumping**: Given two evaluations E_1 and E_2 of an epistemically modalized claim C, if E_1 derives from a stronger epistemic state than E_2, then E_1 is preferred to E_2.

Trumping is not an unproblematic description of the phenomenon—see von Fintel and Gillies (2008a) and Wright (2007) for examples in which speakers reasonably stand by assessments of epistemically modalized claims in the face of superior evidence, and, as well, the usual concerns about properly separating judgments of truth from judgments of assertibility apply—but it does seem to describe a major aspect of our practice.

But trumping has a troubling consequence. Suppose that when an assessment of a claim is preferred to all others, it is, in fact, the correct assessment. Given trumping, a state of perfect information is preferred to all others. But in a state of perfect information, both "might p" and "must p" are equivalent to p. Thus trumping entails that epistemic modals are semantically superfluous.

5. Some Formal Options

Surely epistemic modals are not semantically superfluous, so we need some other options. The most obvious route toward accommodating trumping without modal vacuity is to allow some sort of *variability*, so that the modal is achieving something different when it is first used than it is when it is later assessed in light of full information.

Recent literature has developed two major forms of variability: *contextualism* and *relativism*. The general form of truth condition for epistemically modalized claims that we have been using suggests that one parameter needed to evaluate such claims for truth or falsity is a modal base (a set of epistemically determined possible worlds). Basic features of the behavior of epistemically modalized claims then suggest that the modal base parameter is subject to variation—so much is mandated, for example, by the thought that paradigmatically the use of "might" or "must" is linked to what is epistemically possible *for the speaker*. There are then two broad categories of models for fixing the value of the modal base parameter:

1. **Semantic**: The modal base is part of the content of the proposition expressed by an utterance—the semantic machinery governing the language determines, for any given utterance, what modal base enters into the proposition, and given that proposition, the truth of the utterance (relative to a given world) is fully determined. Contextualism is characterized by semantic determination of the modal base.
2. **Pragmatic**: The modal base is not part of the content of the proposition expressed by an utterance—the semantic machinery governing the language determines a proposition that is silent on the question of modal base, and given that proposition, the truth of the utterance is determined relative to a given world and modal base. Pragmatic mechanisms then determine, in any given situation, with respect to which modal base a proposition is to be evaluated. Relativism is characterized by pragmatic determination of the modal base.

Contextualist accounts of epistemic modals are defended by, for example, DeRose (1991), von Fintel and Gillies (2008a), Schaffer (2009), and Cappelen and Hawthorne (2009). Such accounts owe an explanation of the semantic mechanism by which the modal base is contextually determined. (Of course, one can always posit a "modal base" index in context, and have epistemic modals contextually dependent on that index, but this is to give the problem a name, not a solution—what is wanted is an account of how that dimension of context is determined.) There are numerous options for such a mechanism, such as:

1. **Index-Linked Descriptivism**: The modal base is determined via its descriptive relation to some standard index of (a Kaplan-style) context. The egocentric truth conditions given at the end of section 2 are a form of index-linked descriptivism.
2. **Liberalism**: The modal base is highly unconstrained—for example, the modal base is fully determined by the intentions of the speaker, or there are many simultaneous modal bases (a *multiple content* view).
3. **Dynamicism**: The modal base is shaped by the prior discourse context, so that (for example) a previous assertion that p, or the location of the epistemic modal in the consequent of a conditional whose antecedent is p, requires that the modal base be a subset of the p worlds.

(The taxonomy here is neither exhaustive nor exclusive.) Since contextualist accounts place the modal base in the semantics and thus deliver a truth-evaluable proposition, they have the advantage of wedding nicely with standard accounts of assertion and belief. On the other hand, the account of agreement, disagreement, and assessment tends to be problematic. Consider an instance of trumping: Alice, in a deprived epistemic state E_1, utters "It might be that p," and Barbara, in an enriched epistemic state E_2, assesses Alice's claim as false. Contextualism can straightforwardly explain why Barbara, were she to utter "It might be that p," would utter something false, but explaining why she can assess Alice's claim, which contains an E_1-determined modal base as part of its propositional content, as false is more difficult. Contextualists at this point appeal to a mixture of error theory (with respect to Barbara's assessment), worries about the data underlying trumping, subtleties regarding propositional anaphora, and contextualist mechanisms that create shared content between Alice and Barbara.

Relativist accounts of epistemic modals are defended by, for example, Egan et al. (2005), MacFarlane (2008), Egan (2007), and Stephenson (2007). On such accounts, propositions do not determine a truth value simplicter (relative to a world), but only a truth value relative to a modal base (and a world). Relativist accounts thus owe an explanation of the pragmatic mechanisms by which, in a given situation, the appropriate (for purposes of believing, assessing, or choosing to assert) modal base is determined. There are numerous options for such a mechanism, such as:

1. **Index-Linked Descriptivism**: The relevant modal base is determined via its descriptive relation to some standard index of context. For example, the modal base relevant to an assessment of an epistemically modalized claim might be the epistemic state of the assessor. The descriptive determination can vary for varying pragmatic relations to claims (assessment, assertion, belief, etc.).
2. **Liberalism**: The relevant modal base is highly unconstrained—there is simply a collection of facts, with respect to any epistemically modalized claim, about its truth value with respect to different modal bases.
3. **Dynamicism**: The modal base is shaped by the prior discourse context, so that (for example) an epistemically modalized claim is properly assessed relative to a modal base shaped by what has been asserted in the discourse prior to the assessment.

(Again, the taxonomy is neither exhaustive nor exclusive.) Since relativist accounts provide a propositional content that is shared by all utterances of a particular epistemically modalized claim, they have the advantage of providing smooth explanations of trumping. Alice, in a deprived epistemic state E_1, utters "It might be that p," and her claim is true relative to the modal base determined by E_1, thus (perhaps) licensing her assertion. Barbara, in an enriched epistemic state E_2, assesses Alice's claim as false, which indeed it is relative to the modal base determined by E_2. Barbara's assessment straightforwardly targets the same propositional content that Alice advances. On the other hand, it is a challenge for relativist accounts to integrate with standard accounts of assertion and belief. When a speaker comes to assert a claim of the form *It might be that p*, he will see that the content he intends to advance is true relative to a host of modal bases and false relative to a host of others. The challenge is to find a norm of assertion, responsive to some subset of these bases, that makes it simultaneously reasonable for the speaker to assert and for the audience to update their beliefs with the content of his utterance. Egan (2007) and MacFarlane (2005) both address this challenge.

The extent to which contextualism and relativism are genuinely competing options, rather than notational variants, is not entirely clear. The way the conceptual territory is divided here is not the only option; see MacFarlane (2009) for a careful discussion of variety of other options.

6. Knowledge, Justification, and Belief

The discussion so far has assumed that the epistemic notion to which epistemic modals are sensitive is *knowledge*, with the critical question being *whose knowledge*. However, knowledge is not the only available epistemic notion, and it is worth considering cases designed to test the hypothesis that knowledge is uniquely linked to epistemic modals. Thus consider:

> **Case 7 (Gettierization):** Pauline thinks that Ralph owns a Ford, on the reasonable grounds of having seen him take the keys to a Ford from his pocket. In fact, Ralph does own a Ford, but (by mere chance) happened to have the keys to the Ford of his friend Sam in his pocket at the time. Pauline thus has a justified true belief that Ralph owns a Ford, but a belief that does not amount to knowledge. Pauline then says (intending to say something false):
>
> PAULINE: Ralph might not own a Ford.

A knowledge-based account of epistemic modals naturally predicts that Pauline, despite her intentions, says something true—that Ralph doesn't own a Ford is not, in fact, ruled out by what she *knows*. However, it is at least unclear that this prediction is correct. There is some temptation to say that Pauline does indeed speak falsely.

There are (at least) two complications. First, the trumping phenomenon can interfere with our judgments. Since we, as theorists, are given that the prejacent of Pauline's might claim is false, there is a temptation to let our superior epistemic state drive an assessment of her claim as false. The fan of a knowledge-based account can thus hold that any inclination to judge Pauline's claim false is (inappropriately) driven by trumping. We must therefore strive to avoid trumping, and assess Pauline's claim in the same spirit that allowed us to view Barbara's claim in (8) above as true. It is not clear that we can reliably perform this task, and our judgments are thus suspect in these cases. Second, it is especially crucial to separate issues of truth and assertability in this case. The fan of a knowledge-based account holds that Pauline's claim is true, but agrees that Pauline does not know it to be true (because she thinks she knows that Ralph owns a Ford). If there is an obligation to assert only that which one knows, Pauline violates that obligation, and for that reason we will judge her claim to be deficient at least in terms of assertability. Judgments of truth and of assertability are notoriously difficult to separate, so the knowledge fan can with some plausibility claim that Pauline's assertion is in fact true, but unassertable. This complication can be mitigated by making Pauline's utterance an act other than an assertion—she can merely suppose, or set out for consideration, or offer a bet on the proposition, that Ralph might not own a Ford.

If there is any plausibility to the view that Pauline's claim in Case 7 is false, we have reason to believe that epistemic modals (sometimes?) have their modal base determined not by what is known, but by what is truly and justifiably believed. Once the possibility of weakening the epistemic goal of "might" and "must" is raised, we ought to consider a range of other options. Thus:

Case 8 (Justification Without Truth): Terry thinks there is an apple on the table in front of him. He has every reason to think this, since he is in direct visual contact with the table, and it looks to have an apple on it. However, there is no apple on the table—that it looks to Terry to have an apple on it is a result of an apple hologram. Terry then says (intending to say something false):

TERRY: There might not be an apple on the table.

If epistemic modals have their modal base determined by what is known or by what is truly and justifiably believed, then Terry's claim is true, since neither what he knows nor what he truly and justifiably believes rules out the absence of an apple on the table. But there is some grip to the thought that Terry's claim is indeed false. He can seem to be misrepresenting his situation with his utterance. (Again, truth and assertability must be carefully separated. In this case, trumping promotes the thought that Terry's claim is true, but still must be set aside for proper evaluation.) If his claim is false, we have reason to believe that epistemic modals (sometimes?) have their modal base determined by what is justifiably believed, whether true or not.

Finally, consider:

Case 9 (Mere Belief): Ursula believes quite sincerely but, as she is aware, with absolutely no justification, that there is life on a planet orbiting Vega. She says (intending to say something false):

URSULA: There might not be life on a planet orbiting Vega.

Again, there is some pull to the thought that Ursula does speak falsely. (One can consider the case under both the hypothesis that there is indeed life on a planet orbiting Vega, and on the hypothesis that there is not.) The pull is perhaps less than in the other cases (it is important not to let Ursula's open lack of justification trend into a view that she does not genuinely believe there is life near Vega), but it is there—as with Terry, Ursula seems to be misrepresenting her situation.

What to make of these cases? The data is cloudy at best (and it is hard to get corresponding judgments with "must" constructions), so there is ample room to dig in one's heels at knowledge, or some other epistemic cut-off point. Alternatively, we could abandon the idea that there is anything distinctively epistemic about epistemic modals. One version of this thought returns to the basic Kratzer (1981) position, and holds that there is only one notion of modality—one which then allows differing sorts of specifications of the modal base ("in view of what the laws require," "in view of what is know," "in view of what I believe"), some epistemic and some not. (Schaffer (2009) endorses a position like this, although not on the basis of these sorts of cases.) But this simple position is not without its own difficulties. It does not seem possible, for example, to obtain readings on which the modal base combines deontic and epistemic restrictions ("in view of what is legal and of what is known"). Suppose Walter is obligated to file his tax report today, and we know that to do so, he will need to visit the post office this evening. Now consider the claim:

(11) Walter must visit the post office before midnight.

The modal "must" can be read deontically: Walter's obligation to file his taxes induces an obligation to perform the necessary means. It can also be read epistemically: we add to what we know the tacit assumption that Walter will fulfill his obligations (thereby converting the deontic restriction into an epistemic one). What we cannot do is read the "must" as indicating inevitability in light of a mixture of deontic and epistemic restriction. Despite the tempting simplicity of a unitary view of modality, some form of epistemically, or at least doxastically, flavored modal may be unavoidable.

References

Asher, N.: 1993, *Reference to Abstract Objects in Discourse*. Kluwer.
Cappelen, H. and J. Hawthorne: 2009, *Relativism and Monadic Truth*. Oxford University Press.
DeRose, K.: 1991, "Epistemic Possibilities." *The Philosophical Review* 100(4), 581–605.
Egan, A.: 2007, "Epistemic Modals, Relativism, and Assertion." *Philosophical Studies* 133, 1–22.
Egan, A., J. Hawthorne, and B. Weatherson: 2005, "Epistemic Modals in Context." In: G. Preyer and G. Peter (eds.): *Contextualism in Philosophy*. Oxford University Press.
Hacking, I.: 1967, "Possibility." *The Philosophical Review* 76(2), 143–168.
Hawthorne, J.: 2004, *Knowledge and Lotteries*. Oxford University Press.
Kratzer, A.: 1977, "What 'Must' and 'Can' Must and Can Mean." *Linguistics and Philosophy* 1, 337–355.
Kratzer, A.: 1981, "The Notional Category of Modality." In: P. Portner and B. Partee (eds.): *Formal Semantics: The Essential Readings*. Blackwell.
MacFarlane, J.: 2005, "Making Sense of Relative Truth." *Proceedings of the Aristotelian Society* 105, 321–339.
MacFarlane, J.: 2008, "Epistemic Modals are Assessment-Sensitive." In: B. Weatherson and A. Egan (eds.): *Epistemic Modality*. Oxford University Press.
MacFarlane, J.: 2009, "Nonindexical Contextualism." *Synthese* 166, 231–250.
Schaffer, J.: 2009, "Contextualism for Taste Claims and Epistemic Modals." In: A. Egan and B. Weatherson (eds.): *Epistemic Modality*. Oxford University Press.
Stephenson, T.: 2007, "Judge Dependence, Epistemic Modals, and Predicates of Personal Taste." *Linguistics and Philosophy* 30, 487–525.
Teller, P.: 1972, "Epistemic Possibility." *Philosophia* 2(4), 303–320.
von Fintel, K. and A. Gillies: 2008a, "CIA Leaks." *The Philosophical Review* 117, 77–98.
Wright, C.: 2007, "New Age Relativism and Epistemic Possibility: The Question of Evidence." *Philosophical Issues* 17(1), 262–283.

51
PRAGMATIC ENCROACHMENT
Jeremy Fantl and Matthew McGrath

In his classic article, Richard Rudner claims that

> in accepting a hypothesis the scientist must make the decision that the evidence is *sufficiently* strong or that the probability is *sufficiently* high to warrant the acceptance of the hypothesis. Obviously, our decision regarding the evidence and respecting how strong is 'strong enough', is going to be a function of the *importance*, in the typically ethical sense, of making a mistake in accepting or rejecting the hypothesis . . . *How sure we need to be before we accept a hypothesis will depend on how serious a mistake would be.*
> (Rudner 1953: 2, emphasis Rudner's)

According to Rudner, an adequate account of the conditions of warranted hypothesis acceptance must include reference to an ethical or, more broadly, a pragmatic factor.

Rudner explicitly confines his discussion to the evidence or probability needed to be warranted in accepting a hypothesis, where acceptance for him seems to be subject to voluntary control, at least in certain cases: we *decide* the evidence is sufficiently strong. But in the past decade a number of philosophers have offered views similar to Rudner's about a broader range of epistemic concepts. For example, regarding knowledge, Jeremy Fantl and Matthew McGrath (2002, 2007, and 2009), John Hawthorne (2004), and Jason Stanley (2005) have recommended views according to which, whether a subject knows something to be the case depends on their practical situation.

This sort of conclusion shouldn't strike us as immediately implausible. After all, there are widely acknowledged links between the practical and the epistemic. What you should do in a certain choice situation is widely acknowledged to be determined not merely by how good or preferred certain possible outcomes of your acts would be, but by how probable these outcomes are given that you act in certain ways. Or consider again the importance of not being wrong. This seems obviously relevant to whether you should inquire further into whether *p* and to whether your evidence is strong enough to justify you in ignoring the chance that *p* is false. If your practical situation can be relevant to these matters, it might not seem to be a huge step to think it can be relevant to whether you know.

Some of our intuitions about specific cases seem to support the claim that knowledge can depend on practical factors. Consider DeRose's famous "Bank Cases":

Bank Case A (Low Stakes). My wife and I are driving home on a Friday afternoon. We plan to stop at the bank on the way home to deposit our paychecks. But as we drive past the bank, we notice that the lines inside are very long, as they often are on Friday afternoons. Although we generally like to deposit our paychecks as soon as possible, it is not especially important in this case that they be deposited right away, so I suggest that we drive straight home and deposit our paychecks on Saturday morning. My wife says, "Maybe the bank won't be open tomorrow. Lots of banks are closed on Saturdays." I reply, "No, I know it'll be open. I was just there two weeks ago on Saturday. It's open until noon."

Bank Case B (High Stakes). My wife and I drive past the bank on a Friday afternoon, as in Case A, and notice the long lines. I again suggest that we deposit our paychecks on Saturday morning, explaining that I was at the bank on Saturday morning only two weeks ago and discovered that it was open until noon. But in this case, we have just written a very large and important check. If our paychecks are not deposited into our checking account before Monday morning, the important check we wrote will bounce, leaving us in a *very* bad situation. And, of course, the bank is not open on Sunday. My wife reminds me of these facts. She then says, "Banks do change their hours. Do you know the bank will be open tomorrow?" Remaining as confident as I was before that the bank will be open then, still, I reply, "Well, no. I'd better go in and make sure."

(DeRose 1992: 913)

It looks as if Keith speaks truly in Case A in attributing knowledge to himself that the bank will be open tomorrow, while he also speaks truly in Case B in denying himself knowledge. The only thing that changes in the two cases is how important it is for Keith to be right about whether the bank will be open tomorrow. Therefore, it looks as though how important it is for Keith to be right about whether the bank will be open tomorrow is relevant to whether Keith knows that the bank will be open tomorrow. And relevant in a clear way: holding fixed Keith's evidence concerning whether the bank will be open tomorrow, whether he knows it will be open varies with variations in how important it is for him to be right about this.

If this is the proper lesson to draw from the Bank Cases, it would appear to follow that two subjects can have the same evidence concerning whether the bank will be open tomorrow, even though one of them knows it'll open tomorrow and the other doesn't. One might think this isn't so problematic. Might this just be because in one case Keith believes the bank will be open tomorrow but in the other he doesn't? Belief is of course often taken to be necessary for knowledge. Notice that DeRose includes in his description of Bank Case B that Keith remains "as confident as [he] was before that the bank will be open then." This stipulation seems meant to ensure that he is equally confident in the two Bank Cases. Following Kent Bach (2008), we might question whether, even if Keith retains the same degree of belief in the two cases, his degree of belief in both cases is high enough for outright belief. (Bach's worries are shared and expanded upon by Jennifer Nagel (2008).)

However, if one thinks Keith can't sincerely say "I'd better go in and make sure" if he has an outright belief that the bank will be open tomorrow, then we can alter the case by stipulating that Keith says, "I know it's open tomorrow." We can further emend the case by having Keith's wife say, "No you don't. This is important, Keith. You need to go in and make sure they're open tomorrow." The question would then be whether what Keith said is false. We see no great gulf between the original Case B and this altered one.

The appeal to a difference in belief, then, seems not to explain why there is a difference in knowledge, despite the sameness in evidence. Nor do there seem to be other traditional factors in knowledge to which we can appeal here. What appears to make the difference in knowledge are the stakes. In fact, one subject might have *more* evidence than another that the bank will be open tomorrow—be better informed, have done more checking, etc.—but because much more is at stake for the more well-informed subject, the more well-informed subject can fail to know that the bank will be open tomorrow while the less-informed subject knows that the bank will be open tomorrow. All this is, of course, very hard to swallow.

DeRose draws a different moral from the cases. He grants that Keith speaks truly in Case A when he says "I know it'll be open" and he also speaks truly in Case B when he responds "no" to the question, "Do you know that the bank will be open tomorrow?" But he insists that it does not follow that the Bank Cases show that pragmatic factors can make a difference to knowledge. Why not? DeRose's answer, roughly, is that Keith's pragmatic situation affects what he means by 'know' but makes no difference to whether he knows. More precisely, his answer has two parts. First, there is a *contextualist* claim: which epistemic relation Keith's use of 'know' picks out varies with his pragmatic situation, and so varies across the Bank Cases. If the epistemic relations picked out vary with the pragmatic situation—the higher the stakes, roughly, the more demanding the epistemic relation picked out—what Keith says in Case A might be true while what he said in Case B might be false. That is the first part—the claim that pragmatic factors matter to the content of knowledge attributions. The second part is the denial that they matter to knowledge: for each epistemic relation K that can be picked out by 'know' in some context, pragmatic factors make no difference to whether you stand in K to a proposition. If this is true of all such relations, then the sentence 'Pragmatic factors make no difference to whether one knows' comes out invariantly true.

What is important for our purposes is that the contextualist finds a way to salvage the intuitions in the cases while avoiding some of the problematic consequences of letting knowledge involve the subject's practical situation. Thus, an important motivation for contextualism, it might be thought, is the avoidance of those problematic consequences. (This point is emphasized in DeRose (2009: 107).)

But contextualism comes with problems of its own; for one thing, the problematic consequences remain, but bumped up a level. The contextualist, it seems, must grant that two subjects might have the same evidence that the bank will be open tomorrow, but one could truly self-attribute knowledge while the other truly self-denies knowledge. One subject could have more evidence than the other, be better informed about whether the bank will be open tomorrow, have done more checking into whether it will be open tomorrow, but the less well-informed subject might be able to truly self-attribute knowledge while the better-informed subject cannot. In addition, there are independent difficulties. For example, Stanley (2005) takes the contextualist about knowledge attributions to be positing a sort of context-sensitivity which departs significantly from the familiar sorts.

So, perhaps we should deny contextualism while maintaining our commitment to the intuitions in the Bank Cases—our commitment to the view that whether a subject knows something depends on the subject's practical situation. This is the *subject-sensitive invariantism* of Hawthorne (2004) and Stanley (2005). (Hawthorne calls his view 'sensitive moderate invariantism' and Stanley calls his 'interest-relative invariantism'. The label 'subject-sensitive invariantism' is due to DeRose (2004).) It is a form of *invariantism* because it holds that the proposition expressed by a knowledge-attribution does not vary from attributor context to attributor context. But it is *subject-sensitive* because it holds that whether a subject knows something is sensitive to the practical situation of the subject.

Note, though, that we are not forced to a denial of contextualism simply by an acceptance of subject-sensitivity. If the primary motivation for contextualism is the preservation of the view that a subject's practical situation must be irrelevant to whether that subject knows, then there will be some pressure, upon accepting subject-sensitivity, to reject contextualism. But there might be other pressures in favor of contextualism. For example, as DeRose (2004) and Stanley (2005) both point out, subject-sensitive invariantists have difficulty accommodating third-person cases, in which a high-stakes subject denies knowledge to a low-stakes subject, even though each subject has the same evidence—evidence, when we are thinking about the low-stakes subject alone, we are tempted to think is good enough to give the low-stakes subject knowledge. (Cohen's (1999) airport case is a good example.) We can adopt contextualism to handle these cases, while still accepting subject-sensitivity if we think it is the most natural way to handle cases like the Bank Cases, or if there are independent arguments for subject-sensitivity—for the claim that your practical situation is relevant to whether you know. Contextualism might also provide a way of dealing with some of the counterintuitive consequences we discussed above. If the attributor A has a certain high stakes practical situation in mind, perhaps that tends to affect the content of 'knows' in A's context, so that an attribution of knowledge can be true in her context only if the subject meets suitably high standards. Thus, it is hard to truly utter the likes of 'S1 and S2 have the same evidence concerning whether p but only S1 knows, because S2 is in a high stakes situation.'

One might well ask under what conditions the *relevance* of the practical or pragmatic becomes the fearsome *encroachment* in Jonathan Kvanvig's (2004) label, "pragmatic encroachment." So far, we have treated 'pragmatic' as equivalent to 'practical.' But there is a broader use of the former term, to cover not only factors having to do with action and preference but also features of a speech context that have been standardly taken not to be relevant to the content of what is said but only to the appropriateness of saying it, e.g., the salience of error-possibilities. Since John Hawthorne tentatively proposes that salience of possible error is relevant to knowledge, let us use 'pragmatic' in the broader sense.

We can distinguish at least two grades of pragmatic relevance. We focus on knowledge, but a similar account could be given for any epistemic feature:

> *First grade*: Knowledge has a pragmatic condition. That is, there is some interesting true principle of one or both of the following forms, where PC is pragmatic:
> in order to know that p, you must satisfy condition PC,
> in order to satisfy condition PC, you must know that p.

Thus, examples of such a condition would include: *being rational to act as if p* (Fantl and McGrath 2002), *being rational to ignore in action the chance that p is false* (Fantl and

McGrath 2009), *being appropriate to use p as a premise in practical reasoning* (Hawthorne 2004; Stanley 2005), *being such that no counterpossibilities of error are salient* (Hawthorne 2004).

Notice that Rudner wants to go further than this, with respect to hypothesis acceptability. For him, it's not merely that in order to be warranted in accepting a hypothesis, you must satisfy some pragmatic condition, though that is true; it's that whether a hypothesis is acceptable for you can vary with mere variations in a pragmatic factor, in particular with mere variations in how important it is to be right about the hypothesis. This suggests a second, deeper, grade of pragmatic relevance:

> *Second grade*: Knowledge can vary with mere variation of pragmatic factors. There are cases of knowledge such that if we merely vary a pragmatic factor present in that case, and leave everything else the same (as much as possible), we arrive at a case of ignorance.

The Bank Cases support this thesis: we have merely varied the importance for Keith of being right about whether the bank will be open tomorrow, leaving everything else, as much as possible, the same, and with this pragmatic variation comes a variation in knowledge.

The second grade is certainly more controversial than the first. Suppose there is pragmatic relevance only of the first grade, and not the second. Then we would not have to cope with the peculiarity of statements such as 'I know that p but I wouldn't know that p if more were riding on whether p'. One way to accept the first grade without the second is to accept the claim that knowledge that p requires epistemic certainty, which in turn requires the satisfaction of pragmatic conditions, such as *being rational to ignore the chance that not-p in one's decision-making*. The obvious worry about such a view is that it makes knowledge too hard to come by.

It is clear that, of these two grades of pragmatic relevance, only the second grade should count as pragmatic encroachment on knowledge. In previous work, we have endorsed the second grade—and so endorsed pragmatic encroachment—because we think it is a simple consequence of the denial of a supervenience thesis concerning knowledge, which we have called "epistemological purism":

> *Epistemological purism*: two subjects alike with respect to their strength of epistemic position with respect to p are alike with respect to whether they know that p (or at least with respect to whether they are in a position to know that p).

It is a tricky matter to specify precisely what strength of epistemic position involves. We take it that your strength of epistemic position with respect to p is determined by your standing on truth-relevant dimensions with respect to p, including reliability, strength of evidence, epistemic probability, and the like. Truth-relevant dimensions, intuitively, can be thought of as dimensions a higher standing on which with respect to p places you in a better position with respect to the truth of p. So, how important it is for your life that you are right about whether p doesn't count as a truth-relevant dimension, nor does your standing on it seem to be fixed by your standing on truth-relevant dimensions with respect to p.

We will say more about the grounds on which we reject this thesis later on. For the moment, notice that one could accept the second grade without denying epistemological purism, as Stanley (2005) does. Stanley argues that variations in knowledge that p, due to pragmatic factors, give rise to variations in your standing along the truth-relevant dimensions. So, in Bank Case A, Keith has better evidence for the proposition that the bank will be open tomorrow than he does in Case B: in Case A, part of his evidence is *the bank will be open tomorrow*, which is superbly good evidence for *the bank will be open tomorrow*; in Case B, Keith lacks this evidence. Stanley suggests the same goes for other epistemic concepts we would like to think of as picking out standings on truth-relevant dimensions. If Stanley is right, then, on the one hand, epistemological purism is not threatened by pragmatic encroachment, but on the other, epistemological purism doesn't deserve its name, because there are no purely truth-relevant dimensions of the relevant sort that come even close to providing a supervenience base for knowledge.

One might think that Stanley's position, although it saves one from the denial of epistemological purism, is a more radical form of pragmatic encroachment than ours, which denies purism. For Stanley thinks there is no genuinely epistemic notion that is unsullied by pragmatic factors. Change the stakes and you change not only knowledge but evidence, justification, reasons, probability, etc. There is pragmatic encroachment, in Juan Comesaña's (forthcoming) words, *all the way down*.

One nice feature Stanley's view might appear to have is that it avoids having to explain away the peculiarities such as 'A and B have the same evidence for p, but only A is in a position to know that p'. We say his view 'appears' to have this nice feature. But we doubt it does. Notice that even if there is pragmatic encroachment all the way down, we can still ask whether some epistemic properties supervene on others. For example, consider the following, where evidence is non-factive (with respect to p) iff it is evidence for p which does not entail p:

> Two subjects alike with respect to their non-factive evidence regarding p are alike with respect to whether they are justified in believing that p.

It is not clear to us how Stanley's acceptance of "pragmatic encroachment all the way down" enables him to avoid denying this antecedently plausible claim.

But for the sake of argument, let us assume that Stanley can avoid peculiar statements asserting sameness of evidence but difference in knowledge. Still, Stanley will have to explain away peculiar temporal and modal claims about pragmatic factors making a difference to knowledge, but perhaps these aren't as counterintuitive. Nonetheless, the cost of following Stanley's particular way of explaining these peculiarities seems greater than the cost of the peculiarities explained away. That's because your standing on many epistemic dimensions isn't plausibly affected by mere changes in practical environment. Consider probability: you are offered a high-stakes bet on the proposition this die will come up 6, that doesn't seem to lower its probability for you and it certainly does not raise the probability for you that it will come up 1–5, or any of 1–5 individually. We see no reason to think that matters are different when the probabilities approach 1, and so when it can seem plausible that, before being offered the bet, you know.

Putting Stanley's deep pragmatic encroachment aside, here is what we take to be the simplest and most convincing case for accepting pragmatic encroachment of the second grade.

Think about Keith in Bank Case A. Unless we are willing to accept the claim that knowledge requires epistemic certainty, we should say that he knows the bank will be open tomorrow (or if one doesn't like this claim because it is about the future, make any adjustments to the example you like, but preserve lack of certainty). At any rate, if knowledge doesn't require certainty, there will be some case relevantly like Bank Case A in which the subject has knowledge. So, Keith knows in Bank Case A that the bank will be open tomorrow. Keith also knows that if it will be open tomorrow, the option with the best outcome is to wait until tomorrow. Given how very well Keith knows this conditional, Keith also knows that waiting until tomorrow will have the best outcome of his available options. And this is what he is justified in doing.

Now consider Keith in Bank Case B. Assume, for reductio, that the second grade of pragmatic encroachment fails: knowledge can't vary with mere changes of pragmatic factors. Then, since Keith knows the bank will be open tomorrow in Case A, he knows it in Case B. But he also seems to know that if it will be open tomorrow the available option with the best outcome is to wait until tomorrow to cash the check. Knowing this so very well—just as well as in Case A—Keith will also know that the available option in Case B with the best outcome is to wait until tomorrow. Now ask yourself: if you know that of all your available options, option O will have the best outcome, what should you do? It is hard not to answer: *well*, O! That O will have the best outcome of all your options seems to be a decisive reason to do O, not anything else. Think of what you will know about the other options: that they will have worse outcomes than O. So, if Keith knows that waiting until tomorrow to deposit the check will have the best outcome, he will know that going in to check further will have a worse outcome. Should he do what he knows to be worse than O? That sounds absurd. (Remember here: it's not just that he knows that going in to check further is worse than *some* other actions; he knows which action it is worse than.)

Given that he can't be certain that the bank will be open tomorrow, then assuming the stakes are high enough, and that it is important enough to be right, shouldn't Keith play it safe? Shouldn't he go in and check further and, if necessary, wait in line to deposit the check today? This seems like sound advice, and is likely the advice most decision-theorists will give, at least assuming the stakes are high enough. So, it seems in Case B, Keith isn't justified in waiting until tomorrow to deposit the check; he should rather go in and check further. But we saw that it was absurd to think one should take an option one knows to be worse than a given option. So, our assumption that Keith knows that the bank will be open tomorrow in Case B must be false. (Our argument against what we called evidentialism in Fantl and McGrath (2002) takes roughly this form, using our train case. See also our argument against epistemological purism in our (2007). We should stress: the argument given does not pump intuitions about the Bank Cases in particular. All we need is some case of knowledge without certainty, in which what is known is not irrelevant to the question of what to do.)

What is crucial to this argument are not any intuitions specific to the Bank Cases but, rather, three general claims: (1) the fallibilist thesis that knowledge doesn't require certainty; (2) the assumption that if a subject lacks certainty concerning a proposition relevant to the question of what to do, the lack of certainty can make a difference as to what the subject is justified in doing, if the stakes are high enough; and (3) the assumption that if you know that an option O will have the best outcome of all your available acts then you are justified in doing O. Given these claims, we can show that there is a pair of cases, like the Bank Cases, in which whether a subject knows something varies with mere variations in pragmatic factors.

We take it that assumption (2) is pretty safe. Perhaps in the end (1) should go, though there are serious questions about the skeptical implications of giving it up. There are also hard questions, which we are ignoring here, about how precisely to understand the sort of certainty involved (clearly it is epistemic rather than psychological). Assumption (3) is doing a lot of the work here. One might hope to deny it while explaining away the apparent absurdity of 'I know O will be better than P but I should do P' in terms of a Gricean implicature. We think the prospects for this gambit are poor, but we cannot discuss the matter further here. (We discuss the matter further in our (2007).)

The most serious worry about (3), to our mind, is whether it is just an isolated intuition, or instead can be fitted into a plausible account of the relation between knowledge and what knowledge can justify. So, let's ask: if (3) is right, why might it be? The natural answer is that the proposition that option O will have the best consequences of all your available acts is a decisive reason for doing O. Of course, not all reasons that there are for doing something will justify you in doing it. That there is petrol in the glass is an excellent reason for refraining from drinking what's in the glass. But it only justifies you doing so if you *have* that reason.

What epistemic relation do you have to bear on a reason in order to have it? Our claim is that knowledge of a reason satisfies a sufficient condition on the epistemic relation you have to bear to a reason in order to have it. If you know that r, and r is a good reason for φ-ing, then r is a good reason you have for φ-ing. (See Hawthorne and Stanley (2008) for a similar view. The argument to follow is an abbreviated version of the main argument given in chapter 3 of Fantl and McGrath (2009).)

Surely, this is the case when φ-ing is restricted to believing: if you know that r, and r is a good reason for believing q, then you have that good reason for believing q. Suppose you know that Clinton has already been U.S. president twice and that U.S. presidents can only serve two terms. This is a good reason for believing that Clinton won't be president again. Then you have that good reason for believing that Clinton won't be president again. But knowledge of r satisfies an epistemic condition sufficient for having r, even when what r is a reason for is not restricted to belief.

When trying to determine what is true—that is, in forming beliefs—we draw conclusions from the reasons we have. The same goes for trying to decide what to do. Here, too, we draw conclusions about what to do—we form intentions—from the reasons we have. We bring reasons into our reasoning knowing that we might draw all sorts of conclusions from them along the way, some practical and some theoretical. Suppose your sister calls you on the phone to tell you about plans for her upcoming visit to see you. She tells you, and you thereby come to know, that she'll be arriving at the airport at 8 a.m. and will need a ride to your place. You might well include this proposition in your reasoning and at some point draw a practical conclusion from it, for example, 'I'll be there a little after 8 a.m. with my car', but you might also draw along the way any number of theoretical conclusions as well, e.g., that she'll be ready to be picked up a little after 8 a.m., that she'll be tired when she arrives, that you'll not be able to drop the kids off at preschool, and so on. The bottom line is that we don't segregate reasons by whether they are available for drawing practical or for theoretical conclusions. But if knowledge that r gave us r as a reason for forming beliefs but not for performing actions, we'd expect some degree of segregation, if not always, at least when something significant is at stake.

This is not what we find. Even when the stakes are high there is no segregation; rather, when the stakes are high, we are more careful about drawing theoretical conclusions—as careful as we are about drawing practical conclusions. Do you walk across or walk around the frozen pond? Walking around will take a while, but you don't want to fall through the ice. (Thanks to Mark Migotti for suggesting this example.) How do you decide? Presumably, your decision will depend on whether you think the ice is thick enough to hold you. So, you'll start trying to make your decision about what to do by trying to figure out whether the ice is thick enough. Suppose you do some checking and on the basis of your information, you come to know that the ice is thick enough. So *the ice is thick enough* becomes a reason you have to draw theoretical conclusions on its basis (e.g., that it would be perfectly safe to cross it). It would then be very odd not to allow this knowledge into your practical reasoning. Why did you try to figure out whether the ice was thick enough in the first place? For fun? No, you tried to figure it out because you were (correctly) under the impression that figuring out whether the ice was thick enough would help you decide what to do. When r becomes available as a basis for theoretical conclusions, it is 'barmy' (to use an expression suggested by one of our informants) to just ignore p in one's decision-making and planning.

So, it looks as if whatever we treat as epistemic status sufficient to have r for use in reasoning—as a reason—for beliefs, we also treat as sufficient to have r for use in reasoning—as a reason—for intention and action. Similar remarks can also be applied to emotional states, desires, hopes, and reactive attitudes generally (here the emphasis on reasoning would have to be toned down with regard to some of these states, though there clearly is such a thing as responding to reasons in these cases). These observations support the claim that if knowledge that r qualifies r to be a reason you have for belief, it qualifies r to be a reason you have for any φ.

Clearly, that option O will have the best results of all your available actions is a reason for taking option O. Therefore, when you know this reason to be true, it's a reason you have for taking option O. If it's a reason you have for taking option O, what could stand in the way of it justifying you in taking option O? Well, perhaps it's defeated by some contrary reason—e.g., that there's a chance that option O is not the best option and, if it's not, the consequences will be disastrous. This reason might be true consistent with your knowing that option O is the best option, provided that knowledge does not require certainty. And if it is, perhaps it is natural to reason this way:

> Yes, I do know that waiting until tomorrow to go to the bank is best. Of course, if it's not best, then that means that the bank isn't open tomorrow, and so if I do wait until tomorrow, the consequences will be disastrous. And there's a chance that waiting until tomorrow isn't best. It's just too risky. I'll wait in line now.

Does this reflect the way we reason? In reasoning, do we find ourselves weighing p—a reason for φ-ing—against *there is a serious risk that not-p*—a reason for not φ-ing? Not plausibly. For here's what the weighing of competing reasons feels like in uncontroversial cases:

> Ice cream tastes good, and that's a reason I have to eat it, but it also is unhealthy, so that's a reason I have not to. Which is more important, taste or health?

> The rain will make me wet, so that's a reason I have to bring my umbrella, but the umbrella's also really heavy, so that's a reason I have not to. Which is more important, staying dry or being unencumbered?

> His paper didn't have an argument, so that's a reason I have to give him a bad grade, but also he did work really hard, so that's a reason I have to give him a good grade. Which is more important, quality of work or quality of effort?

Contrast these examples with:

> There's a serious risk that waiting until tomorrow isn't best, so that's a reason I have to wait in line now. But waiting until tomorrow is also best, so that's a reason I have to wait until tomorrow. Which is more important, the serious risk that waiting until tomorrow isn't best, or the fact that waiting until tomorrow is best?

People don't weigh these kinds of reasons in the way we'd expect them to if people could have both of them at once. We'd expect to find people explicitly weighing up reasons concerning actual results against conflicting reasons concerning expected results. We find no such thing. People do vacillate: 'The ice is very thick. Surely it will hold me. But . . . there's a real possibility it won't. I'd better not risk it.' Perhaps even with the right halting tone of voice someone might say, 'The ice will hold me (won't it? *surely* it will, right?). Forget it. I'll play it safe and walk around.' What you don't find is the likes of, 'Hmm, the ice might not hold me. That's one consideration. Another is that it will hold me.'

So, if you have a reason, r, for φ-ing, it seems that the reason can't be defeated by some further reason to the effect that r might be false. And this is for the simple reason that we never have both of these reasons at the same time. Of course, even if we did have O *is best* and O *might not be best* at the same time as reasons for doing contrary things, it's not at all clear that O *might not be best* would be the winning reason. We care about actual results, not expected results, and if we have O *is best* that seems like it should beat out O *might not be best*, regardless of the consequences. But, the fact of the matter is that we don't ever have both reasons at once, and this is reflected in the fact that it is absurd to picture us reasoning by weighing the fact that p against the possibility that not-p.

So, if you know that O is best, then that's a reason you have to do O. And if that's a reason you have to do O, then it can't be defeated by considerations about the chance that O isn't best or any other epistemic considerations with respect to the reason that O is best. And it doesn't seem as though, in this case, any other obstacles could stand in the way of your being justified in doing O. Therefore, if you know that O is best, you are justified in doing O. And this is just premise 3 in the above argument.

Premise 3, then, is not just an arbitrary premise. It is grounded in principles about knowledge and the having of reasons, in particular:

> A) If you know that r, then if r is a reason for φ-ing, r is a reason you have for φ-ing.
>
> B) If r is a reason you have for φ-ing, then r can't be defeated by any consideration to the effect that r might be false.

Suppose you know that O *is best*. That O is best is a reason to do O. By (A) O *is best* is a reason you have do O. By (B), this reason isn't defeated by any consideration to the effect that O might not be best. The only plausible obstacles to O *is best* being a justifying reason you have to do O are considerations about the chance that O might not be best. So, that O is best is a justifying reason you have to do O. If you have a justifying reason to do something then you are justified in doing it. Thus, if you know that O is best, you are justified in doing O.

Once knowledge doesn't require certainty, then, commitment to the second grade of pragmatic relevance—pragmatic encroachment—doesn't just get motivated by our intuitive reactions to hypothetical cases. It is grounded in deep principles about knowledge and reasons.

Bibliography

Bach, Kent. (2008). "Applying Pragmatics to Epistemology." *Philosophical Issues* 18: 68–88.
Cohen, Stewart. (1999). "Contextualism, Skepticism, and the Structure of Reasons." In Tomberlin, J. (Ed.) *Philosophical Perspectives*. Cambridge: Blackwell: 57–89.
Comesaña, Juan. (forthcoming). "Epistemic Pragmatism: An Argument Against Moderation." *Midwest Epistemology Workshop*. University of Nebraska-Lincoln.
DeRose, Keith. (1992). "Contextualism and Knowledge Attributions." *Philosophy and Phenomenological Research* 52: 913–29.
——. (2004). "The Problem with Subject-Sensitive Invariantism." *Philosophy and Phenomenological Research* 68: 346–50.
——. (2009). *The Case for Contextualism*. Oxford: Oxford University Press.
Fantl, Jeremy and McGrath, Matthew. (2002). "Evidence, Pragmatics, and Justification." *The Philosophical Review* 111: 67–94.
——. (2007). "On Pragmatic Encroachment in Epistemology." *Philosophy and Phenomenological Research* 75: 558–89.
——. (2009). *Knowledge in an Uncertain World*. Oxford: Oxford University Press.
Hawthorne, John. (2004). *Knowledge and Lotteries*. Oxford: Oxford University Press.
—— and Stanley, Jason. (2008). "Knowledge and Action." *Journal of Philosophy* 105: 571–90.
Kvanvig, Jonathan. (2004). "Pragmatic Aspects of Knowledge?" Blog. January 29, 2009. <http://fleetwood.baylor.edu/certain_doubts/?p=13>
Nagel, Jennifer. (2008). "Knowledge Ascriptions and the Psychological Consequences of Changing Stakes." *Australasian Journal of Philosophy* 86: 279–94.
Rudner, Richard. (1953). "The Scientist *Qua* Scientist Makes Value Judgments." *Philosophy of Science* 20: 1–6.
Stanley, Jason. (2005). *Knowledge and Practical Interests*. Oxford: Oxford University Press.

Part VIII

FORMAL EPISTEMOLOGY

52
LOGIC AND FORMAL SEMANTICS FOR EPISTEMOLOGY
John Symons

Epistemic expressions such as 'knows that' or 'believes that' have systematic properties that are amenable to formal study. Most obviously, statements containing epistemic expressions sometimes involve logical constants which behave in the usual way. So, for example, if you know *p* and *q* then you know *q*. The conceptual features of statements concerning knowledge and belief become more interesting when one begins to examine the characteristics of general principles governing the use of epistemic concepts. The behavior and interaction of these general principles has been the focus of epistemic logic. For example, as G.E. Moore pointed out, there seems to be something wrong with claiming

(1) "*p* and I do not believe *p*."

Assertions of this kind are self-defeating because of the conceptual features of knowledge or belief and not because of the syntactical features of the sentence or the character of the logical constants that are involved. As Moore noted "'I went to the pictures last Tuesday, but I don't believe that I did' is a perfectly absurd thing to say" (1952: 543). The *perfect absurdity* here is due to a violation of a principle governing epistemic concepts.

Notice that (1) is often a correct description of the state of affairs in question. For instance, since I recognize that I am fallible, I am committed to the possibility that there are cases where it is true that *p* and I do not believe *p*. Furthermore, I can assert, without paradox or contradiction, that there is some proposition *p* such that *p* and I do not believe *p*.

The paradox arises from the peculiarity of the agent in question attesting to particular instances of (1), where the variable *p* is replaced by an assertion concerning some state of affairs. Specifically, it is paradoxical insofar as it is, what John Austin called, an illocutionary act (1975: 133). While I recognize that there might be cases where replacing *p* with some description of some state of affairs is true, I cannot sincerely attest to both parts of the conjunction contained in (1) at a particular moment for any specific instance of (1). In this sense, Moore's paradox sheds light on the properties of epistemic agents and the concept of belief. Reflecting on the *perfect absurdity* of Moore's examples, shows us that an agent's belief and its agency are related. However, we are not restricted to relying on epistemic intuitions in our consideration of Moore's paradox. Exploration of the principles or norms governing epistemic notions can take place in an axiomatic fashion. Jaakko Hintikka, for example, provided a proof of the contradictory nature of the paradoxical form of the Moore statements, the case where the statement asserts that an agent believes p and $not\text{-}p$ (1962: 67). I can take as a rule for instance that it is prohibited or confused to say:

(2) "I know p but it is not the case that p."

If (2) is prohibited, it is due in part to the illocutionary considerations which applied in (1) but unlike assertions of belief, (2) is prohibited by virtue of another general principle, namely the veracity of knowledge.

(3) If one knows p then it is true that p.

If we accept that knowledge implies veracity then we can consider what the implications of taking it as an axiom might be and whether it is consistent with other general epistemic principles we might hold. As discussed below, considerations of this kind have been given an elegant formal framework by epistemic logicians. Wolfgang Lenzen (1978) provided an excellent overview of arguments from the 1960s and 1970s concerning the appropriate axioms for knowledge.

Observations of the kind emphasized by Moore, concerning the behavior of the term "knows that" served as the starting points for the development of modern epistemic logic. G.H. von Wright was the first to sketch an axiomatic treatment of the behavior of epistemic concepts (1951: 29–35). However, modern epistemic logic began in earnest once Hintikka provided a semantic interpretation of epistemic and doxastic notions in the early 1960s.

Hintikka began by supplementing the language of propositional logic with two unary epistemic operators K_a and B_a such that $K_a p$ reads 'Agent a knows p' and $B_a p$ reads 'Agent a believes p' for some proposition p. In this way, candidate epistemic or doxastic axioms can be presented in formal terms. So, for instance, we have already seen that one intuitive axiom which we are likely to accept into our epistemic logic is:

(4) $K_c A \to A$

This is known as axiom T which we saw above as (3). With our modest addition to first-order logic in hand, we can begin to catalog other plausible epistemic axioms.

A standard list of the axioms (following Lemmon (1977), Bull and Segerberg (1984)) that are relevant for epistemic logic run as shown in Table 52.1:

Table 52.1 Axioms of Epistemic Logic

K	$K_c(A \to A') \to (K_c A \to K_c A')$
D	$K_c A \to \neg K_c \neg A$
T	$K_c A \to A$
4	$K_c A \to K_c K_c A$
5	$\neg K_c A \to K_c \neg K_c A$

LOGIC AND FORMAL SEMANTICS FOR EPISTEMOLOGY

.2 $\quad \neg K_c \neg K_c A \to K_c \neg K_c \neg A$
.3 $\quad K_c(K_c A \to K_c A') \lor K_c(K_c A' \to K_c A)$
.4 $\quad A \to (\neg K_c \neg K_c A \to K_c A)$

We can consider the philosophical merits of each axiom to a certain extent without the introduction of additional formalism. However, Hintikka's approach to the semantics of epistemic notions offers an important supplement to our intuitive reflections. In order to begin thinking about the relative merits of these axioms one can begin by considering the familiar interpretation of the K and B operators using possible world semantics along the lines discussed above:

$K_c A$: In all possible worlds compatible with what c knows, it is the case that A
$B_c A$: In all possible worlds compatible with what c believes, it is the case that A

The basic assumption is that any ascription of propositional attitudes such as knowledge and belief, involves dividing the set of possible worlds in two: Those worlds compatible with the attitude in question and those that are incompatible with it.

The central idea in possible worlds semantics is the notion of accessibility. Accessibility is a relation that is defined on the set of possible worlds. In standard modal logic we say that some world w is accessible from some world w' just in case w is *possible* relative to w'. Specifically, the relation can be characterized as a subset of the Cartesian product of the set of possible worlds. As described below, determining the accessibility relation is the most basic step in determining the properties of our semantical framework. So, for example, whether one assumes that the accessibility relation is symmetric, transitive, reflexive, or some combination of the three, will make a significant difference in how one thinks about the modal or epistemic properties of the system in question. In the epistemic context, the set of worlds accessible to an agent (its set of epistemic alternatives) depends on its informational resources at an instant. This dependency is captured via the specification of the accessibility relation, R, on the set of possible worlds. To express the idea that for agent c, the world w' is compatible with his information state, or accessible from the possible world w which c is currently in, it is required that R holds between w and w'. This relation is written Rww' and reads "world w' is accessible from w". The world w' is said to be an *epistemic* or *doxastic alternative* to world w for agent c, depending on whether knowledge or belief is under consideration. We can give this a semantic interpretation, by saying that if a proposition A is true in all worlds which agent c considers possible then c knows A.

A possible world semantics for a propositional epistemic logic with a single agent c then consists of a *frame* $\mathcal{F}$ which in turn is a pair $<W, R_c>$ such that W is a non-empty set of possible worlds and R_c is a binary accessibility relation (relative to agent c) over W. A *model* $\mathcal{M}$ for an epistemic system consists of a frame and a denotation function φ assigning sets of worlds to atomic propositional formulas. Propositions are taken to be sets of possible worlds; namely the set of possible worlds in which they are true. Let *atom* be the set of atomic propositional formulae, then $\varphi: atom \mapsto P(W)$, where P denotes the powerset operation.

The model $\mathcal{M} = <W, R_c, \varphi>$ is called a Kripke-model and the resulting semantics Kripke-semantics (Kripke 1963): An atomic propositional formula, **a**, is said to be true in a world w in $\mathcal{M}$ (written $\mathcal{M}, w \vDash$ **a**) iff w is in the set of possible worlds assigned to **a**, i.e., $\mathcal{M}, w \vDash$ **a** iff $w \in \varphi($**a**$)$ for all **a** $\in atom$. The formula $K_c A$ is true in a world w (i.e.,

$\mathcal{M}, w \models K_c A$) iff $\forall w' \in W$, if $R_c ww'$, then $\mathcal{M}, w' \models A$. The semantics for the Boolean connectives follow the usual recursive recipe. Similar semantics can be formulated for the belief operator. Since a belief is not necessarily true but, rather, probably true, possibly true, or likely to be true, we must modify our approach to the semantics of belief appropriately. For instance, belief can be modeled by assigning a sufficiently high degree of probability to the proposition in question and determining the doxastic alternatives accordingly. The truth-conditions for the doxastic operator are defined in a way similar to that of the knowledge operator and the model can also be expanded to accommodate the two operators simultaneously.

A modal formula is said to be *valid* in a frame if, and only if, the formula is true for all possible assignments in all worlds in the frame.

An important feature of possible world semantics is that the epistemic axioms listed above, correspond to algebraic properties of the frame in the following sense: A modal axiom is valid in a frame if, and only if, the accessibility relation satisfies some algebraic condition (see Hendricks and Symons 2006). For example, the axiom expressing the veridicality property that if a proposition is known by c, then A is true,

(5) $K_c A \to A$,

is valid in all frames in which the accessibility relation is reflexive in the sense that $\forall w \in W: Rww$. Given reflexive accessibility, every possible world is accessible from itself. Similarly if the accessibility relation satisfies the condition that

(6) $\forall w, w', w'' \in W: Rww' \wedge Rw'w'' \to Rww''$

which is also known as transitivity, then the axiom (7) is valid.

(7) $K_c A \to K_c K_c A$

(7) is called axiom 4 and is also known as the axiom of self-awareness, positive introspection, or the KK-thesis. In this case, the axiom captures the idea that if the agent knows p then it has knowledge of its knowledge that p. Other axioms require yet other relational properties to be met in order to be valid in all frames: If the accessibility relation is reflexive, symmetric and transitive, then

(8) $\neg K_c A \to K_c \neg K_c A$

is valid. (8) is called axiom 5, also better known as the axiom of wisdom. This is the much stronger thesis that an agent has knowledge of its own ignorance: If a does not know p, it knows that it doesn't know p. The axiom is also known as the axiom of negative introspection.

One contentious axiom which is valid in all possible frames,

(9) $K_c (A \to B) \to (K_c A \to K_c B)$,

is the closure condition for knowledge, also known as axiom K, or the axiom of deductive cogency: If the agent a knows $p \to q$, then if a knows p, a also knows q. As discussed below, this axiom leads to the most difficult philosophical problem for epistemic logicians, namely the apparent commitment to logical omniscience. It seems that if one accepts this axiom, then an epistemic agent must know everything that follows logically from its knowledge.

Other axioms of epistemic import require yet other relational properties to be met in order to be valid in all frames. When combined in various ways, these axioms make up epistemic modal systems of varying strength. Their strengths vary according to the modal formulas valid in the respective systems and given the algebraic properties assumed for the accessibility relation.

Returning to the axioms listed above, we can begin to see how we might compare their relative strengths. The weakest system of epistemic interest is usually considered to be system **T**. The reader should take care to distinguish the epistemic operator K, the modal axiom K and the system of axioms **K** in what follows. Similarly, we distinguish the axiom T from the system **T**. T is a system of modal logic which is characterized by reflexive frame with the axioms T and K as valid axioms.

Additional modal strength can be obtained by extending **T** with other axioms drawn from the above pool, altering the frame semantics to validate the additional axioms. By way of example, while

(10) $K_c A \to A$

is valid in system **T**,

(11) $K_c A \to A, K_c A \to K_c K_c A$ and $\neg K_c A \to K_c \neg K_c A$

are all valid in **S5** but not in **T**.

System **T** has a reflexive accessibility relation, **S5** has reflexive, transitive and symmetrical accessibility relations. The arrows in Table 52.2 below indicate that the system to which the arrow is pointing is included in the system from which the arrow originates and hence reflect relative strength. Then **S5** is the strongest and **S4** the weakest of the ones listed.

Table 52.2 Relative Strength of Epistemic Systems Between S4 and S5

	Epistemic Systems		
KT4	=	S4	
KT4 + .2	=	S4.2	↑
KT4 + .3	=	S4.3	↑
KT4 + .4	=	S4.4	↑
KT5	=	S5	↑

One of the important tasks of epistemic logic is to catalog all sound and complete systems of such logics in order to allow us to pick the most 'appropriate' ones. The logics range from S4 over the intermediate systems S4.2–S4.4 to S5. By way of example, Hintikka settled for S4 (1962), Kutschera argued for S4.4 (1976), Lenzen suggested S4.2 (1978), van der Hoek has proposed to strengthen knowledge according to system S4.3 (Meyer and van der Hoek 1995). Van Ditmarsch, van der Hoek and Kooi (2007) together with Fagin, Halpern, Moses and Vardi (Fagin et al. 1995) and others assume knowledge to be S5 valid.

In the doxastic context, we can also catalog the completeness properties of the alternative systems in a similar fashion. Of course in doxastic logic we drop axiom T, which is usually replaced by D. This avoids committing doxastic logic to the truth of beliefs while retaining the condition that beliefs be consistent. Replacing T with D generates systems like KD4–KD45. This approach permits the combination of epistemic and doxastic systems and for studying the interplay between knowledge and belief (see Voorbraak 1993). There are some important philosophical concerns with such combined doxastic and epistemic systems. Lenzen (1978) and Stalnaker (1996) point out that such combined systems risk conflating knowledge and belief.

How does semantic formalization relate to epistemology? By way of example, it is worth returning briefly to our discussion of Moore's problem to see what kind of light Hintikka's formalization shed on that case. In *Knowledge and Belief*, he was able to prove that statements of the sort "p and I do not believe p" are *perfect absurdities* not because they run afoul of some kind of epistemic intuition, but because, when properly analyzed, they generate a contradiction. More importantly, the analysis allows us to recognize which epistemic commitments are involved in generating the contradiction. These commitments are formulated as rules for epistemic alternatives in model systems. So, for example, the proof of the absurdity of "p and I do not believe p" (Hintikka 1962: 68) relies on the conditions governing the semantics of sentences concerning belief. The difference between the kind of reasoning we find in Moore and Hintikka with respect to "p and I do not believe p" boils down to difference with respect to the degree of explicitness and control that the philosophers aspire to in their arguments. For Hintikka, unlike Moore, the point is to achieve the same level of explicitness in epistemology as is found in logic:

> The word "logic" which occurs in the subtitle of this work is to be taken seriously. My first aim is to formulate and to defend explicit criteria of consistency for certain sets of statements—criteria which, it is hoped, will be comparable with the criteria of consistency studied in the established branches of logic.
>
> (1962: 3)

Logical Omniscience and Idealized Epistemic Agents

Epistemic logic inevitably traffics in idealizations. As discussed below, the problem of logical omniscience (a product of accepting the axiom of deductive cogency or axiom K and standard possible world semantics) encouraged theorists to craft formal systems which more adequately reflected the actual properties of epistemic agents. Since real epistemic agents modify their beliefs and engage in inquiry, there was some philosophical interest in attempting to formally capture the dynamical features of inquiry. Developments since *Knowledge and Belief*, principally those since Kutchera (1976) and Lenzen (1978), attempted to integrate broader insights from modal logic with epistemic logic and have made it possible to formally model some prominent features of the dynamical nature of epistemic agency. Gärdenfors' (1988) account of belief revision was particularly important in setting the stage for a slew of dynamical models of knowledge.

Logical omniscience is related to closure properties. Axiom K can, under certain circumstances, be generalized to a closure property for an agent's knowledge which is implausibly strong: Whenever an agent c knows all of the formulas in a set Γ and A

follows logically from Γ, then c also knows A. In particular, c knows all theorems (letting $\Gamma = \emptyset$), and he knows all logical consequences of any formula which he knows (letting Γ consist of a single formula).

In response to the threat of logical omniscience, some epistemologists raised the question of whether the very idea of a logic of knowledge makes any epistemological sense. For instance, Hocutt challenged the applicability of logic to any realistic account of knowledge (1972). Because there is no guarantee that a knower will recognize that it is committed to some proposition that is logically equivalent to some proposition to which it readily assents, the very idea of an epistemic logic is on slippery ground.

Some of the first proposals for solving the problem of logical omniscience introduce semantical entities which explain why the agent appears to be, but in fact is not really logically omniscient. These entities were called 'impossible possible worlds' by Hintikka (1975). The basic idea is that an agent might mistakenly count among the worlds consistent with his or her knowledge, some worlds containing logical contradictions. The mistake is simply a product of limited resources; the agent might not be in a position to detect the contradiction and might erroneously count them as genuine possibilities.

'Seemingly possible' worlds are introduced by Veikko Rantala (1975) in his urn-model analysis of logical omniscience. Rantala devised a way of alleviating the mismatch between our model theoretic reasoning about knowledge and our proof theoretic commitments: He asks us to conceive of our epistemic relationship with the world by analogy with an urn from which we can draw balls (individual units of information) one by one over time. With each new piece of information drawn from the urn, we can modify our models. The idea is, simply, that inquiry is a dynamical process in which our model of the world changes with new information. Rantala has provided a formalism which incorporates an intuitively reasonable notion of change in a model. Such change can be understood as a change in the properties of individuals of the model or a change in its universe of discourse.

Representing how the agent's model might dynamically update is one way of thinking about epistemic agency in a more realistic manner. However, on any realistic account of epistemic agency, the agent is likely to consider (albeit inadvertently) worlds in which the classical laws of logic do not hold. In this context, the general problem of establishing a set of epistemic principles for a realistic agent is unavoidable. Rantala's approach provides a way of making the appearance of logical omniscience less threatening, but at the cost of introducing a degree of arbitrariness along with impossible or seemingly possible worlds (see Rantala 1982). In Rantala's discussion of the semantics for impossible worlds (1982) the truth condition is completely free, insofar as any contradiction among an agent's beliefs can be represented by a model containing an impossible world. While logical omniscience is avoided, the price we pay is high, since no real epistemic principles hold broadly enough to encompass impossible and seemingly possible worlds (see Meyer and van der Hoek 1995: 87–88).

Some conditions must be applied to epistemic models such that they cohere with epistemic principles. Computer scientists have proposed that what is being modeled in epistemic logic is not knowledge simpliciter but a related concept which is immune to logical omniscience. The epistemic operator $K_c A$ should be read as 'agent c knows implicitly A,' 'A follows from c's knowledge,' 'A is agent c's possible knowledge,' etc. Propositional attitudes like these should replace the usual 'agent c knows A'. While there exists some variation, the locutions all suggest modeling implicit knowledge or what is implicitly represented in an agent's information state rather than explicit knowledge

(Fagin et al. 1995, and others). The agents neither have to compute knowledge nor can they be held responsible for answering queries based on their knowledge under the implicit understanding of knowledge. Logical omniscience is an epistemological condition for implicit knowledge, but the agent might actually fail to realize this condition.

There are a variety of ways of responding to these kinds of challenges. One rather unpromising approach is to deny that epistemic logic is under any obligation to connect with more general epistemological concerns (see, for example, Lenzen 1978: 34). Rather than treating epistemic logic as a purely formal exercise, a preferable response involves maintaining that epistemic logic does carry epistemological significance but in an inevitably idealized sort of way. One restricts attention to a class of rational agents where rationality is defined by certain postulates. Thus, agents have to satisfy at least some minimal conditions to simply qualify as rational. This is, for example, what Lemmon originally suggests (Lemmon 1959). One such condition would involve assuming that rational agents should acknowledge the laws of logic. For instance, if the agent knows p and $p \to q$, it should be able to recognize that q follows validly.

These 'rationality postulates' for knowledge exhibit a striking similarity to the laws of modal and epistemic logic. One can, in turn, legitimately attempt to interpret the necessity operator in alethic axioms as a knowledge operator and then justify the modal axioms as axioms of knowledge. While Lemmon constructs the rational epistemic agent directly from the axiomatization of the logic, another way of justifying the epistemic axioms involves reference to their semantical features. This is the line of thought that Hintikka pursued in *Knowledge and Belief*. Hintikka stipulated that the axioms or principles of epistemic logic are conditions descriptive of a special kind of general (strong) rationality. The statements that can be proved false by application of the epistemic axioms are not inconsistent, meaning that their truth is logically impossible. They are, rather, rationally 'indefensible.' Indefensibility is fleshed out as the agent's epistemic laziness, sloppiness or perhaps cognitive incapacity whenever to realize the implications of what he in fact knows. Defensibility, then, means not falling victim of 'epistemic negligence' as Chisholm calls it (Chisholm 1963, 1977). The notion of indefensibility gives away the status of the epistemic axioms and logics. Some epistemic statement for which its negation is indefensible is called 'self-sustaining.' The notion of self-sustenance actually corresponds to the meta-logical concept of validity. Corresponding to a self-sustaining statement is a logically valid statement. But this will again be a statement which is rationally indefensible to deny. So, in conclusion, epistemic axioms can be understood to be descriptions of rationality. This argument is spelled out in detail by Hilpinen (2002).

Common Knowledge and Distributed Knowledge

So far, this essay has discussed the epistemic properties of individual agents. However, many recent developments in epistemic logic concern the study of the formal properties of systems of interacting agents. This section introduces two of the most prominent notions in the study of multi-agent systems: common and distributed knowledge.

When we consider agents who are connected via some network we can study the effect of new information, presented to part of the (or made public to the whole) group. Formal grasp of the role of announcements in a complex network of agents has important practical consequences for our understanding of cooperation and competition. The manner in which new information moves through a multi-agent system and how it causes individual agents to modify their beliefs is, in part, dependent on the character of the networks connecting those agents. However, analysis of the cooperative and competitive behavior of agents immediately brings into focus the dependency of these behaviors on a prior shared epistemic medium known as common knowledge.

Common knowledge, as distinguished from shared or mutual knowledge begins with the knowledge that one's fellow agents know that p. However, it is more than that, because not only do all the agents in a group know that p, they also know that *all other* agents know p and, furthermore, that they all know that they all know p, and so on. I know that my fellow drivers know that they ought to stop at the red light and they know that I know that they know that they should stop, etc. Thus, in one sense common knowledge is a very powerful kind of phenomenon. The social role played by common knowledge in a broad range of human activities has long been recognized by philosophers from David Hume (1740) to David Lewis (1969).

Common knowledge became a concern for theoretical computer scientists given the difficulties faced by projects in artificial intelligence which focus too narrowly on the epistemic condition of single agents. These difficulties encouraged theoretical computer scientists to focus on the social and conventional features of knowledge and belief. Common knowledge is the basic background knowledge which supports the kinds of social entanglements that are crucial for sophisticated forms of intelligence; it is what any fool knows (to echo John McCarthy (1979)). Philosophical accounts of common knowledge see it as carrying a great burden; supporting the very possibility of the kind of collaborative activity that defines human intelligence. In order to approach anything resembling human epistemic agency, a significant level of social scaffolding needs to be in place. Clearly, for example, we depend on shared epistemic starting points for most basic social interactions, including, prominently, membership in a linguistic community. As Lewis noted (1969) a convention requires common knowledge among the agents that observe it. Robert Aumann (1995) also emphasized the centrality of common knowledge with respect to norms, social and linguistic practices, agent interactions and games.

A detailed treatment of the various formal techniques for tackling common knowledge is beyond the scope of this essay (see Vanderschraaf and Sillari 2007 for an excellent overview). However, given our account of the logical landscape for single-agent systems above, it is possible to introduce some of the main features of multi-agent systems with just a little oversimplification. The primary difference between the semantics of single- and multi-agent semantics is that more than one accessibility relation is introduced. A modal system for n agents results from combining n modal logics in cases where it can be assumed that the agents are homogeneous in the sense that they can all be described by the same logical system. Thus, in the simplest case, an epistemic logic for n agents consists of n copies of a certain modal logic. In such an extended epistemic logic it is possible to express that some agent in the group knows a certain fact, that an agent knows that another agent knows a certain fact, etc.

It is possible to develop the logic even further: Not only can an agent know that another agent knows a fact, but they can all know this fact simultaneously. From here it is possible to express that everyone knows that everyone knows that everyone knows that everyone knows that ... some fact holds. This is what is meant by common knowledge.

One way of defining common knowledge involves defining common knowledge for the entire group of agents rather than partitioning the group of agents into subsets with different common 'knowledges.' Once multiple agents have been added to the syntax, the language is augmented with an additional operator C. CA is then interpreted as 'It is common knowledge among the agents that A.' Well-formed formulas follow the standard recursive recipe with modifications that account for the multiple agents. So, for instance, the operator E is introduced such that EA means 'Everyone knows that A.' EA is defined as the conjunction $K_{1A} \wedge K_{2A} \wedge \ldots \wedge K_nA$.

To semantically interpret n knowledge operators, binary accessibility relations R_n are defined over the set of possible worlds W. A special accessibility relation, $R°$, is introduced to interpret the operator of common knowledge. The relation must be flexible enough to express the relationship between individual and common knowledge. The idea is to let the accessibility relation for C be the transitive closure of the union of the accessibility relations corresponding to the knowledge operators for the individual agents.

The model $\mathcal{M}$ for an epistemic system with n agents where the agents have common knowledge is a structure $\mathcal{M} = <W, R_1, R_2, \ldots, R_n, R°, \varphi>$, where W is a non-empty space of possible worlds, $R_1, R_2, \ldots, R_n, R°$ are accessibility relations over W for which $R° = (R_1 \cup R_2 \cup \ldots \cup R_n)$ and φ again is the function assigning worlds to atomic propositional formula $\varphi: atom \mapsto P(W)$. The semantics for the Boolean connectives remain intact. The formula K_iA is true in a world w, i.e., $\mathcal{M}, w \vDash K_iA$ iff $\forall w' \in W$: if R_iww', then $\mathcal{M}, w' \vDash A$. So, A is common knowledge in a world w, when $\mathcal{M}, w \vDash CA$ iff $R°ww'$ implies $\mathcal{M}, w' \vDash A$.

Varying the properties of the accessibility relations $R_1, R_2, \ldots, R_n$, results in different epistemic logics. For instance system **K** with common knowledge is determined by all frames, while system **S4** with common knowledge is determined by all reflexive and transitive frames. Similar results can be obtained for the remaining epistemic logics (Fagin et al. 1995).

Informally speaking, the claim that some proposition is common knowledge is extremely strong. Therefore, those propositions for which we can claim common knowledge tend to be very weak. To claim that some proposition is common knowledge, that everyone knows that everyone knows A, implies that everybody knows A, which implies individual knowledge of A.

If we think of common knowledge as involving very strong claims about the epistemic state of a group of agents, at the opposite end of the spectrum is the notion of distributed knowledge. Distributed knowledge is an epistemic property which captures the idea that there is an aggregated store of knowledge in a group, some of which might not necessarily be possessed by any individual member of the group. If even one agent in a group knows A then A is part of the distributed knowledge of the group. Where common knowledge is very strong (and its argument is rather weak), distributed knowledge is weaker, but can be obtained for much stronger facts, as we shall see.

One way to think about distributed knowledge is to recognize its relationship to a communication network. Something is distributed knowledge in a group if it could be known by the individuals were they able to talk to each other. For instance, in a crowd of 100 people, when two people have the same birthday, this might not be individually known, but could be known if the members were able to talk to each other. So, to take a simple case, if A knows that B is older than C or D and E knows that B is not older than D, then while no individual agent knows that A is older than C, that knowledge is distributed throughout the group and could be elicited given the right kinds of communication. This is a kind of knowledge that can be ascribed to some collection of agents (given certain conditions) but which need not necessarily be ascribed to any agent in isolation. Of course the knowledge that an individual agent has is also part of the aggregated store of distributed knowledge.

When we consider the epistemic properties of groups such as corporations or scientific communities, distributed knowledge that the group exhibits is likely to be one of the properties of interest. For instance, if we are entitled to say that the electric company as a whole knows how to maintain the power supply, we do so by reference to the distributed knowledge that exists in the group. Similarly, in debates concerning the nature of cognition which relies on resources beyond the confines of the individual brain and body, those problems related to the possibility of extended cognition, the formal study of distributed knowledge might prove useful. The distribution of knowledge in a community might seem like a rather nebulous or metaphysically extravagant notion until we begin to examine it in a formal setting.

The most famous example of the formal study of features of group knowledge involves scenarios like the muddy children problem. The scenario involves n children and their father. k children have mud on their foreheads. The children can see each other but they cannot see whether they have mud on their own foreheads. The children trust their father, do not cheat, are rational and do not communicate with one another. The scenario involves the effect of the father's announcement on the behavior of the group and on the epistemic states of the members of the group. The father announces: 'There is at least one child with mud on its forehead. Will all the children who know they have mud on their foreheads please step forward?' If k is greater than one, no child steps forward. When their father makes his announcement the k-th time all muddy children step forward.

In order to explain this scenario, we first consider the simplest case. Where $k = 1$ then the child with mud on its head knows that it must be the muddy one since it sees no other child with mud on its head. So, when $k = 1$ the explanation is clear. In the case where $k = 2$ we can imagine the following scenario with two muddy children a and b:

$k = 2.$
$a^* \rightarrow b^*$
$\downarrow$[[points from a* to c]]
c

Muddy child a can see that b is muddy, but it does not know whether it is muddy itself. After the father's first announcement, when b does not step forward, a knows that b does not know whether b has a muddy forehead. This means that b sees at least one muddy forehead on either a or c. Since a can see that c has a clean forehead, a reasons that the muddy forehead that b saw, was a's. b reasons in the same way based on the failure of muddy headed a to step forward after the father's first announcement. So, after the second announcement, both children step forward. By induction from cases with one and two muddy children, we can easily see how cases with greater numbers of muddy children would proceed. A full treatment of the muddy children problem can be found in Meyer and van der Hoek (1995: 56) or in Fagin et al. (1995: 3).

There is a range of cases like these in which we must account for the interaction of multi-agent systems and in which certain collective features of group behavior must be explained. The kinds of epistemic systems under consideration include cases, like the muddy children, which are sensitive to the introduction of new information via public announcement and in which the interactions of the agents contributes another dynamical component which has an effect on the unfolding states of the system. The muddy children problem is a simple example of the kinds of dynamical features that epistemic logic tackled in the 1980s and 1990s.

Game Theory, Belief Revision and the Properties of Agents

In multi-agent settings, it is natural to consider the role of competition and cooperation. Thus, as epistemic logic began to attend to the dynamics of groups, game theory began to play a more prominent role in reflections on epistemic agency. Aumann, van Benthem, Brandenburger, Fagin, Halpern, Keisler, Moses, Stalnaker, Vardi and others have contributed to uncovering important features of agent rationality showing how game theory adds to the general understanding of notions such as knowledge, belief and belief revision. By the end of the 1990s, Baltag, Moss and Solecki had combined epistemic logic with belief revision theory to study actions and belief updates in games (Baltag et al. 1998).

In the 1980s, Alchourrón, Gärdenfors and Makinson developed a theory of belief revision theory (AGM) which provides an account of rational change of belief in light of novel evidence (Alchourrón 1985; Gärdenfors 1988). Expansions, contractions and revisions in an agents' set of belief are characterized formally. 'Revision' here means additions of beliefs to the agent's belief-set which maintain consistency. Revision is distinguished from simple expansion, which takes place without regard for consistency, and contraction, where beliefs are removed from the set. In order to be considered rational, an agent who revises his beliefs must obey the AGM postulates. Taking K to be the agent's initial set of beliefs and * to be the revision operation and letting A be the additional information that the agent encounters, the basic postulates are presented by Robert Koons (2009) as follows:

(1) $K*A$ is closed under logical consequence.
(2) A belongs to $K*A$.
(3) $K*A$ is a subset of the logical closure of $K \cup \{A\}$.
(4) If $\neg A$ does not belong to K, then the closure of $K \cup \{A\}$ is a subset of $K*A$.
(5) If $K*A$ is logically inconsistent, then either K is inconsistent, or A is.
(6) If A and B are logically equivalent, then $K*A = K*B$.
(7) $K*(A \& B)$ is a subset of the logical closure of $K*A \cup \{B\}$.
(8) If $\neg B$ does not belong to $K*A$, then the logical closure of $K*A \cup B$ is a subset of $K*(A \& B)$.

Following Andre Fuhrmann's development of the idea of translating AGM into dynamical modal logic (1988, 1991), de Rijke also showed that the AGM postulates governing expansion and revision can be translated into the object language of dynamic modal logic (de Rijke 1994). At about the same time, Segerberg demonstrated how the theory of belief revision could be formulated in modal logic. Segerberg merged the static first generation doxastic logic with the dynamics of belief change into 'dynamic doxastic logic' (Segerberg 1995). Doxastic operators in the logic of belief like $B_c A$ can be captured by AGM in the sense that 'A is in c's belief-set T', or $\neg B_c \neg A$ becomes '$\neg A$ is not in c's belief-set T.' An immediate difference between the two perspectives is that while

AGM can express dynamic operations on belief-sets like expansions ('A is in c's belief-set T expanded by D,' i.e., $A \in T + D$), revisions ('A is in c's belief-set T revised by D,' i.e., $A \in T*D$), and contractions ('A is in c's belief-set T contracted by D,' i.e. $A \in T - D$), no such dynamics are immediately expressible in the standard language of doxastic logic. On the other hand, action languages include operators like [μ] and <μ> which are prefixed to a well-formed formula A. On Segerberg's interpretation, [μ]A (<μ>A) mean that 'after every (some) way of performing action μ it is the case that A.' By introducing three new operators [+], [*], and [−] into the doxastic language, the three dynamic operations on belief-sets may be rendered as $[+D]B_cA$, $[*D]B_cA$ and $[-D]B_cA$.

After revising the original belief revision theory such that changes of beliefs happen in 'hypertheories' or concentric spheres enumerated according to entrenchment, Segerberg (1999a, 1999b) provided several axiomatizations of the dynamic doxastic logic together with soundness and completeness results. The dynamic doxastic logic paradigm can also be extended to iterated belief revision as studied by Lindström and Rabinowicz (1997) and accommodate various forms of agent introspection. A related approach drawn up by van Ditmarsch, van der Hoek and Kooi's new 'dynamic epistemic logic' studies how information changes and how actions with epistemic impact on agents may be modeled (van der Hoek et al. 2003; van Ditmarsch et al. 2007). For a more detailed discussion of belief revision theory, see André Fuhrmann "Theories of Belief Change," Chapter 56 in this volume.

One might also choose to endow the agents with *epistemic capacities* facilitating special epistemic behaviors. Fagin, Halpern, Moses and Vardi have, for instance, considered 'perfect recall' (Fagin et al. 1995): interacting agents' knowledge in the dynamic system might increase as time goes by but the agents might still store old information. The agent's current local state is an encoding of all events that have happened so far in the run. Perfect recall is, in turn, an epistemic recommendation telling the agent to remember his earlier epistemic states.

There are other structural properties of agents being studied in the literature of dynamic epistemic logics. In an epistemic logic suited for modeling various games of imperfect information, van Benthem (2000) refers to such properties as 'styles of playing.' Properties such as 'bounded memory,' various 'mechanisms for information updates' and 'uniform strategies,' infallibility, consistency etc. have been investigated. Yoav Shoham and Kevin Leyton-Brown's *Multi-Agent Systems* (2009) provides an updated overview of the relevant literature on game theory and belief revision in a multi-agent setting. Agents as explicitly learning mechanisms are also integral parts of Kelly's (1996) computational epistemology and a related approach called modal operator epistemology (Hendricks 2001, 2003). Researchers in artificial intelligence have additionally been trying to describe and specify the behavior of intelligent/rational agents by extensions of epistemic of logic by augmenting logics of time, action and belief with modalities for desires and intentions (see Meyer 2003, in particular, his discussion of the BDI-framework of Rao and Georgeff in Section 5.2).

Acknowledgments

I owe a special debt of gratitude to Wiebe van der Hoek, whose detailed criticism of this chapter has improved it considerably. I am very grateful to Vincent Hendricks for his comments and for graciously permitting me to use some of our previously co-authored material in this chapter. Specifically, pages are largely taken from our co-authored 2006.

Thanks also to Duncan Pritchard, Clifford Hill and Emmanuel Genot for helpful criticism of an earlier draft of this essay.

References

Alchourrón, C.E., Gärdenfors, P. and Makinson, D. (1985). "On the Logic of Theory Change," *Journal of Symbolic Logic* 50: 510–530.
Aumann, R. (1995). "Backward Induction and Common Knowledge of Rationality," *Games and Economic Behavior* 8: 6–19.
Austin, J. (1975). *How To Do Things with Words*. Oxford: Oxford University Press.
Baltag, A., Moss, L.S. and Solecki, S. (1998). "The Logic of Public Announcements, Common Knowledge, and Private Suspicion." *Proceedings of TARK 1998*. Los Altos: Morgan Kaufmann Publishers, 43–56.
Benthem, J.F.A.K. van (2000). "Logic and Game Theory—Close Encounters of the Third Kind," in van Loon, I., Mints, G. and Muskens, R. (eds.), *Proceedings of LLC99*. Stanford: CSLI Publications.
Bull, R. and Segerberg, K. (1984). "Basic Modal Logic," in Gabbay, D. and Guenthner F. (eds), *Handbook of Philosophical Logic*, vol. II: *Extensions of Classical Logic*. Dordrecht: D. Reidel Publishing Company, 1–88.
Chisholm, R. (1963). "The Logic of Knowing," *Journal of Philosophy* 60, 773–795.
Chisholm, R. (1977). *Theory of Knowledge* (2nd ed.). Englewood Cliffs, NJ: Prentice Hall.
Ditmarsch, H. van, van der Hoek, W. and Kooi, B. (2007). *Dynamic Epistemic Logic*. Dordrecht: Springer.
Fagin, R., Halpern, J.Y., Moses, Y. and Vardi, M.Y. (1995). *Reasoning about Knowledge*. Cambridge: MIT Press.
Fuhrmann, A. (1988). *Relevant Logic, Modal Logic and Theory Change*, Ph.D. Thesis, Department of Philosophy and Automated Reasoning Project, Institute of Advanced Studies, Australian National University, Canberra.
Fuhrmann, A. (1991). "On the Modal Logic of Theory Change," in Fuhrmann, A. and Morreau, M. (eds.), *The Modal Logic of Theory Change*. Lecture Notes in Artificial Intelligence 465. Heidelberg-Berlin-New York: Springer.
Gärdenfors, P. (1988). *Knowledge in Flux—Modelling the Dynamics of Epistemic States*. Cambridge: MIT Press.
Gettier, E. (1963). "Is Justified True Belief Knowledge?" *Analysis* 23: 121–123.
Hendricks, V.F. (2001). *The Convergence of Scientific Knowledge—A View from the Limit*. Trends in Logic: Studia Logica Library Series, Dordrecht: Kluwer Academic Publishers.
Hendricks, V.F. (2003). "Active Agents," *Journal of Logic, Language and Information*, van Benthem, J. and van Rooy, R. (eds.), 12, 4: 469–495.
Hendricks, V.F. (2005). *Mainstream and Formal Epistemology*. New York: Cambridge University Press.
Hendricks, V.F. and Symons, J. (2006). "Where's the Bridge? Epistemic Logic and Epistemology," *Philosophical Studies* 128, 1: 2–26.
Hendricks, V.F. and Symons, J. (2007). "Epistemic Logic," *The Stanford Encyclopedia of Philosophy (Spring 2009 Edition)*, Edward N. Zalta (ed.), URL = <http://plato.stanford.edu/archives/spr2009/entries/logic-epistemic/>.
Hilpinen, R. (2002). "Deontic, Epistemic and Temporal Modal Logics," in Jacquette, D. (ed.), *A Companion to Philosophical Logic*. Malden, MA: Blackwell, 491–509.
Hilpinen, R. (2006). "Jaakko Hintikka on Epistemic Logic and Epistemology," in Auxier, R.E. (ed.), *The Philosophy of Jaakko Hintikka*. Chicago: Open Court Publishing Company, 783–818.
Hintikka, J. (1962). *Knowledge and Belief: An Introduction to the Logic of the Two Notions*. Cornell: Cornell University Press.
Hintikka, J. (1975). "Impossible Possible Worlds Vindicated," *Journal of Philosophical Logic* 4: 475–484.
Hintikka, J. (2007). "Epistemology without Knowledge and Without Belief," in Hintikka, J., *Socratic Epistemology: Explorations of Knowledge Seeking by Questioning*. Cambridge: Cambridge University Press, 11–37.
Hocutt, M.O. (1972). "Is Epistemic Logic Possible?" *Notre Dame Journal of Formal Logic* 13, 433–453.
Hoek, W. van der, Ditmarsch, H. van, Kooi, B. (2003). "Concurrent Dynamic Epistemic Logic," in Hendricks, V.F., Jørgensen, K.F. and Pedersen, S.A. (eds.), *Knowledge Contributors*. Synthese Library, vol. 322. Dordrecht: Kluwer Academic Publishers, 105–173.
Hume, D. (1976 [1740, 1888]). *A Treatise of Human Nature*, ed. L.A. Selby-Bigge. Rev. 2nd edn, ed. P.H. Nidditch. Oxford: Clarendon Press.

Kelly, K. (1996). *The Logic of Reliable Inquiry*. New York: Oxford University Press.

Koons, R. (2009). "Defeasible Reasoning," *The Stanford Encyclopedia of Philosophy (Spring 2009 Edition)*, Edward N. Zalta (ed.), URL = <http://plato.stanford.edu/archives/spr2009/entries/reasoning-defeasible/>.

Kripke, S. (1963). "Semantical Analysis of Modal Logic," *Zeitschrift für Matematische Logik und Grundlagen der Matematik* 9: 67–96.

Kutschera, F. von (1976). *Einführung in die intensional Semantik*. Berlin: W. de Gruyter.

Lemmon, E.J. (1959). "Is There Only One Correct System of Modal Logic?," *Aristotelian Society Supplementary*, Volume XXXIII, 23–40.

Lemmon, E.J. (1977). *An Introduction to Modal Logic*, in collaboration with D. Scott. Oxford: Basil Blackwell Publishers.

Lenzen, W. (1978). *Recent Work in Epistemic Logic*, in Acta Philosophica Fennica 30: 1–219.

Lewis, D. (1969). *Convention: A Philosophical Study*. Cambridge: Harvard University Press.

Lindström, S. and Rabinowicz, W. (1997). "Extending Dynamic Logic: Accommodating Iterated Beliefs and Ramsey Conditionals within DLL," in Lindahl, L., Needham, P. and Sliwinski, R. (eds.), *For Good Measure*. Uppsala Philosophical Studies, 46: 123–153.

McCarthy, J. (1979). "Ascribing Mental Qualities to Machines." Technical Report STAN-CS-79-725 Stanford University.

Meyer, J.-J. Ch. (2003). "Modal, Epistemic and Doxastic Logic," in Gabbay, D. and Guenthner, F. (eds.), *Handbook of Philosophical Logic* (2nd edition) Vol. 10, Dordrecht: Kluwer, 1–38.

Meyer, J.-J.Ch. and Hoek, W. van der (1995). *Epistemic Logic for AI and Computer Science*. Cambridge Tracts in Theoretical Computer Science 41. Cambridge: Cambridge University Press.

Moore, G.E. (1952). *The Philosophy of G. E. Moore*. (2nd edition) ed. Paul Arthur Schilpp, New York: Tudor Publishing Company.

Rantala, V. (1975). "Urn Models: A New Kind of Non-Standard Model for First-Order Logic," *Journal of Symbolic Logic* 4: 455–474.

Rantala, V. (1982). "Quantified Modal Logic: Non-Normal Worlds and Propositional Attitudes," *Studia Logica* 41, 1: 41–66.

Rijke, M. de (1994). "Meeting Some Neighbours: A Dynamic Modal Logic Meets Theories of Change and Knowledge Representation," in Eijck, J. van and Visser, A. (eds.), *Logic and Information Flow*, Cambridge: MIT Press, 170–196.

Segerberg, K. (1995). "Belief Revision from the Point of View of Doxastic Logic," *Bulletin of the IGPL*, 3: 535–553.

Segerberg, K. (1999a). "The Basic Dynamic Doxastic Logic of AGM," *Uppsala Prints and Preprints in Philosophy*, 1.

Segerberg, K. (1999b). "A Completeness Proof in Full DDL," in Sliwinski, R. (ed.), *Philosophical Crumbs: Essays Dedicated to Ann-Mari Henschen-Dahlqvist on the Occasion of her Seventy fifth Birthday*, Uppsala Philosophical Studies, 49: 195–207.

Shoham, Y. and Leyton-Brown, K. (2009). *Multiagent Systems: Algorithmic, Game-Theoretic, and Logical Foundations*, Cambridge: Cambridge University Press.

Stalnaker, R. (1996). "Knowledge, Belief and Counterfactual Reasoning in Games," *Economics and Philosophy*, 12: 133–163.

Stalnaker, R. (2006). On Logics of Knowledge and Belief, *Philosophical Studies* 128, 169–199.

Vanderschraaf, P. and Sillari, G. (2007). "Common Knowledge," *The Stanford Encyclopedia of Philosophy (Spring 2009 Edition)*, Edward N. Zalta (ed.), URL = <http://plato.stanford.edu/archives/spr2009/entries/common-knowledge/>.

Voorbraak, F. (1993). *As Far as I Know. Epistemic Logic and Uncertainty*, Dissertation, Utrecht University, Utrecht. Published as volume 7 in *Queastiones Infinitae*. Department of Philosophy, Utrecht University.

Wright, G.H. von (1951). *An Essay on Modal Logic*. Amsterdam: North-Holland Publishing Company.

53
SECOND-ORDER KNOWLEDGE

Christoph Kelp and Nikolaj J.L.L. Pedersen

1. Introduction

Knowledge involves belief. Belief is a propositional attitude, i.e. an attitude that a subject holds towards a proposition. If a subject S knows that P and the proposition P involves no further knowledge attribution, let us say that S possesses *first-order knowledge*. On the other hand, if S knows that P and the proposition P involves a knowledge attribution, let us say that S possesses *higher-order knowledge*. The aim of this article is to shed light on the nature of second-order knowledge, a specific kind of higher-order knowledge. It is worth noting, however, that the kinds of considerations offered here are also relevant to cases of knowledge of higher orders—if properly extended or modified.

An example of second-order knowledge is the following:

(1) Duncan knows that he knows that 4 + 5 = 9

as the proposition within the scope of "knows" involves a further knowledge attribution. We will approach the task of shedding light on second-order knowledge by discussing it in relation to three issues from the epistemological literature:

1. *Internalism/externalism*: according to internalists about warrant, if a subject S is warranted in believing that P, then the reasons that underwrite S's warrant are accessible to S by reflection—that is, by introspection, a priori reasoning, or memory—alone. Externalists deny this idea. (For more on internalism/externalism, see, e.g., BonJour 1992, Pryor 2001, and the articles in Kornblith 2001 and Goldberg 2007. "Warrant" here should not be taken in the sense of Plantinga 1993, i.e. as that which renders knowledge when added to true belief.)
2. *KK-Principle*: if S knows that P, then S knows that S knows that P. We can write this formally as follows: $K_S P \to K_S K_S P$ (where "K_S" is read "S knows that ..." and "..." is to be replaced by a proposition).
3. *Knowledge-Transmission Principle*: if S knows that R knows that P, then S knows that P (formally: $K_S K_R P \to K_S P$).

2. Internalism/Externalism, Monism/Pluralism and Second-Order Knowledge

Before we turn to the task of showing how the internalism/externalism distinction can be used to gain insights into the nature of second-order knowledge, a clarificatory remark is in order. The distinction between internalism and externalism has been introduced as pertaining to *warrant*. How, then, can it be relevant to the nature of second-order *knowledge*?

The answer is this: most epistemologists take warrant to be a necessary condition on knowledge. One cannot know that P without also being warranted in believing that P. For this reason, internalists about warrant are also internalists about knowledge in an interesting sense: knowledge is subject to a substantial internalist warrant constraint. Externalists about warrant, on the other hand, maintain that there is no substantial internalist warrant constraint on knowledge. Typically they hold this view, because they hold the further view that being warranted is grounded in features of the relevant belief-forming method or process (possibly in conjunction with features of the environment) and that these features need not be reflectively accessible to the subject in order to be warrant-conferring. According to Goldman (1979), a prominent advocate of externalism, a belief—if warranted—is so because the relevant belief-forming process is reliable, meaning that it yields a good enough ratio of true to false beliefs. The warrant-giving reason—i.e. reliability—need not be reflectively accessible to the subject. It is enough that the process *is* reliable. For our present purposes, we need not dive into the intricate details of the debate between internalists and externalists. It will suffice to table three views that mark the scope of, respectively, internalism and externalism in rather different ways.

The first view and second view are, respectively, internalist and externalist warrant monism (or, respectively, "IW-monism" and "EW-monism," in short). The opposition between these two views has traditionally fueled the internalism/externalism debate, the articulation of the third view—pluralism—being a more recent development. According to the IW-monist, *all* warrants are subject to an internalist accessibility constraint: warrant-underwriting reasons always have to be accessible to the warranted individual through reflection alone. According to the EW-monist, there is no such thing as internalist warrant. No warrant is such that a subject is excluded from being warranted just because the warrant-underwriting reasons fail to be reflectively accessible. (It might be that these reasons are reflectively accessible in some cases. However, this should not be run together with the internalist idea that this kind of accessibility is *required* for warrant.) EW-monism can be held on various grounds. One might think that no warrant involves any warrant-underwriting reason that has to be reflectively accessible. Alternatively, one could grant that some warrants involve reasons that have to be reflectively accessible, but maintain that these reasons never, by themselves, suffice for warrant. To yield warrant they have to be supplemented by reasons that are not subject to a reflective accessibility constraint—"externalist reasons," as it were. The first incarnation of EW-monism is more radically externalist than the second, but both yield a rather strong form of externalism—one that goes beyond what externalism commits one to, as characterized above. Externalism thus characterized only commits one to saying that there are instances of warrant for which the underwriting reasons are not reflectively accessible. The third view is warrant pluralism (or "W-pluralism," in short). According to W-pluralism, some types of warrants are subject to a reflective accessibility constraint, while others are not. The former types of warrants are thus internalist in nature, while the latter are externalist.

The three views just presented are pairwise incompatible. What we will now do is to assume the truth of each of these views in turn and see what can be said about the nature of second-order knowledge against the background of these assumptions.

Assume that IW-monism is true and consider a case of second-order knowledge—rendered formally: $K_S K_S P$. What can be said about the nature of this instance of knowledge? The assumption of IW-monism enables us to make some progress with respect to this question: both knowledge attributions have to be understood along internalist lines. Formally, we can write this by using a superscript: $K^I_S K^I_S P$.

To get a specific point of focus let us return to the example of second-order knowledge given earlier. Duncan knows that he knows that 4 + 5 = 9. Internalism tells us that whatever warrant-giving reasons are involved in Duncan's first-order knowledge that 4 + 5 = 9 must be accessible via introspection, a priori reasoning, or memory. This constraint could be satisfied by Duncan's knowing that 4 + 5 = 9 on the basis of a proof in elementary arithmetic. In that case Duncan's warrant-giving reasons—provided by the proof—are a priori accessible. He can access them by thinking alone. As for Duncan's second-order knowledge, IW-monism dictates that this, too, be subject to an accessibility constraint. How could this constraint be satisfied? Here is one way: Duncan might introspect and come to believe that he knows that 4 + 5 = 9, because he reflects on the pedigree of his proof and reaches the conclusion that it is a solid one. The reasons that underwrite the warrant for his higher-order belief are the belief-contents *I know that 4 + 5 = 9* and *I know so on the basis of a solid proof*. These contents are reflectively accessible to him, as introspective access is a species of reflective access. The general point to draw from this specific case is that an advocate of IW-monism is committed to saying that *every* case of second-order knowledge is like the one just considered by involving two internalist warrants.

Let us leave IW-monism behind and instead assume that EW-monism is true. What can be said about the nature of second-order knowledge against this assumption? We immediately get that the warrant involved in each of the knowledge attributions has to be externalist in nature. The warrant-underwriting reasons need not be accessible purely via reflection. As before, we can signal this formally by using superscripts: $K^E_S K^E_S P$.

To get a specific point of focus let us suppose that

(2) Sven knows that he knows that there is a bottle of water on the table.

Let us see how the EW-monist can account for (2). We will do so by assuming reliabilism, i.e. the brand of externalism mentioned earlier. Furthermore, assume that Sven believes that there is a bottle of water on the table on the basis of visual perception, that he believes that he knows that there is a bottle of water on the table as a result of introspection, and that both of these belief-forming processes are reliable. This delivers the warrants involved in (2), without the satisfaction of a requirement to the effect that the warrant-underwriting feature—i.e. reliability—be reflectively accessible to Sven. This feature by itself renders Sven warranted on the reliabilist picture. What the EW-monist is committed to is the idea that all instances of second-order knowledge can be accounted for in the same manner as (2)—meaning, in particular, that both ingredient warrants must be of an externalist character. (In showing how an externalist can account for (2) we appealed to reliabilism. However, it is important to note that someone who is a reliabilist—or broader, an externalist—about visual-perceptual warrant and/or introspective warrant by no means is committed to EW-monism.)

Let us now turn to warrant pluralism, the last of the three views. According to the pluralist, some types of warranted belief involve satisfaction of the internalist accessibility constraint, while others do not (Burge (1993, 2003), Goldman (1988), and Wright (2004) are sympathetic to some version of warrant pluralism). As we have seen, the IW-monist and the EW-monist alike are committed to holding that all instances of second-order knowledge have a uniform nature. What is interesting about W-pluralism is that it leaves conceptual room for two kinds of non-uniform second-order knowledge, in addition to the uniform kinds endorsed by IW-monism and EW-monism, respectively. Using the formalism relied on so far, W-pluralism accommodates the following four possibilities:

Uniform second-order knowledge:

- $K^I_S K^I_S P$
- $K^E_S K^E_S P$

Non-uniform second-order knowledge:

- $K^I_S K^E_S P$
- $K^E_S K^I_S P$

The considerations just offered show that what stance one takes with respect to the internalism/externalism and monism/pluralism issues is relevant to the nature of second-order knowledge. On the IW-monist view, second-order knowledge is tied thoroughly to reflection. Both knowledge attributions involved in any case of second-order knowledge are subject to the requirement that the warrant-giving reasons be accessible through reflection alone. According to EW-monism, no instance of second-order knowledge has this nature. The ingredient warrants are not subject to a reflective accessibility constraint. The warrant pluralist begs to differ with both the IW-monist and the EW-monist. Some instances of second-order knowledge might have a reflective character ($K^I_S K^I_S P$), while others might have an externalist character ($K^E_S K^E_S P$). Yet other instances, might have neither of these uniform characters, but be non-uniform or mixed instead ($K^I_S K^E_S P$ or $K^E_S K^I_S P$).

3. The KK-Principle

We will now turn to perhaps the most widely discussed issue in the debate over second-order knowledge, the KK-principle. To begin with, recall the formulation of the principle mentioned earlier:

Strong-KK $\qquad K_S P \to K_S K_S P$

This principle is not obviously true and so it requires defense. A full defense of the KK-principle will show not only why we ought to buy into it, but also that it is validated by one's preferred account of (first-order) knowledge. And already at this stage, there is some reason to believe that Strong-KK does not hold. After all, knowledge requires belief. If it turns out to be so much as possible to know a proposition yet fail to believe that one does, Strong-KK will be refuted. And this does certainly seem possible. For instance, one might fail to register that one knows some proposition—due to a lapse of attention, say—and, in consequence, fail to form the corresponding belief. For that reason, one might think that the prospects for Strong-KK are rather dim.

In view of such difficulties, some have tried to restrict the KK-principle. Perhaps the most common move here is to weaken it: if one knows that P then one is *in a position to know* that one knows that P. Or again, formally (where "$\Diamond K_S$" is read as "S is in a position to know . . ." and ". . ." is to be replaced by a proposition):

Weak-KK $\qquad K_S P \rightarrow \Diamond K_S K_S P$

There are various ways of spelling out the notion of being in a position to know. Crucially, however, all of these ways maintain that being in a position to know does not require belief. This will, of course, remedy the above defect. It remains to be shown whether there is good reason to accept Weak-KK and whether it is validated by the correct first-order account of knowledge.

The answer to the question concerning the KK-principle is often viewed as reflecting the traditional divide between IW-monism and EW-monism (recall that the monism/pluralism divide is a more recent development in the debate). IW-monists tend to be more sympathetic to the KK-principle, while EW-monists tend to reject it (some, e.g. Williams (1991), have gone as far as cashing out the distinction between the two views in terms of their diverging stances on the KK-principle). It is not hard to see why this should be so. Consider reliabilism again. Reliabilists typically reject the KK-principle even in its weak form because they typically construe at least some of the processes that are crucial to the delivery of the first-order beliefs—such as perception, testimony etc.—not only as being different from but also as being independent from the ones that are crucial to the delivery of the second-order beliefs—such as introspection. If these processes are both separate and independent, however, it is possible that one—the first-order process, say—operates in such a way as to deliver the warrant, while no second-order process follows suit. In such a situation the subject could acquire a first-order warrant while not even being in a position to acquire a second-order warrant—hence the reliabilists' rejection of even Weak-KK.

Contrast this position with the one favored by the IW-monist. If, as IW-monists think, the subject's (S's) reasons that underwrite her warrant for P must be accessible to her by reflection alone, then through reflecting S can come to know that she has a warrant for P. If, as some IW-monists are also happy to grant, belief is luminous in the sense that one can know by reflection alone that one believes P on grounds G whenever one does, S also has a warrant that she believes that P and that this belief is suitably grounded in her warrant for P. Since in order to know P S must also have a warrant that P is true, she thus has a warrant (a) that she has a warrant for P, (b) that P is true, (c) that she believes P and (d) that her belief that P is grounded in her warrant for P. Given an IW-monist conception of knowledge according to which one knows that P just in case one truly believes P on the basis of a warrant for P, it follows that S has a warrant that she satisfies all the conditions for knowledge that P. In other words, she has a warrant that she knows that P. Thus, if S knows P, she has a warrant that she knows P (and, of course, it is true that S knows P). Finally, suppose that to be in a position to know that P is to be but a suitably based belief that P away from knowledge that P. By the present IW-monist account of knowledge that means that one is in a position to know P if and only if one has a warrant for P and P is true. On this account of being in a position to know, it follows that if S knows P she is in a position to know that she knows P. Thus we have one way in which an IW-monist conception of knowledge validates Weak-KK.

4. Objections to the KK-Principle

Gettier Cases

Let us now move on to some objections to the KK-principle. Some, including card-carrying internalists (e.g. Chisholm 1986: 90), have thought that the Gettier problem not only constitutes the demise of the kind of IW-monist conception of knowledge sketched above, but also highlights that the prospects even for a weak version of the KK-principle are dim.

One way of articulating their worry is as follows: Gettier cases show that knowledge cannot just be warranted true belief (where warrant is construed along IW-monist lines). They show that a further external condition for knowledge is required. Given that the condition is external, however, it will (at least in some cases) be impossible to come to know by reflection alone that one satisfies it. But, the thought continues, in order to be in a position to know that one knows, one must, by IW-monist lights, at least have a warrant—i.e. an *internalist* warrant—that one satisfies all the conditions for first-order knowledge. So, even the IW-monist will be unable to validate Weak-KK. If even the IW-monist cannot do this, the prospects for Weak-KK might appear to be rather dim.

There are a number of ways in which this worry can be allayed. The one we would like to focus on here concerns the possibility of W-pluralism, discussed briefly above. Let it be agreed that knowledge requires a degettierization condition in addition to internalistically warranted true belief. If we are willing to countenance warrant pluralism, we might be able to rescue Weak-KK by putting to use the idea of an externalist warrant that one has by default—call it "entitlement." (For more on entitlement see, e.g., Burge 1993, 2003 and Wright 2004.) Suppose it can be argued that one is entitled to believe that one's first-order beliefs are not gettierized, which seems plausible if a case can be made that there is any proposition one is entitled to believe. Suppose, furthermore, we are willing to grant warrants constituted, on the one hand, by one's internalist warrant that one satisfies the internalist warrant, truth, belief and grounding condition for knowledge and, on the other hand, by one's entitlement that one satisfies the degettierization condition. Then we might be able to validate a version of the KK-principle after all. For now, at least in the default case, one does have a warrant that one possesses first-order knowledge. Again, if to be in a position to know is to be but a suitably based (and, we must now add, degettierized) belief away from knowledge, and if knowledge is degettierized, internalistically warranted and true belief, then, if one has first-order knowledge, one is also in a position to know that this is so. (Notice, however, that since the second-order warrant contains an externalist component, the second-order knowledge must be externalist in nature, i.e. the KK-principle will be of the form $K^*_S P \to \Diamond K^E_S K^*_S P$.)

What is also interesting about this line is that it is available also to the EW-monist. Just like the W-pluralist, the externalist might wish to countenance the possibility of entitlements to propositions about the satisfaction of the conditions for first-order knowledge and venture to defend an EW-monist version of the KK-principle. So, somewhat surprisingly, even if the prospects of an IW-monist version of the KK-principle are dim, EW-monists who are willing to grant that we have entitlements that the conditions for first-order knowledge are satisfied might be able to countenance a purely externalist version of the KK-principle. (McHugh (2010) exploits the notion of entitlement to defend a version of the KK-principle that he claims to be compatible with both internalist and externalist conceptions of knowledge.)

Children and Animal Knowledge

The second objection to the KK-principle we will discuss is as simple as it is powerful. It starts from the observation that it is plausible that small children and certain animals can have basic first-order knowledge of the world. For instance, a toddler might know of his toy that it is red and a dog might know that his master is approaching. At the same time, children, if they are small enough, and certainly many of the relevant animals, do not possess the reflective abilities and concepts requisite to acquire the corresponding second-order knowledge. For instance, they might lack the very concept of knowledge needed to grasp the proposition that they know. Thus, small children and animals might know things but, since they might also lack the very concept of knowledge, they might not be in a position to know that they know. In consequence, the KK-principle fails (Dretske 2004: 176).

Again, there are moves to be made here for the champion of the KK-principle. Perhaps the most obvious one is to place an additional restriction on the principle to the effect that the agent can grasp the proposition that she knows (e.g. Ginet 1970; McHugh 2010). One disadvantage of this move is that it seems to demote the KK-principle's status: instead of capturing a fundamental truth about *knowledge* it now captures a truth about a certain kind of *cognitive agent*, i.e. those capable of grasping propositions about first-order knowledge. Alternatively, one could insist that even small children and animals are in a position to know that they have knowledge where this means that they are but a suitably based (and degettierized) belief away from second-order knowledge. Of course, small children and animals are in no position to form a belief that they know. It remains true, however, that they are but a suitably based (and degettierized) belief away from knowing that they know. Now, it might be objected that in order to have a warrant for some proposition P one already must have the concepts needed to grasp P (Feldman 2005: 111). While this might be plausible for types of warrant that the subject needs to achieve, it is far from clear that this also needs to be the case for types of warrant that can be held by default. Since entitlement is just such a type of warrant, the champion of the KK-principle can avoid this objection by construing the relevant second-order warrants as entitlements. So, it seems that some version of the KK-principle might remain defensible even in the face of the objection from children and animal knowledge.

Williamson's Anti-Luminosity Argument

The last objection against the KK-principle we will discuss here is due to Timothy Williamson. Williamson (2000) argues against the possibility of "luminous conditions." Roughly, a condition is luminous if and only if it is such that if and when one is in it, one is also in a position to know that one is in it. Alternatively, a condition C is luminous just in case

Luminosity: For all subjects S and times t, if at t S is in C then at t S is in a position to know that S is in C.

The KK-principle can then be interpreted as stating that the condition of knowing a proposition is luminous.

Williamson ventures to show that conditions such that one can gradually move from times at which one is in them to times at which one isn't cannot be luminous. The crucial step in Williamson's argument is to show that in conjunction with a plausible application of the so-called "Safety" condition on knowledge, according to which in order to know a proposition, P, one must avoid false belief in P across relevantly similar situations, *Luminosity* yields the paradoxical result that it is impossible to move gradually from times at which one is in the allegedly luminous condition to times at which one isn't.

In order to see how the argument works, let C be any condition that admits of gradual movement in the relevant sense, S any cognitive agent with limited cognitive capacities and t_i and t_{i+1} any two adjacent instants in a series of instants that describes S's gradual movement from times at which S is in C to times at which S is not in C. Furthermore, let the instants in the series be separated by intervals so small that, due to S's limited cognitive capacities, S cannot distinguish between adjacent instants with respect to whether S is in C. Surely, in this situation any two adjacent instants in the series are relevantly similar to one another. Suppose at t_i S believes that she is in C. By Safety, her belief counts as knowledge only if she avoids false belief at t_{i+1}. How can S achieve this? Suppose at t_{i+1} S is not in C. Of course, ex hypothesi, S cannot achieve avoidance of false belief at t_{i+1} through an ability to distinguish between t_i and t_{i+1} with respect to whether she is in C. The only other way in which S can achieve avoiding false belief here is if between t_i and t_{i+1} S loses her belief for some other reason, for instance, as a result of a decrease in confidence below the threshold for belief. As Williamson points out, however, in that case S's belief at t_i is ill based—in the example just mentioned on misplaced confidence—and therefore does not qualify as knowledge. Thus, if at t_{i+1} S is not in C, S's belief at t_i does not qualify as knowledge. Otherwise put:

Safety: For all subjects S and any two adjacent instants, t_i and t_{i+1}, if at t_i S knows that S is in C then at t_{i+1} S is in C.

Now Williamson assumes a conception of what it takes to be in a position to know that is closely related to but slightly stronger than the one outlined above: "If one is in a position to know P, and one has done what one is in a position to do to decide whether P is true, then one does know P" (Williamson 2000: 95). Supposing, as Williamson might in his example, that S does what she can to determine whether P is true, we get that if at t_i S is in C, then at t_i S knows that S is in C. By *Safety* we can derive: at t_{i+1} S is in C. Since *Luminosity* holds for all times and *Safety* for any two adjacent instants t_i and t_{i+1} in the series, continuous application of the two principles will show that if, at any time, S is in C, at all times S is in C—contrary to the assumption that S can move gradually from times at which S is in C to times at which S isn't in C. So, conditions that admit of such gradual movement cannot be luminous.

In order to put the anti-luminosity argument to work against the KK-principle, it remains to be shown that one can move gradually from the condition of knowing a proposition to not knowing it. Fortunately, this is fairly easily done. Consider the following example: S is looking at a surface the color of which gradually changes from red to orange along the color circle. Suppose, at the outset, S believes on the basis of visual-perceptual evidence that the surface is red. Since the surface is clearly red, surely she also knows that it is red. However, as time passes, the visual-perceptual evidence grounding her belief changes gradually from red to orange. The evidence grounding her belief that the surface is red thus becomes gradually weaker until it is no longer strong enough to give her knowledge that it is red. So, it is possible to gradually move from the condition of knowing a proposition—here, that the surface is red—to the condition of not knowing it. The anti-luminosity argument applies. The KK-principle fails.

Powerful as Williamson's argument might be, it does not go uncontested. There are a variety of responses to it including Neta and Rohrbaugh (2004), who deny the Safety condition on knowledge; Weatherson (2004), who argues that conditions that are constituted by the subjects' believing them are luminous; and Dokic and Égré (2009), who have tried to rescue a version of the KK-principle for certain types of knowledge. For present purposes, however, we would like to develop a response on behalf of champions of the KK-principle that is inspired by Hintikka (1970) and Malcolm (1952). Malcolm and Hintikka respond to objections to the KK-principle by restricting the principle to what they call "a strong sense of the concept of knowledge," the sense of the concept they claim to be at issue in most of the epistemological literature. What Malcolm and Hintikka seem to be suggesting here is that the concept of knowledge is ambiguous. While this proposal might have been understandable and even attractive at the time they were writing, strong reasons against such an ambiguity thesis have since come to light (see, e.g., Stanley 2005: 81). Yet, there is a way of breathing new life into this response by combining it with contextualism, a prominent view in recent epistemology. (For more on contextualism see, e.g., Cohen 1988, DeRose 2009 and Lewis 1996.) According to the contextualist, the term "knows" and its cognates are context-sensitive. They express different relations in different contexts. Crucially, context determines just how strong a warrant one needs to have in order to count as "knowing." We can once again express this suggestion formally by introducing a superscript indicating the strength of warrant needed for "knowledge": $K^0_S P$, $K^1_S P$, $K^2_S P$, etc. The rule here is: the higher the numeral in the superscript, the stronger the warrant needed for "knowledge," i.e. the stronger the knowledge relation. We can now argue, and this is where the present line takes its inspiration from Malcolm and Hintikka's remarks, that the KK-principle holds in contexts in which "knows" expresses a suitably strong knowledge relation. That is to say, we get: $K^n_S P \rightarrow \Diamond K^n_S K^n_S P$ for suitably large n. If Williamson's argument is sound, it is hard to see how any being with limited cognitive capacities could ever stand in such a strong knowledge relation (except perhaps to a very limited range of propositions). However, contextualists are typically happy to grant that at least in some contexts "knows" might express such a strong relation. If so, contextualists might be able to countenance a version of the KK-principle even if Williamson's anti-luminosity argument goes through.

5. The Social Aspect of Second-Order Knowledge

Above, our discussion of second-order knowledge has focused on single-agent cases, i.e. cases where S knows that R knows that P, and S and R are identical. We will now drop the assumption of identity and consider multi-agent cases. The following example involving Fermat's Last Theorem is an example of multi-agent second-order knowledge:

(3) Bob knows that Jack knows that no solution exists for the equation $a^n + b^n = c^n$ for positive integers a, b, c, and n and $n > 2$.

Cases like (3) are interesting for several reasons. One quite simple reason is that it serves to highlight the social nature that second-order knowledge sometimes has. (3) reflects the fact that we—or most of us, anyway—do not live in complete epistemic isolation. We are part of epistemic communities or groups that involve other agents with whom we interact and to whom we bear significant epistemic connections.

An example of this kind of interaction or connection is captured by the following principle of knowledge transmission:

(KTP) $\quad K_S K_R P \to K_S P$

KTP will strike many as plausible, at least to the extent that it is thought that we often gain knowledge by knowing that someone else knows something. Applying this idea to the Bob–Jack example, one might think that, by knowing that Jack knows Fermat's Last Theorem (i.e. the theorem in (3)), *Bob* knows the theorem too. How could this be? Well, perhaps Bob—who has no specialist knowledge about mathematics—has been told by Jack what Fermat's Last Theorem says and that he, Jack, is working on a proof of the theorem (assuming, for the sake of exposition, that he is unaware that Wiles proved it). Bob knows that Jack is an extremely talented mathematician. Over a very extended period of time Bob witnesses Jack work on the proof and eventually hears him utter, "Fermat's Last Theorem is true! I've proved it!" Let us suppose that Jack has in fact proved the theorem, and that he knows that the theorem is true on this basis. Furthermore, suppose that by observing Jack and hearing his utterance, Bob knows that Jack knows Fermat's Last Theorem. But does Bob also know the theorem? This is just another way of asking whether KTP holds in this particular case.

KTP has some prominent advocates—Hintikka (1962), to mention just one. However, even if we suppose that advocates of KTP are right in maintaining that the principle holds, it is important to avoid confusion about what the principle says. In particular, although it is natural to read KTP as saying that subject S knows that P by knowing that subject R does so, the specific warrant involved in R's knowledge is not automatically transmitted to, or inherited by, S. This can be so even if S is fully aware of what the source of R's knowledge—and warrant—is. The Bob and Jack example will serve nicely to drive this point home. Jack's knowledge—and warrant for believing—that Fermat's Last Theorem is true is based on the proof that he has constructed. Bob is fully aware of this. It should be clear, though, that this does not make Bob's warranted belief in the theorem—and his corresponding knowledge—directly proof-based. He is not capable of following the proof, for one. If anything, the warrant possessed by Bob is based on Jack's testimony (for more on testimony, see Burge 1993 and the articles in Lackey and Sosa 2007).

Turn now to internalism/externalism and monism/pluralism, the themes against which our discussion has been cast. Both forms of monism deliver only uniform instances of KTP. For the IW-monist all warrants are internalist, whereas the EW-monist thinks that they are all externalist. What this means in our present context is that KTP must be read uniformly on both of the monist views:

KTP + IW-monism: $\quad K^I_S K^I_R P \to K^I_S P$
KTP + EW-monism: $\quad K^E_S K^E_R P \to K^E_S P$

KTP is a different story from a W-pluralist point of view. As earlier, one reason to find W-pluralism interesting is that it widens conceptual space. This is reflected by the different kinds of instances it leaves room for:

KTP + W-pluralism:

Uniform:
$$K^I_S K^I_R P \to K^I_S P$$
$$K^E_S K^E_R P \to K^E_S P$$

Non-uniform:
$$K^I_S K^I_R P \to K^E_S P$$
$$K^E_S K^E_R P \to K^I_S P$$
$$K^I_S K^E_R P \to K^I_S P$$
$$K^I_S K^E_R P \to K^E_S P$$
$$K^E_S K^I_R P \to K^I_S P$$
$$K^E_S K^I_R P \to K^E_S P$$

That is, W-pluralism leaves room not only for uniform instances of KTP, but also various non-uniform ones.

References

BonJour, L. (1992) "Externalism/Internalism," in J. Dancy and E. Sosa (eds.) *Blackwell Companion to Epistemology*, Oxford: Blackwell.
Burge, T. (1993) "Content Preservation," *The Philosophical Review* 102: 457–88.
—— (2003) "Perceptual Entitlement," *Philosophy and Phenomenological Research* 67: 503–48.
Chisholm, R. (1986) "The Place of Epistemic Justification," *Philosophical Topics* 14: 85–92.
Cohen, S. (1988) "How to Be a Fallibilist," in J. Tomberlin (ed.) *Philosophical Perspectives* 2: 81–123.
DeRose, K. (2009) *The Case for Contextualism*, Oxford: Clarendon.
Dokic, J. and Égré, P. (2009) "Margins for Error and the Transparency of Knowledge," *Synthese* 166: 1–20.
Dretske, F. (2004) "Externalism and Modest Contextualism," *Erkenntnis* 61: 173–86.
Feldman, R. (2005) "Respecting the Evidence," in J. Hawthorne (ed.) *Philosophical Perspectives* 19: 95–119.
Ginet, C. (1970) "What Must be Added to Knowing to Obtain Knowing That One Knows?" *Synthese* 21: 163–86.
Goldberg, S. (2007) *Internalism and Externalism in Semantics and Epistemology*, Oxford: Oxford University Press.
Goldman, A. (1979) "What is Justified Belief?" in G. Pappas (ed.) *Justification and Knowledge*, Dordrecht: D. Reidel: 1–23.
—— (1988) "Strong and Weak Justification," in J. Tomberlin (ed.) *Philosophical Perspectives* 2: 51–69.
Hintikka, J. (1962) *Knowledge and Belief: An Introduction to the Logic of the Two Notions*, Ithaca, NY: Cornell University Press.
—— (1970) "'Knowing that One Knows' Reviewed," *Synthese* 21: 141–62.
Kornblith, H. (2001) *Epistemology: Internalism and Externalism*, Oxford: Blackwell.
Lackey, J. and Sosa, E. (eds.) (2007) *The Epistemology of Testimony*, Oxford: Oxford University Press.
Lewis, D. (1996) "Elusive Knowledge," *Australasian Journal of Philosophy* 74: 549–67.
Malcolm, N. (1952) "Knowledge and Belief," *Mind* 61: 178–89.
McHugh, C. (2010) "Self-knowledge and the KK-Principle," *Synthese* 173: 231–57.
Neta, R. and Rohrbaugh, G. (2004) "Luminosity and the Safety of Knowledge," *Pacific Philosophical Quarterly* 85: 396–406.
Plantinga, A. (1993) *Warrant: The Current Debate*, Oxford: Oxford University Press.
Pryor, J. (2001) "Highlights of Recent Epistemology," *British Journal for the Philosophy of Science* 52: 95–124.
Stanley, J. (2005) *Knowledge and Practical Interests*, Oxford: Clarendon.
Weatherson, B. (2004) "Luminous Margins," *Australasian Journal of Philosophy* 82: 373–83.
Williams, M. (1991) *Unnatural Doubts: Epistemological Realism and the Basis for Scepticism*, Oxford: Blackwell.
Williamson, T. (2000) *Knowledge and Its Limits*, Oxford: Oxford University Press.
Wright, C. (2004) "Warrant for Nothing (Foundations for Free)?" *Proceedings of the Aristotelian Society* 78: 167–212.

54
EPISTEMIC CLOSURE
Peter Baumann

1. The Basic Idea

Do we know everything which is entailed by what we know? This would suggest the following principle:

If S knows that p, and if p entails q, then S knows that q.

(This would hold for all subjects S and all propositions p and q, of course; for the sake of simplicity we can skip this clause in the following.) In other words, knowledge is "closed under entailment." This principle seems much too strong. It would only be true of logically omniscient subjects (who know all the logical consequences of what they know). For instance, everyone who knows certain mathematical axioms would thus also know all the mathematical theorems which follow from the axioms; if one does not know one of these theorems, then one also does not know the axioms.

A more restricted principle seems much more plausible in the case of human subjects:

(C1) If S knows that p, and if S knows that p entails q, then S knows that q.

In other words, knowledge is "closed under known entailment" (or "closed"; see for (C1) and for the principle above, Hintikka 1962: 30–38). If Mary knows that both Paul and Peter are at the party, then she also knows that Peter is at the party (given her knowledge that the latter follows from the former). If we were to deny that Mary knows that Peter is at the party, then we would be ready to deny that she knows that Peter and Paul are at the party (given her knowledge that the latter entails the former).

2. Importance: Skepticism

(C1) and similar principles play an important role in epistemology. Doesn't the possibility of inferential knowledge require the truth of some closure principle? And, apart from that, doesn't closure play an important role in discussions of epistemic skepticism? Here is the template of a typical skeptical argument crucial to the recent discussion about epistemic skepticism (with "~" as the negation sign, "→" as the sign for material implication, "K" for "S knows that," "s" for some skeptical proposition—like *I am a handless brain in the vat merely imagining that I have hands* (see Putnam 1981)—and "o" for some ordinary proposition—like *I have hands*):

(1) ~K ~s
(2) (~K ~s) → (~Ko)
(C) ~Ko

I don't know I have hands because I don't know I am not a brain in a vat and if I don't know the latter, then I don't know the former. The crucial premise (2) follows from (C1) together with the relatively unproblematic assumption that K(o → ~s).—Some anti-skeptics (called "Neo-Mooreans") like to turn this kind of argument on its head, again relying on closure:

(1') Ko
(2') (Ko) → (K ~s)
(C') K ~s.

I know I am not a brain in a vat because I know that I have hands and if I know the latter then I also know the former. Some of those who are not convinced by the latter argument but do not want to give in to skepticism propose to give up (C1) and similar or related principles (see Dretske 2005a but cf. also Brueckner 1985). Whatever option one chooses, it seems that closure—whether in the form of (C1) or of some other principles (see below)—plays an important role for the discussion of at least some important forms of epistemic skepticism (but cf. also Brueckner 1994, Cohen 1998 and David and Warfield 2008).

3. Refinements

The closure principle (C1) requires some refinements and modifications. Suppose Frank knows that the temperature has just fallen below freezing point. Suppose he also knows that if the temperature is below freezing point, then driving can be dangerous. However, it seems perfectly possible that Frank does not "put two and two together" and thus does not know that driving can be dangerous now. Only if Frank makes the relevant inference, does he come to know that driving can be dangerous now. To accommodate such cases, the following modification seems appropriate:

(c2) If S knows that p, knows that p entails q, and deduces from all this that q, then S knows that q.

Now, "p" could stand for a complex proposition of the form "p and (p → q)." This gives us the case of "single-premise closure" which is at the centre of the current discussion about closure (see sec. 7 below for multi-premise closure):

(c3) If S knows that p, and deduces q from p, then S knows that q.

Sometimes people propose to weaken (C1) in the following way rather than moving on to (C2) or (C3):

(C1') If S knows that p, and if S knows that p entails q, then S is in a position to know that q.

However, being in a position to know is not the same as knowing; hence (C1′) is too weak for our purposes; we would not be talking about knowledge closure any more but rather about being-in-a-position-to-know closure. And, apart from that, it is not clear at all what is required for being in a position to know; this idea seems a bit too unspecific to be of much help (see David and Warfield 2008: sec. IV).

Now, the deduction mentioned in (C3) needs to be a correct one and based on a general ability of the subject to draw such a correct inference. Let us say that in such a case the subject "competently" deduces q from p. If Frank makes an invalid inference even to a true conclusion, he might not come to know the conclusion. Also, if he just happens to make a correct inference when he usually fails to get these things right, he also might not come to know the conclusion. Hence, we had better replace (C3) by

(C4) If S knows that p, and competently deduces q from p, then S knows that q.

But what if Frank is the kind of person who simply cannot believe that it could ever be too dangerous for him to drive? Even though he deduces q from p, he does not come to believe that q (and he does not come to believe it on the basis of his deduction; see on this Harman 1986: 11–12). Let us modify (C4) then (see also Bogdan 1985; Hales 1995: 188–192):

(C5) If S knows that p, competently deduces q from p, and believes that q, then S knows that q (see, e.g., Forbes 1984: 43, 49–50 and Williamson 2000: 117 who add that S "thereby" comes to believe that q; see also (T) below).

(C5) expresses not just a contingent fact but a necessity. Hence, we can add that "necessarily" (C5) is the case.—What if S ceases to know that p in the process of deducing q from it? Some (see, e.g., Hawthorne 2004: 29, 33) hold that we have to add a further condition: that S retains knowledge that p throughout the process of deduction.—Kvanvig (2006: 261–262) proposes a further qualification: that S learns of no undefeated defeater for q (e.g., someone extremely trustworthy just told me that not q and even though they are wrong there is no indication of that). Thus we get:

NECESSARILY: If S knows that p, competently deduces q from p while retaining knowledge that p throughout the inference, believes that q and does not learn of any undefeated defeater for q, then S knows that q.

There might be further conditions to be added (see David and Warfield, Ms.; David and Warfield 2008: secs. II–III; Warfield 2004) but we don't need to get into a potentially endless discussion (resembling the post-Gettier discussion about *knowledge*); it is not clear whether one can indicate sufficient conditions for inferential knowledge that q (similar things hold of similar principles below). Anyway, the basic idea should be both clear and robust enough now. (C5) expresses the core of the idea of knowledge closure currently discussed. I will stick with (C5), also for the sake of simplicity and because nothing in the following depends on the added subtleties.

4. Transmission

Closure principles remain silent about where S's knowledge that q comes from: S need not know q on the basis of deduction from p. Now, one might want to stress that S's knowledge that q can be derived from or based upon S's knowledge that p (where p differs from q). This gives us a transmission principle:

(T) If S knows that p, competently deduces q from p, and believes that q, then S knows or comes to know that q on the basis of that deduction (no matter whether q is also known independently from the knowledge that p).

This is a transmission principle in the sense that it specifies the conditions under which knowledge can "transmit" by deduction from one proposition (p) to another (q). Closure principles like the ones above do not say anything about transmission as such. Unfortunately, closure and transmission principles are very often not, or not clearly, distinguished; sometimes it is very difficult to tell whether an author talks about closure or transmission of knowledge (for a clear distinction, see: Wright 1985: 438, fn. 1, 2000: 141; Davies 1998: 325–326, 2000: 393–394, 2003b: 108; McLaughlin 2003: 83; Dretske 2005a: 15, 16).

Very often transmission is explained in terms of transmission of warrant (where warrant is taken as whatever turns true belief into knowledge; but cf., e.g., Williamson 2000). This results in principles of the transmission of warrant across valid inference, like, e.g., the following one:

(TW) If S has warrant for (believing that) p, competently deduces q from p, and believes that q, then S acquires (for the first time or not) warrant for (believing that) q on the basis of that deduction (and S can thus come to know that q).

It does not matter here whether the subject believes or knows she has warrant or whether the subject believes or knows that the warrant supports the relevant proposition. The discussion about the transmission of warrant principles does not seem to depend on what position one takes on such issues.

If having warrant for a true belief is sufficient for turning that belief into knowledge, then every case of a true belief that q which meets a transmission principle like (TW) also meets a closure principle like (C5). The reverse, however, is not true (see above): A case can meet (C5) but not (TW) because the subject's knowledge that q might not be derived from or based upon their knowledge that p. I know that there is an apple in front of me and I also know that this entails that there is no fake apple in front of me; according to many, even if I know that there is no fake apple in front of me, I cannot know this on the basis of my knowledge that there is an apple in front of me (more on such cases below).

5. Denials: Dretske and Nozick

The conviction that some closure (or transmission) principle is true is very widespread in contemporary philosophy. It seems very hard to deny that we can acquire new knowledge by making inferences from what we already know. Denying closure (or transmission) seems to jeopardize the very idea of inferential knowledge. And how abominable does it sound to say, e.g., that "I know that I am sitting on a chair but I don't know that I am not merely dreaming that I am sitting on a chair"?

However, there are dissenters. One of the first philosophers who can be read as denying closure is Ludwig Wittgenstein. In *On Certainty* (1969) he makes remarks which suggest that what we know is based on and presupposes things we don't know (see also, more recently: Greene 2001: 67–71; Harman and Sherman 2004). If we read "based" and "presupposes" as involving some known entailment relation (between what we know and what we presuppose), then all this comes to a denial of closure. I know there is a tree in the yard but I don't know there is an external world. Much more explicit is the denial in the case of some more recent epistemologists, particularly Robert Nozick and Fred Dretske. In Nozick's case, the failure of closure is a consequence of his account of knowledge. His "Sensitivity" or "Tracking Account of Knowledge" has it that (with "iff" for "if and only if" and with "⇒" as the sign for the subjunctive conditional, that is, for a conditional of the form "If p were the case, then q would be the case")

S knows that p iff

(a) p,
(b) S believes that p,
(c) $(\sim p) \Rightarrow$ S does not believe that p, and
(d) $p \Rightarrow$ S believes that p.

S knows that there is a dog over there just in case the following conditions are met: S truly believes this (a, b); furthermore, if there were no dog over there, S would not believe it (c); finally, under different possible circumstances under which there is a dog over there, S would believe it (d). Sure, knowledge does not require that S's belief "tracks" the truth even under the wildest possible circumstances (in the presence of artificial fake-dogs, etc.). Therefore, the subjunctive conditionals (c) and (d) have to be evaluated not with respect to all possible worlds but only to "close" ones—to those which resemble the actual circumstances very much. Furthermore, one has to take into account the way in which the belief was formed (see Nozick 1981: 172ff.). Such details left aside, it becomes clear quickly that this account is not compatible with any of the closure (or transmission) principles mentioned so far (see Nozick 1981: 206, 227–240). Consider this case. Bob knows that he has hands because he has hands, he believes he has hands, in all close possible worlds in which he has hands he believes this, and in all close possible worlds in which he lacks hands (e.g., because of an accident) he does not believe he has hands. Suppose Bob also knows that if he has hands then he is not a handless brain in a vat. Does he or can he also know that he is not a handless brain in a vat? According to Nozick's condition (c), if Bob were a handless brain in a vat, he would have to not believe that he is not a handless brain in a vat. However, given what it means to be a brain in a vat, he would believe that he is not a handless brain in a vat. Hence, Bob does not meet Nozick's condition (c) and thus does not know that he is not a handless brain in a vat. The problem for closure is now obvious: According to Nozick, one can know something even without knowing something else which one knows follows from what one knows. Closure fails (where closure is understood along the lines of (C5) and similar principles). Many philosophers hold the closure principle so dear that they hold the failure of closure against Nozick's account of knowledge. Nozick went the other way and proposed to give up closure principles like (C5). One advantage in the case of skeptical arguments is that Nozick can thus accommodate both our view that we know a lot of ordinary propositions and the skeptical insight that we don't know that we're not brains in a vat. Other modal accounts, of knowledge, like the safety view (see, e.g., Sosa 1999), also have problems with closure (see the dachshund example in Goldman 1983: 84, which has an echo in a well-known similar example by Saul Kripke; Sosa (1999: 292–294) concedes that there is a problem).

Dretske's denial of ordinary closure principles is at least partly motivated by reasons very similar to Nozick's (see Dretske 2003: 113, 2005a: 19–20, 2005b: 43–44). However, it also seems triggered by the discussion of cases. Here is one of Dretske's most well-known examples (see Dretske 1970, 1982; cf. critically Klein 1981: 29–33 and Vogel 1990: 13–15; see, for other examples, Audi 1998: 169 and the debate on it in: Feldman 1995 and Audi 1995; see also Hookway 1989/90: 9–10; Maitzen 1998; Salmon 1989: sec.VI). Suppose Fred is in the zoo and standing in front of the zebra cage. Does he know that he is looking at zebras? There seems to be no reason to deny this. But does he know that he is not looking at cleverly disguised mules (painted as zebras)? It seems clear that he does not know that. However, the latter proposition can be easily known by Fred to be entailed by the former one. Hence, closure fails. Dretske also applies this to contemporary skeptical arguments: One can know that there is a cup in front of one even if one does not know what is known to be entailed by it, e.g., that one is not merely dreaming that there is a cup in front of oneself. Like Nozick, Dretske can thus make peace between the skeptic and the anti-skeptic (see Dretske 2005a: 18, 23). One can also explain all this in terms of Dretske's "relevant alternatives theory of knowledge" (Dretske 1981, 2005a: 19; McGinn 1984: 544; Stine 1976; Lewis 1996; Heller 1999; for Dretske's view on information and closure see Dretske 2003: 115, 2004: 176–177).

It should be stressed that both Dretske and Nozick seem to talk not just about closure but about transmission principles, too (see Nozick 1981: 205–206). More importantly, I should stress that, strictly speaking, neither Dretske nor Nozick opt for an unrestricted denial of any principle of closure (not just (C5)). Dretske accepts closure in cases of (known) conjunction-elimination (Dretske 1970; but cf. Hawthorne 2005: 31–32) while Nozick denies it in those cases (as well as for universal instantiation; see Nozick 1981: 227–229); Nozick accepts closure for cases of (known) equivalence, existential generalization, conjunction-introduction or disjunction-introduction (see Nozick 1981: 229, 230, 236; cf. p. 231 for a restriction of closure rather than its denial). Furthermore, Dretske has later argued in a way which seems to explicitly suggest a restriction of closure principles rather than their abolishment (see Dretske 2005a: 16, 17 or 2003 where he argues that closure breaks down when "q" stands for a "heavyweight" or "limiting proposition"). And Roush (2005) has defended a closure-compatible version of Nozick's theory. Looking at such later modifications, one should conclude that the real controversy is much more about the proper formulation of a closure (or transmission) principle than about the acceptance of any such principle (see Goldman 2008: 478–479; but also Becker 2007: 113–128, who, supporting Nozick, recommends giving up closure, or Adams and Clarke 2005 who defend the tracking account against common counterexamples; see also Luper-Foy 1987).

6. Problems: Lotteries and Easy Knowledge

There are also some serious problems which anyone who wants to defend some closure (or transmission) principle would have to address. The apparent incompatibility of ordinary knowledge claims, closure and the impossibility to know one is not in a skeptical scenario has already been mentioned above. Let us now look at a problem first brought up by Gilbert Harman (see Harman 1973: 161; see also Hawthorne 2004 and Vogel 1990: 15–20). Suppose you believe that you will never be a millionaire. Suppose that this is in fact true and you know it. Now, you also know that if you will never be a millionaire, then you will never win the millionaires' lottery. But how can you know that you won't win that lottery? If we assume—with many contemporary epistemologists—that one cannot know that one won't win a lottery (given normal circumstances, like having bought a ticket for a fair and unrigged lottery, etc.), then it seems very hard to stick with the claim to know that one will never be rich (given closure). This problem easily generalizes to all pairs of propositions such that one proposition is an ordinary proposition we would tend to claim to know and the other proposition is a "lottery" proposition entailed by the first one; a lottery proposition is a proposition which has a high probability of being true but which we would typically not tend to claim to know (for more on the notion of a lottery proposition see Vogel 1990: 16–17). Here is another example, not involving a literal lottery. Frank knows that his children are playing in the garden but he does not know that his children have not been kidnapped and replaced by actors who pretend convincingly to be his children. Since it is hard to think of any ordinary proposition which does not entail some lottery proposition and since such an entailment can easily be known by the subject, our problem is hard to contain and concerns all kinds of propositions we ordinarily think we know. Three main responses are on offer in the current debate. First, one could accept closure as well as the idea that one cannot know a lottery proposition (both plausible); but then one also has to accept the resulting widespread skepticism (not plausible to many). Second, one could accept closure as well as our ordinary knowledge claims (both plausible); but then one would also have to be ready to accept the possibility of knowledge concerning lottery propositions (not plausible to many). Finally, one could accept both skepticism concerning lottery propositions as well as our ordinary knowledge claims (both plausible); but then one would have to reject closure (cf. from the recent debate: Hawthorne 2004). An analogous problem arises, of course, for transmission principles.

Another problem is the problem of "bootstrapping" and "easy knowledge" (see Cohen 2002; Sosa 2009: chs. 4, 5, 9, 10). My speedometer tells me that I am driving at 40 mph. Suppose I am traveling at that speed. It seems hard to deny that I can thus come to know that I am traveling at 40 mph. I can also come to know that the speedometer indicates a speed of 40 mph (by looking at it). From both I can infer that the speedometer is indicating the speed correctly. If I repeat this little exercise many times, I can infer that the speedometer is working reliably. However, these conclusions do not seem to constitute knowledge. But they follow from other things I know and the entailment is also known. Here is another example of the same kind. I look in front of me and thus come to know that there is an apple in front of me. I also know a real apple is not a fake apple made to look like an apple. I can conclude but, it seems, not come to know in this way that there is no such fake apple in front of me. Knowledge cannot be acquired that easily. What has gone wrong? And what ought we to say about such cases? Should we deny knowledge of one of the two premises? Should we allow for bootstrapping and easy knowledge? Or should we deny closure? All three options seem implausible. Again, a parallel problem arises for transmission principles.

One way out would be to restrict the closure principle in a certain way. Here is a rough idea. What is common to such cases of bootstrapping and easy knowledge is that the subject is granted knowledge of the premises but only insofar as the subject is also granted certain assumptions or presuppositions even if they do not constitute knowledge from the outset: that the speedometer is working, that the subject's vision is fine, etc. If we were to not grant the subject these assumptions and presuppositions—if, for instance, we saw good reasons to doubt that everything is fine with the speedometer or the eyes of the subject—then we would not attribute knowledge of the premises to the subject. This suggests the following modification of (C5):

> (C6) If S knows that p, competently deduces q from p, and believes that q, then S knows that q—but not if q is both antecedently unknown by S but taken for granted and presupposed by S's belief and knowledge that p (see Barke 2002: 164–166 and even Dretske 1970: 1014 as well as Nozick 1981: 239–240).

Even if a closure principle like (C6) holds in certain cases, transmission might still fail. In any case, it is good to have a restricted transmission principle which takes care of such potential failures of transmission. Here is a proposal (for the case of transmission of warrant):

> (TW*) If S has warrant for (believing that) p, competently deduces q from p, and believes that q, then S acquires (for the first time or not) warrant for (believing that) q on the basis of that deduction (and may thus come to know that q)—but not if the having of the warrant for (believing that) p depends on antecedent reliance on q (for more along such lines, see Wright 1985: 432–438, 2000, 2002, 2003, 2004, 2007; Davies 1998: 351–355, 2000: 402–412, 2003a: 30–45, 2003b: 122–130, but cf. 2004; see further McLaughlin 2003: 91, 84–91; Brown 2004; Pryor 2004 and forthcoming; Okasha 2004; Silins 2005; Nozick 1981: 239–240; Olin 2005: 237–238, 243).

We can leave the question open whether principles like (C6) or (TW*) can help us deal with the problem of easy knowledge, bootstrapping or with the lottery problem (see Hawthorne 2004). There is some hope but we cannot go into that here.

7. Further Problems: Multi-Premise Closure and Probability

So far we have only considered cases in which the subject deduces one proposition from another proposition. But what about a case like the following? You're throwing a party and have invited all of your 100 friends. Alfonsina has accepted the invitation and promised to come. You believe her because you know her to be extremely reliable; as a matter of fact, she will indeed show up. It seems uncontroversial to say that you can thus come to know that she will come to your party. Similar things are true of Bernie, Claire and all your other friends. You know 100 premises where each premise says of one of your friends (a different one each time, of course) that they will come to the party: You know that $p1$, that $p2$, . . . that $p100$. You also know about conjunction-introduction. You thus make the inference to the conjunction and conclude that all of your 100 friends will attend the party. But even if they all do this hardly seems to be knowable by you. Again, we have a problem: the knowledge of the premises, some closure principle and the lack of knowledge of the conclusion are incompatible with each other.

What creates the problem? Here is an idea. For each individual proposition there is a very high though not maximal (subjective) probability that it is true. Let us assume the probability is .99 in each case. It seems plausible that such a proposition can be known to be true despite the element of fallibility. Let us further assume that all these propositions are probabilistically independent from each other. The probability of the conjunction of all these propositions is then much smaller than .99 (namely less than .37). It is hard to believe that such a relatively unlikely proposition can still be known. However, it follows from all of the highly likely individual propositions, given plausible logical principles (there are obvious parallels here with Kyburg's lottery paradox (Kyburg 1961: 197) as well as with the preface paradox (Makinson 1965; Olin 2005)).

What should one do about this? Skepticism with respect to the individual premises appears too high a price to pay. Even less plausible is it to claim that one can come to know the rather unlikely conclusion. What then about denying multi-premise closure? This principle might seem much more plausible anyway than it ought to. The plausibility of closure principles seems to depend on using simple cases with just one premise; it seems to fade away as soon as we consider cases with more than one premise (see Hawthorne 2004: passim). (A very thorny problem comes with the question of how one should individuate premises: Is it always clear how many premises the subject used? Aren't there cases where one could count premises in more than one way, with different results?)

Perhaps we should then just give up the idea—bitter as it might seem—that there is more than single-premise closure to have (but cf. Stine 1976: 251 and Lasonen-Aarnio 2008). Neither the multi-premise parallel of the simple closure principle (C1),

> (MC1) If S knows that $p1, \ldots$, and that pn, and if S knows that $p1, \ldots$, and pn together entail q, then S knows that q,

nor the multi-premise parallel of the more complex closure principle (C6),

> (MC6) If S knows that $p1, \ldots$, and that pn, competently deduces q from $p1, \ldots$, and pn, and believes that q, then S knows that q—but not if q is both antecedently unknown by S but taken for granted and presupposed by S's belief and knowledge that $p1$ or $\ldots$ by S's belief and knowledge that pn,

are true. The same holds, *mutatis mutandis*, for transmission principles (see also Olin 2005).

Not all acceptable inferences are deductive. Some inferences are "probabilistic" in the sense that the truth of the conclusion is not "guaranteed" by the truth of the premises but made probable by the premises. The probability of such a conclusion might not be extremely high but it can still be high enough for knowledge (again: if a probability less than 1 is compatible with knowledge). Here is an example: Ann's car is parked in front of her flat and she is usually at home when her car is there; hence, Ann is at home. If one knows the premise(s), then one should be able to come to know the conclusion—if it is true—by such an inference. This suggests probabilistic versions of our closure principles. Here is a principle parallel to (C1):

(P1) If S knows that p, and if S knows that p makes q probable (enough), and if q is true, then S knows that q.

And here is the principle parallel to (C6):

(P6) If S knows that p, competently makes a probabilistic inference to q from p, believes that q, and if q is true, then S knows that q—but not if q is both antecedently unknown by S but taken for granted and presupposed by S's belief and knowledge that p.

There will be similar transmission principles. But again, for the kinds of reasons explained above, one should not expect there to be true principles of multi-premise probabilistic closure.

8. Conclusion

The idea of closure of knowledge under known entailment is of great importance for epistemology (we had to leave closure principles for epistemic justification and other relevant notions aside here). There seems to be very widespread agreement—and not without good reason—that some closure principle has to be true. What looks like a contemporary debate between a majority of defenders of closure and a minority of deniers of closure is to a large degree (though not completely) a debate about the right kind of closure principle. It is plausible to assume that several whistles and bells have to be added to the simple closure principle (C1). Furthermore, there is not only a plausible closure principle for the case of deductive inference but also for the case of probabilistic inference. It is much harder to see how a principle of multi-premise closure could be true. There are also problems for principles of single-premise closure awaiting a convincing solution, such as Harman's problem or the problem of bootstrapping and easy knowledge. The related discussion about transmission of failure can give useful impulses to the debate about closure.

References

Adams, F. and Clarke, M. (2005) "Resurrecting the Tracking Theories" *Australasian Journal of Philosophy* 83, 207–221.
Audi, R. (1995) "Deductive Closure, Defeasibility, and Scepticism: a Reply to Feldman" *The Philosophical Quarterly* 45, 494–499.
Audi, R. (1998) *Epistemology: A Contemporary Introduction to the Theory of Knowledge*, London & New York: Routledge.
Barke, A. (2002) *The Closure of Knowledge in Context*, Paderborn: mentis.
Becker, K. (2007) *Epistemology Modalized*, New York & London: Routledge.
Bogdan, R.J. (1985) "Cognition and Epistemic Closure" *American Philosophical Quarterly* 22, 55–63.
Brown, J. (2004) *Anti-Individualism and Knowledge*, Cambridge, MA: MIT Press.
Brueckner, A.L. (1985) "Skepticism and Epistemic Closure" *Philosophical Topics* 13, 89–117.
Brueckner, A.L. (1994) "The Structure of the Skeptical Argument" *Philosophy and Phenomenological Research* 54, 827–835.
Cohen, S. (1998) "Two Kinds of Skeptical Argument" *Philosophy and Phenomenological Research* 58, 143–159.
Cohen, S. (2002) "Basic Knowledge and the Problem of Easy Knowledge" *Philosophy and Phenomenological Research* 65, 309–329.
David, M. and Warfield, T.A. (2008) "Knowledge-Closure and Scepticism," in Q. Smith (ed.) *Epistemology. New Essays*, Oxford: Oxford University Press, 137–187.

David, M. and Warfield, T.A., "Six Possible Counterexamples to One or Two Epistemic Closure Principles," Ms.

Davies, M. (1998) "Externalism, Architecturalism and Epistemic Warrant," in C. Wright, B. Smith and C. Macdonald (eds.) *Knowing Our Own Minds*, Oxford: Clarendon, 321–361.

Davies, M. (2000) "Externalism and Armchair Knowledge," in P. Boghossian and C. Peacocke (eds.) *New Essays on the A Priori*, Oxford: Clarendon, 384–414.

Davies, M. (2003a) "The Problem of Armchair Knowledge," in S. Nuccetelli (ed.) *New Essays on Semantic Externalism and Self-Knowledge*, Cambridge, MA & London: MIT Press, 23–55.

Davies, M. (2003b) "Externalism, Self-Knowledge and Transmission of Warrant," in M.J. Frápolli and E. Romero (eds.) *Meaning, Basic Self-Knowledge, and Mind. Essays on Tyler Burger*, Stanford: CSLI Publications, 105–130.

Davies, M. (2004) "On Epistemic Entitlement: Epistemic Entitlement, Warrant Transmission and Easy Knowledge" *Proceedings of the Aristotelian Society, Supplement* 78, 213–245.

Dretske, F.I. (1970) "Epistemic Operators" *The Journal of Philosophy* 69, 1007–1023.

Dretske, F.I. (1981) "The Pragmatic Dimension of Knowledge" *Philosophical Studies* 40, 363–378.

Dretske, F.I. (1982) "A Cognitive Cul-de-sac" *Mind* 91, 109–111.

Dretske, F.I. (2003) "Skepticism: What Perception Teaches," in S. Luper (ed.) *The Skeptics. Contemporary Essays*, Aldershot: Ashgate, 105–118.

Dretske, F.I. (2004) "Externalism and Modest Contextualism" *Erkenntnis* 61, 173–186.

Dretske, F.I. (2005a) "The Case against Closure," in M. Steup and E. Sosa (eds.) *Contemporary Debates in Epistemology*, Malden, MA: Blackwell, 13–26.

Dretske, F.I. (2005b) "Reply to Hawthorne," in M. Steup and E. Sosa (eds.) *Contemporary Debates in Epistemology*, Malden, MA: Blackwell, 43–46.

Feldman, R.(1995) "In Defence of Closure" *The Philosophical Quarterly* 45, 487–494.

Forbes, G. (1984) "Nozick on Scepticism" *Philosophical Quarterly* 34, 43–52.

Goldman, A. (2008) "Knowledge, Explanation, and Lotteries" *Noûs* 42, 466–481.

Goldman, A.I. (1983) "Review of Nozick, Philosophical Explanations" *The Philosophical Review* 92, 81–88.

Greene, R. (2001) "A Rejection of the Epistemic Closure Principle" *Southwest Philosophy Review* 17, 59–73.

Hales, S.D. (1995) "Epistemic Closure Principles" *Southern Journal of Philosophy* 33, 185–201.

Harman, G. (1973) *Thought*, Princeton: Princeton University Press.

Harman, G. (1986) *Change in View. Principles of Reasoning*, Cambridge, MA: MIT Press.

Harman, G. and Sherman, B. (2004) "Knowledge, Assumptions, Lotteries" *Philosophical Issues* 14, 492–500.

Hawthorne, J. (2004) *Knowledge and Lotteries*, Oxford: Clarendon.

Hawthorne, J. (2005) "The Case for Closure," in M. Steup and E. Sosa (eds.) *Contemporary Debates in Epistemology*, Malden, MA: Blackwell, 26–43.

Heller, M. (1999) "Relevant Alternatives and Closure" *Australasian Journal of Philosophy* 77, 196–208.

Hintikka, J. (1962) *Knowledge and Belief. An Introduction to the Logic of the Two Notions*, Ithaca, NY: Cornell University Press.

Hookway, C. (1989/90) "Scepticism and Autonomy" *Proceedings of the Aristotelian Society* 90, 103–118.

Klein, P.D. (1981) *Certainty: A Refutation of Scepticism*, Brighton: The Harvester Press.

Kvanvig, J.L. (2006) "Closure Principles" *Philosophy Compass* 1/3, 256–267.

Kyburg, H.E. Jr. (1961) *Probability and the Logic of Rational Belief*, Middletown, CN: Wesleyan University Press.

Lasonen-Aarnio, M. (2008) "Single Premise Deduction and Risk" *Philosophical Studies* 141, 157–173.

Lewis, D. (1996) "Elusive Knowledge" *Australasian Journal of Philosophy* 74, 549–561.

Luper-Foy, S. (ed.) (1987) *The Possibility of Knowledge. Nozick and His Critics*, Totowa, NJ: Rowman & Littlefield.

Maitzen, S. (1998) "The Knower Paradox and Epistemic Closure" *Synthese* 114, 337–354.

Makinson, D.C. (1965) "The Paradox of the Preface" *Analysis* 25, 205–207.

McGinn, C. (1984) "The Concept of Knowledge" *Midwest Studies in Philosophy* 9 P.A. French, T.E. Uehling Jr., H.K. Wettstein (eds.), Minneapolis: University of Minnesota Press, 529–554.

McLaughlin, B.P. (2003) "McKinsey's Challenge, Warrant Transmission, and Skepticism," in S. Nuccetelli (ed.) *New Essays on Semantic Externalism and Self-Knowledge*, Cambridge,MA & London: MIT Press, 79–96.

Nozick, R. (1981) *Philosophical Explanations*, Cambridge, MA: Harvard University Press.

Okasha, S. (2004) "Wright on the Transmission of Support: A Bayesian Analysis" *Analysis* 64, 139–146.
Olin, D. (2005) "A Case against Closure" *Veritas* 50, 235–247.
Pryor, J. (2004) "What's Wrong with Moore's Argument?" *Philosophical Issues* 14, 349–378.
Pryor, J. (forthcoming) "When Warrant Transmits," in A. Coliva (ed.) *Wittgenstein, Epistemology and Mind: Themes from the Philosophy of Crispin Wright*, Oxford: Oxford University Press.
Putnam, H. (1981) "Brains in a Vat," in H. Putnam, *Reason, Truth and History*, Cambridge: Cambridge University Press, 1–22.
Roush, S. (2005) *Tracking Truth. Knowledge, Evidence, and Science*, Oxford: Clarendon.
Salmon, N. (1989) "Illogical Belief" *Philosophical Perspectives* 3, 243–285.
Silins, N. (2005) "Transmission Failure Failure" *Philosophical Studies* 126, 71–102.
Sosa, E. (1999) "How to Defeat Opposition to Moore" *Philosophical Perspectives* 13, 141–154.
Sosa, E. (2009) *Reflective Knowledge. Apt Belief and Reflective Knowledge*, vol. II, Oxford: Oxford University Press.
Stine, G.C. (1976) "Skepticism, Relevant Alternatives, and Deductive Closure" *Philosophical Studies* 29, 249–261.
Vogel, J. (1990) "Are there Counterexamples to the Closure Principle?," in M.D. Roth and G. Ross (eds.) *Doubting. Contemporary Perspectives on Skepticism*, Dordrecht etc.: Kluwer, 13–27.
Warfield, T.A. (2004) "When Epistemic Closure Does and Does not Fail: A Lesson from the History of Epistemology" *Analysis* 64, 35–41.
Williamson, T. (2000) *Knowledge and Its Limits*, Oxford: Oxford University Press.
Wittgenstein, L. (1969) *On Certainty*, Oxford: Blackwell.
Wright, C. (1985) "Facts and Certainty" *Proceedings of the British Academy* 71, 429–472.
Wright, C. (2000) "Cogency and Question-Begging: Some Reflections on McKinsey's Paradox and Putnam's Proof" *Philosophical Perspectives* 10 (Skepticism), 140–163.
Wright, C. (2002) "(Anti-) Sceptics Simple and Subtle: G.E. Moore and John McDowell" *Philosophy and Phenomenological Research* 65, 330–348.
Wright, C. (2003) "Some Reflections on the Acquisition of Warrant by Inference," in S. Nuccetelli (ed.) *New Essays on Semantic Externalism and Self-Knowledge*, Cambridge, MA & London: MIT Press, 57–77.
Wright, C. (2004) "Warrant for nothing (and foundations for free?)" *Proceedings of the Aristotelian Society*, Supplement 78, 167–212.
Wright, C. (2007) "The Perils of Dogmatism," in S. Nuccetelli and G. Seay (eds.) *Themes from G.E. Moore: New Essays in Epistemology and Ethics*, Oxford: Oxford University Press, 25–48.

55
BAYESIAN EPISTEMOLOGY

Stephan Hartmann and Jan Sprenger

1. Introduction

Bayesian epistemology addresses epistemological problems with the help of the mathematical theory of probability. It turns out that the probability calculus is especially suited to represent degrees of belief (credences) and to deal with questions of belief change, confirmation, evidence, justification, and coherence. Compared to the informal discussions in traditional epistemology, Bayesian epistemology allows for a more precise and fine-grained analysis which takes the gradual aspects of these central epistemological notions into account. Bayesian epistemology therefore complements traditional epistemology; it does not replace it or aim at replacing it.

Bayesian epistemology can be traced back to the work of Reverend Thomas Bayes (1701–1761) who found an elementary mathematical theorem that plays a central role in Bayesian epistemology. More on this below. Later Bayesian ideas began to surface not only in philosophy, but also in statistics, formal learning theory, and other parts of science. Obviously, the probability calculus finds many applications because of its enormous flexibility, expressive power, and formal simplicity. Bayesian epistemology shares much with these endeavors, including a certain scientific attitude vis-à-vis the problems in question, but it is worth noting that Bayesian epistemology is, in the first place, a philosophical project, and that it is its ambition to further progress in philosophy.

This essay is structured as follows. Section 2 introduces the probability calculus and explains why degrees of belief obey the probability calculus. Section 3 applies the formal machinery to an analysis of the notion of evidence, and highlights potential application. Section 4 discusses Bayesian models of coherence and testimony, and section 5 ends this essay with a comparison of traditional epistemology and Bayesian epistemology.

2. Probability and Degrees of Belief

Bayesian epistemology can be described as the attempt to use an intuitive, but powerful tool—the probability calculus—for tackling longstanding problems in epistemology and philosophy of science. In particular, Bayesian epistemology models degrees of belief as mathematical probabilities. Probability is interpreted subjectively or epistemically (as opposed to the "objective chance" of an event). This section explains the relationship between the different interpretations of probability, the concept of degree of belief, and the application of those tools to epistemological problems. We start with some motivational remarks that draw on the analogy to deductive logic.

Deductive logic is often perceived as the *logic of full rational belief*, in the sense that an agent's set of (fully endorsed) beliefs can be described as a set of first-order propositions. If this set is logically inconsistent, i.e. if there is no joint model of all propositions, then the agent cannot be (epistemically) rational: the propositions cannot hold simultaneously, hence she ought to abandon at least one of her beliefs. The calculus of deductive logic is helpful here: it detects inconsistencies in a set of beliefs by exploring their implications according to a set of inferential rules.

The mathematical theory of probability plays the same role with respect to *partial rational beliefs*, in the sense that the probability calculus is a powerful instrument in order to infer the doxastic implications of a certain set of partial beliefs. To spell out the concept of a rational or irrational degree of belief, Frank Ramsey [1926] (1978) suggested to make use of the standard, economic conception of rationality—irrational degrees of belief would cost us money if we let them guide our actions. The crucial concept is *betting behavior*, or the inclination to accept and reject bets according to our degrees of belief. For fixed betting odds, a bet appears to be more favorable if we have a strong degree of belief in the underlying propositions than if we only weakly believe in them. This suggests to quantify a degree of belief in terms of the betting odds which we consider to be fair. As Ramsey argues, sports events are not the only occasion when we get involved in betting:

> [. . .] all our lives we are in sense betting. Whenever we go to the station we are betting that a train will really run, and if we had not a sufficient degree of belief in this we should decline the bet and stay at home.
> (Ramsey [1926] 1978: 85)

Thus, we can describe our degrees of belief by means of the betting odds which we consider fair. To make this explicit, we need some formalism: A *bet* on the event A is a triple $\langle A \mid x \mid y \rangle$ where x and y are positive real numbers. The bookie pays the bettor y euros if A occurs and the bettor pays the bookie x euros if A does not occur. x is the bettor's *stake*, and the ratio $(x + y)/x$ is called the *betting odds* on A, indicating the bettor's total gain (including the stake) for a successful € 1 euro bet. Such a betting odd is a preliminary quantification of a degree of belief. Naturally, an agent judges the bet $\langle A \mid x \mid y \rangle$ to be fair if it offers no advantage to either side, i.e. if to the agent's mind, neither the bookie nor the bettor have an advantage, and both have the same expected utility. In this case, $(x + y)/x$ are the betting odds corresponding to the agent's degree of belief.

The connection to the probability calculus is quickly made: if x is much greater than y and the bettor takes more risk than the bookie, the agent believes the event A to be *probable*. Conversely, if agent S believes A to occur in $(100*p)\%$ of all possible cases, he will consider the bet $\langle A \mid x \mid y \rangle$ to be fair if and only if there is no advantage for either side and the bet is a zero-sum game:

$$py + (1-p)(-x) = 0. \qquad (1)$$

The only real number that solves equation (1) is $p = x/(x + y) \in [0,1]$. This value p is called the *probability corresponding to S's degree of belief*. It is easy to see that there is an isomorphism between probabilities and betting odds since we can determine the probability from the betting odds by taking the inverse, and vice versa. In the remainder, we will therefore read "the probability of A" as the subjective degree of belief in A. Evidently, 1 denotes maximal and 0 minimal degree of belief. What exactly makes a judgment on the fairness of a bet, or actual betting behavior, irrational? If we accept 1:1 bets on an event A which you know to be highly improbable, we might still be rational. Maybe we have less information than you. Or perhaps there is not enough information available to determine a uniquely rational degree of belief. For instance, if we have a certain degree of belief in the independent propositions A and B, our degree of belief in $A \vee B$ should not be lower. Thus, degrees of belief/betting odds/probabilities are not arbitrary if we proceed from A and B to their truth-functional compounds. Probability theory reflects these entanglements in two simple axioms (Kolmogorov 1933):

> *Definition:* Let $\mathcal{A}$ be a field of propositions (i.e. a set of propositions that is closed under truth-functional combination and contains all tautologies). $P: \mathcal{A} \to [0,1]$ is a *probability function* on $\mathcal{A}$ if and only if
>
> - $P(A) = 1$ for any tautology A.
> - For incompatible (mutually exclusive) propositions A and B, $P(A \vee B) = P(A) + P(B)$.

Any such function P is called a probability. The axioms are natural: Each tautology is assigned maximal degree of belief, and the disjunction of mutually exclusive propositions is assigned the sum of the individual degrees of beliefs. As a corollary, we obtain that $P(\neg A) + P(A) = P(A \vee \neg A) = 1$.

We will see in a minute that these simple equations contain everything that an agent's rational degrees of belief have to satisfy, and vice versa. Here, the famous *Dutch Book Theorem* comes in: if one of the probability axioms is violated, the betting odds implied by the agent's probabilities cannot have been fair altogether—it is possible to construct a system of bets that assures a risk-free gain to the bookie or the bettor, a so-called Dutch Book. Therefore, these degrees of belief cannot have been rational either.

> *Dutch Book Theorem:* Any function $P: \mathcal{A} \to [0,1]$ on a field $\mathcal{A}$ that does not satisfy the axioms of probability allows for a system of bets that is vulnerable to a Dutch Book.

There is a second theorem, the Converse Dutch Book Theorem, which ensures that probability functions are *not* vulnerable to Dutch Books:

> *Converse Dutch Book Theorem:* No probability function $P: \mathcal{A} \to [0,1]$ is vulnerable to a Dutch Book.

> *Proofs:* See Kemeny 1955.

In other words, the Dutch Book Theorem establishes the probability calculus as a logic of partial belief. Probabilistic degrees of belief are immune to Dutch Books, and non-probabilistic degrees of belief aren't. For instance, if your degrees of belief in A, B and $(A \vee B)$ did not conform to the probability axioms, we could offer you a bet on $(A \vee B)$ in a twofold way: directly, or as a bet implied by two single bets on A and B. But the implicit betting odds would be different, leading to a reductio ad absurdum:

> If anyone's mental condition violated these laws [of the probability calculus], his choice would depend on the precise form in which the options were offered him, which would be absurd.
>
> (Ramsey [1926] 1978: 84)

Thus, the Dutch Book Theorem establishes probability as the mathematical model of degrees of belief. However, the axiom of probabilities merely constrains *systems* of degrees of belief. They do not capture the irrationality of *isolated* beliefs. There are some people who *know* that the (objective, ontic) chance that their football club wins the national championship is no more than 0.01, but they continue to accept 1:8 bets on that event. Whatever the reasons for such a behavior, they act against their own knowledge. The inconsistency arises from the gap between the subjective degree of belief and the objective chance of the event. For this reason, we need a principle that supplements the Dutch Book Theorem with an account of the relationship between chances—objective probabilities in the world—and rational degrees of belief. This task is fulfilled by the Principal Principle (PP, Lewis 1980): If an agent knows the objective probability of proposition A to be equal to p and he has no "overruling information" available, then his rational degree of belief in A must also be equal to p. Lewis (1980) argues for the self-evidencing character of (PP), and this is in line with our intuitions: if we know a roulette table to be perfectly fair, we have no reason to play a specific strategy. But as Strevens (1999) points out, it is hard to give a non-circular defense of (PP).

Nevertheless, (PP) gives, together with the Dutch Book Theorem, a comprehensive account of the *statics* of rational belief. But what about the dynamics? We are lacking a principle that asserts how degrees of belief should be *changed* in the light of incoming information. Here, the third and final cornerstone of Bayesian epistemology enters, namely the updating of degrees in the light of new evidence. The degree of belief in proposition A after learning another proposition E is expressed by the conditional probability of A given E, $P(A|E)$. This value is defined as $P(A.E)/P(E)$ and is usually interpreted as the probability of A if we take E for granted.

Bayesian Conditionalization: The rational degree of belief in a proposition A after learning E is the conditional probability of A given E: $P_{new}(A) = P(A|E)$.

By means of the famous Bayes's Theorem (see Joyce 2008), we can reformulate this equation and make it easier to handle in practice:

$$P_{new}(H) = P(H|E) = \frac{P(H)\,P(E|H)}{P(E)}$$

$$= \frac{P(H)\,P(E|H)}{P(H)\,P(E|H) + P(\neg H)P(E|\neg H)} \qquad (2)$$

To give an easy example: A friend of yours has bought a new car. Your prior degree of belief that it is a Ford is about 0.1 (corresponding to the percentages of Fords among newly bought cars). One day, he comes to your place, driving a Ford. If he actually owns a Ford, it is quite likely that you see him in a Ford rather than in his wife's Toyota $P(E|H) \approx 0.8$), whereas, if he did not own a Ford, he would probably have taken his wife's car or public transport rather than borrowing a Ford from someone else ($P(E|\neg H) \approx 0.05$). Using (2), this leads to your new degree of belief $P_{new}(H) \approx 0.94$. In other words, you are now quite convinced that he has bought a Ford.

Together, the Dutch Book Argument, the Principal Principle and Bayesian Conditionalizations are the three pillars of Bayesian epistemology. Let us have a look at what one can do with them.

3. Measuring Evidence

A central concept in modern epistemology and modern science is *evidence*. Something is evidence for a proposition or a scientific theory A, something makes us believe that A, etc. Philosophy of science has, over the past decades, exploited the probabilistic machinery to explicate what it means that a scientific theory is confirmed or undermined. Although this debate mainly took place in philosophy of science journals, it is obviously significant for epistemology: probabilistic confirmation renders a theory more credible, in other words, it is evidence for the theory, and evidence is, in turn, central to justifications and reasons. There are two concepts of evidence that have to be kept apart: the absolute and the relative. According to the absolute concept, E is evidence for a proposition A if and only if, given E, A is highly probable ($P(A|E)$ is high). For instance, a perception is (absolute) evidence for a certain belief if, taking the perception for granted, the belief is highly probable. This understanding certainly captures some ways of using the word "evidence," but on the other hand, E can be absolute evidence for A even if E lowers the probability of E. For instance, let A be the proposition that your favorite football club will *not* be national champion in the next year. Even if they win a league match (E), the probability of A given E is still sufficiently high to make E absolute evidence for A ($P(A|E)$ is still sufficiently high, although lower than $P(A|\neg E)$). At least unless you support Chelsea, Barcelona, or the like.

This unintuitive property of absolute evidence calls for a second, different concept of evidence, namely evidence in the sense of *support*. In the above example, E is evidence for ¬A because it increases the chance of winning the overall competition (though only to a tiny degree). This relative concept of evidence as support is the subject of the rest of the section. Not only is it much more of a *relation* than the absolute concept, it is also fruitful and widely applicable, as we will see later.

> *Definition:* E is (relative) *evidence for a proposition* A if and only if $P(A|E) > P(A)$.

Often, we have to tell good from bad evidence, similar to telling good from bad reasons, or to quantify degree of support, e.g. in order to address famous challenges such as the Duhem-Quine problem (Earman 1992). For these tasks, we need a *measure* of evidence. But what is the most adequate measure of evidence? Which one should we use when judging, for instance, whether "evidence of evidence" is also evidence? Here are some suggestions with both an intuitive appeal and a longstanding tradition (other suggestions have been made by e.g. Crupi et al. 2007):

> **Difference Measure** Takes the difference between the posterior and the prior degree of belief in A as a measure of the support evidence E lends to A: $d(A, E) := P(A|E) - P(A)$. (Earman 1992; Rosenkrantz 1994)

> **Log-ratio Measure** Proposed by Howson and Urbach (1993), this measure is based on the very same quantities, but replaces the difference in d by the logarithmic ratio: $r(A, E) := \log P(A|E)/P(A)$.

Counterfactual Difference Measure Takes quite a different approach and compares the posterior degree of belief in A with the counterfactual degree of belief in A *had ¬E occurred instead of E*: $s(A, E) := P(A|E) - P(A|\neg E)$.

Log-Likelihood Ratio Measures Looks whether A or its negation –A better accounts for observed evidence E: $l(A, E) := \log \frac{P(E|A)}{P(E|\neg A)}$.

The task of explicating evidence thus amounts to making a decision between these measures. This is an intricate task since they also capture different aspects of evidence. Let's come back to the Ford example. If you already knew that your friend had the firm plan to buy a Ford ($P(A) = 0.95$) then the evidence that you see him in a Ford is not very impressive from *d*'s standpoint ($d < 0.1$) since your degrees of belief do not change a lot. Still, A accounts much better for E than ¬A ($l \approx 2.77$). Thus, E remains highly useful to discriminate between A and ¬A, and therefore strong evidence from *l*'s standpoint. Christensen (1999: 438–439) presents a nice analogy: How would we measure the extent to which a candidate for US presidency P is financially supported by a group G? The proportion of G-donations in P's funds? P's relative position in the presidential run as a function of the G-donations? And so on. Christensen conjectures

> Thinking about these different measures of support suggests to me that there is no single clearcut question being asked when we ask "How much support does P get from G?" It would not be surprising if the same were true of the question "How much does evidence E support hypothesis A?"
>
> (Christensen 1999: 439)

Hence, a purely example/intuition-based approach to finding measures of evidence is misguided, since different questions are asked. But one can set up criteria which *all* reasonable measures of evidential support have to satisfy. Then, a lot of measures drop from the list. The remaining ones can be used to model coherence (see the following section), to tackle longstanding philosophy of science puzzles such as the Duhem-Quine problem (see Earman 1992), and they can be connected to empirical evidence in psychology, delivering insights into human reasoning.

To illuminate the strategy, we discuss the *problem of irrelevant conjunctions*. If your watch yields strong evidence that your philosophy seminar is about to begin, this should not be strong evidence for the claim that your philosophy seminar is about to begin *and* that your favorite football club is going to win the national championship. The latter proposition just seems to be irrelevant to the evidential reasoning. Formally, if E is (strong) evidence for A, then E should not always be (strong) evidence for A plus an arbitrary claim X. However, all measures of evidence yield that E is evidence for A.X, too, due to the positive impact of E on A:

> *Proposition 1 (Fitelson 2002)*: Assume that E is evidence for A and that $P(E|A.X) = P(E|A)$ for a sentence X consistent with A. Then E is evidence for A.X, too, for any measure of support.

In other words, if we tack a conjunct to our belief in question that does not change the likelihood of the evidence, then the evidence relation extends to the conjunction as well. For instance, the seminar schedule and the precision of your watch are apparently independent of the results of football matches. And precisely such conjuncts are the ones we would call "arbitrary" or "irrelevant," leading to the counterintuitive Proposition 1, *regardless of the used measure*. Therefore it is important that in such situations, an evidence measure c satisfies $c(A, E) > c(A.X, E)$, i.e. E is weaker evidence for the conjunction $A.X$ than for the original proposition A. It turns out that such a result is available, and that the paradox can be mitigated:

> *Proposition 2 (Hawthorne and Fitelson 2004):* Assume that E is evidence for A and $P(E|A.X) = P(E|A)$ for a proposition X with $P(X|A.K) \neq 1$. Then the evidence E lends to A exceeds the evidence E lends to $A.X$, for d, l, and s, e.g. $d(A, E) > d(A. X, E)$. But for the log-ratio measure r, we always get $r(A, E) = r(A.X, E)$.

Thus, the measure r drops from our list of candidate measures: If E is evidence for A, then E is equally strong evidence for $A.X$ for an irrelevant X, and this is apparently an unacceptable result.

These results do not only affect the debate about evidence measures -- they are important for the psychology of human reasoning as well. You might have heard about the *conjunction fallacy* observed by Tversky and Kahneman (1983): Take the propositions

- E: Linda is 31 years old, single, outspoken, and very bright. She majored in philosophy. As a student, she was deeply concerned with issues of discrimination and social justice, and also participated in anti-nuclear demonstrations.
- A: Linda is a bank teller.
- $A.X$: Linda is a feminist and a bank teller.

Subjects were asked to assess whether A or $A.X$ is more probable given evidence E. Strikingly, they predominantly judged $A.X$ to be more probable, thereby violating the probabilistic law that for each A and X, $P(A.X) \leq P(A)$. Or in other words, a proposition cannot be more credible than one of its consequences. How shall we interpret this result? Are the subjects unaware of elementary logical laws? We need not draw that conclusion. In terms of our measures of evidence, we can tell a story about their judgments (see Crupi et al. 2008; Schupbach 2010). The subjects intuitively judged the *support* relations between E, A and $A.X$. Obviously, E is strong evidence for X ("Linda is a feminist") and by proposition 1, at least weak evidence for $A.X$, whereas E is equally obviously evidence *against* A. This implies a fortiori that E is much stronger evidence for $A.X$ than for A. Thus, the subjects apparently confounded the concepts of high probability and the concept of evidential support, instead of committing a mathematical fallacy (but see the alternative story of Hartmann and Meijs 2010). Note that this formal analysis of the problem is measure-sensitive: as proposition 2 shows, it would not be available if we used r as the measure of support. Similarly, claims of social epistemology can be tackled by means of evidence measures. For instance, Douven (2010) investigates whether "evidence of evidence" is evidence for a proposition, using the different explications of evidence presented in this section. All this illustrates that Bayesian techniques are not (only) a mathematician's delight, but valuable means of tackling traditional epistemological problems. The next section describes Bayesian models of coherence and testimony.

4. Coherence and Testimony

In epistemology, the coherence theory of justification is the main alternative to foundationalism. It says that a set of propositions is justified if it coheres well (BonJour 1985). The theory is attractive as it avoids the problems of foundationalism, but it has its problems as well. Most importantly, it is not clear what it means that a set of propositions coheres. How can this notion be made more precise? The situation is complicated by the observation that coherence is a gradual notion. Some sets of propositions seem more coherent, while others are less coherent. Apparently, we need a measure that specifies how coherent a set of propositions is. Constructing such a measure might also help to get a better grasp of what coherence is. Moreover, the availability of a coherence measure will help addressing longstanding problems in the coherence theory of justification. For example, one might ask if and when coherence is truth-conducive, i.e. under which conditions is the coherence of a set of propositions an indicator of its truth? Bayesian epistemologists have addressed these questions and made substantial progress over the last couple of years. A natural way to start the construction of a measure of coherence is to depart with an epistemological intuition and to formalize it. The following two intuitions about coherence can be identified:

(R) Coherence as positive relevance.
(O) Coherence as relative overlap in probability space.

(R) expresses the intuition that the elements of a coherent set mutually support each other (in the sense of the definition of relative evidence). Such sets of propositions seem to be more coherent than sets of independent propositions or sets whose elements are negatively relevant to each other. (O) expresses the intuition that identical propositions are considered to be coherent. This is especially plausible if one adopts a witness scenario: Imagine that several independent witnesses of a crime give identical reports ("The butler left the crime scene with a bloody knife in his hand."). Obviously, the given reports are maximally coherent and any deviation reduces the coherence accordingly. Probabilistically speaking, identical reports maximally overlap in probability space. So, according to (O), coherence measures the relative overlap of the propositions in probability space. Coherence measures can be classified according to which intuition they formalize. For instance, the *Shogenji measure*, the first explicit coherence measure in the literature, is a pure relevance measure (Shogenji 1999). For two propositions A and B, it is given by the following expression:

$$C_S(A, B) := \frac{P(A|B)}{P(A)} = \frac{P(B|A)}{P(B)} = \frac{P(A.B)}{P(A)P(B)} \qquad (3)$$

$C_S(A, B)$ measures how relevant B is for A, i.e. how much the probability of A is raised if one learns that B is true. Note that the expression is symmetrical in A and B, which is a natural request for a coherence measure. Hence, $C_S(A, B)$ also expresses how relevant A is for B. According to this Bayesian explication, the coherence of a set of propositions is a property of this set *relative* to a probability measure P. Different agents with different probability functions might, therefore, come to different coherence assignments. They might also rank different sets differently according to their coherence. The expression on the right-hand side indicates how the Shogenji measure can be generalized to more than two propositions. This generalization, however, is problematic as Fitelson (2003) has shown. The *Glass–Olsson measure* (Glass 2002: Olsson 2005) is a pure overlap measure:

$$C_O(A, B) := \frac{P(A.B)}{P(A \vee B)} \qquad (4)$$

Also $C_O(A, B)$ can be generalized to more than two propositions in a natural way. It turns out that none of these and related measures always leads to an intuitively satisfactory coherence ordering of sets of propositions (Bovens and Hartmann 2003a; Douven and Meijs 2007). This suggests the search for more complex measures that take both intuitions—positive relevance and overlap—into account. This is achieved by the Bovens–Hartmann measure (Bovens and Hartmann 2003a) and the family of measures that generalize the Bovens–Hartmann measure (Douven and Meijs 2007). Contrary to the Shogenji measure and the Glass–Olsson measure, the construction of these measures does not start with the formalization of an epistemic intuition. It rather starts with the question what the *function* of the coherence of a set of propositions is. One obvious answer is that the coherence of a set of propositions *boosts our confidence in the truth of these propositions*. To make this approach explicit, we need to introduce a *witness scenario*. Consider a set of propositions $S^{(n)} := \{A_1, \ldots, A_n\}$. Assume that each proposition A_i ($i = 1, \ldots, n$) is confirmed by a report E_i of a different witness. The n witnesses are independent and have the same reliability. The construction of a coherence measure then proceeds in three steps:

1. Work out the ratio of the posterior probability $P(A_1, \ldots, A_n | E_1, \ldots, E_n)$ and the prior probability $P(A_1, \ldots, A_n)$. The posterior probability measures the probability of the set of propositions *after* the reports came in. The prior probability measures the probability of the set of propositions *before* the reports came in. The ratio of both, then, measures the confidence boost in $S^{(n)}$. This takes intuition (R) into account.—Notably, Douven and Meijs (2007) replace the ratio measure by alternative evidence measures (e.g. *d* and *l* from section 3), thus obtaining a family of coherence measures.
2. Normalize this ratio to make sure that a set of propositions which fully overlap in probability space, has maximal coherence. This takes intuition (O) into account. It is easy to see that the resulting function cannot be a coherence measure as it depends on the reliability of the witnesses. Coherence, however, is traditionally conceived as an intrinsic property of a set of propositions and independent of the reliability of the witnesses.
3. To solve this problem, it is requested that a set $S^{(n)}$ is more coherent than a set $S'^{(n)}$ if and only if the normalized ratio of posterior and prior probability is greater for $S^{(n)}$ than for $S'^{(n)}$ *for all values* of the reliability of the witnesses. It is easy to see that this entails that there are sets of propositions $X^{(n)}$ and $Y^{(n)}$ that cannot be ordered according to their coherence, which is also intuitively plausible. See Bovens and Hartmann (2003a) and (2003b) for details.

However, it turns out that none of the coherence measures proposed so far is without problems (Meijs and Douven 2005; Bovens and Hartmann 2005). So instead of starting with various armchair intuitions, it might be more promising to go empirical and study the coherence judgments or real people. The results can then be confronted with the coherence measures put forward in the philosophical literature. It is also possible that the data suggest a new coherence measure. For preliminary work in this direction, see Harris and Hahn (2009) (see also Oaksford and Chater 2007). It is hoped that a combination of empirical studies, formal modeling and conceptual analysis will help to resolve the deadlock in the current debate about coherence measures.

Formal analyses of coherence have already been used to examine the relation between coherence and truth. While recent theoretical results seem to rule out a general connection (Olsson 2005), in certain cases coherence is an indicator of truth in the following sense: if two sets of propositions of equal cardinality have the same prior probability and can be ordered according to their coherence, then the more coherent of the two also has the higher posterior probability if all witnesses have the same reliability.

We conclude this section with a discussion of testimony. Epistemologists have stressed that much of our knowledge derives from the testimony of others: parents, teachers, textbooks etc. While this seems true, more specific questions can be asked. For example, how shall the testimonies of several witnesses be combined? And how shall we change our beliefs in the light of testimonial evidence? Bayesian epistemology has the resources to make these questions more precise and to answer them. In *Bayesian Epistemology*, Bovens and Hartmann (2003a) develop a general methodology, using the theory of Bayesian networks (Neapolitan 2003), that facilitate a detailed analysis.

More specifically, models with more or less dependent witnesses of different reliability can be considered and a range of interesting results can be proven. For example, "too-odd-to-be-true" reasoning can be studied: imagine that several independent and partially reliable witnesses give the same report; they all claim that they saw no. 1 in a lineup of n people at the crime scene. We ask: When are we more convinced that the witnesses tell the truth, if the number of suspects is, say, 2 or if it is 100? Most people would say that we are the more convinced in the truth of the reports, the larger the number of suspects is. This makes much sense as it becomes increasingly unlikely that a witness hits the truth by accident if the number of suspects is large. The probability for this is only $1/n$ and decreases if n goes up. From a Bayesian perspective, however, different perspectives on this phenomenon are possible: On the one hand, coinciding reports provide the better relative evidence (cf. section 3) the higher the number of suspects is. This seems to confirm our intuitive judgment. But on the other hand, with increasing number of suspects, the prior probability of no. 1 being responsible for the crime declines. Thus the posterior probability of the witnesses telling the truth falls, too, and the coincidence is "too odd to be true." (Note the analogy to the Linda case!) This example illustrates once more that Bayesian epistemology provides fruitful tools to tackle questions of coherence, testimony and reliable evidence. For detailed models and discussion, see Olsson (2002) and Bovens and Hartmann (2003a: ch. 5).

5. Concluding Remarks

We conclude this essay with a comparison of traditional epistemology and Bayesian epistemology and a few remarks about the future of epistemology. Traditional epistemology typically starts with an *epistemic intuition*, developed, perhaps, by examining an example in some detail. Think about the Gettier cases as an illustration. These intuitions inspire a philosophical theory which, in turn, is criticized by other examples, triggered by different or more fine-grained intuitions.

Bayesian epistemology, on the other hand, draws much of its power from the mathematical machinery of probability theory. It starts with a *mathematical intuition*. The construction of Bayesian models is much triggered by what is mathematically elegant and feasible (e.g. Spirtes et al. 2001). The mathematics develops a life of its own (to adopt a phrase due to Hacking), and the comparison with intuitive examples comes only *after* the Bayesian account is given.

One of the goals of this essay was to show that traditional epistemology and Bayesian epistemology can learn from each other: Bayesian epistemology makes certain debates in traditional epistemology more precise, and traditional epistemology inspires Bayesian accounts.

Both Bayesian epistemology and traditional epistemology do not much consider empirical data. Both are based on intuitions, be they mathematical or epistemological. This might be a problem as privilege is given to the philosopher's intuitions. However, recent work in experimental philosophy (Knobe and Nichols 2008) has shown that non-philosophers might have different intuitions. While it is debatable how seriously these intuitions should be taken (maybe people are simply wrong!), it seems clear that both can profit from taking empirical studies into account so that epistemology becomes, at the end, an endeavor to which philosophers with various tools (conceptual analysis, formal methods, and empirical studies) contribute.

The Bayesian framework is very convenient for these studies. It is easy to use, very powerful, and it comes with principles that can be made plausible on rational grounds (Dutch Book arguments, Principal Principle, Bayesian Conditionalization). Moreover, this framework has been very successful as the various applications in epistemology and philosophy of science demonstrate. It has been a progressive research program, to use Lakatos's terminology. But the Bayesian framework might reach its limits just as a scientific theory has to be given up at some point. It is therefore advisable that philosophers also keep on paying attention to other formal frameworks such as alternative theories of uncertainty (such as the Dempster–Shafer theory; see Haenni and Hartmann 2006) and epistemic logics.

References

BonJour, L. (1985) *The Structure of Empirical Knowledge*. Cambridge, MA: Harvard University Press.
Bovens, L. and S. Hartmann (2003a) *Bayesian Epistemology*. Oxford: Oxford University Press.
Bovens, L. and S. Hartmann (2003b) "Solving the Riddle of Coherence," *Mind* 112: 601–634.
Bovens, L. and S. Hartmann (2005) "Why There Cannot Be a Single Probabilistic Measure of Coherence," *Erkenntnis* 63: 361–374.
Chater, N. and M. Oaksford (eds.) (2008) *The Probabilistic Mind: Prospects for Bayesian Cognitive Science*. Oxford: Oxford University Press.
Christensen, D. (1999) "Measuring Confirmation," *Journal of Philosophy* 96: 437–461.
Crupi, V., B. Fitelson and K. Tentori (2008) "Probability, Confirmation and the Conjunction Fallacy," *Thinking and Reasoning* 14(2): 182–199.
Crupi, V., K. Tentori and M. Gonzalez (2007) On Bayesian Measures of Evidential Support: Theoretical and Empirical Issues. *Philosophy of Science* 74(2): 229–252.
Douven, I. (2010) "Is Evidence of Evidence Evidence?," *under review*.
Douven, I. and W. Meijs (2007) "Measuring Coherence," *Synthese* 156: 405–425.
Earman, J. (1992) *Bayes or Bust?* Cambridge, MA: The MIT Press.
Fitelson, B. (2002) "Putting the Irrelevance Back into the Problem of Irrelevant Conjunction," *Philosophy of Science* 69: 611–622.
Fitelson, B. (2003) "A Probabilistic Theory of Coherence," *Analysis* 63: 194–199.
Glass, D. (2002) "Coherence, Explanation, and Bayesian Networks," in: M. O'Neill et al. (eds.), *AICS 2002*, LNAI 2464, 177–182.

Haenni, R. and S. Hartmann (2006) "Modeling Partially Reliable Information Sources: A General Approach Based on Dempster–Shafer Theory," *Information Fusion* 7: 361–379.

Hájek, A. (2003). What Conditional Probability Could Not Be. *Synthese* 137: 273–323.

Harris, A.J.L. and Hahn, U. (2009) "Bayesian Rationality in Evaluating Multiple Testimonies: Incorporating the Role of Coherence," *Journal of Experimental Psychology: Learning, Memory, and Cognition* 35: 1366–1373.

Hartmann, S. and W. Meijs (2010) "Walter the Banker: The Conjunction Fallacy Reconsidered," to appear in *Synthese* [DOI: 10.1007/s11229-009-9694-6].

Hawthorne, J. and B. Fitelson (2004) "Re-solving Irrelevant Conjunction with Probabilistic Independence," *Philosophy of Science* 71: 505–514.

Howson, C. and P. Urbach (1993) *Scientific Reasoning: The Bayesian Approach*. La Salle: Open Court.

Joyce, J. (2008) "Bayes' Theorem," in: E. Zalta (ed.), *The Stanford Encyclopedia of Philosophy* (Fall 2008 Edition).

Kemeny, J.G. (1955) "Fair Bets and Inductive Probabilities," *Journal of Symbolic Logic* 20: 263–273.

Knobe, J. and S. Nichols (2008) *Experimental Philosophy*. New York: Oxford University Press.

Kolmogorov, A.N. (1933) *Grundbegriffe der Wahrscheinlichkeitsrechnung*. Berlin: Springer. English translation: Foundations of the Theory of Probability. New York: Chelsea 1950.

Lewis, D. (1980) "A Subjectivist's Guide to Objective Chance," in: R. Jeffrey (ed.), *Studies in Inductive Logic and Probability*, Vol II., Berkeley: University of California Press, 263–293.

Meijs, W. and I. Douven (2005) "Bovens and Hartmann on Coherence," *Mind* 114: 355–363.

Neapolitan, R. (2003) *Learning Bayesian Networks*. Upper Saddle River, NJ: Prentice Hall.

Oaksford, M. and N. Chater (2007) *Bayesian Rationality: The Probabilistic Approach to Human Reasoning*. Oxford: Oxford University Press.

Olsson, E. (2002) "Corroborating Testimony, Probability and Surprise," *The British Journal for the Philosophy of Science* 53(2): 273–288.

Olsson, E. (2005) *Against Coherence: Truth, Probability, and Justification*. Oxford: Oxford University Press.

Ramsey, F.P. (1978) "Truth and Probability," in: Hugh Mellor (ed.), *Foundations: Essays in Philosophy, Logic, Mathematics and Economics*, 58–100. London: Routledge. Original article published in 1926.

Reichenbach, H. (1956) *The Direction of Time*. Berkeley: University of California Press.

Rosenkrantz, R.D. (1994) "Bayesian Confirmation: Paradise Regained," *British Journal for the Philosophy of Science* 45: 467–476.

Schupbach, J. (2010) "Is the Conjunction Fallacy tied to Probabilistic Confirmation?," to appear in *Synthese* [DOI: 10.1007/s11229-009-9698-2].

Shogenji, T. (1999) "Is Coherence Truth-Conducive?" *Analysis* 59: 338–345.

Spirtes, P., C. Glymour, and R. Scheines (2001). *Causation, Prediction and Search*. Cambridge, MA: MIT Press.

Strevens, M. (1999) "Objective Probability as a Guide to the World," *Philosophical Studies* 95: 243–275.

Tversky, A. and D. Kahneman (1983) "Extensional versus Intuitive Reasoning: The Conjunction Fallacy in Probability Judgment," *Psychological Review* 90: 293–315.

Further Reading

Carnap, R. (1950) *Logical Foundations of Probability*. Chicago: Chicago University Press. (A classic, nowadays out-of-fashion theory of evidence.)

Fitelson, B. (2001a) *Studies in Bayesian Confirmation Theory*. PhD thesis, University of Wisconsin, Madison. (Comprehensive overview of the debate on measures of evidence.)

Jeffrey, R. (1983). *The Logic of Decision*. 2nd ed. Chicago: University of Chicago Press. (Explicates Jeffrey Conditionalization—a more general version of Bayesian Conditionalization that allows to conditionalize on uncertain evidence.)

Williamson, J. (2005) *Bayesian Nets and Causality: Philosophical and Computational Foundations*. Oxford: Oxford University Press. (An introduction to objective Bayesianism—the position that only one degree of belief is rational in a given information situation.)

56
THEORIES OF BELIEF CHANGE
André Fuhrmann

Synchronic Versus Diachronic Epistemic Justification

Karl sees Peter on a bicycle. He believes that if Peter rides a bicycle, then he owns that bicycle. Thus, Karl believes (at time t) that

(*p*) Peter owns a bicycle.

Here is a traditional epistemological problem: Let K be Karl's state of belief at t. Are all of Karl's beliefs justified? In particular, are the two beliefs

(*a*) Peter rides a bicycle

and

(*b*) If Peter rides a bicycle, than he owns that bicycle

justified? For, if they are, then they jointly entail p.

This is the problem of epistemic justification concerning actual beliefs. We take a time slice of an agent's beliefs and ask whether the beliefs at the given point of time are justified. This problem of *synchronic justification* enjoys such a central status in modern epistemology that it is frequently taken to *define* the subject.

In a way, this is rather unfortunate. For, there is another problem, at least as pressing as the problem of synchronic justification, which besets our states of belief.

Suppose that Karl learns from a source he recognizes as reliable that Peter does not own a bicycle. He therefore resolves to retract his belief that p. In other words, he resolves to move from K to a belief state K-*without*-p. But in K the belief that p is deductively forced by the beliefs a and b (= $a \to p$). So in order to give up p, Karl must give up at least a or b. And backtracking from a and b in the deductive network of K we might find further beliefs involved in producing p. There are thus many candidate states that all satisfy the requirement that p be no longer believed—including the initial Cartesian state, *cogito*. The challenge is to justify a choice of such a candidate state as the unique successor K-*without*-p to K. This is the problem of justifying belief change or of *diachronic justification*, as we shall say.

The above example shows clearly that no unique successor belief state K' is in general determined by a given origin state K, a piece of evidence and a logical consequence relation that calculates the consequences of K and the new evidence or backtracks unwelcome consequences to subsets of K. Transitions to unique successor states essentially involve an element of *choice*.

The problem of synchronic justification consists in finding items that could plausibly replace the variable in the schema

(S) = $x R K$

where R indicates the relation of justification. Prominent candidates for x in (S) are fundamental beliefs, coherent integration of beliefs or reliable causal groundings.

In the diachronic case the schema under consideration is this:

(D) = $x R (K, K')$

where the object of justification is a pair representing a transition from an origin state K to a successor state K'.

One might ask whether the two problems are distinct. This is an intricate question. If we could somehow derive a solution to the problem of diachronic justification from an extant account of synchronic justification the apparent dominance of the synchronic problem in modern epistemology would emerge as well-deserved in retrospect. But there is no plausible such derivation in sight.

By contrast, the reduction of synchronic to diachronic justification seems to be a more promising enterprise. As a first attempt consider the Cartesian proposal: A belief state K (and thereby each belief in K) counts as justified if and only if it is connected by a chain of justified belief changes to an unassailable *urcorpus* of beliefs. The term 'urcorpus' is taken from Levi (see e.g. Levi 1980). It does not matter here what one takes to be part of the *urcorpus*. (Levi, by the way, does not advocate assigning the *urcorpus* a foundational role.) At best, however, the Cartesian proposal affords a partial reduction of justified belief to justified belief change, since the *urcorpus* cannot itself be the result of justified belief changes. Approaches that take their inspiration in a pragmatist theory of inquiry do away with ultimate epistemic foundations. In a way, such approaches could be taken to call into question the very problem of synchronic justification: There is a real problem of legitimately fixing one's beliefs; and there is the bogus problem of legitimizing beliefs already fixed. (See Peirce 1877 and Levi's "Truth, fallibility and the growth of knowledge" in Levi 1984.)

In sum, there are two prima facie problems of epistemic justification: The problem of justifying one's presently held beliefs and The problem of justifying a change in one's present beliefs. It is by no means obvious that the one problem can be reduced to the other. Moreover, in a first person perspective the problem of justifying belief change seems much more pressing than the problem of justifying presently held beliefs. For, on the one hand, a proposition believed is a proposition held to be true. On the other hand, attempts at justification are responses to living doubts. But it is incoherent to doubt something that at the same time is held to be true. Living doubt as to present beliefs arises when hitherto unknown evidence becomes available. Then we face the question how to accommodate the new evidence. Such accommodation needs justification. But the required justification is one that pertains to a belief change, not to the belief state prior to the new evidence.

In the light of these considerations it is all the more surprising that theories of diachronic justification have been largely neglected for a long time, with a few exceptions. Only in the 1980s—again, with a few exceptions—philosophers started to develop systematic approaches to the problem. Since then theories of belief change (or theory change or belief revision) have rapidly progressed to a presently rich field of investigation with many crossconnections to other problems, including some of particular concern to computer scientists.

2. The Classical Theory of Belief Change: AGM

The Fundamental Problem

Let us start by asking how much structure in a belief state we need to invest for an interesting problem of belief change to emerge.

We ascribe beliefs to agents. We usually do this by using language, though what we ascribe, using language, are not linguistic items. When using language to ascribe beliefs, we proceed on the innocuous presupposition that sentences can be used to represent beliefs. When we refer to the beliefs of an agent, we can, therefore, do so by representing these beliefs by a set of sentences. Of course, the language needs to be expressive enough to represent the beliefs we are interested in representing. Should that prove difficult, we might start by restricting our attention to an easily representable kind of beliefs.

Beliefs have consequences. A believer is committed to the consequences of his beliefs. There are believers who fail to live up to their commitments. But we do expect believers to acknowledge their commitments once they are clearly and patiently pointed out to them. This expectation is not of an inductive but of a normative kind: One *ought* to acknowledge the consequences of one's beliefs. Thus belief states—as they ought to be—are closed under consequence.

We are now ready to formulate the fundamental problem of belief change. Suppose an agent's belief state K contains beliefs A and B from which follows (by consequence) a further belief C. By closure under consequence, C is also in K. Suppose now that a decision has been taken to remove C from K. How should this decision be implemented? This is the given change problem. At least one of A or B has to give way. What should the resulting belief state not containing C be like?

At this point we could stop with the simple observation that K without A, or K without B, or K without both, or even the closure under consequence of *cogito* are all successors to K satisfying the condition that C be no longer believed. Belief change would thus be relational rather than functional: There simply is no unique successor to K.

Since relational belief change is unhelpful (though see Lindström and Rabinowicz 1991 for a dissenting view) we need to assume some more structure on belief states which delivers a ranking of possible successors such that each change problem issues in a unique successor.

To summarize, we need two assumptions for posing the problem. First, beliefs must be representable in some language for which we can define a relation of consequence. Equivalently we could represent beliefs by sets of possible worlds, with inclusion doing duty for (the converse of) consequence; see e.g. Grove (1988) or Stalnaker (2009). Second, the beliefs held in a belief state are closed under consequence. Some philosophers have argued that for certain purposes it might be advisable to keep track of the base beliefs from which complete belief states are generated by closing under consequence:

see Fuhrmann (1991b) and Hansson (1992). Even if one prefers base changes over theory changes, the problem of belief change emerges in the same way, i.e. only once we consider logical commitments. Finally, a third assumption is needed for solving the problem: Belief states are not merely closed sets of beliefs; they have further structure ranking some (clusters of) beliefs higher than others.

The Sources of the AGM-Theory

The classical theory of belief change has been developed in the 1980s by Carlos Alchourrón, Peter Gärdenfors and David Makinson (hence AGM for short). The "pure" theory of belief change resulted as an abstraction from two more concrete and well-known problems.

Alchourrón's principal interest lay in the concept of legal derogation. This is the act of a legislator of revoking a regulation from a legal code with the implicit intention of thereby also removing everything from the code that implies that regulation (see Alchourrón and Makinson 1981, p. 127).

Gärdenfors tried to elaborate the idea of belief change implicit in the following much-quoted passage from Frank P. Ramsey:

> If two people are arguing "If p will q?" and are both in doubt as to p, they are adding p hypothetically to their stock of knowledge and arguing on that basis about q.
>
> ("General propositions and causality" (1929), in Ramsey 1931)

Thus the theory of belief change to be developed was thought to be constrained by the acceptance test for conditionals suggested by Ramsey. We shall come back to this constraint below. Gärdenfors (1988) is the first book-length treatment of theory change. The three authors joined forces in the standard exposition, of the AGM-theory (Alchourrón et al. 1985). The development of the AGM-theory has been much inspired and critically accompanied by the work of Isaac Levi (see in particular Levi 1984, 1991, 2004). (Rott (2001) summarizes the rise of the AGM-theory over 20 years, provides important missing links and draws out connections with defeasible and practical reasoning. Hansson (1999) is a textbook-style exposition of the AGM-theory containing also some important extensions.)

In the AGM-theory it is assumed that the language used to represent belief states contains all boolean connectives and that the consequence operation (or relation) under which belief states are to be closed is a closure operation in the usual Tarskian sense, including classical logical consequence. As pointed out in Fuhrmann (1997a) and (1997b), for the most part of the theory no such assumptions are really necessary. In fact, the theory enjoys such a degree of abstraction that it covers not only belief change but changes of any items that can be represented in a closure systems.

The consequence operation Cn is thus expected to satisfy the following conditions (for any sets X and Y of sentences):

$X \subseteq Cn(X)$;
if $X \subseteq Y$, then $Cn(X) \subseteq Cn(Y)$;
$Cn(Cn(X)) = Cn(X)$;
if $A \in Cn(X)$, then $\exists X' \subseteq X$: X' is finite and $A \in Cn(X')$.

Sometimes we may also write relationally:

$X \vdash A$ for $A \in Cn(X)$ and $A \equiv B$ for $Cn(A) = Cn(B)$.

Since belief states K are closed under logical consequence we have (for every sentence A)

$A \in K$ iff $K \vdash A$.

Suppose now that we receive input information that triggers a decision to incorporate A into one's present state of belief K. There are two cases to distinguish.

First, A is consistent with K. In that case incorporation is simple: We add A to K and then close again under consequence. We write $K + A$ for this operation of *expanding* K by A. Expansion is easily defined: $K + A := Cn(K \cup \{A\})$, where Cn is the operation of taking the consequences of a set of beliefs.

Second, A is inconsistent with K, i.e. $\neg A$ is in K. Here simple expansion would result in an inconsistent belief state—of which classically there is only one, the trivial belief state including all beliefs. Thus a more subtle operation is called for which will be called the *revision* of K by A, $K * A$.

It is natural to think of revision as a composed operation: First we have to withdraw beliefs from K so as to make our beliefs compatible with A; then we can add A by expansion. The result of retracting from K to a weaker belief state is called a *contraction*. In the case at hand, we would need to contract K by $\neg A$; then we could expand the result, $K - \neg A$, by A without danger of inconsistency. This reduction of revisions to contractions followed by an expansion is the *Levi Identity*:

$K * A = (K - \neg A) + A$.

Given the Levi Identity the theory of belief changes reduces to a theory of contractions (and expansions). We note in passing that one could also take the other direction, from contractions to revisions, via the so-called Harper (or Gärdenfors) Identity: $K - A = (K * \neg A) \cap K$.

The strategy of the theory is simple. On the one hand we transpose plausible conditions on contractions (or revisions) into the language of set-theory, thereby giving an implicit characterization of the operation. On the other hand, we try to give a recipe for solving a given contraction problem, thereby producing models in which contractions can explicitly be defined. Finally, the two approaches need to be linked by a representation result: An operation satisfies the contraction postulates just in case it can be defined as a contraction in a model. If postulates on the one hand and models on the other hand are independently plausible, such a representation result makes for a prima facie stable theory of contractions and of belief change in general. Of the four models furnished in the AGM-theory we shall here present two: partial meet contractions and systems of spheres. The other two are safe contractions, as in Alchourrón and Makinson (1981), and models in terms of epistemic entrenchment, for which see Gäerdenfors (1988) and Rott (2001).

The AGM-Postulates

The postulates for contraction come in two groups:

Basic

(C1) Closure $\quad K - A = Cn(K-A)$
(C2) Success $\quad A \notin K-A$, if $\not\vdash A$
(C3) Inclusion $\quad K - A \subseteq K$
(C4) Vacuity $\quad$ If $A \notin K$, then $K - A = K$
(C5) Recovery $\quad K \subseteq (K - A) + A$
(C6) Congruence $\quad$ If $A \equiv B$, then $K - A = K - B$

Supplementary

(C7) Conjunction 1 $\quad K - A \cap K - B \subseteq K - (A \wedge B)$
(C8) Conjunction 2 $\quad$ If $A \notin K - (A \wedge B)$, then $K - (A \wedge B) \subseteq K - A$

Likewise the postulates for the revision operation:

Basic

(R1) Closure $\quad K * A = Cn(K * A)$
(R2) Success $\quad A \in K * A$
(R3) Inclusion $\quad K * A \subseteq K + A$
(R4) Preservation $\quad$ If $\neg A \notin K$, then $K * A = K + A$
(R5) Consistency $\quad$ If $\bot \in K * A$, then $\vdash \neg A$
(R6) Congruence $\quad$ If $A \equiv B$, then $K * A = K * B$

Supplementary

(R7) Conjunction 1 $\quad K * (A \wedge B) \subseteq (K * A) + B$
(R8) Conjunction 2 $\quad$ If $\neg B \notin K * A$, then $K * A) + B \subseteq K*(A \wedge B)$

The labels must suffice here to indicate the rationale for each of the postulates; only Recovery (C5) will be considered more closely in a moment.

The postulates harmonize: We can derive the revision postulates from the contraction postulates via the Levi-Identity $K * A = (K - \neg A) + A$. (Note that for this derivation Recovery is not needed.) Conversely we can derive the contraction postulates (including Recovery) from the revision postulates via the Harper Identity $K - A = (K * \neg A) \cap K$.

Recovery requires that in contracting we should avoid gratuitous loss of information. Without such a condition contractions are insufficiently constrained by the other postulates: They could result in too small belief states. For example, the operation defined by $K - A = Cn(\emptyset)$ would satisfy all the remaining C-postulates (Makinson 1987).

The idea that contractions should minimize losses of information is essential to a theory of rational belief changes. Thus the theory requires a condition like Recovery. Yet Recovery stands out in at least three other respects.

First, as pointed out above, Recovery is redundant in deriving revisions from contractions.

Second, unlike the other postulates, Recovery is sensitive to the underlying logic: It depends essentially on closure under *classical* consequence. For every $B \in K$ we have by closure for every A, $\neg A \vee B \in K$. When we then contract by A, there is no logical compulsion to remove $\neg A \vee B$. Thus in the models considered below we invariably have $\neg A \vee B$ in every plausible contraction candidate whence also in $K - A$. But then expanding $K - A$ by A reinstates any B that was previously removed from K. (The last move proceeds by disjunctive syllogism, an inference called into question by relevant logicians among others; see e.g. Dunn 1986.)

Third, under certain circumstances Recovery seems implausible. In order to remove A from K, we typically need to remove stronger beliefs that imply A from K. But when we then reinsert the weaker A, why and how should we then regain those stronger beliefs? The circumstances that call Recovery into question are easily identified: Recovery fails indeed when the objects of contractions are open belief bases instead of closed belief states. For certain purposes it might be preferable to change states of beliefs by making all incisions in an axiomatic, usually finite representation of such a state might see (Fuhrmann 1991b, 1997a; Hansson 1992). This is also the more general format for a theory of belief change. The AGM-theory, however, operates under the assumptions that the units of change are *closed* sets of belief, i.e. theories in the logical sense.

The Ramsey-Test for Conditionals

One of the initial motivations for developing a theory of belief revision was the problem of characterizing the operation of "adding something hypothetically to a stock of belief" such that an acceptance or assertion condition for certain conditionals would result, as suggested by Ramsey. Here then is the *Ramsey Test* for counterfactual conditionals:

RT. $A \sqsupset B \in K$ iff $B \in K * A$.

One might take *RT* either (from right to left) as a recipe for generating a logic of conditionals, given a theory of revisions, or (from left to right) as generating a theory of revisions from a given logic of conditionals, or simply as a bridging principle requiring conditionals and revisions to walk hand in hand.

Any such aspirations have to be laid to rest by observing that *RT* requires revisions to be monotonic:

MR. If $K \subseteq H$, then $K * A \subseteq H * A$.

Monotonicity is not a desirable feature for revisions; counterexamples are not difficult to find. Yet we do not need to remain at the level of assessing intuitions. For, from MR we quickly slip to triviality. It can be shown that MR, Preservation and Consistency are compatible only on pain of triviality. The result was found by Gärdenfors (1988) and will be proved in a moment. It is closely related to Lewis's impossibility theorem (1976) concerning the identification of probabilities of conditionals with conditional probability and Arrow's theorem concerning social choice under certain conditions (see Leitgeb and Segerberg 2007).

We suppose that there are A, B and K such that A and B are independent in K and K is not opinionated as to A and B. That is to say,

(1) neither $A \to B$ nor $B \to A$ is in K, and
(2) neither A, $\neg A$, B nor $\neg B$ is in K.

(1) and (2) give the sense in which the revision task is supposed to be non-trivial.
First step: Let $K' = K + A$ and $K'' = K + B$. Then ...

$$\cfrac{\cfrac{A \in K'}{A \in K' + \neg(A \wedge B)} \quad \cfrac{\cfrac{B \notin K'}{A \wedge B \notin K'}}{K' + \neg(A \wedge B) = K' * \neg(A \wedge B)}}{A \in K' * \neg(A \wedge B)} \text{Preservation}$$

The same reasoning also gives

$B \in K'' * \neg(A \wedge B)$.

Second step: Let $H = K + (A \wedge B)$. Then ...

$$\cfrac{\cfrac{\cfrac{K' \subseteq H \supseteq K''}{K' * \neg(A \wedge B) \subseteq H * \neg(A \wedge B) \supseteq K'' * \neg(A \wedge B)} \text{MR}}{A \in K' * \neg(A \wedge B) \subseteq H * \neg(A \wedge B) \supseteq K'' * \neg(A \wedge B) \ni B} \text{first step}}{\cfrac{A \wedge B \in H * \neg(A \wedge B)}{\text{contradiction!}} \text{Consistency}}$$

Various ways of constraining *RT* in such a way that its spirit is maintained have been explored. The general lesson seems to be this: Caution needs to be exercised when trying to systematically connect factual beliefs ("objectual beliefs") with beliefs reflecting the behavior or content of belief states ("meta-beliefs"). This is confirmed by a similar impossibility result concerning the *Levi Test* for serious possibility. (Levi does not propose such a test. He notes that such a test for epistemic possibility might be suggested and counsels caution.)

LT. $\Diamond A \in K$ iff $\neg A \notin K$.

The modality in *LT* is what is called a reflective modality in Fuhrmann (1989); all such tests of a reflective kind, including *LT* can be shown to be inconsistent.

Partial Meet Contraction

As pointed out above, belief change is fundamentally a choice problem. The partial meet models of AGM model this element of choice by brute force by simply assuming the existence of an appropriate choice function.

Suppose we decide to remove A from K. We might proceed as follows. First we collect all maximal subsets of K that do not entail A. (Let $K \perp A$ denote the family of such *remainders*.) Then we select the "best" of them. (Let s_K be a *choice function* that is defined on the family of subsets of K; if $K \perp A$ happens to be empty, then we let $s(K \perp A) = \{K\}$.)

In the sequel we omit the subscript K to the choice function s. But it is important to remember that the choice functions used represent the theoretical preferences of a given belief set K. These preferences might change after a contraction has been performed. It is for this reason that the AGM-theory does not cover in any interesting way iterated belief changes. For an attempt at tackling iterated changes see Darwiche and Pearl (1997). Finally we take what is common to all such best subsets. Thus

$$K - A := \bigcap s(K \perp A).$$

It is not difficult to verify that this definition of a contraction operation satisfies all the basic C-postulates.

Conversely, every contraction operation satisfying the basic C-postulates can be defined as a partial meet contraction. We prove this in a moment. Together the two observations yield the sought representation result: Essentially the same operation may be characterized implicitly by the postulates (C1–6) or explicitly defined as a partial meet contraction. Thus postulates and models support each other.

To prove that the postulates pick out partial meet contractions we assume that $K - (\ )$ satisfies (C1–6) and define a canonical selection function for K, σ, as follows:

$$(\sigma) \quad \sigma(K \perp A) := \begin{cases} \{X \in K \perp A : K - A \subseteq X\}, & \text{if } K \perp A \neq \emptyset; \\ \{K\}, & \text{otherwise.} \end{cases}$$

We need to show that σ (for K) is a selection function s_K of the above introduced kind. This is done by verifying five claims:

(1) σ is well-defined, i.e. $K \perp A = K \perp B$ entails $\sigma(K \perp A) = \sigma(K \perp B)$.
(2) $\sigma(K \perp A) = \{K\}$, if $K \perp A = \emptyset$.
(3) $\sigma(K \perp A) \subseteq K \perp A$, if $K \perp A \neq \emptyset$.
(4) $\sigma(K \perp A) \neq \emptyset$.
(5) $K - A = \bigcap \sigma(K \perp A)$.

(1–4) are more or less immediate reflections of the C-postulates. It will thus suffice to give the argument for (5). One direction, $K - A \subseteq \bigcap \sigma(K \perp A)$, is immediate from (σ) and Inclusion (C3). It remains to show

(*) If $B \notin K - A$, then $B \notin \bigcap \sigma(K \perp A)$

Case $A \notin K$. Then by Vacuity (C4) $K - A = K$ and so, according to (σ), $K = \bigcap \sigma(K \perp A)$, whence (*) holds.

Case $A \in K$. (*) is trivially true if $B \notin K$. So let us suppose further that $B \in K$. We need to convince ourselves that there will be a set X such that

(a) $K - A \subseteq X$ and (b) $B \notin X$ and (c) $X \in K \perp A$.

We proceed on the basis of a Lemma proved in Alchourrón et al. (1985) (Lemma 2.4):

$$\frac{X \in K \perp C \quad D \in K \quad X \nvdash D}{X \in K \perp D}$$

Then the sought conclusion follows thus:

$$\text{Ad a)}\quad \cfrac{\cfrac{\overline{B \in K}\ \text{Hyp.}}{K - A, A \vdash B}\ (C5) \quad \cfrac{}{K - A \not\vdash B}\ \text{Hyp.}}{\cfrac{K - A, \neg A \not\vdash B}{\cfrac{K - A \not\vdash A \vee B}{\exists X \in K \perp A \vee B\colon K - A \subseteq X}}}$$

$$\text{Ad b)}\quad \cfrac{\cfrac{}{X \in K \perp A \vee B}\ \text{a)}}{\cfrac{X \not\vdash A \vee B}{B \notin X}}$$

$$\text{Ad c)}\quad \cfrac{\cfrac{}{A \in K}\ \text{Hyp.} \quad \cfrac{}{X \in K \perp A \vee B}\ \text{a)} \quad \cfrac{\cfrac{}{X \in K \perp A \vee B}\ \text{a)}}{\cfrac{X \not\vdash A \vee B}{X \not\vdash A}}\ \text{Lemma}}{X \in K \perp A}$$

This concludes the proof that contractions satisfying the basic AGM-postulates represent exactly the partial meet contractions. The result can be extended to the supplementary postulates by generating the selection function from a preference relation (see Alchourrón et al. 1985, §4). The representation result carries over to revisions via the Levi Identity.

Systems of Spheres

The Ramsey Test, even though not tenable in its naive form, suggests a close analogy between counterfactual conditionals and the revision operation. The analogy naturally invites the thought that extant semantics for counterfactuals might be adapted to yield models of belief revision.

The Ramsey Test can be seen as an epistemic version of what one might call the *Stalnaker Test*:

$A \mathbin{\Box\!\!\!\to} B$ in w iff $B\ (w * A)$.

The $*$-operation on the right-hand side takes the world w and sentence A to the least deviation from ("revision" of) w so as to make A true. Perhaps there is no unique such least deviation, whence we might prefer the *Lewis Test*:

$A \mathbin{\Box\!\!\!\to} B$ in w iff B in all worlds in $(w * A)$.

The task at hand is now to determine $w * A$. A system of nested spheres centered around w is the key to modeling $w * A$ in David Lewis' semantics for counterfactuals. Put briefly, in the spheres semantics for counterfactuals worlds are ordered around w in spheres of similarity (see Figure 56.1a). If sphere S_2 is more distant from w than S_1, i.e. if $S_1 \subseteq S_2$, then the worlds in S_1 are more similar to w than the worlds in S_2. To assess $A \mathbin{\Box\!\!\!\to} B$ at w, we look at the closest-to-w sphere S that contains A-worlds; $w * A$ collects the A-worlds in S. To evaluate the conditional we check whether all worlds in $w * A$ satisfy B. If so, the conditional is true at w, otherwise it is false at w. This is the principal case. If there are no A-permitting spheres around w, i.e. if the antecedent is not entertainable when viewed from w, then the conditional is stipulated to be vacuously true at w.

The Ramsey Test, however, does not test for the truth of a conditional in a world w but for acceptance in a belief state K. A belief states can be modeled by the set of worlds not ruled out by what is believed. Thus, in the Ramsey Test,

$$A \sqsupset B \text{ in } K \text{ iff } B \text{ in } K * A,$$

the belief states K and $K * A$ can be interpreted as standing for sets of worlds. We can simply adapt the spheres models for counterfactuals by centering spheres on a *set* of worlds (representing K) and determining the new belief state $K * A$ as before. The spheres represent now fallback positions ordered as to comparative plausibility from the viewpoint of K. The result is shown in Figure 56.1b.

This is the proposal. It remains to verify that it works. That is to say, we need another representation result.

Let W be a universe of possible worlds, let K be a belief state and let $[K] \subseteq W$ be the representation of K in W. A system of spheres for K is a family of subsets of W such that $[K]$ is the smallest and W the largest sphere, all spheres are comparable by set-inclusion, and for any nonempty subset X of W, there is always a smallest sphere, S_X, cutting X nonemptily. Thus a spheres system for K can be pictured as an onion or Russian doll, with $[K]$ in the centre and W as the outermost shell; formal definitions can be found in Grove (1988). We define the set of worlds representing $K * A$ thus:

$$(*) \quad [K * A] := \begin{cases} S_{[A]} \cap [A], & \text{if } A \text{ is consistent;} \\ Cn(\bot) & \text{otherwise.} \end{cases}$$

Then we can prove the following result (Grove 1988): Revisions, as defined in (*), satisfy the revision postulates (R1–8), and any revision operation satisfying (R1–8) can be defined as in (*). An analogous representation result holds for contractions *via* the Harper Identity.

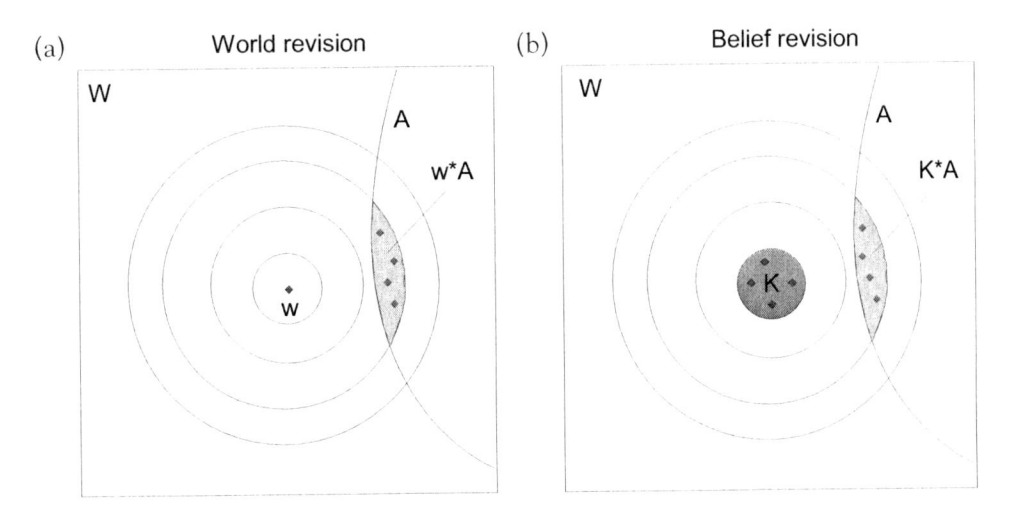

Figure 56.1

Given the correspondence between revision in systems of spheres and revisions satisfying the AGM-postulates, there follows a correspondence between spheres-revisions and partial meet revisions. This should not be surprising. The latter correspondence can be made transparent without detouring via the postulates. It suffices to note a bijection between [¬A] and $K \perp A$. (Here we only look at the principal case that $A \in K$ and A is consistent.) From spheres to remainders we have for every $w \in [¬A]$ a corresponding remainder $|[K] \cup \{w\}|$ in $K \perp A$, where $|X| = \{A: \forall y \in X: y \vDash A\}$, for each subset X of W. Conversely, from remainders to spheres we have for every remainder $X \in K \perp A$ a unique $w \in [¬A]$ such that $w \in [X]$. Thus a system of spheres for K selects among the ¬A-worlds just in case a selection function for K takes its pick in $K \perp A$.

3. Multimodal Theories of Belief Change

A sentence like $B \in K * A$ we read thus:

(1) After revising his beliefs so as to include A, K believes that B.

Perhaps the logical form of (1) can be analyzed in a number of ways. But one particularly natural analysis would be this: There is a sentence B that stands in the skopus of an *epistemic operator* ("K believes that") which in turn stands in the skopus of an *action operator* ("after revising his beliefs") *parameterized* by a sentence ("so as to include A"). This suggests conducting the whole theory of belief change in a multimodal language containing a belief operator **B** and action operators $[a_0], [a_1], [a_2], \ldots$ with each action of the form ∗⟨sentence⟩ (for revision) or −⟨sentence⟩ (for contraction).

The idea of recasting the AGM-theory in a modal language has been aired repeatedly. Early attempts are found in van Benthem (2004b) and Fuhrmann (1991a). There are presently two approaches to belief revision in a modal setting, Public Announcement and Dynamic Epistemic Logic (PAL and DEL), and Doxastic Dynamic Logic (DDL). In the remainder of this survey we give a brief exposition of DDL, as presented in Leitgeb and Segerberg (2007), and then add a few remarks on PAL and DEL.

What are the advantages of presenting a theory of belief change in a modal language? First, we can help ourselves to the rich reservoir of semantical techniques available for modal languages. This is a cheap point and might indeed amount to nothing unless the techniques employed deliver clear benefits. But in one respect at least there is every reason to expect such benefits; they will be indicated in connection with the third point below.

Second, the modal language sketched above is more expressive than the set-theoretic AGM-language. We can express metabeliefs such as that the subject believes that after revision by A she will believe B: **B**[∗A]**B** B. A direct translation back to AGM would render that formula as "$(B \in K * A) \in K$"—which is ill-formed. Alternatively the language of AGM would have to be stratified—a notoriously unwieldy and artificial device.

Third, the modal language is in some respects less expressive and thereby less misleading than the AGM-language. The notation $K * A$ suggests that K and A are arguments *en par* to a revision operation ∗. That is not the case. Perusing the postulates shows that nothing of interest is said about varying the belief state-parameter. Indeed, the only candidate postulate we have considered, Monotonicity for revisions, turned out to lead to disaster. The models showed why this is so. Both the selection functions and spheres determining the new, changed belief state are essentially tied to the belief state to be changed; they unfold the theoretical preferences built into that belief state. The AGM framework has no resources to study interactions or transitions between different theoretical preferences.

However, just like the AGM-language, the modal language allows to chain changes, as in

$$[-A][-B]\mathbf{B}\ C.$$

This is known as iterated belief change. Iterated belief change is difficult precisely because we need to know how the transition from the theoretical preferences of K to those of $K - B$ and in turn to those of $(K - B) - A$ is constrained so as to settle the question whether the latter belief state ought to include C. This is where modal semantics can be beneficial: It might deliver or suggest constraints for iterated modalities and make their evaluation more transparent.

Basic Doxastic Dynamics

We shall simplify the exposition of how belief change can be treated in a multimodal language by confining ourselves to a language in which belief states can only be changed by and can only contain "factual" beliefs. This simplification regrettably takes away the potential of the modal framework for a substantial theory of iterated belief change. We shall indicate prospects and problems for the more general theory in the final section.

The language is based on a set of *atoms* from which we generate the *factual formulae* by Boolean combinations. Every factual formula is a *formula*. The modal formulae are built by employing a belief and a knowledge operator, $\mathbf{B}$ and $\mathbf{K}$, and a revision operator [∗]. If A is factual and B a formula, then $\mathbf{B}A$, $\mathbf{K}A$ and $[*A]B$ are formulae. Contractions, $[-A]B$, are defined in the spirit of the Harper Identity as $B \wedge [* \neg A]B$. Expansions can be introduced in analogy to so-called tests in dynamic logic, i.e. $[+A]B := \mathbf{B}A \rightarrow B$.

The knowledge operator $\mathbf{K}$ appears in **DDL** for mainly technical reasons: it will be used to signal unrevisable beliefs, those belonging to the urcorpus, to use Levi's term again. In particular, the urcorpus contains all logical truths. Note that this notion of knowledge as unrevisable belief is slightly at odds with the more usual notion that requires knowledge to entail truth.

What is the logic of these operators? Usually this depends on the kind of models one aims to describe. But in this case we have yet another clue. If we suppose that the AGM-postulates provide a reliable and complete description of belief revision, we shall be in the vicinity of the desired logic by combining the basic properties of the unary modal operators $\mathbf{B}$, $\mathbf{K}$ and $[*A]$ (for each factual A) with translations of the AGM revision postulates into our modal language. Adjustments need then possibly be made in light of the aimed at models.

Before presenting the system of basic **DDL** (for "Doxastic Dynamic Logic") a cautionary note is in order. We know that the Ramsey Test trivializes the AGM-theory. The Ramsey Test requires a systematic connection between revisions and conditionals. The fact that we do not have a (counterfactual) conditional connective in our language for which the Ramsey Test is plausible is no sufficient reason to relax. We must rule out the possibility that some formula C in our language might step in for the conditional in the Ramsey Test, i.e. that the dangerous schema

D. $BC(A, B) \leftrightarrow [*A]BB$

be derivable for some formula C with constituents A and B. In basic **DDL** this is ruled out by the syntactic formation rules in combination with the Congruence Rule below.

The basic system of **DDL** extends classical propositional logic to a normal modal logic for each of the modalities **B**, **K** and [*A] (where A is factual), i.e. it contains apart from all tautologies the following axiom schemes and schematic rules ($\Box \in \{$**B**, **K**, [*A]: A factual$\}$, $\langle *A \rangle := \neg[*A]\neg$):

Regularity	$\Box(A \wedge B) \leftrightarrow (\Box A \wedge \Box B)$
Necessitation	$\Box \top$
Congruence Rule	$\dfrac{A \leftrightarrow B}{\Box A \leftrightarrow \Box B}$

To these we add the following translations of the AGM-postulates for revision:

Success	$[*A]BA$
Inclusion	$[*\top]BA \to BA$
Preservation	$\neg B\bot \to (BA \to [*\top]BA)$
Consistency	$[*A]B\bot \to K\neg A$
Congruence	$K(A \leftrightarrow B) \to [*A]BC \leftrightarrow [*B]BC$
Supp. 1	$[*(A \wedge B)]BC \to [*A]B(B \to C)$
Supp. 2	$\neg[*A]B\neg B \to ([*A]B(B \to C) \to [*(A \wedge B)BC])$

No translation of the closure postulate is required as it is already built into the first group of axiom schemes. Finally we need to make sure that revision issues in a definite (belief) state and we give a minimal characterization of the required notion of knowledge:

Function	$\langle *A \rangle B \leftrightarrow [*A]B$
KB	$KA \to BA$
K*K	$KA \leftrightarrow [*B]KA$

Spheres Semantics

The interpretation of (normal) multimodal languages generalizes that familiar from simple (normal) modal logic in a straightforward way. Each modality $\Box_i$ is matched by a binary relation R_i (on the set W of evaluation points) such that we have a clause of this form:

$$w \models \Box_i A \text{ iff } \forall v : R_i wv \Rightarrow v \models A.$$

In the case at hand, however, some modalities come with a structure which we should like to make available for logical investigation. Thus in our semantics, we should like the relations concerned to reflect that structure, as in

THEORIES OF BELIEF CHANGE

$w \models [*B]A$ iff $\forall v : R_{[B]} wv \Rightarrow v \models A,$

where [B] is the proposition denoted by B. A clause of this form results on adapting again the spheres semantics.

A *revision structure* on a (nonempty) *universe* W consists of a *family of systems of spheres* in W and for each proposition $P \subseteq W$ a *binary relation* R_P between systems of spheres. The systems of spheres are, as before, families of subsets of W, closed under intersection (so that the system is centered on the smallest sphere, representing one's beliefs in that sphere), completely ordered under set-inclusion (so that the system is nested), and such that for each nonempty proposition P there is a smallest sphere cutting P (so that the system is sufficiently discrete). We let $\mathfrak{S} \bullet P = \{S \in \mathfrak{S}: S \cap P \neq \emptyset\}$ denote the collection of those spheres S in a system $\mathfrak{S}$ that cut P nonemptily.

The structure is subject to four conditions. It is customary to first state these conditions before proceeding to the interpretation of the modal language. Let us here change the official order of exposition; we shall then see how the conditions help the interpretation to deliver the correct results.

Some formulae, the modal ones, receive their truth-values depending on what system of spheres we are considering. For this reason the satisfaction relation $\models$ will link systems of spheres and worlds on the one hand with formulae on the other. For atoms p and Boolean formulae, of course, only the world-coordinate contains relevant information. Let a valuation V distribute atoms over possible worlds. Then

$\mathfrak{S}, w \models p$ iff $w \in V(p),$

and so on for $\neg, \wedge,$

$\mathfrak{S}, w \models BA$ iff $\bigcap \mathfrak{S} \subseteq [A],$

$\mathfrak{S}, w \models KA$ iff $\bigcup \mathfrak{S} \subseteq [A],$

$\mathfrak{S}, w \models [*A]B$ iff $\forall \mathfrak{S}' : R_{[A]} \mathfrak{S} \mathfrak{S}' \Rightarrow , w \models B.$

According to the clause for **B**, the current beliefs of an agent as evaluated in a system of spheres are represented by the innermost sphere. The clause for **K** displays the notion of knowledge used here: unrevisable beliefs, i.e. beliefs that stay, no matter to what sphere we shall retreat.

Now back to the four conditions. First,

$R_p \mathfrak{S}\mathfrak{S}'$, then $\bigcap \mathfrak{S}' = \begin{cases} P \cap \min(\mathfrak{S} \bullet P), & \text{if } (\mathfrak{S} \bullet P) \neq \emptyset \\ \emptyset & \text{otherwise.} \end{cases}$

This *defines* the revision of one's current belief state (in $\mathfrak{S}$) by the sentence representing P: it is the shaded area in the right diagram in the earlier illustration.

The second condition guarantees that systems of spheres are large enough to carry out any revision:

$W \setminus \bigcup \mathfrak{S} = W \setminus \bigcup \mathfrak{S}' \quad (\forall \mathfrak{S}, \mathfrak{S}' \in \Sigma)$

It replaces for technical reasons our earlier and simpler requirement that each system is bounded above by W.

The final two conditions make sure that revision operations are well-defined. The first secures that they always have a value,

635

∀𝔖∃𝔖′ : R𝔖𝔖′,

the second that they always have at most one value:

R𝔖𝔖′ and R𝔖𝔖″, then 𝔖′ = 𝔖″

Segerberg has shown that the theorems of basic **DDL** are exactly those formulae that are true relative to all pairs (𝔖, w) in any interpretation in a revision structure.

4. Current and Future Changes

The transposition of the AGM-theory into a modal framework attempts to address from a different angle certain questions and problems left open in the classical version of that theory. Four such questions arise immediately.

The first three concern higher-order beliefs. If we waive the syntactic restrictions imposed in basic **DDL**, we will be confronted with three types of higher-order beliefs.

First, there will be beliefs about changes, as in B[∗A]B: Karl believes that after revising by A, B is the case, or, counterfactually: Were he to believe that A, then he would believe that B, where the place of B will typically be taken by another belief formula, BC. Now, if it is the case that [∗A] BB, then Karl can know that fact by pure introspection: The result is determined by logic plus his present theoretical preferences. What Karl can know in this way, he should know. Thus it would seem to be quite in order to impose the following condition on how the belief operator should interact with revisions:

B([∗A]BB) ↔ [∗A]BB.

But this is just an instance of the dangerous schema D! Thus adding beliefs about changes to our language amounts to a non-conservative and indeed potentially hazardous extension of the theory.

Second, there will be changes by beliefs, as in [∗BA]B: If Karl were to come to believe that he believes A, then B would be the case. At first sight one would expect that the Success condition for revisions carries over to the extended language and that we thus have in particular [∗BA]BA. But now consider a Moore-sentence like

m. $p \land \neg Bp$.

By Success we expect [∗Bm]Bm from which we get by Regularity both [∗Bm]Bp and [∗Bm]B ¬Bp. Even in very weak logics of belief, the latter gives [∗Bm] ¬Bp, thus contradicting the former. (It suffices to add to the basic axioms above the condition that belief be consistent, B ¬A → ¬BA, and the introspective schema BA → BBA. Jointly these conditions describe a **KD4**-type modal logic.) So one cannot (successfully and consistently) revise one's beliefs so as to include a Moore-sentence. This is as it should be. But it also shows that there are classes of formulae that must be systematically exempted from conditions that otherwise make good sense. For an elaboration of this point as applied to sentences of the form "A and I do not know that A"—which trigger the Fitch-paradox—see van Benthem (2004b).

Third, there will be changes of changed belief states, as in [∗A] ([∗B]C): Were Karl to revise by A, then a further revision by B would make it the case that C. The models of basic **DDL** permit evaluating such formulae; but they have nothing interesting to say on iterated belief changes, just like the original AGM-theory. Iterated belief changes involve possible changes in theoretical preferences. Such changes find no direct representation in the modal languages considered so far. Thus one natural way to proceed is to introduce preference changes into the object language, as in van Benthem (2004a).

Fourth, the methodological restriction to a single-agent perspective must eventually give way to considering belief change in a multi-agent environment. Most of our belief changes are made in response to, or under the influence of, the belief states of others. We have beliefs about what others believe and they are aware of this, and so on.

Beliefs about what other agents believe are the subject matter of Public Announcement Logic (PAL, see Baltag et al. 2006) and the closely related paradigm of Dynamic Epistemic Logic (DEL, see van Ditmarsch et al. 2005, 2008). They study the rational commitments of agents who receive information by public announcements. It would be misleading, however, to think of these theories as logics of belief revision. In their basic forms they study the rather limited scenario of knowledge expansions in a multi-agent environment under the influence of an oracle. As reduction results show, PAL (and DEL) without a "looping" common knowledge modality does not go beyond a multi-epistemic logic. But PAL is open to incorporate genuine belief revision operators; see e.g. Baltag and Smets (2006). It is to be expected that PAL, DEL, DDL and the logic of preference change will merge into a unified and general framework for studying belief change; an outline of such an integrated family of theories may be found in Bentham (2004a).

References

Alchourrón, Carlos, and David Makinson. Hierarchies of regulations and their logic. In R. Hilpinen, editor, *New Studies in Deontic Logic*, pages 123–148. Reidel, Dordrecht, 1981.

Alchourrón, Carlos, Peter Gärdenfors, and David Makinson. On the logic of theory change: Partial meet contraction and revision functions. *The Journal of Symbolic Logic*, 50: 510–530, 1985.

Baltag, Alexandru and Sonja Smets. The Logic of Conditional Doxastic Actions: A theory of dynamic multi-agent belief revision. In Sergei Artemov and Rohit Parikh, editors, *Proceedings of the Workshop on Rationality and Knowledge, ESSLLI 2006*. 2006.

Baltag, Alexandru, Lawrence S. Moss, and Slawomir Solecki. The logic of public announcements, common knowledge, and private suspicions. In *TARK '98: Proceedings of the 7th conference on Theoretical aspects of rationality and knowledge*, pages 43–56. San Francisco, CA, USA, 1998. Morgan Kaufmann Publishers Inc.

Darwiche, Adnan and Judea Pearl. On the logic of iterated belief revision. *Articial Intelligence*, 89: 1–29, 1997.

Dunn, John M. Relevance logic and entailment. Handbook of Philosophical Logic. In D. M. Gabbay and F. Guenthner, editors, *Handbook of Philosophical Logic*, volume 3, pages 117–224. Reidel, Dordrecht, 1986.

Fuhrmann, André. Reflective modalities and theory change. *Synthese*, 81: 115–134, 1989.

Fuhrmann, André. On the modal logic of theory change. Lecture Notes in Articial Intelligence 465, pages 259–281. Springer, Heidelberg-Berlin-New York, 1991a.

Fuhrmann, André. Theory contraction through base contraction. *Journal of Philosophical Logic*, 20: 256–281, 1991b.

Fuhrmann, André. *An Essay on Contraction*. Studies in Logic, Language and Information. CSLI Publications, Stanford, 1997a.

Fuhrmann, André. Everything in flux: Dynamic ontologies. In R. Sliwinski, S. Lindström, and J. Österberg, editors, *Odds and Ends. Philosophical Essays Dedicated to Wlodek Rabinowicz*, pages 111–125. Uppsala, 1997b.

Gärdenfors, Peter. *Knowledge in Flux*. MIT Press, Cambridge, Mass., 1988.

Grove, Adam. Two modellings for theory change. *Journal of Philosophical Logic*, 17: 157–170, 1988.

Hansson, Sven Ove. In defense of base contraction. *Synthese*, 91: 239–245, 1992.
Hansson, Sven Ove. *A Textbook of Belief Dynamics*. Kluwer, Dordrecht, 1999.
Leitgeb, Hannes and Krister Segerberg. Dynamic doxastic logic: why, how, and where to? *Synthese*, 155: 167–190, 2007.
Levi, Isaac. *The Enterprise of Knowledge*. MIT Press, Cambridge, Mass., 1980.
Levi, Isaac. *Decisions and Revisions*. Cambridge University. Press, Cambridge, 1984.
Levi, Isaac. *The Fixation of Belief and Its Undoing*. Cambridge University. Press, Cambridge, 1991.
Levi, Isaac. *Mild Contractions*. Cambridge University. Press, Cambridge, 2004.
Lewis, David. Probabilities of conditionals and conditional probabilities. *The Philosophical Review*, 85: 297–315, 1976.
Lindström, Sten and Wlodek Rabinowicz. Epistemic entrenchment with incomparabilities and relational belief revision. In André Fuhrmann and Michael Morreau, editors, *The Logic of Theory Change*, Lecture Notes in Articial Intelligence 465, pages 93–126. Springer, Heidelberg-Berlin-New York, 1991.
Makinson, David. On the status of the postulate of recovery in the logic of theory change. *Journal of Philosophical Logic*, 16: 383–394, 1987.
Peirce, Charles S. The fixation of belief. *Popular Science Monthly*, 12: 1–15, 1877.
Ramsey, Frank P. *The Foundations of Mathematics*. Routledge and Kegan Paul, Oxford, 1931.
Rott, Hans. *Change, Choice and Inference*. Clarendon Press, Oxford, 2001.
Stalnaker, Robert. Iterated belief revision. *Erkenntnis*, 70: 189–209, 2009.
van Benthem, Johan. *Language in Action: Categories, Lambdas and Dynamic Logic*. Studies in Logic and the Foundations of Mathematics. North-Holland, Amsterdam, 1991.
van Benthem, Johan. Dynamic logic for belief revision. *Journal of Applied Non-Classical Logics*, 14: 1–26, 2004a.
van Benthem, Johan. What one may come to know. *Analysis*, 64: 95–105, 2004b.
van Ditmarsch, Hans, W. van der Hoek, and B. P. Kooi. Playing Cards with Hintikka: An introduction to dynamic epistemic logic. *The Australasian Journal of Logic*, 3: 108–134, 2005.
van Ditmarsch, Hans, Wiebe van der Hoek, and Barteld Kooi. *Dynamic Epistemic Logic*. Springer, Dordrecht, 2008.

57
THE KNOWABILITY PARADOX
Joe Salerno

The paradox of knowability (a.k.a. *Fitch's paradox* or the *Church-Fitch paradox*) is a proof that threatens all too easily to refute various forms of semantic anti-realism and to collapse useful modal epistemic distinctions. The anti-realisms in question are those that advocate an epistemic characterization of truth. They tell us that truth and knowability are necessarily coextensive—or at least that any truth is knowable in principle. We call this the *knowability principle* (KP), which is naturally expressed by the following formula:

(KP) $\neg\forall\varphi(\varphi \to \Diamond K\varphi)$

(KP) says, "for all propositions φ, if φ then it is possible that somebody at some time knows that φ." Interesting versions of the thesis focus on moderately idealized *human* knowability—that is, knowability by subjects whose capacities and resources are only finitely better than our own. Knowability-by-God is too weak of an idealization, since it leaves us with a view that is consistent with realism—namely, the view that truth can outrun the epistemic capacities of subjects like us. Moderate epistemic theories of truth also aim to protect themselves from going in the other direction; the epistemic idealization is meant to distance the theory from naive forms of idealism (NI), which say that something is true only if it is known (by someone at some time):

(NI) $\forall\varphi(\varphi \to K\varphi)$

The thesis is often cited as the "omniscience principle," because it says that for every truth there is someone who knows it. The omniscience in question is group (and not individual) omniscience. It doesn't say that there is someone who knows every truth, but that every truth is known by someone or other. However, allowing infinitary propositions, the conjunction of all truths is itself a truth, and so by (NI), is known by someone. In that case, someone among the humans is indeed omniscient. (For more on the paradox in the context of infinitary propositions, see Humberstone 1985; Bigelow 2005; Fox unpublished ms.)

While linking truth with God's knowledge is vacuous, naive idealism fails to appreciate the objectivity and discoverability of truth. The moderate (KP) is a candidate expression or consequence of various historical non-realisms, including Michael Dummett's semantic anti-realism, Hilary Putnam's internal realism, the logical positivisms of the

Berlin and Vienna Circles, Peirce's pragmatism, Kant's transcendental idealism, and Berkeley's metaphysical idealism.

The *knowability paradox* is naturally characterized as the following result:

(Knowability Paradox) $\forall \varphi(\varphi \to \Diamond K\varphi) \vdash \forall \varphi(\varphi \to K\varphi)$,

where our variables are propositional (suitably regimented); $\Diamond$ is some brand of alethic possibility, and K is the epistemic operator 'somebody at some time knows.'

A very weak normal modal logic and relatively uncontroversial assumptions about knowledge are enough to establish the result. We'll look at a proof in a moment. Note that the converse is trivial, since truth entails possibility.

It should be clear that if the result is valid, then it threatens moderate anti-realism. That is because a natural expression (or consequence) of anti-realism—namely, (KP)—entails a widely implausible brand of idealism—namely, (NI).

The significance of the knowability paradox is not simply that any plausible epistemic theory of truth that has (KP) as a consequence is false. It is more interesting than that. If the proof is valid, then there is no logical distinction between truth being a matter of what can be known and truth being a matter of what in fact is known. So if we merely think there is a significant difference between moderate anti-realism and naive idealism, we have some explaining to do. We have ourselves a paradox.

The first publication of the result appears in its contrapositive form in Frederic Fitch (1963; 2009). There it was called *Theorem 5*, which may be expressed as follows:

(T5) $\exists \varphi(\varphi \,\&\, \neg K\varphi) \vdash \exists \varphi (\varphi \,\&\, \neg \Diamond K\varphi)$,

Under this expression of the proof, we learn that whenever there is an unknown truth, there is an unknowable truth. Again, the converse is trivial. So, if our ignorance (i.e., the existence of an unknown truth) is a contingent matter, then (T5) does the work in collapsing the logical distinction between the existence of contingent ignorance and the existence of necessary ignorance.

The Proof

To demonstrate the knowability paradox, one begins with four modest logical principles. First, knowing a conjunction entails knowing each of the conjuncts:

(A) $K(\varphi \,\&\, \psi) \vdash K\varphi \,\&\, K\psi$

Second, knowledge entails truth:

(B) $K\varphi \vdash \varphi$

Third, the necessitation of a modal epistemic theorem is itself a theorem:

(C) If $\vdash \varphi$, then $\vdash \Box \varphi$.

And finally, things necessarily false are not possible:

(D) $\Box \neg \varphi \vdash \neg \Diamond \varphi$.

A version of the proof goes like this (explanation below):

(1) $\forall\varphi(\varphi \to \Diamond K\varphi)$ (KP)
(2) $K(p \,\&\, \neg Kp)$ Assumption [for reductio]
(3) $Kp \,\&\, K\neg Kp$ from 2, by (A)
(4) $Kp \,\&\, \neg Kp$ from 3, applying (B) to the right conjunct
(5) $\neg K(p \,\&\, \neg Kp)$ from 2–4, by reductio, discharging Assumption 1
(6) $\Box \neg K(p \,\&\, \neg Kp)$ from 5, by (C)
(7) $\neg \Diamond K(p \,\&\, \neg Kp)$ from 6, by (D)
(8) $(p \,\&\, \neg Kp) \to \Diamond K(p \,\&\, \neg Kp)$ instance of (1)
(9) $\neg(p \,\&\, \neg Kp)$ from 7,8
(10) $p \to Kp$ from 9, by classical logic
(11) $\forall\varphi(\varphi \to K\varphi)$ from 10, by generalization

Suppose (KP), and suppose for reductio that a Fitch-conjunction, $p \,\&\, \neg Kp$, is known. Then, by (A), it follows that $Kp \,\&\, K\neg Kp$. By (B) and some trivial logic, $Kp \,\&\, \neg Kp$. The contradiction allows us to negate and discharge our only supposition, giving the theorem, $\neg K(p \,\&\, \neg Kp)$, which we may now necessitate by (C). So, by (D), our supposition is impossible. This together with the relevant instance of the knowability principle, $(p \,\&\, \neg Kp) \to \Diamond K(p \,\&\, \neg Kp)$, jointly entail $\neg(p \,\&\, \neg Kp)$. A classical equivalent is $p \to Kp$, which we can now generalize—giving $\forall\varphi(\varphi \to K\varphi)$. QED.

The first proof of the result originates in a pair of anonymous referee reports authored by Alonzo Church in 1945. The reports appear in their entirety in Church (2009). Fitch was the recipient, and eventually published the result with credit to the unknown referee. He also generalized the finding by showing that the collapse occurs with any monadic propositional operator O that is both factive and distributes over conjunction (i.e., that satisfies the corresponding formulations of principles A and B, substituting O for K). What significance Fitch initially gleaned from the result is not immediately apparent in Fitch's paper (Salerno 2009). Fitch appears not in the business of refuting any particular theory of truth but, rather, seems to be interested in the consequence that unknowable truth has for giving a formal definition of value. It is clear, however, that he does not take the knowability proof or the general result to be paradoxical. Yes, $\forall\varphi(\varphi \to \Diamond O\varphi) \vdash \forall\varphi(\varphi \to O\varphi)$ is valid for any operator O that is factive and conjunction-distributive, but that's not enough for paradoxicality. After all, substituting the S5 necessity operator for O (and reading $\Diamond$ as S5 possibility) leaves us with a non-paradoxical result. That is because in S5 there is indeed no significant distinction between possible necessities and necessities.

On the face of it, a Fitch *paradox* arises for any operator O that satisfies the following four conditions:

1. The O-ability principle is plausible:
   $\forall\varphi(\varphi \to \Diamond O\varphi)$
2. Clearly, some truths are not O-ed:
   $\exists\varphi(\varphi \,\&\, \neg O\varphi)$
3. O is factive:
   $O\varphi \vdash \varphi$
4. O is closed under conjunction-elimination:
   $O(\varphi \,\&\, \psi) \vdash O\varphi \,\&\, O\psi$

But even this isn't general enough. On closer inspection, however, even this list does not capture what is essential to a Fitch paradox, since neither (3) nor (4) is necessary to prove the result. For instance, there is a version of the paradox without conjunction-distributivity in Williamson (1993). And, as is shown in Wright (2000: 356), one can derive an O-ability paradox without an unrestricted O-factivity principle. The application of Factivity (i.e., principle (B)) in the above proof is applied only to higher order O-claims of the form O¬Op. All we really need then is a restricted factivity principle of the form:

(Restricted Factivity Principle): $O\neg O\varphi \vdash \neg O\varphi$

An example of a non-factive operator that arguably satisfies the restricted principle is the reflective belief operator. The corresponding principle says, whenever one reflectively believes that one doesn't reflectively believe φ, then indeed one doesn't reflectively believe φ.

Most generally the paradox then arises when:

1. The O-ability principle is plausible:
   $\forall \varphi (\varphi \rightarrow \Diamond O\varphi)$
2. Clearly, some truths are not O-ed:
   $\exists \varphi (\varphi \& \neg K\varphi)$, and
3. it is a theorem that the conjunction, $\varphi \& \neg O\varphi$, is not O-ed:
   $\vdash \neg O(\varphi \& \neg O\varphi)$

Notice that the well-known *paradox of omnipotence* is an instance of the generalized Fitch paradox. Fitch actually demonstrates his general result with that example. Since 'God brought it about that' is factive and conjunction-distributive, we get the following apparently sound argument:

(i) If a proposition is true, then God could have brought it about. (By definition of Omnipotence.)
(ii) Some truths were not brought about by God.
(iii) Contradiction! [via Fitch's reasoning]

Therefore, by reductio, (ii) is false. So,

(iv) all truths were in fact brought about by God. (So much for freewill and man-made evil.)

The following *paradox of explanation* also fits the template. Read "p is explained" in a factive and conjunction-distributive sense—as in, "the fact that p is (at some time) explained." Then we get the following Fitch paradox:

(i) Any deterministic empirical truth can be explained, but
(ii) some deterministic empirical truths are never explained.
(iii) Contradiction! [via Fitch]

Therefore, (ii) is false. Hence, absurdly,

(iv) every deterministic empirical truth is (at some time) explained.

One other example is a new *paradox of happiness*. It would seem that at least in principle one could be happy about . . ., well, just about anything. The relative arbitrariness of the attitude makes plausible the generalization that (at least in principle) a person could be happy about any truth. More carefully, if φ is true, then it is possible for someone to be happy that φ. Moreover, it is arguable that "happy that" is factive and conjunction-distributive. Necessarily, if s is happy that φ then φ. And one isn't happy that a conjunction is true, unless she is happy that each of the conjuncts are true. The assumption here is that happiness about a conjunct is implicit in happiness about the conjunction. We don't need the more general, and most implausible, principle that happiness is closed under logical entailment—namely, If φ entails ψ and someone is happy that φ, then she is happy that ψ. Finally, it is obvious that there are truths that we are not happy about. So once again a Fitch paradox emerges.

An alternative approach is to accept the weaker restricted thesis that one can be happy that one isn't happy that p, only if one isn't happy that p. Or if even this does not seem plausible, then stipulate a factive sense of the operator—e.g., "happy about the fact that."

Reactions to the Paradox

There are numerous reactions to the knowability proof. The first wave of replies to Fitch's 1963 paper, including Hart and McGinn (1976), Hart (1979), Mackie (1980), and Routley (1981), has a unified theme: Fitch's proof is valid and discredits various forms of verificationism (i.e., the view that all meaningful statements, and so all truths, are knowable). An exception is Walton (1976), whose aim was to draw lessons in the philosophy of religion. It wasn't until the 1980s that the perception in the literature had changed. The perception seems to be that Fitch's result is paradoxical. Compare Rasmussen and Ravnkilde (1982), Williamson (1982, 1988), Edgington (1985) and Wright (1987). The thought being that either the reasoning is subtly invalid, or there is a better (although elusive) formal expression of the epistemic theory of truth.

The first suggestion for blocking the proof is found in one of Church's referee reports (2009: Report 2, pp. 4–5). Here's the background. Church proved (T5). Recall that it roughly says that if there is an unknown truth then there is an unknowable truth:

(T5) $\exists \varphi(\varphi \,\&\, \neg K\varphi) \vdash \exists \varphi(\varphi \,\&\, \neg \Diamond K\varphi)$

More carefully, he proved, "if there is a truth that s doesn't know at time t, then there is a truth that s can't know at t." This had the affect of undermining a certain formal definition of 'value' that Fitch was articulating in the paper submitted for consideration. The paper was called "A Definition of Value." The definition was a natural formal expression of the informed desire characterization. It said, roughly, φ is valuable to s just in case, for some truth ψ, s would desire that φ if she were to know ψ. By the above contrapositive result, whenever s is non-omniscient, there will be a truth that she cannot know. In that case there will be a truth ψ such that, vacuously, if s were to know ψ she would desire φ. That is because conditionals with impossible antecedents are vacuously true. Hence the right-hand side of the analysis of value is satisfied, for arbitrary propositions φ. s values everything!

Church offered Fitch a way of blocking the trivialization objection by appealing to Russell's theory of types for the attitude operators. The key idea is that one might not know$_i$ a proposition φ, if φ contains an operator 'knows$_n$' (or any other attitude operator O$_n$) where n ≥ 0. So, even though it will be impossible to know$_i$ the conjunction, φ but it's not known$_i$ that φ, it will be logically possible to know$_i$ the conjunction, φ but it's not known$_n$ that φ, when n < 0. This has the effect of blocking the reductio in the knowability proof. However, Church dismisses the option of typing the operators as contrary to Fitch's purposes, since so doing would invalidate closure principles central to Fitch's discussion of value. Later defenses of the type-theoretic strategy appear in Linsky (1986; 2009) and Paseau (2008) (cf. Hart 2009).

When Fitch finally published the value paper in 1963, he did not embrace the type-theoretic strategy. Indeed he clearly takes the knowability proof to be valid. So instead Fitch (2009: 27) restricts the right-hand side of his analysis of value to relevant truths that it is possible to know. Hence, the modified analysis roughly says, "it is valuable to s that φ just in case s would desire that φ if she were appraised of the relevant knowable truths."

Interestingly Fitch and Church had already in 1945 discussed (through the editor, Ernest Nagel) the question of whether this sort of restriction blocks the initial trivialization worry. Church did not think that it did, and Fitch ultimately withdrew the 1945 paper owing to "a defect in my definition of value." (See Salerno 2009 for commentary on their discussion.)

The secondary literature on Fitch considers the paradox in an all-together different context, that is, independently of value-theory. However, we find that the restriction strategy is a typical reaction. The restriction is applied directly to the knowability principle. More generally, a typical reaction to Fitch paradoxes is to restrict the dominant quantifier in the O-ability principle. For instance, Aquinas restricts the omnipotence principle to those truths that it is logically possible for God to bring about. Analogously, Neil Tennant (1997) restricts the knowability principle to any truth that it is logically possible for someone to know. The resulting O-ability principle is not circular if the operant notion of possibility is stronger than logical possibility.

(Restricted O-ability) $\forall \varphi (\varphi \rightarrow \Diamond O\varphi)$, where $O\varphi$ does not entail a logical inconsistency.

One might object that the restricted knowability principle is already an abandonment of the anti-realist theory of truth. After all, the restriction is motivated by the admission that there are at least some truths that are not knowable. However, a realism debate might be interesting even if the target class of truths is restricted. For instance, if for the general case, a failure to meet one's obligations warrants blame, then it seems plausible to suppose that all truths of the form, "it is obligatory that φ," are knowable in principle. The interest of a dispute over this deontic knowability principle does not decrease with the concession that truths of that form do not include "it is obligatory that φ, but nobody ever knows that it is obligatory." Such truths are unknowable owing to the placement of the embedded epistemic operator in the compound sentence. Intuitively, such considerations seem more relevant to the metaphysical status of truths expressed by knowledge attributions than they do to the status of truths expressed by attributions of obligation.

One major problem with O-ability principles restricted in the above way is that they remain vulnerable to Fitch-like paradoxes once we grant stronger modal epistemic principles that are attractive to semantic anti-realists (Williamson 2000b, 2009; Brogaard and Salerno 2002; 2008; Rosenkranz 2004; Tennant 2010). Of course, the above restriction is not the only way to restrict the knowability principle. Dummett (2001), for instance, considers restricting it to basic truths, and inductively defines the truth of complex formulas with standard intuitionistic clauses. Since 'φ & $\neg K\varphi$' is not basic, its unknowability does not threaten this brand of anti-realism. Dummett (personal correspondence) does not actually endorse the basicality restriction, but instead proposes it shows that the knowability paradox is not a problem for *every* form of semantic anti-realism. Still, questions about whether '$K\varphi$' is basic and questions about the status of the operant notion of possibility are left open by Dummett. Other Fitch-like paradoxes exploit these facts by way of showing that the basicality restriction is not sufficient to eliminate the problem (Brogaard and Salerno 2002). Jose Burmúdez (2009) argues that the basicality restriction is well-motivated, given Dummettian considerations about how one must clarify the notion of indefinite extensibility of such concepts as set and natural number. He concludes that the basicality restriction provides a principled solution to the knowability paradox.

Dorothy Edgington (1985) argues that one can know from a counterfactual perspective that, as things actually are, φ and it is not known that φ. The temporal analogy is helpful here: One cannot now know both that φ is true and that φ is not now known, but one can know at some time t both that φ is now true and that it is not now known. So long as t and the present moment are not identical, no contradiction emerges. Similarly, one cannot in the actual situation know both that φ is true and that φ is not actually known, but in a counterfactual situation one can (without contradiction) know that, in the actual situation, φ is true but unknown. Edgington's knowability principle can be understood as restricted to truths of the form 'Actually φ':

$$A\varphi \to \Diamond K(A\varphi)$$

The formula says, if it is actually the case that φ then it is possible to know that it is actually the case that φ.

Williamson's objection (2000a: 290–298) to this brand of anti-realism is that it requires *transworld knowability* (i.e., counterfactual knowledge of what is actually the case), which he argues is metaphysically impossible. The reason is that transworld knowability is knowledge de re; it is about the actual world uniquely. To achieve this, a merely possible agent would need to stand in the required causal relations, or relations of acquaintance, to the actual world. But no merely possible agent can stand in these relations to actuality. So a merely possible agent cannot directly refer to, let alone have knowledge of, the actual world. Alternatively, if the reference to the actual world is fixed descriptively, the suggestion might be that our possible thinker can know that the relevant proposition φ is true at the world specified by the description. Williamson contends that such knowledge would be uninterestingly trivial. The description would have to be detailed enough to uniquely specify the actual world. Knowledge that a proposition is true at such a world would be trivial logical knowledge, because it would amount to something like knowing that φ_n is true at the world where '. . . & φ_n & . . .' is true.

Edgington's response (2010) is that one really can have non-trivial counterfactual knowledge of actuality. If we deny that possible-world talk always commits us to maximal specificity and deny a Lewisean metaphysics in which worlds/possibilities stand entirely in causal isolation from one another, then a plausible story can be had. Edgington makes use of the temporal analogy once again. I can refer to the future boiling pot of water, having just turned on the burner, even though the water is not boiling at the time of successful reference. And I can refer to a given future table, even if only the parts lie before me yet to be assembled. Just as the relevant shared temporal history of the thinker and future objects plays an important role in securing reference of those objects, the right kind of overlap between actual and counterfactual possibilities can help us to understand how reference and knowledge is achievable across worlds/possibilities. Edgington's view is that non-trivial counterfactual knowledge of what is actually the case is plausible, when the counterfactual thinker can identify her point of departure from the actual world and know the relevant details about how things would have developed from there.

Others have published developments that are sympathetic to varying extent to Edgington's original proposal (cf. Lindström 1997; Rückert 2004; Proietti and Sandu 2010; Fara 2010). Carlo Proietti and Gabriel Sandu, for instance, focus on a quite different sort of worry that arises for Edgington's strategy. Within the standard semantics for basic modal logic, propositions of the form "Actually p" are necessary—giving

$$\vdash Ap \leftrightarrow \Box Ap.$$

This is problematic if we think that Edgington's knowability principle should tell us something about contingent, as well as necessary, truths. Moreover, when the knowledge operator K is treated as a universal modal operator (such that 'Kp' is true iff 'p' is true in every epistemically accessible possible world), we get the analogous epistemic collapse,

$$\vdash Ap \leftrightarrow K(Ap).$$

That is, we regain the very sort of epistemic determinism (i.e., group omniscience) that Edgington's strategy was designed to avoid. Modeling the knowability paradox in a temporal framework and utilizing ceteris paribus modalities, Proietti and Sandu develop notions of necessity and knowledge that are not susceptible to the above collapses. They go on to formulate knowability principles in the spirit of Edgington's original proposal.

Another traditional strategy for dealing with the paradox is to argue the knowability proof is invalid. For instance, a central theme of Dummett's work is that an epistemic theory of truth carries with it independent reasons for rejecting classical logic in favor of intuitionistic logic. With a semantic foundation that characterizes truth and falsity epistemically, we lose the unrestricted validity of double-negation elimination, $\neg\neg\varphi \vdash \varphi$. For instance, constructing a refutation of the possibility of a disproof of φ leaves open the question of whether we can construct a proof of φ. The penultimate step of our knowability proof, which derives $p \to Kp$ from $\neg(p \& \neg Kp)$, abbreviates a piece of classical reasoning that is not intuitionistically valid, since it employs double-negation elimination (or something intuitionistically equivalent to it). Hence, an anti-realist who has independent reasons for favoring intuitionistic logic over classical need not be moved by the intuitionistically invalid knowability proof (Williamson 1982).

The intuitionist herself only gets as far as proving $p \to \neg\neg Kp$. Generalizing, we get $\forall \varphi \varphi \to \neg\neg K\varphi)$, or the intuitionistic equivalent, $\neg\exists\varphi(\varphi \& \neg K\varphi)$, which appears to say that no truth is forever unknown. An important objection to the intuitionistic strategy is found in the view that such intuitionistic consequences of Fitch's reasoning are as bad, or almost as bad, as the classical consequences (Percival 1990). The main intuitionistic consequence is $\neg\exists\varphi(\varphi \;\&\; \neg K\varphi)$, which apparently says that no truth is forever unknown. Some equivalent formulas include $\forall\varphi(\neg K\varphi \to \neg\varphi)$, which says that anything forever unknown is false, and $\neg\exists\varphi(\neg K\varphi \;\&\; \neg K\neg\varphi)$, which denies that there are any forever undecided statements.

The intuitionistic anti-realist need only reply that these consequences sound bad only when read with a classical semantics. Intuitionistically, they sound harmless (cf. Rasmussen and Ravnkilde 1982; Wright 1987). $\neg\exists\varphi(\varphi \;\&\; \neg K\varphi)$, for instance, says that there is a refutation of the possibility of constructing a proof of the conjunction, $\varphi \;\&\; \neg K\varphi$. Indeed we do have the skeleton of such a refutation in lines (2) through (5) of our presentation of the knowability proof. However, I believe the thrust of the objection is not that the intuitionistic consequences are themselves implausible when understood intuitionistically, but that intuitionism doesn't have the resources to express what seems clearly expressible (and true)—namely, some truths are *never* discovered. It's not that we have a disproof of the possibility of ever discovering them but, rather, that there just so happens to be no time at which they are discovered.

The expressibility objection, which is a focus of Wright (1993: 426–427) and Williamson (1994), can be put this way. The intuitionistic anti-realist lacks the logical constants to express the apparent truism that there might be truths that never in fact will be known, formally $\exists\varphi\,(\varphi \;\&\; \neg K\varphi)$. That is because the inconsistency derivable from the joint acceptance of the knowability principle and $\exists\varphi\,(\varphi \;\&\; \neg K\varphi)$ is intuitionistically valid. There seems to be two ways the intuitionist can go here. Add some constants to the language (for instance, an empirical/contingent negation, $\sim$, such that the joint acceptance of the knowability principle and $\exists\varphi\,(\varphi \;\&\; \sim K\varphi)$ is intuitionistically consistent), or bite the bullet. Arguments against the former approach appear in Williamson (1994). Dummett (2009; and personal correspondence) defends the latter strategy, and happily denies that there is any coherent reading of 'never' other than the reading allowed by the intuitionistic logical constants. (For discussion, see Weiss 2007; Bermúdez 2009; Hand 2009, 2010; Rasmussen 2009; Murzi 2010).

Still others reject classical logic in favor of a paraconsistent logic. Paraconsistent logics allow inconsistency without trivialization, by rejecting the validity of ex falso quadlibet, the principle stating that anything follows from a contradiction. A paraconsistent approach to the paradox was first suggested in Richard Routley (1981; reprint 2010). While considering the liar ('This very statement is not true'), the knower ('This very statement is not known') and Fitch's proposition, $\Diamond K(p \;\&\; \neg Kp)$, Routley entertains a uniform treatment on behalf of the "hardened paraconsistentist"—namely, that these (but not all) inconsistencies are coherent and indeed hold true. Routley does not endorse the strategy, but merely entertains it in a footnote. The paraconsistent approach is first defended in J.C. Beall (2000), where it is argued that the knower sentence provides independent evidence that a proper description of our knowledge is inconsistent. For the knower entails that $Kp \;\&\; \neg Kp$, for some p. Further, it is argued that without a solution to the knower we should accept contradictions of this form and go paraconsistent. On Beall's approach, the inconsistency in the knowability proof then does not license the reductio used ultimately to derive naive idealism. (See also Wansing 2002; Priest 2009; Beall 2009.)

In the only book-length treatment of the paradox, Jonathan Kvanvig (2006) proposes that Fitch's result is invalid, owing to a fallacious substitution into a modal context. The mistake is to be explained by the context-sensitivity of quantified expressions—in particular expressions of the form, 'somebody at some time knows'. On a Russellian view of propositions, the value of a logically proper name enters into the proposition expressed by the sentence in which the name occurs. If, for example, 'Kripke' is a logically proper name, then Kripke himself is a part of the proposition expressed by 'Kripke is a philosopher'. Similarly, on Kvanvig's *neo-Russellian* view, the domain of quantification enters into the proposition expressed by a quantified statement. The proposition expressed by 'all humans are mortal', for example, contains the domain fixed by the context of utterance as a constituent part. Consequently, the proposition expressed by 'all humans are mortal' is sensitive to the modal context in which it is embedded. And so, this *modal indexicality*, as Kvanvig calls it, is a species of non-rigidity. For the case at hand, Kvanvig's neo-Russellian account tells us that 'p but nobody ever knows that p' is non-rigid and the domain of quantification is a constituent of the proposition expressed. As such, the proposition it expresses when embedded in a modal context might differ from the proposition it expresses unembedded. Hence, the substitution of that conjunction for the propositional variable in knowability principle, $\varphi \rightarrow \Diamond K\varphi$, is said to be fallacious.

One immediate cost of Kvanvig's view is that we lose the unrestricted validity of a host of other useful modal principles, such as necessitation (i.e., the principle that every theorem is necessary). However, this sort of loss is a familiar phenomenon in the face of related forms of context-sensitivity. For instance, 'actually' is modally indexical, and the sentence, 'p just in case actually p' (formally, $p \leftrightarrow Ap$), is a theorem even though it is not necessary. That is because there might be worlds where p is false even though p is actually true.

Critical reviews of Kvanvig's approach appear in Jenkins (2006a) and Percival (2007). Brogaard and Salerno (2008) offer a related approach that does not depend on Kvanvig's philosophy of language but does rely on the syntactic approach to quantifier restriction advocated in Stanley and Szabo (2000). A two-dimensional analysis of an alleged modal fallacy appears in Costa-Leite (2006).

Much of what has been written on the knowability paradox comes in the form of attempts to express a relevant form of anti-realism without paradox (cf. Chalmers 2002; Dummett 2009; Edgington 2010; Fara 2010; Hand 2009, 2010; Jenkins 2006b; Kelp and Pritchard 2009; Linsky 2009; Restall 2009; Tennant 2009). David Chalmers, for instance, defends the idea that given enough qualitative information about the world we could in principle know the truth value of any claim. More carefully, his scrutability thesis says, if D is a complete qualitative description of the world, then for all T, it is knowable a priori that D (materially) implies T. Importantly, the knowability paradox does not threaten the claim that true Fitch-conjunctions are derivable a priori from a complete description of the world.

Christoph Kelp and Duncan Pritchard (2009) offer some hope for an anti-realism that endorses a justified believability principle in place of the knowability principle. They evaluate the thesis that, for any true proposition, it must be possible to justifiably believe it. An alternative weakening of the knowability principle is proposed by Greg Restall (2009). His principle states that, for every truth *p*, there is a collection of truths, such that (i) each of them is knowable and (ii) their conjunction is equivalent to *p*. Restall proves that this formulation evades the paradox, and draws lessons about the operant notion of possibility.

There is disagreement about whether the knowability proof is paradoxical at all. Williamson (2000a: Chapter 12; 2009), for instance, considers the result merely surprising, but warns that it is a sign of doom for anti-realist theories of truth. However, that position would best be complemented with an explanation of how moderate anti-realism can so convincingly appear to be distinct from naive idealism. Williamson does not offer such an explanation. How might the explanation begin? One possibility is this. The knowability principle and naive idealism are both necessarily false and, as such, are in fact logically equivalent. Routley (1981) and Rescher (2005), for instance, offer arguments that both the ignorance and the unknowability of some truth are necessary. Importantly, there are plenty of logically equivalent sentences that do not appear to express the same proposition (e.g., '2 + 2 = 4' and 'p → p'). If a rational subject has some attitude toward one without having that attitude toward the other, then that must be because one fails to recognize the equivalence. However, this is not satisfying. We might recognize the equivalence between the knowability principle and idealism, and still think there is no such equivalence between moderate anti-realism and idealism. We simply deny that the knowability principle is the best characterization of the moderate thesis. Intuitively, there really is a difference between understanding truth as idealized knowledge and understanding truth as actual knowledge. Writing off the knowability principle as implausible does nothing to help us to understand the metaphysical difference at the heart of this problem. And it surely does not support the thought that there is no way to formulate that difference. So we are back to where we started, seeking a semantic story about how a moderate epistemic thesis about truth can be distinguished from naive idealism.

So what can we all agree to? Not everyone thinks that the knowability proof is paradoxical, but if it is not then some explaining is still required. Among those who think there is a paradox, there is divergence on whether the knowability proof is valid. Even those who agree that it is not valid cannot seem to agree about which principles are violated. Among those who think the proof is valid but paradoxical, there is little agreement about how to resolve the paradoxicality and express the relevant form of moderate anti-realism. The only consensus there might be is that there is *no* consensus about how properly to deal with the paradox of knowability.

References

Beall, J.C., (2000). "Fitch's Proof, Verificationism, and the Knower Paradox" *Australasian Journal of Philosophy* 78, 241–247.

——, (2009). "Knowability and Possible Epistemic Oddities" in J. Salerno (ed.), *New Essays on the Knowability Paradox*. Oxford University Press, 270–299.

Burmúdez, J., (2009) "Truth, Indefinite Extensibility, and Fitch's Paradox" in J. Salerno (ed.), *New Essays on the Knowability Paradox*. Oxford University Press, 76–90.

Bigelow, J., (2005). "Omnificence" *Analysis* 65: 187–196.

Brogaard, B. and Salerno, J., (2002). "Clues to the Paradoxes of Knowability: Reply to Dummett and Tennant" *Analysis* 62: 143–150.

—— and ——, (2008). "Knowability, Possibility and Paradox" in D. Pritchard and V. Hendricks (eds.), *New Waves in Epistemology*. Palgrave Macmillan, 270–299.

Chalmers, D., (2002). "Does Conceivability Entail Possibility?" in T. Gendler and J. Hawthorne (eds.), *Conceivability and Possibility*. Oxford University Press, 145–200.

Church, A., (2009). "Referee Reports on Fitch's 'A Definition of Value'" in J. Salerno (ed.), *New Essays on the Knowability Paradox*. Oxford University Press, 13–20.

Costa-Leite, A., (2006). "Fusions of Modal Logics and Fitch's Paradox" *Croatian Journal of Philosophy* 6: 281–290.

Dummett, M., (2001). "Victor's Error" *Analysis* 61, 1–2.

——, (2009). "Fitch's Paradox of Knowability" in J. Salerno (ed.), *New Essays on the Knowability Paradox*. Oxford University Press, 51–52.

Edgington, D., (1985). "The Paradox of Knowability" *Mind* 94, 557–568.

——, (2010). "Possible Knowledge of Unknown Truth" *Synthese* 173: 41–52.
Fara, M., (2010). "Knowability and the Capacity to Know" *Synthese* 173: 53–73.
Fitch, F. (1963). "A Logical Analysis of Some Value Concepts" *The Journal of Symbolic Logic* 28: 135–142. Reprinted in J. Salerno (ed.), *New Essays on the Knowability Paradox*. Oxford University Press. 2009.
Fox, J. Unpublished Manuscript. "Fitch-Humberstone Arguments."
Hand, M., (2009). "Performance and Paradox" in J. Salerno (ed.), *New Essays on the Knowability Paradox*. Oxford University Press, 283–301.
——, (2010). "Antirealism and Universal Knowability" *Synthese* 173: 25–39.
Hart, W. D., (1979). "The Epistemology of Abstract Objects: Access and Inference" *Proceedings of the Aristotelian Society*, supp. vol. 53, 153–165.
——, (2009). "Invincible Ignorance" in J. Salerno (ed.), *New Essays on the Knowability Paradox*. Oxford University Press, 320–323.
—— and McGinn, C., (1976). "Knowledge and Necessity" *Journal of Philosophical Logic* 5: 205–208.
Humberstone, I., (1985). "The Formalities of Collective Omniscience" *Philosophical Studies* 48: 401–423.
Jenkins, C., (2006a). "Review of Kvanvig: *The Knowability Paradox*" *Mind* 115: 1141–1147.
——, (2006b). "Anti-Realism and Epistemic Accessibility" *Philosophical Studies* 132: 525–551.
Kelp, C. and Pritchard, D., (2009). "Two Deflationary Approaches to Fitch-Style Reasoning" in J. Salerno (ed.), *New Essays on the Knowability Paradox*. Oxford University Press, 324–338.
Kvanvig, J., (2006). *The Knowability Paradox*. Oxford University Press.
Lindström, S., (1997). "Situations, Truth and Knowability: A Situation-Theoretic Analysis of a Paradox of Fitch" in E. Ejerthed and S. Lindström (eds.), *Logic, Action and Cognition: Essays in Philosophical Logic*. Kluwer Academic Publishers, 183–210.
Linsky, B., (1986). "Factives, Blindspots and Some Paradoxes" *Analysis* 64: 10–15.
——, (2009). "Logical Types in Arguments about Knowability and Belief" in J. Salerno (ed.), *New Essays on the Knowability Paradox*. Oxford University Press, 163–179.
Mackie, J. L., (1980). "Truth and Knowability" *Analysis* 40, 90–92.
Murzi, J., (2010). "Knowability and Bivalence" *Philosophical Studies* 149: 269–281.
Paseau, A., (2008). "Fitch's Argument and Typing Knowledge" *Notre Dame Journal of Formal Logic* 49: 153–176.
Percival, P., (1990). "Fitch and Intuitionistic Knowability" *Analysis* 50, 182–187.
——, (2007). "Review of Jonathan Kvanvig's *The Knowability Paradox*" *Notre Dame Philosophical Reviews*. URL= http://ndpr.nd.edu/review.cfm?id=8924.
Priest, G., (2009). "Beyond the Limits of Knowledge" in J. Salerno (ed.), *New Essays on the Knowability Paradox*. Oxford University Press, 93–104.
Proietti, C. and Sandu, G., (2010). "Fitch's Paradox and Ceteris Paribus Modalities" *Synthese* 173: 75–87.
Rasmussen, S. A., (2009). "The Paradox of Knowability and the Mapping Objection" in J. Salerno (ed.), *New Essays on the Knowability Paradox*. Oxford University Press, 53–75.
—— and Ravnkilde, J., (1982). "Realism and Logic" *Synthese* 52: 379–437.
Rescher, N., (2005). *Epistemic Logic*. University of Pittsburgh Press.
Restall, G., (2009). "Not Every Truth Can be Known (at least not all at once)" in J. Salerno (ed.), *New Essays on the Knowability Paradox*. Oxford University Press, 339–354.
Rosenkranz, S., (2004). "Fitch Back in Action Again?" *Analysis* 64: 67–71.
Routley, R., (1981). "Necessary Limits of Knowledge: Unknowable Truths" in M. Edgar, N. Otto, and Z. Gerhard (eds.) *Essays in Scientific Philosophy. Dedicated to Paul Weingartner/Philosophie als Wissenschaft. Paul Weingartner gewidmet*. Bad Reichenhall: Comes Verlag : 93–115. Reprinted in (2010) *Synthese* 173: 107–122.
Rückert, H., (2004). "A Solution to Fitch's Paradox of Knowability" in S. Rahman, J. Symons, D. Gabbay, and J. van Bendegem (eds.) *Logic, Epistemology and the Unity of Science*. Kluwer Academic Publishers.
Salerno, J., (2009). "Knowability Noir: 1945–1963" in J. Salerno (ed.) *New Essays on the Knowability Paradox*. Oxford University Press, 29–48.
Stanley, J. and Szabo, Z., (2000). "On Quantifier Domain Restriction" *Mind and Language* 15: 219–261.
Tennant, N., (1997). *The Taming of the True*. Oxford: Clarendon Press.
——, (2009). "Revamping the Restriction Strategy" in J. Salerno (ed.), *New Essays on the Knowability Paradox*. Oxford University Press, 223–238.
——, (2010). "Williamson's Woes" *Synthese* 173: 9–23.
Walton, D., (1976). "Some Theorems of Fitch on Omnipotence" *Sophia* 15: 20–27.

Wansing, H., (2002). "Diamonds are a Philosopher's Best Friend: The Knowability Paradox and Modal Epistemic Relevance Logic" *Journal of Philosophical Logic* 31: 591–612.
Weiss, B., (2007). "Truth and the Enigma of Knowability" *Dialectica* 61: 521–537.
Williamson, T., (1982). "Intuitionism Disproved?" *Analysis* 42: 203–207.
——, (1993). "Verificationism and Non-Distributive Knowledge" *Australasian Journal of Philosophy* 71: 78–86.
——, (1994). "Never Say Never" *Topoi* 13: 135–145.
——, (1998). "Knowability and Constructivism" *Philosophical Quarterly* 38: 422–432.
——, (2000a). *Knowledge and its Limits*. Oxford University Press.
——, (2000b). "Tennant on Knowable Truth" *Ratio* 13: 99–114.
——, (2009). "Tennant's Troubles" in J. Salerno (ed.), *New Essays on the Knowability Paradox*. Oxford University Press, 183–204.
Wright, C., (1993 [1987]). *Realism, Meaning and Truth*. 2nd ed., Blackwell.
——, (2000). "Truth as Sort of Epistemic: Putnam's Peregrinations" *Journal of Philosophy* 97: 335–364.

Part IX

THE HISTORY OF EPISTEMOLOGY

58

PLATO

Timothy Chappell

No great philosopher is more centrally concerned to ask questions about knowledge (Greek *epistêmê*) and its definition (Greek *logos*) than one of the first and greatest philosophers of all: the Athenian aristocrat Plato (428–348 BC). Among much else, he is the first philosopher to propose and explore a possible definition of knowledge as justified true belief (in the *Meno*, *Republic*, and *Theaetetus*). He is the first philosopher to suggest and discuss the principle that knowledge can only be based on knowledge (most clearly in *Republic* Book VII). And he is the first philosopher to explore the problems of misrepresentation (most notably in the *Theaetetus*) and of self-knowledge (in the *Charmides* and elsewhere).

Note that I say "propose," "discuss," "explore," not "teach," "assert," or "take the view that." Engaging philosophically with Plato is not a simple matter of displaying a row of propositions, surgically abstracted from the texts, that give us Plato's definitive views. It is more like joining a concrete and particular philosophical conversation, where dead ends and messy digressions are only too possible, and where even the surest conclusions remain tentative and provisional because there is always more to say. How ironic that Plato's most familiar caricature should make him an inhumanly abstract dogmatizer, when in truth the human concreteness of his writings problematizes at every turn the very words "Plato says . . . ."

It is not merely that Plato's journey to the answers that he has to offer us goes a roundabout way. The journey itself—the *dialectic*, to use Plato's word—is what Plato has to offer us (Sedley 2003: 1): "Plato's real reason for persisting with the dialogue form is . . . his growing belief that conversation, in the form of question and answer, is the structure of thought itself."

This conception of the nature of philosophy is already a doctrine in epistemology. The doctrine is that all human "knowledge," all human doctrines, are no more than moments in a continuing conversation which, for all we know, might turn out to refute them at the very next moment.

This doctrine comes within its own scope; as we shall see, it is itself subjected to dialectical examination and development as Plato's career progresses. But it is clearly where he starts. Thus what is probably the earliest picture of Socrates that Plato gives us, in the *Apology*, is dominated by a near-skeptical conception of human knowledge. (It was not for nothing that the ancient skeptics—Pyrrho and Sextus Empiricus for instance—routinely claimed that they, not the Platonists, were the true heirs of Socrates.)

In the *Apology* Socrates tells a (hostile) Athenian jury that his mission in life is to discover whether anyone has any knowledge, by way of the dialectical method: by asking them questions about what they claim to know. But Socrates has found no one who can defend their own knowledge-claims. For instance, he says, politicians have, on examination, nothing to back up their reputation for wisdom—except a resentment if this reputation is undermined. Poets create their works "not by wisdom, but by divine inspiration and something in their natures" (*Apology* 22c1). Even craftsmen, despite their apparent specialist knowledge in particular areas, share with the poets an inability to explain their own expertise, and a brash over-confidence outside that expertise, as if wisdom in one area guaranteed wisdom in all. Socrates thinks that these failings undermine the craftsmen's claim to knowledge even in their own specializations. Hence, concludes Socrates, the truest "knowledge" that humans can have (it might, he speculates, be otherwise for gods) is only self-aware epistemic humility, and a willingness to ask hard questions: "the wisest man among [us] is the one who recognises, like Socrates, that in truth he is worth nothing where wisdom is concerned" (*Apology* 23b1).

One striking thing about this remark from the *Apology* is that it is about as close as Plato gets to the celebrated paradox "All I know is that I know nothing," often attributed to Socrates (following Diogenes Laertius, *Life of Socrates* XVI), but never quite put in his mouth by Plato. A second striking feature is that the passage treats knowledge and wisdom as being, in the final analysis, one and the same thing. This equation of knowledge and wisdom seems to be no linguistic accident, and no passing slip either: it is explicitly argued for in the later dialog the *Theaetetus* (145d7–e7). Part at least of the import of this equation is, surely, to take us away from an emphasis on the propositional. We paradigmatically think of knowledge as justified belief in a true thesis. Where all theses and doctrines are—at least for knowers like us—permanently vulnerable to unexpected refutation, it is perhaps not these shakily provisional claims that most stably deserve the name of knowledge. In the absence of the kind of stable known that, for instance, we might have access to if we could define any of the virtues, the focus shifts to the inquirer: what most deserves to be called (human) knowledge is the best state that that inquirer can reasonably be expected to get himself into. And this is, once more, the epistemic humility described above.

Thus, for Plato, knowledge is not primarily a matter of awareness of doctrines, but of what we nowadays call epistemic virtue. Epistemic virtue, moreover, is the greatest virtue of all. It is Plato's Socrates who first defends the thesis that virtue and knowledge/wisdom are one and the same thing, and that wisdom is the key to everything else. When Plato famously says (*Republic* 473c) that the state cannot be well ruled until it has philosopher-kings, another way of putting this which might have appealed to Socrates would be to say that the truest justice, the true master-virtue, is wisdom.

Returning to the *Apology* passage: what does Socrates think the politicians, poets, and craftsmen of Athens *lacked*? Why exactly didn't they count as having (complete or perfect) knowledge? It is common ground among Plato scholars to reply that what he thought they lacked was the ability to *logon didonai* (*Theaetetus* 175d1). We might translate this as "provide definitions," but that translation is misleading. Plato's point is not the implausible one that Mr Gradgrind makes in *Hard Times*, Chapter II: that if Sissy Jupe cannot define the word "horse," then she cannot know anything about horses (even though she rides a pony every day in her father's circus). Plato is not unaware that a potter does not need to be able to enounce explicitly a formal scientific definition of clay to produce first-rate pots (see *Parmenides* 130c8; *Theaetetus* 147a–c), or that a poet does not need a definition of meter to produce magnificent verse—he can, as the *Apology* passage acknowledges, produce it simply by "inspiration" (whatever that is). And Plato is not claiming that the potter, poet, or any other craftsman needs to be able to produce such definitions in order to perform their own distinctive crafts. What he is claiming is that such crafts cannot be complete or perfect knowledge all on their own. For what is needed for complete and perfect knowledge is a *synoptic understanding* of each and every craft: a coherent overall account of the place of each activity and its aims within the overall aim of living well. An overall account can also show us that something that seems a genuine craft actually is not, because it has no real place in the overall good life. That is part of the message of the *Gorgias*' contrast of false crafts (e.g. cookery, rhetoric) with true crafts (e.g. medicine, dialectic).

When we turn from questions about crafts to questions about virtues, a parallel point is taken even further by Plato. The crafts can at least exist in isolation: one can be a good potter without being a good man, even if knowledge of pottery without an understanding of where it fits into the good life can never be complete or perfect knowledge. By contrast, anyone who lacks a coherent overall account of any given virtue, one which integrates it with all the other virtues, does not really have any knowledge at all, even of that virtue on its own. (This is Plato's famous doctrine of "the unity of the virtues.") In the case of the crafts, we need to "give an account" of them to complete our knowledge of them. In the case of the virtues, our knowledge of them is not even begun, never mind completed, until we can "give an account" of them.

Equipped with this understanding of *logon didonai*, and granted a careful reading of the dialogs, we can divide the victims of Socrates' questioning into three groups. In the first group are those, like the poets, who can provide no answers whatever when he asks them to give an account of their expertise. At least as Socrates reports them, they simply cannot explain at all how they know what they claim to know; they have nothing whatever to say about what makes the difference, for them, between success and failure. This makes their knowledge-claims as mysterious, from a holistic point of view, as a psychic gambler's. Someone who reliably backs the winning horse, but has no idea how he picked the winner out from all the other horses, is plausibly said to have no *knowledge* of which horse will be the winner—he is simply a lucky guesser.

In the second group are those, e.g. Euthyphro and Laches in the eponymous dialogs, who do have *some* sort of answer to Socrates' request for an account (of holiness and courage, respectively). However, the accounts that they offer are not coherent. They include logical contradictions, and their adherents' assent to them is fickle, unstable over time. These features of contradiction and fickleness make their knowledge-claims highly dubious.

On contradiction: someone who says that he knows p, *and* that he knows that p implies q, *and* that he knows that p implies *not*-q, is not in a mental state that we can comfortably and unambiguously describe as knowing p. On fickleness: consider a scenario described to me by Nicholas Denyer. Suppose Nick is sure at 0701 that p, sure at 0702 that *not*-p, not sure one way or the other at 0703 p.m., and back to certainty that p at 0704. At all four times, Nick is not in a mental state that deserves to be called knowing p. (Interestingly, this seems the right thing to say even if Nick's belief that p at 0701 and 0704 is justified true belief; not all counter-examples to "knowledge = justified true belief" are Gettier cases.)

In the third group we find those whose claim to know a given craft, or to understand a given virtue, is compromised when Socrates' questioning reveals that the so-called expert has no idea, or a wrong or inadequate idea, of how the aims of his particular expertise relate to any other aims that he might be expected to have. Evidently Protagoras is meant to exemplify this fault in relation to the virtue of courage (*Protagoras* 349d–351b).

Even if he can give a satisfactory account of what courage is like, he cannot say anything convincing about how the aims of courage relate to the aims of the other virtues. This undermines his right to say that he knows *anything* about courage. For to be ignorant of how courage fits into the good life overall is not an incidental flaw in an account of courage. It spells the collapse of the whole account, from the top downwards.

The basic problem here is one about *isolated* knowledge-claims. Someone who claims to know, say, that they farm ostriches in Aberdeenshire, seems at first sight to have a piece of knowledge. After all, they *do* farm ostriches in Aberdeenshire. But now suppose that this person does not know that ostriches are birds, or where Aberdeenshire is. Do we still feel confident that this person *knows* something as opposed to having a true belief? (Notice, again, that there might be counter-examples here to the equation of knowledge with justified true belief which are quite unlike Gettier's counter-examples.) Suppose, further, that this person does not even know that ostriches are animals, or that Aberdeenshire is a place, or what farming is. By this point we might begin to doubt that such a person even has a belief—never mind a true belief, or a piece of knowledge.

The same point, that knowledge or expertise cannot, in the end, exist in isolation, is made by Plato's notorious critique of poetry in *Republic* Book X. However good poets might be technically, there remains the question what ends their technical mastery really serves. The poets themselves, Plato complains (surely unfairly, but that's another story), are utterly casual about this question. But without an answer to it, there is no guarantee that their sort of goodness is really goodness at all. To get that guarantee, we need to know first that poets have any place in the ideal state, and if so, what that place is. Until we are clear about this, we can no more infer from "x is a good poet" to "x is a good person" than we can infer from "x is a good concentration-camp guard" to "x is a good person." In what we might call the hierarchy of the crafts and virtues, the overarching holistic vision of the good governs everything below it. That is why Plato insists, at *Republic* 352d7–9, that his argument "is not about just any chance question; it is about the question *how life should be lived.*"

It is important not to be distracted here by the largely ethical content of many of the knowledge-claims that Plato assesses. A modern philosophical outlook typically sees ethical discourse as a special case, clearly demarcated from non-ethical discourse, and not even fully truth-apt as non-ethical discourse is. This might tempt us to see Plato's focus on ethical knowledge-claims, and equally his claim that virtue is *identical* to knowledge, as a naive anachronism. We should resist the temptation. Ethical subjectivism was as widespread in Plato's society as in ours, and Plato was anything but naive about it. One aim of the last paragraph's argument is, precisely, to undermine the subjectivist assumption that ethical knowledge *can* ultimately be separated from other sorts of knowledge. To be sure, you can be a good potter without being a good man: you can concern yourself solely with questions such as how hot the kiln should be and what mixture of mud and water makes the best clay, and ignore questions such as how my being a potter fits into the rest of my life or into the rest of the city. The subjectivist wants to call these latter two questions specially ethical ones, and to claim that, unlike the former two, they have no clear or incontestable answers. Plato would reply that every potter is also a human, that all humans face questions like these latter two, and that it would be surprising indeed if there were expertise about small matters like pottery, but no expertise about the greater matters of ethics—not just how pottery is to be practiced, but how life itself is to be lived. In this a fortiori argument, apparently, he would have Aristotle's support (*Nicomachean Ethics* 1094a1–23). For Plato, there simply isn't the sharp distinction between the ethical and the non-ethical that the subjectivist wishes to draw.

The more Plato spells out his negative account of why his own ordinary contemporaries do not count as having knowledge, the more he uncovers, as if by accident, a positive account: an account of what it would be to have knowledge. The transition from Plato's early period to his middle dialogs consists in a growing confidence about this positive account. Plato becomes clearer what the conditions for knowledge must be, and comes to think that there might after all be cases where human cognition actually meets those conditions: cases where humans do actually know.

It was evidently mathematics that led Plato in this more optimistic direction. To see what most struck Plato about mathematics, recall the three marks of those who do not know listed above. At least one of the following is true of the ignorant person: (1) he can say nothing about what makes the difference between cases where he gets it right and cases where he gets it wrong; (2) he cannot spell out and describe what he knows, e.g. to answer (1), without falling into contradiction, or failing to form a stable view, or both; (3) he cannot state the significant interrelations between the parts and wholes of knowledge, or explain how knowledge in his area contributes to and interrelates with knowledge as a whole. Removing the negations from this, we get three marks of someone who *does* know, or of what is known: we can call them (1) perspicuity, (2) consistency, (3) holism. What is striking about mathematicians is how well they display at least the first two marks.

(1) No familiar form of human inquiry exposes faulty methodologies more starkly than mathematics does, or makes it plainer why good methodologies are good. Compare pottery: only practice and trial and error can teach me the knack of using a potter's wheel. Even once I have learned that knack, I might not understand *why* there are some things you can do with a piece of clay, and others you can't—I just recognize that's how it is for potters. By contrast, to understand why a mistake in mathematics—say, the claim that $5 + 7 = 11$—is a mistake is simply to understand the meanings of the terms involved. No one who clearly understands these terms can possibly make that mistake. And there is a crunchy little puzzle, which preoccupies Plato in *Theaetetus* 187–201, about how mathematical and other a priori mistakes are possible at all. How can someone who *knows* 5, 7, 11, addition, and equals, end up thinking that they are connected as above? Isn't it a condition of knowing them that anyone who does know them should be incapable of making this sort of mistake? But then, equally, how can anyone who does *not* know them make such a mistake—since, not knowing them, he can't think about them at all?

To demonstrate the correctness of a mathematical claim, we need only display how the truth of the whole claim follows from the meanings of its parts plus the rules for conjoining them. Likewise, to show where a piece of mathematical reasoning has gone wrong, we need only show where the reasoner has failed to assign the correct meanings to the terms involved, or failed to follow the conjunction-rules, or both. To show this we need no special equipment—only the concepts themselves. Even the person who made the original mistake can be shown where he has gone wrong, provided he at least understands the concepts. That person need be no expert: as Socrates undertakes to demonstrate to his friend Meno, he might be no more than an uneducated slave-boy (*Meno* 82b–86b). Anyone who merely understands the concepts can, with a little coaxing, be led to unearth their interrelations—to 'recollect' what, in truth, he already implicitly knows about them. Hence, Socrates argues, our implicit knowledge of the interrelations of concepts is evidence for the immortality of the soul. In tapping into this knowledge which is part of our souls, we are tapping into something eternal; so there is a part of our souls which is eternal.

(2) Hence, no familiar form of human inquiry is better than mathematics at producing extended trains of reasoning and argument which simply cannot involve inconsistencies—if they did, these inconsistencies would be immediately detectable and eliminable—and which simply cannot be easily changeable. The mathematician's understanding of the reasonings might come and go, but the reasonings themselves are true unchangingly. If the mathematician fully grasps the reasoning, his understanding too will become unchanging in this way (*Meno* 97d–98b).

(3) Mathematics is then for Plato a paradigm of knowledge in its perspicuousness, and in its consistency. It is only in the third respect, holism, that it falls short. We can put the point about holism in two ways. We can say either that mathematics is less than paradigmatic knowledge because we can imagine that someone might give a fairly full specification of the good, the purpose, of mathematics, without being able to say how the good of mathematics fits into the good as a whole: more briefly, a good mathematician is not necessarily a good person, or even a wise one. Or we can put the point as Plato puts it in *Republic* 511b–c, and say that the shortcoming of mathematics—high though it stands in the scale of human cognitive achievements—is that it is a fundamentally *conditional* inquiry: it starts from assumptions, and unfolds the implications of those assumptions, but it never justifies the assumptions themselves. Hence mathematics fails to be fully holistic, fully integrated into knowledge as a whole, in the way that true knowledge must be: "the person who sees things synoptically is a dialectician; the person who does not is not": *Republic* 537d8).

Plato finds a related flaw in the program of science conducted by the philosopher Anaxagoras (*c*.500–428 BC) that Socrates criticizes in *Phaedo* 97c ff. Anaxagoras, he complains, raised high hopes by his slogan "Mind governs all" (DK 59B12). This slogan sounded to Socrates like the announcement of a unitary program of teleological explanation of everything, of the sort that Plato himself was to attempt in the *Timaeus*. But in fact, Socrates reports, Anaxagoras offered no such thing. His use of "Mind" was only sloganeering; his real explanations were ad hoc, messy, and "by way of all sorts of out-of-place agents—'airs' and 'ethers' and 'waters' and so on" (*Phaedo* 98c2–3). Thus Anaxagorean "scientific explanation" does not even get as close as mathematics does to satisfying the requirements for knowledge. Socrates' criticism (whether it is a *fair* criticism is another story) of Anaxagorean science is this: it consists of disjointed, isolated postulates, jammed untidily together without any true holistic unity. That is why, even if such an account is perspicuous and consistent, it still is not true knowledge.

Take a third example of something that falls short of Plato's ideal of true knowledge, the case of the skill of making artifacts such as the bed that Plato mentions in *Republic* 596b5–7. The making of artifacts is a teleological business. Knowing how to make a good table means knowing what a table would be like that perfectly served the specific function of a table. That is, it means looking towards the *ideal* table; which in turn means, in part at least, understanding the truth of (arguably) timelessly true claims like these: "A good table has legs of equal length"; "The perfect table would not be made of thistledown or jelly"; "Ideally, a table will have a flat surface," and so on.

Plato's reason for raising this example is partly to suggest an a fortiori argument. If even a craftsman's technical mastery cannot be fully understood without treating it as involving Plato's famous Ideas or Forms, still less can the much more purely conceptual mastery of the mathematician—or the true science of the dialectician himself. Why then does the craftsman's mastery fail to count as true knowledge? For at least two reasons.

First, because, as before, it is not guaranteed by its content to be holistic. Wisdom or expertise in table-making can exist in isolation, but not as complete or perfect knowledge, because it on its own does not entail wisdom or expertise about everything; a good table-maker might have no idea of how to explain how the good of table-making fits in with the other goods. Contrast the world-maker in the *Timaeus*, who (at least on a neo-Platonist interpretation) *does* have this holistic understanding, and creates the world according to it. What he "looks towards" is not just a single Form but also "the eternal," i.e. the whole of God's own nature; what he makes is "aimed towards what can be understood by reason and wisdom, and what is unchangingly the same" (29a7–8). Hence the world is completely ordered by a single all-encompassing explanation (*Timaeus* 29e–30c).

Secondly, the table-maker's expertise falls short of being knowledge because it is unclear to us, in our state of understanding, that there is any such thing as *the* specific function of a table anyway. A table can be used for eating from; or for resting a computer and books on (like my own just now); or for signing a peace treaty on; or for a game of shove ha'penny; or for dancing on; or to block a doorway; or as an *objet trouvé* in an art gallery. . . . Which of these is *the* function of the table? We do not know. This is not to say that there is no answer; in fact Plato at least outlines what an answer to this question would be like at *Cratylus* 389a–d. But it is to say that the answer can only come from the holistic understanding of everything, and of how the goods of every thing interrelate, that alone Plato is prepared to call knowledge.

All three of these cases, then—mathematics, Anaxagorean science, table-making—are cases of partial understanding, but they do not pass Plato's three tests for complete and perfect knowledge. To remind ourselves of those tests: knowledge, for Plato, is a system of reasoned argument which is, in the senses I have spelled out, (1) perspicuous, (2) consistent, and (3) completely holistic. (1) Real knowledge cannot coexist with ignorance of how epistemic success differs from epistemic failure. (2) Real knowledge cannot coexist with logical inconsistency, or with the different sort of inconsistency that is involved in constantly changing one's mind about what is true or false. (3) Real knowledge cannot be *isolated* knowledge: true knowledge is systematic, indeed the true system of knowledge must be one of maximally integrated logical systematicity.

There is an obvious objection to this conception of knowledge: it is too demanding. If this is what any cognition needs to be to count as knowledge, then hardly anything will count. But (the objection continues) it is a matter of familiar observation that we count *lots* of things as knowledge. So Plato's conditions for knowledge are untenably stringent.

This objection is central to the critique of Plato's epistemology that was already being developed, in Plato's own lifetime, by his great pupil Aristotle (*Nicomachean Ethics* I.6, *Metaphysics* I.9). We can see from *Parmenides* 133b–134e that Plato had arrived at something like this objection on his own account, almost certainly before Aristotle stated it. According to "Parmenides" there, the greatest difficulty for Plato's theory of Forms is that it creates a super-world of super-knowledge, quite unrelated to the needs and realities of *our* world and *our* knowledge.

Plato can say at least four things in response. First, he can observe that his stringent conception of the conditions for knowledge is derived from an examination of the concept of knowledge itself. All along, his project has been to ask what "we," on reflection, are prepared to count as knowledge, and by what criteria. Thus his demanding conception of knowledge is not one that he has plucked out of the air. It is one that Socrates has carefully developed through discussions with other reflective people. (Here again we see the crucial importance of the fact that Plato's method is dialectical, i.e. conversational.) So it is pointless to object that "we" "count *lots of* things as knowledge." That observation merely returns us to the beginning of the Platonic dialectic that was aimed at *refining* what we so count. The critic who makes this objection just isn't keeping up.

Secondly, Plato can concede that something quite close to skepticism is indeed the upshot of his conception of knowledge. That is not itself a good reason for doubting his arguments for that conception; any real philosopher is committed to "following the argument wherever it goes" (*Crito* 46b5), no matter how inconvenient the destination. Moreover, it is not clear that the skepticism is complete. When Socrates famously wonders, at *Republic* 540d3, whether the city that he describes can ever come into being, it is perhaps not too fanciful to suggest that it is not just an ideal *political* system that he thinks it "certainly difficult—yet possible *somehow*" to realize. It is an epistemic system too. It is a striking difference between Plato's way of thinking and our own that for him these possibilities stand or fall together.

Thirdly, Plato can and does accept the thought that naturally follows from the demandingness objection to his epistemic ideal: the thought that if the conditions for knowledge are so hard to satisfy, then perhaps, a lot of the time, the best thing for us to do is to stop worrying about *knowledge*, and accept some lesser epistemic state—true belief or perception, say—as a makeshift (*Meno* 97c5, *Philebus* 58d–62d). This is not to say that Plato would accept the connected thought that a modern reader (such as Kvanvig (2003)) is quite likely to have: that Plato's whole argument is not really about *knowledge* at all, but about some more epistemically exalted state—understanding, perhaps, or science. Certainly, Plato's word for "knowledge," *epistêmê*, is also the classical Greek for "science." And certainly, as I have observed, Plato himself argues that "knowledge" and "wisdom" are synonyms. It is, nonetheless, still knowledge, in just our sense, that Plato is talking about. Thus his point about epistemic isolation, for instance, is not only the point that an isolated cognition cannot be *understanding*. It is also the point that an isolated cognition cannot be *knowledge*; and we have already seen why there is something very plausible about that point. If the point is correct, that lends support to Plato's idea that understanding, wisdom, and knowledge are (at the very least) inextricably connected concepts.

Fourthly, Plato is anyway not entirely negative in his conception of knowledge. In the *Republic* he has a great deal to tell us about what the epistemic system that he envisages might look like—even if what Socrates tells us there is, confessedly and deliberately, expressed only in tantalizing images, by "one who speaks of what he does not know, as if he *did* know" (506c1):

> As to the Good Itself, we should let it be for now; to speak of that would seem to me to be beyond our reach at present. But I am willing to tell you about the offspring of the Good, and of what is most like to it . . .
>
> (506e1–6)

The "offspring of the Good" that Socrates speaks of here are the three magnificent extended metaphors of Sun, Line, and Cave that immediately follow. (Here notice again the pervasive irony of Plato. To speak of the Good *via* these images is to break his own ban on *eikasia*, imitation (*Republic* 598b), a ban imposed because imitation gives us no knowledge of the reality of things. So what knowledge of the Good can we derive from Plato's three metaphors?)

The Sun, Line, and Cave are immensely rich and intricate images, and there is of course no substitute for reading them. But *Republic* 532a–b offers us a fairly brief summary of the central point that at least the Sun and the Cave make about knowledge (the Line is more complicated). Understanding progresses upwards by the criticism of such provisional and incomplete forms of cognition as (say) table-making, physical science, and mathematics. Elsewhere in Plato other examples of incomplete forms of cognition include the science of naming, criticized in the *Cratylus*, and the love of individual beauty criticized in the *Symposium*. To come to understand *why* these are not cases of knowledge, by seeing how they measure up to something like the three criteria for knowledge that I have suggested, is to move beyond them. The ultimate goal of that movement is The Form of the Good. But once that is reached, there is a re-descent (*Republic* 520c2–3). The Form of the Good is the first principle of all reality, and so, likewise, the first principle of all understanding of reality. The person who has once grasped it will therefore understand everything else in the light of it, including all the interrelations of the various other subordinate Forms that are teleologically controlled by The Form of the Good; hence, the person who grasps it will have full knowledge of everything.

Here, in the same spirit as before, we are bound to meet the objection: What is the use of such an ideal of knowledge, if in fact no actual human cognizer can ever satisfy it? The answer to that, I think, is that Plato is interested in how we *approach* this ideal. More generally, he is interested in how the whole of reality, insofar as it is intelligible or knowable at all—even in only a lowly degree and an approximate sense of "knowable"—is bound to be intelligible or knowable via the Forms.

Two of the main arguments that Plato offers for the Forms are relevant here: as they are usually called, the One over Many (*Republic* 596a ff.), and the Argument from Opposites (*Phaedo* 104b ff.; *Republic* 477a ff.). The One over Many gives an explanation of similarities: it says that where two different things X and Y are F, that is no mere coincidence, and not something for which there can be no more explanation than just the brute fact that X and Y are similar. There is a *reason* for the similarity, and the reason lies in the fact that X and Y share in a property, F-ness, this property being by nature one of Plato's Forms. To understand X and Y *as* F is, then, to understand them as being informed (the *mot juste*) by the Form of F-ness.

The Argument from Opposites, on the other hand, gives a resolution of differences and contradictions: it notes that things in the world are full of contradictions, that they never perfectly exemplify the properties of which we baldly take them to be exemplars. There is, for instance, no such thing as a perfect circle in nature; as Plato might rather hyperbolically express it, any natural figure "is just as much a circle as not a circle." Discarding the hyperbole, we can see an important point here about, for instance, geometry. When someone says that the area of the circle is πr^2, they do not mean that the area of *this* circle here o is πr^2. For that circle is not truly a circle at all; it is only an approximation to a circle. What πr^2 applies to, strictly and accurately speaking, is only *the ideal circle*; it applies to actual and imperfect circles only insofar as they approximate that ideal; moreover, the degree to which actual and imperfect circles are rationally intelligible, by geometry, is only the degree to which they approximate that ideal circle. To make rational sense of actual and imperfect circles in the world is, then, only possible insofar as we see them as resembling that ideal circle.

These two arguments for the Forms show how and why Plato came to think that, necessarily, real knowledge at the very least always involves the Forms, and quite possibly is never about anything but the Forms. Plato thinks that an argument can be developed to the same conclusion that *shows* how knowledge necessarily involves the Forms, by trying to construct an account of knowledge that ex hypothesi does not involve the Forms, and demonstrating how it fails.

Just this (at least on my reading: Chappell 2004) is the project that Plato engages in the *Theaetetus*, where his aim is to refute on its own terms the empiricist view (as we might anachronistically call it) that we need nothing more than perception to give a full account of knowledge. Thus the *Theaetetus* first shows that knowledge cannot be identical to perception. Perception, in itself, is no more than unstructured sensation. For us to derive knowledge from such sensation is for us to impose the kind of structure on it that gives it propositional shape. But this is precisely the kind of structure that only the Forms can give to things. Furthermore, if knowledge is only perception, then there could be no distinction between true and false belief: for perception without the Forms is (as we have seen) only unstructured sensation, to which no true/false distinction can apply until it is given propositional structure. Thus the empiricist's problem is not just with *false* belief, but with belief as such: what the empiricist lacks is an account of how the objects of perception can attain semantic structure, so as to become possible objects of knowledge. This he will go on lacking until he becomes a Platonist.

The *Theaetetus* thus exploits another crucial aspect of the Forms—that they are what structures thought and discourse (*Sophist* 259e6; *Theaetetus* 202b6)—to run what is in effect a transcendental argument for the necessity of the Forms for knowledge. So far from the *Parmenides* being (as some have held) the dialog where Plato gives up on the Forms because of the objections to them that are there produced, it already foreshadows this transcendental argument (*Parmenides* 135b7–c2):

> if someone, with an eye on all these and other similar objections, will neither allow there to be Forms of the things that exist, nor define a single Form for each one, then he will have nowhere else to turn his understanding, because he does not allow there to be an eternally-changeless Form for each thing; and so he will completely destroy our capacity for language.

The Forms, on this account, are necessary conditions of our understanding anything at all, or even formulating propositions. And as the Argument from Opposites and the One over Many imply, the world is intelligible and knowable only because it comes to us with intelligibility and knowability built into it, insofar as it is structured by the Forms. In works of the Later period such as *Timaeus*, *Sophist* and *Philebus*, Plato spells out this thesis more fully than it is spelled out by the metaphors of the *Republic* and the purely negative transcendental argument of the *Theaetetus*: he attempts, that is, to give us a more detailed picture of *how* the Forms structure the world and render it intelligible, knowable, and oriented to the Good in the way that the *Phaedo* and *Republic* originally proposed.

Plato's attempt to spell his theory out can lead him into some strange and, to our eye, philosophically unfruitful territories; witness the oddities of physiology and numerology that we find in the *Timaeus*. Many of these oddities in the detail are undoubtedly best understood as early attempts to do science. However they are to be understood, that there are oddities in Plato, particularly at the level of his detailed theorizing, should come as no surprise. Plato is not the only great philosopher to propose with great plausibility, via a brilliant transcendental argument, that reality or some key part of it can only be understood as having a certain structure—and then get into difficulties and awkward over-complications when he tries to say something more positive about what that structure is like. Kant's philosophical psychology is notoriously the most rebarbative part of his critical philosophy. To cite an even closer parallel, Frege's difficulties over what we can *positively* say about the denizens of his *drittes Reich* are equally notorious. At any rate the disappointment is there, and was already reported by Plato's earliest auditors. Most of those who came to Plato's lecture "On the Good," Aristoxenus tells us (Aristoxenus, *Harmonics* 39.8–40.4, apparently reporting a tale he heard from Aristotle), hoped to hear about the conditions of human well-being; what they got instead was "a discussion of the mathematical sciences" and the enigmatic conclusion "that good is one"; "this struck them as utterly paradoxical." The strangeness to us of (at any rate) the detail of Plato's conceptions of the good and of knowledge is not, then, a result merely of the fact that he comes from a radically different philosophical culture; people in his own culture found his theories strange too.

In assessing Plato as an epistemologist, we are missing something if we do not register this strangeness. We are equally missing something if we do not register Plato's extraordinarily creative genius: the sheer number of areas where later philosophy as we know it is simply inconceivable without his contribution.

Acknowledgments

My thanks to Sarah Broadie, Nicholas Denyer, Michel Narcy, Denis O'Brien, David Sedley, and Duncan Pritchard for helpful comments.

References

Timothy Chappell, *Reading Plato's Theaetetus*. Academia Verlag/Hackett, 2004.
Jonathan Kvanvig, *The Value of Knowledge and the Pursuit of Understanding*. Cambridge University Press, 2003.
David Sedley, *Plato's Cratylus*. Cambridge University Press, 2003.

59
ARISTOTLE
Richard Patterson

Aristotle's views concerning knowledge are broad in scope, encompassing accounts of the potential objects of knowledge, the diversity of branches of knowledge and their hierarchical organization, the cognitive processes by which humans achieve knowledge, the embodied nature of virtually all cognitive capacities, the kind of reasoning through which we extend our knowledge by deriving new results from previous knowledge, the varieties of understanding or explanation, and the place of knowledge in a good human life. Although Aristotle does appear to address one or two familiar skeptical arguments (a regress-of-justification argument, *Posterior Analytics* I.3; perhaps a skeptical dream argument, *Metaphysics* 1011a6–7) he does not much concern himself with the dread specter of skepticism that has come to haunt modern epistemology. In his view humans clearly do attain theoretical, practical, and productive knowledge; his main concern is not to show that there is knowledge, but to understand its varieties, acquisition, exercise and value.

Section (A) below provides an overview of Aristotle's classification of branches of knowledge, (B) his theory of scientific understanding proper, and (C) the manner in which we know what to do in situations of choice and action. For present purposes productive expertise (craft, *techne*) does not call for extensive discussion, but will serve (D) to reinforce the overarching conclusion that although all types of knowledge share a broad common framework, Aristotle did not think of science or theoretical understanding as a model the rest should all approximate. Finally (E) considers Aristotle's basic assumptions that (1) the contents of knowledge must somehow enter the mind via sense perception and (2) all thinking is accomplished in or by means of images. These assumptions appear to set significant limits on human knowledge, but in practice Aristotle copes with difficult cases by broadening the range of underlying images beyond those of the five standard senses, and by the use of analogy.

A. The Branches of Knowledge

Aristotle distinguishes two very broad types of knowledge on the basis of their objects or subject matter: (I) knowledge of that which is necessary (i.e., cannot be otherwise) and (II) knowledge of that which is not necessary. The objects of the latter subdivide into (A) things we can affect by action, and (B) products of craft. These two simple bifurcations give rise to the traditional categories of theoretical, practical, and productive knowledge. Theoretical knowledge in turn includes (1) natural science, (2) mathematics and (3) "first philosophy" pertaining, respectively, to things that are "natural" or "by nature" (i.e., that possess a source of change or stability in themselves, such as living things or earth, air, fire, and water); things that exist as embodied in particular objects but are studied "in abstraction" from those bodies (mathematical entities); and the principles of all "being qua being." (The relation between the study of being qua being—metaphysics—and of the eternal pure forms that govern cosmic motion—theology—is still much debated.) Aristotle retains this close tie between epistemology and ontology through further subdivisions—e.g., of natural science into basic physics, biology, zoology, etc., and productive knowledge into poetry, rhetoric, architecture, etc. Each type of knowledge has its own subject domain, whose existence it postulates as one of its "starting points" or "first principles" (*archai*).

B. Theoretical Knowledge

As described in the *Posterior Analytics* (*Apo*), each branch of knowledge has an axiomatic structure resting on necessary "first principles" (*archai*) from which other truths of the science follow deductively. This is not to say that science either discovers or teaches these further truths simply by way of deduction, but rather that the results of a science can be displayed in the form of deductions from first principles. Since there was at the time neither any formal theory nor even any explicit concept of logical consequence, Aristotle had to forge these himself (see below). However, scientific deductions are not merely supposed to establish the truth of their conclusions, but to *explain* why they are true. Science does not aim primarily at justified true belief, or certainty that a body of propositions is true, but at *understanding why* things are as they are. (See, e.g., Kosman 1973; Burnyeat 1981.) Deductions that explain general connections by deriving them from first principles are called "demonstrations" (*epideixeis*) or "scientific deductions" (*syllogismos epistemonikos*, APo I, 71b17–18). Thus scientific understanding is a "demonstrative state" (*hexis apodeiktike*, NE VI, 1139b31–32), and to know a demonstrable truth is just to possess a demonstration of it (APo II, 90b9–13).

In addition to a general existence assumption for its domain (e.g., numbers, animals, heavenly bodies), the first principles of a science include basic definitions (odd and even number, things existing "by nature," animate thing) and further non-definitional assumptions (e.g., the Law of Non-contradiction in First Philosophy, "Equals added to equals . . ." in mathematics, "Nature does nothing in vain" in the natural sciences). To function as foundational and explanatory first principles, these *archai* must be (1) true, (2) necessary, (3) not derived from anything prior to them, (4) prior to all other truths of the science, (5) "better known" than, and (6) explanatory of all other truths of the science (APo I, 71b20–22). How, then, do we know the first principles and how do we construct demonstrations?

Aristotle's formulaic response is that we know scientific *archai* via *epagoge* (usually translated 'induction'; see esp. APo I.18), and other truths via demonstrations from *archai*. This is misleadingly simple, however. On the one hand, while it is true that propositions which in fact are first principles are known via *epagoge* (broadly, movement from apprehension of particulars to a universal, or from more specific to more generic universals), not every proposition or definition reached in that way is a first principle. First principles must meet the six conditions just listed, and this is largely a matter of their larger, systematic role—e.g., that they be explanatorily fundamental.

Similarly, demonstrations are deductions, but not every deduction is a demonstration. Here Aristotle had first to characterize deduction itself, then say how demonstrations constituted a special sort of deduction. Thus prior to the theory of demonstration worked out in the *Posterior Analytics* we find, naturally enough, the *Prior Analytics* (*APr*), in whose first seven chapters Aristotle sets out his system of the plain (i.e., non-modal) syllogism (*syllogismos*, "deduction"), which became the "Traditional Logic" of the West. A deduction is a "discourse in which, if some things are given, something else necessarily follows, . . . and follows because of the things stated" (*APr* I.1, 24b91–22). The most famous syllogism (later nicknamed 'Barbara': three a's signify the syllogism's three universal affirmative propositions) has the form, 'All As are Bs; All Bs are Cs; therefore all As are Cs.' Barbara illustrates the fact that a syllogism concludes to a statement relating two terms (A, C), where the relation asserted between A and C (e.g., *applies to every*, *applies to some*) must obtain if A relates to B (the "middle term") and B relates to C in the way asserted in the premises.

However, Aristotle says in the first sentence of *APr* that the inquiry is "about *demonstration*" (24a10) and, as he will emphasize in *APo*, this involves among other things necessary premises and conclusions. Accordingly Chapters 8–22 of the *APr* set out Aristotle's modal syllogistic, adding to "plain" propositions those in which the predicate relates necessarily or possibly or contingently to the subject. Thus did Aristotle create modal logic. His modal system has its own strengths and weaknesses, both as a logic of alethic modalities and as an instrument of science (see, e.g., Patterson 1985). But Aristotle was typically content in his actual scientific works to leave results unformalized, or simply to suggest an organization into plain syllogisms.

Whence the First Principles of Theoretical Knowledge?

If we come to know other truths by means of syllogistic deductions from first principles, how do we come to know the first principles themselves? *APo* II.19 describes a four-stage process: starting with perceptions of "familiar" things, we build up memories of similar particulars; over time we acquire experience (*empeiria*) in a domain; finally we grasp an *arche* or starting point—a basic concept or connection. We achieve this critical last step by *nous*—usually translated "intellect" or "reason." Aristotle tells us little about *nous*. One common reading takes it to be something like "intuition" or "intuitive insight," which might amount to (1) particular episodes of having intuitive insight, (2) the capacity to have such insight, (3) the state of understanding we enjoy once we have had insight, or (4) all of the above. These alternatives all suggest that *nous* involves a distinctive, immediate apprehension of a basic concept in its simplicity, or of the necessity and self-evidence of a general truth, or both. A more "empiricist" and less "rationalist" reading (e.g., Barnes 1975; Burnyeat 1981; Wedin 1988) makes *nous* more continuous with experience—i.e., something like the final, clarifying and consolidating stage in one's progress toward apprehension of basic truths or concepts.

A third possibility is that *nous* recognizes first principles *as* first principles. Although Aristotle's theories of perception and memory (*De Anima*, *De Sensu*, and *De Memoria*), do not make any clearer than *APo* II.19 exactly *how* multiple memories become experience, or how experience leads to understanding, it is clear that becoming experienced in a field takes time, practice, and often the guidance of a teacher. It also typically involves acquisition of general concepts and connections, rules of thumb and the like, even if not the ability to put these things precisely into words, or to organize them into a system of explanations. *Nous* then becomes the recognition of certain propositions, definitions, etc. *as* explanatorily fundamental starting points rather than simply as primitive universals or necessary co-variations among types of thing (see McKirahan 1992:

Ch. XVIII). On this third reading *nous* is neither intuition, nor the achieving of an explicit, secure generalization; it is, rather, the recognition, as the result of careful observation and critical reflection, that some concept or connection is fundamental—i.e., that it explains without itself having any further explanation. The scholarly debate goes on, but in any event all three conceptions of *nous* have heavily influenced the subsequent history of epistemology.

The "Four Causes" in Theoretical (and Other) Knowledge

A second important framework for theoretical knowledge, and one extending to practical and craft knowledge as well, involves Aristotle's celebrated "four causes" (*aitiai*, factors responsible for, or explanatory of, something's being what it is). *Physics* II.3 describes and illustrates (1) the formal cause—what it is to be a certain kind of thing, as given in a definition; (2) the material cause—that out of which something comes or is made, and which persists; e.g., the bronze of the statue; (3) the final cause—the goal, *telos*, for the sake of which a thing exists or is done or is produced; and (4) the efficient cause—the primary source of the change or stability that results in the coming-to-be of the thing. Aristotle says at *APo* II.11, 94a20–23 that we have understanding when we know the explanation (cf. *Physics* 194b16–20), and cites the four kinds of cause or explanation (although indicating the material cause rather obliquely). He maintains further that "these are proved through the middle term," thus asserting a fundamental link between the theory of the four causes and the theory of demonstration from first principles. Unfortunately his general defense of this assertion is not entirely clear or successful (see esp. Barnes 1994). On the other hand it is often easy to see in practice how the four causes would enter into an explanation of the phenomena of biology, psychology, craft, etc., and why identifying these causes in particular cases would at least implicitly guide a good deal of one's investigative and pedagogical practice. Not every *explanandum* calls for all four causes, but most do, and Aristotle's comprehensive view is that one understands a phenomenon or correlation only when one has worked out all the applicable sorts of *aitia*, and has seen how they function as explanatory syllogistic middle terms.

Scientific Theory and Practice

With these general conceptions of theoretical knowledge in mind we can briefly consider two thorny questions about their adequacy as a description of actual scientific inquiry. First, is syllogistic logic (even putting aside questions about modality) adequate for expressing scientific propositions and deductions? Second, is it even used by Aristotle in his own scientific works, such as the biological treatises? With regard to the first question, Aristotle's comments on mathematics are especially bold and provocative. Although Greek geometers do not express their proofs in syllogistic terms—using instead a combination of natural language and diagrams—Aristotle says that their proofs use syllogisms having the form of Barbara (*APo* II.14). What does he mean by this, and is it even remotely plausible? Two possibilities suggest themselves. First, he might have meant only that syllogistic logic is adequate for expressing the heart of any given proof. Aristotle frequently cites the theorem that *the interior angles of a triangle are equal to two right angles* (call this 2R). He points out that this is true because the *interior angles of a triangle* (A) are in fact *angles equal to the angles around a point* (B), and these in turn are *angles equal to two right angles* (C). This explanation goes easily into a standard syllogism with B (*angles equal to the angles around a point*) as the explanatory middle term.

Another possibility is that Aristotle had in mind the more full-dress mathematical proofs such as one finds in Euclid's *Elements* or its precursors, and more specifically the portion of a proof labeled "demonstration" (*epideixis*)—as opposed to the "setting out" of what is to be proved, the "construction" of the diagram, etc. The *epideixis* section simply uses natural language—while referring to points, lines, etc. in a diagram—to specify inferential steps leading to a desired conclusion. However, these deductive steps are typically expressible as universal affirmative propositions of syllogistic logic (see Mueller 1974 and Mendell 1998; the point is developed in detail in Patterson 1995). So it is clear enough, given the general terms Aristotle had in mind (e.g., *interior angles of a triangle, angles around a point*) why he might reasonably think that the geometers "use syllogisms in Barbara," even as we see clearly today both that there are many gaps, large and small, in Euclid's own proofs, and that Aristotle's own syllogistic logic is far from adequate for completely formalizing plane geometry.

Second, is syllogistic logic adequate for expressing the results of Aristotle's own scientific work, especially when he focuses on finding specific explanations, in zoology, physics, etc.? It is striking that even there one finds hardly a trace of a syllogism. Recent work has shown, however, that Aristotle's explanatory practice does reflect the *Analytics*' conceptions of deduction and demonstration. In zoology, for example, one regular feature of land animals is the possession of lungs, with which they breathe air in and out. But what is the point of that? Aristotle concludes that this is how land animals cool themselves. This gives a syllogism explaining why land animals have lungs: All *land animals* (A) are *animals that cool themselves by respiration* (B); All *animals that cool themselves by respiration* (B) are *animals that have lungs* (C); therefore All *land animals* (A) are *animals that have lungs* (C). The explanatory middle term is (B) *animals that cool themselves by respiration*. Why, then, do animals need to cool themselves? In part, because they need to cool the heart. Why? For one thing, the heart is the place where nutrients are "cooked" into blood. Why do nutrients have to be concocted into blood? And so on. Explanatory answers spread out into widening networks of interconnections among natural "*differentiae*" which themselves fall under four main heads (animal parts, activities, life history, and psychology; Balme 1987: 80). The complex interconnections among these zoological differentiae and their subtypes are typically expressed in universal affirmative propositions (*All As are B*), and can then be arranged into syllogisms in which some connections explain others. In short, one can gather from numerous examples the kinds of syllogistically structured demonstrations Aristotle had in mind, even though he seldom bothered, in the course of ground-level investigation, to stop and cast results in that form. And in fact he is sometimes still working toward such explanations as an ultimate goal (see especially the articles by Lennox, Gotthelf, and Bolton in Section II of Gotthelf and Lennox 1987).

C. Practical Wisdom

Although there are broad parallels between *sophia* in theoretical science and *phronesis* in the realm of good or bad action, the latter is acquired by a different method and has a considerably more complex structure. Since *phronesis* aims at rationally grounded action it must combine elements of what we now call ethics, epistemology, and action theory, and its epistemological interest lies largely in the way it combines these diverse elements. Again there are *archai*, and again we must work our way to them starting out from what is initially familiar—here, *endoxa*, views common to everybody or almost everybody, or to "the (distinguished) few." We investigate *endoxa* critically in order to determine what is correct and useful in them as we develop our own account. From this perspective the "historical" surveys with which many of Aristotle's works begin are crucially important for the initial gathering of *endoxa* and marshaling of problems. If we wind up disagreeing with reputable *endoxa*, we should be able to say why reasonable people might have believed them; and if we manage to resolve the difficulties in the *endoxa*, and of course in our own views, so as to arrive at a position in harmony with the most trustworthy of the (corrected or amended) *endoxa*, this is "adequate proof" (*NE* 1145b2–7). Aristotle calls the whole process "dialectic" (*dialectike*) as opposed to adversarial debate (*eristic*), or *epagoge* in theoretical science.

However, there is no clean separation between the methods of *epagoge* and *dialectic*. *Endoxa* and the questions they generate are important in all sciences: in metaphysics the views of philosophers predominate, since most people (even Greeks) have few opinions about being qua being; in meteorology one can often start with widespread opinions (e.g., thunder is a noise in the clouds); in ethics opinions are plentiful and varied. Nonetheless it is remarkable that in any study *endoxa* should be so methodologically central, and the aim of harmonizing diverse views and resolving difficulties so authoritative. This has raised worries that Aristotle is backsliding toward moral subjectivism, or that he holds a coherence theory of truth in ethics or politics. But probably he means that (1) this is the best sort of support for our views we can get in ethics and politics, which by nature do not afford the exactitude of geometry (*NE* VI.X); (2) it is in fact an adequate basis for our holding our views even if they don't "prove" us right; and (3) we should *act* on the views that enjoy such support. This is in the spirit of Socrates' injunction to put our trust in the *logos* that survives critical scrutiny (*Phaedo* 85c–d), and carries no suggestion that coherence or general agreement is what makes our views true.

Dialectical discussion generates a great deal that we would now see as belonging to ethics rather than epistemology. For example, it seeks definitions of virtue, courage, practical wisdom, deliberation, happiness, *et al.*, formulates and defends fundamental assumptions about the nature of "the good" (e.g., the nature of the best human life is determined by human nature), discusses such difficult notions as weakness of will, voluntariness, pleasure, and so on. But these "theoretical" results are not the primary goal of practical wisdom, which aims at doing the right thing in particular situations. For this to happen, neither holding the right theory nor, pace intellectualist views, recognizing what one should do here and now is sufficient. Thus Aristotle distinguishes *phronesis* from "comprehension" (*sunesis*), which also judges correctly what ought to be done, but merely judges and does not initiate or prescribe action (*NE* VI.9). Moreover *phronesis* also involves the ability to figure out how best to bring about a decided-upon action when intermediate steps are necessary—an ability Aristotle calls mere "cleverness" (*deinotes*) if divorced from *phronesis*. Unlike cleverness, *phronesis* aims at good action all down the line.

It is here that more recognizably epistemological questions emerge: how do we correctly and reliably judge that *this* is the right thing to do; how do we know how to bring about a decided-upon end; and what role does knowledge of first principles play in any of this? Aristotle's simplifying formula is that "virtue makes the end right and deliberation makes what promotes the end correct" (*NE* 1144a9–10). Virtue is "a settled disposition that decides, depending on a mean that is relative to us, in accord with reason—the reason by reference to which the *phronimos* would define it" (*NE* 1106b36 ff.). Deliberation is rational calculation concerning things that in one way or another contribute to achieving the end. (Debate continues as to whether one deliberates about ultimate ends, or only "means" in a broad sense.) But how does virtue make the ends, deliberation the means, correct?

Although our particular decisions are "in accord with" right reason they are not deduced from general principles. This is impossible not just because practical generalizations "can be otherwise," but also because there are no deductive chains of universal or even "for the most part" connections leading down from basic principles to the specific action one ought to perform given one's particular circumstances—e.g., donate five drachma today to the Daughters of Marathon Fund. *Phronesis* involves all-things-considered practical judgments (Broadie and Rowe 2002), and these must consider, well, all things—from the open-ended variety of circumstances and consequences potentially relevant to a particular choice (e.g., agent, patient, means, occasion, as noted at *NE* 1109b14, 23), to one's general conception of the good or happy life. The *phronimos* is the virtuous person who correctly recognizes and assesses the relevant factors, and on this basis sees with "the eye of the soul" (*nous*) the right thing to do. So even if our ethical principles are themselves structured in important ways by logical relationships, as when some conception of human nature implies a specific conception of the good for humans, the space between these general truths and the particular, situated actions we choose or reject is bridged not by deductions, but by a long-developing, well-practiced ability to see how consideration of all things great and small points to doing *this* rather than *that*.

Some interpreters see moral intuition at work here, this time with *nous* operating at the level of particular actions—perhaps in addition to grasping fundamental ethical principles. But once again there are two general readings of *nous*, parallel to the first two of those discussed in connection with theoretical science: first, as a distinct "intuitive" faculty of direct moral apprehension and prescription; second, as the concluding phase of a process of weighing multiple considerations to determine the best option in a particular situation in light of one's principles. Both readings attempt to capture important features of relevant human experience, and both are at least possible interpretations of the pertinent texts. (The term *nous* is itself neutral as regards these options, since it covers more than one psychic act, condition, or process, depending on the context. Nonetheless it appears to be concerned in all its uses with seeing that some item lies at a cognitive limit (whether "upper" or "lower")—a point at which analysis, justification, explanation, or deliberation comes to its proper end.)

D. A General Framework Without a Dominant Model

As noted above, both *sophia* and *phronesis* seek out general first principles by means of a method that starts from what is initially familiar to us, or what appears to be the case—the *phainomena*. Some passages suggest a division of *phainomena* into sensibles (in natural science) and *endoxa* (in action contexts). This is on the whole correct, even though *endoxa* have a significant role in natural science and in First Philosophy as well. Moreover the search for general principles in ethics is driven almost entirely by critical reflection and discussion, and in natural science by the interplay of careful observation and critical theorizing. Nonetheless, at a very general level the pursuit of both *sophia* and *phronesis* occurs within a broadly Socratic framework: gather the *phainomena* and the questions and problems to be addressed; where the *phainomena* are views or opinions (*endoxa*) about a topic, examine them critically and revise or discard them where appropriate as one develops one's own account; at every stage marshal further questions and difficulties and, where applicable, pertinent empirical observations; finally, adopt the view that best resolves these issues while accounting in a convincing way for the *phainomena*, or at least for the fact that people do pre-critically accept the *phainomena*.

At a yet more abstract level there is a framework of *aporia* (puzzlement; the formulation of unanswered questions and unresolved difficulties) and *lusis* (resolution) common to all sorts of knowing. This applies not only to theoretical and practical reflection, but also to productive *techne*, where the goal is to produce some product separate from reflection and from the activity of production (*NE* VI.4). At a less general, more detailed, level one can add that the craftsman needs training, experience, general principles, cleverness at figuring out how to proceed in given circumstances, and a good eye for judging when a work is or is not well done. These elements all have clear parallels in the sphere of *phronesis*. Thus in terms of the two-fold division of knowledge depending on whether or not its subject can or cannot be otherwise, practical and productive knowledge emerge as similarly structured subtypes of knowledge dealing with mutable things.

In sum, while there is a very general (Socratic) framework for pursuit of all forms of knowledge, and while there are important parallels between theoretical and practical inquiry, and between practical and productive knowing, theoretical science does not set "the" model for knowledge in general. Other forms of knowledge need not and should not try to conform to an axiomatic structure, and they must employ somewhat different means to attain their distinctive practical or productive knowledge.

E. Perceptual Sources and the Limits(?) of Knowledge

Aristotle maintains in *De Anima* and elsewhere that the content of thought must enter the mind via sense perception, and that all thinking involves images. Here it is possible only to mention the main features of Aristotle's position, then consider briefly how Aristotle counters, at least in practice, the limits those two assumptions would appear to impose on human knowledge.

Regarding the perceptual sources of cognitive content, *De Anima* (*De An*) characterizes both sense perception and thought in terms of matter and form (*hule* and *morphe*), for these factors are found "in the whole of nature" (*De An* III.5, 430a10–11). Perception of a sense object is "reception of the [perceptible] form [of the object] without the matter," and is thus a "becoming like" the object sensed (e.g., II.12, 424a17–21). To distinguish perception from other cases of such reception, e.g., a stone's being heated by the sun, Aristotle says that the sense organ, but not the stone, is the locus of a certain *logos* (proportion, measure; II.12, 424b1 ff.), which is the sense proper. He says little about this *logos*, but since perceptible properties are themselves combinations of opposites (light/dark, etc., as explained in *De Anima* and *De Sensu*) the *logos* is probably a sort of natural balance or proportion between relevant opposites within the sense organ. Since by definition "natural" things tend to maintain their natural condition unless disturbed and to return to it unless prevented, Aristotle might well have thought of the sensory organ-cum-*logos* as a natural mechanism for monitoring change toward or away from some neutral proportion of sensible opposites.

Similarly, cognition of a universal is reception of [intelligible] form, so that the intellect (*nous*) "becomes all things" (III.4–5). Thus thought is to the thinkable as sense is to the sensible (III.4, 429a13–18). Aristotle distinguishes "active" from "passive" (*poietike* versus *pathetike*) intellect, where active *nous* is somehow like light illuminating the intelligible forms received in passive *nous* (430a10–17). He does not posit a *logos* in the passive or receptive intellect, evidently because it must "become *all* [universal] things" and therefore must be entirely characterless—like, as he fatefully says, a blank tablet (429b29 ff.).

How might these difficult texts be related to the entry-level, perceptual sources of cognitive content? Certainly Aristotle rejects Plato's view that humans can in the exercise of *nous* rise above images to a level of pure conceptual thought (*Republic* VI, 510b, 511b). As Aristotle says, one "never thinks without a phantasm" (*De An* 430a14–16); "it is impossible even to think without a phantasm" (*On Memory* 449b31 ff.); "that which thinks, thinks (*noei*) forms (*eide*) in images (*phantasmata*)" (*De An* 431b1–2). Words are not the fundamental medium of thought, but signify "*pathemata* (affections) in the soul." And while words vary from person to person, these *pathemata* are the same, and are "likenesses" of actual things (*De Interpretatione* 16a4–8). Although some images arise simply as the causal result of sense perception (*De An* 429a1–2; cf. 428b10–16), humans can produce images at will, in the absence of any external sense object (427b17–18). Thus images can be formed as needed—in planning action, recollecting, doing geometry, etc.

But if we must think in (particular) images, how can we think abstractly? And again, are we not thereby limited to knowing things of which we can form an image? For that matter, how do we attain to general truths even about concrete sensibles (horses, bronze spheres) by thinking in particular images?

With regard to the practical sphere, *De An* 431b6 is especially helpful: "At other times one reasons and deliberates (*logidzetai kai bouleuetai*) by images or thoughts (*phantasmasi, noemasi*) in the soul, as if seeing them (*hosper horon*), and deliberates and thinks about the future in relation to the present." This mental simulation of alternative practical scenarios would be basic both to cleverness and to practical wisdom, but in the latter case would both elicit and facilitate judgment of right and wrong at all steps of deliberation and choice by bringing possible actions concretely before the mind's eye. And even if these imaginings involve images of particular people and circumstances (real or imaginary) they could serve in principle as the basis for more general practical reasoning, for seeing the universal in the particular. This is crucial for Aristotle's view of how we attain general knowledge, and is addressed directly in connection with geometric diagrams.

The geometer's diagram is a particular representation, whether external or in the imagination, and the typical Greek mathematical proof ostensibly refers throughout to particular points, lines, etc. in a diagram. The proof nonetheless establishes a general conclusion because, as Aristotle says, although our image might have a determinate size, we "do not use that determinate size in our reasoning" (*De Mem* 449b31 ff.). If we use only the shape of the figure (e.g., the fact that it is a triangle) but not its size, then our proof holds for all figures of any size whatsoever, so long as they have that same shape. In the Greek theory of proportion this universalizing step is even more sweeping, since ancient proofs use drawings of line to prove theorems not just about lengths but about all types of quantities—areas, volumes, temporal durations, weights, etc.

The case of general proportion theory illustrates not just the seeing of the universal in the particular, but also the far-reaching importance of analogy, as in "The length of segment AB is to CD as area G (or volume, duration, weight, age G) is to H." Aristotle himself uses analogies from one sensible analog to another quite frequently in his biological works (e.g., gills:fish :: lungs:land animal), although the importance and mode(s) of functioning of analogy there have yet to be thoroughly investigated (but see Lloyd 1966/1992). Equally important, analogy allows us to extend our understanding from sensible things to "theoretical entities"—as, for example, in the case of animal reproduction. According to Aristotle in *Generation of Animals* (GA), motions in the vital heat of the father's semen shape the matter contributed by the mother (the menses) into a viable embryo. The semen then dissipates without ever becoming part of the developing organism. Human beings do not see these motions in the vital heat, but they can see and imagine other visible motions, and they can form a conception of how motions in the vital heat might work by analogy to the movements, say, of a craftsman bringing determinate form into matter (GA 743b20 ff.; cf. rennet causing milk to curdle or "set"; GA 729a9 ff., 737a12 ff., et al.). Here analogy allows one to form at least a vague image of how semen and menses combine in passing species' form from generation to generation, and even to understand this process in terms of matter (the menses), form (the functional structure of the mature adult that produces the semen), *telos* or goal (reproduction of a new individual according to type) and source of motion (either the adult again, or the motion in the vital heat)—i.e., in terms of the four causes.

By contrast "active intellect" is pure form, and is therefore not something of which we can literally form even a conjectural image. But in its functional role it is analogous to light: as light makes potential colors into actual colors, so active *nous* makes the potentially intelligible actually intelligible (*De An* III.5, 430a14–17). Or again, active intellect is like a craftsman, insofar as it facilitates the bringing of form into matter (i.e., the passive intellect's becoming the object of cognition). It is a serious question how far such analogies can actually advance our understanding of the intellect, even if we accept Aristotle's theories concerning light and color, or the need for active and passive aspects of intellect. The point is simply that whatever we do know of active intellect—including its basic epistemic function—is conveyed, and even conceived, in terms of familiar experiential analogs.

Speaking more generally, Aristotle does offer some analysis of arguments from analogy (*Rhetoric* B.20). But he does not expressly acknowledge the importance of analogy for his own philosophical and scientific practice, or that it is in some key cases essential to our understanding of a subject; nor does he attempt to show that imagistic analogs can in all cases support our conception of entities that cannot be directly and literally imaged. He seems content to devise appropriate analogies as needed, on a case-by-case basis.

Conclusion

Aristotle gives us the general picture of humans starting from particular perceptual experiences of the world and proceeding by way of memory and accumulated experience, by careful observation, critical reflection and discussion, to universal truths, general concepts and ultimately to first principles. The process is driven by the formulation of questions and problems, and aims to resolve these on as firm a basis as possible so as to achieve understanding; for as human beings we "desire to know" (*Metaphysics* A.1, 980a21). Given our human cognitive abilities from sense perception to intellect, we segment, clarify, generalize and organize our experience of the world in somewhat different ways to achieve stable conditions of understanding of various sorts. Despite some important general similarities, the "way up" to first principles and the way down to particular cognitions, actions, or productions, differs significantly from one domain and one sort of knowledge to another in ways dictated by differences in subject matter and aim. But all understanding falls under one of the three great types of knowledge—theoretical, practical, or productive—through which we might achieve a life of distinctively human excellence.

References

Balme, D. M., "Aristotle's Use of Division and Differentiae," in Gotthelf and Lennox, 1987, 69–89.
Barnes, Jonathan, *Aristotle's Posterior Analytics*, 2nd ed., Clarendon Aristotle Series, Oxford: Clarendon Press, 1975, revised edn 1994.
Bolton, Robert, "Definition and Scientific Method in Aristotle's *Posterior Analytics* and *Generation of Animals*," in Gotthelf and Lennox, 1987, 120–166.
Broadie, Sarah, and Rowe, Christopher, *Aristotle, Nicomachean Ethics*, Oxford: Oxford University Press, 2002.
Burnyeat, M. F., "Aristotle on Understanding Knowledge," in Berti, E., ed., *Aristotle on Science: The Posterior Analytics*, Padova: Editrice Antenore, 1981, 97–139.
Gotthelf, Allan, "First principles in Aristotle's Parts of Animals," in Gotthelf and Lennox, 1987, 167–198.
Gotthelf, Allan, and Lennox, James G., eds., *Philosophical Issues in Aristotle's Biology*, Cambridge: Cambridge University Press, 1987.
Kosman, L. A., "Understanding, Explanation and Insight in the Posterior Analytics," in E. N. Lee, A. P. D. Mourelotos, and R. M. Rorty, eds., *Exegesis and Argument*, Phronesis, supp. vol. 1, Assen, 1973.
Lennox, James G., "Divide and Explain: The *Posterior Analytics* in Practice," in Gotthelf and Lennox, 1987, 90–119.
Lloyd, G. E. R., *Polarity and Analogy*, Cambridge: Cambridge University Press, 1966; repr. Bristol: Bristol Classical Press and Indianapolis: Hackett Pub. Co., 1992.
McKirahan, Richard, *Principles and Proofs*, Princeton: Princeton University Press, 1992.
Mendell, Henry, "Making Sense of Aristotelian Demonstration," *Oxford Studies in Ancient Philosophy* 16 (1998), 160–225.
Mueller, Ian, "Greek Mathematics and Greek Logic," in *Ancient Logic and its Modern Interpretations*, John Corcoran, ed., Dordrecht: Kluwer, 1974.
Patterson, Richard, *Aristotle's Modal Logic*, Cambridge, 1985.
Patterson, Richard, "Aristotle and Syllogistic as the Logic of Mathematics," unpublished ms., 1995.

Further Reading

For English translations of all Aristotle's works see *The Complete Works of Aristotle*, Jonathan Barnes, ed. (Princeton, 1984). *The Basic Works of Aristotle*, Richard McKeon, ed. (New York, Modern Library, 2001), and *Aristotle: Selections*, G. Fine and T. Irwin, eds. (Indianapolis: Hackett, 1995) contain substantial selections of Aristotle's work.

For other brief treatments of Aristotle's epistemology see C. C. W. Taylor, "Aristotle's Epistemology," in S. Everson, ed., *Cambridge Companion to Ancient Thought I: Epistemology* (Cambridge, 1990) and D. Modrak, "Aristotle's Epistemology: One or Many Theories?," in *Aristotle's Philosophical Development, Problems and Prospects*, W. Wians, ed. (Lanham, MD: Rowman and Littlefield, 1996).

David Ross's *Aristotle* is the classic exposition of Aristotle's thought as a whole; the 6th edition (London: Routledge, 2004) contains a useful introduction and bibliography by J. L. Ackrill.

For an introduction, translation and incisive critical "running commentary" on the *Posterior Analytics*, see Jonathan Barnes' *Aristotle's Posterior Analytics* (2nd ed., Oxford: Clarendon Press, 1994). Richard McKirahan's *Principles and Proofs* (Princeton: Princeton University Press, 1992) is a consistently interesting examination of the main themes of the *Posterior Analytics*.

Articles on Aristotle 1. Science, R. Sorabji, M. Schofield, and J. Barnes, eds. (London: Duckworth, 1973), and *Aristotle on Science: The Posterior Analytics*, E. Berti, ed. (Padova: Editrice Antenore, 1981) are both excellent collections.

Sarah Broadie's introduction to *Aristotle, Nicomachean Ethics* (with translation by Christopher Rowe, Oxford: Oxford University Press, 2002) is a very helpful introduction to the philosophical themes of the work, including the nature of practical wisdom.

On perception, imagination, and cognition see the relevant items in *Essays on Aristotle's De Anima*, M. Nussbaum and A. Rorty, eds. (Oxford: Clarendon Press, 1992), and the major studies by D. K. Modrak, *Aristotle: The Power of Perception* (Chicago: University of Chicago Press, 1987), M. Wedin's *Mind and Imagination in Aristotle* (New Haven: Yale University Press, 1988), and Steven Everson's *Aristotle on Perception* (Oxford: Oxford University Press, 1997).

For an extensive bibliography see Richard Ingardia's site, aristotlebibliography.com.

60
RENÉ DESCARTES
Stephen Gaukroger

The modern canon for the history of philosophy was provided in Kuno Fischer's multi-volume history of philosophy (Fischer 1852–77). Fischer argued two theses: first, that the core of philosophy in the seventeenth century shifted from metaphysics to epistemology; second that, with this shift, the metaphysical dichotomy between Platonism and Aristotelianism was replaced by the epistemological dichotomy between rationalism and empiricism. Descartes is identified as the source of both these developments, and both Fischer's typology and his assessment of Descartes have been followed by the majority of philosophers since then, at least until recent times. Actually, both his theses are profoundly misleading (see, for example, Garber 1992; Gaukroger 1995a; Kuklick 1984; Loeb 1981), but it remains the case that Descartes did effect a major change in philosophical thinking and that it had to do with epistemology. My task in this chapter is to elucidate what this change consisted in. To this end, I want to begin by contrasting Descartes' approach to epistemology with that of two of his influential predecessors, Montaigne and Bacon, and then to show that a key problem that shaped his thinking was that of representation, before turning to the development of his views on epistemology, and to distinguishing three epistemological enterprises in Descartes: the psychophysiology of perceptual cognition, the development of an adequate methodology for natural philosophy, and the project of legitimating his natural philosophy via a combination of skepticism and foundationalism.

Epistemology in Descartes' Immediate Predecessors

If there are any other contenders for the title of the founding fathers of modern philosophy, they are Montaigne and Bacon, the former not only taking skepticism seriously but transforming our understanding of the nature of subjectivity in such a way that introspection can form a legitimate source of knowledge, and the latter transforming the pursuit of knowledge from a speculative to an observational/experimental enterprise. Both of them had distinctive views on epistemology, but in both cases they rely on traditional understandings of epistemology that differ significantly from that of Descartes.

Montaigne was a key figure in the revival of systematic doubt in the sixteenth century. The term "revival" here is important, because, unlike the systematic skeptical doubt that we (correctly) associate with Descartes, ancient doubt was different from modern skepticism in two respects that bore centrally on its role in epistemology. First, systematic doubt in antiquity was doxastic rather than epistemological. It was directed towards beliefs, not towards knowledge as such: its aim was to show that we are not entitled to our beliefs, and indeed there were forms of systematic doubt, such as Pyrrhonism, associated with a particular kind of ascetic life-style deemed appropriate to someone who had rejected all forms of "dogmatism." Cartesian doubt, by contrast, is epistemological: there could not possibly be a life-style associated with it because its most distinctive form, hyperbolic doubt, explicitly leaves our beliefs untouched: what it questions is whether we are entitled to say that these beliefs constitute knowledge. Indeed, hyperbolic doubt need not even affect our degree of certainty. Our degree of commitment to some knowledge claims, such as that $2 + 3 = 5$, remains unchanged because we do not know what it would be like for such claims to be mistaken: Descartes' argument is that what we can conceive of cannot constrain the ways in which an omniscient God could deceive us, but he has no doubt that it does constrain us. Second, there is a slippage in ancient systematic doubt between skepticism—the view that there is a way the world is, but we are unable to establish in what way it is—and relativism—the view that there is no way the world is independently of our changing perceptions of it (see Gaukroger 1995b). The distinctive form of Cartesian doubt, hyperbolic doubt, has no relativist analog, and is resolutely skeptical. With the revival of Pyrrhonism in the second half of the sixteenth century, we can find both a continuation of relativistically driven doxastic doubt and the beginnings of a skeptically driven epistemological doubt. This is true even of Montaigne's *Essais*, a point that has not been fully appreciated, because of a tendency to assimilate all forms of doubt to skeptical doubt (see, e.g., Popkin 1979: chs 2–3). In fact, the treatment of doubt in the *Essais* shows a clearly relativistic strain of thought. In the first chapter of Part II, for example, we are told that "we change as does that animal that takes the colour of each place it visits" and that:

> Not only does the wind of accidents move me at its will, but I am also moved and disturbed simply as a result of my own unstable posture, and anyone who observes carefully can scarcely find himself in the same state on two occasions. I give my soul now one face now another, depending on the direction in which I turn it. If I speak of myself in different ways, this is because I look at myself in different ways. All contradictions may be found in me by some twist and in some fashion.
> (Montaigne 1962: i. 369–70)

And even when we turn to the *Apologie de Raimond Sebond*, much of what Montaigne writes has a relativistic connotation: many of the examples he gives—what's true on one side of the mountain is false on the other; we hide away while engaging in sexual intercourse, whereas the Indians do it in public; and so on—stick closely to the relativist tone of his Pyrrhonist sources.

Francis Bacon's approach to epistemology, by contrast, was dictated primarily by a combination of natural-philosophical and psychological considerations (see Gaukroger 2001). This is not simply a matter of a different choice of resources, but rather an indication that his project is directed towards different kinds of questions. One way in which one might capture the contrast is between perception and observation. For Aristotle and the Aristotelian tradition, perception and observation are part of the same problem of how we come by knowledge of the world. But by the early-modern era, a gulf has opened up between the two. In Descartes, perception tends to be treated either as an epistemological issue, or one in optics or psycho-physiology, whereas observation is treated as an autonomous methodological issue. Correlatively, whereas perception is treated primarily as something that involves the mind or the brain, observation is something that involves the person as a whole. Hence, for Descartes, the psychological (as opposed to mental or epistemological) dimension is, generally speaking, inappropriate in the epistemology of perception, but of central relevance in accounts of the methodology of observation. Bacon, by contrast, is concerned with observation above all, and questions of perception are subordinate to it, with the result that his account of perceptual cognition is largely psychological rather than epistemological.

In fact, Descartes is concerned with observation as well as epistemological questions of perception, and the approach is not as completely removed from Bacon's concerns as it might first appear, but there is no doubt that his skeptically driven epistemology, which is dictated by how we can respond to systematic hyperbolic doubt, runs along a completely different trajectory.

The Problem of Representation

Descartes' epistemology brings together three different kinds of problem about representation, generated, respectively, by rhetoric, late scholastic theories of perception, and optics.

The importance of rhetoric lies in the fact that we can trace the genealogy of Descartes' key epistemological doctrine of clear and distinct ideas back to its roots in the rhetorical-psychological theories of the Roman rhetorical writers, especially Quintilian (see Gaukroger 1995a: 115–24). Quintilian was concerned with the qualities of the "image," with the search for and presentation of images that are distinctive in their vividness and particularity, above all with the question of what features or qualities they must have if they are to be employed effectively in convincing an audience. Whether one is an orator at court or an actor on stage, Quintilian tells us, our aim is to engage the emotions of the audience, and perhaps to get it to behave in a particular way as a result, and what one needs in order to do this is to employ images that have the quality of *evidentia*—vivid illustration. The core of Quintilian's account is that unless we are already convinced by our own images, we will not be in a position to use them to convince others. So self-conviction is a prerequisite for the conviction of others, and self-conviction, like the conviction of one's audience, depends on the qualities of the image, amongst which must figure clarity and vividness. Note that whether an idea is clear and distinct is manifested in its application: the degree to which it moves us, or moves our audience, is a sign of its clarity and distinctness. In taking up this model of self-conviction, Descartes transforms it from a rhetorical doctrine, in which we amplify some emotion or belief by presenting that belief clearly and distinctly to ourselves, into a cognitive doctrine, in which we assess the truth or falsity of an idea by presenting it to ourselves clearly and distinctly. The first version of this new cognitive doctrine is evident in the *Rules for the Direction of the Intellect*, in Rule 3 for example, where we are told that what we must seek is something we can clearly and evidently intuit, and that the mind that is "clear and attentive" will be able to achieve this (Descartes 1987–91: i. 14). The early *Rules* draw their model of knowledge almost exclusively from mathematics, and the doctrine of clear and distinct ideas is applied to the case of mathematics in what becomes a paradigmatic way. The idea is that by representing arithmetical operations in terms of manipulations of line lengths, rather than in terms of operations on numerals, we grasp the validity of the operation in a clear and distinct way. Here again, the clarity and distinctness of the idea is manifested in its application. At the end of the 1620s, however, Descartes abandons this kind of clear and distinct grasp as a general model and gradually shifts to a metaphysical conception whereby clarity and distinctness, which now require a divine guarantee, are manifested paradigmatically in the *cogito*. This shift into the realm of metaphysics brings with it an inheritance of a number of epistemological/psychological questions that had come to prominence in scholastic philosophy in the later sixteenth century.

In his discussion of sense perception in Books II and III of *De Anima*, Aristotle had argued that in perception, the mind is identical with its object, meaning by this that the form of the thing perceived is in the mind. In his elaboration of this account in the *Summa Theologia*, Aquinas argued that the form of the thing known "must of necessity be in the knower in the same manner as in the known itself" and so the sensible form "is in one way in the thing which is external to the soul, and in another way in the senses." The intelligible species that the intellect receives from objects in sense perception are not forms produced by the mind (they are not mental representations that the mind produces to match the object known, for example) but by the thing itself, and indeed they are these things themselves in the intellect. These things really exist in the intellect, because what the thing is essentially is its form, and when the intellect takes on this form in cognition, what it takes on is the same form as the object. But just what it was that was present to the mind in this kind of account was disputed among Aquinas" successors, particularly Duns Scotus and Suárez and their followers (see Picard 1926). By the late sixteenth century, one pressing issue was what the conformity between the object and our idea of it consisted in: what marked out a true idea of something? Two kinds of concept—a formal concept and an "objective" concept—were postulated, and the question of true ideas was considered to lie in the relation between these (see Dalbiez 1929; Dear 1992). The formal concept of an object was that object as it existed in the intellect, but formal concepts are not necessarily true concepts, for some of them can be mistaken. To say this is to say that they do not conform to the object of which they are the concept, but the object is a material thing: how can the idea conform to something material? The problem was added to by the fact that many scholastic writers denied that we have genuine access to essences, but they had no doubt that we had access to truth. Where could this truth derive from if not from the object itself? What was needed was something immaterial that stood in for the material thing, so that this could be compared with the formal concept. That immaterial thing is the objective concept, and it is the thing "insofar as it is known." So what we compare the formal concept with is not the thing itself but its objective concept. This leaves the question of what the relation between the objective concept and the thing itself is. The relation is labeled "objective being," but what exactly this consists in is obscure. It is initially tempting to think that it is just the relation that we might have supposed to hold between the formal concept and the thing itself, had it not been for the problem of comparing entities that are unlike, in that one is corporeal and one intellectual. In a case where we routinely grasped essences in sense perception, this is indeed what the relation would be, but it is clear that sense perception is fallible, and we hardly ever—if at all—grasp essences in this way. In light of this, the problem is to establish that our formal concepts are not all, or even largely, false.

Descartes connects questions of clarity and distinctness and questions of objective reality in a distinctive way, but to understand how he does this, we need to consider the third area, optics. Kepler's work on optics at the beginning of the seventeenth century shows conclusively that the image in vision is not formed in the crystalline humor, whose liquid volume takes on the form of the thing seen, but on the retina, where the image is inverted and flat. Descartes believed that there was something deeply wrong with the Aristotelian view that we have the sense organs we do because they naturally display to us the nature of the world, and that veridical perception is that in which our ideas exactly resemble those things in the world of which they are the ideas. In place of the Aristotelian account, Descartes offered a representational theory of perception, and the representations do not have to resemble what they represent at all. So, for example, we perceive colors, but our ideas of colors do not resemble colors. On Descartes' account of color, the corpuscles making up the light transmitted from the sun may be given spins of varying speeds on encountering the textured surfaces of objects, and such spins are perceived as colors by us because we are "fitted by nature" ("hard-wired" as we might put it now) to respond to such spins by perceiving the colors correlated with the particular spin speeds.

How, then, do we know which of our representations correspond to how things are in the world? We clearly cannot compare them with things in the world, and it is at this point that we can draw the questions of representation/resemblance, objective reality, and clarity and distinctness together. Basically, in the absence of any means of providing an external comparison with how things are in the world, Descartes uses the criterion of clarity and distinctness to secure veridicality. The criterion tells us something about the quality of the idea independently of its content, and because of this, we can assess first whether an idea of this kind is reliable—by assessing its power to represent—before asking what the content that it represents is. In this way, it connects with the objective reality of ideas. On the scholastic conception of perceptual cognition, comparison of the objective reality of concepts with their formal reality seemed to lock us out of establishing veridicality. Objective reality functions differently in Descartes because of the way in which he conceives of the relation between essence and existence. The standard scholastic view was that we must establish the existence of something before we can ask about its essence, but Descartes reverses this (see Secada 2000). For Descartes, "according to the rules of true logic we must never ask whether something exists unless we already know what it is" (Descartes 1987–91: ii. 190).

Application of the criterion of clarity and distinctness to an idea tells us something crucial about its objective reality. It tells us about the ability of the idea to represent anything at all to us. Only once we have established this can we inquire what it is that corresponds to the idea. The procedure in Meditation VI is to identify only those ideas of the world that satisfy the criterion of clarity and distinctness, and the only such ideas that Descartes tells us he is aware of are those which we conceive geometrically. When he then asks what corresponds to these ideas, we end up with a mechanical world completely different from that which we started out from in Meditation I, one quite distinct from the world of sensation. In the world of sensation, there are colored objects, for example, but there are no colors in the real physical world revealed in Meditation VI. One might ask why our senses have misled us, or, to put the question in a different way, why God has provided us with sense organs that represent the world without resembling it. The answer supplied by Descartes, is that God has given us our sense organs so that we might "preserve our bodies," not so that we might know the world. What reveals the true structure of the world to us is not sensation, but reason (which includes sensations guided by reason, as in scientific observations and experiments).

Descartes' Naturalized Epistemology

For Descartes, the physiological and physical details of what occurs in sense perception are absolutely crucial to our assessment of it as a source of knowledge, and this is what effectively makes sense perception an unsuccessful competitor to the mechanist natural philosophy that he arrives at in Meditation VI. This has been missed in many writers on Descartes, who, mesmerized by the skeptically driven epistemology of the *Meditations*, have assumed that the *Meditations* delivers its results through skepticism alone (e.g. Williams 1978). On such a reading, the unbridgeable gulf between the world of Meditation I and Meditation VI is completely ignored, so that the point of the project now becomes that of showing that our initial reasons for believing in the existence of the external world, for example, cannot survive radical skeptical probing, demonstrating the need for foundations for knowledge, which Descartes provides, in the process rebuilding the world from first principles and putting any further skeptical doubts to rest.

It is worth reminding ourselves of how thoroughly naturalized Descartes' epistemology was in the period prior to his interest in skepticism in the 1630s, and asking why he took up skepticism then. At the end of 1632, Descartes wrote to Mersenne that he was "dissecting the heads of various animals, so that I can explain what imagination, memory, etc. consist in" (Descartes 1987–91: iii. 40). The culmination of this research was the *Treatise on Man* (in Descartes 1998: see Gaukroger 2002: 180–214), an extensive account not just of various topics in physiology—such as nutrition and respiration—but also in developmental physiology—where Descartes has an account of the development of the fetus which excludes goal-directedness—and psycho-physiology. The treatise deals with human physiology to the extent that it shared with animals, and this covers psycho-physiology also. Part II of the *Treatise*, for example, provides a detailed account of perceptual cognition in psycho-physiological terms, explaining in particular how distance perception is possible through a form of innate trigonometry that animals and humans share. What was distinctive about Descartes' approach was not that he introduced two substances—mind and body—where we might have expected one, but that he introduced two whereas earlier and contemporary writers were toying with four: matter, vegetable soul, sensitive soul, and rational soul. The middle two were introduced on the assumption that bare matter could not account either for such phenomena as nutrition, excretion, reproduction, and respiration in plants and animals, or a fortiori for sense perception in animals. Descartes rejected this, arguing that the vegetative and sensitive souls were just empty labels, and that nutritive and sensitive functions could be accounted for in the same mechanical terms that one accounted for ordinary material processes, provided one used these resources in a sufficiently thoughtful way (e.g. in realizing that sense perception was a semantic not a merely causal process). A good deal of perceptual cognition is covered under psycho-physiology: the rational soul comes into play only when we turn to the question of reflection on our cognitive states, a distinctively human activity in Descartes' view, and one that raises questions of truth and veridicality.

In dealing with these latter questions, we might ask why Descartes didn't pursue them in terms of questions of method, as his contemporaries did, and as he himself had done in the *Rules* and the *Discourse on Method* (see Gaukroger 2006). Why, in the early 1630s, did he suddenly move in a completely novel direction, turning to skepticism? Note that he never gave up his psycho-physiological investigations—he summarized these in the early sections of his last work, the *Passions of the Soul*, for example, and continued to work on his *Description of the Human Body*. Even more interesting, in his *Search for the Truth*, he distinguishes between two kinds of procedure. The first is that designed to convince anyone of the truth of his natural-philosophical conclusions, which involves clearing the mind by going through radical doubt then building up knowledge on a new basis. The second, by contrast, concerns what the natural philosopher needs to follow in developing the discipline, and here Descartes turns not just to methodological considerations, but also to psychological ones about the *persona* of the natural philosopher (see Gaukroger 2002: 239–44).

In terms of the traditional distinction between methods of discovery and methods of presentation, the way in which Descartes divides methodological and psychological questions and skeptical/foundational ones indicates that the former fall within the ambit of a method of discovery, whereas the latter fall within the ambit of a method of presentation. Methodological questions cannot be separated from epistemology, and psychological ones had been a vehicle for epistemology in the tradition represented by Quintilian for example, so the divide is not between non-epistemological and epistemological questions. Rather, it is between what might be termed an exploratory epistemology and a legitimatory one. Exploratory epistemology is typically pursued through devising theories of method. Legitimatory epistemology, by contrast, is designed not to help us discover anything but to establish something that we believe we know, and to convince others of its truth. This matches Descartes' concerns at the time that we find him taking an interest in skepticism. In 1633 Descartes abandoned work on his account of a cosmological system, *The World*, begun in 1629. He argued there for a system in which the planets orbited our sun, matched by an indefinite number of other solar systems, and the principal tools in establishing this were his matter theory and his account of centrifugal force, for the theory explained the stability of planetary orbits in terms of a balance between centrifugal forces acting outwards from a center into which the lightest matter had been squeezed, and pressure towards the center caused by matter rotating at a greater speed and pushing the planet inwards. In 1633 Descartes read of the Condemnation of Galileo, in which it was argued that natural-philosophical arguments in themselves were insufficient to establish conclusively a thesis like heliocentrism, which was contrary to the teaching of traditional devotional texts. Descartes' response, as I have argued elsewhere (Gaukroger 1995a: 290–321), was to seek a form of argument that would bypass both natural-philosophical and confessional views because it was so fundamental and certain as to compel assent from any rational person. This was the combination of a skeptically driven epistemology and an account of God, the mind, and the world on new foundations. The strict separation of the natural world from God and the mind removes any notions of intentionality, teleology and, it turns out, internally generated activity from it, and the world that emerges in Meditation VI is one in full accord with Descartes' matter theory, and whose properties are ripe for geometrical exploration. It is this conception of the world, which he had set out in *The World* in 1630, that is now prefaced in the *Principia* by a reworking of the legitimatory metaphysics of the *Meditations*.

Conclusion: The Status of a Legitimatory Epistemology in Descartes

Descartes' statements on the status he accords his legitimatory project in epistemology are not consistent. In a letter to Princess Elizabeth in 1643, he tells her that the principles set out in the *Meditations* need to be understood, but that one should not spend more time than is needed on this. Rather, one should devote one's time to the more important part of the exercise, namely "those thoughts in which the intellect co-operates with the imagination and the senses" (Descartes 1987–91: iii. 228), that is, natural philosophy. Six years later, he tells Burman that he should not waste time on the *Meditations* as this is just a preparation for the main questions, which "concern physical and observable things" (Descartes 1987–91: iii. 346). This suggests that a skeptically driven metaphysics is merely legitimatory, and can perhaps be bypassed by someone who did not need to be convinced in this way, because, being the kind of uncorrupted natural philosopher whom Descartes describes in *The Search for Truth*, they are able to appreciate the truth of the Cartesian system on purely natural-philosophical grounds. For such a person, methodological considerations would be the sole content of their epistemological concerns.

When Descartes' follower Regius promoted the Cartesian system in the first Cartesian textbook (Regius 1646), he proceeded in exactly this way, dispensing with the legitimatory epistemological apparatus and moving straight to the natural philosophy. Descartes reacted against this in the strongest terms (see Verbeek 1993), keen to set out the errors which Regius had opened himself up to by not taking care on foundational questions. In other words, Descartes did think that legitimatory epistemology was a critical part of the exercise, not an added extra. This was not because it was a procedure for generating knowledge. To the extent to which epistemology played a role in the generation of knowledge it was that form of epistemology that accompanied methodological enquiry, not that which began by questioning whether we could claim to know anything.

Yet if on the Cartesian view a skeptically driven epistemology is no more than, but no less than, a necessary prelude to natural philosophy, how do we explain its longevity in the modern era? Much of this longevity is, I believe, illusory. Not only do natural philosophy textbooks outside the Cartesian tradition not include a legitimatory epistemology, none of the Cartesian ones do either. Those identified as Descartes' "rationalist" followers, namely Spinoza and Leibniz, urge the irrelevance of skepticism to epistemology at the earliest opportunity. The one continental successor of Descartes—albeit his most influential one in the early-modern era—who took a skeptically driven epistemology seriously was Malebranche, and it was that British Malebranchean, Berkeley, who helped develop it into such a powerful tool. Locke's moral and political probing was motivated more by worries about relativism than skepticism, and his views on real and nominal essences are not, I believe, motivated by skepticism but by natural-philosophical issues about phenomenal explanations (see Gaukroger 2009). Skepticism is central in Hume, of course, but it is more like a mixture of ancient doxastic skepticism and epistemological skepticism than the straightforward Cartesian/Malebranchean variety, for it does indeed prompt a distinctive way of life in response to it (see Livingston 1998), which epistemological skepticism alone could not do.

The dominant epistemological concerns among Descartes' successors in the modern era were the more traditional methodological ones, to which Descartes himself devoted a great deal of attention. In the debates between Newtonians and Cartesians at the end of the century, Descartes' position was identified with the postulation of hypotheses, and his natural-philosophical system was characterized as speculative and hypothetical, by contrast with the empirical certainties of the Newtonian one (see Laudan 1981). His skeptical epistemology was marginal in the era, outside Malebranche, Berkeley, and (with very significant qualifications) Hume. It was revived, in Humean guise, by Russell at the beginning of the twentieth century, but to understand why this happened, it is twentieth-century philosophy, not that of Descartes, that we need to understand.

References

Dalbiez, R. (1929) "Les sources scolastiques de la théorie cartésienne de l'être objectif," *Revue d'Histoire de la Philosophie* 3: 464–72.
Dear, P. (1992) "From Truth to Disinterestedness in the Seventeenth Century," *Social Studies of Science* 22: 619–31.
Descartes, R. (1987–91) *The Philosophical Writings of Descartes*, trans. J. Cottingham et al., Cambridge: Cambridge University Press.
Descartes, R. (1998) *The World and Other Writings*, trans. S. Gaukroger, Cambridge: Cambridge University Press.
Fischer, K. (1852–77) *Geschichte der neuren Philosophie*, Mannheim: Bassermann & Mathy.
Garber, D. (1992) *Descartes' Metaphysical Physics*, Chicago: University of Chicago Press.
Gaukroger, S. (1995a) *Descartes, An Intellectual Biography*, Oxford: Oxford University Press.
Gaukroger, S. (1995b) "The Ten Modes of Aenesidemus and the Myth of Ancient Scepticism," *British Journal for the History of Philosophy*, 3, 371–87.
Gaukroger, S. (2001) *Francis Bacon and the Transformation of Early-Modern Philosophy*, New York: Cambridge University Press.
Gaukroger, S. (2002) *Descartes' System of Natural Philosophy*, Cambridge: Cambridge University Press.
Gaukroger, S. (2006) "Knowledge, Evidence, and Method," in D. Rutherford (ed.), *The Cambridge Companion to Early Modern Philosophy*, Cambridge: Cambridge University Press.
Gaukroger, S. (2009) "The Role of Natural Philosophy in the Development of Locke's Empiricism," *British Journal for the History of Philosophy*, 17, 57–80.
Kuklick, B. (1984) "Seven Thinkers and How They Grew: Descartes, Spinoza, Leibniz; Locke, Berkeley, Hume; Kant," in R. Rorty, J. B. Schneewind and Q. Skinner (eds.), *Philosophy in History*, Cambridge: Cambridge University Press.
Laudan, L. (1981) *Science and Hypothesis*, Dordrecht: Reidel.
Livingston, D. W. (1998) *Philosophical Melancholy and Delirium*, Chicago: University of Chicago Press.
Loeb, L. E. (1981) *From Descartes to Hume*, Ithaca, NY: Cornell University Press.
Montaigne, M. de (1962) *Essais*, ed. Maurice Rat, Paris: Garnier.
Picard, G. (1926) "Essai sur la connaissance sensible d'après les scolastiques," *Archives de philosophie* 4: 1–93.
Popkin, R. (1979) *The History of Scepticism from Erasmus to Spinoza*, Berkeley: University of California Press.
Regius, H. (1646) *Fundamenta physices*, Amsterdam: Elzevier.
Secada, J. (2000) *Descartes' Metaphysics*, Cambridge: Cambridge University Press.
Verbeek, T. (1993) Ed., *Descartes et Regius*, Amsterdam: Rodopi.
Williams, B. (1978) *Descartes*, Harmondsworth: Penguin.

61
JOHN LOCKE
E. J. Lowe

The most important positive contribution of John Locke (1632–1704) to epistemology consists in Book IV—"Of Knowledge and Opinion"—of his greatest work, *An Essay Concerning Human Understanding*, the first edition of which was published in 1690. To say this is not to detract from the historical importance of Book I of the *Essay*, "Of Innate Notions," in which he roundly rejects the view that we have innate knowledge of any kind, even in the domain of mathematics and logic. But the burden of his argument there, whatever merits or deficiencies it might be deemed to have, is essentially negative. Only in Book IV does he finally attempt to formulate a comprehensive positive account of the nature and sources of human knowledge. It is this account that we shall focus on here, partly because it is less widely known than his famous attack on the doctrine of innate ideas and principles, and partly because it has a relevance to present-day epistemology which that attack now rather lacks, presuming as it does that innate knowledge could have only a divine source, being "Originally printed on the Mind" (Locke 1975: 1.2.1) by our Creator. Modern evolutionary psychology points to a possible explanation for innate knowledge which even Locke, as a good empiricist, would surely have to acknowledge as scientifically respectable, were he alive today (Lowe 1995: 27–33).

1. Locke on Intuitive Knowledge and the "Agreement" and "Disagreement" of Ideas

Locke endorses a tripartite division of human knowledge by reference to its sources in *intuition*, *reason* and *experience*, following a tradition accepted by many other seventeenth-century philosophers. But he notoriously combines it with the idiosyncratic and somewhat puzzling doctrine that knowledge always *consists in* our "Perception of the Agreement, or Disagreement, of any of our *Ideas*" (4.3.1). This seems, on the face of it, at best to be a way of characterizing certain examples of what Locke calls "intuitive" knowledge and is difficult to extend, without considerable strain, to Locke's two other kinds of knowledge. Examples of knowledge of this first kind are provided by Locke in passages such as the following:

> [S]ometimes the Mind perceives the Agreement or Disagreement of two *Ideas* immediately... And this... we may call *intuitive Knowledge*... Thus the Mind perceives, that *White* is not *Black*, That a *Circle* is not a *Triangle*, That *Three* are more than *Two*, and equal to *One* and *Two*. (4.2.1)

Now, the "ideas" of white and black would certainly seem to "disagree," at least in the sense that one cannot perceive a surface as being, at one and the same time, both black and white—though whether this "cannot" expresses a mere psychological impossibility, or something stronger, is open to debate. Such a "disagreement" is apparently not, however, a *logical* disagreement, in the sense that a *formal contradiction* can be derived from the statement "*S* is both black and white," when suitable definitions of "black" or "white" are provided. Indeed, according to Locke, there can be no such definitions, since our ideas of black and white are, according to him, *simple* and hence *unanalyzable*—a claim which does indeed have considerable plausibility. Certainly, "white" clearly does not simply *mean* "not black," since red is neither black nor white. Nor does it mean "not black nor any chromatic color," for—even if we could non-circularly define "chromatic color"—grey is neither black nor white nor any chromatic color. Nor does it mean "not black nor grey nor any chromatic color"—since a transparent surface might come under none of these descriptions and yet not be white either. It seems, then, that no satisfactory *definition* of "white" is available whose *definiens*, when substituted for "white" in "*S* is both black and white," turns the latter into a logical contradiction.

It is worth mentioning, in this connection, the interesting question raised recently by Lex Newman of whether, on Locke's account of knowledge, "[t]ruths are knowable only if they are analytic" (Newman 2007: 339), in the sense of "analytic" in which it involves what Newman calls "idea-containment"—a sense which, I take it, is supposed to be distinct from the semantic one that we have just been examining. Newman's own answer to this question is affirmative and he even tries to defend Locke on this score. Newman's test case is, once more, the proposition that *White is not Black*, concerning which Newman contends on Locke's behalf that "[t]hough not every idea of white explicitly contains an idea of not-black, *when considering them in relation to one another the mind apprehends in the idea of white that it is not black*" (341, emphasis added). Now, it could be said that white and black are, by their very natures, the opposite extremes of the achromatic color-range, with all the shades of grey in between, and so *perhaps* a case can be made out for saying that "white is not black" expresses an "analytic" truth in Newman's sense, since the *relation* in which they stand to one another is precisely that of being these two opposite extremes. Even so, matters are plausibly otherwise with, for example, "Red is not green," a variant of which—"Nothing is both red and green all over"—many philosophers have advanced as the very paradigm of a necessary but non-analytic truth. It is extremely hard to see how Locke—who again took the ideas of red and green to be perfectly *simple* ones—could maintain that the idea of red "contains," *in any sense at all*, the idea of not-green. Rather, I think that he would probably have maintained that, upon becoming perceptually acquainted with both red and green, we simply *directly apprehend* their mutual exclusiveness, as a brute and irreducible fact. Perhaps, in the end, this is really all that Newman himself intends to claim: but in that case I think that his talk of "idea-containment" is misplaced and misleading in this context.

Notice, however, that even as soon as we come to Locke's *second* example of "intuitive" knowledge—that a circle is not a triangle—we no longer have an irreducible disagreement between simple, unanalyzable ideas. A *triangle* can be defined as a plane figure bounded by three straight lines, and a *circle* as a plane figure bounded by a curved line which is everywhere equidistant from a central point—and given further axioms and definitions of Euclidean geometry it would indeed be possible to derive a formal contradiction from the statement "*F* is both a circle and a triangle." Even so, Locke would obviously maintain—again with considerable plausibility—that our "perception" of the "disagreement" between the ideas of a circle and a triangle is "immediate," rather than being grounded in a demonstration from those axioms and definitions. The same applies to his third, arithmetical example that *three equals one plus two*: no proof of this from the axioms and definitions of arithmetic could make us any *more* assured of its truth than we are by simple reflection upon the meaning of the statement itself. (Indeed, we are *less* certain of those axioms and definitions than we are of such simple arithmetical truths as that three equals one plus two.) That some things are indeed known to us by "intuition," as Locke suggests, certainly appears to be at least a truth about our psychological condition—although whether it reflects anything special about the status of the *objects* of that knowledge seems altogether more debatable.

Why are some things knowable by us "intuitively"—such as that a circle is not a triangle—but others only "demonstratively," by inference from other things—such as that any triangle whose base is the diameter of a circle and whose opposite vertex lies on the circumference of that circle is right-angled? Locke himself says that the reason why we do not know intuitively that, for instance, the three internal angles of a triangle equal two right angles is that

> the Mind being willing to know the Agreement or Disagreement in bigness . . . cannot by an immediate view and comparing them, do it . . . Because the three Angles of a Triangle cannot be brought at once, and be compared with any other one, or two Angles. (4.2.2)

But it is far from evident that this is not just a psychological limitation on our part, which could be overcome by other intelligent beings. Might not "demonstrable" truths, such as those just cited, be as "obvious" or "self-evident" to some minds as it is to ours that three equals one plus two?

Once this thought strikes us, however, and we are led to realize that the intuitive self-evidence of a proposition is not an intrinsic property of the proposition itself but, rather, a status that it has only relative to the mind of the knower, we might come to query the reliability of intuition as a supposed source of knowledge. Might there not be beings—benighted, indeed, by *our* standards—for whom it was "obvious" and "self-evident" that a circle might be a triangle and three equal to two plus two? Locke's "psychologistic" approach to knowledge as being a matter of our *perception* of agreement or disagreement between our *ideas* inevitably invites such skeptical and relativistic challenges. At the same time, it makes for a degree of tension with his own repudiation of the doctrine of innate ideas, in Book I of the *Essay*. For if the obviousness *to us human beings* that a circle is not a triangle is a reflection of our own psychological make-up, which might not be duplicated in other species of intelligent creatures, this seems to give succor to the innatist thesis that the basic elements of our conceptual repertoire and their general organization within our cognitive economy is fixed prior to, and independently of, our subsequent experience: that the human mind is not in fact, at birth, the "yet empty Cabinet" (1.2.15) that Locke holds it to be.

So much for knowledge by "intuition." As for knowledge by *reason*—that is, by logical demonstration or proof—Locke supposes, again in line with the prevailing tradition of his time, that each step in a chain of demonstrative reasoning must be perceived as intuitively certain, as must be the initial premises:

> (I)n every step Reason makes in demonstrative Knowledge, there is an intuitive Knowledge of that Agreement or Disagreement, it seeks, with the next intermediate *Idea*, which it uses as a Proof . . . By which it is plain, that every step in Reasoning, that produces Knowledge, has intuitive Certainty. (4.2.7)

Clearly, any doubts we may have about the status of "intuition" as a source of knowledge will extend to the status of "demonstration," at least on this account of reasoning.

2. Locke on "Sensitive" Knowledge

Locke's third and final category of knowledge, knowledge by "sensation"—that is, by *experience*—of the existence of things external to ourselves, is especially difficult to accommodate with his official characterization of knowledge as the perception of the agreement or disagreement of our ideas. This is for the simple reason that, in sensation, the idea ostensibly produced in us by an "external" object does not appear to stand in any relevant relation of "agreement" or "disagreement" with other *ideas* we have, so much as a relation of "agreement" or "disagreement" *with external reality*: and this is a relation that we cannot be said to "perceive" in any sense in which we could be said to perceive relations of "agreement" or "disagreement" *amongst our ideas*. The danger is that we might allow this consideration to persuade us—as it plainly has persuaded some of Locke's critics—that Locke's theory of sense-perception, coupled with his theory of knowledge, condemns his system to vitiation by an insoluble "veil of perception" problem. In fact, however, I think that it is probably a mistake to suppose that Locke's system is inherently any *more* vulnerable to this kind of skeptical problem than is even the most explicit form of "direct" realism (Lowe 1995: 46–7).

In defending Locke on this score, I have no wish to endorse his official doctrine as to the *nature* of knowledge—that it consists in our perception of the agreement or disagreement of our ideas—but I do want to support his common-sense insistence that sense experience *does* constitute a trustworthy source of knowledge concerning the existence and, to some extent, the properties of external objects, as when he says that

> The notice we have by our Senses, of the existing of Things *without* us, though it be not altogether so certain, as our intuitive Knowledge . . . yet it is an assurance that *deserves the name of Knowledge*. If we persuade our selves, that our Faculties act and inform us right, concerning the existence of those Objects that affect them, it cannot pass for an ill-grounded confidence: For I think no body can, in earnest, be so sceptical, as to be uncertain of the Existence of those Things which he sees and feels. (4.11.3)

Perhaps what Locke needs in order to give his confidence a satisfactory theoretical underpinning is what would today be called an "externalist" account of empirical knowledge, whereby states of knowledge are states produced by reliable mechanisms interacting causally in appropriate ways with the objects of knowledge. If our "Faculties" are such mechanisms, then their products—such as our perceptual judgments—qualify as states of knowledge by such an account *irrespective* of whether or not those states are attended by a subjective apprehension of their "certainty." However, writing as he was at a time at which an "internalist" conception of knowledge was dominant, not least through the influence of Descartes, Locke could hardly have been expected to make such an alternative, "externalist" account his official doctrine.

Before moving on, I should mention another interesting suggestion recently made by Lex Newman, this time addressing the difficulty we have just noted of reconciling Locke's general definition of knowledge, couched in terms of our "perception of the agreement or disagreement of our ideas," with his account of sensitive knowledge. Rather ingeniously, Newman defends Locke on this score by contending that, in the case of sensitive knowledge, the required agreement consists not in "an agreement . . . between an idea and an *actual real existence*" (which would ostensibly conflict with Locke's official definition), but rather in "an agreement involving the *idea of* actual existence, not actual existence itself" (Newman 2007: 331). The only trouble with this, it seems to me, is that it appears to commit Locke to some form of *idealism* (as opposed to realism), although Newman takes some pains to defend Locke against this charge by distinguishing on his behalf between "knowledge per se" (as defined by Locke) and "*real* knowledge"—how convincingly, I leave for others to judge.

3. Locke on Reality and Truth

Some passages in the *Essay*—as when Locke says that "the Mind knows not Things immediately, but only by the intervention of the *Ideas* it has of them" (4.4.3)—do indeed make Locke look very much like an "indirect" or "representative" realist, trapped behind the infamous "veil of ideas." But, as has been suggested elsewhere (Yolton 1970: 132; Lowe 1995: 46; Lowe 2005: 43), it might be more helpful to think of the "way of ideas" as Locke's method of explaining how we have *access* to knowledge of the real world rather than as a stumbling block to such knowledge. It could be said, thus, that "ideas," for Locke, are our *bridge* to reality, or *window* upon it, not a veil or wall which screens it off from us. And, after all, no account of our knowledge of things outside us, however "realist" and however "direct," can place those things themselves literally *inside* our minds or heads, unless we are idealists like Berkeley. Knowledge of things beyond us has to be mediated in *some* way by the impact that those things have on us—and the form of that impact will inevitably be conditioned not only by the nature of the things themselves but also by *our* nature and by the nature of our relationship to the things in question. Any account of knowledge which attempted to defy these constraints would either have to be anti-realist or else non-naturalistic—perhaps, indeed, *super*naturalistic. Locke is to be commended, not criticized, for grasping this fact and being prepared to work through its consequences.

In response to his own question, as to how the mind shall know that its ideas "agree with Things themselves" (4.4.3), Locke answers as follows:

> I think there be two sorts of *Ideas*, that, we may be assured, agree with Things . . . The first are simple *Ideas*, which since the Mind . . . can by no means make to it self, must necessarily be the product of Things operating on the Mind in a natural way . . . and so . . . represent to us Things under those appearances which they are fitted to produce in us . . . *Secondly, All our complex* Ideas, *except those of Substances, being Archetypes of the Mind's own making . . . cannot want of any conformity necessary to real Knowledge.* (4.4.3–4.4.5)

Locke's point about simple ideas is, perhaps, not entirely convincing—first because it seems question-begging to contend, as Locke does, that these could not be products of the mind's own operations and secondly because, even granting that they are produced in us by the operation of "external" things, it might be queried whether they need correspond to unitary properties of those things, as opposed to a great variety of heterogeneous properties having the same effect on us in different circumstances. Thus, when Locke asserts that

> the *Idea* of Whiteness, or Bitterness, as it is in the Mind, exactly answering that Power which is in any Body to produce it there, has all the real conformity it can, or ought to have, with Things without us (4.4.4)

it could be objected that, for all we know, what makes one object look white or taste bitter to us is utterly different from what makes another object do this. Indeed, modern color science *does* tell us that precisely this is so as far as perceived colors are concerned (Hardin 1988). Lights with very different mixtures of wavelengths can all *appear* exactly the same hue to a human observer. However, curiously enough, the very fact that this is now empirically well-established shows that, if anything, Locke was *too modest* in his claim about the knowledge we can have of the powers of objects to produce simple ideas in us. We are not restricted to knowing those powers *only* by way of the very ideas in question, since by drawing more widely upon observation and experiment, we can develop well-confirmed theories to *explain* how objects produce sensory effects in us. Of course, we should not criticize Locke for failing to anticipate just how successful science could be in this regard, writing as he was at a time when the scientific revolution had barely begun.

The second class of ideas concerning which Locke believes that we can be assured that they "agree with Things themselves" is that of "*All our complex* Ideas, *except those of Substances*." This might sound as though it is a wildly optimistic claim—until we see what it really amounts to. The examples he gives are of such ideas as the complex mathematical ideas of a rectangle or a circle and complex moral ideas such as those of justice and temperance, remarking

> The Mathematician considers the Truth and Properties belonging to a Rectangle, or Circle, only as they are in *Idea* in his own Mind. For 'tis possible he never found either of them existing mathematically, *i.e.* precisely true, in his Life. But yet the knowledge he has of any Truths or Properties belonging to a Circle . . . are nevertheless true and certain, even of real Things existing: because real Things are no farther concerned . . . than as (they) really agree to those *Archetypes* in his Mind. (4.4.6)

So Locke's point is that in the case of a complex idea like that of a circle and the properties that circles are conceived of as having according to that idea, the "direction of fit"—to deploy that useful modern phrase (see, e.g., Searle 1983: 7)—is not *from ideas to the world* but, rather, *from the world to ideas*. That is to say, we are not under an obligation to show that our idea of a circle conforms to how circles are in reality: rather, whether something existing in reality has the form of a circle depends on whether it conforms to our idea of that shape. Similar considerations apply, Locke seems to suppose, in the sphere of moral ideas.

As far as geometry is concerned, Locke's contention is no longer as acceptable as it might have appeared in his own day. We are now familiar with the fact that there are many consistent alternatives to Euclidean geometry: geometries in which, for instance, the three internal angles of a triangle do *not* sum to two right angles. Locke might be right in supposing that there are, say, truths of Euclidean geometry which obtain, and can be known to obtain, independently of how things are in the real world. But nowadays we are faced with a question, unthinkable to Locke, of *which* geometry, of all those that are *mathematically* possible, best describes the metrical properties of objects located in physical space and time. This *is* an empirical question, involving the idea-to-world direction of fit. Whether anything similar can be said of ideas in the moral sphere is less clear, but arguably it can.

Why does Locke make an exception of our complex ideas of *substances*? Locke explains this as follows:

> (T)o have *Ideas* of *Substances*, which, by being conformable to Things, may afford us *real* Knowledge, it is not enough, as in Modes, to put together such *Ideas* as have no inconsistence . . . But *our Ideas of Substances* being . . . referred to *Archetypes* without us, must . . . be taken from something that does or has existed . . . Herein therefore is founded the *reality* of our Knowledge concerning *Substances*, that all our complex *Ideas* of them must be such, and such only, as are made up of such simple ones, as have been discovered to co-exist in Nature. (4.4.12)

Locke's point, then, is that in the case of substances the "direction of fit" is from ideas to the world, not *vice versa*. Our idea of gold should conform to the properties of something existing in the real world: but whether certain properties *do* co-occur in nature is something that we can only hope to ascertain by observation, lacking as we do—or as in Locke's time we did—any knowledge of the "real essences" of substances, which would serve to explain why some properties occur together while others do not. Locke accordingly makes only a very modest claim about our ability to acquire real knowledge of substances, but does not deny it altogether:

> (O)ur *Ideas* being thus true, though not, perhaps, very exact Copies, are yet the Subjects of *real* . . . Knowledge of them. Which . . . will not be found to reach very far: But so far as it does, it will still be *real knowledge*. (4.4.12)

Here Locke is, again, at once too optimistic and too pessimistic. He is too optimistic because he does not anticipate the problem that Hume was to make of induction—that is, the problem of extrapolating from our observation of the co-occurrence of certain properties in certain instances to a conclusion that those properties *regularly* occur together in nature. On the other hand, he is too pessimistic in that he did not anticipate—through no fault of his own—the degree to which empirical science *is* capable of penetrating to the "real essences" or internal constitutions of substances, with the aid of advanced experimental technology and sophisticated methods of analyzing observational data.

Finally, a word about Locke's theory of *truth*, if indeed it can be called a "theory." He himself seems to consider that there is nothing of substance to be said in terms of truth that is not already said by him elsewhere in terms of "real knowledge." Insofar as truth is a property of *sentences*, it is parasitic upon the truth of the *thoughts* which sentences are used to express, and the latter—"mental truth," as Locke calls it—is nothing other than real knowledge:

> When *Ideas* are so put together, or separated in the Mind, as they, or the Things they stand for do agree, or not, that is, as I may call it, *mental Truth* . . . *Truth of Words* is . . . the affirming or denying of Words one of another, as the *Ideas* they stand for agree or disagree: And this . . . is twofold. Either *purely Verbal*, and trifling . . . *or Real* and instructive; which is the Object of that real Knowledge, which we have spoken of already. (4.5.6)

Most modern philosophers tend to explain the notion of knowledge in terms of a prior notion of truth; in Locke the direction of explanation seems to be the reverse of this.

4. Locke on Reason, Probability and Faith

According to Locke, belief or opinion—which he contrasts with *knowledge*—can be grounded either in *probability* or in *faith*. Since, by Locke's account, the scope of our knowledge is "very narrow" (4.15.2), in most everyday concerns he thinks we have to rely on probability, which is mere "likeliness to be true" (4.15.3), rather than certainty. One frequently reliable ground of probability is *testimony*, on which we depend for a very large proportion of our firm beliefs, even in those matters which are capable of demonstration. Thus Locke gives an example of how a non-mathematician might firmly, and quite properly, *believe* that the three internal angles of a triangle add up to two right angles because a mathematician "of credit" has told him that this is so, though it is only the mathematician who *knows* that it is so, having constructed a proof or demonstration of that proposition (4.15.1). By contrast, in some matters of religion in which intuition, reason and sensation cannot provide us with knowledge, we might justifiably ground our belief in (what we take to be) divine revelation, and assent of this sort Locke calls *faith*. He is emphatic that, rightly understood, reason and faith do not stand in opposition to one another (both, he assumes, being gifts of God), but he is very critical of exaggerated claims of the scope of revelation:

> Whatever GOD hath revealed, is certainly true; no Doubt can be made of it. This is the proper Object of *Faith*: But whether it be a divine Revelation, or no, *Reason* must judge; which can never permit the Mind to reject a greater Evidence to embrace what is less evident, nor allow it to entertain Probability in opposition to Knowledge and Certainty. (4.18.10)

In all of these matters, Locke was broadly representative of the enlightened intellectuals of his time. The divisions that he makes between knowledge and belief, and between reason, probability and faith, are standard ones for his time, and not so very different from standard epistemological distinctions that are still drawn today. Perhaps, though, the biggest gulf between his usage and that of present-day philosophers arises from his much more restrictive application of the term "knowledge," as describing only that of which we are certain:

> And herein lies the *difference between Probability* and *Certainty*, *Faith* and *Knowledge*, that in all the parts of Knowledge, there is intuition; each immediate Idea, each step has its visible and certain connexion; in belief not so. That which makes me believe, is something extraneous to the thing I believe. (4.15.3)

Today we would regard it as very odd to say that we do not *know* that the earth is not flat, that the sun is millions of miles away from us or that Napoleon lost the Battle of

Waterloo—yet, by Locke's standards, we cannot be said to "know" these things, however justifiably assured we might be of their truth, whether through testimony or through scientific or historical research. Thus Locke is apt to sound unduly skeptical to modern ears. But although—as I explained in the previous section—I think he *was* too pessimistic about the scope of human knowledge, we should not misconstrue as skepticism a view that merely deploys the term "knowledge" in a more restrictive sense than would be acceptable today. What *we* mean by saying that we "know" that the earth is not flat is perhaps not so very different from what Locke would mean by saying that we "believe" this, with a high degree of probability. At the same time, we should not be *too* lenient on Locke on this account: for, as I remarked in section 1, there are grounds for supposing that his "internalist" approach to knowledge, which is partly responsible for the connection he insists upon between knowledge and certainty, is not, ultimately, a fruitful one.

5. Locke on the Extent and Limits of Human Knowledge

To what degree can Locke's conception of the scope of human knowledge be defended today? To a surprisingly large degree, I believe—surprising, at least, when one considers the very different world-views taken for granted in seventeenth- and twentieth-century educated circles. Locke was writing at a time when it was implicitly believed even by the vast majority of enlightened thinkers that the world was only several thousand years old, that it had been created in a short period of time by a supremely powerful and intelligent Being, and that the earth, although perhaps not at the centre of the universe, was in all probability the only inhabited region in a universe by no means inconceivably large by human standards. By contrast, almost all educated people today believe that the earth is a tiny, insignificant planet orbiting a very ordinary star, that this star is just one of many millions in a galaxy which is itself only one among a vast number of others spread throughout a universe thousands of millions of years old and unimaginably huge in extent—a universe that appears to have developed in the way it has quite as much by chance as by law, from an initial "singularity" involving stupendously high energies and temperatures but no very obvious trace of divine intervention. Human beings themselves are now thought to be the products of quite purposeless processes of biological evolution, involving chance mutation and natural selection, rather than being the direct handiwork of God. Such "native faculties" as human beings possess—such as a capacity to reason—cannot now be regarded as divine gifts designed to enable us to know and understand the world of our Creator, and hence cannot for that reason be assumed to be reliable and truth-revealing.

At this point, however, we seem to be threatened by paradox: the modern scientific world-view, which leads us to regard our seventeenth-century forebears as radically mistaken in *their* world-view, is one that leads us to regard *ourselves* as erratic products of purposeless evolution, unblessed by any special faculty for revealing the true nature of our world—so what right do we have to our confidence in our own superior knowledge and understanding of nature? Such reflections might persuade us that Locke's humility regarding the scope of our "real" knowledge was more justified than modern "scientific" opinion would perhaps be happy to admit.

It might be helpful at this point to see if we can identify a solid core of commonsense belief about the "external world" which is *stable*, in the sense of being relatively invulnerable to possible future revolutions in science as fundamental as those that have marked the transition from the seventeenth- to the twentieth-century world-views. Some radically relativist philosophers would no doubt contend that it is *impossible* to identify any such "core"—a position that seems to commit them to an all-embracing anti-realism. Locke, I am sure, would resist such extreme skepticism and, in the face of it, defend what might be called a "moderate" or "modest" realism. Such a view holds that we can with complete confidence claim to know that an external world of causally interacting three-dimensional material objects exists, amid which we ourselves are situated, our experience of those objects being a product of their interaction with us and affording us precisely that knowledge of their existence and behavior as has just been claimed. This is a "modest" realism in that it does not claim access to secure and unrevisable knowledge of what Locke calls the "internal constitutions" or "real essences" of physical things, allowing that, for instance, modern quantum physics might in time be discarded as emphatically as classical atomism has been today.

In my view, such a modest realism is probably the most that we can reasonably aspire to, so that I am broadly in agreement with what I take to be Locke's position. In earlier sections I did, it is true, point to the apparent *success* of modern science in probing the microstructure of the physical world as testifying to Locke's *excessive* modesty regarding the accessibility to us of the "real essences" of physical things. But now I need to qualify those remarks rather than retract them. Locke was indeed—unsurprisingly and perfectly excusably—unaware of the degree to which the scientific investigation of nature might be facilitated by advances in technology and experimental method, and so could not have imagined how scientists would eventually devise techniques enabling them to test the empirical implications of different hypotheses concerning the atomic and molecular structure of matter. However, what still has to be acknowledged, despite the remarkable fruitfulness of such techniques, is that they still only leave us with *hypotheses*, however "well confirmed" by experiment. One does not have to espouse Locke's perhaps unduly restrictive sense of the term "knowledge" to contend that our being in possession of such well-confirmed hypotheses need not constitute *knowledge* of the microstructure of matter. (If one is an "externalist" about knowledge, one might allow that it is *possible* that our current scientific beliefs constitute knowledge, while conceding that we cannot *know* that they do.) So one might consistently claim that Locke was excessively modest concerning the *practical* possibilities for extending the scope of scientific research, while agreeing with him on the more fundamental issue of the extent to which we can aspire to achieve a solid and unrevisable core of natural knowledge. With regard to the latter issue, Locke's modest realism does indeed seem to me to be a philosophically defensible position: one that allows us to possess a *real* but *limited* knowledge of the natural world—but a knowledge which nonetheless has, very arguably, "all the real conformity it can, or ought to have, with Things without us" (4.4.4).

References

Hardin, C. L. 1988. *Color for Philosophers*. Indianapolis: Hackett.
Locke, J. 1975. *An Essay Concerning Human Understanding* [1690]. Ed. P. H. Nidditch. Oxford: Clarendon Press.
Lowe, E. J. 1995. *Locke on Human Understanding*. London and New York: Routledge.
Lowe, E. J. 2005. *Locke*. London and New York: Routledge.
Newman, L. 2007. Locke on Knowledge. In L. Newman (ed.), *The Cambridge Companion to Locke's "Essay Concerning Human Understanding."* Cambridge: Cambridge University Press.
Searle, J. R. 1983. *Intentionality*. Cambridge: Cambridge University Press.
Yolton, J. W. 1970. *Locke and the Compass of Human Understanding*. Cambridge: Cambridge University Press.

62
GOTTFRIED WILHELM LEIBNIZ
Nicholas Jolley

Leibniz is generally classified as a successor of Descartes in the Rationalist tradition, but in one way this classification is misleading: it tends to suggest a greater similarity between them in epistemology than really exists. It is true of course that both philosophers urge that genuine knowledge is to be achieved by turning away from the senses, and they emphasize the superiority of the pure intellect over the imagination. But in general Leibniz's approach to epistemology is very different from Descartes'. Unlike Descartes Leibniz was never greatly exercised by the problem of radical skepticism, and he was critical of Descartes' method of doubt as a starting-point in philosophy. Indeed, Leibniz's conception of the role of epistemology in philosophy aligns him more with the third major Rationalist, Spinoza, than with Descartes. In his most important expository works, such as the *Discourse on Metaphysics*, Leibniz, like Spinoza in the *Ethics*, generally seeks to deduce a theory of knowledge from metaphysical premises. Whether or not he was directly influenced by him, Leibniz shares Spinoza's conviction that the proper method in philosophy is to begin with a theory of substance and to derive epistemological consequences from that theory.

Significantly, the most striking area of agreement between Leibniz and Descartes in epistemology involves a doctrine that is by no means uniquely Cartesian: both philosophers revive the ancient doctrine of innate ideas and knowledge found in Plato's *Meno*. Leibniz's indebtedness to the Platonic and Neo-Platonic tradition in philosophy is arguably of vital importance for understanding his whole theory of knowledge. One of the main theses of Leibniz's philosophy, one that is never seriously questioned, is that the human mind is a mirror or image of God; Leibniz also expresses the point by saying that the human mind is a "little God." This Neo-Platonic theme helps not only to explain his commitment to the theory of innate knowledge, which can be seen as an epistemological expression of the "mirror" principle; but also to explain his impatience with the kind of radical skepticism that Descartes took as his point of departure in philosophy.

Leibniz and Descartes

Leibniz's lack of sympathy with Descartes' approach to epistemology is nowhere more apparent than in his response to Descartes' method of doubt; it is of course by means of this famous method that Descartes seeks to rebuild the edifice of knowledge on absolutely firm and lasting foundations. For Leibniz, Descartes' method of doubt is more like a theatrical device designed to win the applause of the ignorant than an indispensable methodological tool for making progress in philosophy (Leibniz 1969: 384). Perhaps because of his conviction that the human mind is a mirror of God, Leibniz is unable to take seriously such distinctively Cartesian themes as what is sometimes called "defective nature doubt"; that is, he dismisses the worry, raised in the First Meditation, that we may have a defective nature that makes us incapable of knowledge. For Leibniz, the only reasonable grounds for fearing that we may have fallen victim to error are such commonplace ones as that our mind is tired, distraught, or insufficiently attentive. More significantly perhaps, Leibniz raises the objection, later developed by Peirce, that Cartesian doubt is not serious; as Leibniz remarks in the *New Essays on Human Understanding,* "to doubt in earnest is to doubt in a practical way" (Leibniz 1996: 445). Cartesian doubt, by contrast, is self-consciously designed to have no implications for practice.

Leibniz may have been an unsympathetic critic of Descartes' method of doubt, but he was also a characteristically shrewd one. Like some modern commentators Leibniz is sharply critical of some of Descartes' less careful formulations of the method. Notoriously Descartes sometimes describes the method of doubt in terms of believing that all one's former opinions are false (e.g. *Discourse on Method* IV). As Leibniz notes, when described in these terms the method is a recipe not for freeing ourselves from error but, rather, for acquiring new errors or false beliefs (Leibniz 1969: 384). For among my former opinions are presumably some true ones; if then I reject all my previous opinions as false, I have simply added to my stock of false beliefs. Obviously Descartes' method of doubt is more carefully characterized by explaining the rejection of previous beliefs in terms of suspension of judgment about them rather than believing that they are all false.

Leibniz's attitude towards Descartes' famous Archimedean point—the *cogito*—is not similarly dismissive, but it is lukewarm and perhaps somewhat insensitive. Certainly Leibniz shows no tendency to accord the *cogito* the privileged status that Descartes claims for it. Leibniz insists that "Various things are thought by me" is no less certain than "I think, therefore I am." Here Leibniz is no doubt alluding to his own metaphysical doctrine that the human mind is a simple substance that perceives many things; indeed, it perceives the whole universe according to its point of view. Leibniz's readiness to put these two principles on a par as primary truths of knowledge suggests a certain insensitivity to the distinctive features of the *cogito*. As many commentators have noticed, the *cogito* is not merely an incorrigible judgment in the sense that necessarily, if I believe it, it is true; it is also self-verifying. To deny one's own thinking and one's own existence is not to say something that is necessarily false in the logical sense, but it is pragmatically self-defeating or self-stultifying. Curiously, Leibniz never shows any signs of appreciating these features of the *cogito*.

Leibniz on Knowledge of Existence of Bodies

One issue that Descartes' method of doubt placed on the agenda for subsequent epistemology was our knowledge of the existence of bodies, or the existence of the external world. This problem, the failure to solve which was regarded by Kant as a scandal to philosophy, was taken up not only by Descartes' Rationalist successors but also, in varying degrees, by Empiricists such as Locke, Berkeley, and Hume. Descartes' formulation of the problem is a major contribution to philosophy, but his own proposed solution to it has been almost universally rejected. Leibniz is no exception to the general chorus of criticism. Indeed, Leibniz makes a memorably damning judgment on Descartes' attempted proof: "The argument by which Descartes tries to prove that material things exist is weak; it would have been better not to try" (Leibniz 1969: 391).

Leibniz's objections to Descartes' attempted proof of the existence of bodies fall into two classes. First, in common with other, more recent critics, Leibniz objects to Descartes' crucial premise that God would be a deceiver if our deeply rooted, instinctive belief in the existence of bodies as causes of our sensations should turn out to be false. However, Leibniz's grounds for objecting to this premise are somewhat different from those that have become familiar. The standard objection today concerns the internal coherence of Descartes' position. In the *Meditations* Descartes argues that God would be a deceiver if our clear and distinct ideas or judgments should prove to be false; he offers no justification for extending this claim to other judgments, no matter how firm and instinctive. Yet Descartes never argues that we have a clear and distinct idea of the existence of bodies as causes of our sensations. Descartes thus seems to have no warrant for this key premise of the argument. Leibniz also focuses on the issue of the epistemic warrant for the key premise, but he does not raise the issue of internal coherence; he objects rather that God might allow us to be deceived on this issue without having the character of a deceiver. Moreover, our being deceived in this matter might be a just punishment for sin in a previous life. Leibniz's other line of objection to Descartes' attempted proof turns on its formal features. Descartes' proof is of the form of an argument by elimination; unfortunately, however, Descartes' enumeration of the alternatives is not complete. According to Leibniz, Descartes overlooks the possibility that while our sensory perceptions are caused by God, our judgment that they are caused by bodies, and hence the deception, originates with us. Leibniz draws an interesting parallel with the situation regarding our pre-reflective judgments about secondary qualities; secondary qualities are not in bodies, but the judgment that they are, and hence the deception, originates with us.

Leibniz's stance with regard to Descartes' proof raises difficult questions that bear on disputed issues in the interpretation of his metaphysics. One strand in Leibniz's critique of Descartes is the observation that Descartes is seeking a greater degree of certainty on this issue than the nature of the subject permits. As Leibniz says, "about sensible things we can know nothing more, nor ought we desire to know more, than that they are consistent with each other as well as with rational principles that cannot be doubted, and hence that future events can to some extent be foreseen from the past" (Leibniz 1969: 384). Elsewhere Leibniz supplements consistency or coherence with vividness and complexity as criteria for judging of the veridicality of our experiences (Leibniz 1969: 363). In contexts such as these it is clear that the criteria Leibniz proposes are supposed to be epistemic ones; that is, he is suggesting that the satisfaction of these criteria allows us to be at least morally certain that bodies exist. On this approach, then, there is a logical gap between our sensory experiences and the existence of bodies; bodies are something over and above such experiences. Yet it must be noted that a different approach to the problem is suggested by one doctrine that has sometimes been attributed to Leibniz. Some readers have found in Leibniz a commitment to phenomenalism of the kind that is more often associated with Berkeley; in other words, bodies are reducible to the contents of our perceptual states. If Leibniz does indeed subscribe to such a doctrine, then, like Berkeley, he would seem to have a ready way of dealing with the skeptical worries that troubled Descartes and some of his successors. Since there is no logical gap between sensory perceptions and bodies, the skeptical problem cannot get off the ground. Moreover, consistency, complexity and vividness would not be merely epistemic criteria for judging of the veridicality of sensory experiences; the existence of bodies would be constituted by sensory experiences that satisfy these criteria. For example, to say that I am perceiving a table would just be to say that I am having a certain sensory experience as of a table that is vivid, complex, and coherent with my own perceptions and those of other perceivers.

Whether Leibniz does indeed subscribe to a phenomenalist account of bodies is a controversial issue that cannot be resolved here. It is true that Leibniz sometimes makes statements that have a distinctively phenomenalist flavor; he tells a correspondent, Des Bosses, for instance, that "we mean nothing else when we say that Socrates is sitting down than that what we understand by 'Socrates' and by 'sitting down' is appearing to us and to others who are concerned" (Leibniz 1969: 605). Elsewhere, he similarly writes that "matter and motion . . . are not so much substances or things as they are the phenomena of percipient beings, whose reality is located in the harmony of the percipient with himself (at different times) and with other percipient beings" (Leibniz 1969: 537). However, in considering the phenomenalist reading of Leibniz, two points need to be kept in mind. First, although Leibniz regularly says that bodies are mere phenomena, it is not clear that he is thereby committed to Berkeley-style phenomenalism that reduces bodies to the contents of harmonized sets of perceptions; more typically, Leibniz combines the thesis that bodies are phenomena with the non-phenomenalist thesis that bodies are aggregates of monads or simple substances. Secondly, even Leibniz's statements that sound most phenomenalistic are not primarily driven by epistemological considerations; they are driven rather by metaphysical issues such as the composition of the continuum. The ontology of bodies was a matter of vital concern for Leibniz throughout his philosophical career; he was deeply interested in the issue of whether any bodies satisfy the conditions for being substances. By contrast, the issue of our knowledge of the existence of bodies did not have anything like the same urgency in his philosophical thought.

Leibniz's Theory of Innate Ideas and Knowledge

The contrasts between Leibniz and Descartes in their approach to epistemology are apparent even when Leibniz is endorsing and developing Descartes' position. The doctrine of innate ideas and knowledge is a case in point. Leibniz self-consciously follows in Descartes' footsteps in reviving the ancient Platonic doctrine, and they both cite Socrates' argument in the *Meno* with approval. But the doctrine occupies a different position in Leibniz's philosophical system from that which it occupies in Descartes'. In the *Meditations* Descartes introduces the doctrine of innate ideas at a key stage in the journey back from the methodic doubt: in reflecting on his causal proof of the existence of God, which plays a crucial role in the reconstruction of knowledge, Descartes argues that God inscribed the idea of himself on the meditator's mind in creating him. Leibniz, by contrast, typically seeks to deduce his theory of innate ideas from metaphysical premises; in the *Discourse on Metaphysics*, for instance, Leibniz argues for a version of the doctrine from the thesis that the human mind is a causally self-sufficient substance which nothing can enter from the outside. By virtue of his metaphysical commitments Leibniz is led to the conclusion that, strictly speaking, all ideas are innate. In some contexts, however, such as the *New Essays on Human Understanding*, Leibniz is prepared to accommodate the intuitive distinction between innate and acquired or "adventitious" ideas; those ideas, namely sensory ideas, are said to be acquired which represent things as external to us.

If Leibniz seeks to argue for the innateness of ideas, it is natural to ask what he means by the term "idea." Fortunately, Leibniz addresses this issue directly, in a short essay that actually bears the title "What is an Idea?" (*Quid sit Idea?*). Here Leibniz explains that an idea is something which is "in the mind" and that it "consists not in some act but in the faculty of thinking, and we are said to have an idea of the thing even if we do not think of it, if only on a given occasion, we can think of it" (Leibniz 1969: 207). With this definition Leibniz seeks to steer a middle course between the positions of Malebranche and Descartes whose teaching was later to be defended against Malebranche by Arnauld. Leibniz agrees with Descartes that ideas are mental or psychological entities; by saying that they are "in the mind," Leibniz is resisting Malebranche's attempt to return to a Platonic-Augustinian conception of ideas as abstract entities in God to which our minds are related in thinking. Yet despite this point of agreement with Descartes (and later Arnauld) over the psychological status of ideas, Leibniz opposes them by treating ideas not as mental episodes or occurrent thoughts but, rather, as dispositions to have such thoughts. Elsewhere Leibniz supplements this analysis of the nature of ideas by insisting that the object of the idea must be internally consistent. Leibniz presses this point into service of his critique of Descartes' version of the ontological argument for God's existence; on Leibniz's analysis, to establish that we have an idea of God it is not sufficient to assert that we can think of God, or a being possessing all perfections. It remains to be shown that the concept of a most perfect being is free from lurking contradictions.

The thesis that ideas are mental dispositions suggests a tight logical connection between the theory of ideas in general and at least Leibniz's best-known version of nativism. If ideas are mental dispositions to think in certain ways, then innate ideas are simply mental dispositions to think in certain ways that we have had at least since birth. Leibniz defends the dispositional version of nativism most prominently, against Locke, in the *New Essays on Human Understanding*. In his own polemic against nativism Locke had sought to confront the defender of the doctrine of nativism with regard to ideas and principle with a dilemma: on a strong interpretation, the doctrine is empirically false, for it ascribes ideas to infants who do not have them, and on a weak interpretation it is condemned to triviality, for it asserts no more than a native capacity to acquire the ideas we have. Leibniz seeks to refute Locke by going through the horns of his dilemma by saying that he is defending a thesis that is weaker than the first horn but stronger than the second: innate ideas are less than fully actual thoughts, but they are more than mere capacities. Leibniz famously illustrates his point through a comparison with a block of marble in which the figure of Hercules is already marked out by the veins; the sculptor's task is thus limited to following the veins in the marble (Leibniz 1996: 52). Descartes made a somewhat similar attempt to defend dispositional nativism through an equally illuminating analogy: ideas are innate in the mind in the same way that certain character traits, like generosity, and diseases, like gout, are said to be congenital in certain families.

Leibniz's dispositional defense of innate ideas is his best-known defense of nativism, but it is arguably not the only one; in several texts it is accompanied by what might seem like an alternative account in terms of the mind's capacity to reflect on its own nature: we can acquire ideas of substance, cause, and identity by turning our mental gaze inwards and coming to recognize that our minds are substances, causes, and self-identical over time. Leibniz often summarizes this account of innateness with the suggestive if somewhat opaque tag that "we are innate to ourselves, so to speak" (Leibniz 1996: 51).

The reflection account of innateness has tended to puzzle Leibniz's critics, and it certainly raises a number of questions and difficulties. First, the reflection account seems to trivialize the nativist claims: to say that an idea is innate on this account is to say simply that its origin is non-sensory; there seems to be no implication that it has been present in the mind at least since birth. Secondly, the reflection account narrows the scope of the nativist thesis to a small set of metaphysical ideas; traditionally, however, nativists have wished to argue for the innateness of mathematical (e.g. geometrical) and other ideas; indeed Leibniz himself sometimes argues for the innateness of all ideas. In view of problems like these it is natural to wonder whether the reflection account is advanced as a genuine alternative to the dispositional version or whether, rather, it is intended to serve as a strand in a larger, overarching version of nativism that also includes a dispositional component.

It is not difficult to see why the reflection account has generally received a bad press, but it also true that the account has more in its favor than has been realized. For one thing, Leibniz might not have been greatly disturbed by the charge that it allows no real sense in which ideas are present in the mind since birth. What Leibniz is most anxious to defend is not so much a temporal account of nativism as, rather, the non-sensory origin of certain ideas. Moreover, it is a mistake to suppose, as some have done, that Leibniz is claiming no more than Locke himself would concede, for though Leibniz is keen to find common ground with Locke, who admits ideas of reflection or introspection, Leibniz goes beyond Locke by claiming that reflection acquaints us with the mind's own nature, and not just with mental operations. Finally, Leibniz might have the resources to broaden the scope of the doctrine in ways that are not easily recognized. For instance, Leibniz, following Descartes himself, can make use of the concept of the eminent possession of a property to show how we can acquire mathematical ideas by reflection on the mind's own nature. To say that a substance possesses a property eminently is to say that it possesses, not the property itself—that is, it does not possess it formally in traditional jargon—but, rather, a grander version of the property. Thus if Smith is six feet tall, then he is eminently five feet ten inches tall. The mind, then, might not be formally triangular, but it is eminently so; in this way the mind can acquire the idea of triangularity by reflection on its own nature.

The reflection account might have a further advantage for Leibniz: it harmonizes better than does the dispositional version of the doctrine with Leibniz's fundamental insistence that the human mind is a mirror of God. From this standpoint the problem with the dispositional version of nativism is that it is not clear that God can have any unactualized dispositional properties, for according to theological orthodoxy God is pure act. Thus the dispositional version of nativism is dubiously consistent with the mirror of God thesis. By contrast, the reflection account emphasizes a capacity of the human mind that seems clearly to align us with God: since Leibniz holds that reflection is a distinctive mark of spirits or higher monads, God can surely reflect on the perfections of his own nature. This defense of the reflection account on this score leads, however, to an interpretative dilemma. For on this approach the reflection account is to be regarded as an alternative to the dispositional version of nativism: the suggestion is that the reflection account is free from one weakness that seems to beset the dispositional version. However, there might be other, more strictly philosophical reasons for holding that the reflection account is simply a strand in an overarching theory of nativism with regard to ideas that includes a dispositional component. For instance, a plausible defense of Leibniz would take the form of saying that reflection on properties of one's own mind is simply a stimulus by means of which an innate mental disposition to think of such properties is activated. This interpretative dilemma is not easily resolved.

Certainly Leibniz himself does little or nothing to explain the relationship between the reflection account and dispositional nativism.

Whatever its relationship to dispositional nativism, it is clear that the reflection account is limited in scope to ideas. More clearly than Descartes, however, Leibniz seeks to extend nativism to principles or propositions, that is, items with a truth-value. In the Preface to the *New Essays on Human Understanding* Leibniz argues that necessary truths are all innate in the mind in the sense that we are predisposed towards occurrent knowledge of these truths. Indeed, Leibniz insists that we cannot establish the necessity of these truths without appealing to their innateness, since the senses do not serve to establish the necessity of general truths. Thus, for Leibniz, it is innateness that in some sense makes a priori knowledge possible.

Leibniz's thesis that we can have a priori knowledge of necessary truths needs to be understood in the light of his distinction between two kinds of truths: truths of reason and truths of fact (*Monadology* 33). Truths of reason are all necessary truths, and their opposite is impossible; they can be proved a priori by reduction to identities in a finite number of steps. Such truths are to be found in logic, mathematics, and even ethics. Truths of fact, by contrast, are all contingent truths, and their opposite is possible; these truths cannot be reduced to identities (at least, not in a finite number of steps), but by virtue of the Principle of Sufficient Reason, there is always a reason why the facts are as they are and not otherwise. Truths of fact, which all concern the actual world, are to be found in the natural sciences and other areas of empirical enquiry. Although truths of fact can be known only a posteriori by human minds, there is a sense in which God can know them a priori; God, for instance, can know the truth of the singular proposition "Julius Caesar crossed the Rubicon" by inspecting the complete concept of Julius Caesar that he finds in his mind.

Leibniz's project of extending nativism to knowledge of necessary truths has antecedents in Plato's *Meno* and less obviously in Descartes as well. Despite its impressive pedigree, however, it seems to face at least two serious philosophical problems. First, Leibniz's dispositional nativism is arguably less persuasive with regard to knowledge of necessary truths than with regard to ideas or concepts. In the case of metaphysical ideas such as *substance* and *cause*, it is rather plausible to maintain that they are innate in Leibniz's dispositional sense; we have a natural tendency to interpret our experience in terms of things with properties rather than clusters of features, just as we have a natural tendency to look for law-like necessary connections between events. It seems less plausible to maintain such a thesis with regard, say, to the laws of logic: in view of the fact that people's reasoning is fallacious much of the time it is difficult to defend the thesis that the rules of the propositional calculus work with the grain of the mind, as it were.

The second difficulty is perhaps more fundamental. Defenders of nativism such as Leibniz have often been criticized for conflating two issues that should be kept distinct. The objection is that it is one thing to appeal to innateness to explain items of occurrent knowledge; it is quite another to appeal to innateness to establish the truth of propositions. Consider the case of the slave boy in Plato's *Meno*. As a result of Socrates' questioning the slave boy comes to have occurrent knowledge of how to double the size of a given square; since the boy made no measurements and received no information from Socrates it might be plausible to explain his occurrent knowledge in this case in terms of an innate disposition. (Plato of course argues further for the doctrine of recollection of a previous existence, a doctrine that Leibniz rejects as a myth.) But in works such as the *New Essays on Human Understanding* Leibniz appeals to nativism to solve not just the explanatory problem of explanation but also the more purely epistemic problem of verification; he seeks to argue that necessary truths are "proved by what lies within, and cannot be established by experience, as truths of fact are" (Leibniz 1996: 79). But it is natural to object that there is no reason to suppose that propositions that are innate in our minds are true, let alone necessarily true: why should not a pack of lies be inscribed on the mind? Descartes might be able to answer such an objection by appealing to the fact of divine benevolence: innate propositions are inscribed on our mind by God who is not a deceiver. Leibniz, however, does not have this avenue open to him, since, as we have seen, he is highly critical of Descartes' attempts to solve epistemological problems by appealing to divine benevolence. Leibniz never seems to address this objection to his doctrine directly, but he might be able to appeal to his mirror of God principle in order to solve it. The mirror of God principle guarantees an isomorphism between the human mind and the divine mind, which in Leibniz's words sets "the pattern for the ideas and truths which are engraved in our souls" (Leibniz 1996: 447).

Leibniz and Kant

Leibniz's doctrine of innate ideas and knowledge is possibly his main contribution to epistemology; it seems to have exerted an influence on Kant's doctrine of categories in the *Critique of Pure Reason*. But although Kant might have responded positively to Leibniz on innate ideas, he was in general a severe critic of Leibniz's epistemology. In the *Critique of Pure Reason* Kant memorably criticizes Locke and Leibniz for complementary errors. Whereas Locke is guilty of sensualizing the pure concepts of the understanding, Leibniz is guilty of intellectualizing appearances; that is, he treats sensory perceptions as if they lie on a continuum with intellectual ideas, and regards the former as simply obscure and confused versions of the latter. For Kant, the truth is that concepts and intuitions are wholly heterogeneous, even if the associated faculties of understanding and sensibility might have a common, though to us unknown, root. In terms of this distinction Kant memorably diagnoses the alleged error behind Leibniz's principle of the Identity of Indiscernibles: the principle is true at the level of concepts, but not at the level of particulars given in sensory experience.

Kant's criticism of Leibniz for treating the sensory and the intellectual as if they lay on a continuum might be unfair. Indeed, Leibniz's position as outlined in the *Meditations on Knowledge, Truth and Ideas* has sometimes been seen as an anticipation of Kant's own distinction between concepts and intuitions. In defense of Leibniz it has been claimed that, far from treating sense-perception as a confused form of thought, Leibniz fairly consistently recognizes a basic distinction between concepts and sense-perception (Wilson 1999: 322–35). Like Descartes, Leibniz employs the terminology of "clarity" and "distinctness," and their contraries "obscurity" and "confusion," to characterize cognition, but unlike Descartes, Leibniz recognizes a wholly distinctive way in which this terminology applies to concepts. In the *Meditations on Knowledge, Truth and Ideas*, Leibniz employs the Cartesian terminology to characterize levels of conceptual ability. An idea of a kingfisher, for example, is said to be clear when it enables a person to identify or pick out kingfishers; an idea is said to be distinct when it enables a person to state distinguishing marks of kingfishers. Leibniz's paradigm example of a distinct idea is the idea that assayers have of gold; it is, as he says, an idea that "enables them to distinguish gold from all other bodies by sufficient marks and observations" (Leibniz 1969: 292). It is important to note that for Leibniz distinct ideas seem to be a proper subset of clear ideas.

Critics of Leibniz have sometimes objected that his account of conceptual abilities is inconsistent with claims that he makes about the ideas of the blind person. In the *Meditations on Knowledge, Truth, and Ideas*, Leibniz says that we cannot explain to a blind man what red is; in another work, he similarly says that a blind man could learn the whole of optics, but not acquire any idea of light (Leibniz 1969: 285). The objection turns on the fact that Leibniz sometimes seems to recognize that sensible qualities, such as redness, can be defined in scientific terms; for instance, to say that a body is red is just to say it reflects light waves of a certain frequency. But if this is the case, then there seems to be no reason in principle why a blind person could not have a distinct idea of red: if the blind person knows the scientific definition of red, then he has a distinct idea of red despite his inability to have any experience of red things. Thus some critics have charged that Leibniz is, after all, blurring the distinction between conceptual abilities and perceptual experiences.

The coherence of Leibniz's position in the *Meditations on Knowledge, Truth, and Ideas* can be defended against these objections. First, Leibniz denies here that it is possible to state distinguishing marks for sensible qualities such as redness; in this work at least, he does not hold that sensible qualities can be defined in scientific terms. Secondly, even if Leibniz concedes that sensible qualities can be so defined, he has a line of defense on which to fall back. For it is clear that for Leibniz the recognitional ability—that is, having a clear idea—is a necessary condition of having a distinct idea. Since the blind person presumably lacks the ability to pick out or recognize red things, he cannot have a distinct idea of red, no matter how much science he knows. (Even if the blind person could unfailingly pick out red things, Leibniz could say that he or she would have to give evidence of following a rule, and it is difficult to see how this could be done.) If there is a remaining problem in Leibniz's account it is not one of internal coherence in the *Meditations*; it is, rather, that Leibniz might vacillate with regard to the issue of whether it is sensible qualities themselves, or their causes, that can be scientifically defined.

Leibniz can to some extent be defended against Kant's criticisms in the *Critique of Pure Reason*. It seems fair to say that his position on concepts and sense-perception represents an advance in philosophical sophistication over Descartes; at least it marks a step in the direction of Kant's famous distinction between intuitions and concepts. Nonetheless, though the gap between them in this area might not be as great as it has sometimes appeared, there is no doubt that they are poles apart on larger issues; they differ widely in their attitude towards the nature of epistemology and its place in philosophy. For Kant, the very possibility of speculative metaphysics needs to be called into question; for this reason among others, he insists on the need for a critique of pure reason. Leibniz, by contrast, never seems to have been seriously troubled by the possibility of speculative metaphysics; as we have seen, to a large extent the theory of knowledge finds its proper place in his philosophy as a deduction from metaphysical principles that are supposedly known a priori.

References

Leibniz, G.W. (1969) *Philosophical Papers and Letters*, L.E. Loemker (trans.), Dordrecht: Reidel (2nd edn)
Leibniz, G.W. (1996) *New Essays on Human Understanding*, P. Remnant and J. Bennett (eds. and trans.), Cambridge: Cambridge University Press (2nd edn)
Wilson, M.D. (1999) *Ideas and Mechanism*, Princeton: Princeton University Press

Further Reading

Jolley, N. (1984) *Leibniz and Locke: A Study of the* New Essays on Human Understanding, Oxford: Oxford University Press. (Emphasizes the metaphysical motivation of Leibniz's critique of Locke's Theory of Knowledge.)

Jolley, N. (1990) *The Light of the Soul: Theories of Ideas in Leibniz, Malebranche, and Descartes*, Oxford: Oxford University Press. (Places Leibniz's theory of ideas in general and his theory of innate ideas in relation to Descartes and Malebranche.)

Kulstad, M. (1991) *Leibniz on Apperception, Consciousness and Reflection*, Munich: Philosophia Verlag. (A careful analytic study.)

MacRae, R. (1976) *Leibniz on Perception, Apperception, and Thought*, Toronto: University of Toronto Press. (An important and sometimes controversial study.)

Simmons, A. (2001) "Changing the Cartesian Mind: Leibniz on Sensation, Representation, and Consciousness," *The Philosophical Review* 110, 31–75. (A penetrating study that emphasizes Leibniz's break with the Cartesian theory of mind.)

63
GEORGE BERKELEY
George Pappas

Berkeley's epistemological views are mainly contained in his three earliest publications: the *Essay Towards a New Theory of Vision* (1709); the *Principles of Human Knowledge* (1710); and *Three Dialogues between Hylas and Philonous* (1713). A few later works also contain some material of epistemological significance. However, *Alciphron* (1732) is primarily a work in the philosophy of religion, and where it touches on epistemological issues it largely repeats what is contained in the *Essay Towards a New Theory of Vision*. The same can be said of the *Theory of Vision Vindicated and Explained* (1733); it is a defense of the doctrines contained in the 1709 book. Another later work, *De Motu* (1721), is mainly concerned with a defense of an instrumentalist version of scientific explanation.

Another important source of information on nearly every aspect of Berkeley's philosophy is the *Philosophical Commentaries*. These are early private notebooks that Berkeley kept in the years 1707–08, and they show his thought developing on a wide variety of issues that find later expression in the published works, though sometimes in forms that are very much modified from those contained in the *Philosophical Commentaries*.

Perception and Knowledge of Distance

In the *New Theory of Vision* (NTV), Berkeley considers how it is that we visually perceive, or see, distance, and also how we are able to see the magnitude and situation of distant objects (NTV, #1). He also considers how it is that we make judgments, based on vision, of the distance objects are from ourselves (NTV, #3). Seeing distance, magnitude and location of objects, we can presume, is somewhat different from judging what the distance, magnitude or location of those objects might be. And we might also presume that Berkeley is interested in justified judgments of distance, magnitude and location, and not merely judgments taken in isolation, since Berkeley thinks that we often know the distance from ourselves to an object based on vision.

A theoretical concern with visual perception and with the questions Berkeley considers had been prominent in the half century prior to Berkeley. Descartes' *Optics* had appeared in 1637, and Isaac Barrow's *Optical Lectures* (1669) was widely consulted. Malebranche's *Search after Truth* (1674) contains a number of chapters on distance and the visual perception of it, and, somewhat closer to Berkeley's own time, William Molyneux had published *Dioptrica Nova* (1692), which is entirely devoted to questions of the sort that interested Berkeley in NTV. Berkeley knew all of these works and it is generally agreed that he drew on all of them in his work in the *New Theory of Vision*.

Berkeley critically examines the "received" view about visual distance perception, a view which held that it involves engaging in some geometrical calculation. Imagine a distant object O at which a stationary person S is looking. The object's facing surface will reflect light to each of S's eyes. We can think of a line connecting each of the points at which the light from O enters each eye; this line, roughly, runs from one eye across the bridge of the nose to the other eye. We can consider this the base line which, together with the lines formed by the incoming light rays, forms a triangle in S's visual perception. According to the theory, S is presumed to know the length of the base line, and also to know the angles that each light ray makes at the respective eye with the base line. Then, by elementary geometry, S can compute the altitude of the triangle formed by these lines and this altitude is the distance from S to object O. It is in this manner that one sees the distance, and also in this manner that one comes to know the distance. Further, S would know the exact distance up to O, given these calculations, provided that S knew the exact degree of the angles and the exact length of the horizontal line. Less exact but still useful information would be gained, according to Berkeley's statement of the theory, depending on the dimensions of the angle formed at the object O. If this angle is large the object is taken to be close to the perceiver and the narrower this angle becomes the farther away the object is judged to be. Berkeley says:

> But when an object is placed at so near a distance as that the interval between the eyes bears any sensible proportion to it, the opinion of speculative men is the two optic axes (the fancy that we see only with one eye at once being exploded) concurring at the object do there make an angle, by means of which, according as it is greater or lesser, the object is perceived to be nearer or farther off.
>
> (Berkeley 1948–57: Vol. 1, 171; *NTV*, #4)

Berkeley has several criticisms of the received theory. Perhaps the most interesting is one that relies on the supposed self-intimating character of the mental. This thesis states that if a person is in some mental state at some time, then the person knows, at that time, that she is in that mental state. This thesis, widely accepted in Berkeley's time, is supposed to be fully general, applying to all persons and times. According to the received theory, a person would know the relevant angles and the length of the relevant line from eye to eye by a kind of perception. Berkeley observes that *he* never occurrently knows those angles and lengths when he is engaged in visual perception, and from this he infers via the self-intimation thesis that he does not perceive those angles and lines. This is enough, he feels, to refute the received theory, though he is confident that very few observers will ever know the relevant angles and lengths of lines. Moreover, of course, even if they possessed this knowledge, a great many observers would be in no position to actually perform the geometrical calculation said to be required by the received theory. In summing up this criticism, Berkeley says: "Since, therefore, those angles and lines are not themselves perceived by sight, it follows ... that the mind doth not by them judge of the distance of objects" (Berkeley 1948–57: Vol. 1, 173; *NTV*, #13).

Berkeley also thinks that the received theory is a priori, in the sense that according to the theory one can have a priori knowledge of the distance. This is not entirely correct, of course; one has to have perceptual experience of the optic angles and of the length of the line between the two eyes. What is a priori in the theory is the geometrical calculation, presumed capable of being performed by anyone who can see distance.

Berkeley's alternative theory dispenses altogether with geometrical calculations and with any a priori elements, and stresses instead experienced correlations between visual and tactile ideas of sense. He explains one of these correlations:

> It is certain by experience that when we look at a near object with both eyes, according as it approaches or recedes from us, we alter the disposition of our eyes, by lessening or widening the interval between the pupils. This disposition or turn of the eyes is attended by a sensation, which seems to me to be that which in this case brings the idea of greater or lesser distance into the mind.
> (Berkeley 1948–57: Vol. 1, 174; *NTV*, #16)

So, to illustrate, upon looking at a distant object one receives some visual ideas or appearances. Depending on the distance of the object, one will either narrow the pupils or widen them, receiving in either case a tactile (or better, bodily) sensation, which one has learned from past experience indicates a certain distance. In this manner one would see the distance, and be able to judge what it might be. Unlike in the received theory, however, this would be, at best, a rough estimate of the distance.

Berkeley also mentions the degree of clarity in the visual ideas; the closer objects are the less clear will be the visual idea, thereby suggesting small distance. There is no bodily sensation here to correlate with the visual ideas. However, in many cases where one sees a close object, one has to strain the eye in the attempt to produce greater clarity in the visual ideas. And here there is a correlation: the greater the bodily sensation of straining, as that correlates with the visual ideas then received, the closer the object is taken to be. However, even with the correlations Berkeley mentions, one will get only a very rough estimate of the distance of some object. A more accurate judgment of an object's distance often will come in a different way.

Suppose one sees a distant small building, thereby experiencing certain visual ideas. Berkeley suggests (*NTV*, #45) that if one were to walk towards this object, having as one does some thought of the number of paces taken, then upon reaching the distant object one might gain certain tactile sensations by touching the object. Berkeley's idea is that the distance would be measured by the number of paces taken, and one would get a more accurate judgment as to the actual distance of the object than from the simple visual and tactile correlations mentioned above.

In this example, Berkeley clearly assumes that there is a distant object which exists independently of any visual or tactile sensation or ideas anyone might receive. He is thus, in the *New Theory of Vision*, assuming that objects exist independently of all perception, contrary to the thesis he defends in the *Principles* and *Three Dialogues*, namely that for all sensible objects, to be is to be perceived. Berkeley mentions this very conflict at *Principles* #44, and there indicates that while he made the assumption of the independent existence of objects in the *New Theory of Vision*, this was merely a matter of convenience. He could have made do without this assumption, but it was easier not to do so. His point is thus that the *New Theory of Vision* contains no real conflict with his idealist thesis that objects exist if and only if they are perceived.

Berkeley's Realist Opponents

In both the *Principles* and *Three Dialogues*, Berkeley discusses theories of his opponents, and claims not only that these theories contain various defects, but also that defects aside, the theories lead to skepticism. He plainly takes the latter fact, if it is one, as a strike against these theories. It is thus important for Berkeley *not* to have the doctrines of the *New Theory of Vision* commit him to objects which exist independently of all perception.

The theory Berkeley is most concerned to attack is the representative realist theory of perception. On this theory, whenever a person perceives an object, she is immediately aware of one or more ideas, themselves causally related to that object. The object is perceived only mediately or indirectly, by way of the immediate perception of these ideas. What makes the theory representational is the fact, as claimed by Locke for example, that some of the immediately experienced ideas resemble some surface features of the object, namely, the object's primary qualities. This is the very point at which Berkeley criticizes the theory, for Berkeley thinks that the resemblance thesis is false. He holds, on the contrary, that an idea can only be like, or resemble, another idea, and of course if this is correct, then the representational realist theory of perception would be defective. Berkeley makes these points in the following passage:

> But say you, though the ideas themselves do not exist without the mind, yet there may be things like them whereof they are copies or resemblances, which things exist without the mind, in an unthinking substance. I answer, an idea can be like nothing but an idea; a colour or figure can be like nothing but another colour or figure. If we look but ever so little into our thoughts, we shall find it impossible for us to conceive a likeness except only between our ideas.
> (Berkeley 1948–57: Vol. 2, 44; *Principles*, #8)

Of course, there are indirect realist theories of perception which do not contain the resemblance thesis, and those theories are immune to this particular criticism from Berkeley.

In the *New Theory of Vision*, Berkeley does hold that distant objects are only *mediately* perceived by sight. Objects are only immediately perceived by touch. One might suspect, then, that the doctrines of the *New Theory of Vision* lead to a form of skepticism about objects, in just the way that Berkeley thinks that representative realism does. Berkeley has a way of disarming this suspicion, however. In the case of the *New Theory of Vision*, objects are immediately perceivable by touch, whereas in the case of representative indirect realism, objects are not immediately perceivable at all. Thus, there really is no strong parallel sufficient to think that the doctrines of the *New Theory of Vision* lead to skepticism in the way that Berkeley thinks that representative realism does.

Skeptical Worries

Berkeley also maintains that the representative realist theory leads to skepticism about the external world, and he takes this to be a decisive mark against the theory. His worry is that the theory would require one to first verify that some form of conformity obtains between one's ideas and external objects, before one could have knowledge of those objects. But Berkeley thinks we would never be in a position to actually carry out this verification, and so knowledge would never be gained. Here is one version of the argument Berkeley presents:

> It is your opinion, the ideas we perceive by our senses are not real things, but images, or copies of them. Our knowledge therefore is no farther real, than as

our ideas are the true representations of those originals. But as these supposed originals are in themselves unknown, it is impossible to know how far our ideas resemble them; or whether they resemble them at all. We cannot therefore be sure we have any real knowledge.

(Berkeley 1948–57: Vol. 2, 246. From *Three Dialogues*)

Most likely, when Berkeley says the "originals are in themselves unknown" he means that the originals are not themselves immediately perceived. That reading would explain why he says it would be impossible to know whether the resemblance, or conformity, obtains between the ideas and the objects. That is, his line of thought would be that in order to know this one would have to compare the two items, ideas and objects; and this comparison would require that both objects be immediately perceived. However, according to the representative realist theory, physical objects are never immediately perceived. Hence, given the theory, the required comparison cannot be carried out and so, given the theory, one would never have perceptual knowledge of objects.

This line of argument is successful only if Berkeley is right that, for the representative realist, one must have knowledge of this conformity between ideas and objects if one is to have perceptual knowledge of objects. It is true that Locke, at whom Berkeley's argument is no doubt directed, encourages this way of thinking. He says:

Where-ever we perceive the Agreement or Disagreement of any of our *Ideas* there is certain Knowledge; and where-ever we are sure those *Ideas* agree with the reality of Things, there is certain real Knowledge.

(Locke 1975: 573; *Essay*, IV, IV, 18)

If this passage expresses Locke's all-things-considered opinion on this matter, then Berkeley's argument would have some force against Locke. Berkeley's argument would be less effective if the representative realist theory held only that there *be* a conformity between ideas and objects, in order for one to gain perceptual knowledge of objects, and not that the cognizer needs to know about this conformity (Pappas 2005: 98–103).

Berkeley has a second argument which is more general in that it can be aimed at any version of indirect realism, and not just those that contain some representational element. The argument, in a nutshell, is that any indirect realist theory of perception would require that any perceptual knowledge we might gain about objects would have to be inferential knowledge. That is, such knowledge would have to be based upon knowledge of immediately experienced ideas. However, according to Berkeley's argument, the required inferences would fail, so that indirect realism would lead to skepticism about objects. The relevant inferences, Berkeley sees, would be either deductive or some form of induction. They would not be deductive, because no proposition about experienced ideas or group of such propositions entails a physical object proposition. As for inductive inferences in this context, the only such inference Berkeley considers is an explanatory one. That is, he considers whether the assumption that there are objects of relevant sorts best explains the ideas we immediately experience. He rejects this explanatory argument because it would presume that we have some accounts of how material bodies causally act upon non-material minds wherein, it is supposed, experienced ideas are to be located. Berkeley claims that nobody, including all of the indirect realists, understands how mind–body causal interaction of that kind operates, and so concludes that inductive inferences from idea-propositions to object-propositions do not succeed (Berkeley 1948–57: Vol. 2, 48–49; *Principles*, #19).

It is clear that this argument by Berkeley has but limited success, however, because it considers just one form of inductive inference and, perhaps more importantly, because it takes no account of those indirect realist theories that do not assume that minds are non-material substances. Moreover, Berkeley's argument assumes that indirect realism entails that perceptual knowledge of objects is always inferential and based upon immediate knowledge of experienced ideas. This assumption is certainly open to challenge, though it is not a matter that Berkeley ever addresses (Pappas 2005: 108–113).

Response to Skepticism

We have noted that Berkeley holds that representative realism, and even non-representative versions of indirect realism, leads to skepticism about objects. He maintains that there are other routes to skepticism, however, and he aims to undermine all of these routes as well. One such route is the thesis that there are abstract general ideas. Of this, Berkeley says that,

> My purpose, therefore is, to try if I can discover what those principles are, which have introduced all that doubtfulness and uncertainty, those absurdities and contradictions into the several sects of philosophy . . . what seems to have had a chief part in rendering speculation intricate and perplexed, and to have occasioned innumerable errors and difficulties in almost all parts of knowledge. And that is the opinion that the mind hath a power of framing *abstract ideas* or notions of things.
> (Berkeley 1948–57: Vol. 2, 26–27; *Principles*, Introduction, #4)

If Berkeley is right that the thesis of abstract general ideas leads to skepticism, then it is important to reject that thesis so that one avenue towards skepticism is closed. This is exactly what he does in the introduction to the *Principles*, where he argues that abstract general ideas are impossible (Berkeley 1948–57: Vol. 2, 27–31; *Principles*, Introduction, #7–10; Pappas 2000: 39–79).

Another route to skepticism, according to Berkeley, is the thesis that objects consist in a material substance or substratum in which qualities inhere. This can be seen in the following exchange between Hylas and Philonous in the *Three Dialogues*, where Philonous acts as a spokesperson for Berkeley:

HYLAS: What! Can anything be more fantastical, more repugnant to common sense, or a more manifest piece of skepticism, than to believe there is no such thing as *matter*?

PHILONOUS: What if I should prove, that you who hold there is, are by virtue of that opinion a greater *skeptic*, and maintain more paradoxes and repugnancies to common sense, than I who believe no such thing?
(Berkeley 1948–57: Vol. 2, 172)

Accordingly, Berkeley tries to show in both the *Principles* and the *Three Dialogues*, that there cannot be any material substratum, either because the very concept of such a thing is contradictory or because that concept is empty. At one point in the *Three Dialogues* Philonous says to Hylas, in summing up what he has to say about material substance, that,

> My business was only to shew, you meant *nothing*; and this you were brought to own. So that in all your various senses, you have been shewed either to mean nothing at all, or if any thing, an absurdity. And if this be not sufficient to prove the impossibility of a thing, I desire you will let me know what is.
>
> (Berkeley 1948–57: Vol. 2, 226)

Yet another route to skepticism that Berkeley identifies is the thesis that objects and their qualities exist independently of all perception. On this point he says that,

> So long as we attribute a real existence to unthinking things, distinct from their being perceived, it is not only impossible for us to know with evidence the nature of any real unthinking being, but even that it exists. Hence it is, that we see philosophers distrust their senses, and doubt the existence of heaven and earth, of every thing they see or feel, or even of their own bodies.
>
> (Berkeley 1948–57: Vol. 2, 79; *Principles* #88)

Berkeley tries to undermine this route to skepticism by establishing that all sensible objects and their qualities exist if and only if they are perceived. This is his famous thesis, for sensible things, of *esse is percipi*, or to be is to be perceived (Berkeley 1948–57: Vol. 2, 50–51; *Principles*, #22–24).

Having blunted all three of these routes to skepticism, and having shown the problems facing representative realism, Berkeley feels that he has undermined all of the principal routes to skepticism.

Berkeley's Positive Epistemology

Like the representative and indirect realist, Berkeley accepts the thesis that in every perceptual experience, one or more ideas are immediately perceived. Unlike the representative and indirect realist, however, he maintains that physical objects are also among the objects that are immediately perceived. The question then becomes how does Berkeley manage to combine the theory of ideas with the thesis that objects are immediately perceived?

There are a number of passages where Berkeley endorses the thesis that objects are immediately perceived, among them these two:

> Wood, stones, fire, water, flesh, iron, and the like things, which I name and discourse of, are things that I know. And I should not have known them, but that I perceived them by my senses; and things perceived by the senses are immediately perceived.
>
> (Berkeley 1948–57: Vol. 2, 230)

and also in a letter to the American philosopher Samuel Johnson:

> I see no difficulty in conceiving a change of state, such as is vulgarly called Death, as well without as with material substance. It is sufficient for that purpose that we allow sensible bodies, i.e., such as are immediately perceived by sight and touch.
>
> (Berkeley 1948–57: Vol. 2, 282; Pappas 2000: 172–178)

Berkeley can accommodate this line of thought if he identifies individual ideas with physical objects, because we know that he holds that ideas of sense are immediately perceived. However, this does not seem to be his considered opinion because he says that,

> A certain colour, taste, smell, figure and consistence having been observed to go together, are accounted one distinct thing, signified by the name *apple*. Other collections of ideas constitute a stone, a tree, a book, and the like sensible things; which as they are pleasing or disagreeable, excite the passions of love, hatred, joy, grief, and so forth.
> (Berkeley 1948–57: Vol. 2, 41; *Principles*, #1)

Thus, his view is that objects are really collections, or groups, of sensible ideas. This sort of metaphysical thesis will allow for immediate perception of objects, so long as Berkeley is willing to agree that by immediately perceiving some of the ideas making up a collection of ideas that is identical to an object O, one thereby immediately perceives O. A rough example of this sort, though not in the terminology of ideas, would be when a person is standing in a doorway looking into a room containing a class of students. From her vantage point in the doorway, she can only see some number of the students, but still we do not hesitate to say that she thereby sees the class of students. It is similar, and more familiar, with parts. If one looks at the front of College Hall, one thereby sees College Hall, even though one sees only some of its connected parts.

Berkeley says very little about what he takes the collections that are identified with objects to be. Presumably we do not want to hold that the sensible ideas immediately perceived by a given person at a time make up the object, even though those sensible ideas form a collection. At a later time that same person immediately perceives a different group of sensible ideas, and so if these later ideas made up an object it would be a different object from what was first perceived. However, Berkeley will surely want to hold that the same person might perceive the same object at different times, and so he will need a concept of collections of sensible ideas that will allow for this.

Notice that, as Berkeley sees it, the fact that objects are always only indirectly perceived, given indirect realism, is what leads those theories to the result that any knowledge one would have of those objects would be inferential. By allowing that objects are immediately perceived, by contrast, Berkeley seems to at least leave the way open to hold that we have immediate, non-inferential knowledge of objects. Indeed, this is a path that he actually takes. Two passages from the *Philosophical Commentaries* bring out this point:

> We have an intuitive Knowledge of the Existence of other things besides our selves & even praecedaneous to the Knowledge of our own Existence. in that we must have Ideas or else we cannot think.
> (Berkeley 1948–57: Vol. 1, 69; *Commentaries*, #547)

and,

> I am the farthest from Scepticism of any man. I know with an intuitive knowledge of the existence of other things as well as my own Soul. This is w^t Locke nor scarce any other Thinking Philosopher will pretend to.
> (Berkeley 1948–57: Vol. 1, 70; *Commentaries*, #563)

GEORGE BERKELEY

Here Berkeley makes use of Locke's term, "intuitive knowledge," and as Locke had used this term, such knowledge is the very paradigm of knowledge which is non-inferential. Moreover, in the second of these passages he contrasts his view with Locke's, and the contrast has to be that intuitive knowledge is not restricted to knowledge of ideas. That is decidedly Locke's position, and so for the contrast to make sense Berkeley's use of the term "other things" must refer to objects and not merely to ideas. The same is almost certainly the case with the first of these passages, as it appears in the same cluster of passages in the *Commentaries*, #547–563, where Locke's position on intuitive knowledge is challenged.

In sum, Berkeley's positive epistemology is supposed to vanquish skepticism about objects outright. This is because it shows, as Berkeley thinks, that we do have knowledge of objects precisely because we have immediate, non-inferential knowledge of objects. We have this sort of privileged knowledge of objects, in turn, because objects are among the things that are immediately perceived. Immediate perception of objects, in the right circumstances where one is attentive and has the relevant conceptual repertoire, is taken by Berkeley to suffice for knowledge. Indeed, Berkeley goes beyond this point and, following Locke, insists that we also have immediate, non-inferential knowledge of ourselves, and that this self-knowledge is not mediated by nor based upon knowledge of ideas (Berkeley 1948–57: Vol. 2, 233).

Foundationalism

It has often been supposed that Berkeley, along with other classical empiricists such as Locke and Hume, adopted an empiricist version of foundationalism about knowledge. That is, Berkeley is often taken to have held that all knowledge, or at least all knowledge of contingent truths, is based upon and derivable from epistemically more basic knowledge of experienced ideas. Whatever might be said about Locke and Hume on this matter, we can now see that this is not the right way to understand Berkeley. Knowledge of external objects and of oneself is not taken by Berkeley to be based upon knowledge of experienced ideas at all. Rather, like our knowledge of experienced ideas, much of our knowledge of objects and of oneself is immediate and non-inferential. Thus Berkeley, if he is to be construed as a foundationalist about knowledge, is not one who accepts the empiricist version of that thesis here described. If he accepts foundationalism, then knowledge of objects and of oneself is every bit as basic as knowledge of experienced ideas.

Certainty and Knowledge

Under the powerful influence of Descartes, many philosophers in Berkeley's time period accepted the thesis that knowledge implies certainty in one's belief, and that the sort of certainty involved was that wherein the logical possibility of mistaken belief was ruled out. If Berkeley accepted, or was committed to, these two principles, then of course he would be in no position to maintain that we have immediate knowledge of objects because he would be in no position to claim that we have *any* knowledge of objects. After all, propositions about objects are not entailed by propositions about ideas, and no belief about objects is immune to error in the way that would be demanded by this concept of certainty.

Berkeley does think that one's knowledge of immediately experienced ideas is certain in just the way that the above concept of certainty lays out. He says, for example, that

> So long as I confine my thoughts to my own ideas divested of words, I do not see how I can easily be mistaken. The objects I consider, I clearly and adequately know. I cannot be deceived in thinking I have an idea which I have not. It is not possible for me to imagine, that my own ideas are alike or unlike, that are not truly so.
> (Berkeley 1948–57: Vol. 2, 39; *Principles*, Introduction #22)

However, when it comes to our knowledge of objects, Berkeley seems to have a different concept of certainty in mind. We can see this in some passages from the *Philosophical Commentaries* and from the *Three Dialogues*. In the former work, Berkeley says,

> I am certain there is a God, tho I do not perceive him have no intuition of him. this not difficult if we rightly understand w^t is meant by certainty.

and then,

> Malbranch in his Illustration differs widely from me. He doubts of the Existence of Bodies I doubt not in the least of this.
> (Berkeley 1948–57: Vol. 1, 96 & 97; *Commentaries*, #813 and 800)

In *Three Dialogues*, we find much the same point:

> Let me be represented as one who trusts his senses, who thinks he knows the things he sees and feels, and entertains no doubt of their existence.
> (Berkeley 1948–57: Vol. 2, 237)

These several passages indicate that Berkeley is content to make use of a very weak concept of certainty when it comes to knowledge of bodies, namely a concept in which one is certain in one's belief about an object just when one has no doubts vis-à-vis one's belief about that object. This is a very different concept of certainty from that employed by Descartes, and even from that employed by Berkeley in other contexts. It should be clear that if he makes use of this weaker notion of certainty, then there is no objection, based on the strong concept of certainty that we trace to Descartes, to Berkeley's claim that we have non-inferential and immediate knowledge of objects.

References

Berkeley, G. (1948–57) *The Works of George Berkeley*, ed. T. Jessop and A. Luce, Edinburgh: Thomas Nelson.
Locke, J. (1975) *An Essay Concerning Human Understanding*, ed. P. Nidditch, Oxford: Clarendon Press.
Pappas, G. (2000) *Berkeley's Thought*, Ithaca: Cornell University Press.
—— (2005) "Berkeley's Assessment of Locke's Epistemology," *Philosophica*, Vol. 76, 91–114.

Further Reading

Atherton, M. (1991) *Berkeley's Revolution in Vision*, Ithaca: Cornell University Press. (A comprehensive treatment of Berkeley's *New Theory of Vision*.)
Pitcher, G. (1977) *Berkeley*, London: Routledge. (Excellent treatment of most of Berkeley's work.)
Stoneham, T. (2002) *Berkeley's World*, Oxford: Oxford University Press. (Focuses on the *Three Dialogues*.)
Winkler, K. (1989) *Berkeley: An Interpretation*, Oxford: Clarendon Press. (Excellent examination of Berkeley's overall work.)

64
THOMAS REID
Ryan Nichols

From the earliest pages of his first book, *Inquiry Into the Human Mind*, epistemology is Reid's major philosophical interest. Reid develops his unconventional epistemological theories in response to his predecessors. Uniquely for his time, Reid theorized about problems of epistemology from a point of view not divorced from his embodied, social and psychological context. After concluding that the skeptics that preceded him—Descartes, Berkeley, Hume—did not appreciate ways that epistemic theories infect other philosophical commitments, Reid articulated and explained the presuppositions of knowledge needed to build an epistemological theory capable of providing knowledge of self and world. Reid's method is governed by common-sense reflection, not Cartesian doubt. He *presupposes* that we have knowledge and seeks to understand how and why. It is far from a coincidence that many of the leading lights of contemporary epistemology—Lehrer, Plantinga and Alston, to name three—have not only studied Thomas Reid's corpus closely but have published papers and books about Reid's epistemology. This essay explains Reid's context and method, the content and epistemic status of his first principles, his arguments against skepticism and his theory of perceptual knowledge.

1. Reid's Context and Method

Thomas Reid (1710–1796) is a Scottish philosopher whose major works are *Inquiry into the Human Mind* (originally published in 1764), *Essays on the Intellectual Powers* (1785) and *Essays on the Active Powers* (1788). Reid was educated in Marischal College, Aberdeen, during which time Scotland was experiencing religious uprisings and tumult. Reid became a parish minister in 1737 (see Wood 1985). In 1751 Reid was appointed professor at King's College, Aberdeen, then in 1764 he replaced Adam Smith as chair of moral philosophy at Glasgow.

Reid constructs his epistemology out of the ruins of the epistemologies of Descartes, Locke, Berkeley and Hume. They all endorsed the 'Way of Ideas,' which can be characterized by the following theses:

> Mind-independent objects are not directly perceived, but rather only mental representations ('ideas' or 'images') are. Sensations are often confused with objects of perception. Our perceptual experience does not yield justification for beliefs about the mind-independent world. Perception and memory are not reliably aimed at forming true beliefs, but the faculty of reason is.

Reid allows for a use of the term 'ideas' to refer to *operations of* or *events in* the mind, but does not believe there are ideas qua mental intermediaries.

In order to correct the mistakes promulgated by the Way of Ideas Reid bridges the gap between philosophy and psychology by drawing his method from Newton's experimentally minded *Opticks* and from the theoretically minded *Principia*. He sought to reorient philosophical method so philosophers would embrace natural science and avoid giving unthinking allegiance to prior philosophical ideas (EIP 1.4, 51). Reid gathers evidence for his conclusions from philosophical argumentation, introspective observation on what happens in his own mind, empirical observations of others, and testimony drawn from scientists (EIP 1.3, 49–50; see EIP 2.8, 120–21; EIP 5.3, 371; and EAP 527a). Proper philosophical explanations, like proper scientific explanations, appeal to laws of nature. Reid's approach to foundationalism is to find laws about patterns of human belief formation in accord with a faculty psychology (Lehrer 1998, 15) then defend them against skeptical attack.

2. Foundations of Knowledge

2.1. *Common Sense First Principles of Contingent Truth*

Reid's approach to the foundations of knowledge—which he calls 'first principles'—resonates with his interest in applying methods from empirical psychology to epistemology. He describes his method saying, "there is but one way to the knowledge of nature's work—the way of observation and experiment," which Reid likens to philosophy conducted in light of Newton's *regulae philosophandi* (INQ 1.1, 11–12; Newton 1999, 794). First Reid observes what people believe, when people come to believe what they do, and how widely these beliefs are disbursed over the population. Second, he attempts to unify this observational data through laws of belief formation, i.e. first principles, much as a field ecologist might attempt to describe and classify observations of a diversity of organisms.

Reid has two sets of first principles. The first set concerns contingent truths and the second necessary truths. The set of necessary truths includes principles about grammar, logic, morality, metaphysics and theology (see EIP 6.6). For example, "that no man ought to be blamed for what it was not in his power to hinder" (EIP 6.6, 494). The foundations in Reid's theory of empirical knowledge are his first principles of contingent truth, which he often describes as his 'first principles of common sense'. Common sense is a faculty of judgment (EIP 6.1, 406–7) whereby we judge of "what is true and what is false in matters that are self-evident, and which he distinctly apprehends" (EIP 6.2, 426). The term 'first principles' refers to

> propositions which are no sooner understood than they are believed.... There is no searching for evidence, no weighing of arguments; the proposition is not deduced or inferred from another; it has the light of truth in itself, and has no occasion to borrow it from another.
> (EIP 6.4, 452; see de Bary 2002, 32–48)

This is a psychological description of these principles as opposed to a normative description of the principles. Reid intends to set them in their cognitive context prior to explaining their epistemic implications.

2.2. Opposition to Classical Foundationalism

Since Reid's own foundationalism follows from his criticisms of Descartes', we examine those criticisms now. First, even if Descartes' *cogito* could be used as a first principle to generate other beliefs, those beliefs would be so narrow in scope that, from it, "very little, if anything, can be deduced by just reasoning" (EIP 6.7, 518). Second, Descartes' appeal to God's goodness and knowledge is viciously circular (EIP 6.5, 481). These criticisms generalize: Reid is opposed 'classical foundationalism,' the theory that foundational beliefs must (i) have epistemic properties—certainty, indubitability—that render them 'skeptic-proof' and (ii) are epistemically self-evident through the light of pure reason. Third, his method of doubt prompts Descartes to search for a solution to skepticism in a vacuum—in which Descartes does not know that he is even embodied. This, though, falls afoul of Reid's insistence on an empirically and psychologically real epistemology. On this point Reid foreshadows responses to skepticism of Moore and Wittgenstein (e.g., see Moore 1959, 226).

Lastly, Reid objects to Descartes' method of doubt:

> How do you know that your consciousness cannot deceive you? You have supposed that all you see, and hear, and handle, may be an illusion. Why, therefore, should the power of consciousness have this prerogative, to be believed implicitly, when all our other powers are supposed fallacious?
> (EIP 6.7, 515)

Descartes' justification for the *cogito* depends upon a dubitable presupposition: that first-person access to thought is transparent and reliable, but that no other belief-forming faculty is (INQ 6.20, 168–9). But reason comes from the same "mint of Nature" as perception, memory and judgment, which leads Reid to a parity argument: if we regard perception as fallible, then we have equal reason to regard reason as fallible. This line of Reid's thinking is aimed at semi-skeptics who assert, of some but only of some circumscribed areas of inquiry, we lack all knowledge. Extrapolating from these focused criticisms, Reid is making a broad criticism of the Enlightenment's elevation of reason over other belief-forming faculties.

2.3. Two Types of First Principles of Contingent Truth

In addition to responding to Descartes' failed foundationalism, Reid's foundationalism is motivated by recognition of a regress argument (EIP 6.7, 522, and 6.4, 455). First principles of contingent truth are necessary in the construction of a body of knowledge because "all knowledge got by reasoning must be built upon first principles" (EIP 6.4, 454) if the regress is to be stopped. While Descartes claimed his foundations for knowledge was indubitable, Reid says his are fallible. While Descartes replies to skepticism by identifying a single, widely applicable principle that guided further reflection, Reid identifies a number of first principles specific to particular domains.

Reid's foundations include principles that state a singular fact and principles that function as recipes for the generation of particular beliefs:

> 4. Another first principle is, Our own personal identity and continued existence, as far back as we remember anything distinctly. (EIP 6.5, 476)

5. Another first principle is, That those things do really exist which we distinctly perceive by our senses, and are what we perceive them to be (EIP 6.5, 476)

(4) asserts individual human beings have diachronic personal identity; (4) says this universal generalization is psychologically self-evident. (5) asserts the veridicality of our distinct perceptual beliefs; it implies that token perceptual beliefs about what we distinctly perceive are psychologically self-evident. (5) is a recipe, i.e. an 'epistemological' first principle. 'Epistemological' first principles include principles of memory, reasoning, testimony and induction. 'Factual' first principles like (4) include principles that we possess free will and that there are other minds. Lastly, in addition to being *psychologically* self-evident, (4) and (5) might also be *epistemically* self-evident so long as the epistemic self-evidence of a statement does not imply that it is necessary that the statement is true or the statement is known indubitably.

3. Externalism and Naturalism

Reid is the first to articulate an externalist theory about the basis of epistemic justification and to adopt a broadly naturalistic method that sees epistemology as a form of psychology (see 'Externalism/Internalism', Chapter 14 in this volume). Reid's epistemology resembles contemporary forms of externalism in two key ways: the key epistemic feature of any belief type is its veridicality, and Reid is more concerned with the psychological and physiological genesis of belief than he is with the deontological justification of belief (Alston 1985). We might laugh at the fact that Reid writes thousands and thousands of words about double vision (INQ 6.15–17), but only by taking this to heart can we understand the as yet unappreciated lengths to which Reid goes to bring epistemology into relationship with psychology. Reid endorses a nuanced form of externalism on the basis of commitments to proper functionalism, theism, and common sense.

3.1. Proper Functionalism and Theism

Reid facilitates his externalism first by endorsing a nascent 'proper functionalism.' Reid says he will "take it for granted that the evidence of sense, when the proper circumstances concur, is good evidence, and a just ground of belief" (EIP 2.20, 229). What Lehrer calls Reid's 'metaprinciple' reflects this commitment: "that the natural faculties, by which we distinguish truth from error, are not fallacious" (EIP 6.5, 480; see de Bary (2002, ch. 5.3) on the 'metaprinciple'). This point suggests an 'innocent until proven guilty' attitude about our noetic equipment (see Davis 2006, 35–59) on Reid's use of legal language and courtroom metaphor). By claiming that justification is natural Reid affects a contrast with internalism. Non-mental matters of fact, including features of the environment and the functioning of one's body and brain, structure one's justification.

As with Alvin Plantinga's proper functionalism (Plantinga 1993), Reid's is *motivated* by his Christian theism. Reid is inspired to adopt externalism on the grounds that human beings have been created by a supremely intelligent, beneficent being to form true beliefs. Whether Reid's externalism is *justified* by way of belief in God is a controversial issue among commentators. Reid appeals to the fact of God's wise creation of our faculties as support for his account of first principles on only a few occasions (INQ 6.24, 196; EIP 2.21, 243–4 and 6.7, 516; EAP 617a). Several scholars conclude that

Reid's anti-skepticism depends firmly upon a prior and unjustified commitment to God's existence (Daniels 1974/1989, 117; Norton 1979, 318; Popkin 1980/1993, 68), but this position faces problems, as research about the 'detachability' of Reid's theism from his epistemology has revealed (DeBary 2001, 65–74, 160 and 165–88; Lehrer and Warner 2000; Somerville 1995, 346).

Reid is aware of Descartes' circular argumentation regarding knowledge and God, and he does not make a mistake of that kind. Perceptual beliefs, for example, are the "inspiration of the Almighty" in the sense that they are "the immediate effect of our constitution, which is the work of the Almighty." But he explicitly says that 'inspiration' does not imply epistemic dependence:

> for a man would believe his senses though he had no notion of a Deity. He who is persuaded that he is the workmanship of God, and that it is a part of his constitution to believe his senses, may think that a good reason to confirm his belief. But he had the belief before he could give this or any other reason for it.
> (EIP 2.20, 232; cf. INQ 6.20, 170; INQ 6.24, 193)

Reid's externalism is unambiguously *motivated by* his theism, but knowledge of beliefs about the external world does not appear to *depend upon* prior justification of belief in God.

3.2. First Principles Are Token Beliefs

Though Reid's use of common sense is wide and varied, the conceptual connection with externalism is unmistakable. His first principles are not principles derived via a priori reason but principles of common sense drawn from observations of human beings. Common sense is construed as a faculty responsible for judging of things self-evident (EIP 6.2, 426–7). So the beliefs yielded by epistemic first principles have prima facie external justification.

By examining an ambiguity in the structure of Reid's epistemological principles we will uncover a key feature of Reid's externalism. James Van Cleve (1999) argues that principles like (5) above can be read in two ways by adjusting the implicit universal quantifier:

> 5.1 It is a first principle that, for all people, every distinct perceptual belief is true.
> 5.2 For all people, every distinct perceptual belief is a first principle for that person.

(5.1) represents a 'methodist' interpretation, while (5.2) represents a 'particularlist' interpretation. The particularist version implies, for example, that my visual belief *I see a tree* is self-evident. In contrast, the generalist reading suggests that such a belief is not self-evident; its justification depends upon prior justification of and/or inference from (5.1). Reid's claim that particular token beliefs are first principles has been analyzed in terms of theses about epistemic directness and reliabilism (Alston 1989; Pappas 1989; Cummins 1974).

This interpretation of Reidian first principles best represents Reid's intent because it offers the contrast with Cartesian methodism Reid seeks and is grounded in empirical psychology. Also, particularism draws together many of Reid's 'signs' and 'indications' of the first principles. He says that first principles are self-evident, believed immediately upon being understood, and universal across cultures (see §4.1 below). Particular token perceptual beliefs—*I see a tree*—fit this description. However, those who interpret Reidian first principles as being general principles, and not particular token beliefs, might argue that (i) those general principles are also self-evident, and that (ii) *I see a tree* is self-evident but not a first principle.

Several texts substantiate attribution of an externalism about justification to Reid. He says token perceptual beliefs are "part of that furniture which Nature hath given to the human understanding" (INQ 7, 215). He says, "There is no reasoning in perception" (INQ 6.20, 172). These commitments are represented in his examples:

> When I hear a certain sound, I conclude immediately, without reasoning, that a coach passes by. There are no premises from which this conclusion is inferred by any rules of logic. It is the effect of a principle of our nature, common to us with the brutes.
>
> (INQ 2.7, 38; see EIP 2.20, 231; cf. EIP 2.5, 98–9)

Sounds are received by our ears. They are non-consciously sorted by our minds into categories. If the sound is familiar from previous experience as being caused by a coach, then I will non-inferentially form a perceptual belief that there is a coach passing by.

4. Indirect Responses to the Semi-Skeptic

The global skeptic who has adopted a Cartesian method of doubt and presupposes a demanding definition of knowledge argues that I can know statements about the mind-independent world only if the statements are incorrigible. Reid has little interest in sparring with such a skeptic because he cannot be refuted through philosophical reasoning (EIP 6.5, 480–1). However, the "semi-skeptical" position can be (INQ 5.7, 71–2). The semi-skeptic argues that without possession of, or access to, second-order justification for beliefs such as *I see a tree*, I do not know *I see a tree*. More modestly, the semi-skeptic might object that, in order to stop a regress, first principles must have positive epistemic status and cannot simply be presupposed without support. In Reid's first reply to the semi-skeptic he marshals epistemic support for his first principles. In the second he makes a dialectical point about the nature of evidence.

4.1. Track-Record Support for First Principles

Reid denies that first principles are or need be incorrigible and affirms fallibilism about the justification of first principles: their justification is defeasible. But Reid does not say that first principles can be proven true; rather, "common principles seldom admit of direct proof, nor do they need it" (EIP 1.2, 39). Nonetheless, "there are certain ways of reasoning even about them, by which those that are just and solid may be confirmed, and those that are false may be detected" (EIP 6.4, 463). The contrast between *directly proving* and *reasoning on behalf of* a first principle hints at his approach (DeBary 2001, 134).

First principles can be given justificatory support in the form of 'indirect proofs,' which include:

(a) denying a first principle yields inconsistency downstream because the first principle will inevitably be presupposed in further cognitive processing;
(b) denying a first principle yields absurdity;
(c) the content of languages supports the structure and content of first principles by representing psychologically real thought processes;
(d) they are formed early in life, and not by ratiocination on evidence;
(e) they are indispensible in practice.

Among the 'signs' that a purported claim is a first principle are that it is: accepted when understood; the result of original powers (not inference); in need of no external evidence to be psychologically compelling; and accessible to ordinary intelligence (EIP 6.4, 463–7).

This support is not non-circular since first principles are principles that must be taken for granted. But evidence gathered through the use of perception cannot be used to justify my prior commitment to its reliability in a non-circular way. Likewise, if we attempt to prove that reasoning is not fallacious we fall into absurdity "since the very point in question is, whether reasoning may be trusted" (EIP 6.5, 480). (Reid is not a coherentist about justification.) Reid offers a type of track-record argument to the semi-skeptic along with a distinction between viciously and non-viciously circular patterns of inference. For example, he says that induction can be given non-viciously circular justification because "when we grow up and observe the course of nature, we can confirm [it] by reasoning" (EIP 6.5, 489). Reid realizes that his indirect arguments are successful *only if* first principles are in fact true.

Note that, like Alston, Moore and Wittgenstein, Reid's use of track-record arguments of this form is primarily dialectical and intended to shift the burden of proof onto the semi-skeptic (see Alston 1985; Wolterstorff 2001). This is why Reid says: that "they require to be handled in a way peculiar to themselves. Their evidence is not demonstrative, but intuitive. They require not proof, but to be placed in a proper point of view" (EIP 1.2, 41; see INQ 2.5, 32).

4.2. Parity of Belief-Forming Faculties Argument

This leads to the second of Reid's indirect replies to the skeptic, foreshadowed above in §2.2: semi-skeptics are inconsistent because they place unjustified confidence in some faculties while withholding confidence in others.

> Reason, says the sceptic, is the only judge of truth, and you ought to throw off every opinion and every belief that is not grounded on reason. Why, Sir, should I believe the faculty of reason more than that of perception; they came both out of the same shop, and were made by the same artist; and if he puts one piece of false ware into my hands, what should hinder him from putting another.
> (INQ 6.20, 169; see EIP 2.22, 244 and 252; EIP 6.4, 463)

When Descartes believes reason is reliable and no other faculty is, Reid charges him with inconsistency. Reid frames a dilemma for the semi-skeptic: either we accept multiple sources of belief as reliable, or we reject them all (EIP 6.5, 480–1). Reid accepts them, relies upon his indirect proofs of the epistemological, belief-generating first principles and grants these particularist first principles prima facie justification.

5. Direct Responses to the Semi-Skeptic

Reid also opposes specific semi-skeptical arguments with direct refutations. The semi-skeptical arguments of most concern are mounted from a commitment to the Way of Ideas. The Way of Ideas asserts that forms of mental awareness are mediated by representations, whether ideas or images or both.

5.1. The Way of Ideas

Reid's arguments against skepticism often take the form of arguments against the Way of Ideas because:

> [the] sceptical system ... leans with its whole weight upon a hypothesis, which is ancient indeed, and hath been very generally received by philosophers, but of which I could find no solid proof. The hypothesis I mean, is, That nothing is perceived but what is in the mind which perceives it.
>
> (INQ Dedication 4)

Reid (i) supports his claim that this claim about the objects of perception on the Way of Ideas (EIP 1.1, 31; cf. EIP 2.7, 105; IHM 1.7, 23); (ii) argues the Way of Ideas implies or suggests skepticism; then (iii) infers that the Way of Ideas is false by reductio. Reid offers other arguments against the Way of Ideas that have the effect of serving as proxy for arguments against skepticism.

5.2. Inferences in Perception

However, not all skeptical arguments in this milieu presuppose the existence of ideas as intermediaries (Greco 2004, 142). One important semi-skeptical argument begins with reflection on the nature of sensations as phenomenal experiences. These experiences are insufficient evidence on which to infer beliefs about the mind-independent world. When a tree-like image appears to my eyes, the visual sensations are insufficient to justify my belief that *I see a tree*. Sensations are events in the mind and they do not represent mind-independent objects. Often they do not suggest true beliefs about the world, as in cases of mirages.

Reid responds to this concern by stressing that perception is a non-inferential process; by denying that sensation resembles what causes it; and by leaning upon his naturalistic account of our sensory experience (Greco 2004, 145). These points are deployed as objections to the foregoing skeptical argument. For example, whereas the semi-skeptic says that we form beliefs about sensations from which we cannot justifiably infer beliefs about the external world, Reid argues that we form no beliefs about sensations in the first place (see §6.2, below).

5.3. Perceptual Relativity Argument

The semi-skeptic might take a different tack in order to argue for the existence of ideas and for perceptual skepticism. Historically the most forceful arguments for mental intermediaries arise from visual experience. For example, Hume says that, contrary to the "universal and primary opinion of all men," philosophy teaches us that nothing can ever be present to the mind but an image or perception, and that the senses are only the inlets through which these images are conveyed, without being able to produce any immediate intercourse between the mind and the object. The table, which we see, seems to diminish, as we remove farther from it: but the real table, which exists independent of us, suffers no alteration: it was, therefore, nothing but its image, which was present to the mind. These are the obvious dictates of reason.

(Hume 2007, 111/12.9; see T 187/1.4.1.12)

Our visual sensations misinform us about the size of the table since our visual sensations are relative to the particular coordinates from which we view the table. So the table is not an immediate object of perception.

Reid has several replies to this argument. First, Hume equivocates on the implicit term 'size of the table' because it refers to both tangible and visible size (EIP 2.14, 182–3; see INQ 6.2, 81–2). Tangible size does not change as I move my eyes relative to the table's location, even though the visible size does. Second, Reid develops an account of visible figure, including discussion of the ontology of the objects of vision, the relationship between visible figure and tangible figure, and a geometry for visible space. Visible figure is not a private mental representation but, rather, a relational property between a pair of eyes and an object's tangible figure (Van Cleve 2002; Nichols 2002c). Thus visible figures are not ideas; they have a foothold in the mind-independent world. They are also unlike ideas by being intersubjective: if anyone occupies the coordinates my eyes are now in, they will see the same figure as did I. Vision still gives us some measure of non-inferential knowledge about the world, even though this is nuanced and subtle.

Third, Reid turns the tables on proponents of the argument from perceptual relativity by arguing that his account and his geometry of visibles are the only plausible ways to explain the uniformity and regularity of visible figures across persons' visual experience (Yaffe 2002). This constancy is difficult to explain in terms of each person being aware of their own private mental ideas. (On visible figure see Yaffe 2003a, 2003b; Falkenstein and Grandi 2003; Nichols 2007, ch. 4). Fourth, Reid argues that even if this argument were sound, it would not imply that the immediate objects of *all perception* are ideas. At most it implies that the immediate objects of *visual perception* are not mind-independent objects. Vision and touch are structured differently (EIP 2.14, 182–3), and touch gets us closer to the mind-independent world than does vision.

6. Perception and Perceptual Learning

As the previous point indicates, understanding Reid's theory of perception is crucial for understanding his epistemology. In this section I explain the fundamentals of Reid's theory of perception, then discuss its relevance for his epistemology.

6.1. The Perceptual Process

The perceptual process has three features: conception, belief and immediacy (EIP 2.5, 111–12; cf. IHM 6.20, 168). Conception and belief are simple operations of the mind and Reid says of them that they are primitive and do not admit of analysis. States of conception are necessarily intentional states (EIP 4.1, 405), as are states of perception.

But one can conceive of things that do not exist (EIP 4.2, 320–3; cf. Nichols 2002a), whereas one cannot perceive things that do not exist.

Conceptions of mind-independent objects like those embedded in acts of perception are not obtained through a process of abstraction from our sensations (Van Cleve and Sosa 2001, 183). This is the principal point of Reid's 'experimentum crucis,' a thought experiment in which a subject is given various tactile sensations (IHM 5.6–7, 65–72). In Reid's judgment, the subject is in principle unable to form the conception of an extended, mind-independent body merely from his reception of tactile sensations. But, contrary to Berkeley, Reid is unwilling to conclude that we lack concepts of mind-independent bodies. Instead, the concept of extension is innate in the sense that we are endowed with a natural capacity to form the concept of extension once cued with the appropriate sensory signs (IHM 5.7, 72; Nichols 2007, ch. 3). The immediate objects of perceptual states are mind-independent bodies and/or their qualities. My conception of the object is not mediated by mental representations, and my perception of the object is not mediated by mental representations.

Reid is the first clearly to distinguish between sensations and perceptions. Reidian sensations are non-intentional sensory events with phenomenal content, such as pains or tastes. He says, "The form of the expression, *I feel pain*, might seem to imply, that the feeling is something distinct from the pain felt; yet, in reality, there is no distinction" (IHM 6.20, 167–8). Sensations play important roles in perceptual events, even though Reid omits sensation from his formal definition of 'perception.' Specifically, sensations signal or suggest perceptions on the proviso that the agent is functioning properly in apt circumstances. Reid offers a complex taxonomy of the roles of sensations for various types of perception (INQ 2.7, 38, INQ 5.3, 59–60 and INQ 6.2, 177–8), though it has inconsistencies (Nichols 2007, Table 1 p. 88).

Reid recognizes that sensations are sometimes immediate objects of conception in acts of perception. But, first, Reid is not asserting every act of perception is direct. Second, perceptions in which we conceive of or think about sensations are typically perceptions of the secondary qualities of objects (IHM 5.5, 63; IHM 5.3, 61). Reid is up front about the way perception yields direct concepts of primary qualities and only yields 'relative' ideas of secondary qualities (EIP 2.17, 252). Third, ideas were originally hypothesized to be imagistic mental resemblances of objects in the world. Like Berkeley (*Principles* 1.8, WGB ii, 44), Reid argues that the ontology of sensations as events implies that sensations are ill-suited to *represent*, which is in part why Reid presses sensations into service as *signs* functioning to suggest conceptions in perception (EIP 2.11, 156). How this process works is difficult to understand and is dealt with in Reid's embryonic theory of suggestion.

6.2. Inference, Reasoning and Conceptual Content

We mentioned an objection from the semi-skeptic to the effect that a perceiver is unjustified in believing *I see a tree* because perceptual experiences occur in the mind. The semi-skeptic might be persuaded to allow as foundational *I see red* or *I seem to see a tree* because the conceptual content of those statements does not require a causal connection to a mind-independent reality. According to the semi-skeptic, belief about a *mind-independent* feature of the world is not non-inferentially known—if it is known at all. In this context contrasting terms *seeing* and *seeing as* illustrate perceptions with poor and rich conceptual content. My distinct perceptual belief *I see a tree* might be irresistible and self-evident in Reid's psychological sense, but it could be produced by hallucination. This drives a wedge between mere psychological self-evidence and perceptual knowledge. Reid does not address skepticism motivated by hallucination cases, but he does discuss the cognitive and non-cognitive stages involved in acquiring perceptual knowledge.

First, Reid works with an implicit account of *defeasible* justification, as his objections to Descartes' standards for knowledge imply (see §2.2). *I see a tree* is prima facie *justified* by virtue of being formed by my perceptual systems. *I know I see a tree* so long as my belief is produced by reliable perceptual systems that bear the appropriate connection to the external world, even if it is dubitable or corrigible. That is, I know I see a tree if it is produced reliably in the proper circumstances, *and* it is undefeated by further facts. If I've ingested something that causes my visual system to produce hallucinations, then Reid's proper function condition fails and I am not justified in believing *I see a tree*.

Malfunctions of my perceptual equipment are relatively rare. But, second, particular first principles are defeated in another way discussed in EIP 2.22—'Of the Fallacy of the Senses': "We are disposed to impute our errors rather to false information than to inconclusive reasoning, and to blame our senses for the wrong conclusions we draw from their testimony" (EIP 2.22, 244–5). This suggests, oddly, that we *do* reason to perceptual beliefs in some cases in which we erroneously form false perceptual beliefs. But, the semi-skeptic would reply, if we reason in those cases, and those cases are phenomenologically identical cases in which we form true beliefs, then, by parity, we also reason to form true perceptual beliefs. This appears inconsistent with Reid's externalism about perceptual knowledge.

This presents a philosophical problem for Reid, and current research has not yet solved it. Nonetheless, Reid's published and unpublished works yield clear evidence of a distinction between two stages of perceptual belief formation, which Reid calls 'original' and 'acquired' perception, that is helpful here. *Original* perceptions are formed without application of universals that allow differentiation and classification of the perceived object with other objects. They are produced "probably before judgment is brought forth; but these first notions are . . . gross and indistinct" (EIP 6.1, 416). Original visual perceptions include perceptions of "extension in two dimensions" (EIP 2.21, 236) and original tactile perceptions include the three-dimensional extension of objects (INQ 6.20, 171). *Acquired* perceptions differ in content from original perceptions, but they also differ in the means by which they are formed. Their content is conceptually robust in comparison because to perceive the apple *as* an apple one must apply the general concept *apple* to the object of perception (INQ 6.24, 192). This requires "some ripeness of understanding" (EIP 2.19, 219; see Nichols 2002b, 2007).

Reid implicitly subdivides the category of acquired perceptions. To motivate this point, consider: he says the belief in the moon's three-dimensionality is a conclusion "not obtained by simple perception, but by reasoning" (INQ 6.20, 172), but also says "Perception, whether original or acquired, implies no exercise of reason; and is common to men, children, idiots, and brutes" (INQ 6.20, 173). In manuscripts and drafts of EIP Reid distinguishes acquired beliefs that *directly involve* reasoning and acquired beliefs formed *on the basis of* prior reasoning. This process is complex. It starts with an original perception of sound waves in the ambient atmosphere. In the stage prior to the establishment of an habituated perception, I actively reason that the sound is caused by the carriage. Once that occurs several times, I automatically and non-inferentially form a belief, upon hearing that tell-tale sound, that a carriage passes by. In the latter stage, once the belief is habituated, I no longer reason. Only inferential perceptions are *formed by* conscious reasoning; habituated perceptual beliefs merely *depend upon* prior reasoning for their justification.

7. Conclusion

Reid's epistemology is naturalistic and is crafted from commitments to empirical psychology. He offers a proto-reliabilist theory of empirical justification, and a fallibilist foundationalism that eschews a priori Cartesian demands on knowledge. His direct realist theory of perception yields non-inferential knowledge of the mind-independent world.

Future work on Reid's epistemology is needed (i) to better understand first principles as psychological generalizations within the context of Reid's Newtonian method, while still making sense of their justificatory status; (ii) to clarify the apparent confusion in Reid's description of the role of reasoning in perception, and its relation to original and acquired perceptual beliefs; and (iii) to understand Reid's account of the intentionality of conception and perception. This final point is only one of many issues surrounding Reid's epistemology (memory knowledge; other minds; self-knowledge) that this cannot address.

Abbreviations

AC	*Animate Creation*, Reid 1995.
EAP	*Essays on the Active Powers*, Reid 1994
EIP	*Essays on the Intellectual Powers*, Reid 2002a
INQ	*Inquiry into the Human Mind*, Reid 1997

Bibliography

Alston, William. (1985). "Thomas Reid on Epistemic Principles," *History of Philosophy Quarterly* 2: 435–52.

——. (1989). "Reid on Perception and Conception." In *The Philosophy of Thomas Reid*. M. Dalgarno and E. Matthews, eds., pp. 34–47. Kluwer: Dordrecht.

Berkeley, George. (1948). *The Works of George Berkeley*, ed. by A. Luce and T. Jessop. London: Nelson and Sons.

Cummins, Phillip. (1974). "Reid's Realism," *Journal for the History of Philosophy* 12: 317–40.

Daniels, Norman. (1974/1989). *Thomas Reid's Inquiry: The Geometry of Visibles and the Case for Realism*. Stanford: Stanford University Press.

Davis, Thomas C. (2006). *Thomas Reid's Ethics: Moral Epistemology on a Legal Foundation*. Continuum Studies in British Philosophy. James Fieser, Series Editor. London: Continuum.

de Bary, Phillip. (2002). *Thomas Reid and Scepticism: His Reliabilist Response*. London: Routledge.

Falkenstein, Lorne and Grandi, Giovanni. (2003). "The Role of Material Impressions in Reid's Theory of Vision: a Critique of Gideon Yaffe's 'Reid on the Perception of the Visible Figure'," *The Journal of Scottish Philosophy* 2: 117–33.

Greco, John. (2004). "Reid's Reply to the Skeptic." In *The Cambridge Companion to Thomas Reid*. T. Cuneo and R. van Woudenberg, eds., pp. 134–55. Cambridge: Cambridge University Press.

Hume, David. (2007). *An Enquiry Concerning Human Understanding*, ed. by Peter Millican. Oxford: Oxford University Press.

Lehrer, Keith. (1998). "Reid, Hume and Common Sense." *Reid Studies* 2: 15–26.

——, and Warner, Bradley. (2000). "Reid, God and Epistemology," *American Catholic Philosophical Quarterly* 74: 357–72.

Moore, G. E. (1959). *Philosophical Papers*. London: George Allen and Unwin.

Newton, Isaac. (1999). *The Principia: Mathematical Principles of Natural Philosophy: A New Translation and Guide*, ed. & trans. by I. B. Cohen and A. Whitman. Berkeley: University of California Press.

Nichols, Ryan. (2002a). "Reid on Fictional Objects and the Way of Ideas," *Philosophical Quarterly* 52: 582–601.
———. (2002b). "Learning and Conceptual Content in Reid's Theory of Perception," *British Journal for the History of Philosophy* 10: 561–90.
———. (2002c). "Visible Figure and Reid's Theory of Visual Perception," *Hume Studies* 28: 49–82.
———. (2007). *Thomas Reid's Theory of Perception*. Oxford: Oxford University Press.
Norton, David Fate. (1979). "Hume and his Scottish Critics." In *McGill Hume Studies*. D. F. Norton et al., eds. San Diego: Austin Hill Press.
Pappas, George. (1989). "Sensation and Perception in Reid," *Noûs* 23: 155–67.
Plantinga, Alvin. (1993). *Warrant and Proper Function*. New York: Oxford University Press.
Popkin, Richard. (1980/1993). *The High Road to Pyrrhonism*. Indianapolis: Hackett Publishing.
Reid, Thomas. (1994). *Essays on the Active Powers of Man*, in *The Works of Thomas Reid*. Vol. 2, ed. by W. Hamilton. Bristol: Thoemmes Press.
———. (1995). *Thomas Reid on the Animate Creation*, ed. by P. Wood. University Park, PA: Pennsylvania State University Press.
———. (1997). *An Inquiry into the Human Mind on the Principles of Common Sense*, ed. by D. Brookes. University Park, PA: Pennsylvania State University Press.
———. (2002a). *Essays on the Intellectual Powers of Man*, ed. by D. Brookes. University Park, PA: Pennsylvania State University Press.
———. (2002b). *The Correspondence of Thomas Reid*, ed. by P. Wood. University Park, PA: Pennsylvania State University Press.
———. (2004). *Thomas Reid on Logic, Rhetoric, and the Fine Arts*, ed. by A. Broadie. University Park, PA: Pennsylvania State University Press.
Somerville, James. (1995). *The Enigmatic Parting Shot*. London: Avebury.
Van Cleve, James. (1999). "Reid on the First Principles of Contingent Truths," *Reid Studies* 3: 3–30.
———. (2002). "Thomas Reid's Geometry of Visibles," *The Philosophical Review* 111: 373–416.
——— and Sosa, Ernest. (2001). "Thomas Reid." In *The Blackwell Guide to the Modern Philosophers*. Steven Emmanuel, ed., pp. 179–200. Blackwell: London.
Wolterstorff, Nicholas. (2001). *Thomas Reid and the Story of Epistemology*. New York: Cambridge University Press.
Wood, Paul. (1985). "Thomas Reid and the Scottish Enlightenment: An Exhibition to Celebrate the 200th Anniversary of the Publication of Thomas Reid's Essays on the Intellectual Powers of Man 1785." Prepared for the Thomas Fisher Rare Book Library, University of Toronto (33 pp.).
Yaffe, Gideon. (2002). "Reconsidering Reid's Geometry of Visibles," *Philosophical Quarterly* 52: 602–20.
———. (2003a). "Reid on the Perception of Visible Figure," *The Journal of Scottish Philosophy* 2: 103–15.
———. (2003b). "The Office of an Introspectible Sensation: A Reply to Falkenstein and Grandi," *The Journal of Scottish Philosophy* 2: 135–40.

65
DAVID HUME
Helen Beebee

1. Introduction

David Hume (1711–76) was an empiricist—the third in the famous trio of British Empiricists, after John Locke and George Berkeley. His aim, as stated in the Introduction to his *Treatise of Human Nature* (1739–40, henceforth "*T*"), is to instigate the "science of man"; and the appropriate method, Hume thinks, is "experimental philosophy": "the only solid foundation we can give to this science . . . must be laid on experience and observation." Hume's science of man, then, is the "application of experimental philosophy to moral subjects" (*T* xx). Hume's contemporary status as a founding father of analytic philosophy in the empiricist tradition thus needs to be approached with a certain amount of caution; indeed, as I shall argue, in the particular case of the Problem of Induction Hume's interests are more psychological than epistemological.

Nonetheless, an important feature of the context of Hume's work is his opposition to what Edward Craig (1987) calls the "Image of God" doctrine, according to which human beings are imperfect versions of God. The Image of God doctrine carries with it substantive epistemological commitments, and at least part of Hume's aim is to show that those commitments are spurious. For example, the Image of God doctrine drives the view that in principle, a priori access to the nature of the world is possible. Such a view naturally leads to a conception of the causal structure of the world that is analogous to logical entailment, so that stages in a causal process are like stages of a mathematical proof: if we could fully comprehend the nature of the cause, we would be able to infer a priori what the next stage in the process would be. Thus, for example, the principle *ex nihilo nihil fit* (nothing comes from nothing) was generally taken to be a conceptual truth, knowable a priori, as was the related principle that a cause must contain at least as much reality as its effect—a principle that Descartes famously used in his "Trademark Argument" for the existence of God in the *Meditations*.

Hume, in opposition to this consequence of the Image of God doctrine, holds that: "If we reason *a priori*, anything may appear able to produce anything. The falling of a pebble may, for aught we know, extinguish the sun; or the wish of a man control the planets in their orbits" (*Enquiry Concerning Human Understanding*, 1748—henceforth "*E*"—164). His discussion of inductive inference is aimed, at least in part, at establishing this claim that the inference from causes to effects cannot be a priori. From a contemporary perspective, this is hardly a claim that needs to be justified; but of course the acknowledged implausibility of the Image of God doctrine is part of the philosophical debt we owe to Hume.

Hume's contribution to epistemology is not, of course, limited to his discussion of induction (the topic of §2 below). Inter alia, he also grapples with the problem of skepticism concerning the external world. I discuss Hume's views about belief in the external world in §3, and conclude, in §4, with a general discussion of Hume's attitude towards skepticism.

2. Inductive Inference (or Causal Reasoning)

Hume is often credited with inventing, and showing to be insoluble, the "Problem of Induction." The Problem of Induction is the problem of justifying the belief that the unobserved resembles the observed. For example, on every previous occasion when I pressed the brake in a car, the car slowed down; and so, this time I press the brake, I expect the car to do the same. But what, if anything, justifies this belief? That the car has slowed down in the past does not *entail* that it will do so on this occasion; so why should we think that my experience of past slowing-downs *justifies* the belief that it will slow down now? Or, in other words, what justifies the *inference* from "all previous brake-pressings have been followed by slowing down" to "this brake-pressing will be followed by slowing down?" An adequate answer to this question would be a solution to the Problem of Induction; unfortunately such an answer turns out to be very hard (and, according to some philosophers, impossible) to come up with.

While, as we shall see, the main elements of the Problem of Induction are certainly present in Hume's discussion, it is not at all clear that he is really concerned with the Problem of Induction—a problem about the *justification* of beliefs about the unobserved—at all. In fact, I shall claim, his concern is rather with the psychological question of *how* belief in the unobserved arises.

2.1. Inductive Inference and Causation

One important difference between the Problem of Induction as standardly understood and Hume's discussion is that for Hume, "inductive" inference is reasoning from causes to effects (he does not use the terms "inductive" and "induction" at all; he merely talks, in the *Enquiry* (E 36), about our being "induced to expect" effects). Indeed, his discussion of what I shall call causal reasoning—the inference from cause to effect—is an essential part of a larger project, that of examining the "idea" of causation (we can think of Hume's "ideas" roughly as concepts). As we shall see, Hume's own view about causal reasoning is that the inference is a matter of mere custom or habit. Having observed sufficiently many Cs being followed by Es, on observing a C we *automatically* come to expect an E to follow—not as a result of any process of "argument or ratiocination" (E 39) but as a result of an associative mechanism: the same psychological mechanism that leads a dog to expect a walk when its lead is taken off its hook. And it turns out, in Hume's famous discussion of the idea of necessary connection (in the *Treatise* Book I, Part III, §14—T 155–73—and the *Enquiry*, §7, E 60–79), that it is the operation of this mechanism—the "determination of the mind to pass from one object to its usual attendant" (T 165)—that provides the impression-source for this idea (Hume being an empiricist, all legitimate ideas must have their source in an element of experience, or an "impression").

So for Hume, (a) judging that one event is the cause of another, and (b) inferring the existence of the second on the basis of past experience of similar events being "constantly conjoined" are very closely connected:

when one species of event has always, in all instances, been conjoined with another, we make no longer any scruple of foretelling one upon the appearance of the other, and of employing that reasoning [namely custom or habit], which can alone assure us of any matter of fact or existence. We then call the one object, *Cause*; the other, *Effect*. (E 75)

Hume's point here is not that, having established, via inductive inference, that the two "species of event" are constantly conjoined, we *infer* that the first is a cause of the second; rather, our inferring the second event and our thinking of it as an effect of the first are two sides of the same coin, the inference supplying the impression of necessary connection on the basis of which we make the causal judgment. This approach contrasts sharply with most contemporary discussions of the Problem of Induction, which tend to focus on the inference from the observed to the unobserved in isolation from any judgments we might happen to make about a causal connection between the relevant events or objects (see, for example, Howson 2000).

2.2. The Argument

Hume's discussion of causal reasoning occurs in Book I, Part III, Section VI of the *Treatise* (T 86–94) and, in a slightly different form, in §4 of the *Enquiry* (E 32–9). Hume himself often talks about looking for a "foundation" for the inference from causes to effects. Note, however, that this can be given an epistemological or a psychological reading: a "foundation" for the inference might be something that confers justification on it, or else it might be something that explains *how* the inference happens. For now, I shall preserve this ambiguity and just focus on sketching the argument; I shall later return to the question of whether we should think of Hume's interest as a psychological or an epistemological interest. Here, then, is how Hume's argument concerning causal reasoning—the inference from causes to effects—proceeds. (I shall follow the *Treatise* version of the overall argument.)

First of all, Hume establishes that "the inference we draw from cause to effect, is not deriv'd merely from a survey of these particular objects, and from such a penetration into their essences as may discover the dependence of the one upon the other" (T 86). In other words, we cannot tell, just by examining one object or event, what its effects will be. We can be sure of this because "[s]uch an inference wou'd amount to knowledge, and wou'd imply the absolute contradiction and impossibility of conceiving any thing different" (T 86–7); whereas clearly it always *is* conceivable that the effect might not occur. It might be a well-established fact that if you drop a wine glass on a stone floor from a great height it will shatter, but we can perfectly well *imagine* it failing to do so (while we cannot similarly imagine, say, Socrates' being a man and all men are being mortal, and yet Socrates not being mortal). Since, according to what is sometimes called Hume's "Conceivability Principle," nothing whose denial is conceivable can be known a priori, it cannot be known a priori, and just on the basis of the observation or examination of c, that e will be one of its effects. Hume concludes from this that it is "by EXPERIENCE only, that we can infer the existence of one object from that of another" (T 87). In other words, it is only when we have experienced several Cs being followed by Es that we are able, on observing a C, to infer that an E will follow.

Having established that inference from causes to effects proceeds on the basis of past observation of constant conjunction, Hume asks "[w]hether experience produces the idea [of the effect] by means of the understanding or of the imagination; whether we are determin'd by reason to make the transition, or by a certain association and relation of perceptions" (*T* 88–9). Hume will eventually conclude that the correct account is the latter; so he needs to rule out the possibility that the inference from cause to effect is founded on some process of reasoning or argument and is therefore the product of the understanding. And, he thinks, there is only one possible way this could work: "If reason determin'd us, it wou'd proceed upon that principle, *that instances, of which we have had no experience, must resemble those, of which we have had experience, and that the course of nature continues always uniformly the same*" (*T* 89). This principle is often known as the "Principle of the Uniformity of Nature" (PUN). So the suggestion Hume is considering is that the inference from cause to effect proceeds something like this:

(P1) Cs have always been followed by Es in my experience.
(P2) A C has just occurred.
(P3) Instances I haven't observed resemble instances I have observed (PUN).

Therefore

(C) An E will occur.

Hume then asks on what (P3) is founded: "let us consider all the arguments, upon which such a proposition [PUN] may be suppos'd to be founded; and as these must be deriv'd either from *knowledge* or *probability*, let us cast our eye on each of these degrees of evidence, and see whether they afford any just conclusion of this nature" (*T* 89). By "knowledge" Hume means a priori knowledge, and by "probability" he means belief derived from experience. His plan is to show that PUN (a) cannot be known a priori, and (b) cannot non-circularly be founded on reasoning from experience.

The first part of the argument, (a), is easy, and simply involves a second appeal to the Conceivability Principle. Since we can easily imagine a change in the course of nature, it is possible that PUN is false, and so it cannot be known a priori.

As for (b), Hume says:

> We have said that all arguments concerning existence are founded on the relation of cause and effect; that our knowledge of that relation is derived entirely from experience; and that all our experimental conclusions proceed upon the supposition that the future will be conformable to the past. To endeavour, therefore, the proof of this last supposition by probable arguments, or arguments regarding existence, must evidently be going in a circle. (*E* 35–6)

In other words, *all* our "experimental conclusions" (that is, beliefs that are founded on reasoning from experience or "probable arguments") presuppose PUN. Hence PUN cannot *itself* be founded on reasoning from experience, because such reasoning presupposes that very principle. (I shall claim in §2.3 below, however, that Hume's complaint here makes better sense when the argument from (P1–3) to (C) is construed as a possible method for forming, rather than justifying, beliefs.)

Hume presents a similar argument against the claim that reasoning from causes to effects proceeds via appeal to an unknown "power of production," present in the cause, which guarantees the occurrence of the effect (*T* 90–2 and *E* 36–8). Grant, for the sake of the argument, that past experience of the constant conjunction of Cs and Es gives us reason to believe in the *past* presence, in Cs, of the "power" to produce Es. Even so, without presupposing PUN, there is no foundation for the required inference to "the current C has the power to produce an E," and so no foundation for the inference to the occurrence of the effect.

That completes Hume's argument—after which he proceeds to provide what he calls a "sceptical solution" to the problem he has been discussing, which is his well-known claim that causal reasoning in fact arises merely as a matter of "Custom or Habit" (*E* 43) or a "principle of association" (*T* 93).

There can be very few other cases of such a short passage—a mere handful of pages—having such a powerful and long-lasting impact on philosophical inquiry. While of course most contemporary philosophers do not work directly on the Problem of Induction, no orthodoxy has emerged concerning the best solution to it. But was the Problem of Induction, conceived as a problem about *justifying* our beliefs about the unobserved, really what Hume was interested in? I shall briefly argue in the next section that it was not.

2.3. Interpretative Issues

The standard interpretation of Hume's discussion of causal reasoning is that he really is raising—and pronouncing insoluble—the Problem of Induction, that is, the problem of *justifying* our beliefs about the unobserved. Hence his "solution" is merely a "sceptical solution": it is not supposed to undermine inductive skepticism, but only to excuse our reliance on induction on the grounds that we cannot help ourselves, our psychological mechanisms being what they are. However, this interpretation is increasingly regarded as controversial. Some interpreters have argued that Hume's intention in his discussion of causal reasoning is merely to show that causal reasoning is not a priori reasoning (see, for example, Flew 1961 and Stove 1965)—something that does not require him to view causal reasoning as unjustified. Others have argued that his aim is to show that belief in the unobserved does not *in fact* arise as a matter of some process of argument *about* causal reasoning (see, for example, Garrett 1997 and Noonan 1999).

My own view is that this latter interpretation is closer to the mark, in that it correctly construes the issue Hume is concerned with as a psychological rather than an epistemological issue. The fact that Hume's stated project, as described in the Introduction to the *Treatise*, is a "science of man" (*T* xvi), provides one reason to think that inductive skepticism is not on his agenda. After all, according to an inductive skeptic, a "science of man" could only deliver completely unwarranted conclusions. The traditional interpretation of his "sceptical solution"—that it excuses, in some sense, our reliance on causal reasoning by showing it to be psychologically mandatory—does not help here, since indulging in "experimental philosophy" of the kind Hume pursues in his science of man is not itself psychologically mandatory. Hume appears both to endorse the experimental method and to regard its pursuit as a distinctly optional enterprise.

I believe that Hume's primary interest in his discussion of causal reasoning is the *origin of belief*. When I have an impression as of, say, depressing the brake pedal, what is the process or mechanism by which I thereby come to believe that the car will slow down? One way in which beliefs can be formed is via a priori reasoning: if I start with the belief that Jane has three apples and June has two apples, I can infer a priori—and hence come to believe—that Jane has more apples than June. But Hume shows that reasoning from causes to effects is not *a priori* reasoning, so belief in the effect, given the impression of the cause, cannot come about in that way. How, then, *does* belief in the effect come about? Crucially, the question here is a general question: not, "how did this particular belief come about?" but "how does belief *in general* come about?" We come into the world with no beliefs about any matter of fact that is not present to our senses, but we end up with plenty; how does this happen?

On this interpretation of the question Hume wants to answer, the problem with the argument invoking PUN is not that it is circular in a justificatory sense, but that it is circular in an *explanatory* sense: the argument from (P1–3) to (C) fails not as an argument one might give in an attempt to justify belief in (C), but as an attempt to provide a model for the formation of belief in general. Hume thinks he has already explained the origin of a priori knowledge, through his account of reasoning concerning "relations of ideas" (*T* 69–73). So if PUN were knowable a priori, belief in the effect could come about as a result of a priori inference from (P1) (an item of memory), (P2) (an impression) and (P3) (an item of knowledge): the mechanism that generates belief would have as input only mental items whose origins Hume takes himself already successfully to have explained. But PUN is not knowable a priori, so its status must be that of a *belief*. But in that case, appeal to PUN is useless in an explanation of how beliefs *in general* arise, for the alleged belief-generating mechanism—the inference from (P1–3) to (C)—itself takes a belief as part of the input. So it can only explain how we can come to have some *particular* belief once we already have *other* beliefs.

The only negative epistemological consequence that Hume intends to draw from his discussion of causal reasoning, on this interpretation, is that causal reasoning cannot be justified by (because it cannot be a result of) a priori inference from premises that are known either a priori or on the basis of immediate sensory experience. Thus he does not intend to raise the issue of whether causal reasoning can be justified empirically at all; indeed, he appears to simply take it for granted that it can be, and frequently refers to causal reasoning as a "just" form of reasoning (though see Beebee 2006: 66–74 for the claim that he actually offers—though does not discuss in any detail—a reliabilist justification of induction).

On the other hand, Hume is not completely unaware of inductive skepticism as a possible philosophical position; but he dismisses it:

> For here is the chief and most confounding objection to *excessive* skepticism, that no durable good can ever result from it; while it remains in its full force and vigour. We need only ask such a sceptic, *What his meaning is? And what he proposes by all these curious researches?* He is immediately at a loss, and knows not what to answer . . . a Pyrrhonian cannot expect, that his philosophy will have any constant influence on the mind: or if it had, that its influence would be beneficial to society. On the contrary, he must acknowledge, if he will acknowledge anything, that all human life must perish, were his principles universally and steadily to prevail. (*E* 159–60)

I discuss the merits of this response, along with Hume's response to external-world skepticism, in §4 below.

3. Skepticism about the External World

Hume's interest in our belief about the external world is, as with the case of causal reasoning, at least partly psychological. He is interested, in the first instance, in *how* we get to have that belief, rather than (as is more usual) being interested solely in whether it is justified. Nonetheless, as with the case of causal reasoning, his psychological investigation has epistemological consequences. And the consequences appear to be rather more serious in the case of belief in the external world, since Hume appears to think that there are positive reasons to think that that belief is *false*.

Hume's account of belief in the external world in the *Treatise* is lengthy and difficult, taking up a good proportion of Book IV. In the *Enquiry*, by contrast, it takes up only a handful of pages (Part I of §12, E 149–55). I shall draw on the *Enquiry* version of the discussion here, first outlining Hume's basic account and then, in §3.2, addressing the question of whether he should be thought of as a skeptic about the existence of the external world.

3.1. Belief in the External World

Hume's account starts out by noting that "men are carried, by a natural instinct or prepossession, to repose faith in their senses; and that, without any reasoning . . . we always suppose an external universe, which depends not on our perception, but would exist, though we and every sensible creature were absent or annihilated" (*E* 151). When "men follow this blind and powerful instinct of nature, they always suppose the very images, presented by the senses, to be the external objects, and never entertain any suspicion, that the one are nothing but representations of the other" (ibid.). So the "natural," pre-reflective view, according to Hume, is that (a) the world we perceive exists independently of our perception of it, but (b) that very independently existing world is nothing more than our perceptions. Not surprisingly, Hume finds this view to be untenable: it is a view that is "destroyed by the slightest philosophy" (*E* 152). For we know full well that, for example, moving further away from a table does not result in any change in the table, while it *does* result in a change in our perception (the table seems smaller). So, on reflection, we know that the table itself cannot be identified with our perception of it: perceptions are "fleeting copies or representations of other existences, which remain uniform and independent" (ibid.). In the *Treatise*, Hume describes the two views just described as the "vulgar" and the "philosophical" views, the latter being a view that postulates a "double existence" (*T* 189) since it is ontologically committed both to perceptions and to external objects that those perceptions represent.

The problem with the "double existence" view, of course, is that we now need an argument to the effect that the postulated mind-independent objects really do exist—that "the perceptions of the mind must be caused by external objects, entirely different from them, though resembling them (if that be possible)" (*E* 152–3). And no such argument is possible. It is a "question of fact" (*E* 153) whether our perceptions are so caused, and so our grounds for belief in external objects must be reasoning from experience—that is, causal reasoning. Unfortunately, on this question "experience is, and must be entirely silent. The mind has never anything present to it but the perceptions, and cannot possibly reach any experience of their connexion with objects. The supposition of such a connection is, therefore, without any foundation in reasoning" (ibid.). In other words, causal reasoning requires—as we saw above—experience of constant conjunction. But no such experience is possible, when one of the conjuncts—the supposed cause (i.e. external objects, considered as distinct from perceptions)—can never be present to the mind. Thus "the opinion of external existence . . . if it rested on natural instinct [the 'vulgar' view], is contrary to reason, and if referred to reason, is contrary to natural instinct [that is, causal reasoning], and at the same time carries no rational evidence with it" (*E* 155).

In fact things appear to be even worse than that. Hume *seems* to endorse Berkeley's argument against the primary–secondary quality distinction. It is "universally allowed" that secondary qualities (heat, color, and so on) "exist not in the objects themselves, but are perceptions of the mind, without any archetype or model, which they represent." But our ideas of supposed primary qualities are equally "entirely acquired from the senses of sight and feeling; and if all the qualities, perceived by the senses, be in the mind, not in the object, the same conclusion must reach the idea of extension" (*E* 154). Thus the opinion of external existence turns out not merely to carry "no rational evidence with it"; it is actually "contrary to reason . . . Bereave matter of all its intelligible qualities, both primary and secondary, and you in a manner annihilate it, and leave only a certain unknown, inexplicable *something*, as the cause of our perceptions; a notion so imperfect, that no sceptic will think it worth while to contend against it" (*E* 155).

3.2. Hume's Response to Skepticism?

Hume confronts skepticism head-on at the end of both Book I of the *Treatise* and (briefly) the *Enquiry*; however, the difference in his attitude towards the skeptical position his own philosophical system has forced him into in the two works is, at least at first sight, quite striking. In the *Treatise*, Hume's tone verges on despair:

> The *intense* view of these manifold contradictions and imperfections in human reason has so wrought upon me, and heated my brain, that I am ready to reject all belief and reasoning, and can look upon no opinion as more probable or likely than another. (*T* 268–9)

Luckily this melancholy state is easily remedied, however, as Hume explains:

> Most fortunately it happens, that since reason is incapable of dispelling these clouds, nature herself suffices to that purpose, and cures me of this philosophical melancholy and delerium . . . I dine, I play a game of back-gammon, I converse, and am merry with my friends . . . Here then I find myself absolutely and necessarily determin'd to live, and talk, and act like other people in the common affairs of life. (ibid.)

Of course, this is hardly a philosophical response to the skeptical problem. (Plagued by doubts about the existence of the external world? Play backgammon!) Does Hume do any better in the *Enquiry*?

Well, in fact, not only is the melancholia of the *Treatise* nowhere to be found; in the *Enquiry* Hume barely even seems to bother with considering the consequences of his own argument that belief in the existence of the external world is "contrary to reason." He does, as we saw in §2.3, complain that "Pyrrhonian" skepticism cannot, as a matter of psychological fact, be maintained in the long term, and even if it could it would have serious consequences ("men [would] remain in total lethargy, till the necessities of nature, unsatisfied, put an end to their miserable existence" (*E* 160).) But, here, he seems to be talking only about inductive skepticism, since this passage is preceded by one in which skepticism is identified as the insistence that the natural instinct by which we reason from causes and effects "may be fallacious and deceitful" (E 159). There seems to be no consideration of the skeptical position on the external world that he himself has generated at all. All Hume directly has to say appears when introducing the Berkeleian argument against the primary–secondary quality distinction. He says of this argument—one he apparently endorses—that it "might merit our attention, were it requisite to dive so deep, in order to discover arguments and reasonings, which can so little serve to any serious purpose" (E 154). So it looks as though he takes external-world skepticism to be in the same boat as "Pyrrhonian" skepticism: it serves no useful purpose, so we should not waste our time worrying about it.

Given all this (not to mention the fact that he sometimes describes himself as a skeptical philosopher), it is easy to see why Hume is traditionally characterized as a skeptic. He is clearly well aware of—and indeed appears to endorse—familiar skeptical arguments; and does not, apparently, so much as attempt to find fault with them. However, several interpreters have argued that Hume is not in fact a skeptic, in the sense of thinking that belief in the external world is unreasonable or unjustified, at all. The fact that he does not think that the skeptical arguments can be faulted in the sense of relying on dubious premises or fallacious reasoning does not, it is argued, amount to his thinking that they cannot be faulted on other grounds.

The source of the non-skeptical conception of Hume's overall position lies in the importance he places on our natural instincts or propensities. In the case of causal reasoning, I argued that Hume sees the custom or habit that underlies that reasoning as being perfectly legitimate, despite the fact that the appeal to custom or habit clearly fails to engage with the inductive skeptic's argument on its own terms. Arguably, his attitude towards external-world skepticism is similar. We know that the "vulgar" belief in the external world, according to which external objects are no more than perceptions, is false and gives way to the "double existence" view. The vulgar view, Hume thinks, is delivered by a "blind and powerful instinct of nature" (E 151). So the double existence view, while not delivered straightforwardly by a blind and powerful instinct, is nonetheless delivered by blind instinct together with a modicum of straightforward reasoning (tables don't get smaller when you move away from them, so they must be distinct from our perceptions). So the double existence view, while different to the "vulgar" view, nonetheless "*acquires all its influence on the imagination from the vulgar one*" (T 213).

This is significant, according to some interpreters, when combined with what Don Garrett calls the "Title Principle" (Garrett 1997: 234): "where reason is lively, and mixes itself with some propensity," Hume says, "it ought to be assented to. Where it does not, it never can have any title to operate upon us" (T 270). In the case of the double existence view, reason *does* "mix itself with some propensity," since it is, precisely, the result of the vulgar view—itself the result of a natural propensity—together with some straightforward reasoning. So the double existence view "ought to be assented to."

Of course, this still leaves the more troublesome Berkeleian argument for skepticism: one according to which belief in the external world is not merely "without any foundation in [causal] reasoning" but "contrary to reason." Peter Kail points out that the Title Principle shows us what is wrong with the Berkeleian argument: unlike the double existence view, the view that primary as well as secondary qualities are merely products of the mind does not "mix itself with some propensity." It is the product of pure philosophical argument, and as such has no "title to operate upon us" (see Kail 2007: 70).

On this view, then, Hume is no skeptic about the external world; he is, rather, an indirect realist. Our perceptions represent external, mind-independent reality. We cannot *know* that this external world exists, or that external objects resemble our perceptions in any way. Indeed, we cannot even reach such a conclusion by deploying probable reasoning. Nonetheless, the existence of mind-independent objects that resemble our perceptions merits our assent because it arises as a result of our natural propensities: belief in the external world is what is sometimes known as a "natural belief."

4. Skepticism, Natural Propensities and the Job of Philosophy

Hume's response to skepticism concerning both causal reasoning and the external world might seem rather unconvincing. After all, why *should* we believe what we are naturally disposed to believe (or corrected versions of these beliefs), when there are perfectly sound philosophical reasons to think that such beliefs are not warranted? Hume *says*, apparently, that we should believe these things; but does he—by his own lights—have any legitimate reasons for saying so?

One way to answer this question in the affirmative connects with Hume's claim that what, fundamentally, is wrong with skepticism is that it is psychologically impossible to live with full-time and serves no useful purpose—and that the best way to deal with it is to get out more. This makes considerably more sense if we think of skepticism not as merely the view that belief in the external world (or in the deliverances of causal reasoning) is unwarranted, but rather as the view that that belief—and the processes that give rise to it—*ought to be abandoned*. Thus conceived, the fact that skepticism is not (as Stephen Buckle puts it) "livable" seems to be a reasonable objection to it (see Buckle 2001: 310–11), since the skeptic has no positive proposal for a *better* set of beliefs or processes of reasoning by which to live.

Hume does explicitly endorse what he calls "a more *mitigated* scepticism" (*E* 161): "a degree of doubt, and caution, and modesty, which, in all kinds of scrutiny and decision, ought for ever to accompany a just reasoner" (*E* 162). In addition, "[a]nother species of *mitigated* scepticism, which may be of advantage to mankind, and which may be the natural result of the Pyhrronian doubts and scruples, is the limitation of our enquiries to such subjects are best adapted to the narrow capacity of human understanding" (ibid.). And we can see this "species" of skepticism as precisely the kind of project that Hume is undertaking. As Buckle puts it:

> From the ashes of unbounded skepticism a new philosophy can arise, a philosophy that is able to draw constructive conclusions—especially about the limits of our rational powers—from the failings of dogmatic and Pyrrhonian philosophy alike; and, by a careful application of the principles of experimental philosophy and its mechanical picture of the world, forge principles of probable judgements on which we can confidently rely in the conduct of life.
>
> (Buckle 2001: 314)

Indeed, this "new philosophy," while it "may be the natural result of the Pyrrhonian doubts and scruples," is also conceived by Hume as "nothing but the reflections of common life, methodized and corrected" (*E* 162). And, in the *Treatise*—after the hand-wringing over whether one ought to spend one's time shut in the study despairing of the foundations for one's opinions or out dining with friends—he settles on essentially the same view:

> Since therefore 'tis almost impossible for the mind of man to rest, like those of beasts, in that narrow circle of objects, which are the subject of daily conversation and action, we ought only to deliberate concerning the choice of our guide, and ought to prefer that which is safest and most agreeable. And in this respect I make bold to recommend philosophy, and shall not scruple to give it the preference to superstition of every kind or denomination. (*T* 271)

The upshot of all of this is that while on the one hand Hume does not provide a philosophical response to skepticism that, as it were, meets it on its own territory, he does provide a response that enshrines a view about the nature and purpose of philosophical inquiry. The arguments that lead to skepticism are legitimate on their own terms. But a philosopher who stops with skepticism, and fails to draw any conclusions about how we ought to proceed in our daily lives, has failed in an important respect, since her own conclusions demonstrate how very little her own, narrow philosophical method contributes to a proper understanding of our beliefs and actions. Such an understanding must include positive recommendations for guiding and correcting those beliefs and actions, taking account of—rather than attempting to undermine—our natural propensities. The failure of skepticism is not that it deploys false assumptions or fallacious reasoning; it is, rather, a failure to provide any positive, livable answer to the question, "what ought we to believe?" (since the answer, "nothing," is clearly not livable). The skeptic's mistake is thus to have downed tools before finishing the philosophical job.

Bibliography

Beebee, H. (2006) *Hume on Causation*. Abingdon: Routledge.
Buckle, S. (2001) *Hume's Enlightenment Tract*. Oxford: Oxford University Press.
Craig, E. (1987) *The Mind of God and the Works of Man*. Oxford: Clarendon Press.
Flew, A. (1961) *Hume's Philosophy of Belief*. London: Routledge & Kegan Paul.
Garrett, D. (1997) *Cognition and Commitment in Hume's Philosophy*. Oxford: Oxford University Press.
Howson, C. (2000) *Hume's Problem: Induction and the Justification of Belief*. Oxford: Clarendon Press.
Hume, D. (1739–40) (*T*), *A Treatise of Human Nature*, ed. L. A. Selby-Bigge, 2nd edition, revised and ed. P. H. Nidditch. Oxford: Clarendon Press (1978).
—— (1748) (*E*), *Enquiry Concerning Human Understanding*, in D. Hume, *Enquiries Concerning Human Understanding and Concerning the Principles of Morals* (1748/51), ed. L. A. Selby-Bigge, 3rd edition, revised and ed. P. H. Nidditch. Oxford: Clarendon Press (1975).
Kail, P. J. E. (2007) *Projection and Realism in Hume's Philosophy*. Oxford: Oxford University Press.
Noonan, H. (1999) *Hume on Knowledge*. London: Routledge.
Stove, D. C. (1965) "Hume, Probability, and Induction," *The Philosophical Review* 74, 160–77.

Further Reading

Beebee, H. (2006) *Hume on Causation*. Abingdon: Routledge. (Chapters 2 and 3 discuss Hume's theories of a priori and causal reasoning.)
Millican, P. (2002) "Hume's Sceptical Doubts Concerning Induction," in his *Reading Hume on the Understanding*. Oxford: Clarendon Press, 107–73. (A detailed and systematic analysis of Hume's argument concerning causal reasoning.)
Noonan, H. (1999) *Hume on Knowledge*. London: Routledge. (An introductory-level textbook. Chapters 3 and 4 discuss causal reasoning and belief in the external world.)
Stroud, B. (1977) *Hume*. London: Routledge. (The classic Hume textbook, though less introductory than Noonan 1999. Chapters III–V discuss causal reasoning and belief in the external world.)

66
IMMANUEL KANT
Eckart Förster

Discussions of Kant's epistemology usually take their departure from his *Critique of Pure Reason* (1781), and justifiably so. Yet in the years preceding its publication, the so-called pre-critical period, Kant made a number of discoveries that became the basis for his mature philosophy. In particular, there are three insights without which the *Critique* itself would have been impossible. The first one concerns the difference between logical and real possibility, the second concerns the differences between the basic elements of our cognition, the third concerns reason as a source of illusions. I will begin with the first two and discuss the third insight at the end of this essay.

Formal and Real Possibility

Early in his career, Kant realized that an ontological proof for God's existence à la Descartes is not possible. Descartes had argued that the concept of God as the most perfect being must include existence, because if God lacked existence, a more perfect being would still be possible, i.e. a God who actually existed. Kant objected: Even if the concept of God is the concept of the most perfect being that has all realities, existence is not a reality (not a 'real' predicate or determination of an object). If we compare the thought of an actual object with the thought of the same object as a possible object that has not yet been actualized, we find that both thoughts employ the same set of predicates. The difference between them is not to be explained in terms of a conceptual difference, but only in relation to possible experience: "Thus existence itself cannot be a [real] predicate" (OPA, 2:74), hence it cannot be included in the mere concept of anything, including that of God.

Nevertheless, at this time Kant thought that a proof for God's existence *was* possible, but only indirectly and in relation to another concept, namely that of possibility. To judge that something is possible is to say that the concepts or representations related in the judgment do not contradict each other. This is the formal condition of possibility. But there is also a material condition. In all comparison, what is to be compared must be given beforehand; if there is nothing to be compared, there can be no comparison and hence no possibility. This means, Kant claimed, that nothing can be conceived as possible unless whatever is real in every possible representation or concept exists. Moreover, it must exist with absolute necessity because, in its absence, nothing at all would be possible. Thus possibility itself would be impossible, which cannot be thought without self-contradiction.

Before long, however, Kant realized that this argument is only valid on condition that there is thought in the first place. The alleged absolute necessity of all possible realities is merely a hypothetical necessity and presupposes that possibilities be entertained. This of course is not itself necessary. As Kant would later put the point in the *Critique of Pure Reason*: "I cannot form the least concept of a thing that, if all its predicates were cancelled, would leave behind a contradiction" (CPR, A 595/B 623).

Thus Kant became convinced that at the bottom of all theoretical proofs for God's existence lies a confusion of the necessity of thought with the necessity of things. But if this is so, one has to distinguish not only a formal and material condition of conceptual possibility, but also a formal and a material component with respect to the possibility of things. There is, in other words, pace the rationalists, a fundamental difference between thinking an object and cognizing it. In order to think an object, its concept must be non-contradictory. In order also to cognize it, one must know that the object that is thought is also objectively real, or "really possible." Otherwise one has thought something, "but not in fact cognized anything through this thinking, but rather merely played with representations" (CPR, A 155). If the concept in question is an empirical concept, experience shows *that* its object is really possible. If the concept is an a priori concept, however, as is the case in philosophy, one must be able to demonstrate *how* its object is possible in order to also know the objective reality of the concept. Is such a priori cognition possible? Can philosophy demonstrate the objective reality of its a priori concepts? To answer this question in a general way is one of the main tasks of Kant's *Critique of Pure Reason*:

> A concept is always possible if it does not contradict itself. That is the logical mark of possibility . . . Yet it may nonetheless be an empty concept, if the objective reality of the synthesis through which the concept is generated has not been established in particular . . . This is a warning not to infer immediately from the possibility of concepts (logical possibility) to the possibility of things (real possibility).
>
> (CPR, A 596, cf. B xxvi fn.)

The "Two Stems of Human Knowledge"

The second result of Kant's pre-critical writings that is essential for an understanding of the epistemology of the *Critique* concerns the fundamental difference between thought and perception (or intuition, as Kant calls it). His rational and empiricist predecessors alike assumed a merely quantitative or gradual difference between them (cf. CPR, A 44, 264, 270–1)—the rationalists in terms of "clear and confused" (Leibniz) representations, the empiricists in terms of the "liveliness and vivacity" (Hume) of representations. At first Kant shared this view. After 1768, however, he became convinced of its falsity. This realization was triggered by a discussion of incongruent counterparts in his essay "On the First Ground of the Distinction of Regions in Space" (1768). Incongruent counterparts are objects which in respect to size, proportion and the positions of their parts are perfectly equal, but which nevertheless can have no boundaries in common and therefore do not coincide—for example, the two human hands. "The right hand is similar and equal to the left, and if we look at one of them alone by itself, at the proportions and positions of its parts relative to one another and at the magnitude of the whole, the complete description of it must also hold of the other in every respect" (*DRS*, 2:381). Although conceptually indistinguishable, left and right hand (like all incongruous counterparts) are nevertheless sensibly distinct and incongruent.

Interestingly, there is also a corresponding case where something that can be conceptually represented cannot be sensibly represented: the presence of the soul in a body. This case was discussed at some length in Leonhard Euler's *Letters to a German Princess* (1768, German transl. 1769), which Kant read. Owing to the soul's effects on the body, its presence in the body can be thought, though it cannot be represented sensibly since the soul, as being non-physical, can have no spatial coordinates. This case is analogous to Kant's example of incongruous counterparts. In the case of the soul, the presence of the soul in the body can be thought but not intuitively represented, while in the case of incongruent counterparts, the difference between them is intuitively clear, while eluding conceptual grasp. From this it seems to follow that thought and intuition cannot differ from each other merely by degree, but that, on the contrary, they must be viewed as two fundamentally different sources of knowledge, with their own peculiar conditions and constraints. This at any rate is the consequence Kant drew in 1769. In the *Critique of Pure Reason*, the fundamental difference between thought and intuition is taken for granted: "By way of introduction or anticipation we need only say that there are two stems of human knowledge, namely, *sensibility* and *understanding*, which perhaps spring from a common, but to us unknown, root. Through the former, objects are given to us; through the latter, they are thought" (*CPR*, A15).

For human cognition, both 'stems' of knowledge are equally necessary, for through mere thought no objects are given, through mere perception no objects are known. Or, as Kant famously claims: "Thoughts without content are empty, intuitions without concepts are blind" (*CPR*, A 51/B 75). If our thoughts were to produce their own corresponding objects, we would have an intellectual intuition that knows only actual objects. But our understanding is not intuitive; it is discursive and can only combine what is given to it from elsewhere. For its knowledge, the understanding is thus dependent on sensibility as a receptive faculty:

> Accordingly, the distinction of possible from actual things . . . arises from the fact that even if something does not exist, we may yet always give it a place in our thoughts, or if there is something of which we have no conception we may nevertheless imagine it given. To say, therefore, that things may be possible without being actual, that from mere possibility, therefore, no conclusion whatever as to actuality can be drawn, is to state propositions that hold true for human reason, without such validity proving that his distinction lies in the things themselves. (*CJ*, 5:402)

Proof of the objective reality of a priori concepts must hence consist in the demonstration of their relation to possible experience.

The Critique of Pure Reason

In the *Critique of Pure Reason*, Kant first looks at both sensibility and understanding separately, then at their cooperation in the formation of knowledge.

"The capacity (receptivity) for receiving representations through the mode in which we are affected by objects, is entitled *sensibility*" (*CPR*, A 19). The effect of this process is a "modification of our mind," a sensation, or an appearance. What is strictly speaking given to us are not objects, but representations "in us." If all representations are modifications of our mind and are thus in us, how is it possible ever to have knowledge of objects outside us?

Kant's first important step toward a solution of this problem is the claim that the concept of space (and of time) cannot be abstracted from outer experience. For assume it could be abstracted from experience, as his empiricist predecessors claimed, how would that take place? At first there would be a mere succession of representations in inner sense, one after the other. In order to gain the representation of space from these impressions, I would have to be able to abstract from them the representations of coexistence of distinct places, and of simultaneity. Now two things, A and B, are simultaneous, if the perception of A and B can reciprocally proceed and succeed each other. In inner sense, however, everything is successive and each new representation is later than its predecessor. In inner sense alone it is impossible to represent a manifold as simultaneous and hence as distinct from me. A distinction between a succession of representations in me and something enduring outside me, between a subjective succession of perceptions and an objective order of co-existing elements, cannot be drawn on the basis of inner sense alone. The representation of space makes experience of simultaneity originally possible and cannot be abstracted from it.

According to Kant, this means that space is a form of human sensibility that allows us to represent sensations as distinct from us, and as outside and alongside one another. At the same time, this form of sensibility constrains us—i.e., I can only represent something as being distinct from me by representing it as being in a different *place*. In this sense, Kant claims, space is "ideal." (To show that space (and time) are *nothing but* forms of human sensibility requires a different argument. For it might be said that space and time, in addition to being forms of intuition, could also exist in themselves and independently of human beings. Kant addresses this objection in the 'Dialectic' of the *Critique of Pure Reason* where he shows that if we take space and time to exist in themselves, antinomies become inevitable. I will return to this point shortly.)

But this is only half the story. Space as the form of outer intuition constrains my attempt to represent something as distinct from me but it does not itself refer. For this, concepts and judgments are needed. It is the task of the understanding to supply them. "All intuitions, as sensible [= passive] rest on affections, concepts rest on functions. By a function, however, I understand the unity of the action of ordering different representations under a common one. Concepts are therefore grounded on the spontaneity of thinking, as sensible intuitions are grounded on the receptivity of impressions" (*CPR*, A 68/B 93).

A concept is a rule that allows me to unite a certain number of representations while excluding others. When I predicate something of a subject that is not contained in its concept, I thereby determine it. The representations involved are no longer viewed as mere 'modifications of my mind,' but as representations of something distinct from me, and cognition becomes possible. Since the understanding can make no other use of concepts than to combine them in judgments, Kant writes: "we can trace all actions of the understanding to judgments, so that the understanding in general can be represented as a faculty for judging" (*CPR*, A 69/B 94).

Since judgments relate concepts or representations to one another, it must be possible to list all the elementary functions of the understanding by giving an exhaustive statement of the functions of unity in judgments. And this, Kant thought, can indeed be done.

If one abstracts from the contents in judgments and merely regards their form, one finds that they can be distinguished in terms of quantity, quality, relation, and modality. With respect to *quantity*, judgments can be universal, particular, or singular. With respect to *quality*, affirmative, negative, or infinite; with respect to *relation*, they can be categorical, hypothetical, or disjunctive; and with respect to *modality*, judgments can be problematic, assertoric, or apodictic.

How do these functions of the understanding make possible a relation to something distinct from the subject? For that to be possible, the manifold of sense must be grasped in such a way that it can be determined with respect to the forms of judgment. It must be subject to fundamental operations of synthesis that allow for the application of judgments, and these fundamental operations of synthesis, the basic concepts, Kant calls categories: "The forms of judgments (converted into a concept of the synthesis of intuitions) yields categories which direct all employment of understanding in experience" (CPR, A 312/B 377). These fundamental concepts, corresponding to the twelve forms of judgment, are the categories of unity, plurality, totality (*Quantity*), of reality, negation, limitation (*Quality*), of substance/accidence, cause/effect, and reciprocity (*Relation*), and of possibility/impossibility, existence/non-existence, of necessity/contingency (*Modality*) (cf. CPR, A 80/B 106).

Since the understanding does not generate any intuitions of its own but is dependent for its activity on a manifold given to it in the senses, it must be able to take together such manifold in such a way that it can be grasped as a something about which judgments can be formed. Generally speaking, then, "the pure categories are nothing other than the representations of things in general insofar as the manifold of their intuition must be thought through one or another of these logical functions" (CPR, A 245).

We can now sketch Kant's argument more fully. Sensibility, as the "capacity (receptivity) for receiving representations" (CPR, A 19/B 33), is a passive faculty. The manifold it contains is consequently, in virtue of this passivity, disconnected. What *we* can distinguish in sensibility *is* distinct and separate, each representation being nothing but "absolute unity." For knowledge to arise from this material, it must initially be run through and held together, or it must be apprehended. This first act Kant calls the "synthesis of apprehension" (CPR, A 99).

In this process, if we were to lose sight of the first impression as we apprehend the second, the second would be the first and only impression and no unity could possibly arise. Hence, when apprehending the second impression, the first must be reproduced as an impression that was encountered but is no more. This second act, the "synthesis of reproduction in imagination," is required even for the representation of spatial extension and temporal duration, just as it is for a representation of a manifold contained in them.

For this manifold to become the representation of *something determinate*, still more is required. What is apprehended and reproduced must not be connected with all and everything that is contained in a given intuition and that has been run through, but only with what belongs to it, i.e. what can be taken up in a concept. To this end, it has to be compared also with other representations not contained in the given intuition. For a concept, we said earlier, is a rule that unites certain representations that belong together, while at the same time excluding those that do not belong to it. For example, the sensible data that I apprehend and subsume under the concept 'dog' do not include the mat on which it currently sleeps; but it must also include past and possible future perceptions of a dog awake, chasing, barking, eating, etc. (cf. Strawson 1974). Thus the third act is a "synthesis of recognition in a concept." The unity of consciousness in this synthesis of different representations Kant calls "apperception." Of it he writes:

It is this apperception that must be added to the pure imagination in order to make its function intellectual. For in itself the synthesis of the imagination, although exercised a priori, is nevertheless always sensible, for it combines the manifold only as it *appears* in intuition . . . Through the relation of the manifold to the unity of apperception, however, concepts that belong to the understanding can come about, but only by means of the imagination in relation to the sensible intuition. (CPR, A 124)

It must be possible for different representations to co-occur in the same consciousness for there to be a concept or a thought. Just as different words need to occur in the same consciousness to form a sentence, different representations must occur in the same consciousness to form a thought of something: "The identity of the consciousness of myself at different times is therefore . . . a formal condition of my thoughts and their connection" (CPR, A 363).

But how exactly is this identity of consciousness of myself to be understood? To begin with, it does not denote the empirical person who I am and who changes and develops over time, but the thinking subject that remains identical throughout: everything that I have ever thought in the past or will be thinking in the future are thoughts of the same subject; myself. I thus have an a priori knowledge of my identity in all my states of consciousness, past as well as future. Of this Kant writes:

> We are conscious a priori of the thoroughgoing identity of ourselves with regard to all representations that can ever belong to our cognition, as a necessary condition of the possibility of all representations (since the latter represent something in me only insofar as they belong with all others to one consciousness, hence they must at least be capable of being connected in it). This principle holds a priori." (CPR, A 116)

We must thus ask: How is such a priori knowledge of one's own identity through time possible? How can I know already that I will be able in the future to connect all thoughts into the unity of my consciousness and proceed from one thought to any other? Such knowledge is only possible, Kant claims, if the forms of transition from one thought to another are themselves a priori, that is, unchanging and independent of the contents of thoughts: "For this unity of consciousness would be impossible if in the cognition of the manifold the mind could not become conscious of the identity of the function by means of which this manifold is synthetically combined into one cognition" (CPR, A 108).

The a priori nature of this knowledge will become clearer if it is contrasted with the empirical knowledge I have of my own biography (cf. Henrich 1976). The latter, I know, will be constituted by a continuous string of episodes and experiences that will define who I am as a person. But what it is that I will encounter in the course of my life I cannot know in advance, or a priori. I have to wait and see what life has in store for me. Moreover, the occurrence of each new episode in the course of my life excludes others that were possible up to this point but are now irretrievably eliminated. There is no going back, as the saying goes. But with respect to the thoughts I might entertain in the future, I know that, in principle, I can pass from any representation to any other representation and initiate an arbitrary number of thoughts. This kind of knowledge is only possible, however, if the rules of relating representations to each other are the same in the future as they are now. They must be unchanging rules and thus independent of empirical conditions: "for the mind could not possibly think its identity in the manifoldness of its representations, and indeed think this a priori, if it did not have before its eyes the identity of its action, which subjects all synthesis of apprehension (which is empirical) to a transcendental unity, and first makes possible their connection in accordance with a priori rules" (CPR, A 108).

When we ask what these 'identical actions' are that unite representations in determinate ways and make possible the unity of consciousness, it is clear that they can be none other than the forms of judgment, so that "the understanding in general can be represented as a faculty for judging" (CPR, A 69/B 94). The unity of consciousness that I designate with the first person pronoun 'I' is brought about by my forming concepts and using them in judgments. The forms of judgments are unchanging, and what is identical in *all* fundamental acts of judging is the reference, by means of the concepts or representations employed in them, to something distinct from me in which these representations are united: "A judgment in general," Kant defines, is "an action through which given representations first become cognitions of an object" (MFNS, 4:475). Consequently, knowledge that there are things outside me is just as certain as the *cogito*, each being a condition of the possibility of the other.

This argument, Kant's 'Transcendental Deduction of the Categories,' is widely regarded as one of the most profound arguments in the history of philosophy. It sets out to prove that all objects of experience are necessarily subject to the categories, because no objects can be thought without them. And it does so by arguing that the identity of self-consciousness, of which we have a priori knowledge, would be impossible without knowledge of objects. Self-consciousness and consciousness of objects outside me are two sides of the same coin. (This is not to deny, of course, that *once I am* conscious of myself, I can then ascribe 'purely subjective' states to myself. Kant's argument only shows that such self-ascription is secondary and presupposes experience of objects.)

"Thus we ourselves bring into the appearances that order and regularity in them that we call *nature*, and moreover we would not be able to find it there if we, or the nature of our mind, had not originally put it there" (CPR, A 125). Kant can consequently agree with Hume, for example, that our knowledge of causal relations between objects and events is empirical, while insisting that there would be no events to be experienced had we not previously synthesized a manifold of representations in accordance with the category of cause. For we could never distinguish the objective temporal order of an event from the merely subjective order of representations in us, Kant argues, unless we thought the order of the representations that constitute the event as being irreversible. And this we can only do if we think that it is causally structured:

> [T]he mere sequence in my apprehension, if it is not, by means of a rule, determined in relation to something preceding, does not justify any sequence in the object. Therefore I always make my subjective synthesis (of apprehension) objective with respect to a rule in accordance with which the appearances in their sequence, i.e., as they occur, are determined through the preceding state, and only under this presupposition alone is the experience of something that happens [i.e. an event] even possible. (CPR, A 195/B 240)

The Illusions of Pure Reason

Thus Kant silences the skeptics who doubt or deny that a priori knowledge of objects is possible. Such knowledge *is* possible, he claims, and the categories *do* have legitimate application, but *only* with respect to possible experience. No less importantly, however, Kant also wants to silence any dogmatic metaphysicians who think they can lay claim to metaphysical knowledge beyond possible experience. Unlike Descartes who had feigned the hypothesis of an evil genius to demonstrate the possibility that we might be deceived in our beliefs about the world and ourselves, Kant believes he can show that reason encounters contradictions through its own legislation as soon as it transgresses beyond possible experience. Early in his career, being puzzled by the fact that opposing philosophical positions were supported with seemingly equally strong arguments, Kant had tried to prove systematically metaphysical propositions *and* their opposites. To his surprise, he found that he succeeded in this task beyond expectation.

This is the third fundamental discovery Kant made in his so-called pre-critical period. Kant regarded this realization as one of his most significant insights: "[T]he Antinomy of pure reason, which becomes evident in its dialectic, is in fact the most beneficial error into which human reason could ever have fallen, in as much as it finally drives us to the search for the key to escape from this labyrinth" (*CPrR*, 5:107). This key is none other than Kant's transcendental idealism with its allied claims of the ideality of space (and time) and the fundamental distinction between appearances and things in themselves. The ostensive self-contradiction of reason in the Antinomies can thus be seen, Kant insists, as an indirect proof of transcendental idealism. For if space and time with the objects in them are viewed as things in themselves, the antinomies arise, and inevitably so.

In the *Critique of Pure Reason*, Kant presents the problem as follows: If reason leaves the realm of appearances and applies itself to what is supposed to exist independently of human cognition, it is equally possible to prove, for example, that the world has a beginning in time and is also limited as regards space, as it is possible to prove its negation: that the world is infinite as regards both time and space (CPR, A 426/B 454). In the like manner, Kant argues, one can prove that every composite substance is made up of simple indivisible parts *and* that it is infinitely divisible (CPR, A 434/B 462). One can also prove that everything in the world takes place in accordance with laws of nature *and* that there is another causality, namely that of freedom (CPR, A 445/B 473). Finally, one can likewise prove that there belongs to the world an absolutely necessary being, *and* that no absolutely necessary being belongs to the world (CPR, A 453/B 481).

In the *Critique*, Kant does not link these propositions with particular philosophers, but it is clear that historical references can easily be provided for each of them. Each of these antinomial propositions has been supported in the past by one philosopher or another and played a significant role in traditional metaphysics. If this is so, one can see why there was no general agreement among the great thinkers of the past, and hence no progress in the history of philosophy. As soon as theoretical reason leaves the realm of possible experience, it can equally 'prove' contradictorily opposed propositions that are each central to reason's own operations. This demonstrates the failure, Kant maintains, of all earlier metaphysics. For any such metaphysics, since it was not grounded in the ideality of space and time, could only claim dogmatically one of the antinomial propositions without being able in principle to refute its contradictory opposite. Such a philosophy is thus not capable of establishing truths and can never acquire the status of a science. Only transcendental idealism, which is established for the first time in the *Critique of Pure Reason*, can make a scientific metaphysics possible: "The critical path alone is still open" (CPR, A 856/B 884). To a reviewer of the *Critique* who doubted the correctness of transcendental idealism, Kant offered this challenge. In the *Critique*, Kant wrote, the reviewer will find eight propositions which are, pair by pair, always in conflict with one another, but each of which belongs necessarily to metaphysics, which must either accept it or refute it (although there is not a single one of them that has not in its day been accepted by some philosopher or other). He now has the freedom to pick any one of these eight propositions he likes, and to assume it without proof (which I concede to him) . . . and then he is to attack my proof of the antithesis. But if I can rescue it, and in this way show that the opposite of the proposition he adopted can be proven exactly as clearly, in accordance with principles that very dogmatic metaphysics must of necessity acknowledge, then by this means it is settled that there is a hereditary defect in metaphysics that cannot be explained, much less removed, without ascending to its birthplace, pure reason itself. (*Prol.* 4:379)

Kant thus likened his *Critique of Pure Reason* to a tribunal of pure reason that settles its disputes once and for all, by striking at the very root of its conflicts. It silences the skeptical challenge by demonstrating that we do indeed have a priori knowledge, but only of those principles that constitute outer experience. And it demonstrates this by showing that without such a constitution of outer experience, self-consciousness would be impossible. Knowledge of outer objects is thus as indisputable as the evidence of the *cogito*. But the *Critique* also silences the dogmatic philosopher who lays claim to knowledge beyond possible experience. It does so by showing that reason, as soon as it employs itself in the realm beyond the senses, is prone to irresolvable antinomies. Its "proposition lies outside the field of possible experience, and therefore also beyond the boundaries of all human insight" (CPR, A 753/B 781).

References

References to Kant's works are given in the text by using an abbreviation for the work cited, followed by volume and page number of the *Akademie* edition of *Kant's gesammelte Schriften*, which can be found in the margins of all translations of his works into English. References to the *Critique of Pure Reason* are to the standard pagination of the first and second editions, indicated as "A" and "B," respectively.

Kant, Immanuel, *Critique of Pure Reason* (CPR). Translated by Paul Guyer and Allen W. Wood. Cambridge/New York: Cambridge University Press 1998.
—— *Critique of Practical Reason* (CPrR). In: Immanuel Kant, *Practical Philosophy*. Translated and edited by Mary J. Gregor. Cambridge/New York: Cambridge University Press 1996.
—— *Critique of the Power of Judgment* (CJ). Translated by Paul Guyer and Eric Matthews. Cambridge/New York: Cambridge University Press 2000.
—— *Metaphysical Foundations of Natural Science* (MFNS). Translated by Michael Friedman. In: Immanuel Kant, *Theoretical Philosophy after 1781*. Cambridge/New York: Cambridge University Press 2002.
—— "The Only Possible Argument in Support of a Demonstration of the Existence of God" (OPA). In: Immanuel Kant, *Theoretical Philosophy, 1755–1770*. Translated and edited by David Walford, in collaboration with Ralf Meerbote. Cambridge/New York: Cambridge University Press 1992.
—— "On the First Ground of the Distinction of Regions in Space" (DRS). Translated by John Handyside. In: *Kant's Inaugural Dissertation and Early Writings on Space*. Westport, Conn: Hyperion Press 1979.
—— *Prolegomena to Any Future Metaphysics* (Prol.) Translated by Gary Hatfield. In: Immanuel Kant, *Theoretical Philosophy after 1781*. Cambridge/New York: Cambridge University Press 2002.
Henrich, Dieter (1976), *Identität und Objektivität*. Heidelberg: Sitzungsberichte der Heidelberger Akademie der Wissenschaften.
Strawson, Peter (1974), "Imagination and Perception," in *Freedom and Resentment*. London: Methuen & Co., 45–65.

67
BERTRAND RUSSELL
William Demopoulos

Introduction: Three Ideas from Logic

Russell's principal contributions to philosophy derived from his logical investigations and the applications he made of them to the philosophy of mathematics and the philosophy of language. All of this work was carried out very early in his career, being completed in all essentials by the time he turned forty. *The Problems of Philosophy*, which appeared in 1912, was written at the culmination of Russell's work in logic and the foundations of mathematics. *Problems* is a deceptive book; it represents itself as an introduction for students and the general reader, covering traditional issues involving perception and our knowledge of the material world, the problem of universals, the scope of a priori knowledge, and the nature of our knowledge of ethics, to name just some of the topics with which it deals. But a closer examination reveals something much more ambitious than a general survey: *Problems* is Russell's first sustained attempt to apply two of his main discoveries in logic to classical philosophical issues, especially to epistemological problems that a philosopher with empiricist leanings would find pressing.

The logical discovery that figures most prominently in the book is the theory of descriptions which Russell announced in 1905 in his most extensively cited paper, "On denoting." *Problems* elaborates the suggestion, made in the closing paragraphs of "On denoting," that the theory of descriptions has important epistemological applications. The book also contains a hint of how Russell saw the introduction of the concepts of structure and structural similarity in his and Whitehead's *Principia Mathematica* (1912) as an event of great significance for the theory of our knowledge of the physical world. The importance of structure is taken up and argued for at much greater length some fifteen years later in *The Analysis of Matter*. But before *AoM* another idea from logic intervened and made a decisive mark on Russell's epistemological work: the method of logical construction. Its relevance for epistemology received its fullest expression in *Our Knowledge of the External World*. While the theory of descriptions and the concept of structure were instrumental to Russell's elaboration of a broadly realist position, one that constituted a sophisticated correction to, and extension of, Lockean representational realism, the method of logical construction was used in defense of a novel formulation of phenomenalism. This phenomenalist interlude was short-lived; it began in 1914, but was called into question by Russell as early as 1919 (see *Introduction to Mathematical Philosophy*, pp. 61–2). Even though for most of his life Russell vigorously defended a realist epistemology, it is the phenomenalism of this relatively brief period with which he was for a long time most often associated.

The theory of descriptions gave formal precision to Russell's broadly empiricist view of concepts, and the method of logical construction gave his phenomenalism its distinctive character. But the contribution of both of these developments in logic was mainly to the formulation of epistemological theses to which Russell had already been led. By contrast with the theory of descriptions and the method of logical construction, the concept of structure was absolutely essential to the theory Russell articulated after its discovery. And although the theory of descriptions retained its importance for Russell's epistemology throughout his career, this was not true of the epistemological interest of the method of logical construction: there are barely any distinctively epistemological applications of the method after his abandonment of phenomenalism. Most later applications, such as the construction of space-time points, were mainly devoted to achieving some sort of ontological economy.

My plan in this chapter is to discuss the three epistemological theories to which Russell made his most original contributions: concept empiricism, phenomenalism, and structuralism. The organizing principle in each case is to highlight the dependence of Russell's articulation of these theories on the logical doctrines to which they are most closely tied. The period of Russell's intellectual life with which we will be concerned begins in 1905, with the appearance of "On denoting," and continues through 1927, the date of publication of AoM. A brief mention of *Human Knowledge: Its Scope and Limits* and its relation to AoM will complete our discussion. It will be noted that I have not included in my list of principal texts Russell's posthumously published *Theory of Knowledge*. This might seem an unjustifiable omission. But ToK is principally concerned with the analysis of the form and constituents of propositions. As such the book falls more properly within the realm of Russell's theory of propositions and philosophical logic.

The Theory of Descriptions and Concept Empiricism

Classical concept empiricism is a theory concerning the origin of concepts, an elaboration and defense of the slogan, "No idea without a corresponding and prior impression." Russell transformed this doctrine into a theory of propositional understanding: his concept empiricism is a rational reconstruction, along empiricist lines, of our understanding of sentences, a reconstruction that is based on an account of our understanding of their least grammatical constituents and our grasp of the manner of their combination into sentences. The connection of such a theory with concept empiricism is based on the premise that our understanding of some of these grammatical constituents is given by our "acquaintance" with their referents. But unlike the classical theory, Russell's notion of acquaintance does not, by itself, require the acceptance of any particular doctrine about the nature of perception or the primacy of impressions. Such commitments are independent additions to Russell's theory of knowledge, and are not part of his "core" theory of propositional understanding. As we will see in greater detail below, failure to appreciate this point is a principal source of misunderstanding of Russell's epistemological views. In particular, the interpretation of Russell as a phenomenalist is encouraged by a widespread misunderstanding of the epistemological applications he made of his theory of descriptions to his theory of propositional understanding.

The notion of a least grammatical constituent presupposes an analysis of the grammatical form of sentences. Russell's analysis of grammatical form was determined by his logical theory and the requirement that the latter should, at the very least, support a theory of inference capable of representing the theorems of classical mathematical analysis and geometry as the product of a process of purely logical reasoning. This is a condition of adequacy for a theory of logical inference; although such a theory must also constrain the logical form of the propositions of mathematics, it is neutral regarding whether or not they are logical truths, and is therefore considerably weaker than the thesis that mathematics is a part of logic. There are other desiderata that also played an important role in Russell's assessment of a logical theory, but this appears to have been the primary motivation.

For Russell, sentences express propositions. Among propositions there are logical relations that are sensitive to the logical form of the propositions they relate. A logical analysis of propositions determines a grammatical analysis of the sentences belonging to some fragment of a natural language; such a logical analysis is expressed by a translation of the sentences of the fragment into a "regimented" version of it, into a language that not only shares the vocabulary of the natural language fragment, but also extends that vocabulary with additional logical devices for the expression of generality and the representation of quantification. The success of a logical theory is measured by the adequacy of the translations it affords, but its success also depends on the interest and significance of the conditions of adequacy the theory imposes on its translations. Russell's conditions of adequacy, as I indicated earlier, rest on a host of epistemological concerns surrounding the nature of proof in mathematics, rather than on the kind of descriptive adequacy that would constrain an empirical theory of natural language. In the case of recovering the inferences of mathematics as logical inferences—though not necessarily logical inferences from purely logical premises—we know Russell's program to have proven highly successful.

There are two respects in which, on Russell's view, the traditional logic was inadequate, both of them connected with its commitment to the thesis that all propositions are of subject-predicate form. The first consequence of the adherence to a subject-predicate analysis was the failure to formulate logic with sufficient generality to deal with relations. The second consequence is more subtle and has really to do with the understanding of quantification, or what Russell called "denoting phrases"—phrases involving the use of the words 'all,' 'some,' 'every,' 'a,' etc., and especially, 'the.' In *The Principles of Mathematics*, Russell had attempted to deal with the analysis of such phrases by the device of denoting concepts, of which *Principles* contains an elaborate and rather difficult theory. The goal of "On denoting" was to achieve a theory of how such phrases contribute to the logical form of the sentences in which they occur without appealing to the notion of a denoting concept. Fortunately, the central theses of the 1905 theory of definite and indefinite descriptions can be explained without going into the details of the theory of *Principles* which it replaced.

To begin with, Russell placed special emphasis on *definite* descriptions, denoting phrases of the form 'the so and so,' where 'the' is used in its singular sense, as in

> The junior author of *Principia* is mortal.

The sentences

> (*) Russell is mortal

and

(**) The teacher of Wittgenstein is mortal,

will be regarded as "in the same form" by anyone who assimilates definite descriptions to proper names. Indeed, on such a view, their form is given by the expression

(§) Pa

which, according to the traditional analysis, attributes to the individual the property P. On Russell's analysis, this is incorrect: (**) is actually a general (i.e. quantified) sentence of the form

(§§) $\exists x \forall y \varphi(x, y)$.

The difference is important, since the logical consequences of (**) will vary according to whether it has the form (§) or (§§), a fact emphasized by Russell in "On denoting."

The Russellian analysis of (**) sees it as involving the predicate expressions

x taught y,
x is mortal,

the proper name

Wittgenstein,

and the logical vocabulary of variables, quantifiers, and sentential connectives of first-order logic with identity. In greater detail, (**) is given the analysis:

$\exists x(x$ taught Wittgenstein & $\forall y(y$ taught Wittgenstein, only if $x = y)$ & x is mortal)

which, by a well-known procedure (the reduction to prenex normal form) can be reduced to a sentence of the form (§§), as claimed.

Of special interest to us is the manner in which Russell combined his theory of descriptions with a principle he discusses in *Problems* and which he endeavored to maintain throughout his philosophical career. In *Problems* (Ch. V), the principle occurs as *The fundamental principle* and is given the formulation:

Every proposition which we can understand must be composed wholly of constituents with which we are acquainted.

Before discussing this principle, it is necessary to recognize that Russell's use of 'proposition' is a special, technical, one. For Russell, a proposition is a structured object

$<a_1, \ldots, a_n; P_1, \ldots, P_m>$

whose "constituents" are generally non-linguistic entities; thus, the a_i are individuals and the P_j are properties and relations (what Russell calls "propositional functions").

The fundamental principle evidently embodies a very simple theory of linguistic meaning: we grasp the meaning of a sentence if we understand the proposition it expresses. The theory of understanding is compositional: our understanding of the whole proposition goes by way of our understanding of its parts (its constituents), and the understanding of a non-logical constituent consists in our acquaintance with it.

The model for acquaintance with propositional constituents is the common-sense notion of personal acquaintance, as when we distinguish between people whose acquaintance we have made, and those we know only by reputation or "description." There is nothing in the notion of acquaintance taken by itself that precludes our acquaintance with other persons (or material objects), which is why Russell frequently cites them as paradigms of objects of acquaintance when illustrating the fundamentals of his theory. Nor is there any restriction to particulars, and in *Problems* Russell allows acquaintance with all manner of universals. (This is a point where Russell's theory of propositional understanding departs from traditional concept empiricism.)

But even with these caveats about the scope of what falls within the range of our acquaintance, on first hearing, the theory seems wildly implausible and subject to obvious counterexamples. Consider again the sentence

(*) Russell is mortal.

How are we to explain our grasp of the meaning of this sentence if, as would seem to be the case, the proposition $\pi(*)$ it expresses is the structured object

$\pi(*)$ <Russell; x is mortal>

consisting of Russell and the property of mortality? Presumably none of us has been acquainted with Russell, and therefore, by the fundamental principle, we should all fail to understand (*). But in fact we do understand (*).

Russell's resolution of this difficulty consists in observing that our knowledge of things is only sometimes knowledge by acquaintance. We know many things only by description. For example, I know Russell as the junior author of *Principia*, in which case a sentence that better reflects my understanding of (*) is given by its translation into

T(*) The junior author of *Principia* is mortal.

When T(*) is analyzed in accordance with the theory of descriptions, the non-logical constituents of the proposition it expresses are seen to be the referents of the predicate expressions

x authored y,
x is junior to y,
x is mortal,

and the proper name

Principia.

My understanding of (*) thus consists in my grasp of its translation T(*), which, according to the fundamental principle and the theory of descriptions, requires my acquaintance with the referents of the above-mentioned predicate expressions and proper name. *Observe that Russell is not among the constituents of the proposition expressed by* T(*); as Russell would say, he has disappeared under analysis.

Notice that although (*) and T(*) might express different propositions—for someone acquainted with Russell, (*) is a perfectly good reflection of the proposition such an individual understands—they have the same assertoric content: on the assumption that Russell *was* the junior author of *Principia*, (*) and T(*) are responsible to the obtaining of the same state of affairs, namely, that there should exist a time when Russell dies. The proposition expressed by T(*) and whose constituents we are acquainted with, contains the constituents of a propositional function which is uniquely true of Russell, who is the individual the proposition is *about*. But although Russell is a constituent of the proposition we *assert*, he is not a constituent of the proposition we *express*, and it is the proposition we express that we understand, since it is its constituents that we are acquainted with. I should note that I am imposing this terminology on Russell, and that although there is a textual basis for the terminology of *expressed* and *asserted* propositions, Russell is not consistent in his use of these terms. That he nevertheless relied on the distinction, both before and *after* his discovery of the theory of descriptions, is incontrovertible, as is the claim that the distinction clarifies many otherwise puzzling aspects of his theory of propositions and theory of propositional understanding.

Russell's account of our understanding of T(*) is intended to show that we can understand propositions that are *about* constituents which fall outside our acquaintance without compromising the fundamental principle of *Problems*. Russell regarded this application of the theory of descriptions as its major epistemological benefit: it gives the key to maintaining a staunchly acquaintance-based theory of propositional understanding while preserving our common-sense belief that our knowledge often extends beyond the limits of our acquaintance.

This brings us to a point noted earlier: taken by itself, the theory of acquaintance is neutral as regards the *objects* of acquaintance; of the cognitive relations we bear to objects, acquaintance is the most direct. But in order to establish what we can legitimately take to be objects of acquaintance, it is necessary to supplement the theory of acquaintance with other considerations. For Russell, it is reflection on the nature of perception, rather than the nature of acquaintance, that leads to the view that material objects and persons are not objects of acquaintance. The considerations that compel this conclusion and "drive acquaintance in," so to speak, are entirely standard, and derive from Russell's understanding of the argument from the relativity of perception and the argument from science. The former is taken to show that material objects cannot be the objects of perception because the sensible qualities with which perception presents us fail to exhibit the objectivity we demand of the properties of the material world. The argument from science excludes material objects because science gives successful explanations of the interactions of things with each other and with us without attributing sensible qualities to the material world. Since sensible qualities are indispensable to our conception of the objects of perception, material objects cannot be what we are acquainted with in perception. Hence our knowledge of the material world must begin from acquaintance with something else—"sense data" or "percepts"—rather than from acquaintance with material objects. (For a further discussion of the considerations which led Russell to sense data see Demopoulos 2003.)

With this conclusion regarding the nature of the objects of perception in place, Russell's epistemological views proceeded in two directions, each representing a different development of the idea that our acquaintance is with sense data rather than material objects and persons. I call the first development "Russell's phenomenalism," and the second, "Russell's structuralism."

Russell's Phenomenalism

Russell's phenomenalism was developed most extensively in *External World*, and is modeled on his definition of the finite cardinal numbers in terms of classes, this being the canonical application of the method of logical construction and Russell's most successful deployment of it. By the time of *Principia*, Russell realized that the success of his definition requires that there should be sufficiently many entities of lowest type, namely, entities of the type of individuals. Assuming that this is the case, *Principia* defines the finite cardinals as certain classes of classes of individuals. And in general the method of logical construction consists in finding *classes* which can be shown to have the properties usually thought to be exhibited by *individuals*. Since for Russell classes belong to logic, such constructions are *logical* constructions. Any difficulty which attaches to our knowledge of such individuals is transformed into a problem involving knowledge of the classes that replace them. Knowledge of classes is in turn explained in terms of knowledge of the propositional functions which determine them, and knowledge of such functions is generally conceded to be unproblematic. This, in outline, is how the method aims to make a contribution to theory of knowledge. Cases of knowledge of epistemically problematic individuals are shown to be explicable as knowledge of propositional functions which ultimately rest on knowledge of propositional functions of individuals, where knowledge of such propositional functions and the individuals they qualify is epistemically unproblematic.

The appeal of the method is directly proportional to the obscurity that is thought to attach to the individuals it seeks to replace. In the case of the cardinal number 2, the proposal is that 2 should be understood as the class of all two-membered classes, where the notion of a two-membered class is, of course, capable of definition without appeal to the notion of number or to the number 2. In fact, the propositional function which determines the class of two-membered classes can be expressed using only the logical apparatus of first-order logic plus identity. So clarity regarding the number 2 only demands clarity regarding the most basic concepts of logic and the general notion of an individual. That the classes corresponding to the finite cardinals are sufficiently numerous depends on the assumption, noted earlier, that there are enough individuals. But our understanding of the logical construction depends only on our grasp of the relevant logical notions.

Russell was always quick to remark that the success of a proposed logical construction does not *prove* that there is nothing answering to the individual for which the construction is supposed to be a replacement. In the case of cardinal numbers, one can consistently accept the logical construction of 2 as a class of classes and continue to assume that in addition to the class of all two-membered classes, there is also the cardinal number 2, which is an entity that, though *correlated* with the logical construction, is not *identical* with it. The method of logical construction does not claim to refute the existence of the objects for which it provides logical constructions, but it does claim to make the assumption of their existence unnecessary. To establish such a dispensability claim, it must be shown that the logical constructions satisfy some generally agreed upon set of conditions. In the case of the finite cardinals, this is straightforward since everyone agrees that the relevant conditions are fully captured by the Peano-Dedekind Axioms.

The application of this method to the theory of perception led Russell in his *External World* to a view that is best explained by comparison with Berkeley's subjective idealism. Berkeley had taken it upon himself to show the incoherence of the view of material objects of his philosophical opponents. At the same time he also sought to show that his own view captured the common-sense notion of a material object, and that it was in fact an *analysis* of what we take ourselves to *mean* by matter. The novelty of Russell's contribution consists in this: suppose we can find suitable logical constructions which fulfill certain requirements currently satisfied by material objects. Then even if we cannot disprove the existence of material objects, we might consider ourselves justified in refraining from assuming their existence. To establish this, it is not necessary to show that the philosophical notion of a material object is incoherent; nor, for the method to succeed, is it necessary to argue that the logical construction should yield a Berkeleian analysis of the common-sense notion of a material object. It is enough to show that our constructed entities fulfill everything we might have demanded of material objects in order for us to make empirically verifiable assertions about them. A successful application of the method of logical construction requires only that there should be clearly recognized criteria that an adequate notion of a material object must fulfill. But fulfilling such criteria might fall far short of capturing everything that we customarily take the notion to involve. By comparison with Berkeley's idealism, the resulting theory is less dogmatic, since it refrains from claiming to have shown the impossibility or incoherence of the notion of a material object, and it refrains from claiming to have captured what common sense takes itself to mean by the notion. It provides an analysis of our conception of a material object by the provision of a logical construction—in the present case a class of classes of sense data—which purport to satisfy agreed upon criteria of adequacy.

Russell's execution of the strategy is general and schematic and can give the appearance of circularity, since it is motivated by reference to our common-sense idea of perceiving material objects from various possible spatial perspectives, and this seems to assume both material objects and a common or public space. If we are permitted such a framework of assumptions it is easy to form a general conception of the collection of all the ways in which an object might (for example) visually appear to us. Russell's logical constructions consist of the collection of these visual appearances "of" material objects. But if this is Russell's strategy, hasn't he assumed what he set out to dispense with? Not if the framework of material objects and the public space in which they lie serve merely as a scaffolding that is appealed to in specifying the criteria an adequate construction of material objects should fulfill. The question of circularity turns on whether the construction can stand by itself when the scaffolding is kicked away, not on whether the scaffolding is essential in guiding the construction.

The principal achievement of Russell's phenomenalism, as well as the respect in which it represents an extension of Berkeley's subjective idealism, is its clarity regarding the nature and status of criteria of adequacy. This, far more than any of Russell's specific proposals, constitutes the philosophical contribution of his phenomenalism. Russell's clarification of the methodological situation opened the field to others—most notably to Rudolf Carnap and Nelson Goodman—for the development and articulation of more detailed phenomenalist analyses in accordance with the method of logical construction.

Russell's Structuralism

Let us turn now to the concept of structure and the theory to which it led. This theory would not have been possible without the foundational investigations that culminated in logicism; and Russell would not have been convinced of its correctness had he not undertaken the extensive study of developments in physics that form the context of *AoM*. But although Russell's structuralism was informed by his reflections on mathematics and physics, the theory was not determined by these reflections but emerged in response to a traditional philosophical problem confronted by indirect or representational theories of perception: What is the character of our descriptive knowledge of the material world, if we lack acquaintance with that world? Since at least 1905, the idea that we lack such acquaintance was not an assumption Russell ever seriously doubted; nor, with the brief exception of his phenomenalist period, did he seriously doubt that there are material events and processes.

As early as *Problems* Russell accepted Berkeley's criticisms of the Lockean view that our knowledge of material objects is divided between knowledge of their primary and secondary qualities. He agreed with Berkeley that Locke had no basis for his claim that we can know the primary qualitative aspects of the constituents of the material world, and he also agreed with Berkeley's assessment that such a claim is in tension with Locke's own account of secondary qualities. (For the sake of simplicity, I am here assuming a dualism of mental and material events. In a complete account of Russell's epistemology and metaphysics this assumption, and the conclusion just attributed to him, would need to be qualified.) But unlike other less sophisticated exponents of similar views, Russell understood this to entail that we know neither the qualitative character of the properties of material events nor that of the relations among them. To have such qualitative knowledge would require acquaintance with the events of which they hold; but by hypothesis, this is precisely what we do not have.

Russell's earliest logical investigations into the concept of number led to the discovery that the notion of a one-one correspondence is expressible with complete generality, being definable in pure second-order logic. *As such, it is capable of being understood without acquaintance with any of the properties whose extensions it relates.* Similarity of properties or "equinumerosity" generalizes to similarity of relations—"structural similarity"—and this captures Russell's discovery of a kind of non-qualitative similarity that can be grasped without acquaintance with the relations whose fields it correlates. In particular we can have knowledge that a relation with which we are acquainted is structurally similar to one with which we are not acquainted. When we know that a relation is structurally similar to a given relation, we are said to have *structural knowledge* of that relation.

On Russell's structuralism, of percepts we know *both* their quality and structure (where Russell's use of the term 'quality' includes relations), while of external events we know only their structure. Structural properties are thus a particular subclass of properties and relations: they are distinguished by the fact that they are expressible in the language of pure logic. Unlike Locke's distinction between primary and secondary qualities, the Structure/Quality distinction does not mark a difference in ontological status: events have both structure and qualities—indeed when we speak of the structure of external events, this is elliptical for the structural properties of their qualities and relations. Neither is it the case that one is "more fundamental" than the other, or that qualities are occurrent while structure is a power. What is claimed is a deficiency in our knowledge.

Of external events we know the structural properties of their properties and relations, but we do not know the properties and relations themselves. The theoretical knowledge of the material world expressed by physics falls within the scope of this claim, so that Russell's theory immediately yields the consequence that physical theories give knowledge of structure and *only* knowledge of structure.

Russell believed that the discovery of structural knowledge yielded a solution to the problem that had eluded Locke, and that Kant had addressed with only limited success. Contrary to Locke, our knowledge of the material world is not qualitative. Contrary to Kant, it is possible to have significant knowledge of the material or "noumenal" world. The correct view is that of the relations of the material world our knowledge is always structural and never qualitative. As Russell says, of the material world we can know its structure, but not its qualitative character. This, in essence, is Russell's structuralism.

There is a difficulty with this view that was elegantly stated by M. H. A. Newman in an article which appeared just one year after the publication of AoM (see Newman 1928 and Russell 1928, p. 176. The significance of Newman's observation was first emphasized in Demopoulos and Friedman 1985.) The observation on which Newman's criticism was based is a very simple one: Newman drew a contrast between the claim that a given relation has a certain structure—satisfies an appropriate condition that is expressible in pure logic or pure mathematics—and the existential claim that there is a relation which satisfies this condition. He then observed that provided such an existential claim is consistent, it is true in any domain of sufficient cardinality. However, this is not the case for claims regarding specific properties and relations: such claims of structural similarity are epistemologically significant precisely because they are assertions concerning the similarity of given relations, rather than bare existential claims to the effect that there is a relation which is similar to a given one.

In the context of Russell's Lockean realism, the difficulty this poses is that an assertion about the structure of relations holding among the individuals of the material world with which we are not acquainted will be true in any extension of the domain that correctly models our knowledge of those things with which we are acquainted, provided only that the extension is large enough. Hence in a theory such as Russell's, except for a cardinality assumption, the content of our judgments regarding the material world virtually coincides with the content of our reports on the objects of our acquaintance. (See Demopoulos 2010 for a full discussion of these issues.) Moreover, the cardinality assumption is the only component of our knowledge of the material world that is not secured by purely logical or purely mathematical considerations. But this is an evident distortion of what, pre-analytically, we take the epistemological significance of our judgments about the material world to be. It is particularly damaging for Russell's claim to have avoided phenomenalism, since it reduces the difference between a phenomenalist and a realist theory to a claim about cardinality, and this too is an evident distortion of the difference between these two philosophical positions.

A possible response to Newman is to argue that the scope of the quantified relation-variables of the existential claims which express our knowledge of the material world should be restricted to *natural* or *real* relations. Then it is by no means obvious that the condition such a claim expresses is satisfied by real or natural relations. However, there are two difficulties with this response. First, it makes a simple fact involving our judgments of epistemic significance depend on metaphysically difficult notions when it is clear that it does not. And secondly, it fails to capture the scope of Newman's observation, which is independent of a relation's "reality" or "naturalness": there is a distinction to be made between significant and non-significant claims regarding the structural similarity of relations even when one or both of the relations is artificial. Russell's theory is incapable of capturing this distinction with the necessary generality.

In Russell's theory the distinction between a claim concerning a given relation and one that is merely about some relation or other reduces to the distinction between a relation that is "given" to us by our acquaintance with it and one that is not. On such a view, it is not possible for an assertion to be of a given relation unless we have acquaintance with that relation, and this means that assertions regarding relations that fall outside our acquaintance are necessarily general claims, claims of the form *there is an R, such that . . . R . . . .* What Russell's empiricism seeks to preserve is unexceptionable, namely the distinction between properties and relations that are given in experience and those that are not. But as Newman's discussion shows, a position according to which claims about given relations can only be made out in terms of acquaintance or its absence is a position that is incapable of capturing the epistemological significance of common judgments about structural similarity. This observation must be addressed by any response to Newman on Russell's behalf.

In order to compare Russell's structuralism with the recent interest in "structural realism," it is necessary to explain the notion of the "Ramsey sentence" of a theory (introduced in Ramsey 1929). This will also facilitate the comparison of *AoM* with Russell's final statement of his theory in *Human Knowledge* (*HK*). On Russell's view, our assertions regarding relations that fall outside our acquaintance are necessarily general claims of the form *there is a relation R such that . . . R . . . .* To make the connection with Ramsey sentences we have only to imagine that our "theory of the world" can be captured by a reconstruction which distinguishes among the primitives of its non-logical vocabulary between those predicates which are true of things with which we are acquainted and those which are true of things that transcend our acquaintance. Our theory is then schematically expressible by a single postulate which is formulated in a language containing two types of primitive non-logical term: the *acquaintance* or *A-terms* and the *transcendent* or *T-terms*. In accordance with Russell's fundamental principle, the A-terms are fully understood, but the T-terms are problematic insofar as we are precluded from being acquainted with the things they qualify.

In this framework there are no primitive vocabulary items that mix items of acquaintance and items of transcendence. If there were such "cross-category" terms, a question would arise as to how they are understood. And if their understanding could be accounted for compatibly with the fundamental principle, it is difficult to see why the transcendent terms should not also be capable of being understood compatibly with this principle. This strongly suggests that our reconstruction of our theory of the world should not contain cross-category terms, which is what its representation by acquaintance and transcendent terms assumes. But then, given that our understanding of the T-terms is completely general, any theory involving them is itself fully captured by its *Ramsey sentence*, that is by the result of replacing the transcendent terms occurring in it by variables of the appropriate logical category, and then existentially closing the formula which results from this replacement. The Ramsey sentence expresses the idea that of the transcendent part of the world our knowledge is purely general knowledge, and that it admits an analysis like the one provided by Russell's structuralism. Whether and to what extent the Ramsey sentence formulations of structural realism that derive from Russell are also subject to Newman's objections is a topic currently very much under discussion. (See Ainsworth 2009 for an overview and references.)

HK is replete with the discussion of *spatio-temporal* structure, which Russell evidently intends as a replacement for *AoM*'s almost complete reliance on *purely logical* structure. From the perspective of Russell's structuralism, we can represent the change in view which marks this transition as the recognition of the necessity of the assumption:

> *Cross-Category*: Some at least of the relations we know to hold among events with which we are acquainted also hold among events with which we are not acquainted; this includes spatio-temporal relations.

Hence, in *HK* the sharp Structure/Quality division—and for the Ramsey sentence formulation, the sharp division between A- and T-terms—is relaxed in order to secure the conclusion which Newman observed we could not reach from the original statement of the theory of *AoM*, namely, the conclusion that our knowledge of the transcendent part of the world is not a mere matter of knowledge of its cardinality but contains many propositions that express significant truths.

The status *HK* assigns to the assumption which secures our knowledge of the transcendent part of the world (namely, *Cross-Category*) is not unlike the status accorded the Axiom of Infinity in the development of Russell's logicism. Russell initially promised an account of mathematical knowledge that would reveal it as a species of logical knowledge. But in light of the paradoxes it emerged that this thesis could not be maintained, and that the correctness of its central logical constructions required an assumption (namely, the Axiom of Infinity) that logic could not justify. A similar limitation afflicts Russell's theory of knowledge: if empiricism is to capture the character of our knowledge of the physical world, it is necessary to assume that we understand at least some cross-category terms. (*Cross-Category*) entitles such knowledge, but it is an assumption that empiricism, in the form of the fundamental principle and Russell's account of the scope of acquaintance, is incapable of securing.

Acknowledgment

I wish to express my gratitude to the Killam Foundation and the Social Sciences and Humanities Research Council of Canada for support of my research.

References

Ainsworth, P. M. (2009). Newman's Objection. *British Journal for the Philosophy of Science* **60**: 1–37.
Demopoulos, W. (2003). Russell's Structuralism and the Absolute Description of the World, in N. Griffin (ed.) *The Cambridge Companion to Russell* (Cambridge, Cambridge University Press) 392–419.
—— (2010). Three Views of Theoretical Knowledge. *British Journal for the Philosophy of Science*.
—— and M. Friedman (1985). Russell's Analysis of Matter: Its Historical Context and Contemporary Interest, *Philosophy of Science* **52**: 621–39.
Newman, M. H. A. (1928). Mr Russell's "Causal Theory of Perception," *Mind* **37**: 137–48.
Ramsey, F. P. (1929). Theories, in R. B. Braithwaite (ed.) *The Foundations of Mathematics and other Logical Essays* (Paterson, NJ, Littlefield and Adams: 1960) 212–36.
Russell, B. (1903). *The Principles of Mathematics* (London, Allen and Unwin).
—— (1905). On Denoting, *Mind* **14**: 479–93.
—— (1912). *The Problems of Philosophy* (Oxford, Oxford University Press, reprint of 1998).
—— (1914). *Our Knowledge of the External World as a Field for Scientific Method in Philosophy* (London, Allen and Unwin).
—— (1919). *Introduction to Mathematical Philosophy* (London, Allen and Unwin).

—— (1927). *The Analysis of Matter* (New York, Dover reprint of 1954).
—— (1928). Letter to M. H. A. Newman of April 24, 1928, reprinted in *The Autobiography of Bertrand Russell*, Volume 2 (London, Allen & Unwin: 1968), 176.
—— (1931). Review of F. P. Ramsey's The Foundations of Mathematics and other Logical Essays, R. B. Braithwaite (ed.), *Mind* **46**: 476–82.
—— (1948). *Human Knowledge: Its Scope and Limits* (London, Allen and Unwin).
—— (1992). *Theory of Knowledge: The 1913 Manuscript*, E. R. Eames and K. Blackwell (eds.) (London and New York, Routledge).
Whitehead A. N. and B. Russell (1912) *Principia Mathematica*, Volume 2 (Cambridge, Cambridge University Press).

68
LUDWIG WITTGENSTEIN
Marie McGinn

Introduction

Wittgenstein's remarks on knowledge present a fragmented and inconclusive picture. However, there are two themes that Wittgenstein returns to again and again: first, that the idea that "I know" describes a state of affairs which "guarantees" what is known is a wrong picture; and second, that there are circumstances in which doubt is excluded and questions of justification do not arise, and in which the use of "I know" is equivalent to "There is no such thing as doubt in this case" (*On Certainty* (henceforward OC) 58). At least some of these remarks focus on the question of what is sometimes called "non-inferential knowledge," that is, on how we are to understand the status of judgments that we make "*straight off*, without any doubt interposing itself" (OC 524). I here focus on Wittgenstein's distinctive treatment of this issue and show how it avoids the problems that arise for the accounts of non-inferential knowledge put forward by Wilfrid Sellars (1997) and John McDowell (1994, 2008).

The Problem of Non-Inferential Knowledge

The idea that some knowledge is non-inferential is prima facie compelling. What is non-inferentially known provides known premises for arguments that justify knowledge based on inference. In this way, non-inferentially acquired knowledge provides both the starting points, and an ultimate court of appeal, within our overall system of empirical knowledge. However, for those who are moved by these reflections to hold that at least some knowledge is non-inferential, there is a question of what the authority of the relevant knowledge claims derives from. On the one hand, the non-inferential nature of the knowledge seems to preclude the idea of a rational base for the relevant claims; on the other hand, the concept of knowledge is internally linked with the idea of being able to justify what one claims to know. An externalist, reliabilist account of the source of the authority of non-inferential knowledge might offer a way out of the apparent tension, but for those who are committed to the view that reliability is not sufficient for knowledge—that knowledge requires a knower who is self-consciously aware of his right to make the relevant knowledge claim—this is not an acceptable way to resolve the problem. The authority of non-inferential knowledge claims must be accounted for in some other way.

Sellars' Account

Sellars' approach to non-inferential knowledge is to separate the source of the positive epistemic status of a non-inferentially acquired belief from its mode of acquisition. According to Sellars, non-inferential beliefs are just beliefs that a subject acquires independently of any process of reasoning. This means there is no a priori limit on the concepts that can figure in non-inferentially acquired perceptual beliefs. Sellars acknowledges the need to account for both the positive epistemic status of such beliefs, and their power to transmit a positive epistemic status to the beliefs that are based on them. He argues that no account in terms of the notion of direct apprehension of facts is possible. One of the objections he makes to such accounts is that in order to make direct apprehension the basis of correct, well-founded perceptual judgments, there would have to be a criterion by which a subject could distinguish genuine apprehendings from mere seemings to apprehend. He argues that it is only if a subject is in a position to distinguish genuine apprehendings from mere seemings that the notion of direct apprehension could explain the source of the positive epistemic status of non-inferentially acquired perceptual beliefs.

Sellars, therefore, abandons the idea that the epistemic status of non-inferentially acquired perceptual beliefs derives from their being somehow self-warranting. Rather, the positive epistemic status of such beliefs derives from the fact that the process of training which speakers undergo when they learn language brings it about that the majority of their spontaneous observation reports are likely to be true. A subject's propensity to report "This is green" is thus a reliable indicator of the presence of a green object. Sellars does not, however, regard reliable indication as sufficient for knowledge. In order for a perceiver's true and reliable observation reports to count as expressions of knowledge, the perceiver must know that, in conditions that are standard for visual perception, his propensity to report "This is green" is a reliable indicator of the presence of a green object. The perceiver is thus in a position to recognize that his propensity to report, straight off, "This is green" gives him a good reason to judge that he is in the presence of a green object.

For a perceptual report to count as an expression of knowledge, its reliability as an indicator of an objective state of affairs must be recognized by the speaker, and available to him as a means to justify the belief that he (non-inferentially) acquired. Sellars avoids the infinite regress that appears to threaten the idea that a knower's justification for any particular claim depends upon his knowing that his claims are, in general, reliable indicators, by claiming that a speaker might know that his previous utterances were reliable indicators, even if, at the time of making them, they did not amount to expressions of knowledge. It is only at the point at which a speaker's reliability becomes self-conscious, and thus available to figure in a justification of his endorsement of reports that he is spontaneously inclined to give, that those reports acquire the positive epistemic status of observational knowledge.

Objections

There are at least two objections to Sellars' account of non-inferential knowledge. First of all, it is phenomenologically implausible. It just seems false to suggest that the positive epistemic status of, say, my current perceptual judgment, "This is a piece of paper," derives from a general belief that my propensity to make this kind of observational report is a reliable indicator of the presence of a piece of paper. In general, if a proposition, p, is to serve as a justification for affirming another proposition, q, then p must be epistemically more secure than q. But the proposition that my observational reports, "This is a piece of paper," are reliable indicators of the presence of a piece of paper does not seem to be epistemically more secure than my current judgment, "This is a piece of paper," and it is implausible to suggest that the latter inherits its epistemic status from the former.

This leads to a second objection. For it seems clear that Sellars' account fails to preserve what makes the idea of non-inferential knowledge compelling. The idea is that non-inferential perceptual judgments provide the starting point for all empirical knowledge, and the test against which all knowledge based on inference is to be judged. The point of holding that perception provides for the acquisition of non-inferential knowledge lies in our recognizing that perception gives us immediate access to the world. Thus, non-inferential perceptual judgments possess their positive epistemic status in virtue of the circumstances in which they are made, independently of the kind of general justification from which Sellars claims it derives. Moreover, it seems that it is only if we hang on to this idea that we could be said to have provided an account of genuinely non-inferential knowledge. If that is correct, then Sellars' account is not a way of making non-inferential knowledge intelligible, but of showing that there is no non-inferential knowledge: all knowledge owes its status qua knowledge to inference. Sellars has abandoned the element of foundationalism implicit in the idea of non-inferential knowledge and accepted a form of coherentism, in which the epistemic status of any belief is a matter of its inferential connections to other beliefs.

McDowell's Account

One of Sellars' objections to an account of non-inferential knowledge that employs the notion of direct apprehension of a fact is that, in order for such direct apprehension to constitute a case of knowing the relevant fact, the subject must be able to know that he is directly apprehending that fact. This, Sellars argues, requires a criterion by which a subject can distinguish genuine apprehendings from mere seemings. McDowell develops an account of non-inferential knowledge which incorporates a form of epistemological disjunctivism as a means to avoid this difficulty. McDowell accepts that it is at least conceivable that there could be mere seemings to apprehend that are phenomenologically indistinguishable from genuine cases. However, he argues that this does not force us to accept that, in the non-deceptive cases, what is apprehended is not the fact itself. Thus, cases of its seeming to me that I see a piece of paper are of two disjoint kinds: cases in which I merely seem to see (or directly apprehend) a piece of paper, and cases in which the fact that a piece of paper is present is making itself perceptually manifest, that is, in which I am directly apprehending the fact that a piece of paper is present. McDowell argues that a subject's epistemic position depends upon whether the good or the bad disjunct is realized. In the good case, when a subject is seeing a piece of paper in front of him, this constitutes his having direct cognitive access to the fact that there is a piece of paper there, and this direct cognitive access entitles him to make the judgment "This is a piece of paper."

According to McDowell, if a subject is undergoing the experience that constitutes the good disjunct, then he is *thereby* warranted in judging that things are as his experience reveals them to be. The idea that judgment is rationally responsive to what is given in experience does, he acknowledges, impose an idea of rational or doxastic responsibility: if a subject has some special reason to think that appearances are deceptive, then the subject is not in a position to take advantage of the warrant for a judgment as to how things are that his experience in fact provides. But where there is no special reason to think that things might be other than they appear, and the subject is actually perceiving his surroundings, then, McDowell claims, he is in a position to form warranted, knowledgeable judgments about what is the case in his environment. The factive state of seeing a piece of paper justifies the judgment, "This is a piece of paper," without any need of support from premises that are available independently of the subject's having a direct cognitive grasp on the relevant fact. The possibility of deceptive cases shows we are fallible, but our fallibility does not, McDowell claims, undermine the idea that, when things go well, we are in possession of an indefeasible experiential warrant that constitutes the judgments we base on the exercise of our perceptual faculties as cases of genuine knowledge.

McDowell accepts Sellars' view that relations of warrant can only hold between conceptually structured items. However, he argues that if we accept the Kantian insight that, in the case of subjects with the relevant conceptual capacities, the content of experience is conceptually structured, then we are in a position to see perceptual judgments concerning matters of fact as both justified and non-inferential: they are warranted by the content of the experience on which they are rationally based. Thus, when things go well, a warrant for judgment is provide by the subject's being confronted by a fact, conceived as a conceptually structured item that constitutes the content of his experience. On McDowell's conception, the idea that judgments based on what is given in experience must be intrinsically certain is unnecessary to the idea that what is given in experience provides an indefeasible warrant for judgment. For if it is the case that the fact that there is a piece of paper before me is making itself manifest in experience, then the warrant that the content of my experience provides for the judgment, "This is a piece of paper," is one that is incompatible with the judgment's being false. The epistemic position I enjoy in virtue of that fact's making itself experientially manifest is one that is incompatible with its turning out that my judgment, "This is a piece of paper," is mistaken.

McDowell argues that his account of non-inferential knowledge does not commit him to the idea that there are cases of unmediated knowledge, or cases of knowledge that do not require the subject to be in a position to justify what he claims to know. He accepts Sellars' view that epistemic descriptions place the episode described within "the logical space of reasons," i.e. they commit the describer to the idea of a subject who can give a reason for judging as he does. However, he holds that this commitment can be met insofar as a subject who judges, "This is a piece of paper," can justify the judgment, by saying "I see that there is a piece of paper." The justification incorporates the judgment that it is used to justify, but the possibility of giving it makes clear that it is only a subject who is self-consciously aware of what he sees—and of the entitlement to judgment that perception provides—who is in a position to acquire non-inferential perceptual knowledge. Moreover, given the requirement of doxastic responsibility which is intrinsic to the idea that a subject is a rational agent, and thus a knower of truths, there is a standing obligation on the subject's part to be aware of possible grounds for doubt, which might put him in a position in which he cannot take advantage of the warrant that his awareness of an objective fact actually provides.

What is crucial for McDowell is that this account of non-inferential knowledge both acknowledges that the world plays a role in determining the goodness of a subject's epistemic position, and at the same time makes the idea of guaranteed, knowledgeable judgment intelligible. This does not, he claims, require him to hold that the non-inferential, knowledgeable judgments to which a speaker is entitled, in virtue of the cognitive access to facts that perceptual experience provides, are unmediated, intrinsically certain, or incapable of being doubted. All that is required, he argues, is that, when things go well, the experiential warrant that awareness of a fact provides is incompatible with the falsity of the judgment that the fact obtains. Thus, the absolute indefeasibility of the warrant, which the notion of direct apprehension is intended to capture, is conceived in a way that makes it independent of the idea that the judgments that are thus warranted are either intrinsically certain or indubitable.

According to McDowell, a subject who is in possession of the relevant sort of experiential warrant and who judges that a fact obtains *cannot* be wrong about it. But this is not to say that the subject's judgment is infallible: a subject might take himself to be apprehending a fact in cases where he merely seems to apprehend a fact. The point is to enable us to see how, despite our fallibility, there can be such a thing as an indefeasible warrant, which grounds a non-inferential, knowledgeable judgment. The picture is not intended to help us to justify a judgment in the face of skeptical doubt, but only to make us comfortable with the idea that, when things go well, no further warrant, over and above the warrant that derives from the perceptual situation itself, is needed.

Objections

McDowell's account tries to make us comfortable with the idea of direct apprehension of a fact as a ground for non-inferential knowledge, and to show why question-begging justifications ("I see that p") are sufficient to vindicate a subject's entitlement to assert the embedded proposition. The picture of indefeasible, experiential warrant for the non-inferential judgment, "This is a piece of paper," that McDowell presents is intended to show how a judgment that I make "straight off" can possess a rational warrant, and why a suitable justification of the judgment does not—cannot—take the form of a non-question-begging argument with the relevant proposition as its conclusion. This picture of non-inferential knowledge is, on the face of it, a version of what Wittgenstein castigates as "the wrong picture," the one he believes to lie at the root of philosophical misunderstanding:

> But isn't there a phenomenon of knowing, as it were quite apart from the sense of the phrase "I know"? Is it not remarkable that a man can *know* something, can as it were have the fact within him?—But that is a wrong picture.
> (*Zettel* (henceforward Z) §408)

At least one reason for Wittgenstein's sense that the picture is misleading is closely related to Sellars' objection to the idea of direct apprehension: the availability of an experiential guarantee is taken to require that a subject can know that he is in possession of such a guarantee, and this would require that he is infallible about whether he knows the relevant proposition. Wittgenstein spells out the objection at length:

> [I]t is said, it's only knowledge if things really are as he says. But that is not enough. It mustn't be just an accident that they are. For he has got to know that he knows: for knowing is a state of his own mind; he can't be in doubt or

error about it—apart from some special sort of blindness. If then knowledge *that* things are so is only knowledge if they *really* are so; and if knowledge is in him so that he cannot go wrong about whether it is knowledge; in that case, then, he is also infallible about things being so, just as he knows his knowledge; and so the fact which he knows must be within him just like the knowledge. (Z §408)

Clearly, McDowell believes that disjunctivism answers this objection. If we accept disjunctivism, then we can see how, in the good case, we are not only in possession of a guarantee of what we claim to know, but the nature of guarantee enables us to see why, when things go well, "I see that *p*" is a proper justification of the embedded proposition. As McDowell sees it, the objection that Sellars and Wittgenstein raise reflects a distorted picture of direct apprehension, insofar as it assumes that direct apprehension entails that a subject must be infallible about whether he is apprehending a fact, and thus about whether he knows it.

Suppose we accept that McDowell has changed the picture of knowledge as a state in which what is known is guaranteed as a fact, in a way which disconnects it from any idea of infallibility, there is still the question of its application. On McDowell's account, the indefeasible warrant for my perceptual judgment, "There is a piece of paper in front of me," consists in the fact that my situation is one in which the fact that there is a piece of paper in front of me is making itself visually manifest. I am in possession of a warrant that guarantees the truth of my judgment insofar as I stand in a certain kind of cognitive relation (that of seeing) to the fact whose obtaining renders the judgment true. How are we to understand the notion of warrant when it is employed in this way? McDowell suggests that the warrant that I'm in possession of is one that underpins a way of justifying the perceptual judgment, "There is a piece of paper in front of me," which is incompatible with that judgment's being false. Thus, if I'm asked, "How do you know there is a piece of paper in front of you?," I can give a reason for my judgment that "fully vindicates" my entitlement to it: "I see that there is a piece of paper in front of me." The justification fully vindicates the judgment insofar as "I see that there is a piece of paper in front of me" logically entails "There is a piece of paper in front of me." However, it is clear that the judgment which McDowell claims fully vindicates the judgment, "There is a piece of paper in front of me," does so *only* if it is true. And the question is what guarantees its truth.

On McDowell's account, what guarantees its truth is the fact that I am currently seeing that there is a piece of paper in front of me, and that is not something that can be true or false, or for which the question of evidence can arise. That's why the fact which, on McDowell's account, is the content of my experience is able to provide an indefeasible warrant for my judgment, that is to say, provide a guarantee that the judgment which asserts that the fact obtains is true. But for precisely this reason, what guarantees my judgment's truth is not something I can give in justification for my assertion "I see that there is a piece of paper in front of me." As far as my assertion goes, the best I can do is say something that is true, and not something whose truth I'm in a position to guarantee. And insofar as what I say is, at best, true, it seems open to someone to ask again, "How do you know that you see a piece of paper in front of you?" And it seems that, on McDowell's account, all I can do, at this point, is dig in my heels and insist that I do see it, that I'm not merely seeming to see it, that it would be ridiculous to doubt it. Thus, it seems that the indefeasible warrants that McDowell's picture introduces can't be connected with the actual business of providing a warrant for a judgment, since a fact is not itself something that can be offered in justification. In trying to extend the idea of a warrant for judgment to what lies outside judgment, McDowell has introduced a picture of justification for what one asserts that has no application in the actual process of justifying what one claims to know.

It might be objected on McDowell's behalf that he never intended his picture of what guarantees perceptual judgments to be applied in the actual business of justifying either perceptual judgments or assertions of the form "I see that . . . ." The whole point of McDowell's picture is to make sense of a notion of indefeasible warrant for judgments that operates independently of the question whether we are ever in a position to provide a justification for what we claim that would satisfy a skeptic. His account is intended to serve merely as a picture by means of which we can, in a position of reflection, reassure ourselves that, when things go well, we are in possession of an indefeasible warrant, and thus in a position to make knowledgeable judgments about the objects in our surroundings. The picture shows how a non-inferential judgment can possess a rational warrant which guarantees its truth. The question is, does this succeed in explaining the source of our entitlement to our basic judgments concerning the objects in our environment?

The idea is that, other things being equal, it is a fact's being given in experience that provides a rational warrant for the judgment that the fact obtains. If we want to say what the fact is that is given in experience and which warrants the judgment that it obtains, then we will, of course, be obliged simply to repeat the proposition that is the content of the judgment that the fact allegedly warrants. But in that case, doesn't the picture amount to this: I am entitled to the observational judgment that there is a piece of paper before me by the fact that there is a piece of paper before me. And how does this differ from saying that I am entitled to make the observational judgment that there is a piece of paper in front of me in virtue of its being correct to say that there is a piece of paper in front of me? McDowell's picture is supposed to show how this correct judgment can be a rational response to something that is given in experience, but when we are asked to say what it is a rational response to, we are obliged simply to repeat the judgment: the judgment "This is a piece of paper" is a rational response to the fact that this is a piece of paper. The question is, what is the criterion of its being a rational response to the fact that this is a piece of paper? In my own case, it is just that this is what I judge it to be. The fact itself cannot tell me what it is correct to judge; what the fact is is something which, for me, is settled (subject to the usual checks) by what I judge to be the case. In the case of others, the criterion of its being a rational response is, in normal circumstances, that the judgment is correct—that is to say, it is the one that they would make—given such background facts as that I am a competent speaker of English.

Thus, the idea that there is something outside judgment that is the source of my entitlement to judge seems either to conjure up the idea of something outside judgment that can inform me what constitutes a correct description of it, or it adds nothing to the idea that, when I judge, I aim to speak truly and whether I succeed is something that can be confirmed, either by means of further checks that I can carry out, or by others. The former idea is mysterious. I can become informed of what the facts are by determining (that is to say, judging) what is the case, but it makes no sense to say that the facts inform me of what is the case. In trying to apply the notion of an indefeasible warrant in the case of basic, non-inferential judgments, McDowell has either to attribute a mysterious power to facts to inform a judger how to judge, or to bring the chain of justifications to an end in a stutter, in which the entitlement to judge that p is held to consist in its being correct to judge that p. And given that the latter is itself something judged (either by me or by others), the latter gets us no further, for the question immediately arises of our entitlement to the judgment that the judgment that p is correct.

Wittgenstein and Non-Inferential Judgments

Wittgenstein does not use the expression "non-inferential knowledge," and he is in general wary of using the term "know" in connection with judgments that we make "straight off," and for which a question of doubt does not normally arise. However, at least part of his response to Moore's defense of common sense reflects his concern to put these judgments in a light which relieves us of the sense that our lack of doubt, or our lack of a justification, concerning them is in some way amiss. His route to putting us philosophically at ease with these judgments is clearly very different from McDowell's, since it explicitly eschews the path of showing how it is that we can *know* them. In order to become clearer about these judgments, Wittgenstein believes, we need to become clearer about the nature of the certainty that characterizes our ordinary relation to them. The central question for Wittgenstein is whether, as McDowell assumes, this certainty is to be understood as belonging to the same species as our certainty concerning such well-established facts as the boiling point of water or the date of the Battle of Hastings. The idea is that we are tempted by such a picture only because we have not undertaken the investigation Wittgenstein wants us to focus on, and which aims to achieve a realistic understanding of the point at which giving grounds comes to an end.

Wittgenstein's approach to philosophical problems and perplexities can be roughly characterized as descriptive. The aim of the description is to overcome the intellectual temptations which Wittgenstein believes to lie at the root of philosophical perplexity: the temptation to idealize, to create abstractions and hypostatize objects. His aim, as he says in *Philosophical Investigations* (henceforward *PI*) 94, is to get us to see that "nothing out of the ordinary is involved." Describing, reporting, naming, inferring, calculating, etc. are all part of human natural history, and he believes that we have only to come to command a clear view of these practices in order to understand their nature. In particular, he wants us to view judging as "as much a part of our natural history as walking, eating, drinking, playing" (*PI* 25), and to resist the temptation to idealize it. His aim is to get us to see our sophisticated language-game, in which doubts about particular judgments are raised and answered, as a refinement of a more primitive form of language-game, in which a child gradually learns to respond unhesitatingly, in which it trusts its teacher implicitly, and in which doubt is not yet a possibility. It is not that he's concerned to provide an explanation of the origins of our language-game, but he hopes that by seeing a certain order in linguistic phenomena, the disquiet which sends us in search of a mental state in which the fact known is somehow guaranteed can be dispelled. It is not that the foundation we are inclined to look for in indefeasible guarantees is provided by natural reactions but, rather, the aim is to dispel our sense that without this form of guarantee our practice of judging lacks something vital.

The aspects of our practice of judging that Wittgenstein draws attention to are all familiar ones. We learn to judge by being taught judgments:

> We do not learn the practice of making empirical judgements by learning rules: we are taught *judgements* and their connexion with other judgements. (OC 140)

> We teach a child "that is your hand," not "that is perhaps (or "probably") your hand." (OC 374)

> I want to say: our learning has the form "that is a violet," "that is a table." (OC 450)

The process by which we are taught how to judge depends upon an unquestioning trust of our teachers, which is entirely natural to us:

> The child learns to believe a host of things. (OC 144)

> As children we learn facts; e.g., that every human being has a brain, and we take them on trust. (OC 159)

> The child learns by believing the adult. (OC 160)

> For how can a child immediately doubt what it is taught? That could mean only that he was incapable of learning certain language games. (OC 283)

The test of our having mastered the language-game of judging is our ability to go on independently, and apply expressions in judgements that are made without any hesitancy or doubt:

> [O]ne is not playing the game, or is playing it wrong, if one does not recognize objects with certainty. (OC 446)

> We say: if a child has mastered language—and hence its application—it must know the meaning of words. It must, for example, be able to attach the name of its colour to a white, black, red or blue object without the occurrence of any doubt. (OC 522)

Thus, trusting the judgements of both myself and others "is part of judging" (OC 150); "our not doubting . . . is simply our manner of judging" (OC 232). We should, he suggests, see doubt emerging as a complication of this more primitive language-game, in which doubt is not yet a possibility.

> A child learns there are reliable and unreliable informants much later than it learns facts which are told it. (OC 143)

> Doubt comes after belief. (OC 160)

> One doubts on specific grounds. (OC 458)

> When a child learns language it learns at the same time what is to be investigated and what is not. (OC 472)

The child is taught judgments and is trained to recognize objects without hesitation. When it reacts to a situation by giving an object its correct name, there is no question of its having a reason or being able to justify what it does. No more does it have a reason not to doubt. It is not that it learns not to doubt; doubt, at this stage, is not a possibility. Later the child learns when doubt is appropriate; it learns to doubt on specific grounds. These reminders draw attention to the fact that our language-game does not have its roots in reason. But clearly, this is not a matter for concern; it does not undermine or falsify our practice. We don't miss the absence of doubt or justification here.

One way to understand the significance of these reminders is to take the process by which we are initiated into our practice as an object of comparison, which helps us to see our ordinary language-game in a less idealized and more naturalistic light. It helps us to accept that what lies at the bottom of our ordinary language-game are responses that are not grounded in reasons, but are confident and unhesitating reactions to our immediate environment. Not only that, they are ones that each of us can confidently predict will be universally and unhesitatingly shared with others who have been initiated into our practice of judging. Regarding these judgments as absolutely solid "is part of our method of doubt and enquiry" (OC 151). The confidence I have in making these judgments "is something universal . . . not just something personal" (OC 440). Wittgenstein's aim is not to show us that these attitudes are justified, or even correct, but to dispel the sense that some other foundation is needed, or can be given. In normal circumstances, trusting our own and others' judgment—our, and their, ability to say straight off what something is—characterizes our practice. Without that trust, the whole system breaks down, in much the way the capacity to learn breaks down if a child does not trust its teachers, or its own ability to go on independently.

One important element in Wittgenstein's attempt to get us to feel at ease with the groundlessness of the judgments that we accept without further question is to get us to see them under the aspect of "acting surely, acting without any doubt" (OC 196). Although there is a difference between our judgments and the reactions of the child, insofar as we are self-conscious judgers who understand what it is we are doing and the possibilities for being called to account, Wittgenstein wants us to resist the temptation to suppose that this leaves us with a choice between regarding our judgments as mere surmises or seeing them as standing in need of a justification. The whole point is that we do not make these judgments on the basis of possessing a justification, and any justification that might be proffered will be less certain than that which it is supposed to justify. With these judgments "I have arrived at the rock bottom of my convictions" (OC 248), and for that reason the idea of giving grounds is not in play. But it is wrong to think that this reduces these judgments to the status of surmises, for this implies that there is a doubt that is being ignored, that these judgments are not as certain as they could be.

The idea that we see this certainty as corresponding "to a *sureness*, not to a knowing" (OC 511) is intended to make clear a distinction between the judgments that we make unhesitatingly, in response to a question or to our environment, and mere presuppositions which we accept as working hypotheses. In a sense, Wittgenstein could be seen as making us feel at ease with the idea of judgments that we are in a position to make straight off, with no question of justification, by resisting the temptation to assimilate these judgments to those for which the question of evidence is apt. Justification does come to an end in judgments that we make straight off, and for which no question of evidence or justification arises, but it is just this feature of these judgments that marks a logical distinction between them and those for which the question of reasons for belief is apt. This does not render these foundational judgments irrational, but their rational status derives from their place in a whole system of beliefs that are connected with one another, and not from their being based on beliefs that justify them.

Wittgenstein does not rule out the use of the words "I know" in the case of these foundational judgments. However, he points out that, in normal circumstances, this use of "I know" can be replaced by the words "I can say [what that is]" (OC 586, 591), or "I cannot be making a mistake" (OC 425), where the latter is understood to mean: the question of a mistake does not arise here; the question of a mistake is "*logically* excluded" (OC 194). It is for this reason that we can see it as an expression of sureness, rather than knowledge. At a number of points, Wittgenstein compares the sureness with which we say what kind of thing an object is with our treating a calculation as sufficiently checked. We might check a calculation by doing it over twice, or by getting someone else to work it out, but this process comes to an end. And at the end, the certainty we have is already as great as it can be, it would not be increased by our repeating the check twenty times or with twenty others. There isn't, he suggests, any reason why this is so. This is what counts as an adequate test in our language-game of calculation: "*This is how we calculate*" (OC 47). In this case, we can see how the whole language-game of calculation depends upon this sureness in our way of operating with mathematical expressions: there would be no such thing as calculation if we did not act with certainty in this way.

It would be wrong to characterize Wittgenstein's description of our practice of judging as a philosophical account of non-inferential knowledge, if this is taken to imply that Wittgenstein has explained how non-inferential knowledge is possible. But if he succeeds in persuading us that no such explanation is needed, then he has done something that achieves the sort of philosophical peace that it was assumed could only be provided by an explanatory account.

References

McDowell, J.H. (1994), *Mind and World*, (Cambridge, MA: Harvard University Press)
—— (2008), "The Disjunctive Conception of Experience as Material for a Transcendental Argument," *Disjunctivism: Perception, Action, Knowledge*, A. Haddock and F. Macpherson (eds.), (Oxford: Oxford University Press)
Sellars, W. (1997), *Empiricism and the Philosophy of Mind*, (Cambridge, MA: Harvard University Press)
Wittgenstein, L. (1967), *Zettel (Z)*, ed. G.E.M. Anscombe and G.H. von Wright, trans. G.E.M. Anscombe, (Oxford: Blackwell)
—— (1977), *On Certainty (OC)*, ed. G.E.M. Anscombe and G.H. von Wright, trans. D. Paul and G.E.M. Anscombe, (Oxford: Blackwell)
—— (1998), *Philosophical Investigations (PI)*, trans. G.E.M. Anscombe, (Oxford: Blackwell)

69
RUDOLF CARNAP
Thomas Uebel

Writing about the epistemological doctrines of Rudolf Carnap (1891–1970) and some other members of the Vienna Circle holds a certain irony. For the doctrines most closely associated with Carnap were rejected by him and his colleagues only a few years after they had been given what appeared to be their definitive formulation. Moreover, Carnap did not then replace these epistemological doctrines with better but less well-known ones. Instead he gave up epistemology and turned to philosophy of science. Carnap's career suggests that, despite their shared concern with knowledge, the concerns of epistemology and philosophy of science need not fully coincide.

1. The Aufbau and Its Standard Interpretation

The epistemological doctrines that Carnap is most closely associated with are those of his early work *Der logische Aufbau der Welt* (1928, trans. *The Logical Structure of the World*, hereafter *Aufbau*). There Carnap tried to establish that all the concepts of empirical science could be "rationally reconstructed" with the help of logic and set theory, step by step on the basis of just one basic relation, "remembered similarity," holding between as yet unanalyzed experiences. Much later, Carnap summarized the complexities of his project as follows.

> I developed a method called "quasi-analysis," which leads, on the basis of the similarity-relation among experiences, to the logical construction of those entities which are usually conceived as components. On the basis of a certain primitive relation among experiences, the method of quasi-analysis leads step by step to the various sensory domains—first to the visual domain, then to the positions in the visual field, the colors and their similarity system, the temporal order, and the like. Later, perceived things in the three-dimensional perceptual space are constructed, among them that particular thing which is usually called my own body, and the bodies of other persons. Still later, the so-called other minds are constructed; that is to say, mental states are ascribed to other bodies in view of their behavior, in analogy to the experience of one's own mental states.
>
> (1963, 17)

Clearly, phenomenalist reductionism does not come any more radical than this: even sense-data were to be constructed. Yet Carnap was adamant that he did not intend this reductionist doctrine to have any ontological consequences: his was but a "methodological solipsism." By showing all scientific concepts and statements to be so reducible in principle (Carnap only claimed to have provided a sketch), he aimed to show that they shared the same type of empirical basis and so sought to re-establish, on a new logico-linguistic basis, the unity of science that had been called into question (1928, §4). Moreover, Carnap stressed that a rational reconstruction of scientific concepts on a physical or materialistic basis was also possible, since "all psychological (and other) objects are reducible to physical objects" (ibid., §59), but he did not pursue this further.

Clearly, it must be asked what prompted Carnap to pursue this strategy of rational reconstruction and what brought about its perceived failure. But it must also be asked what precisely it was that failed, for the interpretation of its philosophical point that is most commonly given to the *Aufbau* has been strenuously argued against in recent Vienna Circle scholarship. Popularized by W.V.O. Quine in his "Two Dogmas of Empiricism," this interpretation stuck not just to the *Aufbau* but to Vienna Circle philosophy generally: epistemological foundationalism.

For Quine, Carnap "was the first empiricist who, not content with asserting the reducibility of science to terms of immediate experience, took serious steps toward carrying out the reduction" (Quine 1951/1980, 39). Accordingly, what failed when the *Aufbau* failed was the project of up-dating, with the tools of mathematical logic, traditional empiricism's attempt to put all of science on the secure basis of sense experience. What doomed this project was a deficit first noted by Quine. When it came to assigning sense qualities to positions in physical space, Carnap was unable to provide an eliminative reduction of the latter. As Quine put it, "the connective 'is at' remains an added undefined connective: the canons [which Carnap provides] counsel us in its use but not in its elimination" (ibid., 40). The reduction of physical object talk to ever so complex logical constructions of remembered similarity relations between originally unanalyzed experiences had failed.

Now Quine noted that "Carnap seems to have appreciated this point afterward," for "reductionism in its radical form since ceased to figure" in his work. Even so, he also claimed that "the dogma of reductionism has, in a subtler and more tenuous form, continued to influence the thought of empiricists," namely, "in the supposition that each statement, taken in isolation from its fellows, can admit of confirmation or infirmation at all" (ibid., 40–1). By his immediate countersuggestion of Duhemian holism and his linkage of the dogmas of reductionism and the analytic-synthetic distinction, Quine convicted Carnap and his colleagues of sticking to an insufficiently liberalized program of atomistic foundationalism. To be sure, Quine did not explicitly call the *Aufbau* foundationalist and in his later "Epistemology Naturalized," he noted that Carnap's project proceeded while "hope of certainty on the doctrinal side was abandoned" (the "side of epistemology" concerned with the truth of statements including universal ones). Yet that meant only the acceptance of the "Humean predicament"; all the while, "Carnap's heroic efforts on the conceptual side of epistemology" (the side concerned with definitions of terms used) continued to aim for "legitimation by elimination" (Quine 1969, 74, 78). Singular physical object statements were still expected to be reduced without remainder to phenomenalistic statements in the complex fashion described above.

So the picture of the *Aufbau* that emerges from Quine's criticism is a foundationalist one, admitting fallibilism at the level of physical generalizations, but affirming certainty all the way below. Yet we must also note that, if so, it was a foundationalism with a difference. By demanding the eliminative reducibility of physical object statements, this type of foundationalism far exceeded the demands of Chisholm's mid-twentieth-century version which gave defeasible rules for ascent to such statements from statements about phenomenal appearances. At the same time, the *Aufbau* sought a basis far below the level at which that foundationalism stopped, beyond what could possibly be expected to be introspectively accessible upon reflection (in the only reconstructively attributable similarity relations between whole experiences that constituted all objects).

Importantly then, the rational reconstruction provided by the *Aufbau* does not provide an epistemology that lends itself to meliorative concerns with knowledge. Cognition was seen from an impersonal perspective inhospitable to epistemic subjects wanting control of their domain. Carnap explicitly dismissed as irrelevant for his purposes the psychologically salient "epistemic value" of mental states of a subject, building his reconstruction instead on the "logical value" that consists of the reduction formulae for those mental contents (1928, §50). (Across all levels of reconstruction mental contents were individuated purely structurally, namely, by the provision of logical reduction formulae, and the very possibility of communication was said to rest on this shared structural constitution of meaning.)

The only concession made to traditional epistemology was Carnap's adherence to the principle of epistemic primacy which determined his order of reduction. Since "the recognition of our own psychological processes does not need to be mediated through the recognition of physical objects, but takes place directly," Carnap determined that "the sequence with respect to epistemic primacy of the four most important object domains is: the autopsychological, the physical, the heteropsychological, the cultural" (ibid., §58). Carnap's reconstruction thus imposed a psychologically inaccessible formal logical structure on an otherwise very traditionally conceived and fixedly ordered domain of the objects of human knowledge. His aim that "the order of construction reflect the epistemic order of objects" motivated his preference for taking the autopsychological language as basic (ibid., §59).

2. The Standard Interpretation Challenged

It might seem that the deficit detected by Quine dealt a fatal blow to the *Aufbau* project. Its radical reductionism is certainly undermined. But while this spells the end of the radical foundationalism that Quine saw in it, it would not rule out a more relaxed foundationalism that allows fallible ascent from the autopsychological to the physical. Just that is allowed for by Carnap's mid-1930s non-eliminative reduction sentences which made it possible to link terms from the physicalist "thing-language" to the phenomenal language as well as disposition terms (and theoretical terms understood as dispositional) to a purely observational thing-language (1936a, cf. 1936–37, §xx). For Quine, this move "renounce[d] the last remaining advantage we suppose rational reconstruction to have over straight psychology" (1969, 78), prompting his own naturalism in turn. Yet having indicated the logical possibility of retaining the phenomenal base in this attenuated fashion, Carnap never employed it for this or other purposes.

The trouble with Quine's diagnosis of the post-*Aufbau* Carnap is manifold. Not only does it overlook that Carnap himself endorsed Duhemian holism already in *Logical Syntax of Language* (1934/1937, §82), but also that soon after Carnap drew the consequence that, given such holism, scientific successor theories can be couched in a language incommensurable with that of its predecessor (and gave an example from recent physics) (1936b/1949, 126). Moreover, the diagnosis also overlooks that Duhemian holism, being of an epistemological and not a semantical kind, is compatible with the retention of the analytic–synthetic distinction, affirming the confirmability or disconfirmability of empirical statements only in suitably large chunks. (Consider also the holism inherent in Carnap's later ramseyfications of scientific theories that still sought to separate the synthetic and analytic components of the theoretical language (e.g., 1966, Chs. 26–28).) Most misleading is the continued attribution of foundationalist ambitions: it overlooks not only the strongly coherentist motive in Carnap's thinking, but also the constructivist impulse with which he approached the logico-linguistic treatment of problems in the philosophy of science ever since his abandonment of methodological solipsism in late 1932.

Quine's diagnosis of the *Aufbau* is equally contestable. Following a lead given by Michael Friedman, it has been the charge of revisionist Vienna Circle scholarship that the *Aufbau*, despite all appearances, is not a foundationalist tract. (See, e.g., Friedman 1987, 1992; Richardson 1998, Chs. 1–3, 8; Pincock 2005; Uebel 2007, Ch. 2. The present and next paragraphs draw on these sources as well as on Mormann 2007.) To be sure, it embodies the perhaps most thorough attempt at phenomenalist reductionism ever undertaken. Yet "certainty" is not a term one can find in the *Aufbau* at all: a central aspect of foundationalism in Carnap's day is missing. (To try to defend the diagnosis by arguing that nowadays foundationalism also merely claims prima facie non-inferential justification for its foundations would be futile. It was, after all, the traditional aim of putting science on the supposedly secure basis of sense experience that Quine imputed to the *Aufbau*.) Moreover, the term "justification" is missing from the text of the *Aufbau* as well, and for good reason: as we saw, Carnap showed no concern for internalist justification. What replaces it is "rational reconstruction": the justification of a knowledge claim became the satisfaction of its reduction formula (of which agents were ignorant). While this looks somewhat "externalist" it would be equally problematical, however, to see an anticipation of contemporary externalism in the *Aufbau*. Carnap was not concerned with reliable belief acquisition processes or modal conditions on knowledge ascription. The epistemology of the *Aufbau*, it must be concluded, does not fit happily into the taxonomy of current work in the field.

So what did motivate Carnap's radical phenomenalist reductionism? Revisionist scholarship detects a variety of motives reflecting different influences, ranging from the provision of a logico-linguistic proof for the unified science thesis to the development of a neo-Kantian conception of objectivity, with multiple other tendencies besides. That some of these interpretations are compatible suggests a strongly integrative ambition at work. For instance, by the very scope of his attempted reduction, Carnap sought to avoid both the bifurcation in scientific terminology and the split into types of scientific reasoning that threatened the unity thesis on two alternative approaches: the postulational approach to theoretical terms of Schlick's *General Theory of Knowledge* (1918/25) left explicitly and implicitly defined scientific terms and their respective languages sharply separated while the neo-Kantian differentiation between generalizing "nomothetic" and individualizing "ideothetic" statements sharply separated the natural from the human sciences and history. And by marrying his logically structuralist method of analysis of mental contents to the methodologically solipsist starting point of his reconstruction, Carnap was also able to defend the objectivity claim of science without abandoning the empiricist perspective: their origin in subjective experiences held no obstacle to the objectivity of scientific knowledge claims since rational reconstruction revealed the structural similarity of all of our concept formations, an invariance across all subjects. Carnap's intention, all this suggests, was to render scientific cognition self-contained.

The significance of the interpretation that Carnap himself later put on the *Aufbau*—an interpretation that does not contradict Quine's analysis—does not lie in the support it seems to lend to the latter, but in the light it casts upon the fate of the *Aufbau* in the Vienna Circle.

> Under the influence of some philosophers, especially Mach and Russell, I regarded in the *Logischer Aufbau* a phenomenalistic language as the best for a philosophical analysis of knowledge. I believed that the task of philosophy consists in reducing all knowledge to a basis of certainty. Since the most certain knowledge is that of the immediately given, whereas knowledge of material things is derivative and less certain, it seemed that the philosopher must employ a language which uses sense-data as a basis. In the Vienna discussions my attitude changed gradually towards a preference for the physicalistic language.
>
> (1963, 50)

If the *Aufbau* was not built to serve foundationalist aims, why did Carnap say so here? The answer is that Carnap himself adopted this perspective on the *Aufbau* after—and only after—he had come to Vienna. It is this take on his *Aufbau* model that Carnap remembered in his autobiography. Just why Carnap adopted this perspective is an interesting question. His acculturation into the Vienna Circle certainly played an important role. (As many commentators noted, most of the *Aufbau* predated that association.) Of particular importance was Carnap's recognition, in Vienna, of the advances that Wittgenstein's conception of logic as tautologous afforded the formulation of a modern empiricism and his subsequent desire to accommodate his *Aufbau* to the demands that the *Tractatus* made of meaningful discourse. So just as Wittgenstein flirted with a phenomenalist interpretation of the elementary propositions of his *Tractatus* in 1929–30, so Carnap was concerned to psychologize his *Aufbau* model during the same period. (And likewise, just as the Circle's Wittgensteinians helped themselves to the concept of strictly speaking meaningless but philosophically necessary "elucidations" to save the *Tractatus* from its meaning-theoretical doctrines, so Carnap appears to have adverted to these "elucidations" to save his *Aufbau* from Wittgenstein's charge of illegitimate metalinguistic discourse.)

What's most important about this for posterity, however, is that the foundationalist reading prompted a sustained debate within the Vienna Circle about the content, form and status of "protocol statements" (statements recording the observational evidence in science serving as checkpoints for theory acceptance). This debate led Carnap to once again abandon foundationalism and soon all traditional, subject-centered epistemological concerns. (For more detailed documentation of the episodes related below and the entire debate see Uebel 2007.)

3. The Vienna Circle's Protocol Sentence Debate

As noted, already in the *Aufbau* Carnap held that the construction system with a physical basis was possible and that it "has the advantage that its basic domain is the only domain (namely the physical) which is characterized by a clear regularity of processes" (1928, §59). By 1930, an additional advantage was noted: the physicalist language "makes intersubjective knowledge possible" (1930/1959, 144). This raised the question, not only of what relation obtained between the physicalist language of unified science and the phenomenalist system of the *Aufbau*, but also of whether the latter was still needed.

Carnap's answer was that both were required, for the latter "corresponds to the epistemological viewpoint because it proves the validity of knowledge by reduction to the given," whereas the former "corresponds to the view point of the empirical sciences" (ibid.). An early draft for his 1932 paper later translated as *Unity of Science* shows that for him both the phenomenalist and the physicalist languages were "universal" languages. (Roughly, a "universal language" was an empirical language into which all other empirical languages were translatable; as in the *Aufbau*, mathematics was presupposed.) What rendered the phenomenal language universal was that it was presupposed by all processes of verification whatsoever. What rendered the physical language universal was that it was presupposed in the verification of all intersubjectively recognizable states of affairs. The division of labor between the two languages was envisaged to be that each played the role of universal language in their respective domain. Epistemologically speaking, all meaningful languages had to be translatable into a subject's phenomenal language, while scientifically speaking, all languages of the empirical disciplines had to be translatable into the physical language. Given their different competencies, neither language could usurp the other.

Otto Neurath disagreed strongly with the epistemological conception Carnap accepted already by 1930. An early draft for his *Empirical Sociology* (1931a) shows that he regarded the foundationalist methodologically solipsist system as deeply mistaken, but as yet was unable to press the point. Beyond finding the notion of elucidations highly suspect, Neurath did not yet possess an argument against Carnap's restriction of the universality of the physicalist language to intersubjectively recognizable states of affairs and the claim that the autopsychological language was indispensable for epistemological purposes. It was not until the Circle meeting on February 26, 1931 that Neurath openly rejected reference to the given as superfluous. Carnap was not yet convinced. At the meeting of 12 March he indicated instead that he was prepared to jettison the *Aufbau*'s method of quasi-analysis and reconsider the nature of elementary propositions by perhaps reintroducing sense-data (he entertained similar ideas in the 1961 Preface to the second edition of the *Aufbau*). Neurath moved in the opposite direction.

Crucial to Neurath's opposition was an argument he first expressed during a private but minuted "Discussion about Physicalism" with, among others, Carnap and Hans Hahn on March 4, 1931, an argument he subsequently invoked repeatedly (e.g. 1932a/1983, 62; 1932b/1983, 96; 1934/1983, 110; 1941/1983, 228–9). As he put it in its first published form:

> only one language comes into question from the start, and that is the physicalist. One can learn the physicalist language from earliest childhood. *If someone makes predictions and wants to check them himself, he must count on changes in the system of his senses, he must use clocks and rulers*; in short, the person supposedly in isolation already makes use of the "intersensual" and "intersubjective" language. The forecaster of yesterday and the controller of today are, so two speak, two persons.
>
> (Neurath 1931b/1983, 54–5, italics added)

Against Carnap's methodologically solipsist protocol language, Neurath argued that a language must be usable by one individual over time. Phenomenal languages do not "come into question from the start" for they do not allow for mechanisms whereby the constancy of an individual's language use can be guaranteed which, in turn, is required for "checking" to take place.

What could be called Neurath's private language argument comes to this. If physicalistic statements such as instrument readings need, themselves, to be translated into phenomenal terms directly related to a scientist's experience in order to be meaningful, then no touchstone at all is available by which the constancy of an individual's language use could be established. The incoherence that threatens experience conceived of in this solipsistic fashion showed that the constancy of the language use of an individual over time can be established only by reference to the spatio-temporal determinations of physical states of affairs that the language spoke about. If language use was so controllable, then that language was already intersubjective. So if the protocol language was to be an epistemically functional language, it could not be a phenomenalist one. (Even a solitary thinker required a system of symbolic representation for the ordering of his experiences over time that is of necessity intersensual—not specific to one particular sense modality—and intersubjective.)

By the time Carnap published the German original of *Unity of Science* in the spring of 1932, the two universal languages of the first draft were reduced to one, the physicalist language. The argument to this conclusion was that, given even a relatively liberal version of verificationism, statements about mental states were unintelligible unless they referred to a person's behavioral disposition or bodily state. Carnap first established that on the assumption of the intertranslatability of the psychological and physical languages, statements about other minds were verifiable and meaningful (1932a/1934, 60–6; 1932b/1959, 170–2). Then he assumed the standpoint of the phenomenalist opponent (which denies such intertranslatability) and established that in this case statements about other minds would be unverifiable and meaningless (1932a/1934, 78–82; 1932b/1959, 173–4). Following Castañeda (1967), we can understand Carnap's argument here as a verificationist private language argument.

What had changed? The phenomenalistic protocol languages were now deemed to be translatable into the physical language. What allowed this change was Carnap's introduction of the concepts of the (potentially misleading) material and the (correct) formal modes of speech. This distinction pertained to metalinguistic discourse: the former mode spoke of (possibly Platonic) meanings of terms and sentences, whereas the latter mode spoke only of syntax and meaning relations insofar as these could be expressed in terms of logical entailments. Given his adoption of the formal mode of speech and its constraints on meaning talk, Carnap was able to drop his previous objections against the physicalization of the phenomenalist language (which had restricted the range of the physical language to intersubjective states of affairs only and which were based on the putative differences in meaning between co-extensive statements of the two languages).

Even so, for Carnap, protocol languages retained their old office. Since "verification is based upon 'protocol statements'" which "include statements belonging to the basic protocol or direct record of the scientists' experience," Carnap's "basic" or "primitive" protocol statements (in the material mode) "refer to the given, and describe directly given experience or phenomena, i.e. the simplest states of which knowledge can be had." Alternatively put in the formal mode, they are "statements needing no justification and serving as the foundation for all the remaining statements of science" (1932a/1934, 42–5; cf. 1932b/1959, 166). So Carnap retained the idea of "primary" protocol languages separate from the physical language. While this epistemic priority now officially no longer necessarily required a phenomenalist language, its de facto retention testifies to Carnap's continued allegiance to the foundationalist ideal, for there remained the following asymmetry in justification. Carnap held that "a protocol sentence, being an epistemological point of departure, cannot be rejected" (1932b/1959, 191).

Yet as Neurath stressed, the idea that an "original" protocol statement could not be rejected, but only its translation into a physical system statement, faced an unenviable and entirely avoidable dilemma. According to Carnap, a person could only take their own protocol statements as checking points (1932a, 461, dropped from 1934). Now, if these protocol languages are construed along phenomenalist lines, a speaker's grasp of their meaning would be incorrigible. This conception retained a sense of privacy that was vulnerable to the private language argument that Neurath had been pressing. For Neurath, the self-understanding of an individual language user was as problematical as was the understanding of other minds. Already an isolated epistemic agent requires the intersubjective language for the coherence of his experience: Robinson required one, Neurath once averred, "even before Friday arrived" (1934/1983, 110). If, on the other hand, these primary protocol languages were construed as already physicalist of sorts, it becomes exceedingly difficult to see what enabled primitive protocols to remain unrevisable. Unable to tie into scientific practice as we know it, Carnap's protocols remained problematic elucidations, after all. Neurath was correct in detecting in Carnap's conception of separate protocol languages vestiges of the atomistic conception of knowledge that the Circle had been ascribing to the *Tractatus*.

Arguing from the standpoint of the intersubjectivity of the physicalist language, Neurath continued to press the point in "Protocol Statements" (1932b) that it did not matter whose protocol statements are used to check scientific claims. Partially in response to him, Carnap abandoned his insistence on methodological solipsism even in its weakened sense and adopted a straightforward physicalistic construal of fallible protocols. But he added: "this is a question not of two mutually inconsistent views, but rather two different methods for structuring the language of science which are both possible and legitimate" (1932c/1987, 457). Carnap here made first use of the famous Principle of Tolerance of *Logical Syntax*: "Everyone is at liberty to build up his own logic, i.e. his own form of language, as he wishes. All that is required of him is that, if he wishes to discuss it, he must state his methods clearly and give syntactical rules instead of philosophical arguments" (1934/1937, §17).

So Carnap did not fully accept Neurath's argument (whose private language argument had a broader scope than his own), nor Neurath's specific proposal for the form that protocol statements should take (either here or in his later "Testability and Meaning" (Carnap 1936–37, 12–13)). The ultimate reason why, it turns out, derives from his only just emerging mature conception of the nature of philosophy: "The logic of science takes the place of the inextricable tangle of problems which is known as philosophy" (Carnap 1934/1937, §72). From about mid-1932 until the fall of 1935, Carnap conceived of philosophy as the study of the "syntax" of the language of science (later semantics was included). This logic of science was continuous with philosophy in its a priori method. Empirical concerns did not play directly into the exploration of the consistency of various logics and of the expressive power of various logico-linguistic frameworks. That human beings cannot employ phenomenalist protocol languages in justificatory capacities would, as Neurath thought, only provide empirical considerations that bear on possible applications of such models in epistemological contexts, but not on their logical probity itself. The logician of science was not debarred from considering them. Yet as Carnap also stressed, the logic of science was not an end in itself and the point was to develop reform proposals that are "useful and productive in practice" for "particular point[s] of the language of science" (ibid., §86). But this only showed that language choice was a pragmatic issue of convenience and instrumental efficiency, not a factual one. Conceptions of a supposed epistemic order no longer dictated the answer to the questions about protocol statements. Instead, physicalistic languages were preferred for the pragmatic advantage they bestowed on reconstructions of scientific theories.

4. After Epistemology: The Logic of Science

Carnap's methodological message now was that after the rejection of speculative metaphysics by Kant and the rejection of his synthetic a priori in empiricist epistemology, a third step needed to be taken: the rejection of the mixture of psychological and logical concerns typical in that epistemology for the adoption of a strict logic of science. When it concerned evidential relations, Carnap's logic of science was concerned no longer with doxastic but with a kind of propositional justification, that is, justification not of individual believings but of propositions in light of available evidence independently of their appreciation by a subject—where evidence is conceived of independently of its appreciation by a subject. Beyond that, philosophy pursued as logic of science could offer but different ways of conceptualizing contested scientific notions: it made "proposals" and explored conceptual possibilities. (Later Carnap called these proposals "explications" (1950, §§3–5).)

In 1932 Neurath had declared that "within a consistent physicalism there can be no 'theory of knowledge,' at least not in the traditional form. It could only consist in defense actions against metaphysics, i.e. unmasking meaningless terms. Some problems of the theory of knowledge will perhaps be transformable into empirical questions so that they can find a place within unified science" (1932a/1983, 67). Two tasks were here assigned to whatever was to be philosophy's successor discipline in unified science: unmasking meaningless terms and asking empirical questions about knowledge production. Both represented different aspects of what unified science contained alongside all of the first-order disciplines: a scientific metatheory. This higher-order theory of science comprised logical inquires as well as empirical ones.

By discarding the epistemological-elucidatory ambitions of his methodological solipsism, Carnap's position was brought into agreement with this conception. Unlike Neurath, however, Carnap stressed an element of continuity in the replacement of traditional philosophy by the logic of science because its methods of inquiry remained a priori. What Carnap was able to add to Neurath's "defensive" task for the logic of science, moreover, was his conventionalist constructivism concerning alternative frameworks. This was a widening of the scope of scientific metatheory that Neurath could accept. That Carnap's position, in turn, did not rule out of the court of scientific metatheory all naturalistic concerns is made clear by his remark that the logic of science is itself but part of a still more comprehensive inquiry, the "theory of science," which comprises also "empirical investigation of scientific activity," namely, "historical, sociological and, above all, psychological inquiries" (Carnap 1934/1937, §72). It was precisely these fields that Neurath differentiated from the logic of science as "the behavioristics of scholars" in which he located his own concerns with protocol statements (1936/1983, 169) and that Philipp Frank later called the "pragmatics of science" (1957/2004, 360) and in which he investigated external determinants of theory choice. So both Carnap and Neurath (and Frank) recognized the need for both logical and empirical branches of scientific metatheory, but they pursued their own detailed work in different branches.

Their final proposals concerning protocols reflect this. For Neurath, protocols were complex statements containing embedded clauses meant to indicate different sets of conditions which the acceptance of scientific observation reports is subject to (see, e.g., his 1932b/1983 and Uebel 2009). By treating protocol statements as testimony whose acceptance is circumscribed in particular ways, Neurath moved away from any concern one might have—and Schlick did have (1934)—about the "foundation of knowledge" in one's own first-hand experience. First-person authority was, if not wholly undermined, then radically subverted: in principle, one's own protocol carried no more weight than another's. Carnap likewise was no longer concerned with personal beliefs but knowledge claims and their objective evidence. Where Neurath sought to outline canons of report acceptance, Carnap's work concentrated on isolating the logical relations of deductive and inductive support that protocols afforded to more theoretical statements. He merely required that protocol statements in the everyday thing-language feature predicates for observable properties, leaving it to psychology to determine exactly what is and is not observable (1936–37, 13). Concern with acceptance conditions lay outside his remit.

So one subject-centered form of epistemology—albeit a non-traditional one that was socio-naturalized and warrant-centered—continued to be practiced as part of metatheory in unified science, but not as Carnap's logic of science which kept still greater distance from the tradition. Of course, already in the epistemological phase of his career Carnap had paid no attention to philosophical skepticism: the *Aufbau*'s defense of the objectivity of science proceeded from intra-scientific worries. His move from epistemology to logic of science in the mid-1930s was a further radicalization. In the *Aufbau* rational reconstructionism meant abstraction from how people in practice justify their knowledge claims and the sole focus on sustaining the extensional validity of their beliefs as reconstructed. When Carnap "cleansed" epistemology (1936c, 36) by rejecting previously held "psychologistic" assumptions, he moved from rational reconstructions of subject-based beliefs to logical explications of knowledge claims independent of particular epistemic subjects. (His later work on the semantic concept of confirmation (1950) is of a piece with this.) What is significant about this move is not so much that he rejected naturalistic reasoning as inapplicable in the logic of science (he allowed it in the empirical part of scientific metatheory), but what he deemed to be so unduly psychological: the notion of doxastic justification and the assumption of the epistemic priority of the phenomenal language and of personal protocol languages.

It is notable that by dropping the doctrine of the epistemic priority of phenomenal over physicalist beliefs, Carnap abandoned traditional epistemology as he understood it. This move leaves open, of course, that he viewed the priority conception as a potentially plausible empirical but philosophically irrelevant thesis. His 1961 *Aufbau* Preface indicates that he saw nothing wrong with it in principle, but also that he still strongly preferred the physical basis of the thing-language for reconstructing the concepts of empirical science. This suggests that for Carnap—as for Neurath but for different reasons—the concerns of epistemology and the philosophy of science were discontinuous. Note, moreover, that for the longest time, the priority conception was challenged only by theorists expressly arguing against the epistemological tradition like Quine (1969) or, differently, Wilfrid Sellars (1956/1997). Philosophers exercised by skepticism, in particular, rarely questioned it until John McDowell's attack on the "highest common factor" element in the argument from illusion (1982) and Michael Williams' attack on "epistemological realism" (1990), both to expose unwarranted skeptical assumptions. By contrast, what prompted Carnap's abandonment of the priority conception was the rediscovery of his own earlier disregard of skepticism and his resolve to still more resolutely understand the complexities of scientific knowledge entirely from within (albeit in purely logical terms). This suggests that for all their differences about how such a program was to be executed, Carnap was much closer to Quine than is often supposed (especially if the complementarity of his own logic of science and Neurath and Frank's pragmatics of science is recognized as intended, however imperfectly so).

References

Ayer, Alfred J. (ed.), 1959, *Logical Positivism*, New York: Free Press.
Carnap, Rudolf, 1928, *Der logische Aufbau der Welt*, Berlin: Bernary, 2nd ed. Hamburg: Meiner, 1961, trans. *The Logical Structure of the World*, Berkeley: University of California Press, 1967, repr. Chicago: Open Court, 2003.
Carnap, Rudolf, 1930, "Die alte und die neue Logik," *Erkenntnis* 1, 12–26, trans. "The Old and the New Logic," in Ayer 1959, 60–81.
Carnap, Rudolf, 1932a, "Die physikalische Sprache als Unversalsprache der Wissenschaft," *Erkenntnis* 2, 432–65, transl. with introductions by the author and M. Black *The Unity of Science*, London: Kegan, Paul, Trench Teubner & Co., 1934.
Carnap, Rudolf, 1932b, "Psychologie in physikalischer Sprache," *Erkenntnis* 3, 107–42, trans. "Psychology in Physicalist Language," in Ayer 1959, 165–98.
Carnap, Rudolf, 1932c, "Über Protokollsätze," *Erkenntnis* 3, 215–28, trans. "On Protocol Sentences" in *Noûs* 21 (1987), 457–70.
Carnap, Rudolf, 1934, *Logische Syntax der Sprache* (Schriften zur wissenschaftlichen Weltauffassung 8), Vienna: Springer, rev. ed. transl. by A. Smeaton, *The Logical Syntax of Language*, London: Kegan, Paul, Trench Teubner & Cie, 1937, repr. Chicago: Open Court, 2002.
Carnap, Rudolf, 1936a, "Über die Einheitssprache der Wissenschaft. Logische Bemerkungen zum Project einer Enzyklopädie," *Actes du Congres Internationale de Philosophie Scientifique, Sorbonne, Paris 1935*, Facs. II, "Unité de la Science," Paris: Herman & Cie, 60–70.
Carnap, Rudolf, 1936b, "Wahrheit und Bewährung," *Actes du Congres Internationale de Philosophie Scientifique, Sorbonne, Paris 1935*, Facs. IV, "Induction et Probabilité," Paris: Hermann & Cie., 18–23, trans. with additions "Truth and Confirmation" in Feigl and Sellars (eds.), *Readings in Philosophical Analysis*, New York: Appleton-Century-Crofts, 1949, 119–27.
Carnap, Rudolf, 1936c, "Von der Erkenntnistheorie zur Wissenschaftslogik," *Actes du Congress Internationale de Philosophie Scientifique, Sorbonne, Paris 1935*, Facs. I "Philosophie Scientifique et Empirisme Logique," Paris: Herman & Cie, 36–41.
Carnap, Rudolf, 1936–37, "Testability and Meaning," *Philosophy of Science* 3, 419–71; 4, 1–40.
Carnap, Rudolf, 1950, *Logical Foundations of Probability*, Chicago: University of Chicago Press.
Carnap, Rudolf, 1963, "Intellectual Autobiography," in P.A. (ed.), *The Philosophy of Rudolf Carnap*, LaSalle: Open Court, 1963, 3–84.
Carnap, Rudolf, 1966, *Philosophical Foundations of Physics*, New York: Basic Books, 2nd rev. ed. *An Introduction to the Philosophy of Science*, 1974, repr. New York: Dover, 1995.
Castañeda, Hector-Neri, 1967, "Private Language Problem," in P. Edwards et al. (eds.), 1967, *Encyclopedia of Philosophy*, New York: Macmillan and The Free Press, 1967, vol. 6, 459–64.
Frank, Philipp, 1957, *Philosophy of Science. The Link between Science and Philosophy*. Englewood Cliffs: Prentice-Hall, repr. New York: Dover: 2004.
Friedman, Michael, 1987, "Carnap's *Aufbau* Reconsidered," *Noûs* 21, 521–45, repr. in Friedman 1999, 89–113.
Friedman, Michael, 1992, "Epistemology in the *Aufbau*," in *Synthese* 93, 15–57, repr. with postscript in Friedman 1999, 114–64.
Friedman, Michael, 1999, *Reconsidering Logical Positivism*, Cambridge: Cambridge University Press.
McDowell, John, 1982, "Criteria, Defeasibility and Knowledge," *Proceedings of the British Academy* 68, 455–79, repr. in McDowell, *Meaning, Knowledge & Reality*, Cambridge, Mass.: Harvard University Press, 1998, 369–94.

Mormann, Thomas, 2007, "Carnap's Logical Empiricism, Values and American Pragmatism," *Journal of General Philosophy of Science* 38, 127–46.
Neurath, Otto, 1931a, *Empirische Soziologie. Der wissenschaftliche Gehat der Geschichte undf Nationalökonomie*, repr. in Neurath, *Gesammelte philosophische und methodologische Schriften* (ed. by R. Haller and H. Rutte), Vienna: Hölder-Pichler-Tempsky, 1981, 423–527, partly trans. "Empirical Sociology," in Neurath, *Empiricism and Sociology* (ed. by M. Neurath and R.S. Cohen), Dordrecht: Reidel, 1973, 391–421.
Neurath, Otto, 1931b, "Physikalismus," *Scientia* 50, 297–303, trans. "Physicalism" in Neurath 1983, 52–7.
Neurath, Otto, 1932a, "Soziologie im Physikalismus," *Erkenntnis* 2, 393–431, trans. "Sociology and Physicalism," in Ayer 1959, 282–320, and "Sociology in the Framework of Physicalism," in Neurath 1983, 58–90.
Neurath, Otto, 1932b, "Protokollsätze," *Erkenntnis* 3, 204–14, trans. "Protocol Sentences," in Ayer 1959, 199–208, and "Protocol Statements," in Neurath 1983, 91–9.
Neurath, Otto, 1934, "Radikaler Physikalismus und 'wirkliche Welt'," *Erkenntnis* 4, 346–62, trans. "Radical Physicalism and 'the Real World'," in Neurath 1983, 100–14.
Neurath, Otto, 1936, "Physikalismus und Erkenntnisforschung," *Theoria* 2, 97–105, 234–236, trans. "Physicalism and Knowledge," in Neurath 1983, 159–171.
Neurath, Otto, 1941, "Universal Jargon and Terminology," *Proceedings of the Aristotel-ian Society* New Series 41, 127–48, repr. in Neurath 1983, 213–29.
Neurath, Otto, 1983, *Philosophical Papers 1913–1946* (ed. by R.S. Cohen and M. Neurath), Dordrecht: Reidel.
Pincock, Christopher, 2005, "A Reserved Reading of Carnap's Aufbau," *Pacific Philosophical Quarterly* 86, 518–43.
Quine, W.V.O., 1951, "Two Dogmas of Empiricism," *The Philosophical Review* 60, 20–43, repr. in Quine *From a Logical Point of View*, rev. ed. 1980, Cambridge, Mass.: Harvard University Press.
Quine, W.V.O., 1969, "Epistemology Naturalized," in Quine *Ontological Relativity and Other Essays*, New York: Columbia University Press, 69–90.
Richardson, Alan, 1998, *Carnap's Construction of the World*, Cambridge: Cambridge University Press.
Schlick, Moritz, 1918, *Allgemeine Erkenntnislehre*, Berlin: Springer, 1918, 2nd rev. ed. 1925, transl. *General Theory of Knowledge*, LaSalle: Open Court, 1974.
Schlick, Moritz, 1934, "Über das Fundament der Erkenntnis," *Erkenntnis* 4, 79–99, transl. "The Foundation of Knowledge," in Ayer 1959, 209–27.
Sellars, Wilfrid, 1956, "Empiricism and the Philosophy of Mind," in H. Feigl and M. Scriven (eds.), *The Foundations of Science and the Concepts of Psychology and Psychoanalysis* (Minnesota Studies in the Philosophy of Science Vol. 2), Minneapolis: University of Minnesota Press. Reprinted in Sellars, *Empiricism and the Philosophy of Mind* (ed. by R. Brandom), Cambridge, Mass.: Harvard University Press, 1997, 13–118.
Uebel, Thomas, 2007, *Empiricism at the Crossroads. The Vienna Circle's Protocol-Sentence Debate*, Chicago: Open Court.
Uebel, Thomas, 2009, "Neurath's Protocol Statements Revisited. Sketch of a Theory of Scientific Testimony," *Studies in History and Philosophy of Science* 40, 4–13.
Williams, Michael, 1990, *Unnatural Doubts*, Oxford: Blackwell.

70
WILLARD VAN ORMAN QUINE
Richard Creath

Willard Van Orman Quine (1908–2000) was one of the most important epistemologists of the twentieth century. His name will be linked, possibly forever, with such prominent themes as empiricism, holism, pragmatism, simplicity, underdetermination, fallibilism, and naturalism. While he was not the first to discuss any of these themes, he brought them together in an intriguing and evolving view that was first sketched in the "Introduction" to *Methods of Logic* of 1950. Especially from 1960 onward, epistemology became increasingly the focus of Quine's work, and his view continued to develop in substantial ways for the rest of his life.

1. The 1930s and 40s

Quine began publishing in 1932. By the beginning of 1950 he had four books, thirty-eight articles, four abstracts, sixteen reviews, and three other miscellaneous publications in print, almost none dealing with epistemological topics. It would not be unreasonable to view Carnap's "Principle of Tolerance," which he sometimes expressed as the principle of the conventionality of language forms, as a central part of Carnap's epistemology in which logic and mathematics are to be treated as true in virtue of the language chosen and hence as, in some sense, conventional. It might therefore seem reasonable to treat Quine's "Truth by Convention" (1936) as also epistemological because he is thought to express doubts there about the idea that logic could be true by convention. But this paper was written when Quine was, in his own words, very much the disciple of Carnap (Quine 1971: xxiii), and on internal grounds the paper seems not to have been directed against Carnap. In fact, Quine shows there how the truths of logic and mathematics to the exclusion of other truths can be held to be conventional. This technique of conventional truth assignment would "forestall awkward metaphysical questions as to our *a priori* insight into necessary truths" (1936: 119), but it would be "idle elaboration to carry the process further" (1936: 120). In this way, construed as a kind of policy (Carnap would have called it a "proposal"), calling logic and mathematics conventional would be neither empty, nor uninteresting, nor false.

Nearly twenty years later (in 1954, when "Carnap and Logical Truth" (1963a) was written), Quine saw in "Truth by Convention" a powerful argument against calling logic true by convention. The argument is that in order to state the conventions and have this statement generate all the myriad such truths, the full resources of logic would already have to be in place at the time the conventions are stated. The 1936 text, however, recognized that this involves no vicious regress, for "the verbal formulation of conventions is no more a prerequisite of the adoption of conventions than the writing of a grammar is a prerequisite of speech; ... explicit exposition of the conventions is merely one of the many important uses of a completed language" (123). As he points out immediately after this, "this account accords well with what we actually do" (123). So as of 1936 Quine saw no argument to show that logic cannot be true by convention, and he embraced the policy of calling logic and mathematics conventional. To be sure, he did wonder what might be the explanatory force of calling something an implicit convention. One might ask in return why a policy or proposal is expected to have explanatory force.

From 1939 onward Quine began to challenge Carnap's analytic/synthetic distinction, abandoning it probably sometime in 1947. But this was in private. His publications, by contrast, were mostly in logic and set theory, fields that Quine tended to separate from his philosophic work. He wrote philosophic papers too, but until 1950 these were not directly about epistemic matters, but instead concerned reference, ontology, indirect discourse, and modality.

2. The 1950s: The Classic Statements

In 1950 Quine published the first edition of *Methods of Logic*. In December he gave "Two Dogmas of Empiricism" as a talk, which was published early the next year. It is in "Empiricism Without the Dogmas," the final section of this paper, that we find the classic statement of Quine's epistemology. The "Introduction" to *Methods of Logic* covers much the same ground, and so it will be useful to consider these two pieces together. We will also consider two other papers written in the 1950s. These are not primarily about epistemology, but are useful for understanding the general view.

The Basic Idea

Quine's central epistemic image in "Two Dogmas" is that of a fabric (or field) containing the totality of our beliefs meeting experience only around the edges and meeting that experience together as a corporate body rather than as separate statements. This Quine calls holism. When there is a conflict with experience, some of the statements in the fabric must change. The required changes can be made in many different ways, and so our beliefs are underdetermined by experience alone without consideration of any extra-evidential factors. This underdetermination is thoroughgoing. Any claim can be revised, including those of logic and mathematics (fallibilism). And any statement can be preserved, *if* we are prepared to make drastic enough changes elsewhere.

Not all changes are equally likely, however. Some statements, pictured as near the periphery, are sensitive to a certain narrow range of experiences but not to others. The statements are said to be germane to the narrow range of experiences, meaning that the relative likelihood that the statements will be abandoned, given an incorrect prediction concerning those experiences, is high. Even here statements as close as you like to the edge can be preserved when prediction goes awry, if changing them would involve a drastic overall cost elsewhere; we can always plead hallucination. Other statements might be less sensitive but to a wider range of experiences. These are pictured as further from the periphery and are described as having a wider empirical reference. In later writings the vocabulary shifts to empirical "focus," though probably with no change to the underlying idea. Finally, there are statements, exemplified by those of logic and mathematics, thought of as at the center of the field. These are equally germane to all experiences, and least likely to be revised.

Beyond this, there are some general principles that guide our revisions. One is conservatism, the idea that we prefer to revise as little as possible. The second is simplicity, though this is not defined. To a certain extent conservatism and simplicity pull in opposite directions, but what is sought is a balance between the two. Both principles are vital to Quine's epistemology, but in different ways.

In *Methods*, but not in "Two Dogmas" he shows how conservatism underwrites the feeling of many that logic and mathematics are necessarily true. Because logic and mathematics bear on so many other areas, changes in logic or mathematics would require many changes in every part of the fabric of our belief. Given conservatism we would prefer not to make such changes if we do not have to. Given that we can save any part of our belief we want, we will make changes in logic and mathematics last if at all. This makes logic and mathematics appear, misleadingly, to be utterly insensitive to whatever happens in experience. Logico-mathematical beliefs can be altered if there is a compensating gain in simplicity, and the principles involved in these changes are the same as for any empirical theory or claim. The differences are only in degree.

Though not defined, simplicity is deployed systematically in "Two Dogmas" to underwrite ontological decisions. Physical objects are introduced "for working a manageable structure into the flux of experience" (1951: 41). In the 1951 version of "Two Dogmas" Quine makes the same case for positing irrational numbers over and above the rationals, but "the factor of simplification is more overwhelming in the case of physical objects than in the numerical case" (42). And it does not stop there for "Objects at the atomic level and beyond are posited to make the laws of macroscopic objects, and ultimately the laws of experience, simpler and more manageable" (42). The attempt in all this is to show, contra Carnap, that all ontological questions are on a par with the questions of natural science.

Quine does nothing in "Two Dogmas" to argue that the more conservative choice of doctrine or the simpler of two alternatives is more likely to be true. Nor does he claim that he needs no such argument. In later years he was to claim for his empiricism that it was simply a result of science, but he does not make a corresponding claim for conservatism or simplicity here. Of course, even if these two principles were vouched for by methods that include the methods themselves, this would hardly convince anyone who was genuinely worried about them. Later Quine himself expressed worries on these topics.

There is one other principle in revising our beliefs that Quine talks about in *Methods*, but not in "Two Dogmas." This is the principle of preferring to preserve statements about physical objects such as 'My pen is in my hand,' that seem closer to possible experience over other statements not so situated. The reason given is that "It is only by such an allocation of priority that we can hope to claim any empirical content or objective reference for the system as a whole" (1950: xiii). As a principle of revision this is extremely interesting and insightful. But despite arguing in later years that observation reports are the opening wedge into reference, Quine did not in later writing return to this as a priority in the revision of our beliefs. We are told in *Methods* that this principle is "somewhat opposed" by conservatism because a change in laws would be more massive than a change of a particular claim at the periphery. But we are also told that despite the apparent opposition between these two principles, one involves the other because "the connection between a statement such as 'My pen is in my hand' and the experiences which are said to verify it is itself a matter of general principles central to the system" (1950: xiii). No attempt is made to explore or resolve this further.

Quine's discussion of logic in "Two Dogmas" is primarily designed to show that it is epistemically on a par with other scientific theories. In "Carnap and Logical Truth," written in 1954, he says a bit more. As indicated above by this point Quine thought that his earlier "Truth by Convention" showed convincingly that logic could not be true by convention. I shall not reargue the case of what the earlier paper showed. Now Quine holds that logic is obvious and set theory is conventional, but he also says that logic could become conventional and set theory could become obvious. It is difficult to tell what his word 'conventional' means, because while logic could not in principle *be* conventional, logic could become conventional. The notion of obviousness is a bit less inscrutable. About the only thing that Quine could mean in calling logic obvious (and by logic Quine means the truths of the first-order predicate calculus classically and extensionally conceived) is that the truths thereof are so far behind the lines of the moving front of science that we do not seriously consider revising them. Obviousness, then, is an epistemic status of sorts not shared by all other scientific theories. But this in no way compromises the kind of parity between logic and recognizably empirical claims that Quine was trying to establish in "Two Dogmas."

This then is Quine's basic epistemology: Our beliefs meet experience together (holism). When revision is required by experience, there are many ways to do this (underdetermination). In undertaking such revisions the twin and sometimes opposing principles of conservatism and simplicity are centrally involved. The idea that all or even most epistemic issues can be addressed by appeal to principles so few in number and so elegant in their expression is surely attractive. Though Quine's basic idea was to be modified somewhat in the remaining fifty years of his life, this general architecture is discernible throughout. Before we get to that, however, there are some general interpretive questions that must be raised about this epistemology.

Interpretive Questions on the Basic Idea

If our theories of the natural world are underdetermined by the flood of evidence that we have or shall have, then the question of what Quine meant by his writings in the 1950s must be even more severely underdetermined by our more sharply limited evidence. It is tempting, therefore, to read Quine's later views back into his earlier works. The temptation should be resisted because Quine's way of speaking and the doctrines themselves continued to evolve. We have no choice, it seems, but to probe the texts themselves. We might not always get a definitive answer. Where we do, this is all to the good, and where we do not, even that limitation is worth knowing.

What sort of thing, for example, does the fabric or field under discussion contain? Beliefs, of course, but these, whether true or false, are sententially expressed. Strictly speaking what admit of truth and falsity are individual acts of utterance because the truth of the sentence itself will vary with context of its utterance. But it simplifies logical theory to abstract via paraphrasing from these individual acts to something whose truth does not vary with the context. These Quine calls statements, and he is quite consistent in representing the fabric or field as made up of statements. These are items that bear logical relations to one another, a fact that is hardly surprising given that Quine first presents his epistemological view in the "Introduction" to a logic book, *Methods of Logic*.

Quine emphasizes these logical relations and speaks often enough as though this is what he has primarily in mind. Indeed, unless this were so it is hard to see how an argument can be made for any interesting version of an underdetermination thesis. Why not stop with the announcement that "Any statement can be held true come what may"? If it is simply a question of what we can be disposed to utter, there should be no need for changes elsewhere in the system, much less drastic changes. But Quine also speaks as though what he has primarily in mind are causal relations among beliefs, that is, among dispositions to make utterances. What relations could there be other than causal ones between experience, which is neither true nor false, and statements, which are supposed to be non-contextually one or the other? Quine speaks of the relative likelihood that a change in the acceptance of one statement would be followed by a change in our acceptance of some other. This sounds causal or, more minimally, merely descriptive in some narrow sense. There is even a third interpretation that makes the revision of statements a matter of social rules and hence normative. He tells us (1950: xiii) that overruling a multiplicity of statements about experience would under certain circumstances "invite criticism." This comment is somehow both normative and descriptive, but it is too fleeting to bear much weight.

Given the interpretive difficulty, it is tempting to appeal to some version of Quine's later defense of naturalism to argue that he always had the causal/descriptive idea in mind. Unfortunately, Quine's later views on naturalism are open to various interpretations and cannot readily help even if we could be sure, which we cannot, that Quine's views had not evolved as the decades passed. He speaks so consistently in "Two Dogmas" in ways that finesse this interpretive issue that he must have been leaving it deliberately open. We shall as well.

In "Two Dogmas" and *Methods* Quine speaks consistently of getting belief to conform to or, at least, not conflict with, experience, and he uses the word 'experience' rather than 'evidence' here. Later he would mean by 'evidence' either observable objects and events or else the stimulation of nerve endings. In the 1950s, however, 'experience' was the word, and he does seem to mean, at least sometimes, private sensory experience. This might have been no more than a verbal concession to his colleagues. But even then he apparently did not see it as in conflict with his overarching physicalism. And it was a form of speech that appeared more rarely in his later writing.

As indicated earlier, underdetermination at this stage seems to be a claim primarily about logical relations rather than about psychological ones. Also in Quine's presentations underdetermination is announced before simplicity and conservatism are invoked. This strongly suggests that he has not committed himself about any general underdetermination if those two principles are invoked. He seems to think that when simplicity is invoked the argument that there are physical objects is pretty convincing.

This suggests another question for those cases that Quine believes are underdetermined in the relevant sense. The choice between two hypotheses might not be completely settled (deductively determined) by all those claims that we might adduce as evidence concerning the choice. Even so, one of the two hypotheses might be favored, even dramatically so, by the evidence we have. Traditionally, philosophers have tried to address this issue by attempts at a probability theory. But Quine explicitly eschews such attempts in "Two Dogmas." What Quine does say about underdetermination in the 1950s simply does not allow us to tell whether there will never be a best among the available alternatives. If there is a best alternative, then the thesis of underdetermination is very much less important, and it will lack the philosophic consequences that Quine will later want to draw from it.

Finally among our interpretive issues is the question of how to understand simplicity. Later Quine says that simplicity is relevant to the thinking up of theories but not to the testing of them afterward. But this is certainly not his view in the 50s. In "Two Dogmas" simplicity is used to compare alternative theories, theories that presumably have already been thought up. And in 1954 Quine wrote "The Scope and Language of Science" (published in 1957) in which he said: "simplicity itself—in some sense of that difficult term—counts as a kind of evidence; and scientists have indeed long tended to look upon the simpler of the two hypotheses as not merely the more likable, but the more likely" (1957: 6). This is a fairly strong conception of what simplicity comes to. It was not to last.

3. Word and Object

Because the broad architecture of the classic 1950s texts remained, we can turn to noting changes that ensued over the next nearly fifty years. One of the most provocative developments in Quine's whole career came in *Word and Object* (WO) (Quine 1960) with his thesis of the indeterminacy of translation. This is the claim that in radical translation not only will there always be a multiplicity of manuals of translation very unlike one another but fully adequate to all the evidence and every other scientific consideration, but there is absolutely no fact of the matter as to which manual is the correct one. The thesis that there is no fact of the matter is not itself an epistemic one. But the claim about a multiplicity of scientifically adequate manuals of translation is certainly epistemic. So Quine begins the book with a largely methodological chapter in which he discusses his general view and especially simplicity and underdetermination. There are changes, which we shall note, and some old issues come out in sharper relief. WO also marks the beginning of a reorientation in Quine's philosophy in which epistemology replaces reference and ontology at center stage.

The basic idea there is his claim that "Scientific method was vaguely seen . . . as a matter of being guided by sensory stimuli, a taste for simplicity in some sense, and a taste for old things" (1960: 23). The reference to stimuli rather than experience as the touchstone of empirical adequacy is an indication of his now much more thorough behaviorism. Evidence is equated with nerve hits, though he is happy to speak of observation sentences, those that are directly conditioned by evidence. The emphasis on sentences rather than statements probably indicates no more than that his concern is with translation rather than logical theory.

Within the connections of some sentences with others, Quine acknowledges that some are logical while others are causal. This distinction can be made only by reference to so-called logical or causal laws, but these he says are just further sentences of the theory. "[B]ut any such interconnections of sentences must finally be due to the conditioning of sentences as responses to sentences as stimuli" (1960: 11). In short, the connections are understood causally. This is even more obvious with what he calls "circumstantial evidence": "What we are doing when we amass and use circumstantial evidence is to let ourselves be actuated as sensitively as possible by chain stimulations as they reverberate through our theory, from present stimulations, via the interanimation of sentences" (1960: 18). This, of course, does not distinguish using evidence well and using it badly.

In *WO* simplicity comes to have a curiously dual character. Its earlier role is still there. It still underwrites the introduction of frameworks of theoretical entities over and above ordinary middle-sized physical objects. It still underwrites the existence of physical objects as things glimpsed over and above the glimpses of them. Apparently, simplicity can help us choose among alternative hypotheses that we have before us.

So far this is not new. But Quine adds: "Yet this supposed quality of simplicity is more easily sensed than described. Perhaps our vaunted sense of simplicity, or of likeliest explanation, is in many cases just a feeling of conviction attaching to the blind resultant of the interplay of chain stimulations in their various strengths" (1960: 19). This seems to say that simplicity is a feature of whatever theory we happen to come up with. If so, it is hard to see how it could do any of the work he is having it do regarding frameworks of theoretical entities and of physical objects. Later he says: "Simplicity is not a desideratum on a par with conformity to observation. Observation serves to test hypotheses after adoption; simplicity prompts their adoption for testing" (19). Quine seems to have demoted simplicity from the context of justification to the context of discovery. In wanting or needing a very strong underdetermination thesis, there might have been reason for desiring to minimize the effectiveness of simplicity. Quine does seem both to minimize simplicity, and also to use it in the old way. This duality on the topic was to continue for the rest of Quine's career.

In view of the indeterminacy thesis noted above, underdetermination looms large in *WO*. Earlier, underdetermination had seemed to be primarily a logical rather than a psychological claim. With Quine's overwhelmingly behavioral presentation, this is no longer clear. The account here seems to aim at the explanation of belief and not at its justification. Besides, the later stages of the indeterminacy argument need a psychological version of underdetermination. In any case, it seems clear that the focus of Quine's attention is in explaining belief rather than in justifying it, though the latter is not entirely gone.

In the 1950s Quine had presented underdetermination before raising principles of simplicity and conservatism, and given simplicity, he did not seem to think that the question of the existence of physical objects was seriously underdetermined. Now, in *WO*, he makes it very clear that our theories of, say, molecules are underdetermined by all the truths at the commonsense level about ordinary things together with an ideal organon of scientific method. Such an organon would include simplicity and other principles. More precisely he says that theory is conceivably underdetermined and then that it is probably so, and then he just takes underdetermination for granted. His only stated reason is "It seems likelier, if only on account of symmetries or dualities, that countless alternative theories would be tied for first place" (1960: 23).

4. Naturalized Epistemology

In 1969 Quine published "Epistemology Naturalized." It captured the attention of the philosophical world: Some marched proudly under its banner, and others bemoaned it. But there was probably no universal agreement as to what naturalism was, in epistemology or elsewhere. For Quine 'naturalism' is a convenient term to represent his whole point of view. It is sometimes represented as a premise in an argument for his views, but that sounds more like first philosophy (foundationalism) than Quine could be comfortable with.

Much of the paper is presented as a negative commentary on Carnap's *Aufbau* and in particular on its aim to provide a rational reconstruction. Probably the most famous passage of Quine's paper comes at this point:

> But why all this creative reconstruction, all this make-believe? The stimulation of his sensory receptors is all the evidence anybody has to go on, ultimately, in arriving at his picture of the world. Why not see how this construction really proceeds? Why not settle for psychology?
>
> (1969a: 75)

He then describes this as "a surrender of the epistemological burden to psychology" (1969a: 75). Given the thoroughly behavioral account in WO, this seems (as it did to many of Quine's readers) to be settling for a purely descriptive account of how the neuro-physiological connections do in fact go, to the exclusion of whether this is done well or badly. A few pages later Quine goes on in the same vein:

> Epistemology, or something like it, simply falls into place as a chapter of psychology and hence of natural science. It studies a natural phenomenon, viz., a physical human subject. This human subject is accorded a certain experimentally controlled input—certain patterns of irradiation in assorted frequencies, for instance—and in the fullness of time the subject delivers as output a description of the three dimensional external world and its history. The relation between the meager input and the torrential output is a relation that we are prompted to study for somewhat the same reasons that always prompted epistemology; namely, in order to see how evidence relates to theory, and in what way one's theory of nature transcends any available evidence.
>
> (1969a: 82–3)

Again this seems aimed at describing the de facto relations of theory to evidence to the exclusion of questions of justification. Whether Quine himself thought that he was abandoning the normative is less clear. Later he was to say that there was still room for the normative, but one must add that Quine's notion of normativity here is somewhat idiosyncratic. Sometime in the 1970s—the publication was much delayed—he wrote:

> Naturalization of epistemology does not jettison the normative and settle for the indiscriminate description of ongoing procedures. For me normative epistemology is a branch of engineering. It is the technology of truth-seeking, or, in a more cautiously epistemological term, prediction.... There is no question here of ultimate value, as in morals; it is a matter of efficacy for an ulterior end, truth or prediction.
>
> (1986: 664–5)

How much of this Quine had in mind already in 1969, we might never know.

Quine's contemporaries drew a number of other readings of naturalized epistemology from Quine's text. They differ from one another, but each was inspired to some extent by Quine's suggestive phrasing. One such reading was that in naturalized epistemology there is no privileged philosophical vantage point from which to criticize the sciences. The old aim of justifying certain beliefs gives way to the bare description of the actual processes of belief acquisition. Similarly, the old aim of distinguishing between good and bad science gives way to describing how science actually is, to presenting the history and sociology of science.

A related interpretation held that naturalized philosophers are to give no instruction to their scientific colleagues. Whether Quine himself meets such a standard is less clear. In WO he is comfortable telling linguists what they can and cannot do. And "Truth by Convention" of 1936 was, in effect, telling one of the world's greatest geometers, David Hilbert, that he was quite wrong about geometry. But whether Quine would have counted himself as a naturalist at that time is open to question.

A further reading of naturalism has it that it is just the rejection that there are any first principles where this, in turn, is equated with denying an analytic/synthetic distinction and embracing holism. Naturalism in this sense adds little to the general point of view that Quine had defended from 1950 onward.

5. Other Late Writings

Quine's views continued to develop throughout his life. And there are a number of shorter and longer works after WO that deserve special mention but are usefully grouped together. The first topic will be simplicity, then *The Web of Belief*, then the more nuanced holism that gets developed in *Pursuit of Truth* and *From Stimulus to Science*, and finally a proposed reconciliation between the traditional focus of epistemology and the trenchant descriptivism of WO and "Epistemology Naturalized."

From 1950 onward simplicity was an important element in Quine's epistemology. In 1963 Quine devoted a short paper, "On Simple Theories of a Complex World," entirely to the topic. He does not try to define simplicity, though he links it here to the uniformity of nature. He recognizes that while truth is objective and in no way formulation dependent, simplicity is somewhat subjective precisely because it is formulation dependent. His rendering of the maxim of simplicity, therefore, is not that the simpler of two theories is more likely to be true but, rather, that "If two theories conform equally to past observations, the simpler of the two is seen as standing the better chance of confirmation in future observations" (1963b: 103). Quine tries to explain, not the truth of the maxim, but why people might believe it. He lists four considerations. These four are somewhat doubtful and all the more so because Quine and J.S. Ullian (1978: 69–73) list four entirely different considerations when they discuss the issue a few years later in *The Web of Belief*. These four are no more compelling than their predecessors.

Thereafter Quine's settled opinion seemed to be that simplicity (and conservatism and any other virtues that a hypothesis might have) is unlike fidelity to observation. Simplicity and the other virtues he calls normative, though not in the usual sense. They are normative only in that they would be heuristic matters relevant to the thinking up of theories but not to the testing of them afterwards. Observation, by contrast, is relevant to the testing of theories, and this is where the truth conditions and empirical content lie. This is pretty much the view that he had floated in WO, and it is plainly at odds with both the view of "The Scope and Language of Science" and with using simplicity as he still does to defend theoretical realism against some sort of instrumentalism or physical realism against phenomenalism.

The Web of Belief, co-authored with Ullian, appeared in 1970 shortly after "Epistemology Naturalized" with a second, much longer edition appearing in 1978. The book is entirely devoted to epistemological matters and enormously engaging. This is in part because it is aimed at undergraduates. But its orientation is also different from Quine's work in the 1960s. That earlier work had seemed severely descriptivist, concentrating on causal relations among nerve hits, behavioral dispositions, and overt speech.

Moreover, it had seemed to make little if any room for distinctions between reasoning well and good scientific practice on one hand and the free rein of prejudice on the other. *The Web of Belief* by contrast talks freely of the confirmation of theories and the distinction between good and bad science. Indeed, these seem to be the guiding themes of the book. We will address later whether this highly prescriptivist character can be reconciled with the descriptivist work.

Earlier work had talked of two principles beyond conformity to observation that guided the revision of theory, namely simplicity and conservatism. This book speaks of six "virtues" of hypotheses of which simplicity and conservatism are only two. The others are modesty, generality, refutability, and precision. These are said to overlap and to grade off into one another, so perhaps listing six is no very profound change from listing two. In any case Quine reverts to just simplicity and conservatism in later work.

Quine and Ullian discuss a wide variety of topics in the book, but given that it is addressed to undergraduates it would perhaps be unfair to think that all of what is said there represents Quine's considered view unless he repeats it in his later work. Because much of that later work also has epistemological matters among its major foci we can turn to that.

One of those matters is a more nuanced holism that Quine presents in *Pursuit of Truth* and elsewhere. It is a modification of his longstanding view with one dramatic departure. He begins by developing the notion of an observation sentence as the vehicle of scientific evidence. This is an occasion sentence that is both firmly associated with stimulation and intersubjective. The association with stimulation is one where the sentence commands assent or dissent outright given the stimulation independent of further investigation or the interests of investigators. The intersubjectivity requires that under relevantly similar stimulation the sentence get the same verdict from all linguistically competent members of the community. 'It is raining' and 'Birds are singing' would be examples.

Quine then introduces the notion of an observation categorical, a sentence compounded of observable sentences and having 'Whenever this, that' as its form. An observation categorical would be a standing sentence and thus suitable for implication from a theory. They are tested by pairs of observations, and 'Whenever it rains, birds are singing' would be an example. Quine claims that these categoricals involve no reification of or quantification over times.

Quine is still a holist though a more modest one. Our beliefs do not in general meet experience by themselves but we do not have to invoke the totality of belief in order to test them. In between the extremes is a chunk just large enough to imply an observation categorical, and this Quine calls a critical semantic mass. This holism is still very much in the spirit of the former one in that when the implied categorical proves to be in error and we must revise, there will in general be many ways to revise the chunk so as to restore conformity to observation. So belief is still underdetermined. Then Quine says something surprising. He tells us (1990: 14) that in making our revision we will exempt any purely logical truth, not on grounds of conservatism, but because the fateful implication would still hold without its help. This gives logic a very special epistemic status and creates in effect a two-tier system of confirmation. Much of Quine's fame rests on his having fashioned a single-tier system, so this is a dramatic departure indeed (cf. 1992: 14; 1995: 352).

Finally we have to see whether the following obvious tension in Quine's work can be resolved. Traditional epistemology and also *The Web of Belief* are frankly normative in that they give advice on how *rightly* to conduct our cognitive lives. They focus on distinctions between good and bad science and between those causes of belief that *do* provide justification and those that do not. *WO* and "Epistemology Naturalized," by contrast, seem to reject all this in favor of a purely descriptive account, that is, an account that makes no room for evaluative or normative claims.

Quine thinks that the two sides of this tension can be reconciled. To borrow some Kantian vocabulary, we can think of epistemic norms and evaluations, not as categorical imperatives, but as hypothetical ones. These hypothetical imperatives can, in turn, be thought of as factual claims linking means and ends. These are the facts of engineering, and this is exactly how Quine describes simplicity and conservatism. So instead of 'Take the MassPike' as a categorical imperative we get 'If you want to drive from Boston to Springfield in the shortest time, take the MassPike' as a hypothetical imperative. And from that we get 'The MassPike is the quickest driving route from Boston to Springfield' as a factual claim. The first is straightforwardly normative, and the last is straightforwardly descriptive. Or so they seem. And the last seems to capture the imperatival character of the second. How to make the corresponding transitions for simplicity and conservatism would be a very delicate business. Moreover, establishing the truth of the resultant descriptive claim will not be easy either. And this task is made more difficult by the fact that the word 'simplicity' is itself undefined. But all that is a separate issue from whether the purely descriptive account can be reconciled with a more frankly normative one. Quine's answer is yes.

References

Quine, W. V. O. (1936) "Truth by Convention" in *Philosophical Essays for A.N. Whitehead*, O.H. Lee, ed., NY: Longmans, 90–124.
—— (1950) *Methods of Logic*, NY: Holt.
—— (1951) "Two Dogmas of Empiricism" *The Philosophical Review*, 60: 20–43.
—— (1957) "The Scope and Language of Science" *British Journal for the Philosophy of Science* 8: 1–17.
—— (1960) *Word and Object*, Cambridge, MA: MIT.
—— (1963a) "Carnap and Logical Truth" in *The Philosophy of Rudolf Carnap*, Paul Schilpp, ed., LaSalle, IL: Open Court, 385–406.
—— (1963b) "On Simple Theories of a Complex World" *Synthese* 15: 107–11.
—— (1969a) "Epistemology Naturalized" in Quine: *Ontological Relativity and Other Essays*, NY: Columbia University Press, 69–90.
—— (1971) "Homage to Carnap" *Boston Studies in Philosophy of Science* 8: xxii–xxv.
—— (1978) *The Web of Belief* (with J.S. Ullian) revised edition, NY: Random House.
—— (1986) "Reply to Morton White" in *The Philosophy of W.V. Quine*, Lewis Hahn and Paul Schilpp, eds., LaSalle, IL: Open Court, 663–65.
—— (1990) *Pursuit of Truth*, Cambridge, MA: Harvard.
—— (1992) *Pursuit of Truth*, revised edition, Cambridge, MA: Harvard.
—— (1995) "Reactions" in *On Quine: New Essays*, Paolo Leonardi and Marco Santambrogio, eds., Cambridge: Cambridge University Press, 347–61.

Further Reading

Barrett, Robert and Roger Gibson, editors (1990) *Perspectives on Quine*, Oxford: Blackwell. (A good collection of essays on Quine with responses by Quine.)
Davidson, Donald and Jaakko Hintikka, editors (1969) *Words and Objections*, Dordrecht: Reidel. (A good collection of papers on Quine with responses by Quine.)
Gibson Jr., Roger F. (1982) *The Philosophy of W.V.O. Quine*, Tampa, FL: University of South Florida Press. (A systematic exposition of Quine's philosophy with emphasis on epistemology from Quine's later position.)

—— (1988) *Enlightened Empiricism*, Tampa, FL: University of South Florida Press. (A presentation of Quine's epistemology from the perspective of Quine's later work.)
—— editor (2004) *The Cambridge Companion to Quine*, Cambridge: Cambridge University Press. (A comprehensive recent collection of essays on Quine.)
Quine, W. V. O. (1969b) "Natural Kinds" in *Essays in Honor of Carl Hempel*, Nicholas Rescher et al. eds., Dordrecht: Reidel, 5–23. (Discusses the learning of natural kind terms.)
—— (1975) "On Empirically Equivalent Systems of the World" *Erkenntnis* 9: 313–28. (Discusses cases relevant to simplicity.)

71
JOHN LANGSHAW AUSTIN
Mark Kaplan

Introduction

John Langshaw Austin, born in 1911, was a major figure at Oxford University from the end of the Second World War until his death in 1961. He did not see a great deal into print. His influence was largely due to his lectures at Oxford and elsewhere, and to informal study groups he led. Indeed, most of the work now in print under his name was published posthumously. Of the thirteen essays in the current (third) edition of his *Philosophical Papers* (Austin 1979b) only seven had reached print by the time Austin died. *How to Do Things with Words* (Austin 1979a) was constructed from the William James lectures he delivered at Harvard University in 1955; *Sense and Sensibilia* (Austin 1962) from notes Austin wrote for (and others took on) his course lectures.

"Other Minds," which Austin delivered and published in 1946, and *Sense and Sensibilia* constitute the sum total of his published work on epistemology (although, as we shall see, attention to some of the rest of his work is important to assessing the value of Austin's contribution to epistemology). These two works are largely critical in nature, each an attempt to counter arguments to the effect that our epistemic situation is more fraught than one would ordinarily have thought—for example, arguments to the effect that we know little if anything of the world around us, and that we never really (or, at least never directly) see such objects as tables and chairs but can at best infer their presence from sense data. The most remarkable thing about how Austin sought to counter these arguments is the extent to which he appealed to what we would ordinarily say and do—the extent to which Austin appears to have presupposed its being a condition of adequacy, on what we say by way of doing epistemology, that it accord faithfully with what we would say in ordinary circumstances.

This commitment to pursuing epistemology (and philosophy in general) in a way that respects some such condition of adequacy—this commitment to what came to be called "ordinary language philosophy" (a term with which Austin was not entirely happy (Austin 1979b: 182))—is, depending on one's point of view, either one of the strengths of his work, or what most undermines it. Not long after his death, the reception of *Sense and Sensibilia* and *Philosophical Papers* pretty much established the latter point of view as the default view. As a consequence, Austin's epistemological work has been relegated to the margins of the field, and (except in one small corner of the literature on skepticism) is not often cited. I will be suggesting that it is a relegation that is undeserved.

In what follows, I mean to trace a (necessarily selective) line of thought that runs through the anti-skeptical struggle of "Other Minds" and *Sense and Sensibilia*—and, in so doing, highlight some of the most important general conclusions Austin drew as to what an epistemology can properly say. I will then ask by what right Austin thought he could base those conclusions, to the extent he did, on appeals to what we would ordinarily say. This will, in turn, lead us to examine more closely exactly how the condition of adequacy those appeals would seem to presuppose is to be understood. I will be suggesting that the condition is more subtle, and his reasons for imposing it far better, than his critics have appreciated.

Knowledge

"Other Minds" is nominally meant to address skeptical concerns about our capacity to know the minds of others. But it consists mostly in an examination of how philosophers have gone wrong on their way to waxing skeptical about knowledge of the world around us. The argument from ignorance receives especially thorough treatment.

By "the argument from ignorance," I mean a form of argument of which Descartes' dream argument in the First Meditation is the most famous instance. There Descartes argues that, because "there are never any sure signs by means of which being awake can be distinguished from being asleep," and so no sure sign that he is not in the midst of a vivid dream, he has sufficient reason to doubt (and so sufficient reason to deny that he knows) even so modest a proposition about the world around him as the one that he is sitting by the fire holding a piece of paper in his hand (Descartes 1984/5, vol. 2: 13). It is a form of argument that can be described as challenging a person's claim to know that P, by (i) fixing on a proposition Q, such that she cannot but admit that, if Q, then she does not know that P, and maintaining that, *if she does not know that not-Q, then she does not know that P*; (ii) arguing (whether on the basis of her never having conducted any inquiry that would rule out the truth of Q, or—as in the case of Descartes' argument—its being impossible for her to have conducted such an inquiry) that, however improbable it might be that Q is true, *she does not know that not-Q*; and (iii) concluding from the foregoing that, therefore, *she does not know that P*. Descartes' dream argument can thus be viewed as just what results from substituting the proposition that Descartes is sitting by the fire with a piece of paper in his hand for P, the proposition that Descartes is in the midst of a vivid dream for Q, and supposing that the person whose claim to knowledge is being challenged is Descartes himself.

Austin's way with the argument from ignorance was to investigate whether, if someone has claimed in ordinary life to know that P, we really *can* pick any hypothesis Q we all recognize as one that would have to be false for her to count as knowing that P, and legitimately demand, before we credit her with the knowledge she has claimed, that we be satisfied that (that she/we can explain how) she knows it is not the case that Q. To that end, Austin imagined his having claimed to know, by its red head, that the bird in his backyard is a goldfinch. He observed that this is a claim that is open to legitimate challenge. We could legitimately say to him,

> "To be a goldfinch, besides having a red head it must also have the characteristic eye-markings": or "How do you know it isn't a woodpecker? Woodpeckers have red heads too."
>
> (Austin 1979b: 84)

If he is to be credited with the knowledge he claims, Austin needs to do enough to show the bird really was a goldfinch (and, if applicable, that he was in a position—he was well-enough situated, well-enough informed about matters avian—to tell it was a goldfinch). But, Austin noted, there are limits to how much he needs to do.

> Enough is enough: it doesn't mean everything. Enough means enough to show that (within reason, and for the present intents and purposes) it "can't" be anything else, there is no room for an alternative, competing, description of it. It does not mean, for example, enough to show it isnt a *stuffed* goldfinch.
>
> (Austin 1979b: 84)

That is not to say that it is *never* in order to demand that the person do enough to show that it is not a stuffed goldfinch. We can surely imagine circumstances (we are in an aviary that has both stuffed birds and live ones) in which that demand would be very much in order. But Austin's thought was that we have an idea (rough to be sure) of what normally counts as enough to establish the propriety of a knowledge claim of a particular sort (where both the content of the claim and the circumstances in which it is made contribute to determining that the claim *is* of that sort). And it is only in special cases, cases in which we have a special reason to suppose that something is amiss, that we can demand that more be done than normally counts as enough. As Austin put it (writing here about what we can claim to know about other people's emotions),

> These special cases where doubts arise and require resolving, are contrasted with the normal cases which hold the field *unless* there is some special suggestion that deceit &c., is involved.
>
> (Austin 1979b: 113)

And what makes a case special? Austin never explicitly said. What he did tell us, however, is that our awareness of our human fallibility is no bar at all to our making the knowledge claims we do: it does not provide, for any particular occasion on which I have made (or might make) the claim to know that P, a special reason to suppose that I am (would be) mistaken. (Actually, Austin in this instance uses the expression, "concrete reason." I read him as regarding the two expressions as interchangeable; Austin (1979b: 98).) So Austin would seem to have told us this much: for R to count as a special reason to suppose things are amiss in a manner incompatible with my knowing that P, R has to be, at the very least, a reason that we don't *always* have (as we do the reason: we are all humanly fallible) in the normal cases—the cases in which my claim to know that P is to be credited.

This suggests that Austin held the following view. A person's claim to know that P is to be credited when she has done what counts as enough in a normal case to prove that P, where doing enough does not require doing *everything one might have done*. Only when we have some special reason to suppose that things have gone amiss is it legitimate for us to demand that she do more than what counts as enough in a normal case. And for something to count as a special reason it must at the very least be a reason we do not *always* have in a normal case.

But it is characteristic of the instances of the argument from ignorance that figure in the literature on philosophical skepticism that they afford no such reason. Consider Descartes' dream argument. Granted: we have vivid dreams. Granted: for anything a person claims to have seen to be true, we can coherently hypothesize that the person merely had a vivid dream that she saw that thing. But these facts are fully in our possession in the normal cases—the cases in which we happily and appropriately credit ourselves and others with knowledge in ordinary life. Thus they cannot properly be thought to constitute any special reason to suppose anything has gone amiss with Descartes—any special reason to suppose he is dreaming. And so it is a mistake for Descartes to suppose that he needs to know (and thus to be able to say how he knows) he is not dreaming, if he is to know that he is holding a piece of paper in his hand.

Austin's view of knowledge counts as contextualist, because he held that whether he has proved the bird "can't" be anything else depends on present intents and purposes. But it is a contextualist view that rejects the thought (endorsed by so many contemporary contextualists—see, for example, DeRose (1995) and Lewis (1996)) that someone's simply posing the question, "How do you know that it wasn't just a stuffed bird?" is sufficient to change the context in such a way that Austin no longer has such a proof for present intents and purposes unless he has proof that the bird was not stuffed. For Austin, unlike these contemporary contextualists, challenges to knowledge claims are themselves subject to epistemic appraisal. Absent any special reason to suppose something is amiss, it is simply illegitimate to demand that a claimant to knowledge do more than is in an ordinary case required by way of proving that she knows what she claims. Any challenge that makes such a demand in the absence of such a special reason—as does the challenge to Austin, "How do you know that it wasn't just a stuffed bird?" made in the circumstances we've imagined—should be treated just as it would be in ordinary life: it should be dismissed as outrageous.

Austin's view thus also counts as a relevant alternatives view, insofar as he holds that he needs only to be able to prove that not-Q for *some* of the Q's he recognizes must be false if he is to know that P (e.g. he has to be able to prove that it's not a red-headed woodpecker), not for *all* (e.g., he doesn't have to be able to prove that it's not a stuffed goldfinch). But, while Austin's appeal to special reasons tells us something about how he thought these Q's are to be distinguished from one another, he never said what premise, of the relevant instance of the argument from ignorance, he was rejecting: whether it is the premise that *if he doesn't know it isn't a stuffed goldfinch, he doesn't know it is a goldfinch*, or the premise that *he doesn't know it is not a stuffed goldfinch*. The relevant alternatives view has usually been associated with the rejection of the first of these two premises. (See, for example, Dretske 1970.) But there is reason to suppose (see Kaplan forthcoming) that, had he addressed the matter, Austin would have opted to reject the second—not on the grounds that he knows the bird is not stuffed, but on the grounds that, in the circumstances at hand, the proposition, *it isn't a stuffed goldfinch*, occupies a third category: it is neither true that he knows it, nor true that he doesn't know it. Austin had already argued, in "The Meaning of a Word" (Austin 1979b: 67–9), that, when asked to handle cases that they aren't normally asked to handle (even if it is just because we don't normally pay much attention to those cases), ordinary-language distinctions that appear to be exhaustive (as the distinction between what Austin knows and what he doesn't know appears to be) can break down.

The Foundations of Knowledge

It is clear that, when Austin wrote, in "Other Minds," of his having to be able to prove (for present intents and purposes and within reason) that the bird "can't" be anything other than a goldfinch, he meant nothing more than that he has to be able to give a satisfactory answer to the question, "How do you know it is a goldfinch?" He has to be able to meet all challenges that would count as legitimate in the circumstances in which he makes his claim to know. And, for Austin, a challenge is to be counted as legitimate for our purposes as epistemologists only if it is a challenge that we would treat as legitimate in ordinary life: "Whenever I say I know, I am always liable to be taken to claim that, in a certain sense appropriate to the kind of statement (and to present intents and purposes), I am able to prove it" (Austin 1979b: 85).

It is thus no surprise that subsequently, in *Sense and Sensibilia*, Austin came out in opposition to the doctrine (which had been championed in Ayer (1940), one of Austin's targets, and was later to be championed by many more) that our knowledge of the world around us must have (because it doesn't count as knowledge if it doesn't have) a foundation in claims that purport to say nothing about how the world around us is, but only about how *it appears or seems to us that* the world around us is, where those claims are meant to be understood as describing nothing beyond our phenomenology. Who among us thinks that, if you were to ask me how I know a mutual friend was at a party I attended but you did not, "I saw him," would *not* be a perfectly adequate answer? Who among us would actually refuse to grant me the knowledge I claim until or unless I had offered you an explanation of how I know that our friend was at the party that makes no ultimate appeal to anything that, for example, implies that our mutual friend was actually at the party?

Of course, in taking the position he did—in holding that "I saw him" provides a perfectly good answer to the question "How do you know he was at the party?"—Austin stood in opposition not just to foundationalists who hold (see, for example, Chisholm 1982a: 45) that our knowledge of the world around us must have foundations in claims that have no implications as to how things are in the world around us. Austin stood in opposition to *anyone* who holds that my claim to know that our mutual friend was at the party requires deeper or more extensive support than "I saw him" provides. This includes coherentists (see, for example, BonJour 1985), who hold that my explanation of how I know our friend was at the party cannot stop with "I saw him," but must ultimately appeal to my entire set of beliefs and how my conviction that I saw him coheres with that set.

Austin recognized that in holding that, "I saw him," might count as a perfectly good explanation of how I know our mutual friend was at the party, he was allowing such explanations to terminate with fallible claims—claims that we are capable of mistakenly holding true, and sometimes find that we have mistakenly held true. But Austin argued that, even were we to insist on an explanation that terminates in more cautious claims—claims about how it appeared or seemed to me that things were—we would still have to accept explanations that terminate in fallible claims. Suppose, for example, I said, "It appeared to me that he [our mutual friend] was wearing a magenta jacket," meaning thereby to be making a strictly phenomenological claim. (As we will see, Austin actually held that it was a mistake to think this a proper way to understand our use of "appear" and "seems." But I set aside this misgiving for the present purpose.) If I am operating under the illusion that I have (when in fact I lack) the discriminatory mastery required for someone reliably to tell magenta from other reds in its vicinity, what I said might easily be mistaken. (See Austin 1962: 111–13. For a voice on the other side, see Chisholm 1982a: sec. 10.)

Not that Austin wanted to deny that there are circumstances in which I say things, by way of describing how I am appeared to, in which there can be no question but that I have the discriminatory mastery sufficient to get them right. But, as Austin pointed out, there are likewise circumstances (there is excellent light, I am in close proximity, no hoaxes are being perpetrated, and so on) in which I say things about the world around me (for example, "There's a telephone on the table"), in which there can be no question but that I have the discriminatory mastery sufficient to get *them* right (Austin 1962: 114). Austin's conclusion: there is no way, by appeal solely to the content of claims, to distinguish those that are, from those that are not, legitimate candidates to terminate an explanation of how you know something about the world around you; nor any way, by appeal solely to the content of claims, to distinguish those that are, from those that are not, fallible and open to revision. The circumstance, the context, in which the claim is made, has an ineliminable role to play (Austin 1962: 123–4).

Perception and Perceptual Experience

Austin was very much aware, however, that there is a view of perception according to which, when I say, "I saw him," I *am*, in fact, terminating my explanation of how I know with a purely phenomenological claim: I am making a purely phenomenological claim as to how it seemed or appeared to me things were (as if I were seeing him), and making an inference from that claim to a second claim as to what was causally responsible for its having seemed or appeared that things were that way (that he and I were causally related in just the manner required for me to count as having seen him). Thus, on this indirect view of perception, it would seem that, insofar as we know anything of the world around us, our knowledge *does* have a foundation in purely phenomenological claims.

Austin, however, thought this indirect view of perception fundamentally mistaken. He held that no phenomenological claims were implied by my claim, "I saw him." He thought (what he took to be) the abuse of language involved required to express the indirect view (for example, he held that talking of how things seem or appear to me isn't a way of describing my phenomenology, it's just a way of making a more hedged claim than I would be making were I to say that things simply *are* that way) is a symptom of the view's misguidedness (Austin 1962, *passim*). More tellingly, he argued that the view was entirely unmotivated.

Proponents of the indirect view had argued that only on such a view is it possible adequately to make sense of the undeniable fact that, were the person I saw at the party actually someone so made up that I simply could not tell him apart from our mutual friend, I would still say in response to your query as to how I know our friend was at the party (and with the same confidence and conviction), "I saw him." After all (they argued), what does this fact show, if not that, for all my having actually seen our mutual friend at the party, I might have had exactly the same experience I had as I saw him, yet have *failed* to have seen him? It is just this experience, common to both the seeing and to the failure to see, that, on the indirect view, is the phenomenological component of perception to which any adequate account of perception must advert.

But Austin denied that the fact that we are subject to illusion does anything to show that some phenomenological experience is involved in perception. That is because he thought it is simply a mistake to conclude (from the fact that I might have been deceived in the way described) that, for all my having actually seen our mutual friend at the party, I might have had exactly the same experience I had as I saw him, yet have *failed* to have seen him. The experience I had at the party was the experience of seeing our mutual friend. Had I been deceived, I would have had a different experience: the experience of seeing the imposter (and taking him for our mutual friend). All that is shown by that fact that I could have been deceived in the way imagined is that there are circumstances in which I would mistake the latter experience for the former. (See Austin (1962: 32), where this point is made with reference to how to describe the experience of a person who is deceived by a mirage.)

In Austin's corner, of course, is the way in which we ordinarily speak of our experiences—the experience of being kissed for the first time, the experience of scoring a winning goal in the final minute of play, and so on: in terms that make what we say apt only if the world around us is a certain way. You haven't had the experience of scoring a goal in the last minute of play unless you *have* scored a goal in the final minute of play. Austin's take on experiences has since been dubbed "disjunctivism." (See Snowdon (2005) for a brief primer, by a prominent champion of disjunctivism, on the various doctrines that have traveled under that label.)

The Reception of Austin's Epistemological Writings

While some of Austin's substantive claims, as to what we would ordinarily say and when we would say it, have been hotly disputed (none more hotly than his claims as to the proper uses of "appear" and "seems"; see, for example, Ayer (1967) and Chisholm (1977: 30–3)) and some would seem to be just plain wrong (for example, his claim that "I know that P" is a performative—i.e., something whose utterance makes it true—and so it is a mistake to think it is making any descriptive claim), the dominant reaction to Austin's epistemological work has not been to dispute what he said we would say and when he said we would say it. It has, rather, been to dispute that facts about what we would ordinarily say and when we would say it can possibly be as important as Austin thought them to assessing the propriety of epistemological doctrines.

Thus it is that the philosophical reception of his epistemological work has been dominated by a body of papers and books that are unanimous in holding that Austin made a fundamental mistake in supposing it a condition of adequacy on an epistemology that it faithfully accord with what we would ordinarily say—books and papers that differ one from the other only in exactly what blunder its author attributes to Austin by way of explaining why Austin would have made so fundamental a mistake. It has been variously said that Austin thought facts about what we would say when are important in the way he did because:

1. he failed to realize that facts about what ordinary people say do not, and cannot, settle philosophical disputes; only philosophical argument settles philosophical disputes (Fodor and Katz 1963: 69–70). [Fodor and Katz attribute Austin's mistake in part to his having had an amateurish and armchair-bound approach to linguistics; had he appreciated how linguistic research is properly to be done, he would never have thought ordinary language as important to philosophy as he did. In this, they echo Mates 1958: 68];
2. he failed to realize that the epistemological doctrines he was criticizing by appeal to what we ordinarily say when were not *meant* to have any implications for what we would ordinarily say when (Chisholm 1964: 1);
3. he failed to realize (for all his having highlighted the role context plays in determining what we would say) that the context in which the epistemological doctrines

he criticized were being put forth is distinct, and understood by the proponents of these doctrines to be distinct, from the context in which we ordinarily speak of what we know and how we know it (McGinn 1989: 62; Williams 1996: 147–8); he failed to realize that these philosophers were putting forward doctrines that implied things that *they themselves* freely acknowledged they wouldn't say in ordinary life (Cavell 1965: 217); he failed to take due notice that the fact that, when philosophically engaged, people ordinarily say things that they would freely acknowledge to be at odds with what they would say in ordinary life, is itself a fact about what we would ordinarily say (and when we would say it) that speaks against his condition of adequacy (Cavell 1979: 57);

4. he failed to realize that it is entirely compatible with, for example, the fact that we would ordinarily say that we know a great deal about the world around us, that what we thereby say is false; he failed to realize that it is the truth of what we ordinarily say, not the propriety of our ordinarily saying it, that is the only thing that is in dispute between the skeptic and the anti-skeptic; thus he failed to realize that the points he was at pains to make, about what we would ordinarily say, are entirely beside the point in dispute between the skeptic and his foe (Stroud 1984: 57–62). [In this, Stroud echoes Grice's more general complaint (Grice 1961) that Austin failed to appreciate that there are sometimes things we wouldn't ordinarily say (because they would be misleading) even as we recognize that they are true—and that, because Austin failed to appreciate this, he did not realize that, in requiring that philosophy be faithful to what we would ordinarily say (i.e., make true what we would ordinarily say, and false what we wouldn't ordinarily say), he was erasing any possibility that we might arrive at a philosophy that is true. For an insightful evaluation of Grice's complaint (and a response on Austin's behalf), see Travis (1991: 237–46).]

In fact, however, none of these explanations of why Austin appealed in the way he did to what we would ordinarily say fits at all well with what he actually wrote. Austin was well aware of the controversy his way of doing philosophy had generated, well aware that many philosophers found his appeals to what we would ordinarily say ill-considered and unconvincing in philosophical debate. In "A Plea for Excuses" (Austin 1956/7) Austin undertook to respond to his critics—to answer the question (as he put it, Austin (1979b: 183)), "Why should what we all ordinarily say be the only or the best or final way of putting it? Why should it even be true?" Here is his answer:

> Certainly ordinary language has no claim to be the last word, if there is such a thing. It embodies, indeed, something better than the metaphysics of the Stone Age, namely, as was said, the inherited experience and acumen of many generations of men. But then, that acumen has been concentrated primarily upon the practical business of life. If a distinction works well for practical purposes in ordinary life (no mean feat, for even ordinary life is full of hard cases), then there is sure to be something in it, it will not mark nothing: yet this is likely enough to be not the best way of arranging things if our interests are more extensive or intellectual than the ordinary. And again, that experience has been derived only from the sources available to ordinary men throughout most of civilized history: it has not been fed from the resources of the microscope and its successors. And it must be added too, that superstition and error and fantasy of all kinds do become incorporated in ordinary language and even sometimes

stand up to the survival test (only, when they do, why should we not detect it?). Certainly, then, ordinary language is not the last word: in principle it can everywhere be supplemented and improved upon and superseded. Only remember, it is the first word.

(Austin 1979b: 185)

It is hard to see in this passage the philosopher who is supposed to have committed the blunders just described. On the contrary, we see a philosopher who acknowledges that what it is appropriate to say when we are engaged in a sophisticated inquiry—when "our interests are more extensive or intellectual than ordinary"—will often answer to different standards than those that govern what we would ordinarily say; who agrees that the mere fact that a distinction is commonly drawn in ordinary life (or ordinary speech) is entirely compatible with its being defective for the purposes of such an inquiry; who agrees that the fact that P is something we would say in ordinary life is entirely compatible with P's being false. [Indeed, Austin repeatedly affirmed that its being appropriate to have said one knows something to be so is entirely compatible with one's *not* in fact having known it to be so. For example (Austin 1979b: 98): "[W]e are often right to say we *know* even in cases where we turn out subsequently to have been mistaken--and indeed we seem always, or practically always, liable to be mistaken"; and "It is naturally always possible ('humanly' possible) that I may be mistaken or may break my word, but that by itself is no bar against using the expressions 'I know' and 'I promise' as we do in fact use them."] We see a philosopher who explicitly denies that the facts as to what we would ordinarily say constitute the last word—the decisive word—in matters philosophical.

Austin's Method Properly Understood

So why *did* Austin appeal to what we would ordinarily say in the way he did? We can grant that what we ordinarily say deserves the pride of place he accords it at the end of the passage above, and for precisely the reason he thinks it does. While doubtless flawed and shot with error, ordinary language works. And it makes sense not to give up something that works except for something that promises to work better. But why would Austin think that an epistemological theory, understood by its champion not to have any implications whatsoever for what we would ordinarily say (and so understood as neither seeking to reform ordinary language, nor demanding that we give up any ordinary way of speaking or acting), could be in any way undermined by its failure to accord with what we would ordinarily say?

Austin never explicitly answered this question. But the answer is, I submit, not very hard to see in his writings. Consider, in particular, the first lecture of *Sense and Sensibilia*, where Austin announces that he will be devoting his lectures to the examination of the view that

> we never see or otherwise perceive (or "sense"), or anyhow we never directly perceive or sense, material objects (or material things), but only sense-data (or our own ideas, impressions, sensa, sense-perceptions, percepts, &c.).
>
> (Austin 1962: 2)

He then proceeds to tell us what he thinks of the view and, in particular, of the way its champions argue in its favor:

> My general opinion about this doctrine is that it is a typically scholastic view, attributable, first, to an obsession with a few particular words, the uses of which are over-simplified, not really understood or carefully studied or correctly described; and second, to an obsession with a few (and nearly always the same) half-studied "facts". (I say "scholastic", but I might just as well have said "philosophical"; over-simplification, schematization, and constant obsessive repetition of the same small range of jejune "examples" are not only not peculiar to this case, but far too common to be dismissed as an occasional weakness of philosophers.)
>
> (Austin 1962: 3)

Here we see Austin (particularly in his second, longer parenthetical remark) issuing a general complaint about how his philosophical colleagues are plying their trade. They appeal to examples to argue for the doctrines they champion. But they do it in a highly selective and not very careful way. They are quick, much too quick, to generalize from the examples to which they appeal—and so arrive at doctrines that are overly simple, and thus defective.

In the light of this, Austin's way of criticizing epistemological doctrines looks to be simply an application of the principle of total evidence. We epistemologists motivate our theories, and we could not possibly do epistemology were we barred from motivating our theories, by appeal to what we would ordinarily say. This is true even of the most skeptical epistemologists, whose mission, after all, is just to convince us that there are things we would ordinarily say as to the extent and nature of our knowledge that lead to the conclusion that we have far less of it than we think (see, for example, Stroud 1984: 23–31). Can there be any question but that the instances of the argument from ignorance that are offered by way of challenging our claims to know anything of the world around us, such as Descartes' dream argument, would not even *seem* to have any force but for the fact that the argument from ignorance has *other* instances that issue legitimate challenges in ordinary life? But if we are going to motivate our epistemological theories by appeal to what we would ordinarily say in certain cases—if we are going to count it in favor of an epistemological theory that it accords with what we would ordinarily say in those cases—it is hard to see how we can fail to count it *against* the theory that it *fails* to accord with what we would ordinarily say in other cases.

After all, as the principle of total evidence rightly says, one cannot evaluate *any* theory on *any* topic by looking only for, and only counting as probative, such evidence as one can find in its favor; one has to evaluate a theory on *all* the evidence. So if we are going to evaluate our epistemological theories according to how they accord with certain things we ordinarily say, if we are going to count our ordinarily saying these things as evidence in favor of our theories, intellectual hygiene would seem to demand that we evaluate these theories according to how well they accord with *everything* we would ordinarily say. Intellectual hygiene would seem to demand that we treat the fact that an epistemological theory would have us say things that we would find outrageous to say in ordinary life exactly as Austin treats it: as providing reason to reject that epistemological theory.

My suggestion, then, is that Austin wrote as he did because he saw anyone who would pursue epistemology in a manner at odds with his own as caught in a dilemma. Either what we would ordinarily say about cases counts as evidence for epistemological theories, or it doesn't. If it doesn't, then we cannot make any appeal to what we would ordinarily say to motivate our epistemological theories, in which case we cannot get any epistemology off the ground. But if what we ordinarily say thus *does* count as evidence for epistemological theories, then we must judge our epistemological theories as we would any others: according to how well they accommodate *all* of the evidence. Thus Austin's conviction that it is a condition, on our responsibly doing epistemology at all, that we do it his way.

Vindicating Austin's conviction would require arguing that there is no way to navigate between the horns of the foregoing dilemma. There is no space for that here (but see Kaplan (2000, 2003, 2006, 2008) for how some of the argument might go). This much, however, is evident: it is simply not credible, the supposition that Austin committed the blunders that his critics have attributed to him. And it is likewise evident that we cannot read his as a mindlessly conservative methodology that would dismiss sophisticated and innovative ways of thinking and talking simply because they do not coincide with what ordinary people think and say.

As we have seen, Austin thought, of what ordinary people think and say, that "in principle it can everywhere be supplemented and improved upon and superseded" (Austin 1979b: 185). In the light of this, it is hard to see how we can possibly read Austin's demand, that epistemology be faithful to what we would say and do in ordinary life, as a requirement that would have epistemology bend slavishly to the contours of what ordinary people say and do. What Austin was demanding, by way of fidelity, appears, rather, to be nothing more or less than this: that our philosophical assessment of our epistemic condition coincide with our ordinary assessment of that condition. (Compare Goodman (1983: 62–5), where a requirement much like this is put forth as the only legitimate constraint we are in a position to impose on the enterprise of trying to arrive at an adequate account of what makes for a good inductive inference.)

Thus, when we find our epistemological inquiries leading us to views at odds with what we would ordinarily say or do, the requirement of fidelity does not tell us to stop. Ordinary language is *not*, after all, the last word. Rather, the requirement tells us that we have two choices. We can either reconsider the path on which those inquiries have led us, or change what we are prepared to say and do in ordinary life to conform to our epistemological views. What the requirement of fidelity rules out is the position Austin's critics want to allow an epistemologist to occupy. They want to allow an epistemologist to occupy a pure, disengaged, detached position from which she might conclude, without thereby in any way challenging the propriety of our continuing to say and do what we say and do in ordinary life, that some (or much) of what we thus say and do is nonetheless unsatisfactory from a philosophical point of view. (This is nowhere better expressed than in Stroud (1984: 64–7).) Given Austin's requirement of fidelity to what we would ordinarily say, this position is simply unavailable.

By the lights of the requirement so understood, an epistemology that would offer a philosophical critique of our claims to knowledge has a much tougher row to hoe. What is at stake is no longer simply what we say in the philosophy seminar room; it is also what we say and do outside. Anyone who would tell us, on philosophical grounds, that we know less than we thought, would tell us that we should stop acting (in thought, speech and deed) as if we know more. If she is to sway us, she had better offer us good reason to think we will be better off for changing our ordinary practices in the way required. It is in this sense that ordinary language, though not the last word, *is* the first: for an epistemologist to convince us that what we ordinarily would say is mistaken, she needs to convince us to stop saying it.

It might be thought, then, that Austin's real blunder (and the blunder to which his critics have been pointing; see especially Chisholm (1977: 18); Stroud (1984: chapter 2); Stroud (1989)) was to have failed to appreciate that epistemological inquiry is only properly *philosophical* insofar as it is conducted from a pure, detached, disengaged perspective. But, I have been suggesting, this is not something Austin failed to appreciate; it is something he considered and rejected. He was convinced (and, I am suggesting, not entirely without reason) that to construe epistemology as a discipline whose doctrines have no consequences for what it is proper for us to say and do when we are not engaged in philosophy is to construe it as no discipline at all. It is to construe epistemology as an inquiry intolerably free from evidential constraint, an inquiry that leaves every epistemologist entirely free to pick and choose as she fancies, and without any cost, what (among the things we would ordinarily say and do) she will consider probative for the evaluation of her theories. It can hardly be any wonder that Austin would find it hard to see the point of an inquiry that proceeds like *that*.

Bibliography

Austin, John L. (1946). "Other Minds," *Proceedings of the Aristotelian Society: Supplementary Volume* 20: 148–87. Reprinted in Austin 1979b, pp. 76–116.

——. (1956/7). "A Plea for Excuses," *Proceedings of the Aristotelian Society* 57: 1–30. Reprinted in Austin 1979b, pp. 175–204.

——. (1961). "The Meaning of a Word," in Austin 1979b, pp. 55–75. First published in the first edition of *Philosophical Papers*; delivered in 1940.

——. (1962). *Sense and Sensibilia*, (ed.) G. J. Warnock. Oxford University Press.

——. (1979a). *How to Do Things with Words* (2nd edn), (eds.) J. O. Urmson and Marina Sbisà. Oxford University Press. First edition published in 1962.

——. (1979b). *Philosophical Papers* (3rd edn), (eds.) J. O. Urmson and G. J. Warnock. Oxford University Press. First edition published in 1964.

Ayer, Alfred J. (1940). *The Foundations of Empirical Knowledge*. Macmillan.

——. (1967). "Has Austin Refuted Sense Data?" *Synthese* 17: 117–40. Reprinted in Fann 1969, pp. 284–308.

BonJour, Laurence. (1985). *The Structure of Empirical Knowledge*. Harvard University Press.

Cavell, Stanley. (1965). "Austin at Criticism," *The Philosophical Review* 74: 204–19. Reprinted in Cavell 1976, pp. 97–144; and in Fann 1969, pp. 59–75.

——. (1976). *Must We Mean What We Say?* Cambridge University Press.

——. (1979). *The Claim of Reason: Wittgenstein, Skepticism, Morality, and Tragedy*. Oxford University Press.

Chappell, Vere C. (ed.). (1964). *Ordinary Language*. Prentice-Hall.

Chisholm, Roderick M. (1964). "Austin's *Philosophical Papers*," *Mind*, new series 73: 1–26; reprinted in Fann 1969, pp. 101–26.

——. (1977). *Theory of Knowledge* (2nd edn). Prentice-Hall.

——. (1982a). "Theory of Knowledge in America," in Chisholm 1982b, pp. 109–93. Originally published in R. M. Chisholm, William K. Frankena, and Manley Thomson, *Philosophy*. Prentice-Hall, 1964, pp. 233–344.

——. (1982b). *The Foundations of Knowing*. University of Minnesota Press.

Descartes, René. (1984/5). *The Philosophical Writings of Descartes*, 2 vols., (ed.) John Cottingham, Robert Stoothoff and Dugald Murdoch. Cambridge University Press.

DeRose, Keith. (1995). "Solving the Skeptical Problem," *The Philosophical Review*: 1–52.

Dretske, Fred. (1970). "Epistemic Operators," *The Journal of Philosophy* 67: 1007–23.

Fann, K. T. (ed.). (1969). *Symposium on J. L. Austin*. Routledge & Kegan Paul.

Fodor, Jerry A. and Katz, Jerrold J. (1963). "The Availability of What We Say," *The Philosophical Review*: 57–71.

Goodman, Nelson. (1983). *Fact, Fiction, and Forecast* (4th edn). Harvard University Press. First edition published in 1954.

Grice, H. Paul. (1961). "The Causal Theory of Perception," *Proceedings of the Arisotelian Society, Supplementary Volume* 35: 121–53.

Kaplan, Mark. (1996). "Skepticism and Pyrotechnics," *Acta Analytica* 16/17: 159–77.

——. (2000). "To What Must an Epistemology Be True?" *Philosophy and Phenomenological Research*, 61: 279–304.

——. (2003). "Chisholm's Grand Move," *Metaphilosophy* 34: 563–81.

——. (2006). "If You Know You Can't be Wrong," in Stephen Hetherington (ed.) *Epistemology Futures*. Oxford University Press, pp. 180–98.

——. (2008) "Austin's Way with Skepticism," in John Greco (ed.) *The Oxford Handbook of Skepticism*. Oxford University Press. pp. 348–71.

——. (Forthcoming). "Tales of the Unknown," in Sørli and Gustafsson (forthcoming).

Lewis, David. (1996). "Elusive Knowledge," *Australasian Journal of Philosophy*: 549–67.

Mates, Benson. (1958) "On the Verification of Statements about Ordinary Language," *Inquiry* 1: 161–71. Reprinted in Chappell 1964, pp. 64–74. Page references are to Chappell.

McGinn, Marie. (1989). *Sense and Certainty: A Dissolution of Scepticism*. Blackwell Publishers.

Snowdon, Paul. (2005). "The Formulation of Disjunctivism: A Response to Fish," *Proceedings of the Aristotelian Society* 105: 129–41.

Sørli, Richard and Gustafsson, Martin (eds). (Forthcoming). *New Essays on the Philosophy of J. L. Austin*. Oxford University Press.

Stroud, Barry. (1984). *The Significance of Philosophical Scepticism*. Clarendon Press.

——. (1989). "Understanding Human Knowledge in General," in *Knowledge and Skepticism*, Marjorie Clay and Keith Lehrer (eds). Westview Press, pp. 31–50. Reprinted in Stroud 2002, pp. 99–121.

——. (2002). *Understanding Human Knowledge*. Oxford University Press.

Travis, Charles. (1991). "Annals of Analysis," *Mind* 100: 237–64.

Williams, Michael. (1996). *Unnatural Doubts: Epistemological Realism and the Basis of Scepticism*. Princeton University Press. First published in 1991.

Part X
METAEPISTEMOLOGICAL ISSUES

72
EPISTEMOLOGY AND THE ROLE OF INTUITIONS
William G. Lycan

1. Intuitions, What

In everyday English, an "intuition" is something somewhere between a judgment call and a hunch, not based on a conscious reason. In cognitive psychology, the term has been used to mean something like, an intuitive as opposed to *counterintuitive* judgment, what seems like the reasonable thing to say about something given just the superficial facts at hand (Wisniewski 1998), or instinctive "sentiments and preferences" (Shafir 1998, p. 59).

But the term has a special use in contemporary philosophy (nearly irrelevant to what Kant meant by it). First and foremost, intuitions are about *cases*, actual or hypothetical—Gettier examples, moral situations, particular sets of sentences. A first pass might be to call an intuition a verdictive judgment on a case, not consciously based on inference or on any other particular reason. But such a characterization would already be controversial.

Plantinga (1993, p. 105) speaks of "finding yourself utterly convinced that the proposition in question is *true* . . . [, and that it] is not only true, but could not have been false." That is consistent with an intuition's being a judgment, but Bealer (1998) and BonJour (1998) question Plantinga's assumption that intuiting is a type of believing. Rather, Bealer calls it an intellectual *seeming*, "a sui generis, irreducible . . . propositional attitude that occurs episodically" (p. 207). BonJour actually assimilates it to perception or apprehending, a matter of "seeing" that a proposition is necessary; the proposition *appears* to be necessarily true. BonJour (2001, 2005) moves even further in the perceptual direction, maintaining that intuitions are not propositional at all but are more like perceptual sensations. As with optical illusions, something X can insuperably continue to seem or appear F to us even though we do not believe that X is F, and even when we know that X is not F. Sosa (1998) points out that when we accept a particular solution to an enduring paradox such as the Liar or the Sorites, rejecting the relevant premise does not make the corresponding intuition go away.

But Plantinga's and BonJour's common focus on the necessity of a proposition as the object of an intuition is unacceptably restrictive: though we do have modal intuitions, and perhaps intuitions of some types do have as their contents the necessity of some proposition, there is no reason to think that a moral intuition or a syntactic one takes that form. (Someone might argue that in the moral case, what is intuited to be necessary is the conditional from the facts of the case to the moral verdict, and in the syntactic case the conditional from the sentence's consisting of its particular string of words to the grammaticality judgment, but (a) this is not the phenomenology in either case, and (b) to say that either conditional was necessary would be at best controversial in the first place.)

Intuitions, then, are intellectual seemings-true. (Williamson (2007) grants this, but offers a deflationary account of it in turn: "For myself, I am aware of no intellectual seeming beyond my conscious inclination to believe" (p. 217). Yet, while we might agree that every seeming-true is a conscious inclination to believe, the latter condition is hardly sufficient for intuitionhood. There are many things I am consciously inclined to believe: that my wife is home right now, that there is a pool of water over there in the sand, that if the coin has come up heads six times in a row it will almost certainly come up tails on the next toss, and that all music departments are snake pits. (Some of these I do also actually believe, some not.) But none would qualify as an intuition in the philosophers' sense. Not all are even seemings of any kind.)

2. Intuitions as Evidence

Philosophers treat intuitions as *data points*, as confirming or supporting some hypotheses while at least presumptively refuting others. This suggests that they take intuitions to be evidence. And it is important to see that appeal to intuitions is ubiquitous and probably indispensable in philosophy, if only because philosophical arguments themselves are based on deductive and ampliative inferences whose legitimacy is attested only by intuition.

In order to assess the claim that intuitions are evidence, we need at least two distinctions. First, as is discussed by philosophers of science, not every defense of an hypothesis is an evidential one (Achinstein 2001); e.g., one might champion H1 over H2 on grounds of H1's explanatory virtues even though the two are supported by exactly the same set of evidence. Even if intuitions justify, they might not qualify as evidence—especially because even if they are quasi-perceptual, they are not perceptual.

Let us waive that issue; it is enough to ask whether intuitions do justify. But here too a distinction is needed. "Justify" normally has a veritistic sense, in which to justify a claim is to support it as being substantively and factually true. In this sense, antirealists about a subject-matter, say, moral or other evaluative judgments, could not grant that those can be justified, by intuitions or by anything else. But sophisticated antirealists agree that moral judgments can be reasonable or unreasonable, well supported or stupid and pigheaded. In a weaker sense, such antirealists agree that moral judgments can be justified, say, by the method of reflective equilibrium (sec. 5 below). Rosenberg (1994) makes this distinction explicit, arguing that an epistemology of reflective equilibrium marks a subject-matter as nonfactual; for questions of substantive fact, harder kinds of specifically perceptual evidence are required.

Two further qualifications. First, intuitions come in several different epistemological types, and we might expect that they will not afford an entirely uniform treatment. There are logical intuitions, such as that the sentence "Alex is beautiful and Bill loves her" entails "Bill loves Alex." Then there are more broadly linguistic-semantical intuitions, such as that "Donald furtively buttered the toast in the bathroom" entails "Donald did something furtive in the bathroom" and "Something happened to the toast." There are (arguably) a priori modal intuitions, such as: that what is known must be believed, that a speaker cannot refer to a physical object if there is no sort of causal contact between the speaker and that object, that abstract entities have no causal powers, that gold could have lacked all the stereotypical features associated with gold, and that W.V. Quine could not have been a ping-pong ball. And there are the empirically tutored modal intuitions called to our attention by Kripke and Putnam: that nothing can be gold without having the atomic number 79, that this very table could not have been made of ice instead of the wood it is made of, and so on.

Second, there is a tradition, exemplified in Descartes, of taking certain intuitions to be epistemically infallible—e.g., modal intuitions held under carefully self-supervised conditions. If intuitions can have that status, then it seems obvious that such intuitions can justify, and in a fairly dramatic way. But few contemporary philosophers would claim infallibility for moral intuitions, or epistemological ones, or even for many metaphysical ones. For one thing, nearly every such intuition has actually been disputed by theorists of demonstrable intellect, effort and sincerity; and even intrapersonally, I might change my mind about a strong intuition I once had. This is true even of some logical intuitions, such as the Law of Excluded Middle or Vel-Introduction. It is possible that some intuitions are infallible, say purely conceptual intuitions held by people who fully possess the relevant concepts and are not distracted or confused by any perturbing mental conditions, but this is far from the norm.

(David Chalmers (1996) and Frank Jackson (1998) have disputed the claim made above, that intuitions come in different epistemological types, and they have explicitly tried to assimilate the alleged merely modal intuitions to species of conceptual ones. Their arguments have some attraction, but remain controversial at best; see Lycan (2009). Williamson (2007) takes a strongly opposing view: that so-called conceptual intuitions are nothing special; they result from ordinary counterfactual thinking as on any everyday subject.)

3. Anti-Intuitionism

Before turning to positive proposals as to how intuitions justify, let us survey a few arguments for the flat claim that they cannot.

(i) Harman (1977) argues that a person's having an intuition is a fact about that person, specifically about what is going on in that person's mind. Consequently, what calls for explanation is only the fact that the person has it; and in many cases—notably that of moral intuitions—the best explanation does not invoke the intuition's truth or correctness. (In other cases perhaps it does, but in those, auxiliary factual assumptions will be needed; the intuition alone does not justify.)

Lycan (1987, Ch. 11) replies that the term "intuition" displays what Sellars called the "-ing"/"-ed" ambiguity: It can be used to mean the intuit*ing* done by the subject, a condition of the subject's mind, or it can mean the intuit*ed*, the putative fact that is the content or object of the intuiting, e.g., that torturing a helpless cat is wrong. Harman has focused on the intuitings, but it is the intuiteds that are the proper explananda for (as here) moral theory—just as in science it is the observeds and measureds rather than the observings and measurings that are the data.

(ii) Nonetheless, in many cases the psychological basis of an intuition might be, not the possession of a concept and clear and perfect grasp of its boundaries, but merely the inability to think of a counterexample. Harman (2003) contends that this inability shows nothing except perhaps about the poverty of the theorist's imagination. He adds that we have all had the experience of thinking something unimaginable but then finding upon reflection that we can conceive the thing quite clearly.

Russell (2007) replies that seasoned philosophers have been extensively trained to sniff out bare possibilities that novices cannot; moreover, we often have sociological evidence that no one else has been able to think of a counterexample either. In such cases, the best explanation is still that there are no counterexamples and the intuition has identified a necessary truth. Of course, this verdict is defeasible.

(iii) DePaul (1998, p. 299) complains that (1) if intuitions are evidence, they function as such through the medium of reflective equilibrium; (2) there is no reason to think that that method is truth-conducive; (3) to abandon truth-conduciveness as a requirement is in effect to fall back on a coherence theory of justification; but (4) mere coherence is too weak a standard for justification. (Evidently DePaul is thinking of justification in the strong, veritistic sense.) This concern will be addressed in sec. 6 below.

(iv) Cummins (1998) compares the role of intuitions to that of observations in science, and argues at length that all philosophical intuitions are "artifacts," where an observation is an artifact if it "carries information about the observational apparatus or process rather than about the target" (p. 116), as in a case of optical illusion. Cummins surveys some possible sources of intuitions, including folk belief, language, concepts, and tacit theories, and argues briefly that each of these collapses into the last: a pre-existing tacit theory of the relevant subject-matter. But if intuitions are driven by tacit theories, their evidential value is only as good as the theories are reliable, and Cummins maintains that our tacit theories are the joint products of evolution and social pressure, which make for adaptiveness and effectiveness but not necessarily for accuracy and truth. Our intuitions reveal more about our coping strategies than they do about the world itself. (Kornblith (1998) agrees that intuitions arise from tacit theories and that they have value only so far as those theories are reliable, but unlike Cummins he opines that the theories are often likely to be true.)

Replies: First, no firm believer in determinate concepts and conceptual truth will be convinced by Cummins' quick Quinean assimilation of conceptual intuitions to fallible tacit theory. Second, even if our tacit theories are inaccurate, it does not follow that intuitions generated by them are evidentially worthless; it means only that appeals to such intuitions should not be given a great deal of weight. Perhaps this varies with the type of intuition: Aesthetic intuitions, perhaps, fall at Cummins' end of the scale, as our aesthetic sense is not likely to have been designed for accurate mapping of the world. It is a little harder to see how logical intuitions are *merely* adaptive and not adaptive because truth-preserving, though we should not dismiss the former possibility.

(v) The point is often made that intuitions are malleable, in some cases highly so. White (1989) presents an ingenious set of examples to show that our intuitions about personal identity through time vary radically depending on which of two different (though equivalent) ways in which a case is described. Shafir (1998) similarly argues that preference orderings shift with description of the options involved.

When intuitions shift in this dramatic way, obviously their evidential value is weak or negligible. But (a) under explicit reflection on the different descriptions, they might stabilize; and, more importantly, (b) it has not even been claimed, much less shown, that all or even most intuitions are thus malleable. Logical, semantical and syntactic intuitions are not, even when they are disputable on other grounds.

Several other arguments have been given against appeal to intuitions, but like (iv) and (v), each of them shows at best that the intuitions' evidential value is small or weak, not that it is in principle nil.

For example: Some intuitions are contested; theorists may be deeply split. In such a case, of course, the intuition contributes little. Cummins (1998) argues that this is the analog of two instances of the same scientific experiment that produce disparate outcomes; in such an event, no evidence at all can be recorded in the collective logbook; the community must await decisive replication of the one result or the other.

But that seems to overdo the analogy between intuitions and scientific observations. Science is a public enterprise that operates by institutional rules, one of which is a strong standard for publicity based on replicability. It would be pleasant, but mistaken, to think that philosophy can aspire to such institutional rigor. True, some intuitions are so contested that they should be considered evidentially worthless and banned from future use (Swampman comes to mind). But majority intuitions carry some weight however little, even though there are those who do not share them. Moreover, either of the rival theorists might have a shot at explaining away the other's having, or their failing to share, the intuition in question.

However, more dramatically, some intuitions might vary across cultures. Weinberg et al. (2001) maintain on the basis of surveys that this is true of the Gettier intuition. They present data they have collected, according to which the intuitions of subjects from different ethnic groups vary statistically: 60 percent of subjects originally from the Indian subcontinent, presented with a Gettier example, judged that its protagonist does "really know" as opposed to "only believe."

Let us ignore doubts about the authors' experimental procedures (starting with the forced choice between "really know" and "only believe"), and suppose that the survey results are impeccably produced and robustly replicated: 60 percent of an Asian ethnic group firmly reject Gettier and insist, clearheadedly and understanding the terms and the issue, that a Gettier subject does know. On that supposition, it seems the most likely explanation is that there is a conceptual difference: In the speech of the 60 percent, the word we translate as "know" really does mean just justified true belief; it thus differs from "know" itself. (It would be interesting to go on to ask those subjects whether they see any important difference between the two kinds of "knowers," the ordinary and the Gettiered. Perhaps they would stigmatize the Gettier victims in some way for which there is no simple convenient expression. Or, less likely, they would see no important difference, and simply have no stronger conception of successful cognition.) Anglo-American philosophers could not then claim to be explicating a concept universally possessed. But, so far as has been shown, the Gettier intuition would nonetheless have constituted evidence bearing on the structure of our own concept. (For a fuller response to Weinberg et al., see Sosa 2006.)

Weatherson (2003) argues that the evidential value of an intuition, even a very strong one, is so slight that it can be ignored in the interest of smooth and elegant theory. Thus, e.g., despite the persistence of the Gettier intuition we should continue to maintain that knowledge is merely justified true belief and insist that Gettier victims do know.

4. Intuitions and Reliability

Reliabilism remains the dominant epistemology of our day, and so we must ask whether we should suppose that intuitions are produced by reliable cognitive processes, or that they reliably indicate states of the universe or the pluriverse. (This question is problematic when an intuition purports to deliver a necessary truth; any such intuition that is in fact correct would eo ipso be reliable in the metaphysical sense.)

We have seen that Cummins and Kornblith appeal to reliability, whether negatively or positively. Goldman and Pust (1998) simply assume that if intuitions are to serve as a "basic evidential source," they must be reliably connected to the truth (p. 180); the authors grant that intuitions can play that role, so long as all they are taken to be evidence for is the structure of concepts in the psychological sense of that term.

But it is George Bealer (1987, 1996a, 1996b, 1998) and Ernest Sosa (1998, 2007) who go out of their way to build a positive reliabilist case for the use of intuitions in obtaining a priori knowledge. Sosa (1998, pp. 262–3) offers an argument reminiscent of Descartes' bootstrapping of the *cogito* into a vindication of clarity and distinctness as guides to the truth: We do take ourselves to know some propositions on the basis of intuition (that Ampersand-Elimination is valid, that "The boy hit the colorful ball" is grammatical, that everything is identical with itself). At the very least these beliefs are justified. It "must be more than a coincidence" that we are right about them; it is fair to say that we would not be believing them if they were not true. But all that justifies them is intuition. Therefore, intuition must to some degree track the truth, even if we do not understand its mechanism. Sosa points out that similar arguments can be, and are, made for the faculties of basic sense perception and introspection. (I know of no theorist who believes that there is a distinctive *faculty* for intuition in the present sense.)

Bealer goes a bit deeper. He argues at some length that intuitions "are evidence," indeed a basic source of evidence, and then he asks how that fact might be explained. (Sosa (2007) also adverts to explanatory considerations.) Bealer surveys several potential explanations, and rejects all but one: "modal reliabilism," the claim that there is a "strong modal tie between [intuition's] deliverances and the truth" (1998, p. 216). (The tie is not infallible, nor would it hold for any very complex proposition or outside an appropriately narrow range of subject-matter.)

Bealer adds a further argument (1998, sec. III): He focuses on the notion of "determinate" (full, perfect) concept possession, and offers an analysis of it. According to the analysis, to possess a concept determinately *just is* to have corresponding intuitions that track the truth, assuming an absence of cognitive perturbation. Bealer continues to assume that truth-tracking justifies; so, for anyone who possesses a concept determinately, the corresponding intuitions are evidence. (See also Goldman 2007.)

Of course, many epistemologists are not reliabilists at all, and they will remain entirely unmoved by the arguments surveyed in this section. Perhaps more to the point, it is incongruous to hold intuitions up to the bar of reliability, because their natural home has always been in the methodology of reflective equilibrium, a coherentist method. To that we now turn.

5. Intuitions and Reflective Equilibrium

The method was introduced by Goodman (1955) and developed by Rawls (1971). It is a way of systematizing our intuitions on a given topic—originally, in Goodman, our intuitions about the validity of deductive inferences and the probity of inductive ones. It consists in taking our original intuitions about particular cases, formulating rules or generalizations that attempt to capture them, testing the further predictions of the proposed rules, accepting some, rejecting others, revising the rules, and most importantly, abandoning original intuitions when they stand in the way of major gains in explanatory coherence for the system as a whole. Nothing, neither an initial intuition nor a rule, is treated as unrevisable. Reflective equilibrium itself is achieved (if ever) when the system settles into a stable configuration high in coherence and there is no net pressure to revise in any direction. (For fuller description and discussion, see Daniels 2003/2008.) The resulting beliefs are justified, it is held, because every one has its place in an explanatory web; every one is in principle answerable to every other one; and each is able to resist challenge by drawing support from the system as a whole.

As a description of deductive logic and inductive logic, this is instantly recognizable (though closely allied considerations such as the fit between proof-theoretic derivability and model-theoretic semantics play a role also). It also fits linguistic theory very well, and can readily be seen in much of epistemology. But if anything, the method is now more popularly associated with ethics and moral philosophy. In one style of theorizing (contrasting sharply with the Kantian a priori deduction of moral principles from Ur-concepts), moral intuitions are systematized, and moral theories built, in much the same way as are logical and syntactic theories.

Practitioners distinguish between "narrow" reflective equilibrium, as just described, and "wide" reflective equilibrium, in which a more diverse range of beliefs are consulted. Moral intuitions and moral rules alike might be brought into confrontation with, e.g., theories of human nature, general theories of rationality, relevant epistemology, relevant metaphysics, psychology, and even neuroscience. As always, the goal is the highest possible degree of explanatory coherence among all those.

In sec. 3 above we heard DePaul maintain that coherence of this sort is too weak a standard for justification, at least for veritistic justification. Evidently he is alluding to standard objections to coherentist epistemologies, particularly those that apply directly to reflective equilibrium. Two in particular come to mind.

First, the method assumes that a moral intuition carries at least some initial evidential weight, even though the intuition might later be marginalized or thrown out entirely. Some theorists dispute this, notably our more skeptical reliabilists such as Cummins. Brandt (1979) complains against Rawls that if the intuitions we begin with have no "initial credibility," which he believes they do not, they cannot then acquire justification merely by being brought to cohere with each other.

Second, Stich (1988, 1990) and others have complained that reflective equilibrium is an objectionably conservative method, privileging what we already believe and in effect insisting that other views be brought into line with that. And some theorists fear a kind of relativism: Practitioners who begin with sharply different sets of initial intuitions might converge to different equilibrium states, with nothing to choose between them. Indeed, a lunatic whose initial intuitions are bizarre could bring them into reflective equilibrium with other loony things s/he believes, but that would not lend any justification to any of the resulting set.

As noted, these objections are special cases of standard anti-coherentist arguments in epistemology. Such arguments have been rebutted by coherentists.

6. Coherentism Defended

Suppose one champions some explanatory coherentist (portmanteau'd "explanationist") sort of epistemology generally; that is, one maintains that most of our beliefs are justified by their plausibly explaining other things we believe, and indeed that *all* justification is explanationist (Harman 1965, 1986; Quine and Ullian 1970; Lycan 1987).

Then one faces a general version of the first objection to reflective equilibrium (Lehrer 1974, Ch. 7; Plantinga 1993): Because explanation is asymmetric and on pain of regress, one must ultimately have some "explained unexplainers" as Lehrer calls them, there must be some data propositions that are not themselves justified by explaining more primitive data in their turn. Yet an explanatory hypothesis is justified by the data it explains only if the data propositions are themselves justified, and so those data propositions must be justified in some way other than by their explaining anything. But the alternative is that the data propositions are justified by themselves being explained; and they can be so justified only if the explaining hypotheses are themselves justified, and so there seems nowhere for justification to get an initial foothold. So how does the whole explanatory enterprise get started in the first place?

Lycan (1987, Ch. 8) holds that the explained unexplainers are justified by a particular application of the "Principle of Credulity," which is, "Accept at the outset each of those things that seems to be true." At any given time we involuntarily find ourselves being seemed to in certain ways, typically though not invariably leading to initial belief—at least those produced by perception and by memory, though the Principle makes no appeal to those faculties per se as justifying. Call such unconsidered beliefs "spontaneous" beliefs; they are mostly about our immediate environment, about past events, perhaps about our own mental states, and probably more. Now, since all their contents are things that seem true to us, the Principle of Credulity tacks those propositions in place long enough for them to serve as data for explanation. And once they are justly available for explaining, most will soon acquire the kinds of coherence that are constituted by a proposition's being explained. (A minority will not, and will be thrown out almost immediately.)

But why should anyone accept the Principle of Credulity? Should it not rather be called the "Principle of Credulousness"? As Lehrer observes, any Reidian "innocent until proven guilty" principle of this kind stops sounding like just plain good sense as soon as one considers cases in which very good or very bad consequences hang on the actual truth-value of the belief in question.

Nonetheless, the Principle is defensible; it is a consequence of the more general characteristically explanationist claim that conservativeness, as Quine and Ullian call it and as they argue, is a theoretical virtue: Hypothesis H1 will and should be preferred to H2 if H1 fits better with what we already believe. If this in its turn sounds dogmatic or bigoted, notice that, inescapably, we never even consider competing hypotheses that would strike us as grossly implausible—invisible alien invaders from the planet Werdna, violations of laws of nature, and such. Granted, epistemic conservatism is itself controversial and in need of defense against those who find it unmotivated, arbitrary, politically disgusting and the like; for such defense, see Sklar (1975) and Lycan (1987, Chs. 7, 8). The key contention is that: Whatever epistemic or justifying status inheres in the other standard pragmatic theoretical virtues—simplicity, testability, fruitfulness, power, and the like—conservativeness shares that same status. (Some philosophers have doubted whether any of the pragmatic virtues eo ipso justifies beliefs at all, but the present point is that whether or not the other virtues have that power, conservativeness stands or falls with the rest of them.)

If we can agree that the Principle of Credulity is a correct epistemological norm, i.e., that appearances are innocent until *at least some slight reason* is given for suspecting them guilty, then there is a very simple alternative explanation of the evidential status of intuitions. Intuitions are seemings-true. By the Principle of Credulity, therefore, they are evidence. There is no need to ask what produces them, or for any bold modal claims (even ones as cautious as Bealer's), or for any weird connection between intuitions and truth. For those reasons, the explanationist account of intuitions' being evidence is at least simpler, more straightforward, and considerably less problematic than reliabilist ones.

What of the conservatism/relativism charge? It would be idle to deny that sometimes a philosopher evinces a truly weird set of intuitions, and with ingenuity is able to ground a whole coherent philosophical theory on it.

As before, this complaint is a special case of a more general objection to coherentisms; but here I doubt that standard replies to the latter will serve (Lycan 1996). Rather, we may return to Cummins' concern for intersubjectivity (sec. 3 above). Philosophy is a communal discipline, and it matters whether one's intuitions are widely shared. If the weirdo's intuitions are shared by virtually no one, then, as argued above, they have negligible justifying power

7. Empirical Approaches

The recent industry, "experimental philosophy" (Knobe and Nichols 2008), has been at work testing the epistemological intuitions of ordinary subjects as opposed to those of professional philosophers. Weinberg et al. (2001), addressed above, was a leading early example; for discussion of it and more recent work, see "Experimental Epistemology," Chapter 73 in this volume.

Some cognitive scientists have begun investigating the psychological foundations of moral intuitions, with interesting and controversial results; see, for example, Haidt (2001) and Greene (2007).

References

Achinstein, P. (2001). *The Book of Evidence* (Oxford: Oxford University Press).
Bealer, G. (1987). "The Philosophical Limits of Scientific Essentialism," in J.E. Tomberlin (ed.), *Philosophical Perspectives 1: Metaphysics* (Atascadero, CA: Ridgeview Publishing), 289–365.
Bealer, G. (1996a). "A Priori Knowledge and the Scope of Philosophy," *Philosophical Studies* 81: 121–42.
Bealer, G. (1996b). "On the Possibility of Philosophical Knowledge," in J.E. Tomberlin (ed.), *Philosophical Perspectives 10: Metaphysics* (Atascadero, CA: Ridgeview Publishing), 1–34.
Bealer, G. (1998). "Intuition and the Autonomy of Philosophy," in DePaul and Ramsey (1998).
BonJour, L. (1998). *In Defense of Pure Reason* (Cambridge: Cambridge University Press).
BonJour, L. (2001). "Précis" and "Replies," in a Book Symposium on BonJour (1998), *Philosophy and Phenomenological Research* 63: 625–31, 673–98.
BonJour, L. (2005). "In Defense of the A Priori," in M. Steup and E. Sosa (eds.), *Contemporary Debates in Epistemology* (Malden, MA: Blackwell Publishing).
Brandt, R. (1979). *A Theory of the Good and the Right* (Oxford: Oxford University Press).
Chalmers, D. (1996). *The Conscious Mind* (Oxford: Oxford University Press).
Cummins, R. (1998). "Reflection on Reflective Equilibrium," in DePaul and Ramsey (1998).
Daniels, N. (2003/2008). "Reflective Equilibrium, *The Stanford Encyclopedia of Philosophy* (Fall 2008 Edition), E.N. Zalta (ed.), URL = <http://plato.stanford.edu/archives/fall2008/entries/reflective-equilibrium/>.

DePaul, M. (1998). "Why Bother with Reflective Equilibrium?," in DePaul and Ramsey (1998).
DePaul, M., and W. Ramsey (1998). *Rethinking Intuition* (Lanham, MD: Rowman & Littlefield).
Goldman, A. (2007). "Philosophical Intuitions: Their Target, Their Source, and Their Epistemic Status," *Grazer Philosophische Studien* 74: 1–25.
Goldman, A., and J. Pust (1998). "Philosophical Theory and Intuitional Evidence," in DePaul and Ramsey (1998).
Goodman, N. (1955). "The New Riddle of Induction," in *Fact, Fiction and Forecast* (Cambridge, MA: Harvard University Press).
Greene, J.D. (2007). "Why are VMPFC Patients more Utilitarian?: A Dual-Process Theory of Moral Judgment Explains," *Trends in Cognitive Sciences* 11: 322–3.
Haidt, J. (2001). "The Emotional Dog and Its Rational Tail: A Social Intuitionist Approach to Moral Judgment," *Psychological Review* 108: 814–34.
Harman, G. (1965). "The Inference to the Best Explanation," *The Philosophical Review* 74: 88–95.
Harman, G. (1977). *The Nature of Morality* (Oxford: Oxford University Press).
Harman, G. (1986). *Change in View* (Cambridge, MA: MIT Press).
Harman, G. (2003). "The Future of the A Priori," in *Philosophy in America at the Turn of the Century* (American Philosophical Association Centennial Supplement to the *Journal of Philosophical Research*). (Charlottesville, VA: Philosophy Documentation Center.)
Jackson, F. (1998). *From Metaphysics to Ethics* (Oxford: Oxford University Press).
Knobe, J., and S. Nichols (2008). *Experimental Philosophy* (New York: Oxford University Press).
Kornblith, H. (1998). "The Role of Intuition in Philosophical Inquiry: An Account with No Unnatural Ingredients," in DePaul and Ramsey (1998).
Lehrer, K. (1974). *Knowledge* (Oxford: Clarendon Press).
Lycan, W.G. (1987). *Judgment and Justification* (Cambridge: Cambridge University Press).
Lycan, W.G. (1996). "Plantinga and Coherentisms," in J. Kvanvig (ed.), *Warrant and Contemporary Epistemology* (Totowa, NJ: Rowman & Littlefield.)
Lycan, W.G. (2009). "Serious Metaphysics: Frank Jackson's Defense of Conceptual Analysis," in I. Ravenscroft (ed.), *Minds, Worlds and Conditionals: Essays in Honour of Frank Jackson* (Oxford: Oxford University Press).
Plantinga, A. (1993). *Warrant and Proper Function* (Oxford: Oxford University Press).
Quine, W.V., and J.S. Ullian (1970). *The Web of Belief* (New York: Random House).
Rawls, J. (1971). *A Theory of Justice* (Cambridge, MA: Harvard University Press).
Rosenberg, J.F. (1994). *Beyond Formalism* (Philadelphia: Temple University Press).
Russell, B. (2007). "A Priori Justification and Knowledge," *The Stanford Encyclopedia of Philosophy* (2007 Edition), E.N. Zalta (ed.), URL = <http://plato.stanford.edu/entries/apriori/>.
Sosa, E. (1998). "Minimal Intuition," in DePaul and Ramsey (1998).
Sosa, E. (2006). "A Defense of the Use of Intuitions in Philosophy," in M. Bishop and D. Murphy (eds.), *Stich and His Critics* (Oxford: Basil Blackwell).
Sosa, E. (2007). "Intuitions: Their Nature and Epistemic Efficacy," in *Grazer Philosophische Studien*, special issue: C. Beyer and A. Burri (eds.), "Philosophical Knowledge: Its Possibility and Scope" (Amsterdam: Rodopi).
Shafir, E. (1998). "Philosophical Intuitions and Cognitive Mechanisms," in DePaul and Ramsey (1998).
Sklar, L. (1975). "Methodological Conservatism," *The Philosophical Review* 84: 374–400.
Stich, S.P. (1988). "Reflective Equilibrium, Analytic Epistemology and the Problem of Cognitive Diversity," *Synthese* 74: 391–413.
Stich, S.P. (1990). *The Fragmentation of Reason* (Cambridge, MA: Bradford Books/MIT Press).
Weatherson, B. (2003). "What Good are Counterexamples?" *Philosophical Studies* 115: 1–31.
Weinberg, J., S. Stich and S. Nichols (2001). "Normativity and Epistemic Intuitions," *Philosophical Topics*, 29: 429–60.
White, S. (1989). "Metapsychological Relativism and the Self," *Journal of Philosophy* 86: 298–323.
Williamson, T. (2007). *The Philosophy of Philosophy* (Oxford: Basil Blackwell).
Wisniewski, E.J. (1998). "The Psychology of Intuition," in DePaul and Ramsey (1998).

73
EXPERIMENTAL EPISTEMOLOGY

Jonathan M. Weinberg

I. What is Experimental Philosophy?

In recent years a growing number of philosophers have begun to deploy some of the methods of the sciences as a component of their philosophical methods. Although this chapter is particularly concerned with experimental epistemology, the work so far in this area shares a number of traits with experimental philosophy on the whole, including:

- a primary concern with *intuitions* in large part paralleling traditional analytic philosophical practice, while rejecting the epistemic authority of the armchair;
- use of the methods of social psychology, in particular in the form of surveys;
- almost all work involves contrasting either different versions of the surveys themselves, varying in the content of the cases, or their framing, or their order; or looking for differences across different subject populations;
- the predominant statistical tools and norms are also taken from social psychology, such as null hypothesis testing, with $p<0.05$ being the critical threshold for significance; the number of subjects tends towards the few-dozen to the low hundreds;
- a generally exploratory attitude towards the empirical findings themselves, and about the philosophical conclusions to be drawn from them.

Some philosophers take the judgments as revealed in the experiments to provide evidence for or against substantive philosophical theses, either for first-order epistemological claims or at least for our folk epistemological theories, perhaps without going on to endorse those folk theories; following a usage suggested (in unpublished work) by Farid Masrour, call this the *positive program*. Others, however, do not seek to use the experimental results as a basis for any such claims, and aim instead only to undermine the practice of appealing to intuitions in the first place; call this the *negative program*.

II. The Positive Program

A. *Contextualism Under Scrutiny*

The bulk of work conducted in the positive program of experimental epistemology has been concerned with debates about contextualism and various forms of sensitive invariantism. It is an inviting target, as the various accounts at play in the literature make clear predictions about what factors should or should not be expected to produce different patterns in ordinary judgments about the application of "knows." Of particular interest have been versions of the "Bank Cases" (DeRose 1992; Stanley 2005; Schaffer 2006). Joshua May et al. (2010) deploy four such cases, contrasting along the dimensions of the stakes involved and whether any uneliminated alternatives have been made explicitly salient:

Low Stakes-No Alternative (LS-NA)
Hannah and her wife Sarah are driving home on a Friday afternoon. They plan to stop at the bank on the way home to deposit their paychecks. It is not important that they do so, as they have no impending bills. As they drive past the bank, they notice that the lines inside are very long, as they often are on Friday afternoons. Hannah notes that she was at the bank two weeks before on a Saturday morning, and it was open. Realizing that it isn't very important that their paychecks are deposited right away, Hannah says, "I know the bank will be open tomorrow. So we can deposit our paychecks tomorrow morning."

High Stakes-No Alternative (HS-NA)
Hannah and her wife Sarah are driving home on a Friday afternoon. They plan to stop at the bank on the way home to deposit their paychecks. Since they have an impending bill coming due, and very little in their account, it is very important that they deposit their paychecks by Saturday. As they drive past the bank, they notice that the lines inside are very long, as they often are on Friday afternoons. Hannah notes that she was at the bank two weeks before on a Saturday morning, and it was open. Hannah says, "I know the bank will be open tomorrow. So we can deposit our paychecks tomorrow morning."

Low Stakes-Alternative (LS-A)
Hannah and her wife Sarah are driving home on a Friday afternoon. They plan to stop at the bank on the way home to deposit their paychecks. It is not important that they do so, as they have no impending bills. As they drive past the bank, they notice that the lines inside are very long, as they often are on Friday afternoons. Hannah notes that she was at the bank two weeks before on a Saturday morning, and it was open. Sarah points out that banks do change their hours. Still, realizing that it isn't very important that their paychecks are deposited right away, Hannah says, "I know the bank will be open tomorrow. So we can deposit our paychecks tomorrow morning."

High Stakes-Alternative (HS-A)
Hannah and her wife Sarah are driving home on a Friday afternoon. They plan to stop at the bank on the way home to deposit their paychecks. Since they have an impending bill coming due, and very little in their account, it is very important that they deposit their paychecks by Saturday. As they drive past the bank, they notice that the lines inside are very long, as they often are on Friday afternoons. Hannah notes that she was at the bank two weeks before on a Saturday morning, and it was open. Sarah points out that banks do change their hours. Hannah says, "I know the bank will be open tomorrow. So we can deposit our paychecks tomorrow morning."

May et al. claim that a relevant-alternatives epistemology (like Schaffer's) would predict differences between the NA and A versions, with less knowledge attributed in the A versions. A pragmatic encroachment epistemology (like Stanley's) would predict differences between the LS and HS versions, with less knowledge attributed in the HS versions. Their aim is to canvass the folk, and see to what extent the attributions of the folk do or do not line up with these epistemologies' predictions. They found the following mean responses, on a 7-point Likert scale in which 1 represented a strong disagreement with a knowledge attribution to Hannah, 7 strong agreement with such an attribution, and 4 a neutral response: LS-NA = 5.33, LS-A = 5.30, HS-NA = 5.07, and HS-A = 4.60. The difference between the NA and A versions were not significant, which seems problematic for the relevant-alternatives view.

Their findings were also inconsistent with the standardly reported pattern judgments in the LS and HS versions. The typical attributions in the literature would attribute knowledge in the LS version, and deny it in the HS version. But May et al.'s subjects generally attributed knowledge in *both* cases—that is, their means were statistically above the 4.0 value for a neutral response. However, they did find a difference in that the subjects in the LS groups were on the whole *more enthusiastic* in their attributions of knowledge than were the subjects in the HS groups. They interpret this as a disconfirming finding for claims of stakes-sensitivity, though here we run into one of the still-unsettled methodological questions in experimental philosophy: how ought we interpret mean responses of groups of subjects? We traditionally speak fairly unequivocally of *the* intuition about a particular case, a yea or a nay, and if we know what predictions different epistemologies are supposed to make about the case, then we can simply tell whether it is or is not a problem case for which epistemologies. But what does it mean if, say, 30 percent of subjects withhold knowledge, and 70 percent attribute it—what is 'the' intuition in that case? The idea of 'majority rule' seems tempting, but it is unclear on what basis the 30 percent minority can really be ruled *wrong* just in virtue of their minority status. Relativism might be no more tempting here, either.

Positive experimental epistemology might succeed best at evaluating, not what 'the' folk intuition is about particular cases—there just might not be any fact to be reported in such a form—but, rather, what factors do or do not make a difference in folk intuitions. So if proponents of stakes-sensitivity are willing to yield authority on the particular cases that have been their stock-in-trade, they might yet find some confirmation in May et al.'s findings.

Several other researchers have also been examining folk intuitions for contextualist/sensitivist effects, and thus far they have fairly consistently found no evidence of substantial stakes-sensitivity. Wesley Buckwalter (2010) also used variants on the bank cases, and uncovered neither a stakes-based difference nor a relevant-alternatives difference. Adam Feltz and Chris Zarpentine (manuscript) used a different sort of case, involving an agent crossing over a rickety-looking bridge. They report a *very* weak stakes effect, and as with May et al., all of the mean scores were on the positive side of neutral. Their findings are suggestive of what they call an "attributer effect," in that their data were consistent with the hypothesis that people are more reluctant to agree with third-person knowledge attributions than first-person attributions. Similarly, Ram Neta and Mark Phelan (manuscript) used a different sort of case, concerning an agent's knowledge of whether they were on the correct city street, and found no stakes differences in judgments about how confident an agent should be.

That the data thus far have been so uniform should not lead one to infer that contextualism in any of its various forms has been anything liked *disproved*. But the results thus far do seem at least to impose that much of a burden on any contextualists who expect their theory to reflect ordinary usage.

B. Knowledge-How

Another epistemological question that has received recent experimental attention is that of intellectualism about knowledge-how. John Bengson et al. (2009) examined a number of hypotheses about the relationship between attributions of knowledge-how and attributions of ability, in particular "neo-Ryleanism": the claim that the ability to do X is necessary and sufficient for knowing how to do X. The necessary sub-condition they term "anti-intellectualism," and the sufficient, "praxism." Their materials included scenarios like the following:

> Pat has been a ski instructor for 20 years, teaching people how to do complex ski stunts. He is in high demand as an instructor, since he is considered to be the best at what he does. Although an accomplished skier, he has never been able to do the stunts himself. Nonetheless, over the years he has taught many people how to do them well. In fact, a number of his students have won medals in international competitions and competed in the Olympic games. (391)

Subjects were asked both whether Pat knows how to do the stunts, and whether he is able to do them. "Contrary to anti-intellectualism, the vast majority (81%) judged both that Pat knows how to perform the stunts and that he is unable to do them" (392). They also did an experimental test of "praxis," using the following scenario (395–6):

> Sally, who is an inexperienced hiker with extremely poor vision, decides to go snow shoeing through the mountains in February. As she is hiking along, an avalanche suddenly starts and a rush of snow sweeps down the mountain and over Sally. Sally, however, mistakenly takes the snow to be a body of water (she believes incorrectly that a nearby damn has broken) and so she responds by making rapid swimming motions. Sally aims to swim through the water towards the surface. Though Sally has never heard of this fact before, making swimming motions is a way to escape avalanches. As a result of her lucky mistake, Sally is able to escape from the avalanche.

Subjects were asked both whether Sally knows how to escape avalanches and whether she is able to do so. Since the answer to the latter question is rather explicitly provided in the scenario, praxism predicts that subjects will generally respond in the affirmative to both questions. However, 75 percent of the subjects attributed to Sally the ability, but not the know-how. The remaining subjects were evenly split between those who withheld both attributions, and those who made the praxism-predicted double attributions.

In short, Bengson et al.'s results indicate that folk patterns of knowledge-how and ability attributions are not particularly coupled in the way that neo-Ryleanism would predict. Using a further set of questions, however, they also found that subjects in these studies *did* make a link between knowledge-how and *understanding*, in particular, understanding how to perform the action in question. They take their results to be strong prima facie evidence for a rejection of neo-Ryleanism, at least as an account of folk attributive practices (398).

C. Epistemic Side-Effects

The positive experimental work described thus far has taken on existing epistemological debates, and the various predictions of the different positions in those debates, and has deployed experimental methods to apply some new evidential pressure on them. That is, their hypotheses about which sorts of cases will or will not produce similar intuitions have all come from the non-experimental literature. But much of the work in experimental philosophy more generally has put into play novel hypotheses—ones unanticipated in the armchair-produced literature—as to what sorts of patterns might be found in intuitions about cases. One recent research project in positive experimental epistemology has attempted to do just that, by exploring whether there are epistemic parallels to a now well-documented pattern of intuitions in the literature on agency, the 'side-effect effect', or 'Knobe effect' (Knobe 2003, 2006). The original version of the side-effect effect concerns attributions of "intentionally" to consequences of an action that are foreseen but not in themselves desired: when those consequences are evaluated by subjects as positive, subjects are on balance less willing to say that the agents brought about those consequences intentionally, but when those consequences are evaluated as negative, subjects are much more willing to say that the agents brought about those consequences intentionally.

James Beebe and Wesley Buckwalter (forthcoming) hypothesized that a similar effect might be found using materials drawn from epistemology instead of action theory, and presented subjects with a similar pair of cases:

> The vice-president of a company went to the chairman of the board and said, "We are thinking of starting a new program. We are sure that it will help us increase profits, and it will also *help/harm* the environment." The chairman of the board answered, "I don't care at all about *helping/harming* the environment. I just want to make as much profit as I can. Let's start the new program." They started the new program. Sure enough, the environment was *helped/harmed*. Did the chairman know that the new program would *help/harm* the environment?

They found that subjects in the "harm" condition were more likely to attribute knowledge to the chairman than were the subjects in the "help" condition. Roughly speaking, the mean response to the "help" condition was a bit less than +1 on a 7-point Likert scale of −3 to +3, whereas the mean response to the "harm" condition was a bit above +2. The effect was also statistically significant when different subjects were asked to answer the question as an all-or-nothing matter, instead of on a scale.

The authors interpret these findings as suggestive of a hitherto-unexamined variety of pragmatic encroachment, in which standards of attributing knowledge to an agent might be raised or lowered by the moral status of the agent's actions.

III. The Negative Program

Adherents of the negative program in experimental epistemology seek to dethrone the centrality of the appeal to intuitions in philosophical methodology. The primary sort of finding appealed to is that of *inappropriate variation*: intuitions in some philosophical domain D are shown to vary with some factor F which does not itself vary with the facts in D.

A. The Main Troublemaking Results

With knowledge, primarily there are two classes of results: ethnicity effects, and order effects. Inspired by work like that of Richard Nisbett and his collaborators (e.g., Nisbett et al. 2001; Nisbett 2003) that found systematic and surprising cognitive variation between East Asian and American/European subjects, Weinberg et al. (2001) looked for divergence in attributions of knowledge between Asian- and European-descended subjects (all of whom were native English speakers attending college in New Jersey, however). One result concerned a version of a Gettier case:

> Bob has a friend, Jill, who has driven a Buick for many years. Bob therefore thinks that Jill drives an American car. He is not aware, however, that her Buick has recently been stolen, and he is also not aware that Jill has replaced it with a Pontiac, which is a different kind of American car. Does Bob really know that Jill drives an American car, or does he only believe it?

As one might expect, close to 80 percent of subjects of European descent said, as most epistemologists surely would, that Bob does not really know. Surprisingly, though, slightly over half of the subjects of East Asian descent judged that Bob *does* really know. Following Nisbett, Weinberg et al. hypothesize that this difference might be explained by the East Asian judgments being more similarity-based, and less causation-based, than corresponding Western judgments.

Weinberg et al. also report an ethnicity-based difference in patterns of answers to a range of different "Truetemp"-like cases (Lehrer 1990). Different sets of subjects each were given a version of the Truetemp case, one in which the human thermometer ability is acquired by a freak accident, another in which the ability is implanted by a team of well-meaning scientists, and yet another in which the ability is acquired by an entire community of people. European-descended subjects showed no differences across the three cases, but East Asian subjects were somewhat more willing to attribute knowledge in the latter two sorts of cases. This difference might be explainable in terms of the cognition of subjects of East Asian descent being more influenced by contextual and community factors, again consistent with the cross-cultural findings of psychologists.

Swain et al. (2008) pursued a different line of worry, about not interpersonal variation of intuitive judgments but intrapersonal stability of those judgments. Each of their subjects offered knowledge judgments on the same set of four cases: a Truetemp case (the same as used in Weinberg et al.), a fake-barn case, a chemist using the scientific information of her profession, and a person making a lucky guess about the flip of a coin. The latter two cases were expected to count as clear cases of knowledge and non-knowledge, respectively. What varied from subject to subject was the order in which the cases were presented. Swain et al. hypothesized, based on an earlier pilot study, that judgments about the Truetemp case would be sensitive to order, and they indeed found that attributions of knowledge, as registered on a 5-point Likert scale, were highest when the case followed the coin-flip case; lowest when it followed the chemist case; and unaffected by the fake-barn case.

These results support the *restrictionist challenge*: philosophers ought to restrict, perhaps in a radical way, their reliance on such intuitions (Alexander and Weinberg 2007).

B. The Argument

There is some history of empirically-*nonspecific* challenges to the philosophical practice of appealing to intuitions about cases (e.g., Stich 1990; Cummins 1998). However, the nonspecificity of those challenges has meant that they have needed very heavy-duty epistemological premises, of a sort that defenders of armchair intuitive practices have objected can lead to skeptical conclusions, because the epistemological premise will apply to too many other putative sources of evidence, very likely including those that the challenger would look to use in her own arguments (Bealer 1992; Pust 2000; D. Sosa; 2006; Williamson 2007). But experimental philosophy results have a specific empirical content, so maybe they can succeed with a weaker, more targeted epistemological argument—and indeed they had better do so, or else the same sorts of anti-skeptical concerns will apply to them (E. Sosa 2006). I will offer two such candidate premises for consideration here.

First, one might offer an argument very similar in its basic structure to a classical skeptical argument, but in which one distinguishes between *merely* possible sources of error, and what we might call *live* possibilities of error—possibilities for which we have at least some evidence for their actuality, where that evidence must cross some moderate but still nontrivial threshold. Allowing the existence of the merely possible sources of error to undermine a source of evidence might well lead to skeptical conclusions, but the existence of live possibilities for error present legitimate challenges to a source of evidence—challenges that must be met before further appeals to that source can be considered legitimate. What the experimental results provide, on this view, is just that requisite evidence for the claim that these sorts of errors are a live possibility. Until philosophers can demonstrate that their intuitions are actually sufficiently immune to such errors, the argument goes, they cannot legitimately rely on them. And it will not do to protest, as Ernest Sosa does (2006, 105), that these results only mean that philosophers should simply be careful when using their intuitions, as the restrictionist challenge reveals just how little we know about what kinds of care are actually required of us, if we are to deploy our intuitions responsibly.

A different approach here is to take the experimental results to indicate a kind of deficiency not in intuitions *in general*, but rather in the *particular practices* that philosophers typically engage in when they deploy such intuitions as premises in what might be called the "method of cases." This approach has the advantage of adopting a more restricted target, one that does not obviously include either more ordinary or more scientific deployments of intuitions, and which would thus avoid *immediately* running into skeptical dangers. Nonetheless, such an approach would still need to show how those dangers do not recur at a later stage of consideration. That is, whatever it is that is supposed to be deficient about the "method of cases," if the same worries can be raised about ordinary or scientific uses of intuition—or, for that matter, about perception, memory, and the like—then we would again have the unwanted skeptical result. What the negative experimental philosopher needs to do, therefore, is to identify a deleterious epistemic characteristic which *does* apply to the method of cases, but which does *not* apply to (at least most of) ordinary and scientific evidential practices.

One proposal for a deleterious epistemic characteristic that can thread this needle appeals not to the initial risk of error, but rather to what resources a given evidential practice has available in order to *mitigate* such a risk of error when it arises. That is, we can attend not only to how likely a given practice is to make errors in the first place, but also how good a job it can do at either removing such errors, or at least minimizing their impact on the rest of our theories. We can tolerate the danger of error in, say, ordinary uses of perception, precisely because we are reasonably able to monitor for such errors, and to correct for or at least quarantine such errors when they arise. To the extent that an evidential practice possesses such resources for detecting, correcting, and quarantining errors as they might arise, let us call such a practice *hopeful*.

We can thus propose the following candidate for a deleterious epistemic characteristic that might apply to the method of cases, but which does not seem to apply to most of our ordinary and scientific evidential practices: hopelessness. What the experimental results indicate, and moreover what the *surprising* nature of those results underscore, is just how limited is armchair philosophy's resources of discerning these particular sorts of errors as they might afflict our practices. That these sources of error are live threats is perhaps not enough by itself to raise deep worries about armchair philosophical practice; but that these sources of error are live threats *for which we currently possess no good means of remedying*, might well be.

C. Armchair-Defending Responses

The master argument for the restrictionist challenge thus has three main parts. First, there are the experimental results themselves, which at this point in time overwhelmingly concern 'ordinary' subjects (typically, but not entirely, university undergraduates). In particular, there is the claim that the studies in question reveal a worrisome pattern of responses in those subjects, such as ethnic variation or sensitivity to the order of presentation of the cases. Second, there is an ampliative inference from the patterns disclosed concerning the ordinary subjects to the predicted occurrence of those patterns in professional philosophers. Third, there is a metaphilosophical claim that these patterns are not truth-tracking, with regard to the philosophical domains in question.

We can thus organize responses to this argument in terms of which step any such response is aimed at.

C.1. Direct Empirical Responses

One might object to the experimental philosophers' findings themselves, or at least their interpretations of them, and thereby cut off the negative argument at the knees. This has not yet proved a particularly popular strategy, perhaps because philosophers do not (yet) generally have the requisite training in experimental methods to undertake such critiques. Because of this, what few attempts have been made by philosophers to address the empirical findings directly have tended to fail to rise to the general adequacy conditions of such critiques—in particular, in proposing a confound to an experimental finding, one must both (i) provide some minimal empirical motivation for the confound and, moreover, (ii) at least sketch how the proposed confound could actually have produced the observed data. Kirk Ludwig (2007), for example, suggests that Machery et al.'s (2004) subjects might not have been uniformly distinguishing between speaker's reference and semantic reference—but he fails to suggest why one should find systematic confusions among subjects in that regard, and worse, he does not provide any reason why one might expect East Asian and Western subjects to display systematic asymmetry in this regard. His proposal thus fails both of those necessary conditions on a proposed confound.

Somewhat more successful critiques can be found in Justin Sytsma and Jonathan Livengood (2009) and Simon Cullen (2010), who admirably undertake to substantiate their critiques with further experimental work of their own. Sytsma and Livengood's own studies indicate that the effect that Machery et al. interpreted as a general difference in semantic intuitions about cases across East Asian and Western subjects might better be understood as a difference in preferred perspective adopted when considering those cases. They found that conditions that induce subjects to take on the speaker's perspective ("When John uses the name 'Gödel,' does John think he is talking about . . .?") in the scenario led to a substantially higher proportion of those subjects giving the "descriptivist" judgment. However, inducing subjects to take on the narrator's perspective ("When John uses the name 'Gödel,' is he actually talking about . . .?") produces a higher proportion of "Kripkean" judgments. Their results go some distance towards providing the empirical motivation lacking in Ludwig's proposal, and thus succeeding on the first, 'empirical plausibility' condition on proposing confounds). Nonetheless, they do not indicate why this difference should be found asymmetrically across ethnic groups, and thus do not yet have a finding that predicts the actual results reported by Machery et al.

Similarly, Cullen's research indicates some ways in which incidental aspects of survey design, such as the wording of the instructions or whether a binary or Likert-scale judgment is requested, can substantially influence experimental subjects' responses, which usefully confirms some common-but-untested assumptions. For example, asking subjects whether an agent "really knows" a given proposition generates fewer attributions of knowledge than simply asking whether or not an agent knows, simpliciter. He goes on to suggest that at least some of the order effects reported by Swain et al. might be due to such pragmatic instructional factors. However, as with Sytsma and Livengood, he does not quite generate predictions of the overall pattern of results reported by the negative experimental philosophers, and thus does not quite manage to propose a real confound.

C.2. *Blocking the Inference from the Folk to the Philosophers*

If one grants for the sake of argument that the experimentalists interpretation of their findings are correct then there are at least two ways that one might attempt to block the inference from that interpretation to the further claim that philosophers' intuitions are similarly susceptible. First, the intuitions offered by the folk might not have the benefit of *reflection* that philosophers typically devote to their own judgments. Second, the folk lack the *philosophical expertise* that would be reflected in the superior performance of trained philosophers in the production of intuitions.

Antti Kaupinnen (2007) has offered an argument along the first of those lines, suggesting that intuitions that are the product of due consideration and reflection on the cases will produce *robust* intuitions that are immune to the sorts of effects studied by negative empirical philosophers; similar concerns are offered by S. Matthew Liao (2008). That reflection will affect, and in at least some ways improve, intuitive judgments is not a claim that experimental philosophers will want to have to disagree with.

One worry about this response, however, is that Kaupinnen needs the stronger claim that such reflection will *immunize* intuition from the sort of variation that experimental philosophers have been concerned with. But it is hard to see how, for example, considered reflection will protect philosophers from any culturally local influences on their judgments. Moreover, there are some recent experimental findings indicating that subjects likely to give more thought to their judgments are not, as a matter of fact, shielded from effects like the order effects reported by Swain et al. It appears that ordinary subjects high in "need for cognition" (NFC)—a personality trait indicating strong intrinsic motivation towards thought and reflection—demonstrate an order effect similar to that of the Swain et al. subjects, but in the opposite direction. Sometimes greater reflection might aid intuitive judgment; but sometimes it might also lead such judgments astray in novel directions. Such findings are not unanticipated in the scientific literature (Reber 1993; Gigerenzer et al. 1999; Petty et al. 2001; cf. Bishop 2000; Kornblith 2002, chapter 4).

The appeal to philosophical expertise has been by far the most popular response to the negative experimental challenge. Timothy Williamson offers the following straightforward version of it:

> Much of the evidence for cross-cultural variation in judgments on thought experiments concerns verdicts by people without philosophical training. Yet philosophy students have to learn how to apply general concepts to specific examples with careful attention to the relevant subtleties, just as law students have to learn how to analyze hypothetical cases. Levels of disagreement over thought experiments seem to be significantly lower among fully trained philosophers than among novices.
>
> (Williamson 2007, 191; cf. Ludwig 2007)

The truth of such claims to expertise is a complicated matter, and there is a large and complex literature on the psychology of expertise that could be brought to bear. But it is a literature that *needs* to be brought to bear. Among the central results of that literature is that our untutored sense of where expertise might be expected to develop is not actually very accurate—where expertise will or will not develop is not, it seems, something we can judge well from the armchair (Camerer and Johnson 1991; Shanteau 1992). Another result from the research on expertise that should unsettle philosophers' confidence in their status as expert intuiters concerns how narrowly defined most expert competences are; for example, medical expertise is highly specific to particular types of cases (Feltovich et al. 2006). So philosophers' manifest expertise in areas such as logic does not translate over into any special skill at applying general concepts to specific cases (Weinberg et al. forthcoming).

C.3. Relativism/Contextualism

Another avenue of response would be to defend the variation documented by the experimental philosophers as actually truth-tracking. Perhaps the different patterns of attribution simply reflect different extant concepts in different cultural groups, and each group's intuitions are correct for that group's main epistemic concepts (Goldman 2001; Jackson 2001; Lycan 2006). Moreover, if different groups care about different epistemic matters, this argument goes, then it is not problematic if their intuitions track different sorts of epistemic facts as well. Here, for example, is E. Sosa (2006, 109) responding to the Weinberg et al. (2001) data:

> I wonder how it is any better than saying to someone who values owning money banks that since others mean river banks by 'banks' his valuing as he does is now in doubt, and that he needs to show how owning money banks is better than owning river banks. Why need he suppose that owning money banks is better? He just thinks it's quite good as far as it goes. Maybe owning river banks is also good, maybe even better in many cases. And the same would seem reasonable when the commodities are all epistemic. The fact that we value one commodity, called 'knowledge' or 'justification' among us, is no obstacle to our also valuing a different commodity, valued by some other community under that same label.

Stich (1998, 235) has responded that

> While Sosa is baffled by our argument, I am baffled by his bafflement, . . . If a Yanomamö intuitively judges that it is morally permissible to kill men who are not members of his tribe, take their possessions, rape their wives and enslave their children, while I intuitively judge that it is not morally permissible to do these things, and if the disagreement can't be attributed to confusion, then the Yanomamö and I are invoking different concepts of moral permissibility. And if . . . this case is entirely parallel to the knowledge case, presumably Sosa would deny that there is any conflict here.

Philosophers pursuing these lines of response to the restrictionist challenge will need to consider whether epistemic relativism is any more acceptable than such radical forms of moral skepticism.

Where relativism might be an appropriate kind of response to evidence of variation across ethnicities, contextualism might similarly seem attractive as a response to order effects such as those reported by Swain et al. Confronting subjects with cases in which an agent clearly knows might raise the standards for knowledge, whereas confronting them with cases in which an agent clearly fails to know might similarly lower those standards. This predicts, therefore, that subjects will attribute more knowledge to intermediate sorts of cases such as Truetemp when it is presented right after a coin-flip case than when it is presented right after a scientific-knowledge case—which is what Swain et al. reported. However, it is not clear how this approach would explain why the Truetemp-style case showed this contextual effect but a similarly borderline fake-barn case did not; it also cannot accommodate the reverse-direction order effect in high-NFC subjects.

References

Alexander, J. and Weinberg, J. (2007) "Analytic Epistemology and Experimental Philosophy," *Philosophy Compass*, 2.1, 56–80.
Bealer, G. (1992) "The Incoherence of Empiricism," *Proceedings of the Aristotelian Society, Supplementary Volume* 66, 99–138.
Beebe, J. and Buckwalter, W. (Forthcoming) "The epistemic side-effect," *Mind and Language*.
Bengson, J., Moffet, M., and Wright, J. (2009) "The Folk on Knowing How," *Philosophical Studies* 142, 387–401.

Bishop, M. (2000) "In Praise of Epistemic Irresponsibility: How Lazy and Ignorant Can You Be?" *Synthese* 122, 179–208.

Buckwalter, W. (2010) "Knowledge Isn't Closed on Saturday: A Study in Ordinary Language," *Review of Philosophy and Psychology* 1.2, 395–406.

Camerer, C. F. and Johnson, E. J. (1991) "The process-performance paradox in expert judgment: How can experts know so much and predict so badly?" in K. A. Ericsson and J. Smith (eds.), *Towards a General Theory of Expertise: Prospects and Limits* (pp. 195–217). New York: Cambridge University Press.

Cullen, S. (2010) "Survey-Driven Romanticism," *Review of Philosophy and Psychology* 1.2, 275–296.

Cummins, R. (1998) "Reflections on Reflective Equilibrium," in *Rethinking Intuition: The Psychology of Intuition and its Role in Philosophical Inquiry*, ed. M. DePaul and W. Ramsey, Lanham, MD: Rowman and Littlefield.

DeRose, K. (1992) "Contextualism and Knowledge Attributions," *Philosophy and Phenomenological Research* 52, 913–29.

Feltz, A. and Zarpentine, C. (Unpublished manuscript) "Do You Know More When It Matters Less?"

Feltovich, P. J., Prietula, M. J. and Ericsson, K. A. (2006) "Studies of Expertise from Psychological Perspectives," in K. A. Ericsson, N. Charness, P. Feltovich, and R. R. Hoffman, R. R. (eds.), *Cambridge Handbook of Expertise and Expert Performance* (pp. 39–68). Cambridge, UK: Cambridge University Press.

Gigerenzer, G., Todd, P., and the ABC Research Group (1999) *Simple Heuristics that Make Us Smart*. Oxford: Oxford University Press.

Goldman, A. (2001) "Replies to Contributors," *Philosophical Topics* 17, 131–45.

Kaupinnen, A. (2007) "The Rise and Fall of Experimental Philosophy," *Philosophical Explorations* 10, 95–118.

Knobe, J. (2003) "Intentional Action in Folk Psychology: An Experimental Investigation," *Philosophical Psychology* 16, 309–23.

——. (2006) "The Concept of Intentional Action: A Case Study in the Uses of Folk Psychology," *Philosophical Studies* 130, 203–31.

Kornblith, H. (2002) *Knowledge and Its Place in Nature*. Oxford: Oxford University Press.

Lehrer, K. (1990) *Theory of Knowledge*. Boulder, CO: Westview Press.

Liao, S. M. (2008) "A Defense of Intuitions," *Philosophical Studies* 140, 247–62.

Ludwig, K. (2007) "The Epistemology of Thought Experiments: First vs. Third Person Approaches," *Midwest Studies in Philosophy* 31.1, 128–159.

Lycan, W. (2006) "The Gettier Problem Problem," in *Epistemology Futures*, ed. S. Hetherington, Oxford: Oxford University Press.

Machery, E., Mallon, R., Nichols, S., and Stich, S. P. (2004) "Semantics, Cross-cultural Style," *Cognition* 92, 3, B1–B12.

May, J., Sinnott-Armstrong, W., Hull, J. and Zimmerman, A. (2010) "Practical Interests, Relevant Alternatives, and Knowledge Attributions: An Empirical Study," *Review of Philosophy and Psychology* 1.2, 265–273.

Murphy, D., and Bishop, M., eds. (2009) *Stich and His Critics*. Oxford: Blackwell.

Neta, R. and Phelan, M., Unpublished manuscript, "Evidence That Stakes Don't Matter for Evidence."

Nisbett, R. (2003) *The Geography of Thought: How Asians and Westerners Think Differently . . . and Why*. New York: Free Press.

——, Kaiping, P., Incheol, C., and Norenzayan, A. (2001) "Culture and Systems of Thought: Holistic Versus Analytic Cognition," *Psychological Review* 108, 291–310.

Petty, R., Tormala, Z., Hawkins, C., and Wegener, D. (2001) "Motivation to Think and Order Effects in Persuasion: The Moderating Role of Chunking," *Personality and Social Psychology Bulletin*, 27, 332–44.

Pust, J. (2000) *Intuitions as Evidence*. New York: Garland.

Reber, A. (1993) *Implicit Learning and Tacit Knowledge: An Essay on the Cognitive Unconscious*. Oxford: Oxford University Press.

Schaffer, J. (2006) "The Irrelevance of the Subject: Against Subject-Sensitive Invariantism," *Philosophical Studies*, 127, 87–107.

Shanteau, J. (1992) "Competence in Experts: The Role of Task Characteristics," *Organizational Behavior and Human Decision Processes*, 53, 252–266.

Sosa, D. (2006) "Scepticism About Intuition," *Philosophy* 81, 633–47.

Sosa, E. (2006) "Experimental Philosophy and Philosophical Intuition," *Philosophical Studies* 132, 99–107.

Stanley, J. (2005) *Knowledge and Practical Interests*. Oxford: Clarendon Press.

Stich, S. (1990) *The Fragmentation of Reason*. Cambridge, MA: MIT.

——. (1998) "Reflective Equilibrium, Analytic Epistemology, and the Problem of Cognitive Diversity," in *Rethinking Intuition: The Psychology of Intuition and its Role in Philosophical Inquiry*, ed. M. DePaul and W. Ramsey, Lanham, MD: Rowman and Littlefield.

Swain, S., Alexander, J., and Weinberg, J. (2008) "The Instability of Philosophical Intuitions: Running Hot and Cold on Truetemp," *Philosophy and Phenomenological Research* 76, 138–55.

Sytsma, J., and Livengood, J. (2009) "A New Perspective concerning Experiments on Semantic Intuitions," presented as "The Case for Divergent Descriptions," to American Philosophical Association Pacific Division 83rd Annual Meeting, Vancouver, British Columbia.

Weinberg, J., Nichols, S., and Stich, S. (2001) "Normativity and Epistemic Intuitions," *Philosophical Topics* 29, 429–60.

——, Gonnerman, C., Buckner, C., Alexander, J. (Forthcoming) "Are Philosophers Expert Intuiters?" to appear in *Philosophical Psychology*.

Williamson, T. (2007) *The Philosophy of Philosophy*. Oxford: Blackwell.

Further Reading

Bealer, G. (1996) "A priori knowledge and the scope of philosophy," *Philosophical Studies* 81, 121–42.

——. (1998) "Intuition and the Autonomy of Philosophy," in *Rethinking Intuition: The Psychology of Intuition and its Role in Philosophical Inquiry*, ed. M. DePaul and W. Ramsey, Lanham, MD: Rowman and Littlefield.

Feltz, A. (2008) "Problems with the Appeal to Intuition in Epistemology," *Philosophical Explorations* 11, 131–41.

Jackson, F. (2001) "Responses," *Philosophy and Phenomenological Research* 62, 653–64.

Knobe, J. and Burra, A. (2006) "The Folk Concept of Intention and Intentional Action: A Cross-cultural Study," *Journal of Culture and Cognition* 6, 113–32.

Sosa, E. (2009) "A Defense of the Use of Intuitions in Philosophy," in Murphy and Bishop (2009).

Stich, S. (2009) "Replies," in Murphy and Bishop (2009).

Weinberg, J. (2007) "How to Challenge Intuitions Empirically Without Risking Skepticism," *Midwest Studies in Philosophy* 31(1), 318–43.

74
NATURALISTIC EPISTEMOLOGY
Klemens Kappel

1. Introduction

Naturalistic epistemology names a cluster of views according to which epistemology should be reconciled with, or even draw upon, empirical science. By contrast, traditional epistemology assumes that epistemology is prior to and independent of empirical science, both in terms of its subject matter and in terms of its methods. The details of this are complicated and there are now many different views championed under the heading of naturalistic epistemology.

It is useful to make a rough distinction between two enterprises in epistemology. The *descriptive project* aims to understand the basic nature of matters epistemic, that is, the nature of epistemic properties, states, norms, aims, concepts, expressions, practices of epistemic evaluations (henceforth I will just write "epistemic notions"). Thus the descriptive project asks questions such as: What is knowledge? What is it for a belief to be justified? What is an epistemic norm? What is it to say that a belief is known? The *normative project*, by contrast, seeks to advance and justify epistemic evaluations. Do our beliefs really qualify as justified? Are the beliefs usually regarded as known rightly so judged? Are we doing right in adopting the epistemic norms that we rely upon in our epistemic practices? What would improved epistemic practices be? Note that the normative project includes, but is not exhausted by, what is sometimes called *meliorative epistemology*, the attempt to improve on our ways of reasoning.

Corresponding to the descriptive and the normative project, one can discern two distinct classes of naturalistic views, which I will refer to as *descriptive naturalism* and *normative naturalism* (Laudan 1990).

Traditionally, epistemology has been conducted using *philosophical methods*, that is methods that allegedly proceed by means of conceptual analysis, linguistic analysis, a priori insights, considered intuitions about how to classify possible cases, and attempts to reach reflective equilibrium between these possibly conflicting inputs and other theoretical commitments. Philosophical methods are non-empirical in that they appeal only to what can be justifiably believed or known without conducting empirical investigations of the external world.

By contrast, *methodological naturalism* is the view that empirical investigations should partly or entirely *replace* philosophical methods. So, a methodological naturalist about the descriptive project thinks that, roughly, when determining what knowledge is, we should in part or entirely turn to empirical investigations, say in cognitive science or psychology. Methodological naturalism about the normative project advocates making use of empirical findings when addressing questions within the normative project.

These different forms of naturalisms are typically related in being motivated by a more general naturalistic outlook, but they are nonetheless logically distinct. One can be a descriptive naturalist without being a normative naturalist, and vice versa. And one can accept methodological naturalism about the normative project, without endorsing it about the descriptive project, or conversely.

2. Quine's "Epistemology Naturalized"

The recent history of the subject dates back to W.V. Quine's widely read paper "Epistemology Naturalized" (1969). Here Quine famously held that epistemology should fall "into place as a chapter of psychology," confining itself to the study of how subjects generate beliefs about the world as a function of the input they receive. For Quine, this study of the "relation between the meager input and the torrential output" should be undertaken for "somewhat the same reasons that always prompted epistemology; namely, in order to see how evidence relates to theory, and in what ways one's theory of nature transcends any available evidence."

As has often been observed, it is difficult to see how Quine's naturalism could plausibly be a successor discipline to traditional epistemology (Kim 1988; BonJour 1994: 287). The descriptive project asks about the nature of epistemic notions such as knowledge or justified belief. Studying the "relation between the meager input and the torrential output" could be an attempt to eliminate such questions, but would hardly settle them. A crucial part of the normative project is to decide if our everyday and scientific beliefs about the world are in fact justified. Again, it is hard to see how a mere description of how we in fact proceed when forming beliefs could be a new way of answering those questions. In later writings Quine has, however, clarified his position and explicitly asserted a normative role of epistemology, saying in one place that normative epistemology is "a branch of engineering," seeking to aid the "technology of truth-seeking" (Quine 1986; Foley 1994).

Irrespective of perceived weaknesses of Quine's "Naturalized Epistemology," many influential epistemologists endorse naturalistic views (Goldman 1986; Kitcher 1992; Kornblith 2002; Bishop and Trout 2005). Prominent critics of naturalistic epistemology are plentiful, and include Laurence BonJour, Richard Feldman, Michael Williams, Barry Stroud, Donald Davidson and Robert Brandom, just to mention a few (see Kornblith 2002: chapters 3–5).

3. Descriptive Naturalism

Descriptive naturalism claims that the nature of epistemic notions can be accounted for in natural terms, i.e. terms referring exclusively to natural objects and properties. Natural objects and properties are such as would figure in our best scientific understanding of the world.

Descriptive naturalism remains a controversial position. Knowledge is, by most accounts, true belief acquired or sustained for good epistemic reasons, with sufficient evidence, or in non-accidental ways (ignoring Gettier complications). However, notions such as having a good epistemic reason, or sufficient evidence for holding a belief do not figure as a part of psychology or cognitive science, and neither does a belief's property of being non-accidentally acquired. So states of knowledge do not immediately seem to be composed entirely of natural objects and properties. Similarly, a complete naturalistic description of a cognitive process would seem to leave open whether this process would count as embodying a proper epistemic norm or not.

Those inclined to naturalism about the descriptive project have responded to this set of questions in a variety of rather different ways. Eliminativists have repudiated the normative side of epistemic notions altogether, in favor of an enterprise that merely seeks to describe the ways in which beliefs are actually formed. Quine (1969) held this sort of view (see Maffie 1990 for an overview and further references).

Since eliminativism could be said to repudiate rather than account for epistemic notions, this position might not be considered a form of naturalistic epistemology at all. Other strategies do not seek to eliminate the normative dimension of epistemic properties, but to account for them. To provide a less abstract presentation of some basic ideas within this family of strategies, it might be helpful to consider a more specific theory of justification and knowledge:

> *Reliabilism.* Beliefs are justified to the extent that they are acquired or sustained by a reliable process. Beliefs are known when true and sufficiently justified.

Reliabilism and similar views have been defended by Alvin Goldman (1979, 1986, 1992b) and many others. Reliabilism is but one member of a wider class of *externalist* theories which hold that beliefs can be justified (or known if true) in virtue of features that are external to the purview of the subject, but, for present purposes, we need not consider the wider class of externalist theories. It is important to note though, that nothing in descriptive naturalism per se forces one to be an externalist about knowledge or justification. It is just that many proponents of descriptive naturalism have adopted some form of reliabilism or externalism about knowledge and justification, whereas those opposed to naturalism tend to be internalists about knowledge and justification.

A descriptive naturalist who accepts reliabilism might propose this view as a naturalistically acceptable *analysis* of our concepts of justification and knowledge. Closely related, one might consider reliabilism as offering a *reduction* of epistemic to natural properties. Recently, Kornblith (2002) has defended the view that knowledge is a natural kind, just as water or aluminum are natural kinds. Reliabilism, on Kornblith's view, figures as a part of the account of the natural properties that constitute knowledge as a natural kind. A less ambitious option is to view reliabilism in *criterialist* terms. According to this view, reliabilism specifies the conditions for the proper application of epistemic predicates, but refrains from providing an analysis or reduction of those predicates. Hence, the criterialist concedes that "epistemic predicates cannot be naturalistically defined or reduced without loss of their essential content" (Maffie 1990: 285). In later work, Goldman (1992a) has embedded reliabilism in an empirically supported naturalistic view of how epistemic evaluators apply the concepts of knowledge and justification.

All non-eliminativist versions of descriptive naturalism agree that epistemic properties depend on natural properties:

> *Supervenience.* For any epistemic property E, and any agent x and y, if x has E, there is a set of natural properties N, such that x has N, and necessarily, whatever agent y has N y also has E.

Supervenience, or similar views, has been widely endorsed (Van Cleve 1985, 1999; Kim 1988; Goldman 1994), though there are noteworthy dissenters (Lehrer 1999). It is important to realize, however, that while involving some degree of naturalism, supervenience is compatible with epistemic properties being genuine but non-natural, and hence not analyzable or reducible to natural objects and properties.

Accounting for the Normativity of the Epistemic

Non-eliminativist forms of descriptive naturalism might seem to face a problem accounting for the distinctive normative dimension of the epistemic. There is a sense in which one ought to acquire beliefs in certain ways, or ought to believe certain things when in possession of particular evidence or reasons. How is this "to-do-ness" or the "ought-to-believe-ness" supposed to flow from an austere account of the natural properties that epistemic properties consist of? This problem is, of course, reminiscent of the problem J. L. Mackie (1977) pointed out in ethics (cf. Kornblith 2002: chapter 5).

For simplicity, consider the problem specifically in terms of epistemic norms. Let us say that an *epistemic norm* is a directive, principle or rule stating a way to adopt, revise or sustain beliefs. Epistemic norms might be embodied in an individual subject's modes of reasoning and methods of inquiry, or they could be embodied in socially embedded epistemic practices, such as those found in science or public debate. We might rely on particular epistemic norms even when we are not aware of doing so, or are unable to explain what, if anything, justifies us in doing so.

Let us say that a *proper* epistemic norm is one that we are epistemically permitted to make use of, given appropriate circumstances. Induction is a proper epistemic norm (or set of norms), whereas crystal ball gazing or affirming the consequent is not. So, proper epistemic norms exert some sort of normative force: given appropriate conditions, one ought to make use of them. Any view in epistemology must account for the purported normative force of proper epistemic norms. What is the descriptive naturalist account of the normative force of proper epistemic norms?

A common option is to think of epistemic norms as hypothetical imperatives. Relative to particular ends, certain ways of reasoning or acquiring beliefs might be more or less expedient in various circumstances. So, for example, one might say that for a subject S and some appropriate end E, epistemic norm EN is proper just in case relying on EN makes S sufficiently adept at arriving at E under the conditions in which S would normally use EN to arrive at E.

Quine (1986) subscribed to this sort of view, holding that epistemic norms are instruments relative to the aim of finding truth, which on Quine's view appears to be a purely contingent aim. Stephen Stich (1990: 131–2) advocates a very general form of pragmatism according to which an agent's set of epistemic norms should be assessed in terms of their contribution to the total set of things the agent values. Kornblith (2002: 158) has criticized both of these views and argued that while epistemic norms are indeed hypothetical imperatives, the merits of a system of epistemic norms should be assessed not relative to contingent aims, but relative to the aim of truth, which we are bound to care about "whatever we may otherwise care about."

Another and quite different strategy that might suit the descriptive naturalist is to adapt the expressivist account of normativity that is well-known from ethics (Gibbard 1990, 2003; Blackburn 1998). This view, which is only sparsely elaborated, is now referred to as *epistemic expressivism*. Epistemic expressivism holds that epistemic expressions are not fully descriptive but at least partly expressive. Thus, uttering sentences of the form "S knows that p" normally serves to express a distinct kind of pro-attitude to subjects' holding certain beliefs. Similarly, saying that some epistemic norm is proper is expressing one's pro-attitude towards the use of that norm. Hartry Field (1998) is a proponent of epistemic expressivism (though he calls it non-factualism), and a similar view has been defended in Chrisman (2007). Recently, epistemic expressivism has been criticized in Cuneo (2007) and Kvanvig (2003)

4. Normative Naturalism

The normative project concerns the epistemic evaluation of our ways of reasoning and conducting inquiry. When we judge that beliefs are justified or known, are we right? When we rely on specific modes or forming beliefs or patterns of inference, are we doing right? Could we improve on our ways of reasoning? Note that issuing and justifying epistemic evaluations of beliefs and epistemic norms is different from accounting for the normative dimension of epistemic properties, which is part of the descriptive project.

Normative naturalism holds that when addressing the questions of the normative project, we can in certain ways appeal to everyday beliefs about the world, as well as to empirical findings from disciplines such as psychology and cognitive science. This position is controversial and, to understand why, we need to consider the ways in which the normative project has traditionally been pursued in epistemology.

The Privileged Class Constraint

The normative project has, to a large extent, evolved around two more specific sets of issues: a range of skeptical challenges, and the problem of how to justify our epistemic norms, where this includes epistemology's meliorative project.

The most prominent of the skeptical challenges, the Cartesian challenge, is this: How can one rule out the possibility of being a brain in a vat, devoid of genuine perceptual contact to the external world? The Lockean challenge is slightly different, and asks roughly: How can we have knowledge about the external world, given all we have to go on are beliefs about our own perceptual experience?

It is quite crucial for these skeptical challenges that they come with the following restriction in permissible responses: one cannot appeal to premises the knowledge of which is rendered in doubt by the skeptical challenge in question. So, when responding to the Cartesian challenge, one cannot appeal to empirical facts about how extremely unlikely the scenario in question is, or indeed to what would normally count as observations incompatible with being a brain in a vat. When responding to the Lockean challenge, one cannot appeal to putative empirical facts about correlations between the character of one's sense experience and the external world. Thus, the common structure of the skeptical challenges is that they grant that while we are justified in accepting members of a fairly small class of beliefs (*the privileged class*), we are not justified in a certain other class of beliefs (*the target class*). The skeptic then charges us with the task of explaining how we are, after all, justified in accepting members of the target class, while appealing only to members of the privileged class. Call this the *privileged class constraint*.

Clearly, different specific skeptical challenges vary with respect to the extensions of the target class and the privileged class. Very general skeptical challenges admit only a priori justified beliefs in the privileged class (or perhaps only a subclass of these), whereas less general skeptical problems might admit reflectively accessible beliefs, including beliefs about the nature of certain perceptual experiences or memory experiences. The problem of other minds admits beliefs about the overt behavior of others in the privileged class, while beliefs about the mental life of others are to be found in the target class.

Consider then the other part of the normative project, that of justifying our epistemic norms. Is there a cogent argument to the effect that we should trust sense perception? Are we justified in relying on inductive inferences, and if so, in virtue of what? Again, a version of the privileged class constraint is assumed to apply. When replying to the question whether we are justified in relying on some epistemic norm EN, we cannot appeal to EN or otherwise make use of EN. So, when explaining why certain forms of inductive inferences are reasonable, we cannot make use of induction. When explaining why we are permitted to trust sense perception, we cannot rely on the deliverances of sense perception, or on beliefs the justification of which depends on sense perception.

Note that the problem of justifying epistemic norms remains distinct from the problem of responding to skeptical challenges. For example, one might think that one can reject as incoherent the possibility that one might be a brain in a vat, and yet still be at a loss to explain why we are permitted to rely on inferences to best explanations. But of course, one can mount a skeptical challenge by arguing that some class of our epistemic norms are not reliable, or that we have no reason to consider them reliable.

Ignoring the Privileged Class Constraint

Throughout the history of epistemology, tremendous efforts have been invested in the attempt to address skeptical challenges and justify epistemic norms while observing the privileged class constraint. For example, many writers have pursued the strategy of mounting transcendental arguments purporting to show that, on a priori grounds, the idea that one might be a brain in a vat is incoherent. Others have attempted to argue on a priori grounds that we should trust sense perception, memory, or rely on induction. For example, P. F. Strawson (1952: 257) once held it to be an a priori knowable truth that we are permitted to rely on induction, since the use of induction under appropriate circumstances is part of "what 'being reasonable' means in such a context." BonJour (1998) has recently offered a general defense of a priori reasoning which includes an a priori defense of induction. Such strategies would, if otherwise successful, provide a vindication of certain of our epistemic norms, while still observing the privileged class constraint.

Perhaps the single most important and controversial contribution of naturalistic epistemology is to advocate *ignoring* the privileged class constraint. When facing skeptical challenges, and when evaluating epistemic norms, we are not obliged to observe the privileged class constraint.

There are different ways of pursuing this strategy. One example is Strawson (1985) who advocated thinking of "skeptical arguments and rational counter-arguments as equally idle—not senseless, but idle—since what we have here are original, natural inescapable commitments which we neither choose nor could give up" (27–8). Strawson here seems to concede to the skeptic that, properly speaking, we are not really justified in a range of our beliefs, just as we are incapable of providing a satisfactory demonstration that our epistemic norms are proper. It is just, says Strawson, that we cannot really change our minds on these issues. In this sense, Strawson recommends ignoring the privileged class constraint.

Another example is, again, Quine (1975), who insisted on "the point that sceptical doubts are scientific doubts," which for Quine meant that they can and should be answered by scientific means (68). Goldman (1978) says something very similar: "In studying and criticizing our cognitive procedures, we should use whatever powers and procedures we antecedently accept. There is no starting 'from scratch'" (522). Kitcher (1992) concurs, when he concedes that on "naturalism's own ground, there are bound to be unanswerable forms of skepticism," and adds that the "naturalists should therefore decline blanket invitations to play the game of synchronic reconstruction." Rather, "parts of our current scientific beliefs must be assumed in criticizing others" (90–1).

An important question raised by these normative naturalist strategies concerns their wider epistemological implications. Here one can distinguish two views. *Weak* normative naturalism urges that we can ignore the privileged class constraint and make use of empirical findings and ordinary beliefs about the world when pursuing the normative project. But, the weak normative naturalist concedes, one does beg the question against the skeptic by violating the privileged class constraint. In consequence we should give up the hope of providing a genuine justification of our epistemic norms and a genuine demonstration that much of what we take to be known is indeed so. What we have is a kind of naturalistic *ersatz* for the normative judgments that (naive) traditional epistemology in vain sought to underpin while observing the privileged class constraint. Strawson, Quine and possibly Kitcher seem to acquiesce to this view; Bishop and Trout (2005b: 161) explicitly endorse it.

Strong normative naturalism, by contrast, insists that thus begging the question against the skeptic has no wider epistemological implications. The fact that we cannot, without begging the question, demonstrate the propriety of our epistemic norms in the face of a skeptical challenge, does nothing to show that we are not epistemically justified in relying on those epistemic norms. The fact that we cannot rule out a skeptical scenario to the skeptic's satisfaction does not imply that we have virtually no knowledge or justified beliefs about the world.

Is Strong Normative Naturalism Tenable?

To see how strong normative naturalism might be a defensible position, return again to reliabilism. Part of the normative project is to explain the epistemic status of our beliefs and the epistemic norms we use or might use. Consider what reliabilism implies about these questions. When our beliefs are formed by reliable processed, they are justified. When true, in addition, our beliefs are known. Now, in many cases, we have, or are in a position to acquire, justified beliefs to the effect that specific beliefs of ours are indeed reliably formed and true, and thus instances of knowledge. So, granted reliabilism and certain seemingly innocuous beliefs about the world, we can easily reject certain conclusions that seem to be looming in the face of skeptical challenges.

Consider then the problem of evaluating our epistemic norms. Assume that according to reliabilism, an epistemic norm is proper just if reliable under the conditions of its normal use. So certifying that some epistemic norm is proper requires canvassing empirical evidence of its reliability under those circumstances. Explaining the features in virtue of which the norm is proper would be accomplished by pointing to the features that make it reliable. Say that some subject S is justified in relying on an epistemic norm just in case doing so results from a reliable process for the *selection* of proper epistemic norms to rely upon. So, explaining that S is justified in relying on a particular epistemic norm would require identifying such processes that led to trusting this norm. Finally, a belief to the effect that some epistemic norm is proper is itself justified just if acquired and sustained by a reliable process. So for the reliabilist to explain how we can be justified in believing certain epistemic norms to be proper requires pointing to such processes. The explanation, of course, fails to respect the privileged class constraint.

Unsurprisingly, many epistemologists have objected that the violation of the privileged class constraint is question-begging. Here is Fumerton (1994: 337–8; cf. 1996):

> None of this, of course, will make the skeptic happy. You cannot *use* perception to justify the reliability of perception! You cannot *use* memory to justify the reliability of memory! You cannot *use* induction to justify the reliability of induction! Such attempts to respond to the skeptic's concerns involve blatant, indeed pathetic, circularity.

The strong normative naturalist can offer a response to this worry, however. For simplicity, consider just the problem of evaluating epistemic norms. The strong normative naturalist can distinguish several parts of this enterprise. One is the task of providing a *dialectically satisfactory* response to a challenge posed by someone who is assumed—if only for the sake of argument—to seriously doubt the propriety of a particular epistemic norm EN. Clearly, in this kind of enterprise one cannot assume EN to be a proper epistemic norm. Indeed, this stems from a general feature of argumentative debate. When proposing an argument to someone who seriously questions whether there are reasons to accept some proposition *p*, one cannot appeal to *p* itself, or to premises the truth or justification of which depend on *p*. So, we can understand what motivates the privileged class constraint, and see why it applies to the problem of providing a dialectically appropriate response to a skeptic.

However, the strong normative naturalist can insist that the crucial task is not that of convincing a presumed skeptic, but the different one of explaining the epistemic status of our epistemic norms. Providing a successful explanation of this kind is very different from providing a dialectically acceptable argument to someone who is assumed to seriously question the propriety of some epistemic norm. Suppose that, as reliabilists we seek to explain the epistemic properties of a certain epistemic norm EN. And suppose that, when providing such reliabilist explanation of the features of EN, we rely on the use of EN. Would this epistemic circularity (Alston 1986), as it is often called, invalidate the explanation we seek to mount? It seems not. Explanations generally appeal to facts that we know or justifiably believe. When, as is generally the case, we know or justifiably believe facts by relying on epistemic norms, they must be proper norms. So, successful explanations require reliance on proper epistemic norms. Clearly, this requirement applies to the epistemic circularity at hand. So, if the explanation of how we can be justified in relying on EN or in believing that EN is a proper epistemic norm itself trades on beliefs whose justification depends on the use of EN, then the explanation presupposes that EN is indeed a proper norm. So, if EN is in fact a proper norm, that is, if EN is reliable under the appropriate circumstances, then the explanation is successful, at least as far as EN is concerned, despite the epistemic circularity. So, the epistemic circularity at hand need not invalidate the explanation we seek.

What the presence of this kind of epistemic circularity does show, however, is that someone doubting the propriety of EN should not let herself rationally convince by the explanation we offer, since she rejects part of the basis for the explanation. But, as we have seen, the strong normative naturalist can insist that the success of the explanation on offer is unaffected by this.

How is Knowledge Possible?

Barry Stroud has, in many writings, pressed what is effectively a related objection to strong normative naturalism. He poses a transcendental question: How is knowledge possible? As we have seen, the reliabilist has a simple answer. Knowledge just is true belief formed by a reliable process under appropriate circumstances (ignoring Gettier complications). So, knowledge is possible because we are beings equipped with a range of ways of forming beliefs that are reliable and regularly lead to true beliefs under the appropriate circumstances. This explanation of how knowledge is possible relies heavily on matters known, of course. But it is not thereby invalidated. One cannot explain a fact by itself. But clearly one can explain the fact that we are capable of knowing facts by appealing to other facts, knowledge of which are presupposed in the explanation. Explaining how knowledge is possible is not convincing to a skeptic.

Stroud (2000) finds this deeply unsatisfactory. As he says: "The difficulty in understanding how sense-perception gives us knowledge […] is that it seems at least possible to perceive what we do without thereby knowing something about the things around us." According to Stroud, the transcendental question invites us to explain how we nevertheless can have knowledge of the world. As he says, "Given the apparent 'obstacle,' how is our knowledge possible?" (5–6). In other places Stroud says that a philosophical theory of knowledge must provide "an account of our knowledge of the world that would make all of it intelligible to us all at once" (8).

Stroud seems to assume that a satisfactory answer to the transcendental question must also answer a skeptical challenge, or a range of them. Thus, when explaining how knowledge is possible we are permitted to appeal only to features that could feature in a dialectically acceptable answer to a skeptic. This, in turn, means observing the privileged class constraint. On this construal of the question "How is knowledge possible?" strong normative naturalism fails to provide a satisfactory answer.

Clearly, however, the strong normative naturalist can respond that Stroud conflates the dialectical requirements relevant when responding to a skeptic with requirements reasonably imposed on an explanation of what knowledge is and how it is possible. Thus, strong normative naturalism promises a non-skeptical explanation of how we can have knowledge and justified belief, but one that cannot convince a presumed skeptic. What is decisive is that failing to respect the privileged class constraint carries no dramatic epistemological consequences.

Note that the fate of strong and weak normative naturalism is independent of descriptive naturalism. One might reject descriptive naturalism, and still advocate lifting the privileged class constraint. Note also that, contrary to what is often assumed, normative naturalism does not depend on the rejection of the a priori. One can concede that some propositions can be known a priori and yet advocate normative naturalism. One can even accept that the propriety of some epistemic norms can be known a priori, and yet adopt the general strategy of normative naturalism. And there might be a very good reason to do so. Even if the propriety of some epistemic norms could be established a priori, this is unlikely to provide us with the epistemic advice that we need. We need to establish, it seems, which specific epistemic norms are best (or at least good enough) given the actual "powers and limits of the human cognitive system" (Goldman 1978: 510), and given our wider non-epistemic interests and concerns. Even on the most optimistic views about what might be known a priori, it is hard to see how this could be accomplished without resorting to empirical investigations.

5. Naturalism about Methodology in Epistemology

A second dimension of naturalistic epistemology concerns the method by which epistemological questions should be pursued. The methodological naturalist rejects the exclusive commitment to philosophical methods in epistemology, and holds that we should include methods and empirical findings from various parts of science, including biology, cognitive psychology and many other disciplines.

Note that one can advocate the use of non-empirical methods as a necessary supplement to philosophical methods, or one can reject philosophical methods as entirely unsuitable for epistemology. Note also that methodological naturalism can be applied selectively to the various projects of epistemology. For example, one can reject methodological naturalism regarding the descriptive project, but accept it regarding the normative project.

Kornblith is a prominent advocate of methodological naturalism with respect to the descriptive project. According to Kornblith, a theory of knowledge should provide a correct account of the nature of knowledge, as distinct from an account of the concept of knowledge. And just as an analysis of the concept of aluminum will hardly reveal the nature of aluminum, analysis of the concept of knowledge is unhelpful for understanding what knowledge is. Rather, we should "examine apparently clear cases of knowledge to see what it is that they have in common." We must, says Kornblith (1999: 161; cf. 2002: chapters 1–2), "examine the various psychological mechanisms by which knowledge is produced and retained in order to see what, if anything, they have in common."

Kornblith's view remains quite controversial, even among philosophers otherwise sympathetic to naturalism. One cause of concern is the very idea that the concept of knowledge is a natural kind concept. This seems highly contentious—there might be no underlying theoretical unity to cases of knowledge, apart from the fact that they, at least according to reliabilism, all involve true belief formed by reliable processes (Goldman 2005: 405).

Kornblith is indeed sympathetic to reliabilism. But reliabilism seems best defended by philosophical methods, or at any rate this is how the view has been defended in recent epistemology. Reliabilism is justified by the fact that this theory (allegedly) captures a broad range of our considered epistemic judgment concerning putative cases of knowledge and justified belief. Empirical investigations could, of course, have some role in providing counterexamples to proposed analyses of knowledge and justification, thereby forcing revisions. The problem, however, is that the counterexamples needed would seem to be readily available anyway (Feldman 1999). So, it is not clear that methodological naturalism could be a vital part of the descriptive project.

However, others have questioned precisely the role of considered epistemic judgments are assumed to have in philosophical methods, and this points to a different form of methodological naturalism. Weinberg et al. (2001) call attention to the fact that considered epistemic judgments might vary across cultures and social strata. And indeed, preliminary empirical findings did suggest some interesting differences in considered epistemic judgment. For example, students of Indian, Pakistani and Bangladeshi descent were found to be significantly less willing to characterize a typical Gettier case as one in which one does not have knowledge than were their Western counterparts.

One might, of course, question the specific findings and methods in Weinberg et al. However, assuming that considered epistemic judgments are indeed relevant for understanding our epistemic concepts and the nature of epistemic properties, it seems that empirical surveys of the actual set of judgments that people have would be indispensable for more robust relevant information. At least such empirical surveys would seem necessary to establish that the considered epistemic judgments of professional epistemologists are not merely idiosyncratic and therefore beyond general interests, as indeed Bishop and Trout (2005a) suspect.

Even if this problem is overcome Bishop and Trout's discussion points to a wider methodological issue concerning the relevance of the descriptive project for the normative concerns in epistemology. It is often, if only tacitly, assumed that since epistemic notions such as knowledge and justification are essentially normative, understanding their nature will immediately lead to prescriptions regarding how to reason and conduct inquiry. It is not obvious, however, that standard theories of knowledge and justification such as fundamentalism, coherentism, reliabilism, and contextualism really are prescriptive in this way. These theories are, at their core, descriptive theories aiming to capture our considered epistemic judgment, or providing accounts of the content of our epistemic concepts. But why pay so much attention to our actual considered set of epistemic judgments, or our actual epistemic concepts? Why not turn directly to the problem of devising better ways of reasoning and conducting inquiry?

References

Alston, W. P. (1986) Epistemic Circularity. *Philosophy and Phenomenological Research*, 47, 1–30.
Bishop, M. and Trout, J. D. (2005a) The Pathologies of Standard Analytic Epistemology. *Noûs*, 39, 696–714.
—— (2005b) *Epistemology and the Psychology of Human Judgment*, Oxford, Oxford University Press.
Blackburn, S. (1998) *Ruling Passions: A Theory of Practical Reasoning*, Oxford, Clarendon Press.
BonJour, L. (1994) Against Naturalized Epistemology. *Midwest Studies in Philosophy*, 19, 283–300.
—— (1998) *In Defense of Pure Reason*, Cambridge, Cambridge University Press.
Chrisman, M. (2007) From Epistemic Contextualism to Epistemic Expressivism. *Philosophical Studies*, 135, 225–54.
Cuneo, T. (2007) *The Normative Web: An Argument For Moral Realism*, Oxford, Oxford University Press.
Feldman, R. (1999) Methodological Naturalism in Epistemology. In Greco, J. and Sosa, E. (Eds.) *The Blackwell Guide to Epistemology*.
Field, H. (1998) Epistemological Nonfactualism and the A Prioricity of Logic. *Philosophical Studies*, 92, 1–24.
Foley, R. (1994) Quine and Naturalized Epistemology. In French, P. A., Uehling, J., Theodore, E. & Wettstein, H. K. (Eds.) *Midwest Studies in Philosophy. Philosophical Naturalism*. Notre Dame, IN, University of Notre Dame Press.
Fumerton, R. A. (1994) Skepticism and Naturalistic Epistemology. In French, P. A., Uehling, J., Theodore, E. and Wettstein, H. K. (Eds.) *Midwest Studies in Philosophy. Philosophical Naturalism*. Notre Dame, IN, University of Notre Dame Press.
—— (1996) *Metaepistemology and Skepticism*, Lanham, MD, Rowman & Littlefield.
Gibbard, A. (1990) *Wise Choices, Apt Feelings: A Theory of Normative Judgement*, Oxford, Clarendon.
—— (2003) *Thinking How to Live*, Cambridge, MA; London, Harvard University Press.
Goldman, A. (1978) Epistemics: The Regulative Theory of Cognition. *Journal of Philosophy*, 75, 509–23.
—— (1979) What Is Justified Belief? in Papas, G. (ed.) *Justification and Knowledge*, Dordrecht, D. Reidel, 1–23.

—— (1986) *Epistemology and Cognition*, Cambridge, MA, Harvard University Press.
—— (1992a) Epistemic Folkways and Scientific Epistemology. In Goldman, A. (Ed.) *Liaisons: Philosophy Meets the Cognitive and Social Sciences*. Cambridge, MA, MIT Press.
—— (1992b) *Liaisons: Philosophy Meets the Cognitive and Social Sciences*, Cambridge, MA, MIT Press.
—— (1994) Naturalistic Epistemology and Reliabilism. In French, P. A., Uehling, J., Theodore, E. and Wettstein, H. K. (Eds.) *Midwest Studies in Philosophy. Philosophical Naturalism*. Notre Dame, IN, University of Notre Dame Press.
—— (2005) Kornblith's Naturalistic Epistemology. *Philosophy and Phenomenological Research*, 71, 403–10.
Kim, J. (1988) What Is "Naturalized Epistemology"? In Tomberline, J. E. (Ed.) *Philosophical Perspectives, Epistemology*. Atascadero, CA, Ridgeview Publishing Co.
Kitcher, P. (1992) The Naturalists Return. *The Philosophical Review*, 101, 53–114.
Kornblith, H. (1999) In Defense of a Naturalized Epistemology. In Greco, J. & Sosa, E. (Eds.) *The Blackwell Guide to Epistemology*. Blackwell.
—— (2002) *Knowledge and its Place in Nature*, Oxford, Clarendon.
Kvanvig, J. L. (2003) *The Value of Knowledge and the Pursuit of Understanding*, Cambridge, UK; New York, Cambridge University Press.
Laudan, L. (1990) Normative Naturalism. *Philosophy of Science*, 57, 44–59.
Lehrer, K. (1999) Reply to Van Cleve. *Philosophy and Phenomenological Research*, 59, 1068–71.
Mackie, J. L. (1977) *Ethics: Inventing Right and Wrong*, Harmondsworth, Penguin.
Maffie, J. (1990) Recent Work on Naturalized Epistemology. *American Philosophical Quarterly*, 281–93.
Quine, W. V. (1969) *Epistemology Naturalized. Ontological Relativity and Other Essays*. New York, Columbia University Press.
—— (1975) The Nature of Natural Knowledge. In Guttenplan, S. (Ed.) *Mind and Language*. Oxford University Press.
—— (1986) Reply to Morton White. In Hahn, L. and Schilpp, P. (Eds.) *The Philosophy of W.V. Quine*. LaSalle, IL, Open Court.
Stich, S. P. (1990) *The Fragmentation of Reason: Preface to a Pragmatic Theory of Cognitive Evaluation*, Cambridge, MA, MIT Press.
Strawson, P. F. (1952) *Introduction to Logical Theory*. London, Methuen & Co.; New York, John Wiley & Sons.
—— (1985) *Skepticism and Naturalism: Some Varieties: The Woodbridge Lectures 1983*, London, Methuen.
Stroud, B. (2000) *Understanding Human Knowledge: Philosophical Essays*. Oxford, Oxford University Press.
Van Cleve, J. (1985) Epistemic Supervenience and the Circle of Belief. *Monist: An International Quarterly Journal of General Philosophical Inquiry*, 68, 90–104.
—— (1999) Epistemic Supervenience Revisited. *Philosophy and Phenomenological Research*, 59, 1049–55.
Weinberg, J., Nichols, S. and Stich, S. (2001) Normativity and Epistemic Intuitions. *Philosophical Topics*, 29, 429–60.

75
EVOLUTIONARY EPISTEMOLOGY
Michael Bradie

Historical Sketch

The seeds of evolutionary epistemology were planted by Charles Darwin in the *Descent of Man*. He there attempted to make good on his throw-away line from the *Origin of Species* to the effect that, from an evolutionary point of view, "light would be thrown on the origin of man and his history." Among the first to exploit and question the epistemological implications of Darwinism were the American pragmatists.

Charles Sanders Peirce accepted the view that the emergence of modern science was a result of instinctive beliefs that were originally the product of natural selection but he resisted the idea that natural selection is a useful tool for explaining which of a number of alternative theories might survive (Skagestad 1979). William James, in the *Principles of Psychology* (1983 [1890]), endorsed Darwin's selectionist account of the development of the biological structures underlying human mental capacities. Chauncey Wright (1971) had no hesitation in employing natural selection and the "struggle for existence" to explain the harmonization of beliefs with circumstances. Finally, John Dewey (1910) saw the specific import of the Darwinian revolution as radically reshaping the philosophical landscape by calling into question traditional epistemological norms and projects such as the search for certainty.

In the twentieth century, the psychologist Donald Campbell (1960) is credited with coining the term "evolutionary epistemology." Campbell's basic idea is that there exists a hierarchy of interlocking "blind variation and selective retention processes" that explain not only the evolutionary development of the biological bases of human knowledge but the evolutionary development of modern science as well. He saw an affinity between his view and Karl Popper's (1962) "conjecture and refutation" model of the growth of scientific knowledge. Both Popper and Campbell argued that theories and concepts were "shaped" by the environmental circumstances that they represented (Lorenz 1982). Popper goes so far as to suggest that biological organs are embodied "theories" and scientific theories are disembodied "organs." One advantage, he claims, that human beings have over non-theorizing animals is that theoretical mistakes usually only result in the "death" of a theory whereas biological "mistakes" often result in the death of the organism.

Both Campbell and Popper see the development of science as "progressing" toward a better—i.e., more complete and more accurate—representation of the world. This has elicited some criticism of the Darwinian bone fides of their views on the grounds that, for Darwin, natural selection is a "directionless" process that has no aim or goal. Stephen Toulmin and Thomas Kuhn are two who embrace the Darwinian implications and reject the idea that science is "progressive" over the long run. Toulmin (1972) adopts a "populational" approach to conceptual change. At any given stage in the historical development of an intellectual lineage, there are competing hypotheses and conceptual frameworks that are subject to selective pressures. The net result is some notion of "local" progress as judged by the prevailing standards of the age but as these themselves are in a population subject to selective processes, no long-term notion of "progress" is viable. Kuhn's thesis in *The Structure of Scientific Revolutions* (1962: 172f.) can be understood along similar lines.

Two Distinctions

EEM versus EET

Evolutionary epistemology is concerned with two fundamentally different aspects of what can be broadly called the "theory of knowledge." Traditionally, this has meant an investigation into the conceptual status of knowledge and belief, the nature and status of rules of evidence and justification, the nature of conceptual change, and the like. An evolutionary perspective, however, draws attention to the biological substrate underlying the acquisition and evaluation of beliefs. It is convenient, therefore, to separate issues concerned with the *Evolution of Epistemic Mechanisms* (EEM) from issues concerned with the *Evolution of Epistemic Theories* (EET) (Bradie 1986). EEM projects address questions concerning the evolution and development of brain structures and psychological mechanisms involved in epistemic processes. EET projects address questions concerning the growth of human knowledge and the development of epistemic norms. One rationale for making this distinction is that evolutionary analyses of EEM questions have an initial plausibility that evolutionary analyses of EET questions do not. This follows from the fact that, from a Darwinian point of view, there is an evolutionary and, presumably, selective explanation of the development of biological and psychological cognitive capacities. We might not be in a position to completely verify such accounts but we can be relatively confident that some such stories are broadly correct. The situation is different with respect to the "evolution" of human knowledge or scientific theories, on the one hand, and epistemic norms on the other. Of course, no one denies that the corpus of human knowledge is constantly changing or that norms of acceptability have changed over time. What is problematic is the presumption that this process is adequately represented as a "Darwinian" selective process. In particular, one must be careful not to conclude that just because there is a Darwinian account of the evolution of the underlying biological and psychological mechanisms there is a plausible Darwinian account of the growth of the intellectual products of those mechanisms.

Ontogeny Versus Phylogeny

Cutting across the *EEM/EET* distinction is the distinction between *ontogenetic* questions dealing with the development of individuals from embryo to adult and *phylogenetic* questions dealing with the development of what Popper (1972) called "objective knowledge" over historical time periods. The net result is a four-fold division of issues. Some representative samples are given below.

EEM/Ontogenetic

The issues here involve first the development of the brain structures that enable cognitive and epistemic activity. Recent work by Jean-Pierre Changeux (1985), Gerald Edelman (1987) and others suggests that the embryological development of neural tissue involves processes of variation and selection. The architecture of the adult brain is not completely determined by inherited genetic "programs" but reflects modulations due to the ambient environments of the developing individual. In addition, recent work by evolutionary psychologists suggests that the development of inherited psychological dispositions imposes constraints on human cognitive abilities (Barkow et al. 1992).

EEM/Phylogenetic

The evolution of the nervous system and the brain emerge as the central concerns of phylogenetic EEM projects. Since the brain and its complex substructures are organs, there is presumably a broadly Darwinian account of their evolutionary development. Of especial importance in this historical story is the emergence of consciousness and the capacity for language. That these structures and capacities have evolved is a straightforward implication of the presumption that the original life forms were not more than complex replicating molecular systems. Unfortunately, it is not clear how much more can be said about these significant developments. The phylogenetic emergence of conscious organisms is shrouded in the deep past. There is no relevant fossil evidence and no prospects for discovering any. Given the current adaptive value of having a neocortex, being conscious with the capacity for language, it is often assumed that these features are adaptations, that is, that they were selected for on the basis of the functional capabilities that they provided. But, as has been pointed out many times, it is a mistake to infer that because some organ or capacity has a present utility, therefore that organ or capacity was selected for in the distant past (Gould and Lewontin 1979). So, although Darwinian solutions to phylogenetic EEM questions have the most prima facie plausibility, it is not clear that they can remain much more than vague sketches. As such, any light they might be thought to throw on epistemological concerns is likely to be dim indeed.

More recently, evolutionary psychologists have pursued the development of phylogenetic reconstructions of psychological capacities (Barkow et al. 1992). Their working hypothesis is often that such and such a psychological capacity is an adaptation, that is, was selected for by environmental pressures in the distant past—usually the Pleistocene era (1.8 million–10,000 years ago). Their work is both promising and controversial. One potentially important epistemological implication is the possibility of accounting for various cognitive biases as the results of dispositions that were advantageous in the Pleistocene but which are disadvantageous in modern societies. However, this work is controversial and has polarized both the philosophical and psychological communities. Some critics contend that the fundamental methodology is seriously flawed (Buller 2005; Richardson 2007). One problem is that the Pleistocene covered a long period of time and critics suggest that it is impossible to determine exactly what the social and natural environmental conditions that allegedly led to the selection of various psychological dispositions were. In addition, there is a serious methodological worry about the fact that investigators are not in a position to conduct comparative studies. Without such evidence, it is reckless to conclude that some feature developed in early humans was selected for *because* it conferred a selective advantage in the environments in which early humans found themselves.

EET/Ontogenetic

Organisms acquire knowledge as they mature through a process of learning and assimilation. How are we to model this process? B. F. Skinner explicitly notes the parallels between the behaviorist theory of operant conditioning, Edward Thorndike's "Law of Effect" and Darwin's theory of natural selection (Skinner 1981; Edelman 1987).

Recent work in evolutionary psychology suggests that human beings have inherited psychological dispositions that, when triggered by environmental stimuli, influence the knowledge we acquire, the conclusions we come to and the inferences that we make. Radical behaviorism, insofar as it assumes a "blank slate" model of the newborn mind, is not an adequate model for understanding the acquisition of knowledge in the growing organism. Nevertheless, there is a strong analogy between operant conditioning where an organisms emits a behavior that is reinforced or not by the environment and the method of "trial and error" whereby an organism makes a "conjecture" that is either confirmed or refuted. The exact details of how learning occurs are still unknown. In addition to inherited constraints and individual initiative information is transmitted "laterally" from parents, teachers and peers.

Dan Sperber (1996) has argued for what he calls an "epidemiological" model of the transmission of cultural information. The basic idea is that ideas in people's brains give rise to behaviors that cause ideas in other people's brains. People communicate with one another by means of this process of transmission. If the ideas that arise in the listener resemble the ideas in the transmitter, then the latter has been understood by the latter. The spread of ideas through a culture is analogous to the spread of a contagious disease and warrants, in Sperber's brain, the medical metaphors he uses to characterize his approach.

Sperber's epidemiological model has certain affinities with memetic approaches to the spread of cultural information but Sperber sees his model as emphasizing the importance of inherited psychological mechanisms in ways that other selectionist models do not. Which approach turns out to be most promising in explaining the ontogenesis of knowledge remains to be seen but all the current evidence suggests that Darwinian mechanisms are not likely to be the whole story.

EET/Phylogenetic

The phylogenetic analysis of the evolution of human knowledge involves a consideration along two dimensions. On the one hand, there is the evolution of specific bits of human knowledge, that is, the acquisition of specific facts and the generation and validation of specific theories. On the other, there is the evolution of epistemic methodologies and norms. In principle, one can provide different selectionist accounts for both processes. Nicholas Rescher (1990), accordingly, distinguishes between what he calls "thesis Darwinism" and "methodological Darwinism." He rejects the selectionist accounts of the growth of scientific knowledge but argues for a selectionist account of the development of scientific methods. Popper and Campbell remain the *loci classici* of twentieth-century selectionist accounts of the phylogenetic development of human knowledge. This view was extended to all forms of learning and innovation by Gary Cziko (1995) who defended a view that he called "Universal Darwinism" following Richard Dawkins (1983) and Daniel Dennett (1995).

The Evolutionary Metaphor

To what extent does knowledge "evolve" in a way that is appropriately represented as a Darwinian selection process or, for that matter, any evolutionary process found in biological systems? Is evolutionary biology an appropriate model for epistemic change or is it merely a metaphor, useful for certain points but misleading for others? As noted above, Popper and Campbell, as well as the "Universal Darwinists," argue that the process of change in both biology and epistemology is the same (Toulmin 1967, 1972, 1981; Popper 1972; Popper and Eccles 1977; Hull 1988). Critics argue that the idea of "evolutionary" epistemology is only a metaphorical (i.e., non-literal and at best suggestive) extension of evolutionary biology (Thagard 1980; Kary 1982, Lewontin 1982, Bunge 1983).

In a series of publications, David Hull (1973, 1975, 1982, 1988) has argued that neither biological evolution nor the growth of knowledge serves as the primary model in terms of which we are to understand the other. Hull prefers to develop a general analysis of "evolution through selection processes which applies equally to biological, social and cultural evolution" (1982: 275).

Almost all critics and defenders alike agree that in one important respect conceptual evolution differs from biological evolution. In science, it is claimed, there is progress toward a goal; in biological evolution, there are no goals. Kuhn (1962: 172f.) is one of the few who sees a virtue where others see a flaw. Under pressure to clarify the sense in which his position did or did not avoid relativism, Kuhn argued that "scientific development is, like biological evolution, unidirectional and irreversible" (Lakatos and Musgrave 1970: 264). Toulmin (1972: 322ff.) objected to this reformulation as illegitimately attributing unidirectionality to biological evolution and as a throwback to a providential view of evolutionary theory rather than a populational view which, Toulmin argued, is characteristic of Darwinism. Toulmin argued for a "local" or "ecological" concept of contextual rationality. The recognition of the populational nature of concept change leads us to the conclusion that there are no universal criteria for rationality and no "global" selection criteria (Toulmin 1972: 317; 1981: 31; Blackwell 1973; Hull 1973).

That the progress of science implies some such "global" criteria whereas natural selection does not has, in fact, been taken as a strong point of disanalogy between conceptual and biological evolution (e.g., Elster 1979; Thagard 1980; Blackwell 1973). Hull (1982) and Robert Bechtel (1984) have argued that scientific progress need not involve a commitment to global criteria if it is recognized that the regularities of nature and the "laws of nature" exert a transcontextual constraint on the development of scientific theories.

The progress issue is a problematic test for the adequacy of evolutionary models of scientific development. If the views of Kuhn and Toulmin are correct then our notion of progress needs to be re-evaluated. For all we know, progress in science could turn out to be as chimerical as we now take immanent purpose in nature to be. Leading intellectuals 300 years ago might have disagreed. An appeal to realism, in and of itself, does not seem to me to be sufficient to guarantee that science can be progressive (see discussion on "convergent" realism below). Popperian realism might appear to provide such guarantees but that approach leads to will-o'-the-wisp chases after measures of progress such as "verisimilitude." The fact of the matter is that judgments of progress in science are always "local" judgments. Even if "global" criteria exist we are never in a position to know what they are except by a local presumption or fiat. The history of science and the history of ideas should give us pause when we contemplate reifying a contemporary standard as an inviolable canon.

Evolutionary epistemology is not merely the attempt to understand knowing via the use of metaphors drawn from evolutionary biology, but also the attempt to understand biological processes in terms of metaphors drawn from epistemology (Campbell 1960). Vittorio Somenzi (1980) credits Samuel Butler with first introducing the metaphor of organisms as problem solvers and it is of interest to note that Samuel Butler is hailed by Popper as the most astute nineteenth-century philosopher of biology.

Richard Lewontin (1982) and Toulmin (1967, 1972, 1981) have both noted that contemporary evolutionary models of the growth of knowledge based on "Darwinian" models do not represent the introduction of biological considerations into epistemology but, rather, a shift from one underlying metaphor to another. Lewontin sees two central growth metaphors permeating biology and the social sciences: unfolding (a transformational model characteristic of embryology, classically understood) and trial and error (a variational model characteristic of Darwinian evolution). The distinction between transformational models and variational models of development corresponds roughly to Toulmin's distinction between providential and populational processes. Lewontin explicitly (and Toulmin, implicitly) argues that "unfolding" is as much a metaphor for embryology and "trial and error adaptation" is as much a metaphor for biological evolution, as they are allegedly metaphors for the evolution of knowledge or culture. Lewontin (1982: 155) goes on to argue that both metaphors are bad metaphors for embryology and organic evolution, so, he thinks, "little wonder that they have failed to resolve the contradictions in the theory of cognition." The argument against treating organic evolution as a process of trial and error adaptations rests on pointing out the limitation of viewing organisms as optimality-seeking problem-solvers (157–159).

Lewontin proposes, instead, a metaphor of "dialectical interdependence" which involves the "interpenetration of organism and environment" (159–163). Niches exist and can be identified only in virtue of the organisms that occupy them. Organisms and environments are constantly shaping and reshaping each other. The separation of organism from its environment can be, one is led to think, only conceptual and not real.

The implications of this metaphor for epistemology are potentially, quite profound. For one thing, if niches are "created" by organisms, and do not exist independently of them, this suggests that perhaps problems might not properly exist independently of their tentative solutions. Taking Lewontin's dialectical metaphor seriously suggests that the theory–problem distinction could turn out to be as problematic as the theory–observation distinction. More radical consequences follow. If the organism–environment coupled pair is the analog of the knower–known pair, then the problems loom for many forms of realism (Fleck 1979; Lewontin 1982).

Realism

Campbell (1979: 195f.) argued that descriptive epistemology, which studies how organisms acquire and process knowledge, leads to the "debunking of the value of 'hard facts'." Nevertheless, he concluded, the ideology of "stubborn facts" has a functional truth. Evolutionary epistemology, in turn, abandons "literal truth" while retaining the "goal of truth." For Campbell, the central epistemological issues concern how organisms interact with their environments to produce knowledge. Evolutionary and processing considerations suggest that knowledge is analogous to a mosaic mural, "a compromise of vehicular characteristics and of referent attributes" (183). We find ourselves committed to an "epistemological relativity." Amoebas know what they know, frogs know other things, and humans still more. Each organism comes to know what it does through processing by cognitive structures which are the product of evolutionary development. We might know more things than other creatures or different things but each kind of organism constructs, as it were, an image of reality based on its own needs and capacities. However, Campbell, with Popper, is unwilling to push this epistemological relativism to an ontological relativism even though, as he says, "The language of science is subjective, provincial, approximate, and metaphoric, never the language of reality itself" (Campbell 1975: 1120).

That reality itself does have a "language" is embodied in Campbell's presumptive ontological view which he calls "hypothetical realism." The basic postulate of hypothetical realism is that there is an objective world of objects and relations which exists independently of any knowing and perceiving organisms. The organisms which inhabit and interact with this world, however, have only indirect, fallible knowledge, which is "edited" by the "objective referent" (Brewer and Collins 1981; Lorenz, 1977, 1982).

Hypothetical realism, then, is the view that there is a real world which scientific theories only approximately "fit." As science "progresses," it converges on a "true description" of that world. The notion of "approximate fit" captures the sense in which the view of Campbell and Konrad Lorenz is a "transcendental" as well as a "hypothetical" realism. As such it controverts certain forms of instrumentalism, pragmatism and relativism. That our theories change and might even converge locally, in itself, does not entail the Campbellian conclusion (via Peirce and Popper) that an ultimate consensus at the end of scientific inquiry is a legitimate goal.

On the other hand, an evolutionary argument for a convergence-free version of realism can be constructed as follows. Biological evolution is opportunistic. Organisms exploit their local environments and the longevity of lineages is contingent not only on issues of selective advantage but also upon historical accidents (Gould 1989). Most evolutionary epistemologists (Toulmin excepted) are unwilling to accept the implications of this for cognitive or conceptual evolution. They will admit that the local, intellectual, social, and cultural background out of which new ideas emerge is a relevant factor in forming the selective forces which determine which of those ideas will survive and which will not, but they are unwilling to accept the radical implication that the direction of conceptual evolution and change need not be leading anywhere in particular. They are unwilling to abandon the eschatological vision of a terminal-consensus "in the long run" (cf. Hull 1988).

To be sure, there are good philosophical motives for their recalcitrance having to do with the virtues of "objectivity" and "truth." But, there is no biological rationale for convergence to consensus, at least insofar as it draws upon Darwinism. Hypothetical realism, in and of itself, neither suggests nor guarantees convergence. There is a long inferential leap from general coping with the environment, which all successful lineages must develop, to consensus of structure, content and function of knowledge. The appeal to laws or regularities of nature to force convergence assumes that the constraints "reality" imposes on how and what we think are sufficient, in the long run, to wash out the social and cultural differences, which, for all we know, operate to induce divergence. Even if a global or galactic community eventually reached consensus, shared bias and mutual reinforcement could not be ruled out as major contributory causes. Accepting a non-convergent form of realism means that the difficult issues of how to construe rationality and objectivity remain to be dealt with. But convergent forms of realism face these problems as well.

The Question of Norms

Traditional epistemology is, in large part, a normative discipline. Evolutionary epistemologies in particular, and naturalistic epistemologies in general, insofar as they construe epistemology as continuous with science would seem to be purely descriptive. Can such enterprises deal with normative questions? How one approaches this question depends upon how one construes the relationship of evolutionary epistemology to traditional epistemology. If evolutionary epistemology is seen as a "successor" discipline to traditional epistemology then one might be well prepared to write off many of the traditional questions that epistemology set for itself to answer. Other naturalized theories of knowledge, e.g. Laudan's (1990), involve reinterpreting normative claims in terms of empirical hypotheticals. Willard Van Orman Quine (1990) also argues that naturalizing epistemology does not lead to a rejection of norms; "normative epistemology gets naturalized into a chapter of engineering: the technology of anticipating sensory stimulation" (19).

Deriving epistemological norms from the facts of human knowledge acquisition would seem to commit some version of the naturalistic fallacy. It is open to evolutionary epistemologists to challenge the contention that the naturalistic fallacy (or at least any attempt to base norms on facts) is a fallacy. An argument of this form can be found in Robert Richards (1987) with respect to the naturalistic fallacy in ethics. Richards argues that not all derivations of moral norms from facts are fallacious. The general idea is that norms need to be calibrated against intuitively clear cases. If some evolutionary account is forthcoming as to why we are inclined to argue in certain ways with respect to morality (or logic or epistemology) then we can ground our normative principles in these evolutionary considerations. A similar argument should be constructible for epistemological norms (Munz 1985; Vollmer 1987; Bartley 1987; Bradie 1989). In any case, even if some evolutionary account of the emergence of epistemological norms is forthcoming, it is very unlikely that specific norms are going to be derivable or justifiable from biological or genetic considerations alone. The specific form of the epistemological norms that are accepted by communities of cognizers will most certainly reflect local cultural contingencies in much the same way that specific moral codes reflect local cultural contingencies.

Evolutionary Epistemology and the Skeptic

Next to worries about the ability of evolutionary epistemology to deal with the problem of epistemic norms the most serious objection to an evolutionary approach to epistemology is that it fails to provide a convincing answer to the skeptic. The problem is this. Evolutionary or naturalized epistemologies, drawing as they do on the results of the natural sciences, appear to beg the question against the skeptic who demands an epistemic warrant before allowing the use of scientific knowledge to account for and ground knowledge. The philosophical question of how knowledge is possible at all in the first place goes unanswered (Stroud 1981).

The strategy of the evolutionary epistemologist is to adopt what Campbell (1974b) called the "epistemology of the other one." Instead of adopting a Cartesian point of view that requires that a knower first justify first-person knowledge claims, we shift the focus to the empirical question of how humans (and other organisms) in general acquire and process knowledge. Quine (1981) endorses this approach by challenging the transcendental Cartesian perspective in favor of an approach that involves routine appeals to "analogies and causal hypotheses within our scientific theories." In such a way, Quine thinks, we can get from an epistemology of the other to traditional epistemology. Quine's move might appear to just beg the question against the skeptic again. However, the sting of traditional skepticism can be defused by dividing skeptics into two groups: those who will not accept anything and those who argue for skepticism on the basis of arguments from illusion or the fallibility of science or the like. To the former, we can say nothing and must leave them at the crossroads. To the latter, Quine's point is, in effect, a rejection of the skeptic's move to "transcendentalize" objections which, after all, were derived from intersubjective comparisons and errors in the first place. Both the skeptic and the epistemologist of the other start from the same intersubjective considerations but the skeptic gives the argument a transcendental turn and then complains that appeals to intersubjective experience are question-begging. The epistemologist of the other seeks to block the transcendental turn that leads to all the "veil of illusions" objections which have plagued post-Cartesian epistemology. The solution is to avoid being seduced behind the veil in the first place.

Descriptive Versus Prescriptive Epistemology or Evolutionary Epistemology and the Tradition

For Campbell (1974a: 413), evolutionary epistemology minimally takes cognizance of and is compatible with "man's status as a product of biological and social evolution." Campbell characterizes his approach to epistemology as "descriptive" rather than "analytic" or prescriptive. A descriptive epistemology is "descriptive of man as knower." Descriptive epistemologies, minimally, put constraints on prescriptive epistemologies. So, Campbell argues, an evolutionary picture of human development rules out (1) the view that truth is divinely revealed to humans; (2) direct realism, which assumes that human beings have veridical perception of the world; and, (3) epistemologies based on ordinary language analysis. Descriptive epistemology is a branch of science rather than traditional philosophy (Campbell 1974b: 141). As such, it is both hypothetical and contingent (Brewer and Collins 1981: 12).

Fred Dretske (1971: 586) agrees that evolutionary considerations *might* be construed as explanations for why organisms, in general, get things right but he argues that this has *no* particular *epistemological* significance, just as the fact that well trained rats invariably find their way through mazes does not entail that the rats *know* their way through the maze. Human beings, unlike rats, make judgments. Evolutionary theory and, by implication, evolutionary epistemology fails to address the central issues of "true" epistemology such as what counts as the right to be sure, what counts as adequate evidence, what counts as a good or the best explanation, and how to distinguish between conclusive and inconclusive reasons (Dretske 1971; Kim 1988).

Campbell does not disagree with this assessment. Descriptive epistemology, in his view, is trying to do something different from traditional epistemology (1974b: 140). What then is the relationship between evolutionary epistemology and traditional epistemology? There are three possibilities:

1. Descriptive epistemology is a *competitor* to traditional epistemology. On this view, both are trying to address the same concerns and offering competing solutions (Riedl 1984). Dretske and Jaegwon Kim, among others, argue that descriptive epistemology in this sense fails to touch the traditional questions and thereby, is epistemologically irrelevant. The force of this argument is tempered by the extent to which one rejects the "tradition" as irrelevant or uninteresting.
2. Descriptive epistemology might be seen as a *successor* discipline to traditional epistemology. On this reading, descriptive epistemology does not address the questions of traditional epistemology because it deems them irrelevant or unanswerable or uninteresting (Dewey 1910; Quine 1969; Davidson 1973; Bartley 1976, 1987; Dennett 1978; Harman 1982; Munz 1985; Kornblith 1985).
3. Descriptive epistemology might be seen as *complementary* to traditional epistemology. This appears to be Campbell's view. Campbell admits that descriptive epistemology, in his sense, does beg the traditional epistemological question of how knowledge is possible. Descriptive epistemology, as he sees it, attempts to explore the problem of knowledge from "within the framework of contingent knowledge, and by assuming such knowledge" (1974b: 141).

Assessment and Future Prospects

The heyday of constructive and critical work in evolutionary epistemology was the period from the 1970s through the 1990s. For a while, memetics was the rage but this, for the moment, seems to have run its course as well. Evolutionary psychologists have made contributions to our understanding of the phylogenetic development of cognitive mechanisms but that work, although promising, is in its infancy and still controversial. Its lasting significance remains to be determined.

It is still an open question whether an evolutionary epistemology can shed any interesting light on the emergence and nature of epistemic norms. Recent work relying on computer simulations of evolving populations by Brian Skyrms (1996, 2004) and Bill Harms (2004) holds open the possibility of explaining how we come to adopt the epistemic norms and methodologies that we do. It is less clear, however, whether such work will be able to serve as the basis for any more than a pragmatic justification of these norms and methods. From an evolutionary perspective, this might be the best we can or ought to hope for.

Finally, much of the work in evolutionary epistemology to date has focused on selectionist scenarios. But, natural selection, although it might be the major factor in biological evolution is by no means the only factor. In addition, traits can become fixed through a process of random drift or as a result of developmental constraints, among other options. Our cognitive and epistemic capacities are adaptive complex features that are perhaps unlikely to be the result of drift or chance. However, if these capacities are the product of physiological or psychological developmental constraints or are the byproducts of selection for other traits, this has potentially serious implications for our understanding of what we know and how we know it. At the very least, the adequacy of some EEM accounts would need to be re-evaluated. The implication of such possibilities for EET accounts remains to be explored.

References

Barkow, J. H., Cosmides, L. and Tooby, J. (Eds.) (1992) *The Adapted Mind: Evolutionary Psychology and the Generation of Culture*, New York, Oxford University Press.

Bartley, W. W. (1976) The Philosophy of Karl Popper: Part I: Biology and Evolutionary Epistemology. *Philosophia* 6, 463–494.

—— (1987) Philosophy of Biology versus Philosophy of Physics. In Radnitzky, G. and Bartley III, W. W. (Eds.) *Evolutionary Epistemology: Theory of Rationality and the Sociology of Knowledge*, LaSalle, IL, Open Court.

Bechtel, W. (1984) The Evolution of the Understanding of the Cell: A Study in the Dynamics of Scientific Progress. *Studies in the History and Philosophy of Science* 15, 304–356.

Blackwell, R. J. (1973) Toulmin's Model of an Evolutionary Epistemology. *Modern Schoolman: A Quarterly Journal of Philosophy*, 51, 62–68.

Bradie, M. (1986) Assessing Evolutionary Epistemology. *Biology & Philosophy*, 4, 401–459.

—— (1989) Evolutionary Epistemology as Naturalized Epistemology. In Hahlweg, K. & Hooker, C. A. (Eds.) *Issues in Evolutionary Epistemology*, Albany, NY, SUNY.

Brewer, M. B. and Collins, B. E. (1981) *Scientific Inquiry and the Social Sciences*, San Francisco, Jossey-Bass.

Buller, D. (2005) *Adapting Minds: Evolutionary Psychology and the Persistent Quest for Human Nature*, Cambridge, MA, MIT.

Bunge, M. (1983) *Treatise on Basic Philosophy, V. 5: Epistemology and Methodology I: Exploring the World*, Dordrecht, Reidel.

Campbell, D. T. (1960) Blind Variation and Selective Retention in Creative Thought as in Other Knowledge Processes. *Psychological Review*, 67, 380–400.

—— (1974a) Evolutionary Epistemology. In Schilpp, P. A. (Ed.) *The Philosophy of Karl Popper*. LaSalle, IL, Open Court.

—— (1974b) Unjustified Variation and Selective Retention in Scientific Discovery. In Ayala, F. J. & Dobzhansky, T. (Eds.) *Studies in the Philosophy of Biology*. London, MacMillan.

—— (1975) On the Conflicts between Biological and Social Evolution and between Psychology and Moral Tradition. *American Psychologist*, 30, 1103–1126.

—— (1979) A Tribal Model of the Social System Vehicle Carrying Scientific Knowledge. *Knowledge*, 2, 181–201.

Changeux, J.-P. (1985) *Neuronal Man: The Biology of Mind*, NY: Pantheon.

Cziko, G. (1995) *Without Miracles: Universal Selection Theory and the Second Darwinian Revolution*, Cambridge, MA, MIT.

Davidson, D. (1973) On the Very Idea of a Conceptual Scheme. *Proceedings of the American Philosophical Association*.

Dawkins, R. (1983) Universal Darwinism. In Bendal, D. S. (Ed.) *Evolution from Molecules to Men*. Cambridge, Cambridge University Press.

Dennett, D. (1978) *Brainstorms: Philosophical Essays on Mind and Psychology*, Montgomery, VT, Bradford.

—— (1995) *Darwin's Dangerous Idea*, New York, Simon & Schuster.

Dewey, J. (1910) *The Influence of Darwin on Philosophy and Other Essays in Contemporary Thought*, New York, Henry Holt.

Dretske, F. (1971) Perception from an Epistemological Point of View. *Journal of Philosophy*, 68, 584–591.

—— (1985) Machines and the Mental. *Proceedings and Addresses of the American Philosophical Association*, 59, 23–33.

Edelman, G. M. (1987) *Neural Darwinism: The Theory of Neuronal Group Selection*, New York, Basic.

Elster, J. (1979) *Ulysses and the Sirens: Studies in Rationality and Irrationality*, New York, Cambridge University Press.

Fleck, L. (1979) *Genesis and Development of a Scientific Fact*, Chicago, University of Chicago Press.

Gould, S. J. (1989) *Wonderful Life: The Burgess Shale and the Nature of History*. New York, W. W. Norton and Co.

—— and Lewontin, R. C. (1979) The Spandrels of San Marco and the Panglossian Paradigm: A Critique of the Adaptationist Programme. *Proceedings of the Royal Society of London*, **B**, 205.
Harman, G. (1982) Metaphysical Realism and Moral Relativism. *Journal of Philosophy*, 79, 568–575.
Harms, W. F. (2004) *Information and Meaning in Evolutionary Processes*, New York, Cambridge University Press.
Hull, D. (1973) A Populational Approach to Scientific Change. *Science*, 182, 1121–1124.
—— (1975) Central Subjects and Historical Narratives. *History and Theory*, 14, 253–274.
—— (1982) The Naked Meme. In Plotkin, H. C. (Ed.) *Learning, Development and Culture*. New York, Wiley & Sons.
—— (1988) *Science as a Process: An Evolutionary Account of the Social and Conceptual Development of Science*, Chicago, University of Chicago Press.
James, W. (1983 [1890]) *Principles of Psychology*, Cambridge, MA, Harvard University Press.
Kary, C. (1982) Can Darwinian Inheritance be Extended from Biology to Epistemology? In Asquith, P. D. & Nickles, T. (Eds.) *Psa 1982*. Philosophy of Science Association.
Kim, J. (1988) What is "Naturalized Epistemology"? *Philosophical Perspectives*, 381–405.
Kornblith, H. (1985) *Naturalizing Epistemology*, Cambridge, MA, MIT.
Kuhn, T. S. (1962) *The Structure of Scientific Revolutions*, Chicago, University of Chicago Press.
Lakatos, I. and Musgrave, A. (1970) *Criticism and the Growth of Knowledge*, Cambridge, Cambridge University Press.
Laudan, L. (1990) Normative Naturalism. *Philosophy of Science*, 57, 44–59.
Lewontin, R. C. (1982) Organism and Environment. In Plotkin, H. C. (Ed.) *Learning, Development and Culture*. New York, Wiley and Sons.
Lorenz, K. (1977) *Behind the Mirror*, London, Methuen.
—— (1982) Kant's Doctrine of the A Priori in the Light of Contemporary Biology. In Plotkin, H. C. (Ed.) *Learning, Development, and Culture: Essays in Evolutionary Epistemology*. New York, Wiley & Sons.
Munz, P. (1985) *Our Knowledge of the Growth of Knowledge: Popper or Wittgenstein?*, London, Routledge.
—— (1993) *Philosophical Darwinism: On the Origin of Knowledge by Means of Natural Selection*, London, Routledge.
Plotkin, H. (1993) *Darwin Machines and the Nature of Knowledge*, Cambridge, MA, Harvard University Press.
Popper, K. (1961) *The Logic of Scientific Discovery*, New York, Science Editions.
—— (1962) *Conjectures and Refutations*, New York, Basic.
—— (1972) *Objective Knowledge: An Evolutionary Approach*, Oxford, Clarendon.
—— (1984) Evolutionary Epistemology. In Pollard, J. W. (Ed.) *Evolutionary Theory: Paths into the Future*. London, Wiley & Sons.
Popper, K. and Eccles, J. (1977) *The Self and Its Brain*, New York, Springer.
Quine, W. V. (1969) *Ontological Relativity, and Other Essays*, New York, Columbia University Press.
—— (1981) *Theories and Things*, Cambridge, MA, Harvard University Press.
—— (1990) *Pursuit of Truth*, Cambridge, MA, Harvard University Press.
Radnitzky, G. and Bartley III, W. W. (1987) *Evolutionary Epistemology, Rationality, and the Sociology of Knowledge*, LaSalle, Illinois, Open Court.
Rescher, N. (1977) *Methodological Pragmatism*, Oxford, Blackwell.
—— (1990) *A Useful Inheritance: Evolutionary Aspects of the Theory of Knowledge*, Savage, MD, Rowman & Littlefield.
Richards, R. J. (1987) *Darwin and the Emergence of Evolutionary Theories of Mind and Behavior*, Chicago, University of Chicago Press.
Richardson, R. C. (2007) *Evolutionary Psychology as Maladapted Psychology*, Cambridge, MA, MIT.
Riedl, R. (1984) *Biology of Knowledge: The Evolutionary Basis of Reason*, New York, Wiley & Sons.
Ruse, M. (1986) *Taking Darwin Seriously*, Blackwell: Oxford.
Skagestad, P. (1979) C. S. Peirce on Biological Evolution and Scientific Progress. *Synthese*, 41, 85–114.
Skinner, B. F. (1981) Selection by Consequences. *Science*, 213, 501–504.
Skyrms, B. (1996) *Evolution of the Social Contract*, New York, Cambridge University Press.
—— (2004) *The Stag Hunt and the Evolution of Social Structure*, New York, Cambridge University Press.
Somenzi, V. (1980) Scientific Discovery from the Viewpoint of Evolutionary Epistemology. In Grmk, M. D., Cohen, R. S. and Cimino, G. (Eds.) *On Scientific Discovery*. Dordrecht, Reidel.
—— (1981) Discovery from the Viewpoint of Evolutionary Epistemology. *On Scientific Discovery: The Erice Lectures 1977*. Boston, Reidel.

Sperber, Dan. (1996) *Explaining Culture: A Naturalistic Approach*, Oxford, Blackwell.
Stroud, B. (1981) The Significance of Naturalized Epistemology. In French, P. A., Uehling, T. G. J. and Wettstein, H. K. (Eds.) *Midwest Studies in Philosophy VI*. Minneapolis, University of Minnesota Press.
Thagard, P. (1980) Against Evolutionary Epistemology. In Asquith, P. D. and Giere, R. N. (Eds.) *Psa 1980*. Philosophy of Science Association.
Toulmin, S. (1967) The Evolutionary Development of Natural Science. *American Scientist*, 55, 456–467.
—— (1972) *Human Understanding: The Collective Use and Evolution of Concepts*, Princeton, Princeton University Press.
—— (1981) Evolution, Adaptation, and Human Understanding. In Brewer, M. B. and Collins, B. E. (Eds.) *Scientific Inquiry and the Social Sciences: A Volume in Honor of Donald T. Campbell*. San Francisco, Jossey-Bass.
Vollmer, G. (1987) On Supposed Circularities in an Empirically Oriented Epistemology. In Radnitzsky, G. and Bartley III, W. W. (Eds.) *Evolutionary Epistemology: Theory of Rationality and the Sociology of Knowledge*. LaSalle, IL, Open Court.
Wright, C. (1971) *Philosophical Discussions*, New York, Franklin.

76
PRAGMATIST EPISTEMOLOGY
Cheryl Misak

1. Introduction

The thought at the heart of pragmatism is that we must look to the consequences of a concept in order to fully understand it. This pragmatic maxim gives rise to its inquiry-centered, anti-foundationalist account of truth, on which truth is not a relationship between our beliefs and the believer-independent world but, rather, is the best we human inquirers could do. It also gives rise to the central themes running through pragmatist epistemologies: empiricism, naturalism, fallibilism, and holism.

Pragmatists are empiricists in that they require beliefs and theories to be linked to experience; they are naturalists in that they want their philosophical explanations down-to-earth (natural as opposed to supernatural)—they require philosophical theories and norms to arise from our everyday practices; they are fallibilists in that they think that none of our beliefs provide us with a certain foundation for knowledge; and they are holists in that they take their view of truth and inquiry to encompass all areas of inquiry.

This is not to say that pragmatists form one happy family. A debate within pragmatism that began between James and Peirce continues to this day. The debate arises between those who take pragmatism to suggest that there is no truth and objectivity to be had anywhere and those who take pragmatism to promise an account of truth that preserves our cognitive aspiration to get things right. On the one side of the debate we have Richard Rorty and his classical predecessors (James) saying that there is no truth, as we usually understand it, at which we might aim—only what works for me, or secures solidarity for our community.

On the other side of the divide, we have those who think of pragmatism as rejecting ahistorical, transcendental, or metaphysical theories of truth, but nonetheless being committed to doing justice to the fact that those engaged in deliberation and investigation take themselves to be aiming at getting things right, avoiding mistakes, and improving their beliefs and theories.

This more objective kind of pragmatism emanates from the founder of the doctrine, Charles Sanders Peirce. On this view, the fact that our inquiries are historically situated does not entail that they lack objectivity. Neither does the fact that standards of objectivity themselves come into being and evolve. The trail of the human serpent is over everything (to use James' phrase), but (as James himself might or might not have seen) this does not toss us into a sea of arbitrariness, where there is no truth or where truth varies from person to person or community to community. In what follows, Peirce's epistemology will be articulated, followed by accounts of how the epistemological views of other core pragmatists—William James, John Dewey, W.V.O. Quine, and Richard Rorty—merge with it or diverge from it.

2. C.S. Peirce and the Empiricist Background

Peirce (1839–1914) tries to get us to see the difference between three respectable tasks: (i) providing an analytic definition of a concept, which might be useful to someone who has never encountered the concept before; (ii) knowing how to pick out instances of the concept; and (iii) providing a pragmatic elucidation of it—an account of the role the concept plays in practical endeavors.

His interest of course lies in the third project. His best expressions of the maxim are of the following sort: we "must look to the upshot of our concepts in order to rightly apprehend them" (Peirce 1934: vol. 5, s. 4); in order to get a complete grasp of a concept, we must connect it to that with which we have "dealings" (Peirce 1934: vol. 5, s. 416). Perhaps the most elegant is this:

> we must not begin by talking of pure ideas,—vagabond thoughts that tramp the public roads without any human habitation,—but must begin with men and their conversation.
>
> (Peirce 1958: vol. 8, s. 112)

There is a clear whiff of verificationism here and, indeed, the early pragmatists were intensely interested in the verificationism of Auguste Comte's. But Peirce's maxim is not designed to give us a tidy principle to demarcate the spurious from the non-spurious. It is not a semantic principle about the very meaning of our concepts—it is not designed to capture a full account of meaning. David Wiggins gets Peirce's considered view of the pragmatic maxim exactly right. When a concept is "already fundamental to human thought and long since possessed of an autonomous interest," it is pointless to try to define it (Wiggins 2002: 316; see also Misak 1991[2004]). Rather, we ought to attempt to get leverage on the concept, or a fix on it, by exploring its connections with experience and practice. This is the empiricist insight at the heart of pragmatism.

Peirce worried over what kinds of consequences counted—over what kinds of things we must expect from our beliefs. In one of the few papers he published in his stunted career ("How to Make Our Ideas Clear") he says those that count must be consequences, "direct or indirect," for the senses (Peirce 1986: vol. 3, 266). But for the most part, he tries to divert our focus from sensory experience and direct it to a broader notion of experience that would have been an anathema to the logical empiricists.

Experience, for Peirce, is that which is compelling, surprising, unchosen, brute, involuntary, or forceful:

> anything is ... to be classed under the species of perception wherein a positive qualitative content is forced upon one's acknowledgment without any reason or pretension to reason. There will be a wider genus of things *partaking* of the

> character of perception, if there be any matter of cognition which exerts a force upon us.
>
> (Peirce 1958: vol. 7, s. 623)

This extremely broad conception of experience is clearly going to allow for a criterion of legitimacy that allows beliefs other than those which are directly verifiable by the senses.

There is no claim in this account of experience that reports of experience are a kind of introspection about which the experiencer cannot be mistaken. Nothing is implied, that is, about being given something pure or unadulterated. Experience is the tribunal wherein beliefs are tested, but it does not give us access to a truth unclothed by human cognitive capacities and interests. This fallibilism and aversion to the "Given" is an essential platform of any pragmatist's epistemology.

Peirce was clear, however, that fallibilism does not entail that we ought to follow Descartes and try to bring into doubt all beliefs about which error is conceivable. Such doubts would be, Peirce argued, "paper" or "tin"—not the genuine article. He says:

> there is but one state of mind from which you can 'set out', namely, the very state of mind in which you actually find yourself at the time you do 'set out'—a state in which you are laden with an immense mass of cognition already formed, of which you cannot divest yourself if you would . . . Do you call it doubting to write down on a piece of paper that you doubt? If so, doubt has nothing to do with any serious business.
>
> (Peirce 1933: vol. 5, s. 416)

Our body of background beliefs is susceptible to doubt on a piecemeal basis, if that doubt is prompted by surprising or recalcitrant experience. We must *regard* our background beliefs as true, until some surprising experience throws one or some group of them into doubt.

So on the Peircean epistemology, an inquirer has a fallible background of "commonsense" belief which is not in fact in doubt. Only against such a background can a belief be put into doubt and a new, better, belief be adopted. All our beliefs are fallible but they do not come into doubt all at once. Those which inquiry has not thrown into doubt are stable and we should retain them until a reason to doubt arises.

The scientific method, Peirce argues, is the method which pays close attention to the fact that beliefs fall to the surprise of recalcitrant experience. Here is his metaphor for science or inquiry: It "is not standing upon the bedrock of fact. It is walking upon a bog, and can only say, this ground seems to hold for the present. Here I will stay till it begins to give way" (Peirce 1934: vol. 5, s. 589).

The first step in the scientific method is what Peirce called an abductive inference: a hypothesis or a conjecture is identified that explains some surprising experience. Consequences are then deduced from this hypothesis and are tested by induction. If the hypothesis passes the test of experience, then it is accepted—it is stable and believed until upset by experience.

What is the source of the authority of experience on this view? We clearly have no recourse to the idea that the authority of experience comes via its incorrigibility. Rather, our experiential judgments are authoritative in that we have no choice but to pay attention to them. They arrive uncritically and then we subject them to reason and scrutiny.

When we are careful in evaluating our experiential judgments, they tend not to lead us astray and hence our taking them seriously seems wise as well as necessary.

So unlike the logical empiricists, Peirce was not interested in narrowing the scope of legitimate inquiry to the empirical sciences. But like them, he was concerned to set out some principles that would indeed allow one to distinguish the legitimate from the illegitimate. His treatment of mathematical and logical beliefs is the most interesting example of what he was trying to achieve. In it, we see the beginnings of the project of holism.

The history of empiricism is littered with attempts to show how mathematical and logical statements, although apparently unconnected to experience, are nonetheless legitimate. Most of those attempts (think of Hume and the logical empiricists) trade on the idea that mathematics and logic are somehow exempt from the rigors of the empiricist criterion.

Peirce argued that mathematical and logical hypotheses are indeed connected to experience in the requisite way. They meet the requirement set out in the pragmatic maxim: we expect certain things to be the case if they are true. Not only might we have practical or applied or bridge-building expectations about mathematics, but even hypotheses in pure mathematics and logic have consequences. They have consequences, Peirce argued, in diagrammatic contexts. Diagrams provide us with a forum for matters to impinge upon us.

Peirce put considerable effort into trying to get this thought right. (Indeed, he developed his first-order quantified logic using a diagrammatic proof system just as Frege was developing his own logic.) Mathematical and logical inquiry:

> involves an element of observation; namely, [it] consists in constructing an icon or diagram the relation of whose parts shall present a complete analogy with those of the parts of the object of reasoning, of experimenting upon this image in the imagination, and of observing the result so as to discover unnoticed and hidden relations among the parts.
>
> (Peirce 1986: vol. 3, 41)

The mathematician's "hypotheses are creatures of his own imagination; but he discovers in them relations which surprise him sometimes" (Peirce 1958: vol. 5, s. 567). This surprise is the force of experience.

Of course, one thing that needs attention is the matter of saying just which kinds of 'ideal' experiences count and which do not. Peirce struggled with this problem, never getting it quite right. But we shall see below that he certainly thought that James got it wrong.

3. Peirce and the Pragmatist Account of Truth

The concept of truth is one of those concepts, fundamental to human thought, in which we have a long-standing autonomous interest. Peirce thinks that it can be illuminated by looking at our practices—the practices of doubt, belief, inquiry and assertion, which are the human dealings relevant to truth. His is thus a naturalist account of truth—we should not add anything metaphysical to science, or to any other first-order inquiry. We have to extract the concept of truth, as it were, from our practices of inquiry, reason-giving, and deliberation.

When Peirce turns his pragmatic maxim on the concept of truth, the upshot is an aversion to 'transcendental' accounts of truth, such as the correspondence theory, on which a true belief is one that gets right or mirrors the believer-independent world (Peirce 1934: vol. 5, s. 572). Such accounts of truth are examples of those "vagabond thoughts." They make truth "the subject of metaphysics exclusively." For the very idea of the believer-independent world, and the items within it to which beliefs or sentences might correspond, seem graspable only if we could somehow step outside of our corpus of belief, our practices, or that with which we have dealings.

So, for instance, once we see that truth and assertion are intimately connected—once we see that to assert that p is true is to assert p—we can look to our practices of assertion to see what commitments they entail. As Wiggins puts it, hard on the heels of the thought that truth is internally related to assertion comes the thought that truth is also internally related to inquiry, reasons, evidence, and standards of good belief (Wiggins 2004). If we unpack the commitments we incur when we assert, we find that we have imported all these notions.

Peirce argues that when we think of how truth engages with our practices, we shall see that we need to think of a true belief as the very best that inquiry could do—a belief that would be "indefeasible"; or would not be improved upon; or would never lead to disappointment; or would forever meet the challenges of reasons, argument, and evidence. A true belief is a belief we would come to, were we to inquire as far as we could on a matter (Peirce 1934: vol. 5, s. 569; Peirce 1935: vol. 6, s. 485).

He initially put this idea in the following unhelpful way: a true belief would be agreed upon at the hypothetical or "fated" end of inquiry (Peirce 1986: vol. 3, 273). But his considered and much better formulations are the ones above. A true belief would withstand doubt, were we to inquire as far as we fruitfully could into the matter. On the whole, he tries to stay away from unhelpful ideas such as the final end of inquiry, perfect evidence, and the like.

This is not to say that truth has now been *identified* as that which satisfies our aims in assertion and inquiry. We must be careful to not take these elucidations of truth to be attempts at analytic definition. A dispute about definition, he says, is usually a "profitless discussion" (Peirce 1958: vol. 8, s. 100).

One way of describing this project is to say that Peirce deflates the idea of truth by linking it to belief, assertion, experience, and inquiry. What we do when we offer a justification of 'p is true' is to offer a justification for the claim that p. If we want to know whether it is true that Toronto is north of Buffalo, there is nothing additional to check on ("a fact," "a state of affairs")—nothing over and above our consulting maps, driving or walking north from Buffalo to see whether we get to Toronto, etc. The question of the *truth* of the statement does not involve anything more than investigating the matter in our usual ways.

On Peirce's view, we aim at beliefs which would be forever stable; we aim at getting the best beliefs we can. We have in our various inquiries and deliberations a multiplicity of local aims—empirical adequacy, coherence with other beliefs, simplicity, explanatory power, getting a reliable guide to action, fruitfulness for other research, greater understanding of others, increased maturity, and the like. When we say that we aim at the truth, what we mean is that, were a belief really to satisfy all of our local aims in inquiry, then that belief would be true. There is nothing over and above the fulfillment of those aims, nothing metaphysical, to which we aspire. Truth is not some transcendental, mystical thing which we aim at for its own sake.

4. William James on Truth and Consequences

James (1842–1910) was America's most famous intellectual at the turn of the 1900s—in psychology as well as philosophy—and hence, his version of pragmatism has spread far and wide. It attracted critical attention (famously from Bertrand Russell and G.E. Moore) and was very much the view identified as pragmatism. But the epistemology and view of truth put forward by James, while on the surface very similar to Peirce's, was in fact significantly different.

James calls himself a "radical empiricist." All inquiry must begin with, and then advance through, experience. The "postulate" of radical empiricism is this: "the only things that shall be debatable among philosophers shall be things definable in terms drawn from experience" (James 1909[1914]: 138). He adopts the anti-foundationalist epistemology characteristic of all pragmatists and offers us this kind of pragmatist metaphor for the growth of knowledge. One can liken the change in belief to house renovations: "You may alter your house *ad libitum*, but the ground plan of the first architect persists—you can make great changes, but you can not change a Gothic church into a Doric temple" (James 1907[1949]: 170).

But another part of what he means by 'radical empiricism' is that he intends to bring together empiricism and religion. James thinks that religious belief is grounded in experience—in mystical feelings. He says that although he cannot feel what the mystics felt, he has to rely on their reports, just as he relies on the reports of scientific experts who tell him what they saw. The experience had in trances, dreams, and the like are legitimate by James' lights. These experiences are direct perceptions of fact for those who have them, just as the five senses deliver direct perceptions of fact for the majority (James 1907[1949]: 336). James infamously argued in 'The Will to Believe' that if a religious hypothesis has consequences for a believer's life, it is acceptable. James' holism has it that religious hypotheses, like all hypotheses, need to be verified, but the verification in question involves finding out only what works best for the believer:

> If religious hypotheses about the universe be in order at all, then the active faiths of individuals in them, freely expressing themselves in life, are the experimental tests by which they are verified, and the only means by which their truth or falsehood can be wrought out. The truest scientific hypothesis is that which, as we say, 'works best'; and it can be no otherwise with religious hypotheses.
>
> (James 1897[1979]b: 8)

James' view of truth and objectivity thus: "Any idea upon which we can ride ... any idea that will carry us prosperously from any one part of our experience to any other part, linking things satisfactorily, working securely, simplifying, saving labor, is ... true *instrumentally*" (James 1907[1949]: 58). "Satisfactorily," for James, "means more satisfactorily to ourselves, and individuals will emphasize their points of satisfaction differently. To a certain degree, therefore, everything here is plastic" (James 1907[1949]: 61).

Sometimes he puts his position as follows: "True ideas are those that we can assimilate, validate, corroborate and verify"; "truth *happens* to an idea" (James 1907[1949]: 20). He rather infamously suggested in "The Will to Believe" that if the belief in God made a positive or a good impact on someone's life, then it could reasonably be taken as true by that person.

It is this kind of statement of pragmatism that inspired so much vitriol. As Russell argued, one can take 'works' or 'pays' in two very different ways. In science, a hypothesis works if we can deduce a number of verifiable hypotheses from it. But for James, a hypothesis works if

> the effects of believing it are good, including among the effects . . . the emotions entailed by it or its perceived consequences, and the actions to which we are prompted by it or its perceived consequences. This is a totally different conception of 'working', and one for which the authority of scientific procedure cannot be invoked.
>
> (Russell 1966[1992]: 210)

Peirce levels the same kind of objection at James. He tells him in a 1909 letter: "I thought your *Will to Believe* was a very exaggerated utterance, such as injures a serious man very much" (Skrupskelis and Berkekey (eds) 1992–2004: vol. 12, 171). James' view amounts to: "Oh, I could not believe so-and-so, because I should be wretched if I did" (Peirce 1934: vol. 5, s. 378).

G.E. Moore also interrogated the linkage between the true and the useful. If usefulness is a property that might come and go (in James' own words), then "a belief, which occurs at several different times, may be true at some of the times at which it occurs, and yet untrue at others" (Moore 1907[1992]: 183). The truth of a belief, that is, seems to vary from time to time and from culture to culture. Truth is not a stable property of beliefs and that is an anathema, in Moore's view.

James railed against these often harshly put objections, claiming that they had a "fantastic" and "slanderous" character and were based on willful misinterpretation (James 1909[1914]: xv; 180). His protests, however, had very little impact, as he tended to utter the obvious absurdities in his less careful moods.

James Pratt in 1909 makes a distinction that can help to think about the various kinds of pragmatist accounts of truth. Pragmatism, Pratt says,

> seeks to prove the truth of religion by its good and satisfactory consequences. Here, however, a distinction must be made; namely between the 'good', harmonious, and logically confirmatory consequences of religious concepts as such, and the good and pleasant consequences which come from believing these concepts. It is one thing to say a belief is true because the logical consequences that flow from it fit in harmoniously with our otherwise grounded knowledge; and quite another to call it true because it is pleasant to believe.
>
> (Pratt 1909: 186–7)

The difference between the views of Peirce and James can be nicely summarized by Pratt's distinction, with two caveats. Peirce holds that "a belief is true because the logical consequences that flow from it fit in harmoniously with our otherwise grounded knowledge" and James at times seems to hold that a belief is true "because it is pleasant to believe." The first caveat is that Peirce insisted on a subjunctive formulation: a belief is true if the logical consequences *would* fit harmoniously with our otherwise grounded knowledge, were we to pursue our investigations as far as they could fruitfully go. Hence, Peirce preserves the stability of truth—it is not a property that comes and goes.

The second caveat is that James, as his protests suggest, sometimes put forward a more careful and subtle account of truth, one that was much closer to Peirce's. He was concerned to characterize truth as something that was of human value, without making a true belief what this or that human finds valuable at this or that time. The true, he says, is "the expedient," but the expedient "in the long run and on the whole, of course" (James 1909[1914]: vii). That is, James too wants to argue that true beliefs are beliefs that survive because they deserve to survive.

5. John Dewey and Instrumentalism

John Dewey (1859–1952) was younger than Peirce and James and outlived them by four decades. After James' death in 1910, Dewey became the standard-bearer for pragmatism. Like James, he was an extremely high-profile public intellectual in America, thoroughly enmeshed in the important debates of his time.

His over-riding mission was to encourage scientific thought in all branches of philosophy. He argued that as thought becomes more scientific, it becomes more rational and progressive. In every realm of inquiry, beliefs are to be tested by experience. Political, social, and ethical questions fall under the scope of experimental science. But unlike some of his empiricist successors, Dewey placed great emphasis on the fact that all science is conducted in a context in which social and psychological factors play significant roles.

For Dewey, epistemology is the "theory of inquiry" or "experimental logic." He adopts, pretty much wholesale, Peirce's doubt-belief model of inquiry. Inquirers begin with a problematic situation, arrive at hypotheses which might explain or solve that problematic situation, and then test these hypotheses in action. If the candidate hypotheses are successfully employed in action, enabling us to meet our goals, they are true or, as Dewey later put it, we can assert them with warrant.

The quest for certainty, he later argued, following through on this pragmatist epistemology, is not only a fruitless quest, but in fact isn't the quest that we are engaged in. No one investigating this or that problem aims for certainty. What we aim at is "security" or a reliable solution to the problem at hand (Dewey 1981: vol. 4, Ch. 1). Knowledge isn't a relationship between a proposition, a speaker, and the world; rather, knowledge is a process involving an inquirer and his or her environment. This is Dewey's special twist on the Peircean account of inquiry. He takes as his focus the idea of an organism trying to maintain stability or harmony in its environment—hence his famous attack on "the spectator theory of knowledge" (Dewey 1929[1984]: vol. 4, 18–19, 163, 195).

Philosophers, Dewey argues, have thought of knowledge in terms of a visual metaphor. This has resulted in the dominant view of knowledge being the Spectator Theory, which has it that knowing is a relation between a person and an object—a relationship that can be characterized as a passive seeing of the object by the subject. Pragmatists, on the other hand, argue that everything that we experience comes laden with active cognition.

With James, Dewey thinks that we make truth. Truth is not a "ready-made" property of propositions:

> The pragmatist says that since every proposition is a hypothesis referring to an inquiry still to be undertaken (a proposal in short) its truth is a matter of its career, of its history: that it becomes or is made true (or false).
> (Dewey 1911[1998]: 114)

Again with James, he takes pragmatism to be a species of empiricism. But unlike British empiricism, Dewey argues that pragmatism

> does not insist upon antecedent phenomena but upon consequent phenomena; not upon the precedents but upon the possibilities of action. And this change in point of view is almost revolutionary in its consequences.
> (Dewey 1925: 8)

So for Dewey, as for James, truth and knowledge are not static phenomena—it is not the case that our beliefs either mirror reality (and are hence true) or fail to do so (and are hence false). Peirce, on the other hand, thought that truth was static in the sense that a belief either would or would not survive the rigors of inquiry. But all three of the classical pragmatists speak with one voice when they suggest that we are always immersed in a context of inquiry, where the decision to be made is a decision about what to believe from here, not what to believe were we able to start from scratch—from certain infallible foundations.

Where Dewey most distinguishes himself from his fellow pragmatists is in the extension of his views of truth and objectivity to ethics and politics. He argues that "the problems of men" can be brought under the sweep of science or inquiry. Thus Dewey characterized his view as being experimentalist, through and through.

He also tries to offer the beginnings of an answer to a pressing problem for all naturalist epistemologies. How is it possible to derive norms from practice? Dewey's answer to this query is to challenge the idea that physical science is normless (Welchman 1995: 2). It is a mistake to think that science is purely descriptive. Science is a rule-governed activity—one of developing hypotheses, predictions, and explanations, of deciding what is to count as evidence for or against a hypothesis or prediction, of deciding which explanations should be adopted and acted upon, etc. It is shot through with methodological principles about how it ought to conduct itself; it is shot through with normativity. Similarly, the science of ethics is normative. We develop hypotheses and predictions about what people desire, approve, disapprove and we develop prescriptions about what they ought to desire, approve, disapprove. We develop prescriptions about how people ought to conduct themselves as part and parcel of the science of morals.

6. Willard van Orman Quine

Quine (1908–2000), more than any other twentieth-century thinker, most strikingly combines the pragmatist pillars of empiricism, naturalism, and holism. Indeed, when he first put his position forward, he was happy placing it in the pragmatist camp. He later started to distance himself from pragmatism, as James' radical position was identified with pragmatism.

In the abstract of the 1951 "Two Dogmas of Empiricism," he asserts that one upshot of the paper is "a shift towards pragmatism" (Quine 1980: 20). In the same year, he is easy talking about science as being a tool for managing the flux of experience that could be right out of James and which could not have failed to bring Dewey to mind:

> As an empiricist I continue to think of the conceptual scheme of science as a tool, ultimately for predicting future experience in the light of past experience. Physical objects are conceptually imported into the situation as convenient

intermediaries—not by definition in terms of experience, but simply as irreducible posits comparable, epistemologically, to the gods of Homer. For my part I do, qua lay physicist, believe in physical objects and not in Homer's gods... But in point of epistemological footing the physical objects and the gods enter our conceptions only as cultural posits. The myth of physical objects is superior to most in that it has proved more efficacious than other myths as a device for working a manageable structure into the flux of experience.

(Quine 1980: 44)

Quine argues that our entire belief system must be seen as an interconnected web. Mathematics and logic are at the center, gradually shading into the theoretical sentences of science, and then to specific observation sentences at the periphery. When faced with recalcitrant evidence, we must choose where to make adjustments in our web of belief—and no observation sentence is immune from revision. It was Quine who made famous Neurath's metaphor: we are like sailors adrift at sea, never able to return to dry dock to reconstruct our boat out of the finest materials. We work with what we have, replacing our boat of knowledge plank by plank, as required by the surprise of experience. The resonances with the metaphors offered by the early pragmatists are striking. So is the following:

The naturalistic philosopher begins his reasoning within the inherited world theory as a going concern. He tentatively believes all of it, but believes also that some unidentified portions are wrong. He tries to improve, clarify and understand the system from within.

(Quine 1981: 28)

Indeed, it is a perfect summary of the pragmatism that Peirce, James and Dewey were so keen to articulate.

7. Contemporary Pragmatism: The Influence of Rorty and the Return to Peirce

In the 1970s Richard Rorty (1931–2007) put forward a pragmatist view that tended "to center around James's version (or, at least, certain selected versions out of the many that James casually tossed off) of the pragmatic theory of truth" (Rorty 1995: 71). Rorty argues that we must cease thinking of the mind as a great mirror which holds representations of the world. If we look at the practices of first-order inquiry, we see that such notions of truth and objectivity are irrelevant to inquirers. What we aim at is not truth, but solidarity or agreement with our peers.

Along with every pragmatist, Rorty thinks that our concept of truth cannot outrun our practices of inquiry or our current and ongoing 'conversations' in the context of which we must form our beliefs, make our decisions, and live our lives. "[T]here is nothing deep down inside us except what we have put there ourselves, no criterion that we have not created in the course of creating a practice, no standard of rationality that is not an appeal to such a criterion, no rigorous argumentation that is not obedience to our own conventions" (Rorty 1982: xlii).

Unlike Peirce, who thinks that he can extract a concept of truth from our practices, when Rorty examines our practices of inquiry, he finds that truth plays no role whatsoever. He thinks that we should abandon the idea in inquiry and that in philosophy: truth is "not the sort of thing one should expect to have an interesting philosophical theory about" (Rorty 1982: xiii).

What Rorty finds when he looks at our practices is that the transcendental account of truth, which has beliefs or sentences corresponding to something non-human, plays no role whatsoever. The yearning for an unconditional, impossible, indefinable, sublime thing like truth comes at the price of "irrelevance to practice" (Rorty 2000: 2). Inquirers simply do not aim at that sort of thing. Here, of course, he is in line with every other pragmatist.

Rorty then takes his step away from Peirce and towards James. Inquirers aim not at truth, but at solidarity or what we have come to take as true. Truth and objectivity are what our peers will let us get away with saying (Rorty 1979: 176). What Rorty would like to see is a "post-philosophical culture" in which there are no appeals to authority of any kind, including appeals to truth and rationality (Rorty 1982: xlii; see also 1995: 71). We are to "substitute the idea of 'unforced agreement' for that of 'objectivity'" in every domain of inquiry—science as well as morals and politics (Rorty 1991: 36, 38).

The kinds of criticisms that were put to James are put to Rorty. The charge is that Rorty really is a relativist, holding that one belief is no better than another, and that one must "treat the epistemic standards of any and every epistemic community as on a par" (Haack 1995: 136). Like James, Rorty leaves us with no way of adjudicating claims. It is argued that this is not only an unsatisfactory view, but also that it is incompatible with Rorty's commitment to his own set of beliefs and with his practice of arguing or giving reasons for them.

Rorty's response to the charge of relativism is that once we drop the vocabulary of truth, reason, and objectivity, we shall see that both relativism and its opposites are spurious doctrines. The very idea of a claim's being relative or having only relative validity makes sense only if we have something against which to contrast it—something like absolute validity (Rorty 1989: 47). Rorty is not putting forward a theory of truth, hence he is not putting forward a relativist theory of truth (Rorty 1991: 24; 1989: 53).

One might argue that the dangers of relativism do not disappear so easily. Calling for the dissolution of a dualism, such as that between relativism and absolutism, does not guarantee that one succeeds in escaping the pitfalls of one or the other of the two positions. After the call for the abandonment of a way of looking at things, one must replace the problematic mode of thinking with a new way which really does undercut the problems endemic in the old view. This can be seen as the project at the heart of the best kind of pragmatist epistemology. It tries to replace the old dichotomy of "objective standards or no standards at all" with low-profile, non-absolutist conceptions of truth and objectivity which can guide us in our inquiries and deliberations.

Peirce and all his pragmatist successors stress that we are always immersed in a context of inquiry, where the decision to be made is a decision about what to believe from here, not what to believe were we able to start from scratch or from certain infallible foundations. As one of those successors, Arthur Fine puts it, we of course do not go forward arbitrarily (Fine 2007: 56). The central and deep pragmatist challenge is how we should go from present practice to a future practice, where our very standards themselves might be thrown into question.

References

Dewey, John (1911[1998]) "The Problem of Truth," in L. Hickman and T. Alexander (eds.), *The Essential Dewey: Pragmatism, Education, Democracy*, vol. 2, Bloomington: Indiana University Press.
—— (1925) "The Development of American Pragmatism," in L. Hickman and T. Alexander (eds.), *The Essential Dewey: Pragmatism, Education, Democracy*, vol. 1, Bloomington: Indiana University Press.
—— (1929[1984]) *The Quest for Certainty*, in J.A. Boydston (ed.), *The Later Works of John Dewey 1925–1953, Vol. iv*, Carbondale, IL: Southern University Press.
—— (1981) "Creative Democracy: The Task Before Us," in J.A. Boydson (ed.), *The Later Works of John Dewey 1925–1953, vol. 14, Essays*, Carbondale, IL: Southern Illinois University Press.
Fine, Arthur (2007) "Relativism, Pragmatism, and the Practice of Science," in C. Misak (ed.), *New Pragmatists*, Oxford: Oxford University Press.
Haack, Susan (1995) "Vulgar Pragmatism: An Unedifying Prospect," in H.J. Saakamp, (ed.), *Rorty and Pragmatism: The Philosopher Responds to his Critics*, Nashville: Vanderbilt University Press.
James, William (1897[1979]a) "The Moral Philosopher and the Moral Life," in *The Will to Believe and Other Essays in Popular Philosophy*, Cambridge, MA: Harvard University Press.
—— (1897[1979]b) *The Will to Believe and Other Essays in Popular Philosophy*, in *The Works of William James*, volume 6, Cambridge, MA: Harvard University Press.
—— (1907[1949]) *Pragmatism: A New Name for Some Old Ways of Thinking*, New York: Longmans, Green and Co.
—— (1909[1914]) *The Meaning of Truth: A Sequel to Pragmatism*, New York: Longmans Green and Co.
Misak, Cheryl ([1991] 2004) *Truth and the End of Inquiry: A Peircean Account of Truth*, 2nd edition, Oxford: Oxford University Press.
—— (ed.) (2007) *New Pragmatists*, Oxford: Oxford University Press.
Moore, G.E. (1907[1992]) "Professor James's 'Pragmatism'," *Proceedings of the Aristotelian Society*, 8, 33–77. Reprinted in Olin (1992), 161–195.
Olin, Doris (1992) *William James: Pragmatism in Focus*, London: Routledge.
Peirce, Charles Sanders (1931–1935; 1958) *Collected Papers of Charles Sanders Peirce*, Vols. 1–6, C. Hartshorne and P. Weiss (eds.), 1931–35; Vols. 7 and 8, A. Burks (ed.), 1958, Cambridge MA: Belknap Press.
—— (1981–2000) *The Writings of Charles S. Peirce: A Chronological Edition*, 1–6 Peirce Edition Project, eds., Bloomington: Indiana University Press.
Pratt, J.B. (1909) *What is Pragmatism*, New York: Macmillan.
Quine, Willard van Orman (1980) "Two Dogmas of Empiricism," in *From a Logical Point of View*, 2nd edition, Cambridge, MA: Harvard University Press.
—— (1981) "The Pragmatist's Place in Empiricism," in R. Mulvaney and P. Zeltner (eds.), *Pragmatism: Its Sources and Prospects*, University of South Carolina Press.
Rorty, Richard (1979) *Philosophy and the Mirror of Nature*, Princeton: Princeton University Press.
—— (1982) *Consequences of Pragmatism (Essays 1972–80)*, Minneapolis: University of Minnesota Press.
—— (1989) *Contingency, Irony, and Solidarity*, New York: Cambridge University Press.
—— (1991) *Objectivity, Relativism, and Truth: Philosophical Papers*, vol. 1, Cambridge: Cambridge University Press.
—— (1995) "Response to Richard Bernstein," in H.J. Saakamp (ed.), *Rorty and Pragmatism: The Philosopher Responds to his Critics*, Nashville: Vanderbilt University Press,
—— (2000) "Universality and Truth," in R. Brandom (ed.), *Rorty and his Critics*, Oxford: Oxford University Press.
Russell, Bertrand (1966[1992]) "William James's Conception of Truth," in *Philosophical Essays*, London: Allen and Unwin. Reprinted in Olin (1992), 196–211.
Skrupskelis, K., Berkekey, E.M. (eds.) (1992–2004) *The Correspondence of William James*, 12 vols., Charlottesville, VA: University Press of Virginia.
Welchman, Jennifer (1995) *Dewey's Ethical Theory*, Ithaca: Cornell University Press.
Wiggins, David (2002) "An Indefinibilist cum Normative View of Truth and the Marks of Truth," in R. Schantz (ed.), *What Is Truth?*, New York: De Gruyter.
—— (2004) "Reflections on Inquiry and Truth Arising from Peirce's Method for the Fixation of Belief," in C. Misak (ed.), *The Cambridge Companion to Peirce*, Cambridge: Cambridge University Press.

77
SOCIAL EPISTEMOLOGY
Martin Kusch

Introduction

"Social epistemology" (SE) can be understood broadly or narrowly. On the broad understanding, the expression covers all systematic reflection on the social dimension or nature of cognitive achievements such as knowledge, true belief, justified belief, understanding, or wisdom. The sociology of knowledge, the social history of science, or the philosophy of the social sciences are among the key parts of SE thus construed. Many contributors to Pragmatism, Marxism, Critical Theory or Hermeneutics also qualify. On the narrow understanding, SE dates from the 1980s, is primarily a philosophical enterprise, and has its roots in Anglo-American epistemology, in feminist theory, as well as in the philosophy of science. The perspective of this chapter lies between the narrow and the broad renderings.

Knowledge in a Social World

Goldman's *Knowledge in a Social World* (KSW) (1999) has been crucial in giving structure and inspiration to the contemporary field of philosophical SE. The book is divided into three parts. Part One lays "foundations." Goldman points out that SE can take different forms, depending on whether individuals or groups are taken as knowers. Adopting the former perspective, KSW investigates how individuals gain knowledge in and through their interactions with one another. Knowledge is taken in the "weak" sense of (merely) "true belief." Goldman's focus is on the evaluation of the truth-conduciveness ("veritistic quality") of social practices. In order to develop "veritism" systematically, Goldman develops a semi-formal measure of "veritistic value." One way to spell out this value involves defining the V-value of a true belief as 1.0; the V-value of a rejection of a true proposition as .0; and the V-value of withholding judgment regarding a true proposition as .5. An epistemic practice π_1 has a higher V-value than another epistemic practice π_2 if using π_1 leads to bigger increases in V-value than using π_2.

Having introduced his framework, Goldman turns to the veritistic analysis of "generic social practices" in Part Two. Such generic social practices are testimony, argumentation and communication. KSW's main idea concerning second-hand knowledge is that our normal practice for assessing testimony can be improved by relying on Bayes Theorem. KSW goes on to distinguish fourteen standards for good argumentation. Goldman puts much emphasis on what he calls the "truth-in-evidence principle": "A larger body of evidence is generally a better indicator of the truth-value of a hypothesis than a smaller, contained body of evidence, as long as all the evidence propositions are true and what they indicate is correctly interpreted" (1999: 145). Part Two concludes with a wide-ranging discussion of "the technology and economics of communication." Goldman seeks to refute the idea that "more total V-value will be achieved if speech is regulated only by free market mechanisms rather than by other forms of regulation" (1999: 194). Goldman shows that economic theory does not support this view and that non-market regulation is needed to prevent false but persuasive speech.

Part Three turns from "generic social practices" to the "special domains" of science, law, democracy, and education. Concerning science Goldman covers inter alia "sources of scientific success," "the distribution of scientific research" (centralized agencies might be needed to make sure that different problem-solving methods are pursued), "scientific publication" (editors should aim to publish papers that produce the greatest increase in knowledge), and "recognizing authority" (novices can recognize authorities via observational verification and argumentation). KSW criticizes the veritistic credentials of the common-law tradition. Veritistic epistemology cannot accept that certain types of evidence (e.g. statistical data) are excluded simply because juries are unable to comprehend them. KSW also makes provocative claims concerning democracy. Goldman urges voters to acquire such knowledge as would enable them to decide which of the candidates would, if elected, produce the best outcome. Finally, regarding education, Goldman demands, among other things, that schools enable students to identify truths, that postmodern relativism be kept away from children, and that the curriculum must respect established scientific expertise.

Social Epistemology and the Classical Tradition

Goldman's KSW is an intriguing intervention into several contemporary philosophical and political debates, a useful summary of much earlier work in SE, a clear map of the terrain (as Goldman sees it), and a stimulating outline of possible future directions. Many of these suggestions have been taken up in subsequent work both by Goldman himself and by many others. Since these developments have already been reviewed extensively elsewhere (e.g. Goldman 2002b, 2006, 2009b), I shall concentrate on the question of how SE should relate to epistemology as a whole. I shall use Goldman's stance on this issue as a foil for my own view.

Goldman wants to convince the traditionalist—that is, the "classical epistemologist"—that SE deserves to be counted as "*real* epistemology" (2009b, 2010). To that end, Goldman distinguishes between three forms of SE: "revisionist," "preservationist," and "expansionist." The three forms differ in how they relate to the basic assumptions of classical epistemology; to wit, that epistemic agents are exclusively individuals; that epistemology clarifies key concepts of epistemic evaluation (such as knowledge or justification); that these concepts are of universal validity; and that concepts of epistemic achievement are linked to an objective and mind-independent truth.

As far as *revisionist* SE is concerned, Goldman suggests, the traditionalist is right: it does not belong within *real* epistemology. Revisionists give up most or all of the assumptions of classical epistemology and aim for a "successor" project. Metaphorically speaking, revisionists tear down the building of classical epistemology and build themselves an altogether new intellectual home. "Postmodernism, deconstructionism, social constructionism, relativism, and social studies of science, including the 'strong programme' in sociology of science" belong here (Goldman 2010). Goldman pays closer attention only to the last-mentioned approach. Its two leading figures, Barry Barnes and David Bloor deny that there are "context-free or super-cultural norms of rationality" (Barnes and Bloor 1982: 27) and they redefine knowledge as "institutionalized belief"; knowledge is a "collective representation of the world [that is] ... held by the group as a convention" (Bloor 1991: 169). Bloor's "Strong Programme" in the sociology of scientific knowledge is defined by an insistence on a number of "symmetries": natural and mathematical sciences *as well as* the humanities and social sciences can be analyzed sociologically, and true *as well as* false beliefs are open to sociological explanation. Indeed, Bloor writes that "the same types of causes would explain, say, true and false beliefs" (Bloor 1991: 7).

Goldman claims that Strong Programmers intend to "debunk the epistemic authority of science" by showing that political interests and power—rather than good evidence—determine theory choice. Goldman objects that this position undermines itself. The empirical-historical case studies produced by Strong Programmers seek to present empirical evidence for the claim that empirical evidence is always outweighed by political interests (Goldman 2006).

Preservationist SE is a *conservative* extension of classical epistemology—and thus it counts as *real* epistemology. The preservationist adds a new storey to the epistemological house but sees no need for laying new foundations. Preservationist SE follows the tradition in restricting its interest to understanding and evaluating "doxastic decision making" by single epistemic agents: that is, to understanding and evaluating how a single epistemic agent adopts or retains attitudes of belief, disbelief, or suspension of belief towards a proposition based on perceptions, memories, or prior beliefs. Preservationist social epistemology goes beyond classical epistemology, however, in reminding us that we often gain vital information or evidence from other human agents. The most important phenomena thereby brought into the purview of epistemology are testimony and cognitive disagreement.

Expansionist SE proposes bolder forays into new territory—but it, too, is *real* epistemology. The expansionist builds a new wing to the old edifice of classical epistemology and this endeavor calls for the laying of some new foundations. A relatively modest expansion concerns the epistemic norms of assertion and argumentation. Three bolder steps are the assessment of scientific experts in terms of their track records (cf. Goldman 2001/2002), sensible ways of diversifying scientific research efforts (Kitcher 1993), and the introduction of collective believers and knowers (Pettit 2003; Schmitt 1994, 2006).

Sociology of Scientific Knowledge

I agree with Goldman that SE is *real* epistemology. But I disagree with him over two crucial points: I find his portrayal of the sociology of scientific knowledge (SSK) inadequate, and I regard his attitude towards classical epistemology as far too deferential. Both issues are significant since they influence which ideas and research programs we count as relevant to SE, or as part of it.

Correcting Goldman's misunderstanding of SSK is important for two reasons. First, SSK must have a central role within, or opposite, social epistemology: after all, SSK is dedicated to the empirical investigation of social dimensions of knowledge. Second, philosophical forms of SE tend to use SSK as a foil. Goldman is a case in point. But for this to be an adequate maneuver, philosophers must get SSK right.

Goldman assumes that SSK is in the business of motivating skepticism about science. Or, as another influential philosophical critic puts it: SSK seeks to establish that science "is just another social institution clamoring for power" (Brown 2001: 143). It is hard to square this interpretation with any of the existing historical SSK case studies. These studies aim to identify the *differences* between scientific and other institutions, and they are *not* concentrating on issues of social power. Consider, for example, the single most influential idea in SSK, Harry Collins' "Experimenters' Regress" (Collins 1985). Collins shows that in cutting-edge experimental science researchers face at least two kinds of uncertainty: they do not know which kinds of phenomena exist, and they do not know whether their detection instruments work. The one form of ignorance feeds into the other: their lack of knowledge about what exists prevents the experimenters from properly calibrating their instruments; and their lack of knowledge about how best to calibrate their instruments prevents the experimenters from having much confidence in their ability to detect. Collins goes on to document, on the basis of numerous interviews with scientists, that the latter seek to break the resulting regress on the basis of a wide variety of different considerations. Such considerations prominently include information about the social standing and the track record of different experimenters and their laboratories.

Philosophers who treat Collins as a skeptical "debunker" regarding scientific knowledge attribute roughly the following argument to him (cf. Godin and Gingras 2002):

[1] If scientists (at the cutting edge of research) assess each others' contributions in light of the social criteria Collins mentions, then cutting-edge science does not produce knowledge.
[2] Scientists (at the cutting edge of research) *do* assess each others' contributions in light of the social criteria Collins identifies.
[3] Ergo: Cutting-edge science does not produce knowledge.

Collins' critics usually take issue with [2]. They contend that the experimental data plus relevant theories are always sufficient to break the Experimenters' Regress. Call this the "direct" response to the skeptical argument [1–3]. Collins rejects the direct response. But this does not mean that he accepts the skeptical argument (Collins 2002). Using terms familiar from philosophical treatments of skepticism, we might say that Collins favors a "diagnostic" response to skepticism about science. The diagnostic response rejects [1]; it denies that the possibility of scientific knowledge in cutting-edge science depends upon the absence of social criteria for the assessment of knowledge-claims.

The point generalizes to other case studies and theoretical writings in SSK. Their goal is not to undermine science; their goal is to convince the reader of the social nature of all central scientific phenomena, from observation to experiment, theory choice to calibration. Or consider how Bloor tackles Saul Kripke's (Wittgenstein's) famous meaning-skeptical argument (Kripke 1982; Bloor 1997). Again the response is diagnostic: Bloor holds that the meaning-skeptical argument is compelling only as long as we have a single and isolated rule-follower in mind. Once we replace the individual with a group, meaning skepticism is defeated.

But what about SSK's commitment to a "nihilistic" relativism (Goldman 2009a), and Bloor's alleged view that "our epistemic reasons never make *any* contribution whatsoever to the causal explanation of our beliefs, so that the correct explanation is always exclusively in terms of our social interests" (Boghossian 2006: 112)? The answers are straightforward. The relativism of Barnes and Bloor is methodological not substantive. Their view "is not that all beliefs are equally true or equally false, but that regardless of truth and falsity the fact of their credibility ... calls for empirical investigation" (Barnes and Bloor 1982: 23). Boghossian's charge is refuted by Bloor's statement according to which SSK is committed to the thesis that "our perceptual and thinking faculties are two different things and that our perceptions influence our thinking more than our thinking our perception" (Bloor 1991: 33). Bloor also rejects the suggestion that "knowledge is purely social": "The strong programme does say that the social component is always present and always constitutive of knowledge. It does not say that it is the *only* component, or that it is the component that must necessarily be located as the trigger of any and every change: it can be a background condition" (1991: 166).

Diagnostic Social Epistemology

Goldman's attitude towards classical epistemology is deferential. He deems its central assumptions fully adequate to its traditional task of understanding the socially isolated knower. And Goldman is eager to show that his favorite examples of SE remain true to many if not most of these assumptions. The two modes of deference result in too narrow a conception of SE: Goldman has no space for what one might call "diagnostic" programs of SE. Diagnostic epistemology tries to analyze, explain and criticize the foundations of classical epistemology. Or, to return once more to the housing metaphor: diagnostic epistemology studies the structure of the building, its central pillars and cornerstones, and the rock (or swamp) on which it rests. Diagnostic *social* epistemology does all this in social or political terms.

This can take a variety of forms. An *analytic* version aims to establish that classical epistemology is incoherent, and that—properly understood and reworked—it points towards SE. The problem with classical epistemology might be located in how it interprets or selects from our pre-theoretical intuitions. Or the problem might be in how the various core assumptions of classical epistemology fit together.

A *genealogical* SE offers an imaginary social history of the development of our current epistemic concepts. In constructing such "just-so" history, the genealogist treats classical epistemology both as a resource and as a target of criticism. Genealogy is speculative history. This is because it concerns itself with pre-historical events of which no records survive. The starting point of the narrative is a hypothetical pre-historical "state-of-nature." Genealogy explains why "proto-epistemic" concepts were first introduced and how they related to human needs and interactions. And the social dimension does not end here: every step of the route from epistemic proto-concepts to our concepts is at least in part social. Conceptual change *is* social change.

Eventually the genealogical narrative will reach a stage from which historical records do survive. At this point genealogy turns into *historical epistemology*. This is the project of writing the social history of our current epistemic intuitions, practices, and theories. This social history can, but need not, discredit classical epistemology.

Political epistemology aims to unveil the political costs of classical epistemology and some of our current epistemic practices. This might take the form of convincing us that classical epistemology has the ideological function of excluding certain kinds of people (e.g. women, ethnic minorities) from qualifying as knowers or true believers.

Finally, *naturalistic* SE challenges the individualism of classical epistemology in the light of results in the natural or social sciences. This can come in two flavors. On the one hand, the naturalistic critic points out that some of our best scientific theories routinely attribute knowledge to *groups* of animals or humans. On the other hand, the naturalist insists that we can only understand the possibility of contemporary scientific knowledge if we dismiss the individualistic intuitions upon which classical epistemology is built.

Analytic Social Epistemology

I shall now add some flesh to the skeleton of diagnostic positions. It is hard to think of a better representative of analytic social epistemology than Donald Davidson's "Three Varieties of Knowledge" (1991/2001). Davidson argues that knowledge of my own mind, knowledge of the (physical) world, and knowledge of other minds "form a tripod: if any leg were lost, no part would stand" (1991/2001: 220). For present purposes the most important upshot of this argument is the idea that a social isolate is unable to know anything. The central strand of Davidson's reasoning goes as follows. The starting point is the claim that, at least in the case of our simplest perceptual beliefs, their content is determined by their causes. But how can we pick out the *relevant* causes, given that every belief has an infinite number of causes—all the way *out* to the Big Bang, all the way *in* to unobservable brain processes? Davidson maintains that the problem is intractable as long as we consider a single perceiver in isolation. Only a second person, interacting with the first, is able to determine the right cause. The relevant, content-fixing cause is the "last common" cause in the chains of causes that end in the minds or brains of two people facing the same object or event in the external physical world. Davidson recognizes that his thought here is close to Wittgenstein's idea according to which our concepts of objective truth and knowledge depend on interpersonal communication. The point is worth emphasizing since Wittgenstein has been a central resource or inspiration for other analytic social epistemologists as well. For instance, Wittgenstein is clearly a key influence for authors favoring a "dialectical" approach to justification. According to this approach, "being justified" is social status granted by others to the believer (see Annis 1978; Rorty 1979; Williams 2001; Kusch 2002; cf. Goldberg 2007).

Genealogical Social Epistemology

The modern classic of genealogical SE is Edward Craig (1990). Craig offers a hypothetical social account of the prehistory of our concept of knowledge. His narrative is constrained by two ideas. The first idea is that of an epistemic "state-of-nature," that is, of an imaginary, early, social community composed of language-using human beings who are co-operative though not kin, and whose conceptual and reflective powers are somewhat weaker than our own. The genealogical narrative must make intelligible why these creatures found it useful or valuable to introduce an ancestor of our concept of knowledge. The second constraint is social-developmental: the genealogical narrative must explain—*invoking social change as the central cause*—why the ancestor concept was eventually replaced by our concept. For ease of reference, I shall refer to the ancestor concept and word (and their cognates) as *protoknowledge*, "protoknowledge," etc.

Craig's genealogy can be summed up as follows. In the state of nature, individuals depend upon one another for information. "Inquirers" need information they are currently unable to directly obtain themselves; "informants" offer such information. Inquirers must be able to separate good from bad informants. And it is natural to assume that meeting this need will involve concepts. Assume that *protoknower* is the central conceptual tool for dealing with this problem. Which conceptual components should *protoknower* contain? What should we hypothesize our imaginary ancestors to want this concept for? Craig's answers are that our ancestors want this concept as a tag for good informants and that the concept *protoknower (whether p)* comprises the following elements: (i) being as likely to be right about *p* as the inquirer's current needs require; (ii) being honest; (iii) being able to make the inquirer believe that *p*; (iv) being accessible to the informant here and now; (v) being understandable to the inquirer; and (vi) being detectable as a good informant concerning *p* by the inquirer. Craig is adamant that (i) to (vi) are not necessary and sufficient conditions. Finally, *protoknowledge* differs from *knowledge* in that: (a) only the former is closely tied to testimony; (b) *protoknowledge* is not a fully public concept insofar as it is indexed to the capacities and needs of specific inquirers; (c) *protoknowledge* can be ascribed only to others but not to oneself; and (d) protoknowledge is not undermined by accident or luck.

This brings us to the hypothetical social-historical narrative that takes us from *protoknowledge* to *knowledge*. Craig speaks of this development as a process of "objectivization" of *protoknowledge*. Key steps in this objectivization are the following. First, *protoknowledge* comes to be used in self-ascription. In response to the question "who knows whether *p*?" group members start to investigate themselves. Second, inquirers begin to recommend informants to others. This can be done in a helpful manner only if the perspectival or indexical character of *protoknowledge* is weakened. Recommending an informant to ever more inquirers makes protoknowledge increasingly harder to get. Third, inquirers begin to use "being recommended" as a property that indicates a good informant. This move dilutes the original detectability requirement. Fourth, in the context of group action inquirers cease to care whether the needed information is accessible to them as individuals; they are satisfied if it is accessible to someone in the group. As a result they will speak of protoknowledge even outside the context of testimony. And thus we reach our concept of *knowledge*.

Craig's important book has inspired a number of other authors: Bernard Williams (2002) provides a genealogy of the epistemic virtues of truthfulness and accuracy; Miranda Fricker (2007) a genealogy of virtues of epistemic justice; and Martin Kusch (2009) a genealogy of epistemic value. Melissa Lane (1999) seeks to close the gap between epistemic and political states of nature.

Historical Epistemology

The development of our epistemic concepts and practices did not end in prehistory. Historical epistemology takes up the story from the point where written sources are available. Most exercises in historical epistemology are histories of the sciences. Spoiled for choice, I shall concentrate on one aspect of Steven Shapin's social history of testimony (1994). This allows me to illustrate the contribution of SSK-inspired history of science to SE.

Bernard Williams (2002) suggests that epistemic concepts and virtues need to be studied in the context of other values and ideas. For instance, Williams proposes that there are important conceptual links between knowledge and freedom (2002: 146). Shapin's study might be read as a social-historical contribution to understanding this link. Shapin's topic is the role of testimony and gentility in the shaping of the investigative culture of English natural philosophy during the lifetime of Robert Boyle. Natural philosophers of seventeenth-century England accepted—notwithstanding the Royal

Society's motto *"Nullius in verba"* (on no man's word)—that testimony was needed to make natural knowledge, and that finding good testifiers was a difficult practical problem. Seventeenth-century literature on the topic suggested any number of maxims, such as "(i) assent to testimony which is plausible; (ii) assent to testimony which is multiple" or "(iii) assent to testimony which is consistent" (1994: 212). Alas, no sooner was a maxim proposed than critics found it to be of only limited help. For instance, maxim (i) could potentially and incorrectly exclude true reports that conflicted with dominant false beliefs; maxim (ii) was of limited value in cases where the multiple reports derived from one another; or maxim (iii) did not account for the experience that "too great a display of internal consistency" might be a signal "that a polished performance had been prepared" (1994: 233). Only one maxim was never challenged: "assent to testimony from sources of acknowledged integrity and disinterestedness" (1994: 212). On first sight, this might not sound like a helpful maxim; how were practitioners of the new science supposed to know who the disinterested reporters were?

This is where gentility and freedom became important. Shapin's major historical thesis is that "English experimental philosophy . . . emerged partly through the purposeful relocation of the conventions, codes, and values of gentlemanly conversation into the domain of natural philosophy" (1994: xvii). And one of the central beliefs about the gentleman was that he was a natural truth-teller. The gentleman was thought to be a natural truth-teller primarily on the grounds of his possessing a special "disinterestedness" (1994: 83). This disinterestedness was taken to derive in good part from the gentleman's economic circumstances. As Henry Peacham put it in his influential treatise *The Complete Gentleman* at the time: "whosoever labour for their livelihood and gain have no share at all in nobility or gentry" (Shapin 1994: 50). In other words, to be a gentleman was to be financially independent and secure. And a life that was independent and secure in this sense was equated with a free life. The overarching thought linking freedom, gentry, and testimony together was thus as follows: "Gentlemen were truth-tellers because nothing could work upon them that would induce them to be otherwise" (1994: 84).

The conventions of gentlemanly experimental philosophy did not allow for anyone to openly express disbelief in a report coming from a gentleman. The situation was very different for all those who did not make the gentry grade: women, servants, "the poor and the mean in general," merchants, Catholics, Continental gentry, Italians and politicians. In the cases of all of these groups, their "unreliable truthfulness . . . was pervasively referred to their constrained circumstances" (1994: 86). This obviously did not mean that no one but a gentleman was ever believed: given that much of, say, Boyle's experimental work was carried out by "domestics" such widespread distrust would have destroyed the whole enterprise of natural philosophy. One has to see the link between freedom and truthfulness as a resource: citing the constrained circumstances of domestics-technicians was a way in which a gentleman could explain experimental failures. And whatever information the domestics produced, it became knowledge, and thus a property of the gentlemanly community of natural philosophers, only once it was vouched for by Boyle (or another gentleman) (1994: Ch. 8).

Other SSK-inspired contributions to historical SE include Shapin and Simon Schaffer's (1985) investigation into the social origins of the development of "the experimental form of life"; Donald McKenzie's (2001) social history of attempts to mechanize proof; or Martin Kusch's (1995, 1999) philosophical-historical accounts of self-knowledge and anti-naturalism. Lorraine Daston and Peter Galison (2007) owe little to SSK but illustrate elegantly that epistemic virtues have a social history. Many of Ian Hacking's (e.g., 1992/2002) historical-philosophical investigations also belong here.

Political Social Epistemology

Feminist epistemology is arguably the most important contemporary instance of political social epistemology. I shall here mention only one prominent view in this regard: Sandra Harding's "standpoint theory."

Standpoint epistemology has its roots in the Marxist tradition, especially in the thought of Georg Lukács. Lukács believed that one's position in the process of production constrains what one is able to learn about society. Some social positions, or "standpoints," are more limiting than others. The capitalist understands important aspects of the economic process but he is unable to recognize the workers' essential humanity. The proletarian has no such blinkers. His standpoint is therefore superior to that of the capitalist, both epistemically and politically.

A number of feminists have adapted Lukács' idea for the relationship between men and women. In Harding's (1991) influential treatment, a standpoint is an "objective location" in society. Women's lives constitute one such location. Only few standpoints are able to meet the standard of "strong objectivity": to be strongly objective a standpoint must not only be highly truth-conducive but also be known to be so to its occupants. The latter knowledge must be based on systematic research into the social history of the standpoint. For instance, Harding insists that natural science can be strongly objective only if its core assumptions have been investigated and found acceptable by social-scientific research. She even goes so far as to write that "the natural sciences are illuminatingly conceptualized as part of the social sciences" (1991: 14). Strong objectivity contrasts with "weak objectivity" or "objectivism." The latter position reduces objectivity to mere value-neutrality. As far as knowledge of the social world and some parts of the natural world are concerned, women's standpoint is epistemically superior to men's. This is because women are "strangers" to the social order; women are "outsiders within"; women have a strong interest in understanding oppressive social circumstances; women experiment with social reality; women are closer to basic material conditions; and women are forced to mediate the dualism of nature and culture.

Once the role of standpoints is understood, Harding suggests, it is easy to see what is wrong about classical epistemology. Classical epistemology assumes that knowers are "interchangeable," and that social position and one's embodiment are irrelevant to one's epistemic position. Classical epistemology is therefore unable to support an *epistemic* case for affirmative action. Standpoint theory is a diagnosis and a criticism of this failing.

Naturalistic Social Epistemology

John Hardwig (1985, 1991) raises the possibility that the existence of our most cherished knowledge in the natural sciences remains obscure as long as we stick to the idea—central to classical epistemology—of individual knowers. Hardwig's example is a highly collaborative experiment in high-energy physics of the 1980s. This research resulted in an article with 99 co-authors, many of which will "not even know how a given number in the article was arrived at" (1985: 347). Needless to say, producing the data for such a joint paper presupposes that scientists exchange information, and that they take each others' reports concerning measurements as evidence for these measurements. Empirically, it could not be otherwise. It is clear that such experiments could not be done by one person. None of the participating physicists could replace his knowledge based on testimony with knowledge based on perception—to do so would require too many lifetimes.

Hardwig brings out the importance of "epistemic dependence" to knowledge by asking *who* should be said to *know* the results reported in the co-authored physics paper. There seem to be three alternatives. Hardwig does not label them; I suggest "strict individualism," "relaxed individualism," and "communitarianism." Strict individualism insists that knowledge is the possession of the individual, and that knowledge presupposes evidence based on one's own "onboard resources." A philosopher adopting this option would have to deny that *anyone* knows the results of the physicists' paper. Relaxed individualism allows that individuals know "vicariously," that is, "without possessing the evidence for the truth of what [they] know, and perhaps without even fully understanding what [they] know." Communitarianism sees the community as the primary knower. Thus it is the community of physicists, perhaps the 99 co-authors, that constitutes the epistemic subject of the knowledge reported in the paper. Communitarianism allows us to retain the idea that a knower must be in "direct" possession of the evidence but it breaks with the assumption that such a knower must be, or can be, an individual. Hardwig regards both relaxed individualism and communitarianism as viable options, but he favors the latter: "The latter conclusion may be the more epistemologically palatable; for it enables us to save the old and important idea that *knowing* a proposition required understanding the proposition and possessing the relevant evidence for its truth" (1985: 349).

Conclusion

While no one has done more for establishing SE as a vibrant field in epistemology than Goldman, in some respects his vision of the field is too limiting. He shows too little interest in social-historical and sociological studies of (scientific) knowledge and subsumes diagnostic approaches under revisionism, where this is couched as postmodernism and deconstructionism. It is true that some diagnostic theories end up rejecting the pillars of classical epistemology. But that should not disqualify them from being "*real* epistemology." If SE is to grow not just in width but also in depth, then diagnostic contributions will have to become more central in the future.

References

Annis, D. B. (1978) "A Contextualist Theory of Epistemic Justification," *American Philosophical Quarterly* 15: 213–19.
Barnes, B. and D. Bloor (1982) "Relativism, Rationalism and the Sociology of Knowledge," in M. Hollis and S. Lukes (eds.), *Rationality and Relativism*, Oxford: Basil Blackwell, 21–47.
Bloor, D. (1991) *Knowledge and Social Imagery*, 2nd ed., Chicago: Chicago University Press.
—— (1997) *Wittgenstein, Rules and Institutions*, London: Routledge.
Boghossian, P. (2006) *Fear of Knowledge: Against Relativism and Constructivism*, Oxford: Oxford University Press.
Brown, J. (2001) *Who Rules in Science: An Opinionated Guide to the Wars*, Cambridge, MA: Harvard University Press.
Collins, H. M. (1985) *Changing Order: Replication and Induction in Scientific Practice*, London: Sage.
—— (2002) "The Experimenters' Regress as Philosophical Sociology," *Studies in History and Philosophy of Science A* 33: 149–56.

Craig, E. (1990) *Knowledge and the State of Nature: An Essay in Conceptual Synthesis*, Oxford: Clarendon Press.
Daston, L. and P. Galison (2007) *Objectivity*, New York: Zone Books.
Davidson, D. (1991/2001) "Three Varieties of Knowledge," repr. in Davidson, *Subjective, Intersubjective, Objective*, Oxford: Oxford University Press, 205–20.
Fricker, M. (2007) *Epistemic Injustice: Power and the Ethics of Knowing*, Oxford: Oxford University Press.
Godin, B. and Y. Gingras (2002) "The Experimenters' Regress: From Skepticism to Argumentation," *Studies in History and Philosophy of Science A* 33: 133–48.
Goldberg, S. C. (2007) *Anti-Individualism: Mind and Language, Knowledge and Justification*, Cambridge: Cambridge University Press.
Goldman, A. I. (1999) *Knowledge in a Social World*, Oxford: Clarendon Press.
—— (2001/2002) "Experts: Which Ones Should You Trust?" repr. in Goldman 2002a: 139–63.
—— (2002a) *Pathways to Knowledge: Private and Public*, Oxford: Oxford University Press.
—— (2002b) "What is Social Epistemology? A Smorgasbord of Projects," in Goldman 2002a: 182–204.
—— (2006) "Social Epistemology," *Stanford Encyclopedia of Philosophy*. Online at http://plato.stanford.edu/entries/epistemology-social/ (accessed June 1, 2009).
—— (2009a) "Epistemic Relativism and Reasonable Disagreement," in R. Feldman and T. Warfield (eds.), *Disagreement*, Oxford: Oxford University Press.
—— (2009b) "Social Epistemology," *Blackwell Companion to Epistemology*, Oxford: Blackwell.
—— (2010) "Why Social Epistemology is Real Epistemology," forthcoming in A. Haddock, A. Millar and D. Pritchard (eds.), *Social Epistemology*, Oxford: Oxford University Press.
Hacking, I. (1992/2002) "'Style' for Historians and Philosophers," repr. in Hacking, *Historical Ontology*, Cambridge, MA: Harvard University Press, 178–99.
Harding, S. (1991) *Whose Science? Whose Knowledge? Thinking from Women's Lives*, Milton Keynes: Open University Press.
Hardwig, J. (1985) "Epistemic Dependence," *Journal of Philosophy* 82: 335–49.
—— (1991) "The Role of Trust in Knowledge," *Journal of Philosophy* 88: 693–704.
Kitcher, P. (1993) *The Advancement of Science: Science without Legend, Objectivity without Illusions*, Oxford: Oxford University Press.
Kripke, S. (1982) *Wittgenstein on Rules and Private Language*, Oxford: Blackwell.
Kusch, M. (1995) *Psychologism: A Case Study in the Sociology of Philosophical Knowledge*, London: Routledge.
—— (1999) *Psychological Knowledge: A Social History and Philosophy*, London: Routledge.
—— (2002) *Knowledge by Agreement: The Programme of Communitarian Epistemology*, Oxford: Oxford University Press.
—— (2009) "Testimony and the Value of Knowledge," in A. Millar, A. Haddock and D. H. Pritchard (eds.), *Epistemic Value*, Oxford: Oxford University Press, 60–94.
Lane, M. (1999) "States of Nature, Epistemic and Political," *Proceedings of the Aristotelian Society* 99: 211–24.
McKenzie, D. (2001) *Mechanizing Proof: Computing, Risk, and Trust*, Cambridge, MA: MIT Press.
Pettit, P. (2003) "Groups with Minds of their Own," in F. Schmitt (ed.), *Socializing Metaphysics*, Lanham, MD: Rowman and Littlefield, 167–93.
Rorty, R. (1979) *Philosophy and the Mirror of Nature*, Oxford: Blackwell.
Schmitt, F. F. (1994) "The Justification of Group Belief," In F. F. Schmitt (ed.), *Socializing Knowledge: The Social Dimensions of Knowledge*, Lanham, MD: Rowman and Littlefield, 257–80.
—— (2006) "Testimonial Justification and Transindividual Reasons," in J. Lackey and E. Sosa (eds.), *The Epistemology of Testimony*, New York: Oxford University Press, 193–224.
Shapin, S. (1994) *A Social History of Truth*, Chicago: University of Chicago Press.
Shapin, S. and S. Schaffer (1985) *Leviathan and the Air-Pump*, Princeton, NJ: Princeton University Press.
Williams, B. (2002) *Truth and Truthfulness: An Essay in Genealogy*, Princeton and Oxford: Oxford University Press.
Williams, M. (2001) *Problems of Knowledge: A Critical Introduction to Epistemology*, Oxford: Oxford University Press.

Further Reading

Two journals are dedicated to all areas of SE: *Social Epistemology* and *Episteme*.
Barnes, B., D. Bloor, and J. Henry (1996) *Scientific Knowledge: A Sociological Analysis*, London, Athlone Press. (The definitive statement of the Strong Programme in SSK.)

Brandom, R. (1994) *Making it Explicit: Reasoning, Representing, and Discursive Commitment*, Cambridge, MA: Harvard University Press. (Although Brandom is not normally classified as a social epistemologist, there are numerous themes here that are relevant for the foundations of SE.)

Coady, C. A. (1992) *Testimony: A Philosophical Study*, Oxford: Clarendon Press. (In addition to being the modern study of testimony, Coady's book also contains many themes that are relevant for SE more generally.)

Collins, H. and R. Evans (2007) *Rethinking Expertise*, Chicago: University of Chicago Press. (A normative political epistemology by a leading sociologist of knowledge.)

Fuller, S. (1988) *Social Epistemology*, Bloomington and Indianapolis: Indiana University Press. (Fuller's version of SE is a form of science policy with the goal of making science more democratic and accountable to the public.)

Gilbert, M. (1989) *Social Facts*, London: Routledge. (Gilbert's defense of collective intentionality is a key resource for authors defending the idea of collective knowers.)

Hutchins, E. (1995) *Cognition in the Wild*, Cambridge, MA: MIT Press. (This is one of the most important empirical studies defending the idea that cognition is embodied and distributed over many individuals.)

Kvanvig, J. L. (1992) *The Intellectual Virtues and the Life of the Mind: On the Place of the Virtues in Epistemology*, Savage, MD: Rowman and Littlefield. (This book defends a social form of virtue epistemology.)

Lehrer, K. and C. Wagner (1981) *Rational Consensus in Science and Society*, Reidel: Dordrecht. (A semi-technical study of rational consensus formation in science.)

List, C. (2005) "Group Knowledge and Group Rationality: A Judgment Aggregation Perspective," *Episteme: A Journal of Social Epistemology* 2: 25–38. (List builds on Pettit's work on groups as persons and as knowers.)

Longino, H. (1990) *Science as Social Knowledge*, Princeton, NJ: Princeton University Press. (Longino defends an intersubjective conception of knowledge and objectivity.)

Schmitt, F. F. (1994) *Socializing Epistemology: The Social Dimension of Knowledge*, Lanham, MD: Rowman and Littlefield. (A highly influential collection of essays on testimony and SE more broadly.)

Selinger, E. and R. P. Crease (eds.) (2006) *The Philosophy of Expertise*, New York: University of Columbia Press. (A collection of papers addressing the problem of how laypersons might assess scientific experts.)

Shera, J. (1970) *Sociological Foundations of Librarianship*, New York: Asia Publishing House. (The earliest text to use the expression "social epistemology.")

Tuomela, R. (1995) *The Philosophy of Sociality: The Shared Point of View*, Oxford: Oxford University Press. (One of the key texts in social ontology, this book also contains discussions of group knowledge and group justification.)

Zagzebski, L. T. (1996) *Virtues of the Mind: An Inquiry into the Nature of Virtue and the Ethical Foundations of Knowledge*, Cambridge: Cambridge University Press. (This book defends a social form of virtue epistemology.)

78
FEMINIST EPISTEMOLOGY
Alessandra Tanesini

One of the generally unquestioned assumptions of modern epistemology is that knowledge knows no gender. More specifically, it has been typically presumed that the gender of the knower *is* and *should be* irrelevant to the philosophical study of knowledge. Feminist epistemologists over the last thirty years have exposed these claims as assumptions and have questioned, in some respects, their truth. First, feminist scholars have pointed out that the gender of the knower, as a matter of fact, has not been irrelevant to epistemology. On the contrary, assumptions about gender and other social characteristics of individuals have influenced the development of epistemology in numerous ways which, for the most part, have had detrimental effects for women and, for example, people from under-privileged backgrounds. Second, feminist scholars have claimed that gender should not be considered irrelevant to the philosophical study of knowledge. They have not usually defended this view by arguing that there are distinctively male and female styles of reasoning, although—especially in the early 1980s—the view that there are styles of knowing and moral thinking which are specific to women enjoyed significant popularity (cf. Belenky et al., 1986). Instead, they have based their claim on the thesis that knowledge is, typically, value-laden. More specifically, they have argued that political values, and especially feminist values, can play a positive role in the justification of claims to knowledge.

This essay consists of two sections. In the first, I offer a discussion of some of the ways in which theories and claims that have been presented as gender neutral have, as a matter of fact, been partly shaped by unhelpful gender biases. In particular, I explain how feminist epistemologists have shown that the choice of some forms of knowledge as paradigmatic of knowledge in general depends on the implicit coding of some kinds of individual as paradigmatic knowers. In the second section, I present the view, held by all feminist epistemologists, that gender should not be thought as irrelevant to the philosophical study of knowledge. I show how feminist epistemologists defend the claim that knowledge and justification are best understood as value-laden in light of the criticisms developed by some of their critics. In the context of this discussion of the importance of gender to knowledge I will also present a brief survey of some of the most influential versions of feminist epistemology to date.

1. Uncovering Gender Biases

The uncovering of hidden gender biases is a staple of feminist scholarship in many fields, and epistemology is no exception. Some of the earliest work in the area has been precisely dedicated to this purpose. In particular, feminist scholars have pointed out that the selection of some forms of knowledge over others as paradigmatic of knowledge in general, despite its pretence of gender neutrality, depends on biased assumptions about the character of the ideal knower. They also noted that it has had significant implications for the status of women as credible knowers and experts.

Analytic epistemology since Chisholm has inherited a tradition that privileged propositional knowledge (so-called "knowledge that") over practical knowledge (so-called "knowledge how") and knowledge by acquaintance of people and places. Such privileging is still in place. Most textbooks in epistemology are almost exclusively concerned with propositional knowledge. Another feature of this tradition which has been inherited by contemporary epistemology is the assumption that only a limited range of states can play a positive role in the justification of belief. For instance, it has been presumed that emotions and desires can only interfere with the process of justification without offering any positive contribution to knowledge or rationality.

While analytic epistemology is in these ways only the latest development of a long tradition of Western thought about knowledge, it also differs in equally important ways from that tradition. In particular, a lot of work in contemporary epistemology has focused primarily on beliefs or other states that might count as knowledge. It has, therefore, been almost exclusively concerned with issues of warrant, evidence and justification. This focus is a break with the past. The dominant tradition in ancient, medieval and even early modern times has been virtue epistemology in its various forms. The traditional concerns of epistemologists were the intellectual virtues and vices of knowers and the training required for the cultivation of an epistemically virtuous character.

This break from the tradition is significant because it has obscured the original motivation for some assumptions that contemporary epistemology shares with that tradition. As a result it has become difficult to appreciate fully some of the complaints made by feminist epistemologists about androcentric bias, because these, although relevant to contemporary debates, have been formulated in the terms of a virtue epistemology. The selection of propositional knowledge as paradigmatic of all knowledge is the result of a tradition for which theoretical knowledge is a superior form of knowledge, a more significant cognitive achievement than any other kind of knowledge. It is also a tradition according to which emotions can only be an impediment to knowledge. These views were, in the past, explicitly motivated by accounts of the sort of intellectual character that fitted the ideal knower. These accounts were developed in ways that associated intellectual virtue with masculinity (cf. Lloyd, 1984). Contemporary epistemology has preserved the assumptions about propositional knowledge and emotions but lost sight of their initial motivations. It has thereby made it harder to reveal their harmful nature.

Several feminists have pointed out that this privileging of propositional over practical knowledge, of theory over practice, has had negative effects on traditional forms of knowledge possessed by under-privileged individuals and communities (Harding, 1986, 1991). The negative effects of this devaluation of practical knowledge have been numerous. In some cases women have been harmed. For example, the number of women dying in childbirth initially increased when home births assisted by a midwife were discouraged in favor of hospital births in the care of a medical doctor (cf. Ginzberg, 1987, pp. 98–100). This devaluation of the practical is linked, as Ruth Ginzberg has noted, to denying the honorific title of "science" to women's traditional activities (1987, p. 91). Thus, forms of knowledge possessed by women have been suppressed and delegitimized. As a result a conception of women as individuals who are less capable than men in the acquisition of knowledge has taken root (Anderson, 1995a, p. 63).

The origins of this phenomenon have been analyzed by Genevieve Lloyd in her hugely influential book *The Man of Reason* (1984). She traces the devaluation of practical knowledge to various accounts of reason. Lloyd is quite explicit from the start that hers is an investigation into the character ideals, centered on the notion of reason, advanced in the philosophical tradition. She is not primarily concerned with reason as it figures in the assessment of belief. Instead her focus is on reason as it plays a role in the assessment of character (1984, p. ix). Further, it is important to emphasize that Lloyd is not concerned with reason itself as a trait of character but with various philosophical accounts of this faculty. When Lloyd claims that reason has been constructed as masculine, she is not to be read as saying that reason itself has this feature. Her claims are about theories about reason, which she claims, attribute to reason features that, either by the theorists themselves or by their societies, are associated exclusively or primarily with masculinity.

Lloyd's account is a detailed history of philosophical theories of reason. She traces various continuities and differences among these accounts. For our purposes here three stages in this history are particularly significant. In the first stage, characterized by the work of philosophers in antiquity and late antiquity such as Aristotle, Plato and Augustine among others, theories of reasons are embedded in ethical accounts of what makes a life well-lived. The ideal life is thought to be the contemplative life, and the use of reason is central to living such a life. Ancient philosophers thought of reason as comprising several capacities, including some which are practical. Some of them ranked these practical uses of reason lower than the more theoretical and contemplative uses. They also either explicitly associated these practical uses with women (Augustine) or associated them with traits which were commonly understood as feminine (Plato) (Lloyd, 1984, p. 31 and pp. 18–22). These same philosophers described as masculine the virtuous character necessary for living a good life and in which reason plays a dominant role (1984, p. ix). These views did not prohibit the attribution of the ideal character to some women. Such a possibility was left open because at least some ancient philosophers thought that women can be as manly as any man.

The second stage is characterized by Descartes' novel conception of reason. Descartes offers an account that narrows the faculty of reason to the employment of only one form of reasoning: abstract reasoning. He also draws a clear divide between the reasoning mind and the body. Descartes' intentions are egalitarian. He clearly states that all are endowed with the light of reason. However, contrary to his intentions, reason as he conceives of it becomes associated with masculinity because of the previous cultural associations between femininity and the practical realm as well as the body (Lloyd, 1984, pp. 46–50). This development marks a difference with ancient conceptions. In those views women were associated with lesser forms of rationality. After Descartes they become associated with traits that are other than rationality, and often conceived as irrational.

This last point characterizes the third stage, dominated by views such as those held by Hegel and Rousseau. It is at this stage that the idea emerges that there is not one single kind of virtuous character ideal for all human beings, but at least two, one for each gender. Lloyd points out that these two ideals map neatly into the public private distinction (1984, p. 78). Men are expected to be ideal public citizens, engaged in public lives, they are therefore expected to develop the intellectual virtues required to carry out their civic duties. Women, on the other hand, are expected to be good mothers and homemakers and to develop the moral and intellectual virtues required for these tasks.

As a result, knowledge and rationality are important features of the sort of person men should aspire to become, while caring and selflessness are seen as important features of the ideal woman (Lloyd, 1984, p. 37).

These considerations illustrate the continuing centrality of issues of virtue and character to knowledge as conceived from the ancient to modern times. It is instructive to note that, despite differing views about the intellectual virtues of rationality, these accounts are not neutrally specified; they are gender coded. More specifically, the ideal is formulated in terms that associate anything which in the philosophers' societies was coded as feminine or as lower class as either an inferior form of rationality or as something outside rationality (Lloyd, 1984, p. 37). Thus, the accounts embody androcentric biases because they treat masculinity as the norm and treat femininity as either inferior or abnormal.

It might be argued that even if the history of theories of reason is marred by androcentric bias and sexism, we have now developed accounts that do not suffer from the same shortcomings. Such a claim would seem premature. It is true that there have been positive changes. For instance, recent years have witnessed work on the positive contributions of emotions and other affective states to rationality (Jaggar, 1992). But many of the prejudices of traditional accounts have been inherited without much questioning. These include assumptions about the nature of rationality and about the paradigmatic status of propositional knowledge. Contemporary epistemologists have, on the whole, done very little to challenge the perception of women as either less suited to knowledge and rationality than men or as having a different style of thinking, one which is more caring.

It is important to realize that the problem highlighted here is not merely political. Issues of social justice are pertinent, but the problem is fundamentally epistemological. To see that this is the case, we need to consider that the solution to the problem does not lie in claiming that women are simply as rational as men. Personally I would be surprised if women do not turn out to be as rational as men when non-sexist standards are applied. But to make this claim now before scrutinizing current ideals of rationality would be a mistake. If current ideals of rationality are still distorted by androcentric biases, it might simply be false that women match those standards as well as men. However, what would follow from this conclusion is not that women are less rational than men, but that there might be something wrong with the adopted standards. So the solution would lie in the revision of our ideals of rationality which, of course, will need to be combined with political activity.

A question might arise naturally at this point. Suppose it is granted that epistemology has historically been damaged by an androcentric bias. It would seem that the role of feminist epistemology must be limited to exposing the existence of such a bias. There cannot be anything positive for feminist epistemology to do. After all, if feminist epistemology bears its political commitments on its sleeve, it is inevitably biased. How could it, therefore, be desirable? This question, which Louise Antony has called the "bias paradox," has vexed all feminist epistemologists. Their answers on the whole have relied on the idea that not all biases are bad, but that some are positively good (Antony, 1993, pp. 188–9). It is to this question that I turn in the second section.

2. Gender Matters

There is widespread agreement on the claim that all kinds of values might, even in quite bizarre ways, lead individuals or communities to formulate theories and hypotheses or to acquire beliefs that happen to have quite a lot of epistemic mileage. In other words, it is undisputed that contextual values, of all sorts, might play helpful or not so helpful roles in the so-called context of discovery. A scientist, who values her own success, might be spurred on by her desire for fame to a great discovery, or the same desire might blind her from recognizing the clear superiority of another's point of view. Another scientist might simply assume that male primate behavior must be determinant of primate social organization because of his implicit endorsement of male superiority in primates. These values from selfish to sexist can inform for good or for ill the discovery of theories and the acquisition of beliefs. Feminist values and commitments to the promotion of women's interests can play the same roles. For example, they might motivate the development of gynocentric models of primate social organization which take female competition over food to determine whether females are organized in kin-related groups or whether they are isolated. Male organization is then determined by the need to gain optimum access to females (Hrdy 1999, pp. 122–7).

As the examples illustrate there is no necessary relation between the endorsability of the values driving a bit of research and the epistemic value of the theories or beliefs produced as a result. Good values can lead to bad theories—that is, theories that are false or empirically inadequate or with little explanatory power. Bad values, on the other hand, can lead to good theories. Hence, the mere fact that bad values played a role in the formulation of a view is not sufficient to determine that the theory is epistemically bankrupt (Anderson, 1995a, p. 76). It appears reasonable, however, to take the bad history of a theory to license the need for a thorough scrutiny of its empirical adequacy.

The need for scrutiny in such cases does not imply that values can or should always be screened out when we consider the justification of theories or beliefs. Quite the opposite might be true, if, as feminist epistemologists hold, enquiry is inevitably value-laden in the sense that allows for the unavoidable presence of values in the justification of theories and beliefs. The value-ladenness of justification in the natural sciences is a consequence of the under-determination of scientific theories by all available empirical data (Quine, 1980). Often whether any given observation conflicts with, or offers evidence in support of, a given theory might well depend on the background assumptions of the theorist. Hence, for instance, the perihelion precession of Mercury was taken by astronomers, who subscribed to Newtonian mechanics, as evidence for the existence of a small planet "Vulcan" inside the orbit of Mercury. The same phenomenon was, instead, interpreted by Einstein as evidence that Newtonian mechanics must be false, given the failure to find Vulcan, because his theory of relativity could explain perihelion precession as an effect of the sun's gravitational field.

It is not just factual assumptions that feature in the background and contribute to justification, values can play the same role. Cognitive values might directly lead one to prefer a theory to another on grounds such as simplicity, ease of applicability, or prospect of future explanatory fruitfulness. But contextual values can also play a similar role; they might offer support to background assumptions which are not at stake when the justification for specific theories is being considered. For example, Barbara McClintock's and Evelyn Fox Keller's preference for ontological heterogeneity and complexity in relationships is relevant to the justifications they offer for their theories in genetics (cf. Longino, 1994, pp. 477–8; 1995, pp. 387–8).

In the same vein Linda Fedigan showed that the tendency to think of dominance as a unified category in primatology led to theories that supported the claim that male primates dominate females. Once the category is split into different notions of aggressiveness, victory in conflicts, suppression of conflict, initiation of group movement or direction of such movement, a different picture emerges (cf. Anderson, 1995b, p. 30). All of these examples indicate that contextual values can be as significant in the justification of theories as they are in the series of events leading to their discovery.

This point can be further strengthened if we note that much knowledge, including scientific knowledge is concerned with social kinds. This is especially true in the social sciences, but it is equally applicable to medicine where many of the classifications used are driven by a concern with promoting human health. The very distinction between a pathogenic and non-pathogenic element, for example, is drawn so as to track human health rather than reproductive fitness alone. Hence, some organisms that are relevant to fitness because they make individuals less attractive (e.g., bad breath) are not classified as pathogenic, while some pathogenic organisms only cause ailments so trivial that they do not have any effect on reproductive fitness (Anderson, 1995b, p. 44). In this way, contextual values become embedded in the very content of theories, since the very concepts used in the theory reflect these values. Therefore, the influence of the values goes well beyond the mere context of discovery.

This claim is denied by Susan Haack. Haack argues that the sole purpose of scientific inquiry is the accumulation of significant truths and that contextual values bear no evidential relation to the truth of any scientific factual claim (1997). Haack's criticism of the view that scientific inquiry is inevitably value-laden is wholly dependent on her views about the goal of inquiry. It is these views that typically are denied by feminist epistemologists. For instance, Anderson argues that the constitutive goals of scientific inquiry should be understood more broadly, and that—when they are—these goals are themselves properly subjected to moral and political evaluation (1995b, p 34).

In what follows I articulate the disagreements among feminist epistemologists in terms of their contrasting answers to Antony's "bias paradox." Since to be a feminist is, at least, to be committed to a cluster of political and ethical values about the injustice of discrimination against women, feminists cannot claim value neutrality for their inquiries. The task of feminist epistemology, then, is to offer a defense of value-laden enquiry. In order to do so, it must offer criteria for the demarcation of good from bad biases, and a justification for that demarcation.

The idea that we need criteria for distinguishing good from bad biases only makes sense if the notion of a good bias is intelligible. In this context I use "bias" to refer to all contextual values including those which are moral or political. Thus, good biases are those contextual values which, in a given context, contribute positively to the acquisition of knowledge and the justification of belief. Bad biases are those whose influence on the progress of enquiry is negative. It is highly possible, of course, that some values might function as good biases in some contexts and bad biases in others.

This conception of the task of feminist epistemology as offering criteria for demarcating good from bad biases is a basis for the classification of four varieties of feminist epistemology: empiricism, standpoint, virtue and postmodernism.

Feminist empiricists are committed to the claim that the grounds for accepting a theory should only make a reference to factual evidence and to cognitive values. This position is best understood in terms of the notion of impartiality as developed by Hugh Lacey (2005). A theory's acceptance is said to be in accordance with impartiality when the theory is best supported by the empirical evidence and manifests the cognitive values to a higher degree than its rivals (p. 230). Thus, impartiality requires that moral and political values do not appear among the grounds for accepting a theory so that its justification is rationally binding on all irrespective of the contextual values they might endorse. Contextual values, however, are permitted to play numerous roles in accordance with impartiality. First, they are embedded in the research programs or strategies that lead to the formulation of any theory. Second, contextual values are crucial to an assessment of whether applying the theory in practical contexts is at all useful. That is to say, these values are essential to assessing the significance of the theory. Third, contextual values play a role in the selection and classification of the empirical data that can count for or against a theory. Thus, for instance, interest in the promotion of human health is at the basis of the classification of some agents as pathogenic. This is a classification that is deployed in the description of the phenomena that can count as evidence for or against medical theories about the causes and natures of some diseases. Fourth, since contextual values play a role in the selection of the factual data against which the theory is measured, and since supporters of different values might use different data as the phenomena that might confirm or disconfirm their theories, if the domain of study is amenable to study under more than one research program, then before any theory can be accepted more than one program needs to be developed so that the theory that is finally accepted is better confirmed by the data selected under its research program (and manifests the cognitive values more highly) than any other competitor theory is confirmed by the data selected under its own program (Lacey, 2005, p. 230).

Impartiality is compatible with the value-ladenness of enquiry because it is independent of value neutrality, where the latter is understood as the requirement that values play no role in the justification of theories (Lacey, 2005, pp. 240–7; Anderson, 2004, 3). Impartiality requires that cognitive values and factual considerations alone count as evidence for or against the truth of a theory. However, impartiality permits that contextual values are relevant to an assessment of the significance of a theory. In this manner, contextual values can play a positive role in theory choice in accordance with impartiality.

Impartiality is the trademark of empiricism understood as the view that theory acceptance should proceed in accordance with the virtue of impartiality and that experience provides all the evidence we can possibly have about the world. So defined, empiricism is one of the most varied and developed forms of feminist epistemology. This characterization of feminist empiricism differs from Harding's account of it as opposed to value-laden enquiry. In her view feminist empiricism proposes to ameliorate the situation of women by stricter adherence to a value-neutral methodology (1986, p. 24). Most self-proclaimed feminist empiricists, such as Antony, Anderson and Longino would reject Harding's characterization of this position, but I think that they would accept, perhaps subject to qualifications, impartiality as an important feature of their views.

Antony appeals to truth-conducivity to distinguish good from bad biases. For her, maximizing truth and minimizing falsity are the dual aims of enquiry. Values and interests are good insofar as they make our belief-forming processes more reliable than they would be if we did not adopt them. Antony does not consider the possibility that a theory that is a collection of claims or beliefs which are individually true might, nevertheless, be collectively highly misleading. This is a possibility considered by Anderson. It is particularly lively in those areas of enquiry which, like history, require selecting some among many facts as particularly relevant.

For this reason Anderson proposes that significant truth rather than truth per se should be the aim of enquiry. Her view still subscribes to the virtue of impartiality because she is committed to separating out assessments of the significance of a theory from assessments of its truth. The facts alone are allowed to play a role in the determination of truth, but values play a role in the determination of significance (2004, p. 23). In her view, what makes the difference between good and bad biases is the epistemic virtue of open-mindedness. What matters is that value judgments are not held dogmatically so that they do not drive enquiry to a pre-determinate conclusion, irrespective of the empirical evidence (2004, p. 11).

Open-mindedness, however, will not by itself be sufficient to promote impartiality as defined above. This is because impartiality in many areas requires that different theories driven by different values be compared to each other both in terms of their manifestation of the cognitive values and in terms of their confirmation by the evidence judged to be relevant in accordance with the program that has led to the formulation of each theory. What is also required is the ability to foster different research programs whose resulting theories can be subsequently compared.

Helen Longino's account takes these considerations at its core (1994, 1995). Her proposal amounts to an endorsement of democratic pluralism in epistemology. In particular she argues that the way to control for the influence of bad biases in science is to foster criticism which proceeds from as many points of view as possible (1995, p. 384). To this end Longino wishes to promote enquiry guided by feminist theoretical virtues which she identifies as: empirical adequacy, novelty, ontological heterogeneity, complexity of relationship, applicability to current human needs, and diffusion of power (1994, pp. 476-9; 1995, p. 386-90). She does not claim that these virtues are the exclusive preserve of feminists but simply that they are particularly helpful in the attempts to reveal both androcentric biases and sexist assumptions (1995, p. 391). Longino also wishes to promote the democratization of the scientific community. This would involve the recruitment in the scientific community of individuals from a more diverse background, and the acknowledgment that lay members of the community should also be granted some cognitive authority to criticize the claims of the so-called experts.

While Antony and Anderson think of impartiality as an achievable goal for epistemic practices, Longino treats this value at best as a regulative ideal; something which is desirable but which cannot ever be fully achieved. In places, however, Longino appears to shy away even from this moderate support for impartiality. There she holds that there are legitimate grounds for accepting theories that are not binding on all discussants (1997, pp. 28-9). There are, however, other versions of feminist epistemology, which are quite explicit in their rejection of both value-neutrality and impartiality. Feminist standpoint epistemology is best understood as belonging to this camp.

Crucial to standpoint epistemology is the view that at least some social phenomena are not amenable to successful investigation from every perspective. On the contrary, these features of social reality can be revealed and understood only by those who investigate them from some perspective but not from others. A standpoint is a perspective which is epistemically privileged in a domain of investigation because it is conducive to developing an understanding of that domain which is better (in an epistemic sense) than that permitted by research adopting a different perspective. Some cash out the sense in which the understanding afforded by the standpoint is better in terms of improved truthfulness. More commonly, it is cashed out in terms of its empirical adequacy and its applicability in ways that help the needs of human beings.

The idea that there are epistemically privileged standpoints is especially plausible when it concerns aspects of social reality that can be transformed by the process of formulating theories about them (Haslanger, 2007). For example, the description of some forms of eccentricity and rebellion as mental illness has led to the institutionalization of many women in the past, thus causing genuine changes in their behavior.

Standpoint epistemologists typically argue that the perspective of social groups which are crucial to the continuation of some system of social relations but whose members do not benefit from it, offers a better insight into the true workings of the social system than that afforded by the viewpoint of those who have a vested interest in the continuation of the system. Thus, Nancy Hartsock (1983) has argued that, in the same way in which the perspective of the working class is epistemically privileged with regard to understanding capitalism, a feminist perspective is privileged with regard to understanding those features of the social system that are responsible for the continuation of women's oppression.

For our purposes in this context three points are especially significant. First, a standpoint is an achievement. It is not something that pertains to under-privileged individuals automatically just in virtue of being oppressed. Instead, only those individuals who view social reality through the lenses offered by the values and interests of the underprivileged can be said to have taken up a standpoint. Hence, for instance, not all women, and not only women, view social reality from a feminist standpoint.

Second, a standpoint epistemology entails that values and interests play an essential role in the classification of social phenomena into kinds and in the justification of the theories developed to explain such a social reality. It is also typically formulated so as to include among the goals of enquiry, beyond mere empirical adequacy, the suitability of the theory for deployment in the context of political action and debate.

Third, it follows from the two observations above that standpoint epistemology does not subscribe to the value of impartiality. Instead, it is committed to the view that contextual (moral and political) values can figure among the grounds for accepting a theory (Haraway, 1991). It is beyond the scope of this chapter to assess fully the plausibility of standpoint epistemology's rejection of the value of impartiality. It is important to notice, however, that some quick dismissals of the position are far too hasty. In order to refute the view it is not sufficient to point out that unless research is based on impartial grounds then it is not rationally binding on all enquirers, as some critics of standpoint theory appear to think. This consideration would only be devastating if there was no scope for rational disagreement and discussion about the contextual values themselves. If we insist, instead, that values can be subject to rational scrutiny, the quick argument provided above offers no refutation of epistemologies that do not require grounds for accepting theories to be impartial. What the approach entails is that consideration of the facts alone might not be sufficient to settle even factual disputes.

I have so far discussed several ways in which feminist epistemologists have drawn the distinction between good and bad bias. These ways of drawing the distinction presume that it applies primarily to beliefs or theories held by individuals or communities. Feminist virtue epistemology takes the distinction to be best applied to stable dispositions and character traits of individuals and to structural features of institutions. So it is biased traits of character, or dispositions, which are being assessed for their legitimacy. In her pioneering work Lorraine Code (1987) argued that epistemic responsibility is the primary intellectual virtue, and more recently both Anderson (1995a) and Miranda Fricker (2007) have given prominence to the idea that justice is a fundamental intellectual virtue. These accounts do not only include open-mindedness, carefulness, honesty and so forth among the epistemic virtues, but they also add some specifically feminist theoretical virtues, such as those promoted by Longino (1994 and 1995).

It must be noted that not all feminists are willing to draw a distinction between good and bad biases. Some, often called postmodern skeptics, have claimed that the idea that there is a genuine distinction between different kinds of bias is mistaken (Flax, 1990, p. 56). Instead, they claim that we must give up any pretence that conflicts can be resolved by rational means. In their view, what dresses up as rational disagreement over justification is, in reality, a power struggle for the satisfaction of one's own group interests.

To conclude, this brief survey of various forms of feminist epistemology shows that the most important debate within feminist epistemology is about the desirability of impartiality. It also demonstrates that all versions of feminist epistemology reject value neutrality and accept that contextual values, including feminist values, have a positive role to play in empirical enquiry. In this sense they all support the view that gender should matter to epistemology.

References

Anderson, E. 1995a: Feminist Epistemology: An Interpretation and a Defense. *Hypatia*, 10 (3), 50–84.
Anderson, E. 1995b: Knowledge, Human Interests, and Objectivity in Feminist Epistemology. *Philosophical Topics*, 23 (2), 27–58.
Anderson, E. 2004: Uses of Value Judgments in Science: A General Argument, with Lessons from a Case Study of Feminist Research on Divorce. *Hypatia*, 19 (1), 1–24.
Antony, L. M. 1993: Quine as Feminist: The Radical Import of Naturalised Epistemology. In L. Antony and C. Witt (eds), *A Mind of One's Own: Feminist Essays on Reason and Objectivity*, Boulder: Westview Press, 185–225.
Belenky, M., Clinchy, B., Tarule, J. and Goldberger, N. 1986: *Women's Ways of Knowing: The Development of Self, Voice and Mind*. New York: Basic Books.
Code, L. 1987: *Epistemic Responsibility*. Hanover: Brown University Press.
Flax, J. 1990: Postmodernism and Gender Relations in Feminist Theory. In L. J. Nicholson (ed.), *Feminism/Postmodernism*, New York and London: Routledge, 39–62.
Fricker, M. 2007: *Epistemic Injustice*. Oxford: Clarendon Press.
Ginzberg, R. 1987: Uncovering Gynocentric Science. *Hypatia*, 2, 89–105.
Haack, S. 1997: Science as Social?—Yes and No. In L. Hankinson Nelson and J. Nelson (eds), *Feminism, Science and the Philosophy of Science*, Dordrecht: Kluwer Academic Publishers, 79–93.
Haraway, D. 1991: Situated Knowledges: The Science Question in Feminism and the Privilege of Partial Perspective. In *Simians, Cyborgs and Women: The Reinvention of Nature*, London: Free Association Books, 183–201.
Harding, S. G. 1986: *The Science Question in Feminism*. Ithaca: Cornell University Press.
Harding, S. G. 1991: *Whose Science? Whose Knowledge?: Thinking from Women's Lives*. Ithaca: Cornell University Press.
Hartsock, N. 1983: The Feminist Standpoint: Developing the Ground for a Specifically Feminist Historical Materialism. In S. G. Harding and M. B. Hintikka (eds), *Discovering Reality*, Dordrecht: Reidel, 283–310.
Haslanger, S. 2007: "But Mom, Crop-Tops Are Cute." Social Knowledge, Social Structure and Ideology Critique. *Philosophical Issues*, 17, 70–91.
Hrdy, S. B. 1999: *The Woman That Never Evolved*: With a New Preface and Bibliographical Updates. Rev. ed. Cambridge, MA: Harvard University Press.
Jaggar, A. M. 1992: Love and Knowledge: Emotion in Feminist Epistemology. In A. Garry and M. Pearsall (eds), *Women, Knowledge and Reality: Explorations in Feminist Philosophy*, New York and London: Routledge, 129–55.
Lacey, H. 2005: *Is Science Value Free?: Values and Scientific Understanding*. London: Routledge.

Lloyd, G. 1984: *The Man of Reason: "Male" and "Female" in Western Philosophy*. Minneapolis: University of Minnesota Press.
Longino, H. E. 1994: In Search of Feminist Epistemology. *Monist*, 77 (4), 472–85.
Longino, H. E. 1995: Gender, Politics, and the Theoretical Virtues. *Synthese*, 104 (3), 383–97.
Longino, H. E. 1997: Feminist Epistemology as a Local Epistemology. *Aristotelian Society* Supp, no. 71, 19–35.
Quine, W. V. 1980: Two Dogmas of Empiricism. In *From a Logical Point of View: 9 Logico-philosophical Essays*, Cambridge: Harvard University Press, 20–46.

INDEX

Page numbers in **bold** refer to the chapter of the book dedicated to that topic.

abductive inference 275–7, 863–4
absolutist relativism 79–82
abstraction 359–60
Academic skepticism 433
access 145, 146, 211–13, 307, 308–14, 428–31
accessibility 573
access internalism 31, 146–50, 491–2
accuracy 538–9
acquaintance 60, 148, 309, 374, 428–31, 492–3, 751, 753–5, 758–60
acquaintance foundationalism 60
action, reasons for 213–14, 385–8
actual access internalism 491
Adler, Jonathan 168, 532
Aenesidemus of Cnossos 403, 409, 410
aesthetic cognitivism 376–7
aesthetic holism 372
aesthetic knowledge **369–77**
aesthetic particularism 371–2
aesthetic reasons 372–3
aesthetic testimony 374–5
Against the Ethicists (Sextus Empiricus) 406, 410
Against the Logicians (Sextus Empiricus) 406–7, 409
Against the Physicists (Sextus Empiricus) 406
AGM theory of belief revision 582–3, 623–7, 636–7
agreement of ideas 687–91
Agrippan trilemma 411
airport scenario 526–7
Alchourrón, Carlos 582–3, 624, 625
Alciphron (Berkeley) 707
alethic pluralism 11
alethic relativism 78–9
Alexander, Joshua 828, 831
alien cognizers problem 179–80
Alston, William 117, 147–8, 162, 182–3, 246–7, 396, 504: *Epistemic Justification* 246
ambiguity 551, 594
analogy 674–5; argument from 437–8, 439
The Analysis of Matter (Russell) 750, 751, 758, 759, 760–61
analyticity 284–5, 289–90, 293, 470
analytic social epistemology 877, 878
Anaxagoras 660

Anderson, Elizabeth 890, 891–2, 893
Angere, Staffan 266
Annis, David 523
anti-intellectualism 826–7
anti-intuitionism 815–17
anti-luck epistemology 91–3, **187–97**, 226–7
Antinomies 748
anti-realism 351–2, **477–87**, 639, 644–9
Antony, Louise 888, 890, 891
Apologie de Raimond Sebond (Montaigne) 679
Apology (Plato) 96, 104, 655–6
apperception 745–6
apprehension 88–90, 745, 764, 765, 767–8
a priori justification 283–93
a priori knowledge **283–93**, 470–71, 703, 734–5, 746–7, 818
Aquinas, Thomas 681
archai 667, 668–9, 671
archery scenario 225–6, 229–30
argument from analogy 437–8, 439
argument from depression 97
argument from evil 97–8
argument from examples 285–6
argument from ignorance 799–801
argument from illusion 295–6
argument from natural evil 162
argument from opposites 663–4
argument from silence 64–5
Aristotle **666–76**; on conditions for knowledge 661; *De Anima* 673–5, 681; formal and efficient causes 222; *Generation of Animals* 675; on induction 271; *Metaphysics* 246, 249; and moral knowledge 408; on perception 296, 673–5, 681; *Posterior Analytics* 247, 249, 667–9; practical wisdom 670–72, 887; *Prior Analytics* 668; and skepticism 246–7, 249; theoretical knowledge 666–70; on truth 3; on wisdom 96, 99–101, 670–72, 887
Armstrong, David M. 176
assertion 214–15, 527
assessment sensitivity 536, 537–9
atomism 21, 484
Audi, Robert 331
Augustine, Saint 887

INDEX

Aumann, Robert 579
austere reliabilism 249–50
Austin, John Langshaw 571, **798–809**: *How to Do Things With Words* 798; "Other Minds" 798, 799, 801–2; "The Meaning of a Word" 801; *Philosophical Papers* 798; "A Plea for Excuses" 805–6; *Sense and Sensibilia* 798, 799, 802, 806–7
authority 394–5, 397–8, 426
availability 145, 298–9; *see also* access
Avramides, Anita 433
Ayer, A.J. 119, 438, 458, 483, 489

Bach, Kent 531–2, 559
Bacon, Francis 281, 679–80
Baker, Lynne Rudder 90–91
Baltag, Alexandru 582
bank cases 540, 541–2, 558–64, 824–6
Barnes, Barry 874–5, 876–7
Barrow, Isaac: *Optical Lectures* 707
basic beliefs 236, 237
basing relation 27–8, **109–18**
Bayes, Thomas 448–9, 609
Bayesian conditionalization 29, 80–82, 612–13
Bayesian epistemology **609–19**; and belief change 29, 80–82, 612–13; and coherence 616–18; and confirmation theories 277–8, 448–9, 450–52, 613–15; and degrees of belief 609–13; and evidence 59–60, 65–6, 613–15; and inductive inference 447, 448–9, 450–52; and relativism 80–82
Bayesian Epistemology (Bovens and Hartmann) 618
Bealer, George 301, 813, 818
Beall, J.C. 647
Bechtel, Robert 852
Beebe, James 827
behaviorism 309–10, 851
belief **14–23**; degrees of 42–5, 609–13; epistemic reasons for 40–42, 54–5; knowledge rule for 214–15; non-epistemic reasons for 40–42, 54–5; norm of 8–9; origins of 734–6; and pragmatism 40–42, 48–9, 54–5; and rationality 42–5; transparency of 53–4
belief change 29, 80–82, 156, 582–3, **621–37**, 787–91
Bender, John W. 258
Bengson, John 826–7
Bennett, Jonathan 428
Benthem, Johan van 583, 632
Bergmann, Michael 148
Berkeley, George 295, 435–6, 438–40, 482, 685, 699–700, **707–16**, 757–8; *Alciphron* 707; *New Theory of Vision* 707–10; *Philosophical Commentaries* 707, 714–15, 716; *Principles of Human Knowledge* 707, 709–10, 712–13, 714; *Theory of Vision Vindicated and Explained* 707; *Three Dialogues between Hylas and Philinous* 707, 709, 710–11, 712–13
better-self theories 203
bias paradox 888–94
binding theory 336–7
Bishop, Michael 842, 846
Blackburn, Simon 434

Blanshard, Brand 485
Bloor, David 874–5, 876–7
Boghossian, Paul 876–7
BonJour, Laurence 28, 146–9, 151, 154, 180–81, 250, 258, 259, 813, 841
Boolos, George 360
bootstrapping 451, 603–4
Bovens, Luc 265, 617–18
Bovens-Hartmann measure 617
Braddon-Mitchell, David 16
Bradley, Francis Herbert 28, 485
brain-in-a-vat scenario 20, 32, 190–91, 418–19, 446, 480, 500–506
Braithwaite, R.B. 292
Brandt, Richard 819
Brogaard, Berit 85, 648
Brueckner, Anthony 169
Buckle, Stephen 739
Buckwalter, Wesley 825, 827
Burge, Tyler 111, 307, 312–13, 339
Burmúdez, Jose 645
Burnyeat, Myles 433
Butler, Samuel 853

Campbell, Donald 848, 852, 854, 856–7
Cappelen, Herman 528
Carnap, Rudolf 273, 275, 447, 757, **774–84**, 786–7: *Logical Syntax of Language* 776, 781; *Der Logische Aufbau der Welt* 774–9, 783; *Unity of Science* 779–80
"Carnap and Logical Truth" (Quine) 786, 789
Carneades 132
Carrier, Leonard S. 135, 138
Carroll, Lewis 51, 288
Cartesian doubt 38, 122, 678–9, 697–8, 719, 770–73
Cartesian insight 139–40
Cartesian rationalism 346–7
Cartesian skepticism 133, 138–40, **414–23**, 434, 479–80, 500–501, 685, 799
Cassam, Quassim 441, 442
categorical imperative 387, 471
categories 704, 745–7
causal chains 115
causal theories: action 213–14; basing relation 111–14; beliefs 37–8; and Gettier cases 124–5; inductive inference 731–5; knowledge 150, 176; memory 328; reasoning 731–5; responses to skepticism 419; truth 4–5
Cavell, Stanley 805
certainty 346–7, 416–18, 422, 480, 563–4, 694–5, 715–16
Chalmers, David 180, 648
Changeux, Jean-Pierre 850
character traits 199–201, 202–4
charity, principle of 507–9
children 149, 202, 204, 319–21, 428–31, 592, 770–72
Chisholm, Roderick 27, 119, 498, 578, 775–6, 802, 804
Chomsky, Noam 337, 338, 341
Chrisman, Matthew 840

INDEX

Christensen, David 614
Church, Alonzo 641, 643–4
Church-Fitch paradox *see* knowability paradox
Churchland, Patricia 20
Churchland, Paul 20
circularity 257–8, 289–81, 291–2, 408, 411, 843–4
circularity, mode of 408, 411
circumstantial relativism 388
clairvoyant scenario 146–7, 151, 181–2
clarity 680–83, 699–700, 704
Clifford, William K. 52, 54, 167, 172
closure *see* epistemic closure
Code, Lorraine 199, 201, 893
Cogito ergo sum 284, 425, 621, 681, 698, 719, 818
cognitivism 48, 55, 389–90, 466–8
Cohen, Stewart 134–5, 138, 140, 178, 497, 526, 530–31
coherence: and Bayesianism 616–18; defining nature of 28–9, 258–61, measures of 260–61, 265–6, 616–18; and memory 332; and reflective equilibrium 819; and sensory experiences 699–700; and truth 261–3, 472–3, 485
coherentism **257–66**; emergent 250–52; and intuitions 820–21; and justification 26–30, 169, 472–3, 485; and probability 265–6; and rationality 41; and regress 237, 250–52; and skepticism 250–52, 263–5, 423
Collins, Harry 876
Comesaña, Juan 174, 183, 192–3, 563
common knowledge 578–80
common sense 212–3, 436, 478, 718, 721–2
competing reasons 566–8
complex ideas 691, 692–4
Comte, Auguste 862
conceivability principle 732, 733
concept empiricism 751–6
concepts: and intuitions 704–5, 744–5; and norms 50–52
conditional fallacy 5–6, 203
conditionalization 29, 80–82, 612–13
Conee, Earl 167–8, 170–71, 172, 181, 182–3
confirmation theories 266, 271–8, 448–51, 613–15
conjunction fallacy 615
conjunction rule 43–4
consciousness 217; identity of 746–7
conservatism 788, 794
constructivism 308–12, 389–90
content externalism 502–3
content relativism 539
contextualism 33–4, **523–33**, 539–40, 553–4, 560–61, 594, 799–801, 823–6
contingent propositions 284
contingent truths 718, 719–20
contrastivism **513–22**
correspondence theory of truth 3–5, 484
cosmology 684
Costa-Leite, Alexandre 648
counterfactual difference measure 614
counterfactual theories 114–16, 150, 203, 440, 645–6
craftsmanship 660–61, 673

Craig, Edward 730, 878–9
Cratylus (Plato) 661, 663
credulity, principle of 820–21
"Criteria, Defeasibility, and Knowledge" (McDowell) 299
Critique of Pure Reason (Kant) 704, 705, 741–9
Cross, Charles B. 265
Cruz, Joseph 51
Cullen, Simon 831
cultural variation 817, 828, 831
Cummins, Robert 816, 817, 819
Cuneo, Terence 840
Cyrenaics 433–4

Darwin, Charles 848–9: *Descent of Man* 848; *Origin of Species* 848
Datson, Lorrane 880–81
Davidson, Donald 18, 19, 21, 111–13, 312, 337, 434, 438, 506–9, 878; "Three Varieties of Knowledge" 878
Dawkins, Richard 852
De Anima (Aristotle) 673–5, 681
de dicto beliefs 21–2
deduction 346–7, 667–8
default and challenge model 164–5
defeasibility 124, **156–65**, 317–18, 727
defeater-defeaters 161–2, 317
defensibility 578
definite descriptions 752–3
deflationary theories, of truth 6–10, 484–5
degrees of belief 42–5, 609–13
demon worlds *see* evil demon scenario
demonstrations 667–8
Demopoulos, William 759
Dennett, Daniel 18–19, 21, 852
DePaul, Michael 816, 819
dependence thesis 236
depression, argument from 97
de re beliefs 21–2
DeRose, Keith 191–2, 526–7, 528, 530, 551, 558–61
Descartes, René **678–86**; cogito 284, 425, 621, 681, 698, 719, 818; *Descriptions of the Human Body* 684; *Discourse on Method* 683; and doubt 38, 122, 678–9, 697–8, 719, 770–73; dream argument 799, 800–801; existence of God 741; foundationalism 394–5, 719; and Leibniz 697–701, 703–4; and material existence 698–701; *Meditations on First Philosophy* 394, 416, 434, 438, 479, 500, 682, 683, 684–5, 699, 700, 730; *Optics* 707; on other minds 438; *Passions of the Soul* 684; on perception on 679–80, 681–2, 683; *Principles of Philosophy* 347; rationalism 346–7, 887; *Rules for the Direction of the Mind* 346–7, 680, 683; *Search for the Truth* 684, 685; on self-knowledge 305, 307, 425; and skepticism 133, 138–40, **414–23**, 434, 479–80, 500–501, 685, 799; *Treatise on Man* 683; *The World* 684
Descent of Man (Darwin) 848
descriptions, theory of 750–56
Descriptions of the Human Body (Descartes) 684

899

descriptive epistemology 854, 856–7
descriptive naturalism 836, 837–40
determination 342–4
deviant causal chains 112–13, 125
Devitt, Michael 292
Dewey, John 848, 868–9
diachronic justification 621–3
diagnostic social epistemology 877–82
dialectic 655, 662, 671
dialectical defeaters 164
Dietrich, Franz 266
difference measure 613
Diogenes Laertius: *Life of Pyrrho* 403, 409, 410
Dioptrica Nova (Molyneux) 707
direct apprehension 764, 765, 767–8
direct realism 295, 296, 299–301, 327–8, 481
disagreement 61, **68–74**, 384, 748–9
disagreement of ideas 687–91
Discourse on Metaphysics (Leibniz) 697, 700
Discourse on Method (Descartes) 683
discriminatory capacities 515–16
disjunctivism 216, 299–301, 493, 503–4, 765, 768, 804
dispositional theories 17–18, 456–7, 701–3
distance, knowledge of 707–9
distinctive value 223
distinctness 680–83, 699–700, 704
distributed knowledge 548–51, 580–82
Ditmarsch, Hans van 583
Dodd, Dylan 135
dogmatic invariantism 537
dogmatism: and fallibilism 133, 134, 135, 137–8; and skepticism 404, 406, 409, 411
Dokic, Jérôme 594
doubt 38, 122, 678–9, 697–8, 719, 770–73
Dougherty, Trent 135, 142
Douven, Igor 615
doxastic defeaters 158, 159
doxastic dynamic logic 632, 633–4, 636–7
doxastic justification 28, 168
dreaming scenario 479–80, 799, 800–801
Dretske, Fred 15–16, 122, 177, 420, 441, 513–15, 602, 856–7
Duhem, Pierre 351–2, 449–51
Duhem–Quine problem 613
Duhemian holism 775, 776–7
Dummett, Michael 645, 646, 647
Dutch book theorem 278, 611–13
dyadic relation 536, 537, 539
dynamic epistemic logic 632, 637
dynamicism 553, 554

easy knowledge 497–8, 603–4
Edelman, Gerald 850
Edgington, Dorothy 645–6
efficient cause 669
Egan, Andy 554
Égré, Paul 594
eliminative induction 271, 281–2
eliminativism 20, 48, 838

embellished reliabilism 249–50
emergent coherentism 250–52
eminent properties 702
emotivism 458
empirical knowledge 362–4
empirical psychology 718, 721–2
empirical research *see* experimental epistemology
Empirical Sociology (Neurath) 779
empiricism 289–92, 718, 721–2, 730, 862–4
"Empiricism Without the Dogmas" (Quine) 787
endoxa 671, 672
Enlightenment 394–8
Enquiry Concerning Human Understanding (Hume) 730, 731–2, 736–7
entailment 337–8, 469–70, 597
entitlement 51, 591
enumerative induction 272–3
environmental luck 92
epagoge 667
epistemic boost problem 331
epistemic closure 137–8, 236–7, **597–606**
epistemic expressivism 839–40
epistemic justification *see* justification
Epistemic Justification (Alston) 246
epistemic modals *see* modals
epistemic normativity *see* normativity
epistemic permissiveness 82
epistemic pluralism 76, 77–8
epistemic privilege 470–71
epistemic purism 562–3
epistemic rationality *see* rationality
epistemic relationism 76
epistemic standards 536, 537–9
epistemic relativism *see* relativism
epistemological constructivism 389
epistemological determination 342–3
epistemological skepticism 455
"Epistemology Naturalized" (Quine) 775, 792–4, 837
error theories 467–8, 526, 529–31
Essays (Montaigne) 679
An Essay Concerning Human Understanding (Locke) 687–8, 689, 691
Essays on the Active Powers (Reid) 717
Essays on the Intellectual Powers (Reid) 717
eternalism 538
ethical naturalism 382
ethical relativism 388–9
Ethics (Spinoza) 697
ethnicity, and intuitions 828, 831
Euler, Leonhard: *Letters to a German Princess* 743
Evans, Gareth 311
evidence **58–66**; absence of 64–5; and Bayesianism 59–60, 65–6, 613–15; and coherence 261–2; and defeasibility 158; extraordinary 65–6; forgotten 173–4; and foundationalism 60–61; and Gettier cases 123–4; and independence 66, 262, 264; interpretation 63–4; and intuitions 814–15; measuring 613–15; nature of 58–9, 168–9; and norms 52, 54–5; objectivity constraint 61–3; possession of 169–80;

principle of total 807; propositional 59–60; relevance of 451–2; and social epistemology 873–4; and testimony 65–6
evidence-gathering 172–3
evidentialism 52, 54–5, 61–3, **167–74**, 181–2
evidentialist reliabilism 161, 183–4
evidential support 171–2
evil, argument from 97–8
evil demon scenario 32, 137, 138–9, 152–3, 177–8, 434, 479–80, 500; *see also* new evil demon problem
evolutionary epistemology **848–58**
evolution of epistemic mechanisms (EEM) 849, 850–51
evolution of epistemic theories (EET) 849, 851–2
Ewing, A.C. 258–9
examples, argument from 285–6
expansionist social epistemology 875
experience 169, 283–4, 286–7, 690–91, 732–4, 862–4, 866
experiential foundationalism 241–3
experimental epistemology 125–6, 817, **823–33**
experimenters' regress 876
explicit beliefs 16–17
explicit endorsement 22
exploratory epistemology 684
expressivism 48, 55, 380, 839–40
externalism **144–54**; and belief 20–21; content 502–3; and defeasibility 160–61; and evidence 60–61; and justification 29–32, 38, 144–5, 150–53, 492–8; and norms 51–2; and Reid 720–22; responses to skepticism 153–4, 415, **488–99**; and second-order knowledge 587–91, 595–6; semantic 210–11, **500–509**
extraordinary evidence 65–6

faculties: parity of 723; virtues as 204–6
fake barn scenario 120–21, 122, 127, 205, 226–7, 229–30, 828
Fagin, Ronald 583
fallibilism 121, 122, **131–42**, 362, 787, 863
falsificationism 278, 351–2, 447–9, 450
fancy intensions 536, 537–9
Fantl, Jeremy 558
Fedigan, Linda 889–90
Feldman, Richard 123, 134, 135, 138, 142, 167–8, 170–71, 172–3, 181, 182–3
Feltz, Adam 825
feminist empiricism 890–92
feminist epistemology 881, **885–94**
feminist virtue epistemology 893–4
Feyerabend, Paul 352–4
Field, Hartry 840
final cause 669
Fine, Arthur 871
finite minds 253
Fintel, Kai von 552
first-person authority 306–14
first principles: Aristotle 667–9, 671; Reid 436–7, 441, 718–20, 721–3
Fischer, Kuno 678

Fitch, Frederic 640–44
Fitch's paradox *see* knowability paradox
Fitelson, Branden 266, 617
five modes of Agrippa 408–9, 411
Fodor, Jerry 15, 21, 339, 804
Fogelin, Robert 411–12
Foley, Richard 149, 153, 508–9
forgotten evidence 173–4, 331
formal semantics **571–83**
form of the good 663
formal cause 669
formal possibility 741–2
Forms 661, 663–4
Forrest, Peter 301
Foster, John 296
foundational beliefs 236
foundationalism **235–44**; and Austin 801–3; and Berkeley 715; and Carnap 775–8; and Descartes 394–5, 719; and evidence 60–61; and infinitism 246–50, 254; and justification 26–7, 164; and moral beliefs 468–70; and perception 297; and rationality 41; and Reid 718–20; and religious knowledge 394–5; and skepticism 248–50
foundations thesis 236, 237
four causes 669
Fox Keller, Evelyn 889
Fraassen, Bas van 278, 352, 520
Frank, Philipp 782–3
Frege, Gottlob 284–5, 289, 338, 359–60, 665
Fricker, Miranda 879, 893
Friedman, Michael 759, 777
Fuhrmann, André 582, 624, 628, 632
Fumerton, Richard 309, 491, 496, 497, 508–9, 843
functionalism 10–12, 19–20, 31
fundamental principle 753–5

Galison, Peter 880–81
game theory 582–3
Gärdenfors, Peter 576, 582–3, 624, 625, 627
gargabe chute scenario 192–3
Garrett, Don 738
Garrett, Richard 98
Garron, Joseph 20
Geach, Peter 337
Gemes, Kenneth 451
Gendler, Tamar Szabó 23
genealogical social epistemology 877, 878–9
general normative principle 9
generalized quantifier theory 337
General Theory of Knowledge (Schlick) 777
generality 52, 55, 121–2
generality problem for reliabilism 141–2, 182–4, 493–4
Generation of Animals (Aristotle) 675
generativism 331–2
genetic construtivism 389
genuine overdetermination 115
Gertler, Brie 23
Gettier, Edmund 37, 176, 209: "Is Justified True Belief Knowledge?" 37, 187

INDEX

Gettier cases 29, **119–29**; and causality 124–5, 176; and defeasibility 124, 156–7; and evidence 123–4; and fallibility 121, 122, 137; and intuitions 125–6, 817, 828; and knowledge-first epistemology 214–15, 220; and luck 92, 121, 122–3, 126–8, 187–9; and second-order knowledge 591–2; and virtue epistemology 205–6
Gillies, Anthony 552
Ginzberg, Ruth 886
Glass, David H. 261, 266, 617
Glass-Olsson measure 617
global reductionism 319–20
global skepticism 488–9
Glymour, Clark 451
Gödel, Kurt 360–62
Goldbach's conjecture 141
Goldman, Alvin: causal theory of knowledge 150; on education 95; on intuitions 818; *Knowledge in a Social World* 873–4; reliabilism 30, 38, 150–53, 176–7, 179–82, 493, 587, 838, 842; social epistemology 873–5, 877; weak sense of knowledge 92
Goodman, Nelson 275, 342, 757, 818–19: "New Riddle of Induction" 275
Gorgias (Plato) 657
gradualism 127–8
grasping 88–90; *see also* apprehension
Greco, John 195–6, 200, 205
Grice, H. Paul 805
Griffin, James 84
grue 274–5, 342
gypsy lawyer case 113–14, 115

Haack, Susan 132–4, 139, 890
Hacking, Ian 549, 881
Halpern, Joseph Y. 583
Hamilton, William 437
Harding, Sandra 881, 891
Hardwig, John 881–2
Harman, Gilbert 297, 350, 420–21, 603, 815–16: "The Intrinsic Quality of Experience" 297
Harms, William F. 857
Harper identity 625
Hartmann, Stephan 265, 617–18
Hartsock, Nancy 893
Hattiangadi, Anandi 461
Hawthorne, John 92, 169, 518–19, 528, 542, 551, 558, 561
hedonism 472
Hegel, Georg Wilhelm Friedrich 887
Heller, Mark 182
Hempel, Carl Gustav 274, 447, 485
Hetherington, Stephen 135–6, 139, 140
Higginbotham, James 336
high stakes cases 525–7, 540, 558–68, 824–5
higher-order knowledge 586
Hilpinen, Risto 578
Hintikka, Jaakko 572–3, 576, 577, 578, 594: *Knowledge and Belief* 576, 578
historical epistemology 877, 879–81

Hocutt, Max O. 577
Hoek, Wiebe van der 583
holism: aesthetic 372; and belief 21; Carnap 776–7; Duhem 449–51, 776–7; Plato 659, 660–61; Quine 258, 291–2, 449–51, 775, 787–91, 795–6; and skepticism 449–51
Horwich, Paul 7
Howson, Colin 613
How to Do Things With Words (Austin) 798
Huemer, Michael 112, 265, 266
Hull, David 852
Human Knowledge: Its Scope and Limits (Russell) 751, 760–61
Hume, David **730–40**; on aesthetic knowledge 370; on cause and effect 328, 481; *Enquiry Concerning Human Understanding* 730, 731–2, 736–7; on inductive inference 278–81, 445–6, 481, 731–5; non-cognitivism 381, 465; on perception 724–5; on self-knowledge 305–6; and skepticism 735–40; on testimony 35, 65–6, 319; *Treatise of Human Nature* 730, 732–4, 736–7, 739–40
Hume's principle 359–60
Hume's problem 278–81, 445–6, 731–5
humility 656
Hungerford's objection to inference to the best explanation 277
hyper-realist contrastivism 520
hypotheses 273–4, 350–51, 447–52, 863–4
hypothesis, mode of 408, 411
hypothetical realism 854–5
hypothetico-deductivism 273–4, 351, 447–9
Hyslop, Alec 439

ideal critic 371
idealism 153, 295, 757; *see also* phenomenalism
ideality of space 744
idealized agents 576–8
ideal knowers 886–8
identity of consciousness 746–7
ignorance, argument from 799–801
illusion, argument from 295–6
image of God doctrine 730; *see also* mirror of God principle
immanence 12
impartiality 890–91
implicit beliefs 16–17
implicit reactions 22–3
incongruent counterparts 742–3
incorrigibility 307–8
indefeasibility 162–4
independence 66, 262, 264
independent warrant 355
indeterminacy of translation 791–2
indexical content relativism 539
indexical contextualism 539–40
indexicals 537
index-linked descriptivism 553, 554
indirect realism 295–9, 481–2, 710–13, 738–9
inductive knowledge **271–82**; skepticism about **245–52**; *see also* inference

902

inductivism 347–9
infallibility 122, 162–3, 239–40, 287–8, 307–8, 426
inference: and the basing relation 111; to best explanation 63–4, 172, 275–7; Hume on 731–5; and interpretation of evidence 63–4; and perception 726–8; scientific 347–50, 353–4; *see also* inductive knowledge
inferential internalism 492
inferential justification 492, 496
infinite regress, mode of 408, 411
infinitism 26–7, 237, **245–55**
inheritance principle 248, 252
innate ideas 700–704
Inquiry Into the Human Mind (Reid) 717
instrumentalism 351–2, 868–9
intellectual egalitarianism 395
intension 147–9
intentionality 296–7
internalism **144–54**; access internalism 31, 146–50, 491–2; analysis of knowledge 210; and belief 20; and defeasibility 160–61; and evidence 60; inferential internalism 492; internal state internalism 491; and justification 29–32, 38, 144–50; mentalism 31, 145; and norms 51–2; responses to skepticism 153–4, 491–2; and second-order knowledge 587–91, 595–6
internal state interalism 491
interpersonal view, testimony 321–2
interpretational theories 17, 18–19
"The Intrinsic Quality of Experience" (Harman) 297
introspection 284, 310–11; *see also* access; self-knowledge
intuition 125–6, 346–7, 360–62, 618–19, 687–90, 714–15
intuitionism 383–4, 385–7, 471, 646–7
intuitions 704–5, 744–5, **813–21**, 823–33
invariantism 33–4, 537, 539, 540–42
irrelevant conjunctions 614–15

Jackson, Frank 16, 481
James, William 53, 54, 327, 848, 861–2, 866–8, 870–71: *Principles of Psychology* 848; "The Will to Believe" 866–7
Jeffrey, Richard C. 134, 138, 140–41: *The Logic of Decision* 134; "Probability and the Art of Judgment" 134; "Probable Knowledge" 134
Jenkins, Carrie 648
Joachim, Harold Henry 485
job/coins scenario 120, 122, 123, 125, 126, 187–8, 190
Johnston, Mark 301
judgement: non-inferential 764–73; stability of 828; suspension of 404–6, 407, 409, 411
justification **25–35**; a priori 283–93; and coherentism 26–30, 169, 472–3, 485; default and challenge model 164–5; diachronic 621–3; doxastic 28, 168; and experience 169; and externalism 29–32, 38, 150–53, 492–8; and foundationalism 26–7, 164, 236–44; and indefeasibility 162–4; inferential 492, 496; and

internalism 29–32, 38, 144–50; and luck 187–8; and memory 330–32; and moral beliefs 468–73; non-inferential 492–6; and norms 51–2; objective 152–3; and pragmatism 33–4; and probabilism 28–9; propositional 28, 168, 203–4; relation to knowledge 37–9; and reliabilism 30–31, 38, 150–53, 177–82, 493–4, 497–8; second-level 496–8; subjective 152–3, 200, 202; synchronic 621–3; and testimony 36, 319–22; and virtue epistemology 31, 32–3, 202–6; weak and strong 152; *see also* warrant
justified true belief, knowledge as 37, 119, 209, 214–15
"Is Justified True Belief Knowledge?" (Gettier) 37, 187

Kahneman, Daniel 615
Kail, Peter 738
Kant, Immanuel **741–9**; on aesthetic judgement 374; categorical imperative 387, 471; categories 704, 745–7; contrastivism 519–20; *Critique of Pure Reason* 704, 705, 741–9; and Leibniz 704–5; on moral knowledge 387, 389–90, 471; and structural knowledge 759; transcendental idealism 743–9
Kantian contrastivism 519–20
Kaplan, David 180
Kaplan, Mark 126, 219
Katz, Jerrold R. 804
Kaupinnen, Antti 831–2
Kelly, Kevin 583
Kelp, Christoph 648
Kepler, Johannes 681–2
Kim, Jaegwon 857
Kitcher, Philip 842
KK-principle 589–94
Klein, Peter D. 27, 157, 265
Knobe, Joshua 827
knowability paradox **639–49**
knowability principle 639
knowledge: as achievement 224–30; aesthetic 369–77; analysis of 209–11; a priori **283–93**, 470–71, 703, 734–5, 746–7, 818; Aristotle's classification 666–7; causal theories 150, 176; by experience 690–91; higher-order 586; inductive **271–82**; by intuition 687–90, 714–15; as justified true belief 37, 119, 209, 214–15; limits of 695–6; logical **358–68**; mathematical **358–68**, 659–60, 669–70; and memory 328–30; moral **380–91**; non-inferential 763–73; perceptual **294–304**; practical 100–105, 670–73, 826–7, 886, 887; by reason 689–90; religious 162, **393–400**; scientific 346–57, 660, 669–70, 875–7; second-order **586–96**; self- 22, 211–13, **305–14**; semantic 335–44; testimonial **316–22**; theoretical 666–70, 672–3; and understanding 85–8, 90–93; value of 205, 219–30; and virtue epistemology 202–6; and wisdom 656, 662
Knowledge and Belief (Hintikka) 576, 578
Knowledge and its Limits (Williamson) 32
knowledge attributions: and contextualism **523–33**; and contrastivism **513–22**; and

knowledge attributions (*cont.*):
  epistemic modals **545–67;** and pragmatic encroachment **558–68;** and relativism **536–43**
knowledge externalism 440
knowledge-first epistemology 32, 61, 169, 177, **208–17,** 494–5
knowledge-how 826–7, 886, 887
knowledge internalism 440
Knowledge in a Social World (Goldman) 873–4
knowledge transmission 316–18, 594–6, 600
Kompa, Nikola 528
Kooi, Barteld 583
Koons, Robert 582
Korcz, Keith 117–18
Kornblith, Hilary 816, 838, 839, 845
Kratzer, Angelika 550, 556
Kripke, Saul 341–4, 454–5, 456–9, 573–4, 815
Kripke-semantics 573–4
Kuhn, Thomas 353, 354, 849, 852: *The Structure of Scientific Revolutions* 353, 849
Kusch, Martin 879, 880
Kvanvig, Jonathan 91–3, 113, 199, 201, 219, 221, 561, 599, 647–8, 840

Lacey, Hugh 890–91
Lackey, Jennifer 128, 226, 318
Lane, Melissa 879
language-like representations 16
Laudan, Larry 855
legitimatory epistemology 684–5
Lehrer, Keith 113–14, 115, 122, 123–4, 258, 265, 720, 820
Leibniz, Gottfried Wilhelm **697–705**: *Discourse on Metaphysics* 697, 700; *Meditations on Knowledge, Truth and Ideas* 704–5; *New Essays on Human Understanding* 698, 700, 703
Lemmon, E.J. 578
Lenzen, Wolfgang 572, 576
Lepore, Ernest 21, 528
Letters to a German Princess (Euler) 743
Levi, Isaac 624
Levi identity 625
Lewis, C.I. 259, 263, 264–5, 332
Lewis, David 16, 135, 527, 579, 612, 627, 630
Lewis test 630
Lewontin, Richard 853
Leyton-Brown, Kevin 583
Liao, S. Matthew 831
liberal dispositionalism 18
liberalism 553, 554
Life of Pyrrho (Diogenes Laertius) 403, 409, 410
Lindström, Sten 583
linguistic convention 290
linguistic-semantic intuitions 814–15
linguistic theory 340–41
Linsky, Bernard 644
Lipton, Peter 277, 350
Livengood, Jonathan 831
living well 97–8, 101–5, 657, 658
Lloyd, Genevieve 887–8: *The Man of Reason* 887

local invariantism 536, 537, 539
local reductionism 319–20
local skepticism 488–9, 722–5
Locke, John 481, 685, **687–96,** 701–2, 704, 711, 714–15, 758, 759; *An Essay Concerning Human Understanding* 687–8, 689, 691
logic **571–83**
logical construction 750–51, 756–7
logical empiricism 34
logical intuitions 814
logical knowledge **358–68**
logical monism 367
logical omniscience 576–8
logical pluralism 367–8
logical positivism 34
logical possibility 741–2
Logical Syntax of Language (Carnap) 776, 781
The Logic of Decision (Jeffrey) 134
logic of science 782–4
Der Logische Aufbau der Welt (Carnap) 774–9, 783
log-likelihood ratio measures 614
log-ratio measure 613
Longino, Helen 892, 894
loose use theory 541
Lorenz, Konrad 854
lottery scenarios 29, 43–4, 157, 184–5, 188, 190, 195, 518–19, 603
loveliness 277, 281
low stakes cases 526–7, 540, 558–68, 824–5
luck: and Gettier cases 91–2, 121, 122–3, 126–8, 187–9; and justification 187–8; *see also* anti-luck epistemology
lucky disjunction scenario 120
Ludlow, Peter 337, 338–9, 528
Ludwig, Kurt 830–31
Lukács, Georg 881
luminosity 212, 307–8, 590, 592–4
Lycan, William G. 124, 815, 820
Lynch, Michael P. 12

McClintock, Barbara 889
McDowell, John 299–300, 765–70, 783–4: "Criteria, Defeasiblity, and Knowledge" 299
MacFarlane, John 538, 554–5
McGinn, Marie 804–5
McGrath, Matthew 331, 558
Machery, Edouard 830–31
McKenzie, Donald 880
Mackie, J. L. 839
Makinson, David 582–3, 624, 625
Malcolm, Norman 328–9, 333, 594
Malebranche, Nicolas 435, 436, 685, 701: *Search after Truth* 707
Mallon, Ron 830–31
The Man of Reason (Lloyd) 887
map-like representations 16
Marcus, Ruth Barcan 17–18
Margalit, Avishai 329
Markie, Peter 497–8
Masrour, Farid 823

INDEX

material cause 669
mathematical knowledge **358–68**, 659–60, 669–70
Maxwell, James Clerk 355–6
May, Joshua 824–5
May, Robert 337
meaning nihilism 457–62
"The Meaning of a Word" (Austin) 801
Meditations on First Philosophy (Descartes) 394, 416, 434, 438, 500, 682, 683, 684–5, 699, 700, 730
Meditations on Knowledge, Truth and Ideas (Leibniz) 704–5
meliorative epistemology 836
memory 215–16, 243, 263–5, 317, **326–33**, 489–90, 492–8
memory markers 327
Meno (Plato) 32, 205, 220–24, 697, 700, 703
Menssen, Sandra 396
mentalism 31, 145
metaphysical constructivism 390
metaphysical determination 343–4
Metaphysics (Aristotle) 246
methodological naturalism 836–7, 845–6
Methods of Logic (Quine) 786, 787–91
Mill, John Stuart 347, 348–9, 350, 382, 386, 437–8, 439, 471–2, 483: *A System of Logic* 347
mirror of God principle 702, 704; *see also* image of God doctrine
misleading defeaters 157, 161
modal bases 550–51, 553–7
modal epistemology 31, **187–97**
modal intuitions 815
modals **545–67**
mode of circularity 408, 411
mode of hypothesis 408, 411
mode of infinite regress 408, 411
mode of relativity 408–10
mode of undecidable dispute 408
moderate empiricism 289–90
moderate foundationalism 164
moderate generativism 331–2
moderate realism 696
Moffett, Marc A. 826–7
Molyneux, William: *Dioptrica Nova* 707
monism, and warrant 587–9, 595–6
Montaigne, Michel de 678–9: *Apologie de Raimond Sebond* 679; *Essays* 679
Montmarquet, James 199–200, 201–2
Moore, G.E. 382–3, 421–2, 466, 469–70, 571–2, 576, 867
Moore's paradox 214–15, 571–2, 576
moral intuitionism 471
moral knowledge **380–91**
moral skepticism **464–73**
Moran, Richard 321–2
Moretti, Luca 266
Moses, Yoram 583
Moss, Lawrence S. 582
motivation 381, 465–6
Mott, Peter 133
muddy children scenario 581

multiple agents 548–51, 578–82, 594–6
multi-premise closure 604–6

naive unificationism 551
nativism 701–4
natural evil, argument from 162
natural propensities 739–40, 764–5
naturalistic fallacy 855
naturalistic social epistemology 877–8, 881–2
naturalized epistemology 30, 48, 292, 382–3, 683–4, 720–22, 792–4, **836–46**
necessary propositions 284
necessary truths 703–4, 718
neo-Ryleanism 826–7
Neta, Ram 196, 594, 825
Neurath, Otto 485, 779–84: *Empirical Sociology* 779
New Essays on Human Understanding (Leibniz) 698, 700, 703
new evil demon problem 177–80, 204
Newman, Lex 688, 691
Newman, Max H.A. 759
"New Riddle of Induction" (Goodman) 275
New Theory of Vision (Berkeley) 707–10
Newton, Isaac 347–9, 718: *Optics* 718; *Principia* 347–8, 718
Nichols, Shaun 125–6, 817, 828, 830–31, 845–6
Nicod's criterion 272, 273
nihilism 457–62
Nisbett, Richard 828
no-defeater conditions 124, 151–2, 159–60
no false evidence proposal, Gettier cases 123–4
nominalism 358–9, 365–6
non-cognitivism 380–81, 465–6
non-factualism 48, 458–62
non-indexical contextualism 537, 538, 539, 540
non-inferential justification 492–6
non-inferential knowledge 763–73
non-occurrent mental states 170
non-operational epistemology 211
non-originating principle 248, 252
non-reductionism 319
non-reductive realism 382–5
non-reflective justification 149–50
non-trivial mental states 212–13
normal worlds 152, 179–80
normative defeaters 158–60, 317
normative naturalism 836, 840–45
normative objectivity 48
normative principle 9, 80
normative relativism 79–80, 81
normativity **47–56**, 77–82, 90–93, 456–7, 839–40, 855
normativity problem 77, 78–9
norms 8–9, **47–56**, 82
Norton, John D. 353, 354, 452
nous 100, 668–9, 672, 674
Nozick, Robert 98, 150, 177, 189–91, 420, 440, 601–2

objective justification 152–3
objective understanding 90–91

INDEX

objectivity 3–5, 48, 61–3
objectivity constraint 61
observation 679–80
observation categoricals 795
occurrent mental states 170
O'Hanlon, Hugh F. 438, 439
Okasha, Samir 446
Olsson, Erik J. 261, 265–6, 617
omniscience principle 639, 642, 644
On Certainty (Wittgenstein) 601, 770–73
"On Denoting" (Russell) 750, 751, 752
one over many 663, 664
"On Other Minds" (Austin) 798, 799, 801–2
"On Simple Theories of a Complex World" (Quine) 794
ontogenetic evolution 849, 850, 851
ontological skepticism 455
opacity, referential 22
operational epistemology 211–12
opposites, argument from 663–4
Optical Lectures (Barrow) 707
optics 681–2, 707–9; *see also* perception
Optics (Descartes) 707
Optics (Newton) 718
ordinary language philosophy 798, 804–9
Origin of Species (Darwin) 848
other minds 799; skepticism about 433–43
Our Knowledge of the External World (Russell) 750, 756–7
Outlines of Pyrrhonism (Sextus) 404–6
over-intellectualization 149–50, 171–2

paraconsistent logic 647
paradox of explanation 642
paradox of happiness 643
paradox of omniscience 642
Pargetter, Robert 439
Parmenides (Plato) 661, 664
Parsons, Charles 361–2
Partee, Barbara 528
partial meet contraction 628–30
Pascal, Blaise 54
Paseau, Alexander 644
Passions of the Soul (Descartes) 684
patterns 364–5
Paxson, Thomas D. 124
Peirce, Charles 5, 132–4, 139, 486, 698, 848, 861–5, 867, 870–71
perception **294–304**, 481–2; Aquinas on 681; Aristotle on 296, 673–5, 681; Austin on 803–4; Berkeley on 707–15; Descartes on 679–80, 681–2, 683; distinguished from sensation 726; distinguished from thought 742–3; and foundationalism 238–44; Hume on 481, 736–7; Kant on 742–7; and knowledge-first epistemology 215–16; Leibniz on 704–5; Locke on 481, 690–91; and mathematical knowledge 360–62; and other minds 436, 439–40, 441; Plato on 664; Reid on 724–8; Russell on 758–61

Percival, Philip 648
perfect induction 271
permissiveness 82
Phaedo (Plato) 660, 664
Phelan, Mark 825
phenomenalism 153, 437–8, 482–4, 699–700, 750–51, 756–7
phenomenalist reductionism 774–6, 777–8
phenomenal principle 295–6
Philosophical Commentaries (Berkeley) 707, 714–15, 716
Philosophical Investigations (Wittgenstein) 454, 770
Philosophical Papers (Austin) 798
philosophy of language 30, 33, 454, 457–62, 546
philosophy of science 612–5, 778–84; *see also* scientific knowledge
phronesis 99–101, 670–73
physical speculation, method of 355–6
Photius: *Pyrrhonist Discourses* 403, 410
phylogenetic evolution 849–52
Plantinga, Alvin 31, 132, 141, 151, 160, 162, 398–400, 495, 720, 813
Plato 376, 411, **655–65**, 887: *Apology* 96, 104, 655–6; *Cratylus* 661, 663; *Gorgias* 657; *Meno* 32, 205, 220–24, 697, 700, 703; *Parmenides* 661, 664; *Phaedo* 660, 664; *Republic* 411, 658, 660, 662–3, 664; *Symposium* 663; *Theaetetus* 656, 659, 664; *Timaeus* 660–61, 665
Platonism 358–9, 362–4
"A Plea for Excuses" (Austin) 805–6
pluralism 11–12, 76, 77–8, 154, 587–9, 591, 595–6
pluralistic relativism 388–9
political social epistemology 877, 881
Pollock, John L. 51, 331
Popper, Karl 278, 351–2, 447–9, 451, 848, 852–3
positivist contrastivism 519–20
possibility 741–2
possible world semantics 573–6
Posterior Analytics (Aristotle) 247, 249, 667–9
postmodernism 874, 882, 890, 894
potential access internalism 491
powers, virtues as 204–6
practical knowledge 100–105, 670–73, 826–7, 886, 887
practical value 223
practical wisdom 100–105, 670–73, 826–7, 886, 887
pragmatic encroachment 33–4, **558–68**
pragmatic relevance 561–2
pragmatism 5–6, 33–4, 40–42, 48–9, 54–5, 532, **861–71**
Pratt, James 867
praxism 826–7
prediction theories 448–51
premise-circularity 280–81, 292
prescriptivism 380
preservationism 317, 330–31
preservationist social epistemology 875
principal principle 612–13
Principia (Newton) 347–8, 718
Principia Mathematica (Whitehead & Russell) 750, 756

906

principle of charity 507–9
principle of credulity 820–21
principle of sufficient reason 703
principle of tolerance 781, 786
principle of total evidence 807
principle of uniformity of nature 733–5
principle of utility 385, 386
Principles of Human Knowledge (Berkeley) 707, 709–10, 712–13, 714
The Principles of Mathematics (Russell) 752
Principles of Philosophy (Descartes) 347
Principles of Psychology (James) 848
Prior Analytics (Aristotle) 668
Pritchard, Duncan 91–2, 122, 189, 194–6, 219, 221, 225–30, 489, 648
privileged class constraint 840–42
probabilism 28–9, 265–6
probability: and belief 609–13; and closure 605–6; and evidence 59–60, 62, 65–6; and fallibilism 140–42; and inductive inference 447–9; Locke on 694; *see also* Bayesian epistemology
"Probability and the Art of Judgment" (Jeffrey) 134
"Probable Knowledge" (Jeffrey) 134
problem of induction 278–81, 445–6, 731–5
The Problem of Perception (Smith) 295
The Problems of Philosophy (Russell) 264, 750, 753–5, 738
process reliabilism *see* reliabilism
Proietti, Carlo 646
proliferation, principle of 352–4
proper function theories 151, 160, 161
proper functionalism 720–21
properly basic beliefs 237–9
propositional anaphora 551–2
propositional attitudes 14, 306
propositional content 78
propositional evidence 59–60
propositional justification 28, 168, 203–4
protocol statements 778–83
Pryor, James 136, 138
pseudo-overdetermination 115–16
psychological defeaters 317
psychology 88–90, 95, 339, 718, 721–2, 793
public announcement logic 632, 637
Pursuit of Truth (Quine) 795
Pust, Joel 818
Putnam, Hilary 5–6, 20–21, 418–19, 486, 501–6, 520, 815
Pyrrhonian modes 407–11
Pyrrhonian skepticism 248–9, **403–12**, 415, 433, 678–9, 737–8
Pyrrhonist Discourses (Photius) 403, 410
Pyrrho of Elis 403

Quine, W.V.O. **786–96**; on a priori knowledge 290–92; on Carnap 775, 776–8, 783–4; "Carnap and Logical Truth" 786, 789; "Empiricism Without the Dogmas" 787; "Epistemology Naturalized" 775, 792–4, 837; fallibilism 156, 787; falsificationism 448; Gavagai example 507; holism 21, 258, 291–2, 449–51, 775, 787–91, 795–6; on intuitions 820; *Methods of Logic* 786, 787–91; naturalized epistemology 792–4, 837, 838, 839, 842, 855; "On Simple Theories of a Complex World" 794; Platonism 362–4; and psychology 30; pragmatism 869–70; *Pursuit of Truth* 795; "The Scope and Language of Science" 791, 794; "Truth by Convention" 786–7, 789; "Two Dogmas of Empiricism" 775, 787–91, 869–70; underdetermination 787–91, 792; *The Web of Belief* 794–6; web of belief metaphor 258, 291, 794–6, 870; *Word and Object* 791–2
Quinean Platonism 362–4
Quintilian 680

Rabinowicz, Wlodek 583
radical empiricism 290–92, 866
radical generativism 331
radical interpretation 18, 506–9
radical skepticism 479–80
"The Raft and the Pyramid" (Sosa) 199
Ramsey, Frank P. 176, 610, 612, 624, 627, 760
Ramsey, William 20
Ramsey sentences 760–61
Ramsey test 627–8, 630–31, 633
Rantala, Veikko 577
rational recognition principle 399–400
rational reconstruction 774–6, 777–8, 783
rationalism 287–8, 346–7
rationality **37–45**, 49–50, 399–400
ravens paradox 274, 516
Rawls, John 389–90, 818–19
Read, Stephen 367
realism: and anti-realism 477–9, 814; and evolutionary epistemology 854–5; and memory 326–8; and moral knowledge 382–5; and perception 295–301, 481; and truth 484–5
real possibility 741–2
reason, knowledge by 689–90
reasonable belief 398–400
reason-defeating defeaters 158
reasoning 287
rebutting defeaters 158
reductionism 289, 319–21, 774–6, 777–8
reductive realism 382
Reed, Baron 136–7, 139, 140, 141
referential opacity 22
referential transparency 22
reflection account 701–3
reflective equilibrium 384–5, 814, 818–19
Regius, Henricus 685
regress 26–7, 51, 147–8, 237, 245–52, 257–8, 288, 415, 719
Reichenbach, Hans 447
Reid, Thomas 35, 319, 328, 436–7, 438–9, 440–42, **717–28**: *Essays on the Active Powers* 717; *Essays on the Intellectual Powers* 717; *Inquiry Into the Human Mind* 717
relational content relativism 539
relational contextualism 537, 539–40

INDEX

relationism 76, 539–40
relativism **75–82**; and contextualism 539–40; ethical 388–9; and invariantism 540–42; and knowledge attributions **536–43**; and modals 554; and synthesis 542–3
relativity, mode of 408–10
relevance, evidence 451–2
reliabilism **176–85**; austere 249–50; and defeaters 160–61; embellished 249–50; and evidence 61; and induction 279–81; and intuitions 818; and justification 30–31, 38, 150–53, 177–82, 493–4, 497–8; and naturalism 838, 842–4, 845; and non-inferential knowledge 763; and norms 52; and second-order knowledge 588–9, 590; and skepticism 493–4, 497–8; and virtue epistemology 201, 204
reliabilist contrastivism 520
reliabilist foundationalism 242–3
reliability 262–3, 264, 333, 764–5, 818
religious knowledge 162, **393–400**
Remarks on the Foundations of Mathematics (Wittgenstein) 454
representational theories: belief 15–17; Descartes 680–82; memory 326–7; perception 680–82, 710–13; truth 4–5
representative realism 326–7, 710–13
Republic (Plato) 411, 658, 660, 662–3, 664
Rescher, Nicholas 257, 265, 649, 851–2
Resnik, Michael 364–5
responsibility 199–200, 201–2
Restall, Greg 648
revisionist social epistemology 874–5
rhetoric 680–81
Richards, Robert 855
Riggs, Wayne 95
Rijke, Maarten de 582
Roberts, Robert C. 200, 202
Robinson, Howard 296
Rohrbaugh, Guy 196, 594
Rorty, Richard 35, 76, 861, 870–71
Rosen, Gideon 82
Rosenberg, Jay F. 814
Ross, William David 383–6
Rott, Hans 625
Roush, Sherrilyn 602
Rousseau, Jean-Jacques 887
Routley, Richard 647, 649
Rudner, Richard 558, 562
rule-circularity 280–81, 292
rule-following skepticism **454–62**
Rules for the Direction of the Mind (Descartes) 346–7, 680, 683
Russell, Bertrand **750–61**; *The Analysis of Matter* 750, 751, 758, 759, 760–61; on coherence 264; correspondence theory of truth 3; *Human Knowledge: Its Scope and Limits* 751, 760–61; on intuitions 816; on memory 327, 332–3; "On Denoting" 750, 751, 752; *Our Knowledge of the External World* 750, 756–7; phenomenalism 756–7; pragmatism 867; *Principia Mathematica* 750, 756;

The Principles of Mathematics 752; *The Problems of Philosophy* 264, 750, 753–5, 738; sense-datum theory 295, 756–7; and skepticism 685–6; structuralism 758–61; theory of descriptions 751–6; *Theory of Knowledge* 751
Russell's paradox 359–60
Ryan, Sharon 97–8
Ryle, Gilbert 18
Rysiew, Patrick 135, 142

safe indication theory 422–3
safety theories 193–7, 593
Sagan, Carl 64, 65
Salerno, Joe 648
Salmon, Wesley 91
Sandu, Gabriel 646
scatter problem 200
Schaffer, Jonathan 521
Schaffer, Simon 880
Schiffer, Stephen 525, 530, 540
Schlick, Moritz: *General Theory of Knowledge* 777
Schlosser, Markus 113
Schubert, Stefan 266
Schwitzgebel, Eric 23
science, logic of 782–4
scientific knowledge **346–57**, 660, 669–70; sociology of 875–7
scope, problems of 4–5, 6
"The Scope and Language of Science" (Quine) 791, 794
Search after Truth (Malebranche) 707
Search for the Truth (Descartes) 684, 685
second-level justification 496–8
second-order knowledge **586–96**
Segerberg, Krister 582–3
self-blindness 313
self-evidence 383–4, 470, 719, 721–2
self intimation *see* luminosity
self-justifying beliefs 238
self-knowledge 22, 211–13, **305–14**; skepticism about **425–32**
self-verifying thoughts 425–7
Sellars, Wilfrid 27, 147–8, 764–5, 783
semantic anti-realism 644–5
semantic externalism 210–11; and skepticism **500–509**
semantic knowledge **335–44**
semantic transparency 7–8
semi-skepticism *see* local skepticism
sensation, distinguished from perception 726
Sense and Sensibilia (Austin) 798, 799, 802, 806–7
sense-datum theory 295–9, 481–4
sensitivity theories 189–93
sensory experiences 238–44; *see also* perception
Sextus Empiricus 132, 246–7, 403–10, 433–4; *Against the Ethicists* 406, 410; *Against the Logicians* 406–7, 409; *Against the Physicists* 406; *Outlines of Pyrrhonism* 404–6
Shafir, Eldar 816
Shah, Nishi 172

INDEX

Shapin, Steven 879–80
Sherman, Brett 420–21
Shoemaker, Sydney 311, 313–14, 333
Shogenji, Tomoji 261, 265, 616–17
Shogenji measure 616–17
Shoham, Yoav 583
Shope, Robert 203
Sibley, Frank 369–70
side-effect effect 827
silence, argument from 64–5
simple ideas 691–92
simplicity 788, 791, 792, 794
simultaneity 744
singularity 300–301
Sinnott-Armstrong, Walter 412, 824–5
skeptical scenarios *see* brain-in-a-vat-scenarios; evil demon scenarios
skeptical solution 457–62
skepticism: Academic 433; and anti-realism **477–487**; Cartesian 133, 138–40, **414–23**, 434, 479–80, 500–501, 685, 799; and closure 597–8; and coherentism 250–52, 262–5, 423; and contextualism 525–6; and contrastivism 517–18; epistemological 455; and evolutionary epistemology 855–6; and externalism 153–4, 415, **488–99**; and fallibilism 133, 134, 135, 137–8; and foundationalism 248–50; global 488–9; and Hume 735–40; and idealism 153; about inductive knowledge **445–52**; and infinitism 253–4; and internalism 153–4, 491–2; and knowledge-first epistemology 212–13, 494–5; local 488–9, 722–5; and memory 332–3; moral **464–73**; and normative naturalism 840–42; ontological 455; about other minds **433–43**, 799; and phenomenalism 153; Pyrrhonian 248–9, **403–12**, 415, 433, 737–8; radical 479–80; and regress 246–7; and Reid 722–5; and reliabilism 493–4, 497–8; and representative realism 710–13; about rule-following **454–62**; about self-knowledge **425–32**; and semantic externalism **500–509**; and semantic knowledge 341–4
Skinner, B.F. 851
Skyrms, Brian 271, 857
Smith, A.D. 295–6: *The Problem of Perception* 295
Soames, Scott 342–4
social epistemology 35, 55, 615, **873–82**
social psychology 823
sociology of scientific knowledge 875–7
Socrates 32, 96, 205, 221, 305, 655–7, 659–60, 662–3, 700
Solecki, Slawomir 582
Somenzi, Vittorio 853
sophia 99–101, 666–70, 672–3
sophisticated unificationism 551
Sosa, Ernest: anti-skepticism 529; garbage chute case 192–3; on intuitions 813, 818, 829, 833; new evil demon problem 178–9, 204; pluralism 154; "The Raft and the Pyramid" 199; safety theories 194; on self-knowledge 249; virtue epistemology 154, 199, 200

space, ideality of 744
special consequence principle 274
speckled hen scenario 297–9
Sperber, Dan 851
spheres semantics 630–32, 634–6
Spinoza, Baruch 697: *Ethics* 697
stability, judgements 828
Stainton, Rob 528
Stalnaker, Robert 576
Stalnaker test 630
standard invariantism 537
standpoint epistemology 881, 892–3
Stanley, Jason 135, 137, 528, 542, 558, 560–61, 563, 648
status relativism 388
Stich, Stephen 20, 125–6, 340–41, 817, 819, 828, 830–31, 833, 839, 845–6
stoicism 411
Strawson, Peter F. 4, 841–2
Strevens, Michael 612
strong access internalism 146–50
strong justification 152
strong normative naturalism 842–4
strong objectivity 881
strong programme in sociology of science 874–5
strong safety 195–6
Stroud, Barry 805, 844
structuralism 364–5, 750–51, 758–61
structural realism 520, 760
The Structure of Scientific Revolutions (Kuhn) 353, 849
subjective Bayesianism 80–82
subjective idealism 757
subjective justification 152–3, 200, 202
subjective understanding 90–91
subject-sensitive invariantism 537, 541–2, 561
sufficient reason, principle of 703
Sullivan, Thomas D. 396
Summa Theologia (Aquinas) 681
superstructure beliefs 236
supervenience 838–9
superwarrant 6
suspension of judgement 404–6, 407, 409, 411
Swain, Marshall 114–16
Swain, Stacey 828, 831
swamping problem 32–3, 206, 219
Swampman scenario 19
syllogistic logic 668, 669–70
Symposium (Plato) 663
synchronic justification 621–3
synthetic propositions 284
A System of Logic (Mill) 347
systems of spheres 630–32, 634–6
Sytsma, Justin 831
Szabo, Zoltán 648

tacit knowledge 338
Tarski, Alfred 4
taste 369–71
Teller, Paul 551
ten modes of Aenesidemus 408–11

Tennant, Neil 644
testimony **316–22**; and achievement 226; and aesthetic knowledge 374–5; and coherence 261–2; and evidence 65–6; Hume on 35, 65–6, 319; and independence 262; and justification 35, 319–22; and probability 618, 694; and religious knowledge 397–8; and social epistemology 879–80
Thagard, Paul 265
Theaetetus (Plato) 656, 659, 664
theoretical wisdom 100–105, 666–70, 672–3
theory of descriptions 750–56
Theory of Knowledge (Russell) 751
Theory of Vision Vindicated and Explained (Berkeley) 707
Thorndike, Edward 851
Three Dialogues between Hylas and Philonous (Berkeley) 707, 709, 710–11, 712–13
"Three Varieties of Knowledge" (Davidson) 878
Timaeus (Plato) 660–61, 665
title principle 738
token beliefs 721–2
token functionalism 19
token processes 182
tolerance, principle of 781, 786
Tolliver, Joseph 116–17
Tom Grabit scenario 156–7, 161, 205–6
total evidence, principle of 807
Toulmin, Stephen 849, 852, 853
tracking theories 150, 420, 601–2
track-record arguments 722–3
Tractatus (Wittgenstein) 778
traditional foundationalism 239–40, 241–3
tranquility 404–6
'Transcendental Deduction of the Categories' (Kant) 743–7
transcendental idealism 743–9
transcendental realism 520
translation 791–2
transmission 316–18, 594–6, 600, 604
transparency 7–8, 22, 53–4, 307
Treatise of Human Nature (Hume) 730, 732–4, 736–7, 739–40
Treatise on Man (Descartes) 683
Trout, J.D. 842, 846
Truetemp cases 828
trumping 552
truth **3–12**, 484–6; and coherence 261–3, 472–3, 485; correspondence theory 3–5, 484; deflationary theories 6–10, 484–5; functionalist theories 10–12; Locke on 693–4; and moral beliefs 466–8; norm of 52–4; pluralist theories 11–12; pragmatic theories 5–6, 864–71; and realism 484–5; and relativism 78–9
"Truth by Convention" (Quine) 786–7, 789
truth-conducivity 146, 149, 265–6, 873, 891
truth relativism 537, 539
Tversky, Amos 615
twin earth scenarios 20–21, 418
"Two Dogmas of Empiricism" (Quine) 775, 787–91, 869–70

twofold consequentialism 101–5
Tye, Michael 300–301
type functionalism 19
type processes 182
type theory 643–4

Ullian, J.S. 794–5, 820
undecidable dispute, mode of 408
undefeated defeaters 318
underconsideration 277, 280
undercutting defeaters 158
underdetermination 445–6, 447, 449–51, 787–91, 792
understanding **84–93**, 202, 225, 374–5, 662, 744–5
Unger, Peter 122, 417, 513
uniformity of nature, principle of 733–5
uniqueness 82
Unity of Science (Carnap) 779–80
Universal Darwinism 852
unsophisticated agents 149, 202, 204, 319–21, 428–31, 592, 770–72
Urbach, Peter 613
utilitarianism 386
utility, principle of 385, 386

validation 332–3
validity 11
value problem **219–30**
value theory 643–4
values 47, 55–6,
Van Cleve, James 721
Vardi, Moshe Y. 583
variation thesis 420–21
verificationism 442, 643, 780, 862
veritic epistemic luck 189
Vienna Circle 775, 778–82
virtue epistemology 31, 32–3, **199–206**, 224–30, 893–4
virtues 99–101, 656–8
Virtues of the Mind (Zagzebski) 96, 199
Voltaire's objection to inference to the best explanation 277, 280

Warfield, Ted A. 265
warrant 248–50, 252, 255, 355, 587–9, 595–6, 765–70; *see also* justification
warrant monism 587–9, 595–6
warrant pluralism 587–9, 591, 595–6
way of ideas 717–18, 724
weak justification 152
weak normative naturalism 842
weak objectivity 881
weak safety 196
Weatherson, Brian 594, 817
web of belief 258, 291, 794–6, 870
The Web of Belief (Quine & Ullian) 794–6
Wedgwood, Ralph 113
Weinberg, Jonathan 125–6, 817, 828, 831, 845–6
Whewell, William 149–50
White, Roger 82
White, Stephen 816

INDEX

Whitehead, Alfred North: *Principia Mathematica* 750, 756
Wiggins, David 862, 864
"The Will to Believe" (James) 866–7
Williams, Bernard 433, 879
Williams, Michael 165, 411, 507, 523, 784, 804–5
Williamson, Timothy: on experimental epistemology 832; on intuitions 340, 814; on knowability paradox 642, 645, 647, 648–9; *Knowledge and its Limits* 32; knowledge-first epistemology 32, 61, 169, 177, 220, 221, 494–5; on luminosity 212, 307, 592–4; on memory 330–31
wisdom **95–105**, 202, 225, 397, 656–8, 662, 666–73
witnesses 261–2, 618; *see also* testimony
Wittgenstein, Ludwig **763–73**; on closure 601; correspondence theory of truth 3; on justification 35, 878; on non-inferential knowledge 770–73; *On Certainty* 601, 770–73; *Philosophical Investigations* 454, 770; and Pyrrhonian skepticism 412; and regress 26; *Remarks on the Foundations of Mathematics* 454; on rule-following 454–5; on semantic knowledge 341–4, 454–5; and skepticism 341–4, 412, 442–3; social epistemology 35, 878; *Tractatus* 778; *Zettel* 767–8
Wood, W. Jay 200, 202
Word and Object (Quine) 791–2
The World (Descartes) 684
Wright, Chauncey 848
Wright, Crispin 6, 11, 454–5, 462, 552, 642, 646
Wright, Georg Henrik von 572
Wright, Jennifer C. 826–7

Zagzebski, Linda 96, 100–101, 199, 200–201, 203–4, 206, 219; *Virtues of the Mind* 96, 199
Zarpentine, Chris 825
Zettel (Wittgenstein) 767–8
Zimmerman, Aaron 23, 824–5

eBooks – at www.eBookstore.tandf.co.uk

A library at your fingertips!

eBooks are electronic versions of printed books. You can store them on your PC/laptop or browse them online.

They have advantages for anyone needing rapid access to a wide variety of published, copyright information.

eBooks can help your research by enabling you to bookmark chapters, annotate text and use instant searches to find specific words or phrases. Several eBook files would fit on even a small laptop or PDA.

NEW: Save money by eSubscribing: cheap, online access to any eBook for as long as you need it.

Annual subscription packages

We now offer special low-cost bulk subscriptions to packages of eBooks in certain subject areas. These are available to libraries or to individuals.

For more information please contact webmaster.ebooks@tandf.co.uk

We're continually developing the eBook concept, so keep up to date by visiting the website.

www.eBookstore.tandf.co.uk